Shooter's Bible ®

ABOUT OUR COVER

The two custom shotguns featured on our front cover are Krieghoff K-80 Trap Combos. The one on the left was custom-stocked by Brent Umberger, Master Stockmaker of Sportsman's Haven, Cambridge, Ohio. The deep engraving in art deco style, done by Gerhard Ruppert, has 24-carat gold line work and coin finish. The custom K-80 on the right has deep relief engraving accented with fine clusters of 3-tone gold flower inlays; engraved by Gino Cargnel. Both firearms are privately owned and were sold thru Jaqua's Fine Guns of Findlay, Ohio. The shooting glasses were provided courtesy of Allan Lehman Optical of Phoenix, Arizona.

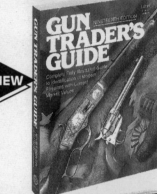

NO. 88
1997 EDITION

EDITOR:
William S. Jarrett

PRODUCTION EDITOR:
Charlene Cruson Step

PRODUCTION & DESIGN:
Loretta Luongo

EDITORIAL ASSISTANT:
Susan Baldassano

FIREARMS CONSULTANTS:
Bill Meade
Vincent A. Pestilli
Paul Rochelle

COVER PHOTOGRAPHER:
Ray Wells

PUBLISHER:
David C. Perkins

PRESIDENT
Brian T. Herrick

Shooter's Bible ®

STOEGER PUBLISHING COMPANY

Every effort has been made to record specifications and descriptions of guns, ammunition and accessories accurately, but the Publisher can take no responsibility for errors or omissions. The prices shown for guns, ammunition and accessories are manufacturers' suggested retail prices (unless otherwise noted) and are furnished for information only. These were in effect at press time and are subject to change without notice. Purchasers of this book have complete freedom of choice in pricing for resale.

Published by Stoeger Publishing Company
5 Mansard Court
Wayne, New Jersey 07470

Library of Congress Catalog Card No.: 63-6200
International Standard Book No.: 0-88317-192-9

Manufactured in the United States of America

In the United States:
Distributed to the book trade and to the sporting goods trade by
Stoeger Industries
5 Mansard Court
Wayne, New Jersey 07470
Tel: 201-872-9500 Fax: 201-872-2230

In Canada:
Distributed to the book trade and to the sporting goods trade by
Stoeger Canada Ltd.
1801 Wentworth Street, Unit 16
Whitby, Ontario, L1N 8R6, Canada

Contents

FOREWORD

If SHOT Show attendance is any indication of how well the firearms industry is doing these days, then 1996-97 should be a banner year. Speaking of which, gun owners everywhere can give themselves a real treat by attending one of these annual events. The 1997 show is scheduled for January 30-February 2 in Las Vegas, Nevada, so jot that down on your calendar and join us at this annual exhibit. You'll learn a lot about what's going on, what's new, and what's not so new.

This 88th edition of SHOOTER'S BIBLE falls somewhere in that same category—something old, something new. We begin by backtracking to the 1947 edition of SHOOTER'S BIBLE for our 10th rendition of "50 Years Ago in Shooter's Bible." This annual feature is not only popular with our readers, it also happens to be a subject no other gun annual can offer. Other articles you should check out include Jim Casada's continuing series of biographies of the world's great hunters and outdoor writers, this time the story of Elmer Keith. He was truly "A Man For All Seasons" who wrote, among many titles, the legendary *Hell, I Was There!* Ralph Quinn, a regular contributor to these pages, has covered the fascinating but seldom touched subject of gun engraving ("Artistry in Steel"). Another old friend, Wilf Pyle, offers sage advice on how to reduce recoil by choosing "soft-shooting" rifles. Next comes news about hunting with in-line muzzleloaders by Toby Bridges, a longtime veteran of the blackpowder world. Gene Gangarosa Jr., whose books on handguns have been published under the Stoeger imprint for several years, weighs in with "The Forgotten Walthers: Models 4 and 5," which all serious handgunners will want to read. Steve Irwin's piece on Indian rifles makes a nice change of pace, covering in depth the weapons used by North American Indians, including their decorations, ammunition and the like. And finally, we urge you to take a look at Wayne von Zwoll's article on choosing the right rifle cartridge for hunting big game.

After you've gone through the articles, feel free to do some serious shopping in the Manufacturers' Showcase, featuring all kinds of firearms products not found in the Specifications Section. In the Spec Section you'll find important information on new and current guns of all kinds, starting with handguns. This year we welcome such new manufacturers as Brolin, J.O. Arms and Safari, while lamenting the loss of Anschutz, Dan Wesson and Texas Arms. The Rifle Section adds Arnold Arms, Harris Gunworks, K.B.I., Kongsberg, Lazzeroni Arms, Magtech, and Rifles, Inc., but unfortunately loses Benton & Brown, Feather, McMillan, Ruko, Lakefield and Voere. Likewise, in the Shotgun category we will miss Rizzini and Ithaca while welcoming Dakota Arms. Our Blackpowder Section rounds out the firearms category with Mountain State, Prairie River Arms, Colt and Cabela's as noteworthy additions, although UFA Teton is no longer listed.

The Sights and Scopes section continues to grow—with many new products offered by most of the established manufacturers. That leads us to the Ammunition and Ballistics area, in which readers will find what's new at Remington, Federal, Winchester, Fiocchi and others. Then comes the Reloading Section, featuring bullets, gunpowder and all kinds of equipment and tools essential to gunsmiths/handloaders of various degrees of expertise.

And last, but far from least, is the Reference Section. It includes two vital indexes—the Caliberfinder and Gunfinder—to help you find perhaps a bolt-action rifle that shoots a 270 Winchester cartridge. You'd look for that caliber in the Caliberfinder, select the gun you'd want to review, then check it out in the Gunfinder for the page number. It's that easy. Should you want to contact one of the companies featured in SHOOTER'S BIBLE, there's a complete Directory of Manufacturers and Suppliers, listing addresses and phone/fax numbers. And this year for the first time we're including a new Product Index, which canvasses all the products in this edition and lists them by manufacturer and page number.

We offer a lot in this 88th edition of America's longest-running gun annual. We hope you find it a useful and important addition to your library all year long.

William S. Jarrett
Editor

Articles

50 YEARS AGO
IN SHOOTER'S BIBLE

With the demands and shortages of World War II slowly fading into the history books, the firearms industry in the year 1947 continued its fast recovery. The pipelines were full, and waiting lists for parts and ammunition had already become relics of the recent past. Wartime ceiling prices had been lifted and most of the major gunmakers—Remington, Parker and Fox among them—looked forward to the new year with high expectations. At the same time, while unsettled economic conditions prevailed in Europe, foreign gunmakers found it increasingly difficult to export firearms to the States.

For U.S. manufacturers, 1947 was something worth waiting for. A new Browning automatic Skeet shotgun sold for $132.35 (with an extra $8.85 for a beavertail forearm). Smith & Wesson's .38/.44 Heavy Duty revolver went for $51.70, and Harrington & Richardson was busy selling the "Leatherneck" Model 165 in semiautomatic rifle .22 caliber for only $57.44.

On the following pages you'll find other examples of what was available in 1947 as we continue our popular series, "50 Years Ago in Shooter's Bible." At the top of each page, representing each of the 12 months, we've added brief summaries of important news and sports events that took place half a century ago. (Did you know that a rookie second baseman named Jackie Robinson led the Brooklyn Dodgers into the 1947 World Series against the mighty New York Yankees?)

Now that the world had been made safe for democracy, it was indeed time to return to the good life. We trust you'll get a glimpse of what we're talking about in the next 12 pages.

SMITH & WESSON

.38/44 HEAVY DUTY

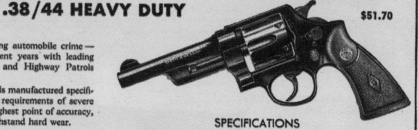

$51.70

An ideal gun for combatting automobile crime — particularly popular in recent years with leading State Police Departments and Highway Patrols from coast to coast.

The .38/44 Heavy Duty is manufactured specifically to meet the exacting requirements of severe usage and represents the highest point of accuracy, efficiency and ability to withstand hard wear.

Chambered for the entire line of .38 Special Cartridges right up to and including the ultra-modern High-Velocity, Metal-Piercing .38 Specials. This gun delivers tremendous power. Yet it has a marvelous "feel" and wonderful ease in shooting due to the weight and superb balance given by its .44 caliber frame and heavy, reinforced barrel.

SPECIFICATIONS

CALIBER: .38 S & W Special
NUMBER OF SHOTS: 6
BARREL: 4 or 5 inch
LENGTH: With 5-inch barrel, 10¼ inches
WEIGHT: With 5-inch barrel, 40 ounces
SIGHTS: Fixed, 1/10-inch service type front; square notch rear
STOCKS: Checkered Circassian walnut with S & W Monograms.

Choice of square or Magna type
FINISH: S & W Blue or Nickel

AMMUNITION
.38 S & W Special High-Speed
.38 S & W Special Super Police
.38 S & W Special
.38 S & W Special Mid-Range
.38 Short Colt
.38 Long Colt
.38 Colt Special

$51.70

1926 MODEL .44 MILITARY

SPECIFICATIONS

CALIBER: .44 S & W Special
NUMBER OF SHOTS: 6
BARREL: 4, 5 or 6½ inches
LENGTH: With 6½-inch barrel, 11¾ inches
WEIGHT: With 6½-inch barrel, 39¼ ounces
SIGHTS: Fixed, 1/10-inch service type front; square notch rear
STOCKS: Checkered Circassian walnut with S & W Monograms. Choice of square or Magna type
FINISH: S & W Blue or Nickel

AMMUNITION
.44 S & W Special
.44 S & W Russian

Immensely popular in the Southwest where Police, Sheriffs and Border Patrol traditionally prefer a heavy caliber, long range sidearm.

The large frame gives the 1926 Military all the weight it needs to handle the powerful .44 S & W Special cartridge with ease and comfort, while the reinforcing lug on the barrel contributes exceptional strength and perfect balance.

The .44 Military is justly considered by many as the finest large caliber revolver ever made. Its .44 S & W Special cartridge gives it all the muzzle energy and shock power of the .45, but with far greater accuracy and ranging power.

.45 CAL. 1917 ARMY

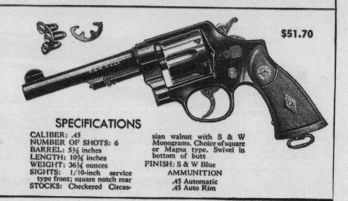

$51.70

The 1917 Army designed for use with the .45 Auto Rim cartridge or the regular .45 Auto cartridge in semi-circular clips, was chosen by the United States Army for use by American troops in the last war.

In actual Government test it gave greater penetration, velocity and accuracy than any other gun tested. In fact, the greater accuracy possible with this arm raised the former qualifying score in the National Pistol Course of the N. R. A. several points over that required when the Automatic Pistol was used.

A very powerful, fast handling gun for practical shooting up to 100 yards. Without doubt the quickest loading, safest and accurate arm made for the Service Cartridge.

SPECIFICATIONS

CALIBER: .45
NUMBER OF SHOTS: 6
BARREL: 5½ inches
LENGTH: 10¾ inches
WEIGHT: 36¼ ounces
SIGHTS: 1/10-inch service type front; square notch rear
STOCKS: Checkered Circas-

sian walnut with S & W Monograms. Choice of square or Magna type. Swivel in bottom of butt
FINISH: S & W Blue

AMMUNITION
.45 Automatic
.45 Auto Rim

H&R .22 CALIBER RIFLES

THE "LEATHERNECK!" MODEL 165

This new H&R .22 caliber semi-automatic rifle is patterned and designed after the famous H&R Marine Corps .22 cal. Training Rifle, (Model 65).

Several of these rifles are officially credited with firing over 100,000 rounds during tests, with many on their training program having passed the 40,000 rounds mark with no defects or loss of accuracy.

To assure continued safety against premature firing, every H&R "Leatherneck" has an adjustment with which wear, caused by years of usage, can be taken care of.

Dry firing has long been the bug-a-boo of rim firing arms. Now, for the first time, H&R has produced, patented, and proven a new firing pin. You can aim and dry-fire all you want—without the slightest possibility of damage to the pin or chamber.

SPECIFICATIONS
Overall Length: 43 inches.
Caliber: Chambered for .22 cal. Long Rifle Cartridges, regular or hi-speed.
Clip Loading: 10 shots.
Barrel: 23 inches, crowned muzzle, one turn in 16 inches.
Sights: Front, ramp with blade. Rear, Redfield Micrometer.
Stock: Polished American Walnut, Sporter Type.
Weight: 7 to 7½ lbs.
Bolt Stop: Manually operated on right side of receiver, locks bolt open for inspection and cleaning.
Finish: Standard Blue.
Sling swivels, web sling strap.
Safety on right side, positive disengaging of trigger mechanism from sear.
PRICE $57.44

"TARGETEER" NEW BOLT ACTION MODEL 265

The H&R "Regular" is the expert's rifle you can afford. For the first time, at the right price, here is a 10 shot repeating .22 caliber rifle of extremely fine workmanship, ruggedness and dependability, heretofore found only in high-priced, hand-made, custom-built guns. The H&R "Regular" matches the best afield or on the range in accuracy, balance and reliability. It surpasses all others in the medium price class.

SPECIFICATIONS
Overall Length: 40 inches.
Caliber: Chambered for .22 cal. Long Rifle Cartridges, regular or hi-speed.
Clip Loading: 10 shots.
Barrel: 22 inches, one turn in 16 inches, crowned muzzle.
Sights: Front, ramp with blade. Rear, Lyman Receiver Sight.
Stock: Polished American Walnut.
Weight: 6½ to 6¾ lbs.
Finish: Standard Blue.
Bolt Release: Spring type, on left side of Receiver.
Safety: Rear and under Receiver for Thumb operation.
PRICE $34.19

"REG'LAR" NEW SINGLE SHOT MODEL 365

The H&R "Ace" is the all-around .22 rifle for all-around sport and skill.

Proven features are yours today with the H&R "Ace". Engineered into this rifle is dependability and accuracy and a ruggedness never before available in a moderately priced rifle. You can dry-fire with the H&R "Ace" all you want. The exclusive firing pin is contained entirely within the bolt head-space and *positively* cannot hit the edge of the chamber, therefore cannot deform or burr edges.

SPECIFICATIONS
Overall: 40 inches.
Caliber: Chambered for .22 cal. Long Rifle Cartridges, regular or hi-speed. Single Shot.
Barrel: 22 inches, one turn in 16 inches, crowned muzzle.
Sights: Front, ramp with blade. Rear, Lyman Receiver Sight.
Stock: Polished American Walnut.
Weight: 6½ lbs.
Finish: Standard Blue.
Bolt Release: Spring type, on left side of Receiver.
Safety: Rear and under Receiver for Thumb operation.
PRICE $28.24

"TARGETEER SPECIAL" MODEL 465

In the H&R Target Model 465, marksmen at last can have full advantage of all the exclusive patented H&R features. This new .22 caliber bolt action 10 shot repeater is designed especially for target shooters giving them perfect balance, necessary weight (insuring "holding on target") and extreme accuracy. This rifle is the heavy target shooter model of the H&R 265 shown above. It has a longer, heavier barrel and a heavier stock. The H&R 465 is designed especially for target shooters who demand a heavier model rifle.

SPECIFICATIONS
Overall Length: 41¼ inches.
Caliber: Chambered for .22 cal. Long Rifle Cartridges, regular or hi-speed.
Clip Loading: 10 shots.
Barrel: 25 inches, crowned muzzle, one turn in 16 inches.
Sights: Front, ramp with blade. Rear, Lyman 57 E Receiver.
Stock: Polished American Walnut Target Type.
Weight: Approx. 9 lbs.
Finish: Standard Blue.
Bolt Release: Spring type, on left side of Receiver.
Safety: Rear and under Receiver for Thumb operation.
Sling swivels, web sling strap.
PRICE $52.96

A COMPLETE NEW LINE OF 22 CALIBER RIFLES

L. C. SMITH SHOTGUNS

IDEAL GRADE

The hankering for a custom-built gun is satisfied by the Ideal Grade Smith. Here is the balance and "fit" you seek . . . the sheen and decorative grain of specially selected walnut, matched in stock and fore-end . . . the beauty of rich engraving. The Ideal Grade has all the useful features of the Field Grade . . . and it is a gun to make the real gun fancier glow with pride.

IMPROVED FIELD GRADE

In its price class, this staunch and dependable model continues to reign as the favored selection of double gun users throughout the world.

For rough work in timber and brush, for the strain of incessant shooting on the skeet field and over the traps, for long range and "to bring 'em down"—an L. C. Smith *Improved* Field Grade! Complete with the SINGLE SIGHTING PLANE rib.

SPECIFICATIONS AND PRICES

GAUGES

12. 16 or 20

BARRELS

12 Gauge	...............30"—28"—26"
16 Gauge	......................28"—26"
20 Gauge	......................28"—26"

WEIGHTS

12 Gauge	..............approx. 6⅞ lbs.
16 Gauge	..............approx. 6⅝ lbs.
20 Gauge	..............approx. 6¼ lbs.

BARREL CHOKES

Right	*Left*
30" Modified	.....................Full
28" Modified	.....................Full
26" Improved Cylinder	.......Modified

Proof tested, bored by the Smith system for penetration and uniform pattern.

STOCKS

Field Grade: Approx. Length 14"—drop at comb. 1½"—drop at heel 2½". Full pistol grip.
Ideal Grade: Approx. Length 14"—drop at comb. 1½"—drop at heel 2½". Full pistol grip.

PRICES

Field Grade..................	$ 83.45
Ideal Grade	112.00
Automatic Ejectors — Field or Ideal. add	19.00
Selective Single Trigger Field or Ideal, add...........	27.30
Beavertail Forend (Ideal only), add	21.10

EXTRAS

| Standard Recoil Pad fitted.... | 6.37 |
| Standard Ivory Sights fitted... | 1.67 |

OTHER L. C. SMITH GUNS AVAILABLE AGAIN LATER

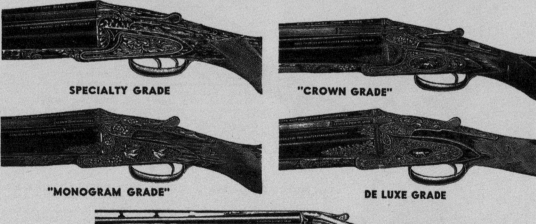

SPECIALTY GRADE

"CROWN GRADE"

"MONOGRAM GRADE"

DE LUXE GRADE

OLYMPIC GRADE
SINGLE BARREL TRAP GUN

GUNS YOU WILL BE PROUD TO OWN

MARLIN .22 CAL. RIFLES

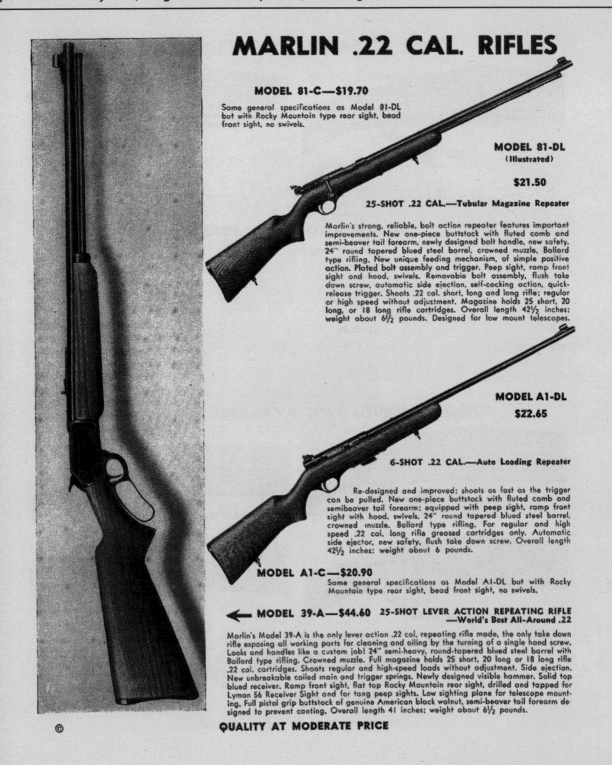

MODEL 81-C—$19.70

Same general specifications as Model 81-DL but with Rocky Mountain type rear sight, bead front sight, no swivels.

MODEL 81-DL
(Illustrated)

$21.50

25-SHOT .22 CAL.—Tubular Magazine Repeater

Marlin's strong, reliable, bolt action repeater features important improvements. New one-piece buttstock with fluted comb and semi-beaver tail forearm, newly designed bolt handle, new safety. 24" round tapered blued steel barrel, crowned muzzle. Ballard type rifling. New unique feeding mechanism, of simple positive action. Plated bolt assembly and trigger. Peep sight, ramp front sight and hood, swivels. Removable bolt assembly, flush take down screw, automatic side ejection, self-cocking action, quick-release trigger. Shoots .22 cal. short, long and long rifle; regular or high speed without adjustment. Magazine holds 25 short, 20 long, or 18 long rifle cartridges. Overall length 42½ inches; weight about 6½ pounds. Designed for low mount telescopes.

MODEL A1-DL
$22.65

6-SHOT .22 CAL.—Auto Loading Repeater

Re-designed and improved; shoots as fast as the trigger can be pulled. New one-piece buttstock with fluted comb and semibeaver tail forearm; equipped with peep sight, ramp front sight with hood, swivels. 24" round tapered blued steel barrel, crowned muzzle. Ballard type rifling. For regular and high speed .22 cal. long rifle greased cartridges only. Automatic side ejector, new safety, flush take down screw. Overall length 42½ inches; weight about 6 pounds.

MODEL A1-C—$20.90

Same general specifications as Model A1-DL but with Rocky Mountain type rear sight, bead front sight, no swivels.

← **MODEL 39-A—$44.60** **25-SHOT LEVER ACTION REPEATING RIFLE —World's Best All-Around .22**

Marlin's Model 39-A is the only lever action .22 cal. repeating rifle made, the only take down rifle exposing all working parts for cleaning and oiling by the turning of a single hand screw. Looks and handles like a custom job! 24" semi-heavy, round-tapered blued steel barrel with Ballard type rifling. Crowned muzzle. Full magazine holds 25 short, 20 long or 18 long rifle .22 cal. cartridges. Shoots regular and high-speed loads without adjustment. Side ejection. New unbreakable coiled main and trigger springs. Newly designed visible hammer. Solid top blued receiver. Ramp front sight, flat top Rocky Mountain rear sight, drilled and tapped for Lyman 56 Receiver Sight and for tang peep sights. Low sighting plane for telescope mounting. Full pistol grip buttstock of genuine American black walnut, semi-beaver tail forearm designed to prevent canting. Overall length 41 inches; weight about 6½ pounds.

QUALITY AT MODERATE PRICE

AUTOMATIC PISTOLS OF THE WORLD WAR

WALTHER H-P (P-38) DOUBLE ACTION

This pistol which represents one of the most advanced designs in automatic pistol manufacture, was used by the Germans in World War II equally with the Luger. The outstanding feature is the outside hammer with double action. It shoots the regular 9m/m Luger cartridge. Has a barrel 4⅞ inches in length and the overall length is 8½ inches. Weighs 34 ounces. Magazine has a capacity of eight shots.

GERMAN SAUER DOUBLE ACTION

Magazine capacity: 8 shot. Barrel length: 3⅝ inches. Overall length: 6½ inches. Weight: 22 ounces. Cartridge .32 Colt Automatic. Probably the most advanced design in pistol manufacture in the world today.

STEYR MODEL 1911

This pistol was the official pistol of the Austro-Hungarian Army in the First World War, but many were used in World War II. The cartridge is a special 9m/m, rather a cross between the 9m/m Luger and the .38 Super Automatic, neither of which, however, is suitable for use in this gun. The cartridges are fed on a strip of eight and inserted from the top. It does not have a detachable magazine. The barrel is 5 inches long, and the pistol has an overall length of 8½ inches. Weighs 18½ ounces.

MAUSER "H Sc" DOUBLE ACTION

This pistol probably represents the very latest in automatic pistol design being completely streamlined. Has double action feature as well as outside hammer and extremely simple takedown. Shoots the regular .32 automatic cartridge. Has 3⅜ inch barrel, overall length 6½ inches. Weighs 20½ ounces.

MAUSER MILITARY PISTOL

WEBLEY .455

This pistol shoots the special .455 Webley automatic cartridge, similar to but larger than the .45 Colt Automatic. Has a capacity of 7 cartridges, with 5 inch barrel, overall length 8½ inches. Weighs 36 ounces.

This pistol has been made in three calibers, of which two are common, the special 7.63m/m Mauser and 9m/m Luger. It has also been made in a special long 9m/m, which is, however, quite rare. To distinguish between the two 9m/m's, the one chambered for the 9m/m Luger usually has a red "9" carved into the wooden grip. This pistol is regularly made with a combination wooden stock and holster and the design has been changed several times, particularly as to magazine capacity, type of safety, and full or semi-automatic fire feature.

FOR COMPLETE INFORMATION ON ALL MILITARY ARMS

STEVENS-SPRINGFIELD BOLT ACTION .22 CALIBER RIFLES

MODEL 416-2 STEVENS TARGET RIFLE

For .22 R. F. Long Rifle Cartridges

A NEW MATCH RIFLE
Fully Equipped—Guaranteed Accuracy

This new rifle represents the most recent offering in the .22 target line and is a genuine contribution by the Stevens factory to the small bore shooter. For the first time a really substantial, well proportioned match rifle with proper weight, balance, trigger pull, target sights and great accuracy is available at a price within reach of many who formerly had to content themselves with inferior rifles.

No. 416-2 Specifications:

Barrel—26-inch. Heavy Tapered Round. .22 Long Rifle. A five shot machine rest group with each rifle guarantees extreme accuracy.

Action—Bolt Action. Five Shot Clip Magazine. Speed Lock. Adjustable Trigger Pull. Bolt Handle of design to permit telescope sight in low position giving same sighting plane as regular sights. Independent Safety with Red Dot Indicator.

Stock—American Walnut. Oil Finish. Adjustable Front Sling Loop. Fitted with 1¼-inch Neats-foot Oil Treated Leather Sling. Checkered Steel Butt Plate.

Sights—New Stevens No. 25 Hooded Front Sight with Five Removable Inserts, and No. 106 Peep Sight. Telescope Blocks.

Weight—With Sling Strap about 9½ pounds.

Ammunition—.22 Long Rifle Regular or High Speed.

No. 416-2	$48.40
No. 416-3 (without sights)	41.20
Extra 5 Shot Clip	1.20
Extra 10 Shot Clip	1.35

NO. 417

for Target Shooting

STEVENS "WALNUT HILL" HEAVY TARGET RIFLE

For HiSpeed or regular cartridges. BARREL—28 inch heavy, round, tested for accuracy. FRAME—Casehardened. ACTION—Original Stevens "Ideal" Breech Block. Automatic Ejector. Lever Action. Short, Fast Hammer Fall. STOCK—American Walnut 13½-inch. Oil Finish. High Comb. Full Pistol Grip Target Model Stock and Forearm. Fitted with 1¼-inch military Style. Neatsfoot Oil Treated Sling Strap, Shotgun Butt with Steel Butt Plate. SIGHTS—Standard Equipment Lyman No. 17A Front. Telescope Blocks, Lyman No. 48L Receiver Sight. WEIGHT—about 10½ pounds. AMMUNITION—.22 Long Rifle.

No. 417-1, fitted with Lyman No. 48L Sight	$87.75
No. 417-2, fitted with Lyman No. 144 Sight in place of No. 48L	77.70
No. 417-3, without front or rear sights	69.45
Extra heavy 29 inch barrel add to above prices	49.40

MODEL 084   FOR TARGET SHOOTING AND SMALL GAME

Caliber .22 Long Rifle, .22 Long and .22 Short

Barrel—Tapered, Round, 24-inch, with Crowned Muzzle for .22 L. R. .22 L. or .22 S. Regular or High Speed Cartridges. Take-down. 5 shot Detachable Clip Magazine. Action—Self Cocking. Bolt Action with Independent Safety. Chromium Plated Bolt and Trigger. Stock—Full size. Oval Military Style. Full Pistol Grip, Walnut Finish. Rubber Butt Plate.

Sights—Hooded Ramp Front sight with removable hood and three interchangeable inserts. Receiver rear with three sighting discs, also folding sporting middle sight. Ammunition—Any .22 L. R. .22 L. or .22 S., High Speed or Regular Cartridge. Weight—About 6 pounds. Length over all, 43½ inches.

Price Model 84 Open Sights	$15.65
	14.75
Extra 5 Shot Clip	1.10
Extra 10 Shot Clip	1.35

MODEL 086   FOR TARGET SHOOTING AND SMALL GAME

Caliber .22 Long Rifle, .22 Long and .22 Short

Action—Self Cocking, Bolt Action, with Independent Safety, Chromium Plated Bolt and Trigger.

Stock—Turned. Walnut Finish. Rubber Butt Plate.

Sights—Hooded Ramp Front Sight with three interchangeable inserts. Receiver rear sight with sighting disc, also folding sporting middle sight. Weight—5½ pounds. Length over all, 41½ inches.

Barrels—24-inch. Round, Tapered. Take-down. The rifle has a tubular magazine with capacity of fifteen .22 long rifle, seventeen .22 long, or twenty-one .22 short, High Speed or Regular Cartridges.

Price	$19.70
Price Model 86 Open Sights	18.80

© **TELL OTHERS ABOUT STOEGER'S CATALOG**

COLT TARGET REVOLVERS

Only the most carefully designed and perfectly manufactured target arm can hold its own on the modern target ranges of America—and it must be designed to meet the rigid requirements for accuracy demanded by today's highly skilled target shooters.

Colt target revolvers have been designed by experts and are flawlessly manufactured by skilled workmen, who thoroughly understand the needs and desires of the modern shooter. Their graceful lines, perfect balance, comfortable grip and super accuracy have earned the confidence of target shooters everywhere. Their match winning ability is being proven on target ranges constantly in every part of the country.

The standard sight equipment of Colt Target Arms—New Service Target, Shooting Master, Officer's Model Target and Police Positive Target Revolvers, "Camp Perry" Model Cal. .22 single shot Target Pistol and "Woodsman" and "ACE" .22 caliber Automatic Pistols are the square or "Patridge" front and square cut rear as shown in the accompanying illustrations. Regulation Bead sights will be supplied on any of these models (except "ACE") when so specified, at no extra cost. Ivory Bead or Gold Bead front sights may be had at an extra cost of $1.00. Unless otherwise specified, the square or "Patridge" sights will be fitted to all Target Arms ordered.

OFFICERS' MODEL TARGET

The Colt Officers' Model Target Revolver is recognized as America's premier target arm—combining perfect balance, smooth, fast action and full, comfortable grip—making possible higher and more consistent scores, for beginners and experts alike. It is the arm chosen by leading target shooters everywhere—the target revolver that makes champions!

Shooters can shift from the .22 to the .38 Caliber model without changing method of sighting, grip or hold. Same balance, same trigger pull and operation.

.22 Cal. Price $47.25
.32 or .38 Cal. 45.75

SPECIFICATIONS: .38 Special Model

Ammunition—.38 Caliber Model: .38 Short Colt; .38 Long Colt; .38 Colt Special; .38 S. & W. Special (full and mid-range loads); .38 Colt Special High Speed; .38 S. & W. Special High Speed; .38-44 S. & W. Special cartridges.

Lengths of Barrel: Caliber .38, 4½, 6 inches. Heavy barrel, 6 inch length only.

Length Over All: With 6 inch barrel, 11¼ inches.

Weight: Caliber .38, with 6 inch heavy barrel, 36 ounces.

Sights: Adjustable, Bead or Patridge. Stippled.

Back Strap: Checked.

Stocks: Checked Walnut.

Trigger and Hammer Spur: Checked.

Finish: Blued. Top and back of frame stippled to prevent light reflection.

CALIBERS: .22 Long Rifle; .38 Special

This is the model that target shooters depend on for serious target shooting. It is built on a .41 caliber frame with its medium weight perfectly distributed. Equipped with adjustable Bead or Patridge target sights, both stippled to prevent light reflection. Flat type top of frame, stippled. Back strap is checked to provide firm grip and stocks are checked walnut. Trigger and hammer spur are checked and non-slipping. The .22 Caliber model is furnished with 6 inch barrel only, and has the new Colt Embedded Head Cylinder, making this model safe for use with high speed or regular ammunition.

SPECIFICATIONS:

.22 Caliber Model

Ammunition: .22 Long Rifle cartridges. Regular or High Speed.

Length of Barrel: 6 inches only.

Length Over All: 11¼ inches.

Weight: 38 ounces.

Sights: Adjustable, Bead or Patridge. Stippled.

Cylinder: Embedded Head Type.

Stocks: Checked Walnut.

Back Strap: Checked.

Trigger: Checked.

Hammer Spur: Checked.

Finish: Blued. Top of frame stippled to prevent light reflection.

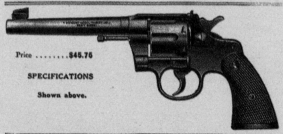

Price $45.75

SPECIFICATIONS

Shown above.

OFFICERS' MODEL TARGET
WITH HEAVY BARREL

CALIBER: .38 Special

An important change was made some time ago in the Colt Officers' Model by furnishing this world famous target revolver with a heavy barrel—similar in design and weight to the barrel used in the Shooting Master Revolver. This heavy barrel adds two ounces to the weight of the gun, steadying it for rapid fire shooting and balancing the arm perfectly. Shooters have already recorded a number of World's Records with the new Officers' Model.

POLICE POSITIVE TARGET REVOLVER

CALIBERS:
.22 Long Rifle

The Police Positive Target Model is lighter in weight than the Officers' Model, being built on a .38 Caliber frame. Its grip is smaller and is ideal for those with small hands as well as for ladies. This model has all target refinements, including hand finished action, adjustable target sights, stippled frame top and deeply checked trigger. Can be furnished with either Bead or Patridge sights. The action of this model is smooth and fast and the trigger pull crisp and clean. Furnished with Colt Embedded Head Cylinder, for use with high speed or regular ammunition.

Ammunition—.22 Caliber Model: .22 long Rifle cartridges. Regular or High Speed.
Sights: Adjustable, Bead or Patridge Stippled.
Length of Barrel: 6 inches only.
Length Over All: 10½ inches.
Weight: .22 Caliber, 26 oz.
Action: Hand finished.
Sights: Adjustable, Bead or Patridge. Stippled.
Back Strap: Checked.
Stocks: Checked Walnut.
Cylinder: Embedded Head Type.
Trigger and Hammer Spur: Checked.
Finish: Blued. Top of frame stippled to prevent light reflection.

Price $42.00

© **SOON AVAILABLE AGAIN AT REVISED PRICES**

GENUINE BROWNING AUTOMATIC SHOTGUNS

SKEET MODEL
12, 16 and 20 GAUGES.

**With Cutts Compensator.
All gauges chambered for 2¾" shells.**

The Browning Automatic "Skeet Model" has proved itself to be an ideal skeet gun. The popularity of the Browning Automatic at skeet shooting, together with the outstanding records of thousands of Browning shooters is evidence of its performance and satisfaction.

A careful study by our technicians has developed the present Browning Skeet Model, which has proven to be the ideal skeet gun. Its dependability, perfect balance, "quick handling" and performance has earned for it a following among experienced skeet shooters unequalled by any other gun.

STOCK SPECIFICATIONS—Half pistol grip—drop at comb 1⅝ inches—drop at heel 2½ inches—length 14¼ inches.

Special Skeet Model, Either Gauge, 5- or 3-Shot, equipped with ventilated rib (as illustrated), and Cutts Compensator in 26" length only......**$132.35**
(Blued Steel Compensator with skeet and full choke tubes regularly supplied or blued aluminum furnished when specified).

Extra for Beavertail Forearm.................... 8.85

Cutts Compensator fitted to any other Browning Automatic Shotgun, blued steel or blued aluminum with skeet and full choke tubes (add to price of gun).... 24.50

Additional Pattern Control Tubes—each........ 3.60

Extra for barrel length other than 26", including Compensator with skeet tube (add to price of gun 4.85

UTILITY FIELD GUN
12, 16 and 20 GAUGES.

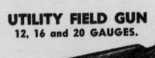

**With Aero-Dyne Super Poly Choke.
All gauges chambered for 2¾" shells.**

The Browning Utility Field Gun has been produced to meet the demand of field shooters. The utility feature of the Poly Choke which provides varying degrees of chokes is desirable to many.

The Browning Utility Field Gun now combines this flexible feature with all the advantages of the Browning Automatic described on pages 2 and 3.

STOCK SPECIFICATIONS—Half pistol grip—drop at comb 1⅝ inches—drop at heel 2½ inches, length 14¼ inches.

5 OR 3 SHOT

5-Shot is Adjustable to 3-Shot with Browning Magazine Adaptor (3-shot magazine plug) Furnished at no extra cost with all new 5-shot guns.

Utility Field Gun with Poly Choke, striped matted barrel without rib, 26 inches only including Poly Choke **$100.55**

Poly Choke supplied on any other new or used Browning Automatic Shotgun................. 14.75

EXTRAS
(On New Guns Only)

Oil Finishing Stock............................... $3.00
Oil Finishing Forearm........................... 2.00
Recoil Pad. any standard type, fitted (no extra charge for shortening stock) 6.75
Beavertail Forearm 8.85
Stock shortened up to 1 inch.................... 3.75
Stocks made to special dimensions other than regular specifications of standard American Walnut.......................... 19.80
Sights, Ivory or Red, fitted, each................ 1.50
Sights, Ivory or Red, fitted, per set front and middle........... 2.65
Sling Straps, leather, including swivels, fitted on new Automatic Shotguns 2.20

THE FINEST IN FIREARMS

DAISY AIR RIFLES

No. 111 RED RYDER 1000-SHOT CARBINE
Fred Harman (famous cowboy-artist who draws and writes the exciting Red Ryder comic strip) helped design this new business-like Red Ryder carbine. So, it looks, feels and handles like a real western saddle gun. Genuine leather thong knotted to Carbine Ring! **$3.95**

NO. 25 PUMP REPEATER, KING OF ALL AIR RIFLES. (TAKE DOWN MODEL) **$5.95**

BULLS EYE copperized steel shot per tube ....5¢

Benjamin Super Single Shot Target Pistols

With Hand Pump

Breech Loading - Bolt Action - Hammer Fire
Hair Trigger - Safety Lock

BENJAMIN TARGET PISTOLS are really practical, accurate and economical for Indoor or Outdoor Recreation.

THE NEW STREAMLINE HAND PUMP and larger pump barrel reduces pumping effort. A longer shot barrel increases muzzle velocity and accuracy. Additional size and weight of grip improves effectiveness.

BENJAMIN TARGET PISTOLS are practical for indoor practice shooting or outdoor sports, at lowest ammunition cost. Shooting force is adjustable depending upon air pressure—with amazing maximum power and accuracy—will penetrate up to ¼" in soft pine. No fouling or cleaning.

EASY TO PUMP while camping or fishing and hunting; or around the house for killing rats or other pests—without noise, smoke or fumes. Five or six pump strokes supply ample power for average use.

Length overall 11 inches. Shot barrel 8 inches long. Patridge type sights; distance between sights is 10 inches. Rear sight is adjustable for elevation and windage. Gun metal finish barrel and butt with genuine walnut stocks and pump handle. Very fine trigger pull 1½ to 3 pounds. Net weight 1¾ pounds.

©   **New Prices and Delivery on Benjamins to be Announced When Ready**

No. 130. BENJAMIN SUPER SINGLE SHOT TARGET PISTOL—smooth bore—for shooting lead or steel air rifle shot and Caliber .177 darts; will group 2" from rest at 10 yards; including one pound Benjamin Lead or Steel Air Rifle Shot. Domestic shipping weight 4 lbs. Price **$9.00**

No. 132. BENJAMIN SUPER SINGLE SHOT TARGET PISTOL—rifled—for shooting Caliber .22 lead pellets which fit tight in rifled grooves, giving maximum power and accuracy; will group 1" from rest at 10 yards; including 500 Caliber .22 BENJAMIN H-C PELLETS. Domestic shipping weight 4 lbs. Price......... **$10.50**

No. 137. BENJAMIN SUPER SINGLE SHOT TARGET PISTOL—rifled—for shooting Caliber .177 lead pellets which fit tight in rifled grooves, giving maximum power and accuracy; will group 1" from rest at 10 yards; including 500 Caliber .177 BENJAMIN H-C PELLETS. Domestic shipping weight 3 lbs. Price......... **$10.50**

No. 160. BENJAMIN SUPER 8-SHOT AIR PISTOL—smooth bore—for shooting steel air rifle shot; will group 2" from rest at 10 yards; including one pound Benjamin Steel Air Rifle Shot. Domestic shipping weight 4 lbs. Price.................................... **$12.00**

SAVAGE COMBINATION RIFLES AND SHOTGUNS

The Savage Arms Corporation has filled herewith a long felt demand for a low priced combination of High powered Rifle and Shotgun for those who cannot spend a great deal of money for more expensive equipment of such design. Construction of these guns is modern and of the best in material and expert workmanship such as the name Savage stands for.

MODEL 219 SINGLE SHOT RIFLE

Calibers .30/30, .32/20, .25/20 and .22 Hornet

Tapered, medium weight, round barrel with raised ramp front sight base, length 26 inches. Proof tested. Barrel and lug forged in one piece. Hammerless action with Automatic Top Tang Safety. Automatic ejector, insuring positive extraction and ejection. Polished and blued frame. Barrel bolted to frame with large beveled locking bolt. Forearm fastens with tension of heavy steel spring against hinge pin and forearm barrel lug. Both features designed to automatically take up wear. Selected American Walnut stock and forearm, full pistol grip stock with fluted comb. Hard rubber butt plate. Sights, adjustable flat top rear sight. Bead front sight. Weight about 6 pounds.

Model 219 ....Price $23.80

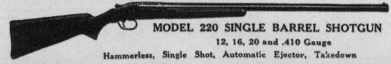

MODEL 220 SINGLE BARREL SHOTGUN

12, 16, 20 and .410 Gauge

Hammerless, Single Shot, Automatic Ejector, Takedown

Barrel made of selected forged gun barrel steel. Proof tested. Barrel and lug forged in one piece. Barrel lengths: 12 gauge, 28, 30, and 32 inch (50 cents extra for 34 and 36 inch); 16 gauge, 28, 30 and 32 inch; 20 gauge, 26, 28, 30 and 32 inch; .410 gauge, 26 and 28 inch. Hammerless action with Automatic Top Tang Safety. All working parts made of long wearing special alloy steel and operated by strong coil springs. Automatic ejector is ½ inch wide, insuring positive extraction and ejection. Frame polished and blued. Barrel bolted to frame with large beveled locking bolt. Forearm fastens with tension of heavy steel spring against hinge pin and forearm barrel lug. Both features designed to automatically take up wear. Walnut stock and forearm, stock full pistol grip and forearm large wide design. Hard rubber butt plate. Weight about 6 lbs.

Model 220 ....Price $17.95

Rifle Barrel

Shotgun Barrel

SAVAGE UTILITY GUN RIFLE and SHOTGUN

Model No.	Rifle-Barrel	Shotgun Barrel		Model No.	Rifle Barrel	Shotgun Barrel	
221	.30/30 caliber	12 gauge	30"	227	.22 Hornet	12 gauge	30"
222	.30/30 caliber	16 gauge	28"	228	.22 Hornet	16 gauge	28"
223	.30/30 caliber	20 gauge	28"	229	.22 Hornet	20 gauge	28"

THE SAVAGE UTILITY GUN is made up of the Model 219 Rifle described below and a shotgun barrel and fore-end carefully fitted to the rifle frame. Packed complete as a single unit, one in a box.

Price $30.85

MODEL 220-P SINGLE BARREL SHOTGUN WITH POLY CHOKE

12, 16 and 20 Gauge

Same specifications as Model 220 above with following extras:

Special Poly Choke built integral with barrel.

Metal Bead front sight.

Special Recoil Pad.

Barrel lengths: 12 ga., 30"; 16 ga., 28"; 20 ga., 28".
The Poly Choke is a device at the muzzle of barrel with finger adjustable sleeve so the shooter can instantly change to any choke desired. Nine distinct adjustments can be obtained from cylinder to full choke.

Price $25.75

© **ORDER BLANK IN MIDDLE AND INDEX IN BACK OF CATALOG**

Remington

MODEL 720. BOLT ACTION HIGH POWERED RIFLE
FOR BIG GAME AND TARGET SHOOTING

Not Available in 1946

CALIBERS
30-06 Springfield
270 Winchester
257 Remington-Roberts

MODEL 720A (With 22" bbl.)

MODEL 720SR (With 24" bbl. and Receiver Sight)

SPECIFICATIONS

Round, tapered barrel of ordnance steel with choice of 24, 22 or 20-inch length. Carefully bored and rifled for extreme accuracy. New style sporting stock of genuine American walnut. Properly shaped pistol grip. Long, full, well rounded fore-end of semi-beavertail type. Fine checkering on grip and fore-end. Shotgun style steel butt plate, checkered to prevent slipping. Swivel loops for 7/8-inch sling strap—loops easily removed, leaving wide screw eyes for quick release swivels. Rifle cocks on opening movement of bolt. Top of receiver matted. Short, snappy, light, single trigger pull—option of double military pull. Side-placed thumb operated safety. Magazine holds five cartridges. Copper bead front sight mounted on matted ramp. Step adjustable sporting rear sight. Receiver tapped and drilled for Redfield, Marble and Lyman micrometer receiver sights. Weight about 8 pounds. Length over-all (No. 720A) 42½".

STYLES AND PRICES

No. 720A (22-inch barrel) open sights $97.40
No. 720AR with Redfield No. 70RST micrometer receiver sight 106.65
No. 720AM with Marble-Goss receiver sight. 110.90
No. 720AL with Lyman No. 48 receiver sight. 115.00
No. 720S (24-inch barrel) open sights 97.40

No. 720SR with Redfield No. 70RST micrometer receiver sight 106.65
No. 720SM with Marble-Goss receiver sight. 110.90
No. 720SL with Lyman No. 48 receiver sight. 115.00
No. 720R (20-inch barrel) open sights 97.40
No. 720RR with Redfield No. 70RST micrometer receiver sight 106.65

No. 720RM with Marble-Goss receiver sight. 110.90
No. 720RL with Lyman No. 48 receiver sight. 115.00
7/8" Leather Sling Strap, Whelen type, extra. 3.40
7/8" Leather Sling Strap, Whelen type, with quick release swivels, extra 5.85

Model 720 gives knockdown wallop for big or medium game.

All-weather reliability in hot, cold, wet, or dry climates.

Sturdy construction for tough going.

Long range accuracy for those thrilling long shots.

THE MODERN BIG GAME RIFLE

WINCHESTER
MODEL 24

DOUBLE-BARREL HAMMERLESS SHOTGUN
STANDARD GRADE. CHAMBERED FOR 2¾" SHELLS. 12, 16 AND 20 GAUGES.

With new modern streamline styling, Model 24 is the latest in standard double-barrel hammerless shotgun design. Built to sell at a very moderate price, a distinct new contribution to the long era of double-barrel hammerless shotgun popularity, it is a remarkable value. A surprisingly nice handling, finely balanced, hard shooting gun, for the shooter who has his heart set on a finely styled double gun yet must buy in the moderate-price bracket. Receiver, barrels and all important parts are made of high-grade steel. There are no castings anywhere. Frame is machined from a solid steel forging, and extra strong. Extra strength is carried out in the action design, combining locking bolt, barrel lug, hinge pin, forearm shoe, and forearm lug. Barrels fit down deep and snugly in the receiver, giving the whole gun breech an especially attractive rounded contour. Locking bolt, barrel lug and hinge pin are wide and sturdy, with large bearing surfaces. Lug fits snugly in a deep recess in the receiver. Bolting is exceptionally strong, simple, dependable. Firing action is exceedingly fast. Barrels are of Winchester selected steel, with matted rib: 12 ga., 30", 28" or 26"; 16 ga. and 20 ga. 28" or 26". Extractors, cam operated, with supplemental spring action. Stock is genuine American walnut, with full-rounded low, streamlined comb and full pistol grip; streamlined to receiver. Dimensions: 14½" x 1½" x 2½", with 2" down pitch. Streamlined semi-beavertail forearm of matching walnut, shaped to the barrels, coming up high at the sides, and accurately fitted. Automatic safety. Take down. Weight approximately 7¼ lbs.

Order by symbol shown below

Symbol	Gauge	Barrel Length	CHOKE Right	Left	Each
G2402B	12	30"	Modified	Full	
G2403B	12	28"	Modified	Full	
G2405B	12	28"	Cylinder	Modified ...	
G2404B	12	26"	Cylinder	Modified ...	$47.95
G2423B	16	28"	Modified	Full	
G2424B	16	26"	Cylinder	Modified ...	
G2443B	20	28"	Modified	Full	
G2444B	20	26"	Cylinder	Modified ...	

WINCHESTER
MODEL 37

STEELBILT SEMI-HAMMERLESS SINGLE SHOTGUN
MADE IN 12, 16, 20 AND 28 GAUGES AND .410-BORE.

To meet the growing demand for a strong, quick-operating single-shot Winchester shotgun, shooting all standard ammunition, at a price comparable to that of an ordinary .22 rim fire rifle, Winchester developed an altogether new gun-building method for the production of its Steelbilt Model 37. This gun is steel in all metal parts. Its frame is of an ingenious new Winchester design—super-strong—with corresponding ingenuity and strength in bolting, lock construction and assembly with the super-strong steel barrel. The all-steel bolting parts and forged barrel lug are doubly large. Action, top-lever breakdown with pivot bolting. Semi-hammerless lock with low safety cocking lever located well forward on tang. Double-action automatic ejection, starts shell extraction by positive mechanical force as gun is opened, and ejects by spring power. Genuine American walnut stock with pistol grip and composition butt plate; dimensions 14" x 1½" x 2¼". Large, full, rounded forearm, same diameter entire length, fits any reach. Winchester proof-marked steel barrel is full choke. Barrel lengths: 12, 16 and 20 gauges. 32", 30" or 28"; 28 gauge, 30" or 28"; 410 gauge, 28" or 26". Chambered for 2¾-inch shells, in 12, 16 and 20 gauges, 2⅞" in 28 gauge and 3" in .410, shooting all standard loads. Single shot. Weight, 12 gauge, 30" barrel, approx. 6½ lbs. Take down.

Order by symbol shown below

Symbol	Gauge	Barrel	Each
G3701S	12	32 inch full choke........	
G3702S	12	30 inch full choke........	
G3703S	12	28 inch full choke........	
G3710S	16	32 inch full choke........	
G3711S	16	30 inch full choke........	
G3712S	16	28 inch full choke........	
G3720S	20	32 inch full choke........	$14.55
G3721S	20	30 inch full choke........	
G3722S	20	28 inch full choke........	
G3731S	28	30 inch full choke........	
G3732S	28	28 inch full choke........	
G3740S	410	28 inch full choke........	
G3741S	410	26 inch full choke........	

STEELBILT—LOW IN PRICE—HARD SHOOTING

THE CARTRIDGE MAKES THE DIFFERENCE

by Wayne van Zwoll

Typically, many avid hunters these days insist on carrying two or even three rifles into the field. The problem is that too often these same people use their rifles as machines, not as tools. A machine works for you. A tool assists you.

In buying rifles chambered for powerful cartridges, then topping them with scopes the size of caulking guns, many hunters get the idea that triggering a shot is all that's required to kill game. This makes about as much sense as hopping in your automobile, shifting into drive, and expecting to end up in Cincinnati. Indeed, a lot of hunters buy rifles to do what they're supposed to do as hunters. But you can't simply turn a rifle on and watch it work. You must manipulate it—like a violin, not a radio. You get the most from any tool or instrument when it's used a lot. And you're more apt to use it often when doing so is fun. A rifle that makes your gums ache and your ears ring is no fun to shoot. Neither is one that denies you the satisfaction of hitting. On the other hand, your bullets must be a match for your quarry, killing quickly no matter what the range or shot angle may be.

The first step in shooting big game, it would seem, lies in the intelligent selection of a rifle. Sometimes when hunters talk about rifles, they mean cartridges, and vice versa. A rifle is a launcher. To one shooter, a ".70 Winchester" may actually be a Winchester rifle; but to another shooter, it's a cartridge, and the rifle may be a Ruger. When someone mentions a .30-06, a modern scoped rifle comes to mind, not a cartridge. We'd all be better off being more specific. Rifles properly go by make and model; cartridge designations are generally by bore or bullet diameter, along with the parent company. Thus, the "Savage Model 110 in 7mm Remington Magnum" is specific; but a "7mm Savage" rifle could as well be chambered for a 7mm Mauser (7x57) cartridge.

When shopping for a hunting rifle, it's a good idea to consider rifle and cartridge separately. The best approach is to choose the cartridge first, then find a rifle that's chambered for it. Enough versatile rounds are on the market nowadays to give you plenty of rifle choices. The ideal whitetail cartridge isn't the best round for moose or even a mule deer, given differences in terrain. Still, the notion that a different rifle is required for each animal is utter nonsense. One well-chosen rifle can serve for whitetail and mule deer, sheep, goats, pronghorns, black bears, elk, moose and even African plains game.

THE .30-06: STILL THE ALL-AROUND BEST
The .30-06 has often been called the best all-around big-game cartridge. Some writers attribute this to the wide range of bullet weights available

Major ammunition firms now make the .30-06 even more versatile by loading "controlled-expansion" bullets for tough game. Federal offers Nosler Partitions as well as Trophy bonded bullets. These .30-06 rounds feature 165-grain Trophy Bondeds.

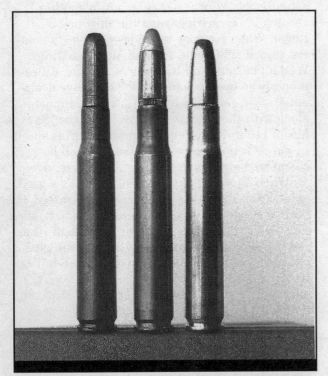

The .30-06 (left), a top all-around big-game cartridge since 1906, was necked up in the 1920s to form the .35 Whelen. It remained a wildcat cartridge until 1988, when Remington took over production. The .338-06 (center) is still used mostly by handloaders. All three are fine choices for deer and elk hunting.

in factory ammunition: 125 to 250 grains. And yet, few shooters vary bullet weights or types in their .30-06s. They've found that one bullet can work well for a variety of game; and by sticking with only one, they don't have to fret over sight changes.

Why shouldn't some other cartridge be as versatile as the .30-06 without the smorgasbord of bullet options? Good question. The versatility of the .30-06 does not derive from a candy store array of 30-caliber bullets. It comes from a combination of tolerable recoil and mid-weight bullets with the proper diameter, velocity and sectional density to kill game big enough to satisfy most hunters. Moreover, it's inherently accurate, easy to handload and, because it served as a military round for many years, it provides access to cheap surplus ammunition. But when all is said and done, the .30-06 continues to shine because it's easy to shoot—and it's deadly.

Topping the list of alternative cartridges are the .270 Winchester, .280 Remington and .35 Whelen, with the .308 Winchester and 7mm-08 Remington heading up the roster in short rifle actions. As for long-range deer cartridges, the .270 and .280 are probably the best ever developed (they're also good for elk in most situations). The fat 250-grain .35 Whelen bullet is hard to beat for

close-cover elk, flying as flat as 180-grain .30-06 bullets at normal hunting ranges and striking only an inch and a half lower at 200 yards. Remington's .350 Magnum offers similar results, but unfortunately it is no longer commercially chambered. Adding the .338-06, as Remington did with the .35 Whelen, should be seriously considered by one of the cartridge companies. The .338-06 can drive a 200-grain bullet about as fast as a

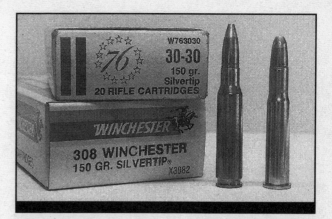

The .308 Winchester, while not much bigger than the .30-30, has a lot more punch. Hornady's "Light Magnum" .308 ammunition equals the down-range performance of many .30-06 loads.

The 7x57 Mauser dates back to 1893 and yet it ranks among the worlds most versatile rounds. Traditionally, it has been throttled to modest performance levels in order to ease the strain on early military actions.

.30-06 can push one in the 180 range.

The .308 and 7mm-08 are essentially short versions of the .30-06 and .280 Remington, with velocity differences amounting to 100 fps or so. The .284 Winchester, with its fat case and rebated rim, is more potent, providing roughly the same powder capacity and performance of the .280. Because .284 ammunition is hard to find, however, few rifles now chamber it. Another cartridge deserving accolades is the 103-year-old 7x57; but this factory round is usually throttled to pressures that won't strain early military actions. Cartridges less potent than the 7x57 are of limited use on game bigger than deer.

Bullet weight and velocity both count when making a hit—but knowing how much is enough depends on many variables. A reasonable minimum for deer-size game would be a 100-grain bullet traveling 2000 fps at impact. That combination offers little more than 900 foot-pounds of energy (for elk, figure on a bullet of 140 grains at the same strike speed producing about 1250 foot-pounds). Using a heavier bullet, of course, can trim velocity and achieve the same punch. Reducing bullet weight as the speed accelerates can also keep energy at that level, but decelerating too far can impede bullet upset. Light bullets can fail to drive through big bones or muscle and are more susceptible to wind deflection.

As a measure of killing power, foot-pounds fail because speed figures so heavily in its calcu-

The 7mm Remington Magnum, introduced in 1962, now rivals the .30-06 in popularity. It outsells the similar .264 Winchester Magnum, partly because its range of bullet weights reaches well beyond the .264, making the 7mm more suitable for elk.

The .25-06 Remington and .257 Weatherby Magnum deliver a lot more energy, but again most of the ballistic advantage is due to high speed. The tough hide, thick muscles and bones that frame a half-ton animal can stop small bullets like windshields eat bugs. Fast, frangible bullets will swat light-boned game to the ground, but 19th-century hunters found high sectional density—essentially, the ratio of bullet length to diameter—crucial for large animals.

Conversely, long, heavy bullets couldn't be launched fast enough. Penetration was sure and deep, though, so when a bullet was well-placed, death came quickly. In Africa, ivory hunters used to bring down elephants with 215-grain bullets fired from British .303 military rifles. And a backwoodsman in British Columbia armed with a .303 Savage once killed 18 animals, including two grizzlies, with a single box of 20 cartridges.

Hunters soon learned that higher speed gave bullets flatter trajectories and more punch at distant targets. Around 1904, in an attempt to boost velocity, the Germans exchanged their 236-grain 8mm military bullet for the new and lighter 154-grain spitzer. This left the muzzle at 2800 fps, thereby achieving a net gain of nearly 700 fps. The U.S. Army took note and switched from a 220-grain bullet in the .30-03 to the 150-grain

lation, at the expense of bullet weight. A 52-grain bullet fired from a .22-250 is ill-suited for elk; still, it develops more foot-pounds of energy than a 190-grain .303 Savage bullet loaded by the same company. Knowledgeable big-game hunters reject both fly-weight bullets at high speed and heavy bullets that leave the muzzle at a shuffle.

While the .243 Winchester, 6mm Remington and .257 Roberts are popular for deer, they don't have enough bullet weight to take elk effectively.

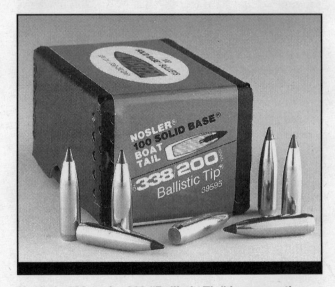

Nosler's 200-grain .338 "Ballistic Tip" is among the author's top bullet choices for the .338-06. It also excels as an open-country bullet for the .338 Winchester Magnum.

These Swift A-Frame 30-caliber Spitzer bullets, which are loaded by Remington, are similar in design to Nosler Partitions.

.30-06 load. Earlier, Charles Newton and other experimenters had worked hard to increase the speed of bullets in sporting cartridges, leading to Savage's .250-3000 ("3000" designating the velocity of its 87-grain bullet).

THE APPEAL OF MAGNUMS

High speed meant light weight until the 1940s, when Roy Weatherby came up with the first of his belted magnum cartridges. Since then, magnums have appealed to hunters who stalk big game at great distances. Weatherby's, incidentally, was a headspacing device, a "stop" that kept the case from entering the chamber too far. The rims found on contemporary .30-30 cases, along with the shoulders on rimless rounds like the .30-06, serve the same purpose.

Belted magnums were derived from the famous British .375 Holland and Holland round, introduced in 1912. "Short" magnums are designed to work through standard actions (.375, .300 Weatherby and other full-length magnums are too long). Hawked aggressively by their developer, Weatherby Magnums got lots of pub-

licity; but because they were proprietary rounds—i.e., chambered only in Weatherby rifles—sales grew slowly. Then, in 1956, Winchester announced its .458 Magnum, the first in a series of short magnums, followed shortly by the .264 and .338 Winchester Magnums. Remington unveiled its 7mm Magnum in 1962, and a year later Winchester countered with its .300, both rounds becoming hugely popular. In fact, the 7mm Remington Magnum now rivals the .30-06 in popularity.

Not long ago, Winchester and Remington added a few Weatherby chamberings to their Model 70 and 700 rifles. Both firms, as well as Federal Cartridge, now manufacture Weatherby ammunition. The .270 and 7mm Weatherby Magnums are loaded by Norma to performance levels not quite matched by the .264 Winchester and 7mm Remington, though case capacities are close. Because they can accommodate heavier bullets, the 7mms have a slight edge over the .264 and .270 magnums.

Perhaps the most versatile big-game cartridges fall in the magnum 30 category, i.e., the

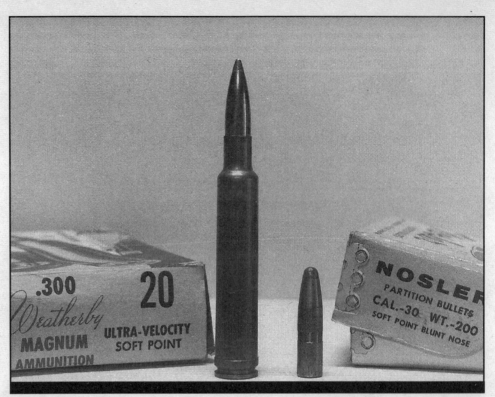

Weatherby's .300 Magnum carries more muscle than any 30-caliber cartridge. It ranks among the best long-range elk rounds.

.300 Holland and Holland, .308 Norma and .300 Winchester. The .300 H&H, a 1925 derivative of the .375, requires long actions and is chambered in only a few rifles. The .308 Norma and .300 Winchester offer slightly more power and recoil in shorter cases. The Winchester is more popular because it is widely chambered with factory loads available from U.S. companies. The most potent of all— the Weatherby .300 — reaches far and kicks hard.

Some shooters who favor powerful cartridges insist they are good insurance against bad bullet placement. But consider this: a hunter who cripples a buck with a .300 Weatherby has just fired 4,350 foot-pounds of energy downrange, nearly three times that expended by a .303 Savage. The wound from the Weatherby was indeed severe, but this hypothetical deer traveled over a mile from where it had been shot before a fortuitous sighting enabled another hunter to bag the injured animal.

Powerful rifles do help with long shots, when greater bullet weight and speed reduce the effects of wind and gravity. They also offer deeper penetration up close, enabling quartering shots to be taken with confidence. But an animal that is hit in the leg or paunch by bullets from magnums can still escape. The bottom line is, these magnums simply enable incompetent people to injure game at greater distances. The fault is not mechanical—it's human. Magnums do offer more energy, but that extra energy must be properly directed. Moreover, hunters don't enjoy the pounding that magnums dish out, so they practice as little as possible. Consequently, they're poor marksmen.

Recently this writer watched a hunter with a .30-06 ease up behind a bush and shoot a bull elk squarely through both lungs at 200 yards. The elk died instantly. Later, a fellow with a magnum shot a bull at about the same distance, breaking the spine quite far back. He emptied his rifle at the downed animal without a hit. Still another hunter missed an elk at about 150 yards, then clipped the animal on the run and fired nearly a box of cartridges at the poor struggling beast before killing it at long range with his magnum. In short, magnums are deadly only when used by

skilled marksmen.

Another thing to keep in mind when choosing a cartridge is that, in most cases, bullets in the middle of the weight range perform most efficiently. For example, a .264 Winchester Magnum with 160-grain bullets in 6.5mm (.264) diameter can launch the same mass as a 7mm Remington Magnum. But a 160-grain bullet is in the *middle* of the 7mm weight range, not at the top. Handloaders aren't likely to experience erratic pressures, and the hunter will be able to drive the 7mm bullet faster with lower pressure, even though the case capacity is almost identical. Mid-

weight bullets usually afford the best combination of sectional density, velocity and accuracy.

Choosing a bullet is increasingly more difficult because so many good ones are available. It's a good idea to pick a narrow weight range and bullet type, then test several loads for accuracy. And it's not necessary to be a handloader to acquire good bullets. Federal, Remington and Winchester cartridges have marketed effective deer bullets for decades, and now all three firms offer "controlled-expansion" bullets for tough game like elk. Federal loads Trophy Bonded and Nosler; Remington offers Swifts; and Winchester

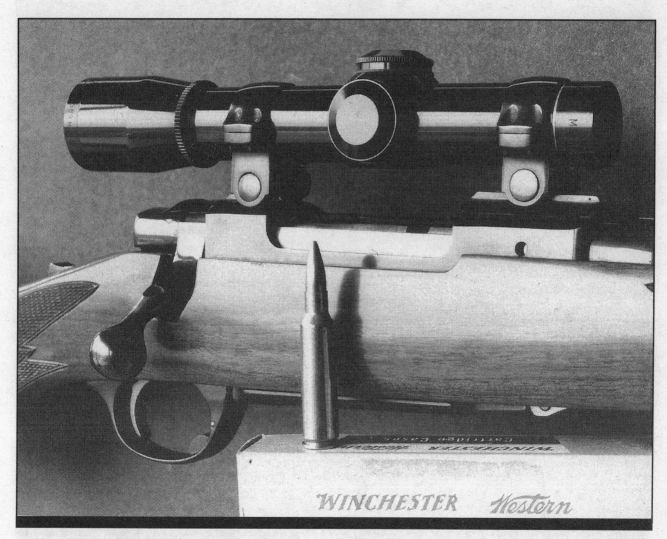

This short-action Ruger 77, chambered in .250 Savage, is topped by a Leupold 2.5x Compact scope. This combination is ideal for deer hunting in close cover.

Compromise dictates proper barrel length and rifle weight. The 22-inch barrel on this 8.5 pound rifle makes it easy to carry and quick to point.

sells its Fail Safe. True, handloaders have more options, including Elkhorn, Blue Mountain, Plainsbond, Hawk and Jensen. But factory ammunition featuring bullets once used by handloaders only has drawn applause from elk hunters everywhere. Some don't shoot as accurately, however, as standard softnose bullets.

A bullet designer for one of the major firms states that his company's top seller is *not* the most accurate bullet, nor was it designed to be. Its behavior in game was so good, though, that both the company and its customers were pleased. Minute-of-angle accuracy is not required to shoot big game. Groups twice that size mean your bullets won't wander outside a deer's vitals until that deer is 500 yards away! That's at least 100 yards farther than most hunters can hold their crosswire inside a tractor tire from a hunting position.

Finally, when testing a rifle, try several factory loads before going to the loading bench. A rifle that shoots well with handloads generally will shine with at least one factory load. It's also a good idea to try cartridges from less-known firms, such as PMC and Hansen. Hornady's "Light Magnum" series also offers a substantial ballistic edge.

IS THE BOLT-ACTION RIFLE FOR YOU?

Cartridges and bullets may generate more debate than do rifles, but the rifle is just as important because it helps direct bullets to an animal's vitals. In the West, where bolt guns outnumber all others by a huge margin, action-type rifles are hardly a consideration. Even in the East — where lever-actions, pumps and autoloaders provide quick second chances at whitetails — the bolt rifle has made great gains. That's true partly because almost everyone hunts with a scope these days. Hunters seem to think they must be prepared to shoot far away. On average, bolt-action rifles are more rugged and accurate; they're also more forgiving of handloads that don't quite meet factory specs.

Trigger. Another advantage shared by some bolt-action shooters is a finely adjustable trigger. Triggers on other repeating rifles can't be as closely fitted. Sadly, the threat of lawsuits by people who don't know how to use rifles has prompted the development of attorney-proof triggers on

rifles that would be exceedingly more effective with a crisp 3-pound trigger pull. Yanking the trigger used to be a fault in form; increasingly, it's become a requisite for releasing the sear. Without an acceptable trigger pull, accuracy must suffer; after all, half of a rifle's accuracy is built into its barrel, action and bedding—what you might call intrinsic accuracy. The other half—called "woods accuracy" by some—is derived from stock fit, balance and trigger pull. An accurate barrel is of little use if the stock doesn't fit or the trigger pull is off. So, when buying a rifle, have the trigger adjusted to your satisfaction; or contact a reputable trigger manufacturer about installing an adjustable trigger.

Barrel. A barrel is harder to replace; moreover, there's no way to test one without shooting several types of ammunition. Fortunately, the barrels found on modern sporting rifles are, almost without exception, more than accurate enough for big-game hunting. For target shooters who like to drill prairie dogs at 300 steps, a custom barrel may be worth the extra expense. One major U.S. rifle manufacturer buys barrels from its supplier for about $20 apiece. They may not be match grade, but they've sent bullets into lots of deer and elk.

While a barrel's accuracy can't be predicted, its length and weight can be specified. Most barrels on hunting rifles range in length from 22 to 26 inches. Carbine barrels of 18 and 20 inches are handy, but they increase muzzle blast and reduce bullet speed. Barrels of 24 and 25 inches are preferable on most rifles, partly because they're a little muzzle-heavy and hold steadier. For example, compare the stability of an old muzzleloading rifle with that of a modern carbine. Muzzle brakes that are installed to reduce recoil may add ballast, but they offer no extra velocity because the gas leaves the bullet base as soon as it's free of the barrel. In addition to increasing overall rifle length, brakes boost enough muzzle blast to damage unprotected ears.

Balance. Balance depends on a barrel's weight and contour, not just its length. Barrel blanks for sporting rifles are numbered 1 through 4, with 1 being the lightest. Most commercial big-game rifles wear No. 3 barrels, though a few are contoured from No. 4 blanks. Many hunters choose a standard-weight Ruger,

Nikon's 3-9x variable is the most popular and reasonably priced big-game scope. This one is mounted in Conetrol rings on a Remington 700 with synthetic stock.

Remington or Winchester rifle over the Ultra Light, Mountain and Featherweight models with their short, light barrels. True, it's harder to carry a heavier rifle for several miles just to make one shot; but once that shot is made, the hunt is over.

Rifles have been getting lighter in general because hunters want whatever it takes to make hunting more comfortable. The proliferation of carrying straps as wide as hammocks also indicates that an easy day on the trail matters more than an accurate shot. But for serious hunting, a 7.5-pound rifle with scope, shooting sling and a full magazine is about right for most hunting.

Stock. Since rifle stocks are built for average people, they're not likely to fit anyone to perfection. Surprisingly, though, most modern stocks are comfortable. So when shopping, don't be too concerned about measurements. Rather, bring the preferred rifle to your shoulder as you would in the field. Aim with it from different positions. Hang it on your shoulder. Cradle it. Swing it into action quickly from the carry. Now lay it on the counter, close your eyes, then pick it up, cheek it, and open your eyes.

Are the sights lined up? Is the scope field centered and full? Comb dimensions determine eye placement. Find a rifle with a stock that puts your eye where you want it without making you work. If a powerful cartridge has been selected, pay attention to where the bolt handle falls in relation to the trigger finger. How close does the thumb knuckle come to your nose during recoil?

Regarding stock material, synthetic stocks have become more popular with hunters who imagine themselves trudging through a snowstorm on Bighorn Mountain with a great ram's head on the packboard, blood on the rifle and facing a nine-mile hike back to the tent. In truth, walnut stocks have endured these conditions, and worse, for centuries. They're not as stable or durable as synthetics, but for most hunters they're good enough.

Grip. A grip that pleases one hunter probably won't please another. Those with large hands want a grip more like that found on a fine upland shotgun than that of a competition rifle. True, grips can be changed by sanding; but getting a

grip that feels good is trickier than it may appear. Moreover, unless you're a skilled woodworker, you'll end up with an ugly rifle. It's best to look at lots of rifles and find one with a grip that is suitable as is. Grips used to vary significantly within any given model, but stock-shaping is done almost entirely by machine now, and differences between stocks for the same rifle have become minimal.

Scope. Ounces pared from rifle barrels and stocks have been replaced by optics. Fat, powerful scopes have become the rage, their pie-plate objective lenses promising brighter sight pictures in poor light. Variables have all but buried fixed-power scopes. But adding weight and bulk to the top of a rifle at the expense of barrel weight is nonsense. A 3x or 4x scope works fine for most hunters, while a 6x is preferable for pronghorns and other creatures that are usually shot at long range. As for variables, it's hard to beat a 1.5-6x or 2-7x scope. In any event, there are plenty of useful scopes around that weigh less than 12 ounces.

Big objective lenses increase the diameter of

Practice, not cartridge size, makes a skilled marksman. Here the author brushes up on his offhand shooting with a Springfield rifle in .30-06 Improved. Inset: It's a good idea to shoot at both short and long ranges. This group, while it looks loose, is really quite good for a sporting rifle at 250 yards (less than a minute of angle).

Among variable scopes with modest power, this Leupold Vari-X III, 1.75-6x, is a popular choice. It's light in weight and compact enough to mount low.

the exit pupil, which is the pencil of light one sees in a lens when the scope is held at arm's length. To determine this diameter (in millimeters), divide the objective lens diameter by the magnification. Thus, a 6x scope with a 42mm objective has an exit pupil of 7mm, or about as much light as the human eye can use in total darkness. In bright light, of course, a much smaller exit pupil is sufficient. Oversize objective lenses only pay their way when one aims at high magnification in very poor light. A standard 3-9x scope with a 40mm objective provides enough exit pupil needed up to about 6x, which is normally all the magnification a hunter will need.

Also, because small scopes are lighter in weight and can be mounted lower, they don't impair rifle balance like some big scopes. They make it easier to stow a rifle in a case or scabbard, and they're less susceptible to knocks. And, because they lie tight to the rifle, light scopes allow the hunter to aim faster.

Someone once wrote that a Winchester Model 70 or Remington 721 .30-06 rifle with a 4x scope was probably the most versatile big-game gun for hunting in North America. Since then, a lot of people have written and talked about other cartridges and other scopes, and about exotic rifles built of materials that weren't even on the market a few years ago. Now the 721 has been

replaced by the 700 and Savage and Ruger are offering bolt rifles. Better bullets and wider selection of cartridges are available. And yet, that writer's observation rings as true now as it did on the heels of World War II.

The only thing the writer didn't mention was practice. In a day when rifles were accepted even by people who didn't shoot, perhaps nobody needed this reminder. Sadly, such is not the case today. Our rifles, ammunition and optics are better than ever, but few marksmen are practiced enough to take advantage of them. Remember, the most deadly big-game rifle is the one that sits on the shoulder of a skilled marksman.

WAYNE VAN ZWOLL is a writer known for his expertise on big-game hunting and the technical aspects of shooting. He has written for most of the major sporting magazines, including Field & Stream, Sports Afield, *and* Rifle and Bugle. *He has authored three books:* Mastering Mule Deer *(1988, North American Hunting Club),* Americas's Great Gunmakers, *(1992, Stoeger Publishing) and* Elk Rifles, Cartridges and Hunting Tactics *(1993). Van Zwoll has been a wildlife agent with the Washington State Dept. of Game and a field director for the Rocky Mountain Elk Foundation. He has also served as editor of* Kansas Wildlife *magazine.*

The only autoloader that softens the blow

here...

and here.

The Soft Shooting System™ that handles target loads to 3″ Mags without ever changing barrels.

Now, one autoloader can cover every shot-gunner's game. When the season changes, you only change chokes, not barrels. Mossberg's exclusive gas compensation system is the key. Its simple, yet rugged, design vents excess pressure while operating the action. The result is a substantial reduction in recoil without any reduction in reliability. You'll also like the reduction in cost compared to other autoloaders.

A. gas from barrel
B. action movement
C. vents excess gas

Camo, Slugs and Combos make the Model 9200 the most versatile autoloader.

Mossy Oak® Treestand, new Realtree® All Purpose Gray and affordable OFM Woodland… turkey hunters and water-fowlers can find a Model 9200 for the cover they hunt. Slug hunters enjoy less recoil and still get all of the accuracy of a scope mounted, fully rifled barrel with the Trophy Slugster™ version. With both a 28″ vent rib barrel and a 24″ rifled slug barrel, the Model 9200 Combo is Mossberg's best deal.

Even the new, more affordable Viking Grade™ Model 9200 has a Lifetime Limited Warranty.

The new Viking Grade™ Model 9200 delivers soft shooting, gas operated performance in an even more attractively priced model. Outfitted with a rugged, good looking Moss green synthetic stock and a Mil-Spec Parkerized barrel, the Viking Grade Model 9200 is loaded with Mossberg Value. Just like every other Model 9200, it's backed by Mossberg's Lifetime Limited Warranty.

MOSSBERG

LIFETIME WARRANTY 9200

NEW! Viking Grade™ Model 9200 Autoloader

O.F. Mossberg & Sons, Inc. • 7 Grasso Avenue • P.O. Box 497 • North Haven, CT 06473-9844

© 1996, O.F. Mossberg & Sons, Inc.

Safety and safe firearms handling is everyone's responsibility.

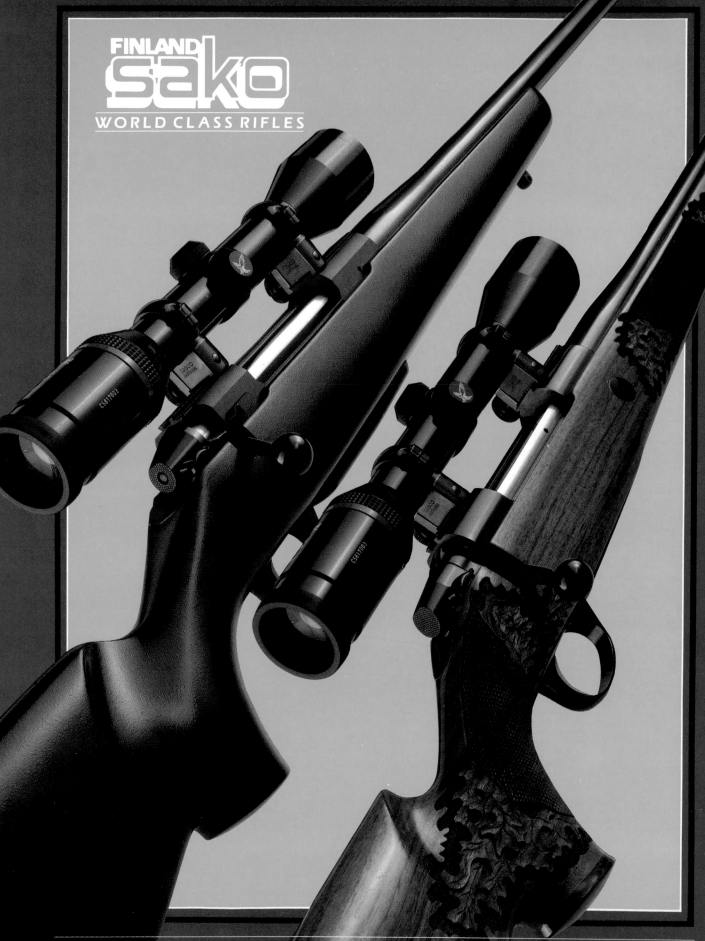

FINLAND SAKO
WORLD CLASS RIFLES

COMMITMENT TO EXCELLENCE—A SAKO TRADITION

When you have to be quick, you need a gun that won't slow you down.

Beretta Field Grades: the fastest over-and-unders you can own.

Silver Pigeon

S686 Onyx

S686 Essential

It happens in an instant: an explosion of sound and color and more speed than you're ready for. And yet, you *are* ready for it. You swing, mount and fire in one smooth, continuous motion, as though

the Beretta Field Grade in your hands is actually a part of you.

It's a sensation Beretta shooters never tire of...the result of over a century of refining the Beretta Over-and-Unders into the world's finest – and fastest – production shotguns.

This is a gun that's built for speed. Its low profile, special steel alloy closed receiver and chrome-nickel-moly

tri-alloy steel barrels provide remarkable strength without burdensome bulk. Its compact fore-end design contributes to proper hand-eye alignment, near-perfect balance and lighter weight.

Yet, this is also a gun that's built to last. Beretta's dual conical locking lugs adjust automatically, and our bores are hard-chromed for maximum strength and corrosion-resistance. So your Beretta Field Grade will keep locking snugly and firing dependably year after year.

Beretta Field Grades: you'll never know how fast you can be until you try one. See your authorized Beretta dealer, or contact Beretta U.S.A. Corp., 17601 Beretta Dr., Accokeek, MD 20607, (301) 283-2191.

Beretta

A tradition of excellence since 1526.

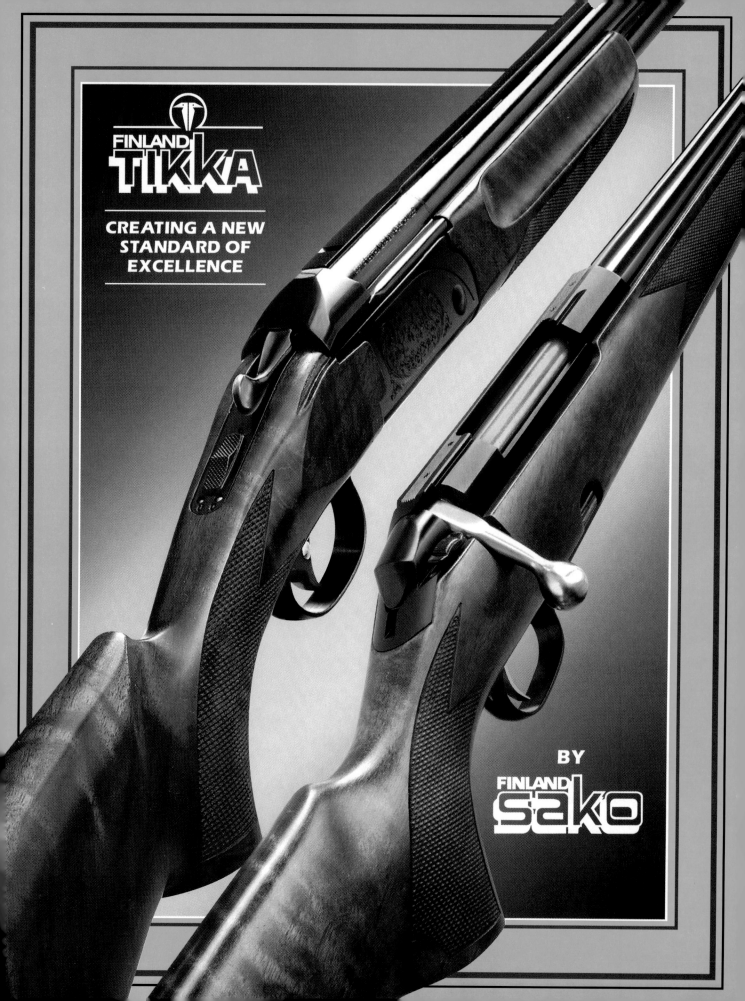

THE FORGOTTEN WALTHERS

by Gene Gangarosa Jr.

The Carl Walther Waffenfabrik of Germany ranks among the most famous firearms firms in the world. Today its Models PP, PPK and P38 handguns are known and respected worldwide. But long before their appearance in the 1920s and 1930s, Walther was already acquiring an international reputation with two earlier pistols: the Models 4 and 5. These were the guns that put Walther on the map as a global leader in handgun manufacture.

The pre-World War I history of Walther's handgun development and production that led to Models 4 and 5 is confusing, partly because the company factory records were lost in 1945. We do know that Carl Walther (1858–1915) founded his factory as the Venuswaffenwerke as early as 1886. The original manufacturing by Walther and a handful of employees was limited to hunting and target rifles and a few shotguns. Nevertheless, the factory prospered and quickly gained an enviable reputation for making arms of high quality.

From the beginning of the company's experimentation with handguns, Carl Walther's son, Fritz (1889-1966), provided most of the company's expertise in pistol design. During the early 1900s, the success of several new automatic pistols, particularly the pocket models made by John Browning for Fabrique Nationale of Belgium,

aroused interest at the Walther plant. By 1908, the Walther plant had developed two pistols: a .32 ACP (7.65mm) medium-frame model and a .25 ACP (6.35mm) pocket pistol. Both used the calibers developed by John Browning and the engineers at Fabrique Nationale. Even at that early date, these calibers were considered world standards in small pistol ammunition.

The first Walther pistol to reach production status was the .25-caliber model—later called the Model 1—which probably went into production in 1910. It proved reasonably successful, with some 30,000 produced over a five-year period. But the Walthers, dissatisfied with the gun's complicated construction, began a major simplification process almost immediately. This redesign led to the Models 2, 3 and 4. The .25-caliber Model 2, a smaller version of the Model 3, appeared around 1914. The .32-caliber Models 3 and 4 went into production sometime during the 1913–14 period. The six-shot Model 3, which was intended as a concealment pistol, packed a powerful cartridge for its small size. The holster-sized Model 4 was identical to the Model 3, but its deeper frame held a larger eight-shot magazine, a longer barrel and matching barrel extension.

Construction of the Models 2, 3 and 4 featured a recoil spring placed around, rather than underneath, the barrel. The spring was secured by a

bushing, an arrangement similar to that of the John Browning-designed FN Model 1910. What influence, if any, the FN design had on Walther's efforts remains unclear. The sticking point appears to be the date of each pistol's introduction. The FN Model 1910, although patented in 1909, did not go into full production until 1912. Sales of FN's Model 1900 pistol were still so strong that the company hesitated to introduce a competing product until it was absolutely necessary.

The official Walther history claims that the Models 3 and 4 appeared in 1910; the evidence now suggests, however, that the FN pistol appeared at least a year before the Walther designs. If so, and even supposing Walther copied from FN, the Belgian company returned the favor in 1922 when it created the Model 1922 pistol. This new gun was derived from the Model 1910 exactly the same way Walther had created the Model 4—by enlarging the Model 3. One noteworthy difference between the Walther and FN designs is that the Walther Models 2, 3, 4 and 5 all used a concealed hammer, whereas the FN Model 1910 employed a striker. Another differ-ence involved the safety arrangements on the Walther models, which were quite different from the FN pistols.

THE MODEL 4 COMES INTO ITS OWN

By the beginning of World War I in 1914, the Models 2, 3 and 4 were well on their way to becoming commercial successes. The Walther company then employed 75 people, working with 50 powered machines. The Model 4 was especially successful, having become a top police pistol in Germany before and during the war. It had also made company history by receiving the first large-scale German government order when, in May 1915, the Prussian government ordered 250,000 Model 4s for its armed forces. Walther's pistol quickly became popular among soldiers who did not want or need a full-sized handgun (such as the Luger Parabellum P 08). Judging by the serial numbers, as many as 275,000 Model 4s may have served in the wartime German army.

So successful was the Model 4 that Walther outgrew its original factory in an attempt to produce enough pistols to satisfy the demand. Shortly after the war began, the Walther compa-

Walther's Model 4 (center) was appreciably smaller than its World War II-era P. 38 (top), but larger than the Model 5 pocket pistol (bottom).

ny sold its Venuswerke and moved to a new factory, the Carl Walther Waffenfabrik. This facility remained the center of all Walther manufacture until 1945.

The year 1915 was crucial for the Walther family and company, for Carl Walther, founder of the firm and its driving force, died that year. Fortunately, three of his five sons continued the firearms business, with the eldest son, Fritz, taking over the day-to-day management of the operation. He also continued to design new firearms, notably pistols, for the German war effort.

THE MODEL 5 AND THE POSTWAR ERA

The Model 5, which was simply an improved and simplified Model 2, appeared around 1915. This small, .25-caliber, seven-shot pistol was highly popular as a concealment pistol among German soldiers. The Model 5 also served as the basis for the Model 7, which featured a deeper frame and extended barrel. In the absence of detailed factory records (destroyed in 1945), exact numbers of a particular model built are impossible to determine with absolute certainty. However, firearms researcher James Stewart, after carefully examin-

ing large numbers of surviving pistols, reconstructed a likely serial number progression for Walther handguns up to 1945. He estimates that combined production of Models 4, 5 and 7 during the WW I years approached 356,000 pistols. Certainly the Walther factory grew tremendously during that period in response to government orders for its handguns. By 1918 more than 500 people worked with 750 machines in the new and larger plant.

This all changed after the Armistice was signed in November. Walther continued production for a brief time before it was forced to close its doors in 1919. Production resumed in 1920, with only the Model 4 used primarily by the police and possibly a few civilians. Remarkably long-lived, it remained in production until 1929, at which time the more advanced Model PP supplanted it. Of similar size, caliber and ammunition capacity, the Model PP featured a much more sophisticated firing mechanism, including a double-action trigger. By 1920s' standards, though, the Model 4 was well suited for police work, thus encouraging Walther to continue to manufacture it until the more advanced PP and

The extent to which FN's Model 1910 (top) influenced the design of Walther's Model 4 (bottom) is open to dispute, but the similarities in mechanical characteristics, size, shape and operational features are considerable.

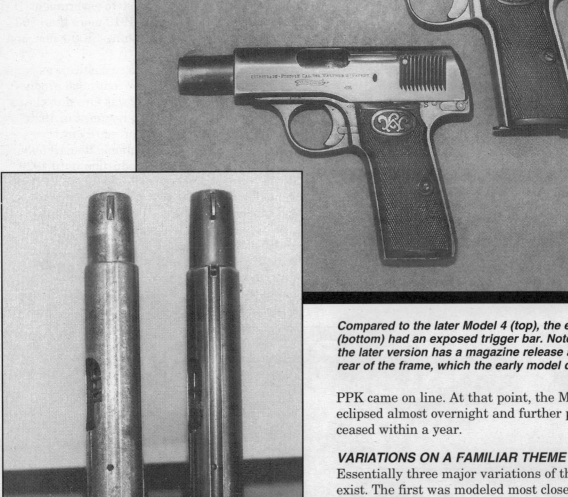

Compared to the later Model 4 (top), the early Model 4 (bottom) had an exposed trigger bar. Note also that the later version has a magazine release at the bottom rear of the frame, which the early model does not.

The earlier Model 4 lacked a separate raised rear sight (right), which later Model 4s (left) included. Note also that the early Model 4 uses a different method for attaching the barrel extension.

PPK came on line. At that point, the Model 4 was eclipsed almost overnight and further production ceased within a year.

VARIATIONS ON A FAMILIAR THEME

Essentially three major variations of the Model 4 exist. The first was modeled most closely after the Model 3. This first variation had no rear sight; instead, a groove that ran along the top of the slide offered a view of the ramped front sight. This same Model 4 variant also featured a Model 3-type release catch on the right front portion of the slide for removal of the barrel extension. The trigger bar, which connected the trigger to the sear, was exposed on the left side of the trigger.

The second variation of the Model 4 had a small rear sight, a rounded hemispherical front sight, and no external release for the barrel extension. Like the first variation, this Model 4 had an exposed trigger bar and a company

address on the slide—*Zella-St. Basil*—indicating that production took place prior to 1919.

The third variation featured slide serrations that were finer and closer together than those found on the two earlier variations, plus a return to the ramped front sight and no exposed trigger bar. The company address on the slide was *Zella-Mehlis*, indicating manufacture took place from 1919 on.

The Model 5 resumed production from 1920 until about 1923, at which time the new Walther Models 8 and 9 replaced it. During the postwar period, the Model 5 was sold primarily to civilians and possibly some high-ranking officers as well. Postwar Model 5 production (according to James Stewart's analysis of serial numbers) consisted of approximately 10,000 pistols. This was doubtless a much smaller number than had been produced during the war years.

The Model 5 was available in two major varia-

tions. The first had coarse slide serrations, eight on each side of the slide, with the Carl Walther name and pre-1919 address—*Zella St. Basil*—appearing on the right side of the slide. The second variation, which was produced from 1919 on, also had slide serrations, but they were much finer and closer together than those found on the earlier variation. The slide was now marked in large letters: *WAFFENFABRIK WALTHER ZELLA-MEHLIS*.

The direct influences of the Models 4 and 5 on later Walther pistols were limited, at least from a design standpoint. Virtually none of the construction techniques or methods used in the Models 4 and 5 appear in Walther pistols made after the late 1920s. What does remain is their high quality, sleek lines and rugged functionality. The tactical niches filled by the Models 4 and 5 are today supplied by more advanced Walther designs, principally in the small service pistol category.

Walther's Model 4 is capable of producing good accuracy. This rapid-fire offhand group fired from a distance of 25 feet measures only 1¹⁄₂ inches across.

In 1929 the similar but much more advanced Model PP (top) replaced the Model 4 (bottom) in the Walther lineup.

THE OLD VS. THE NEW

How do the "forgotten Walthers" perform today? Any fair evaluation of the handling and shooting characteristics of these two pistols must allow for the fact that they are extremely old. Even the most recent examples are approaching their 70th year. Despite this, the guns hold up remarkably well, being well-made and having many positive qualities with only a few negative traits. Indeed, the Model 4 in particular handles reasonably well even by modern standards. It's handy, light in weight (20 oz. fully loaded) and has clean, simple lines that make it unlikely to snag on the

draw. These characteristics combine to make the Model 4 easy to carry and point well. At distances up to 50 feet, it produces acceptable accuracy. Two test pistols examined recently by this writer proved completely reliable with military full-metal-jacket (ball) ammunition; jams occurred only on rare occasions with modern hollowpoint ammunition.

Less welcome characteristics of the Model 4 include undersized sights, a fairly difficult trigger pull, and surprisingly brisk recoil for such a low-powered gun. Also, operation of the manual safety once the gun has been cocked leaves some-

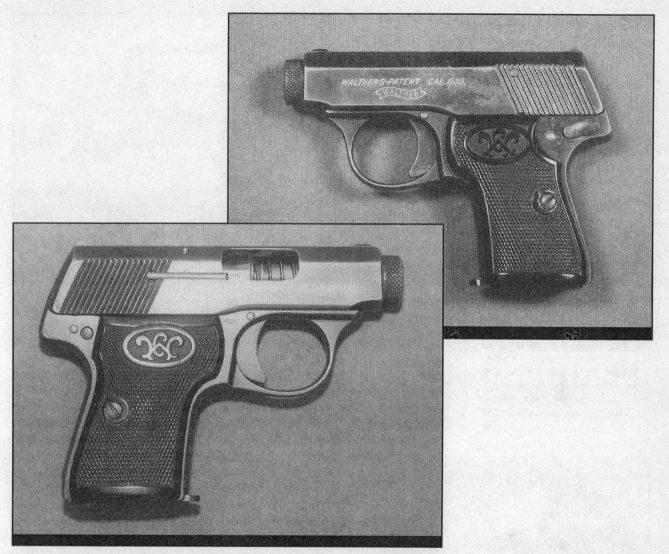

On this Model 5, the 6,35mm (.25 ACP) caliber marking appears on the left side of the slide (top right). Occasionally a portion of the recoil spring on the Model 5 can be seen exposed in the ejection port (bottom). Note also the magazine release in the heel position of the frame, as on other handguns of European design.

thing to be desired. Located at the left rear of the frame, the Model 4's safety catch must be moved up and back (covering the letter F) before the gun will fire, an awkward motion even for a right-handed shooter. As single-action designs, both the Models 4 and 5 must be cocked manually by the shooter before firing the first shot.

The Model 5 proved less capable as a shooting tool compared to the Model 4—no surprise. Its design was, after all, made as small in size as

possible for optimum concealability. Making an automatic pistol that small usually leads to a reduction in functional reliability, which test-firing affirmed. The pistol tested for this article displayed repeated tendencies to jam; on the other hand, it also proved acceptably accurate at short ranges and was easy to carry and point.

There's no questioning the fact that the Models 4 and 5 were extremely important to the early success of the Carl Walther company. They

The Model 5 (bottom) is an extremely compact pocket pistol. Note how the modern Intratec Pro-Tec (top), which is not a large gun by any means, seems to dwarf the Model 5.

The Model 5 can produce acceptable accuracy at point-blank distances, which is vital for a pocket pistol. This rapid-fire offhand group, spanning 1.4 inches, was shot from a distance of 10 feet.

established this famous manufacturer firmly in the handgun business and, in doing so, helped create a climate in which all future Walther pistols could flourish and become known throughout the world.

GENE GANGAROSA JR. is a teacher and technical writer who lives in Florida with his wife and two children. His long association with, and fascination for, handguns began in the U.S. Navy (1977–1981) as a helicopter rescue crewman operating in the Pacific and Indian Oceans. Since 1988, he has written more than 100 articles about firearms for such publications as Guns, Gun World, Combat Handguns, Pocket Pistol Handbook, Sportsman's Gun Annual *and* Handgun Testfire. *This is Gangarosa's first appearance in* SHOOTER'S BIBLE. *His new* Encyclopedia of Handguns *is soon to be published by Stoeger Pub. Co. His two earlier books — P38 Automatic Pistol: The First 50 Years (1993) and Modern Beretta Firearms (1994) — were also published by Stoeger.*

INDIAN RIFLES:
PRACTICAL AND PERSONAL

by R. Stephen Irwin, M.D.

Before the Europeans arrived, the Native American hunter relied on the spear and the bow and arrow. Generally, bows of the Western Plains tribes were shorter so they could be used more easily from horseback. The stone-tipped spears naturally had greater antiquity than the bows. Their effectiveness as weapons was greatly enhanced by the invention of the spear thrower, or *atlatl*. Essentially a wooden handle with a bone-tipped projection on the ends, the atlatl was retained in the hand as the spear was thrown. This clever device increased the velocity and range of the spear by effectively lengthening the casting arc of the thrower's arm.

During the mid-17th century when European firearms were introduced, Indian reliance on "stone-age" weapons ended. In 1660 some French fur traders rebelled against the French-Canadian government and pledged their allegiance to England. A London-financed expedition to Hudson Bay ensued, bringing in a huge cargo of furs, whereupon King Louis XIV ordered the Hudson's Bay Company to commence trade with the natives. At the time, steel traps, knives, pots, axes, food and whiskey were all standard fare when trading with Indians for furs. And, while few early examples still exist, guns and ammunition were also traded by the thousands to the Indians.

The standard Hudson's Bay Company trade gun was a muzzleloading, smoothbore flintlock that could handle either shot or ball. The company hired up to 16 gunsmiths at a time to produce these guns according to a pattern supplied by the company. Upon delivery, the company's "gunviewer" inspected the arms and gave them a company proof, or viewer's mark, as a seal of approval. The gun viewers may have used their own marks to indicate that the guns had been inspected, or their marks may have been used together with a company mark. Not enough early Hudson's Bay Company guns have been found with these identifiable marks to clarify this point. At any rate, later Hudson's Bay Company gun marks were standardized in the form of a sitting fox depicted above the initials "HB" on the barrel. This system of purchasing trade guns remained unchanged almost throughout the history of the company.

By 1761, trade guns of the Hudson's Bay Company had evolved into a definite and recognizable style known throughout the area as the "North West Gun." Made in .50 and .60 caliber, they featured large, over-sized trigger guards, and an octagonal breech (although the mid-section of the barrel and the muzzle were round). About 1748, the sideplate, located on the opposite side of the stock from the lock mechanism, began sporting a dragon or sea serpent design. Made of

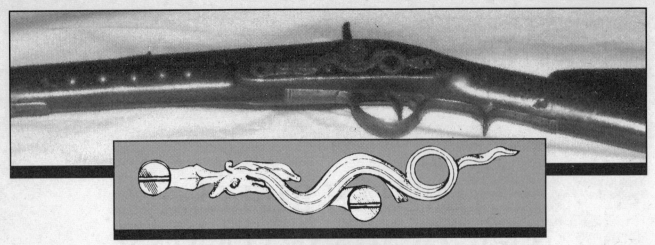

This early example of the dragon, or sea serpent, design (inset) was found on the sideplates of many North West Guns. Accepted as a mark of authenticity, the serpent was believed to hold special powers according to the Indians. The North West Gun shown here with its serpent sideplate may have belonged to a band led by Chief Joseph.

brass, this attractive decoration became not only the trademark but the distinguishing feature of the North West Gun. The design has no known significance, but similar animals had embellished European armament for years. Once the serpent sideplate had appeared on a few shipments of trade guns, it was accepted as a mark of authenticity, even though it was eventually copied by many different gunmakers. Nonetheless, the Indians attributed special powers to the serpent sideplate and insisted on it.

Recent excavations of 17th-century sites in upper New York State have shed interesting information on how the North West Guns influenced the everyday life of the local Indians during that period. Locks, having been detached from the guns, were found in a number of graves. Strike-a-lights, thought to be an important item for use in the after-life, were also commonly found, but never in graves containing one of the detached flintlock mechanisms. Indeed, these mechanisms may have been valued more as fire-starters than as parts of a gun. Also revealed in the Seneca excavations were substantial caches of spare gun parts, suggesting that within a relatively short time following the introduction of guns to the Indians they had already established a lively trade among themselves in repair parts.

Most of the North West Guns in North America were distributed by traders and Indians alike throughout the Western states and provinces. In fact, Lewis and Clark, during their expedition in 1804-1806, found North West Guns and their look-alikes in the hands of Native Americans on the upper Missouri and, later on, at the mouth of the Columbia River. In another instance, Ned Frost, a famous big-game guide in Wyoming, discovered a North West Gun leaning against the wall of a cave high on the side of Heart Mountain in Wyoming. This gun may have belonged to a Crow, a Blackfoot, a Gros Ventre or a Shoshone, and it was probably sold at Fort Union or some other post along the Missouri River. This gun can now be seen at the Museum of the Fur Trade in Chadron, Nebraska.

PLAIN NEED LEADS TO THE PLAINS RIFLE

Expansion of the fur trade west of the Mississippi during the first half of the 19th century spurred production of an American-made trade gun. The prototype was the "Kentucky" rifle made in Lancaster, Pennsylvania. Some of these early rifles were traded to the Indians and given as gifts or as treaty rifles. Unlike the North West Gun, they had spiraled or rifled inner barrels to improve accuracy. Available mostly in .52 caliber, they were solid, well-made guns that had been thoroughly tested by the fur companies. While initially they followed the basic lines of the Kentucky rifle—which was already legendary in

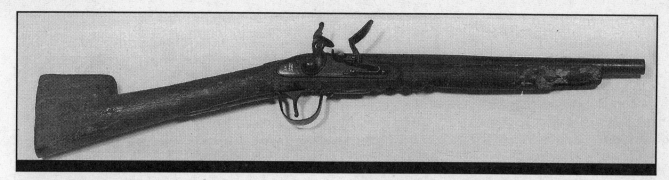

This flintlock North West Gun was found along Montana's Yellowstone River. (Photo courtesy of Museum of the Fur Trade, Chadron, NB, Charles E. Hanson, Jr., Director.)

the eastern forests—they became larger in caliber, thicker at the waist, with shorter barrels. Their full stocks were reduced to save weight. About 1860, the transition from flintlock to percussion ignition was complete. Unlike the Kentucky rifles, which were made individually by gunsmiths, hence essentially one-of-a-kind rifles, the "plains rifle" was a production piece made in small gun shops under the auspices of a gunsmith who typically had several apprentices in his employ.

One trait common among the Plains Indians in particular was a readiness to modify their rifles according to their basic need; i.e., a short rifle easily managed on horseback. For that reason, they usually cut 4–6 inches off the barrel and shortened the stock. To buffalo hunters, loss

of the front sight posed no disadvantage because their shooting was at near pointblank range. Once the stock was shortened, the buttplate would no longer fit, so these extraneous items were often pressed into service as hide scrapers.

Barrel rings were highly prized as personal adornments or jewelry and were frequently removed from the Indian guns. The stock could be reattached to the barrel by stitching wet rawhide around the forepiece and barrel. Upon drying, the rawhide shrank until it had made a strong bond. Such hide-wrapping was characteristic of many Indian rifles; stocks were frequently split because of overloading, falls or lack of a buttplate and thus needed this repair. Stocks were broken intentionally when the Indians went on reservations, where guns were banned. They would sur-

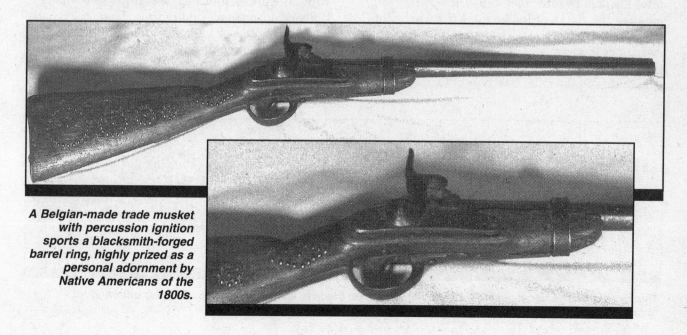

A Belgian-made trade musket with percussion ignition sports a blacksmith-forged barrel ring, highly prized as a personal adornment by Native Americans of the 1800s.

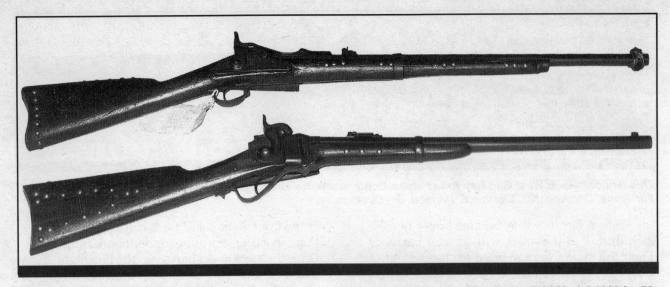

These two percussion rifles show the individual nature of Indian-"owned"arms. The Springfield Model 1869 in .50-.70 (top) is embellished with leather and a front sight made of deer horn. (Photo courtesy of Father Louis Taelman of St. Ignatius, Montana.) The Sharps Model 1859 in .52 caliber (bottom) was taken from the Nez Perce Reservation in 1862. Note the difference in the tack patterns.

render just enough obsolete weapons to divert suspicion, then break the stocks, hiding the parts under the skirts of their squaws. They knew they could always mend the broken stocks with their rawhide wraps.

Another distinguishing feature of Indian rifles was the brass tack patterns that decorate their stocks, first practiced by the Plains tribes but later adopted by others as well. These tacks adorned the stocks of Indian guns in an array of geometric designs that had "appeared" to their owners in the form of a dream or vision. Their presence was believed to lend a special power or spirituality to the rifle. One type of tack, used to

fasten the lids on ammunition boxes, featured humped backs so that air could circulate between the stacked boxes. Their presence on a rifle stock added a little extra flair. Occasionally, decorative "drippings"—such as beaded leather panels, bullet pouches or swatches of horsehair—were suspended from the stock.

New technology was, and remains, fraught with difficulties, and such was the case of the Indians' dependence on firearms. They knew nothing about forges or molten metals, and they were seldom able to repair anything except to hide-wrap a split stock or perhaps switch parts from one rifle to another. Keeping powder dry was

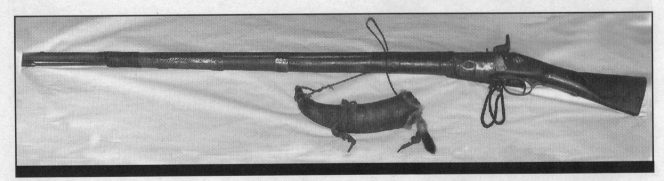

This Enfield percussion musket (c. 1859) with shortened stock is tacked and wrapped with leather and tin obtained from U.S. food tins. The rear peep sight was handmade.

always a concern; moreover, flintlocks were susceptible to the vagaries of prairie winds, which often swept powder right out of the pan before it could ignite the charge, rendering the weapon useless. Percussion caps, when they became available, were impervious to this problem; but there remained the difficulty of supply and the hazard of dropping these caps in the tall grass, effectively putting the hunter out of commission.

Because smoothbore muskets proved more adaptable to Indian needs, they were often preferred by the Indians even after the introduction of the rifled barrel. For one thing, the smoothbore could fire single or multiple balls of most any caliber. Lead shot was also used but was difficult to obtain because, unlike balls, it could not be molded by hand. Smoothbore muskets were easier to load than rifled barrels, but all muzzleloading weapons took too much time to load. About 30 seconds were required to prime, patch-load, aim

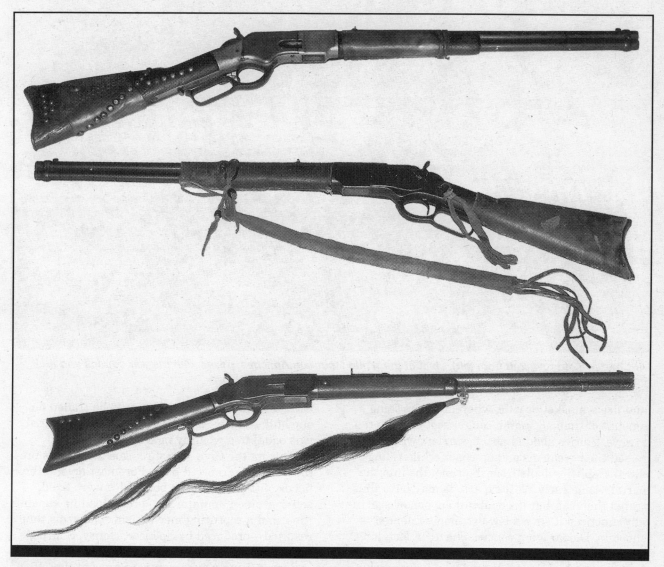

Winchester lever-actions were favorites among Indian hunters, especially the Winchester "Yellowboy" Model '66 carbine (top). Decorated rifles demonstrated great individuality, and the meaning to each owner represented by the patterns should not be underestimated. The Winchester Model 1873 carbine in .44-.40 caliber (center) was hidewrapped with a bullet pouch and decorated with Indian Chief beads. The bottom model, also an 1873 Winchester, is tacked and wears horsehair "drippings."

Al-Che-Say (2nd row, 2nd from left), chief of the White Mountain Apaches, poses with his war council and their prized rifles (c. 1890).

and fire a musket or rifle, whereas in the same amount of time an Indian could shoot eight to ten arrows. Stories abound about warriors who could reload their weapons on horseback while riding full tilt, spitting balls from their mouths into the barrel. Some early Western artists may have illustrated this feat, but it's doubtful anyone ever actually practiced it save a few extremely talented shooters. Disparaging remarks have, in fact, long been made about the Native Americans' competence as marksmen. Aside from their remarkable ability to shoot from horseback—a salute to their equestrian skills as much as their marksmanship—a major factor was most likely the scarcity of ammunition. Records indicate that as few as

three rounds of ammunition could be traded for one buffalo robe. At such a price, each shot fired was equal to a wealthy man's luxury.

During the Civil War, firearms inventions proliferated at a frenzied pace. Foremost among the needs of the military on both sides were fixed, self-contained ammunition, breechloading capabilities, and a repeating mechanism. The arms that resulted—produced by Spencer, Henry, Sharps, Winchester and Remington—have become legendary, setting a sure course to present-day American firearms manufacture. It was only a matter of time before these modern repeating carbines and rifles fell into Indian hands. They were particularly drawn to the brass-framed, short-bar-

reled Winchester carbine, which first appeared in 1866. It was called the "Yellowboy," and the Indians would give almost anything to obtain one.

With the push westward by white settlers, encroachment on traditional Indian land caused new conflicts. Laws were passed to prohibit the trading of guns to Indians, but they were flagrantly ignored. Different types of guns found their way into Indian camps in various ways, mostly through trade, theft, capture, smuggling and as gifts. According to Thomas E. Mails in his book, *The Mystic Warriors of the Plains*, the Cheyenne obtained Sharps military rifles and carbines from wagon trains traveling along the South Platte River between 1858 and 1865. During the late 1860s, Cheyenne warriors also captured Spencer repeating rifles after derailing a handcar in Nebraska. In 1862, a Sioux chief named Bear Ribs came into possession of a double-barreled shotgun. And in 1869, Canadian and American traders who specialized in liquor became the first to trade breechloading firearms and cartridges to the Blackfeet. At the conclusion of the Fort Rice Treaty in 1868, the new Indian Peace Commission gave guns as gifts to several Sioux tribesmen. Later, these same weapons were turned against U.S. soldiers. Thus did the Indians gradually come to possess an odd assortment of firearms. This fact became apparent in 1970 when B. William Henry, former historian at Custer Battlefield National Monument, completed a study of rifles and cartridge cases located by metal detectors along battle positions once occupied by Indian warriors. Among them were .45-.55 Springfield carbines, .44 Henry R.F., .50-.70 government issue Springfield models, .56-.56 Spencer R.F., .45 Colt government issue, .44-.40 Winchester, and an assortment of .44 and .58 caliber balls.

Along with their acquisition of modern firearms, the Indians faced the constant problem of replenishing ammunition. To this end, and to the consternation of military forces, they exhibited considerable ingenuity in reloading cartridges.

Rimfire shells were reprimed with phosphorus taken from match heads. Percussion caps—the kind used in cap-and-ball muzzleloaders—were used to prime spent shell cases. And finally, powder and lead obtained by breaking up cartridges of another, unwanted caliber, were used to reload shells.

Among the major accouterments of Indian rifles were their majestic, beaded buckskin cases. These often dazzling pieces of work featured a long buckskin fringe extending from the barrel portion to the rear opening. Typically, a geometric beaded design was applied only around the front and rear ends of the case. Some tribes attached a shoulder sling, while others carried the cased rifle in the crook of their arm.

Highly figured walnut stocks, 24-lines-to-the-inch checkering and ornate metal engraving do not fall into the realm of the Indian rifles. These guns were heavily used—even misused—and they show it. Rather, Indian rifles portray the fur trade and the exploration and settlement of a continent. They represent proud hunting peoples in the waning days of their traditional lifestyle. They also represent their confrontation with a government that forever changed that lifestyle. Few authentic examples exist, true, but the ones that do, speak volumes about our nation's past.

DR. STEPHEN IRWIN, *a practicing family physician, combines his love of hunting and fishing with an artistic eye and talent for writing. From his Montana home, he writes on the history of hunting/fishing as well as such specialized topics as antique fishing lures and firearms, duck decoys and sporting art. His articles have appeared in many outdoor publications. He is currently working on a book about sporting collectibles (to be published by Stoeger Pub. Co.), and is the author of* Indian Hunters: Hunting and Fishing Methods of North American Natives. *This is Dr. Irwin's eighth in a series of articles for* SHOOTER'S BIBLE.

SOFT SHOOTING:
KICKING THE FLINCH

by Wilf E. Pyle

What's the word that best describes the bane of every rifle shooter's existence? The answer is simple: *Recoil, recoil, recoil*. Unfortunately, when selecting a rifle and cartridge combination, few shooters stop to consider recoil. They plunk down their money, confident they've finally found that dream rifle in the caliber of their choice, without regard to the nasty effects recoil — even light recoil — can produce. They forget that recoil leads to such accuracy spoilers as flinching and trigger jerking, not to mention less pleasure from their favorite shooting sport. Clearly, recoil is here to stay. In the early years, a .40-82 Winchester Model '86 produced 12 ft.-lbs. of free recoil, while in the 1950s a .30-06 in a Winchester Model 70 offered 15. Today, a .458 Winchester Magnum can produce up to 24 ft.-lbs. of free recoil.

Throughout the history of American firearms, sharp recoil and sensitivity to its cumulative effect led to the creation of several medium to intermediate cartridges. In the 1800s, the .32-20 was popular, and by the 1950s the .222 Remington had bloomed, almost overtaking the sales of harder shooting calibers. Now we have all those early choices, plus the .223 and others that offer the shooting public soft shooting and low recoil choices for field shooting and small-game hunting.

From a practical standpoint, what can shooters do to reduce recoil effect, maximize striking power and still keep the fun in shooting? Must shooters sacrifice striking power and trajectory on the altar of bruised shoulders? Fortunately, the modern shooter can, through wise choices, stay in the game and at the same time save his shoulder from turning into mincemeat. We can keep shooting without sacrificing the kind of performance needed to take most North American big game.

SWITCH TO LIGHTWEIGHT RIFLES?
The key lies in selecting the right cartridge, using a heavier rifle and perhaps adding a muzzle brake. One persistent problem, however, remains in the selection of lightweight rifles. A few years ago, gun writers issued a collective cry for the return of the lightweight rifle, which has always enjoyed a kind of shooting-culture mystique. This probably relates to the high adventure and exotic locals with which these rifles have often been associated. In the early years, they were known as mountain rifles and carbines. Others gained the obnoxious moniker of "saddle guns" at a time when hardly any hunting was done from the back of a horse. Winchester was the first to experiment with a true lightweight rifle when it modified a pre-1964 Model 70. The rifle had a short life, simply because nobody was interested at the time. Lightweights didn't go away, though, and slowly grew in popularity until they'd earned a legitimate place at the shooter's breakfast table. Today

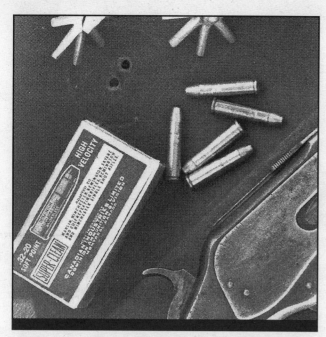

Throughout firearms history, shooters who are sensitive to recoil have influenced the development of medium cartridges like these .32-20s.

military lines for nearly 30 years.

For all practical purposes, modern shooters who seek an easy answer to handling recoil should select sporter-weight rifles that are on the heavy side, an expedient that works well for experienced shooters as well as beginners. A cautionary note to sport shooters: don't take this advice to the extreme. Heavy-barreled rifles, or those with target or semi-target stocks, definitely add weight and provide all the shock absorption needed to distribute felt recoil. However, these rifles are difficult to shoot well under field conditions.

there are more so-called lightweights—including trappers, classics, mountain, scout, "boy's" or saddle types—than sporting models or those rifles variously referred to as "express, African or standard."

The late Colonel Townsend Whelen once commented that a hunting rifle should weigh no less than nine pounds. This weight was generally considered enough to counter much of the recoil developed by standard hunting cartridges—especially the military look-alikes familiar to Whelen. For many years, this belief was accepted until more women and young people began to get involved in sport rifle shooting. In Whelen's day, a fully configured sporting rifle typically bent the scale at 10 pounds, especially with a scope, mount, sling and full magazine. Some combinations were often closer to 11 or 12 pounds, varying somewhat in stock density. This weight effectively counterbalanced recoil, or at least allowed for the kind of felt recoil that athletic outdoorsmen like Whelen could handle. Interestingly, the gun manufacturing industry agreed with Whelen: what was good enough for the colonel was certainly good for the shooting public. And so, sporting rifles remained noticeably heavy and curiously configured along

Colonel Townsend Whelen once noted that a standard hunting rifle, similar to the one shown here, should weigh no less than nine pounds, enough to counter much of the recoil generated by standard hunting cartridges.

Until women and youths began taking up sport rifle shooting, heavy rifles predominated. Now rifles like Sako's AI Lightweight Hunter are widely used by small-framed shooters.

Carry around a Parker-Hale Varminter any distance, for example, and your entire body will be screaming with pain, especially after you've been moving quickly through bush and fence country.

For such shooters—those who spend more time carrying their rifles than firing them—thoughts soon turn to lightweight rifles that shoot high-velocity cartridges. There's a trade-off, though. A seven-pound .30-06 rifle firing 150-grain bullets develops 22 ft.-lbs. of recoil. The same cartridge shot in a standard 10-pound model produces only 13 ft.-lbs. This reduction is significant when one realizes that the shooter has absorbed the entire difference. In going from a standard-weight rifle with a medium-power cartridge to a lightweight rifle in a magnum class cartridge, recoil increases. While most hunters don't consider this a major problem, excessive recoil does cause the human body to develop a strong reaction reflex, more commonly known as flinch, causing the shooter to jerk the trigger rather than squeezing it and closing one's eyes instead of focusing on the target. What happens, essentially, is that the body begins to anticipate the shot and builds neural tension, or fear, of the impending recoil. This automatic reaction, delivered without any conscious thought process, soon trains the body to

respond adversely.

Once a shooter develops a flinch with one particular load and a single rifle, this instant reaction soon extends to all shooting with other rifles and loads. Indeed, recoil affects some shooters in

Lightweight rifles like this Sako Mannlicher carbine are prized by hunters who seek high adventure and exotic locales.

For all practical purposes, shooters who seek an easy answer to handling recoil should select a sporter-weight rifle that tends toward the heavy side. This veteran Model 70 Winchester with scope tips the scale at 10 pounds.

such a negative way that they flinch even when firing mild .22 rimfires. Thus does the reflex action destroy the ability to shoot accurately— and if nothing else, it certainly dampens a shooter's enthusiasm for shooting! To test your own recoil influence, ask a friend to load your rifle and hand it to you before shooting. Then, at some point during the shooting session, have that friend pass, unknown to you, an unloaded rifle. The severity of your reaction upon squeezing off the imaginary round may well astound you as the firing pin falls on the empty chamber.

Recovering from a case of flinch takes conscious effort. For most shooters, this mean *practice.* One good way to proceed is to switch to soft-shooting rifle/cartridge combinations. Besides selecting heavier sporting-type rifles to thwart recoil, you'll need light but deadly loads. Among the first cartridges thought to be easy shooters was the 7X57mm Mauser. In the U.S., the slightly longish 140-grain softpoint bullet proved exceptionally fine on game. Originally, the load used a 175-grain bullet at a velocity of approximately 2200 fps. Designed as a military round for the Spanish government for use in various Mausers, it made an excellent, inexpensive off-the-rack deer rifle, even with iron sights. Thanks in large measure to the writings of Jack O'Connor, the 7X57mm Mauser cartridge received some atten-

tion, although it was years after his death before an American rifle for the round ever came to market. O'Connor wrote convincingly about its reasonable ballistics combined with good performance on game. In particular, he noted the mild recoil and low report offered by the round, which he considered an ideal cartridge for women and youths. Today, the Savage 110LE bolt action is found in this caliber, as are the Remington 700 and Ruger's M-77 MKII.

POPULAR SOFT-SHOOTING CARTRIDGES

Without a doubt, the most popular soft-shooting cartridges today are the .243 Winchester and 6mm Remington. Both appeared at the same time and continue to treat shooters exceptionally well. There's nothing quite like the joy of shooting cartridges that leave behind anywhere from 8 ft.-lbs. of recoil in a 10-pound rifle to 12 ft.-lbs. in a 7-pound rifle. In many respects, these cartridges are considered the best choice for those who actively seek a soft-shooting rifle. Indeed, these cartridges are so well-known for accuracy now that many shooters don't recognize them as cures for flinching or protection from recoil.

.243 Caliber. The 6mm or .243 caliber owes its origins to Fred Huntington of RCBS fame, who experimented with it at a time when the only cases were a leftover 6mm Lee Navy or a British

Heavy-barreled rifles, or those with target stocks, have enough weight to dampen recoil, but they are difficult to shoot well under field conditions. Shooting a Parker-Hale Varminter like this one is difficult without a rest because the added weight hinders ease of movement.

.240 Apex. Today, versatility characterizes these cartridges. There's a good supply of bullets for reloaders, plus a good commercial selection of loads with varmint or deer bullets, enabling both cartridges to earn the rank of "soft shooting." Shooters also recognize them as dual-purpose cartridges that have proven themselves useful for varmint hunting as well as white-tailed deer and antelope.

It's a tribute to gun writers that these cartridges are so popular. Warren Page, firearms editor of *Field and Stream* magazine, was an early exponent of the cartridge. In 1954, he urged gun manufacturers to look seriously at the .243, because he was convinced the cartridge offered superior deer-killing power. The .243 caliber originated from necking down the .308, which was really nothing more than the commercialization of the military 7.62 NATO round for the M14 battle rifle. Here commercialization means more open specifications, especially in terms of neck thickness, bullet tension, primer crimping and tightness. Winchester struggled in the early 1960s to get this round out to the public in the Model 70 Lightweight, and a year later in the Model 88. Both remain excellent soft shooters, although the Model 88 lever rifle is now difficult to find. Savage still chambers its time-honored Model 99 lever for this round (which, by the way, features a very handy clip magazine). Another good choice is Browning's Model 81 BLR High Power, which also features a clip magazine.

When it comes to bolt-action rifles, nearly every company has at least one model in .243, including Remington, Winchester, Browning, Dakota, Kimber, Ruger and Sako. Lightweight models include a Remington 700 Mountain rifle that weighs a scant 6¾ pounds, and an ultra-light Ruger M-77RL that weighs 6 pounds. Ruger's International Mannlicher and the Sako Hunter both ranked for many years as the lightest wood-stocked rifles ever produced. The point being, many different models are available for shooters who seek a soft-shooting, yet lightweight rifle.

.257 Roberts. No discussion of soft-shooting options could exclude the .257 Roberts, which comes close to accomplishing maximum power with minimum recoil. Beyond that, the pendulum begins to shift toward cartridges that produce more recoil or to rifles that are too heavy for the field. The .257 Roberts wasn't always popular, but somehow it hung on in the minds of shooters, especially deer hunters. In 1975, Ruger made a production run of slightly more than 1,000 rifles in .257 Roberts, baiting would-be aficionados with a taste of the past. Ruger's promotional literature stressed the accuracy of the round and its historical acceptance by shooting greats from a bygone era. Little mention was made, however, of the fact that the .257 made a great compromise between power and recoil.

In 1982, Winchester brought out a Model 70 Featherweight featuring the .257 Roberts. Rifles continued to abound in this caliber for some years to follow, especially after Remington brought out its Model 700 Classic. For in doing so, it helped breathe new life into what was then a moribund round. The +P .257 Roberts ammunition added

100 fps to the factory load and 130 fps to the traditional 117-grain roundnose load, making them particularly useful for most hunting applications. The 100 grain +P load has virtually identical downrange ballistics to the .243, which allows .25 calibers to compete. Until recently, several rifle models were available in .257 Roberts, but catalogs now fail to show any such models. For now, the second-hand market is the best place to look, at least until the .257 Roberts has gone into another resting phase.

.250 Savage. Another good low recoil package is the .250 Savage. For savvy shooters who seek a light report/low recoil round, the .250 Savage is a good choice. Originally called the .250-3000, it was the first round to travel over 3,000 fps. When Savage placed it on the market in 1915, the round developed only 6 ft.-lbs. of recoil in a 10-pound rifle—light enough for even the most recoil sensitive shooter. Savage continues to list its Model 110 bolt-action in .250 Savage. As a standard-weight sporter, this well-balanced rifle produces just over 9 ft.-lbs. of free recoil, making it perfectly acceptable for hunting white-tailed deer at 250 yards with minimum recoil. Savage made this cal-

iber available for many years in its carbine, one of the first lightweight, soft-shooting rifles available. And while the rifle enjoyed limited popularity among horse-mounted hunters, those shooters who kept their rifles behind the kitchen door liked it. Nevertheless, Savage dropped the gun unceremoniously in the mid-1980s—another example of a cartridge that served specific purposes and met important needs but lacked enough support among shooters.

7mm-08. Another modern cartridge with a wildcat background—one that offers light recoil and updated ballistics—is the 7mm-08. Fired from a Browning BLR lever rifle, this combination yields (depending on scope weight) around 12 ft.-lbs. of recoil. In some areas of North America the 7mm-08 is surprisingly popular for deer. Many gun writers in the late 1970s considered it a ready replacement for the 7mm Mauser. Indeed, that's exactly what happened: more American rifles are now chambered for the 7mm-08 than the 7mm Mauser. Among the recommended rifle selections are Browning's BLR Model 81, Remington's Mountain Rifle Model 700, and the standard BDL bolt-action.

Note how this shooter handles recoil by placing the butt squarely on his shoulder, forming a pressure triangle across the butt, grip and comb.

Other Recoil-Reducing Rounds. Although most shooters do not consider them as low-recoil contenders, the following cartridges are all easy on the shooter: .307 Winchester, .356 Winchester, .44 Magnum and the 7.62X39mm. The Winchester rounds, which duplicate the old .38-55 in performance, are limited to the Model 94 Big Bore rifle. The .44 Magnum was also once available in the Model 94 Winchester and Ruger's versatile Model 44 semiautomatic rifle. The 7.62X39mm, despite being light on recoil and highly accurate, is still trying to find its place in the U.S. cartridge line-up.

In addition to the ones listed here, there's a growing number of back-listed cartridges that produce intermediate velocities and good accuracy: .300 Savage, .30-40 Craig, .303 British, 6.5X55mm Swedish, .32 Special, .35 Remington and .38-55. Plenty of second-hand rifles are available for these rounds and some have begun to appear as prized collector items, proving that our forefathers had the right idea about light recoil cartridges.

OTHER WAYS TO REDUCE RECOIL

Some shooters are more sensitive to recoil than others. For them, no amount of advice or coaching can change their innate levels of sensitivity or the natural fear of receiving a kick in the shoulder. Having recognized these personal levels of recoil sensitivity, it's important to learn a few fundamentals beyond the choice of rifle and cartridge.

Shooters have long observed that big men tend to shoot big calibers better than their lighter-framed counterparts. Their meatier shoulders seem to absorb recoil better, whereas leaner shooters are often bent backwards by a punishing recoil. Some of this response lies in the way one holds the rifle. First, the butt must be placed squarely on the shoulder and a "pressure triangle" maintained across the butt, grip and comb. Typically, a larger person with larger hands and greater strength can pull the rifle into the shoulder more easily once the butt has been placed squarely.

In general, however, being able to handle recoil relates more to how one holds and positions the stock, regardless of physique. The stock itself is critical as well. Stocks found on most sporting rifles today are nearly above reproach, thanks in

The custom recoil pad on this Winchester Model 70 dampens recoil and helps prevent the rifle from falling over when placed against a wall or fence in the field.

part to the endless harping by Colonel Whelen and Jack O'Connor during the 1950s. Essentially, they promoted the modern sporter-stock design and, while not the first to recognize the importance of scopes, identified which stocks were best suited for scope use with high-powered cartridges. The drop at heel and comb are also critical factors in delivering recoil. Stocks with good drop allow the shooter to take the recoil through the center of the butt. Early lever rifles featured excessive drop, which tended to drive the toe of the stock into the shoulder even under mild recoil conditions.

Muzzle Brake. Another major factor in recoil reduction is a modern invention called a "muzzle brake." Although the time is coming when every factory-made rifle will have a built-in muzzle brake, for now it's an add-on, after-market feature. Muzzle brakes were originally designed for artillery pieces to control flash and report, not recoil; but in recent years it's been found that redistributing the muzzle blast at the time of firing can dampen the recoil effect. It's been estimated that muzzle brakes reduce recoil by as much as 80 percent. They are most efficient with high-velocity cartridges simply because there's more gas to redistribute. Interestingly, they're more popular on shotguns than on rifles, perhaps because of the cost of installation, or because a rifle's front sight is often removed to accommodate installation of a muzzle brake. Most hunters still feel that a rifle without a front sight looks strange.

Muzzle brakes can also raise and sharpen the report level to ear-piercing heights, a fact that should be considered when shooting in bush or along a valley. Some kind of ear protection on the firing range is recommended, and even those going afield should use ear plugs or modern sound arrestors. For some, report can be far more disturbing than recoil. One muzzle brake that has received accolades among hunters is the Quiet Muzzle Brake. David Gentry, its designer, has angled the holes in the brake sleeve more toward the front, thereby redirecting the passing gases. Other examples of current muzzle brakes include the KDF Recoil Arrestor, Barnes Straight Line, Gentry Quiet and the New Answer System brake.

Recoil Pad. The recoil pad is another add-on, after-market feature. At one time hundreds of models were available, from custom-fitted kinds to simple slip-on types. Whole articles were written about recoil pads, which redistribute felt recoil over the entire shoulder area and spread it over a longer time span. Recoil pads feature a matrix construction that collapses within milliseconds of recoil, then rebounds to retain its shape. Pads do indeed remain a good bet for sensitive shooters. In addition, the rubber (or similar) material used provides a good non-slip base, enabling shooters to lean a rifle against a wall or a fence without fear of its falling over. At least one manufacturer provides a factory-made, soft buttplate for this reason.

Because recoil pads are difficult to install, the services of a professional gunsmith are usually required. Some of the material can be of poor quality, though, causing the pad to decompose or crack. Mosquito repellents can also break down the material used on most recoil pads, a fact worth remembering for those who hunt in the northern states. Make sure the length of pull remains the same once the pad is in place; most gunsmiths will shorten the stock if necessary, but poor quality work is frequently a problem.

Based on the criteria presented here, hunters who seek the softest shooting rifle with maximum power should strongly consider a .243 Model 7400 Remington or Browning BAR outfitted with a soft-rubber recoil pad, heavy scope, military sling and muzzle brake. On the other hand, a standard-weight, bolt-action rifle similarly outfitted might help increase power. The important thing to remember is: learn all you can about recoil and understand your own reactions to this ever-present problem.

WILF PYLE is an avid sportsman who has hunted nearly all game species with a wide variety of firearms. A well-known authority on sporting arms and reloading, he has a passion for sporting rifles, hence his expertise on "soft shooting." His books include Small Game and Varmint Hunting *and* Hunting Predators for Hides and Profit *(Stoeger Publishing). He has also co-authored* The Hunter's Book of the Pronghorn Antelope *(New Century).*

ELMER KEITH:
A MAN FOR ALL SEASONS

by Jim Casada

The title of Elmer Keith's autobiography, *Hell, I Was There!*, could not have been better chosen. A cowboy, guide, outfitter, horseman, gunsmith, expert marksman, outdoor writer, hunter and shooter for all seasons, Keith was a man who had, as the saying goes, "Been there and done that." Controversial, often cantankerous and always colorful, he ranks among America's greatest gun writers.

He was also a noted inventor and innovator, often called, justifiably, the "Father of the .44 and .41 Magnum." Keith was a consummate handloader whose work in this field helped popularize a number of new loads. He was perhaps the leading six-gunner of this century and a tireless advocate of big-bore rifles. These interests and accomplishments, among a host of others, have endeared him to three generations of gun enthusiasts. Still, he is much less well known today than his accomplishments and his impact on the gun world merit. What follows will, we trust, help introduce today's gun lovers to this fascinating man.

Elmer Merrifield Keith was born on March 8, 1899, in Hardin, Missouri. Adventure ran through his bloodlines, for ancestors on both sides of the family had been Kentucky pioneers in the days of Daniel Boone. Later they traveled west to Missouri, but Keith, continuing that family tradition, spent most of his life in Montana and Idaho.

There's little doubt that he was heavily endowed with the restlessness and love of the wild that had characterized his forebears, including Captain William Clark, an explorer who was commissioned by President Thomas Jefferson to explore the lands acquired in the Louisiana Purchase of 1803.

Even as a small lad, Keith lived close to and loved the good earth. His early years were spent on a farm, growing up with the prairie for a backyard. It was during these formative years that he developed a lifelong passion for horses. He could ride almost as soon as he could walk, and in time he became an acknowledged expert about what constituted a good horse, saddle or tack. Also, in keeping with that time and place, he had an early introduction to shooting. As he later wrote in his autobiography (first published in 1976 as *Keith: An Autobiography)*: "From my earliest years I seem to have been more interested in guns and ammunition than other things." Certainly his career reflected these dual interests, because virtually all of the various career paths he took involved, in one way or another, shooting and horses.

In 1905, the Keith family left Missouri and moved to the Montana mining community of Marysville. Their stay lasted only a couple of years before they returned to Missouri, and it was

With the hills of his Idaho home as a backdrop, Elmer Keith shows off a favorite revolver. In 1973 he won the first Outstanding American Handgunner award ever presented. Note the ten-gallon hat and dangling cigar—his trademarks. (All photos courtesy of Petersen Publishing)

then that Keith obtained the first gun he could call his own: a .22 Hopkins & Allen rifle. Before long he was an expert marksman, able to contribute to the family larder through his squirrel and rabbit hunting. Soon young Keith became adept at handling a shotgun, but not until he'd learned a lesson the hard way. Accustomed to firing his little .22, he took aim at a fox squirrel without taking into account the heavy recoil of a single-shot shotgun. As he later wrote: "What part of the gun hit me, I don't know. But it cut my upper lip clear through to my teeth, and when I woke up about three hours later there was blood all over the side of my face." Typically, this misfor-

tune did nothing to deter Keith's enthusiasm, just as he never let his slender figure interfere with his love for shooting big-bore rifles.

By the time the Keith family moved to Montana permanently in 1911, young Elmer was already an exceptionally accomplished shot and a fine woodsman. A rambunctious lad in his teens, there's no question that, for Keith, the veneer of civilized society wore thin early on. Throughout his life, in fact, his forthrightness and often abrasive tongue got him into far more than his fair share of scrapes, contentious arguments and fights. He became a salty, even pugnacious character, as witness his well-known dispute with

The storyteller works at his typewriter in his trophy-laden office. Keith wrote many articles and several noteworthy books that earned him his place in the literature and lore of American gunning.

Jack O'Connor over the relative merits of big-bore versus smaller bore rifles. Keith's short temper and transparent honesty were in some sense among his most redeeming qualities. A man always knew precisely where he stood with Elmer Keith. He rarely minced words.

While in Montana, the Keith family lived a somewhat peripatetic existence, with frequent moves back and forth between Missoula and Helena. During one of these moves, young Elmer was terribly burned in a hotel fire, and it took the better part of a decade for him to recover fully. Still, he managed to do some bronco busting, trapping, hunting, and competitive rifle shooting.

In the summer of 1915, Keith worked at a bakery, feeding coal to the oven furnace, and with money saved from his wages he bought a hammerless double-barrel Ithaca shotgun. Soon he became a masterful wingshot, adding to the status he'd already acquired with pistol and rifle. By his late teens he'd become a tough, seasoned young man. At the time, Montana was still a real frontier. As Keith put it: "Those were rough times in Montana and a man carried his law with him. If he didn't, he might not last too long." Far from being an overstatement, his view was in reality not too far-fetched. Indeed, for most of his adult life he made it a practice to carry a sixgun at his

A big-bore advocate for big game, Keith battled for years with Jim O'Connor, another popular outdoor writer. Here Keith sights in a rifle with a 375 H&H Magnum.

side when at home, and there's little doubt about his willingness and ability to use it should the occasion arise.

By his early 20s, Keith was a bonafide "gun nut," with most of his earnings from a variety of jobs going toward the beginnings of what eventually became an impressive arsenal. Otherwise, he was footloose and fancy free, despite a bout with influenza in the early 1920s that nearly killed him. At this juncture, the Keith family pulled up stakes again and moved to Idaho.

Once he had fully recovered from the flu, Keith took several steps that loomed large in shaping his career. It began in 1922, when he joined the National Rifle Association (NRA). Anxious to try his hand at match shooting, he signed up for the Montana National Guard and in 1924 represented the state in the national matches held annually at Camp Perry, Ohio. There he met such renowned gun writers and authorities as James V. Howe, Townsend Whelen, Julian S. Hatcher and others. While there's no indication Keith had even thought about a writing career, it seems fair to assume that getting to

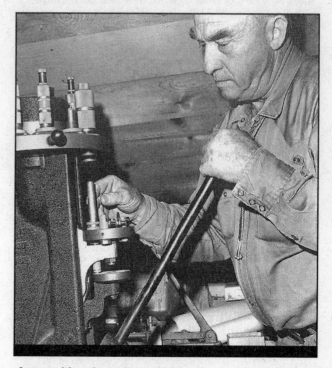

Among his other talents, Keith was a proficient handloader.

After 50 years of marriage, Keith's wife Lorraine became skilled with a rifle, too. Here the couple proudly display an antelope she brought down in 1976.

know these men and their way of life made a strong impression.

Following the matches in Ohio, Keith visited his parents at their new home in Idaho, and it was there he met his future bride, Lorraine Raddall. The following year he returned to Camp Perry, where he performed well in several competitive venues. By then, he had also made his first appearance in print in the form of a letter to Thomas G. Samworth, editor of *American Rifleman* magazine. This contact with Samworth, a gun genius in his own right as well as a highly skilled editor, was to prove quite significant for Elmer. While at Camp Perry in 1925, Keith was asked to write up that year's matches for the NRA's house publication, and by so doing he launched his career as an outdoor writer. Although many years would pass before he made enough money to call it a full-time profession, this assignment represented the heart of what Keith was to do from that point on.

Meanwhile, in the summer of 1926, Elmer

and Lorraine were married, honeymooning for 10 days at a camp alongside Idaho's Weiser River. Over the next few years, the Keiths tried their hand at ranching, along with a lot of hunting and shooting. During this period, Elmer wrote an account of an elk hunt he had taken recently and won $100 in a writing contest run by *American Rifleman*. That was considered big money during the Great Depression. The reason Keith won the contest, in addition to his in-depth knowledge, was his natural talent as a storyteller. His tales carried an aura of authenticity just as his technical pieces were noted for their accuracy.

And yet, Keith was anything but a skilled "wordsmith." In truth, he was in some ways an editor's nemesis, especially in later years after he'd become solidly established as a gun-writing legend. Should an eager young editor dare to revise one of his grammatical and stylistic nightmares, Keith would pick up the phone and subject the poor man to a tirade full of epithets. Anecdotes of this sort abound in the outdoor writing fraternity. Ludo Wurfbain, head of the Safari Press and a noted collector of sporting memorabilia, including a wealth of Keith material, recalls that Elmer's personal correspondence indicates he was barely literate. As a result, over the years a series of editors took Keith's exceedingly rough prose and managed somehow to maintain its wit and wisdom while vastly improving its literary quality.

Once he began writing on guns and the outdoors, Keith worked at the task with a passion. He sold his first piece to *Outdoor Life* in 1926 and was soon making regular contributions to *American Rifleman*. As his career blossomed, Elmer invested his and Lorraine's meager savings in a ranch on the North Fork of Idaho's Salmon River, a place they called home for the rest of their lives. In 1930, with the economic depression in full swing, Keith made a monumental decision: to make his living writing about and guiding big-game hunters and fishing parties. One of the first parties he guided was hosted by Zane Grey and a handful of his angling cronies. Over the next several years, guide work became Keith's primary source of income, although he did gradually expand his writing endeavors to the point where he had earned

national recognition as a gun scribe.

Keith published his first book in 1936 with Thomas Samworth's Small-Arms Technical Publishing Company. Keith's blunt commentary on this effort, written many years later, left no doubt that for him the undertaking was singularly distasteful.

> T.G. Samworth . . . commissioned me to write three manuals, which I did. The first one was to be on six-gun cartridges and loads; the second one on big game rifles and cartridges; and the third one varmint rifles. I wrote the three manuals which were to sell at a dollar apiece. He [Samworth] never did publish the last one. He paid me $250 down on it, and $250 on each of the others. The others sold all right, and plenty good. He later sold the Big Game and Cartridges to the Stackpole Company and it published a lot more of them. However, I never did get the final payment on either book that he published and, of course, not on the one that he didn't publish.

All of this may be true, and certainly *Sixgun*

The consummate hunter, Keith enjoyed the African safari. Here he is with guide and a prized kudu.

Cartridges and Loads followed close on the heels of *Big Game Rifles and Cartridges,* both appearing in 1936. The third volume, entitled *Varmint and Small Game Rifles,* was never printed because, according to Samworth, the first two volumes did poorly. In Samworth's defense, ample evidence exists—in the form of 40 other books he published—that he ran a generally clean business. The bitter taste of that first venture as a book author notwithstanding, writing became increasingly important to Keith. In 1936, he became gun editor for *The Outdoorsman,* a position he kept for more than a decade.

As his writing fortunes prospered, Keith consciously cultivated a distinct "character." He favored huge ten-gallon hats and invariably had an oversized cigar clamped between his teeth. A small man in stature, he always thought big, delighting in the most visible examples of his preoccupations with large things: his love of big-bore rifles, for example. Indeed, he waged a long and bitter battle with Jack O'Connor over what constituted the proper guns for big game, repeatedly ridiculing his adversary's preference for the .243 and .270. O'Connor, for his part, was considerably more restrained, perhaps sensing that personality differences concerning matters of gun preference went beyond the pale. No matter, Keith approached everything he did in life with a passion, and doubtless he reveled in such controversy. Conversely, he had a real talent for making friends, many of whom recall Elmer with great fondness as a warm, caring man.

As things turned out, Keith needed all of his allies, including his own strength of character. During the 1940s, despite a solidly established national reputation, he suffered great personal adversities. For one thing, at age 41, following the outbreak of World War II, he tried to join the military, but was forced to settle for an advisory position at a government arsenal in Ogden, Utah. Meanwhile, his daughter, Druzilla, was badly injured in a car accident and eventually died from its effects. Keith himself was acutely ill at the time, having fallen victim to a serious bout of emphysema.

Somehow he persevered. He wrote another book, *Keith's Rifles for Large Game,* published in 1946 by Standard Publishing Company (which soon thereafter sold out to Stackpole Books).

Unfortunately, half of the edition of 2500 was destroyed in a warehouse fire. Keith could not have earned much in the way of royalties; and given his track record with books, it seems surprising that he continued writing them. Nonetheless, he kept on until new, more successful books followed. He had, meanwhile, assumed an editorial position on the staff of *American Rifleman,* a job that he dearly loved. Most of his duties focused on answering readers' questions, many of them highly technical and complex.

In 1950, Keith wrote *Shotguns by Keith* for Stackpole, followed in 1955 by *Sixguns by Keith.* Interestingly, many of Keith's books bore his name in the title. While ego may have played a

Believed to be the most dangerous beast to hunt, this Cape Buffalo was brought down by Keith with a .500 Nitro Express.

Surrounded by ivory during one of his African safaris, Keith catches up on some reading.

role, it was also a calculated promotional effort to play on the author's reputation. For by then Keith had become, along with O'Connor, one of America's most widely respected gun writers.

During the final 25 years of his life, Keith traveled widely, savoring his success to the fullest and generally enjoying his hard-earned place as a gun sage. To be sure, several career changes took place over the years, but that was and remains characteristic of the outdoor writer's life. He served for several years as executive editor of *Guns and Ammo* and its sister publication, *Petersen's Hunting.* Petersen also published four of his later books, although there was a long period covering the last half of the 1950s and the first half of the 1960s when he did not write a single book. Keith's final works were, in order of publication, *Guns and Ammo for Hunting Big Game, Safari, Keith: An Autobiography,* and *Hell, I Was There!* In many ways these were his best books, including as they did words of wisdom from a writer who was now widely considered the grand

old man of the gun world. For those who love Africa, *Safari* was especially delightful, while his autobiographical efforts were at once titillating and tempestuous, retaining the essence of the storyteller at his best.

As he approached 70, Keith's health began to suffer, beginning with a serious heart attack in 1967. It is a testament to the man's inherent toughness that he lived another 16 years, although his natural drive and stamina waned noticeably. Shortly before his 80th birthday he revealed some of his feelings about the ravages of age: "I have no intention of retiring. You retire, you become a vegetable and usually last six months to three years. I don't care for that kind of an end. I'd rather keep working and die with my boots on if necessary."

In 1973, Keith won the first Outstanding American Handgunner award ever given, and from then on he rejoiced in holding center stage whenever gun-related matters were at issue. No doubt he sensed the end was near when he wrote

BOOKS BY ELMER KEITH

Many of Keith's books have now become collector's items in their original editions or have been reprinted. All are listed below in chronological order according to their original appearance. Most show up regularly in lists and catalogs published by dealers in our-of-print sporting books. Keith is so popular with both sporting book collectors and gun enthusiasts, however, that buyers must be prepared to pay a hefty sum for most of these titles:

Big Game Rifles and Cartridges (Onslow County, N.C.: Small Arms Technical Publishing Company, 1936). A second issue was made in 1943 and a second printing in 1946. Wolfe Publishing did a deluxe reprint of 1500 copies, and in 1985 Gun Room Press put out a facsimile reprint.

Sixgun Cartridges and Loads: A Manual (Onslow County, N.C.: Small Arms Technical Publishing Co., 1936) A second impression came out in 1945. A facsimile reprint was issued by Gun Room Press in the 1980s.

Shotguns by Keith (New York: Stackpole, Heck, 1950; 2nd edition, 1961). Reprinted by Bonanza Books, 1967; reprinted in the Firearms Classic Library (with an Editor's Note by Jim Casada) in 1995.

Big Game Hunting (Boston: Little, Brown, 1948; 2nd printing, 1954).

Sixguns by Keith (Harrisburg, PA: Stackpole, 1955). 2nd edition published by Bonanza Books, 1961.

Guns and Ammo for Hunting Big Game (Los Angeles: Petersen, 1965). Safari (La Jolla, CA: Safari Publications, 1968).

Keith: An Autobiography (New York: Winchester Press, 1976).

Hell, I was There! (Los Angeles: Petersen, 1979)

Gun Notes: Elmer Keith's "Guns & Ammo" Articles of the 1960s, with a Foreword by Ross Seyfried (Long Beach, CA: Safari Press, 1995).

(in *Hell, I Was There!)* the following words: "Life is a fleeting thing, and one realizes how short it is only after he begins to reach old age." Right up to his death, which came on Valentine's Day, 1983, Keith remained the amusing, abrasive and oft-times endearing character he had always been.

Looking back, it's clear that Elmer Keith received less than his full due while he was alive. The truth is, despite his controversial and argumentative ways, he was closer to the mark than even he could possibly have known when he penned these words: "All my life I have tried to dodge trouble as much as possible, yet for some reason it seems to follow me." Despite all the tragedies and encounters he experienced along life's road, there's no denying his place in the literature and lore of American guns and gunning.

JIM CASADA has been contributing profiles of noted sportsmen and gun scribes to SHOOTER'S BIBLE for several years. A Senior Editor for Sporting Classics magazine and editor-at-large for Turkey & Turkey Hunting, he writes weekly columns for two newspapers and serves on the staffs of several other outdoor publications, including Southern Outdoors, Deer & Deer Hunting, Carolina Adventure, TroutSouth, and Tennessee Valley Outdoors. His most recent book is The Lost Classics of Robert Ruark, a collection of works never before published in book form. Casada is also the editor of a trilogy comprising the writings of Archibald Rutledge: Hunting & Home in the Southern Heartland, Tales of Whitetails, and America's Greatest Game Bird. (Inscribed copies are available by contacting Casada, 1250 Yorkdale Drive, Rock Hill, SC 29730.)

P228 9mm

When the U.S. Army needed a compact sidearm, both for special duty and for concealment, its first choice was the SIG SAUER P228. Similarly, the FBI has chosen the P228 as a compact sidearm for its agents. Despite its small size, this compact pistol packs a *10 round magazine in an easy-pointing, superbly balanced package that's ideal for both law enforcement and personal protection.

ARTISTRY IN STEEL

by Ralph F. Quinn

To engrave or not to engrave? Most gun fanciers ponder this question at some point. The reasons for having a favorite firearm engraved run the gamut—from simply the desire to create a one-of-a-kind gun to adding the crowning touch to a superbly crafted classic rifle. Should the gun fancier happen to be in the gunsmithing trade, then the inclination to engrave may well stem from the need to pass on a signature firearm to family or friend. Whatever the reason, the first step is to find a professional engraver with the technical skill to transfer the art work to a piece of ordnance-grade steel.

Even though the 4140 chrome-moly and 416R stainless used in the receivers and actions of modern firearms rank among the toughest, most unyielding substances known to man, they can become one of the finest artistic mediums when placed in the hands of a talented engraver. Take a close look, for example, at the formal engraving found on American currency, particularly on the backs and corners. There you'll find exquisite borders and scroll work, often with foliate engravings surrounding scenes and numbers. This type of engraving may not be the same style used in adorning firearms, but gun engraving is nonetheless "artistry in steel." Indeed, some gun engravers work entirely in the Bulino style. That way, entire scenes can be created in a thin-point, bank-note style.

How an engraver works has a definite effect on the price one must pay. Some engraving techniques are faster than others; the bottom line depends on how quickly so many square inches of metal can be covered with a pattern. But even the simplest of engraved designs are likely to start at $350 and up. Add the fact that only 300 or so professional engravers are listed in the American Engravers Guild and it becomes a numbers game. With demand for quality engraving at an all-time high, and with a limited number of artisans available, the supply-and-demand continues to spiral costs ever upward. True, you may reduce costs by ferreting out a skilled engraver of little repute, but as with all things in the world of art you will get only what you pay for. Some engravers of lesser talent will execute extensive background stippling amid limited border scrolling and call it "engraving." Such individuals are to be avoided at all costs.

To provide a better understanding of the engraver's art, let's look at the craft closely from start to finish, keeping in mind that an engraver is an artist first and a technician second. The technical aspects of executing scrolls, borders and shading can be mastered with time; but blending these lines into a flowing, well-balanced design is something that cannot be taught. The engraver's

This Bulino (bank-note engraving) scene depicts three generations of gunsmithing. Note the ornate gold framework.

artistry is simply inborn, a gift from the heavens. Ask a master engraver what his or her final work will look like and the answer usually sounds something like this: "Wait until I'm finished."

In general, engravers define their work as light, fine scroll (English), deep-cut relief (Germanic) or something in between, perhaps a combination of English and Bulino, or Germanic and leaflets. American engravers seem to prefer simple, understated designs combined with initials or monograms and game animal inlays. The bottom line is: both design and layout must fit the character of the gun being engraved.

Judging any style of engraving in terms of quality takes time and a critical eye for line and form. The best way to achieve that goal is to look at as many engraved firearms as possible. An-

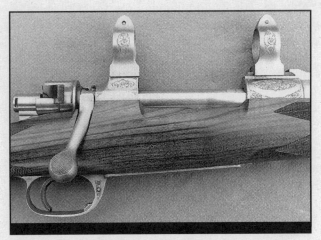

Metalwork embellishment on a high-grade classic stock sets this rifle apart as a truly custom firearm.

other is to review the many gun catalogs that feature engraved firearms. Most examples can be found on European shotguns made by such firms as AyA, Beretta, Francotte, Garbi, Marocchi, Merkel, Perazzi, Piotti and Rizzini. The lone exception is A. H. Fox's DE grade double shotgun, which is produced in the U.S. by Connecticut Shotgun Mfg. Co. (New Britain, CT). Remington, Winchester and Weatherby also offer U.S.-built factory-engraved rifles that are tastefully done.

In assessing any gun engraving, one must first study the arcs, which should be portions of true circles. Leaves, as they cascade across a receiver or floorplate, should have dimension and depth. Patterns should grow within the space occupied and not be crammed in. Shading and background should be done with finesse, augmenting the major elements without detracting from them. The real artists among today's engravers are able to adapt the character of their work to suit both the owner and his or her gun.

For some, a fine scroll in arabesque style done on a classy sidelock double is simply wrong for a rifle or semiauto shotgun. Rosettes and fine scrolls on a rifle are simply out of place. These days, it's not uncommon to embellish bolt-action floorplates with scroll and leaf patterns, coupled with sculpted animal figures in either gold or silver. But with a fine hunting rifle, it's best to let the metal work/stock design do the talking, and limit the engraving to the grip cap and floorplate.

Once an engraver has settled on a design with the client, the next step is to transfer the art work to the metal. If the artist is a talented professional capable of turning out symmetrical designs, he'll simply coat the cleaned metal with Damar (a special thin, quick-drying varnish) and sketch the art directly on the work with a special mark-on-anything pencil. Typically, master engravers often create the design and pattern as the metal is cut, with positive and negative areas having been evaluated before the work begins. Through intense concentration and years of practice, the work is then shaped by one's sense and mastery of style, design and technique. Some engravers learn more quickly than others, however. A top engraver observed at a recent SHOT Show was a young man in his mid-20s. The speed at which the work emerged under his skilled hands was amazing, and the results were excep-

tional. Less skilled but still competent engravers typically work up a design on a scaled template of the part to be engraved. Whether it's a shotgun or rifle, the key word is simplicity. By using clean, well-executed lines, the artist ensures himself enough room for expansion and added dimensions.

Before any engraving can begin, all original finish, bluing and plating must be stripped, making sure that all edges are kept square and screw holes true. Otherwise, they could spell big headaches in the work ahead. Then comes the transfer of the design to the polished steel (320 grit). Perhaps the easiest and most simplistic method of transposing is to use carbon paper as a transfer medium layered between the design (or tracing) and steel. Another method is to stipple the entire design outline into the floorplate and elsewhere. This method is similar to that of the sign painter who uses a pounce wheel to outline paint areas.

A third method used by top professionals involves a thin celluloid sheet to transfer base

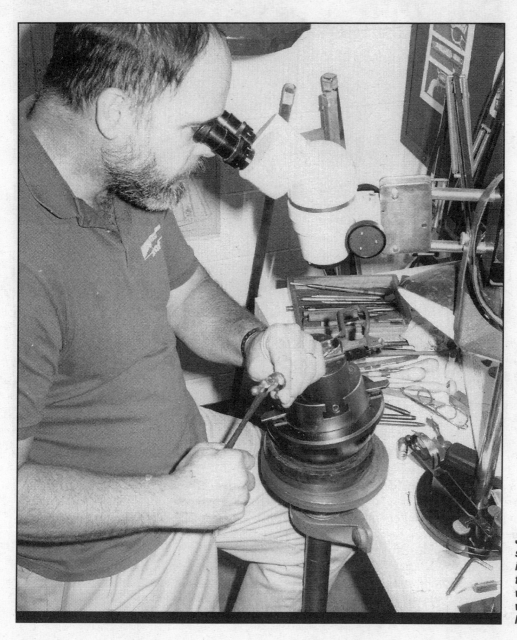

Jesse Houser, a professional engraver and instructor, operates a turntable with his foot while examining his work through a binocular scope.

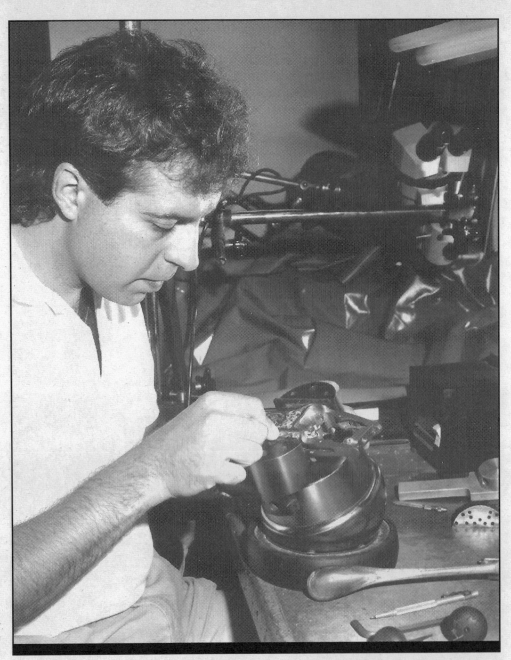

Firearms Guild member Rex Pedersen works on a Remington "Ducks Unlimited" action shotgun. Professionals use an engraving block for both flexibility and stability.

lines to the metal. A piece of clear plastic (overhead transparencies are ideal) is placed over the final paper design. Using a polished needlepoint scribe, the outline is then carefully scratched into the celluloid, producing a powder-holding furrow into the clear plastic. A thin layer of Damar varnish is applied to the gun part and allowed to dry to the tacky stage. The engraver then rubs a bright, dry pigment into the scribed surface. The

trick here is to keep the powder inside the furrows without leaving smudges on the celluloid surface. The engraver's index finger is ideal for keeping the grooves filled when making the final pass.

Using a piece of masking tape as a hinge, the plastic is attached to the metal floorplate or other part of the gun and turned onto the varnished metal. The surface is then burnished (rubbed)

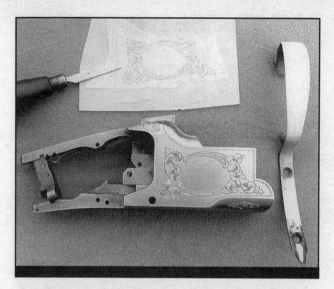

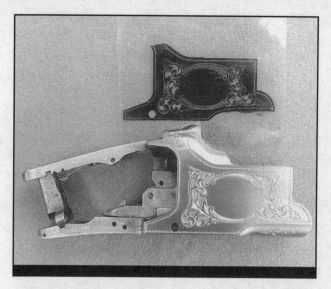

This work-in-progress shows a pattern design overlaid with tracing paper (top). An onglette or scribe is used to transfer the pattern. A triggerguard is shown coated with Damar varnish (right). The engraved over-under action has a basic outline cut.

It's possible to lift an engraved pattern by "smoking" or inking the action sideplate and covering it with wide tape. Such plates help the engraver evaluate his work, past and present.

with a piece of polished steel. When the celluloid is removed, there should be an exact copy of the scribed pattern transferred to the metal part. After the varnish has cured, the design is re-scribed onto the surface with a carbide stylus (otherwise, the pigment will rub off during the engraving process). Keep in mind that when an engraver creates a design he begins with the big elements first; i.e., the size of the scrolls and the way they flow together or intertwine. Once complete, the fine details fall quickly into place. If the basic design is not correct, however, no amount of fill detail can conceal lopsided scrolls and uneven transitions.

The tools needed for basic engraving work are few. They include a square (1/16") or incise die sinker's chisel for cutting individual single lines; and an onglette or knife graver for hand-etching. Many professionals prefer the onglette (or point graver) because it produces cuts quite similar to the square (or lozenge) graver and is suitable for hand-graving as well. Add a couple of line gravers for cutting parallel lines in backgrounds, a beading (or dot) punch .010, and a chase hammer (11/8" face). Finally, two stones—an India stone and a medium-hard Arkansas stone—are needed for renewing points and sharpening cutting edges.

The engraver's easel must provide enough flexibility and stability to ensure a workplace free of

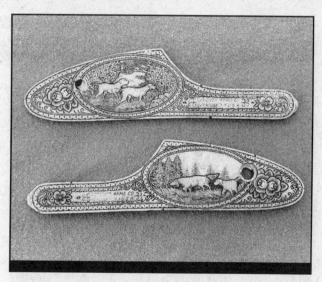

Epoxy casts from a small-gauge double shotgun provide a permanent record of past work. India ink highlights the delicate Bulino art in these center panels.

vibration. According to Jesse Houser, a noted engraver, the best engraving setup would be a vise mounted to a tree trunk firmly anchored in our mother earth! In actuality, he prefers a professional engraving-block vise mounted on a foot-operated, bench-mounted turntable.

With the work held firmly by the vise, the straight borders on all four sides of the design are

This pair of Smith & Wesson revolvers was completed by a 68-year-old retiree after attending an engraving class at a Community College program sponsored by the NRA.

cut (using the incise graver), making sure the graver tip bevels to the inside. The master lines of the scrolls are then cut with the onglette or incise graver, the line being beveled to the inside of each scroll. All master lines representing the leaves and inner stems are cut with the incise graver. The appearance of roundness is achieved by cutting parallel lines. The closer and deeper the cuts, the greater the feeling of curvature and dimension. The design is made to stand out by cutting away portions of the background with a chisel graver. Adding shallow lines near the edges of the leaves and other features produces a modeled effect. The bead (or dot) punch is used to produce background areas within the scrolls and between scrolls and borders. The line graver blends the elements and enhances the design perspective.

So the cutting goes. After mastering the design phase, cutting the major elements should pose no problem. Since an engraver is evaluated or graded on how well these principal lines are executed, it's extremely important to perfect these cuts through great diligence. Once the large

elements have been completed, the artist can finish each of the parts in turn. A good rule-of-thumb is to start in the corners and work separately within each element, thereby avoiding unsightly tool marks. The fine shading lines come last.

One of the biggest problems novice engravers face lies in finding the best angle for holding the graver while working with different metals. Softer metals incise best with a flatter angle; but graver position also depends on the angle that's ground on the tool heel. How easily the graver cuts depends on lubrication, sharpness and how well the tip is polished. The slightest flaw in the tip can cause the tool to wander, creating an unsightly mess, particularly in the border areas.

For most, practice is the key to finding the proper graver angle and the touch needed to drive the tool forward. A common error occurs when the back of the chisel is raised too high, causing the tip to bury itself. The result is an unsightly start-stop appearance in the finished line. Moreover, many aspiring engravers become discouraged early on because they select a design

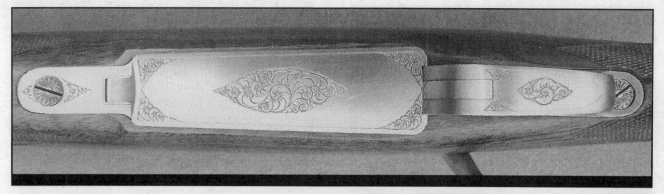

Custom-rifled floorplates and trigger guards are typically engraved in tasteful scrolls with an occasional animal inlay of gold or silver. Note the checkered bolt knob, a form of functional engraving.

that's too complicated or overly intricate. The motto here is: "Start at the beginning, keep it simple, and be patient." By practicing with hammer and chisel, any novice can increase the control needed to prevent slips and develop the power necessary for heavier cuts.

Once the tool basics have been mastered, the artist may want to consider using a "power" graver, such as the air-driven GRS Gravermeister, Foredom's Power-Graver or the NGraveR electric engraving tool. Rex Pedersen, longtime board member of the Firearms Engravers Guild of America, uses the GRS Gravermax almost exclusively to speed up production and still maintain a quality product. Using a Gravermeister, choppy lines in scroll work are virtually eliminated, with smooth-flowing lines and curves guaranteed from start to finish. Border cuts are made of uniform depth.

For gun enthusiasts with a strong desire to learn the engraver's art, J. B. Meek's book, *The Art of Engraving*, is highly recommended. Video fans are urged to view Layton McKenzie's "Beginning Engraving." The GRS Corporation, manufacturer of the air-powered Gravermeister and Gravermax, has an excellent video, entitled "GRS Engraving Methods & Techniques," which demonstrates the proper use of their highly regarded equipment. Suppliers include:
—Brownells, Inc.
200 S. Front, Montezuma, IA 50171
—Hand Engraver's Supply
601 Springfield Dr., Albany, GA 31707
—Jantz Supply
309 W. Main, Davis, OK 73030
—The Ngraver Co.
67 Wawecus Hill Rd., Bozrah, CT 06334

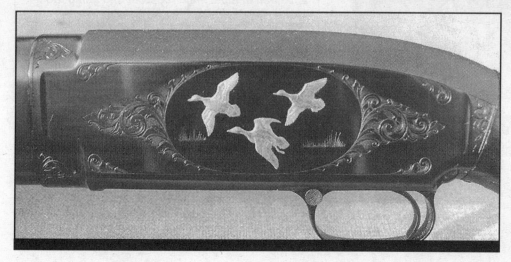

Waterfowl are often engraved on shotgun receivers simply because they "fit" the firearm theme. Well-executed, balanced scrollwork like this displays inlays nicely.

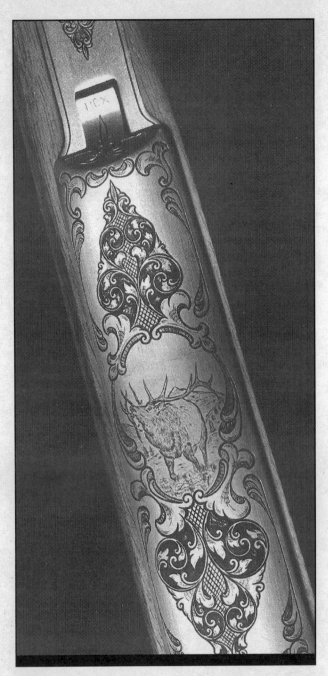

In-the-white rifle floorplate shows scrolls and foliate work in arabesque style. The fluer-de-lis add balance, while crosshatching and background stippling lend extra dimension.

Indeed, within hours an amateur engraver can produce work that once took years using the traditional chase hammer technique. Master engravers, who know the value of time, appreciate full well how the power engraver makes their work more competitive. Depth of cut and impact, all controlled by a foot throttle and handpiece, provide the full range of cutting, from delicate hairline strokes to those with enough power to remove heavy background metal.

As with any artistic endeavor, it's wise for engravers—beginner and advanced alike—to use honest criticism when evaluating their own progress or the work of a professional engraver. Don't let high praise cloud critical judgment. Review earlier work and make comparisons periodically. The important thing is to improve your technique. Regardless of the time involved, almost anyone can experience success as an engraver, although few will ever attain the rank of professional. There are no dark secrets or magic words needed to achieve the prize, only patience and hard work. Anyone who aspires to be an engraver, or who has admired the works of the truly great artists, can appreciate the words of the immortal master engraver Arnold Griebel: "Hard work, with the will to better what has gone on before, is what will eventually make an artist in steel."

RALPH F. QUINN has been a full-time freelance writer for the past 20 years. His articles have appeared in most major outdoor and gun periodicals, including Rifle, Rifle & Shotgun Sport Shooting, Petersen's Hunting, Wing & Shot, American Rifleman, Aquafield Accuracy & Shooting, Sigarms Quarterly *and* Handgunning. *A dedicated riflesmith and collector, he regularly upgrades his inventory of skills through NRA Gunsmithing Schools. Much of the information in this article stems from engraving courses offered by Pine Tech (Pine City, MN) and Montgomery Commercial College (Troy, NC).*

TOP PERFORMANCE FROM IN-LINE MUZZLELOADERS

by Toby Bridges

Only a few decades ago, many hunters turned to the muzzleloader for the first time simply out of curiosity, while an equal number did so merely to learn firsthand what it was like to hunt with a firearm the way their ancestors did. Today, the hunters—especially those who prefer whitetail deer—definitely outnumber the nostalgia buffs. In most states, the special "muzzleloader only" deer days now offer legitimate "third-season" opportunities for dedicated whitetail hunters.

To take advantage of this bonus season, the modern blackpowder hunter has turned to a new breed of percussion in-line ignition rifles—a far cry from the long-barreled originals carried by early American settlers and adventurers. These guns also perform a lot better than the more traditional muzzleloaders equipped with equally traditional projectiles (regulations in most states allow hunters to go as modern or as traditional as they wish).

Unfortunately, several muzzleloading manufacturers have made some pretty outlandish claims about the performance of their frontloading rifles. One claims energy levels that are comparable to what a .338 Winchester Magnum can generate, while another insists that its rifle retains more energy at 200 yards than most others can produce at the muzzle. These claims notwithstanding, a muzzleloading rifle is capable of producing only so

much velocity with even the heaviest loads of blackpowder or Pyrodex. Anyone who claims an energy level exceeding 3,000 foot-pounds at the muzzle is stretching the truth.

When it comes to selecting a bullet for hunting big game, the modern blackpowder hunter has three basic choices: the patched round ball, the heavy pure-lead conical bullet or the saboted projectile. Of the three, the patched round ball is the least effective because it loses velocity so fast, thereby shedding much-needed downrange energy levels. Generally speaking, a patched round ball will hit a game animal at 100 yards with only about one-third of the energy generated at the muzzle. Let's assume that a .50-caliber rifle has a 100-grain charge of FFg or Pyrodex "RS" or "Select." That means a 178-grain .490-inch ball smacks the target at 100 yards with only 450 foot-pounds of energy, hardly a real big-game stopper.

On the other hand, a heavy lead conical bullet, with its elongated shape and weight about twice that of a round ball for the same caliber rifle, will maintain an extremely high energy level downrange. Take, for example, a 385-grain conical bullet developing 1,582 ft.-lbs. of energy at the muzzle of a .50-caliber rifle with a 100-grain charge of FFg blackpowder or Pyrodex "RS"/"Select." That projectile can still hit home with 1,187 ft.-lbs. of energy at 100 yards, which is more than enough

Today's in-line percussion rifle looks more like a modern centerfire than a muzzleloader. As proof that it can outperform the centerfire, note this excellent specimen: a caribou taken at 160 yards with a saboted handgun bullet.

energy to take any big-game animal walking around the North American continent.

One major complaint about the conical lead bullet lies with its fragile "driving" or "bearing" bands and, in some designs, the skirts of its hollow base. Lead has no memory, so once a pure-lead conical is shoved down the bore at a crooked angle, even if only slightly, the rifling is bound to shave off a small amount of lead. By the time the bullet reaches the powder charge, its fit with the bore will be loose at best. As a result, at the moment of ignition gases can force past the bullet, producing inaccuracy. Moreover, a bullet that fits this loosely in the bore creates a dangerous situation. Any bullet that practically falls down to the powder charge can just as easily work its way forward when the rifle is carried with the muzzle down. Should the bullet move forward even a fraction of an inch, accuracy can be affected adversely. Worse still, should the bullet move forward as much as a foot or more, dangerous pressures can occur, the same as with a barrel obstruction. The result: a burst barrel and serious injury to the shooter.

Another problem with slow-moving conical bullets (which can weigh as much as 500 to 600 grains for a .50- or .54-caliber muzzleloading rifle) is their terrible rainbow trajectory. Even with a hefty 100- to 120-grain charge of FFg blackpowder or Pyrodex "RS"/"Select," a conical bullet containing only 400 or so grains can drop more than 10 inches from 100 to 150 yards. At that point, the big slugs have the trajectory of a thrown brick. They're also notorious for poor expansion at longer ranges.

SABOTED BULLETS: THE BEST COMBO

The best of both worlds can be achieved by shooting the saboted bullet, easily the most versatile and effective system available to the muzzleloading hunter. A growing variety of these hard-hitting bullets is now available, all designed specifically for shooting with a sabot out of a muzzleloader. Moreover, commercial bullet manufacturers currently offer several hundred or more different handgun bullets, all of which can be fired from a muzzleloader using one of the plastic sabots. Not all of these handgun bullets offer the kind of performance needed to take deer and other big game cleanly. Knowing which bullet to use for the game in question is the real key to success with saboted handgun bullets.

Most of the .44- and .45-caliber jacketed handgun slugs now on the market have been designed to expand and transfer energy at velocities which are, for all practical purposes, the same as those

produced by a muzzleloading hunting rile and a hunting charge of either blackpowder or Pyrodex (those with muzzle velocities of around 1,400 to 1,600 feet per second). Modern Muzzleloading, Hornady, Thompson/Center and a few others market sabots and jacketed handgun bullets already matched. Shooters who seek the best combination for whitetail or mule deer need only visit their local sporting goods store and "pick up a pack." Those who need to know exactly which bullet gives the best terminal performance and accuracy can purchase the sabots alone and match them up with a bullet of the proper diameter. By doing so, an unbelievable variety of bullets, ranging from lightweights of about 180 grains to heavyweights of around 400 grains, are available for firing from a .50- or .54-caliber muzzleloader. Speer, Nosler, Hornady, Sierra, Barnes, Accuracy Unlimited, among others, offer good selections of .44- and .45-caliber handgun bullets.

Tony Knight, designer of the popular Knight in-line percussion rifles, has established several loads for hunting whitetail deer. With a .50-caliber rifle, he favors the 310-grain Knight lead bullet loaded into the bore with a black Knight "Hi-Per Shock" sabot. With a 100-grain charge of FFg blackpowder or Pyrodex "RS"/"Select," this bullet develops 1,477 fps at the muzzle and gener-

ates 1,441 ft.-lbs. of energy. Downrange at 100 yards, the projectile still moves along at 1,297 fps with 1,158 ft.-lbs. of energy left over. At this distance, the bullet will take even the biggest whitetail. In fact, at 150 yards this load can still hit the target with 1,011 ft.-lbs. of energy.

When shooting a .54-caliber rifle, most knowledgeable shooters switch to the slightly heavier 325-grain jacketed hollowpoint bullet, which has proven extremely accurate and powerful, especially when used with a purple Knight "Hi-Per Shock" sabot. The same 310-grain lead bullet used with a .50-caliber rifle can be fired with great accuracy from a .54 caliber by switching to a red Knight "Hi-Per Shock" sabot. That's because the big .50-caliber 325-grain jacketed bullet is closer to the bore size of the .54 Knight rifle, thereby allowing the use of the purple sabot with its thinner petals. The closer a bullet is to the bore size of the rifle, the greater accuracy is generally produced. For that reason, a .45-caliber bullet tends to produce the best accuracy out of a .50-caliber rifle, while a .50-caliber bullet turns in the best accuracy from a .54 caliber. Knight has found that a 325-grain .50-caliber jacketed hollowpoint can be a real tack driver out of a .54 rifle.

A 100-grain charge of FFg blackpowder or Pyrodex "RS"/"Select" can push a 325-grain bullet

This fine Missouri whitetail was taken at 100 yards with a saboted Speer 260-grain .45 jacketed hollowpoint from a .50-caliber Black Knight muzzleloader. The gun's designer, Tony Knight, is shown at left.

In the past, muzzleloading hunters were forced to choose between the patched round ball (left) or the heavy lead conical bullet (right). Today's blackpowder hunter has a much better choice: the saboted handgun bullet.

Big lead conical bullets like this Thompson/Center "Maxi-Ball" develop tremendous energy levels, but they also produce rainbow trajectories. The recovered bullet (right) was taken from a buck dropped at 120 yards.

Buffalo Bullet's hollow-pointed "Maxi" bullet is made from pure lead to ensure easy loading and high energy levels.

from the muzzle of a 24-inch Knight rifle barrel at about 1,420 fps and will generate 1,455 ft.-lbs. of muzzle energy. At 100 yards this bullet smacks home with close to 1,150 ft.-lbs. of energy. The additional 15-grain weight offers no significant advantage, but when a .50-caliber bullet hits a whitetail or any other big-game animal with that much energy—and the shot is where it should be—the animal will definitely go down. When hunting with a .54-caliber Knight rifle using a load of 110 grains of Pyrodex "Select," the energy level at 100 yards is increased by another 100 ft.-lbs. or so. That's stopping power!

When hunting everything from pronghorn antelope to moose with a .50-caliber Knight rifle, a different bullet is needed for each. For antelope, the primary concern is to maintain a flat trajectory. For moose, proper penetration and transfer of energy are paramount. The availability of .429" and .451" (and even .500") handgun bullets offers an optimum choice for any game found on this planet.

Most experienced muzzleloading hunters who've made the switch to hunting with saboted bullets have discovered that, in terms of energy and knockdown power, the .50-caliber rifles will do everything a .54-caliber rifle can. And because a wider range of .44- and .45-caliber bullets is available to shoot with accuracy from a .50-caliber bore, due in part to the thinner sabot needed to load and shoot these bullets, the .50-caliber reigns in popularity. When hunting deer-sized game, most .50-caliber rifle shooters who've switched to saboted bullets tend to prefer bullets that weigh between 240 and 260 grains. With a 100-grain charge of Pyrodex "Select" or FFg blackpowder, a saboted 260-grain bullet leaves the muzzle of a 24-inch barrel at 1,600 fps and hits home at 1,400 ft.-lbs. of energy. At 100 yards, a modern, well-designed jacketed hollowpoint conical bullet will still hit the target with 1,050 ft.-lbs. or so of energy. And at 150 yards, the same bullet can reach the target with 900 ft.-lbs. of energy.

A modern in-line percussion hunting rifle sighted in at 100 yards will only print this load about 6½ inches low at 150 yards. To compensate for some of this drop, hunters in open country are now beginning to sight their rifles two to three inches high at 100 yards. This allows them to hold center on a whitetail buck at any range from 75

to 150 yards and still put a jacketed hollowpoint bullet into the kill zone.

Fortunately, the popularity of saboted bullets for muzzleloading hunting rifles has finally resulted in bullets designed specifically for that purpose. Barnes Bullets (American Fork, Utah) markets a very effective all-copper saboted bullet, which it calls the Expander-MZ bullet. And for the slightly longer all-copper bullet, Barnes has designed a new, longer plastic sabot as well. Currently, the company markets 250- and 300-grain saboted .45-caliber bullets for .50-caliber muzzleloading rifles, and 275- and 325-grain bullets for shooting with a .54 frontloader. Reports from a number of experienced blackpowder hunters indicate that these bullets are devastating on big game. This writer used a Knight .50-caliber muzzleloader and 100 grains of Pyrodex "Select" with a 300-grain Expander-MZ bullet for a clean one-shot, 45-yard kill on a huge bull elk weighing close to 900 pounds. And another outdoor writer—John Sloan of Lebanon, TN— took his muzzleloader to Quebec for caribou recently and dropped a nice bull at 168 yards with one of the 250-grain Barnes bullets. Both recovered slugs were perfectly expanded.

ENSURING OPTIMUM ACCURACY

Not every modern muzzleloader can shoot saboted handgun bullets accurately, however. Most hunters should concentrate on rifles with a relatively fast rate of rifling twist, such as 1 turn in 20–32 inches. Anything slower generally won't produce acceptable accuracy. To help ensure optimum accuracy from a muzzleloader, you should consider the following tips:

1. Buy the very best quality rifle you can afford. Yes, bargains do exist on the muzzleloading market, but they are few and far between. Normally, you get what you pay for in quality and performance.

2. If your rifle won't shoot the type of projectile it's supposed to, check the rifling for rough spots or overly sharp edges. Either condition will greatly affect accuracy. If you feel a rough spot when wiping the bore with a cleaning patch, or if you notice slits in the patch made by sharp rifling edges, you may have to lap the bore to remedy the problem. Most of the time, though, this condition can be taken care of simply by sprinkling a common bathroom scouring powder

This MK-95 Magnum Elite from Modern Muzzleloading is one of the new breed of muzzleloading hunting rifles. It relies on hot target rifle primers for sure-fire ignition.

on a wet, tight-fitting cleaning patch and running it through the bore a hundred or more times. The scouring powder isn't so abrasive that it can wear the rifling, but it will work effectively on rough spots and dull those sharp rifling edges.

3. Always use projectiles of proper diameter. Any changes in the diameter, or even the brand of projectiles, can affect accuracy. For example, if you've been shooting a saboted 260-grain .45-caliber Speer bullet, but then you start loading with Nosler, Hornady, Sierra or any other bullet of the same diameter and weight, don't be surprised if your rifle produces shots that are entirely different.

4. Always wipe the bore clean of oils and solvents before loading your rifle. And before dump-

The modern in-line percussion rifle is now used by serious hunters who seek game once reserved only for flat-shooting centerfire rifles. Outdoor writer Jim Shockey is shown here with a stone sheep he took out with a single shot from his in-line rifle.

dex are both forgiving when it comes to being a grain or two off from shot to shot, but a five-grain difference can cause relevant inconsistencies. Also, always use the same powder measure. It's not uncommon for weighted charges to vary as much as 10 grains, even though two different measures have the same setting.

6. To ensure that a powder charge is properly seated, do not bounce the ramrod on the projectile after it's been pushed down over the powder charge. You'll only deform the nose of the bullet and ruin accuracy. When seating a bullet, push down hard enough so that the projectile is properly seated, and use the same procedure each and every time. Consistency has its rewards—and better accuracy is one of them.

7. When shooting for accuracy, be sure to wipe the bore with a damp patch after each shot—not every other shot, or every third shot, but after *every* shot. Whether you use blackpowder or Pyrodex, it's important to do this. Many hunters use Pyrodex in the field because they feel they can load a second, third, or even fourth follow-up shot without having to wipe the bore. In doing so, accuracy will suffer. When using blackpowder, there's no choice but to wipe fouling from the bore after each shot, even out in the field.

A final tip: For better hunting performance from any muzzleloader, be sure to get out and shoot often. Don't be afraid to experiment. Many successful hunting loads have been developed simply by trying bullet and sabot combinations that are not readily available on the market. Taking a good buck with a load that has been custom-tailored for your own rifle adds to the enjoyment and satisfaction of the hunting experience.

ing in a powder charge, always snap several caps on a percussion rifle to blow out any oil that may exist in the ignition system. Oil residue in the barrel or the ignition system itself can cause a hangfire or misfire. This usually occurs only on the first shot—but that could well be the only one you get at a good buck.

5. When loading, always use a reliable powder measure, and be sure to load with consistent charges from shot to shot. Blackpowder and Pyro-

TOBY BRIDGES is one of the country's most respected authorities on blackpowder hunting. Armed with a variety of muzzleloading rifles, he has collected nearly a hundred whitetails and a wide range of other North American big game. He is the author of Advanced Muzzle Loaders Guide *(Stoeger Pub. Co.), now under revision, and has written for many shooting and hunting publications. He is presently head of market development for Modern Muzzleloading, Inc. (Centerville, IA).*

A NEW ERA IN HOMEMADE BALLISTICS

by Don Lewis

Sometime during the 13th century, Friar Roger Bacon worried that his black dust—a mixture of charcoal, sulphur and saltpeter—was too dangerous for mankind. He wrote, "If used in large amounts, no one could stand the terror of the noise and flash." Bacon knew well that his black dust, later known as gunpowder, caused an alarming sound and produced an unseen force that couldn't be explained. And so, to protect mankind, he hid his formula in a code so complex that it has never been fully deciphered. But Bacon's efforts to protect mankind from gunpowder were to no avail: gunpowder had come to stay.

In one sense, gunpowder is the substance that makes firearms possible; but it's the unseen force created by the burning powder that seals the cartridge against the chamber walls and bolt face, then drives the bullet through the bore. This force, known as "chamber pressure," is produced by large volumes of rapidly expanding carbon dioxide and nitrogen gases. When confined, as in a cartridge case, tremendous pressure is generated. The barrel (chamber) and bolt are strong enough to contain this pressure, hence the only movable part of the combination is the bullet, which lies in front of the powder charge and seals the bore. Pushed forward by the violently expanding gas, the bullet gains velocity rapidly until its exit from the muzzle, at which point the gunpowder has done its job.

To do this obviously requires a great deal of pressure, but not so much as to go beyond the safety limits of the firearm itself. For that reason, the pressure output of factory ammunition is carefully controlled, making it safe to fire in firearms in good condition. Remember, though, that any factory pressure figure indicated for a particular shell is the average pressure reading. It does not indicate the extreme spread among the shots fired. Let's assume a figure of 56,300 psi (pounds per square inch) is the average for a 10-shot test. It's possible that one or more shots will hit 60,000 psi or more, but several low readings may fall in the 57,000 psi range, making the average velocity 58,300 psi. Even though every aspect of the shells in the test group could be called identical, chamber pressures and velocities will vary. No matter how exact handloaders may assemble their rounds, it's literally impossible to get identical chamber pressure readings shot after shot.

Pressure readings should also fall within a reasonable extreme pressure spread. For example, if a five-shot test produces a low reading of 42,000 psi and a high reading of 55,000 psi—or an average pressure of 50,380—there's simply too much difference in pressure to consider that load combination acceptable. Keeping peak pressure under 60,000 psi, with an extreme pressure spread as low as possible, should be the goal of

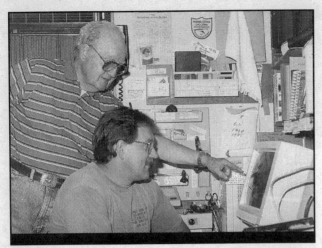
The author and computer expert Steve Hamilton discuss data provided by the Oehler Model 43 unit.

every handloader. Uniformity is the name of the game, for sure.

As an example, a suggested book load for a Model 700 Remington 6mm is 38 1/2 grains of IMR 4895 behind a 70-grain Sierra HP bullet fired by a Remington 9 1/2 primer. This combination produced an average pressure for five shots of 66,800 psi. The high reading was 67,800 psi and the low 65,000, a difference of 2,800 psi. Average muzzle velocity for the total group was 2,917 fps. In reality, there's no such thing as "just a little extra pressure." Pushing this powder charge another grain could increase pressure output considerably. It's a cardinal rule in handloading never to-exceed, even by a half grain, the maximum suggested powder charges as published in any current reloading manual.

For decades, measuring chamber pressure was the sole property of firearms companies, ammunition makers, ballistics laboratories and a handful of ballistics experts. The general consensus over the years held that measuring chamber pressure in one's own rifle was beyond the technical and financial reach of most handloaders. Furthermore, the methods used for measuring pressure, such as the crusher and transducer systems, required drilling a hole into the chamber, a move that automatically ruined a rifle for hunting or target purposes.

The only system that could possibly have been used by handloaders was the strain gage, consist-

ing of a fine wire embedded in a thin material cemented tightly around the outside of the barrel. When the cartridge fired, the barrel expanded ever so slightly, stretching the wire and creating a change in its electrical resistance that was proportional to the pressure. This resistance is measurable with the aid of sophisticated and expensive electrical equipment. In fact, the high expense alone kept the strain gage system out of the hands of handloaders (for some reason, "gauge" in pressure measuring devices has always been spelled "gage").

When Roger Bacon's black dust mixture was first used by the military in cannons (and later shoulder weapons), there was no way of knowing whether the device would fire the projectile or simply explode. According to historical records, military forces in that era prayed to their patron, St. Barbara, to protect them in case their weapons detonated when fired. Gunmakers in the 1300s had no alternative but to increase the thickness of metal in the barrel. Not being able to measure chamber pressure was indeed the Achilles heel of early gun builders.

Sometime around 1850—more than 500 years after the gun was invented—Sir Alfred Noble designed the first practical instrument for measuring chamber pressure inside a gun. This "crusher gage," as it came to be known, required

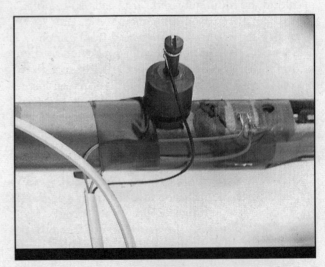
A strain gage is shown glued onto a Savage Model 23D .22 Hornet. Note the tape holding the wires (to prevent them from being pulled away from the barrel).

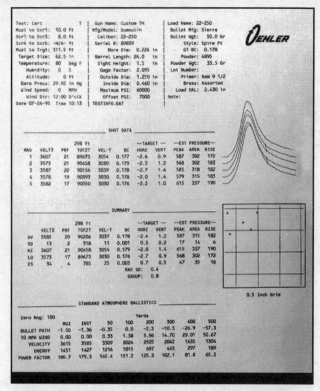

In this screen printout from the M-43 PBL, note the pressure curve for each shot. The tiny vertical line on each curve represents the point when the bullet left the muzzle. The enlarged grid below the pressure curves indicates where the bullets hit. Average pressure for the group shown was 58,700 psi.

drilling a small hole into the chamber area and fitting the hole with a sliding piston. This allowed the piston to crush a small piece of lead against an anvil once the gun was fired. The higher the pressure, the more lead was deformed by the piston.

This crushed lead cylinder was measured against lead cylinders from the same batch having the same specific height and diameter. These "proof" cylinders were then subjected to static compression tests, which yielded a chart showing the deformed height as opposed to the applied force (or pressure) equivalent. Once a shot was fired, the deformed cylinder from the crusher gage was measured and the chart translated the height of the crushed cylinder to the pressure of the shot.

More than a century later, the lead crusher gage continued to measure peak pressures falling within blackpowder and shotgun ranges.

The picture changed, though, when smokeless powder came on the scene. According to Dr. Kenneth Oehler (Oehler Research, Inc., manufacturer of the Model 43 Personal Ballistic Laboratory), smokeless powders in modern cartridges produce much higher pressures. Because these higher pressures caused the lead to deform to an unacceptable level, lead was replaced by a copper cylinder. During the last 20 years or so, however, ever higher and unmeasurable pressures have caused the copper crusher to be replaced by piezoelectric transducers in most chamber pressure measurements.

Oehler further points out that whereas two systems now exist for measuring pressure, the readings don't agree. As a result, pressure readings that were formerly accepted as gospel became suspect. Copper crusher readings that once represented peak pounds per square inch were now superseded by another system that also measured peak pounds per square inch. "Copper crusher" readings and "peak psi" readings taken from transducers are not interchangeable. As Dr. Oehler points out, ballistics charts may appear to offer a conversion between CUP (copper units of pressure) readings and peak PSI (pounds per square inch), but that conversion isn't easy. Military ballisticians have fired thousands of rounds seeking an easy answer. They haven't found it yet—and they won't. As a result, readings taken with copper crushers are tagged with the designation CUP, while the PSI designation is reserved for readings taken with transducers,

William C. Davis, Jr., Ballistic Editor for *American Rifleman* and a noted ballistic authority, reports that small arms pressures, as measured by crusher gages, range from 5–20 percent below true peak pressures, depending more or less on the characteristics of the load and the type of crusher gage used. It's called a "systematic error," because it's consistent from shot to shot. Because of this systematic error, some ballisticians feel it's academically inaccurate to refer to crusher-gage measurements as pressures in pounds per quare inch. Because of these objections, it has become the practice in U.S. commercial parlance to speak of crusher gage measurements in terms of "copper units of pressure (c.u.p.)" and "lead units of pressure (l.u.p.)". These new terms are used to distinguish crusher gage

measurements from those made by electronic-transducer gages, which are now expressed in psi or psia (pounds per square inch absolute).

WELCOME TO A NEW ERA!

Obviously, measuring chamber pressure is a highly complicated task that for years required special equipment and trained ballistics technicians. No wonder it was commonly felt that measuring chamber pressure in hunting and target rifles was an "impossible dream" for most gunsmiths, amateur and professional alike. Enter the Oehler Model 43 Personal Ballistic Laboratory. For the first time, thanks to the computer, shooters could make measurements of pressure available, along with muzzle and downrange velocities, flight times and measured ballistic coefficients. Most of what we could only guess at previously could now be measured and recorded.

Previously, chronographs told shooters what was going on in front of a gun, but they had no idea what was going on inside the gun. If the gun held together, we assumed the load was safe. If a cartridge case showed visible signs of excessive pressure, or it couldn't be reloaded, it was considered borderline. From a viewpoint of personal safety, that kind of thinking was completely unacceptable. Smart shooters tried to "read" indications of excess pressure by paying particular

attention to a case after it had been fired. A load combination that generated too much pressure was considered reloadable by common standards for such pressure signs as hard-to-lift bolt handles, excessive recoil and case stretching, not to mention case-head expansion, primer leakage, cratered primers and signs of incipient case cracking.

Traditionally, shooters have expressed concern about pressure, but they often haven't given pressure the respect it deserves. Until now, they've had no equivalent to a chronograph to help them. That's where Oehler's M-43 PBL comes into play. It offers a lot of ballistics data, true, but the emphasis here is on pressure measurements. Unlike crusher gages and some transducers that require drilling holes in the chamber and cartridge case, the M-43 PBL uses a small (1/2") thin strain gage that glues onto the barrel. Instead of a wire wrapped around the barrel, this new electrical path forms a zigzag path, making it possible for a longer wire to be used in a smaller package. The longer the wire, the more sensitive the gage. This tiny zigzag circuit is connected to larger, copper-coated tabs where lead wires are soldered to the barrel.

When a shot is fired, pressure causes the chamber to stretch, or strain. With a strain gage glued over the chamber area, it's possible to mea-

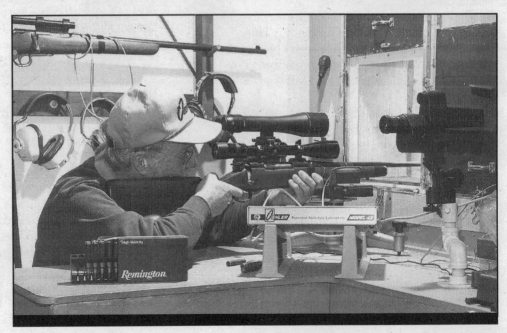

The author fires a Model 700 Mountain rifle chambered for the 280 Remington. Note the strain gage emerging from the rifle barrel and connected to the M-43 PBL

The amplifier and downrange cable reel are shown after the acoustic target has been hung on a target board. Each corner of the triangle contains a microphone which picks up the bullet's sonic boom and also measures its velocity and ballistic coefficient.

sure the stretch. Assuming the chamber is a simple steel cylinder, with no "end effects," the M-43 measures the inside and outside diameters of the cylinder and estimates the pressure required to produce the stretch or strain previously observed. The M-43's instruction manual goes into detail on how to install a strain gage, and also how to install and operate its ballistic program in the computer. A laptop computer powered by a battery works best because it can then be used out at the range. All skyscreen and range measurements, barometric pressure, altitude, wind direction, temperature, humidity, etc., are then entered in the first column of the program. The second column contains data on the firearm used, including outside (measured with a dial caliper) and inside chamber measurements.

The second column also includes information on sight height (usually 1$\frac{1}{2}$ inches for scopes), gage factor, maximum PSI (60,000 psi or less) and offset PSI (the amount of pressure required to expand the cartridge case against the sidewall of the chamber). The M-43 recommends 7,000 psi for metallic cartridges, 500 psi for shotguns and zero for muzzleloaders. Offset pressure is included in the pressure readout.

The last column contains data on primer/powder/bullet combinations, including the overall length of a complete cartridge. The ballistic coefficient of a given bullet is measured automatically when either downrange skyscreens or an acoustic target is used. Ballistic coefficient (when using an acoustic target) is obtained by measuring the distance between the rifle muzzle and the acoustic target to within one-tenth of a foot.

Gluing a strain gage to a rifle barrel is an extremely precise procedure. But by following the step-by-step method in the M-43's instruction manual anyone can obtain a perfect bond between barrel and gage. For the tests used for this article an area roughly $3/4" \times 3/4"$ was sanded white (to remove the bluing) slightly ahead of the recoil lug. Detailed instructions are provided on how to make strain gage cables, including tips on soldering. The M-43 kit comes complete with muzzle skyscreens, five strain gages, a modular cable and connectors for making strain gage cables, tapes, glues and tools.

If an acoustic target is ordered separately, be sure to order $1/2$-inch Schedule 40 PVC plastic pipe (do not use metal pipe). The acoustic target is a 60-inch triangle (a 40-inch triangle is recommended for 17 and 22 calibers) of plastic pipe containing three microphones, one at each corner. These microphones pick up the Mach cone (sonic boom) of the bullet and transmit downrange velocity, time of flight and ballistic coefficient through an amplifier and range cable back to the M-43. The major benefit of the acoustic target lies in its measurement of ballistic coefficients for each bullet fired— an important asset, Dr. Oehler reminds us. With a 200-yard zero, a significant change in the ballistic coefficient may alter the point of impact slightly at 400 yards; but the same change in the ballistic coefficient can change 400-yard energy and wind deflection significantly. As William C. Davis, Jr., points out: "The BC is a quantitative indicator of a bullet's ability to maintain its velocity as it flies through the air. Mathematically, it's expressed as $C = W/(I*D2)$, where "W" is the bullet's weight in pounds; "D" is its diameter in inches, and "I" is a so-called form factor which depends on the bullet's shape.

We know that book pressure readings represent the average peak pressures obtained from the testing procedure, and there's no guarantee that a handloader will achieve the same peak pressure in his or her rifle. For one thing, ammu-

nition makers use new brass along with specifically selected components that have been fired under controlled conditions. Generally speaking, handloaders use brass that has been fired at least once—possibly many times—plus components purchased over the counter. Almost any change in brass (i.e., from one brand to another) or components can change pressure readings significantly. IMR4350 powder is not necessarily the same as H4350, and each should be used with its own loading data. That's why it is imperative never to start with a maximum suggested load. Start low and work up.

Measuring slightly over 11 inches wide, 9 inches deep and 1 1/2 inches thick, the M-43 PBL unit is surprisingly small. It contains a rechargeable battery for range use and a DC adapter for electric power. Receptacles and jacks are found on the rear panel for plugging in muzzle sky-screens, downrange connector, computer RS232 receptacle, strain gage and a power supply jack.

The main thrust of our tests for this article was to accumulate pressure data on similar primer/powder/bullet combinations in rifles of the same chambering. They were not for checking against book pressure readings on the same loads. One test involved three 22-250 caliber rifles with the same load combinations. Our purpose was to show how three chambers react with nearly identical primer/powder/bullet combinations. The loads were carefully assembled with standard RCBS 22-250 full-length sizing dies, Rockchucker press and automatic primer seating tool. Each powder charge was weighed to plus-or-minus 1/10 grain of powder on an RCBS electronic scale.

Rifles selected for the test included a Dumoulin Custom, Ithaca LSA 55 and Remington Model 700 BDL. The first test used 33 1/2 grains of H4895 powder, 50- grain Sierra bullets and 9 1/2 Remington primer. Peak pressure was 428PSI(M-43) (42,800 psi) in the Dumoulin; 45,800 psi in the LSA 55, and 33,100 psi in the Remington 700. A maximum book load of 36 1/2 grains of H4895 produced the following peak pressure readings: Dumoulin Custom=56,400 psi; Ithaca LSA 55=63,200 psi; and Remington 700=41,800 psi.

Interestingly, the Ithaca LSA 55 registered the highest peak pressure in each test. Conversely, the Remington Model 700 produced far lower pressures than the other rifles tested. With the LSA 55 registering an average peak pressure reading above 60,000 psi (63,200 psi), this load was not used in the Ithaca. The pressure readings for the 5-shot test in the LSA 55 were: 61,200 psi, 63,900 psi, 66,600 psi, 62,000 psi and 62,500 psi. Every shot produced a pressure reading above 60,000 psi, which is considered maximum pressure in a rifle chamber (handloaders generally prefer pressure readings in the low 50,000 psi category). Throughout our tests, using an assortment of hunting rifles and many different load combinations, it became evident that increasing the powder charge does increase velocity; but, in some cases, this detracted from accuracy and created pressure readings above the 60,000 psi maximum limit. The M-43 PBL proved emphatically that maximum powder charges should be approached with caution.

In conclusion, the M-43 PBL offers handloaders a wealth of ballistic data from conventional hunting and target rifles that heretofore was available only from firearm and ammunition manufacturers using special barrels. Handloaders have speculated for decades about chamber pressure, velocity, downrange velocity, time of flight, bullet path, energy, impact of wind, and ballistic coefficients. These facts are now readily available on the M-43 PBL printout in the form of a complete ballistic data sheet covering all load combinations used from a given test firing. The old days of guesswork for the amateur handloader are past, and a new era in home ballistics has definitely arrived.

DON LEWIS is a retired corporate credit manager who now tests and evaluates firearms and shooting equipment. A regular contributor to SHOOTER'S BIBLE, *Lewis writes gun-related articles for several publications, including* Handloader's Digest *and* Pennsylvania Game News, *for which he has served as gun columnist for the past 31 years. He also regularly contibutes to* Leader Times, Varmint Hunter, AquaField Publications, Precision Shooting *and* Pennsylvania Sportsman.

MANUFACTURERS' SHOWCASE

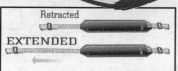

RETRACTA-SLING BY HUNTER:

The Sling with a Memory

RETRACTA-SLING is the greatest advancement in sling development since the rifle was invented. When slung, RETRACTA-SLING affords a firm comfortable fit, with plenty of shock-absorbing comfort no matter how little or how much clothing is worn. When unslung, it retracts to a taut position for clean, no-slop, no-adjust ease of carrying, storing and retrieving of the rifle. No more snagging on brush and limbs. No more "Squeaky Swivels." Incredibly strong yet ultra-lightweight. Non-slip backing. Lifetime warranty. For a complete catalog of HUNTER accessories, call or write:

HUNTER COMPANY
3300 West 71st Ave.,Westminster, CO 80030
1-800-676-4868 (Toll Free)

AMTEC 2000 REVOLVER

AMTEC 2000, INC. is a unique joint venture that brings together two of the world's foremost makers of fine firearms: Erma Werke and Harrington & Richardson. These firms have united German engineering skill and American manufacturing skill to create a new company that is greater than the sum of its parts. This AMTEC 2000 Double Action model in 38 S&W Special is a five-shot revolver with swing-out cylinder and shell ejector. Offered in high-polish blue, matte electroless nickel or stainless steel finish. The grips are Pachmayr composition with finger grooves. For further information, contact:

AMTEC 2000, INC.
P.O. Box 1191, Gardner, MA 01440

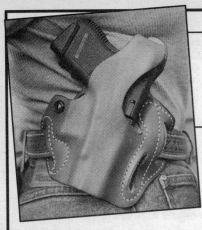

DeSANTIS THUMB BREAK SCABBARD

A perennial favorite with law-enforcement professionals, the DeSANTIS Thumb Break Scabbard carries the weapon high and at an optimum angle of presentation. Its thumb break and exact molding, together with a new screw tensioning device, allow for secure and highly concealed carry. Dual belt slots allow wearers to choose their own carry angle. The DeSANTIS Thumb Break Scabbard is available for medium and large autos as well as medium and large revolvers. It comes in tan or black, plain lined or basket-weave lined. Please note some models have no tension screw. Call or write:

DeSANTIS HOLSTER & LEATHER GOODS, INC.
P.O. Box 2039, New Hyde Park, NY 11040-0701
Tel: 516-354-8000 Fax: 526-354-7501

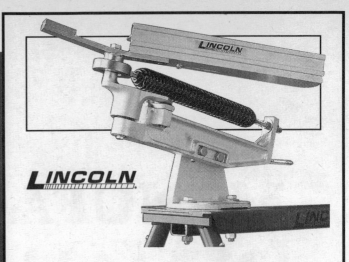

LINCOLN Traps define quality, durability and reliability. Crafted in the USA, they are built to last, with an unbeatable factory warranty. Three whisper-quiet models are priced from **$249.00**. Accessories are available to customize your individual shooting needs, including a new variety of throwing arms. LINCOLN stands for quality. "Discover the Difference" today.

SHYDA'S SERVICES, INC.
"Home of the Lincoln"
1009 S. Lincoln Ave., Lebanon, PA 17042
Tel: 717-274-8676

MANUFACTURERS' SHOWCASE

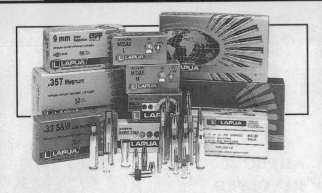

LAPUA AMMO NOW AVAILABLE

The world-famous LAPUA ammunition is now available in the U.S. LAPUA has been making top-quality ammunition and components since 1923 and is one of the leading brands in Europe. LAPUA ammunition is used by top national teams in shooting competitions throughout the world. A complete selection of .22 rimfire, centerfire rifle and centerfire pistol ammunition is available, along with a wide variety of brass and bullets. Specialized loads are made for competition, hunting and self-defense/law-enforcement applications. Imported exclusively by:

KENG'S FIREARMS SPECIALTY, INC.
875 Wharton Drive, S.W., Atlanta, GA 30336-2125

TAURUS BRINGS BACK ITS POPULAR MODEL 85

Thanks to popular demand, TAURUS announces the re-introduction of its .38 Special Model 85 five-shot revolver (discontinued when Taurus brought out its 357 Magnum Model 605 revolver in 1996). Each Model 85, either a standard or concealed-hammer version, whether blued or stainless steel, is now equipped with a pair of the famous Uncle Mike's Boot Grips designed by Craig Spegal. This enhancement further reduces the configuration of the M85's already compact snubnose and adds value to perhaps the most affordable quality .38 Special on the market today!

TAURUS INTERNATIONAL FIREARMS
16175 N.W. 49th Avenue, Miami, FL 33014-6314
Tel: 800-327-3776 (TollFree) or 305-624-1115
Fax: 305-623-7506

NEW BULL BARREL YOUTH SLUG GUN BY HARRINGTON & RICHARDSON®

HARRINGTON & RICHARDSON introduces the Model SB1-925 ULTRA™ Youth Slug Hunter— the first 20-gauge rifled slug gun with dimensions appropriate for young adults. This new gun uses a 12-ga. barrel blank under-bored to 20 ga. and shortened to 22". Features a factory-mounted Weaver-style scope base and a reduced Monte Carlo stock forend. For further information, see your Harrington & Richardson Gold Star Dealer or write:

H&R 1871, INC.
60 Industrial Rowe, Gardner, MA 01440
Tel: 508-632-9393 Fax: 508-632-2300

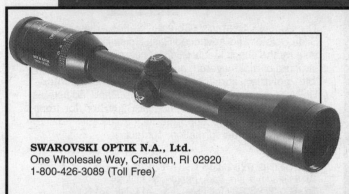

SWAROVSKI OPTIK N.A., Ltd.
One Wholesale Way, Cranston, RI 02920
1-800-426-3089 (Toll Free)

THE ULTIMATE FOR BIG GAME: PREMIUM 3-10X42mm RIFLESCOPE

This American-style scope from SWAROVSKI OPTIK is engineered for bean field, black timber and Eastern brush and hill hunting. The 42mm objective lens and Swarotop™ multi-coatings and all lens surfaces transmit more light in the early morning or late afternoon than regular scopes with a 50mm objective lens. The scope is light in weight, fully shockproof and waterproof/submersible with a great reputation for precision and accuracy— plus a warranty to back it up. Call for a catalog and the name of your nearest dealer.

MANUFACTURERS' SHOWCASE

DeSANTIS APACHE ANKLE RIG

The Apache's wide, elasticized leg band largely eliminates the unwanted rocking motion commonly associated with ankle holsters. It is a sensible choice for discreet carry by law-enforcement officers and legally armed civilians for whom a second gun just might save the day. The DeSANTIS Apache is made for small, medium and large-frame autos as well as small revolvers. There are also models designed specifically for the Glock Model 26/27 handguns as well as the Kahr Arms Model K9 and the S&W Sigma .380. Available in black only. Call or write:

DeSANTIS HOLSTER & LEATHER GOODS, INC.
P.O. Box 2039, New Hyde Park, NY 11040-0701

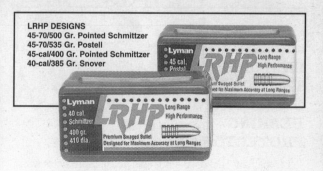

LRHP DESIGNS
45-70/500 Gr. Pointed Schmittzer
45-70/535 Gr. Postell
45-cal/400 Gr. Pointed Schmittzer
40-cal/385 Gr. Snover

LYMAN'S "LRHP"—LONG-RANGE HIGH-PERFORMANCE BULLETS

LYMAN finally brings to market the high-performance lead rifle bullets that competition shooters have sought for years. LRHP designs have been proven in competition— some have even won long-range matches before the turn of the century. All bullets are premium cast with special LYMAN-developed alloy. Bullets are sized to exact specifications and lubed with LYMAN's Orange Magic. Ideal for blackpowder or smokeless powder use, with proven accuracy out to 550 yards. For more information, please write to:

ED SCHMITT, LYMAN PRODUCTS CORPORATION
475 Smith St., Middletown, CT 06457
Tel: 1-800-22-LYMAN (Toll Free)

PHOENIX ARMS OFFERS
COMPACT PISTOLS

PHOENIX ARMS® introduces its new compact semiautomatic HP series pistols in two calibers—the HP-22-LR (.22 caliber) and the HP-25-ACP (.25 caliber). Both measure only 4.1 inches by 5.5 inches and weigh less than 20 ounces. Features include adjustable rear sights, quick-release takedowns, manual hold open, magazine interlocks and firing-pin block safeties. Can also be converted into a target gun using the 2-in-1 Extended Target Barrel and Magazine Conversion Kit™ .

PHOENIX ARMS
1420 South Archibald Ave., Ontario, CA 91761
Tel: 909-947-4843 Fax: 909-947-6798

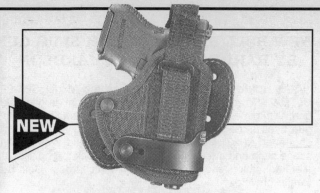

NEW CONTOUR HOLSTER
FROM SHOOTING SYSTEMS GROUP INC.

The SHOOTING SYSTEMS' "Contour" Series Advanced Belt Slide Holster and Advanced Back Holster are now available for the Glock Model 26/27. These holsters are constructed of multi-layered, quilted ballistic nylon and flexible polymer composite materials. The "Contour" Holsters feature the patented PowerBand adjustable tension system, patented Nichols SightStrip for front- and rear-sight protection, and fully adjustable retainer straps. For more information, contact:

SHOOTING SYSTEMS GROUP, INC.
1075 Headquarters Park, Fenton, MO 63026
Tel: 800-325-3049 (Toll Free) Fax: 314-349-3311

MANUFACTURERS' SHOWCASE

PELTOR'S TACTICAL 6 ELECTRONIC HEARING PROTECTOR

PELTOR'S new Tactical 6 electronic hearing protector was designed for every user of a shotgun or long gun. The electronics built into this hearing protector virtually eliminate interference from any gun stock. This product was developed to ensure ease of communication while still providing hearing protection. The Tactical 6 suppresses sound above 79db with a response time under two milliseconds. This stereo system contains two microphones each with independent volume controls that enable the wearer to balance the volume, making it ideally suited for those with impaired hearing. Lightweight (7.3 oz.) and compact, it folds for safe storage and transportation. AAA batteries provide over 150 hours of service. Replacement ear cushions and foam dampers available. Call or write:

PELTOR
41 Commercial Way, East Providence, RI 02914
Tel: 401-438-4800 Fax: 401-434-1708

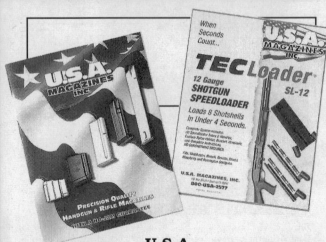

U.S.A.
MAGAZINES, INC.

Order precision-quality magazines with a **NO-JAM GUARANTEE**. Available for most rifles and handguns. Full line of 10-round magazines, PLUS stainless steel extended capacity magazines for law enforcement, and the one and only TEC-LOADER shotgun speedloader. Catalog and Video, only **$5.00**.

U.S.A. MAGAZINES, INC.
21833 De La Luz Ave., Woodland Hills, CA 91364
Tel: 818-346-9752 Fax: 818-346-9753

NEW BIPOD MODELS

B-SQUARE bipods are now available in several models. The Rigid Bipod is available with Swivel Stud "Sporter" or Barrel Clamp "Service" attachment. The "Tilt" Bipod provides the same rigid support "canting" from side to side for fine-tuning your aim. "Tilt" bipods are also available with both swivel stud and barrel clamp attachment. The "Roto-Tilt" Bipod offers everything you could want in a bipod: rigid support, side-to-side "canting," swivels in a 30-degree angle, enabling the shooter to follow perfectly aimed shots. Available with swivel stud attachment only. All bipods available in blue or stainless and feature an Unlimited Leg Extension System with 7-inch leg extenders (sold separately). For more info, call or write:

B-SQUARE CO.
P.O. Box 11281, Fort Worth, TX 76110
Tel: 1-800-433-2909 (Toll Free) or 817-923-0964

COMPACT MINI LASERS

B-SQUARE introduces the little laser that is big on performance. At only 1.1″ x 1.1″ x .6″, the Compact Mini Laser delivers 5mW of power (Class IIIa), while operating on common A76 size batteries (lithium or alkaline). Visibility is 1.0″ at 25 yards. Features an omnidirectional screw-type aiming method with windage and elevation adjustments and is the only laser with an "Air-Lock" feature. Moisture-proof and shock-resistant, the B-SQUARE Compact Mini Laser carries a lifetime warranty. Service is available simply by calling B-SQUARE. Mounting systems are available for trigger guard, under barrel, and long guns. The vertical T-Slot design makes them quick-detachable and ensures no change in zero. Contact:

B-SQUARE CO.
P.O. Box 11281, Fort Worth, TX 76110
Tel: 1-800-433-2909 (Toll Free) or 817-923-0964

MANUFACTURERS' SHOWCASE

B-SQUARE
SHOTGUN SADDLE MOUNTS

B-SQUARE Shotgun Saddle Mounts are now available for most popular 12-gauge guns. These newly designed mounts straddle the receiver and fit the top of the gun tightly. All mounts have a standard dovetail base and "see-thru" design allowing continued use of the gun's sight. Standard dovetail rings can be used. B-SQUARE shotgun mounts do not require gunsmithing, have a blued finish, and attach to the gun's side with included hardware. Mounts available for: Remington 870/1100; Mossberg 500, 5500 and 835; Winchester 1400/1300/1200; Ithaca 37/87; and Browning A-5 shotguns. The mounts retail for **$49.95** at your local dealer, or call B-SQUARE toll-free for a FREE catalog.

B-SQUARE CO.
P.O. Box 11281, Fort Worth, TX 76110
Tel: 1-800-433-2909 (Toll Free) or 817-923-0964

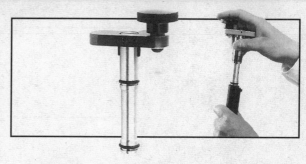

CHOKE TUBE SPEED WRENCH

The Texas Twister© Choke Tube Speed Wrench from B-SQUARE is currently available for most 12-gauge shotguns. The wrench inserts into the choke tube so it can be cranked out of the bore. A bore guide prevents crooked starts and damaged threads. The T-handle is designed to break stubborn tubes loose so they can be cranked out quickly and easily. Texas Twister© wrenches are available for Briley, Beretta, Browning, Mossberg, Weatherby, Remington, Ruger, SKB and Winchester 12-gauge shotguns. Retail price is **$29.95** at your local dealer, or call B-SQUARE toll-free. A catalog featuring the complete line of B-SQUARE products is available on request.

B-SQUARE CO.
P.O. Box 11281, Fort Worth, TX 76110
Tel: 1-800-433-2909 (Toll Free) or 817-923-0964

HIGHLANDER™ RIFLE SLING

Dress up your stock with BUTLER CREEK's new Highlander™ Rifle sling. Designed with the shooter and hunter in mind, it offers comfort, quality and style—all in one package. A patented stretch material placed between two pieces of neoprene offer a super controlled stretch design; Non-Slip Grippers on the underside keep the sling on your shoulder. For an extra touch of class, the edges have been finished and leather panels have been added. Mention this ad when you call or write for a **FREE** catalog of BUTLER CREEK products.

BUTLER CREEK CORP.
290 Arden Drive, Belgrade, Montana 59714
Tel: 406-388-1356 Fax: 406-388-7204

CLASSIC

CLASSIC IVORY-LIKE & STAL-LIKE GRIPS

"CLASSIC" Ivory-like grips are made of a polyurethane that is perfect for reproducing rare and beautiful grips from the days of the frontier. Screws included. Dealer discounts. Will not chip or shrink. Specify make and model: **$30**/pair plus **$3.00** (S&H). Send **$2.00** for 8-page list of over 350 U.S. and foreign grips, buttplates, marbled axe handles and repro bison skulls.

N.C. ORDNANCE
Classic Steer Head Grips for all Colts and Rugers
P.O. Box 3254, Wilson, NC 27895

MANUFACTURERS' SHOWCASE

NAVY ARMS REPLICA CATALOG

Send **$2.00** for our full-color catalog packed with black-powder and cartridge reproductions, ranging from the 18th century to the Old West era. Featured in this new edition are the new 1873 Trapdoor Springfield and 1875 Schofield replicas. A complete line of military surplus arms and ammunition is also represented. Dealers: Send a copy of your FFL for a **FREE** catalog and inclusion on our dealer flyer mailing list.

NAVY ARMS CO.
689 Bergen Blvd., Dept. SB, Ridgefield, N.J. 07657
Tel: 201-945-2500 Fax: 201-945-6859

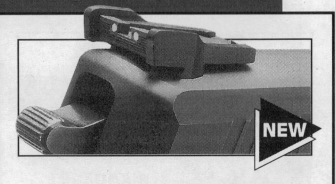

NEW MILLETT ULTRA-SIGHT

With MILLETT'S new Ultra-Sight, you can put a precision adjustable rear sight on your favorite automatic pistol without having to change the front sight! All parts are fabricated from nickel steel and carbon fiber using a totally new cam principal, providing maximum incremental adjustments in a compact space. The Ultra-Sight is offered in Target Black, 3-Dot and the famous MILLETT White Outline blade style. Avail. for the Colt 1911, CZ75-TA, Beretta 92 Series, Browning Hi-Power, Llama, Taurus PT 92, Firestar, EAA Witness, S&W Second & Third Generation Autos, Ruger P85, H&K USP Pistols, Glock, Sig/Sauer and others.

MILLETT SIGHTS
7275 Murdy Circle, Huntington Beach, CA 92647
Tel: 714-842-5575 Fax: 714-843-5707

HARRINGTON & RICHARDSON'S SIDEKICK REVOLVER

HARRINGTON & RICHARDSON's new Model 929 Sidekick® revolver is a complete beginner's package that includes an Uncle Mike's ballistic nylon holster and a trial-size package of TETRA® Gun oil and grease. It features a square butt frame with cinnamon laminate grips and fixed sights. The swing-out, nine-shot cylinder handles 22 Short, 22 Long and 22 LR cartridges interchangeably. For more information, see your HARRINGTON & RICHARDSON Gold Star Dealer or write:

H&R 1871, INC.
60 Industrial Rowe, Gardner, MA 01440
Tel: 508-632-9393 Fax: 508-632-2300

KAHLES SCOPES
TRADITION - VALUE - PRECISION

Because KAHLES of Vienna, Austria, has been making riflescopes for over 100 years, its engineers have perfected the art of making premium-quality, variable-power riflescopes at the lowest possible price. This means great value for anyone who buys or owns a KAHLES. These scopes are rugged, extremely accurate, dependable and as bright—or brighter—than any other traditional European riflescopes. KAHLES variable-power riflescopes come in 1.5-6X42, 2.2-9X42 and 3-12X56 with a variety of reticles. Call for a catalog and the name of your nearest dealer.

KAHLES
A Swarovski Company
Swarovski Optik N.A., Ltd.
One Wholesale Way, Cranston, RI 02920
Tel: 1-800-426-3089 (Toll Free)

MANUFACTURERS' SHOWCASE

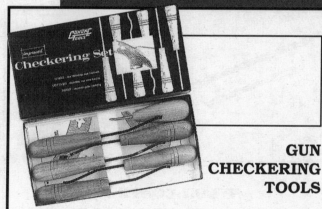

GUN CHECKERING TOOLS

GUNLINE Checkering Tools are precisely made and come with illustrated instructions and easy-to-follow sample checkering patterns. Easy to use as well, the cutting qualities and simple design of these tools are useful for hobbyists and professional gunstockers alike. GUNLINE offers a full line of medium and fine replaceable cutters from 16 to 32 lines per inch, in 60° and 90°, in short or long sizes. Three types of handles are available, one with an offset rear-view feature. Tool set prices start at **$37.50**, plus **$4** shipping charge. The Camp Perry Set of six tools lists for **$57.50**. For a brochure, send a self-addressed stamped envelope to:

GUNLINE TOOLS
P.O. Box 478, Placentia, CA 92670
Tel: 714-993-5100 Fax: 714-572-4128

TRIUS 1-STEP
"Setting the Standard for 41 Years"

The new TRIUS 1-Step is almost effortless to use: (1) Set arm; (2) Place target on arm without tension; (3) Step on pedal to put tension on arm and release target in one motion. Adjustable without tools. Easy cocking, lay-on loading, singles, doubles, plus piggy-back doubles offer unparalleled variety. **Birdshooter**: quality at a budget price—now with high-angle retainer. **Model 92**: a best-seller with high-angle clip and can thrower. **TrapMaster**: sit-down comfort plus pivoting action. TRIUS also offers Sporting Clay traps.

TRIUS PRODUCTS INC.
P.O. Box 25, Cleves, OH 45002
Tel: 513-941-5682 Fax: 513-941-7970

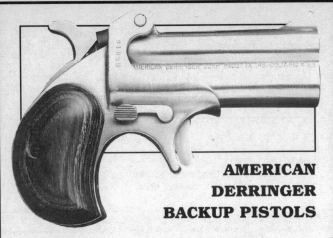

AMERICAN DERRINGER BACKUP PISTOLS

Designed to be the ultimate in short-range backup pistols, this gun has no equal. Over 10 years were spent in developing and refining this pistol to make it the finest derringer ever manufactured. The smallest and most powerful pocket pistol ever made, it is built from the finest high-tensile strength stainless steel — strong enough to handle the 44-Magnum cartridge if you are man enough to shoot it! Over 60 different rifle and pistol calibers are available. Classic styling and smooth lines give these derringers a classic look.

AMERICAN DERRINGER CORPORATION
127 N. Lacy Drive, Waco, Texas 76705
Tel: 800-642-7817 (Toll Free) Fax: 817-799-7935

RUGER 10/22 MG-42 KIT

Transform your Ruger 10/22 into a 2/3 replica WWII MG-42 with GLASER's new stock kit. Requires only simple tools, 15 minutes and no permanent alterations to your rifle. The assembled MG-42 has adjustable sights and weighs no more than the stock rifle. GLASER's Featherweight Bipod adds the final authentic touch to your new MG-42. This bipod is the strongest, lightest one made and comes with a LIFETIME warranty, plus all the hardware needed to mount it on Colt AR series rifles or any sporter rifle with a sling swivel mount. Hidden and quick detachable mounting accessories are also available. For a brochure, contact:

GLASER SAFETY SLUG, INC.
P.O. Box 8223, Foster City CA 94404
Tel: 1-800-221-3489 (Toll Free)

MANUFACTURERS' SHOWCASE

BENCH MASTER RIFLE REST

The Bench Master Rifle Rest is a rugged, compact and highly adjustable rifle-shooting accessory— one that offers precision line-up and recoil reduction when sighting in a rifle, testing ammunition or shooting varmints. It features three course positions totaling 5½″, with 1½″ fine adjustment in each course position, plus leveling and shoulder height adjustments for maximum control and comfort. Because of its unique design, the Bench Master can easily double as a rifle vise for scope mounting, bore sighting and cleaning. It comes with a LIFETIME Warranty and a list price of only **$119.95**. For a free brochure, call or write:

DESERT MOUNTAIN MFG.
P.O. Box 2767, Columbia Falls, MT 59912-2767
Tel: 800-477-0762 (Toll Free)

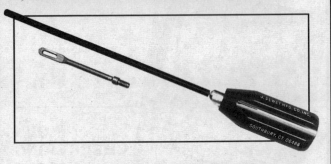

NYLON-COATED GUN CLEANING RODS

J. DEWEY cleaning rods have been used by the U.S. Olympic shooting team and the benchrest community for over 20 years. These one-piece, spring-tempered, steel-based rods will not gall delicate rifling or damage the muzzle area of front-cleaned firearms. Each nylon-coated rod comes with a non-breakable plastic handle supported by ball-bearings for ease of cleaning. The brass cleaning jags are designed to pierce the center of the cleaning patch or wrap around the knurled area to keep the patch centered in the bore. Available from 17-caliber to shotgun bore size in several lengths. For more information, contact:

J. DEWEY MANUFACTURING CO., INC.
P. O. Box 2014, Southbury, CT 06488
Tel: 203-264-3064   Fax: 203-262-6907

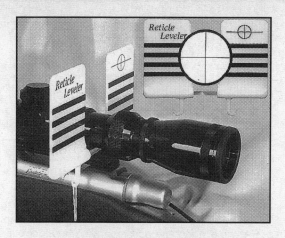

SEGWAY INDUSTRIES
RETICLE LEVELER

This newly patented device is just the thing to end scope-mounting frustration. Usable with virtually any scoped firearm, it sits on the base, under the scope, and shows you when your scope is level. Taking only seconds to mount and remove, it's a jewel of a tool.

SEGWAY INDUSTRIES
P.O. Box 783, Suffern, NY 10901-0783
Tel: 914-357-5510 Fax: 914-357-5510

ERMA SR-100 PRECISION RIFLE

AMTEC 2000, Inc. offers the ERMA SR-100 Precision Rifle for sale in the U.S. A Mil spec. precision rifle of uncompromising accuracy, the SR-100 is a box-fed, bolt-action rifle with a detachable magazine, a quick-detachable barrel and a fully adjustable tactical stock. The receiver is made of forged alloy consisting of two parts, with the lower section acting as a massive bedding block. Lock-up strength is assured because the bolt lugs lock into the barrel and not the receiver, ensuring exceptional strength and the most precise headspace possible. In calibers: 308 Win., 300 Win. Mag. and 338 Lapua Magnum. The trigger assembly is fully adjustable for take-up, weight of pull, length of pull, preload and overtravel. Production is extremely limited and intended primarily for military and law-enforcement use.

AMTEC 2000, INC.
P.O. Box 1191, Gardner, MA 01440
Tel: 508-632-9608

MANUFACTURERS' SHOWCASE

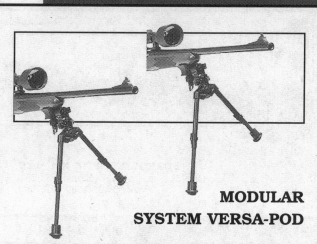

MODULAR
SYSTEM VERSA-POD

The Versa-Pod is a modular system of shooting rests. It is composed of two prone-position bipods—a sitting position bipod and a shooting stick/monopod. A wide variety of adapters are available to fit almost any production rifle. With an adapter installed, mounting any of the shooting supports onto a rifle is a snap. Removing the bipod is just as easy, so you can carry your rifle and your bipod separately. The Versa-Pod models all have built-in tilting, canting and panning movements. The bipods have legs that feature true one-touch operation.

KENG'S FIREARMS SPECIALTY, INC.
875 Wharton Drive, S.W., Atlanta, GA 30336-2125

BLUE BOOK OF
GUN VALUES

The new 17th edition of the BLUE BOOK OF GUN VALUES by S. P. Fjestad contains 1,360 pages and includes pricing and detailed technical information on domestic, foreign and military guns (both new and discontinued), plus major trademark antiques, commemoratives, special editions, and most new models. Included in the 17th edition is a revised 40-page, full-color section of high-resolution photographs showing rifles, shotguns and handguns in various percentages of condition from zero to 100 percent. The retail price is **$27.95** (add **$3.00** for shipping and handling). To order, call:

BLUE BOOK PUBLICATIONS, INC.
8009 34th Ave. So., Minneapolis, MN 55425
1-800-877-4867 (Toll-Free) OR 612-854-5229 Fax: 612-853-1486

LE-500
ELECTRONIC SCALE

LYMAN's new LE-500 Electronic Scale offers state-of-the-art reloading technology that most reloaders can afford. This handy compact unit has real capacity of over 650 grains, perfect for powder or large bullets. The compact size takes up little room at the reloading bench and is easily transported to the range. Storage/carry case is included. The LE-500 operates on four AAA batteries and is accurate to 1/10 grain. Powder pan and calibration weight are also included. For more information, please write to:

ED SCHMITT, LYMAN PRODUCTS CORPORATION
475 Smith St., Middletown, CT 06457
Tel: 1-800-22-LYMAN (Toll Free)

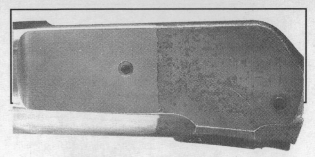

HOW-TO VIDEO FOR
QUALITY METAL PREPARATION

This 37-minute video and accompanying handbook outline the steps needed to do a quality metal preparation job on your own gun—not just the steps in polishing, but the first steps you need to know to do a quality job. The tape also shows the various finishes used by the manufacturers on their original parts, giving you complete guidelines to follow so you can do a professional job yourself and save money. Most important, it will give you the satisfaction of doing your own quality job. **$19.95** plus **$3.00** S&H. Contact:

DOUG TURNBULL RESTORATION
6426 County Rd. 30, P.O. Box 471, Bloomfield, NY 14469
Tel: 716-657-6338

MANUFACTURERS' SHOWCASE

THE ULTIMATE 6-24X50 (30mm)
RIFLESCOPE From Swarovski

This remarkable scope is designed for long-range competition, hunting and varmint shooting. Its precise 1/8" click adjustments and large, internal optics yield optimum accuracy and twilight performance. The light, one-piece alloy tube has a 50mm to infinity parallax adjustment ring and an exclusive reticle suspension system for extreme accuracy with any rifle caliber. The reticle is positioned in the second image plane and holds the same size at all power settings. The 6-14x50 scope is nitrogen filled and waterproof/submersible with the target turret caps removed. Warranty backup. Call for a catalog and the name of your nearest dealer.

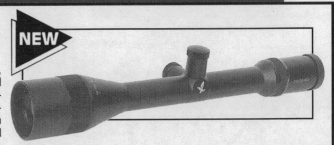

SWAROVSKI OPTIK N.A., LTD.
One Wholesale Way, Cranston, RI 02920
1-800-426-3089 (Toll Free)

GUNSMITH'S MAINTENANCE
CENTER FROM MTM CASE-GARD

The Gunsmith's Maintenance Center is a "must have" tool for those who want to keep their rifles and shotguns in top working condition. Each gun fork can be adjusted to a high, low or narrow-wide position. This is important when cleaning with the more aggressive solvents or mounting scopes. Special molded compartments are provided to hold solvents, oils and sprays to help prevent spillage. The large deep bottom compartment is big enough to hold most of your essential tools. Write for our free catalog!

**MTM
CASE-GARD CORP.**
P.O. Box 14117, Dept. SB97
Dayton, OH 45413 Tel: 513-890-7461

LAZZERONI ARMS MODEL 2000 RIFLE

This new state-of-the-art rifle features a 4340 chrome-moly steel receiver with two massive locking lugs, a match-grade 416R stainless steel barrel, a fully adjustable benchrest trigger and a Lazzeroni-designed synthetic or wood stock that is hand-bedded using aluminum pillar blocks. Included is a precision-machined floorplate/triggerguard assembly. The L2000 is chambered in one of four Lazzeroni calibers to provide the flattest shooting, hardest hitting hunting rifle available—with guaranteed accuracy at minute of angle or less. Call or write for our free catalog.

LAZZERONI ARMS CO.
P.O. Box 26696
Tucson, AZ 85726-6696
Tel: 520-577-7500   Fax: 520-624-4250

LOHMAN'S POPULAR SIGHT-VISE SSV-2

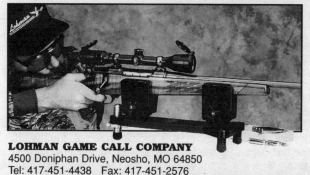

LOHMAN GAME CALL COMPANY
4500 Doniphan Drive, Neosho, MO 64850
Tel: 417-451-4438   Fax: 417-451-2576

Ideal for all caliber guns, the Sight-Vise SSV-2 from LOHMAN is a precision instrument that makes accurate rifle sighting and shotgun patterning easy. Adjustable dual clamps hold the gun stock firmly, regardless of size or shape, while the unit's soft, padded jaws prevent stock-marring. An adjustable rear post is provided for precise aiming.

The U.S.-made Sight Vise SSV-2 is extremely sturdy. Its wide, stable base helps reduce recoil and increase the shooter's confidence and accuracy. Extra lead shot can be added to the base for extra support and stability. The Sight-Vise can also be used to secure the gun for cleaning, scope mounting and repair work.

MANUFACTURERS' SHOWCASE

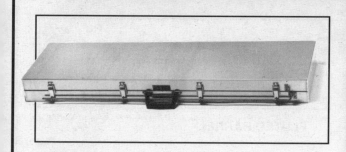

PROTECTIVE METAL CASES

A complete line of Protective Metal Transport/Shipping Cases are available through ICC (IMPACT CASE COMPANY) and KK AIR INTERNATIONAL. Both lines are products of KNOUFF & KNOUFF, INC. In addition to the "flat case" design, three-piece and "Trunk"-style cases are part of the standard lines. KK AIR also manufactures customized cases to each owner's sizing and specifications. These case products are designed for STRENGTH, with third-party handling in mind, and are "proven." For detailed specification sheets, contact:

KNOUFF & KNOUFF, INC.
P.O. Box 9912, Spokane, WA 99209
Tel: 1-800-262-3322 (Toll Free)

GLASER SAFETY SLUG AMMO

GLASER SAFETY SLUG's state-of-the-art professional-grade personal defense ammunition is now offered in two bullet styles: BLUE uses a #12 compressed shot core for maximum ricochet protection, and SILVER uses a #6 compressed shot core for maximum penetration. The manufacturing process results in outstanding accuracy, with documented groups of less than an inch at 100 yards! That's why GLASER is the top choice among professional and private law enforcement agencies worldwide. Currently available in every caliber from 25 ACP-30-06, including 40 S&W, 10mm, 223 and 7.62 × 39. For a free brochure contact:

GLASER SAFETY SLUG, INC.
P.O. Box 8223, Foster City, CA 94404
Tel: 1-800-221-3489 (Toll Free)

RUGER 10/22 COMBO TARGET BARREL AND STOCK

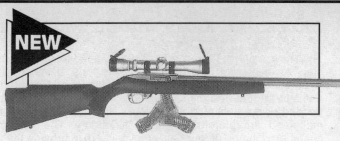

BUTLER'S CREEK'S new 20" Drop-in Target Barrel includes a Bentz/Match chamber to ensure better accuracy with all 22 Long Rifle ammo. A recessed target crown and six-groove button rifling with 1:14" twist further enhances accuracy. The barrel—fluted or standard—is available in stainless steel or blued finish. The matching Target Stock features a semi-Monte Carlo comb for scoped shooting, a fuller forearm, checkering, swivel studs and adult trigger pull. For a **FREE** catalog of BUTLER CREEK products, mention this ad when you call or write:

BUTLER CREEK CORP.
290 Arden Drive, Belgrade, Montana 59714
Tel: 406-388-1356 Fax: 406-388-7204

**HARRIS
ENGINEERING, INC.**
Barlow, Kentucky 42024
Tel: 502-334-3633

HARRIS BIPODS

HARRIS bipods clamp securely to most stud-equipped bolt-action rifles and are quick-detachable. With adapters, they can fit other guns as well. HARRIS bipods are the result of time-proven design and quality, and are made with heat-treated steel and hard alloys. Folding legs have completely adjustable spring-return extensions (except Model LM). The sling swivel attaches to the clamp. Series S Bipods rotate 45° for instant leveling on uneven ground. The hinged base has tension adjustment and buffer springs to eliminate tremor or looseness in the crotch area of the bipod. Otherwise, all series S models are similar to the non-rotating Series 1A2.

MANUFACTURERS' SHOWCASE

QUARTON OUTSHINES ALL OTHERS

QUARTON'S BEAMSHOT is a top-of-the-line laser sight that easily attaches to a rifle, shotgun, pistol or revolver. Constructed of aircraft aluminum, this sturdy unit is powered with an easily obtainable 3-volt lithium battery, giving the operator a 20-hour constant "on" usage. The unit weighs only 3.8 ounces, is activated by a simple pressure switch, and has a range of 300 to 800 yards. In addition to the laser sight, the BEAMSHOT kit includes a lithium battery, a 5-inch pressure switch, a mount for the gun of your choice, and a one-year warranty. All at an incredibly competitive price! Call, fax or write:

QUARTON USA, LTD. CO.
7042 Alamo Downs Pkwy., Suite 250, San Antonio, TX 78238
Tel: 210-520-8430 Fax: 210-520-8433

FLUTED BARREL

PRO SERIES 95

Destined to be among the world's most popular competitive pistols, the PRO SERIES 95 pistols are precision target handguns designed for the knowledgeable, advanced target shooter. Features include: military grip *interchangeable barrels *fully adjustable target sights *trigger pull adjustment *trigger travel adjustment *automatic slide lock and Pachmayr rubber grips. The fluted barrel model features the military bracket rear sight acclaimed by many competitive shooters as the most reliable sighting system developed. Contact:

STOEGER INDUSTRIES
5 Mansard Court, Wayne, NJ 07470
Tel: 201-872-9500 Fax: 201-872-2230

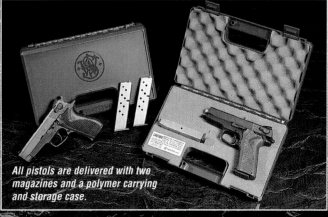

FINLAND TIKKA
CONTINENTAL VARMINT AND LONG - RANGE

SYNONYMOUS WITH ACCURACY

TIKKA IS PLEASED TO ANNOUNCE THE DEVELOPMENT OF THEIR CONTINENTAL VARMINT AND LONG-RANGE HUNTING RIFLES. DESIGNED AND CRAFTED BY SAKO OF FINLAND, THESE NEW MODELS FEATURE A HEAVY 26" BARREL FOR IMPROVED VELOCITY AND PERFORMANCE. BOTH NEW MODELS ALSO FEATURE A BEAVERTAIL FOREND TO PROVIDE ADDED STABILITY AND SUPPORT.

OTHER SUPERIOR FEATURES INCLUDE

- "SMOOTH AS SILK" BOLT
- TRAVEL-FREE ADJUSTABLE TRIGGER
- FREE FLOATING, COLD HAMMER-FORGED BARREL • QUICK-RELEASE DETACHABLE MAGAZINE • INTEGRAL SCOPE MOUNT RAILS
- MATTE LACQUER WALNUT STOCK WITH PALM SWELL • RECOIL PAD SPACER SYSTEM.

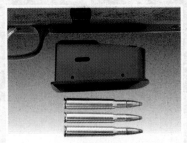

DETACHABLE MAGAZINE

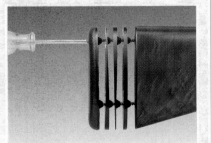

CUSTOMIZED SPACER SYSTEM

BY

FINLAND sako

AT BROLIN ARMS WE BELIEVE
"A PISTOL IS NOT JUST A FIREARM
BUT A PIECE OF FINE ART."

Brolin Arms

Brolin Arms™
PATRIOT SERIES
Made in the U.S.A.

Brolin Arms   P.O. Box 698 La Verne, Calif. 91750-0698 U.S.A.
Tel: 1-888-8 BROLIN

AMERICAN EAGLE

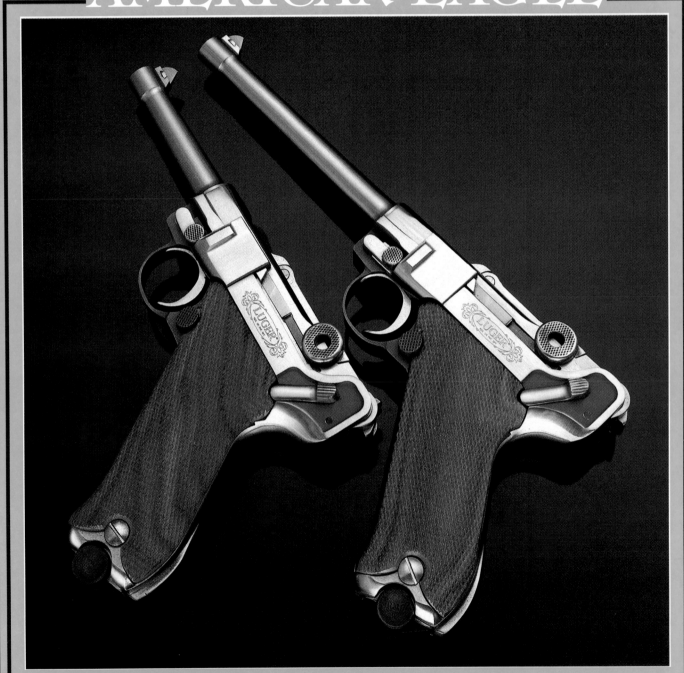

YESTERDAY'S TRADITION - TODAY'S TECHNOLOGY

Handguns

For addresses and phone/fax numbers of manufacturers and distributors included in this section, please turn to DIRECTORY OF MANUFACTURERS AND SUPPLIERS on page 554.

AMERICAN ARMS

**ESCORT .380 ACP
$349.00**

SPECIFICATIONS
Caliber: .380 ACP
Action: DA **Capacity:** 7-shot magazine
Barrel length: 3³/₈" **Overall length:** 6¹/₈"
Width: ¹³/₁₆" **Weight:** 19 oz.
Sights: Fixed; low profile
Features: Stainless steel frame, slide & trigger; nickel-steel
   barrel; soft polymer grips; loaded chamber indicator

**AUSSIE SEMIAUTO
$425.00**

SPECIFICATIONS
Calibers: 9mm, 40 S&W
Capacity: 10 rounds
Barrel length: 4³/₄" **Overall length:** 7⁷/₈"
Weight: 23 oz.
Features: Polymer frame w/nickeled steel slide & barrel;
   five safeties; beveled magazine; ergonomically designed
   grip w/finger grooves; checkered sides and back; extend-
   ed slide release

**UBERTI .454 SINGLE ACTION (not shown)
$869.00**

SPECIFICATIONS
Caliber: .454
Barrel lengths: 6", 7¹/₂"
Features: Top ported barrels; satin nickel finish; fully adj.
   sight; hammer block safety; hardwood grips

**MODEL P-98 CLASSIC
SEMIAUTO $209.00**

SPECIFICATIONS
Caliber: 22 LR
Capacity: 8-shot clip
Barrel length: 5" **Overall length:** 8¹/₈"
Weight: 26 oz. (empty)
Sights: Fixed blade front; adjustable square-notch rear
Grip: Black polymer

**MODEL PK-22 CLASSIC
DA SEMIAUTO $199.00**

SPECIFICATIONS
Caliber: 22 LR
Capacity: 8-shot clip
Barrel length: 3¹/₃" **Overall length:** 6¹/₃"
Weight: 22 oz. (empty)
Sights: Fixed blade front, "V"-notch rear
Grip: Black polymer

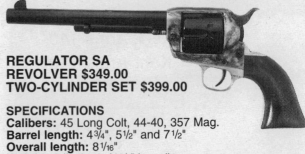

**REGULATOR SA
REVOLVER $349.00
TWO-CYLINDER SET $399.00**

SPECIFICATIONS
Calibers: 45 Long Colt, 44-40, 357 Mag.
Barrel length: 4³/₄", 5¹/₂" and 7¹/₂"
Overall length: 8¹/₁₆"
Weight: 2 lb. 3 oz. (4³/₄" barrel)
Sights: Fixed **Safety:** Half cock
Features: Brass trigger guard and backstrap; two-cylinder
   combos avail. (45 L.C./45 ACP and 44-40/44 Special)
Also available:
BUCKHORN TARGET. Same as Regulator but with
   stronger frame for 44 Rem. Mag.; front/rear target
   sights **$379.00**
REGULATOR DELUXE w/blued steel backstrap and
   trigger guard; hammer block safety **$395.00**

AMERICAN DERRINGER PISTOLS

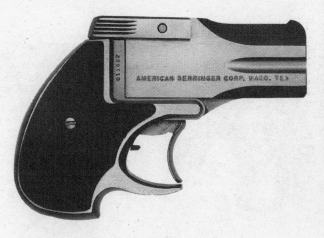

MODEL 1

SPECIFICATIONS
Calibers: See below
Action: Single action w/automatic barrel selection
Capacity: 2 shots
Barrel length: 3" **Overall length:** 4.82"
Weight: 15 oz. (in 45 Auto)

Calibers:	Prices
22 Long Rifle w/rosewood grips	$245.00
32 Magnum/32 S&W Long	255.00
32-20	245.00
357 Magnum w/rosewood grips	257.00
357 Maximum w/rosewood grips	265.00
38 Special w/rosewood grips	245.00
38 Super w/rosewood grips	253.00
38 Special +P+ (Police)	253.00
38 Special Shot Shells	253.00
380 Auto, 9mm Luger	245.00
10mm Auto, 40 S&W, 45 Auto, 30 M-1 Carbine	257.00
45-70 (single shot)	312.00
45 Colt, 2 1/2" Snake (45-cal. rifled barrel), 44-40 Win., 44 Special	320.00
45 Win. Mag., 44 Magnum, 41 Magnum	385.00
30-30 Win., 357 Mag., 45/.410, 223 Rem., Comm. Ammo dual calibers	375.00

MODEL 7 Ultra Lightweight Single Action (7 1/2 oz.)
(not shown)

22 LR, 22 Mag. Rimfire, 32 Mag./32 S&W Long, 38 Special, 380 Auto	$240.00
44 Special	500.00

MODEL 10 Stainless Steel Barrel (10 oz.) **(not shown)**

38 Special	$240.00
45 Auto	257.00
45 Colt	320.00

MODEL 11 Lightweight Double Derringer (11 oz.)

22 LR, 22 Mag. Rim., 32 Mag./SW, 38 Special, 380 Auto	$225.00

38 DOUBLE ACTION DERRINGER (14.5 oz.)

SPECIFICATIONS
Calibers: See below   **Capacity:** 2 shots
Barrel length: 3" **Overall length:** 4.85"
Weight: 14.5 oz.
Height: 3.3"   **Width:** 1.1"
Finish: Stainless steel
Safety: Hammerblock thumb

Calibers	Prices
22 LR, 38 Special	$300.00
9mm Luger	325.00
357 Magnum, 40 S&W	350.00

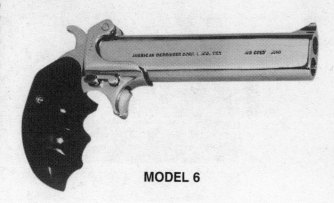

MODEL 6

MODEL 6
STAINLESS STEEL DOUBLE DERRINGER

SPECIFICATIONS
Calibers: See below   **Capacity:** 2 shots
Barrel length: 6" **Overall length:** 8.2"
Weight: 21 oz.

Calibers:	Prices
22 Win. Mag.	$300.00
357 Mag.	300.00
45 Auto	345.00
45/.410, 45 Cal.	363.00

AMERICAN DERRINGER PISTOLS

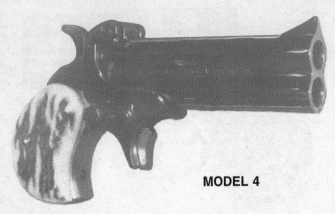

MODEL 4

MODEL 4
STAINLESS STEEL DOUBLE DERRINGER

SPECIFICATIONS
Calibers: 45 Colt and 3".410
Capacity: 2 shots
Barrel length: 4.1"
Overall length: 6"
Weight: 16.5 oz.
Finish: Satin or high-polish stainless steel
Price:. $352.00
    With oversized grips 382.00

Also available:
In 45 Auto, 357 Mag., 357 Maximum $369.00
In 45-70 w/oversized grips, both barrels 495.00
In 44 Mag. w/oversized grips 422.00
MODEL M-4 ALASKAN SURVIVAL
    in 45-70/45-.410, 45-70/45 Colt 388.00

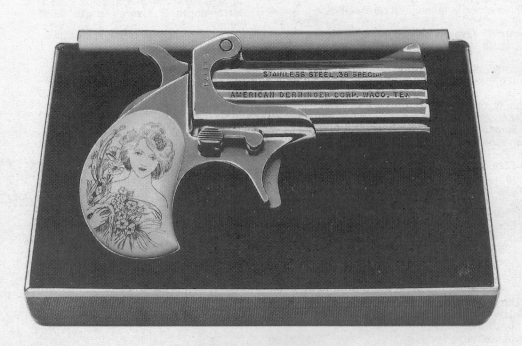

LADY DERRINGER
STAINLESS STEEL DOUBLE

LADY DERRINGER (Stainless Steel Double)

Calibers:	Prices
38 Special	$260.00
32 Mag.	280.00
357 Mag.	300.00
45 Colt	345.00

TEXAS DOUBLE DERRINGER
COMMEMORATIVE
(not shown)

Calibers:	Prices
38 Special (Brass)	$280.00
44-40 or 45 Colt (Brass)	345.00

AMT PISTOLS

BACKUP

SPECIFICATIONS
Calibers: 357 SIG, 380 ACP (9mm Short), 38 Super, 40
  S&W, 45 ACP
Capacity: 5-shot (40 S&W, 45 ACP); 6-shot (other calibers)
Barrel length: 3"
Overall length: 5 3/4"
Weight: 23 oz.
Width: 1"
Features: Locking-barrel action, checkered fiberglass grips,
  grooved slide sight
Prices:
In 380 ACP **$329.99**
Other calibers. **449.99**

BACKUP
(380 or 9mm Short)

380 BACKUP II

SPECIFICATIONS
Caliber: 380 ACP
Capacity: 5 shots
Barrel length: 2 1/2"   **Overall length:** 5"
Weight: 18 oz.   **Width:** 11/16"
Sights: Open
Grips: Carbon fiber
Prices:
Single Action **$309.99**
Double Action. **329.95**

1911 GOVERNMENT
45 ACP LONGSLIDE (not shown)

SPECIFICATIONS
Caliber: 45 ACP
Capacity: 7 shots
Barrel length: 7" **Overall length:** 10 1/2"
Weight: 46 oz.
Sights: 3-dot, adjustable
Features: Wide adjustable trigger; Neoprene wraparound
  grips
Price:. **$595.99**
Also available:
Conversion Kit **299.99**

380 BACKUP II

1911 GOVERNMENT MODEL

SPECIFICATIONS
Caliber: 45 ACP **Capacity:** 7 shots
Barrel length: 5" **Overall length:** 8 1/2"
Weight: 38 oz. **Width:** 1 1/4"
Sights: Fixed
Features: Long grip safety; rubber wraparound Neoprene
  grips; beveled magazine well; wide adjustable trigger
Price:. **$489.99**

Also available:
1911 **HARDBALLER**. Same specifications as Standard
  Model, but with adjustable sights and matte rib.
  .**$549.99**
Conversion Kit **$279.00**

1911 GOVERNMENT

AMT PISTOLS

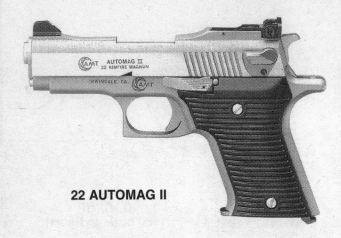

22 AUTOMAG II

22 AUTOMAG II RIMFIRE MAGNUM

The only production semiautomatic handgun in this caliber, the Automag II is ideal for the small-game hunter or shooting enthusiast who wants more power and accuracy in a light, trim handgun. The pistol features a bold open-slide design and employs a unique gas-channeling system for smooth, trouble-free action.

SPECIFICATIONS
Caliber: 22 Rimfire Magnum
Barrel lengths: 3³/₈", 4¹/₂" or 6"
Magazine capacity: 9 shots (4¹/₂" & 6"), 7 shots (3³/₈")
Weight: 32 oz. (6"), 30 oz. (4¹/₂"), 24 oz. (3³/₈")
Sights: Adjustable 3-dot
Finish: Stainless steel
Features: Squared trigger guard; grooved carbon fiber grips; gas channeling system
Price:. $405.95

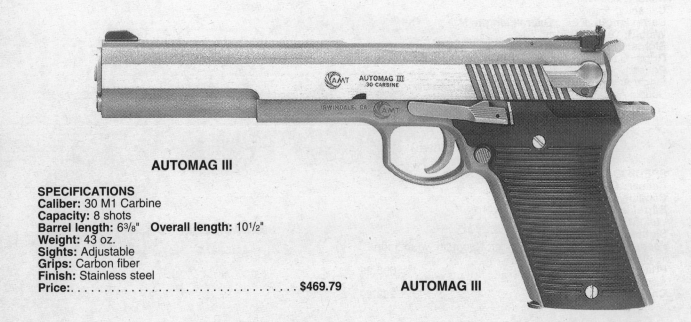

AUTOMAG III

AUTOMAG III

SPECIFICATIONS
Caliber: 30 M1 Carbine
Capacity: 8 shots
Barrel length: 6³/₈"   **Overall length**: 10¹/₂"
Weight: 43 oz.
Sights: Adjustable
Grips: Carbon fiber
Finish: Stainless steel
Price:. $469.79

AUTOMAG IV

AUTOMAG IV

SPECIFICATIONS
Caliber: 45 Win. Mag.
Capacity: 7 shots
Barrel length: 6¹/₂"   **Overall length**: 10¹/₂"
Weight: 46 oz.
Sights: Adjustable
Grips: Carbon fiber
Finish: Stainless steel
Price:. $699.99

AUTO-ORDNANCE PISTOLS

MODEL 1911A1 THOMPSON

SPECIFICATIONS
Calibers: 45 ACP, 9mm, 10mm and 38 Super
Capacity: 9 rounds (9mm, 10mm & 38 Super); 7 rounds
    (45 ACP)
Barrel length: 5" **Overall length:** 8½"
Weight: 39 oz.
Sights: Blade front; rear adjustable for windage
Stock: Checkered plastic with medallion
Prices:
9mm and 38 Super $427.00
38 Super, satin nickel 445.50
10mm. 435.00
45 ACP, blued 397.50
45 ACP, satin nickel 425.95
45 ACP, Duo-Tone finish 435.00
PIT BULL MODEL (45 ACP w/3½" barrel). 455.00
WW II PARKERIZED PISTOL (45 cal. only) 389.95
DELUXE MODEL (45 cal. only) 425.95
    9mm and 38 Super 435.00

**MODEL 1911A1
THOMPSON (9mm)**

**MODEL 1911A1
DUO-TONE**

MODEL 1911A1 COMPETITION

SPECIFICATIONS
Calibers: 45 ACP and 38 Super
Weight: 42 oz.
Barrel length: 5"
Overall length: 10"
Stock: Rubber wraparound
Sights: White 3-dot system
Features: Full-length recoil spring guide system, Videcki
    adjustable speed trigger; extended combat ejector; Hi-
    ride beavertail grip safety
Prices:
38 Super $645.75
45 ACP 635.50

MODEL 1911 "THE GENERAL"
(not shown)

SPECIFICATIONS
Calibers: 45 ACP and 38 Super
Capacity: 7 rounds
Barrel length: 4½" **Overall length:** 8"
Weight: 37 oz.
Stock: Black textured, rubber wraparound with medallion
Sights: White 3-dot system
Feature: Full-length recoil guide system
Prices:
38 Super $479.75
45 ACP 465.00

**MODEL 1911A1
COMPETITION**

BERETTA PISTOLS

COMPACT FRAME PISTOLS

COUGAR SERIES
MODEL 8000 (9mm) MODEL 8040 (40 cal.)

Beretta's 8000/8040 Cougar Series semiautomatics use a proven locked-breech system with a rotating barrel. This design makes the pistol compact and easy to conceal and operate with today's high-powered 9mm and 40-caliber ammunition. When the pistol is fired, the initial thrust of recoil energy is partially absorbed as it pushes slide and barrel back, with the barrel rotating by cam action against a tooth on the rigid central block. When the barrel has turned about 30 degrees, the locking lugs on the barrel clear the locking recesses, which free the slide to continue rearward. The recoil spring absorbs the remaining recoil energy as the slide extracts and ejects the spent shell casing, rotates the hammer, and then reverses direction to chamber the next round. By channeling part of the recoil energy into barrel rotation and by partially absorbing the barrel and slide recoil shock through the central block before it is transferred to the frame, the Cougar shows an unusually low felt recoil.

**MODEL 8000/8040
COUGAR**

SPECIFICATIONS
Calibers: 9mm and 40 semiauto
Capacity: 10 rounds
Action: Double/Single or Double Action only
Barrel length: 3.6"
Overall length: 7"
Weight: 33.5 oz.
Overall height: 5.5"
Sight radius: 5.2"
Sights: Front and rear sights dovetailed to slide
Finish: Bruniton/Plastic
Features: Firing-pin block; chrome-lined barrel; short recoil, rotating barrel; anodized aluminum alloy frame
Prices:
Double action only $663.00
Double or Single action 699.00

SMALL FRAME PISTOLS

MODEL 3032 TOMCAT

SPECIFICATIONS
Caliber: 32 Auto
Capacity: 7-shot magazine
Barrel length: 2.45"
Overall length: 5"
Weight: 15 oz.
Sights: Blade front, drift-adjustable rear
Features: Double action, thumb safety, tip-up barrel for direct loading/unloading, blued or matte finish
Prices:
Matte/Plastic. $240.00
Blued/Plastic 299.00

MODEL 3032 TOMCAT

BERETTA PISTOLS

SMALL FRAME PISTOLS

MODEL 21 BOBCAT DA SEMIAUTOMATIC

A safe, dependable, accurate small-bore pistol in 22 LR or 25 Auto. Easy to load with its unique barrel tip-up system.

SPECIFICATIONS
Caliber: 22 LR or 25 ACP. **Magazine capacity:** 7 rounds 22 LR); 8 rounds (25 ACP). **Overall length:** 4.9". **Barrel length:** 2.4". **Weight:** 11.5 oz. (25 ACP); 11.8 oz. (22 LR) **Sights:** Blade front; V-notch rear. **Safety:** Thumb operated. **Grips:** Plastic or Walnut. **Frame:** Forged aluminum.
Prices:
Matte/Plastic. $194.00
Blued/Plastic 244.00
Nickel/Plastic 254.00
Blued/Engraved/Wood 294.00

MODEL 21 BOBCAT

MODEL 950 JETFIRE

MODEL 950 JETFIRE
SINGLE-ACTION SEMIAUTOMATIC

SPECIFICATIONS
Caliber: 25 ACP. **Barrel length:** 2.4". **Overall length:** 4.7". **Overall height:** 3.4". **Safety:** External, thumb-operated **Magazine capacity:** 8 rounds. **Sights:** Blade front; V-notch rear. **Weight:** 9.9 oz. **Frame:** Forged aluminum.
Prices:
Matte/Plastic. $159.00
Blued/Plastic 187.00
Nickel/Plastic 221.00
Blued/Engraved/Wood 267.00

MEDIUM-FRAME PISTOLS

MODEL 84 CHEETAH

This pistol is pocket size with a large magazine capacity. The first shot (with hammer down, chamber loaded) can be fired by a double-action pull on the trigger without cocking the hammer manually.

The pistol also features a favorable grip angle for natural pointing, positive thumb safety (designed for both right- and left-handed operation), quick takedown (by means of special takedown button) and a conveniently located magazine release. Black plastic grips. Wood grips extra.

SPECIFICATIONS
Caliber: 380 Auto (9mm Short). **Magazine capacity:** 10 rounds. **Barrel length:** 3.8". (approx.) **Overall length:** 6.8". (approx.) **Weight:** 23.3 oz. (approx.). **Sights:** Fixed front; rear dovetailed to slide. **Height overall:** 4.85" (approx.).
Prices:
Bruniton/Plastic $529.00
Bruniton/Wood 557.00
Nickel/Wood 599.00

MODEL 84 CHEETAH

BERETTA PISTOLS

MEDIUM-FRAME PISTOLS

MODEL 85 CHEETAH

This double-action semiautomatic pistol features walnut or plastic grips, Bruniton or nickel finish on steel slide, barrel and anodized forged aluminum, ambidextrous safety and a single line 8-round magazine.

SPECIFICATIONS
Caliber: 380 Auto (9mm Short). **Barrel length:** 3.8". **Weight:** 21.9 oz. (empty). **Overall length:** 6.8". **Overall height:** 4.8". **Capacity:** 8 rounds. **Sights:** Blade integral with slide (front); square-notched bar, dovetailed to slide (rear).
Prices:
Bruniton/Plastic $499.00
Bruniton/Wood 530.00
Nickel/Wood 599.00

Also available:
Model 87 in 22 LR. **Capacity:** 7 rounds. Straight blow-back, open slide design. **Width:** 1.3". **Overall height:** 4.7". **Weight:** 20.1 oz. **Finish:** Blued with wood. $493.00

MODEL 85 CHEETAH

MODEL 86 CHEETAH

SPECIFICATIONS
Caliber: 380 Auto. **Barrel length:** 4.4". **Overall length:** 7.3". **Capacity:** 8 rounds. **Weight:** 23.3 oz. **Sight radius:** 4.9". **Overall height:** 4.8". **Overall width:** 1.4". **Grip:** Walnut. **Features:** Same as other Medium Frame, straight blow-back models, plus safety and convenience of a tip-up barrel (rounds can be loaded directly into chamber without operating the slide).
Price:
Bruniton/Wood Grips $514.00

MODEL 86 CHEETAH

MODEL 89 GOLD STANDARD

This sophisticated single-action, target pistol features an eight-round magazine, adjustable target sights, and target-style contoured walnut grips with thumbrest.

SPECIFICATIONS
Caliber: 22 LR. **Capacity:** 8 rounds. **Barrel length:** 6". **Overall length:** 9.5". **Height:** 5.3". **Weight:** 41 oz. **Price** $736.00

MODEL 89 GOLD STANDARD

BERETTA PISTOLS

LARGE FRAME PISTOLS

MODELS 92FS (9mm) & 96 (40 Cal.)

SPECIFICATIONS
Calibers: 9mm and 40 cal.
Capacity: 10 rounds
Action: Double/Single
Barrel length: 4.9" **Overall length:** 8.5"
Weight: 34.4 oz.
Overall height: 5.4" **Overall width:** 1.5"
Sights: Integral front; windage adjustable rear; 3-dot or tritium night sights
Grips: Wood or plastic
Finish: Bruniton (also available in blued, stainless, silver or gold)
Features: Chrome-lined bore; visible firing-pin block; open slide design; safety drop catch (half-cock); combat trigger guard; external hammer; reversible magazine release

Also available:
MODELS 92D (9mm) and **96D** (40 cal.). Same specifications but in DA only and with Bruniton finish and plastic grips only. Also features chamber loaded indicator on extractor; bobbed external hammer; "slick" slide (no external levers)
MODEL CENTURION (9mm and 40 cal.). Same as above but with more compact upper slide and barrel assembly. **Barrel length:** 4.3". **Overall length:** 7.8". **Weight:** 33.2 oz.

MODEL 92D/ 96D

MODEL 96

Models	Prices
Model 92FS Plastic w/3-Dot sights	$626.00
For wood grips, **add**	20.00
For tritium sights, **add**	90.00
Model 92F Stainless w/3-dot sights	757.00
Model 92FS Plastic Centurion	
9mm/40 cal. w/3-dot sights	626.00
w/tritium sights	716.00
Model 92D (DA only, bobbed hammer)	
w/3-dot sights	586.00
w/tritium sight	676.00
Model 92F Deluxe gold-plated engraved	5429.00
Model 92F-EL Stainless	1243.00
Model 96 w/3-dot sights	643.00
w/tritium sights	733.00
Model 96D (DA only)	607.00
w/tritium sights	697.00
Model 96 Centurion	643.00
w/tritium sights	733.00

BRIGADIER

The Brigadier is a variant of the Beretta 92/96 Series of 9mm and 40-caliber pistols. It features removable front sights and a reconfigured high slide wall profile that reduces felt recoil and improves sight alignment between shots.

SPECIFICATIONS
Calibers: 9mm and 40 cal.
Capacity: 10 rounds
Barrel length: 4.9"
Weight: 35.3 oz.
Sights: 3-dot sight system
Finish: Matte black Bruniton
Price: On request

MODEL 92/96 BRIGADIER

BERNARDELLI PISTOLS

MODEL P.018 TARGET PISTOL
$725.00 (Black Plastic)
$780.00 (Chrome)

SPECIFICATIONS
Caliber: 9mm
Capacity: 16 rounds
Barrel length: 4.8"
Overall length: 8.25"
Weight: 34.2 oz.
Sights: Low micrometric sights adjustable for windage and elevation
Sight radius: 5.4"
Features: Thumb safety decocks hammer; magazine press button release reversible for right- and left-hand shooters; hardened steel barrel; can be carried cocked and locked; squared and serrated trigger guard and grip; frame and barrel forged in steel and milled with CNC machines; manual thumb, half cock, magazine and auto-locking firing-pin block safeties; low-profile 3-dot interchangeable combat sights

**MODEL P.018
TARGET PISTOL**

MODEL P.018 COMPACT TARGET PISTOL
$725.00 (Black Plastic)
$780.00 (Chrome)

SPECIFICATIONS
Calibers: 380, 9mm, 40 S&W (chrome only)
Capacity: 14 rounds
Barrel length: 4"
Overall length: 7.44"
Weight: 31.7 oz.
Sight radius: 5.4"
Grips: Walnut or plastic
Features: Same as Model P.018

**MODEL P.018
COMPACT TARGET**

MODEL P.010 TARGET PISTOL
$899.00

SPECIFICATIONS
Caliber: 22 LR
Capacity: 5 or 10 rounds
Barrel length: 5.9"
Weight: 40 oz.
Sights: Interchangeable front sight; rear sight adjustable for windage and elevation
Sight radius: 7.5"
Features: All steel construction; external hammer with safety notch; external slide catch for hold-open device; inertia safe firing pin; oil-finished walnut grips for right- and left-hand shooters; matte black or chrome finish; pivoted trigger with adjustable weight and take-ups

**MODEL P.010
TARGET**

BERSA AUTOMATIC PISTOLS

THUNDER 9 DOUBLE ACTION
$458.95 (Duo-Tone) $475.00 (Satin Nickel)
$448.95 (Matte)

SPECIFICATIONS
Caliber: 9mm **Capacity:** 10 rounds
Action: Double
Barrel length: 4" **Overall length:** 7³/₈"
Weight: 30 oz. **Height:** 5.5"
Sights: Blade front (integral w/slide); fully adjustable rear
Safety: Manual, firing pin and decocking lever
Grips: Black polymer
Finish: Matte blue, satin nickel or duo-tone
Features: Reversible extended magazine release; adjustable trigger release; "Link-Free" design system (ensures positive lockup); instant disassembly; ambidextrous slide release

THUNDER 9 DOUBLE ACTION

THUNDER 22

THUNDER 380

SERIES 95

THUNDER 22
$249.95 (Blue) $266.95 (Satin Nickel)

SPECIFICATIONS
Caliber: 22 LR **Capacity:** 10 rounds
Action: Double
Barrel length: 3.5" **Overall length:** 6⁵/₈"
Weight: 24.5 oz.
Sights: Notched-bar dovetailed rear; blade integral with slide front
Safety: Manual firing pin
Grips: Black polymer

THUNDER 380
$249.95 (Blue) $266.95 (Satin Nickel)

SPECIFICATIONS
Caliber: 380 ACP **Capacity:** 7 rounds
Barrel length: 3.5" **Overall length:** 6⁵/₈"
Weight: 25.75 oz.
Sights: Notched-bar dovetailed rear; blade integral with slide front
Safety: Manual firing pin
Grips: Rubber
Finish: Blue, satin nickel, duo-tone
Also available:
THUNDER 380 PLUS (26 oz.; 10 shots) **Prices: $316.95** (Matte); **$349.00** (Satin Nickel)

SERIES 95
$224.95 (Matte) $241.95 (Nickel)

SPECIFICATIONS
Caliber: 380 ACP **Capacity:** 7 rounds
Action: Double
Barrel length: 3.5" **Overall length:** 6⁵/₈"
Weight: 23 oz.
Sights: Notched-bar dovetailed rear; blade integral with slide front
Safety: Manual firing pin
Grips: Black polymer

BROLIN ARMS

PRO SERIES

MODEL PRO-COMP PISTOL
$909.00 ($929.00 Stainless or Two-Tone)

SPECIFICATIONS
Caliber: 45 ACP **Capacity:** 8+1
Action: Single
Barrel length: 4" **Overall length:** 8.5"
Weight: 37 oz.
Finish: Blue, Stainless or Two-Tone
Features: Signature wood grip; beveled magazine well; beavertail grip safety; adj. rear sight; black ramp front sight; recoil guide rod; adj. aluminum match trigger; slotted commander hammer; dual-port compensator

Also available:
MODEL PRO-STOCK. Same specifications as the Pro-Comp Pistol, except without dual-port compensator.
Price: $779.00 ($799.00 in Stainless or Two-Tone)

PRO SERIES
PRO-COMP

PATRIOT SERIES

MODEL P45C COMP COMPACT
$679.00 ($699.00 Stainless or Two-Tone)

SPECIFICATIONS
Caliber: 45 ACP **Capacity:** 7+1
Action: Single
Barrel length: 3.25" **Overall Length:** 7.5"
Weight: 33 oz.
Features: DPC Compensator w/conical lock-up match barrel; orange- ramp front sight, white-outline rear sight; slotted commander hammer; beavertail grip safety; checkered wood grip; adj. aluminum match trigger; dual recoil springs

Also available:
MODEL P45 COMP STANDARD. Same specifications as the P45C Comp Compact, except w/o DPC Compensator and dual recoil springs. **Price: $649.00 ($669.00** Stainless or Two-Tone)

MODEL P45C COMP
COMPACT

LEGEND SERIES

MODEL L45 STANDARD
$449.00

SPECIFICATIONS
Caliber: 45 ACP **Capacity:** 7+1
Action: Single
Barrel length: 5" **Overall length:** 8.5"
Weight: 46 oz.
Finish: Matte blue
Features: Throated match barrel; orange-ramp front sight; white-outlined rear sight; beveled magazine well; checkered walnut grip; aluminum match trigger

Also available:
MODEL L45C COMPACT. Same specifications as the L45 Standard, except with integral conical lock-up. **Price: $459.00**

LEGEND SERIES L45
STANDARD

BROWNING AUTOMATIC PISTOLS

**9mm HI-POWER
SINGLE ACTION**

HI-POWER SINGLE ACTION

Both the 9mm and 40 S&W models come with either a fixed-blade front sight and a windage-adjustable rear sight or a nonglare rear sight, screw adjustable for both windage and elevation. The front sight is an 1/8-inch-wide blade mounted on a ramp. The rear surface of the blade is serrated to prevent glare. All models have an ambidextrous safety. See table below for specifications and prices.

HI-POWER SPECIFICATIONS 9mm & 40 S&W

Model	Sights	Grips	Barrel Length	Overall Length	Overall Width	Overall Height	Weight*	Mag. Cap.	Prices
Mark III	Fixed	Molded	4.75"	7.75"	1 3/8"	5"	32 oz.	10	$550.95
Standard	Fixed	Walnut	4.75"	7.75"	1 3/8"	5"	32 oz.	10	584.95
Standard	Adj.	Walnut	4.75"	7.75"	1 3/8"	5"	32 oz.	10	635.95
HP-Practical	Fixed	Pachmayr	4.75"	7.75"	1 3/8"	5"	36 oz.	10	629.95
HP-Practical	Adj.	Pachmay	4.75"	7.75"	1 3/8"	5"	36 oz.	10	681.95
Silver Chrome	Adj.	Pachmayr	4.75"	7.75"	1 3/8"	5"	36 oz.	10	650.95
Capitan (9mm only)	Adj.	Walnut	4.75"	7.75"	1 3/8"	5"	32 oz.	10	692.95

* 9mm weight listed. Overall weight of the 40 S&W Hi-Power is 3 oz. heavier than the 9mm.

MODEL BDM 9mm DOUBLE ACTION

Browning's Model BDM (for Browning Double Mode) pistol provides shooters with convenience and safety by combining the best advantages of double-action pistols with those of the revolver. In just seconds, the shooter can set the BDM to conventional double-action "pistol" mode or to the all-new double-action "revolver" mode.

SPECIFICATIONS
Caliber: 9mm Luger
Capacity: 10 rounds
Barrel length: 4.73"
Overall length: 7.85"
Weight: 31 oz. (empty)
Sight radius: 6.26"
Sights: Low-profile front (removable); rear screw adjustable for windage; includes 3-dot sight system
Finish: Matte blue
Features: Dual-purpose ambidextrous decocking lever/safety designed with a short stroke for easy operation (also functions as slide release); contoured grip is checkered on all four sides
Price: $612.95

**MODEL BDM
9mm DOUBLE ACTION**

BROWNING AUTOMATIC PISTOLS

**MODEL
BDA-380**

MODEL BDA-380

A high-powered, double-action semiautomatic pistol with fixed sights in 380 caliber.

SPECIFICATIONS
Capacity: 10 shots
Barrel length: $3^{13}/_{16}$"
Overall length: 6.75"
 Weight: 23 oz.
Sights: Fixed
Grips: Walnut
Prices:
Nickel Finish $606.95
Blued Finish 563.95

**BUCK MARK STANDARD
(5.5" Barrel)**

**BUCK MARK
PLUS NICKEL**

BUCK MARK SPECIFICATIONS

BUCK MARK MODELS	Mag. Cap.	Barrel Length	Overall Length	Weight	Overall Height	Sight Radius	Grips	Prices
Standard	10	5.5"	9.5"	36 oz.	$5^5/_8$"	8"	Molded Composite, Ambidextrous	$256.95
Micro Standard	10	4"	8"	32 oz.	$5^3/_8$"	$9^9/_{16}$"	Molded Composite, Ambidextrous	256.95
Nickel	10	5.5"	9.5"	36 oz.	$5^3/_8$"	8"	Molded Composite, Ambidextrous	301.95
Micro Nickel	10	4"	8"	32 oz.	$5^3/_8$"	$9^9/_{16}$"	Molded Composite, Ambidextrous	301.95
NEW Plus Nickel	10	5.5"	9.5"	36 oz.	$5^3/_8$"	8"	Laminated Hardwood	342.95
NEW Micro Plus Nickel	10	4"	8"	32 oz.	$5^3/_8$"	$9^9/_{16}$"	Laminated Hardwood	342.95
Plus	10	5.5"	9.5"	36 oz.	$5^3/_8$"	8"	Laminated Hardwood	313.95
Micro Plus	10	4"	8"	32 oz.	$5^3/_8$"	$9^9/_{16}$"	Laminated Hardwood	313.95

BROWNING AUTOMATIC PISTOLS

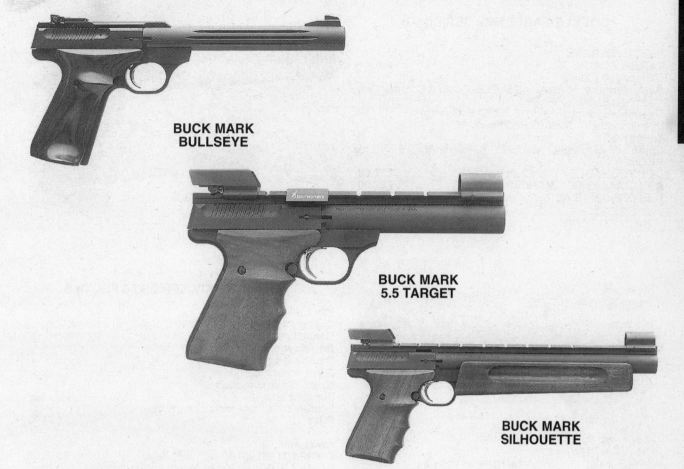

**BUCK MARK
BULLSEYE**

**BUCK MARK
5.5 TARGET**

**BUCK MARK
SILHOUETTE**

BUCK MARK SPECIFICATIONS (cont.)

NEW	**Bullseye, Standard**	10	7.25"	11⁵/₁₆"	36 oz.	5³/₈"	9⁷/₈"	Molded Composite, Ambidextrous	$376.95
NEW	**Bullseye, Target**	10	7.25"	11⁵/₁₆"	36 oz.	5³/₈"	9⁷/₈"	Contoured Rosewood	484.95
		10	7.25"	11⁵/₁₆"	36 oz.	5³/₈"	9⁷/₈"	Wraparound fingergroove	484.95
5.5 Field		10	5.5"	9⁵/₈"	35.5 oz.	5⁵/₁₆"	8.25"	Contoured walnut	411.95
		10	5.5"	9⁵/₈"	35.5oz.	5⁵/₁₆"	8.25"	Wraparound fingergroove	411.95
5.5 Target		10	5.5"	9⁵/₈"	35.5 oz.	5 ⁵/₁₆"	8.25"	Contoured walnut	411.95
		10	5.5"	9⁵/₈"	35.5 oz.	5 ⁵/₁₆"	8.25"	Wraparound fingergroove	411.95
5.5 Nickel Target		10	5.5"	9⁵/₈"	35.5 oz.	5 ⁵/₁₆"	8.25"	Contoured walnut	462.95
		10	5.5"	9⁵/₈"	35.5 oz.	5⁵/₁₆"	8.25"	Wraparound fingergroove	462.95
5.5 Gold Target		10	5.5"	9⁵/₈"	35.5 oz.	5⁵/₁₆"	8.25"	Contoured walnut	462.95
		10	5.5"	9⁵/₈"	35.5 oz.	5⁵/₁₆"	8.25"	Wraparound fingergroove	462.95
Silhouette		10	9⁷/₈"	14"	53 oz.	5⁵/₁₆"	13"	Contoured walnut	434.95
		10	9⁷/₈"	14"	53 oz.	5⁵/₁₆"	13"	Wraparound fingergroove	434.95
Unlimited Silhouette		10	14"	14"	64 oz.	5⁵/₁₆"	15"	Contoured walnut	535.95
		10	14"	18¹¹/₁₆"	64 oz.	5⁵/₁₆"	15"	Wraparound fingergroove	535.95
Varmint		10	9⁷/₈"	14"	48 oz.	5⁵/₁₆"		Contoured walnut	390.95
		10	9⁷/₈"	14"	48 oz.	5⁵/₁₆"		Wraparound fingergroove	390.95
Extra Magazine									24.95

COLT AUTOMATIC PISTOLS

DOUBLE EAGLE MKII SERIES 90

SPECIFICATIONS
Caliber: 45 ACP
Capacity: 8 rounds
Barrel lengths: 5" (Std.); 4.25" (D.E. Combat Commander);
   3.5" (D.E. Officer's ACP)
Overall length: 8.5" (Std.); 7.75" (D.E. Combat
   Commander); 7.25" (D.E. Officer's ACP)
Weight: 35 to 39 oz. (approx.)
Sights: WDS w/sight radius 5.25" (Officer's ACP)-6.5" (Std.)
Prices:
DOUBLE EAGLE $727.00
D.E. COMBAT COMMANDER 727.00
D.E. OFFICER'S ACP 727.00

DOUBLE EAGLE

MODEL M1991A1

M1991A1 MKIV SERIES 80 PISTOLS

SPECIFICATIONS
Caliber: 45 ACP
Capacity: 7 rounds
Barrel length: 5"
Overall length: 8.5"
Sight radius: 6.5"
Grips: Black composition
Finish: Parkerized
Features: Custom-molded carry case
Price: $538.00

Also available:
COMPACT M1991A1 with 3.5" barrel $538.00
COMMANDER M1991A1 with 4.25" barrel and
   7-round capacity 538.00
   Stainless with 5" barrel 590.00

COMBAT COMMANDER MKIV SERIES 80

The semiautomatic Combat Commander, available in 45 ACP and 38 Super, features an all-steel frame that supplies the pistol with an extra measure of heft and stability. This Colt pistol also offers 3-dot high-profile sights, lanyard-style hammer and thumb and beavertail grip safety. Also available in lightweight version with alloy frame (45 ACP only). **Barrel length:** 4.25".

SPECIFICATIONS

Caliber	Weight (ounces)	Overall Length	Magazine Rounds	Finish	Price
45 ACP	36	7.75"	8	Blue	$735.00
45 ACP	36	7.75"	8	Stainless	789.00
45 ACP LW	27.5	7.75"	8	Blue	735.00
38 Super	37	7.75"	9	Stainless	789.00

COMBAT COMMANDER
4¹/4" barrel only

COLT AUTOMATIC PISTOLS

MKIV SERIES 80

GOLD CUP NATIONAL MATCH

SPECIFICATIONS
Caliber: 45 ACP
Capacity: 7 and 8 rounds
Barrel length: 5"   **Overall length**: 8.5"
Weight: 39 oz.
Sights: Colt Elliason sights; adjustable rear for windage and elevation
Hammer: Serrated rounded hammer
Stock: Rubber combat
Finish: Colt blue, stainless or "Ultimate" bright stainless steel
Prices: $ 937.00 Blue
 1003.00 Stainless steel
 1073.00 Bright stainless
Also available:
COMBAT ELITE in 45 ACP or 38 Super; features Accro Adjustable sights, beavertail grip safety. **Price: $895.00**
COMBAT TARGET in 45 ACP. **Price: $768.00** Matte
 $820.00 Stainless

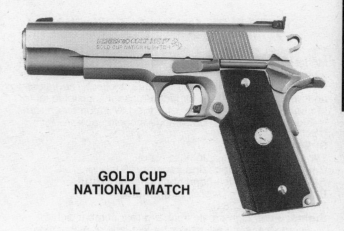

**GOLD CUP
NATIONAL MATCH**

GOVERNMENT MODEL
MKIV SERIES 80 SEMIAUTOMATIC

These full-size automatic pistols with 5-inch barrels are available in 45 ACP and 38 Super. The Government Model's special features include high-profile 3-dot sights, grip and thumb safeties, and rubber combat stocks.

SPECIFICATIONS
Calibers: 38 Super and 45 ACP
Capacity: 9 rounds (38 Super); 8 rounds (45 ACP)
Barrel length: 5"   **Overall length**: 8.5"
Weight: 38 oz. (45 ACP), 39 oz. (38 Super)
Prices: $735.00 45 ACP blue
 789.00 45 ACP stainless
 863.00 45 ACP bright stainless
 735.00 38 Super blue
 789.00 38 Super stainless
 863.00 38 Super bright stainless

GOVERNMENT MODEL

GOVERNMENT MODEL 380
MKIV SERIES 80 SEMIAUTOMATIC

This scaled-down version of the 1911A1 Colt Government Model does not include a grip safety. It incorporates the use of a firing-pin safety to provide for a safe method to carry a round in the chamber in a "cocked-and-locked" mode. Available in matte stainless-steel finish with black composition stocks.

SPECIFICATIONS
Caliber: 380 ACP
Magazine capacity: 7 rounds
Barrel length: 3.25"   **Overall length**: 6"
Height: 4.4"   **Weight**: 21.75 oz. (empty)
Sights: Fixed ramp blade front; fixed square-notched rear
Grip: Composition stocks
Prices: $462.00 Blue
 493.00 Stainless steel
Also available:
POCKETLITE MODEL (14.75 oz.) blued finish only. **$462.00**

**380 GOVERNMENT
POCKETLITE**

COLT AUTOMATIC PISTOLS

MKIV SERIES 80

DELTA ELITE AND DELTA GOLD CUP

The proven design and reliability of Colt's Government Model has been combined with the powerful 10mm auto cartridge to produce a highly effective shooting system for hunting, law enforcement and personal protection. The velocity and energy of the 10mm cartridge make this pistol ideal for the serious handgun hunter and the law enforcement professional who insist on downrange stopping power.

SPECIFICATIONS
Type: 0 Frame, semiautomatic pistol
Caliber: 10mm   **Magazine capacity:** 8 rounds
Rifling: 6 groove, left-hand twist, one turn in 16"
Barrel length: 5"   **Overall length:** 8.5"
Weight (empty): 38 oz.
Sights: 3-dot, high-profile front and rear combat sights; Accro rear sight adjustable for windage and elevation (on Delta Gold Cup only)
Sight radius: 6.5" (3-dot sight system), 6.75" (adjustable sights)
Grips: Rubber combat stocks with Delta medallion
Safety: Trigger safety lock (thumb safety) is located on left-hand side of receiver; grip safety is located on backstrap; internal firing-pin safety
Price: **$807.00** (**$860.00** Stainless)

DELTA GOLD CUP

Also available:
DELTA GOLD CUP. Same specifications as Delta Elite, except 39 oz. weight and 6.75" sight radius. Stainless.
Price: $1027.00

COLT MUSTANG .380

This backup automatic has four times the knockdown power of most 25 ACP automatics. It is a smaller version of the 380 Government Model.

SPECIFICATIONS
Caliber: 380 ACP   **Capacity:** 6 rounds
Barrel length: 2.75"   **Overall length:** 5.5"
Height: 3.9"   **Weight:** 18.5 oz.
Prices: **$462.00** Standard, blue
         493.00 Stainless steel
Also available:
MUSTANG POCKETLITE 380 with aluminum alloy receiver; 12" shorter than standard Govt. 380; weighs only 12.5 oz.
Prices: $462.00 (**$493.00** in nickel).
MUSTANG PLUS II features full grip length (Govt. 380 model only) with shorter compact barrel and slide (Mustang .380 model only). **Weight:** 20 oz. **Prices: $462.00** (blued); **$493.00** (stainless steel).

COLT MUSTANG .380

COLT OFFICER'S 45 ACP

SPECIFICATIONS
Caliber: 45 ACP   **Capacity:** 6 rounds
Barrel length: 3.5"   **Overall length:** 7.25"
Weight: 34 oz.
Prices: **$789.00** Stainless steel
         735.00 Standard blue
         863.00 Ultimate stainless
Also available:
OFFICER'S LW w/aluminum alloy frame (24 oz.) and blued finish. **Price: $735.00**

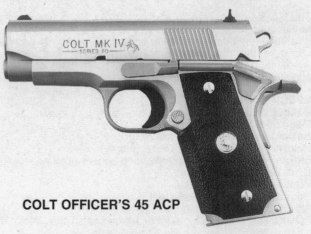

COLT OFFICER'S 45 ACP

COLT PISTOLS/REVOLVERS

COLT .22 SEMIAUTOMATIC DA

SPECIFICATIONS
Caliber: 22 LR   **Capacity:** 10 rounds
Barrel length: 4.5"   **Overall length:** 8⅝"
Weight: 33.5 oz.
Sight radius: 5.75"
Grips: Rubber polymer
Finish: Stainless steel
Price: $248.00
Also available:
COLT .22 TARGET w/6" barrel. **Weight:** 40.5 oz. **Sight radius:** 9.25". **Sights:** Removable front, adjustable rear.
Price: $377.00

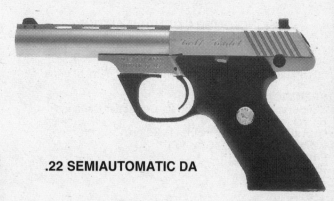

.22 SEMIAUTOMATIC DA

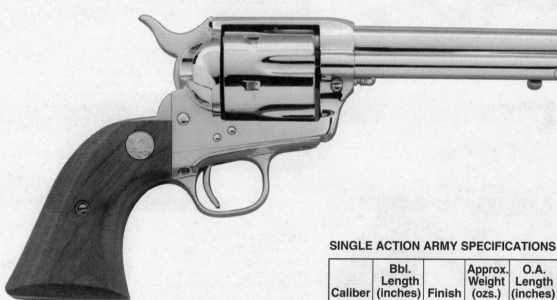

SINGLE ACTION ARMY
(Nickel Finish)

SINGLE ACTION ARMY REVOLVER

Colt's Custom Gun Shop maintains the tradition of quality and innovation that Samuel Colt began more than a century and a half ago. Single Action Army revolvers continue to be highly prized collectible arms and are offered in full nickel finish or in Royal Blue with color casehardened frame, without engraving, unless otherwise specified by the purchaser. Grips are American walnut.
Price: **$1213.00**

SINGLE ACTION ARMY SPECIFICATIONS

Caliber	Bbl. Length (inches)	Finish	Approx. Weight (ozs.)	O.A. Length (inches)	Grips	Medal-lions
45LC	4.75	CC/B	40	10.25	BCE	Gold
45LC	4.75	N	40	10.25	BCE	Nickel
45LC	5.5	CC/B	42	11	BCE	Gold
45LC	5.5	N	42	11	BCE	Nickel
45LC	7.5	CC/B	43	13	BCE	Gold
45LC	7.5	N	43	13	BCE	Nickel
44LC	7.5	CC/B	43	13	BCE	Gold
44LC	7.5	N	43	13	BCE	Nickel
44-40	4.75	CC/B	40	10.25	BCE	Gold
44-40	4.75	N	40	10.25	BCE	Nickel
44-40	5.5	CC/B	42	11	BCE	Gold
44-40	5.5	N	42	11	BCE	Nickel
38-40	4.75	CC/B	40	10.25	BCE	Gold
38-40	4.75	N	40	10.25	BCE	Nickel
38-40	5.5	CC/B	42	11	BCE	Gold
38-40	5.5	N	42	11	BCE	Nickel

N—Nickel   CC/B—Colorcase frame/Royal Blue cylinder & barrel   BCE—Black Composite Eagle

COLT REVOLVERS

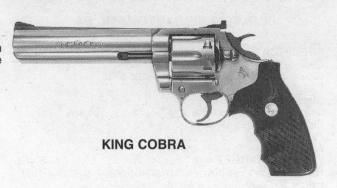

KING COBRA

KING COBRA DOUBLE ACTION

This "snake" revolver features a solid barrel rib, full-length ejector rod housing, red ramp front sight, white outline adjustable rear sight and "gripper" rubber combat grips.

SPECIFICATIONS
Calibers: 357 Mag./38 Special **Capacity:** 6 rounds
Barrel length: 4" or 6"
Overall length: 9" (4" bbl.); 11" (6" bbl.)
Weight: 42 oz. (4"); 46 oz. (6")
Finish: Stainless
Price: $455.00

ANACONDA (6" barrel)

ANACONDA DOUBLE ACTION

SPECIFICATIONS
Calibers: 44 Magnum/44 Special and 45 Colt (6" and 8"
   barrel only)
Capacity: 6 rounds
Barrel length: 4", 6" or 8"
Overall length: $9^5/_8$", $11^5/_8$", $13^5/_8$"
Weight: 47 oz. (4"), 53 oz. (6"), 59 oz. (8")
Sights: Red insert front; adjustable white outline rear
Sight radius: 5.75" (4"), 7.75" (6"), 9.75" (8")
Grips: Black neoprene combat-style with finger grooves
Finish: Matte stainless steel
Price: $612.00
Also available:
REALTREE ANACONDA in 44 Mag./44 Special w/8" barrel. **Price: $740.00 ($999.00 w/rings, scope)**

MODEL 38SF-VI

COLT MODEL 38 SF-VI

SPECIFICATIONS
Caliber: 38 Special **Capacity:** 6 rounds
Barrel lengths: 2" and 4"
Overall length: 7" w/4" bbl.
Weight: 21 oz. **Sight radius:** 4"
Grips: Black composition
Finish: Stainless steel
Price: $408.00
Also available:
COLT SPECIAL LADY w/bobbed hammer (2" barrel).
Price: To be determined

PYTHON PREMIUM DOUBLE ACTION

The Colt Python revolver, suitable for hunting, target shooting and police use, is chambered for the powerful 357 Magnum cartridge. Python features include ventilated rib, fast cocking, wide-spur hammer, trigger and rubber grips, adjustable rear and ramp-type front sights, grooved.

SPECIFICATIONS
Calibers: 357 Mag./38 Special
Barrel length: 4", 6" or 8"
Overall length: 9.5", 11.5", 13.5"
Weight: 38 oz. (4"); 43.5 oz. (6"); 48 oz. (8")
Stocks: Rubber combat (4") or rubber target (6", 8")
Finish: Colt high-polish royal blue, stainless steel and "Ultimate" bright stainless steel

PYTHON (8" barrel)

Prices: $815.00 Royal Blue
      904.00 Stainless steel
      935.00 "Ultimate" Bright Stainless Steel

COONAN ARMS

357 MAGNUM PISTOL
5" Barrel (top)
6" Barrel (middle)
Compensated Barrel (bottom)

357 MAGNUM PISTOL

SPECIFICATIONS
Caliber: 357 Magnum
Magazine capacity: 7 rounds + 1
Barrel length: 5" (6" or Compensated barrel optional)
Overall length: 8.3"
Weight: 48 oz. (loaded)
Height: 5.6"
Width: 1.3"

Sights: Ramp front; fixed rear, adjustable for windage only
Grips: Smooth black walnut (checkered grips optional)
Finish: Stainless steel and alloy steel
Features: Linkless barrel; recoil-operated; extended slide catch and thumb lock
Prices:
With 5" barrel $720.00
With 6" barrel 755.00
With Compensated barrel 999.00

"CADET" COMPACT MODEL

SPECIFICATIONS
Caliber: 357 Magnum
Magazine capacity: 6 rounds + 1
Barrel length: 3.9"
Overall length: 7.8"
Weight: 39 oz.
Height: 5.3"
Width: 1.3"
Sights: Ramp front; fixed rear, adjustable for windage only
Grips: Smooth black walnut
Features: Linkless bull barrel; full-length guide rod; recoil-operated (Browning falling-block design); extended slide catch and thumb lock for one-hand operation
Price: $841.00

"CADET" COMPACT

CZ PISTOLS

The firearms manufacturer CZ, established in 1936 and located in the town of Uhersky Brod in the eastern part of the Czech Republic, is now Europe's second largest manufacturer of sporting, hunting and competitive firearms. The classic CZ 75 design of the early 1970s has been widely used by police departments in more countries around the world than any other firearm. It has been unavailable in the U.S. for many years because of government prohibitions against importing arms from Communist countries. With the lifting of the Iron Curtain, CZ pistols can now be sold in this country once again.

CZ 75

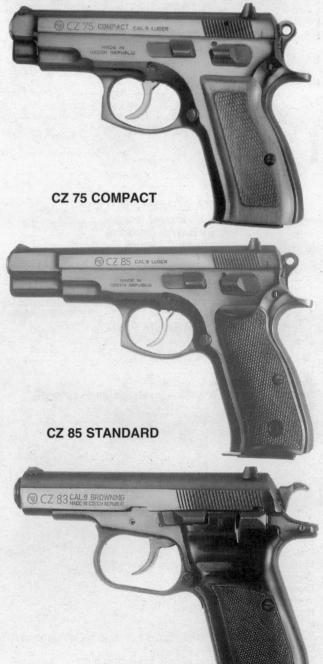

CZ 75 COMPACT

CZ 85 STANDARD

CZ 83

MODEL CZ 75
$539.00 ($569.00 in Nickel)

SPECIFICATIONS
Caliber: 9mm Luger
Capacity: 10 shots
Barrel length: 4.7"   **Overall length:** 8.1"
Weight: 35.27 oz.   **Height:** 5.4"
Grips: Black polymer
Finish: Black polymer or nickel
Also available:
MODEL CZ 75 COMPACT. Capacity: 10 shots. **Barrel length:** 3.94". **Weight:** 32.38 oz. **Grips:** Checkered walnut
Price:. $539.00
MODEL CZ 85. Same as above, except for ambidextrous slide release and safety levers.
Price:. $549.00
MODEL CZ 85 COMBAT. Same as above, but w/adj. rear sight, extended magazine release button, no magazine break, trigger blacklash adjustment w/trigger stop.
Price:. $649.00

MODEL CZ 83
$409.00

SPECIFICATIONS
Caliber: 380 (9mm Browning)   **Capacity:** 10 shots
Barrel length: 3.8"   **Overall length:** 6.77"
Weight: 33.86 oz. **Height:** 5"
Finish: High-polish blue
Also available:
MODEL CZ 100. In 9mm and 40 S&W Luger. **Capacity:** 10 shots. **Barrel length:** 3.7". **Overall length:** 6.9". **Weight:** 23.8 oz.
Price:. $489.00

DAEWOO PISTOLS

MODEL DP51 (not shown)
$400.00

SPECIFICATIONS
Caliber: 9mm Parabellum
Capacity: 10 rounds
Barrel length: 4.1" **Overall length:** 7.5"
Weight: 28 oz.
Muzzle velocity: 1150 fps
Sights: Blade front (1/8"); square notch rear, drift adjustable with 3 self-luminous dots
Safety: Ambidextrous manual safety, automatic firing-pin block
Feature: Patented Fastfire action with light 5-6 lb. trigger pull for first-shot accuracy

MODEL DP51C
COMPACT

MODEL DH380

Also available:
MODEL DP51C COMPACT. Barrel length: 3.6". **Overall length:** 7". **Weight:** 26 oz. **Height:** 4.5". **Price:** $445.00
MODEL DP51S. Barrel length: 3.6". **Overall length:** 7". **Weight:** 27 oz. **Height:** 4.8". **Price:** $420.00

MODEL DH380
$410.00

SPECIFICATIONS
Caliber: 380 ACP **Capacity:** 8 rounds
Barrel length: 3.8" **Overall length:** 6.7"
Weight: 24 oz. **Height:** 4.1"
Width: 1.2"

MODEL DH40
$450.00

MODEL DP52 PISTOL
$380.00

SPECIFICATIONS
Caliber: 40 S&W
Capacity: 10 rounds
Barrel length: 4.1" **Overall length:** 7.5"
Weight: 32 oz. **Height:** 4.8"
Width: 1.38"
Firing mode: Double, single or FastFire, Tri-Action

SPECIFICATIONS
Caliber: 22 LR
Capacity: 10 rounds
Barrel length: 3.8" **Overall length:** 6.7"
Weight: 23 oz. **Width:** 1.18"
Sights: 1/8" front blade; drift adjustable rear (3 white-dot system)

DAVIS PISTOLS

MODEL D-25 DERRINGER

D-SERIES DERRINGERS
$75.00

SPECIFICATIONS
Calibers: 22 LR, 22 Mag., 25 Auto, 32 Auto
Capacity: 2 shot
Barrel length: 2.4" **Overall length:** 4"
Height: 2.8" **Weight:** 9.5 oz.
Grips: Laminated wood
Finish: Black teflon or chrome

LONG-BORE D-SERIES
$104.00 ($110.00 9mm only)

SPECIFICATIONS
Calibers: 22 Mag., 9mm, 32 H&R Mag., 38 Special
Capacity: 2 rounds
Barrel length: 3.5" **Overall length:** 5.4"
Height: 3.31" **Weight:** 16 oz.

Also available:
BIG-BORE 38 SPECIAL D-SERIES. Calibers: 22 WMR, 9mm, 32 H&R Mag., 38 Special. **Barrel length:** 2.75". **Overall length:** 4.65". **Weight:** 14 oz.
Price: . . . .$98.00 ($104.00 9mm only)

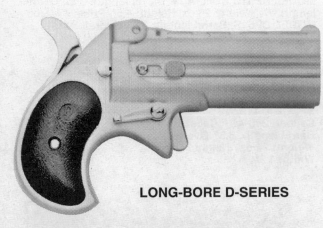

LONG-BORE D-SERIES

MODEL P-32
$87.50

SPECIFICATIONS
Caliber: 32 Auto
Magazine capacity: 6 rounds
Barrel length: 2.8" **Overall length:** 5.4"
Weight (empty): 22 oz. **Height:** 4"
Grips: Laminated wood
Finish: Black teflon or chrome

MODEL P-380
$98.00

SPECIFICATIONS
Caliber: 380 Auto
Magazine capacity: 5 rounds
Barrel length: 2.8" **Overall length:** 5.4"
Height: 4"
Weight: 22 oz. (empty)

MODEL P-32

MODEL P-380

EMF/DAKOTA

SINGLE-ACTION REVOLVERS

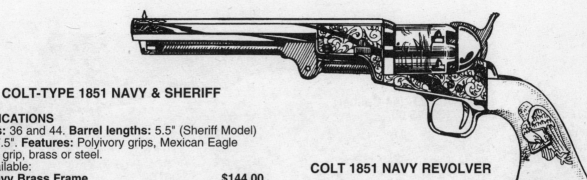

COLT-TYPE 1851 NAVY & SHERIFF

SPECIFICATIONS
Calibers: 36 and 44. **Barrel lengths:** 5.5" (Sheriff Model)
and 7.5". **Features:** Polyivory grips, Mexican Eagle
Head grip, brass or steel.
Also available:

COLT 1851 NAVY REVOLVER

1851 Navy Brass Frame	$144.00
Engraved	197.00
With nickel trim	184.00
1851 Navy Steel Frame	192.00
Engraved	280.00
1851 Sheriff Brass Frame	144.00
With steel frame	192.00
1861 Navy Steel Frame (36 Cal.)	240.00

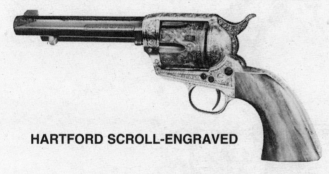

HARTFORD SCROLL-ENGRAVED

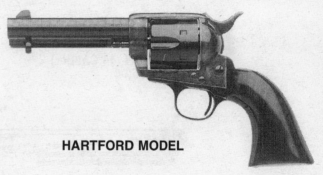

HARTFORD MODEL

HARTFORD SCROLL-ENGRAVED SINGLE-ACTION REVOLVER
$840.00 ($965.00 in Nickel)

SPECIFICATIONS
Calibers: 22, 45 Long Colt, 357 Magnum, 44-40. **Barrel lengths:** 4⅝", 5.5" and 7.5". **Features:** Classic original-type scroll engraving.

HARTFORD MODELS
$600.00 ($725.00 in Nickel)

EMF's Hartford Single Action revolvers are available in the following calibers: 32-20, 38-40, 44-40, 44 Special and 45 Long Colt. **Barrel lengths:** 4¾", 5.5" and 7.5". All models feature steel back straps, trigger guards and forged frame. Identical to the original Colts.

HARTFORD MODELS
"CAVALRY COLT" AND "ARTILLERY"
$700.00

The Model 1873 Government Model Cavalry revolver is an exact reproduction of the original Colt made for the U.S. Cavalry in caliber 45 Long Colt with barrel length of 7.5". The Artillery Model has 5.5" barrel.
Also available:
Sheriff's Model (3.5" barrel) $700.00

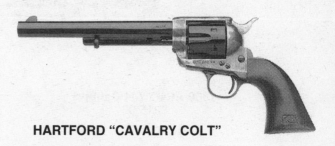

HARTFORD "CAVALRY COLT"

EMF/DAKOTA

NEW HARTFORD PERCUSSION REVOLVERS

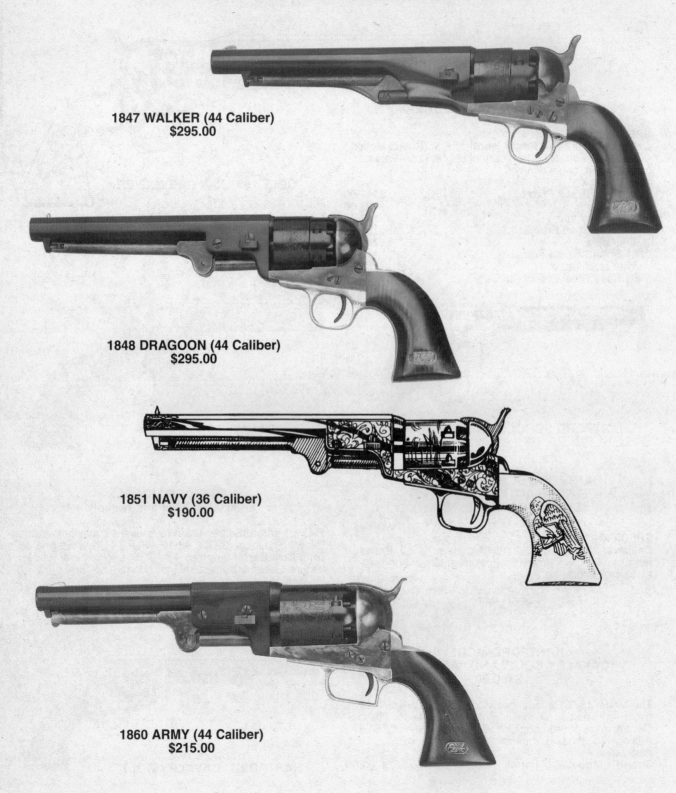

1847 WALKER (44 Caliber)
$295.00

1848 DRAGOON (44 Caliber)
$295.00

1851 NAVY (36 Caliber)
$190.00

1860 ARMY (44 Caliber)
$215.00

EMF/DAKOTA

1873 DAKOTA SINGLE ACTION

1873 DAKOTA SINGLE ACTION
$410.00
$525.00 in Nickel

SPECIFICATIONS
Calibers: 357 Mag., 44-40, 45 Long Colt. **Barrel lengths:** 4.75", 5.5" and 7.5". **Finish:** Blued, casehardened frame. **Grips:** One-piece walnut. **Features:** Set screw for cylinder pin release; parts are interchangeable with early Colts.

MODEL 1875 "OUTLAW"

MODEL 1875 "OUTLAW"
$550.00 w/Brass Trigger Guard
$640.00 in Nickel

SPECIFICATIONS
Calibers: 44-40, 45 Long Colt, 357. **Barrel lengths:** 5.5"and 7.5". **Finish:** Blue or nickel. **Special features:** Casehardened frame, walnut grips; an exact replica of the Remington No. 3 revolver produced from 1875 to 1889.
Factory Engraved Model (7.5" bbl.)............ $600.00
   In nickel................................ 710.00
With steel trigger guard 475.00

PINKERTON DETECTIVE SA

PINKERTON DETECTIVE SA
$700.00

SPECIFICATIONS
Caliber: 45 Long Colt. **Barrel length:** 4". **Grip:** Bird's-head.

MODEL 1890 REMINGTON POLICE

MODEL 1890 REMINGTON POLICE
$570.00 w/Brass Trigger Guard
$665.00 in Nickel

SPECIFICATIONS
Calibers: 44-40, 45 Long Colt and 357 Magnum. **Barrel length:** 5.75". **Finish:** Blued or nickel. **Features:** Original design (1891–1894) with lanyard ring in buttstock; casehardened frame; walnut grips.
Engraved Model............................$815.00
In nickel................................. 910.00
With steel trigger guard 585.00

ERMA TARGET ARMS

MODEL 777 SPORTING REVOLVER

SPECIFICATIONS
Caliber: 357 Magnum
Capacity: 6 cartridges
Barrel length: 4" and 5.5"
Overall length: 9.7" and 11.3"
Weight: 43.7 oz. w/5.5" barrel
Sight radius: 6.4" and 8"
Grip: Checkered walnut
Price: $1019.00

Also available:
MODEL 773 MATCH (32 S&W Wadcutter). Features 6" barrel, 6-shot capacity, adjustable match grip, micrometer rear sight (adjustable for windage and elevation), interchangeable front and rear sight blades, adjustable trigger and polished blued finish. **Weight:** 47.3 oz.
Price: **$1068.00**

MODEL 777 STANDARD

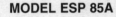

MODEL ESP 85A

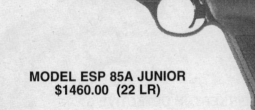

MODEL ESP 85A JUNIOR
$1460.00 (22 LR)

MODEL ESP 85A AUTOLOADING COMPETITION PISTOLS

SPECIFICATIONS
Caliber: 22 LR or 32 S&W Wadcutter
Action: Semiautomatic
Capacity: 5 cartridges (8 in 22 LR optional)
Barrel length: 6"
Overall length: 10"
Weight: 37 oz.
Sight radius: 7.8"
Sights: Micrometer rear sight; fully adjustable interchangeable front and rear sight blade (.13/.16")
Grip: Checkered walnut grip with thumbrest

Prices:
ESP 85A MATCH 32 S&W **$2110.00**
Target adjustable grip, **add** 258.75
   Left hand, **add** 302.25
ESP 85A MATCH 22 LR 1895.00
   In 32 S&W 2000.00
ESP 85A CHROME MATCH 22 LR 2110.00
   In 32 S&W 2325.00
ESP 85A CHROME SPORT PISTOL 22 LR 2000.00
   In 32 S&W 2215.00
Conversion Units 22 LR 980.00
   In 32 S&W 1185.00
Chrome Slide 22 LR 1185.00
   In 32 S&W 1390.00

EUROPEAN AMERICAN ARMORY

ASTRA MODEL A-70
$360.00 (Blue)
$385.00 (Nickel or Stainless Steel)

SPECIFICATIONS
Calibers: 9mm and 40 S&W
Capacity: 8 rounds (9mm), 7 rounds (40 S&W)
Barrel length: 3.5"
Overall length: 6.5"
Weight: 29.25 oz.
Finish: Blue, nickel or stainless steel

ASTRA MODEL A-70
Blued

ASTRA MODEL A-75
$415.00 (Blue)
$445.00 (Nickel or Stainless Steel)

SPECIFICATIONS
Calibers: 9mm, 40 S&W and 45 ACP
Capacity: 8 rounds (7 in 45 ACP & 40 S&W)
Barrel length: 3.5" (3.7" in 45 ACP)
Overall length: 6.5" (6.75" in 45 ACP)
Weight: 31 oz.; 23.5 oz.(Featherweight Model); 34.4 oz.
 (45 ACP steel)
Finish: Blued, nickel or stainless steel
Also available:
Featherweight 9mm **$445.00**

ASTRA MODEL A-75
Blued

ASTRA MODEL A-100
$445.00 (Blue)
$475.00 (Nickel)

SPECIFICATIONS
Calibers: 9mm, 40 S&W and 45 ACP
Capacity: 17 rounds (9mm); 10 rounds (40 S&W); 9
 rounds (45 ACP)
Barrel length: 3.8"
Overall length: 7.5"
Weight: 34 oz. (steel); 26.5 oz. (9mm)
Finish: Blued, nickel or stainless steel

Also available:
MODEL A-100 CARRY COMP. Same specifications as
Model A-100 (w/o compensator) but with 1" compensator;
blued finish only. **Price:** **$520.00**

ASTRA MODEL A-100
Blued

EUROPEAN AMERICAN ARMORY

WITNESS DOUBLE-ACTION PISTOLS

SPECIFICATIONS
Calibers: 9mm, 38 Super,
   40 S&W and 45 ACP
Capacity: 10 rounds (40 S&W or 45 ACP); 16 rounds
   (9mm); 19 rounds (38 Super);
Barrel length: 4.5" **Overall length:** 8.1"
Weight: 33 oz.
Finish: Blued, chrome or stainless steel
Prices:
9mm Blue $410.00
Chrome or blue/chrome 437.00
Stainless steel 480.00
40 S&W Blue 437.00
Chrome or blue/chrome 465.00
Stainless steel 508.00
45 ACP or 38 Super Blue 525.00
Chrome or blue/chrome 550.00
Stainless steel 595.00

WITNESS SUBCOMPACT (not shown)

SPECIFICATIONS
Calibers: 9mm, 40 S&W, 45 ACP. **Capacity:** 10 rounds
(9mm); 9 rounds (40 S&W); 8 rounds (45 ACP). **Barrel
length:** 3.66". **Overall length:** 7.24". **Weight:** 30 oz. **Finish:**
Blued, chrome or stainless steel.
Prices:
9mm Blue $410.00
Chrome 425.00
40 S&W Blue 415.00
Chrome 445.00
45 ACP Blue 525.00

WITNESS FAB-92

This all-steel semiautomatic pistol
features a special ambidextrous hammer drop safety/decocker system now
required by many law enforcement agencies.

SPECIFICATIONS
Calibers: 9mm, 40 S&W, 45 ACP (full size only)
Capacity: 10 rounds
Barrel length: 4.5" (3 5/8" Compact)
Overall length: 8.1" (4.5" Compact)
Weight: 33 oz. (30 oz. Compact)
Finish: Blue, hard chrome or Duo-Tone
Optional: Tritium night sights; extended magazine release;
   rubber grips
Prices:
9mm Blue (full and Compact) $395.00
40 S&W Blue (full and Compact) 425.00
45 ACP Blue 475.00

WITNESS GOLD TEAM

WITNESS GOLD TEAM

SPECIFICATIONS
Calibers: 9mm, 40 S&W, 38 Super, 9X21mm, 45 ACP
Capacity: 10 rounds; 16 rounds (9mm); 19 rounds (38
Super)
Barrel length: 5.25" **Overall length:** 10.5"
Weight: 38 oz.
Finish: Hard chrome

Features: Triple chamber comp, S/A trigger, extended safety competition hammer, checkered front strap and backstrap, low-profile competition grips, square trigger guard
Price: $2150.00
Also available:
WITNESS SILVER TEAM. Same calibers as above.
Features double chamber compensator, competition hammer, extended safety & magazine release, blued finish. **O.A.
length:** 9.75". **Weight:** 34 oz. **Price:** $967.45

PRO SERIES 95

MATCH GRADE TARGET PISTOLS

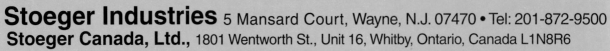

EUROPEAN AMERICAN ARMORY

EUROPEAN SINGLE-ACTION COMPACT

SPECIFICATIONS
Calibers: 380 ACP and 32 ACP
Capacity: 7 rounds
Barrel length: 3.2" **Overall length:** 6.5"
Weight: 26 oz.
Finish: Blued or chrome
Features: All-steel construction; automatic ejection; single-action trigger; European wood grips; rear sight adj. for windage; positive sighting system
Prices:
Blued finish **$160.00**
Chrome finish. **175.00**

EUROPEAN SA COMPACT

WINDICATOR DOUBLE ACTION (STANDARD GRADE)

SPECIFICATIONS
Calibers: 22 LR, 22 LR/22 WMR, 38 Special, 357 Mag.
Capacity: 6 rounds (centerfire); 8 rounds (rimfire)
Barrel length: 2" or 4" (centerfire); 4" or 6" (rimfire)
Finish: Blued only
Features: Swing-out cylinder; black rubber grips; hammer block safety
Prices:
38 Special w/2" barrel **$180.00**
38 Special w/4" barrel **207.00**
357 Magnum w/2" barrel **195.00**
357 Magnum w/4" barrel **225.00**

WINDICATOR REVOLVER

**BIG BORE
BOUNTY HUNTER
SINGLE ACTION**

SPECIFICATIONS
Calibers: 357 Mag., 45 Long Colt and 44 Mag.
Capacity: 6 rounds
Barrel length: 4.5" or 7.5"
Sights: Fixed
Weight: 2.45 lbs. (4.5" bbl.); 2.7 lbs. (7.5" bbl.)
Finish: Blued or color casehardened
Features: Transfer bar safety, 3-position hammer; hammer-forged barrel; walnut grips
Prices:
Blued **$300.00**
Color casehardened receiver **310.00**

BENELLI MODEL MP95E (not shown)

SPECIFICATIONS
Calibers: 22 LR & 32 WC
Capacity: 5 rounds (WC) or 9 rounds (22LR)
Barrel length: 4.25"
Overall length: 11.44" **Width:** 1.69"
Weight: 2.2 lbs.
Finish: Blue or chrome
Features: Single-stage trigger; adj. rear sight w/removable blade; 3/8" integral scope mount rails; ambidextrous safety & European walnut grip; several grip & magazine options (w/tool kit)
Prices:
Blued, 9-shot **$552.50**
Blued, 5-shot **595.00**
Chrome, 9-shot **595.00**

FREEDOM ARMS

MODEL 252 REVOLVER
SILHOUETTE CLASS 10" BARREL

SPECIFICATIONS
Caliber: 22 LR (optional 22 Magnum cylinder)
Barrel lengths: 5.13", 7.5" (Varmint Class) and 10" (Silhouette Class)
Sights: Silhouette competition sights (Silhouette Class); adjustable rear express sight; removable front express blade
Grips: Black micarta (Silhouette Class); black and green laminated hardwood (Varmint Class)
Finish: Stainless steel
Features: Dual firing pin; lightened hammer; pre-set trigger stop; accepts all sights and/or scope mounts
Prices:
Silhouette Class (10" barrel) $1509.00
Varmint Class (5.13" & 7.5" barrels) 1454.00
22 Mag. Cylinder 253.00

SILHOUETTE/COMPETITION MODELS
(not shown)

SPECIFICATIONS
Calibers: 357 Magnum and 44 Rem. Mag.
Barrel lengths: 9" (357 Mag.) and 10" (44 Rem. Mag.)
Sights: Silhouette competition **Grips:** Pachmayr
Trigger: Pre-set stop; trigger over travel screw
Finish: Field Grade
Price: $1347.35

MODEL 353 REVOLVER
FIELD GRADE 7½" BARREL

SPECIFICATIONS
Caliber: 357 Magnum
Action: Single action **Capacity:** 5 shots
Barrel lengths: 4.75", 6", 7.5", 9"
Sights: Removable front blade; adjustable rear
Grips: Pachmayr Presentation grips (Premier Grade has impregnated hardwood grips
Finish: Nonglare Field Grade (standard model); Premier Grade brushed finish (all stainless steel)
Prices:
Field Grade $1253.00
Premier Grade 1627.00

454 CASULL FIELD GRADE

MODEL 555
PREMIER GRADE (50 AE)

454 CASULL & MODEL 555
PREMIER & FIELD GRADES

SPECIFICATIONS
Calibers: 454 Casull, 44 Rem. Mag.
Action: Single action **Capacity:** 5 rounds
Barrel lengths: 4.75", 6", 7.5", 10"
Overall length: 14" (w/7.5" barrel)
Weight: 3 lbs. 2 oz. (w/7.5" barrel)
Safety: Patented sliding bar
Sights: Notched rear; blade front (optional adjustable rear and replaceable front blade)
Grips: Impregnated hardwood or rubber Pachmayr
Finish: Brushed stainless
Features: Patented interchangeable forcing cone bushing (optional); ISGW silhouette, Millett competition and express sights are optional; SSK T'SOB 3-ring scope mount optional; optional cylinder in 454 Casull, 45 ACP, 45 Win. Mag. ($311.50)
Prices:
MODEL FA-454AS Premier Grade
W/adjustable sights $1677.00
W/fixed sights. 1568.00
44 Remington w/adjustable sights. 1627.00
W/fixed sights. 1521.00
MODEL FA-454FGAS Field Grade
With stainless-steel matte finish, adj. sight,
   Pachmayr presentation grips 1301.00
W/fixed sights. 1207.00
44 Remington w/adjustable sights. 1253.00
MODEL 555 Premier 50 Action Express 1677.00
MODEL 555 Field 1301.00

GLOCK PISTOLS

MODEL 17L COMPETITION

MODEL 17L COMPETITION
$790.00 (Fixed Sight)

SPECIFICATIONS
Caliber: 9mm Parabellum
Magazine capacity: 10 rounds (17 and 19 rounds optional)*
Barrel length: 6.02"
Overall length: 8.85"
Weight: 23.35 oz. (without magazine)
Sights: Fixed (adjustable rear sights **$28.00** add'l)

MODEL 17 (Not Shown)
$606.00 (Fixed Sight)

SPECIFICATIONS
Caliber: 9mm Parabellum
Magazine capacity: 10 rounds (17 and 19 rounds optional)*
Barrel length: 4.5" (hexagonal profile with right-hand twist)
Overall length: 7.32"
Weight: 22 oz. (without magazine)
Sights: Fixed (adjustable rear sights **$28.00** add'l)

MODEL 19 COMPACT
$606.00 (Fixed Sight)

SPECIFICATIONS
Caliber: 9mm Parabellum
Magazine capacity: 10 rounds (15 and 17 rounds optional)*
Barrel length: 4"
Overall length: 6.85"
Weight: 21 oz.
Also available:
MODEL 21. Caliber: 45 ACP. **Capacity:** 10 rounds (13 rounds optional)*. **Price: $658.00** (Fixed Sight)

MODEL 19 COMPACT

MODEL 20
$658.00 (Fixed Sight)

SPECIFICATIONS
Caliber: 10mm
Magazine capacity: 10 rounds (15 rounds optional)*
Action: Double action
Barrel length: 4.6" **Overall length:** 7.59"
Height: 5.47" (w/sights)
Weight: 27.68 oz. (empty)
Sights: Fixed (adjustable **$29.00** add'l)
Features: 3 safeties, "safe-action" system, polymer frame

*For law enforcement and military use only

MODEL 20

GLOCK PISTOLS

MODEL 23 COMPACT
SPORT/SERVICE MODEL
$606.00

SPECIFICATIONS
Caliber: 40 S&W
Capacity: 10 rounds (15 rounds optional)*
Barrel length: 4.5"
Overall length: 7.32"
Weight: 23 oz.

Also available:
MODEL 22 (Sport and Service models). **Caliber:** 40 S&W.
Capacity: 10 rounds (15 rounds optional)*. **Overall
length:** 7.32". **Price: $606.00** (Fixed Sight)

MODEL 23 COMPACT

MODEL 24 COMPETITON
$790.00 ($830.00 w/Compensated
Barrel, Fixed Sights)

SPECIFICATIONS
Caliber: 40 S&W
Capacity: 10 rounds (15 rounds optional)*
Barrel length: 6.02"
Overall length: 8.85"
Weight: 26.5 oz. (empty)
Safety: Manual trigger safety; passive firing block and drop
   safety
Finish: Matte (Tenifer process); nonglare

**MODEL 24
COMPETITION**

MODEL 26
$606.00 (Fixed Sight)

SPECIFICATIONS
Caliber: 9mm **Action**: DA
Capacity: 10 rounds
Barrel length: 3.47"
Overall length: 6.3"
Weight: 19.77 oz.
Finish: Matte (Tenifer process); nonglare
Features: 3 safeties; Safe Action trigger system; poly-
   mer frame

Also available:
MODEL 27. Same specifications as Model 26 but in .40
S&W. **Capacity:** 9 rounds. **Price: $606.00** (Fixed Sight)

* For law enforcement and military use only.

MODEL 26

HÄMMERLI U.S.A. PISTOLS

MODEL 160 FREE PISTOL
$2085.00

SPECIFICATIONS
Caliber: 22 LR
Barrel length: 11.3"   **Overall length:** 17.5"
Height: 5.7"   **Weight:** 45 oz.
Trigger action: Infinitely variable set trigger weight; cocking lever located on left of receiver; trigger length variable along weapon axis
Sights: Sight radius 14.8"; micrometer rear sight adj. for windage and elevation
Locking action: Martini-type locking action w/side-mounted locking lever

**MODEL 160
FREE PISTOL**

Barrel: Free floating, cold swaged precision barrel w/low axis relative to the hand
Ignition: Horizontal firing pin (hammerless) in line w/barrel axis; firing pin travel 0.15"
Grips: Selected walnut w/adj. hand rest for direct arm to barrel extension

MODEL 162 ELECTRONIC PISTOL
$2295.00

SPECIFICATIONS
Same as **Model 160** except trigger action is electronic.
Features: Short lock time (1.7 milliseconds between trigger actuation and firing pin impact), light trigger pull, and extended battery life.

**MODEL 162
ELECTRONIC PISTOL**

MODEL 208S STANDARD PISTOL
$1925.00

SPECIFICATIONS
Caliber: 22 LR   **Capacity:** 8 rounds
Action: Single
Barrel length: 5.9"   **Overall length:** 10"
Height: 5.9"   **Weight:** 36.7 oz.
Sight radius: 8.2"
Sights: Micrometer rear sight w/notch width; adj. for windage & elevation; standard front blade
Trigger: Adj. for pull weight, travel, slackweight & creep
Safety: Rotating knob on rear of frame

**MODEL 208S
STANDARD PISTOL**

MODEL 280 TARGET PISTOL
$1565.00 ($1765.00 in 32 S&W)

SPECIFICATIONS
Calibers: 22 LR and 32 S&W
Capacity: 6 rounds (22 LR); 5 rounds (32 S&W)
Action: Single
Barrel length: 4.58"   **Overall length:** 11.8"
Height: 5.9"
Weight: (excluding counterweights) 34.6 oz. (22 LR); 41.8 oz. (32 S&W)
Sight radius: 8.7"   **Sights:** Micrometer adjustable
Grips: Orthopedic type; stippled walnut w/adj. palm shelf
Features: 3 steel & 3 carbon fiber barrel weight; combination tool; 4 Allen wrenches; dry fire plug; magazine loading tool; extra magazine
Also available:
MODEL 280 TARGET PISTOL COMBO
With carrying case $2595.00
Conversion Unit (22 LR) 748.00
In 32 S&W 928.00

**MODEL 280
TARGET PISTOL**

HARRINGTON & RICHARDSON

MODEL 929 SIDEKICK REVOLVER

The Model 929 Sidekick® 22 LR revolver is a complete beginner's package, including a lockable plastic storage case, an Uncle Mikes ballistic nylon holster, and a trial-size package of TETRA® gun oil and grease. The 9-shot Sidekick has a square butt frame with cinnamon laminate grips. The entire revolver is high polished and hot blued, giving it a color and finish similar to pre-war guns. Sights are fixed with a blade front and a notch rear milled into the top strap. Safety is provided by a transfer bar system for safe carry even with all nine chambers loaded or in case of a blow to the hammer. Steel and select hardwood laminate ensure an exceptional service life.
Calibers: 22 Short, Long and Long Rifle
Capacity: 9-shot swing-out cylinder
Price: $159.95

MODEL 929 SIDEKICK REVOLVER

AMTEC 2000 DA REVOLVER

AMTEC 2000, Inc., is a unique joint venture that brings together two of the world's foremost makers of fine firearms: Erma Werke and Harrington & Richardson. These firms have united German engineering skill and American manufacturing skill to create a new company that is greater than the sum of its parts. This AMTEC 2000 Double Action model in 38 S&W Special is a five-shot revolver with a swing-out cylinder, shell ejector and the following specifications.

SPECIFICATIONS
Caliber: 38 S&W Special   **Action:** Double
Capacity: 5-shot w/swing-out cylinder and shell ejector
Barrel length: 2"or 3"
Overall length: 7 1/8" (2" barrel); 8 1/2" (3" barrel)
Weight: 24 oz. (2" barrel); 25.5 oz. (3" barrel)
Height: 5 1/4"
Sights: Fixed notch rear, ramp front
Safety: Transfer bar safety system
Grips: Pachmayr composition with finger grooves
Finish: High polish blue, matte electroless nickel or stainless steel
Price: On request

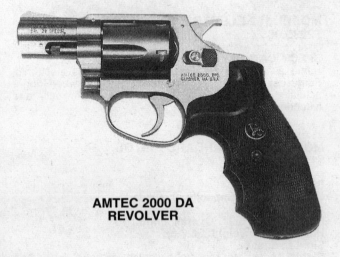

AMTEC 2000 DA REVOLVER

COMPETITOR PISTOL (Not Shown)

This single-shot pistol is completely ambidextrous with interchangeable barrels in over 250 calibers, ranging from small rimfire to large belted magnums. Competitor barrels can be changed within three minutes. Standard Competitor pistols are available with synthetic grips, black oxide finish and 14-inch barrel with adjustable sights (or standard scope mount). Features include nickel finish, muzzle brake, natural or laminated grips, cammed rotary ejection and optional non-standard barrels from 10.5" to 23".

SPECIFICATIONS
Action: Single shot
Type: Rotary cannon, self-cocking
Calibers: Rimfire-belted Magnum interchangeable barrel system (over 250 calibers available)

Barrel length: 14" standard (10.5", 12", 14 7/8", 16"–23" available)
Overall length: 15 1/8" (w/14" barrel)
Weight: 2 lbs. 9 oz. (w/synthetic grip and 14" barrel in .223 caliber); 2. lbs. 4 oz. (w/walnut grip)
Ejection: Rotary style cammed to initiate removal of stuck cases (6 ejectors for most calibers from RF to belted mag.)
Safety: Dual safety (sliding thumb safety in rear and one in trigger)
Grip: Ambidextrous, synthetic, laminated or natural wood
Sights: Fixed ramp front, all-steel click adjustable
Finish: Matte blue, electroless nickel optional (all critical parts made from hardened 4140 or 8620 steel)
Prices:
Competitor Pistol (standard calibers w/14" barrel, sights or standard scope mount, synthetic grip $399.95
  With laminated wood 439.95
Competitor barreled action only
  (standard calibers) 244.95
Spare 14" barrel (standard calibers w/sights) . . 149.95
Rimfire or Centerfire Conversion Kit (incl. barrel w/sights and ejector) 209.20
Universal scope mount 27.95
Standard scope mount 15.95

HARRINGTON & RICHARDSON

MODEL 939 PREMIER TARGET REVOLVER
$184.95

The Model 939 Premier is a single- and double[-action]
revolver with nine-shot swing-out cylinder and feat[ures a]
heavy target-grade barrel with barrel rib.

MODEL 939 PREMIER TARGET REVOLVER

SPECIFICATIONS
Calibers: 22 Short, Long, Long Rifle
Capacity: 9 rounds
Barrel length: 6"
Weight: 36 oz.
Grips: Walnut hardwood; nickel medallion
Sights: Fully adjustable rear; fixed front
Features: Two-piece walnut-stained hardwood western-styled grip frame profile, transfer bar system; made of high-quality ferrous metals

MODEL 949 CLASSIC WESTERN REVOLVER

MODEL 949 CLASSIC WESTERN REVOLVER
$184.95

With true Western styling, the single- and double-action Model 949 features a color casehardened frame and back-strap, loading gate, shrouded ejector rod and transfer bar safety system.

SPECIFICATIONS
Calibers: 22 Short, Long and Long Rifle
Capacity: 9 rounds
Barrel length: 5.5" or 7.5" (case colored)
Weight: 36 oz. (5.5" barrel); 38 oz. (7.5" barrel)
Sights: Fixed front; drift-adjustable rear
Grips: Two-piece walnut-stained hardwood; nickel medallion

SPORTSMAN 999 REVOLVER
$279.95

SPECIFICATIONS
Calibers: 22 Short, Long, Long Rifle
Action: Single and double
Capacity: 9 rounds
Barrel lengths: 4" and 6" (both fluted)
Weight: 30 oz. (4" barrel); 34 oz. (6" barrel)
Sights: Windage adjustable rear; elevation adjustable front
Grips: Walnut-finished hardwood
Finish: Blued
Features: Top-break loading with auto shell ejection

SPORTSMAN 999 REVOLVER

HECKLER & KOCH PISTOLS

MODEL HK USP

MODEL USP45 UNIVERSAL SELF-LOADING PISTOL

SPECIFICATIONS
Calibers: 9mm, 45 ACP and 40 S&W
Capacity: 10 + 1
Operating system: Short recoil, modified Browning action
Barrel length: 4.25" **Overall length:** 7.64"
Weight: 1.74 lbs. (40 S&W); 1.66 lbs. (9mm)
Height: 5.35" **Sights:** Adjustable 3-dot
Grips/stock: Polymer receiver and integral grips
Prices:
9mm & 40 S&W **$636.00**
   W/control lever on right 656.00
45 ACP 696.00
   W/control lever on right 716.00
Universal Tactical Pistol Light (UTL) 255.00

SPECIFICATIONS
Caliber: 45 ACP **Capacity:** 10 rounds
Action: DA/SA or DAO
Barrel length: 4.41" **Overall length:** 7.87"
Height: 5.55" **Weight:** 1.90 lbs.
Grips/Stock: Polymer frame & integral grips
Prices:
Variants* 1, 3, 5, 7, 9 . . . . **$696.00**
Variants* 2, 4, 6, 10 . . . . 716.00
Stainless steel, **add** 45.00
* Variants refers to availabilty of control lever options for
  right- or left-hand shooters

Also available in 9mm and 40 S&W. **Barrel length:** 4.25".
Overall length: 7.64". **Weight:** 1.75 lbs. **Price: $681.00**
(**$701.00** w/control lever on right)

MODEL P7M8 SELFLOADING PISTOL

MARK 23 SPECIAL OPERATIONS PISTOL (SOCOM)

SPECIFICATIONS
Caliber: 9mmx19 (Luger) **Capacity:** 8 rounds
Barrel length: 4.13" **Overall length:** 6.73"
Weight: 1.75 lbs. (empty)
Sight radius: 5.83" **Sights:** Adjustable rear
Grips/Stock: Plastic
Finish: Blue or nickel
Operating System: Recoil-operated; retarded inertia slide
Price: **$1187.00**

SPECIFICATIONS
Caliber: 45 ACP **Capacity:** 10 rounds
Operating system: Short recoil, modified Browning action
Barrel length: 5.87" **Overall length:** 9.65"
Height: 5.9" **Weight:** 2.66 lbs.
Sights: 3-dot
Grips/Stock: Polymer frame & integral grips
Price: **$1995.00**

HERITAGE MANUFACTURING

**SENTRY
DOUBLE ACTION**

**ROUGH RIDER SA
w/ Bird's-Head Grip**

ROUGH RIDER SA

SPECIFICATIONS
Caliber: 38 Special   **Capacity:** 6 rounds
Barrel length: 2"   **Overall length:** 6.5"
Weight: 21 oz.
Sights: Ramped front, fixed rear
Grips: Black polymer   **Finish:** Blued or nickel
Features: Internal hammer block; additional safety plug in
   cylinder, transfer bar safety.
Prices:
Blued **$129.95**
Nickel. **139.95**

SPECIFICATIONS
Caliber: 22 LR or 22 LR/22 WMR
Capacity: 6 rounds   **Weight:** 31 to 38 oz.
Barrel lengths: 4.75", 6.5", 9" (regular grip); 2.75", 3.75",
   4.75" (Bird's-Head grip)
Sights: Blade front, fixed rear
Grips: Exotic hardwood   **Finish:** Blued or nickel
Features: Rotating hammer block safety; brass accent
   screws
Prices:
22 LR (4.75", 6.5" bbl.) blued, regular grip **$109.95**
22 LR/22 WMR
   W/blued finish, regular grip:
   4.75" & 6.5" barrels **129.95**
   9" barrel. **139.95**
   W/nickel finish, regular grip:
   4.75" & 6.5" barrels **149.95**
   9" barrel. **169.95**
   W/blued finish, Bird's-head grip:
   2.75", 3.75" & 4.75" barrels **129.95**
   W/nickel finish: Bird's-head grip:
   2.75", 3.75" & 4.75" barrels **149.95**

**STEALTH
COMPACT PISTOL**

MODEL H25S (not shown)

SPECIFICATIONS
Caliber: 9mm   **Capacity:** 10 rounds
Barrel length: 3.9"   **Overall length:** 6.3"
Weight: 20 oz.   **Height:** 4.2"
Triggerpull: 4 lbs.
Frame: Black polymer
Styles: Model C-1000 17-4 Stainless steel slide
   Model C-2000 17-4 Black stainless steel slide
   Model C-1010 17-4 Two-tone stainless steel slide
Features: Striker-fire trigger; gas-delayed blow back action;
   frame-mounted ambidextrous trigger safety; drop safety;
   closed breech safety; magazine disconnect safety
Price: all styles **$299.95**

SPECIFICATIONS
Caliber: 25 ACP
Capacity: 6 rounds
Action: Single
Barrel length: 2.25"   **Overall length:** 4.58"
Weight: 13.5 oz.
Safety: Frame-mounted trigger safety; magazine discon-
   nect safety
Trigger pull: 5 lbs.
Features: All-steel frame and slide; exposed hammer
Prices:
Blued. **$149.95**
Nickel. **159.95**

HI-POINT FIREARMS

MODEL 9mm

380 POLYMER

MODEL 9mm
$139.95

SPECIFICATIONS
Caliber: 9mm Parabellum
Capacity: 9 shots
Barrel length: 4.5"
Overall length: 7.72"
Weight: 39 oz.
Sights: 3-dot type
Features: Quick on-off thumb safety; nonglare military black finish

MODEL 380 POLYMER
$79.95

SPECIFICATIONS
Caliber: 380 ACP
Capacity: 8 shots
Barrel length: 3.5"
Also available:
MODEL 45 in 45 ACP. Same specifications as the 9mm, except w/7-shot capacity and two-tone Polymer finish.
Price: **$148.95**
MODEL 40 in 40 S&W. Same specifications as the 45 ACP w/8-shot capacity. **Price:** **$148.95**
MODEL 9mm COMPACT w/3.5" barrel. **Price:**. . .**$124.95**

HIGH STANDARD

**OLYMPIC
RAPID FIRE**

OLYMPIC
RAPID FIRE
$1995.00

SPECIFICATIONS
Caliber: 22 Short   **Capacity:** 5 rounds
Barrel length: 4"
Overall length: 11.5"
Weight: 46 oz.
Sights: Click-adjustable for windage and elevation (rear); mounted on vent aluminum rib
Grips: Special International
Finish: Matte blue
Features: Push-button barrel takedown system; trigger adj.for weight of pull and travel; gold-plated trigger, slide stop, safety and magazine release
Also available:
OLYMPIC MILITARY w/5.5" barrel **$536.00**

HIGH STANDARD

SUPERMATIC CITATION
$446.00

SPECIFICATIONS
Caliber: 22 LR **Capacity:** 10 rounds
Barrel length: 5.5" **Overall length:** 9.5"
Weight: 44 oz.
Finish: Blued or Parkerized
Features: Optional Universal Mount to replace open-sight
   rib (deduct $30.00)
Also available:
CITATION MS. Recoil-operated semiautomatic. **Barrel
length:** 10". **Overall length:** 14". **Weight:** 49 oz. Gold-plat-
ed trigger; slide lock lever; push-button takedown system;
adjustable trigger; drilled and tapped for Weaver-style scope
base **$695.00**
SUPERMATIC CITATION MS. Similar to Citation above,
except 10" barrel (14" overall), 49 oz. weight, RPM sights
click-adjustable for windage and elevation, checkered right-
hand thumbrest and matte blue finish **$695.00**
TROPHY/CITATION 22 Short Conversion Kit (incl. barrel
w/sight, slide, 2 magazines) **$309.00**

SUPERMATIC TROPHY
$516.00 (5.5" Barrel)
$536.00 (7.25" Barrel)

SPECIFICATIONS
Caliber: 22 LR **Capacity:** 10 rounds
Action: Recoil-operated semiautomatic
Barrel length: 5.5" bull or 7.25" fluted
Overall length: 9.5 (w/5.5" bbl.) and 11.25" (w/7.25" bbl.)
Weight: 44 oz. (w/5.5" bbl.) and 46 oz. (w/7.25" bbl.)
Sights: Click-adjustable rear for windage/elevation; under-
   cut ramp front
Grips: Checkered American walnut with right-hand thumb-
   brest (left-hand optional)
Features: Gold-plated trigger; slide lock lever; push-button
   takedown system; magazine release
Also available:
22 Short Conversion Kit (see left)

SUPERMATIC
TOURNAMENT
$399.00

SPECIFICATIONS
Caliber: 22 LR
Capacity: 10 rounds
Barrel length: 5.5"
Overall length: 9.5"
Weight: 44 oz.
Finish: Matte frame
Features: Fully adjustable rear sight; non-adjustable trigger

VICTOR 22 LR
$532.00

SPECIFICATIONS
Caliber: 22 LR **Capacity:** 10 rounds
Barrel lengths: 4.5" and 5.5"
Overall length: 8.5" and 9.5"
Weight: 45 oz. (w/4.5" bbl.); 46 oz. (w/5.5" bbl.)
Finish: Blued or Parkerized frame
Features: Optional steel rib; click-adjustable sights for
   windage and elevation; optional barrel weights and
   Universal Mount (to replace open-sight rib)
Also avaliable:
22 Short Conversion Kit 5.5" barrel w/vent rib, slide, two
magazines **$397.00**

J.O. ARMS

KAREEN MK II COMPACT
$496.50

SPECIFICATIONS
Caliber: 9mm
Capacity: 10 rounds
Barrel length: 3.82"
Overall length: 6"
Height: 5.07" **Weight:** 2 lbs.
Features: Ambidextrous safety; rubberized grips; 41/40 steel; extended hammer protection: improved trigger guard
Also available:
KAREEN MK II. Single-action semiautomatic with the same specifications as the Kareen MK II Compact, except 4.6" barrel (7.72" overall) and weight 2.11 lbs.
Price:. $410.50

GOLAN DA
$649.50 (9mm) $684.50 (40 S&W)

SPECIFICATIONS
Calibers: 9mm, 40 S&W
Capacity: 10 rounds
Barrel length: 3.9"
Overall length: 7"
Height: 5.4" **Weight:** 29 oz.
Features: Double action; forged steel slide; ambidextrous controls; drop proof safety; chromed barrel; internal automatic safety
Also available:
GOLAN COMPACT. In 45 ACP, 8 shots, 4.25" barrel (7.75" overall), weight 36 oz. rubberized wraparound grip, forged-steel frame and slide, competition trigger, hammer, slide stop, standard two-tone.
Price:. $525.00

KAHR ARMS

MODEL K9 PISTOL
$595.00

All key components of the Kahr K9-frame, slide, barrel, etc.-mare made from 4140 steel, allowing the pistol to chamber reliably and fire virtually any commercial 9mm ammo, including +P rounds. The frame and sighting surfaces are matte blued, and the sides of the slide carry a polished blue finish. The grips are crafted from exotic wood.

The unique trigger system holds the striker in a partially cocked state; then, a pull of the trigger completes the cocking cycle and releases the striker. Recoil on firing partially cocks the striker for the next trigger pull. This design allows a lighter-than-normal "DA" pull that is consistent from shot to shot. A trigger-activated firing-pin block prevents accidental discharge. Like a double-action revolver, no other safeties are needed.

SPECIFICATIONS
Calibers: 9mm and 9mm+P **Capacity:** 7 rounds
Barrel length: 3.5" **Overall length:** 6"
Height: 4.5" **Weight:** 25 oz. (empty)
Sights: Drift-adjustable, low-profile white bar-dot combat sights
Grips: Textured polymer
Finish: Nonglare black finish on slide, frame & sighting surfaces (electroless nickel model available)
Features: Trigger cocking safety; passive firing-pin block; no magazine disconnect; locked breech

KBI PISTOLS

FEG GKK-45 AUTO PISTOL
$349.00

SPECIFICATIONS
Calibers: 45 ACP and 40 S&W
Capacity: 8 rounds (9 rounds in 40 S&W)
Barrel length: 4¹/₈"
Overall length: 7.75"
Weight: 36 oz.
Sights: 3-dot, blade front; rear adjustable for windage
Stock: Hand-checkered walnut
Features: Double action; polished blue or hard chrome finish; combat trigger guard; two magazines and cleaning rod standard

**FEG GKK-45
AUTO PISTOL**

FEG MODEL PJK-9HP
$295.00 ($375.00 Chrome)

SPECIFICATIONS
Caliber: 9mm Luger Parabellum
Magazine capacity: 10 rounds
Action: Single
Barrel length: 4.75"
Overall length: 8"
Weight: 21 oz.
Grips: Hand-checkered walnut
Safety: Thumb safety
Sights: 3-dot system
Finish: Blue or chrome
Features: One 10-round magazine, cleaning rod

**FEG MODEL
PJK-9HP**

FEG MODEL SMC-380
$259.00

SPECIFICATIONS
Calibers: 22 LR, 380 ACP, 9mm Makarov (9X18)
Capacity: 6 rounds (10 rds in 22 LR)
Action: Double
Barrel length: 3.5"
Overall length: 6¹/₈"
Weight: 18.5 oz.
Safety: Thumb safety w/decocking
Grips: Black composite
Features: High-luster blued steel slide; blue anodized aluminum alloy frame

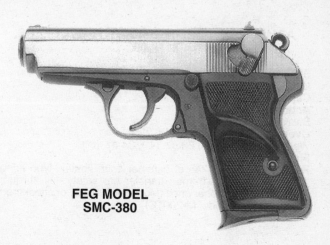

**FEG MODEL
SMC-380**

KBI HANDGUNS

FEG SMC-22 AUTO PISTOL
$259.00

SPECIFICATIONS
Calibers: 22 LR and 380 ACP
Capacity: 6 rounds (380 ACP) or 8 rounds (22 LR)
Barrel length: 3.5"
Overall length: 6 1/8"
Weight: 18.5 oz.
Stock: Checkered composition w/thumbrest
Sights: Blade front; rear adjustable for windage
Features: Alloy frame; steel slide; double action; blue finish; two magazines and cleaning rod standard

FEG SMC-22

ARMSCOR MODEL M1911-A1P
$399.00

SPECIFICATIONS
Caliber: 45 ACP
Action: Semiauto
Capacity: 7 or 10 rounds
Barrel length: 5"
Overall length: 8.75"
Weight: 38 oz.
Finish: Parkerized
Features: Ambidextrous positive thumb safety; extended slide release; beavertail grip safety; skeletonized combat hammer & trigger

**ARMSCOR MODEL
M1911-A1P**

ARMSCOR MODEL M-200DC/TC REVOLVERS
$199.00

SPECIFICATIONS
Calibers: 22 LR, 22 Mag. RF, 38 Super
Capacity: 6 rounds
Action: Double
Barrel lengths: 2.5", 4", 6"
Overall lengths: 8 3/8", 8 7/8", 10 7/8"
Weight: 22 oz. (2.5"), 28 oz. (4"), 34 oz. (6")
Finish: Blued
Features: Serrated target hammer spur; floating-type firing pin (mounted in frame); transfer bar safety; full shroud; combat style rubber grips (Model M-200 DC) or checkered wood grips (Model M-200TC)

**ARMSCOR MODEL
M-200DC/TC**

KIMBER PISTOLS

CLASSIC .45
CUSTOM

CLASSIC .45
GOLD MATCH

KIMBER CLASSIC .45

This Chip McCormick-inspired pistol is made in the U.S.A. by the famous rifle-maker, Kimber. The new firearm comes in four versions—Custom, Stainless, Custom Royal and Gold Match—according to differences in sights, grips, capacity and finish.

SPECIFICATIONS
Caliber: 45 ACP
Capacity: 8 (10 in Gold Match)
Barrel length: 5"   **Overall length:** 8.5"
Weight: 38 oz.
Sights: McCormick low-profile combat type (Bo-Mar sights only in Gold Match model)
Finish: Polished blue (Custom Royal & Gold Match); matte black (Custom); stainless steel (Custom Stainless)
Features: Lowered and flared ejection port; slide machined from solid steel; premium match-grade hammer-forged- barrel and bushing; front and rear serrations; ultra-light-weight composite premium match trigger; relief cut under trigger guard; extended combat-style thumb safety; flat main spring housing; beveled magazine well

Models	Prices
CUSTOM	$575.00
CUSTOM STAINLESS	650.00
CUSTOM ROYAL	715.00
GOLD MATCH	925.00

CLASSIC .45
CUSTOM ROYAL

CLASSIC .45
CUSTOM STAINLESS

L.A.R. GRIZZLY

MARK I GRIZZLY
45 Win Mag $1000.00   357 Magnum $1014.00

This semiautomatic pistol is a direct descendant of the tried and trusted 1911-type .45 automatic, but with the added advantage of increased caliber capacity.

SPECIFICATIONS
Calibers: 45 Win. Mag., 45 ACP, 357 Mag., 10mm
Magazine capacity: 7 rounds
Barrel lengths: 5.4" and 6.5"
Overall length: 10.5"
Weight (empty): 48 oz.
Height: 5.75"
Sights: Fixed, ramped blade (front); fully adjustable for elevation and windage (rear)

Grips: Checkered rubber, nonslip, combat-type
Safeties: Grip depressor, manual thumb, slide-out-of-battery disconnect
Materials: Mil spec 4140 steel slide and receiver with non-corrosive, heat-treated, special alloy steels for other parts

Also available:
Grizzly 44 Magnum Mark IV w/adj. sights $1014.00
Grizzly Win Mag Conversion Units
   In 45 Win. Mag., 45 ACP, 10mm 233.00
   In 357 Magnum 248.00
Win Mag Compensator 119.00
   In 50 caliber 130.00

GRIZZLY WIN MAG
6.5" BARREL

MARK IV
GRIZZLY 44 MAG.

GRIZZLY 50 MARK 5
$1152.00

SPECIFICATIONS
Caliber: 50 AE   **Capacity:** 6 rounds
Barrel lengths: 5.4" and 6.5"
Overall length: 10⁵/₈"
Weight: 56 oz.   **Height:** 5.75"
Sights: Fixed front; fully adjustable rear
Features: Browning–type short recoil; locked breech

GRIZZLY 50 MARK 5

LASERAIM TECHNOLOGIES

LASERAIM SERIES I PISTOLS

SPECIFICATIONS
Calibers: 45 ACP, 10mm
Capacity: 7+1 (45 ACP) and 8+1 (10mm)
Barrel lengths: 3⁷/₈" and 5.5"
Overall length: 8.75" (3⁷/₈") and 10.5"
Weight: 46 oz. (3 ⁷/₈") and 52 oz.
Features: Adjustable Millet sights, ambidextrous safety, beavertail tang, non-glare slide serration, beveled magazine well, extended slide release
Price:. **$629.00**
(w/Adjustable Sights) **659.00**

Also available:
DREAM TEAM w/Laseraim Laser, fixed sights,
   HOTDOT **$794.95**

The Series I pistol features a dual port compensated barrel and vented slide to reduce recoil and improve control. Other features include stainless-steel construction, ramped barrel, accurized barrel bushing and fixed sights (Laseraim's "HOT-DOT" sight or Auto Illusion electronic red dot sight available as options).

LASERAIM SERIES III PISTOLS

SPECIFICATIONS
Calibers: 45 ACP and 10mm
Capacity: 8+1 (10mm) and 7+1 (45 ACP)
Barrel length: 5"   **Overall length:** 7⁵/₈"
Weight: 43 oz.
Overall height: 5⁵/₈"
Features: Same as Series I
Price:. **$599.00**
   w/Adjustable Sights **629.00**

Also available:
SERIES II w/3³/₈" or 5" barrel, fixed sights **$499.00**
   w/Adjustable sights, add **30.00**

The Series III pistol features a ported barrel and slide to reduce recoil and improve control. Includes stainless-steel construction, ramped barrel, accurized barrel bushing and comes with adjustable and laser sights (optional).

LLAMA AUTOMATIC PISTOLS

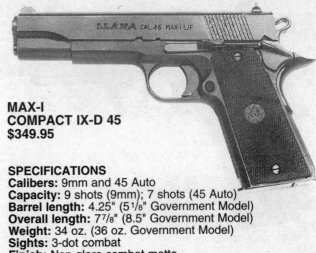

**SMALL-FRAME
380 AUTOMATIC
(Deep Blue Finish)
$291.95**

**MAX-I
COMPACT IX-D 45
$349.95**

SPECIFICATIONS
Calibers: 9mm and 45 Auto
Capacity: 9 shots (9mm); 7 shots (45 Auto)
Barrel length: 4.25" (5¹/₈" Government Model)
Overall length: 7⁷/₈" (8.5" Government Model)
Weight: 34 oz. (36 oz. Government Model)
Sights: 3-dot combat
Finish: Non-glare combat matte
Price:. **$349.95**
10-shot Model **399.95**
7-shot 45 Govt. Model **366.95**

LLAMA AUTOMATIC PISTOL SPECIFICATIONS

Type:	Small-Frame	Compact-Frame	Government Model
Calibers:	380 Auto	45 Auto	45 Auto
Frame:	Precision machined from high-strength steel	Precision machined from high-strength steel	Precision machined from high-strength steel
Trigger:	Serrated	Serrated	Serrated
Hammer:	External; wide spur, serrated	External; military style	External; military style
Operation:	Straight blow-back	Locked breech	Locked breech
Loaded Chamber Indicator:	Yes	Yes	Yes
Safeties:	Extended manual & grip safeties	Extended manual & grip safeties	Extended manual & grip safeties
Grips:	Matte black polyme	Anatomically designed rubber grips	Anatomically designed rubber grips
Sights:	Patridge-type front; sq.-notch rear	3-dot combat sight	3-dot combat sights
Sight Radius:	4¹/₄"	6¹/₄"	6¹/₄"
Magazine Capacity:	7 shots	10 shots	10 shots
Weight:	23 oz.	39 oz.	41 oz.
Barrel Length:	3¹¹/₁₆"	4¹/₄"	5¹/₈"
Overall Length:	6¹/₂"	7⁷/₈"	8¹/₈"
Height:	4³/₈"	5⁷/₁₆"	5⁵/₁₆"
Finish:	Standard:High-polished, deep blue. Deluxe: Satin chrome	Non-glare combat matte	Non-glare combat matte

AMERICAN EAGLE LUGER®

AMERICAN EAGLE LUGER®

9mm AMERICAN EAGLE LUGER®
STAINLESS STEEL

It is doubtful that there ever was a pistol created that evokes the nostalgia or mystique of the Luger pistol. Since its beginnings at the turn of the 20th century, the name Luger® conjures memories of the past. Stoeger Industries is indeed proud to have owned the name Luger® since the late 1920s and is equally proud of the stainless-steel version that graces this page.

The "American Eagle" name was introduced around 1900 to capture the American marketplace. It served its purpose well, the name having become legendary along with the Luger® name. The "American Eagle" inscribed on a Luger® also distinguishes a firearm of exceptional quality over some inexpensive models that have been manufactured in the past.

Constructed entirely of stainless steel, the gun is available in 9mm Parabellum only, with either a 4" or 6" barrel, each with deeply checkered American walnut grips.

The name Luger®, combined with Stoeger's reputation of selling only quality merchandise since 1918, assures the owner of complete satisfaction.

SPECIFICATIONS
Caliber: 9mm Parabellum
Capacity: 7 + 1
Barrel length: 4" (P-08 Model); 6" (Navy Model)
Overall length: 8.25" (w/4" bbl.), 10.25" (w/6" bbl.)
Weight: 30 oz. w/4" barrel, 32 oz. w/6" barrel
Grips: Deeply checkered American walnut
Features: All stainless-steel construction
Price:. $695.00
In matte black. 760.00

MAGNUM RESEARCH

MARK XIX COMPONENT SYSTEM

MARK XIX w/10" Barrel

MARK XIX w/6" Barrel

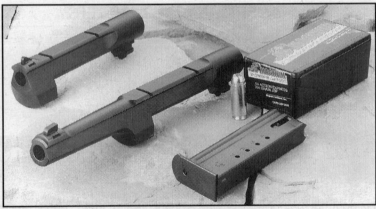

The new Mark XIX Component system allows for three caliber changes in two different barrel lengths.

The Desert Eagle Pistol Mark XIX Component System is based on a single platform that transforms into six different pistols—three Magnum calibers, each with a 6-inch or 10-inch barrel. Changing calibers is a simple matter of switching barrels and magazines. (Converting to or from .357 Magnum also involves changing the bolt.)

The barrel design alone sports several improvements. Each barrel is now made of a single piece of steel instead of three. All six barrels, including the optional 10-inch barrels, have a 7/8" dovetailed design with cross slots to accommodate scope rings; no other scope mounts are required. The .50 A.E.'s new 10-inch barrel will fit existing .50s, as well as the new Mark XIX platform.

Hogue soft rubber grips are standard equipment on the new gun. The pistol's well-known gas operation, polygonal rifling, low recoil and safety features remain the same, as do the Mark VII adjustable trigger, slide release and safety levers.

SPECIFICATIONS
Calibers: 357 Magnum, 44 Magnum and 50 A.E.
Capacity: 9 rounds (357 Mag.); 8 rounds (44 Mag.);
   7 rounds (50 A.E.)
Barrel lengths: 6" and 10"
Overall length: 10.75" (w/6" bbl.); 14.75" (w/10" bbl.)
Weight: 4 lbs. 6.5 oz. (w/6" bbl.); 4 lbs. 15 oz. (w/10" bbl.)(empty)
Height: 6.25" **Width:** 1.25"
Finish: Standard black
Prices:
357 Mag. w/6" barrel . . . . $ 979.00
357 Mag. w/10" barrel 1029.00
44 Mag. w/6" barrel 999.00
44 Mag. w/10" barrel 1049.00
50 A.E. w/6" barrel 1049.00
50 A.E. w/10" barrel 1099.00

MAGNUM RESEARCH

BABY EAGLE PISTOL
$569.00 $659.00 (Chrome)

SPECIFICATIONS
Calibers: 9mm, 40 S&W
Capacity: 10 rounds
Barrel length: 4.72" **Overall length:** 8.14"
Weight: 35.27 oz. (empty)
Sights: Combat
Features: Double action; extra-long slide rail; combat-style trigger guard; decocking safety; polygonal rifling; ambidextrous thumb safety; all-steel construction

BABY EAGLE 9mm PISTOL VARIATIONS
$569.00 (10-round capacity)

1. With Frame-mounted safety, black finish
2. With Frame-mounted Safety & Short Barrel (3.62")
3. With Frame-mounted Safety, Short Barrel & Short Grip

BABY EAGLE

MOUNTAIN EAGLE
(Not Shown)
$239.00

This affordable, lightweight triangular-barreled pistol with minimum recoil is ideal for plinkers, target shooters and varmint hunters. The barrel is made of hybrid injection-molded polymer and steel, and the standard 15-round magazine is made of high-grade, semitransparent polycarbonate resin. It uses a constant force spring to load all 15 rounds easily. The receiver is made of machined T-6 alloy.

SPECIFICATIONS
Caliber: 22 LR
Barrel length: 6" **Overall length:** 10.6"
Weight: 21 oz. (unloaded)
Sights: Standard orange in front, black in rear (adjustable for windage and elevation
Grip: One-piece injection-molded, checkered conventional contour side panels, horizontally textured front and back panels
Also available:
TARGET EDITION with 8" barrel, 2-stroke target trigger, jeweled bolt, adj. sights, range case **$279.00**

MOUNTAIN EAGLE
COMPACT EDITION
$199.00

Same specifications as the standard Mountain Eagle, except with 4.5" barrel. **Weight:** 19.3 oz.

LONE EAGLE SINGLE
SHOT BARRELED ACTION
$289.00

This specialty pistol is designed for hunters, silhouette enthusiasts, long-range target shooters and other marksmen. The pistol can fire 14 different calibers of ammo. Available w/interchangeable 14-inch barreled actions. Calibers: 22 Hornet, 22-250, 223 Rem., 243 Win., 30-06, 30-30, 308 Win., 35 Rem., 357 Maximum, 358 Win., 44 Mag., 444 Marlin, 7mm-08, 7mm Bench Rest. Features ambidextrous grip, new cocking indicator and lever.

LONE EAGLE

Also available:
LONE EAGLE with barreled action in calibers 7mm-08, 308 or 30-06. Features integral muzzle brake, silver matte Ecoloy II satin finish, satin scope mount and travel case **$399.00**

MITCHELL ARMS

45 ACP GOLD SERIES SINGLE-COLUMN MODELS

STANDARD MODEL
$675.00

STANDARD MODEL
(Wide Body)
$840.00

Mitchell Arms offers two models of its new competition 45-caliber pistols: a standard 8-round model and a "wide body" 10-round model. Innovations include a bull barrel/slide lock-up, adjustable trigger, replaceable front sights and beveled magazine wells. Plus the same grip angle as the original 1911 pistols, that matches Mitchell's 22-caliber competition target pistols.

The Gold Series standard model accepts virtually every 8-round single-stack 1911-type 45 ACP magazine (pistols acquired by law-enforcement agencies and U.S. Military also accept double-stack 13-round magazines). Options include stainless steel or high blue finish, fixed or fully adjustable rear sights, replaceable combat-type front sights, American walnut or blue rubberized competition grips.

SPECIFICATIONS
Action: Single Action **Caliber:** 45 ACP
Capacity: 8 or 10 shots (13 shots in Wide Body model avail. for law-enforcement use only)
Barrel length: 5" **Weight:** 32 oz.
Sights: Fixed or adjustable, with optional ghost ring
Stocks: Rubber or walnut
Features: M1911 Government Model, heavy barrel (no bushing), ambidextrous safety, extended slide lock, adjustable trigger, beavertail grip safety, beveled magazine well
Also available:
IPSC LIMITED MODEL
With Ghost Ring sight. $1240.00
With adjustable sight 1195.00

TACTICAL MODEL
$735.00 (Fixed Sights)
$775.00 (Adjustable Sights)

BULLSEYE MODEL
$950.00

MITCHELL ARMS

22 LR TARGET PISTOLS

SOVEREIGN MODEL
(5.5" Bbl., Stainless w/Vent Rib)
$595.00

SOVEREIGN MODEL
(4.5" Bbl., Stainless w/Weaver Rib)

SOVEREIGN MODEL
(w/Weaver Rib and Scope)

SOVEREIGN MODEL

SPECIFICATIONS
Caliber: 22 LR   **Capacity:** 10 shots
Action: Single action
Barrel lengths: 4.5", 5.5"
Weight: 36–42 oz.
Sights: Fully adjustable
Stocks: Checkered American walnut or rubber; competition
  stocks available
Finish: Stainless or two-tone
Features: Optional full-length ventilated or weaver rib;
  adjustable trigger

MONARCH MODEL
$489.00

SPECIFICATIONS
Caliber: 22 LR   **Capacity:** 10 shots
Action: Single action
Barrel lengths: 5.5" (Bull); 7.25" (Fluted)
Weight: 42 oz.
Sights: Fully adjustable frame mounted
Stocks: Checkered American walnut
Finish: Satin finish with nickel trim
Features: Adjustable trigger

MONARCH MODEL
(w/5.5" Bull Barrel)

MITCHELL ARMS

22 LR TARGET PISTOLS

BARON MODEL
$395.00

SPECIFICATIONS
Caliber: 22 LR
Capacity: 10-shot magazine
Action: Single action
Barrel length: 5.5"
Weight: 42 oz.
Sights: Fully adjustable
Stocks: Checkered American walnut
Finish: Satin finish with black trim
Features: Standard trigger

**BARON
TARGET PISTOL**

SPORTSTER MODEL
$325.00

SPECIFICATIONS
Caliber: 22 LR
Capacity: 10 shot-magazine
Action: Single action
Barrel length: 4.5"
Weight: 36 oz.
Sights: Blade front; rear drift adjustable
Stocks: Rubber
Finish: Stainless steel

**SPORTSTER
TARGET PISTOL**

MEDALLION TARGET PISTOL
(w/7.25" Fluted Barrel)

MEDALLION MODEL
$498.00

SPECIFICATIONS
Caliber: 22 LR
Capacity: 10 shot-magazine
Action: Single action
Barrel length: 5.5" (Bull); 7.25" (Fluted)
Weight: 42 oz.
Stocks: Checkered American Walnut with thumb rest
Finish: Polished stainless steel frame with gold trim
Features: Adjustable trigger

Also available:
MEDALIST in 22 Short or 22 LR. **Barrel length:** 6.75".
Price:. $599.00

MEDALIST

MITCHELL ARMS

"JEFF COOPER" SIGNATURE MODELS
$795.00

SPECIFICATIONS
Caliber: 45 ACP
Barrel length: 5"   **Weight:** 32 oz.
Sights: Cooper sights
Stocks: Special slender stocks
Finish: Satin blue
Features: Heavy barrel; slenderized all-steel frame with Jeff Cooper signature engraved in slide on both sides
Also available:
Jeff Cooper Commemorative Model $1895.00

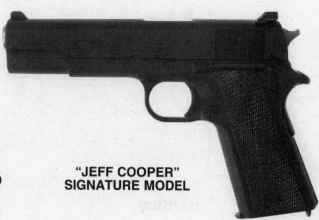

"JEFF COOPER" SIGNATURE MODEL

44 MAGNUM PISTOL

44 MAGNUM PISTOL
$1190.00

SPECIFICATIONS
Caliber: 44 Magnum
Barrel length: 5.5"
Weight: 46 oz.
Sights: All steel, fully adjustable rear sights with dove-tailed front sight
Stocks: Checkered walnut grips
Features: Semiautomatic pistol in Gold Series style; front and rear slide serrations; skeleton fast hammer

GUARDIAN ANGEL
DOUBLE-ACTION PISTOLS

SPECIFICATIONS
Calibers: 22 LR, 22 Magnum
Barrel length: 2"   **Overall length:** 5"
Sights: Channel sights
Stocks: Black
Finish: Nickel, black nickel, satin steel and gold
Features: Compact and lightweight. Standard or deluxe models (deluxe models shipped in a velvet jewelry box with Guardian Angel keychain charm). Each pistol shipped with one 2-shot breech block; interchangeable blocks available.
Price: . . . . $142.95-$199.95

GUARDIAN ANGEL
DA PISTOL

MOA MAXIMUM PISTOLS

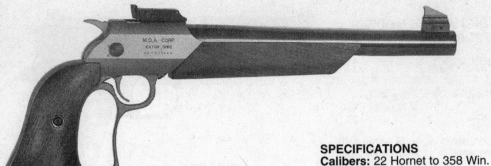

**MAXIMUM
SINGLE SHOT**

MAXIMUM

This single-shot pistol with its unique falling-block action performs like a finely tuned rifle. The single-piece receiver of stainless steel is mated to a Douglas barrel for optimum accuracy and strength.

SPECIFICATIONS
Calibers: 22 Hornet to 358 Win.
Barrel lengths: 8.5", 10.5" and 14"
Weight: 3 lbs. 8 oz. (8.5" bbl.); 3 lbs. 13 oz. (10.5" bbl.);
    4 lbs. 3 oz. (14" bbl.)
Prices:
Stainless receiver, blued barrel $653.00
Stainless receiver and barrel 711.00
Extra barrels (blue) 164.00
   Stainless 222.00
Muzzle brake 125.00

NAVY ARMS REPLICAS

1873 SINGLE ACTION

1873 COLT-STYLE SINGLE-ACTION REVOLVERS

The classic 1873 Single Action is the most famous of all the "six shooters." From its adoption by the U.S. Army in 1873 to the present, it still retains its place as America's most popular revolver. **Calibers:** 44-40 or 45 Long Colt. **Barrel lengths:** 3", 4.75", 5.5" or 7.5". **Overall length:** 10.75" (5.5" barrel). **Weight:** 2.25 lbs. **Sights:** Blade front; notch rear. **Grips:** Walnut.
Price: $390.00

1873 U.S. CAVALRY MODEL
(not shown)

An exact replica of the original U.S. Government issue Colt Single-Action Army, complete with Arsenal stampings and inspector's cartouche. **Caliber:** 45 Long Colt. **Barrel length:** 7.5". **Overall length:** 13.25". **Weight:** 2 lbs. 7 oz. **Sights:** Blade front; notch rear. **Grips:** Walnut.
Price: $480.00

1895 U.S. ARTILLERY MODEL (not shown)

Same specifications as the U.S. Cavalry Model, but with a 5.5" barrel as issued to Artillery units. **Caliber:** 45 Long Colt.
Price: $480.00

1875 SCHOFIELD REVOLVER

1875 SCHOFIELD REVOLVER

A favorite side arm of Jesse James and General George Armstrong, the 1875 Schofield revolver was one of the legendary handguns of the Old West. **Caliber:** .44-40, 45 LC. **Barrel lengths:** 5" (Wells Fargo Model) or 7" (U.S. Cavalry Model). **Overall length:** 10.75" or 12.75". **Weight:** 2 lbs. 7 oz. **Sights:** Blade front; notch rear. **Features:** Top-break, automatic ejector single action.
Price: $795.00

NEW ENGLAND FIREARMS

STANDARD REVOLVER
$134.95 ($144.95 in Nickel)

SPECIFICATIONS
Calibers: 22 S, L or LR
Capacity: 9 shots
Barrel lengths: 2.5" and 4"
Overall length: 7" (2.5" barrel) and 8.5" (4" barrel)
Weight: 25 oz. (2.5" bbl.) and 28 (4" bbl.)
Sights: Blade front; fixed rear
Grips: American hardwood, walnut finish, NEF medallion
Finish: Blue or nickel

Also available:
In 5-shot, calibers 32 H&R Mag., 32 S&W, 32 S&W Long.
Weight: 23 oz. (2.5 barrel); 26 oz. (4" barrel). Other specifications same as above.
Blued finish **$134.95**
Nickel finish (2.5" bbl. only). 144.95
STARTER REVOLVER (pull pin cylinder & lanyard ring) in 22 cal. **Capacity:** 5 and 9 shot. **Finish:** Blued.
Price:. **$104.95**

STANDARD MODEL
(22 LR, 2.5" Barrel)

ULTRA MAG.

ULTRA MODEL
(6" Barrel)

ULTRA AND ULTRA MAG. REVOLVERS
$169.95

SPECIFICATIONS
Calibers: 22 Short, Long, Long Rifle (Ultra); 22 Win. Mag. (Ultra Mag.)
Capacity: 9 shots (22 LR); 6 shots (22 Win. Mag.)
Barrel length: 6"
Overall length: $10^5/_8$"
Weight: 36 oz.
Sights: Blade on rib front; fully adjustable rear
Grips: American hardwood, walnut finish, NEF medallion

Also available:
LADY ULTRA in 5-shot 32 H&R Magnum. **Barrel length:** 3". **Overall length:** 7 1/4". **Weight:** 31 oz. **Price:** . $169.95

LADY ULTRA

NORTH AMERICAN ARMS

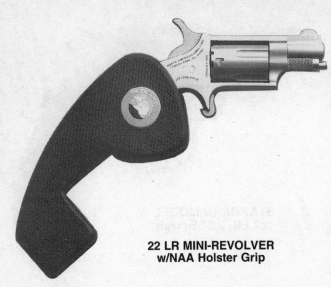

22 LR MINI-REVOLVER
w/NAA Holster Grip

MINI-REVOLVERS

SPECIFICATIONS (Standard on all models)
Calibers: 22 Short (1¹/8" bbl. only), 22 LR and 22 Magnum
Capacity: 5-shot cylinder **Grips:** Laminated rosewood
Safety: Half-cock safety
Sights: Blade front (integral w/barrel); fixed,[ql~notched rear
Material: Stainless steel **Finish:** Matte with brushed sides

COMPANION CAP & BALL MINI-REVOLVER
(Not Shown)
$160.00 (1¹/8" Barrel) $180.00 (1⁵/8" Barrel)

SPECIFICATIONS
Calibers: 22 LR and 22 Magnum (#11 percussion caps)
Capacity: 5-shot cylinder
Barrel lengths: 1¹/8" (22 LR); 1⁵/8" (22 Mag.)
Overall length: 4⁵/16" (22 LR); 5⁷/16" (22 Mag.)
Weight: 5.12 oz. (22 LR); 7.02 oz. (22 Mag.)
Finish: Stainless steel
Features: Includes 50-30 gr. lead bullets; powder charge
measure; bullet seater; leather clip holster; lockable
gun rug

SPECIFICATIONS: MINI-REVOLVERS & MINI-MASTER SERIES

Model	Weight	Barrel Length	Overall Length	Overall Height	Overall Width	Price
NAA-MMT-M	10.7 oz.	4"	7³/4"	3⁷/8"	7/8"	$279.00
NAA-MMT-L	10.7 oz.	4"	7³/4"	3⁷/8"	7/8"	279.00
*NAA-BW-M	8.8 oz.	2"	5⁷/8"	3⁷/8"	7/8"	235.00
*NAA-BW-L	8.8 oz.	2"	5⁷/8"	3⁷/8"	7/8"	235.00
NAA-22LR**	4.5 oz.	1¹/8"	4¹/4"	2³/8"	13/16"	157.00
NAA-22LLR**	4.6 oz.	1⁵/8"	4³/4"	2³/8"	13/16"	157.00
*NAA-22MS	5.9 oz.	1¹/8"	5"	2⁷/8"	7/8"	178.00
*NAA-22M	6.2 oz.	1⁵/8"	5³/8"	2⁷/8"	7/8"	178.00

* Available with Conversion Cylinder chambered for 22 Long Rifle ** Available with holster grip **($188.00)**

MINI-MASTER SERIES

SPECIFICATIONS (Standard on all models)
Calibers: 22 LR (NAA-MMT-L, NAA-BW-L) and 22
Magnum (NAA-MMT-M, NAA-BW-M)

Barrel: Heavy vent
Rifling: 8 land and grooves, 1:12 R.H. button broach twist
Grips: Oversized black rubber
Cylinder: Bull
Sights: Front integral with barrel; rear Millett adjustable
white outlined (elevation only) or low-profile fixed

MINI-MASTER NAA-MMT-M
(22 Mag. 4" Barrel)
$279.00 ($264.00 w/Fixed Sight)

MINI-MASTER NAA-BW-MA/LA
BLACK WIDOW
$249.00 (w/Adj. Sights)

PARA-ORDNANCE

P-SERIES PISTOLS

MODEL P12•45 ACP
(3.5" Barrel, Stainless)

P16•40 S&W
(5" Barrel, Duotone)

P-SERIES SPECIFICATIONS

Model	Caliber	Barrel Length	Weight (Oz.)	Overall Length	Height (w/mag.)	Receiver Type	Matte Finish	Prices
P12•45ER	45 ACP	3.5"	3	7 1/8"	5"	Steel	Black	$750.00
P12•45RR	45 ACP	3.5"	26	7 1/8"	5"	Alloy	Black	705.00
P12•45TR	45 ACP	3.5"	34	7 1/8"	5"	Stainless	Duotone	785.00
P12•45SR	45 ACP	3.5"	34	7 1/8"	5"	Stainless	Stainless	799.00
P13•45ER	45 ACP	4.25"	36	7.75"	5.25"	Steel	Black	750.00
P13•45RR	45 ACP	4.25"	28	7.75"	5.25"	Alloy	Black	705.00
P13•45TR	45 ACP	4.25"	36	7.75"	5.25"	Stainless	Duotone	785.00
P13•45SR	45 ACP	4.25"	36	7.75"	5.25"	Stainless	Stainless	799.00
P14•45ER	45 ACP	5"	40	8.5"	5.75"	Steel	Black	750.00
P14•45RR	45 ACP	5"	31	8.5"	5.75"	Alloy	Black	705.00
P14•45TR	45 ACP	5"	40	8.5"	5.75"	Stainless	Duotone	785.00
P14•45SR	45 ACP	5"	40	8.5"	5.75"	Stainless	Stainless	799.00
P14•40ER	40 S&W	3.5"	34	7 1/8"	5"	Steel	Black	750.00
P14•40RR	40 S&W	3.5"	26	7 1/8"	5"	Alloy	Black	705.00
P14•40TR	40 S&W	3.5"	34	7 1/8"	5"	Stainless	Duotone	785.00
P14•40SR	40 S&W	3.5"	34	7 1/8"	5"	Stainless	Stainless	799.00
P15•40ER	40 S&W	4.25"	36	7.75"	5.25"	Steel	Black	750.00
P15•40RR	40S&W	4.25"	28	7.75"	5.25"	Alloy	Black	705.00
P15•40TR	40 S&W	4.25"	36	7.75"	5.25"	Stainless	Duotone	785.00
P15•40SR	40 S&W	4.25"	36	7.75"	5.25"	Stainless	Stainless	799.00
P16•40ER	40 S&W	5"	40	8.5"	5.75"	Steel	Black	750.00
P16•40TR	40 S&W	5"	40	8.5"	5.75"	Stainless	Duotone	785.00
P16•40SR	40 S&W	5"	40	8.5"	5.75"	Stainless	Stainless	799.00

For recreational purposes, magazine capacities are restricted to 10 rounds.

PRECISION SMALL ARMS

MODEL PSA-25
$249.00

SPECIFICATIONS
Type: Single action, self-loading, blow-back, semiautomatic; all-steel construction; manufactured in the U.S.
Caliber: 25 ACP   **Capacity:** 6+1 round in chamber
Ignition system: Striker fired
Barrel length: 2.13"
Rifling: 6 lands and grooves; right-hand twist
Overall length: 4.11"   **Height:** 2.88"
Weight (unloaded): 9.5 oz.
Radius: 3.54"
Safety Systems: Manual frame-mounted safety; magazine safety; cocking indicator
Sights: Blade front, 0.03" width (0.9mm); fixed V-notched rear
Trigger: Smooth faced, single stage, draw bar; 0.20" width; 5.25 lbs. pull weight
Grips: Composition; black polymer
Finish: Highly polished black oxide (traditional)
Options: Polished stainless-steel frame, slide and barrel; industrial hard chrome, chromium nitrate and gold finish; various grips; engraved limited editions

PSA-25

ROSSI REVOLVERS

MODEL 68
$255.00

MODEL 88
$255.00

SPECIFICATIONS
Caliber: 38 Special
Capacity: 5 rounds
Barrel lengths: 2" and 3"
Overall length: 6.5" (2" barrel); 7.5" (3" barrel)
Weight: 22 oz. (2" barrel); 23 oz. (3" barrel)
Grips: Wood or rubber
Finish: Blued or nickel
Features: Frames machined from chrome-molybdenum SAE 4140

SPECIFICATIONS
Caliber: 38 Special
Capacity: 5 rounds, swing-out cylinder
Barrel lengths: 2" and 3"
Overall length: 6.5" (2" barrel); 7.5" (3" barrel)
Weight: 22 oz. (2"); 23 oz. (3")
Sights: Ramp front, square-notched rear adjustable for windage
Grips: Wood or rubber (2" barrel only)
Finish: Stainless steel

ROSSI REVOLVERS

MODEL 88 "THE LADY ROSSI"
$285.00

SPECIFICATIONS
Caliber: 38 Special
Capacity: 5 rounds
Barrel length: 2"
Overall length: 6.5"
Weight: 21 oz.
Grips: Rosewood
Finish: Stainless steel
Features: Fixed sights, velvet bag

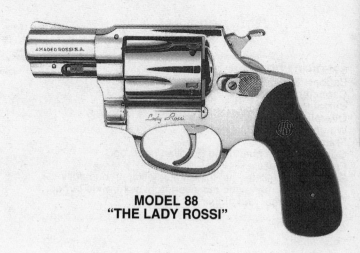

MODEL 88
"THE LADY ROSSI"

MODELS 515/518
$255.00 (22 LR, 518)
$270.00 (22 Mag., 515)

SPECIFICATIONS
Calibers: 22 LR (Model 518) and 22 Mag. (Model 515)
Capacity: 6 rounds
Barrel length: 4"
Overall length: 9"
Weight: 30 oz.
Grips: Checkered wood and rubber wraparound supplied

MODEL 515
22 MAG.

MODEL 720 (Not Shown)
$290.00

SPECIFICATIONS
Caliber: 44 S&W Special
Capacity: 5 shots
Barrel length: 3"
Overall length: 8"
Weight: 30 oz.
Sights: Adjustable rear; red insert front
Finish: Stainless steel
Features: Rubber combat grips; full ejector rod shroud

Also available:
MODEL 720 COVERT SPECIAL. Double action only, shrouded hammer, fixed sights, 3" barrel, full-length ejector shroud.
Price: $290.00

MODEL 720
COVERT SPECIAL

ROSSI REVOLVERS

MODEL 851
$255.00

SPECIFICATIONS
Caliber: 38 Special
Capacity: 6 rounds
Barrel length: 4"
Overall length: 7.5"
Weight: 31 oz.
Frame: Medium
Grips: Full-size checkered Brazilian hardwood
Finish: Stainless
Features: Ventilated rib; full-length ejector shroud; fully adjustable rear sight; red insert front sight; wide target-style hammer and trigger

MODEL 851

MODEL 877
$290.00

SPECIFICATIONS
Caliber: 357 Magnum
Capacity: 6 rounds
Barrel length: 2" heavy
Weight: 26 oz.
Grips: Rubber
Features: Fully enclosed ejector rod; serrated ramp front sight

MODEL 877

MODEL 971(not shown)
$290.00

SPECIFICATIONS
Caliber: 357 Magnum   **Capacity:** 6 rounds
Barrel lengths: 2.5", 4" and 6"
Overall length: 8⁵/₁₆" w/2.5" bbl.; 9³/₁₆" w/4" bbl.; 11³/₁₆" w/6" bbl.
Weight: 22 oz. (2.5" bbl.); 35.4 oz. (4" bbl.); 40.5 oz. (6" bbl.)
Finish: Blued (4" barrel only) or stainless steel

Also available:
MODEL 971 COMPACT GUN. 357 Magnum only with 3" barrel. **Capacity:** 6 shots. **Weight:** 32 oz. **Finish:** Stainless steel only.
Price:. $255.00
MODEL 971 VCR. In 357 Magnum, stainless, rubber grips.
Weight: 30.4 oz. (2.5"); 34.7 oz. (4"); 38.9 oz. (6").
Price:. $340.00

**MODEL 971 VCR
357 MAG. STAINLESS**

RUGER REVOLVERS

BLUED REDHAWK REVOLVER

BLUED STEEL REDHAWK REVOLVER

The popular Ruger Redhawk® double-action revolver is available in an alloy steel model with blued finish or high-gloss standard steel in 44 Magnum caliber. Constructed of hardened chrome-moly and other alloy steels, this Redhawk is satin polished to a high luster and finished in a rich blue. **Capacity: 6 rounds.**

Catalog Number	Caliber	Barrel Length	Overall Length	Approx. Weight (Ounces)	Price
RUGER BLUED REDHAWK REVOLVER					
RH-445	44 Mag.	5.5″	11″	49	$490.00
RH-44	44 Mag.	7.5″	13″	54	490.00
RH-44R*	44 Mag.	7.5″	13″	54	527.00

* Scope model, with Integral Scope Mounts, 1″ Ruger Scope rings.

**MODEL KRH-44
STAINLESS REDHAWK**

STAINLESS REDHAWK DOUBLE-ACTION REVOLVER

There is no other revolver like the Ruger Redhawk. Knowledgeable sportsmen reaching for perfection in a big bore revolver will find that the Redhawk demonstrates its superiority at the target, whether silhouette shooting or hunting. The scope sight model incorporates the patented Ruger integral Scope Mounting System with 1″ stainless steel Ruger scope rings. Available also in high-gloss stainless steel w/ scope model. Case and lock included.

Catalog Number	Caliber	Barrel Length	Overall Length	Approx. Weight (Ounces)	Price
RUGER STAINLESS REDHAWK REVOLVER					
KRH-445	44 Mag.	5.5″	11″	49	$547.00
KRH-44	44 Mag.	7.5″	13″	54	547.00
KRH-44R*	44 Mag.	7.5″	13″	54	589.00

* Scope model, with Integral Scope Mounts, 1″ Stainless Steel Ruger Scope rings.

**STAINLESS REDHAWK
w/Scope (KRH-44R)**

SUPER REDHAWK STAINLESS DOUBLE-ACTION REVOLVER

The **Super Redhawk** double-action revolver in stainless steel features a heavy extended frame with 7.5″ and 9.5″ barrels. Cushioned grip panels contain Goncalo Alves wood grip panel inserts to provide comfortable, nonslip hold. Comes with case and lock, integral scope mounts and 1″ stainless steel Ruger scope rings.

SPECIFICATIONS
Caliber: 44 Magnum
Barrel length: 7.5″ and 9.5″
Overall length: 13″ w/7.5″ bbl.; 15″ w/9.5″ bbl.
Weight (empty): 53 oz. (7.5″ bbl.); 58 oz. (9.5″ bbl.)
Sight radius: 9.5″ (7.5″ bbl.); 11.25″ (9.5″ bbl.)
Finish: Stainless steel; satin polished

KSRH-7 (7.5″ barrel)	$589.00
KSRH-9 (9.5″ barrel)	589.00
GKSRH-7 & 9 (high-gloss stainless steel)	589.00

**MODEL KSRH-9
SUPER REDHAWK STAINLESS**

RUGER SINGLE-ACTION REVOLVERS

SPECIFICATIONS: VAQUERO SINGLE-ACTION REVOLVER

VAQUERO SINGLE ACTION
$434.00 (All Models)

Catalog Number	Caliber	Barrel Length	Overall Length	Weight (Ounces)	Finish*
BNV40	44-40	4⅝"	10.25"	39	CB
KBNV40	44-40	4⅝"	10.25"	39	SSG
BNV405	44-40	5.5"	11.5"	40	CB
KBNV405	44-40	5.5"	11.5"	40	SSG
BNV407	44-40	7.5"	13⅛"	41	CB
KBNV407	44-40	7.5"	13⅛"	41	SSG
BNV475	44 Mag.	5.5"	11.5"	40	CB
KBNV475	44 Mag.	5.5"	11.5"	40	SSG
BNV477	44 Mag.	7.5"	13⅛"	41	CB
KBNV477	44 Mag.	7.5"	13⅛"	41	SSG
BNV44	45 LC	4⅝"	10.25"	39	CB
KBNV44	45 LC	4⅝"	10.25"	39	SSG
BNV455	45 LC	5.5"	11.5"	40	CB
KBNV455	45 LC	5.5"	11.5"	40	SSG
BNV45	45 LC	7.5"	13⅛"	41	CB
KBNV45	45 LC	7.5"	13⅛"	41	SSG

* Finish: high-gloss stainless steel (SSG); color-cased finish on steel cyl. frame w/blued steel grip, barrel, cylinder (CB). LC = Long Colt.

SPECIFICATIONS: NEW MODEL BLACKHAWK AND BLACKHAWK CONVERTIBLE*

Cat. Number	Caliber	Finish**	Bbl. Length	O.A. Length	Weight (Oz.)	Price
BN31	.30 Carbine	B	7.5"	13⅛"	44	**$360.00**
BN34	.357 Mag. ++	B	4⅝"	10⅜"	40	360.00
KBN34	.357 Mag. ++	SS	4⅝"	10⅜"	40	443.00
BN36	.357 Mag. ++	B	6.5"	12.25"	42	360.00
KBN36	.357 Mag. ++	SS	6.5"	12.5"	42	443.00
BN34X*	.357 Mag. ++	B	4⅝"	10⅜"	40	380.00
BN36X*	.357 Mag. ++	B	6.5"	12.25"	42	380.00
GKBN34	.357 Mag. ++	HGSS	4⅝"	10⅜"	40	443.00
GKBN36	.357 Mag. ++	HGSS	6.5"	12.25"	42	443.00
BN41	.41 Mag.	B	4⅝"	10.25"	38	360.00
BN42	.41 Mag.	B	6.5"	12⅛"	40	360.00
BN44	.45 Long Colt	B	4⅝"	10.25"	39	360.00
KBN44	.45 Long Colt	SS	4⅝"	10.25"	39	443.00
BN455	.45 Long Colt	B	5.5"	11⅛"	39	360.00
BN45	.45 Long Colt	B	7.5"	13⅛"	41	360.00
KBN45	.45 Long Colt	SS	7.5"	13⅛"	41	443.00
GKBN44	.45 Long Colt	HGSS	4⅝"	10.25"	39	443.00
GKBN45	.45 Long Colt	HGSS	7.5"	13⅛"	41	443.00

* Convertible: Designated by an X in the Catalog Number, this model comes with an extra 9mm Parabellum cylinder, which can be instantly interchanged without the use of tools. Price includes the extra cylinder.
** Finish: blued (B); stainless steel (SS); high-gloss stainless steel (HGSS); color-cased finish on the steel cylinder frame with blued steel grip, barrel, and cylinder (CB).
++ Revolvers chambered for the .357 Magnum cartridge also accept factory-loaded .38 Special cartridges.

RUGER REVOLVERS

NEW MODEL SUPER BLACKHAWK SINGLE-ACTION REVOLVER

SPECIFICATIONS
Caliber: 44 Magnum; interchangeable with 44 Special
Barrel lengths: 4⁵/₈″, 5.5″, 7.5″, 10.5″
Overall length: 13³/₈″ (7.5″ barrel)
Weight: 45 oz. (4⁵/₈″ bbl.), 46 oz. (5.5″ bbl.), 48 oz. (7.5″ bbl.) and 51 oz. (10.5″ bbl.)
Frame: Chrome molybdenum steel or stainless steel
Springs: Music wire springs throughout
Sights: Patridge style, ramp front matted blade ¹/₈″ wide; rear sight click-adjustable for windage and elevation
Grip frame: Chrome molybdenum or stainless steel, enlarged and contoured to minimize recoil effect

Trigger: Wide spur, low contour, sharply serrated for convenient cocking with minimum disturbance of grip
Finish: Polished and blued or brushed satin stainless steel
Features: Case and lock included
Prices:

KS45N	5.5″ bbl., brushed or high-gloss stainless	**$450.00**
KS458N	4⁵/₈″ bbl., brushed or high-gloss stainless	**450.00**
KS47N	7.5″ bbl., brushed or high-gloss stainless	**450.00**
GKS47N	7.5″ bbl., steel grip frame, high-gloss stainless	**450.00**
GKS459	5.5″ bbl., steel grip frame, high-gloss stainless	**450.00**
GKS458N	4⁵/₈″ bbl., steel grip frame, high-gloss stainless	**450.00**
KS411N	10.5″ bull bbl., stainless steel	**450.00**
S45N	5.5″ bbl., blued	**413.00**
S458N	4⁵/₈″ bbl., blued	**413.00**
S47N	7.5″ bbl., blued	**413.00**
S411N	10.5″ bull bbl., blued	**413.00**

FIXED SIGHT NEW MODEL SINGLE-SIX (W/Extra Cylinder)

NEW MODEL SINGLE-SIX REVOLVER

SPECIFICATIONS
Caliber: 22 LR (fitted with 22 WMR cylinder)
Barrel lengths: 4⁵/₈″, 5.5″, 6.5″, 9.5″; stainless steel model in 5.5″ and 6.5″ lengths only
Weight (approx.): 33 oz. (with 5.5″ barrel); 38 oz. (with 9.5″ barrel)
Sights: Patridge-type ramp front sight; rear sight click adjustable for elevation and windage; protected by integral frame ribs. Fixed sight model available with 5.5″ or 6.5″ barrel (same prices as adj. sight models).
Finish: Blue, stainless steel or high-gloss stainless
Features: Case and lock included
Prices:
In blue **$313.00**
In brushed or high-gloss stainless steel
(convertible 5.5″ and 6.5″ barrels only) **393.00**

NEW MODEL SUPER SINGLE-SIX

NEW MODEL SUPER SINGLE-SIX REVOLVER

SPECIFICATIONS
Caliber: 32 Magnum; also handles 32 S&W and 32 S&W Long
Barrel lengths: 4⁵/₈″, 5.5″, 6.5″, 9.5″
Weight: (approx.) 34 oz. (with 6.5″ barrel)
Price: (includes case and lock) **$313.00**

RUGER REVOLVERS

MODEL SP101 SPURLESS DA
$443.00

GP-100 357 MAGNUM
6″ Heavy Barrel

SPECIFICATIONS SP101 REVOLVERS

Catalog Number	Caliber	Cap.*	Sights	Barrel Length	Approx. Wt. (Oz.)
KSP-221	22 LR	6	A	2.25″	32
GKSP-221	22 LR	6	A	2.25″	32
KSP-240	22 LR	6	A	4″	33
KSP-241	22 LR	6	A	4″	34
GKSP-241	22 LR	6	A	4″	34
KSP-3231	32 Mag.	6	A	3¹/₁₆″	30
GKSP-3231	32 Mag.	6	A	3¹/₁₆″	30
KSP-3241	32 Mag.	6	A	4″	33
GKSP-3241	32 Mag.	6	A	4″	33
KSP-921	9mm×19	5	F	2.25″	25
GKSP-921	9mm×19	5	F	2.25″	25
KSP-931	9mm×19	5	F	3¹/₁₆″	27
GKSP-931	9mm×19	5	F	3¹/₁₆″	27
KSP-821	38+P	5	F	2.25″	25
GKSP-821	38+P	5	F	2.25″	25
KSP-821L	38+P	5	F	2.25″	26
GKSP-821L	38+P	5	F	2.25″	26
KSP-831	38+P	5	F	3¹/₁₆″	27
GKSP-831	38+P	5	F	3¹/₁₆″	27
KSP-321X**	357 Mag.	5	F	2.25″	25
GKSP-321X**	357 Mag.	5	F	2.25″	25
KSP-321XL**	357 Mag.	5	F	2.25″	25
GKSP-321XL**	357 Mag.	5	F	2.25″	25
KSP-331X**	357 Mag.	5	F	3¹/₁₆″	27
GKSP-331X**	357 Mag.	5	F	3¹/₁₆″	27

* Indicates cylinder capacity   ** Revolvers chambered for .357 Magnum also accept 38 Special cartridges.
    Model KSP-240 has short shroud; all others have full. Spurless hammer models are designated by "L" in catalog no. "G" before a catalog no. indicates high-gloss finish models.

GP-100 DA 357 MAGNUM

The GP-100 is designed for the unlimited use of 357 Magnum ammunition in all factory loadings; it combines strength and reliability with accuracy and shooting comfort. (Revolvers chambered for the 357 Magnum cartridge also accept the 38 Special cartridge.)

SPECIFICATIONS

Catalog Number	Finish	Sights†	Shroud††	Barrel Length	Wt. (Oz.)	Price
GP-141	B	A	F	4″	41	**$440.00**
GP-160	B	A	S	6″	43	**440.00**
GP-161	B	A	F	6″	46	**440.00**
GPF-331	B	F	F	3″	36	**423.00**
GPF-340	B	F	S	4″	37	**423.00**
GPF-341	B	F	F	4″	38	**423.00**
KGP-141	SS	A	F	4″	41	**474.00**
GKGP-141	SSG	A	F	4″	41	**474.00**
KGP-160	SS	A	S	6″	43	**474.00**
KGP-161	SS	A	F	6″	46	**474.00**
GKGP-161	SSG	A	F	6″	46	**474.00**
KGPF-330	SS	F	S	3″	35	**457.00**
KGPF-331	SS	F	F	3″	36	**457.00**
GKGPF-331	SSG	F	F	3″	36	**457.00**
KGPF-340	SS	F	S	4″	37	**457.00**
KGPF-341	SS	F	F	4″	38	**457.00**
GKGPF-341	SSG	F	F	4″	38	**457.00**
KGPF-840*	SS	F	S	4″	37	**457.00**
KGPF-841*	SS	F	F	4″	38	**457.00**

* 38 Special only. B = blued; SS = stainless; SSG = high-gloss stainless. † A = adjustable; F = fixed. †† F = full; S = short.

RUGER REVOLVERS

**BISLEY SINGLE-ACTION
TARGET GUN**

BISLEY SINGLE-ACTION TARGET GUN

The Bisley single-action was originally used at the British National Rifle Association matches held in Bisley, England, in the 1890s. Today's Ruger Bisleys are offered in two frame sizes, chambered from 22 LR to 45 Long Colt. These revolvers are the target-model versions of the Ruger single-action line.

Special features: Unfluted cylinder rollmarked with classic foliate engraving pattern; hammer is low with smoothly curved, deeply checkered wide spur positioned for easy cocking.

Prices:
22 LR or 32 Magnum $360.00
357 Mag., 41 Mag., 44 Mag., 45 Long Colt **430.00**

BISLEY SPECIFICATIONS

Catalog Number	Caliber	Barrel Length	Overall Length	Sights	Approx. Wt. (Oz.)
RB22AW	22 LR	6½″	11½″	Adj.	41
RB32W	32 Mag.	6½″	11½″	Fixed*	41
RB32AW	32 Mag.	6½″	11½″	Adj.	41
RB35W	357 Mag.	7½″	13″	Adj.	48
RB41W	41 Mag.	7½″	13″	Adj.	48
RB44W	44 Mag.	7½″	13″	Adj.	48
RB45W	45 Long Colt	7½″	13″	Adj.	48

* Dovetail rear sight adjustable for windage only.

THE NEW BEARCAT

THE NEW BEARCAT
$298.00 (Blued)

Originally manufactured between 1958 and 1973, the 22-rimfire single-action Bearcat features an all-steel precision investment-cast frame and patented transfer-bar mechanism. The New Bearcat also has walnut grips with the Ruger medallion.

SPECIFICATIONS
Caliber: 22 LR
Capacity: 6 shots
Barrel length: 4″
Grips: Walnut
Finish: Blued chrome-moly steel

RUGER P-SERIES PISTOLS

MODEL P93 (not shown)

SPECIFICATIONS: (See also table below)
Barrel length: 3.9″   **Overall length:** 7.3″
Height: 5.75″   **Width:** 1.5″
Weight: 31 oz.
Sights: 3-dot system; square-notch rear, drift adjustable for windage; square post front (both sights have white dots)
Mechanism: Recoil-operated, double action, autoloading
Features: Oversized trigger guard with curved triggerguard bow; slide stop activated automatically on last shot (w/ magazine in pistol); all stainless steel models made with "Terhune Anticorro" steel for maximum corrosion resistance

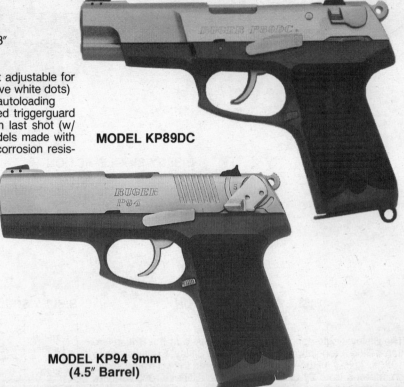

MODEL KP89DC

MODEL P94

SPECIFICATIONS (see also table below)
Barrel length: 4.5″
Capacity: 10 rounds
Overall length: 7.5″
Weight: 33 oz. (empty magazine)
Height: 5.5″   **Width:** 1.5″
Sight radius: 5″
Sights: 3-dot system
Features: See Model P93

MODEL KP94 9mm
(4.5″ Barrel)

SPECIFICATIONS: P-SERIES PISTOLS

Cat. Number	Model	Finish	Caliber	Mag. Cap.	Price
P89	Manual Safety	Blued	9mm	10	$410.00
KP89	Manual Safety	Stainless	9mm	10	452.00
P89DC	Decock-Only	Blued	9mm	10	410.00
KP89DC	Decock-Only	Stainless	9mm	10	452.00
KP89DAO	Double-Action-Only	Stainless	9mm	10	452.00
KP90	Manual Safety	Stainless	45 ACP	7	488.65
KP90DC	Decock-Only	Stainless	45 ACP	7	488.65
KP93DC	Decock-Only	Stainless	9mm	10	520.00
KP93DAO	Double-Action-Only	Stainless	9mm	10	520.00
KP94	Manual Safety	Stainless	9mm	10	520.00
KP94DC	Decock-Only	Stainless	9mm	10	520.00
KP94DAO	Double-Action-Only	Stainless	9mm	10	520.00
KP944	Manual Safety	Stainless	40 Auto	10	520.00
KP944DC	Decock-Only	Stainless	40 Auto	10	520.00
KP944DAO	Double-Action-Only	Stainless	40 Auto	10	520.00
KP95DC	Decock-Only	Stainless	9mm	10	351.00
KP95DAO	Double-Action-Only	Stainless	9mm	10	351.00
P95DC	Decock-Only	Blued, Stainless Frame	9mm	10	351.00
P95DAO	Double-Action-Only	Blued, Stainless Frame	9mm	10	351.00

RUGER 22 AUTOMATIC PISTOLS

MK II STANDARD MODEL

MARK II STANDARD MODEL

The Ruger Mark II models represent continuing refinements of the original Ruger Standard and Mark I Target Model pistols. More than two million of this series of autoloading rimfire pistol have been produced since 1949.

The bolts on all Ruger Mark II pistols lock open automatically when the last cartridge is fired, if the magazine is in the pistol. The bolt can be operated manually with the safety in the "on" position for added security while loading and unloading. A bolt stop can be activated manually to lock the bolt open.

The Ruger Mark II pistol uses 22 Long Rifle ammunition in a detachable, 10-shot magazine (standard on all Mark II models except Model 22/45, whose 10-shot magazine is not interchangeable with other Mark II magazines). Designed for easy insertion and removal, the Mark II magazine is equipped with a magazine follower button for convenience in reloading.

For additional specifications, please see the chart on the next page.

MARK II GOVERNMENT MODEL

MARK II TARGET MODEL

RUGER 22 AUTOMATIC PISTOLS

MARK II BULL BARREL

MARK II 22/45
w/Zytel Frame

22/45 TARGET
MODEL P-512
(w/11-degree angle)

SPECIFICATIONS: RUGER 22 MARK II PISTOLS

Catalog Number	Model*	Finish **	Barrel Length	Overall Length	Approx. Wt. (Oz.)	Price
MK-4	Std.	B	4³/₄″	8⁵/₁₆″	35	$252.00
MK-4B	Bull	B	4″	8.25″	38	336.50
KMK-4	Std.	SS	4³/₄″	8⁵/₁₆″	35	330.25
KP-4***	Std.	SS	4³/₄″	8¹³/₁₆″	28	280.00
MK-6	Std.	B	6″	10⁵/₁₆″	37	252.00
KMK-6	Std.	SS	6″	10⁵/₁₆″	37	330.25
MK-678	Target	B	6⁷/₈″	11¹/₈″	42	310.50
KMK-678	Target	SS	6⁷/₈″	11¹/₈″	42	389.00
P-512***	Bull	B	5.5″	9³/₄″	35	237.50
MK-512	Bull	B	5.5″	9³/₄″	42	310.50
KMK-512	Bull	SS	5.5″	9³/₄″	42	389.00
KP-512***	Bull	SS	5.5″	9³/₄″	35	330.00
MK-10	Bull	B	10″	14⁵/₁₆″	51	294.50
KMK-10	Bull	SS	10″	14⁵/₁₆″	51	373.00
MK-678G	Bull	B	6⁷/₈″	11¹/₈″	46	356.50
KMK-678G	Bull	SS	6⁷/₈″	11¹/₈″	46	427.25
KMK-678GC	Bull	SS	6⁷/₈″	11¹/₈″	45	441.00

* Model: Std. = standard   ** Finish: B = blued; SS = stainless steel   *** 22 cartridge, 45 grip angle and magazine latch

SAFARI ARMS PISTOLS

MATCHMASTER
$770.00

SPECIFICATIONS
Caliber: 45 ACP
Capacity: 7 rounds
Barrel length: 5″
Overall length: 8.25″
Weight: 40 oz.
Finish: Stainless steel or black Parkerized carbon steel
Features: Extended safety & slide stop; wide beavertail grip safety; LPA fully adjustable rear sight; full-length recoil spring guide; squared trigger guide & finger-groove front strap frame; laser-etched walnut grips

ENFORCER
$800.00

SPECIFICATIONS
Caliber: 45 ACP
Capacity: 6 rounds
Barrel length: 4″ conical
Overall length: 7″
Height: $4^{7}/_{8}$″
Weight: 35 oz.
Sight radius: 5.75″
Finish: Stainless steel or black Parkerized carbon steel

COHORT
$840.00

SPECIFICATIONS
Caliber: 45 ACP
Capacity: 7 rounds
Barrel length: 4″ conical
Overall length: 7″
Height: 5.5″
Weight: 37 oz.
Finish: Stainless steel or black Parkerized carbon steel

SIG-SAUER PISTOLS

MODEL P220 "AMERICAN"

MODEL P220 "AMERICAN"

SPECIFICATIONS
Calibers: 38 Super, 45 ACP
Capacity: 9 rounds; 7 rounds in 45 ACP
Barrel length: 4.4″
Overall length: 7.79″ **Height:** 5.6″
Weight (empty): 26½ oz.; 25.7 oz. in 45 ACP
Finish: Blue, K-Kote or Two-tone
Prices:
Blued $805.00
   W/"Siglite" night sights 905.00
W/K-Kote finish 850.00
   W/K-Kote and "Siglite" night sights 950.00

MODEL P210 (Not Shown)

SPECIFICATIONS
Single-action 8-round pistol in 9mm Luger. **Barrel length:** 4.75″.
Overall length: 8.5″. **Weight:** 32 oz. **Height:** 5.4″. **Sights:** Blade
front; notch rear (drift adjustable for windate). **Safety:** Thumb-
operated manual safety lever; magazine safety. **Finish:** Blue
only. Long Rifle conversion kit available (**add $600.00**). **Price:**
$2300.00

MODEL P225

SPECIFICATIONS
Caliber: 9mm Parabellum
Capacity: 8 rounds
Barrel length: 3.9″
Overall length: 7.1″
Trigger: DA/SA or DA only
Weight (empty): 26.1 oz. **Height:** 5.2″
Finish: Blue, K-Kote or Two-tone
Prices:
Blued finish $780.00
Blued w/"Siglite" night sights 880.00
W/K-Kote 850.00
W/K-Kote and "Siglite" night sights 950.00

MODEL P225

MODEL P226

MODEL P226

SPECIFICATIONS
Calibers: 9mm Parabellum and 357 SIG
Capacity: 10 rounds
Barrel length: 4.4″ **Overall length:** 7.7″
Weight (empty): 26.5 oz.; 30.1 oz. in 357 SIG
Triggers: DA/SA or DA only **Height:** 5.5″
Finish: Blue, K-Kote or Two-tone
Prices:
9mm, Blued finish $825.00
   Blued w/"Siglite" night sights 925.00
   W/K-Kote 875.00
   K-Kote w/"Siglite" night sights 975.00
357 SIG 875.00
   w/"Siglite" night sights 975.00

SIG-SAUER PISTOLS

MODEL P228

MODEL P229

MODEL P229

SPECIFICATIONS
Calibers: 9mm, 357 and 40 S&W
Capacity: 10 rounds
Barrel length: 3.8″
Overall length: 7.1″
Weight (empty): 27.5 oz.
Trigger: DA/SA or DA only
Finish: Blackened stainless steel or Two-tone
Features: Stainless steel slide; automatic firing-pin lock; wood grips (optional)
Prices:
Model P229 . . . . **$875.00**
  W/"Siglite" night sight **975.00**
  W/Nickel slide **900.00**
  W/Nickel slide/"Siglite" night sight **995.00**

MODEL P228

SPECIFICATIONS
Caliber: 9mm
Capacity: 10 rounds
Barrel length: 3.9″
Overall length: 7.1″
Weight (empty): 26.1 oz.
Trigger: DA/SA or DA only
Finish: Blue, K-Kote or Two-tone
Prices:
Blued finish **$825.00**
Blued w/"Siglite" night sights **925.00**
W/K-Kote **875.00**
W/K-Kote and "Siglite" night sights **975.00**

MODEL P230

MODEL P230

SPECIFICATIONS
Calibers: 9mm Short (380 ACP) and 32 ACP
Action: DA/SA or DAO
Capacity: 7 rounds (380 ACP); 8 rounds (32 ACP)
Barrel length: 3.6″ **Overall length:** 6.6″
Height: 4.7″
Weight (empty): 16.2 oz.; 20.8 oz. in stainless steel
Safety: Automatic firing-pin lock
Finish: Blued or stainless steel
Prices:
Blued finish **$510.00**
Stainless steel **595.00**
  With Stainless slide **545.00**

MODEL P239 (Not Shown)

SPECIFICATIONS
Caliber: 9mm Luger and 357 SIG
Action: DA/SA or DA only
Capacity: 7 rounds (357 SIG); 8 rounds (9mm)
Barrel length: 3.6″ **Overall length:** 6.6″
Weight: 25.2 oz.
Finish: Blackened stainless steel
Features: Mechanically locked, reoil-operated semiauto; automatic firing-pin lock
Prices: **$575.00**
w/"Siglite" night sight **675.00**

SMITH & WESSON PISTOLS

COMPACT SERIES

MODEL 3900 COMPACT SERIES

SPECIFICATIONS
Caliber: 9mm Parabellum DA Autoloading Luger
Capacity: 8 rounds
Barrel length: 3 1/2"
Overall length: 6 7/8"
Weight (empty): 25 oz.
Sights: Post w/white dot front; fixed rear adj. for windage only w/2 white dots. Adjustable sight models include micrometer click, adj. for windage and elevation w/2 white dots. Deduct $25 for fixed sights.
Finish: Blue (Model 3914); satin stainless (Model 3913)
Prices:
MODEL 3913 . . . . $622.00
MODEL 3913 LADYSMITH (stainless) 640.00
MODEL 3953 (Double action only, stainless) 622.00

MODEL 3913 DA
Stainless

MODEL 4000 COMPACT SERIES (not shown)

SPECIFICATIONS (MODELS 4013 and 4053)
Caliber: 40 S&W
Capacity: 8 rounds
Barrel length: 3 1/2"
Overall length: 7"
Weight: 27 oz.
Sights: White dot front; fixed w/2-dot rear
Price: $722.00

MODEL 4500 COMPACT SERIES

SPECIFICATIONS (MODEL 4516)
Caliber: 45 ACP
Capacity: 7 rounds
Barrel length: 3 3/4"
Overall length: 7 1/4"
Weight: 34 oz.
Sights: White dot front; fixed w/2-dot rear
Price: $774.00

MODEL 4516 COMPACT

MODEL 6900 COMPACT SERIES

SPECIFICATIONS
Caliber: 9mm Parabellum DA Autoloading Luger
Capacity: 10 rounds
Barrel length: 3 1/2"
Overall length: 6 7/8"
Weight (empty): 26 1/2 oz.
Sights: Post w/white dot front; fixed rear, adj. for windage only w/2 white dots
Grips: Delrin one-piece wraparound, arched backstrap, textured surface
Finish: Blue (Model 6904); clear anodized/satin stainless (Model 6906)
Prices:
MODEL 6904 . . . . $614.00
MODEL 6906 . . . . 677.00
MODEL 6906 Fixed Novak night sight 788.00
MODEL 6946 DA only, fixed sights 677.00

MODEL 6906 DA
Stainless

SMITH & WESSON PISTOLS

FULL-SIZE DOUBLE-ACTION PISTOLS

Smith & Wesson's double-action semiautomatic Third Generation line includes the following features: fixed barrel bushing for greater accuracy • smoother trigger pull plus a slimmer, contoured grip and lateral relief cut where trigger guard meets frame • beveled magazine well • ambidextrous safety lever • low-glare bead-blasted finish.

MODEL 4506-1
Adjustable Sight

MODEL 4046

MODEL 4586
Fixed Sight

MODEL 4006
With Fixed Sight

MODEL 4500 SERIES

SPECIFICATIONS
Caliber: 45 ACP Autoloading DA
Capacity: 8 rounds
Barrel lengths: 5″ (Model 4506); 4¼″ (Models 4566 & 4586)
Overall length: 8⅝″ (Model 4506)
Weight (empty): 38½ oz. (Model 4506); 34½ oz. (Model 4566 & 4586)
Sights: Post w/white-dot front; fixed rear, adj. for windage only. Adj. sight incl. micrometer click, adj. for windage and elevation w/2 white dots. Add **$29.00** for adj. sights.
Grips: Delrin one-piece wraparound, arched backstrap, textured surface
Finish: Satin stainless
Prices:

MODEL 4000 SERIES

SPECIFICATIONS
Caliber: 40 S&W   **Capacity:** 10 rounds
Barrel length: 4″   **Overall length:** 7⅞″
Weight: 38½ oz. (with fixed sights)
Sights: Post w/white dot front; fixed or adjustable w/white 2-dot rear
Grips: Straight backstrap, Xenoy wraparound
Finish: Stainless steel
Prices:

MODEL 4006 w/fixed sights	$745.00
Same as above w/adj. sights	775.00
w/fixed night sight	855.00
MODEL 4043 Double action only	727.00
MODEL 4046 w/fixed sights, DA only	745.00
Double action only, fixed Tritium night sight	855.00

MODEL 4506 w/adj. sights, 5″ bbl.	$806.00
With fixed sights	774.00
MODEL 4516 DA, 3.75″ bbl., fixed sights	774.00
MODEL 4566 w/4.25″ bbl., fixed sights	774.00
MODEL 4586 DA only, 4.25″ bbl., fixed sights	774.00

SMITH & WESSON PISTOLS

FULL-SIZE DOUBLE-ACTION PISTOLS

MODEL 5900 SERIES

SPECIFICATIONS
Caliber: 9mm Parabellum DA Autoloading Luger
Capacity: 10 rounds
Barrel length: 4″
Overall length: 7¹/₂″
Weight (empty): 28¹/₂ oz. (Models 5903, 5904, 5946);
  37¹/₂ oz. (Model 5906); 38 oz. (Model 5906 w/adj. sight)
Sights: Front, post w/white dot; fixed rear, adj. for windage
  only w/2 white dots. Adjustable sight models include mi-
  crometer click, adj. for windage and elevation w/2 white
  dots.
Finish: Blue (Model 5904); satin stainless (Models 5903 and
  5906)
Prices:
MODEL 5903 Satin stainless $690.00
MODEL 5904 Blue 642.00
MODEL 5906 Satin stainless 742.00
  With fixed sights 707.00
  With Tritium night sight 817.00
MODEL 5946 Double action only 707.00

**MODEL 5906 DA
Stainless**

MODEL 410

MODEL 410

SPECIFICATIONS
Caliber: 40 S&W
Capacity: 10 rounds
Barrel length: 4″
Overall length: 7¹/₂″
Weight: 28.5 oz.
Sights: 3-dot sights
Grips: One-piece Xenoy wraparound
Features: Right-hand slide-mounted manual safety; decocking
  lever; aluminum alloy frame; blue carbon steel slide; non-
  reflective matte finish; beveled edge slide
Price: $490.00

MODEL 900 SERIES

SPECIFICATIONS
Caliber: 9mm
Capacity: 8 rounds (Model 908); 10 rounds (Model 910)
Barrel lengths: 3.5″ (Model 908); 4″ (Model 910)
Overall length: 7³/₈″
Weight: 28 oz.
Sights: Post front; fixed rear
Grips: Straight backstrap
Safety: External, single side
Finish: Matte blue
Features: Carbon steel slide; alloy frame
Price: $443.00
Also available:
MODEL 909 (9 rounds) w/curved backstrap. **Price:** $443.00

MODEL 910

SMITH & WESSON PISTOLS

SIGMA SERIES

Smith & Wesson's Sigma Series is the product of several years' effort to produce a series of pistols that has resulted in 12 patent applications. These pistols are a combination of traditional craftsmanship and the latest technological advances that allow the guns to be assembled without the usual "fitting" process required for other handguns, a method that results in complete interchangeability of parts.

The polymer frame design for the Sigma Series provides unprecedented comfort and pointability. The low barrel centerline combined with the ergonomic design means low muzzle flip and fast reaction for the next shot.

**SIGMA SERIES MODEL SW40F
FULL SIZE DA**

**SIGMA SERIES SW380
COMPACT DA**

FULL-SIZE SIGMA SERIES DA
$593.00 (9mm) $697.00 (40 S&W)

SPECIFICATIONS
Calibers: 40 S&W and 9mm   **Capacity:** 10 rounds
Barrel length: 4 1/2″   **Overall length:** 7.4″
Weight (empty): 25.4 oz. (9mm); 25.8 oz. (40 S&W)
Height: 5.6″   **Width:** 1.3″
Sight radius: 6.4″
Sights: 3-dot system (Tritium night sights available)
Features: Custom carrying case standard; internal striker firing system; corrosion-resistant slide; field-stripping to four components only; front and backstrap checkering; carbon steel magazine w/Teflon-filled electroless-nickel coating; integral thumbrest

MODEL 457 DA
$490.00

SPECIFICATIONS
Caliber: 45 ACP
Capacity: 7 rounds
Barrel length: 3.75″
Overall length: 7.25″
Weight: 29 oz.
Grips: Straight backstrap
Sights: White dot front; fixed 2-dot rear
Finish: Blued
Features: Carbon steel slide and alloy frame; .260″ bobbed hammer; single side external safety

SIGMA COMPACT SERIES DA
$308.00 (380 ACP)

SPECIFICATIONS
Caliber: 380 ACP
Capacity: 6 rounds
Barrel length: 3″
Overall length: 5.8″
Weight: 14 oz.
Sights: Recessed groove in top of slide
Finish: Blued
Features: Lightweight polymer frame with integral thumbrest; two-piece trigger; corrosion-resistant steel slide

MODEL 457 DA

SMITH & WESSON TARGET PISTOLS

MODEL NO. 41 RIMFIRE
$753.00 (Blue Only)

SPECIFICATIONS
Caliber: 22 LR **Magazine capacity:** 10 rounds
Barrel lengths: 5¹/₂″ and 7″ **Weight:** 44 oz. (5¹/₂″ barrel)
Overall length: 9¹/₁₆″ (5¹/₂″ bbl.); 10¹/₂″ (7″ bbl.)
Sights: Front, ¹/₈″ Patridge undercut; rear, S&W micrometer
click sight adjustable for windage and elevation
Grips: Hardwood target
Finish: S&W Bright blue
Trigger: .365″ width; S&W grooving, adj. trigger stop
Features: Carbon steel slide and frame

MODEL NO. 41

MODEL 422 RIMFIRE 22 SA
$235.00 (Fixed Sight)
$290.00 (Adjustable Sight)

SPECIFICATIONS
Caliber: 22 LR **Capacity:** 10 rounds (magazine furnished)
Barrel lengths: 4¹/₂″ and 6″
Overall length: 7¹/₂″ (4¹/₂″ barrel) and 9″ (6″ barrel)
Weight: 22 oz. (4¹/₂″ barrel) and 23 oz. (6″ barrel)

Grips: Black polymer (fixed sight); wood-grained polymer (adj. sight)
Front sight: Serrated ramp w/.125″ blade (field version); Patridge w/.125″ blade (target version)
Rear sight: Fixed sight w/.125″ blade (field version): adjustable sight w/.125″ blade (target version)
Hammer: .250″ internal **Trigger:** .312″ serrated
Also available:
MODEL 622. Same specifications as Model 422 in stainless steel. **Price: $284.00.** (Add **$53.00** for adj. sights). With vent rib, 6″ barrel, adj. sights **$310.00**

MODEL 622 VR

MODEL 2213
"SPORTSMAN"

MODEL 2206
$385.00 (Adj. Sights)

SPECIFICATIONS
Caliber: 22 LR. **Capacity:** 10 rounds. **Barrel length:** 6″. **Overall length:** 9″. **Weight:** 39 oz. **Finish:** Stainless steel.
Also available:
Model 2206 TARGET w/adj. target sight, drilled and tapped.
Price: $433.00

MODEL 2213/2214 RIMFIRE "SPORTSMAN"
$269.00 (Blue) $314.00 (Stainless)

SPECIFICATIONS
Caliber: 22 LR. **Capacity:** 8 rounds. **Barrel length:** 3″. **Overall length:** 6¹/₈″. **Weight:** 18 oz. **Finish:** Stainless steel slide w/alloy frame (**Model 2214** has blued carbon steel slide w/alloy frame)

MODEL 2206 TARGET

SMITH & WESSON REVOLVERS

SMALL FRAME

MODEL 60LS LADYSMITH
38 S&W Special

LADYSMITH HANDGUNS
MODEL 36-LS $408.00 (Blue)
MODEL 60-LS $461.00 (Stainless)

SPECIFICATIONS
Caliber: 38 S&W Special   **Capacity:** 5 shots
Barrel length: 2″   **Overall length:** $6^5/_{16}$″
Weight: 20 oz.
Sights: Serrated ramp front; fixed notch rear
Grips: Contoured laminated rosewood, round butt
Finish: Glossy deep blue or stainless
Features: Both models come with soft-side LadySmith
   carry case

MODEL 37
CHIEFS SPECIAL AIRWEIGHT
38 S&W Special

MODEL 36
38 CHIEFS SPECIAL
$377.00

SPECIFICATIONS
Caliber: 38 S&W Special   **Capacity:** 5 shots
Barrel length: 2″   **Overall length:** $6^5/_{16}$″
Weight: $19^1/_2$ oz.
Sights: Serrated ramp front; fixed, square-notch rear
Grips: Checkered walnut Service
Finish: S&W blue carbon steel or nickel
Features: .312″ smooth combat-style trigger; .240″ service
   hammer
MODEL 37 CHIEFS SPECIAL AIRWEIGHT: Same as Model
   36, except finish is blue or nickel aluminum alloy; **weight:**
   $13^1/_2$ oz.; 2″ barrel only. **Price:** **$412.00**
MODEL 637 CHIEFS SPECIAL AIRWEIGHT. With 2″ barrel,
   synthetic round butt, stainless finish. **Price:** **$428.00**

MODEL 60
38 CHIEFS SPECIAL
STAINLESS

MODEL 60
38 CHIEFS SPECIAL, STAINLESS
$431.00 (2″ Barrel) $458.00 (3″ Barrel)

SPECIFICATIONS
Calibers: 38 S&W Special and 357 Mag.
Capacity: 5 shots
Barrel lengths: $2^1/_8$″ (357 Mag.); 3″ full lug (38 S&W Spec.)
Overall length: $6^5/_{16}$″ ($2^1/_8$″ bbl.); $7^1/_2$″ (3″ bbl.)
Weight: 23 oz. ($2^1/_8$″ barrel); $24^1/_2$ oz. (3″ full lug barrel)
Sights: Micrometer click rear, adj. for windage and elevation;
   pinned black front (3″ full lug model only); standard sights
   as on Model 36
Grips: Checkered walnut Service with S&W monograms;
   Santoprene combat-style on 3″ full lug model; $2^1/_8$″ bbl.
   model has sythetic round-butt grip
Finish: Stainless steel
Features: .312″ smooth combat-style trigger (.347″ serrated
   trigger on 3″ full lug model); .240″ service hammer (.375″
   semitarget hammer on 3″ full lug model)

SMITH & WESSON REVOLVERS

SMALL FRAME

38 CENTENNIAL "AIRWEIGHT"
MODEL 442
$427.00

SPECIFICATIONS
Caliber: 38 S&W Special
Capacity: 5 rounds
Barrel length: 2″
Overall length: 6⁷/₁₆″
Weight: 15.8 oz.
Sights: Serrated ramp front; fixed, square-notch rear
Finish: Matte blue
Also available:
MODEL 642 CENTENNIAL AIRWEIGHT. With 2″ barrel, synthetic round butt grip, double-action only.
Price: $442.00
LadySmith Model 471.00

MODEL 442 38 SPECIAL

38 BODYGUARD "AIRWEIGHT"
MODEL 38 (not shown)
$444.00 Blue $460.00 Nickel

SPECIFICATIONS
Caliber: 38 S&W Special
Capacity: 5 shots
Barrel length: 2″
Overall length: 6³/₈″
Weight: 14 oz.
Sights: Front, fixed ¹/₁₀″ serrated ramp; square-notch rear
Grips: Checkered walnut Service with S&W monograms
Finish: S&W blue or nickel aluminum alloy

38 BODYGUARD MODEL 49
$409.00 (not shown)

SPECIFICATIONS
Caliber: 38 S&W Special
Capacity: 5 shots
Barrel length: 2″
Overall length: 6¹/₄″
Weight (empty): 20 oz.
Grips: Synthetic round-butt grip
Sights: Serrated ramp front; fixed, square-notch rear
Finish: S&W blue

MODEL 649 BODYGUARD
$469.00

SPECIFICATIONS
Caliber: 38 S&W Special
Capacity: 5 shots
Barrel length: 2″
Overall length: 6¹/₄″
Weight: 20 oz.
Sights: Serrated ramp front; fixed, square-notch rear
Grips: Round butt, synthetic
Finish: Stainless steel

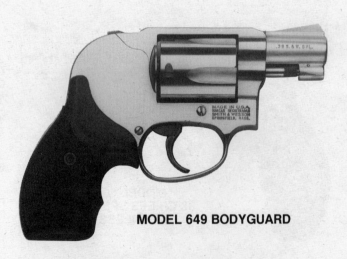

MODEL 649 BODYGUARD

SMITH & WESSON REVOLVERS

SMALL FRAME

MODEL 63

MODEL 640

MODEL 63 22/32 KIT GUN
$458.00 (2″ Barrel)
$462.00 (4″ Barrel)

SPECIFICATIONS
Caliber: 22 Long Rifle   **Capacity:** 6 shots
Barrel lengths: 2″ and 4″
Weight: 22 oz. (2″ barrel); 24$1/2$ oz. (4″ barrel)
Sights: $1/8$″ red ramp front sight; rear sight is black stainless
    steel S&W micrometer click, square-notch, adjustable for
    windage and elevation
Grips: Synthetic round butt
Finish: Satin stainless

MODEL 640 CENTENNIAL
$469.00

SPECIFICATIONS
Calibers: 357 Magnum and 38 S&W Special
Action: Double action only
Capacity: 5 rounds
Barrel length: 2$1/8$″   **Overall length:** 6$3/4$″
Weight: 25 oz.
Sights: Pinned black ramp front; fixed, square-notch rear
Features: Fully concealed hammer; smooth hardwood service
    stock; stainless steel finish; round-butt synthetic grips

MODEL 940 CENTENNIAL

MODEL 940 CENTENNIAL
$474.00

SPECIFICATIONS
Caliber: 9mm Parabellum   **Capacity:** 5 rounds
Action: Double action only
Barrel length: 2″   **Overall length:** 6$7/16$″
Weight: 23 oz.
Sights: Serrated ramp front; fixed, square-notch rear
Grips: Synthetic round-butt grips
Feature: Fully concealed hammer

MODEL 651
22 MAGNUM KIT GUN

22 MAGNUM KIT GUN MODEL 651
$460.00

SPECIFICATIONS
Caliber: 22 Magnum   **Capacity:** 6 shots
Barrel length: 4″   **Overall length:** 8$11/16$″
Weight: 24$1/2$ oz.
Sights: Red ramp front; micrometer click rear, adjustable for
    windage and elevation
Grips: Synthetic round-butt grips
Finish: Stainless steel
Features: .375″ hammer; .312″ smooth combat trigger

SMITH & WESSON REVOLVERS

MEDIUM FRAME

MODEL 10 HEAVY BARREL

38 MILITARY & POLICE
MODEL 10
$383.00 (2″ Bbl.) $390.00 (4″ Bbl.)

SPECIFICATIONS
Caliber: 38 S&W Special   **Capacity:** 6 shots
Barrel lengths: 2″; 4″ heavy barrel
Weight: 28 oz. (2″ bbl.); 33½ oz. (4″ heavy barrel)
Sights: Front, fixed ⅛″ serrated ramp; square-notch rear
Grips: Checkered walnut Service with S&W monograms, round
    or square butt
Finish: S&W blue

357 MILITARY & POLICE
MODEL 13 (HEAVY BARREL)
$394.00

SPECIFICATIONS
Calibers: 357 Magnum and 38 S&W Special
Capacity: 6 shots
Barrel lengths: 3″ and 4″   **Overall length:** 9¼″ (w/4″ bbl.)
Weight: 34 oz. (w/4″ bbl.)
Sights: Front, ⅛″ serrated ramp; square-notch rear
Grips: Synthetic square butt (3″ barrel has round butt)
Finish: S&W blue

MODEL 65

38 MILITARY & POLICE STAINLESS
MODEL 64
$415.00 (2″ Bbl.) $423.00 (3″ & 4″ Bbl.)

SPECIFICATIONS
Caliber: 38 S&W Special
Capacity: 6 shots
Barrel lengthS: 4″ heavy barrel, square butt; 3″ heavy barrel,
    round butt; 2″ regular barrel, round butt
Overall length: 9¼″ w/4″ bbl.; 7⅞″ w/3″ bbl.; 6⅞″ w/2″ bbl.
Weight: 28 oz. w/2″ barrel; 30½ oz. w/3″ bbl.; 33½ oz. w/4″
    bbl.
Sights: Fixed, ⅛″ serrated ramp front; square-notch rear
Grips: Checkered walnut Service with S&W monograms
Finish: Satin stainless

MODEL 64

MODEL 13

357 MILITARY & POLICE
MODEL 65 (HEAVY BARREL)
$427.00

SPECIFICATIONS
Same specifications as Model 13, except **Model 65** is stainless
steel. Available with matte finish.
Also available:
MODEL 65 LADYSMITH. Same specifications as **Model 65**
but with 3″ barrel only (weighs 31 oz.) and rosewood laminate
stock, glass- beaded finish. **Price:** $461.00

SMITH & WESSON REVOLVERS

MEDIUM FRAME

K-38 MASTERPIECE
MODEL 14
$465.00

SPECIFICATIONS
Caliber: 38 S&W Special
Barrel length: 6″ full lug barrel
Overall length: 11⅛″
Weight: 47 oz.
Sights: Micrometer click rear, adjustable for windage and elevation; pinned black Patridge-style front
Grips: Synthetic square butt (on round-butt frame)
Finish: Blue carbon steel
Features: .500 target hammer; .312″ smooth combat trigger

38 COMBAT MASTERPIECE
MODEL 15
$419.00

SPECIFICATIONS
Caliber: 38 S&W Special
Capacity: 6 shots
Barrel length: 4″
Overall length: 9⁵⁄₁₆″
Weight (loaded): 32 oz.
Sights: Serrated ramp front; S&W micrometer click sight adjustable for windage and elevation
Grips: Synthetic square butt (on round-butt frame)
Finish: S&W blue
Features: .375″ semitarget hammer; .312″ smooth combat-style trigger

MODEL 17
$490.00

SPECIFICATIONS
Caliber: 22 LR   **Capacity:** 10 rounds
Action: Single/Double
Barrel length: 6″
Overall length: 11⅛″
Weight: 42 oz.
Sights: Pinned Patridge front; adjustable black blade rear
Grips: Hogue rubber
Finish: Blued carbon steel
Features: .312″ smooth combat trigger; .375″ semi-target hammer

K-22 MASTERPIECE
MODEL 617
$460.00 (4″ barrel) $490.00 (6″ barrel)
$501.00 (8¾″ barrel)

SPECIFICATIONS
Caliber: 22 Long Rifle
Capacity: 6 shots
Barrel length: 4″, 6″ or 8⅜″
Overall length: 9⅛″ (4″ barrel); 11⅛″ (6″ barrel); 13½″ (8⅜″ barrel)
Weight (loaded): 42 oz. with 4″ barrel; 48 oz. with 6″ barrel; 54 oz. with 8⅜″ barrel
Sights: Front, ⅛″ plain Patridge; rear, S&W micrometer click sight adjustable for windage and elevation
Grips: Synthetic square butt (on round-butt frame)
Finish: S&W blue
Features: Target hammer and trigger; drilled and tapped for scope

MEDIUM FRAME

MODEL 19

357 COMBAT MAGNUM
MODEL 19
$416.00 (2¹/₂″ Bbl.) $426.00 (4″ Bbl.)
$430.00 (6″ Barrel)

SPECIFICATIONS
Caliber: 357 S&W Magnum (actual bullet dia. 38 S&W Spec.)
Capacity: 6 shots
Barrel lengths: 2¹/₂″, 4″ and 6″
Overall length: 9¹/₂″ w/4″ bbl.; 7¹/₂″ w/2¹/₂″ bbl.;
  11³/₈″ w/6″ bbl.
Weight: 30¹/₂ oz. (2¹/₂″ bbl.); 36 oz. (4″ bbl.); 39 oz. (6″ bbl.)
Sights: Front, ¹/₈″ Baughman Quick Draw on 2¹/₂″ or 4″ bbl.,
  ¹/₈″ Patridge on 6″ bbl.; rear, S&W Micrometer Click, adjustable for windage and elevation
Grips: Synthetic round butt (2¹/₂″ bbl.); square butt on round-butt frame (4″ and 6″ bbls.)
Finish: S&W bright blue

MODEL 66

357 COMBAT MAGNUM
MODEL 66
$466.00 (2¹/₂″ Bbl.) $471.00 (4″ & 6″ Bbl.)

SPECIFICATIONS
Caliber: 357 Magnum (actual bullet dia. 38 S&W Spec.)
Capacity: 6 shots
Barrel lengths: 4″ or 6″ with square butt; 2¹/₂″ with round butt
Overall length: 7¹/₂″ w/2¹/₂″ bbl.; 9¹/₂″ w/4″ bbl.; 11³/₈″ w/6″ bbl.
Weight: 30¹/₂ oz. w/2¹/₂″ bbl.; 36 oz. w/4″ bbl.; 39 oz. w/6″ bbl.
Sights: Front, ¹/₈″; rear, S&W Red Ramp on ramp base, S&W Micrometer Click, adjustable for windage and elevation; white outline rear
Grips: Uncle Mike's Combat
Trigger: .312″ Smooth Combat
Finish: Satin stainless
Also available:
MODEL 67 in 38 S&W Special, 4″ barrel, stainless steel, synthetic square-butt grip. **Price:** **$467.00**

MODEL 586

DISTINGUISHED COMBAT MAGNUM
MODEL 586
$461.00 (4″ Bbl.) $466.00 (6″ Bbl.)

SPECIFICATIONS
Calibers: 357 Magnum and 38 S&W Special
Capacity: 6 shots
Barrel lengths: 4″ and 6″
Overall length: 9⁹/₁₆″ w/4″ bbl.; 11⁵/₁₆″ w/6″ bbl.
Weight: 41 oz. w/4″ bbl.; 46 oz. w/6″ bbl.
Sights: Front, S&W Red Ramp; rear, S&W Micrometer Click, adjustable for windage and elevation; white outline notch
Grips: Synthetic, square butt on round-butt frame
Finish: S&W Blue

SMITH & WESSON REVOLVERS

MEDIUM FRAME

MODEL 686

MODEL 686 POWERPORT

MODEL 686 (2¹/₂″ Barrel)
$481.00 – $530.00

Same specifications as **Model 586** (see preceding page), except also available with 2¹/₂″ barrel (35¹/₂ oz.) and 8³/₈″ barrel (53 oz.). All models have stainless steel finish, combat or target stock and/or trigger; adjustable sights optional.

MODEL 686 POWERPORT

Same general specifications as the **Model 686,** except this revolver features 6″ full lug barrel with integral compensator, Hogue rubber grips and black-pinned Patridge front sight. Also available:
MODEL 686 PLUS. Capacity: 7 rounds. **Barrel lengths:** 2.5″, 4″ or 6″ full lug. **Overall length:** 7.5″–11¹⁵/₁₆″. **Weight:** 34.5 oz.–45 oz. **Prices: $409.00** (2.5″ bbl.); **$506.00** (4″ bbl.); **$514.00** (6″ bbl.)

LARGE FRAME

MODEL 29

MODEL 625 MOUNTAIN GUN

44 MAGNUM MODEL 29
$554.00 (6″ Bbl.) $566.00 (8³/₈″ Bbl.)

SPECIFICATIONS
Caliber: 44 Magnum   **Capacity:** 6 shots
Barrel lengths: 6″ and 8³/₈″
Overall length: 11³/₈″ with 6″ bbl.; 13⁷/₈″ with 8³/₈″ bbl.
Weight: 47 oz. w/6″ bbl.; 51¹/₂ oz. w/8³/₈″ bbl.
Sights: Front, Red Ramp on ramp base; rear, S&W Micrometer Click, adjustable for windage and elevation; white outline notch
Grips: Hogue rubber
Hammer: Checkered target type
Trigger: .400″ Smooth
Finish: Blued carbon steel

MODEL 625 (Not Shown)
$597.00

SPECIFICATIONS
Caliber: 45 ACP   **Capacity:** 6 shots
Barrel length: 5″ full lug barrel   **Overall length:** 10³/₈″
Weight (empty): 45 oz.
Sights: Front, Patridge on ramp base; S&W Micrometer Click rear, adjustable for windage and elevation
Grips: Synthetic, round butt
Finish: Stainless steel, glass beaded
Also available:
MODEL 625 MOUNTAIN GUN (LTD. EDITION). With 4″ tapered barrel, Hogue round-butt rubber monogrip; satin stainless steel finish; drilled and tapped. **Price on request.**

SMITH & WESSON REVOLVERS

LARGE FRAME

MODEL 629

MODEL 629
$587.00 (4″ Bbl.) $592.00 (6″ Bbl.)
$606.00 (8³/₈″ Barrel)

SPECIFICATIONS
Calibers: 44 Magnum, 44 S&W Special
Capacity: 6 shots
Barrel lengths: 4″, 6″, 8³/₈″
Overall length: 9⁵/₈″, 11³/₈″, 13⁷/₈″
Weight (empty): 44 oz. (4″ bbl.); 47 oz. (6″ bbl.); 51¹/₂ oz. (8³/₈″ bbl.)
Sights: S&W Red Ramp front; white outline rear w/S&W Micrometer Click, adjustable for windage and elevation; drilled and tapped
Grips: Checkered hardwood target or synthetic
Finish: Stainless steel
Features: Combat trigger, target hammer

MODEL 629 CLASSIC
$629.00 (5″ & 6¹/₂″ Bbl.)
$650.00 (8³/₈″ Bbl.)

SPECIFICATIONS
Calibers: 44 Magnum, 44 S&W Special
Capacity: 6 rounds
Barrel lengths: 5″, 6¹/₂″, 8³/₈″
Overall length: 10¹/₂″, 12″, 13⁷/₈″
Weight: 51 oz. (5″ bbl.); 52 oz. (6¹/₂″ bbl.); 54 oz. (8³/₈″ bbl.)
Grips: Hogue rubber

Also available:
MODEL 629 CLASSIC DX. Same features as the **Model 629 Classic** above, plus interchangeable front sights.
With 6¹/₂″ barrel $811.00
With 8³/₈″ barrel 838.00
MODEL 629 POWERPORT w/6.5″ barrel (12″ overall length), weighs 52 oz. Patridge front sight, adjustable black blade rear sight. **Price:** $629.00

MODEL 629 CLASSIC DX

MODEL 657

MODEL 657 STAINLESS
$528.00

SPECIFICATIONS
Caliber: 41 Magnum   **Capacity:** 6 shots
Barrel length: 6″   **Overall length:** 11³/₈″
Weight (empty): 48 oz.
Sights: Front, serrated ramp on ramp base; black blade rear, adjustable for windage and elevation; drilled and tapped
Grips: Hogue rubber
Finish: Satin stainless steel
Features: Combat trigger, target hammer

SPRINGFIELD PISTOLS

MODEL 1911-A1 PISTOLS

MIL-SPEC 1911-A1

MIL-SPEC

SPECIFICATIONS
Calibers: 45 ACP and 38 Super
Capacity: 7 rounds (45 ACP); 9 rounds (38 Super)
Barrel length: 5" **Overall length:** 8⁵/₈"
Trigger pull: 5–6¹/₂ lbs.
Sight radius: 6¹/₄"
Weight: 35.6 oz.
Finish: Parkerized
Features: Black plastic grips; military hammer; 3-dot fixed combat sights
Price: $476.00

**MODEL 1911-A1
STANDARD**

STANDARD & LIGHTWEIGHT

SPECIFICATIONS
Calibers: 45 ACP, 9mm
Capacity: 8 rounds (45 ACP), 9 rounds (9mm & 38 Super)
Barrel length: 5" **Overall length:** 8⁵/₈"
Weight: 35.6 oz.
Finish: Blued or stainless (Standard), matte w/alloy frame (Lightweight)
Features: Walnut grips; Bo-Mar-type sights optional (add **$102.00**)
Prices:
45 ACP Blued or Matte **$527.00**
45 ACP Stainless **572.00**
9mm Blued **557.00**
9mm Stainless **587.00**

**MODEL 1911-A1
TROPHY MATCH BI-TONE**

TROPHY MATCH

SPECIFICATIONS
Caliber: 45 ACP **Capacity:** 7 rounds
Barrel length: 5" **Overall length:** 8⁵/₈"
Weight: 35.6 oz.
Trigger pull: 4–5¹/₂ lbs.
Sights: Fully adjustable target sights
Sight radius: 6³/₄"
Finish: Blued, bi-tone or stainless
Features: Match grade barrel; Videcki speed trigger; extended thumb safety; serrated front strap & top of slide
Prices:
Blued $954.00
Bi-Tone **940.00**
Stainless **985.00**

SPRINGFIELD PISTOLS

MODEL 1911-A1 CHAMPION SERIES

**MODEL 1911-A1
CHAMPION**

MIL-SPEC CHAMPION

MIL-SPEC CHAMPION

SPECIFICATIONS
Caliber: 45 ACP   **Capacity:** 7 rounds
Barrel length: 4″   **Overall length:** 7³/₄″
Weight: 33.4 oz.
Finish: Parkerized
Price: **$476.00**

SPECIFICATIONS
Caliber: 45 ACP   **Capacity:** 8 rounds
Barrel length: 4″   **Overall length:** 7³/₄″
Weight: 33.4 oz.
Trigger pull: 5–6¹/₂″
Sights: 3-dot fixed combat sights
Sight radius: 5¹/₄″
Finish: Blued or stainless
Blued **$543.00**
Stainless 582.00

**MODEL 1911-A1
MIL-SPEC COMPACT**

**MODEL 1911-A1
LIGHTWEIGHT COMPACT**

COMPACT & LIGHTWEIGHT COMPACT

SPECIFICATIONS
Caliber: 45 ACP   **Capacity:** 7 rounds
Barrel length: 4″   **Overall length:** 7³/₄″
Weight: 32 oz. (27 oz. alloy)
Trigger pull: 5–6¹/₂″
Sights: 3-dot fixed combat sights
Sight radius: 5¹/₄″
Finish: Blued, stainless or matte
Prices:
Compact & Lightweight Blued **$543.00**
Compact Stainless 582.00

SPECIFICATIONS
Caliber: 45 ACP   **Capacity:** 6 rounds
Barrel length: 4″   **Overall length:** 7³/₄″
Weight: 32 oz.
Trigger pull: 5–6¹/₂ lbs.
Sights: 3-dot fixed combat sights
Sight radius: 5¹/₄″
Finish: Parkerized
Price: **$476.00**

SPRINGFIELD PISTOLS

MODEL 1911-A1 HIGH-CAPACITY SERIES

**1911-A1 HIGH-CAPACITY
STANDARD**

1911-A1 STANDARD

SPECIFICATIONS
Calibers: 45 ACP and 9mm
Capacity: 10 rounds (13-round & 17-round capacity available for law enforcement and military use only)
Barrel length: 5″
Trigger pull: 5–6¹/₂ lbs.
Sight radius: 6¹/₄″
Finish: Blued, stainless or Parkerized
45 ACP Parkerized **$629.00**
45 ACP & 9mm Blued **659.00**
45 ACP & 9mm Stainless **696.00**

HIGH-CAPACITY
ULTRA COMPACT MODEL (not shown)

SPECIFICATIONS
Caliber: 45 ACP
Capacity: 10 rounds (11-round capacity available for law enforcement and military use only)
Barrel length: 4″
Sight radius: 5¹/₄″
Trigger pull: 5–6¹/₂ lbs.

Finish: Blued or stainless
Features: 3-dot fixed combat sights; flared ejection port; beveled magazine well
Prices:
Blued **$659.00**
Stainless **696.00**

ULTRA COMPACT SERIES

**1911-A1 V10 COMPACT
BI-TONE**

**1911-A1 ULTRA COMPACT
BI-TONE**

SPECIFICATIONS
Caliber: 45 ACP **Capacity:** 7 rounds
Barrel length: 3¹/₂″ **Overall length:** 7¹/₈″
Weight: 30 oz.
Sights: 3-dot fixed combat sights
Sight radius: 5¹/₄″
Trigger pull: 5–6¹/₂ lbs.
Finish: Bi-Tone or stainless
Prices:
Bi-Tone **$659.00**
Stainless **679.00**

SPECIFICATIONS
Caliber: 45 ACP **Capacity:** 7 rounds
Barrel length: 3¹/₂″ **Overall length:** 7¹/₈″
Weight: 31 oz.
Finish: Bi-Tone or stainless
Features: Additional specifications same as V-10 Ultra Compact
Prices:
Bi-Tone **$569.00**
Stainless **585.00**

SPRINGFIELD PISTOLS

MODEL 1911-A1 PDP SERIES

CHAMPION COMP

**LIGHTWEIGHT
COMPACT COMP**

**HIGH-CAPACITY
FACTORY COMP**

CHAMPION COMP

SPECIFICATIONS
Caliber: 45 ACP   **Capacity:** 8 rounds
Barrel length: 4¹/₂″   **Overall length:** 8″
Weight: 38.2 oz.
Finish: Blued
Features: Single port expansion chamber
Price: $871.00

LIGHTWEIGHT COMPACT COMP

SPECIFICATIONS
Caliber: 45 ACP   **Capacity:** 8 rounds
Barrel length: 4¹/₂″   **Overall length:** 8″
Weight: 30.4 oz. (alloy frame)
Finish: Matte
Price: $871.00

DEFENDER (not shown)

SPECIFICATIONS
Caliber: 45 ACP   **Capacity:** 8 rounds
Barrel length: 5″   **Overall length:** 9″
Weight: 40 oz.
Sight radius: 6³/₈″
Finish: Bi-Tone
Features: Adjustable sights, Videcki speed trigger, extended
safety
Price: $993.00

FACTORY COMP (not shown)

SPECIFICATIONS
Calibers: 45 ACP and 38 Super   **Capacity:** 8 rounds
Barrel length: 5⁵/₈″   **Overall length:** 10″
Weight: 40 oz.
Sights: Adjustable 3-dot rear; ramp front
Finish: Blued
Features: Videcki speed trigger; checkered walnut grips; ex-
tended thumb safety; skeletonized hammer
Prices:
45 ACP **$947.00**
38 Super **984.00**

HIGH-CAPACITY FACTORY COMP

SPECIFICATIONS
Calibers: 45 ACP and 38 Super
Capacity: 10 rounds (13 rounds and 17 rounds available for
law-enforcement and military use only)
Barrel length: 5¹/₂″   **Overall length:** 10″
Weight: 40 oz.
Finish: Blued
Features: Triple port comp, skeletonized hammer and grip
safety; match barrel & bushing; extended thumb safety;
lowered & flared ejection port
Prices:
45 ACP **$1075.00**
38 Super **1112.00**

STAR AUTOMATIC PISTOLS

MODELS M40, M43 & M45 FIRESTAR
9mm Parabellum, 40 S&W or 45 ACP

This pocket-sized Firestar pistol features all-steel construction, a triple-dot sight system (fully adjustable rear) and ambidextrous safety. The Acculine barrel design reseats and locks the barrel after each shot. Checkered rubber grips.

SPECIFICATIONS
Capacity: 7 rounds (9mm); 6 rounds (40 S&W and 45 ACP)
Barrel lengths: 3.39″ (3.6″ 45 ACP)
Overall length: 6½″ (6.85″ 45 ACP)
Weight: 30 oz. (9mm); 31.2 oz. (40 S&W); 35 oz. (45 ACP)
Prices:
Firestar M40 Blued finish, 40 S&W $445.00
  Starvel finish 465.00
Firestar M43 Blued finish, 9mm 430.00
  Starvel finish, 9mm 450.00
Firestar M45 Blued finish, 45 ACP 470.00
  Starvel finish, 45 ACP 490.00

M43 FIRESTAR

FIRESTAR PLUS

The new Firestar Plus featues enlarged magazine capacity, lightweight alloy frame, fast button-release magazine, large grip and ambidextrous safety. It also has a triple-dot sight system, tight-lock Acculine barrel for positive barrel/slide alignment and an all-steel slide that glides on internal rails machined inside the frame.

SPECIFICATIONS
Caliber: 9mm Parabellum
Capacity: 10 rounds
Barrel length: 3.39″
Overall length: 6.5″
Weight: 24 oz.
Finish: Blued or Starvel
Prices:
9mm blued $460.00
  Starvel finish 485.00

FIRESTAR PLUS

ULTRASTAR

The Ultrastar features a slim profile, light weight and first-shot, double-action speed. The use of polymers makes this pistol exceptionally strong and durable. Other features include a triple-dot sight system, ambidextrous two-position manual safety (safe and safe decock), all-steel internal mechanism and barrel, slide-mounted on rails inside frame.

SPECIFICATIONS
Calibers: 9mm Parabellum and 40 S&W
Capacity: 9 rounds (9mm); 8 rounds (40 S&W)
Barrel length: 3.5″   **Overall length:** 7″
Weight: 26 oz.
Price: $490.00

ULTRASTAR

STOEGER PISTOLS

PRO SERIES 95

The PRO SERIES 95 are precision target pistols designed for the knowledgeable, advanced target shooter. Destined to be among the world's most popular competitive pistols, the PRO SERIES 95 features 10-round capacity in 22 Long Rifle caliber, plus:

- interchangeable barrels
- fully adjustable target sights
- trigger pull adjustment
- trigger travel adjustment
- automatic slide lock
- Pachmayr military-style rubber grips
- stainless-steel finish

The vent-rib model features a full-length vent rib that produces the most positive sighting plane for the advanced competitor.

The bull-barrel and fluted-barrel models feature the military bracket rear sight, acclaimed by many competitive shooters as the most reliable sighting system developed.

Optional:
Walnut target grips with thumbrest **$40.00**
Stainless-steel magazine (10 rounds): **32.00**

VENT-RIB MODEL
$565.00

BULL-BARREL MODEL
$460.00

FLUTED-BARREL MODEL
$490.00

SPECIFICATIONS PRO SERIES 95

MODEL	BBL. LGTH.	O.A. LGTH.	REAR SIGHT	SIGHT RADIUS	WT./OZ.
Vent Rib	5 1/2"	9 3/4"	ON RIB	8 3/4"	47
Bull Barrel	5 1/2"	9 3/4"	ON BRACKET	8 3/4"	45
Fluted Barrel	7 1/4"	11 3/4"	ON BRACKET	10"	45

TAURUS PISTOLS

MODEL PT-58
$429.00 (Blue) $470.00 (Stainless)

SPECIFICATIONS
Caliber: 380 ACP
Action: Semiautomatic double action
Capacity: 10 + 1
Barrel length: 4″
Overall length: 7.2″
Weight: 30 oz.
Hammer: Exposed
Sights: Front, drift adjustable; rear, notched bar dovetailed to slide, 3-dot combat
Grips: Smooth Brazilian walnut
Finish: Blue or stainless steel
Features: Tri-position safety system

MODEL PT-58

MODEL PT-92 AF
$449.00 (Blue) $493.00 (Stainless)

Caliber: 9mm Parabellum
Action: Semiautomatic double action
Capacity: 10 + 1
Hammer: Exposed
Barrel length: 5″   **Overall length:** 8½″
Height: 5.39″   **Width:** 1.45″
Weight: 34 oz. (empty)
Rifling: R.H., 6 grooves
Sights: Front, fixed; rear, drift adjustable, 3-dot combat
Safeties: (a) Ambidextrous manual safety locking trigger mechanism and slide in locked position; (b) half-cock position; (c) inertia-operated firing pin; (d) chamber-loaded indicator
Slide: Hold open upon firing last cartridge
Grips: Smooth Brazilian walnut
Finish: Blue or stainless steel

Also available:
MODEL PT-99. Same specifications as Model PT 92, but has micrometer click-adjustable rear sight. **$471.00** Blue; **$518.00** Stainless
MODEL PT-99AFD Deluxe Shooter's Pak w/extra magazine & custom case. **$500.00** Blue; **$546.00** Stainless

MODEL PT-92 AF

MODEL PT-92 AFC
$449.00 (Blue) $493.00 (Stainless)

SPECIFICATIONS
Caliber: 9mm Parabellum   **Capacity:** 10 + 1
Barrel length: 4″
Weight: 31 oz.
Sights: Fixed front; drift-adjustable rear, 3-dot combat
Grips: Brazilian hardwood
Slide: Last shot held open
Safety: Manual, ambidextrous hammer drop; inertia firing pin; chamber load indicator
Finish: Blue or stainless steel

MODEL PT-940
$453.00 (Blue) $497.00 (Stainless)

SPECIFICATIONS
Caliber: 40 S&W
Action: Semiautomatic double
Capacity: 9 rounds
Barrel length: 4¼″   **Overall length:** 7.48″
Weight: 30 oz.
Finish: Blue or Stainless
Grips: Santoprene II
Also available:
MODEL 940D Deluxe Shooter's Pak w/extra magazine & custom case. **Prices: $476.00** (Blue); **$520.00** (Stainless)

TAURUS PISTOLS

MODEL PT 22
$187.00 (Blue)
$195.00 (Nickel)

SPECIFICATIONS
Caliber: 22 LR
Action: Semiautomatic (DA only)
Capacity: 8 shots
Barrel length: 2³/₄″
Overall length: 5¹/₄″
Weight: 12.3 oz.
Sights: Fixed
Grips: Brazilian hardwood
Finish: Blue or nickel
Also available:
MODEL PT 25. Same prices and specifications as Model PT 22, except magazine holds 9 rounds in 25 ACP.

MODEL PT 101
$491.00 (Blue)
$537.00 (Stainless)

SPECIFICATIONS
Caliber: 40 S&W
Capacity: 10 + 1
Barrel length: 5″   **Overall length:** 8¹/₂″
Weight: 34 oz. (empty)
Sights: Micrometer click-adjustable rear sight
Grips: Brazilian hardwood
Finish: Blue or stainless steel
Also available:
MODEL PT 100. Same specifications as Model PT 101, but has fixed sights. **Prices: $469.00** Blue; **$514.00** Stainless
MODEL PT-101D Deluxe Shooter's Pak w/extra magazine & custom case. **Prices: $519.00** Blue; **$565.00** Stainless

MODEL PT-908
$435.00 (Blue)
$473.00 (Stainless)

SPECIFICATIONS
Caliber: 9mm Parabellum
Action: Double action
Capacity: 8 shots
Barrel length: 3.8″   **Overall length:** 7.05″
Weight: 30 oz.
Sights: Drift adjustable front and rear, 3-dot combat
Grips: Santoprene II
Finish: Blue or stainless steel
Also available:
MODEL PT-908D Deluxe Shooter's Pak w/extra magazine & custom case. **Prices: $459.00** Blue; **$496.00** Stainless
MODEL PT-910 in 9mm. **Capacity:** 10 shots. **Barrel length:** 4.25″. **Overall length:** 7.48″   **Weight:** 30 oz. **Grips:** Santoprene II. **Price:** TBD.

MODEL PT-945
$453.00 (Blue)
$497.00 (Stainless)

SPECIFICATIONS
Caliber: 45 ACP   **Capacity:** 8 shots
Barrel length: 4.25″   **Overall length:** 7.48″
Weight: 29.5 oz.
Action: Semiautomatic double
Sights: Drift-adjustable front and rear; 3-dot combat
Grips: Santoprene II
Safety features: Manual safety; ambidextrous; chamber load indicator; intercept notch; firing-pin block; floating firing pin
Finish: Blue or stainless

TAURUS REVOLVERS

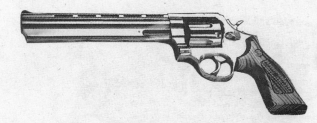

MODEL 44

SPECIFICATIONS
Caliber: 44 Mag.   **Capacity:** 6 rounds
Barrel length: 4″ (heavy, solid); 6¹/₂″ and 8³/₈″ (vent. rib)
Weight: 44 oz. (4″); 52¹/₂ oz. (6¹/₂″); 57¹/₄ oz. (8³/₈″)
Sights: Serrated ramp front; rear micrometer click, adjustable for windage and elevation
Grips: Santoprene II
Finish: Blue or stainless steel
Features: Compensated barrel; transfer bar safety
Prices:

4″ barrel blue	$425.00
stainless steel	484.00
6¹/₂″ and 8³/₈″ blue	443.00
stainless steel	504.00

MODEL 65 (2¹/₂″ Barrel)
$290.00 (Blue)
$357.00 (Stainless)

SPECIFICATIONS
Caliber: 357 Magnum
Capacity: 6 shot
Action: Double
Barrel lengths: 2¹/₂″, 4″
Weight: 34 oz. (4″)
Sights: Rear square notched; serrated front ramp
Grips: Brazilian hardwood
Finish: Royal blue or stainless

MODEL 66
$318.00 (Blue)
$392.00 (Stainless)

SPECIFICATIONS
Caliber: 357 Magnum
Action: Double
Capacity: 6 shot
Barrel lengths: 2¹/₂″, 4″, 6″
Weight: 35 oz. (4″ barrel)
Sights: Serrated ramp front; rear, micrometer click adjustable for windage and elevation
Grips: Brazilian hardwood
Finish: Royal blue or stainless steel

MODEL 83
$265.00 (Blue)
$309.00 (Stainless)

SPECIFICATIONS
Caliber: 38 Special
Action: Double
Capacity: 6 shot
Barrel length: 4″
Weight: 34 oz.
Sights: Serrated ramp front; micrometer-click rear adjustable for windage and elevation
Grips: Brazilian hardwood
Finish: Blue

TAURUS REVOLVERS

MODEL 80
$252.00 (Blue)
$299.00 (Stainless)

SPECIFICATIONS
Caliber: 38 Special
Capacity: 6 shot
Action: Double
Barrel lengths: 3″, 4″
Weight: 30 oz. (4″ barrel)
Sights: Notched rear; serrated ramp front
Grips: Brazilian hardwood
Finish: Blue or stainless

MODEL 80

MODEL 82
$252.00 (Blue)
$299.00 (Stainless)

SPECIFICATIONS
Caliber: 38 Special
Capacity: 6 shot
Action: Double
Barrel lengths: 3″, 4″
Weight: 34 oz. (4″ barrel)
Sights: Notched rear; serrated ramp front
Grips: Brazilian hardwood
Finish: Blue or stainless

MODEL 82

MODEL 94
$293.00 (Blue)
$339.00 (Stainless)

SPECIFICATIONS
Caliber: 22 LR
Number of shots: 9
Action: Double
Barrel lengths: 3″, 4″, and 5″
Weight: 25 oz. (w/4″ barrel)
Sights: Serrated ramp front; rear micrometer click
adjustable for windage and elevation
Grips: Brazilian hardwood
Finish: Blue or stainless steel

Also available:
MODEL 941 in 22 Magnum, 8-shot capacity; ejector shroud.
In blue **$315.00**
In stainless steel 366.00

MODEL 941

TAURUS REVOLVERS

MODEL 85
$239.00 (Blue)
$287.00 (Stainless Steel)

SPECIFICATIONS
Caliber: 38 Special
Capacity: 5 shot
Action: Double
Barrel length: 2″ and 3″
Weight: 21 oz. (2″ barrel)
Sights: Notched rear, serrated ramp front
Grips: Brazilian hardwood
Finish: Blue or stainless steel
Also available:
MODEL 85CH. Same specifications and prices as Model 85, except has concealed hammer and 2″ barrel only.

MODEL 96
$358.00

SPECIFICATIONS
Caliber: 22 LR
Capacity: 6 shot
Action: Double
Barrel length: 6″
Weight: 34 oz.
Sights: Patridge-type front; rear, micrometer click adjustable for windage and elevation
Grips: Brazilian hardwood
Finish: Blue only
Features: Target hammer; adjustable target trigger

MODEL 431
$286.00 (Blue)
$350.00 (Stainless)

SPECIFICATIONS
Caliber: 44 Special
Capacity: 5 shot
Action: Double
Barrel lengths: 2¹/₂″, 3″ or 4″ w/ejector shroud; heavy, solid rib barrel
Weight: 35 oz. (4″ barrel)
Sights: Notched rear; serrated ramp front
Safety: Transfer bar
Grips: Brazilian hardwood
Finish: Blue or stainless steel

MODEL 441
$298.00 (Blue)
$374.00 (Stainless)

SPECIFICATIONS
Caliber: 44 Special
Capacity: 5 shot
Action: Double
Barrel lengths: 3″, 4″ or 6″ w/ejector shroud; heavy, solid rib barrel
Weight: 40¹/₄ oz. (6″ barrel)
Sights: Serrated ramp front; rear, micrometer click adjustable for windage and elevation
Safety: Transfer bar
Grips: Brazilian hardwood
Finish: Blue or stainless steel

TAURUS REVOLVERS

MODEL 605

MODEL 607

MODEL 605
$262.00 (Blue)
$312.00 (Stainless)

SPECIFICATIONS
Caliber: 357 Magnum/38 Special
Capacity: 5 shot
Barrel lengths: 2¼" and 3"
Weight: 24.5 oz.
Sights: Notched rear; serrated ramp front
Grips: Santoprene I
Safety: Transfer bar
Finish: Blue or stainless

MODEL 607
$425.00 (Blue 4")
$443.00 (Blue 6½")
$484.00 (Stainless 4")
$504.00 (Stainless 6½")

SPECIFICATIONS
Caliber: 357 Magnum/38 Special
Capacity: 7 shot
Barrel lengths: 4" (heavy solid rib) and 6½" (vent rib)
Weight: 44 oz. (w/4" barrel)
Sights: Notched rear; serrated ramp front
Safety: Transfer bar
Grips: Santoprene I
Finish: Blue or stainless
Feature: Compensated barrel

MODEL 669

MODEL 689 STAINLESS

MODEL 669
$327.00 (4" and 6" Blue)
$401.00 (4" and 6" Stainless)

SPECIFICATIONS
Caliber: 357 Magnum
Capacity: 6 shot
Action: Double
Barrel lengths: 4" and 6"
Weight: 37 oz. (4" barrel)
Sights: Serrated ramp front; rear, micrometer click adjustable for windage and elevation
Grips: Brazilian hardwood
Finish: Royal blue or stainless
Optional feature: Recoil compensator **$346.00** blue; **$421.00** stainless

MODEL 689
$341.00 (Blue)
$415.00 (Stainless)

The Model 689 has the same specifications as the Model 669, except vent rib is featured.

THOMPSON/CENTER

CONTENDER HUNTER

BULL BARREL

CONTENDER HUNTER

Chambered in the most popular commercially loaded cartridges available to handgunners.

SPECIFICATIONS
Calibers: 7-30 Waters, 223 Rem., 30-30 Win., 35 Rem., 45-70 Government, 375 Win. and. 44 Rem. Mag.
Barrel length: 14"
Overall length: 16"
Weight: 4 lbs. (approx.)
Features: T/C Muzzle Tamer (to reduce recoil); a mounted T/C Recoil Proof 2.5X scope w/lighted reticle, QD sling swivels and nylon sling, plus suede leather carrying case
Prices:

Blued Steel	$798.00
Stainless	$829.00
Extra barrel (44 Rem. Mag.)	244.50

CONTENDER BULL BARREL MODELS

These pistols with 10-inch barrel feature fully adjustable Patridge-style iron sights. All stainless-steel models (including the Super "14" and Super "16" below) are equipped with Rynite finger-groove grip with rubber recoil cushion and matching Rynite forend, plus Cougar etching on the steel frame.

Standard and Custom calibers available:
22 LR, 22 Hornet, 223 Rem., 300 Whisper, 30-30 Win., 7mm T.C.U., 357 Mag., 44 Mag. and 45 Colt/.410

Bull Barrel Blue	$468.60–473.80
Bull Barrel Stainless	494.40–499.60
Standard calibers w/internal choke 45 Colt/.410	455.00
Vent Rib Model	515.00
With **Match Grade Barrel** (22 LR only)	460.00

CONTENDER OCTAGON BARREL MODELS (Not Shown)

This standard blued-steel barrel is interchangeable with any model listed here. Available in 22 LR 10-inch length, it is supplied with iron sights. Incl. Match Grade Chamber. No external choke.

Price:	$473.80

CONTENDER SUPER "14" STAINLESS STEEL

CONTENDER SUPER "14" MODELS

Chambered in 10 calibers (22 LR, 22 LR Match Grade Chamber, 22 Hornet, 223 Rem., 7-30 Waters, 300 Whisper, 30-30 Win., 35 Rem., 375 Win. and 44 Mag.), this gun is equipped with a 14-inch bull barrel, fully adjustable target rear sight and Patridge-style ramped front sight with 13 1/2-inch sight radius.
Overall length: 18 1/4".   **Weight:** 3 1/2 lbs.
Prices:

Blued	$460.00–490.00
Stainless	504.70–515.00
14" Vent Rib Model in 45 Colt/.410, blue	490.00
Stainless	535.60

CONTENDER SUPER "16" VENTILATED RIB/INTERNAL CHOKE MODELS (Not Shown)

Featuring a raised ventilated (7/16-inch wide) rib, this Contender model is available in 45 Colt/.410 caliber. A patented detachable choke (1 7/8 inches long) screws into the muzzle internally.
Barrel length: 16 1/4" inches.

Prices:

Blued	$495.00
Stainless	540.80
10" Vent Rib Model w/internal choke, blue	470.00
Stainless	500.00

UBERTI REPLICAS

1871 ROLLING BLOCK TARGET PISTOL

SPECIFICATIONS
Calibers: 22 LR, 22 Magnum, 22 Hornet, 357 Mag., 45 L.C.
Capacity: Single shot
Barrel length: 9¹/₂″ (half-octagon/half-round or full round Navy Style)
Overall length: 14″ **Weight:** 2.75 lbs.
Sights: Fully adjustable rear; ramp front or open sight on Navy Style barrel
Grip and forend: Walnut
Trigger guard: Brass
Frame: Color casehardened steel

**1871 ROLLING BLOCK
TARGET PISTOL
$380.00**

1873 CATTLEMAN S.A.

SPECIFICATIONS
Calibers: 357 Magnum, 44-40, 45 L.C., 45 ACP
Capacity: 6 shots
Barrel lengths: 3″, 4³/₄″, 5¹/₂″, 7¹/₂″ round, tapered; 18″ (Bunt-line)
Overall length: 10³/₄″ w/5¹/₂″ barrel
Weight: 2.42 lbs.
Grip: One-piece walnut
Frame: Color casehardened steel; also available in charcoal blue or nickel
Also available:
45 L.C./45 ACP Convertible $395.00

**1873 CATTLEMAN
$410.00–475.00**

1875 "OUTLAW"/1890 POLICE

SPECIFICATIONS
Calibers: 357 Magnum, 44-40, 45 ACP, 45 Long Colt
Capacity: 6 shots
Barrel lengths: 5¹/₂″, 7¹/₂″ round, tapered
Overall length: 13³/₄″ **Weight:** 2.75 lbs.
Grips: Two-piece walnut
Frame: Color casehardened steel
Also available:
In nickel plate $450.00
45 L.C./45 ACP Convertible 450.00

**1875 "OUTLAW"/1890 POLICE
$435.00**

BUCKHORN 1873 SINGLE ACTION TARGET

SPECIFICATIONS
Caliber: 44 Rem. Mag.   **Capacity:** 6 shots
Barrel length: 4³/₄″, 6″ or 7¹/₂″ round, tapered
Overall length: 11³/₄″ (6″ bbl.)
Weight: 2 lbs. 12 oz. (6″ bbl.)
Sights: Target
Finish: Black
Also available:
In nickel plate $455.00
44-40 Mag. Convertible 460.00
BUCKHORN TARGET (7¹/₂″ barrel) 415.00
BUCKHORN BUNTLINE 448.00
   Convertible 499.00

**BUCKHORN 1873 SA
TARGET
$410.00 (4³/₄″ Barrel)
$415.00 (7¹/₂″ Barrel)**

UNIQUE PISTOLS

MODEL DES 69U
$1325.00

SPECIFICATIONS
Caliber: 22 LR
Capacity: 5- or 6-shot magazine
Barrel length: 5.9″
Overall length: 11.2″
Weight: 40.2 oz. (empty)
Height: 5.5″
Width: 1.97″
Sights: Micrometric rear; lateral and vertical correction by clicks
Safety: Manual
Features: Orthopedic French walnut grip with adjustable hand rest; external hammer

Also available:
Model DES 32U in 32 S&W Long Wadcutter. Designed for centerfire U.I.T. and military rapid fire. Other specifications same as Model DES 69U. **Price:** **$1350.00**

MODEL I.S. INTERNATIONAL SILHOUETTE
$1145.00

SPECIFICATIONS
Calibers: 22 LR, 22 Magnum, 7mm TCU, 357 Magnum, 44 Magnum
Barrel length: 10″
Overall length: 14.5″
Weight: 38 oz.
Height: 6.5″
Width: 1.5″
Sights: Micrometric rear; lateral and vertical correction by clicks; interchangeable front sight; dovetailed grooves for scope
Features: French walnut grip; interchangeable shroud/barrel assembly; external hammer; firing adjustments

Also available:
International Sport w/light alloy frame in 22 LR and 22 Mag.
Price: **$795.00**

MODEL DES 2000U
$1375.00

SPECIFICATIONS
Caliber: 22 Short
Barrel length: 5.9″
Overall length: 11.4″
Weight: 43.4 oz. (empty)
Height: 5.3″
Width: 1.97″
Sights: Micrometric rear; lateral and vertical correction by clicks

Features: French walnut grips with adjustable hand rest; left-hand grips available; external hammer; dry firing device; slide stop catch; antirecoil device

WALTHER PISTOLS

The Walther double-action system combines the principles of the double-action revolver with the advantages of the modern pistol without the disadvantages inherent in either design.

Models PPK and PPK/S differ only in the overall length of the barrel and slide. Both models offer the same features, including compact form, light weight, easy handling, and absolute safety. Both models can be carried with a loaded chamber and closed hammer, but ready to fire either single- or double-action. Both models are provided with a live round indicator pin to signal a loaded chamber. An automatic internal safety blocks the hammer to prevent accidental striking of the firing pin, except with a deliberate pull of the trigger. Sights are provided with white markings for high visibility in poor light. Rich Walther blue/black finish is standard, and each pistol is complete with an extra magazine with finger-rest extension.

MODEL PPK & PPK/S

MODEL PPK & PPK/S

SPECIFICATIONS
Caliber: 380 ACP
Capacity: 6 rounds (PPK), 7 rounds (PPK/S)
Barrel length: 3.35″
Overall length: 6.5″
Weight: 21 oz. (PPK); 23 oz. (PPK/S)
Finish: Walther blue or stainless steel
Price: $540.00

MODEL PP

MODEL PP DOUBLE ACTION

SPECIFICATIONS
Calibers: 32 ACP and 380 ACP
Capacity: 7 rounds
Barrel length: 3.8″
Overall length: 6.7″
Weight: 25 oz.
Finish: Walther blue
Price: $999.00

MODEL TPH DOUBLE ACTION

Walther's Model TPH is considered by government agents and professional lawmen to be one of the top undercover/backup guns available. A scaled-down version of Walther's PP-PPK series.

SPECIFICATIONS
Calibers: 22 LR and 25 ACP
Capacity: 6 rounds
Barrel length: 2.85″
Overall length: 5.5″
Weight: 14 oz.
Finish: Walther blue or stainless steel
Price: $440.00

MODEL TPH

WALTHER PISTOLS

MODEL P 88 COMPACT

The Walther P 88 Compact is a double-action, locked-breech, semiautomatic pistol with an external hammer. Its compact form, light weight and easy handling are combined with the superb performance of the 9mm Luger Parabellum cartridge. The P 88 Compact boasts target-grade accuracy, dual-function controls and comes with two 10-shot double-column magazines.

SPECIFICATIONS
Caliber: 9mm Parabellum   **Capacity:** 10 rounds
Barrel length: 3.93″   **Overall length:** 7½″
Weight: 28 oz.
Finish: Blue
Price: **$900.00**

MODEL P 88 COMPACT

MODEL P 5 DOUBLE ACTION

SPECIFICATIONS
Caliber: 9mm Parabellum
Capacity: 8 rounds
Barrel lengths: 3.2″ (Compact) and 3.62″
Overall length: 6.6″ (Compact) and 7″
Weight: 26 oz. (3.1″ barrel); 28 oz. (3.5″ barrel)
Finish: Blue
Features: Four automatic built-in safety functions; lightweight alloy frame; supplied with two magazines
Price: **$900.00**

MODEL P 5 DA

**MODEL P5 COMPACT
w/3.2″ Barrel**

WICHITA ARMS PISTOLS

SPECIFICATIONS
Calibers: 308 Win. F.L., 7mm IHMSA and 7mm×308
Barrel length: 14¹⁵/₁₆″
Weight: 4½ lbs.
Action: Single-shot bolt action
Sights: Wichita Multi-Range Sight System
Grips: Right-hand center walnut grip or right-hand rear walnut grip
Features: Glass bedded; bolt ground to precision fit; adjustable Wichita trigger
Also available:
WICHITA CLASSIC SILHOUETTE PISTOL. Barrel: 11¼″. **Weight:** 3 lbs. 15 oz. **Grips:** AAA grade walnut, glass bedded. **$3450.00**
Engraved Model **4850.00**

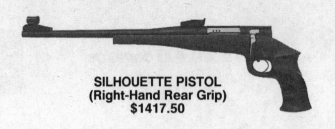

SILHOUETTE PISTOL
(Right-Hand Rear Grip)
$1417.50

SPECIFICATIONS
Calibers: 7-30 Waters, 7mm Super Mag., 7R (30-30 Win. necked to 7mm), 30-30 Win., 357 Mag., 357 Super Mag., 32 H&H Mag., 22 RFM, 22 LR
Barrel lengths: 10″ and 14″ (10½″ for centerfire calibers)
Weight: 3 lbs. 2 oz. (10″ barrel); 4 lbs. 7 oz. (14″ barrel)
Action: Top-break, single-shot, single action only
Sights: Patridge front sight; rear sight adjustable for windage and elevation
Grips and Forend: Walnut
Safety: Crossbolt

INTERNATIONAL PISTOL
$735.00 (10″ Barrel)
$813.75 (14″ Barrel)

WILDEY PISTOLS

WILDEY PISTOLS

These gas-operated pistols are designed to meet the needs of hunters who want to use handguns for big game. The Wildey pistol includes such features as: • Ventilated rib • Reduced recoil • Double-action trigger mechanism • Patented hammer and trigger blocks and rebounding fire pin • Sights adjustable for windage and elevation • Stainless construction • Fixed barred for increased accuracy • Increased action strength (with 3-lug and exposed face rotary bolt) • Selective single or autoloading capability • Ability to handle high-pressure loads

SPECIFICATIONS
Calibers: 45 Win. Mag., 475 Wildey Mag.
Capacity: 7 shots
Barrel lengths: 5″, 6″, 7″, 8″, 10″, 12″, 14″
Overall length: 11″ with 7″ barrel
Weight: 64 oz. with 5″ barrel
Height: 6″

SURVIVOR MODEL in 45 Win. Mag.   **Prices**
    5″, 6″ or 7″ models **$1295.00**
    8″, 10″ or 12″ barrels **1316.00**
SURVIVOR MODEL in 475 Wildey Mag.
    8″, 10″ or 12″ barrels **1316.00**

HUNTER MODEL in 45 Win. Mag.
    5″, 6″ or 7″ barrels **$1413.00**
    8″, 10″ or 12″ barrels **1677.00**
HUNTER MODEL in 475 Wildey Mag.
    8″ or 10″ barrels **1677.00**
    12″ barrel **1803.00**

Also available:
Interchangeable barrel extension assemblies **$523.00** (5″ barrel); **$648.95** (12″ barrel); **$1148.00** (14″ barrel).

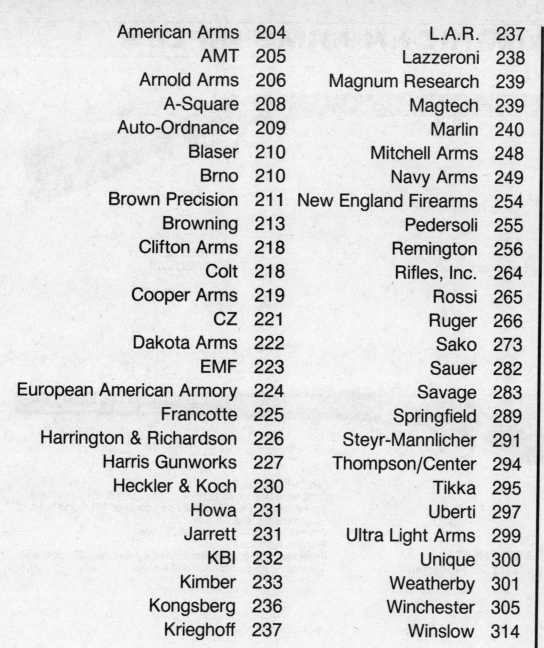

Rifles

For addresses and phone/fax numbers of manufacturers and distributors included in this section, please turn to DIRECTORY OF MANUFACTURERS AND SUPPLIERS on page 554.

AMERICAN ARMS RIFLES

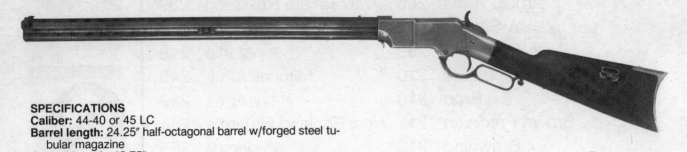

SPECIFICATIONS
Caliber: 44-40 or 45 LC
Barrel length: 24.25″ half-octagonal barrel w/forged steel tubular magazine
Overall length: 43.75″
Weight: 9.25 lbs.
Features: Brass frame, elevator, magazine follower and buttstock; straight-grip walnut buttstock

1860 HENRY
$996.00

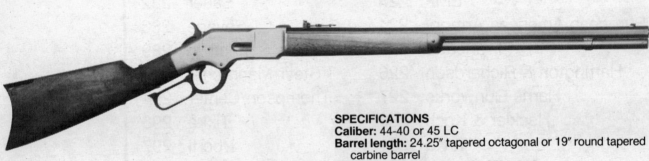

1866 WINCHESTER
$829.00   ($797.00 19″ barrel)

SPECIFICATIONS
Caliber: 44-40 or 45 LC
Barrel length: 24.25″ tapered octagonal or 19″ round tapered carbine barrel
Overall length: 43.25″ (w/24.25″ barrel)
Weight: 8.15 lbs.
Features: Tubular magazine; brass frame, elevator and buttplate; walnut buttstock and forend

SPECIFICATIONS
Caliber: 44-40 or 45 LC
Barrel length: 24.25″ tapered octagonal barrel (tubular magazine)
Features: Color casehardened steel frame with ejection port cover; brass elevator; walnut buttstock with steel buttplate

1873 WINCHESTER
$984.00

AMT RIFLES

22 RIMFIRE MAGNUM

22 RIMFIRE MAGNUM

AMT's rimfire magnum rifle delivers big-bore velocity with minimum cost ammunition. Jacketed bullets combine with magnum velocity to yield high impact. Greater power flattens trajectory and improves accuracy.

SPECIFICATIONS
Caliber: 22 Rimfire Magnum
Capacity: 10 rounds
Barrel length: 20″
Weight: 6 lbs.
Sights: No sights; drilled and tapped for 87-A Weaver scope mount base
Features: Stainless steel construction
Price: (scope not included) **$549.99**

CHALLENGE EDITION 22 LR
(not shown)

SPECIFICATIONS
Caliber: 22 Long Rifle
Capacity: 10-shot automatic
Barrel lengths: 18″ or 22″
Stock: Fiberglass stock with floating barrel and action
Features: Threaded bull barrel; stainless steel match grade; custom trigger (2–4 lbs.) and extended magazine release; scope mount
Price: **$899.00**

BOLT ACTION STANDARD REPEATER

STANDARD RIFLES (Single Shot & Repeater)

SPECIFICATIONS
Calibers: *Single Shot*—22 Hornet, 222, 223, 22-250, 243 Win., 243 A, 22 PPC, 6 PPC, 6.5X08, 708, 308
Repeaters—223, 22-250, 243, 243A, 6 PPC, 25-06, 6.5×08, 270, 30-06, 308, 7mm Mag., 300 Win. Mag., 338 Win. Mag., 375 H&H, 416 Rem. 458 Win. Mag., 416 Rigby, 7.62×39, 7×57, 7.62mm
Action: Push feed post-64 Win. Type
Magazine: Mauser type
Barrels: Match grade up to 28″ long #3
Weight: Approximately 8.5 lbs.
Trigger: Custom-type adjustable
Safety: Three position pre-64 Model 70-type
Stock: Classic Composite
Pull: 13.5″ stock length

Features: Pillar bedding; sliding ejector 2/30° cone bolt; stainless and chrome moly steel; sights drilled and tapped for scope mount
Also available:
DELUXE RIFLES (Single Shot & Repeater). Same as Standard models, but action is Mauser type control feed and stock is custom Kevlar; also features plunger ejector and claw type extractor
Prices:
Standard Single Shot **$1109.99**
Standard Repeater 1109.99
Deluxe Single Shot 2399.99
Deluxe Repeater 1595.99
Actions (Left-Hand models available)
  Single Shot 550.00
  Repeater 650.00
    Magnum actions 690.00

ARNOLD ARMS RIFLES

AFRICAN SERIES

Arnold Arms Company introduces a full line of rifles built on its "Apollo" action with the strongest and hardest chrome-moly and stainless steels available. Alignment of bolt face, receiver and barrel centerline axis results in optimum accuracy. Lapping the bolt lugs, squaring the bolt and truing the receiver are unnecessary—the Apollo action assures perpendicular alignment and equal pressure lock-up. A perfect mating of the receiver, recoil lug and stock, achieved only through the pro-cess of glass bedding, assures uniformity of recoil bearing points shot after shot. The revolutionary positive feed and extraction features designed and machined into the "Apollo" bolt face assure full extraction and ejection as well as next cartridge feeding with every complete bolt cycling. The 3-position positive-lock safety locks up the bolt and firing pin to prevent accidental discharge until the rifle is ready to fire.

AFRICAN SAFARI
w/AA English Walnut & Whitworth Express Sights
$6350.00

AFRICAN SAFARI

SPECIFICATIONS
Calibers: .243 to .458 Win. Magnum
Barrel length: 22″ to 26″ (Contours #2 to #7 C-M; #4 to #7 S.S.)
Sights: Scope mount standard or with optional M70 Express sights
Finish: Chrome-moly in matte blue, polished or stainless steel matte finish
Stock: A and AA Fancy Grade English walnut stock w/#5 standard wraparound checkering pattern (patterns 1-4 & 6-10 available at extra charge.); includes ebony forend tip

Prices:
With "A" Grade English Walnut
Matte Blue	$4987.00
Std. Polish	5337.00
Hi-Luster	5612.00
Stainless Steel Matte	5117.00

With "AA" Grade English Walnut
C-M Matte Blue	5125.00
Std. Polish	5475.00
Hi-Luster	5750.00
Stainless Steel Matte	5255.00

AFRICAN TROPHY (Not Shown)

Same as African Safari but with AAA Extra Fancy English walnut stock with #9 checkering.
Prices:
C-M Matte	$6072.00
Std. Polish	6422.00
Hi-Luster	6697.00
Stainless Steel Matte	6202.00

GRAND AFRICAN (Not Shown)

Same as above but in calibers .338 Magnum to .458 Win. Mag. Other standard features include: Exhibition Grade stock with #10 checkering pattern; choice of ebony or Cape Buffalo forend tip; barrel band; scope mount w/Express sights w/front ring & hood. **Barrel length:** 24″–26″.
Prices:
C-M Hi-Luster Polish only	$8219.00
Stainless Steel Matte	7694.00

AFRICAN SYNTHETIC (Not Shown)

Same as above but in fibergrain stock with or without cheek-piece and traditional checkering pattern or stipple finish (Camo colors also available); Whitworth Express folding leaf optional w/front hood sight.
Prices:
C-M Matte	$3528.00
Std. Polish	3878.00
Stainless Steel Matte	3658.00

SERENGETI SYNTHETIC (Not Shown)

Same as above but in calibers .243 to .300 Magnum; choice of classic or Monte Carlo cheekpiece; scope mount only. **Barrel length:** 22″–26″ (Contours Featherweight to #5 C- M, #4 to #6S.S.
Prices:
C-M Matte	$3528.00
Std. Polish	3878.00
Stainless Steel Matte	3658.00

ARNOLD ARMS RIFLES

ALASKAN SERIES

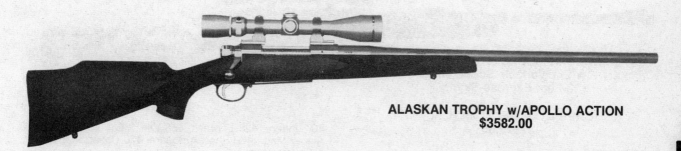

ALASKAN TROPHY w/APOLLO ACTION
$3582.00

ALASKAN TROPHY

Features stainless steel or chrome-moly Apollo action with fibergrain or black synthetic stock; barrel band (.357 H&H and larger magnums); scope mount with Express sights standard. **Calibers:** .300 Magnum to .458 Win. Mag. **Barrel length:** 24″–26″ (contours #4 to #7 C-M, #4 to #7 S.S.)

Prices:
C-M Matte	$4064.00
Std. Polish	4414.00
Stainless Steel Matte	4194.00

ALASKAN RIFLE (Not Shown)

Features stainless steel or chrome-moly Apollo action with black, woodland, or Artic camo stock; scope mount only. **Calibers:** .300 Magnum to .458 Win. Mag. **Barrel length:** 24″–26″ (Contours #4 to #7 C-M, #4 to #7 S.S.)
Prices:
C-M Matte	$3315.00
Std. Polish	3665.00
Stainless Steel	3445.00

ALASKAN SYNTHETIC RIFLE (Not Shown)

Same as above but with fibergrain stock; scope mounts or Express sights optional. **Calibers:** .257 to .338 Magnum.
Prices:
C-M Matte	$4110.00
Std. Polish	4460.00
Stainless Steel Matte	4240.00

GRAND ALASKAN (Not Shown)

Same as above but with AAA fancy select or Exhibition grade English walnut, barrel band and ebony forend; Express sights & scope mount standard. **Calibers:** .300 Magnum to .458 Win. Mag.
Prices:
"AAA" Grade Select English Walnut
C-M Matte	$6667.00
Std. Polish	7017.00
Stainless Steel Matte	6797.00

"Exhibition" Grade, Extra Fancy Select English Walnut
C-M Matte	$7594.00
Std. Polish	7944.00
Hi-Luster	8219.00
Stainless Steel Matte	7724.00

ALASKAN GUIDE (Not Shown)

Same as above but with choice of either "A" English walnut or snythetic stock; scope mount only. **Calibers:** .257 to .338 Magnum. **Barrel length:** 22″–26″ depending on caliber (Contours #4 to #6 C-M, #4 to #6 S.S.)
Prices:
C-M Matte	$5031.00
Std. Polish	5381.00
Stainless Steel Matte	5161.00

RIFLES

A-SQUARE RIFLES

**CAESAR MODEL (416 Hoffman)
w/2x7 Variable Scope and
3-Leaf Express Sights**

**CAESAR MODEL (Left Hand)
$2995.00**

SPECIFICATIONS
Calibers: 7mm Rem. Mag., 7mm STW, 300 Win. Mag., 300 Wby. Mag., 8mm Rem. Mag., 338 Win. Mag., 340 Wby. Mag., 338 A-Square Mag., 358 Norma, 358 STA, 9.3×64mm, 375 H&H, 375 Weatherby, 375 JRS, 375 A-Square Mag., 416 Taylor, 416 Hoffman, 416 Rem. Mag., 404 Jeffery, 425 Express, 458 Win. Mag., 458 Lott, 450 Ackley Mag., 460 Short A-Square, 470 Capstick and 495 A-Square Mag.
Features: Selected Claro walnut stock with oil finish; three-position safety; three-way adjustable target trigger; flush detachable swivels; leather sling; dual recoil lugs; coil spring ejector; ventilated recoil pad; premium honed barrels; contoured ejection port

**HANNIBAL MODEL (416 Rigby)
w/2xLER Scope and 3-Leaf
Express Sights**

**HANNIBAL MODEL
$2995.00**

SPECIFICATIONS
Calibers: 300 Pegasus, 8mm Rem. Mag., 338 Win., 340 Wby., 338 A-Square Mag., 338 Excalibur, 358 Norma Mag., 358 STA, 9.3×64, 375 A-Square, 375 JRS, 375 H&H, 375 Wby., 378 Wby., 404 Jeffery, 416 Hoffman, 416 Rem., 416 Rigby, 416 Taylor, 416 Wby., 425 Express, 450 Ackley, 458 Lott, 458 Win., 460 Short A-Square, 460 Weatherby, 470 Capstick, 495 A-Square, 500 A-Square, 577 Tyrannosaur

Barrel lengths: 20″ to 26″
Length of pull: 12″ to 15¼″
Finish: Deluxe walnut stock; oil finish; matte blue
Features: Flush detachable swivels, leather sling, dual recoil lugs, coil spring ejector, ventilated recoil pad, premium honed barrels, contoured ejection port, three-way adjustable target-style trigger, Mauser-style claw extractor and controlled feed, positive safety

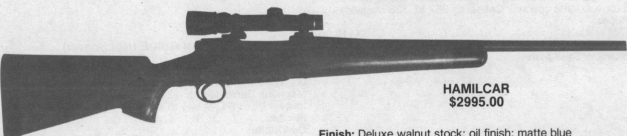

**HAMILCAR
$2995.00**

Finish: Deluxe walnut stock; oil finish; matte blue
Features: Flush detachable swivels; leather sling, coil spring ejector, vent. recoil pad; honed barrels; contoured ejection port; target-style adjustable trigger; Mauser-style claw extractor; controlled feed; positive safety
Also available:
GENGHIS KHAN MODEL in 22-250, 243 Win., 25 Souper, 6mm Rem., 25-06, 257 Wby., 6.5-06, 6.5-08, 264 Win. Features benchrest-quality heavy taper barrel and coil-chek stock. **Price:** **$2895.00**

SPECIFICATIONS
Calibers: 25-06, 257 Wby., 6.5×55 Swedish, 6.5-06, 264 Win., 270 Win., 270 Wby., 7×57 Mauser, 280 Rem., 7mm Rem., 7mm Wby., 7mm STW, 30-06, 300 Win., 300 Wby., 338-06, 9.3×62
Barrel lengths: 20″ to 26″
Length of pull: 12″ to 15¼″

AUTO-ORDNANCE

SEMIAUTOMATIC RIFLES

THOMPSON MODEL M1 CARBINE
$772.50

SPECIFICATIONS
Caliber: 45 ACP
Barrel length: 16½"   **Overall length:** 38"
Weight: 11½ lbs.
Sights: Blade front; fixed rear
Stock: Walnut stock and horizontal foregrip
Features: Side cocking lever; frame and receiver milled from solid steel

THOMPSON DELUXE MODEL 1927 A1
$795.00 (45 Cal.)

SPECIFICATIONS
Caliber: 45 ACP
Barrel length: 16½"   **Overall length:** 41"
Weight: 13 lbs.
Sights: Blade front; open rear adjustable
Stock: Walnut stock; vertical foregrip

Also available:
THOMPSON 1927A1C LIGHTWEIGHT (45 cal.). Same as the 1927A1 model, but weighs only 9½ lbs. **Price:** **$767.00**

VIOLIN CARRYING CASE (for gun, drum & extra magazines) $112.75

BLASER RIFLES

MODEL R 93

MODEL R 93 BOLT ACTION

SPECIFICATIONS
Calibers: (interchangeable)
   Standard: 22-250, 243 Win., 270 Win., 30-06, 308 Win.
   Magnum: 257 Weatherby Mag., 264 Win. Mag., 7mm Rem.
      Mag., 300 Win. Mag., 300 Wby. Mag., 338 Win.
      Mag., 375 H&H, 416 Rem. Mag.
   Varmint: 222 Rem., 223
Barrel lengths: 22″ (Standard) and 24″ (Magnum)
Overall length: 40″ (Standard) and 42″ (Magnum)
Weight: (w/scope mounts) 7 lbs. (Standard) and 7¼ lbs.
   (Magnum)
Safety: Cocking slide
Stock: Two-piece Turkish walnut stock and forend; solid black
   recoil pad, hand-cut checkering (18 lines/inch, borderless)

Length of pull: 13¾″
Prices:
Standard Model $2800.00
Interchangeable barrels 550.00
Deluxe Model 3100.00
Super Deluxe Model 3500.00

Also available:
Safari Model. 375 H&H and 416 Rem. Mag. only. 24″ heavy
barrel (42″ overall); open sights. **Weight:** 9½ lbs. **$3300.00**

BRNO RIFLES

MODEL ZKM 611

MODEL ZKM 611
$569.00

This premium semiautomatic rifle in 22 WMR caliber features
a hammer-forged barrel, 6-round magazine, checkered walnut
stock and forend, single thumb-screw takedown, and a
grooved receiver for scope mounting. The rear sight is mid-
mounted and the front sight is hooded. The action has a lightweight precision spring and large bolt to improve accuracy
while practically eliminating felt recoil. Beechwood stock available: **$499.00.**

SPECIFICATIONS
Caliber: 22 WMR
Capacity: 6 rounds
Barrel length: 20″
Overall length: 37″
Weight: 6 lbs. 2 oz.
Features: High cheekpiece stock; sling swivels; quick-detach
   magazine

BROWN PRECISION RIFLES

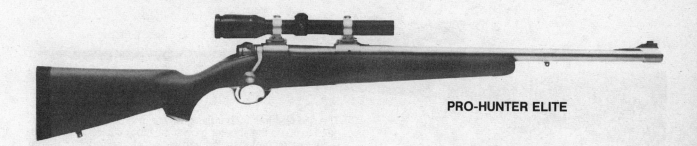

PRO-HUNTER ELITE

PRO-HUNTER ELITE

Designed for the serious game hunter or guide, this version of Brown Precision's Pro-Hunter rifle is custom built, utilizing standard features and equipment. The rifle begins as a Winchester Model 70 Super Grade action with controlled feed claw extractor. The action is finely tuned for smooth operation, and a Speedlock firing-pin spring is installed. The trigger is tuned to crisp let-off at each customer's specified weight. A Shilen Match Grade stainless-steel barrel is custom crowned at the desired barrel length and hand-fitted to the action. A barrel band front QD sling swivel is attached permanently to the barrel.

The Pro-Hunter Elite features the customer's choice of express rear sight or custom Dave Talley removable peep sight and banded front ramp sight with European dovetail and replaceable brass bead. An optional flip-up white night sight is also available, as is a set of Dave Talley detachable T.N.T.

scope mount rings and bases installed with Brown's Magnum Duty 8×40 screws.

All metal parts are finished in either matte electroless nickel or black Teflon. The barreled action is glass bedded to a custom Brown Precision fiberglass stock. Brown's Alaskan configuration stock features a Dave Talley trapdoor grip cap designed to carry the rear peep sight and/or replacement front sight beads. A premium 1″ recoil-reducing buttpad is installed, and the stock painted according to customer choice. Weight ranges from 7 to 15 lbs., depending on barrel length, coutour and options.

Optional equipment includes custom steel drop box magazine, KDF or Answer System muzzle brake, Mag-Na-Port, Zeiss, Swarovski or Leupold scope and Americase aluminum hard case.
Price: **$3565.00**

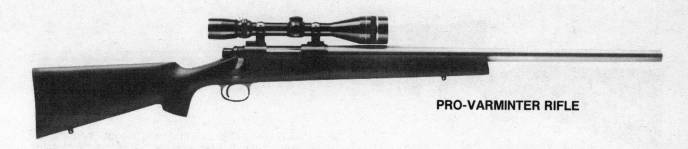

PRO-VARMINTER RIFLE

PRO-VARMINTER RIFLE

The standard Pro-Varminter is built on the Remington 700 or Remington 40X action (right or left hand) and features a hand-fitted Shilen Match Grade Heavy Benchrest stainless-steel barrel in bright or bead-blasted finish. The barreled action is custom-bedded in Brown Precision's Varmint Special Hunter Bench or 40X Benchrest-style custom fiberglass, Kevlar or graphite stock.

Other standard features include custom barrel length and

contour, trigger tuned for crisp pull to customer's specified weight, custom length of pull, and choice of recoil pad. Additional options include metal finishes, muzzle brakes, Leupold target or varmint scopes and others.
Prices:
Right-hand Model 700 Action **$1965.00**
For Left-hand Model, **add** **120.00**
40X Action **2450.00**

BROWN PRECISION RIFLES

HIGH COUNTRY YOUTH RIFLE

This custom rifle has all the same features as the standard High Country rifle, but scaled-down to fit the younger or smaller shooter. Based on the Remington Model 7 barreled action, it is available in calibers .223, .243, 7mm-08, 6mm and .308.

The rifle features a fiberglass, Kevlar or graphite stock shortened to fit. As the shooter grows, the stock can be lengthened, a new recoil pad installed and the stock refinished. Custom features and options include choice of actions, custom barrels, chamberings, muzzle brakes, metal finishes, scopes and accessories.

All Youth Rifles include a deluxe package of shooting, reloading and hunting accessories and information to increase a young shooter's interest.
Price: starts at **$1340.00**

TACTICAL ELITE RIFLE

Brown Precision's Tactical Elite is built on a Remington 700 action and features a bead-blasted Shilen Select Match Grade Heavy Benchrest Stainless Steel barrel custom-chambered for .223 Remington, .308 Winchester, .300 Winchester Magnum (or any standard or wildcat caliber). A nonreflective custom black Teflon metal finish on all metal surfaces ensures smooth bolt operation and 100 percent weatherproofing. The barreled

action is bedded in a target-style stock with high rollover comb/cheekpiece, vertical pistol grip and palmswell. The stock is an advanced, custom fiberglass/Kevlar/graphite composite for maximum durability and rigidity. QD sling swivel studs and swivels are included on the stock. Standard stock paint color is flat black (camouflage patterns are also available).

Other standard features include: three-way adjustable buttplate/recoil pad assembly with length of pull, vertical and cant angle adjustments, custom barrel length and contour, and trigger tuned for a crisp pull to customer's specifications. Options include muzzle brakes, Leupold or Kahles police scopes, and others, and are priced accordingly.
Price: **$2750.00**

CUSTOM TEAM CHALLENGER

This custom rifle was designed for use in the Chevy Trucks Sportsman's Team Challenge shooting event. It's also used in metallic silhouette competition as well as in the field for small game and varmints. Custom built on the Ruger 10/22 semiautomatic rimfire action, which features an extended magazine release, a simplified bolt release and finely tuned trigger, this rifle is fitted with either a Brown Precision fiberglass or Kevlar stock with custom length of pull up to 15″. The stock

can be shortened at the butt and later relengthened and repainted to accommodate growing youth shooters. Stock color is also optional. To facilitate shooting with scopes, including large objective target or varmint scopes, the lightweight stock is of classic styling with a high comb. The absence of a cheekpiece accommodates either right- or left-handed shooters, while the stock's flat-bottom, 1³/₄″-wide forearm ensures maximum comfort in both offhand and rest shooting. Barrels are custom-length Shilen Match Grade .920″ diameter straight or lightweight tapered.

Prices:

With blued action/barrel	**$ 975.00**
With blued action/stainless barrel	1050.00
With stainless action/stainless barrel	1095.00

BROWNING RIFLES

MODEL BL-22 LEVER-ACTION RIFLE
GRADE II $376.95 ($329.95 GRADE I)

RIMFIRE RIFLE SPECIFICATIONS

Model	Caliber	Barrel Length	Sight Radius	Overall Length	Average Weight	Prices
A-Bolt 22 Mag Gr. I	22 WMR	22″	—	40¼″	5 lbs. 4 oz.	$492.95
A-Bolt 22 Mag Gr. I w/sights	22 WMR	22″	17⅝″	40¼″	5 lbs. 4 oz.	503.95
A-Bolt 22 Gold Medallion[1]	22 Long Rifle	22″	—	40¼″	5 lbs. 4 oz.	566.95
A-Bolt 22 Grade I	22 Long Rifle	22″	—	40¼″	5 lbs. 4 oz.	424.95
A-Bolt 22 Gr. I w/sights	22 Long Rifle	22″	17⅝″	40¼″	5 lbs. 4 oz.	438.95
Semi-Auto 22 Grade I & Grade VI	22 Long Rifle	19¼″	16¼″	37″	4 lbs. 12 oz.	398.95*
BL-22 Grade I & Grade II	22 Long Rifle, Long, Short	20″	15⅞″	36¾″	5 lbs.	395.95

[1] No sight models only.   * $819.00 Grade VI

STOCK DIMENSIONS

	Semi-Auto	BL-22	A-Bolt 22
Length of Pull	13 3/4"	13 1/2"	13 3/4"
Drop at Comb	1 3/16"	5/8"	3/4"
Drop at Heel	2 5/8"	2 1/4"	1 1/2"

GRADE VI ENGRAVED
(24-Karat Gold Plated)

22 SEMIAUTOMATIC RIMFIRE RIFLES
GRADES I AND VI

SPECIFICATIONS (See also table above)
Safety: Cross-bolt type. **Capacity:** 11 cartridges in magazine, 1 chamber. **Trigger:** Grade I is blued; Grade VI is gold colored.
Sights: Gold bead front, adjustable folding leaf ear; drilled and tapped for Browning scope mounts.
Stock & Forearm: Grade I, select walnut with checkering (18 lines/inch); Grade VI, high-grade walnut with checkering (22 lines/inch). See table above for prices.

BROWNING RIFLES

**MODEL 1885 LOW WALL RIFLE
$939.95 (High & Low Wall Models)**

SPECIFICATIONS MODEL 1885 LOW WALL or HIGH WALL

Calibers	Barrel Length	Sight Radius	Overall Length	Approximate Weight	Rate of Twist (R. Hand)
High Wall					
22-250 Rem.	28"	—	43 1/2"	8 lbs. 13 oz.	1 in 14"
270 Win.	28"	—	43 1/2"	8 lbs. 12 oz.	1 in 10"
30-06 Sprg.	28"	—	43 1/2"	8 lbs. 12 oz.	1 in 10"
7mm Rem. Mag.	28"	—	43 1/2"	8 lbs. 11 oz.	1 in 9½"
45-70 Govt.	28"	21 1/2"	431/2"	8 lbs. 14 oz.	1 in 20"
Low Wall					
22 Hornet	24"	—	39 1/2"	6 lbs. 4 oz.	1 in 16"
223 Rem.	24"	—	39 1/2"	6 lbs. 4 oz.	1 in 12"
243 Win.	24"	—	39 1/2"	6 lbs. 4 oz.	1 in 10"

**MODEL 1885 BPCR
(BLACK POWDER CARTRIDGE RIFLE)
$1664.95**

Calibers: 40-65, 45-70 Govt. **Barrel length:** 30″. **Overall length:** 46⅛″. **Sight radius:** 34″. **Weight:** 11 lbs. (45-70 Govt.); 11 lbs. 7 oz. (40-65). **Rate of twist:** 1 in 16″ (R.H.).

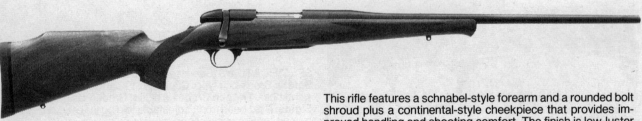

**A-BOLT II EURO-BOLT
$823.95 (No Sights) $921.95 (w/BOSS)**

This rifle features a schnabel-style forearm and a rounded bolt shroud plus a continental-style cheekpiece that provides improved handling and shooting comfort. The finish is low-luster blued and satin-finished walnut. **Calibers:** 243 Win., 30-06, 308 Win. and 7mm Rem. Mag. No Sights. See table on following page for additional specifications and A-Bolt II models.

BROWNING RIFLES

**A-BOLT II BOLT-ACTION
CENTERFIRE RIFLES**

BOSS (Ballistic Optimizing Shooting System) is now optional on all A-Bolt II models (except standard on Varmint). BOSS adjusts barrel vibrations to allow a bullet to leave the rifle muzzle at the most advantageous point in the barrel oscillation, thereby fine-tuning accuracy with any brand of ammunition regardless of caliber.

Scopes: Closed. Clean tapered barrel. Receiver is drilled and tapped for a scope mount; or select **Hunter** model has open sights.

A-BOLT II SPECIFICATIONS (See following page for additional prices)

Caliber	Twist (R. Hand)	Magazine Capacity	Hunter	Gold Medal.	Medal.	Micro-Medal.	Stainless Stalker	Comp. Stalker	Varmint	Eclipse
LONG ACTION MAGNUM CALIBERS										
375 H&H	1 in 12"	3			●		●			
338 Win. Mag.	1 in 10"	3	●		●		●	●		
300 Win. Mag.	1 in 10"	3	●	●	●		●	●		
7mm Rem. Mag.	1 in 9 1/2"	3	●	●	●		●	●		●
LONG ACTION STANDARD CALIBERS										
25-06 Rem.	1 in 10"	4	●	●	●		●	●		●
270 Win.	1 in 10"	4	●	●	●		●	●		●
280 Rem.	1 in 10"	4	●		●		●	●		
30-06 Sprg.	1 in 10"	4	●	●	●		●	●		●
SHORT ACTION CALIBERS										
243 Win.	1 in 10"	4	●		●	●	●	●		
308 Win.	1 in 12"	4	●		●	●	●	●	●	●▼
7mm-08 Rem.	1 in 9 1/2"	4	●		●	●	●	●		
22-250 Rem.	1 in 14"	4	●		●	●	●	●	●	●▼
223 Rem.	1 in 12"	6*	●		●	●	●	●	●	▼
22 Hornet	1 in 16"	4				●				

* Magazine capacity of 223 Rem. models is up to 5 rounds on Micro-Medallion (up to 6 on other models).
▼ = Also available in Varmint version of new Eclipse.

A-BOLT II GEN. DIMENSIONS

Length	Overall Length	Barrel	Sight Radius*
Long Action Mag. Cal.	46 3/4"	26"	18"
Long Action Std. Cal.	42 3/4"	22"	18"
Short Action Cal.	41 3/4"	22"	16"
Micro-Medallion	39 9/16"	20"***	—
Varmint Models	44 1/2"	26"	—

*Open sights available on A-Bolt Hunter and all models in 375 H&H.
**22 Hornet Micro-Medallion has a 22" barrel.
BOSS equipped rifles have the same dimensions.

A-BOLT II AVG. WEIGHT

Model	Long Action Magnum Calibers	Long Action Standard Calibers	Short Action Calibers
Composite/ Stainless Steel	7 lbs. 3 oz.	6 lbs. 11 oz.	6 lbs. 4 oz.
Micro-Medallion			6 lbs. 1 oz.
Gold Medallion	7 lbs. 11 oz.	7 lbs. 3 oz.	
Medallion & Hunter	7 lbs. 3 oz.	6 lbs. 11 oz.	6 lbs. 7 oz.
Varmint			9 lbs.
Eclipse	8 lbs.	7 lbs. 8 oz.	7 lbs. 10 oz.
Eclipse Varmint			9 lbs. 1 oz.

A-BOLT II STOCK DIMENSIONS

	Micro-Med.	Gold Med.	Hunter	Varmint	Stalker	Eclipse
Length of Pull	13 5/16"	13 5/8"	13 5/8"	13 3/4"	13 5/8"	14"
Drop at Comb	3/4"	3/4"-1"	3/4"	9/16"	5/8"	7/16"
Drop at Heel	1 1/8"	1 3/4"	1 1/8"	7/16"	1/2"	1 1/16"

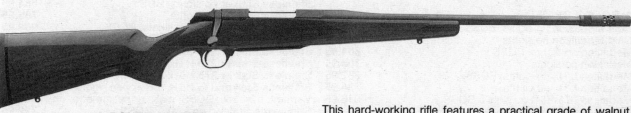

**A-BOLT II HUNTER
$703.95 (w/BOSS, No Sights)
$605.95 (No Sights)**

This hard-working rifle features a practical grade of walnut and low-luster bluing ideal for rugged conditions. Includes the standard A-Bolt II fast-cycling bolt, crisp trigger, calibrated rear sights and ramp-style front sights. Optional BOSS.

BROWNING RIFLES

A-BOLT II ECLIPSE VARMINT

NEW A-BOLT II ECLIPSE MODELS WITH THUMBHOLE STOCK

Some of the most advanced, specialized developments of the A-Bolt II have evolved into the new A-Bolt II Eclipse Series. Each rifle is fitted with a newly designed thumbhole stock configuration. To hold accuracy under changing humidity and pre-cipitation conditions the stock itself is crafted from rugged gray/black, multi-laminated hardwood. This gives the Eclipse a camouflaged look. The custom thumbhole-style stock provides a solid grip and secure feel that adds up to accuracy. The Eclipse is available in two versions: long and short action hunting model with standard A-Bolt II barrel, and a short action varmint version with a heavy barrel. All are BOSS equipped.

A-BOLT II STAINLESS STALKER

The barrel, receiver and bolt are machined from solid stainless steel for a high level of corrosion and rust resistance and also to prolong the life of the rifle bore. The advanced graphite-fiberglass composite stock shrugs off wet weather and rough handling and isn't affected by humidity. A palm swell on both right- and left-hand models offers a better grip. A lower comb directs recoil away from the face. Barrel, receiver and stock have a durable matte finish. The BOSS is optional in all calibers.

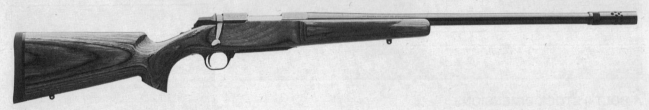

A-BOLT II VARMINT

The A-bolt II Varmint's heavy varmint/target-style barrel provides a steady hold and is less affected by breathing, cross winds and barrel vibrations. A flat forend provides a solid con-tact surface on a sandbag or bench. A palm swell helps position the hand and trigger finger. The laminated wood stock is stronger and less likely to warp than walnut. All Varmint Models are equipped with the BOSS accuracy device. Available with a satin or high-gloss finish.

A-BOLT II SERIES	Prices
Gold Medallion no sights, BOSS	$1047.95
Gold Medallion no sights	949.95
Medallion no sights, BOSS	804.95
Medallion no sights	706.95
Medallion L.H., no sights, BOSS	832.95
Medallion L.H., no sights	734.95
Medallion 375 H&H no sights, BOSS	916.95
Medallion 375 H&H open sights	818.95
Medallion 375 H&H L.H., no sights, BOSS	944.95
Medallion 375 H&H L.H., open sights	846.95
Micro Medallion no sights	706.95

A-BOLT II SERIES	Prices
Stainless Stalker no sights, BOSS	$ 884.95
Stainless Stalker no sights	786.95
Stainless Stalker L.H., no sights, BOSS	909.95
Stainless Stalker L.H., no sights	811.95
Stainless Stalker 375 H&H, BOSS	993.95
Stainless Stalker 375 H&H, open sights	895.95
Stainless Stalker 375 H&H, L.H., BOSS	1021.95
Stainless Stalker 375 H&H, L.H., open sights	811.95
Varmint, hvy. bbl., BOSS, gloss or satin/matte	939.95
Composite Stalker, no sights, BOSS	722.95
Composite Stalker, no sights	624.95
Eclipse no sights, BOSS	1024.95
Eclipse Varmint no sights, BOSS	1054.95

BROWNING RIFLES

LIGHTNING BLR
$576.95 (Short Action)
$608.95 (Long Action)

LIGHTNING BLR SPECIFICATIONS

Calibers	Barrel Length	Magazine Capacity[1]	Sight Radius	Overall Length	Approximate Weight	Rate of Twist (R. Hand)
Long Action Calibers						
270 Win.	22"	4	17 3/4"	42 7/8"	7 lbs. 4 oz.	1 in 10"
30-06 Sprg.	22"	4	17 3/4"	42 7/8"	7 lbs. 4 oz.	1 in 10"
7mm Rem. Magnum	24"	3	19 3/4"	44 7/8"	7 lbs. 12 oz.	1 in 9 1/2"
Short Action Calibers						
223 Rem.	20"	5	17 3/4"	39 1/2"	6 lbs. 8 oz.	1 in 12"
22-250 Rem.	20"	4	17 3/4"	39 1/2"	6 lbs. 8 oz.	1 in 14"
243 Win.	20"	4	17 3/4"	39 1/2"	6 lbs. 8 oz.	1 in 10"
7mm-08 Rem.	20"	4	17 3/4"	39 1/2"	6 lbs. 8 oz.	1 in 9 1/2"
308 Win.	20"	4	17 3/4"	39 1/2"	6 lbs. 8 oz.	1 in 12"

[1]Number of cartridges the magazine holds when locked in the rifle with the bolt closed. The maximum magazine capacity can vary when outside of the rifle.

BAR MARK II SAFARI

BAR MARK II SAFARI SEMIAUTOMATIC RIFLES

The BAR has been upgraded to include an engraved receiver, a redesigned bolt release, new gas and buffeting systems, and a removable trigger assembly. Additional features include: crossbolt safety with enlarged head; hinged floorplate, 4-shot capacity in Standard models (1 in chamber); gold trigger; select walnut stock and forearm with cut-checkering and swivel studs; 13¾" length of pull; 2" drop at heel; 1⅝" drop at comb; and a recoil pad (magnum calibers only).

SPECIFICATIONS BAR MARK II SAFARI

Model	Calibers	Magazine Capacity	Barrel Length	Sight Radius*	Overall Length	Average Weight	Rate of Twist (Right Hand)
Magnum	338 Win. Mag.	3	24"	19 1/2"	45"	8 lbs. 6 oz.	1 in 12"
Magnum	300 Win Mag.	3	24"	19 1/2"	45"	8 lbs. 6 oz.	1 in 9 1/2"
Magnum	7mm Rem Mag.	3	24"	19 1/2"	45"	8 lbs. 6 oz.	1 in 9 1/2"
Standard	30-06 Sprg.	4	22"	17 1/2"	43"	7 lbs. 6 oz.	1 in 9 1/2"
Standard	270 Win.	4	22"	17 1/2"	43"	7 lbs. 9 oz.	1 in 9 1/2"
Standard	308 Win.	4	22"	17 1/2"	43"	7 lbs. 9 oz.	1 in 12"
Standard	243 Win.	4	22"	17 1/2"	43"	7 lbs. 10 oz.	1 in 9 1/2"

Non-BOSS models are available with or without open sights. All models drilled and tapped for scope mounts. BOSS-equipped BAR's not available with open sights.

BAR Mark II specifications are the same with or without the BOSS, except the 338 Win. Mag. which is 5 1/2 ozs. heavier and has a 26" barrel.

BAR MARK II SAFARI	Prices
Standard Calibers	
No sights, BOSS	$811.95
Open sights, no BOSS	729.95
No sights, no BOSS	713.95
Magnum Calibers	
No sights, BOSS	863.95
Open sights	765.95
No sights, no BOSS	781.95

CLIFTON ARMS

SCOUT RIFLE
$3100.00

Several years ago, in response to Colonel Jeff Cooper's concept of an all-purpose rifle, which he calls the "Scout Rifle," Clifton Arms developed the integral, retractable bipod and its accompanying state-of-the-art composite stock. Further development resulted in an integral butt magazine well for storage of cartridges inside the buttstock. These and other components make up the Clifton Scout Rifle.

SPECIFICATIONS
Calibers: 30-06, 308, 35 Whelen, 416 Rem.
Barrel length: 19″ to 22″ (longer or shorter lengths available; made with Shilen stainless premium match-grade steel)
Weight: 7 to 8 lbs.
Sights: Forward-mounted Burris 2³/₄X Scout Scope attached to integral scope base pedestals machined in the barrel; Warne rings; reserve iron sight is square post dovetailed into a ramp integral to the barrel, plus a large aperture "ghost ring" mounted on the receiver bridge.
Features: Standard action is Ruger 77 MKII stainless; metal finish options include Poly-T, NP3 and chrome sulphide; left-handed rifles available.

COLT RIFLES

LIGHTWEIGHTS
$987.00

The Colt Match Target Lightweight semiautomatic rifle fires from a closed bolt, is easy to load and unload, and has a buttstock and pistol grip made of tough nylon. A round, ribbed handguard is fiberglass-reinforced to ensure better grip control. **Calibers:** 223 Rem., 7.62×39mm and 9mm. **Barrel length:** 16″. **Overall length:** 34¹/₂″ (35¹/₂″ in 7.62×39mm). **Weight:** 7.1 lbs. (9mm). **Capacity:** 5 rounds (7.62×39mm); 8 rounds (223 Rem. and 9mm).

MATCH TARGET RIFLES

The Colt Target and H-Bar rifles are range-selected for top accuracy. They have a 3-9x rubber armored variable-power

scope mount, carry handle with iron sight, Cordura nylon case and other accessories. **Caliber:** 223 Rem. **Barrel length:** 20″ (16″ H-BAR II). **O.A. length:** 39″ (34.5″ H-BAR II). **Weight:** 8.5 lbs. (Competition/Match H-Bar); 8 lbs. (Target H-BAR); 7.5 lbs. (Target); 7.1 lbs. (H-Bar II). **Capacity:** 8 rounds.
Prices:

MATCH TARGET	$1019.00
MATCH TARGET H-BAR	1067.00
COMPETITION H-BAR	1073.00
COMPETITION H-BAR II	1044.00

COOPER ARMS RIFLES

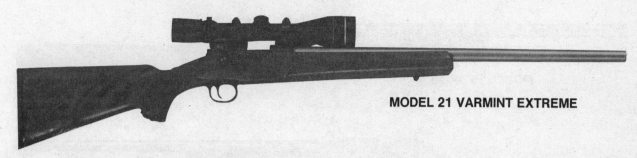

MODEL 21 VARMINT EXTREME

MODEL 21 VARMINT EXTREME

SPECIFICATIONS
Calibers: 17 Rem., 17 Mach IV, 221 Fireball, 222 Rem., 222 Rem. Mag., 22 PPC, 223
Barrel length: 24″
Stock: AAA Claro walnut; flared oval forearm
Other specifications same as Model 36 RF.
Price **$1675.00**

Also available:
MODEL 21 BENCHREST. Same as above, but in 223 and 22 PPC only; competition step crown and match chamber, chrome-moly barrel. **$2140.00**
MODEL 21 CUSTOM CLASSIC 1960.00

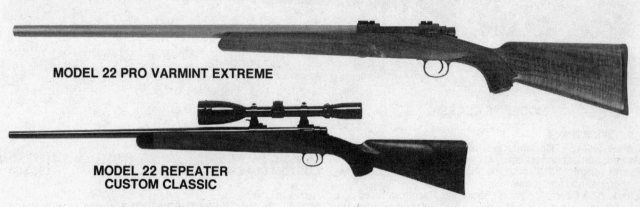

MODEL 22 PRO VARMINT EXTREME

MODEL 22 REPEATER CUSTOM CLASSIC

MODEL 22 SINGLE SHOT PRO VARMINT EXTREME

SPECIFICATIONS
Calibers: 22-250, 220 Swift, 243, 25-06, 308, 6mm PPC
Capacity: Single shot
Barrel length: 24″
Action: 3 front locking lug; glass-bedded
Trigger: Single-stage Match, fully adjustable; Jewell 2-stage (optional)
Stock: McMillan black-textured synthetic, beaded, w/Monte Carlo cheekpiece; 4-panel checkering print; Pachmayr recoil pad

MODEL 22 SINGLE SHOT	Prices
PRO VARMINT EXTREME	**$1785.00**
BR-50 BENCH REST (w/Jewell Trigger)	2140.00
BLACK JACK (Synthetic Sporter)	1785.00

Also available:
MODEL 22 REPEATER. Calibers 22-250, 243, 7mm-08 and 308. Clip-fed 3-shot repeater w/23³/₄″ barrel. **Classic: $2400.00; Custom Classic: $2675.00.**

MODEL 22 BR-50 SINGLE SHOT

COOPER ARMS RIFLES

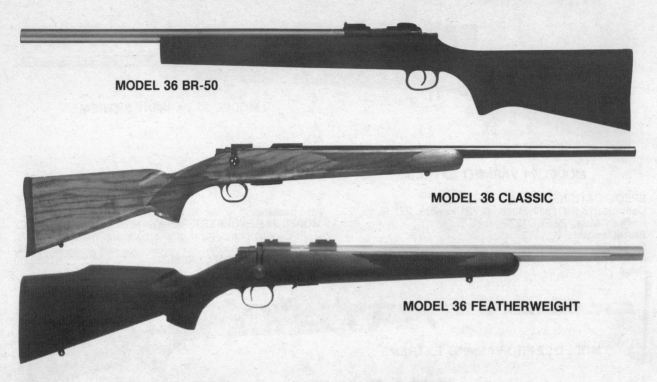

MODEL 36 BR-50

MODEL 36 CLASSIC

MODEL 36 FEATHERWEIGHT

MODEL 36 CLASSIC

SPECIFICATIONS
Caliber: 22 LR **Capacity:** 5-shot magazine
Action: bolt-action repeater
Barrel length: 23¾" (chrome moly); free-floated barrel w/ competition step crown
Stock: AAA Claro, side panel checkering, Pachmayr recoil pad, steel grip cap (Classic Model); AAA Claro, wraparound custom checkering, beaded cheekpiece, ebony tip, steel grip cap (Custom Classic)
Features: Glass-bedded adjustable trigger; bases and rings optional; 3 mid-locking lugs

Prices:
CLASSIC $1675.00
CUSTOM CLASSIC 1960.00

Also available:
MODEL 36 RF/CF FEATHERWEIGHT: Same specifications as Model 36 RF, but weighs 6½ lbs. **$1850.00**
MODEL 36 RF BR-50: Same specifications as Model 36 RF, but w/22" stainless steel bbl. 6.8 lbs. **1850.00**

MODEL 40 CUSTOM CLASSIC

MODEL 40 CUSTOM CLASSIC

SPECIFICATIONS
Calibers: 17 Ackley Hornet, 22 Hornet, 22K Hornet
Capacity: 4-shot clip
Action: 3 mid-locking lug, bolt-action repeater; glass-bedded
Barrel length: 23.75"
Trigger: Single-stage match, fully adjustable (Jewell two-stage optional)
Rate of twist: 1-in-14" (22 cal.); 1-in-10" (17 cal.)

Features: Chrome-moly Match-Grade barrel, free floated; competition step crown
Stock: Oil-finished AAA Claro walnut w/steel grip cap, Pachmayr recoil pad and 22-LPI borderless wraparound ribbon checkering
Prices:
CLASSIC $1825.00
CUSTOM CLASSIC 2025.00

CZ RIFLES

MODEL CZ527

MODEL CZ527
SPECIFICATIONS
Calibers: 22 Hornet, 222 Rem., 223 Rem.
Capacity: 5 rounds
Barrel length: 23.6″ (standard or heavy)

MODEL CZ527
Overall length: 42.4″
Weight: 6.2 lbs. (unloaded)
Sights: Open (grooved to accept scope)
Stock: Luxury sport stock w/cheekpiece
Features: Mauser-type bolt and non-rotating claw extractor; hammer-forged barrel; integral dovetail scope bases with recoil stop; detachable 5-round magazine; silent safety
Price: $629.00

MODEL CZ550
SPECIFICATIONS
Calibers: 243 Win., 270 Win., 30-06, 308 Win., 7mm Rem., 300 Win. Mag.
Capacity: 4 rounds

MODEL CZ550
Barrel length: 23.62″
Weight: 7.26 lbs.
Sights: None
Stock: High comb
Features: Single-set trigger; 3-position safety
Prices:
Standard $649.00
  With full stock 849.00
Magnum 679.00

MODEL ZKK602
SPECIFICATIONS
Calibers: 375 H&H, 416 Rem./Rigby and 458 Win. Mag.
Capacity: 4 rounds.

MODEL ZKK602
Barrel length: 25″.   **Overall length:** 45.28″.
Weight: 9.25 lbs.
Stock: Walnut   **Sight radius:** 19.5″
Sights: Open (grooved to accept scope mount)
Features: Single-stage trigger
Price: $799.00

MODEL ZKM452
SPECIFICATIONS
Calibers: 22 LR, 22 Win. Mag.
Capacity: 5 or 10 rounds (22 LR); 6 or 10 rounds (22 Win .Mag.)
Barrel length: 24.82″   **Overall length:** 42.64″

MODEL ZKM452 LUX
Weight: 6.56 lbs. (unloaded)
Sights: Mechanical sights; machined receiver for custom ring mounts
Stock: Beechwood (Standard); walnut (Lux)
Finish: Lacquer
Prices:
Standard Model 22 LR $299.00
  22 Win. Mag. 379.00
Lux Model 22 LR 329.00
  22 Win. Mag. 399.00

RIFLES

DAKOTA ARMS

DAKOTA 76 RIFLES

SPECIFICATIONS
Calibers:
   Safari Grade: 338 Win. Mag., 300 Win. Mag., 375 H&H Mag., 458 Win. Mag.

   Classic Grade: 22-250, 257 Roberts, 270 Win., 280 Rem., 30-06, 7mm Rem. Mag., 338 Win. Mag., 300 Win. Mag., 375 H&H Mag., 458 Win. Mag.

   African Grade: 404 Jeffery, 416 Dakota, 416 Rigby, 450 Dakota

   Varmint Grade: 22 Hornet, 22 PPC, 22-250, 220 Swift, 222 Rem. Mag., 223, 6mm PPC

Barrel lengths: 21″ or 23″ (Classic); 23″ only (Safari); 24″ (Varmint and African)

Weight: 7½ lbs. (Classic); 9½ lbs. (African); 8½ lbs. (Safari)

Safety: Three-position striker-blocking safety allows bolt operation with safety on

DAKOTA 76 AFRICAN GRADE

Sights: Ramp front sight; standing-leaf rear

Stock: Choice of X grade oil-finished English, Bastogne or Claro walnut (Classic); choice of XXX grade oil-finished English or Bastogne walnut w/ebony forent tip (Safari)

Prices:

Varmint Grade(semifancy walnut)	$2500.00
Classic Grade	2850.00
Safari Grade	3750.00
African Grade	4275.00
Barreled actions:	
Classic Grade	1950.00
Varmint Grade	1950.00
Safari Grade	2200.00
African Grade	2750.00
Actions:	
Classic Grade	1650.00
Varmint Grade	1650.00
Safari Grade	1750.00

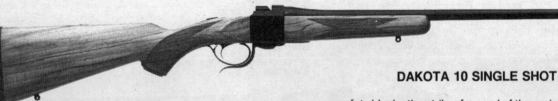

DAKOTA 10 SINGLE SHOT

SPECIFICATIONS
Calibers: Most rimmed/rimless commercially loaded types

Barrel length: 23″ **Overall length:** 39½″ **Weight:** 6 lbs.

Features: Receiver and rear of breech block are solid steel without cuts or holes for maximum lug area (approx. 8 times more bearing area than most bolt rifles); crisp, clean trigger pull; removable trigger plate allows action to adapt to single-set triggers; straight-line coil-spring action and short hammer fall combine for fast lock time; smooth, quiet top tang

safety blocks the striker forward of the main spring; strong, positive extractor and manual ejector adapted to rimmed/rimless cases. XX grade oil-finished English, Bastogne or Claro walnut stock.

Price:	$2900.00
Barreled actions	1950.00
Actions only	1650.00
Also available:	
DAKOTA 10 MAGNUM SINGLE SHOT	$3150.00
Barreled actions	1995.00
Actions only	1750.00

DAKOTA 22 LR SPORTER

SPECIFICATIONS
Calibers: 22 LR **Capacity:** 5-round clip

Barrel length: 22″ (chrome-moly, 1 turn in 16″)

Weight: 6½ lbs.

Stock: X Claro or English walnut with hand-cut checkering

Features: Plain bolt handle; swivels and single screw studs; ½-inch black pad; 13⁵/₈″ length of pull

Price:	$1795.00
Barreled actions	1200.00

EMF REPLICA RIFLES

1860 HENRY RIFLE
$1110.00

This lever-action rifle was patented by B. Tyler Henry and produced by the New Haven Arms Company, where Oliver Winchester was then president (he later gave his name to future models and the company itself). Production was developed between 1860 and 1865, with serial numbers 1 to 12000 (plus 2000 additional units in 1866, when the Winchester gun first appeared).

SPECIFICATIONS
Calibers: 44-40 and 45 LC
Barrel length: 24¼"; upper half-octagonal w/magazine tube in one-piece steel
Overall length: 43¾"   **Weight:** 9¼ lbs.
Stock: Varnished American walnut wood
Features: Polished brass frame; brass buttplate

MODEL 1866 YELLOW BOY RIFLE & CARBINE
$848.00 (Rifle) $825.00 (Carbine)

These exact reproductions of guns used over 100 years ago are available in 45 Long Colt, 38 Special and 44-40. Both carbine and rifle are offered with blued finish, walnut stock and brass frame.

MODEL 1873 SPORTING RIFLE
$1050.00

SPECIFICATIONS
Calibers: 357, 44-40, 45 Long Colt
Barrel length: 24¼" octagonal   **Overall length:** 43¼"
Weight: 8.16 lbs.
Features: Magazine tube in blued steel; frame is casehardened steel; stock and forend are walnut wood

Also available:
MODEL 1873 CARBINE. Same features as the 1873 Sporting Rifle, except in 45 Long Colt only with 19" barrel, overall length 38¼" and weight 7.38 lbs. **Price: $1050.00; $1050.00** Casehardened
MODEL 1873 SHORT RIFLE in 45 Long Colt, 20" barrel.
Price: **$1050.00**

REMINGTON ROLLING BLOCK CARBINE
$960.00

Includes walnut stock, brass trim, blued finish and casehardened frame.
Calibers: 45 Long Colt
Barrel length: 30", full octagonal
Overall length: 48"
Weight: 8 lbs.

EUROPEAN AMERICAN ARMORY

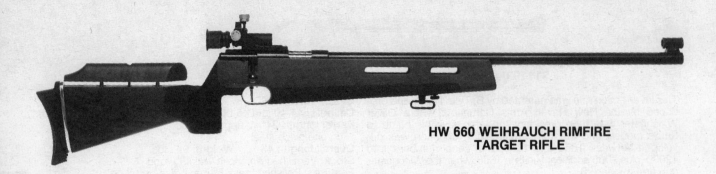

**HW 660 WEIHRAUCH RIMFIRE
TARGET RIFLE**

HW 660 WEIHRAUCH RIMFIRE
TARGET RIFLE (SINGLE SHOT)
$874.95

SPECIFICATIONS
Caliber: 22 LR
Barrel length: 26"   **Overall length:** 45.33"
Weight: 10.8 lbs.
Finish: Blue
Stock: European walnut w/adjustable black rubber buttplate
and comb

Features: Adjustable match trigger; left-handed stock available; aluminum adjustable sling swivel; adj. vertical and lateral cheekpiece; rear sight click-adjustable for windage and elevation; aluminum forend rail; polished feed ramp; external thumb safety

SABATTI MODEL SP1822

SABATTI MODEL SP1822H

SPECIFICATIONS
Caliber: 22 LR
Capacity: 10 rounds (detachable magazine)
Barrel length: 18 1/2"   **Overall length:** 37 1/2"
Weight: 7.15 lbs.   **Sights:** None

Features: Hammer-forged heavy non-tapered barrel; scope-mounted rail (no open sights); flush-mounted magazine release; alloy receiver w/non-glare finish; manual bolt lock; wide claw extractor; blowback action; cross-trigger safety
Price: **$204.95**

FRANCOTTE RIFLES

August Francotte rifles are available in all calibers for which barrels and chambers are made. All guns are custom made to the customer's specifications; there are no standard models. Most bolt-action rifles use commercial Mauser actions; however, the magnum action is produced by Francotte exclusively for its own production. Side-by-side and mountain rifles use either boxlock or sidelock action. Francotte system sidelocks are back-action type. Options include gold and silver inlay, special engraving and exhibition and museum grade wood. Francotte rifles are distributed in the U.S. by Armes de Chasse (see Directory of Manufacturers and Distributors for details).

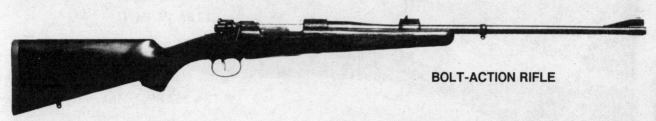

BOLT-ACTION RIFLE

SPECIFICATIONS
Calibers: 17 Bee, 7×64, 30-06, 270, 222R, 243W, 308W, 375 H&H, 416 Rigby, 460 Weatherby, 505 Gibbs
Barrel length: To customer's specifications
Weight: 8 to 12 lbs., or to customer's specifications
Stock: A wide selection of wood in all possible styles according to customer preferences; prices listed below do not include engraving or select wood
Engraving: Per customer specifications
Sights: All types of sights and scopes

BOLT-ACTION RIFLES
	Prices
Standard Bolt Action (30-06, 270, 7×64, etc.)	$7000.00
Short Bolt Action (222R, 243W, etc.)	8500.00
Magnum Action (300 WM, 338 WM, 375 H&H, 458 WM	8000.00

BOXLOCK SIDE-BY-SIDE DOUBLE RIFLES
	Prices
Std. boxlock double rifle (9.3×74R, 8×57JRS, 7×65R, etc.)	$14,000.00
Std. boxlock double (Magnum calibers)	19,000.00
Optional sideplates, **add**	1,400.00

SIDELOCK S/S DOUBLE RIFLES
Std. sidelock double rifle (9.3×74R, 8×57JRS, 7×65R, etc.)	$28,000.00
Std. sidelock double (Magnum calibers)	33,000.00
Special safari sidelock	**Price on request**

MOUNTAIN RIFLES
Standard boxlock	$12,000.00
Std. boxlock (Mag. & rimless calibers)	**Price on request**
Optional sideplates, **add**	1,400.00
Standard sidelock	25,000.00

MOUNTAIN RIFLE
w/Elaborate Engraving

HARRINGTON & RICHARDSON

ULTRA VARMINT

ULTRA 357 REM. MAX.

ULTRA SINGLE-SHOT RIFLES
$249.95

SPECIFICATIONS
Calibers: 223 Rem. (Varmint), 25-06, 308 Win. and 357 Rem. Max.
Action: Break-open; side lever release; positive ejection
Barrel length: 22" (308 Win., 357 Rem. Max.); 22" bull barrel (223 Rem. Varmint); 26" (25-06)
Weight: 7 to 8 lbs.
Sights: None (scope mount included)
Length of pull: 14¹⁄₄"
Drop at comb: 1¹⁄₄"   **Drop at heel:** 1¹⁄₈"

Forend: Semibeavertail
Stock: Monte Carlo; hand-checkered curly maple; Varmint model has light laminate stock
Features: Sling swivels on stock and forend; patented transfer bar safety; automatic ejection; hammer extension; rebated muzzle

Also available: **ULTRA HUNTER** w/Cinnamon Laminate Stock.
 Caliber: 25-06 (26" barrel); 308 Win. (22" barrel)

ROCKY MOUNTAIN ELK FOUNDATION COMMEMORATIVE (RMEF) RIFLE $269.95

Stock: Monte Carlo buttstock; American hardwood in cinnamon color impregnated w/dark brown laminate strip
Features: Heat-tested investment-cast steel frame; scope rail, sling swivel studs, premium recoil pad; RMEF medallion inlayed in stock; stock and forend carved, sanded and cut-checkered

SPECIFICATIONS
Caliber: 35 Whelen
Capacity: Single shot
Barrel length: 26"

WESSON & HARRINGTON BRAND 125th ANNIVERSARY RIFLE
$349.95

In 1871 Frank Wesson and Gilbert Harrington set about the manufacture of firearms in Worcester, MA. Now, 125 years have passed and H&R 1871, Inc. (owners of the current Wesson & Harrington trademark) celebrates the achievements of these important armsmakers with a limited edition rifle, cham-

bered for the 45-70 Government cartridge. This unique firearm will be made by craftspersons who share in one of the richest gunmaking heritages to remain in existence.

Based on the Wesson & Harrington Buffalo Classic rifle, this special 125th edition features a hand-engraved receiver and a full set of steel furniture. The barrel, highly polished blue, is 32 inches long and is dovetailed at the muzzle end. Stock and schnabel forend are of hand-checkered American black walnut. The exposed hammer action is color casehardened as is the crescent steel buttplate that is individually fitted. No sights are supplied. Wesson & Harrington™ brand firearms are manufactured by H&R 1871, Inc.; see Directory of Manufacturers for complete address.

HARRINGTON & RICHARDSON

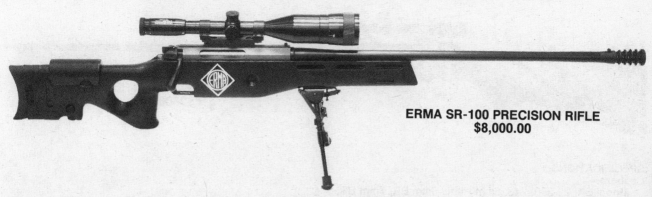

ERMA SR-100 PRECISION RIFLE
$8,000.00

The SR-100 is a box-fed, bolt-action rifle with a detachable magazine, a quick-detachable barrel and a fully adjustable tactical stock. The receiver is made of forged alloy consisting of two parts, with the lower section acting as a massive bedding block. Lock-up strength is assured because the bolt lugs lock into the barrel and not the receiver, ensuring strength and extra precise headspace. The trigger assembly is fully adjustable for take-up, weight of pull, length of pull, preload and overtravel.

SPECIFICATIONS
Calibers: 308 Win., 300 Win. Mag., 338 Lapua Mag.
Capacity: 10 shots (308 Win.); 8 shots (300 Win. Mag); 5 shots (308 Lapua Mag.)
Barrel length: 25.35″ (.308 Win.); 29.25″ (300 Win., 338 Lapua Mag.)
Twist: 1:12″ (308 Win.); 1:10″ (300 Win. Mag., 338 Lapua Mag.)
No. of grooves: 4 (308 Win.); 6 (300 Win. Mag., 308 Lapua Mag.)
Overall length: 49″ (.308 Win.); 53″ (300 Win. Mag., 338 Lapua Mag.)
Weight: 7 lbs. (308 Win.); 7.5 lbs. (300 Win. Mag., 338 Lapua Mag.)

HARRIS GUNWORKS RIFLES

SAFARI
$3663.00 (Magnum)
TALON SAFARI $3963.00 (Super Magnum)

SPECIFICATIONS
Calibers:
   Magnum: 300 Win. Mag., 300 Weatherby, 300 H&H, 338 Win. Mag., 340 Weatherby, 375 H&H, 404 Jeffrey, 416 Rem., 458 Win.
   Super Magnum: 300 Phoenix, 338 Lapua, 378 Wby., 416 Rigby, 416 Wby., 460 Wby.

Other specifications same as the Classic Sporter, except for match-grade barrel, positive extraction Harris Safari action, quick detachable 1″ scope mounts, positive locking steel floorplate, multi-leaf express sights, barrel band ramp front sight, barrel band swivels, and Harris Safari stock.

HARRIS BENCHREST RIFLE
$2600.00 (not shown)

SPECIFICATIONS
Calibers: 6mm PPC, 243, 6mm BR, 6mm Rem., 308
Built to individual specifications to be competitive in hunter, light varmint and heavy varmint classes. Features solid bottom or repeating bolt action, Canjar trigger, fiberglass stock with recoil pad, stainless steel match-grade barrel and reloading dies. Right- or left-hand models.

HARRIS GUNWORKS RIFLES

CLASSIC SPORTER
$2600.00

SPECIFICATIONS
Calibers:
   Model SA: 22-250, 243, 6mm Rem., 6mm BR, 7mm BR, 7mm-08, 284, 308, 350 Rem. Mag.
   Model LA: 25-06, 270, 280 Rem., 30-06
   Model MA: 7mm STW, 7mm Rem. Mag., 300 Win. Mag., 300 Weatherby, 300 H&H, 338 Win. Mag., 340 Weatherby, 375 H&H, 416 Rem.

Capacity: 4 rounds; 3 rounds in magnum calibers
Weight: 7 lbs; 7 lbs. 9 oz. in long action
Barrel lengths: 22″, 24″, 26″
Options: Wooden stock, optics, 30mm rings, muzzle brakes, steel floor plates, iron sights

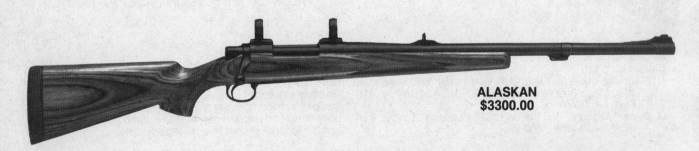

STAINLESS SPORTER
$2800.00

Same basic specifications as the Classic and Standard Sporters, but with stainless steel action and barrel. It is designed to withstand the most adverse weather conditions. Accuracy is guaranteed (3 shot in ½″ at 100 yards). Choice of wood, laminate or Gunworks fiberglass stock.

ALASKAN
$3300.00

SPECIFICATIONS
Calibers:
   Model LA: 270, 280, 30-06
   Model MA: 7mm Rem. Mag., 300 Win. Mag., 300 H&H, 300 Weatherby, 358 Win., 340 Weatherby, 375 H&H, 416 Rem.

Other specifications same as the Classic Sporter, except Harris action is fitted to a match-grade barrel, complete with single-leaf rear sight, barrel band front sight, 1″ detachable rings and mounts, steel floorplate, electroless nickel finish. Monte Carlo stock features cheekpiece, palm swell and special recoil pad. Also available: Stainless Steel Receiver, **add** $150.00

HARRIS GUNWORKS RIFLES

TALON SPORTER
$2600.00

The all-new action of this model is designed and engineered specifically for the hunting of dangerous (African-type) game animals. Patterned after the renowned pre-64 Model 70, the Talon features a cone breech, controlled feed, claw extractor, positive ejection and three-position safety. Action is available in chromolybdenum and stainless steel. Drilled and tapped for scope mounting in long, short or magnum, left or right hand.

Same basic specifications as Harris Signature series, but offered in the following **calibers:**
Standard Action: 22-250, 243, 6mm Rem., 6mm BR, 7mm BR, 7mm-08, 284, 308, 350 Rem. Mag.
Long Action: 25-06, 270, 280 Rem., 30-06
Magnum Action: 7mm STW, 7mm Rem. Mag., 300 Win. Mag., 300 Weatherby, 300 H&H, 338 Win. Mag., 340 Weatherby, 375 H&H, 416 Rem.

VARMINTER
$2600.00

SPECIFICATIONS
Calibers: 223, 22-250, 220 Swift, 243, 6mm Rem., 25-06, 7mm-08, 308, 350 Rem. Mag.
Other specifications same as the Classic Sporter, except the Super Varminter comes with heavy contoured barrel, adjustable trigger, field bipod and hand-bedded fiberglass stock.

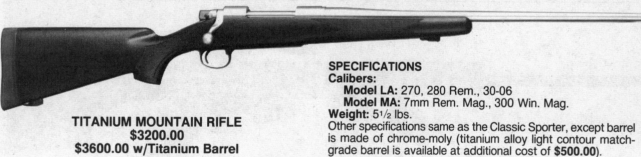

TITANIUM MOUNTAIN RIFLE
$3200.00
$3600.00 w/Titanium Barrel

SPECIFICATIONS
Calibers:
    Model LA: 270, 280 Rem., 30-06
    Model MA: 7mm Rem. Mag., 300 Win. Mag.
Weight: 5½ lbs.
Other specifications same as the Classic Sporter, except barrel is made of chrome-moly (titanium alloy light contour match-grade barrel is available at additional cost of **$500.00**).

.300 PHOENIX
$2600.00

Caliber: 300 Phoenix. **Barrel length:** 27½". **Weight:** 12½ lbs. **Stock:** Fiberglass with adjustable cheekpiece. **Feature:** Available in left-hand action.

RIFLES

HARRIS GUNWORKS RIFLES

NATIONAL MATCH RIFLE
$2600.00

SPECIFICATIONS
Calibers: 308, 7mm-08   **Mag. Capacity:** 5 rounds
Weight: Approx. 11 lbs. (12½ lbs. w/heavy contour barrel)
Available for right-hand shooters only. Features Harris fiberglass stock with adjustable buttplate, stainless steel match barrel with barrel band and Tompkins front sight; Harris repeating bolt action with clip shot and Canjar trigger. Barrel twist is 1:12″.

LONG RANGE RIFLE
$2600.00

SPECIFICATIONS
Calibers: 300 Win. Mag., 300 Phoenix, 7mm Mag., 338 Lapua
Barrel length: 26″   **Weight:** 14 lbs.
Available in right-hand only. Features a fiberglass stock with adjustable butt plate and cheekpiece. Stainless steel match barrel comes with barrel band and Tompkins front sight. Harris solid bottom single-shot action and Canjar trigger. Barrel twist is 1:12″.

HECKLER & KOCH RIFLES

MODEL HK PSG-1 HIGH PRECISION
MARKSMAN'S RIFLE
$10,497.00

SPECIFICATIONS
Caliber: 308 (7.62mm)
Capacity: 5 rounds
Barrel length: 25.6″
Rifling: 4 groove, polygonal
Twist: 12″, right hand
Overall length: 47.5″

Weight: 17.8 lbs.
Sights: Hensoldt 6×42 telescopic
Stock: Matte black, high-impact plastic
Finish: Matte black, phosphated
Features: Aluminum case; tripod; sling; adj. buttstock and contoured grip

HOWA LIGHTNING RIFLES

LIGHTNING BOLT-ACTION RIFLE

The rugged mono-bloc receivers on all Howa rifles are machined from a single billet of high carbon steel. The machined steel bolt boasts dual-opposed locking lugs and triple relief gas ports. Actions are fitted with a button-release hinged floorplate for fast reloading. Premium steel sporter-weight barrels are hammer-forged. A silent sliding thumb safety locks the trigger for safe loading or clearing the chamber. The stock is ultra-tough polymer.

SPECIFICATIONS
Calibers: 22-250, 223, 243, 270, 308, 30-06, 300 Win. Mag., 338 Win. Mag., 7mm Rem. Mag.
Capacity: 5 rounds (3 in Magnum)
Barrel length: 22″ (24″ in Magnum)
Overall length: 42″
Weight: 7.5 lbs. (7.75 lbs. in Magnum)
Price:

Standard Model	**$425.00**
In Magnum calibers	**445.00**
Barreled Actions	**325.00**
In Magnum calibers	**345.00**

JARRETT CUSTOM RIFLES

MODEL NO. 1
$2850.00

Jarrett's Standard Hunting Rifle uses McMillan's fiberglass stock and is made primarily for hunters of big game and varmints.

Also available:
MODEL NO. 3 Coup de Grace. Same specifications as the Standard model, but can use a Remington or Winchester receiver. Includes a muzzlebreak kit. Serial No. 1-100.
Price: **$3495.00**

MODEL NO. 2

MODEL NO. 2
$2850.00

This lightweight rifle—called the "Walkabout"—is based on Remington's Model 7 receiver. It is available in any short-action caliber and is pillar-bedded into a McMillan Model 7-style stock.

MODEL NO. 4 (not shown)
$6000.00

This model—the "Professional Hunter"—is based on a Winchester controlled round-feed Model 70. It features a quarter rib and iron sights and comes with two Leupold scopes with quick-detachable scope rings. A handload is developed for solids and soft points (40 rounds each). It is then pillar-bedded into a McMillan fiberglass stock. Available in any Magnum caliber.

RIFLES

KBI ARMSCOR RIFLES

MODEL M-2000SC SUPER CLASSIC SEMIAUTOMATIC

MODEL M-1800S CLASSIC BOLT ACTION

SUPER CLASSIC
MODELS M-1400SC, M-1500SC, M-1800SC, M-2000SC

SPECIFICATIONS
Calibers: 22 LR, 22 Mag. RF, 22 Hornet
Action: Bolt and semiauto
Capacity: 10 rounds (22 LR); 5 rounds (22 Mag. RF and 22 Hornet)
Barrel length: 22⅝"; 20¾" in semiauto
Overall length: 41¼"; 40½" in semiauto)
Weight: 6.4 lbs. (semiauto); 6.5 lbs. (22 Mag. RF); 6.6 lbs. (22 Hornet); 6.7 lbs. (22 LR)
Finish: Blue
Features: Oil-finished American walnut stock w/hardwood grip cap & forend tip; checkered Monte Carlo comb and cheek-piece, high polish blued barreled action w/damascened bolt; dovetailed receiver and iron sights (ramp front sight, fully adjustable rear sight); recoil pad; QD swivel posts

Prices:
22 Long Rifle	$339.00
22 Mag. Rimfire	349.00
22 Hornet	429.00
22 LR Semiauto	319.00

Also available:
CLASSIC 22 LR. Same specifications as the Super Classic but with walnut-finished hardwood stock and cut checkering.
Prices:
M-1400S	$189.00
M-1500S	209.00
M-1800S	339.00
M-2000S	195.00

STANDARD M-20P SEMIAUTOMATIC

MODEL M-12Y YOUTH BOLT ACTION

STANDARD 22 RIFLES
$119.00

SPECIFICATIONS
Caliber: 22 Long Rifle
Action: Bolt and semiauto
Capacity: 10 rounds
Barrel length: 20¾" (Model M-20P); 22⅝" (Model M-14P)
Overall length: 40½" (Model M-20P); 41" (Model M-14P)
Weight: 6 lbs. 3 oz. (Model M-20P); 6 lbs. 8 oz. (Model M-14P)

Finish: Blue
Features: Walnut-finished hardwood stocks; dovetailed receiver; iron sights (hooded front and leaf-adjustable rear)

Also available:
MODEL M-12Y YOUTH RIFLE. Single shot. **Barrel length:** 17½". **Overall length:** 34⅜". **Weight:** 4 lbs. 13 oz. **Price:** $99.00

KIMBER RIFLES

MODEL 82C 22 LR CLASSIC

MODEL 82C 22 LR SPECIFICATIONS

		Model 82C Classic	Model 82C Stainless Classic	Model 82C Varmint Synthetic	Model 82C SVT	Model 82C SuperAmerica	Model 82C Custom Match
Caliber		.22LR	.22LR	.22LR	.22LR	.22LR	.22LR
Weight (pounds)		6 1/2	6 1/2	7 1/2	7 1/2	6 1/2	6 3/4
Overall Length (inches)		40 1/2	40 1/2	38 1/2	36 1/2	40 1/2	40 1/2
Action:	Type	Rear Locking Repeater	Rear Locking Repeater	Rear Locking Repeater	Rear Locking Single Shot	Rear Locking Repeater	Rear Locking Repeater
	Capacity	4 Shot Clip 5 & 10 Shot (opt.)	4 Shot Clip 5 & 10 Shot (opt.)	4 Shot Clip 5 & 10 Shot (opt.)		4 Shot Clip 5 & 10 Shot (opt.)	4 Shot Clip 5 & 10 Shot (opt.)
Trigger:		Fully Adjustable	Fully Adjustable	Fully Adjustable	Fully Adjustable	Fully Adjustable	Fully Adjustable
	Pressure (pounds)	Set at 2 1/2	Set at 2 1/2	Set at 2 1/2	Set at 2 1/2	Set at 2 1/2	Set at 2 1/2
Barrel:	Length (inches)	22	22	20 (Fluted)	18 (Fluted)	22	22
	Grooves	6	6	6	6	6	6
	Twist (inches)	16	16	16	16	16	16
Stock:	Grade Walnut	A Claro	A Claro	Synthetic	A Claro	AAA Claro	AA French
	Checkering (LPI)	18	18	18	None	22	22
	Coverage	Side Panel	Side Panel	Side Panel	NA	Full Coverage Wrap Around	Full Coverage Wrap Around
Length of Pull (inches)		13 5/8	13 5/8	13 5/8	13 5/8	13 5/8	13 5/8
Metal Finish		Polished & Blued	Stainless Steel Barrel, Matte Blued Action	Stainless Steel Barrel, Matte Blued Action	Stainless Steel Barrel, Matte Blued Action	Polished & Blued	Matte "rust" type blue

MODEL 82C 22 LR — Prices

Classic	$ 785.00	Varmint Synthetic	$ 885.00
Stainless Classic	899.00	SuperAmerica	1326.00
SVT	785.00	Custom Shop SuperAmerica	1550.00
		Custom Match	2075.00

MODEL 82C 22 LR SUPERAMERICA

KIMBER RIFLES

MODEL 84C SINGLE SHOT VARMINT

MODEL 84C

The Kimber Model 84C is a scaled-down mini-Mauser with controlled round feeding. Like other Kimber rifles, the 84C action is machined from solid steel. Designed for the .223 Rem. family of cartridges, it is available in both single shot and repeater versions. Every Model 84C is test-fired for accuracy at the factory. Each rifle must shoot a 5-shot group measuring .400″ or less center-to-center at 50 yards.

MODEL 84C	Prices
Single Shot Varmint	$ 999.00
Classic	1145.00
SuperAmerica	1595.00
Custom Match	starts at 1750.00

MODEL 84C SPECIFICATIONS

	Model 84C Single Shot Varmint	Model 84C Classic	Model 84C SuperAmerica	Model 84C Custom Match
Calibers	.17 Rem. .223 Rem.	.222 Rem. .223 Rem.	.17 Rem. .222 Rem. .223 Rem.	.17 Rem. .222 Rem. .223 Rem.
Weight (pounds)	7 1/2	6 3/4	6 3/4	7
Overall Length (inches)	43 1/2	40 1/2	40 1/2	40 1/2
Action Type	Front Locking Single Shot	Front Locking Controlled Feed Repeater Hinged floor plate, 5 shot box magazine	Front Locking Controlled Feed Repeater Hinged floor plate, 5 shot box magazine	Front Locking Controlled Feed Repeater Hinged floor plate, 5 shot box magazine
Trigger: Pressure (pounds)	Fully Adjustable Set at 2 1/2	Fully Adjustable Set at 2 1/2	Fully Adjustable Set at 2 1/2	Fully Adjustable Set at 2 1/2
Barrel: Length (inches)	25 (Fluted)	22	22	22
Grooves	6	6	6	6
Twist (inches)	.17 Rem.-10 .223 Rem.-12	.222 Rem.-12 .223 Rem.-12	.17 Rem.-10 .222 Rem.-12 .223 Rem.-12	.17 Rem.-10 .222 Rem.-12 .223 Rem.-12
Stock: Grade Walnut	A Claro	A Claro	AAA Claro	AA French
Checkering (LPI)	18	18	22	22
Coverage	Side Panel	Side Panel	Full Coverage Wrap Around	Full Coverage Wrap Around
Length of Pull (inches)	13 5/8	13 5/8	13 5/8	13 5/8
Metal Finish	Stainless Steel Barrel, Matte Blue Action	Polished & Blued	Polished & Blued	Matte "rust" type blue

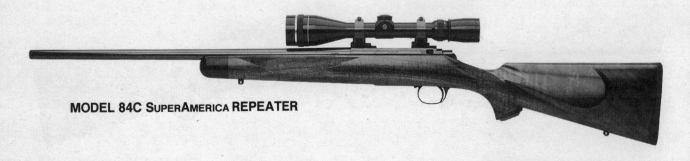

MODEL 84C SuperAmerica REPEATER

KIMBER RIFLES

SWEDISH MAUSER 96 SPORTER

SWEDISH MAUSER 96

SPECIFICATIONS
Calibers: *Sporters*—243 Win., 6.5×55mm, 7mm-08, 308 Win.; *Heavy Barrel Models*—22-250 and 308 Win. (SS Varmint)
Capacity: 5 shots
Action: Mauser, front-locking bolt action, cock on closing
Barrel length: 22″ (Sporters); 25″ (Heavy barrel models)
Overall length: 41.5″ (Sporters); 44.5″ (Heavy barrel models)
Weight: 7.25 lbs. (Sporters); 8.25 lbs. (SS Varmint)
Trigger: Two-stage military trigger
Stock: Ramline™ Syn-Tech™ synthetic plastic "krinkle" finish; lifetime guarantee; length of pull 13.5″

Finish: Satin silver or matte blue (Sporters); stainless barrel w/matte blue action (SS Varmint)
Prices:
SPORTERS
243, 7mm-08 or 308 (matte blue) $415.00
   Same as above in satin silver 465.00
6.5×55mm matte blue 340.00
   Same as above in satin silver 370.00
HEAVY BARREL MODELS
22-250 SS Varmint 505.00
308 SS Varmint 520.00

MAUSER 98 SPORTER

MAUSER 98 SPORTER

The Mauser 98 Sporter features a new match-grade stainless steel fluted barrel with a heavy sporter contour. To compliment the barrel finish, the action is finished in a deep matte blue. Each rifle also incorporates a high- quality synthetic stock with a 1″ recoil pad and comes with scope mounts. To permit proper scope mounting, Kimber installs a new steel Buehler-style safety and repositions the bolt handle. **Calibers:** 220 Swift, 257 Roberts, 270 Win., 280 Rem., 30-06 Spfd., 7mm Rem. Mag., 300 Win. Mag., 338 Win. Mag.
Prices:
Standard calibers $535.00
Magnum calibers 560.00

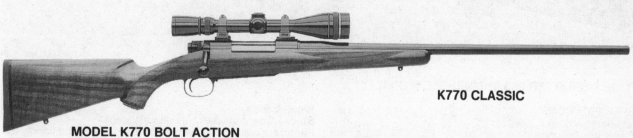

K770 CLASSIC

MODEL K770 BOLT ACTION

The Kimber K770 is a new repeater version of a single-shot target rifle designed by Jack Warne, co-founder of Kimber of Oregon. The K770 design contains several features that enhance accuracy. The front-locking improved bolt has three lugs that lock directly into the barrel breech instead of the receiver. This provides cartridge alignment and support, thus increasing accuracy. Each K770 is test-fired for accuracy at the factory. Five-shot group size of .500″ or less center-to-center at 50 yards is required.

Calibers: 270 Win. and 30-06 Spfd. **Barrel length:** 24″. The **Classic** model has a rich claro-walnut stock, 18 LPI side panel hand-cut checkering, polished steel grip cap and hinged floorplate. The **SuperAmerica** model features a AAA claro-walnut stock with ebony forend tip and beaded cheekpiece (22 LPI full coverage wraparound checkering). Both are finished in matte blue and have two-position Model 70-type safeties.
Prices:
Classic . . . . $ 745.00
SuperAmerica 1260.00

RIFLES

KONGSBERG RIFLES

MODEL 393 CLASSIC

HUNTER 393 MODELS

SPECIFICATIONS
Calibers: 243 Win., 6.5mm×55 Swedish, 270 Win., 30-06, 308 Win., 7mm Rem. Mag., 300 Win. Mag., 338 Win. Mag.
Capacity: 4 rounds (3 rounds in Magnum calibers)
Barrel length: 22.8″
Muzzle diameter: 0.63″
Weight: 7.5 lbs.
Stock: Turkish walnut; Select and Deluxe Models have Monte Carlo stock

Prices:
Select (Standard) Model	$ 980.00
Left Hand	1118.00
In Magnum calibers	1093.00
Classic Model	995.00
In Magnum calibers	1109.00
Deluxe Model	1124.00
Left Hand	1261.00
In Magnum calibers	1236.00

SPORTER 393 THUMBHOLE

SPORTER 393 THUMBHOLE MODEL

SPECIFICATIONS
Calibers: 308 Win., 30-06
Capacity: 4 rounds
Barrel length: 22.4″
Muzzle diameter: 0.75″

Weight: 9 lbs.
Stock: American walnut thumbhole stock
Features: Adjustable comb, release in front of bolt handle for easy bolt removal
Price: $1579.00

KRIEGHOFF DOUBLE RIFLES

CLASSIC SIDE-BY-SIDE DOUBLE RIFLE
$7850.00 (Standard)
$9450.00 (Big Five)

Kreighoff's new Classic Side-by-Side offers many standard features, including: Schnabel forearm . . . classic English-style stock with rounded cheekpiece . . . UAS anti-doubling device . . . extractors . . . 1″ quick- detachable sling swivels . . . decelerator recoil pad . . . short opening angle for fast loading . . . compact action with reinforced sidewalls . . . sliding, self-adjusting wedge for secure bolt . . . large underlugs . . . automatic hammer safety . . . horizontal firing-pin placement . . . Purdey-style extension between barrels.

SPECIFICATIONS
Calibers: *Standard*—7×65R, 308 Win., 30-06, 8×57JRS, 8×75RS, 9.3×74R; *Big Five*—375 H&H, 375 Flanged Mag. N.E., 458 Win. Mag., 416 Rigby, 470 N.E., 500 N.E., 500/ .416 N.E.

Action: Cocking device for optimum safety
Barrel length: 23.5″
Trigger: Double triggers with hinged front set trigger standard (Big Five only); steel trigger guard
Weight: 7.5 to 11 lbs. (depending on caliber and wood density)
Options: 21.5″ barrel; Combi-Cocking Device; double-set triggers; automatic set trigger release; engraved sideplates
Prices:
STANDARD $7850.00
Interchangeable barrels (installed, w/extra
   forearm) 3995.00
BIG FIVE 9450.00
Interchangeable barrels 4995.00

L.A.R. GRIZZLY RIFLE

BIG BOAR COMPETITOR

SPECIFICATIONS
Caliber: 50 BMG
Capacity: Single shot
Action: Bolt action, bull pup, breechloading
Barrel length: 36″
Overall length: 45½″
Weight: 30.4 lbs.
Safety: Thumb safety
Features: All-steel construction; receiver made of 4140 alloy steel, heat-treated to 42 R/C; bolt made of 4340 alloy steel; low recoil (like 12 ga. shotgun)

BIG BOAR COMPETITOR
$2570.00
$2670.00 (Parkerized)
$2820.00 (Nickel Frame)
$2920.00 (Full Nickel)

LAZZERONI RIFLES

These new, state-of-the-art rifles feature 4340 chrome moly steel receivers with two massive locking lugs, a match grade 416R stainless steel barrel, fully adjustable bench rest style trigger and a Lazzeroni-designed synthetic or wood stock that is hand bedded using aluminum pillar blocks. Included is a precision-machined floorplate/trigger guard assembly.

MODEL L2000ST-F
$3695.00

SPECIFICATIONS
Calibers: 6.53 (.257) Scramjet™; 7.21 (.284) Firehawk™; 7.82 (.308) Warbird™; 8.59 (.338) Titan™
Capacity: 3 rounds (one in chamber)
Barrel length: 27″
Overall length: 47.5″
Weight: 8.1 lbs.
Stock: Lazzeroni fiberglass sporter; right or left hand available

MODEL L2000ST-W
$4795.00

SPECIFICATIONS
Calibers: 6.53 (.257) Scramjet™; 7.21 (.284) Firehawk™; 7.82 (.308) Warbird™; 8.59 (.338) Titan™
Capacity: 3 rounds (one in chamber)
Barrel length: 27″
Overall length: 47.5″
Weight: 9.5 lbs.
Stock: Lazzeroni black laminated wood sporter; right or left hand available

MODEL L2000SP-F
$3695.00

SPECIFICATIONS
Calibers: 6.53 (.257) Scramjet™; 7.21 (.284) Firehawk™; 7.82 (.308) Warbird™; 8.59 (.338) Titan™
Capacity: 3 rounds (one in chamber)
Barrel length: 23″
Overall length: 43.5″
Weight: 7.8 lbs.
Stock: Lazzeroni fiberglass thumbhole; available right hand only

MAGNUM RESEARCH

MOUNTAIN EAGLE

VARMINT MODEL
w/Stainless Steel Krieger Barrel

MOUNTAIN EAGLE BOLT-ACTION RIFLE
$1369.00 $1459.00 Left Hand

SPECIFICATIONS
Calibers: 270 Win., 280 Rem., 30-06 Springfield, 7mm Mag., 300 Wby. Mag., 300 Win. Mag., 338 Win. Mag., 340 Wby. Mag., 375 H&H Mag., 416 Rem. Mag.
Capacity: 5-shot magazine (long action); 4-shot (Magnum action)
Action: SAKO-built to MRI specifications
Barrel length: 24″ with .004″ headspace tolerance
Overall length: 44″   **Weight:** 7 lbs. 13 oz.
Sights: None

Stock: Fiberglass composite   **Length of pull:** 13⅝″
Features: Adjustable trigger; high comb stock (for mounting and scoping); one-piece forged bolt; free-floating, match-grade, cut-rifles, benchrest barrel; recoil pad and sling swivel studs; Platform Bedding System front lug; pillar-bedded rear guard screw; lengthened receiver ring; solid steel hinged floorplate
Also available:
VARMINT EDITION. In 222 Rem. and 223 Rem. with stainless steel Krieger barrel. **Price:** $1429.00

MAGTECH RIFLES

MODEL MT 122.2R

MODEL MT 122.2S/R/T BOLT-ACTION RIFLE
$100.00

SPECIFICATIONS
Calibers: 22 Short, Long, Long Rifle
Capacity: 6- or 10-shot clip
Action: Bolt action
Barrel length: 25″ (8-groove rifling), free-floating
Overall length: 43″   **Weight:** 6.5 lbs.
Safety: Double locking bolt, red cocking indicator, safety lever (disconnects trigger from firing mechanism in "safe" position)

Finish: Brazilian hardwood
Features: Double extractors; beavertail forearm; sling swivels. No mechanical sight (for mounting scope or sight later) on Model 122.2S.
Also available:
MODEL MT 122.2R. With adjustable rear sight and post front sight. **Price:** $115.00
MODEL MT 122.2T. With adjustable micrometer-type rear sight and ramp front sight; positive click stops for precise adjustment. **Price:** $120.00

MARLIN 22 RIFLES

MODEL 60
$158.50

SPECIFICATIONS
Caliber: 22 Long Rifle
Capacity: 14-shot tubular magazine with patented closure system

Barrel length: 22″
Overall length: 40 1/2″
Weight: 5 1/2 lbs.
Sights: Ramp front sight with brass bead and Wide-Scan hood; adjustable open rear, receiver grooved for scope mount
Action: Self-loading; side ejection; manual and automatic "last-shot" hold-open devices; receiver top has serrated, nonglare finish; crossbolt safety
Stock: One-piece Maine birch Monte Carlo stock, press-checkered, with full pistol grip; Mar-Shield® finish

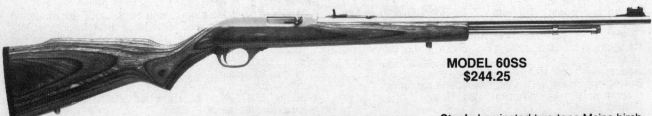

MODEL 60SS
$244.25

SPECIFICATIONS
Caliber: 22 Long Rifle
Capacity: 14 rounds
Barrel length: 22″

Overall length: 40 1/2″
Weight: 5 1/2 lbs.
Sights: Adjustable folding semibuckhorn rear; ramp front sight with high-visibility post and removable Wide Scan™ hood
Stock: Laminated two-tone Maine birch with nickel-plated swivel studs and rubber rifle buttpad
Features: Micro-Groove® rifling; side ejection; manual bolt hold-open; automatic last-shot bolt hold-open; crossbolt safety

MODEL 70PSS "PAPOOSE"
$255.25

SPECIFICATIONS
Caliber: 22 Long Rifle
Capacity: 7-shot clip
Barrel length: 16 1/4″
Overall length: 35 1/4″

Weight: 3 1/4 lbs.
Action: Self-loading; side ejection; manual bolt hold-open; crossbolt safety; stainless-steel breech bolt and barrel

Sights: Screw adjustable open rear; ramp front; receiver grooved for scope mount
Stock: Black fiberglass-filled synthetic with abbrev. forend, nickel-plated swivel studs and molded-in checkering

MARLIN RIFLES

MODEL 922 MAGNUM
$410.75

SPECIFICATIONS
Caliber: 22 Win. Mag. Rimfire
Capacity: 7-shot clip magazine
Barrel length: 20½"
Overall length: 39¾"

Weight: 6½ lbs.
Sights: Adjustable semibuckhorn rear; ramp front sight with brass bead and removable Wide-Scan hood™

Stock: Monte Carlo checkered American black walnut with rubber rifle buttpad and swivel studs
Features: Side ejection; manual bolt hold-open; automatic last-shot bolt hold-open; magazine safety; Garand-type safety; Micro-Groove® rifling

MODEL 995SS
$237.60

SPECIFICATIONS
Caliber: 22 Long Rifle
Action: Self-loading
Capacity: 7-shot nickel-plated clip magazine
Barrel: 18" stainless steel with Micro-Groove® rifling (16 grooves)

Overall length: 37"
Weight: 5 lbs.
Stock: Black fiberglass-filled synthetic with nickel-plated swivel studs and molded-in checkering

Sights: Screw-adjustable open rear; ramp front with high-visibility orange post; cutaway Wide-Scan™ hood
Features: Receiver grooved for tip-off scope mount; stainless-steel breech-bolt and barrel; crossbolt safety

MODEL MR-7
$610.00

SPECIFICATIONS:
Caliber: 30-06 Sprfd. or 270 Win.
Action: Bolt action
Capacity: 4-shot detachable box magazine

Barrel length: 22" (6-groove rifling), recessed muzzle
Overall length: 43"
Weight: 7½ lbs.
Sights: Rear, optional Williams streamlined ramp w/brass bead; front, Williams blade

Stock: American black walnut w/cut checkering; Mar-Shield™ finish
Features: 3-position safety; shrouded striker; red cocking indicator; drilled and tapped receiver, rubber recoil pad

MARLIN BOLT-ACTION RIFLES

**MARLIN 15YN "LITTLE BUCKAROO®" Single Shot
22 Beginner's Rifle
$171.80**

SPECIFICATIONS
Caliber: 22 Short, Long or Long Rifle
Capacity: Single shot
Action: Bolt action; easy-load feed throat; thumb safety; red cocking indicator

Barrel length: 16¼" (16 grooves)
Overall length: 33¼"
Weight: 4¼ lbs.
Sights: Adjustable open rear; ramp front sight

Stock: One-piece walnut-finished press-checkered Maine birch Monte Carlo w/full pistol grip; tough Mar-Shield® finish

**MODEL 25MN
$198.25**

SPECIFICATIONS
Caliber: 22 WMR (not interchangeable w/other 22 cartridges)
Capacity: 7-shot clip magazine

Barrel length: 22" with Micro-Groove® rifling
Overall length: 41"
Weight: 6 lbs.

Sights: Adjustable open rear, ramp front sight; receiver grooved for scope mount
Stock: One-piece walnut-finished press-checkered Maine birch Monte Carlo w/full pistol grip; Mar-Shield® finish

**MODEL 25N
$173.50**

Same specifications as Model 25MN, except **caliber** 22 LR and **weight** 5½ pounds.

**MARLIN 880
$240.25**

Sights: Adj. folding semibuckhorn rear; ramp front w/Wide-Scan™ hood; receiver grooved for scope mount
Overall length: 41"   **Weight:** 5½ lbs.
Stock: Checkered Monte Carlo American black walnut with full pistol grip; Mar-Shield® finish; rubber buttpad; swivel studs

SPECIFICATIONS
Caliber: 22 Long Rifle
Capacity: 7-shot clip magazine
Action: Bolt action; positive thumb safety; red cocking indicator
Barrel: 22" with Micro-Groove® rifling (16 grooves)

Also available: **MODEL 880SS.** Same as Model 880, in stainless steel. **Weight:** 6 lbs. **$256.75**
MODEL 881. Same as Model 880, except w/tubular mag.; holds 17 22-LR rounds. **Weight:** 6 lbs. **$250.25**
MODEL 880SQ SQUIRREL RIFLE. With heavy 22" barrel, recessed muzzle; black synthetic stock w/molded-in checkering, swivel studs; no sights. **Weight:** 7 lbs. **$263.75**

MARLIN BOLT-ACTION RIFLES

MODEL 882
$264.90

MODEL 882SS

Overall length: 41" **Weight:** 6 lbs.
Sights: Adj. semibuckhorn folding rear; ramp front w/brass bead and Wide-Scan™ front sight hood
Stock: Monte Carlo American black walnut with swivel studs; full pistol grip; classic cut-checkering; rubber rifle buttpad

SPECIFICATIONS
Caliber: 22 Win. Mag.
Action: Bolt action; thumb safety; red cocking indicator
Capacity: 7-shot clip
Barrel length: 22"

Also available: **MODEL 882SS.** Same as Model 882, except stainless-steel barrel, receiver front breechbolt striker knob and trigger stud; orange front sight post; black fiberglass-filled synthetic stock w/nickel-plated swivel studs and molded-in checkering.
$282.75

MODEL 882L
$280.75

SPECIFICATIONS
Caliber: 22 WMR (not interchangeable with other 22 cartridges)

Capacity: 7-shot clip magazine
Barrel length: 22" Micro-Groove®
Overall length: 41" **Weight:** 6¼ lbs.
Sights: Ramp front w/brass bead and removable Wide-Scan™ hood; adj. folding semibuckhorn rear

Stock: Laminated hardwood Monte Carlo w/Mar-Shield® finish
Features: Swivel studs; rubber rifle butt pad; receiver grooved for scope mount; positive thumb safety; red cocking indicator

MODEL 883 MAGNUM
$274.50

SPECIFICATIONS
Caliber: 22 WMR (not interchangeable with other 22 cartridges)
Capacity: 12-shot tubular magazine with patented closure system

Action: Bolt action; positive thumb safety; red cocking indicator
Barrel length: 22" with Micro-Groove® rifling (20 grooves)
Overall length: 41" **Weight:** 6 lbs.
Sights: Adjustable folding semibuckhorn rear; ramp front with Wide-Scan™

hood; receiver grooved for scope mount
Stock: Checkered Monte Carlo American black walnut with full pistol grip; rubber buttpad; swivel studs; tough Mar-Shield® finish

MODEL 883SS (Stainless Steel)
$292.25

Same as Model 883, except with stainless barrel and receiver, laminated two-tone brown Maine birch stock with nickel-plated swivel studs and rubber rifle buttpad.

MARLIN RIFLES

MODEL 2000L TARGET
$602.50

SPECIFICATIONS
Caliber: 22 Long Rifle
Capacity: Single-shot; 5-shot Summer Biathlon adapter kit available
Action: Bolt action, 2-stage target trigger, red cocking indicator

Barrel length: Heavy 22″ Micro-Groove w/match chamber, recessed muzzle
Overall length: 41″ **Weight:** 8 lbs.
Sights: Hooded Lyman front sight with 10 aperture inserts; fully adjustable Lyman target rear peep sight

Stock: High-comb "Carbelite" (fiberglass/Kevlar) w/stipple-finished forearm and pistol grip. Blue baked epoxy enamel finish. Buttplate adjustable for length of pull, height and angle. Aluminum forearm rail with forearm stop and quick-detachable swivel

MODEL 9 CAMP CARBINE
$424.50

SPECIFICATIONS
Caliber: 9mm
Capacity: 10-shot clip (12-shot avail.)
Action: Self-loading. Manual bolt hold-open. Garand-type safety, magazine safety, loaded chamber indicator.

Solid-top, machined steel receiver is sandblasted to prevent glare, and is drilled/tapped for scope mounting.
Barrel length: 16½″ with Micro-Groove® rifling
Overall length: 35½″ **Weight:** 6¾ lbs.

Sights: Adjustable folding rear, ramp front sight with high-visibility, orange front sight post; Wide-Scan™ hood.
Stock: Walnut finished hardwood with pistol grip; tough Mar-Shield™ finish; rubber rifle buttpad; swivel studs

MODEL 45
$424.50

SPECIFICATIONS
Caliber: 45 Auto
Capacity: 7-shot clip
Barrel length: 16½″

Overall length: 35½″
Weight 6.75 lbs.
Sights: Adjustable folding rear; ramp front sight with high-visibility, orange

front sight post; Wide-Scan™ hood
Stock: Press-checkered walnut-finished Maine birch with pistol grip; rubber rifle buttpad; swivel studs

MARLIN LEVER-ACTION CARBINES

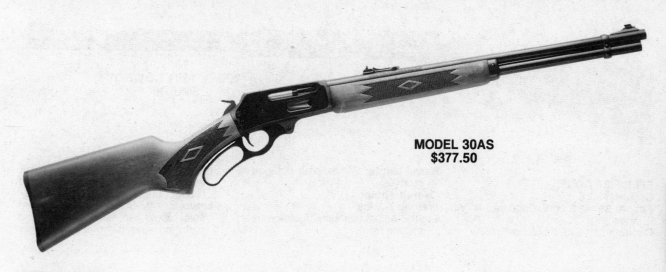

MODEL 30AS
$377.50

SPECIFICATIONS

Caliber : 30-30
Capacity: 6-shot tubular magazine
Action: Lever w/hammer block safety; solid top receiver w/side ejection

Barrel length: 20″ w/Micro-Groove®
Overall length: 38¼″ **Weight:** 7 lbs.
Sights: Tapped for scope mount and receiver sight; also available in combi-

nation w/4x, 32mm, 1″ scope
Stock: Walnut-finished Maine birch stock w/pistol grip; pressed checkering; Mar-Shield® finish

MARLIN GOLDEN 39AS
$444.95

Introduced in 1891, the Marlin lever-action 22 is the oldest shoulder gun still being manufactured.

Solid Receiver Top. You can easily mount a scope on your Marlin 39 by screwing on the machined scope adapter base provided. The screw-on base is a neater, more versatile method of mounting a scope on a 22 sporting rifle. The solid top receiver and scope adapter base provide a maximum in eye relief adjustment. If you prefer iron sights, you'll find the 39 receiver clean, flat and sandblasted to prevent glare. Exclusive brass magazine tube

Micro-Groove® Barrel. Marlin's famous rifling system of multi-grooving has consistently produced fine accuracy be-

cause the system grips the bullet more securely, minimizes distortion, and provides a better gas seal.

And the Model 39 maximizes accuracy with the heaviest barrels available on any lever-action 22.

SPECIFICATIONS

Caliber: 22 Short, Long and Long Rifle
Capacity: Tubular magazine holds 26 Short, 21 Long and 19 LR cartridges
Action: Lever; solid top receiver; side ejection; one-step takedown; deeply blued metal surfaces; receiver top sandblasted to prevent glare; hammer block safety; rebounding hammer

Barrel: 24″ with Micro-Groove® rifling (16 grooves)
Overall length: 40″ **Weight:** 6½ lbs.
Sights: Adjustable folding semibuckhorn rear, ramp front sight with new Wide-Scan™ hood; solid top receiver tapped for scope mount or receiver sight; scope adapter base; offset hammer spur for scope use—works right or left
Stock: Two-piece cut-checkered American black walnut w/fluted comb; full pistol grip and forend; blued-steel forend cap; swivel studs; grip cap; white butt and pistol-grip spacers; Mar-Shield® finish; rubber buttpad

MARLIN LEVER-ACTION CARBINES

MODEL 1894 COWBOY
$668.00

SPECIFICATIONS:
Caliber: 45 LC
Action: Lever action w/squared finger lever
Capacity: 10-shot tubular magazine

Barrel length: 24″ tapered octagon (6 grooves)
Overall length: 41½″
Weight: 7½ lbs.
Sights: Adjustable semi-buckhorn rear; carbine front

Stock: Straight-grip American black walnut w/cut-checkering and hard rubber buttplate
Features: Mar-Shield™ finish; blued steel forend cap; side ejection; blued metal surfaces; hammer block safety

MARLIN 1894S
$459.25

SPECIFICATIONS
Calibers: 44 Rem. Mag./44 Special, 45 Colt
Capacity: 10-shot tubular magazine
Action: Lever action w/square finger lever; hammer block safety

Barrel length: 20″ w/ Micro-Groove®
Sights: Ramp front sight w/brass bead; adjustable semibuckhorn folding rear and Wide-Scan™ hood; solid-top receiver tapped for scope mount or receiver sight

Overall length: 37½″
Weight: 6 lbs.
Stock: Checkered American black walnut stock w/Mar-Shield™ finish; blued steel forend cap; swivel studs

MARLIN 1894CS 357 MAGNUM
$459.25

SPECIFICATIONS
Calibers: 357 Magnum, 38 Special
Capacity: 9-shot tubular magazine
Action: Lever action w/square finger lever; hammer block safety; side ejection; solid top receiver; deeply blued metal surfaces; receiver top sandblasted to prevent glare

Barrel length: 18½″ with Micro-Groove® rifling (12 grooves)
Sights: Adjustable semibuckhorn folding rear, ramp front w/brass bead and Wide-Scan™ hood; solid top receiver tapped for scope mount or receiver sight; offset hammer spur for scope use—adjustable for right or left hand

Overall length: 36″
Weight: 6 lbs.
Stock: Cut-checkered straight-grip two-piece American black walnut w/white buttplate spacer; Mar-Shield® finish; swivel studs

MARLIN LEVER-ACTION CARBINES

MARLIN 1895SS
$522.50

SPECIFICATIONS
Caliber: 45-70 Government
Capacity: 4-shot tubular magazine
Action: Lever action; hammer block safety; receiver top sandblasted to prevent glare

Barrel: 22″ Micro-Groove® barrel
Sights: Ramp front sight w/brass bead; adjustable semibuckhorn folding rear and Wide-Scan™ hood; receiver tapped for scope mount or receiver sight

Overall length: 40 1/2″
Weight: 7 1/2 lbs.
Stock: Checkered American black walnut pistol-grip stock w/rubber rifle buttpad and Mar-Shield® finish; white pistol grip, butt spacers; swivel studs

MARLIN 336CS
$443.50 (Without Scope)

SPECIFICATIONS
Calibers: 30-30 Win., and 35 Rem.
Capacity: 6-shot tubular magazine
Action: Lever action w/hammer block safety; deeply blued metal surfaces; receiver top sandblasted to prevent glare

Barrel: 20″ Micro-Groove® barrel
Sights: Adjustable folding semibuckhorn rear; ramp front sight w/brass bead and Wide-Scan™ hood; tapped for receiver sight and scope mount; off-set hammer spur for scope use (works right or left)

Overall length: 38 1/2″
Weight: 7 lbs.
Stock: Checkered American black walnut pistol-grip stock w/fluted comb and Mar-Shield® finish; rubber rifle buttpad; swivel studs

MODEL 444SS
$522.50

SPECIFICATIONS
Caliber: 444 Marlin
Capacity: 5-shot tubular magazine
Barrel: 22″ Micro-Groove®

Overall length: 40 1/2″
Weight: 7 1/2 lbs.
Stock: Checkered American black walnut pistol grip stock with rubber rifle buttpad; swivel studs

Sights: Ramp front sight with brass bead and Wide-Scan® hood; adjustable semibuckhorn folding rear; receiver tapped for scope mount or receiver sight

MITCHELL ARMS

SEMIAUTOMATIC LIGHTWEIGHT CARBINES

MODEL LW22

MODEL LW22

SPECIFICATIONS
Caliber: 22 LR
Sights: Peep rear sight; guarded post front
Stocks: Skeleton fixed or black foam stock
Features: Blued finish; removable stock; removable barrel

Prices:
Skeleton Stock Model $274.95
Black Foam Stock Model 304.95

MODEL LW9

MODEL LW9

SPECIFICATIONS
Caliber: 9mm Luger
Sights: Peep rear sight; guarded post front
Stocks: Skeleton fixed or black foam stock
Features: Blued finish, removable stock; removable barrel

Prices:
Skeleton Stock Model $499.95
Black Foam Stock Model 534.95

NAVY ARMS REPLICA RIFLES

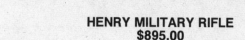

HENRY MILITARY RIFLE
$895.00

This Civil War replica features a highly polished brass frame and blued barrel; sling swivels to the original specifications are located on the left side.

SPECIFICATIONS
Caliber: 44-40 **Capacity:** 13 rounds
Barrel length: 24″ **Overall length:** 43″
Weight: 9¼ lbs.
Stock: Walnut

IRON FRAME HENRY
$945.00

SPECIFICATIONS
Caliber: 44-40 **Capacity:** 13 rounds
Barrel length: 24″ **Overall length:** 43″
Weight: 9 lbs.

Stock: Walnut
Finish: Blued or casehardened
Feature: Iron frame

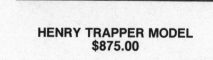

HENRY CARBINE
$875.00

The arm first utilized by the Kentucky Cavalry, with blued finish and brass frame.

SPECIFICATIONS
Caliber: 44-40 **Capacity:** 11 rounds
Barrel length: 22″ **Overall length:** 41″
Weight: 8¾ lbs.

HENRY TRAPPER MODEL
$875.00

This short, lightweight lever-action arm is ideal for the hunter.

SPECIFICATIONS
Caliber: 44-40 **Capacity:** 8 rounds

Barrel length: 16½″
Overall length: 34½″
Weight: 7 lbs. 7 oz.

NAVY ARMS REPLICA RIFLES

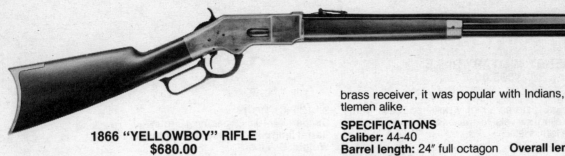

1866 "YELLOWBOY" RIFLE
$680.00

The 1866 model was Oliver Winchester's improved version of the Henry rifle. Called the "Yellowboy" because of its polished brass receiver, it was popular with Indians, settlers and cattlemen alike.

SPECIFICATIONS
Caliber: 44-40
Barrel length: 24" full octagon   **Overall length:** 42½"
Weight: 8½ lbs.
Sights: Blade front; open ladder rear
Stock: Walnut

1866 "YELLOWBOY" CARBINE
$670.00

This is the "saddle gun" variant of the rifle described above.

SPECIFICATIONS
Caliber: 44-40
Barrel length: 19" round   **Overall length:** 38¼"
Weight: 7¼ lbs.
Sights: Blade front; open ladder rear
Stock: Walnut

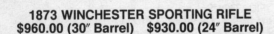

1873 WINCHESTER SPORTING RIFLE
$960.00 (30" Barrel) $930.00 (24" Barrel)

This replica of the state-of-the-art Winchester 1873 Sporting Rifle features a checkered pistol grip, buttstock, casehardened receiver and blued octagonal barrel.

SPECIFICATIONS
Caliber: 44-40 or 45 LC
Barrel length: 24" or 30"
Overall length: 48¾" (w/30" barrel)
Weight: 8 lbs. 14 oz.
Sights: Blade front; buckhorn rear

1873 WINCHESTER-STYLE RIFLE
$820.00

Known as "The Gun That Won the West," the 1873 was the most popular lever-action rifle of its time. This fine replica features a casehardened receiver.

SPECIFICATIONS
Caliber: 44-40 or 45 Long Colt
Barrel length: 24"   **Overall length:** 43"
Weight: 8¼ lbs.
Sights: Blade front; open ladder rear
Stock: Walnut
Also available: 1873 WINCHESTER-STYLE CARBINE
  (19" barrel) $800.00

NAVY ARMS REPLICA RIFLES

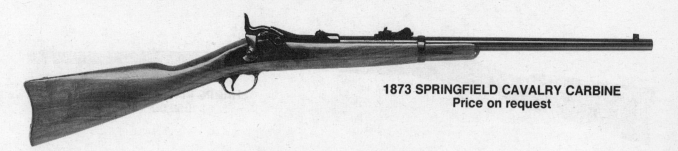

1873 SPRINGFIELD CAVALRY CARBINE
Price on request

A reproduction of the classic U.S. "Trapdoor" Springfield carbine used by the 7th Cavalry at The Battle of Little Big Horn.

SPECIFICATIONS
Caliber: 45-70 Government
Barrel length: 22"

Overall length: 40½"
Weight: 7 lbs.
Sights: Blade front, military ladder rear
Stock: Walnut
Features: Saddle bar with ring

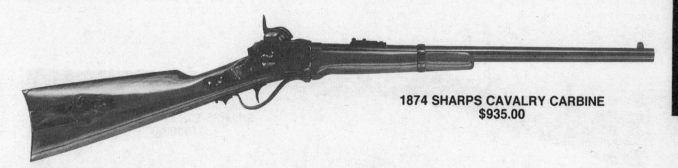

1874 SHARPS CAVALRY CARBINE
$935.00

This cavalry carbine version of the Sharps rifle features a side bar and saddle ring.

SPECIFICATIONS
Caliber: 45-70 percussion
Barrel length: 22"   **Overall length:** 39"

Weight: 7¾ lbs.
Sights: Blade front; military ladder rear
Stock: Walnut

1874 SHARPS INFANTRY RIFLE
$1115.00

Renowned for its accuracy, this replica of the 1874 three-band sharpshooter's rifle was a popular target rifle at the Creedmoor military matches and was the issue longarm of the New York State Militia.

SPECIFICATIONS
Caliber: 45-70
Barrel length: 30"   **Overall length:** 46¾"

Weight: 8 lbs. 8 oz.   **Stock:** Walnut
Features: Double-set triggers; casehardened receiver; patch-box and furniture
Also available:
Single Trigger Infantry Model $1060.00

NAVY ARMS REPLICA RIFLES

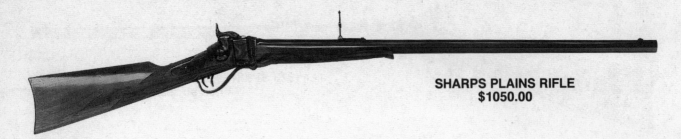

SHARPS PLAINS RIFLE
$1050.00

SPECIFICATIONS
Caliber: 45-70
Barrel length: 32″ octagonal   **Overall length:** 49″
Weight: 9 lbs. 8 oz.

Sights: Blade front, ladder rear (optional tang sight avail.)
Stock: Walnut
Features: Color casehardened receiver and furniture; double-set triggers

SHARPS BUFFALO RIFLE
$1080.00

SPECIFICATIONS
Caliber: 45-70 or 45-90
Barrel length: 28″ octagonal   **Overall length:** 46″
Weight: 10 lbs. 10 oz.

Sights: Blade front, ladder rear (tang sight optional w/set triggers only—$65.00)
Stock: Walnut
Features: Color casehardened receiver and furniture; double-set trigger

KODIAK MK IV DOUBLE RIFLE
$3125.00

SPECIFICATIONS
Caliber: 45-70
Barrel length: 24″   **Overall length:** 39³/₄″
Weight: 10 lbs. 3 oz.
Sights: Bead front, folding-leaf express rear
Stock: Checkered European walnut

Features: Color casehardened locks, breech and hammers; semi-regulated barrels

Also available:
DELUXE KODIAK MK IV DOUBLE RIFLE w/browned barrels and hand-engraving on satin frame and fittings **$4000.00**

NAVY ARMS REPLICA RIFLES

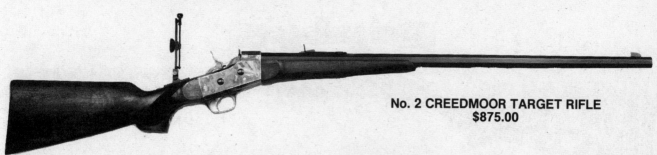

No. 2 CREEDMOOR TARGET RIFLE
$875.00

This reproduction of the Remington No. 2 Creedmoor Rifle features a color casehardened receiver and steel trigger guard, tapered octagon barrel, and walnut forend and buttstock with checkered pistol grip.

SPECIFICATIONS
Caliber: 45-70
Barrel length: 30″, tapered   **Overall length:** 46″
Weight: 9 lbs.
Sights: Globe front, adjustable Creedmoor rear
Stock: Checkered walnut stock and forend

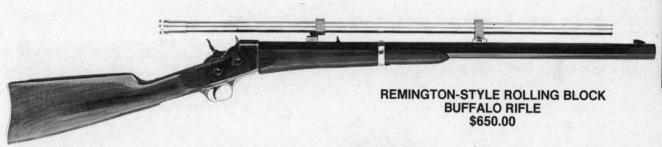

REMINGTON-STYLE ROLLING BLOCK
BUFFALO RIFLE
$650.00

This replica of the rifle used by buffalo hunters and plainsmen of the 1800s features a casehardened receiver, solid brass trigger guard and walnut stock and forend. The tang is drilled and tapped to accept the optional Creedmoor sight.

SPECIFICATIONS
Caliber: 45-70
Barrel length: 26″ or 30″; full octagon or half-round
Sights: Blade front, open notch rear
Stock: Walnut stock and forend
Feature: Shown with optional 32½″ Model 1860 brass telescopic sight **$210.00**; Compact Model (18″) is **$200.00**

GREENER LIGHT MODEL
HARPOON GUN
$995.00

Designed for large game fish, the Greener Harpoon gun utilizes the time-proven Martini action. The complete outfit consists of gun, harpoons, harpoon lines, line release frames, blank cartridges and cleaning kit—all housed in a carrying case.

SPECIFICATIONS
Caliber: 38 Special (blank)
Barrel length: 20″   **Overall length:** 36″
Weight: 6 lbs. 5 oz.   **Stock:** Walnut

NEW ENGLAND FIREARMS RIFLES

HANDI-RIFLE

HANDI-RIFLE

SPECIFICATIONS
Calibers: 22 Hornet, 223 Rem., 243 Win., 270 Win., 280 Rem., 30-06, 30-30 Win., 45-70 Govt., 44 Rem. Mag.
Action: Break-open; side lever release; positive ejection
Barrel length: 22″
Weight: 7 lbs.
Sights: Ramp front; fully adjustable rear; tapped for scope mounts (22 Hornet, 30-30 Win. and 45-70 Govt. only)
Length of pull: 14 1/4″
Drop at comb: 1 1/2″ (1 1/4″ in Monte Carlo)
Drop at heel: 2 1/8″ (1 1/8″ in Monte Carlo)

Stock: American hardwood, walnut finish; full pistol grip
Features: Semi-beavertail forend; patented transfer bar safety; automatic ejection; rebated muzzle; hammer extension; sling swivel studs on stock and forend

Prices:
In 223 Rem., blued	$209.95
In 223 Rem., Bull barrel, blued	209.95
In 22 Hornet, 243 Win., 270 Win., 30-06, 30-30 Win., 44 Rem. Mag., 45-70 Govt.	209.95
In 280 Rem. (26″ barrel), blued	214.95

SURVIVOR RIFLE (357 Magnum)

SURVIVOR RIFLE

This first rifle in New England Firearms's **Survivor** line features a moderate to very mild recoil level, even though the 357 Magnum chambering is effective for medium game as well as a defensive round (it can also be used with more inexpensive 38 Special ammo for training and informal target practice). The single-shot break action is durable and easy to operate.

SPECIFICATIONS
Caliber: 357 Mag. (3″ chamber)
Action: Break action **Capacity:** Single shot
Barrel length: 22″ **Overall length:** 36″
Weight: 6 lbs.

Stock: High-impact synthetic thumbhole stock with beavertail forend
Finish: Matte blue or electroless matte nickel
Features: Fully adjustable rifle sights; drilled and tapped for scope; transfer bar safety
Prices:
Blued	$219.95
Nickel	234.95

Also available in 223 Rem. Specifications are the same but this model has a scope rail instead of the adjustable rifle sight.

PEDERSOLI REPLICA RIFLES

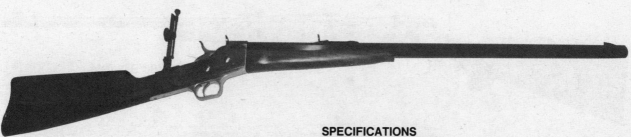

ROLLING BLOCK TARGET RIFLE
$725.00   ($810.00 w/Creedmoor Sight)

SPECIFICATIONS
Calibers: 45-70 and 357
Barrel length: 30″ octagonal (blued)
Weight: 9½ lbs. (45-70); 10 lbs. (357)
Sights: Adjustable rear sight; tunnel modified front (all models designed for fitting of Creedmoor sight)

Also available:
Cavalry, Infantry, Long Range
    Creedmoor . . . .$650.00–$875.00

SPECIFICATIONS
Caliber: 54
Barrel length: 22″ round (6 grooves)
Overall length: 39″
Weight: 7½ lbs.
Sights: Fully adjustable rear; fixed front

Also available:
Sharps 1859 Military Rifle (set trigger, 30″ barrel, 8.4 lbs.).
    Price: $1095.00

SHARPS CARBINE MODEL 766
$885.00 w/Patchbox

SPECIFICATIONS
Calibers: 45-70, 9.3×74R, 8×57JSR
Barrel length: 22″ (24″ 45-70)
Overall length: 39″ (40½″ 45-70)
Weight: 8.24 lbs. (9.7 lbs. 45/70)

Also available:
Kodiak Mark IV w/interchangeable 20-gauge barrel
    Price: $4125.00

KODIAK MARK IV DOUBLE RIFLE
$2495.00

REMINGTON BOLT-ACTION RIFLES

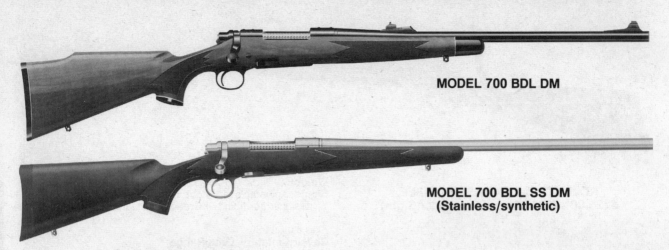

MODEL 700 BDL DM

MODEL 700 BDL SS DM (Stainless/synthetic)

MODEL 700 BDL DM
$629.00   ($656.00 Magnum)

The new Model 700 DM (Detachable Magazine) models feature detachable 4-shot magazines (except magnum-caliber models, which have 3-shot capacity), stainless-steel latches, latch springs and magazine boxes. Model 700 BDL DM rifles feature the standard Remington BDL barrel contour with 22″ barrels on standard caliber models and 24″ barrels on magnum caliber rifles. All barrels feature a hooded front sight and adjustable rear sight. Polished blued-metal finish is used throughout, along with a high-gloss, Monte Carlo-style cap, white line spacers and 20 lines-to-the-inch skipline checkering. Recoil pad and swivel studs are included. **Calibers:** Standard—6mm Rem., 25-06 Rem., 243 Win., 270 Win., 280 Rem., 7mm-08 Rem., 30-06, 308 Win.; Magnum—7mm Rem. Mag., 300 Win. Mag., 338 Win. Mag.

MODEL 700 BDL SS

MODEL 700 BDL

This Model 700 features the Monte Carlo American walnut stock finished to a high gloss with fine-cut skipline checkering. Also includes a hinged floorplate, sling swivels studs, hooded ramp front sight and adjustable rear sight. Also available in stainless synthetic version (Model 700 BDL SS) with stainless-steel barrel, receiver and bolt plus synthetic stock for maximum weather resistance. For additional specifications, see Model 700 table on the following page.

Model 700 BDL	Prices
In 17 Rem., 7mm Rem. Mag., 300 Win. Mag.	$603.00
In 222 Rem., 22-250 Rem., 223 Rem., 243 Win.,	
25-06 Rem., 270 Win., 30-06	576.00
Left Hand in 270 Win., 30-06	603.00
Left Hand in 7mm Rem. Mag.	629.00
Model BDL SS (Stainless Synthetic) in 270 Win.	
30-06	623.00
In 7mm Rem. Mag., 300 Win. Mag.	649.00

MODEL 700 BDL SS DM B
$762.00

Available in **calibers:** 7mm Rem. Mag., 300 Win. Mag., 300 Wby. Mag. and 338 Win. Mag. **Barrel length:** 25½″ (magnum contour barrel). Stainless synthetic detachable magazine with muzzle brake.

REMINGTON BOLT-ACTION RIFLES

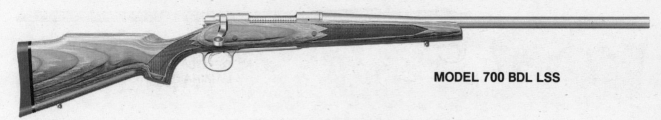

MODEL 700 BDL LSS

MODEL 700 BDL LSS
$676.00

The new Model 700 BDL LSS features a stainless barrel, laminated synthetic stock, hinged magazine floorplate and sling swivel studs. **Calibers:** 270 Win., 30-06, 7mm Rem. Mag., 300 Win. Mag. **Barrel length:** 24″. **Overall length:** 44½″. **Weight:** 7½ lbs. (Magnum); 7⅜ lbs. (Long Action). **Length of pull:** 13⅜″. **Drop at comb:** ½″. **Drop at heel:** ⅜″

MODEL 700 "SENDERO SPECIAL"

MODEL 700 SENDERO
$686.00   ($713.00 Magnum)

Remington's Sendero rifle combines the accuracy features of the Model 700 Varmint Special with long action and magnum calibers for long-range hunting. The 26-inch barrel has a heavy varmint profile and features a spherical concave crown. For additional specifications, see table on the following page.

MODEL 700 SENDERO SF

MODEL 700 SENDERO SF
$826.00 (25-06 Rem.)
$853.00 (7mm Rem. Mag. and 300 Win. Mag.)

This new version of the Model 700 Sendero features a stainless steel barrel, receiver and bolt, and a 26-inch barrel with six longitudinal flutes to improve heat dissipation and reduce gun weight (8½ lbs.). A new spherical, concave crown protects the muzzle.

MODEL 700 ADL (not shown)
$472.00 ($412.00 Synthetic)

See table on the following page for specifications. Synthetic model has a fiberglass-reinforced synthetic stock, positive checkering, straight comb, raised cheekpiece and black rubber recoil pad. Stock and blued metalwork have a non-reflective black matte finish.

REMINGTON BOLT-ACTION RIFLES

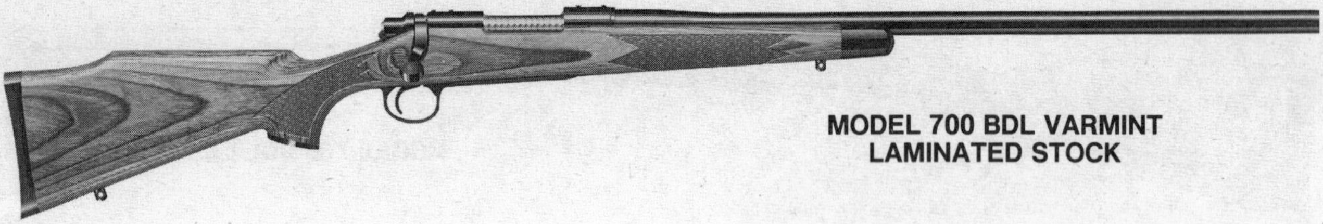

MODEL 700 BDL VARMINT
LAMINATED STOCK

MODEL 700 VS VARMINT SYNTHETIC BOLT-ACTION CENTERFIRE RIFLE

With heavy barrel, synthetic stock and aluminum bedding block **$686.00**
With stainless fluted barrel and synthetic stock in 220 Swift, 22-250 Rem. 223 Rem., 308 Win. . . **826.00**

Also available:
MODEL 700 BDL VARMINT LAMINATED STOCK (VLS) in 222 Rem., 22-250 Rem., 223 Rem., 243 Win. and 308 Win. **$609.00**

SPECIFICATIONS MODEL 700

			Overall Length/Avg. Wt. (lbs.)									
										Varmint Synthetic[1]		Twist
Calibers	Magazine Capacity	Barrel Length	Mtn Rifle (DM)	Sendero™ [1] (26" Barrel)	BDL Stainless Synthetic (DM)	BDL Stainless Synthetic	ADL & BDL	BDL (DM)	VLS (Varmint Laminated Stock)[1]	(26" Heavy BBL)	(26" Stainless Fluted BBL)	R-H, 1 turn in
17 Remington	5	24"	—	—	—	—	43 ⅝"/ 7 ¼	—	—	—	—	9"
220 Swift	4	26"	—	—	—	—	—	—	—	45 ¾"/ 9	45 ¾"/ 8 ½	14"
222 Remington	5	24"	—	—	—	—	43 ⅝"/ 7 ¼	—	45 ½"/ 9 ⅜	—	—	14"
22-250 Remington	4	24"	—	—	—	—	43 ⅝"/ 7 ¼	—	45 ½"/ 9 ⅜	45 ¾"/ 9	45 ¾"/ 8 ½	14"
	4	24"	—	—	—	—	43 ⅝"/ 7 ¼	—	—	—	—	14"
223 Remington	5	24"	—	—	—	—	43 ⅝"/ 7 ¼	—	45 ½"/ 9 ⅜	45 ¾"/ 9	45 ¾"/ 8 ½	12"
6mm Remington	4	22"	—	—	—	—	—	41 ¾"/ 7 ¼	—	—	—	9 ⅛"
	4	24"	—	—	43 ½"/ 7	—	—	—	—	—	—	9 ⅛"
243 Win.	4	22"	41 ¾"/6 ⅜	—	—	—	41 ⅝"/ 7 ¼	41 ¾"/ 7 ¼	—	—	—	9 ⅛"
	4	22"	—	—	—	—	41 ⅝"/ 7 ¼	41 ¾"/ 7 ¼	—	—	—	9 ⅛"
	4	24"	—	—	43 ½"/ 7	—	—	—	45 ½"/ 9 ⅜	—	—	9 ⅛"
25-06 Remington	4	24"	—	45 ¾"/ 9	44 ½"/ 7 ⅜	—	44 ½"/ 7 ¼	44½"/ 7 ⅜	—	—	—	10"
	4	22"	42 ½"/6 ⅜	—	—	—	—	—	—	—	—	10"
270 Win.	4	22"	42 ½"/6 ⅜	—	—	—	42 ½"/ 7 ¼	42 ½"/ 7 ⅜	—	—	—	10"
	4	22"	—	—	—	—	42 ½"/ 7 ¼	42 ½"/ 7 ⅜	—	—	—	10"
	4	24"	—	45 ¾"/ 9	44 ½"/ 7 ⅜	44 ½"/7 ¼	—	—	—	—	—	10"
280 Remington	4	22"	42 ½"/6 ⅜	—	—	—	42 ½"/ 7 ¼	42 ½"/ 7 ⅜	—	—	—	9 ¼"
	4	24"	—	—	44 ½"/ 7 ⅜	44 ½"/7 ¼	—	—	—	—	—	9 ¼"
7mm-08 Remington	4	22"	41 ¾"/6 ⅜	—	—	—	—	41 ¾"/ 7 ¼	—	—	—	9 ¼"
	4	22"	—	—	—	—	—	41 ¾"/ 7 42 ½"/ 7 ⅜	—	—	—	9 ¼"
	4	24"	—	—	43 ½"/ 7	—	—	—	—	—	—	9 ¼"
7mm Rem. Mag.	3	24"	—	45 ¾"/ 9	44 ½"/ 7 ½	44 ½"/ 7 ½	44 ½"/ 7 ½	44 ½"/ 7 ¾	—	—	—	9 ¼"
	3	24"	—	—	—	—	44 ½"/ 7 ½	44 ½"/ 7 ¾	—	—	—	9 ¼"
30-06	4	22"	42 ½"/6 ⅜	—	—	—	42 ½"/ 7 ¼	42 ½"/ 7 ⅜	—	—	—	10"
	4	22"	—	—	—	—	42 ½"/ 7 ¼	42 ½"/ 7 ¼	—	—	—	10"
	4	24"	—	—	44 ½"/ 7 ⅜	44 ½"/7 ¼	—	—	—	—	—	10"
308 Win.	4	22"	—	—	—	—	41 ⅝"/ 7 ¼	41 ¾"/ 7 ¼	—	—	—	10"
	4	24"	—	—	43½"/ 7	—	—	—	45 ½"/ 9 ⅜	45 ¾"/ 9	45 ¾"/ 8 ½	12"
	4	22"	—	—	—	—	41 ⅝"/ 7 ¼	—	—	—	—	10"
300 Win. Mag.	3	24"	—	45 ¾"/ 9	44½"/ 7 ½	44 ½"/ 7 ½	44 ½"/ 7 ½	44½"/ 7 ¾	—	—	—	10"
	3	24"	—	—	—	—	—	44½"/ 7 ¾	—	—	—	10"
300 Wby. Mag.	3	24"	—	—	44½"/ 7 ½	—	—	—	—	—	—	12"
338 Win. Mag.	3	24"	—	—	44½"/ 7 ½	—	—	—	—	—	—	10"
	3	24"	—	—	—	—	—	44½"/ 7 ¾	—	—	—	10"
Stock Length of Pull			13 ⅜"	13 ⅜"	13 ⅜"	13⅜"	13 ⅜"	13 ⅜"	13 ½"	13 ⅜"	13 ⅜"	
Dimensions: Drop at Comb (from centerline of bore)			⅜"	⅝"	½"	½"	½"	½"	15/16"	⅝"	⅝"	
Drop at Heel (from centerline of bore)			⅜"	⅝"	⅜"	⅜"	1 ⅜"	1 ⅜"	13/16"	⅝"	⅝"	

[1]Sendero™, Varmint Laminated Synthetic, Varmint Synthetic Stainless Fluted and Varmint Synthetic equipped with a 26" barrel only. LH = Left Hand. All Model 700™ and Model Seven™ rifles come with sling swivel studs. The BDL, ADL, and Seven™ (except Seven™ chambered for 17 Remington) are furnished with sights. The BDL Stainless Synthetic, Mountain Rifle, Classic, and Varmint guns have clean barrels. All Remington centerfire rifles are drilled and tapped for scope mounts.

REMINGTON BOLT-ACTION RIFLES

MODEL 700 CLASSIC (375 H&H)
$623.00

Since Remington's series of Model 700 Classics began in 1981, the company has offered this model in a special chambering each year. The 300 Win. Mag. was introduced in 1963 for the Model 70 bolt-action rifle following the development of the 338 Win. Mag., 30-338 Wildcat and 308 Norma Mag. The 300 Win. Mag. has a slightly longer body and a shorter neck than its predecessors and is recommended for all North American big-

game hunting. The 375 H&H shown above was introduced in 1996.

The Model 700 Classic features an American walnut, straight-comb stock without a cheekpiece for rapid mounting, better sight alignment and reduced felt recoil. A hinged magazine floorplate, sling swivel studs and satin wood finish with cut-checkering are standard, along with 24″ barrel and 1:10″ twist. Receivers drilled/tapped for scope mounts.

MODEL 700 MOUNTAIN DM
(DETACHABLE MAGAZINE) RIFLE
$629.00

The Remington Model 700 MTN DM rifle features the traditional mountain rifle-styled stock with a pistol grip pitched lower to position the wrist for a better grip. The cheekpiece is designed to align the eye for quick, accurate sighting. The American walnut stock has a hand-rubbed oil finish and comes with a brown recoil pad and deep-cut checkering. The Model 700 MTN DM also features a lean contoured 22″ barrel that helps

reduce total weight to 6.75 pounds. (no sights). All metalwork features a glass bead-blasted, blued-metal finish. **Calibers:** 243 Win., 25-06 Rem., 270 Win., 7mm-08 Rem., 280 Rem and 30-06 Springfield.
Also available:
Left Hand in 270 and 30-06 . . . . **$656.00**
Left Hand in 7mm Rem. Mag. and 300 Win. Mag. . **682.00**

MODEL 700 ALASKAN WILDERNESS RIFLE (AWR)
$1318.00

This custom-built rifle has the same rate of twist and custom magnum barrel contour as the African Plains Rifle below, but features a Kevlar-reinforced composite stock. **Calibers:** 7mm

Rem. Mag., 300 Win. Mag., 300 Wby. Mag., 338 Win. Mag., 375 H&H Mag. **Capacity:** 3 shots. **Barrel length:** 26″. **Overall length:** 46¹/₂″. **Weight:** 7³/₄ lbs.

MODEL 700 AFRICAN PLAINS RIFLE (APR)
$1466.00

The custom-built Model 700 APR rifle has a laminated classic wood stock and the following specifications. **Calibers:** 7mm Rem. Mag., 300 Win. Mag., 300 Wby. Mag., 338 Win. Mag., 375 H&H Mag. **Capacity:** 3 shots. **Barrel length:** 24″. **Overall**

length: 44¹/₂″. **Weight:** 6³/₄ lbs. **Rate of twist:** R.H. 1 turn in 9¹/₄″ (7mm Rem. Mag.); 10″ (300 Win. Mag. and 338 Win. Mag.); 12″ (300 Wby. Mag. and 375 H&H Mag.).

REMINGTON BOLT-ACTION RIFLES

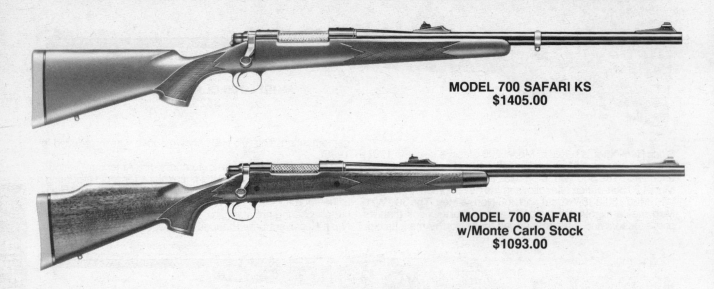

MODEL 700 SAFARI KS
$1405.00

MODEL 700 SAFARI
w/Monte Carlo Stock
$1093.00

Model 700™ Safari Grade bolt-action rifles provide big-game hunters with a choice of either wood or synthetic stocks. Model 700 Safari Monte Carlo (with Monte Carlo comb and cheekpiece) and Model 700 Safari Classic (with straight-line classic comb and no cheekpiece) are the satin-finished wood-stock models. Both are decorated with hand-cut checkering 18 lines to the inch and fitted with two reinforcing crossbolts covered with rosewood plugs. The Monte Carlo model also has rose-wood pistol-grip and forend caps. All models are fitted with sling swivel studs and 24″ barrels. Synthetic stock has simulated wood-grain finish, reinforced with Kevlar® (KS). **Calibers:** 8mm Rem. Mag., 375 H&H Magnum, 416 Rem. Mag. and 458 Win. Mag. **Capacity:** 3 rounds. **Avg. weight:** 9 lbs. **Overall length:** 44½″. **Rate of twist:** 10″ (8mm Rem. Mag.); 12″ (375 H&H Mag.); 14″ (416 Rem. Mag., 458 Win. Mag.).

MODEL 40-XR KS SPORTER
Target Rimfire Position Rifle w/Kevlar Stock
$1428.00

Action: Bolt action, single shot
Caliber: 22 Long Rifle rimfire **Capacity:** Single loading
Barrel: 24″ medium weight target barrel countersunk at muzzle. Drilled and tapped for target scope blocks. Fitted with front sight base
Bolt: Artillery style with lockup at rear; 6 locking lugs, double extractors
Overall length: 43½″ **Average weight:** 10½ lbs.
Sights: Optional at extra cost; Williams Receiver No. FPTK and Redfield Globe front match sight
Safety: Positive serrated thumb safety
Receiver: Drilled and tapped for receiver sight
Trigger: Adjustable from 2 to 4 lbs.

Stock: Position style with Monte Carlo, cheekpiece and thumb groove; five-way adj. buttplate and full-length guide rail

Also available:
MODEL 40-XR BR with 22″ stainless-steel barrel (heavy contour), 22 LR match chamber and bore dimensioms. Receiver and barrel drilled and tapped for scope mounts (mounted on green, Du Pont Kevlar reinforced fiberglass benchrest stock. Fully adjustable trigger (2 oz. trigger optional).
Price: **$1470.00**
(Additional target rifles are available through Remington's Custom Shop.)

REMINGTON BOLT-ACTION RIFLES

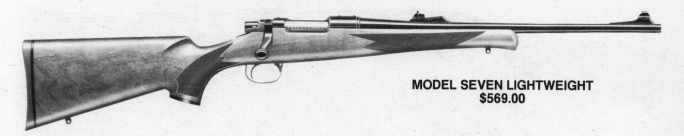

MODEL SEVEN LIGHTWEIGHT
$569.00

MODEL SEVEN RIFLES

Every **Model Seven** is built to the accuracy standards of the famous Model 700 and is individually test fired to prove it. Its tapered 18½" Remington special steel barrel is free floating out to a single pressure point at the forend tip. And there is ordnance-quality steel in everything from its fully enclosed bolt and extractor system to its steel trigger guard and floorplate. Ramp front and fully adjustable rear sights, sling swivel studs are standard. The Youth Model features a hardwood stock that is 1 inch shorter for easy control. Chambered in 243 Win. and 7mm-08 for less recoil. See table at right for additional specifications.

SPECIFICATIONS MODEL SEVEN™

Calibers	Clip Mag. Capacity	Barrel Length	Overall Length	Twist R-H 1 Turn In	Avg. Wt. (lbs.)
223 Rem.	5	18½"	37¾"	12"	6¼
243 Win.	4	18½"	37¾"	9⅛"	6¼
	4	18½"	36¾" (Youth)	9⅛"	6
	4	20"	39¼"	9⅛"	6¼
6mm Rem.	4	18½"	37¾"	9⅛"	6¼
7mm-08 Rem.	4	18½"	37¾"	9¼"	6¼
	4	18½"	36¾" (Youth)	9¼"	6
	4	20"	39¼"	9¼"	6¼
308 Win.	4	18½"	37¾"	10"	6¼
	4	20"	39¼"	10"	6¼

Stock Dimensions: 13³⁄₁₆" length of pull, ⁹⁄₁₆" drop at comb, ⁵⁄₁₆" drop at heel. Youth gun has 12½" length of pull. 17. Rem. provided without sights.
Note: New Model Seven Mannlicher and Model Seven KS versions are available from the Remington Custom Shop through your local dealer.

MODEL SEVEN YOUTH
$465.00

MODEL SEVEN
STAINLESS SYNTHETIC
$623.00 (243 Win., 7mm-08 Rem., 308 Win.)

RIFLES

REMINGTON REPEATING RIFLES

MODEL 7400 (High Gloss Stock)
$573.00

Calibers: 243 Win., 270 Win., 280 Rem., 30-06, 308 Win., 35 Whelen
Capacity: 5 centerfire cartridges (4 in the magazine, 1 in the chamber); extra 4-shot magazine available
Action: Gas-operated; receiver drilled and tapped for scope mounts
Barrel lengths: 22″ (18½″ in 30-06 Carbine)
Weight: 7½ lbs. (7¼ lbs. in 30-06 Carbine and 35 Whelen)

Overall length: 42″
Sights: Standard blade ramp front; sliding ramp rear
Stock: Satin or high-gloss (270 Win. and 30-06 only) walnut stock and forend; curved pistol grip; also available with Special Purpose nonreflective finish (270 Win. and 30-06 only)
Length of pull: 13⅜″
Drop at heel: 2¼″ **Drop at comb:** 1¹³/₁₆″

MODEL 7600 (High Gloss Stock)
$540.00

The Model 7600 shares nearly the same specifications as the Model 7400 featured above, except the 7600 is pump action.
Drop at heel: ¹⁵/₁₆″. **Drop at comb:** ⁹/₁₆″.

Also available:
MODELS 7400 and 7600 with new fine-line engravings of game scenes on right receiver panels (includes scrollwork).
Prices:
F Grade **$5377.00**
F Grade w/gold inlay **8062.00**

MODEL 7400
w/New Engraving

MODEL 7600
Close-up of Left Side of Receiver
w/New Engraving

REMINGTON RIMFIRE RIFLES

MODEL 522 VIPER (22 LR)
$165.00

Remington's autoloading rimfire rifle utilizes a strong lightweight stock of PET resin that is impervious to changing temperatures and humidity. The receiver is made of a Du Pont high-tech synthetic. All exposed metalwork, including barrel, breech bolt and trigger guard, have a nonglare, black matte finish. Stock shape with slim pistol grip and semibeavertail forend is proportioned to fit the size and stature of younger or smaller shooters. Other features include: factory-installed centerfire-type iron sights, detachable clip magazine, safety features, primary and secondary sears in trigger mechanism and a protective ejection port shield.

MODEL 541-T BOLT ACTION
$455.00
$481.00 (Heavy Barrel)
$239.00 (Model 581-S)

RIMFIRE RIFLE SPECIFICATIONS

Model	Action	Barrel Length	Overall Length	Average Wt. (lbs.)	Magazine Capacity
522 Viper	Auto	20″	40″	4⅝	10-Shot Clip
541-T	Bolt	24″	42½″	5⅞*	5-Shot Clip
581-S	Bolt	24″	42½″	5⅞	5-Shot Clip
552 BDL Deluxe Speedmaster	Auto	21″	40″	5¾	15 Long Rifle
572 BDL Deluxe Fieldmaster	Pump	21″	40″	5½	15 Long Rifle

* 6½ lbs. in Heavy Barrel model

MODEL 552 BDL DELUXE SPEEDMASTER
$340.00

The rimfire semiautomatic 552 BDL Deluxe sports Remington custom-impressed checkering on both stock and forend.

Tough Du Pont RK-W lifetime finish brings out the lustrous beauty of the walnut while protecting it. Sights are ramp-style in front and rugged big-game type fully adjustable in rear.

MODEL 572 BDL DELUXE FIELDMASTER
$353.00

Features of this rifle with big-game feel and appearance are: Du Pont's tough RK-W finish; centerfire-rifle-type rear sight fully adjustable for both vertical and horizontal sight alignment; big-game style ramp front sight; Remington impressed checkering on both stock and forend.

RIFLES, INC.

CUSTOM RIFLES

CLASSIC MODEL

CLASSIC MODEL
$1550.00

SPECIFICATIONS
Calibers: Customized for varmint, target or hunter specifications, up to 375 H&H
Action: Remington or Winchester stainless steel Control-round with lapped bolt

Barrel length: 26″–28″ depending on caliber; stainless-steel match grade, lapped
Weight: 6½ lbs. (approx.)
Stock: Pillar glass bedded; laminated fiberglass, finished with textured epoxy
Features: Fine-tuned and adjustable trigger; hinged floorplate trigger guard

SAFARI MODEL

SAFARI MODEL
$1950.00   ($2970.00 with Options)

SPECIFICATIONS
Action: Winchester Model 70 Control-round feed; hand lapped and honed bolt; drilled and tapped for 8×40 base screws
Barrel length: 23″–25″ depending on caliber; stainless-steel match grade, lapped

Weight: 9 lbs. (approx.)
Muzzle break: Stainless Quiet Slimbrake
Metal finish: Matte stainless or black Teflon
Stock: Pillar glass bedded; double reinforced laminated fiberglass/graphite; finished with textured epoxy
Features: Fine-tuned and adjustable trigger; hinged floorplate
Options: Drop box for additional rounds; express sights; barrel band; quarter ribs

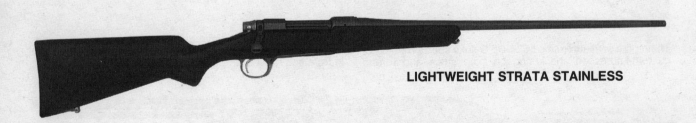

LIGHTWEIGHT STRATA STAINLESS

LIGHTWEIGHT STRATA STAINLESS MODEL
$2150.00

SPECIFICATIONS
Calibers: Up to 375 H&H
Action: Stainless Remington; fluted, tapped and handle-hollowed bolt; aluminum bolt shroud

Barrel length: 22″–24″ depending on caliber; stainless-steel match grade
Weight: 4.75 lbs. (approx.)
Stock: Pillar glass bedded; laminated Kevlar/Boron/Graphite, finished with textured epoxy
Features: Matte stainless metal finish; aluminum blind or hinged floorplate trigger guard; custom Protektor pad

ROSSI RIFLES

PUMP-ACTION GALLERY GUNS

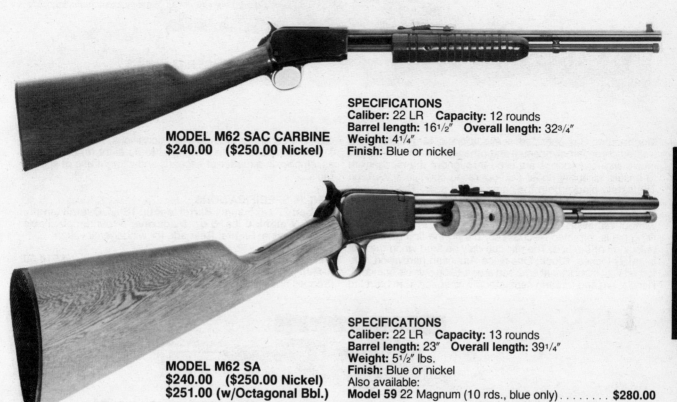

MODEL M62 SAC CARBINE
$240.00   ($250.00 Nickel)

SPECIFICATIONS
Caliber: 22 LR   **Capacity:** 12 rounds
Barrel length: 16½"   **Overall length:** 32¾"
Weight: 4¼"
Finish: Blue or nickel

MODEL M62 SA
$240.00   ($250.00 Nickel)
$251.00 (w/Octagonal Bbl.)

SPECIFICATIONS
Caliber: 22 LR   **Capacity:** 13 rounds
Barrel length: 23"   **Overall length:** 39¼"
Weight: 5½" lbs.
Finish: Blue or nickel
Also available:
Model 59 22 Magnum (10 rds., blue only) **$280.00**

LEVER-ACTION OLD WEST CARBINES

MODEL M92 SRC

MODEL M92 SRS
$360.00 (not shown)

SPECIFICATIONS
Caliber: 38 Special or 357 Magnum
Capacity: 8 rounds
Barrel length: 16"
Overall length: 33"
Weight: 5¾ lbs.
Finish: Blue

MODEL M92 SRC
$360.00

SPECIFICATIONS
Caliber: 38 Special or 357 Magnum   **Capacity:** 10 rounds
Barrel length: 20"   **Overall length:** 37"
Weight: 6 lbs.
Finish: Blue
Also available:
Model M92 (44-40 and 45 L.C.) **$364.00**

RIFLES

RUGER CARBINES

RUGER MINI-14/5

Mechanism: Gas-operated, semiautomatic. **Materials:** Heat-treated chrome molybdenum and other alloy steels as well as music wire coil springs are used throughout the mechanism to ensure reliability under field-operating conditions. **Safety:** The safety blocks both the hammer and sear. The slide can be cycled when the safety is on. The safety is mounted in the front of the trigger guard so that it may be set to Fire position without removing finger from trigger guard. **Firing pin:** The firing pin is retracted mechanically during the first part of the unlocking of the bolt. The rifle can only be fired when the bolt is safely locked. **Stock:** One-piece American hardwood reinforced with steel liner at stressed areas. Sling swivels standard. Handguard and forearm separated by air space from barrel to promote cooling under rapid-fire conditions. **Field stripping:** The Carbine can be field-stripped to its eight (8) basic sub-assemblies in a matter of seconds and without use of special tools.

MINI-14 SPECIFICATIONS
Caliber: 223 (5.56mm). **Barrel length:** 18½". **Overall length:** 37¼". **Weight:** 6 lbs. 8 oz. **Magazine:** 5-round, detachable box magazine. **Sights:** Rear adj. for windage/elevation.
Prices:
Mini-14/5 Blued **$516.00**
K-Mini-14/5 Stainless Steel **569.00**
(Scopes rings not included)

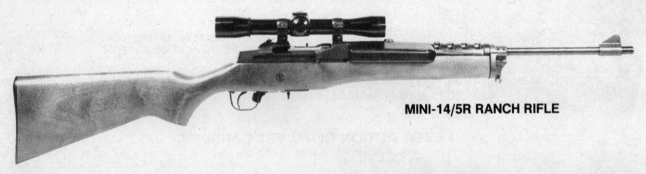

MINI-14/5R RANCH RIFLE

SPECIFICATIONS
Caliber: 223 (5.56mm). **Barrel length:** 18½". **Overall length:** 37¼". **Weight:** 6 lbs. 8 oz. **Magazine:** 5-round detachable box magazine. **Sights:** Fold-down rear sight; 1" scope rings
Prices:
Mini-14/5R Blued **$556.00**
K-Mini-14/5R Stainless Steel **609.00**

MINI-THIRTY

This modified version of the Ruger Ranch rifle is chambered for the 7.62 × 39mm Soviet service cartridge. Designed for use with telescopic sights, it features low, compact scope-mounting for greater accuracy and carrying ease, and a buffer in the receiver. Sling swivels are standard.

SPECIFICATIONS
Caliber: 7.62×39mm. **Barrel length:** 18½". **Overall length:** 37⅛". **Weight:** 6 lbs. 14 oz. (empty). **Magazine capacity:** 5 shots. **Rifling:** 6 grooves, R.H. twist, 1:10". **Finish:** Blued or stainless. **Stock:** One-piece American hardwood w/steel liners in stressed areas. **Sights:** Blade front; peep rear.
Prices:
In Blue **$556.00**
In Stainless steel **609.00**

RUGER CARBINES

STANDARD 10/22 CARBINE

DELUXE 10/22 SPORTER

MODEL K10/22RBI INTERNATIONAL CARBINE STAINLESS

MODEL 10/22T TARGET

MODEL 10/22 CARBINE 22 LONG RIFLE

Construction of the 10/22 Carbine is rugged and follows the Ruger design practice of building a firearm from integrated sub-assemblies. For example, the trigger housing assembly contains the entire ignition system, which employs a high-speed, swinging hammer to ensure the shortest possible lock time. The barrel is assembled to the receiver by a unique dual-screw dovetail system that provides unusual rigidity and strength—and accounts, in part, for the exceptional accuracy of the 10/22.

SPECIFICATIONS
Mechanism: Blow-back, semiautomatic. **Caliber:** 22 LR, high-speed or standard-velocity loads. **Magazine:** 10-shot capacity, exclusive Ruger rotary design; fits flush into stock. **Barrel:** 18½", assembled to the receiver by dual-screw dovetail mounting for added strength and rigidity. **Overall length:** 37¼". **Weight:** 5 lbs. **Sights:** 1/16" brass bead front; single folding-leaf rear, adjustable for elevation; receiver drilled and tapped for scope blocks or tip-off mount adapter (included). **Trigger:** Curved finger surface, 3/8" wide. **Safety:** Sliding cross-button type; safety locks both sear and hammer and cannot be put in safe position unless gun is cocked. **Stocks:** 10/22 RB is birch; 10/22 SP Deluxe Sporter is American walnut. **Finish:** Polished all over and blued or anodized or brushed satin bright metal.

Model 10/22 RB Standard (Birch carbine stock) . . $213.00
Model 10/22 DSP Deluxe (Hand-checkered
   American walnut) 274.00
Model K10/22 RB Stainless 255.00
Model K10/22 RBI International Carbine w/full-
   length hardwood stock, stainless-steel bbl. 282.00
MODEL 10/22 RBI International Carbine
   w/blued barrel 262.00
MODEL 10/22T TARGET (no sights) Hammer-
   forged barrel, laminated target-style stock 392.50

RUGER SINGLE-SHOT RIFLES

The following illustrations show the variations currently offered in the Ruger No. 1 Single-Shot Rifle Series. Ruger No. 1 rifles have a Farquharson-type falling-block action and select American walnut stocks. Pistol grip and forearm are hand-checkered to a borderless design. Price for any listed model is **$665.00** (except the No. 1 RSI International Model: **$688.00**). Barreled Actions (blued only): **$450.00**

NO. 1A LIGHT SPORTER

Calibers: 243 Win., 270 Win., 30-06, 7×57mm. **Barrel length:** 22″. **Sights:** Adjustable folding-leaf rear sight mounted on quarter rib with ramp front sight base and dovetail-type gold bead front sight; open. **Weight:** 7¼ lbs.

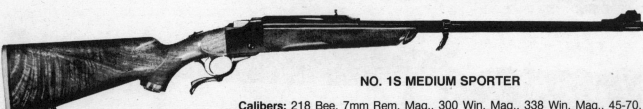

NO. 1S MEDIUM SPORTER

Calibers: 218 Bee, 7mm Rem. Mag., 300 Win. Mag., 338 Win. Mag., 45-70. **Barrel length:** 26″ (22″ in 45-70). **Sights:** (same as above). **Weight:** 8 lbs. (7¼ lbs. in 45-70).

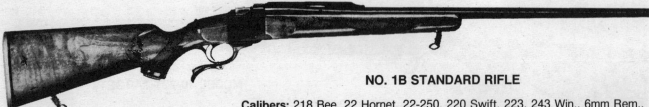

NO. 1B STANDARD RIFLE

Calibers: 218 Bee, 22 Hornet, 22-250, 220 Swift, 223, 243 Win., 6mm Rem., 25-06, 257 Roberts, 270 Win., 270 Wby. Mag., 7mm Rem. Mag., 280, 30-06, 300 Win. Mag., 300 Wby. Mag., 338 Win. Mag. **Barrel:** 26″. **Sights:** Ruger 1″ steel tip-off scope rings. **Weight:** 8 lbs.

NO. 1V SPECIAL VARMINTER

Calibers: 22 PPC, 22-250, 220 Swift, 223, 25-06, 6mm, 6mm PPC. **Barrel length:** 24″ (26″ in 220 Swift). **Sights:** Ruger target scope blocks, heavy barrel and 1″ tip-off scope rings. **Weight:** 9 lbs.

Also available:
NO. 1H TROPICAL RIFLE (24″ heavy barrel) in 375 H&H Mag., 458 Win. Mag., 416 Rigby and 416 Rem. Mag.
NO 1. RSI INTERNATIONAL (20″ lightweight barrel) in 243 Win., 270 Win., 30-06 and 7×57mm

RUGER BOLT-ACTION RIFLES

MODEL 77/22RH HORNET

MODEL 77/22RH HORNET
$489.00   ($499.00 w/Sights)

The Model 77/22RH is Ruger's first truly compact centerfire bolt-action rifle. It features a 77/22 action crafted from heat-treated alloy steel. Exterior surfaces are blued to match the hammer-forged barrel. The action features a right-hand turning bolt with a 90-degree bolt throw, cocking on opening. Fast lock time (2.7 milliseconds) adds to accuracy. A three-position swing-back safety locks the bolt; in its center position firing is blocked, but bolt operation and safe loading and unloading are permitted. When fully forward, the rifle is ready to fire. The American walnut stock has recoil pad, grip cap and sling swivels installed. One-inch diameter scope rings fit integral bases.

SPECIFICATIONS
Caliber: 22 Hornet
Capacity: 6 rounds (detachable rotary magazine)
Barrel length: 20"   **Overall length:** 40"
Weight: 6 lbs. (unloaded)
Sights: Single folding-leaf rear; gold bead front
Length of pull: 13³/₄"
Drop at heel: 2³/₈"   **Drop at comb:** 2"
Finish: Polished and blued, matte, nonglare receiver top
Also available: MODEL K77/22VH. Varmint model w/stainless-steel heavy barrel, laminated American hardwood stock. **Price:** (w/o sights) **$535.00**

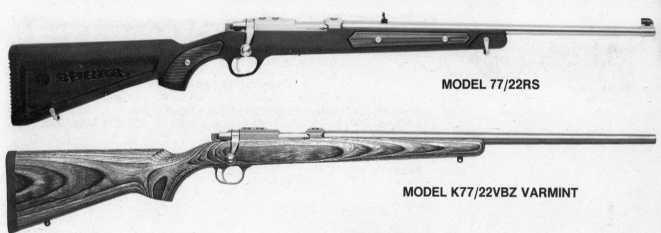

MODEL 77/22RS

MODEL K77/22VBZ VARMINT

MODEL 77/22 RIMFIRE RIFLE

The Ruger 22-caliber rimfire 77/22 bolt-action rifle has been built especially to function with the patented Ruger 10-Shot Rotary Magazine concept. The magazine throat, retaining lips, and ramps that guide the cartridge into the chamber are solid alloy steel that resists bending or deforming.

The 77/22 weighs just under six pounds. Its heavy-duty receiver incorporates the integral scope bases of the patented Ruger Scope Mounting System, with 1-inch Ruger scope rings. With the 3-position safety in its "lock" position, a dead bolt is cammed forward, locking the bolt handle down. In this position the action is locked closed and the handle cannot be raised.

All metal surfaces are finished in nonglare deep blue or satin stainless. Stock is select straight-grain American walnut, hand checkered and finished with durable polyurethane.

An All-Weather, all-stainless steel **MODEL K77/22RS** features a stock made of glass-fiber reinforced Zytel. **Weight:** Approx. 6 lbs.

SPECIFICATIONS
Calibers: 22 LR and 22 Magnum. **Barrel length:** 20". **Overall length:** 39¹/₄". **Weight:** 6 lbs. (w/o scope, magazine empty). **Feed:** Detachable 10-Shot Ruger Rotary Magazine.
Prices:

77/22R Blue, w/o sights, 1" Ruger rings	**$473.00**
77/22RM Blue, walnut stock, plain barrel, no sights, 1" Ruger rings, 22 Mag.	**473.00**
77/22RS Blue, sights included, 1" Ruger rings	**481.00**
77/22RSM Blue, American walnut, iron sights	**481.00**
K77/22-RP Synthetic stock, stainless steel, plain barrel with 1" Ruger rings	**473.00**
K77/22-RMP Synthetic stock, stainless steel, plain barrel, 1" Ruger rings	**473.00**
K77/22-RSP Synthetic stock, stainless steel, gold bead front sight, folding-leaf rear, Ruger 1" rings	**481.00**
K77/22RSMP Synthetic stock, metal sights, stainless	**481.00**
K77/22VBZ Varmint Laminated stock, scope rings, heavy barrel, stainless	**499.00**

RUGER BOLT-ACTION RIFLES

MARK II SERIES

MODEL M-77R MKII

Integral Base Receiver, 1″ scope rings. No sights.
Calibers: (Long action) 6mm Rem., 6.5×55mm, 7×57mm, 257 Roberts, 270, 280 Rem., 30-06 (all with 22″ barrels); 7mm Rem. Mag., 300 Win. Mag., 338 Win. Mag. (all with 24″ barrels); and (Short Stroke action) 223, 243, 308 (22″ barrels).
Weight: Approx. 7 lbs.

Price: **$574.00**
Also available: **M-77LR MKII** (Left Hand).
Calibers: 270, 30-06, 7mm Rem. Mag., 300 Win. Mag. 574.00

MODEL M-77RS MKII

Integral Base Receiver, Ruger steel 1″ rings, open sights.
Calibers: 243, 25-06, 270, 7mm Rem. Mag., 30-06, 300 Win. Mag., 308, 338 Win. Mag., 458 Win. Mag.
Weight: Approx. 7 lbs.

Price: **$635.00**

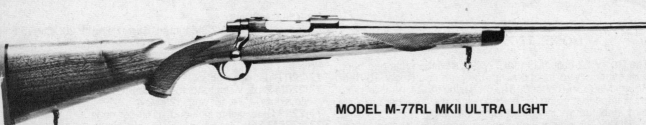

MODEL M-77RL MKII ULTRA LIGHT

This big-game, bolt-action rifle encompasses the traditional features that have made the Ruger M-77 one of the most popular centerfire rifles in the world. It includes a sliding top tang safety, a one-piece bolt with Mauser-type extractor and diagonal front mounting system. American walnut stock is hand-checkered in a sharp diamond pattern. A rubber recoil pad, pistol-grip cap and studs for mounting quick detachable sling swivels are standard. Available in both long- and short-action versions, with Integral Base Receiver and 1″ Ruger scope rings.
Calibers: 223, 243, 257, 270, 30-06, 308.
Barrel length: 20″.   **Weight:** Approx. 6 lbs.

Price: **$610.00**

RUGER BOLT-ACTION RIFLES

MARK II SERIES

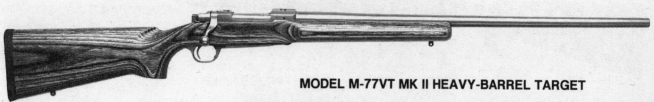

MODEL M-77VT MK II HEAVY-BARREL TARGET

Features Mark II stainless-steel bolt action, gray matte finish, two-stage adjustable trigger. No sights.
Calibers: 22 PPC, 22-250, 220 Swift, 6mm PPC, 223, 243, 25-06 and 308.
Barrel length: 26″, hammer-forged, free-floating stainless steel. **Weight:** 9³/₄ lbs.
Stock: Laminated American hardwood with flat forend.

Price: KM-77VT MK II **$684.00**

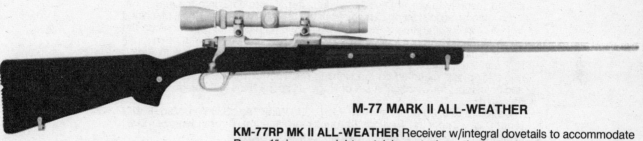

M-77 MARK II ALL-WEATHER

KM-77RP MK II ALL-WEATHER Receiver w/integral dovetails to accommodate Ruger 1″ rings, no sights, stainless steel, synthetic stock.
Calibers: 223, 22-250, 243, 270, 280, 30-06, 7mm Rem. Mag.,
300 Win. Mag., 308, 338 Win. Mag. **$574.00**
KM-77RSP MK II ALL-WEATHER Receiver w/integral dovetails to accommodate Ruger 1″ rings, metal sights, stainless steel, synthetic stock.
Calibers: 243, 270, 7mm Rem. Mag., 30-06, 300 Win. Mag.,
338 Win. Mag. **635.00**

RUGER 77RSM MK II MAGNUM RIFLE

This ''Bond Street'' quality African safari hunting rifle features a sighting rib machined from a single bar of steel; Circassian walnut stock with black forend tip; steel floorplate and latch; a new Ruger Magnum trigger guard with floorplate latch designed flush with the contours of the trigger guard (to eliminate accidental dumping of cartridges); a three-position safety mechanism (*see* illustrations); Express rear sight; and front sight ramp with gold bead sight.
Calibers: 375 H&H, 416 Rigby. **Capacity:** 4 rounds (375 H&H) and 3 rounds (416 Rigby). **Barrel length:** 22″. **Overall length:** 42¹/₈″. **Barrel thread diameter:** 1¹/₈″. **Weight:** 9¹/₄ lbs. (375 H&H); 10¹/₄ lbs. (416 Rigby).

Price: **$1550.00**

RIFLES

RUGER BOLT-ACTION RIFLES

MODEL M-77EXP MARK II EXPRESS RIFLE

For shooters who prefer a sporting rifle of premium quality and price, Ruger offers the M-77 Mark II Express rifle. Its stock is precision machined from a single blank of French walnut. Forend and pistol grip are hand-checkered in a diamond pattern with 18 lines per inch. Hardened alloy steel grip cap, trigger guard and floorplate plus a black buttpad of live rubber, black forend cap and steel studs for quick detachable sling swivels are standard.

Action is standard short or long length in blued chrome-moly steel with stainless-steel bolt. A fixed blade-type ejector working through a slot under the left locking lug replaces the plunger-type ejector used in the earlier M-77 models. A three-position wing safety allows the shooter to unload the rifle with safety on. The trigger guard houses the patented floorplate latch, which holds the floorplate closed securely to prevent accidental dumping of cartridges into the magazine.

An integral, solid sight rib extends from the front of the receiver ring. Machined from a solid chrome-moly steel barrel blank, the rib has cross serrations on the upper surface to reduce light reflections. Each rifle is equipped with open metal sights. A blade front sight of blued steel is mounted on a steel ramp with curved rear surface serrated to reduce glare. Rear sights (adjustable for windage and non-folding) are mounted on the sighting rib. The forward rear sight is folding and adjustable for windage. A set of Ruger 1″ scope rings with integral bases is standard.

Calibers: 270, 30-06, 7mm Rem. Mag., 300 Win. Mag., 338 Win. Mag. **Barrel length:** 22″. **Capacity:** 4 rounds (3 rounds in Magnum). **Overall length:** 42$\frac{1}{8}$″. **Weight:** 7$\frac{1}{2}$ lbs. (avg., loaded). **Length of pull:** 13$\frac{1}{2}$″.

Price: **$1550.00**

MODEL M-77RSI INTERNATIONAL MANNLICHER

Mannlicher-type stock, Integral Base Receiver, open sights, Ruger 1″ steel rings. **Calibers:** 243, 270, 30-06, 308. **Barrel length:** 18″. **Weight:** Approx. 6 lbs.

Price **$642.00**

SAKO RIFLES

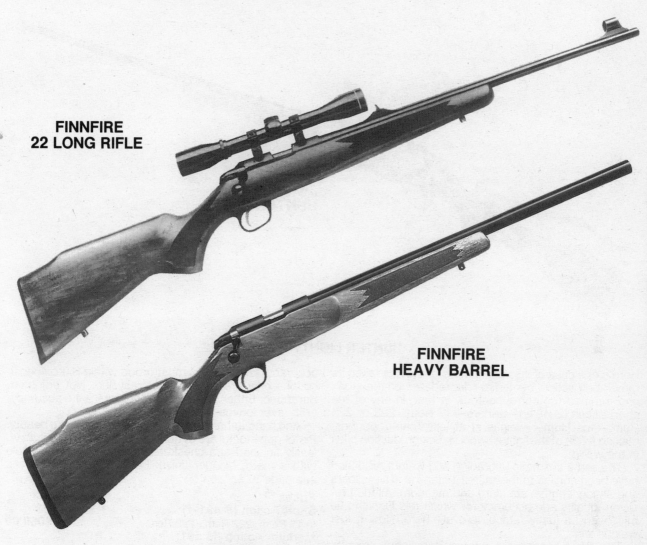

**FINNFIRE
22 LONG RIFLE**

**FINNFIRE
HEAVY BARREL**

FINNFIRE 22 LR BOLT-ACTION RIFLE
$732.00 $815.00 (Heavy Barrel)

SAKO of Finland, acclaimed as the premier manufacturer of bolt-action centerfire rifles, presents its .22 Long Rifle Finnfire. Designed by engineers who use only state-of-the-art technology to achieve both form and function and produced by craftsmen to exacting specifications, this premium grade bolt-action rifle exceeds the requirements of even the most demanding firearm enthusiast.

The basic concept in the design of the Finnfire was to make it as similar to its "big brothers" as possible—just scaled down. For example, the single-stage adjustable trigger is a carbon copy of the trigger found on any other big-bore hunting model. The 22-inch barrel is cold-hammered to ensure superior accuracy. **Overall**

length: 39¹/₂". **Weight:** 5¹/₄ lbs.; 7¹/₂ lbs. (w/heavy barrel). **Rate of twist:** 16¹/₂".

Other outstanding features include:
- European walnut stock
- Luxurious matte lacquer finish
- 50° bolt lift
- Free-floating barrel
- Integral 11mm dovetail for scope mounting
- Two-position safety that locks the bolt
- Cocking indicator
- Five-shot detachable magazine
- Ten-shot magazine available
- Available with open sights

COMMITMENT TO EXCELLENCE — A SAKO TRADITION

SAKO RIFLES

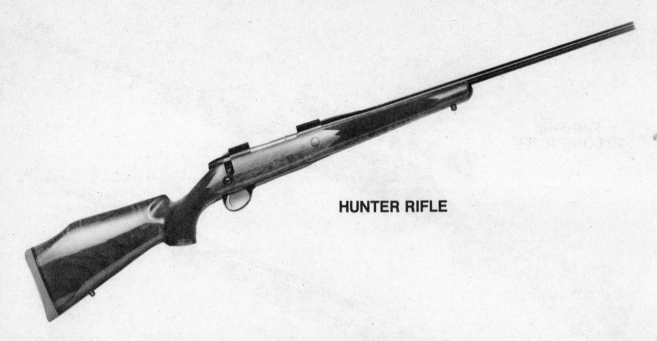

HUNTER RIFLE

HUNTER LIGHTWEIGHT

Here's one case of less being more. SAKO has taken its famed bolt-action, centerfire rifle, redesigned the stock and trimmed the barrel contour. In fact, in any of the short action (S 491-1) calibers—17 Rem., 222 or 223 Rem.—the Hunter weighs in at less than 7 pounds, making it one of the lightest wood stock production rifles in the world.

The same cosmetic upgrading and weight reduction have been applied to the entire Hunter line in all calibers and action lengths, standard and magnum. All the precision, quality and accuracy for which this Finnish rifle has been so justly famous are still here. Now it just weighs less.

The SAKO trigger is a rifleman's delight—smooth, crisp and fully adjustable. If these were the only SAKO features, it would still be the best rifle available. But the real test that sets SAKO apart from all others is its truly outstanding accuracy.

While many factors can affect a rifle's accuracy, 90 percent of any rifle's accuracy potential lies in its barrel. And the creation of superbly accurate barrels is where SAKO excels.

The care that SAKO takes in the cold-hammer processing of each barrel is unparalleled in the industry. For example, after each barrel blank is drilled, it is diamond-lapped and then optically checked for microscopic flaws. This extra care affords the SAKO owner lasting accuracy and a finish that will stay "new" season after season.

You can't buy an unfired SAKO. Every gun is test fired using special overloaded proof cartridges. This test ensures the SAKO owner total safety and uncompromising accuracy. Every barrel must group within SAKO specifications or it's scrapped. Not recycled. Not adjusted. Scrapped. Either a SAKO barrel delivers SAKO accuracy, or it never leaves the factory.

And hand-in-hand with SAKO accuracy is SAKO beauty. Pistol-grip stocks are of genuine European walnut, flawlessly finished and checkered by hand. Also available with a matte lacquer finish. For Left-handed Models, see page 279.

Prices:
Short Action (S 491-1)
In 17 Rem., 222 Rem., 223 Rem. **$1050.00**
Medium Action (M 591)
In 22-250 Rem., 7mm-08, 243 Win. &
  308 Win. **1050.00**
Long Action (L 691)
In 25-06 Rem., 270 Win., 280 Rem., 30-06 . . . . . **1085.00**
In 7mm Rem. Mag., 300 Win. Mag.,
  338 Win. Mag. **1100.00**
In 270 Wby. Mag., 300 Wby. Mag., 7mm Wby. Mag.,
  340 Wby. Mag, 375 H&H Mag., 416 Rem. Mag. **1120.00**

LEFT-HANDED MODELS (Matte Lacquer Finish)
Medium Action (M 591)
In 22-250 Rem., 7mm-08, 243 Win. and
  308 Win. **$1135.00**
Long Action (L 691)
In 25-06 Rem., 270 Win., 280 Rem., 30-06 . . . . . **1165.00**
In 7mm Rem. Mag., 300 Win. Mag.,
  338 Win. Mag. **1180.00**
In 300 Wby. Mag., 375 H&H Mag.,
  416 Rem. Mag. **1200.00**

SAKO RIFLES

**DELUXE
BOLT-ACTION RIFLE**

DELUXE BOLT-ACTION

All the fine-touch features you expect of the deluxe grade SAKO are here—beautifully grained French walnut, superbly done high-gloss finish, hand-cut checkering, deep rich bluing and rosewood forend tip and grip cap. And of course the accuracy, reliability and superior field performance for which SAKO is so justly famous are still here too. It's all here—it just weighs less than it used to. Think of it as more for less.

In addition, the scope mounting system on these SAKOs is among the strongest in the world. Instead of using separate bases, a tapered dovetail is milled into the receiver, to which the scope rings are mounted. A beautiful system that's been proven by over 20 years of use. SAKO Original Scope Mounts and SAKO scope rings are available in short/medium, and high in one-inch and 30mm.

Prices:
Short Action (S 491)
In 17 Rem., 222 Rem. & 223 Rem. **$1475.00**
Medium Action (M 591)
In 22-250 Rem., 243 Win., 7mm-08
   and 308 Win. **1475.00**
Long Action (L 691)
In 25-06 Rem., 270 Win., 280 Rem., 30-06 . . . . . **1510.00**
In 7mm Rem. Mag., 300 Win. Mag. and
   338 Win. Mag. **1525.00**
In 300 Wby. Mag., 375 H&H Mag.,
   416 Rem. Mag. **1545.00**

SUPER DELUXE

SAKO offers the Super Deluxe for the most discriminating gun buyer. This one-of-a-kind beauty is available on special order.

SUPER DELUXE **$3100.00**

SAKO RIFLES

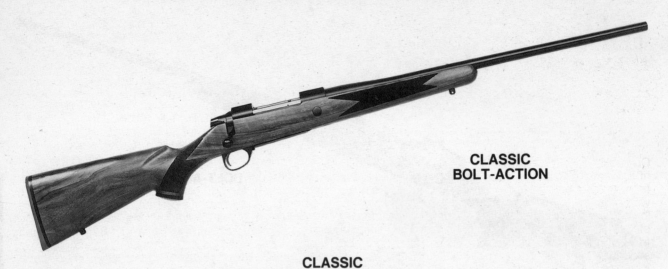

CLASSIC BOLT-ACTION

CLASSIC

Classic elegance best describes one of SAKO's latest models—the CLASSIC—designed for discriminating shooters who demand quality and the traditional clean, graceful lines of the classic style. Available in two action lengths and the most popular calibers (see below). Also available in a left-handed model.

SPECIFICATIONS
Calibers: 243 Win., 270 Win., 30-06, 7mm Rem. Mag.
Barrel length: 22″ and 24″ (Magnum action only)
Capacity: 5 rounds (Medium and Long action); 3 rounds (Magnum action)

Overall length: 42″ and 44″ (Magnum action only)
Weight: 6⅞ lbs. (243 Win.); 7 lbs. (270 Win. and 30-06); 7¼ lbs. (7mm Rem. Mag.)
Finish: Matte lacquer

Prices:
Medium Action (M 591)
In 243 Win. **$1050.00**
Long Action (L 691)
In 270 Win., 30-06 .... 1085.00
In 7mm Rem. Mag. 1100.00

LONG-RANGE HUNTER

NEW LONG-RANGE HUNTING MODELS

Proudly acclaimed as the premier manufacturer of bolt-action rifles, SAKO is pleased to introduce its new long-range hunting rifle. SAKO's legendary out-of-the-box accuracy is further enhanced with this new rifle's 26-inch free-floating heavy barrel. The barrel is fluted to reduce weight while maintaining rigidity. SAKO designed a wide beavertail forend for additional stability and support. The European walnut stock features SAKO's custom recoil-pad spacer system. A fixed magazine with hinged floor-plate has a 4-plus-1 round magazine capacity in 25-06 and 270, while the magnum calibers have a 3-plus-1 capacity. Trigger pull is adjustable from 2 to 4 pounds. Other standard features include mechanical ejection, integral dovetailed scope mount rails, one-piece forged bolt and a matte lacquer stock with palm swell.

Prices:
25-06, 270 Win. **$1275.00**
7 mm Rem. Mag., 300 Win. Mag. 1290.00

SAKO RIFLES/CARBINES

SAFARI GRADE

Crafted in the tradition of the classic British express rifles, Safari Grade is truly a professional's rifle. Every feature has been carefully thought out and executed with one goal in mind: performance. The magazine allows four belted magnums to be stored inside (instead of the usual three). The steel floorplate straddles the front of the trigger guard bow for added strength and security.

An express-style quarter rib provides a rigid, non-glare base for the rear sight, which consists of a fixed blade. The front swivel is carried by a contoured barrel band to keep the stud away from the off-hand under the recoil of big calibers. The front sight assembly is also a barrel-band type for maximum strength. The blade sits on a non-glare ramp, protected by a steel hood.

The Safari's barreled action carries a subtle semi-matte blue, which lends an understated elegance to this eminently practical rifle. The functional, classic-style stock is of European walnut selected especially for its strength of grain orientation as well as for its color and figure. A rosewood forend tip, rosewood pistol grip cap with metal insert suitable for engraving, an elegant, beaded cheekpiece and presentation-style recoil pad complete the stock embellishments.

In Calibers: 338 Win. Mag., 375 H&H Mag. and 416 Rem. Mag. See also Specifications Table on page 280.

Price: **$2765.00**

MANNLICHER-STYLE CARBINE

SAKO's Mannlicher-style Carbine combines the handiness and carrying qualities of the traditional, lever-action "deer rifle" with the power of modern, high-performance cartridges. An abbreviated 18½-inch barrel trims the overall length of the Carbine to just over 40 inches in the Long Action (L 691) calibers, and 38 inches in the Medium Action (M 591) calibers. Weight is a highly portable 7 pounds and 6½ pounds, respectively (except in the 338 and 375 H&H calibers, which measure 7½ pounds).

As is appropriate for a rifle of this type, the Carbine is furnished with an excellent set of open sights; the rear is fully adjustable for windage, while the front is a non-glare, serrated ramp with protective hood.

The Mannlicher Carbine is available in the traditional wood stock of European walnut done in a contemporary Monte Carlo style with hand-rubbed oil finish. Hand-finished checkering is standard. The Mannlicher-style full stock Carbine wears SAKO's exclusive two-piece forearm, which joins beneath the barrel band and also features an oil finish. This independent forward section of the forearm eliminates the bedding problems normally associated with the full forestock. A blued steel muzzle cap puts the finishing touches on this European-styled Carbine.

Prices:
Medium Action (M 591)
In 243 Win. and 308 Win. **$1275.00**
Long Action (L 691)
In 270 Win. and 30-06 . . . . **1310.00**
In 338 Win. Mag. **1335.00**
In 375 H&H Mag. **1350.00**

SAKO RIFLES

MODEL TRG-21
$4265.00

SAKO, known for manufacturing the finest and most accurate production sporting rifles available today, presents the ultimate in sharpshooting systems: the sleek **TRG-21 Target Rifle.** Designed for use when nothing less than total precision is demanded, this new SAKO rifle features a cold-hammer forged receiver, "resistance-free" bolt, stainless-steel barrel and a fully adjustable polyurethane stock. Chambered in .308 Win. A wide selection of optional accessories is also available. Designed, crafted and manufactured in Finland. For additional specifications, see the table on page 280.

- Cold-hammer forged receiver
- "Resistance-free" bolt
- Cold-hammer forged, stainless steel barrel
- Three massive locking lugs
- 60° bolt lift
- Free-floating barrel
- Detachable 10-round magazine

- Fully adjustable cheekpiece
- Infinitely adjustable buttplate
- Adjustable two-stage trigger pull
- Trigger adjustable for both length and pull
- Trigger also adjustable for horizontal or vertical pitch
- Safety lever inside the trigger guard
- Reinforced polyurethane stock

Optional features:
- Muzzle brake
- Quick-detachable one-piece scope mount base
- Available with 1" or 30mm rings
- Collapsible and removable bipod rest
- Quick-detachable sling swivels
- Wide military-type nylon sling

Also available:
TRG-41 in 338 Lapua Mag. **$4825.00**

MODEL TRG-S
$790.00 (Standard Calibers)
$830.00 (Magnum Calibers

The TRG-S has been crafted and designed around SAKO's highly sophisticated and extremely accurate TRG-21 Target Rifle (above). The "resistance-free" bolt and precise balance of the TRG-S, plus its three massive locking lugs and short 60-degree bolt lift, are among the features that attract the shooter's attention. Also of critical importance is the cold-hammer forged receiver—unparalleled for strength and durability. The detachable 5-round magazine fits securely into the polyurethane stock. The stock, in turn, is molded around a synthetic skeleton that provides additional support and maximum rigidity. **Calibers:** *Standard*—25-06 Rem., 270 Win., 6.5×55, 30-06; *Magnum*—7mm Rem. Mag., 7mm STW, 270 Wby. Mag., 300 Win. Mag., 300 Wby., 338 Win. Mag., 338 Lapua Mag., 340 Wby. Mag., 375 H&H Mag., 416 Rem. Mag.

For additional specifications, page 280.

SAKO RIFLES

FIBERCLASS MODEL

In answer to the increased demand for SAKO quality and accuracy in a true "all-weather" rifle, this fiberglass-stock version of the renowned SAKO barreled action has been created. Long since proven on the bench rest circuit to be the most stable material for cradling a rifle, fiberglass is extremely strong, light in weight, and unaffected by changes in weather. Because fiberglass is inert, it does not absorb or expel moisture; hence, it cannot swell, shrink or warp. It is impervious to the high humidity of equatorial jungles, the searing heat of arid deserts or the rain and snow of the high mountains. Not only is this rifle lighter than its wood counterpart, it also appeals to the performance-oriented hunter who seeks results over appearance.

Prices:
Long Action (L 691)

In 25-06 Rem., 270 Win., 280 Rem., 30-06 . . . . . **$1388.00**
In 7mm Rem. Mag., 300 Win. Mag. and
    338 Win. Mag. **1405.00**
In 375 H&H Mag., 416 Rem. Mag. **1425.00**

LEFT-HANDED MODELS

SAKO's Left-Handed models are based on mirror images of the right-handed models SAKO owners have enjoyed for years; the handle, extractor and ejection port all are located on the port side. Naturally, the stock is also reversed, with the cheekpiece on the opposite side and the palm swell on the port side of the grip.

Otherwise, these guns are identical to the right-handed models. That means hammer-forged barrels, one-piece bolts with integral locking lugs and handles, integral scope mount rails, adjustable triggers and Mauser-type inertia ejectors.

SAKO's Left-Handed rifles are available in all Long Action models, while the Hunter grade is available in both Medium and Long Action. The Hunter Grade carries a durable matte lacquer finish with generous-size panels of hand-cut checkering, a presentation-style recoil pad and sling swivel studs installed.

Prices:
Hunter Lightweight (Medium Action)
In 22-250 Rem. 243 Win., 308 Win., 7mm-08 . . . **$1135.00**
Hunter Lightweight (Long Action)
In 25-06, 270 Win., 280 Rem. & 30-06 . . . . **1165.00**
In 7mm Rem. Mag., 300 Win. Mag. and
    338 Win. Mag. **1180.00**
In 300 Wby. Mag., 375 H&H Mag. and
    416 Rem. Mag. **1200.00**

VARMINT

The SAKO Varmint is specifically designed with a prone-type stock for shooting from the ground or bench. The forend is extra wide to provide added steadiness when rested on sandbags or makeshift field rests.

Calibers:
    Short Action—17 Rem., 222 Rem., 223 Rem.
    Medium Action—22-250, 243 Win., 7mm-08, 308 Win.

Price: **$1240.00**

RIFLES

SAKO RIFLES

		LONG RANGE HUNTING	SUPER DELUXE	TRG-21****	SAFARI	CARBINE MANNLICHER STYLE	VARMINT	FIBERCLASS	TRG-S*** MAGNUM	TRG-S	DELUXE	CLASSIC	HUNTER**	FINNFIRE*
Model	Action	L691	M591, L691, L691	*	L691	M591, L691, L691	M591, L691	L691, L691	*	*	S491, M591, L691, L691	M591, L691	S491, M591, L691, L691	*
	Left-handed										■ ■ ■	■	■ ■ ■ ■	
Dimensions	Total length (inches)	48	41½, 42½, 44, 46, 46	46½	44	39½, 40½, 40½	43½, 43½, 46	44, 46, 46	47½	45½, 46	41½, 42½, 44, 46, 46	42½, 44	41½, 42½, 44, 46, 46	39½
	Barrel length (inches)	26	21¼, 21¾, 22, 24, 24	25¾	23¼	18½, 18½, 18½	23, 23	22, 24, 24	*24	22	21¼, 21¾, 22, 24, 24	23¼, 24	21¼, 21¾, 22, 24, 24	22
	Weight (lbs)	9½	6¼, 6½, 7¾, 8¼	10½	8¼	7¾	6, 8½	7¼, 7¼, 8	7¾	7¾	6¼, 6½, 7¾, 8¼	7½	6¼, 6½, 7¾, 8¼	5¼
Caliber/Rate of Twist	17 Rem/10"		■				■				■			■
	22 LR/16.5" (Finnfire)													■
	222 Rem/14"		■								■			■
	223 Rem/12"										■			■
	22-250 Rem/14"		■				■				■		■	
	243 Win/10"		■				■				■	■	■	
	308 Win/12"		■	■			■				■		■	
	7mm-08/9½"						■				■			
	25-06 Rem/10"	■	■								■		■	
	270 Win/10"	■	■			■	■	■		■	■	■	■	
	280 Rem/10"		■								■			
	30-06/10"		■								■		■	
	7mm/Rem Mag/9½"	■	■					■		■	■	■	■	
	300 Win Mag/10"	■	■					■		■	■			
	300 Wby Mag/10"							■		■				
	338 Win Mag/10"		■		■	■		■		■	■			
	338 Lapua/12"			■				■		■				
	375 H&H Mag/12"		■		■	■					■			
	416 Rem Mag/14"	■			■			■		■	■		■	
Stock Finish	Lacquered		■ ■ ■ ■								■ ■ ■ ■ ■			
	Matte Lacquered	■										■ ■	■ ■ ■ ■ ■	■
	Oiled				■	■ ■ ■	■ ■ ■							
	Reinforced polyurethane			■					■	■				
Sights	Without sights	■	■ ■ ■ ■				■ ■ ■				■ ■ ■ ■		■ ■ ■ ■	■
	Open sights				■	■ ■ ■							■ ■	■
	Scope mount rails	■	■ ■ ■ ■	■	■	■ ■ ■	■ ■ ■	■	■	■	■ ■ ■ ■	■	■ ■ ■ ■	■
Mag.	Magazine capacity		6, 5, 5, 4	10	4	6, 5, 5	6, 5	5, 4, 3	**	5	6, 5, 5, 4	5, 4	6, 5, 5, 4	5***
Buttplate	Rubber recoil pad	■	■ ■ ■ ■	■	■	■ ■ ■	■ ■ ■	■ ■ ■	■	■	■ ■ ■ ■	■	■ ■ ■ ■ ■	■

*Also available w/heavy barrel (weight: 7½ lbs.).

**Also available in 270 Wby. Mag., 7mm Wby. Mag., 340 Wby. Mag.

***Also available in 6.5 × 55, 270 Wby. Mag., 7mm Wby. Mag., 340 Wby. Mag., 7mm STW (26" barrel)

****Available in 338 Lapua Mag. (as Model TRG-41)

SAKO ACTIONS

Only by building a rifle around a SAKO action do shooters enjoy the choice of three different lengths, each scaled to a specific family of cartridges. The S 491-1 (Short) action is miniaturized in every respect to match the 222 family, which includes everything from 17 Remington to 223 Remington. The M 591 (Medium) action is scaled down to the medium-length cartridges of standard bolt face—22-250, 243, 308, 7mm-08 or similar length cartridges. The L 691 (Long) action is offered in either standard or Magnum bolt face and accommodates cartridges of up to 3.65 inches in overall length, including rounds like the 300 Weatherby and 375 H&H Magnums. **For left-handers, the Medium and Long actions are offered in either standard or Magnum bolt face.** All actions are furnished in-the-white only.

S 491 SHORT ACTION (formerly AI-1)
$544.00
CALIBERS:
17 Rem., 222 Rem.
222 Rem. Mag.
223 Rem.

S 491-PPC SHORT ACTION
HUNTER: $544.00
$620.00 SINGLE SHOT
CALIBERS:
22 PPC
6 PPC

M 591 MEDIUM ACTION (formerly AII-1)
$544.00
CALIBERS:
22-250 Rem. (M 591-3)
243 Win.
308 Win.
7mm-08

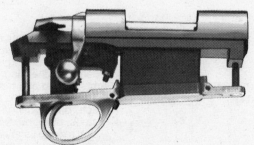

L 691 LONG ACTION (formerly AV-4)
$544.00
CALIBERS:

25-06 Rem. (L 691-1)
270 Win. (L 691-1)
280 Rem. (L 691-1)
30-06 (L 691-1)
7mm Rem. Mag. (L 691-4)
300 Win. Mag. (L 691-4)
300 Wby. Mag. (L 691-4)
338 Win. Mag. (L 691-4)
375 H&H Mag. (L 691-4)
416 Rem. Mag. (L 691-4)

Also available:
LEFT-HANDED ACTIONS
Medium and Long: $582.00

SAUER RIFLES

MODEL 90

MODEL 90
$1595.00 (Standard) $1649.00 (Magnum)

SPECIFICATIONS
Calibers: 243 Win., 25-06, 270, 30-06, 308 Win., 7mm Rem. Mag., 300 Win. Mag., 300 Wby. Mag. and 375 H&H
Barrel length: 23.6″ or 26″
Overall length: 42.5″ (standard calibers); 46.5″ (Magnum calibers)
Weight: 7.5 lbs. to 7.7 lbs.
Sights: None furnished; drilled and tapped for scope mount
Stock: Monte Carlo cut with sculptured cheekpiece, hand-checkered pistol grip and forend, rosewood pistol grip cap and forend tip, black rubber recoil pad, and fully inletted sling swivel studs.
Features: Rear bolt cam-activated locking lug action; jeweled bolt with an operating angle of 65°; fully adjustable gold-plated trigger; chamber loaded signal pin; cocking indicator; tang-mounted slide safety with button release; bolt release button (to operate bolt while slide safety is engaged); detachable 3 or 4-round box magazine; sling side scope mounts; leather sling (extra)
Engravings: Four distinctive hand-cut patterns on gray nitride receiver, trigger housing plate, magazine plate and bolt handle (extra). **Prices on request.**

MODEL 90 ENGRAVING #2

MODEL 202 BOLT ACTION (not shown)
$383.00

SPECIFICATIONS
Calibers: 243 Win., 270 Win., 308., 30-06 S'field; 7mm Rem. Mag., 300 Win. Mag., 375 Win. Mag.
Action: Bolt takedown
Capacity: 3 rounds
Barrel lengths: 23.6″; 26″
Overall length: 44.3″ and 46″
Weight: 7.7 lbs. to 8.4 lbs.
Stock: Select American claro walnut with high-gloss epoxy finish and rosewood forend and grip caps; Monte Carlo comb with checkpiece; 22 line-per- inch diamond pattern, hand-cut checking
Sights: Drilled and tapped for sights and scope bases
Features: Adjustable two-stage trigger; polished and jeweled bolt; quick-change barrel; tapered bore; QD sling swivel studs; black rubber recoil pad; Wundhammer palm swell; dual release safety; six locking lugs on bolt head; removable box magazine; fully enclosed bolt face; three gas relief holes; firing-pin cocking indicator on bolt rear

SAUER .458 SAFARI

SAUER .458 SAFARI

The Sauer .458 Safari features a rear bolt cam-activated locking-lug action with a low operating angle of 65°. It has a gold plated trigger, jeweled bolt, oil finished bubinga stock and deep luster bluing. Safety features include a press bottom slide safety that engages the trigger sear, toggle joint and bolt. The bolt release feature allows the sportsman to unload the rifle while the safety remains engaged to the trigger sear and toggle joint. The Sauer Safari is equipped with a chamber loaded signal pin for positive identification. Specifications include: **Barrel Length:** 24″ (heavy barrel contour). **Overall length:** 44″. **Weight:** 10 lb. 6 oz. **Sights:** Williams open sights (sling swivels included). **Price:** $1995.00

SAVAGE RIFLES

MODEL 93G MAGNUM
$145.00

SPECIFICATIONS
Caliber: 22 WMR
Capacity: 5-shot clip
Barrel length: 20¾"
Overall length: 39½"

Weight: 5¾ lbs.
Stock: Cut-checkered walnut-stained hardwood
Sights: Bead front; sporting rear with step elevator
Feature: Free-floated precision button rifling

MODEL 99C LEVER ACTION
$650.00

Clip magazine allows for the chambering of pointed, high-velocity big-bore cartridges. **Calibers:** 243 Win., 308 Win. **Action:** Hammerless, lever action, top tang safety. **Magazine:** Detachable clip; holds 4 rounds plus 1 in the chamber. **Stock:** Select walnut with high Monte Carlo and deep-fluted comb.

Cut-checkered stock and forend with swivel studs. Recoil pad and pistol grip cap. **Sights:** Detachable hooded ramp front sight, bead front sight on removable ramp adjustable rear sight. Tapped for top mount scopes. **Barrel length:** 22". **Overall length:** 42¾". **Weight:** 7¾ lbs.

MODEL 110 FP TACTICAL
$429.00

SPECIFICATIONS
Calibers: 223 Rem., 25-06 Rem., 30-06 Spfd., 308 Win., 7mm Rem. Mag., 300 Win. Mag.
Capacity: 5 rounds (1 in chamber)
Barrel length: 24" (w/recessed target-style muzzle)
Overall length: 45½"

Weight: 8½ lbs.
Sights: None; drilled and tapped for scope mount
Features: Black matte nonreflective finish on metal parts; bolt coated with titanium nitride; stock made of black graphite/fiberglass-filled composite with positive checkering; left-hand model available

MODEL 110CY (not shown)
$362.00

SPECIFICATIONS
Calibers: 223 Rem., 243 Win., 270 Win., 308 Win.
Capacity: 5 rounds (1 in chamber); top-loading internal magazine

Barrel length: 22" blued
Overall length: 42½"
Weight: 6½ lbs.
Sights: Adjustable: drilled and tapped for scope mounts
Stock: High comb, walnut-stained hardwood w/cut checkering and short pull

RIFLES

SAVAGE RIFLES

MODEL 111GC CLASSIC HUNTER
$407.00

SPECIFICATIONS
Calibers: 270 Win., 30-06 Springfield, 7mm Rem. Mag., 300 Win. Mag.
Capacity: 5 rounds (4 rounds in Magnum calibers)
Overall length: 43½″ (45½″ Magnum calibers)
Weight: 6⅜ lbs.

Sights: Adjustable
Stock: American-style walnut-finished hardwood; cut checkering
Features: Detachable staggered box-type magazine; left-hand model available

MODEL 111FC CLASSIC HUNTER
$418.00

Same specifications as Classic Hunter above, except stock is lightweight graphite/fiberglass-filled composite w/positive checkering. Left-hand model available. **Calibers:** 270 Win., 30-06 Spfld., 7mm Rem. Mag. and 300 Win. Mag.

MODEL 111G CLASSIC HUNTER
$362.00

Same specifications as Model 111GC Classic Hunter, except available also in **calibers** 22-250 Rem., 223 Rem., 243 Win., 25-06, 270 Win., 7mm-08, 7mm Rem. Mag., 30-06 Sprgfld., 300 Win. Mag., 308. Stock is American-style walnut-finished hardwood with cut-checkering. Lef-hand model available.

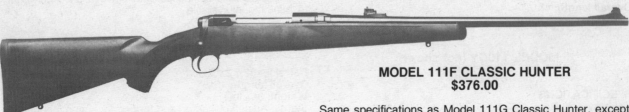

MODEL 111F CLASSIC HUNTER
$376.00

Same specifications as Model 111G Classic Hunter, except stock is black nonglare graphite/fiberglass-filled polymer with positive checkering. Left-hand model available.

SAVAGE CENTERFIRE RIFLES

**MODEL 112FVSS STAINLESS
LONG-RANGE RIFLE
$510.00**

**MODEL 112BVSS VARMINT
$535.00 (not shown)**

SPECIFICATIONS
Calibers: 22-250 Rem., 223 Rem., 25-06 Rem., 30-06, 308 Win., 7mm Rem. Mag., 300 Win. Mag. (single-shot model available in 220 Swift)
Capacity: 5+1
Barrel length: 26" fluted, stainless steel
Overall length: 47 1/2"
Weight: 8 7/8 lbs.
Sights: Graphite/fiberglass-filled composite w/positve checkering
Also available:
MODEL 112FV in 223 Rem. and 22-250 only

SPECIFICATIONS
Calibers: 22-250 Rem., 223 Rem., 25-06, 7mm Rem. Mag., 300 Win Mag., 30-06 Sprgfld., 308 Win. (single-shot model also available in 220 Swift)
Capacity: 5+1
Barrel length: 26" fluted heavy barrel, stainless steel
Overall length: 47 1/2"
Weight: 8 7/8 lbs.
Sights: None; drilled and tapped
Stock: Laminated hardwood w/high comb; ambidextrous grip

**MODEL 112FV VARMINT
w/Graphite Fiberglass Polymer Stock
$400.00**

**MODEL 112 BT COMPETITION GRADE
$1000.00**

SPECIFICATIONS
Calibers: 223 Rem. and 308 Win. (single-shot available in 300 Win. Mag.)
Capacity: 5+1

Barrel length: 26"; blackened stainless steel w/recessed target-style muzzle
Overall length: 47 1/2"   **Weight:** 10 7/8 lbs.
Stock: Laminated brown w/straight comb

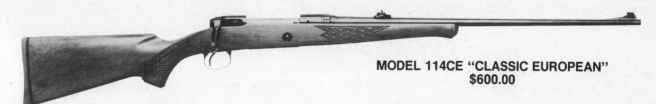

**MODEL 114CE "CLASSIC EUROPEAN"
$600.00**

SPECIFICATIONS
Calibers: 270 Win., 30-06 Sprgfld., 7mm Rem. Mag., 300 Win. Mag.
Capacity: 3 rounds (magnum); 4 rounds (standard)
Barrel length: 22" (standard); 24" (magnum)
Overall length: 43 1/2" (standard); 45 1/2" (magnum)
Weight: 7 1/8 lbs. (approx.)
Finish: Oil-finished walnut stock w/schnabel tip, cheekpiece and French skip-line checkering on grip and forend

Features: Rubber recoil pad; pistol-grip cap with gold medallion; high-luster blued finish on receiver barrel and bolt handle; side button release; adjustable metal sights; precision rifled barrel; drilled and tapped
Also available:
MODEL 114CU CLASSIC ULTRA. Same price and specifications as Model 114CE, except capacity 4 rounds in magnum, 5 rounds in standard and straight American walnut stock. **Price: $525.00**

SAVAGE CENTERFIRE RIFLES

MODEL 116FSS "WEATHER WARRIOR"
$491.00

Savage Arms combines the strength of a black graphite fiberglass polymer stock and the durability of a stainless-steel barrel and receiver in this bolt-action rifle. Major components are made from stainless steel, honed to a low reflective satin finish. Drilled and tapped for scope mounts, the 116FSS is offered in popular long-action calibers. Packed with gunlock, ear puffs and target. Left-hand model available.

SPECIFICATIONS
Calibers: 223, 243, 270, 30-06, 308 Win., 7mm Rem Mag., 300 Win. Mag., 338 Win. Mag.
Capacity: 4 (7mm Rem. Mag., 300 Win. Mag., 338 Win. Mag.); 5 (223, 243, 270, 30-06)
Barrel length: 22" (223, 243, 270, 30-06); 24" (7mm Rem. Mag., 300 Win. Mag., 338 Win. Mag.)
Overall length: 43½"–45½"   **Weight:** 6½ lbs.

MODEL 116FCS "WEATHER WARRIOR"
$554.00

This bolt-action rifle has the same quality features as the Model 116FSS plus a removable box magazine with recessed push-button release for ease in loading and unloading. Left-hand model available.

MODEL 116SE SAFARI EXPRESS
$900.00

Overall length: 45½"   **Weight:** 8½ lbs.
Sights: 3-leaf express
Stock: Classic-style select-grade walnut w/cut checkering; ebony tip; stainless-steel crossbolts; internally vented recoil pad

SPECIFICATIONS
Calibers: 300 Win. Mag., 338, 458 Win. Mag.
Capacity: 4 rounds (1 in chamber)
Barrel length: 24" stainless steel w/AMB

MODEL 116FSK "WEATHER WARRIOR"
$554.00

Features a compact barrel with "shock suppressor" that reduces average linear recoil by more than 30% without loss of Magnum stopping power. Left-hand model available.

SPECIFICATIONS
Calibers: 270 Win., 30-06 Sprg., 7mm Rem. Mag., 300 Win. Mag., 338 Win. Mag.

Capacity: 5 rounds (4 in Magnum)
Barrel length: 22"   **Overall length:** 43½"
Weight: 6½ lbs.

Also available:
MODEL 116FSAK. Same specifications as above except includes adj. muzzle brake. **Price:** $581.00

SAVAGE SPORTING RIFLES

Formerly Lakefield

MODEL 900B BIATHLON
$498.00

MODEL 900S SILHOUETTE
$346.00

SPECIFICATIONS

Model:	900B	900S
Caliber:	.22 Long Rifle Only	.22 Long Rifle
Capacity:	5-shot metal magazine	5-shot metal magazine
Action:	Self-cocking bolt action, thumb-operated rotary safety	Self-cocking bolt action, thumb-operated rotary safety
Stock:	One-piece target-type stock with natural finish hardwood; comes with clip holder, carrying & shooting rails, butt hook and hand stop	One-piece high comb, target-type with walnut finish hardwood
Barrel Length:	21″ w/snow cover	21″
Sights:	Receiver peep sights with 1/4 min. click micrometer adjustments; target front sight with inserts	None (receiver drilled and tapped for scope base)
Overall Length:	39⁵/₈″	39⁵/₈″
Approx. Weight:	8¼ lbs.	8 lbs.

MARK I-G SINGLE SHOT
$119.95

MODEL 64G SEMIAUTO
$138.95

Also available:
MARK I-G "SMOOTHBORE" (20³/₄″ barrel) $119.00
MARK I-G YOUTH (19″ barrel) 119.00
MARK II-G & MARK II-G YOUTH (19″ barrel) 126.00
MARK II-G LEFT HAND (20¹/₂″ barrel) 126.00

SPECIFICATIONS

Model:	MARK I-G	MARK II-G	64G
Caliber:	.22 Short, Long or Long Rifle	.22 Long Rifle Only	.22 Long Rifle Only
Capacity:	Single shot	10-shot clip magazine	10-shot clip magazine
Action:	Self-cocking bolt action, thumb-operated rotary safety	Self-cocking bolt action thumb-operated rotary safety	Semiautomatic side ejection, bolt hold-open device, thumb-operated rotary safety
Stock:	One Piece, Walnut Finish Hardwood, Monte Carlo Type with Full Pistol Grip. Checkering on Pistol Grip and Forend.		
Barrel Length:	20³/₄″	20³/₄″	20¹/₄″
Sights:	Open Bead Front Sight, Adjustable Rear Sight, Receiver Grooved for Scope Mounting.		
Overall Length:	39¹/₂″	39¹/₂″	40″
Approx. Weight:	5¹/₂ lbs.	5¹/₂ lbs.	5¹/₂ lbs.

SAVAGE SPORTING RIFLES

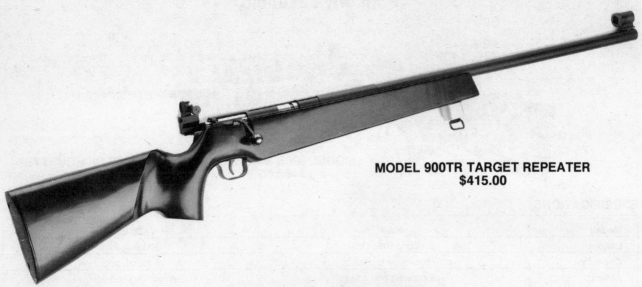

MODEL 900TR TARGET REPEATER
$415.00

SPECIFICATIONS
Caliber: 22 Long Rifle
Capacity: 5-shot clip magazine
Action: Self-cocking bolt action, thumb-operated rotary safety
Overall Length: 43⁵/₈″

Approx. Weight: 8 lbs.
Stock: One-piece, target-type with walnut finish hardwood (also available in natural finish); comes with shooting rail and hand stop
Sights: Receiver peep sights with ¹/₄ min. click micrometer adjustments, target front sight with inserts

SAVAGE MODEL 24F COMBINATION
RIFLE/SHOTGUN
$400.00

SPECIFICATIONS MODEL 24F COMBINATION RIFLE/SHOTGUN

O/U Comb. Model	Gauge/ Caliber	Choke	Chamber	Barrel Length	O.A. Length	Twist R.H.	Stock
24F-20 24F-12	12 or 20/22 LR	Modified Barrel	3″	24″	40¹/₂″	1 in 14″	Black Graphite Fiberglass Polymer
	12 or 20/22 Hornet					1 in 14″	
	12 or 20/223					1 in 14″	
	12 or 20/30-30					1 in 12″	

SPRINGFIELD RIFLES

M1A STANDARD

SPECIFICATIONS
Calibers: 308 Win./7.62mm NATO (243 or 7mm-08 optional)
Capacity: 5- or 10-round box magazine
Barrel length: 22″ **Rifling:** 6 groove, RH twist, 1 turn in 11″
Overall length: 44⅓″ **Weight:** 9 lbs.
Sights: Military square post front; military aperture rear, adjustable for windage and elevation
Sight radius: 26¾″

Prices:
Standard w/walnut stock $1381.00
w/Brown laminated stock 1466.00
w/Black laminated stock 1440.00
w/Camo fiberglass stock 1249.00

Also available:
BASIC M1A RIFLE w/painted black fiberglass stock, caliber 308 only. **$1249.00**; w/bipod and stabilizer **$1381.00**

M1A NATIONAL MATCH

SPECIFICATIONS
Caliber: 308 Win.
Barrel length: 22″
Overall length: 44.375″
Trigger pull: 4½ lbs.
Weight: 10 lbs. (11 lbs. in Super Match)

Features: Comes with National Match barrel, flash suppressor, gas cylinder, special glass-bedded walnut stock and match-tuned trigger assembly.
Price: $1729.00

Also available:
M1A SUPER MATCH. Features heavy match barrel and permanently attached figure-8-style operating rod guide, plus special heavy walnut match stock, longer pistol grip and contoured area behind rear sight for better grip. **$2050.00**

M1A-A1 BUSH RIFLE

SPECIFICATIONS
Calibers: 308 Win./7.62mm, 243 or 7mm-08 Win.
Barrel length: 18″ (w/o flash suppressor)
Overall length: 40.5″
Weight: 8.75 lbs. **Sight radius:** 22″

Prices:
w/Walnut stock $1410.00
w/Black fiberglass stock 1396.00
w/Black laminated stock 1466.00

SPRINGFIELD RIFLES

MODEL SAR-8 SPORTER RIFLE
$1204.00

SPECIFICATIONS
Calibers: 308 Win., 7.62mm
Barrel length: 18″ (1:12″ twist, 4-groove)
Overall length: 40.38″
Weight: 8.7 lbs.

Sights: Protected front post; rotary-style adjustable rear aperture
Features: Recoil-operated w/delayed roller-lock locking system; synthetic thumbhole stock

MODEL SAR-4800 SPORTER RIFLE
$1249.00

SPECIFICATIONS
Calibers: 308 Win., 7.62mm, 5.56mm
Barrel length: 21″ (1:12″ R.H. twist, 4-groove)
Overall length: 43.3″
Weight: 9.5 lbs.

Sights: Protected front post; adjustable rear
Features: Forged receiver and bolt; hammer-forged chrome-lined barrel; adjustable gas system; synthetic thumbhole stock

MODEL M-6 SCOUT RIFLE/SHOTGUN COMBO
$160.00   ($190.00 Stainless Steel)

SPECIFICATIONS
Calibers: 22 LR/.410 and 22 Hornet/.410
Barrel length: 18.25″ (1:15″ R.H. twist in 22 LR; 1:13″ R.H. twist in 22 Hornet)
Overall length: 32″

Weight: 4 lbs.
Finish: Parkerized or stainless steel
Features: .410 shotgun barrel (2½″ or 3″ chamber) choked Full; drilled and tapped for scope mount with Weaver base; lockable plastic carry case (**$24.00**)

STEYR-MANNLICHER RIFLES

SPORTER SERIES

SPORTER HALF STOCK

SPORTER FULL STOCK

SPORTER SERIES

All Sporter models feature hand-checkered wood stocks, a five-round detachable rotary magazine, and a choice of single or double-set triggers. M actions are available in left-hand models. S (Magnum) action are available in half stock only.

SPECIFICATIONS
Calibers: See table on the following page
Barrel length: 20″ (Full Stock); 23.6″ (Half Stock)
Overall length: 39″ (Full)
Weight:
    Model SL—6.16 lbs. (Full) and 6.27 lbs. (Half Stock)
    Model L—6.27 lbs. (Full) and 6.38 lbs. (Half)
    Model M—6.82 lbs. (Full) and 7 lbs. (Half).
Features: SL and L Models have rifle-type rubber butt pad

Prices:

Models SL, L, M Full Stock	$2450.00
Models SL, L, M Half Stock	2250.00
Model MIII Left Hand Full Stock	2850.00
Model MIII Left Hand Half Stock	2650.00
Model MIII Professional (w/black synthetic half stock, 23.6″ barrel and no sights)	995.00
Same as above w/stippled checkered European wood stock (270 Win. and 30-06 calibers)	1125.00
Varmint Rifle Half stock, 26″ heavy barrel	2450.00
Jagd Match Laminated half stock, 23.6″ barrel in 222 Rem., 243 Win., 308 Win.	2450.00
Magnum, Half stock, 26″ barrel in 7mm Rem. Mag., 300 Win. Mag., 375 H&H	2550.00

MODEL M PROFESSIONAL

STEYR-MANNLICHER RIFLES

SPORTER SERIES

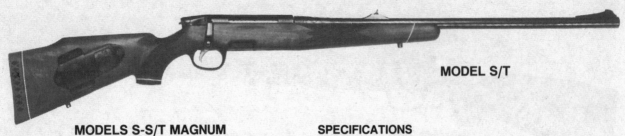

MODEL S/T

MODELS S-S/T MAGNUM

The S/T is a heavy-barreled version of the Sporter S Model designed specifically for big game hunting. It features a hand-checkered walnut stock, five-round rotary magazine, optional butt stock magazine, and double-set or single trigger.

SPECIFICATIONS
Calibers: See table below. **Barrel length:** 26″.
Weight: 8.36 lbs. (Model S); 9 lbs. (Model S/T).
Prices:
Model S (Half stock w/26″ barrel) $2850.00
Model S/T (w/optional butt magazine) 3045.00

SPORTER & LUXUS SERIES CALIBERS SPECIFICATIONS

MODELS:	222 Rem.	222 Rem. Mag.	223 Rem.	243 Win.	25-06	308 Win.	6.5 × 55	6.5 × 57	270 Win.	7 × 64	30-06 Spr.	9.3 × 62	6.5 × 68	7mm Rem. Mag.	.300 Win. Mag.	8 × 685S	9.3 × 64	.375 H & H Mag.	458 Win. Mag.
Sporter (SL)	●	●	●																
(L)				●		●													
(M)							●	●	●	●	●	●							
S													●	●	●	●	●	●	
S/T																		●	●
Mill Professional						●			●	●	●								
Luxus (L)				●		●													
(M)							●	●	●	●	●	●							
(S)													●	●	●	●			
Varmint (not shown)	●																		
Jagd Match	●				●	●													

* Also available in 9.3 × 64

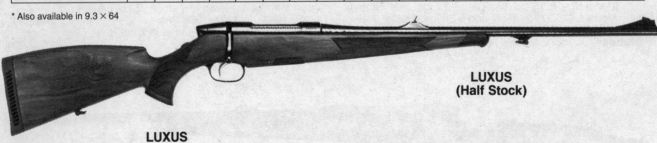

LUXUS
LUXUS (Half Stock)

The Luxus is the premier rifle in the Steyr lineup. It features a hand-checkered walnut stock, smooth action, combination shotgun set trigger, steel in-line three-round magazine (detachable), rear tang slide safety, and European-designed receiver. **Calibers:** See table above. **Barrel length:** 20″ (Full Stock); 23.6″ (Half Stock).

Prices:
Luxus Models
  Half Stock w/23.6″ barrel $2950.00
  Full Stock w/20″ barrel 3150.00
Luxus S (Magnum) Models (26″ barrel,
  Half Stock only) 3250.00

STEYR-MANNLICHER RIFLES

STEYR SSG

The Steyr SSG features a black synthetic Cycolac stock (walnut optional), heavy Parkerized barrel, five-round standard (and optional 10-round) staggered magazine, heavy-duty milled receiver. **Calibers:** 243 Win. and 308 Win. **Barrel length:** 26″. **Overall length:** 44.5″. **Weight:** 8.5 lbs. **Sights:** Iron sights; hooded ramp front with blade adjustable for elevation; rear standard V-notch adjustable for windage. **Features:** Sliding safety; 1″ swivels.

Prices:
Model SSG-PI Cycolac half-stock (26″ bbl. in 308 Win.) $2195.00
Model SSG-PII (20″ or 26″ heavy bbl. in 308 Win.) 2195.00
Model SSG P-IV Urban in 308 Win. w/16¾″ heavy barrel 2660.00
Model SSG Match Scope Mount (1″) 269.00

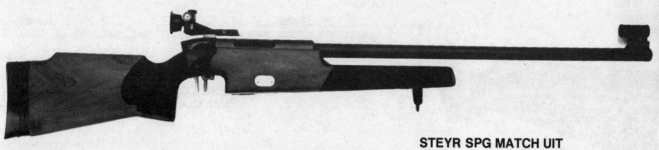

STEYR SPG MATCH UIT

Designed especially for target competition, the Steyr Match UIT features a walnut competition stock, stipple-textured pistol grip, adjustable straight and wide trigger, adjustable first-stage trigger pull, enlarged bolt handle for rapid fire, cold hammer-forged barrel, and non-glare band for sighting.
Caliber: 308 Win. **Overall length:** 44″. **Weight:** 10 lbs.

Prices:
Steyr Match SPG-UIT $3995.00
  10-shot magazine 143.00
Model SPG-CISM 4295.00
Model SPG-T 3695.00

AUG S.A. SEMIAUTOMATIC RIFLE

SPECIFICATIONS
Caliber: 223   **Capacity:** 30-round magazine
Barrel length: 16″
Price: $1685.00
Also available: **AUG** Special Receiver w/Stanag Scope Mount 695.00

THOMPSON/CENTER RIFLES

THE CONTENDER CARBINE
$460.00

Available in 7 **calibers:** 17 Rem., 22 LR Match, 22 Hornet, 223 Rem., 7×30 Waters, 30-30 Win. and 375 Win. **Barrels** are 21 inches long and are interchangeable, with adjustable iron sights and tapped and drilled for scope mounts. **Weight:** Only 5 lbs. 3 oz.

Also available:
Contender Vent Rib Carbine
With standard walnut stock in 22 Hornet, 223 Rem.
   7×30 Waters, 30-30 Win., 375 Win. **$515.00**
With 21″ 17 Rem. barrel 546.00
In .410 smoothbore 535.60
Contender Youth Model Carbine (22 LR and 223 Rem.)
With 16¼″ bbl., walnut Youth stock **$479.00**
Contender Carbine
With Match Grade 22 LR barrel 525.00

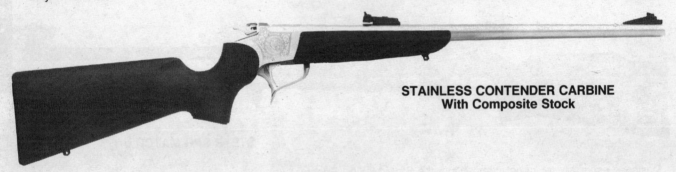

STAINLESS CONTENDER CARBINE
With Composite Stock

CONTENDER CARBINE STAINLESS

Available in 22 LR Match, 22 Hornet, 223 Rem., 7×30 Waters, 30-30 Win., 375 Win., and .410 bore. Same specifications as standard model, with walnut or composite stock. All stainless-steel components interchange readily with blued components (barrels and frames can be mixed or matched).

Prices:
Stainless Carbine, Standard **$509.00**
In 22 LR Match 520.00
Stainless Carbine w/vent rib (.410 ga.) 535.50

CONTENDER CARBINE KIT
Walnut Stock

CONTENDER CONVERSION KIT

Available in 22 LR Match, 22 Hornet, 223 Rem., 30-30 Win. and .410 smoothbore. Each kit contains a buttstock, blued 21″ barrel, forend and sights.

Prices:
Walnut stock **$309.00**
In 22 LR Match 319.50
Composite stock, stainless steel barrel 329.50
In 22 LR Match 340.00
In .410 smoothbore 355.50

TIKKA RIFLES

MODEL 512S DOUBLE RIFLE
$1800.00

The renowned Valmet 512S line of fine firearms is now being produced under the TIKKA brand name and is being manufactured to the same specifications as the former Valmet. As a result of a joint venture entered into by SAKO Ltd., the production facilities for these firearms are now located in Italy. The manufacture of the 512S series is controlled under the rigid quality standards of SAKO Ltd., with complete interchangeability of parts between firearms produced in Italy and Finland. TIKKA'S double rifle offers features and qualities no other action can match: rapid handling and pointing qualities and the silent, immediate availability of a second shot. As such,

this model overcomes the two major drawbacks usually associated with this type of firearm: price and accuracy. Automatic ejectors on 9.3×74R only.

SPECIFICATIONS
Calibers: 308 Win., 30-06, 9.3×74R
Barrel length: 24″
Overall length: 40″
Weight: 8¹/₂ lbs.
Stock: European walnut
Barrel sets only: $990.00

WHITETAIL HUNTER
$559.00   ($589.00 Magnum)

SPECIFICATIONS
Calibers: 22-250, 223, 243, 308 (Medium); 25-06, 270, 30-06 (Long); 7mm Mag., 300 Win. Mag., 338 Win. Mag.
Capacity: 3 rounds (5 rounds optional); detachable magazine
Barrel length: 22¹/₂″ (24¹/₂″ Magnum)
Overall length: 42″ (Medium); 42¹/₂″ (Long); 44¹/₂″ (Magnum)

Weight: 7 lbs. (Medium); 7¹/₄ lbs. (Long); 7¹/₂ lbs. (Magnum)
Sights: No sights; integral scope mount rails; drilled and tapped
Safety: Locks trigger and bolt handle
Features: Oversized trigger guard; short bolt throw; customized spacer system; walnut stock with palm swell and matte lacquer finish; cold hammer-forged barrel

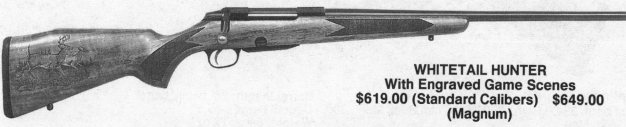

WHITETAIL HUNTER
With Engraved Game Scenes
$619.00 (Standard Calibers) $649.00
(Magnum)

Same specifications as the standard Whitetail Hunter, except with deer or elk scenes engraved on stock.

TIKKA RIFLES

CONTINENTAL VARMINT
$644.00

Finish: Matte lacquer walnut stock w/palm swell
Features: Recoil pad spacer system; quick-release detachable magazine; beavertail forend; cold hammer-forged barrel; integral scope mount rails; adjustable trigger

SPECIFICATIONS
Calibers: 22-250, 223, 308
Capacity: 3 rounds (5 rounds optional)
Barrel length: 26″
Overall length: 46″
Weight: 8 lbs. 10 oz.

CONTINENTAL LONG-RANGE HUNTING RIFLE
$664.00 ($674.00 in Magnum calibers)

SPECIFICATIONS
Calibers: 25-06 Rem., 270 Win., 7mm Rem. Mag., 300 Win. Mag.
Capacity: 3 rounds (5 rounds in standard calibers, 4 rounds in magnum calibers)

Barrel length: 26″ heavy barrel
Overall length: 46.5″
Weight: 8 lbs. 12 oz.
Finish: Matte lacquer walnut stock w/palm swell
Features: Same as Continental Varmint model

UBERTI REPLICAS

ALL UBERTI FIREARMS AVAILABLE IN SUPER GRADE, PRESTIGE AND ENGRAVED FINISHES

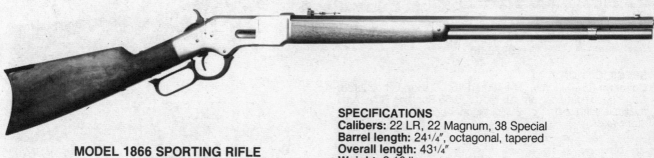

**MODEL 1866 SPORTING RIFLE
$840.00**

SPECIFICATIONS
Calibers: 22 LR, 22 Magnum, 38 Special
Barrel length: 24¼″, octagonal, tapered
Overall length: 43¼″
Weight: 8.16 lbs.
Frame: Elevator and buttplate in brass
Stock: Walnut
Sights: Vertically adjustable rear; horizontally adjustable front

**MODEL 1866 YELLOWBOY CARBINE
$760.00**

The first gun to carry the Winchester name, this model was born as the 44-caliber rimfire cartridge Henry and is now chambered for 22 LR and 44-40.

SPECIFICATIONS
Calibers: 22 LR, 22 Magnum, 38 Special, 44-40
Barrel length: 19″, round, tapered
Overall length: 38¼″
Weight: 7.380 lbs.
Frame: Brass
Stock and forend: Walnut
Sights: Vertically adjustable rear; horizontally adjustable front

**MODEL 1871 ROLLING BLOCK
BABY CARBINE
$460.00**

SPECIFICATIONS
Calibers: 22 LR, 22 Hornet, 22 Magnum, 357 Magnum
Barrel length: 22″
Overall length: 35½″
Weight: 4.85 lbs.

Stock & forend: Walnut
Trigger guard: Brass
Sights: Fully adjustable rear; ramp front
Frame: Color-casehardened steel

UBERTI REPLICAS

MODEL 1873 SPORTING RIFLE
$970.00

SPECIFICATIONS
Calibers: 357 Magnum, 44-40 and 45 LC. Hand-checkered. Other specifications same as Model 1866 Sporting Rifle. Also available with 24¼" or 30" octagonal barrel and pistol-grip stock (extra).

1873 CARBINE
$920.00

SPECIFICATIONS
Calibers: 357 Mag., 44-40, 45 LC
Barrel length: 19" round, tapered
Overall length: 38¼"
Weight: 7.38 lbs.
Sights: Fixed front; vertically adjustable rear

HENRY RIFLE
$950.00

SPECIFICATIONS
Calibers: 44-40, 45 LC
Barrel length: 24¼" (half-octagon, with tubular magazine)
Overall length: 43¾"
Weight: 9.26 lbs.
Frame: Brass
Stock: Varnished American walnut

HENRY CARBINE (not shown)
$950.00

SPECIFICATIONS
Caliber: 44-40   **Capacity:** 12 shots
Barrel length: 22¼"   **Weight:** 9.04 lbs.

Also available:
HENRY TRAPPER. Barrel length: 16¼" or 18". **Overall length:** 35¾" or 37¾". **Weight:** 7.383 lbs. or 7.934 lbs. **Capacity:** 8 or 9 shots. **Price:** $950.00
HENRY RIFLE w/Steel Frame (24¼" barrel; 44/40 cal.). **Price:** $960.00

ULTRA LIGHT ARMS

**MODEL 20
MOUNTAIN RIFLE**

MODEL 28

MODEL 20 SERIES
$2500.00 ($2600.00 Left Hand)

SPECIFICATIONS
Calibers (Short Action): 6mm Rem., 17 Rem., 22 Hornet, 222
Rem., 222 Rem. Mag., 22-250 Rem., 223 Rem., 243 Win.,
250-3000 Savage, 257 Roberts, 257 Ackley, 7×57 Mauser,
7×57 Ackley, 7mm-08 Rem., 284 Win., 300 Savage, 308
Win., 358 Win.
Barrel length: 22″
Weight: 4.75 lbs.
Safety: Two-position safety allows bolt to open or lock with
sear blocked
Stock: Kevlar/Graphite composite; choice of 7 or more colors

Also available:
MODEL 24 SERIES (Long Action) in 270 Win.,
30-06, 25-06, 7mm Express **Weight:** 5¼ lbs.
Barrel length: 22″ $2600.00
Same as above in Left-Hand Model 2700.00
MODEL 28 SERIES (Magnum Action) in 264 Win.,
7mm Rem., 300 Win., 338 **Weight:** 5¾ lbs.
Barrel length: 24″ 2900.00
Same as above in Left-Hand Model 3000.00
MODEL 40 SERIES (Magnum Action) in 300 Wby.
and 416 Rigby. **Weight:** 7½ lbs.
Barrel length: 26″ 2900.00
Same as above in Left-Hand Model 3000.00

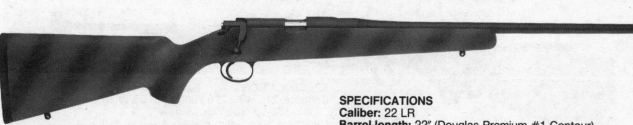

**MODEL 20 RF
$800.00 (Single Shot) $850.00 (Repeater)**

SPECIFICATIONS
Caliber: 22 LR
Barrel length: 22″ (Douglas Premium #1 Contour)
Weight: 5¼ lbs.
Sights: None (drilled and tapped for scope)
Stock: Composite
Features: Recoil pad; sling swivels; fully adjustable Timney
trigger; 3-function safety; color options

UNIQUE RIFLES

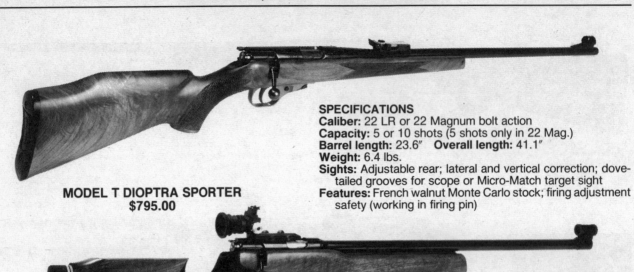

MODEL T DIOPTRA SPORTER
$795.00

SPECIFICATIONS
Caliber: 22 LR or 22 Magnum bolt action
Capacity: 5 or 10 shots (5 shots only in 22 Mag.)
Barrel length: 23.6″   **Overall length:** 41.1″
Weight: 6.4 lbs.
Sights: Adjustable rear; lateral and vertical correction; dove-tailed grooves for scope or Micro-Match target sight
Features: French walnut Monte Carlo stock; firing adjustment safety (working in firing pin)

MODEL T UIT STANDARD RIFLE
$1695.00

SPECIFICATIONS
Caliber: 22 LR
Barrel length: 25.6″   **Overall length:** 44.1″
Weight: 10.4 lbs.
Sights: Micro-Match target sight
Stock: French walnut
Features: Adjustable buttplate and cheek rest; fully adjustable firing; left-hand stock and action available

MODEL T/SM SILHOUETTE
$850.00

SPECIFICATIONS
Caliber: 22 LR or 22 Magnum
Capacity: 5- or 10-shot magazine (5-shot only in 22 Mag.)
Barrel length: 20.5″   **Overall length:** 38.4″
Weight: 6.6 lbs.
Sights: Dovetailed grooves on receiver for scope or Micro-Match target sight
Stock: French walnut Monte Carlo stock (left-hand stock available)

MODEL TGC CENTERFIRE
$1295.00

SPECIFICATIONS
Calibers: 243 Win., 270 Win., 7mm-08, 7mm Rem. Mag., 308 Win., 30-06, 300 Win. Mag.
Capacity: 3- or 5-shot magazine
Barrel length: 24″ bolt action (interchangeable barrel)
Overall length: 44.8″   **Weight:** 8.4 lbs.
Sights: Dovetailed grooves on receiver for scope
Stock: French walnut Monte Carlo stock (left-hand stock available)

WEATHERBY MARK V RIFLES

LAZERMARK

LAZERMARK

LAZERMARK   Prices
26″ Barrel
In Weatherby Magnum calibers 240, 257, 270,
7mm, 300, 340, 378, 416, and 460 . . . . **$1499.00**

MARK V STAINLESS

MARK V STAINLESS

Features 400 Series stainless steel. The action is hand-bedded
to a lightweight, injection-molded synthetic stock. A custom
floorplate on stainless-steel trigger guard with engraved flying
''W'' monogram is standard.

MARK V STAINLESS   Prices
26″ Barrel
In Weatherby Magnum calibers 240, 257, 270,
7mm, 300 and 340 . . . . **$ 999.00**
24″ Barrel
In 270 Win., 7mm Rem. Mag., 30-06 Sprgfld.,
300 Win. Mag., 338 Win. Mag., 375 H&H Mag.   **999.00**

MARK V SYNTHETIC

MARK V SYNTHETIC

Features an injection-molded synthetic stock with dual-tapered
checkered forearm. Comes with custom floorplate release/
trigger guard assembly and engraved flying ''W'' monogram.

MARK V SYNTHETIC   Prices
26″ Barrel
In Weatherby Magnum calibers 240, 257, 270,
7mm, 300 and 340 . . . . **$749.00**
24″ Barrel
In 270 Win., 7mm Rem. Mag., 30-06 Sprgfld.,
300 Win. Mag., 338 Win. Mag., 375 H&H Mag.   **749.00**

FOR COMPLETE SPECIFICATIONS ON THE ABOVE RIFLES, PLEASE SEE THE TABLES ON THE FOLLOWING PAGES.

WEATHERBY MARK V RIFLES

MARK V DELUXE RIFLE

MARK V DELUXE

The Mark V Deluxe stock is made of hand-selected American walnut with skipline checkering, traditional diamond-shaped inlay, rosewood pistol-grip cap and forend tip. Monte Carlo design with raised cheekpiece properly positions the shooter while reducing felt recoil. The action and hammer-forged barrel

are hand-bedded for accuracy, then deep blued to a high-luster finish. See also specifications tables below and on the following page.

Calibers
26″ Barrel:
In 240 Wby. Mag., 257 Wby. Mag., 270 Wby. Mag.,
   7mm Wby. Mag., 300 Wby. Mag. (L.H. also),
   340 Wby. Mag. **$1399.00**
In 378 Wby. Mag. **1475.00**
In 416 Wby. Mag. **1534.00**
In 460 Wby. Mag. **1892.00**

SPECIFICATIONS MARK V RIFLES

Caliber	Model	Barrelled Action	Weight *	Overall Length	Magazine Capacity	Barrel Length/ Contour	Rifling	Length of Pull	Drop at Comb	Monte Carlo	Drop at Heel
.240 WBY Mag.	Mark V Sporter	RH 26″	8 1/2 lbs.	46 5/8″	4+1 in chamber	26″ #2	1-10″ twist	13 5/8″	1″	1/2″	1 5/8″
	Eurosport	RH 26″	8 1/2 lbs.	46 5/8″	4+1 in chamber	26″ #2	1-10″ twist	13 5/8″	1″	1/2″	1 5/8″
	Mark V Deluxe	RH 26″	8 1/2 lbs.	46 5/8″	4+1 in chamber	26″ #2	1-10″ twist	13 5/8″	7/8″	3/8″	1 3/8″
	Euromark	RH 26″	8 1/2 lbs.	46 5/8″	4+1 in chamber	26″ #2	1-10″ twist	13 5/8″	7/8″	3/8″	1 3/8″
	Lazermark	RH 26″	8 1/2 lbs.	46 5/8″	4+1 in chamber	26″ #2	1-10″ twist	13 5/8″	7/8″	3/8″	1 3/8″
	Synthetic	RH 26″	8 lbs.	46 5/8″	4+1 in chamber	26″ #2	1-10″ twist	13 5/8″	7/8″	1/2″	1 1/8″
	Stainless	RH 26″	8 lbs.	46 5/8″	4+1 in chamber	26″ #2	1-10″ twist	13 5/8″	7/8″	1/2″	1 1/8″
.257 WBY Mag.	Mark V Sporter	RH 26″	8 1/2 lbs.	46 5/8″	3+1 in chamber	26″ #2	1-10″ twist	13 5/8″	1″	1/2″	1 5/8″
	Eurosport	RH 26″	8 1/2 lbs.	46 5/8″	3+1 in chamber	26″ #2	1-10″ twist	13 5/8″	1″	1/2″	1 5/8″
	Mark V Deluxe	RH 26″	8 1/2 lbs.	46 5/8″	3+1 in chamber	26″ #2	1-10″ twist	13 5/8″	7/8″	3/8″	1 3/8″
	Euromark	RH 26″	8 1/2 lbs.	46 5/8″	3+1 in chamber	26″ #2	1-10″ twist	13 5/8″	7/8″	3/8″	1 3/8″
	Lazermark	RH 26″	8 1/2 lbs.	46 5/8″	3+1 in chamber	26″ #2	1-10″ twist	13 5/8″	7/8″	3/8″	1 3/8″
	Synthetic	RH 26″	8 lbs.	46 5/8″	3+1 in chamber	26″ #2	1-10″ twist	13 5/8″	7/8″	1/2″	1 1/8″
	Stainless	RH 26″	8 lbs.	46 5/8″	3+1 in chamber	26″ #2	1-10″ twist	13 5/8″	7/8″	1/2″	1 1/8″
	Accumark	RH 26″	8 lbs.	46 5/8″	3+1 in chamber	26″ #3	1-10″ twist	13 5/8″	1″	9/16″	1 1/2″
.270 WIN.	Mark V Sporter	RH 24″	8 lbs.	44 5/8″	4+1 in chamber	24″ #2	1-10″ twist	13 5/8″	1″	1/2″	1 5/8″
	Eurosport	RH 24″	8 lbs.	44 5/8″	4+1 in chamber	24″ #2	1-10″ twist	13 5/8″	1″	1/2″	1 5/8″
	Euromark	RH 24″	8 lbs.	44 5/8″	4+1 in chamber	24″ #2	1-10″ twist	13 5/8″	1″	1/2″	1 5/8″
	Synthetic	RH 24″	8 lbs.	44 5/8″	4+1 in chamberr	24″ #2	1-10″ twist	13 5/8″	7/8″	1/2″	1 1/8″
	Stainless	RH 24″	8 lbs.	44 5/8″	4+1 in chamber	24″ #2	1-10″ twist	13 5/8″	7/8″	1/2″	1 1/8″
.270 WBY Mag.	Mark V Sporter	RH 26″	8 1/2 lbs.	46 5/8″	3+1 in chamber	26″ #2	1-10″ twist	13 5/8″	1″	1/2″	1 5/8″
	Eurosport	RH 26″	8 1/2 lbs.	46 5/8″	3+1 in chamber	26″ #2	1-10″ twist	13 5/8″	1″	1/2″	1 5/8″
	Mark V Deluxe	RH 26″	8 1/2 lbs.	46 5/8″	3+1 in chamber	26″ #2	1-10″ twist	13 5/8″	7/8″	3/8″	1 3/8″
	Euromark	RH 26″	8 1/2 lbs.	46 5/8″	3+1 in chamber	26″ #2	1-10″ twist	13 5/8″	7/8″	3/8″	1 3/8″
	Lazermark	RH 26″	8 1/2 lbs.	46 5/8″	3+1 in chamber	26″ #2	1-10″ twist	13 5/8″	7/8″	3/8″	1 3/8″
	Synthetic	RH 26″	8 lbs.	46 5/8″	3+1 in chamber	26″ #2	1-10″ twist	13 5/8″	7/8″	1/2″	1 1/8″
	Stainless	RH 26″	8 lbs.	46 5/8″	3+1 in chamber	26″ #2	1-10″ twist	13 5/8″	7/8″	1/2″	1 1/8″
	Accumark	RH 26″	8 lbs.	46 5/8″	3+1 in chamber	26″ #3	1-10″ twist	13 5/8″	1″	9/16″	1 1/2″
7mm Rem. Mag.	Mark V Sporter	RH 24″	8 lbs.	44 5/8″	3+1 in chamber	24″ #2	1-9 1/2″ twist	13 5/8″	1″	1/2″	1 5/8″
	Eurosport	RH 24″	8 lbs.	44 5/8″	3+1 in chamber	24″ #2	1-9 1/2″ twist	13 5/8″	1″	1/2″	1 5/8″
	Euromark	RH 24″	8 lbs.	44 5/8″	3+1 in chamber	24″ #2	1-9 1/2″ twist	13 5/8″	1″	1/2″	1 5/8″
	Synthetic	RH 24″	8 lbs.	44 5/8″	3+1 in chamber	24″ #2	1-9 1/2″ twist	13 5/8″	7/8″	1/2″	1 1/8″
	Stainless	RH 24″	8 lbs.	44 5/8″	3+1 in chamber	24″ #2	1-9 1/2″ twist	13 5/8″	7/8″	1/2″	1 1/8″
	Accumark	RH 26″	8 lbs.	46 5/8″	3+1 in chamber	26″ #3	1-9 1/2″ twist	13 5/8″	1″	9/16″	1 1/2″
7mm WBY Mag.	Mark V Sporter	RH 26″	8 1/2 lbs.	46 5/8″	3+1 in chamber	26″ #2	1-10″ twist	13 5/8″	1″	1/2″	1 5/8″
	Eurosport	RH 26″	8 1/2 lbs.	46 5/8″	3+1 in chamber	26″ #2	1-10″ twist	13 5/8″	1″	1/2″	1 5/8″
	Mark V Deluxe	RH 26″	8 1/2 lbs.	46 5/8″	3+1 in chamber	26″ #2	1-10″ twist	13 5/8″	7/8″	3/8″	1 3/8″
	Euromark	RH 26″	8 1/2 lbs.	46 5/8″	3+1 in chamber	26″ #2	1-10″ twist	13 5/8″	7/8″	3/8″	1 3/8″
	Lazermark	RH 26″	8 1/2 lbs.	46 5/8″	3+1 in chamber	26″ #2	1-10″ twist	13 5/8″	7/8″	3/8″	1 3/8″
	Synthetic	RH 26″	8 lbs.	46 5/8″	3+1 in chamber	26″ #2	1-10″ twist	13 5/8″	7/8″	1/2″	1 1/8″
	Stainless	RH 26″	8 lbs.	46 5/6″	3+1 in chamber	26″ #2	1-10″ twist	13 5/8″	7/8″	1/2″	1 1/8″
	Accumark	RH 26″	8 lbs.	46 5/8″	3+1 in chamber	26″ #3	1-10″ twist	13 5/8″	1″	9/16″	1 1/2″
.30-06 Springfield	Mark V Sporter	RH 24″	8 lbs.	44 5/8″	4+1 in chamber	24″ #2	1-10″ twist	13 5/8″	1″	1/2″	1 5/8″
	Eurosport	RH 24″	8 lbs.	44 5/8″	4+1 in chamber	24″ #2	1-10″ twist	13 5/8″	1″	1/2″	1 5/8″
	Euromark	RH 24″	8 lbs.	44 5/8″	4+1 in chamber	24″ #2	1-10″ twist	13 5/8″	1″	1/2″	1 5/8″
	Synthetic	RH 24″	8 lbs.	44 5/8″	4+1 in chamber	24″ #2	1-10″ twist	13 5/8″	7/8″	1/2″	1 1/8″
	Stainless	RH 24″	8 lbs.	44 5/8″	4+1 in chamber	24″ #2	1-10″ twist	13 5/8″	7/8″	1/2″	1 1/8″

WEATHERBY MARK V RIFLES

MARK V SPORTER

MARK V SPORTER

Calibers
26" Barrel:
In 240 Wby. Mag., 257 Wby. Mag., 270 Wby. Mag.,
7mm Wby. Mag., 300 Wby. Mag., 340
Wby. Mag. **$899.00**

24" Barrel:
In 270 Win., 7mm Rem. Mag., 30-06 Sprgfld.,
300 Win. Mag., 338 Win. Mag., 375 H&H Mag. **$899.00**
Also available:
EUROSPORT. Same specifications and prices but with hand-
rubbed satin oil finish.

RIFLES

SPECIFICATIONS MARK V RIFLES (CONT.)

Caliber	Model	Barrelled Action	Weight *	Overall Length	Magazine Capacity	Barrel Length/ Contour	Rifling	Length of Pull	Drop at Comb	Monte Carlo	Drop al Heel
.300 Win Mag.	Mark V Sporter	RH 24"	8 lbs.	44 5/8"	3+1 in chamber	24" #2	1-10" twist	13 5/8"	1"	1/2"	1 5/8"
	Eurosport	RH 24"	8 lbs.	44 5/8"	3+1 in chamber	24" #2	1-10" twist	13 5/8"	1"	1/2"	1 5/8"
	Euromark	RH 24"	8 lbs.	44 5/8"	3+1 in chamber	24" #2	1-10" twist	13 5/8"	1"	1/2"	1 5/8"
	Synthetic	RH 24"	8 lbs.	44 5/8"	3+1 in chamber	24" #2	1-10" twist	13 5/8"	7/8"	1/2"	1 1/8"
	Stainless	RH 24"	8 lbs.	44 5/8"	3+1 in chamber	24" #2	1-10" twist	13 5/8"	7/8"	1/2"	1 1/8"
	Accumark	RH 26"	8 lbs.	46 5/8"	3+1 in chamber	26" #3	1-10" twist	13 5/8"	1"	9/16"	1 1/2"
.300 WBY Mag.	Mark V Sporter	RH 26"	8 1/2 lbs.	46 5/8"	3+1 in chamber	26" #2	1-10" twist	13 5/8"	1"	1/2"	1 5/8"
	Eurosport	RH 26"	8 1/2 lbs.	46 5/8"	3+1 in chamber	26" #2	1-10" twist	13 5/8"	1"	1/2"	1 5/8"
	Mark V Deluxe	RH 26"	8 1/2 lbs.	46 5/8"	3+1 in chamber	26" #2	1-10" twist	13 5/8"	7/8"	3/8"	1 3/8"
	Euromark	RH 26"	8 1/2 lbs.	46 5/8"	3+1 in chamber	26" #2	1-10" twist	13 5/8"	7/8"	3/8"	1 3/8"
	Lazermark	RH 26"	8 1/2 lbs.	46 5/8"	3+1 in chamber	26" #2	1-10" twist	13 5/8"	7/8"	3/8"	1 3/8"
	Synthetic	RH 26"	8 lbs.	46 5/8"	3+1 in chamber	26" #2	1-10" twist	13 5/8"	7/8"	1/2"	1 1/8"
	Stainless	RH 26"	8 lbs.	46 5/8"	3+1 in chamber	26" #2	1-10" twist	13 5/8"	7/8"	1/2"	1 1/8"
	Accumark	RH 26"	8 lbs.	46 5/8"	3+1 in chamber	26" #3	1-10" twist	13 5/8"	1"	9/16"	1 1/2"
.338 Win Mag.	Mark V Sporter	RH 24"	8 lbs.	44 5/8"	3+1 in chamber	24" #2	1-10" twist	13 5/8"	1"	1/2"	1 5/8"
	Eurosport	RH 24"	8 lbs.	44 5/8"	3+1 in chamber	24" #2	1-10" twist	13 5/8"	1"	1/2"	1 5/8"
	Euromark	RH 24"	8 lbs.	44 5/8"	3+1 in chamber	24" #2	1-10" twist	13 5/8"	1"	1/2"	1 5/8"
	Synthetic	RH 24"	8 lbs.	44 5/8"	3+1 in chamber	24" #2	1-10" twist	13 5/8"	7/8"	1/2"	1 1/8"
	Stainless	RH 24"	8 lbs.	44 5/8"	3+1 in chamber	24" #2	1-10" twist	13 5/8"	7/8"	1/2"	1 1/8"
.340 WBY Mag.	Mark V Sporter	RH 26"	8 1/2 lbs.	46 5/8"	3+1 in chamber	26" #2	1-10" twist	13 5/8"	1"	1/2"	1 5/8"
	Eurosport	RH 26"	8 1/2 lbs.	46 5/8"	3+1 in chamber	26" #2	1-10" twist	13 5/8"	1"	1/2"	1 5/8"
	Mark V Deluxe	RH 26"	8 1/2 lbs.	46 5/8"	3+1 in chamber	26" #2	1-10" twist	13 5/8"	7/8"	3/8"	1 3/8"
	Euromark	RH 26"	8 1/2 lbs.	46 5/8"	3+1 in chamber	26" #2	1-10" twist	13 5/8"	7/8"	3/8"	1 3/8"
	Lazermark	RH 26"	8 1/2 lbs.	46 5/8"	3+1 in chamber	26" #2	1-10" twist	13 5/8"	7/8"	3/8"	1 3/8"
	Synthetic	RH 26"	8 lbs.	46 5/8"	3+1 in chamber	26" #2	1-10" twist	13 5/8"	7/8"	1/2"	1 1/8"
	Stainless	RH 26"	8 lbs.	46 5/8"	3+1 in chamber	26" #2	1-10" twist	13 5/8"	7/8"	1/2"	1 1/8"
	Accumark	RH 26"	8 lbs.	46 5/8"	3+1 in chamber	26" #3	1-10" twist	13 5/8"	1"	9/16"	1 1/2"
.375 H&H Mag.	Mark V Sporter	RH 24"	8 1/2 lbs.	44 5/8"	3+1 in chamber	24" #3	1-12" twist	13 5/8"	1"	1/2"	1 5/8"
	Eurosport	RH 24"	8 1/2 lbs.	44 5/8"	3+1 in chamber	24" #3	1-12" twist	13 5/8"	1"	1/2"	1 5/8"
	Euromark	RH 24"	8 lbs.	44 5/8"	3+1 in chamber	24" #3	1-12" twist	13 5/8"	1"	1/2"	1 5/8"
	Synthetic	RH 24"	8 lbs.	44 5/8"	3+1 in chamber	24" #3	1-12" twist	13 5/8"	7/8"	1/2"	1 1/8"
	Stainless	RH 24"	8 lbs.	44 5/8"	3+1 in chamber	24" #3	1-12" twist	13 5/8"	7/8"	1/2"	1 1/8"
.378 WBY Mag.	Mark V Deluxe	RH 26"	9 1/2 lbs.	46 5/8"	2+1 in chamber	26" #3	1-12" twist	13 7/8"	7/8"	3/8"	1 3/8"
	Euromark	RH 26"	9 1/2 lbs.	46 5/8"	2+1 in chamber	26" #3	1-12" twist	13 7/8"	7/8"	3/8"	1 3/8"
	Lazermark	RH 26"	9 1/2 lbs.	46 5/8"	2+1 in chamber	26" #3	1-12" twist	13 7/8"	7/8"	3/8"	1 3/8"
**.416 WBY Mag.	Mark V Deluxe	RH 26"	9 1/2 lbs.	46 3/4"	2+1 in chamber	26" #3	1-14" twist	13 7/8"	7/8"	3/8"	1 3/8"
	Euromark	RH 26"	9 1/2 lbs.	46 3/4"	2+1 in chamber	26" #3	1-14" twist	13 7/8"	7/8"	3/8"	1 3/8"
	Lazermark	RH 26"	9 1/2 lbs.	46 3/4"	2+1 in chamber	26" #3	1-14" twist	13 7/8"	7/8"	3/8"	1 3/8"
**.460 WBY Mag.	Mark V Deluxe	RH 26"	10 1/2 lbs.	46 3/4"	2+1 in chamber	26" #4	1-16" twist	14"	7/8"	3/8"	1 3/8"
	Lazermark	RH 26"	10 1/2 lbs.	46 3/4"	2+1 in chamber	26" #4	1-16" twist	14"	7/8"	3/8"	1 3/8"

Safari Grade, Custom and Crown Custom rifles are also available. Consult your Weatherby dealer or the Weatherby Custom Shop for specifications.

*Weight approximate. Varies due to stock density and bore diameter.   **Available with Weatherby Accubrake only.

WEATHERBY MARK V RIFLES

MARK V EUROMARK

The Euromark features a hand-rubbed oil finish and Monte Carlo stock of American walnut, plus custom grade, hand-cut checkering with an ebony pistol-grip cap and forend tip.

MARK V EUROMARK

26″ Barrel
In Weatherby Magnum calibers 240, 257, 270,
7mm, 300 and 340 . . . . **$1449.00**
In 378 Wby. Mag. **1472.00**
In 416 Wby. Mag. **1581.00**
24″ Barrel
In 270 Win., 7mm Rem. Mag., 30-06 Sprgfld.,
300 Win. Mag., 338 Win. Mag., 375 H&H Mag. **1449.00**

ACCUMARK

ACCUMARK
$1199.00

The new Accumark joins the ranks of other legendary Weatherby Mark V rifles, featuring the flat-shooting hard-hitting performance and accuracy that is the Weatherby trademark.

Built on the proven performance of the Mark V action, the Accumark is a composite of several field-tested features that help make it the utmost in accuracy, including a specially designed, hand-laminated raised-comb Monte Carlo synthetic stock by H-S Precision (a combination of Kevlar, unidirectional fibers and fiberglass). There's also a molded-in, CNC-machined aluminum bedding plate that stiffens the receiver area of the rifle when the barreled action is secured to the block, providing a solid platform for the action. To give the Accumark stock a distinctive look, a matte black gel coat finish is accented with faint grey "spider web" patterning.

The Accumark also features a cold hammer-forged, heavy contour stainless steel barrel with a special longitudinal fluting system and a .705 diameter muzzle with recessed target crown. The flutes deliver 40% more barrel surface to help dissipate heat, while the recessed target crown assures pinpoint accuracy. The custom trigger assembly ranks among the finest. Each trigger is fully adjustable with sear engagement preset at between .012 to .015 and a letoff weight of 4 lbs.

The new Accumark is available in Weatherby Magnum calibers from 257 through 340, 7mm Rem. Mag. and .300 Win. Mag.

Please see the specifications on the previous pages for additional information.

Accuracy

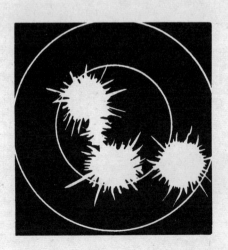

Guarantee

WINCHESTER BOLT-ACTION RIFLES

**MODEL 70 CUSTOM CLASSIC
SHARPSHOOTER**

MODEL 70 CUSTOM CLASSICS

The Model 70 Ultimate Classic features a stock configuration with slimmer, classic styling and special rounded forend. The design offers ideal eye-to-scope alignment without using a Monte Carlo or cheekpiece configuration. The fluted barrel option gives the barrel the stiffness of that of a larger diameter barrel with greatly reduced weight. Both blued steel or all-stainless-steel versions are offered. Other options include:

- Pre-'64 type action
- Choice of round, round fluted, half-octagon, half-round or full- tapered octagon barrels
- Fancy Grade American walnut stock
- Hand-crowned, match-grade barrel

- Special Custom Shop serial numbers and proof stamp
- Inletted swivel bases
- Red 1/2" or 1" recoil pad, depending on caliber
- 70-point cut-checkering
- Hard case

For additional specifications, see table below.

Prices:
Ultimate Classic $2386.00
Custom Express. 2612.00
Sharpshooter II 1994.00
Sporting Sharpshooter II 1875.00

RIFLES

SPECIFICATIONS MODEL 70 CUSTOM CLASSICS

Catalog Number	Caliber	Mag. Cap.*	Barrel Length	Overall Length	Nom. Length of Pull	Nom. Drop at Comb	Heel	Nom. Weight (lbs.)	Rate of Twist 1 turn in	Bases Rings or Sights	BOSS Option
MODEL 70 ULTIMATE CLASSIC											
13918	25-06 Rem.	5	24"	44-3/4"	13-3/4"	5/8"	9/16"	7-1/2	10"	B&R	YES
13919	264 Win. Mag	3	26	46-3/4	13-3/4	5/8	9/16	7-3/4	9	B&R	YES
13920	270 Win.	5	24	44-3/4	13-3/4	5/8	9/16	7-3/4	10	B&R	YES
13921	270 Weath. Mag.	3	26	46-3/4	13-3/4	5/8	9/16	7-3/4	10	B&R	YES
13931	280 Rem.	5	24	44-3/4	13-3/4	5/8	9/16	7-3/4	10	B&R	N/A
13922	30-06 Spfld.	5	24	44-3/4	13-3/4	5/8	9/16	7-3/4	10	B&R	YES
13923	7mm Rem. Mag.	3	26	46-3/4	13-3/4	5/8	9/16	7-3/4	9-1/2	B&R	YES
13924	7mm S.T.W	3	26	46-3/4	13-3/4	5/8	9/16	7-3/4	10	—	N/A
13925	300 Win. Mag.	3	26	46-3/4	13-3/4	5/8	9/16	7-3/4	10	B&R	YES
13932	300 H&H	3	26	46-3/4	13-3/4	5/8	9/16	7-3/4	10	—	N/A
13926	300 Weath. Mag.	3	26	46-3/4	13-3/4	5/8	9/16	7-3/4	10	—	YES
13927	338 Win. Mag.	3	26	46-3/4	13-3/4	5/8	9/16	7-3/4	10	B&R	YES
MODEL 70 CUSTOM CLASSIC EXPRESS											
13771	375 H&H	3	24"	44-3/4"	13-3/4"	9/16"	13/16	10	12"	Adj. Sights	N/A
13805	375 J.R.S	3	24	45	14	9/16	13/16	10	10	Adj. Sights	N/A
13797	416 Rem. Mag.	3	24	44-3/4	13-3/4	9/16	13/16	10	14	Adj. Sights	N/A
13813	458 Win. Mag.	3	22	44-3/4	13-3/4	9/16	13/16	10	14	Adj. Sights	N/A
MODEL 70 CUSTOM CLASSIC SPORTING SHARPSHOOTER II											
24367	7mm S.T.W.	3	26"	46-3/4"	13-5/8"	11/16"	7/8"	8-1/2	10"	—	N/A
24342	300 Win. Mag.	3	26	46-3/4	13-5/8	11/16	7/8	8-1/2	10	B&R	N/A
MODEL 70 CUSTOM CLASSIC SHARPSHOOTER II (STAINLESS STEEL)											
23424	22-250 Rem.	5	26"	46-3/4"	13-3/4"	3/8"	1/8"	11	14"	—	N/A
23426	308 Win.	5	24	44-3/4	13-3/4	3/8	1/8	11	12	—	N/A
NEW 23427	30-06 Spfld.	5	24	44-3/4	13-3/4	3/8	1/8	11	10	—	N/A
23428	300 Win. Mag.	3	26	46-3/4	13-3/4	3/8	1/8	11	10	—	N/A

*For additional capacity, add one round in chamber. Drops are measured from center line of bore. B&R=Bases and rings included. Twist is right hand. Certain combinations of barrel type, stainless steel option, stock grade and DBM availability vary with models. Details are available on request. N/A=BOSS accuracy system not available.

WINCHESTER BOLT-ACTION RIFLES

CLASSIC FEATHERWEIGHT
$620.00 $735.00 w/BOSS (Shown)

SPECIFICATIONS MODEL 70 CLASSIC FEATHERWEIGHT

Model	Caliber	Magazine Capacity*	Barrel Length	Overall Length	Nominal Length Of Pull	Nominal Drop At Comb	Nominal Drop At Heel	Nominal Weight (Lbs.)	Rate of Twist 1 Turn In
70 WALNUT CLASSIC FEATHERWEIGHT	22-250 Rem.	5	22"	42"	13 1/2"	9/16"	7/8"	7	14"
	243 Win.	5	22	42	13 1/2	9/16	7/8	7	10
	308 Win.	5	22	42	13 1/2	9/16	7/8	7	12
	7mm-08 Rem.	5	22	42	13 1/2	9/16	7/8	7	10
	270 Win.	5	22	42	13 1/2	9/16	7/8	7 1/4	10
Standard Grade Walnut	280 Rem.	5	22	42	13 1/2	9/16	7/8	7 1/4	10
Controlled Round Feeding	30-06 Spfld.	5	22	42	13 1/2	9/16	7/8	7 1/4	10
MODEL 70 CLASSIC FEATHERWEIGHT ALL-TERRAIN™ (SYNTHETIC COMPOSITE STOCK)	270 Win.	5	22	42 1/2	13 3/4	9/16	13/16	7 1/4	10
	30-06 Spfld.	5	22	42 1/2	13 3/4	9/16	13/16	7 1/4	10
	7mm Rem. Mag	3	24	44 3/4	13 3/4	9/16	13/16	7 1/4	9 1/2
	300 Win. Mag	3	24	44 3/4	13 3/4	9/16	13/16	7 1/4	9 1/2
BOSS · **MODEL 70 CLASSIC FEATHERWEIGHT ALL-TERRAIN™ (SYNTHETIC COMPOSITE STOCK)**	270 Win.	5	22	42 1/2	13 3/4	9/16	13/16	7 1/4	10
	30-06 Spfld.	5	22	42 1/2	13 3/4	9/16	13/16	7 1/4	10
	7mm Rem. Mag.	3	24	44 3/4	13 3/4	9/16	13/16	7 1/4	9 1/2
	300 Win. Mag	3	24	44 3/4	13 3/4	9/16	13/16	7 1/4	9 1/2

* For additional capacity, add one round in chamber when ready to fire. Drops are measured from center line of bore. Rate of twist is right-hand.

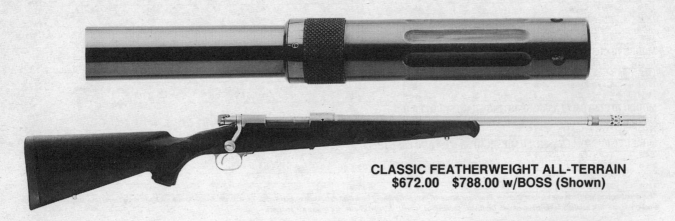

CLASSIC FEATHERWEIGHT ALL-TERRAIN
$672.00 $788.00 w/BOSS (Shown)

WINCHESTER BOLT-ACTION RIFLES

MODEL 70 CLASSIC SM
(Synthetic Composite Stock, Matte)
$620.00
$735.00 w/BOSS System
$672.00 (375 H&H Magnum)

SPECIFICATIONS MODEL 70 CLASSIC

Caliber	Magazine Capacity	Barrel Length	Overall Length	Nominal Length Of Pull	Nominal Drop At		Nominal Weight (Lbs.)	Rate of Twist 1 Turn In	Bases Rings or Sights
					Comb	Heel			
MODEL 70 CLASSIC SM (SYNTHETIC STOCK; CONTROLLED ROUND FEED)									
270 Win.	5	24"	44 3/4"	13 3/4"	9/16"	7/8"	7 3/8	10"	
30-06 Spfld.	5	24	44 3/4	13 3/4	9/16	7/8	7 3/8	10	
7mm Rem. Mag.	3	26	44 3/4	13 3/4	9/16	7/8	7 5/8	9 1/2	
300 Win. Mag.	3	26	44 3/4	13 3/4	9/16	7/8	7 5/8	10	
338 Win. Mag.	3	26	44 3/4	13 3/4	9/16	7/8	7 5/8	10	
375 H&H Mag.*	3	24	44 3/4	13 3/4	9/16	7/8	8	12	Sights
MODEL 70 CLASSIC SM (SYNTHETIC COMPOSITE STOCK, MATTE)									
270 Win.	5	24"	44 3/4"	13 3/4"	9/16"	13/16"	7 1/4	10"	—
30-06 Spfld.	5	24	44 3/4	13 3/4	9/16	13/16	7 1/4	10	—
7mm Rem. Mag.	3	26	46 3/4	13 3/4	9/16	13/16	7 1/2	9 1/2	—
300 Win. Mag.	3	26	46 3/4	13 3/4	9/16	13/16	7 1/2	10	—
338 Win. Mag.	3	26	46 3/4	13 3/4	9/16	13/16	7 1/2	10	—
375 H&H Mag.	3	24	44 3/4	13 3/4	9/16	13/16	7 1/4	12	Sights
BOSS · **MODEL 70 CLASSIC SM (SYNTHETIC COMPOSITE STOCK, MATTE)**									
270 Win.	5	24"	44 3/4"	13 3/4"	9/16"	13/16"	7 1/4	10"	—
30-06 Spfld.	5	24	44 3/4	13 3/4	9/16	13/16	7 1/4	10	—
7mm Rem. Mag.	3	26	46 3/4	13 3/4	9/16	13/16	7 1/2	9 1/2	—
300 Win. Mag.	3	26	46 3/4	13 3/4	9/16	13/16	7 1/2	10	—
338 Win. Mag.	3	26	46 3/4	13 3/4	9/16	13/16	7 1/2	10	—
BOSS · **MODEL 70 CLASSIC STAINLESS (SYNTHETIC COMPOSITE STOCK)**									
22-250 Rem.	5	22"	42 1/4"	13 3/4"	9/16"	13/16"	6 3/4	14"	—
243 Win.	5	22	42 1/4	13 3/4	9/16	13/16	6 3/4	10	—
308 Win.	5	22	42 1/4	13 3/4	9/16	13/16	6 3/4	12	—
270 Win.	5	24	44 3/4	13 3/4	9/16	13/16	7 1/4	10	—
30-06 Spfld.	5	24	44 3/4	13 3/4	9/16	13/16	7 1/4	10	—
7mm Rem. Mag.	3	26	46 3/4	13 3/4	9/16	13/16	7 1/2	9 1/2	—
300 Win. Mag.	3	26	46 3/4	13 3/4	9/16	13/16	7 1/2	10	—
300 Weath. Mag.	3	26	46 3/4	13 3/4	9/16	13/16	7 1/2	10	—
338 Win. Mag.	3	26	46 3/4	13 3/4	9/16	13/16	7 1/2	10	—

* Not available in BOSS models

WINCHESTER BOLT-ACTION RIFLES

MODEL 70 CLASSIC SUPER GRADE
$840.00 $956.00 w/BOSS Option

The Winchester Model 70 Classic Super Grade features a bolt with true claw-controlled feeding of belted magnums. The stainless-steel claw extractor on the bolt grasps the round from the magazine and delivers it to the chamber and later extracts the spent cartridge. A gas block doubles as bolt stop, and the bolt guard rail assures smooth action. Winchester's 3-position safety and field-strippable firing pin are standard equipment. Other features include a satin-finish select walnut stock with sculptured cheekpiece; all-steel bottom metal; and chrome molybdenum barrel with cold hammer-forged rifling for optimum accuracy. Now available with BOSS System. Specifications are listed in the tables below.

SPECIFICATIONS MODEL 70 CLASSIC SUPER GRADE/SUPER EXPRESS RIFLES

Caliber	Magazine Capacity*	Barrel Length	Overall Length	Nominal Length of Pull	Nominal Drop at Comb	Heel	MC	Nominal Weight (Lbs.)	Rate of Twist 1 Turn in	Bases & Rings or Sights
270 Win.	5	24″	44³/₄″	13³/₄″	9/16″	13/16″	—	7³/₄	10″	B + R
30-06 Spfld.	5	24	44³/₄	13³/₄	9/16	13/16	—	7³/₄	10	B + R
7mm Rem. Mag.	3	26	46³/₄	13³/₄	9/16	13/16	—	8	9¹/₂	B + R
300 Win. Mag.	3	26	46³/₄	13³/₄	9/16	13/16	—	8	10	B + R
338 Win. Mag.	3	26	46³/₄	13³/₄	9/16	13/16	—	8	10	B + R

MODEL 70 CLASSIC SUPER EXPRESS $865.00

Caliber	Magazine Capacity*	Barrel Length	Overall Length	Nominal Length of Pull	Nominal Drop at Comb	Heel	MC	Nominal Weight (Lbs.)	Rate of Twist 1 Turn in	Bases & Rings or Sights
375 H&H Mag.	3	24″	44³/₄″	13³/₄″	9/16″	1⁵/₁₆″		8¹/₂	12″	Sights
416 Rem. Mag.	3	24	44³/₄	13³/₄	9/16	1⁵/₁₆		8¹/₂	14	Sights
458 Win. Mag.	3	22	42³/₄	13³/₄	9/16	1⁵/₁₆		8¹/₄	14	Sights

MODEL 70 CLASSIC
STAINLESS w/BOSS OPTION ($788.00)

MODEL 70 CLASSIC STAINLESS (SYNTHETIC COMPOSITE STOCK) $672.00 ($724.00 in 375 H&H Mag.)

Caliber	Magazine Capacity	Barrel Length	Overall Length	Nominal Length Of Pull	Nominal Drop At Comb	Heel	Nominal Weight (Lbs.)	Rate of Twist 1 Turn In	Bases & Rings or Sights
22-250 Rem.	5″	22″	42¹/₄″	13³/₄″	9/16″	13/16″	6³/₄	14″	—
243 Win.	5	22	42¹/₄	13³/₄	9/16	13/16	6³/₄	10	—
308 Win.	5	22	42¹/₄	13³/₄	9/16	13/16	6³/₄	12	—
270 Win.	5	24	44³/₄	13³/₄	9/16	13/16	7¹/₄	10	—
30-06 Spfld.	5	24	44³/₄	13³/₄	9/16	13/16	7¹/₄	10	—
7mm Rem. Mag.	3	26	46³/₄	13³/₄	9/16	13/16	7¹/₂	9¹/₂	—
300 Win. Mag.	3	26	46³/₄	13³/₄	9/16	13/16	7¹/₂	10	—
300 Wby. Mag.	3	26	46³/₄	13³/₄	9/16	13/16	7¹/₂	10	—
338 Win. Mag.	3	26	46³/₄	13³/₄	9/16	13/16	7¹/₂	10	—
375 H&H Mag.*	3	24	44³/₄	13³/₄	9/16	13/16	7¹/₄	12	Sights

* Not available with BOSS System

WINCHESTER BOLT-ACTION RIFLES

MODEL 70 CLASSIC SPORTER w/BOSS

MODEL 70 CLASSIC SPORTER
$613.00 ($651.00 w/Sights)
$728.00 w/BOSS

SPECIFICATIONS MODEL 70 CLASSIC SPORTER

Caliber	Magazine Capacity A	Barrel Length	Overall Length	Nominal Length Of Pull	Nominal Drop At Comb	Nominal Drop At Heel	Nominal Weight (Lbs.)	Rate of Twist 1 Turn In	Sights
70 SPORTER									
25-06 Rem.	5	24"	44³/₄"	13³/₄"	9/16"	13/16"	7³/₄	10"	
264-Win. Mag.	3	26	46³/₄	13³/₄	9/16	13/16	8	9	
270 Win.	5	24	44³/₄	13³/₄	9/16	13/16	7³/₄	10	Sights
270 Win.	5	24	44³/₄	13³/₄	9/16	13/16	7³/₄	10	
270 Wby. Mag.	3	26	46³/₄	13³/₄	9/16	13/16	8	10	
30-06 Spfld.	5	24	44³/₄	13³/₄	9/16	13/16	7³/₄	10	Sights
30-06 Spfld.	5	24	44³/₄	13³/₄	9/16	13/16	7³/₄	10	
7mm Rem. Mag.	3	26	46³/₄	13³/₄	9/16	13/16	8	9¹/₂	Sights
7mm Rem. Mag.	3	26	46³/₄	13³/₄	9/16	13/16	8	9¹/₂	
300 Win. Mag.	3	26	46³/₄	13³/₄	9/16	13/16	8	10	Sights
300 Win. Mag.	3	26	46³/₄	13³/₄	9/16	13/16	8	10	
300 Wby. Mag.	3	26	46³/₄	13³/₄	9/16	13/16	8	10	
338 Win. Mag.	3	26	46³/₄	13³/₄	9/16	13/16	8	10	Sights
338 Win. Mag.	3	26	46³/₄	13³/₄	9/16	13/16	8	10	

MODEL 70 HEAVY BARREL VARMINT
w/Composite Stock, Matte Finish

SPECIFICATIONS MODEL 70 HEAVY BARREL VARMINT RIFLE $764.00

Caliber	Magazine Capacity (A)	Barrel Length	Overall Length	Nominal Length Of Pull	Nominal Drop At Comb	Nominal Drop At Heel	Nominal Weight (Lbs.)	Rate of Twist 1 Turn In	Sights
220 Swift	5	26"	46"	13¹/₂"	3/4"	1/2"	10³/₄	14"	—
22-250 Rem.	5	26	46	13¹/₂	3/4	1/2	10³/₄	14	—
223 Rem.	6	26	46	13¹/₂	3/4	1/2	10³/₄	9	—
243 Win.	5	26	46	13¹/₂	3/4	1/2	10³/₄	10	—
308 Win.	5	26	46	13¹/₂	3/4	1/2	10³/₄	12	—

(A) For add'l. capacity, add one round in chamber when ready to fire. Drops are measured from center line of bore. R.H. rate of twist.

RIFLES

WINCHESTER BOLT-ACTION RIFLES

MODEL 70 CLASSIC LAREDO w/BOSS
$879.00 $764.00 w/o BOSS

Features heavy 26″ barrel H-S Precision gray synthetic stock with full-length "Pillar Plus Accu-Block" in 7mm Rem. Mag. and 300 Win. Mag.

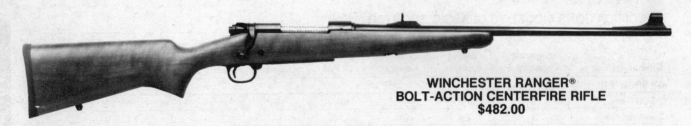

WINCHESTER RANGER®
BOLT-ACTION CENTERFIRE RIFLE
$482.00

The Ranger Bolt-Action Rifle comes with an American hardwood stock, a wear-resistant satin walnut finish, ramp bead-post front sight, steel barrel, hinged steel magazine floorplate, three-position safety and engine-turned, anti-bind bolt. The receiver is drilled and tapped for scope mounting; accuracy is enhanced by thermoplastic bedding of the receiver. Barrel and receiver are brushed and blued.

WINCHESTER RANGER®
LADIES'/YOUTH BOLT-ACTION CARBINE
$482.00

This carbine offers dependable bolt-action performance combined with a scaled-down design to fit the younger, smaller shooter. It features anti-bind bolt design, jeweled bolt, three-position safety, contoured recoil pad, ramped bead front sight, semibuckhorn folding-leaf rear sight, hinged steel magazine floorplate, and sling swivels. Receiver is drilled and tapped for scope mounting. Stock is of American hardwood with protective satin walnut finish. Pistol grip, length of pull, overall length and comb are all tailored to youth dimensions (see table).

SPECIFICATIONS RANGER & LADIES' YOUTH RIFLES

Model	Caliber	Magazine Capacity	Barrel Length	Overall Length	Nominal Length Of Pull	Nominal Drop At Comb	Heel	Nominal Weight (Lbs.)	Rate of Twist 1 Turn in	Bases & Rings Sights
70 RANGER	223 Rem.	6	22″	42″	13$\frac{1}{2}$″	$\frac{9}{16}$″	$\frac{7}{8}$″	6$\frac{3}{4}$	12″	Sights
	243 Win.	5	22	42	13$\frac{1}{2}$	$\frac{9}{16}$	$\frac{7}{8}$	6$\frac{3}{4}$	10	Sights
	270 Win.	5	22	42$\frac{1}{2}$	13$\frac{1}{2}$	$\frac{9}{16}$	$\frac{7}{8}$	7	10	Sights
	30-06 Spfld.	5	22	41$\frac{1}{2}$	13$\frac{1}{2}$	$\frac{9}{16}$	$\frac{7}{8}$	7	10	Sights
70 RANGER LADIES/ YOUTH	243 Win.	5	22	41	12$\frac{1}{2}$	$\frac{3}{4}$	1	6$\frac{1}{2}$	10	Sights
	308 Win.	5	22	41	12$\frac{1}{2}$	$\frac{3}{4}$	1	6$\frac{1}{2}$	12	Sights

For add'l. capacity, add one round in chamber when ready to fire. Drops are measured from center line of bore. R.H. rate of twist.

WINCHESTER RIFLES

LEVER-ACTION CARBINES/RIFLES

MODEL 94 STANDARD WALNUT RIFLE

The top choice for lever-action styling and craftsmanship. Metal surfaces are highly polished and blued. American walnut stock and forearm have a protective stain finish with precise-cut wraparound checkering. It has a 20-inch barrel with hooded blade front sight and semibuckhorn rear sight.

Prices:

30-30 Win., checkered	**$393.00**
w/o checkering	**363.00**

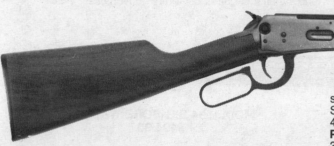

MODEL 94 WALNUT TRAPPER CARBINE

With 16-inch short-barrel lever action and straight forward styling. Compact and fast handling in dense cover, it has a 5-shot magazine capacity (9 in 45 Colt or 44 Rem. Mag./44 S&W Special). **Calibers:** 30-30 Win., 357 Mag., 45 Colt, and 44 Rem. Mag./44 S&W Special.

Prices:

30-30 Winchester	**$363.00**
357 Mag., 45 Colt, 44 Rem. Mag./44 S&W Spec.	**384.00**

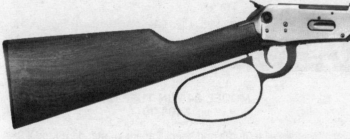

MODEL 94 WRANGLER
$384.00 (30-30 Win.)
$404.00 (44 Rem., 44 S&W Spec.)
MODEL 94 LEGACY (Not Shown)
$393.00

MODEL 94 SPECIFICATIONS (with 100th Anniversary Receiver Inscription)

Model	Caliber	Magazine Capacity (A)	Barrel Length	Overall Length	Nominal Length Of Pull	Nominal Drop At Comb	Nominal Drop At Heel	Nominal Weight (Lbs.)	Rate of Twist 1 Turn in	Rings Sights
94 CHECKERED WALNUT	30-30 Win.	6	20″	37 3/4″	13 1/2″	1 1/8 ″	1 7/8″	6 1/2	12″	Rifle
94 STANDARD	30-30 Win.	6	20	37 3/4	13 1/2	1 1/8	1 7/8	6 1/2	12	Rifle
94 TRAPPER CARBINE	30-30 Win.	5	16	33 3/4	13 1/2	1 1/8	1 7/8	6 1/8	12	Rifle
	357 Mag.	9	16	33 3/4	13 1/2	1 1/16	1 7/8	6 1/8	16	Rifle
	44 Rem. Mag .44 S&W Spec.	9	16	33 3/4	13 1/2	1 1/8	1 7/8	6	38	Rifle
	45 Colt	9	16	33 3/4	13 1/2	1 1/8	1 7/8	6	38	Rifle
94 WRANGLER	30-30 Win.	5	16	33 3/4	13 1/2	1 1/8	1 7/8	6 1/8	12	Rifle
	44 Rem. Mag .44 S&W Spec.	9	16	33 3/4	13 1/2	1 1/8	1 7/8	6	38	Rifle
94 LEGACY	30-30 Win.	6	20	37 3/4	13 1/2	1 1/8	1 7/8	6 1/2	12	Rifle

(A) For additional capacity, add one round in chamber when ready to fire. Drops are measured from center line of bore. Rate of twist is right-hand.

WINCHESTER RIFLES

LEVER ACTION

MODEL 94 RANGER
$320.00   ($376.00 with Scope)

Model 94 Ranger is an economical version of the Model 94. Lever action is smooth and reliable. In 30-30 Winchester, the rapid-firing six-shot magazine capacity provides two more shots than most other centerfire hunting rifles.

MODEL 94 BIG-BORE WALNUT
$404.00

Winchester's powerful 307 and 356 hunting calibers combined with maximum lever-action power and angled ejection provide hunters with improved performance and economy.

MODEL 94 WIN-TUFF RIFLE
$404.00

Includes all features and specifications of standard Model 94 plus tough laminated hardwood styled for the brush-gunning hunter who wants good concealment and a carbine that can stand up to all kinds of weather.

MODEL 94 SPECIFICATIONS

Model	Caliber	Magazine Capacity (A)	Barrel Length	Overall Length	Nominal Length Of Pull	Nominal Drop At Comb	Heel	Nominal Weight (Lbs.)	Rate of Twist 1 Turn in	Sights
94 WIN-TUFF	30-30 Win.	6	20″	37³/₄″	13¹/₂″	1¹/₈″	1⁷/₈″	6¹/₂	12″	Rifle
94 BIG BORE WALNUT	307 Win.	6	20	37¹/₄	13¹/₂	1¹/₈	1⁷/₈	6¹/₂	12	Rifle
	356 Win.	6	20	37³/₄	13¹/₂	1¹/₈	1⁷/₈	6¹/₂	12	Rifle
RANGER	30-30 Win.	6	20	37³/₄	13¹/₂	1¹/₈	1⁷/₈	6¹/₂	12	Rifle
Scope 4X32 and see-through mounts	30-30 Win.	6	20	37³/₄	13¹/₂	1¹/₈	1⁷/₈	6¹/₂	12	R/S

(A) For additional capacity, add one round in chamber when ready to fire. Drops are measured from center line of bore. R/S-Rifle sights and Bushnell® Sportview™ scope with mounts. Rate of twist is right-hand.

WINCHESTER RIFLES

MODEL 9422 LEVER-ACTION RIMFIRE RIFLES

These Model 9422 rimfire rifles combine classic 94 styling and handling in ultra-modern lever action 22s of superb craftsmanship. Handling and shooting characteristics are superior because of their carbine-like size.

Positive lever action and bolt design ensure feeding and chambering from any shooting position. The bolt face is T-slotted to guide the cartridge with complete control from magazine to chamber. A color-coded magazine follower shows when the brass magazine tube is empty. Receivers are grooved for scope mounting. Other functional features include exposed hammer with half-cock safety, hooded bead front sight, semi-buckhorn rear sight and side ejection of spent cartridges.

Stock and forearm are American walnut with checkering, high-luster finish, and straight-grip design. Internal parts are carefully finished for smoothness of action.

MODEL 9422 WALNUT

Considered one of the world's finest production sporting arms, this lever-action rimfire (shown above) holds 21 Short, 17 Long or 15 Long Rifle cartridges.

Model 9422 Walnut Magnum gives exceptional accuracy at longer ranges than conventional 22 rifles. It is designed specifically for the 22 Winchester Magnum Rimfire cartridge and holds 11 cartridges.

Model 9422 Win-Cam Magnum features laminated nonglare, green-shaded stock and forearm. American hardwood stock is bonded to withstand all weather and climates. **Model 9422 Win-Tuff** is also availale to ensure resistance to changes in weather conditions, or exposure to water and hard knocks.

MODEL 9422 TRAPPER

SPECIFICATIONS MODEL 9422

Model	Caliber	Magazine Capacity	Barrel Length	Overall Length	Nominal Length Of Pull	Nominal Drop At Comb	Heel	Nominal Weight (Lbs.)	Rate of Twist 1 Turn in	Sights	Prices
9422 WALNUT	22 S, L, LR 22 WMR	21 S,17 L, 15 LR11	20½"	37⅛"	13½"	1⅛"	1⅞"	6¼	16"	Rifle	$407.00 424.00
9422 WIN-TUFF	22 S, L, LR 22 WMR	21 S, 17 L, 15 LR11	20½	37⅛	13½	1⅛	1⅞	6¼	16	Rifle	407.00 424.00
9422 WIN-CAM	22 WMR	11	20½	37⅛	13½	1⅛	1⅞	6¼	16	Rifle	424.00
9422 TRAPPER	22 S, L, LR	15 S, 12 L, 11 LR	16½	33⅛	13½	1⅛	1⅞	5½	16	Rifle	407.00
9422 HIGH GRADE	22 S, L, LR	22 S, L, LR 21 S, 17 L, 15 LR	20½	37⅛	13½	1⅛	1⅞	6	16	Rifle	489.00

WMR = Winchester Magnum Rimfire. S=Short, L=Long, LR=Long Rifle. Drops are measured from center line of bore.

WINSLOW RIFLES

SPECIFICATIONS

Stock: Choice of two stock models. **The Plainsmaster** offers pinpoint accuracy in open country with full curl pistol grip and flat forearm. **The Bushmaster** offers lighter weight for bush country; slender pistol with palm swell; beavertail forend for light hand comfort. Both styles are of hand-rubbed black walnut. Length of pull—13½ inches; Plainsmaster ³⁄₈ inch castoff; Bushmaster ³⁄₁₆ inch castoff; all rifles are drilled and tapped to incorporate the use of telescopic sights; rifles with receiver or open sights are available on special order; all rifles are equipped with quick detachable sling swivel studs and white-line recoil pad. All Winslow stocks incorporate a slight castoff to deflect recoil, minimizing flinch and muzzle jump.

Magazine: Staggered box type, four shot. (Blind in the stock has no floorplate).

Action: Mauser Mark X Action.

Overall length: 43″ (Standard Model); 45″ (Magnum).

Barrel: 24″ or 26″ Douglas barrel premium grade, chrome moly-type steel; all barrels, 20 through 35 caliber, have six lands and grooves; barrels larger than 35 caliber have eight lands and grooves. All barrels are finished to (.2 to .4) micro inches inside the lands and grooves. All Winslow rifles have company name and serial number and grade engraved on the action and caliber engraved on barrel.

Total weight (without scope): 7 to 7½ lbs. with 24″ barrel in standard calibers 243, 308, 270, etc; 8 to 9 lbs. with 26″ barrel in Magnum calibers 264 Win., 300 Wby., 458 Win., etc.

Calibers:

Standard cartridges: 22-250, 243 Win., 244 Rem., 257 Roberts, 308 Win., 30-06, 280 Rem., 270 Win., 25-06, 284 Win., 358 Win., and 7mm (7×57).

Magnum cartridges: 300 Weatherby, 300 Win., 338 Win., 358 Norma, 375 H.H., 458 Win., 257 Weatherby, 264 Win., 270 Weatherby, 7mm Weatherby, 7mm Rem., 300 H.H., 308 Norma.

Left-handed models are available in most calibers.

WINSLOW BASIC RIFLE

The Basic Rifle, available in the Bushmaster stock, features one ivory diamond inlay in a rose-wood grip cap and ivory trademark in bottom of forearm. Grade 'A' walnut jeweled bolt and follower.

Price:	from $1750.00
With **Plainsmaster stock, add**	100.00
Left-hand model	from 1850.00

WINSLOW VARMINT

This 17-caliber rifle is available with Bushmaster stock or Plainsmaster stock, which is a miniature of the original with high roll-over cheekpiece and a round leading edge on the forearm, modified spoon billed pistol grip. Available in 17/222, 17/222 Mag., 17/223, 222 Rem. and 223. Regent grade shown.

Prices:	
With **Bushmaster stock**	from $1750.00
With **Plainsmaster stock, add**	100.00
Left-hand Model	from 1850.00

Shotguns

For addresses and phone/fax numbers of manufacturers and distributors included in this section, please turn to DIRECTORY OF MANUFACTURERS AND SUPPLIERS on page 554.

AMERICAN ARMS SHOTGUNS

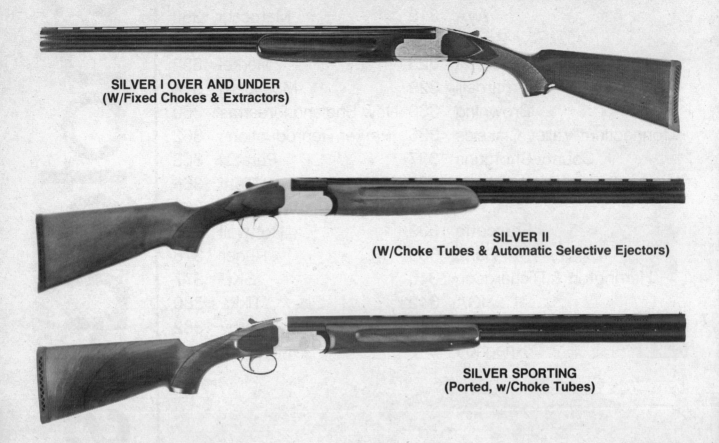

SILVER I OVER AND UNDER
(W/Fixed Chokes & Extractors)

SILVER II
(W/Choke Tubes & Automatic Selective Ejectors)

SILVER SPORTING
(Ported, w/Choke Tubes)

SPECIFICATIONS

Model	Gauge	Bbl. Length	Chamber	Chokes	Avg. Weight	Prices
Silver I	12	26"–28"	3"	IC/M-M/F	6 lbs. 15 oz.	**$599.00**
	20	26"–28"	3"	IC/M-M/F	6 lbs. 12 oz.	
	28	26"	2¾"	IC/M	5 lbs. 14 oz.	625.00
	.410	26"	3"	IC/M	6 lbs. 6 oz.	
Silver II	12	26"–28"	3"	CT-3	6 lbs. 15 oz.	699.00
	16	26"	2¾"	IC/M	6 lbs. 13 oz.	
	20	26"	3"	CT-3	6 lbs. 12 oz.	
	28	26"	2¾"	IC/M	5 lbs. 14 oz.	725.00
	.410	26"	3"	IC/M	6 lbs. 6 oz.	
Silver Upland Lite (not shown)	12	26"	3"	CT-3	6 lbs. 4 oz.	899.00
	20	26"	3"	CT-3	5 lbs. 12 oz.	
	28	26"	2¾"	IC/M	6 lbs.	
Sporting	12	28"–30"	2¾"	CTS	7 lbs. 6 oz.	899.00
	20	28"	3"	CTS	7 lbs. 3 oz.	

CT-3 Choke Tubes IC/M/F   Cast Off = ³/₈"   CTS = SK/SK/IC/M
Silver I and II: Pull = 14 ¹/₈"; Drop at Comb = 1 ³/₈"; Drop at Heel = 2 ³/₈"
Silver Sporting: Pull = 14 ³/₈"; Drop at Comb = 1 ¹/₂"; Drop at Heel = 2 ³/₈"

AMERICAN ARMS SHOTGUNS

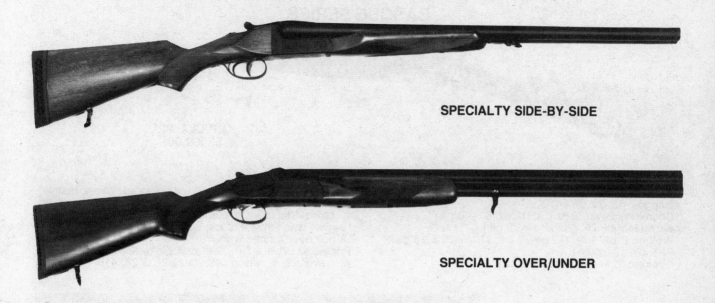

SPECIALTY SIDE-BY-SIDE

SPECIALTY OVER/UNDER

SPECIFICATIONS

Model	Gauge	Bbl. Length	Chamber	Chokes	Avg. Wgt.	Prices
WT/OU	10	26″	3¹/₂″	CT-2	9 lbs. 10 oz.	**$950.00**
WS/OU	12	28″	3¹/₂″	CT-3	7 lbs. 2 oz.	725.00
TS/OU	12	24″	3¹/₂″	CT-3	6 lbs. 14 oz.	725.00
TS/SS	12	26″	3¹/₂″	CT-3	7 lbs. 6 oz.	750.00

CT-3 = Choke tubes IC/M/F.   CT-2 = Choke tubes F/F.   Drop at Comb = 1¹/₈″.   Drop at Heel = 2 ³/₈″.

BASQUE SERIES

BRITTANY
$849.00

SPECIFICATIONS
Gauges: 12, 20
Chamber: 3″   **Chokes:** CT-3
Barrel length: 26″
Weight: 6 lbs. 7 ozs. (20 ga.); 6 lbs. 15 oz. (12 ga.)

Features: Engraved case-colored frame; single selective trigger with top tang selector; automatic selective ejectors; manual safety; hard chrome-lined barrels; walnut English-style straight stock and semi-beavertail forearm w/cut checkering and oil-rubbed finish; ventilated rubber recoil pad; and choke tubes with key

AMERICAN ARMS SHOTGUNS

BASQUE SERIES

GRULLA #2
$3099.00

SPECIFICATIONS
Gauges: 12, 20, 28, .410
Chambers:2³/₄″ (28 ga.); 3″ (12, 20 & .410 ga.)
Barrel length: 26″ (28″ also in 12 ga.)
Weight: 6 lbs. 4 oz. (12 ga.); 5 lbs. 11 oz. (20 & 28 ga.);
   5 lbs. 13 oz. (.410)
Chokes: IC/M (M/F also in 12 ga.)

Features: Hand-fitted and finished high-grade classic double; double triggers; automatic selective ejectors; fixed chokes; concave rib; case-colored sidelock action w/engraving; English-style straight stock; splinter forearm and checkered butt of oil rubbed walnut
Prices: All Grulla #2 models available by special order only. Also available in sets in calibers 20/28 or 28/.410.

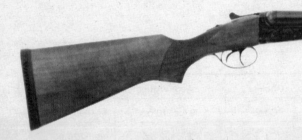

GENTRY SIDE-BY-SIDE
$725.00 (12 or 20 Ga.) $757.00 (28 or .410 Ga.)

Features boxlocks with engraved English-style scrollwork on side plates; one-piece, steel-forged receiver; chrome barrels; manual thumb safety; independent floating firing pin.

SPECIFICATIONS
Gauges: 12, 20, 28, .410
Chambers: 3″ (except 28 gauge, 2³/₄″)

Barrel lengths: 26″, choked IC/M (all gauges); 28″, choked M/F (12 and 20 gauges)
Weight: 6 lbs. 15 oz. (12 ga.); 6 lbs. 7 oz. (20 and .410 ga.); 6 lbs. 5 oz. (28 ga.)
Drop at comb: 1³/₈″   **Drop at heel:** 2³/₈″
Other features: Fitted recoil pad; flat matted rib; walnut pistol-grip stock and beavertail forend with hand-checkering; gold front sight bead

AMERICAN ARMS/FRANCHI

MODEL 48AL (Recoil)
$649.00

SPECIFICATIONS
Gauges: 12/20, 28 gauge   **Chamber:** 2³/₄″
Action: Single Action

Barrel lengths: 24″, 26″, 28″
Choke: Full; fixed (IC) (28 ga. only)
Weight: 5¹/₂ to 6¹/₂ lbs.
Length of pull: 14¹/₄″
Drop at comb: 1¹/₂″   **Drop at heel:** 2³/₈″

AYA SHOTGUNS

SIDELOCK SHOTGUNS

AYA sidelock shotguns are fitted with London Holland & Holland system sidelocks, double triggers with articulated front trigger, automatic safety and ejectors, cocking indicators, bushed firing pins, replaceable hinge pins and chopper lump barrels. Stocks are of figured walnut with hand-cut checkering and oil finish, complete with a metal oval on the buttstock for engraving of initials. Exhibition grade wood is available as are many special options, including a true left-hand version and self-opener. Available exclusively through Armes de Chasse (*see* Directory of Manufacturers and Suppliers).

Barrel lengths: 26″, 27″, 28″, 29″ and 32 ″. **Weight:** 5 to 7 pounds, depending on gauge.

Model	Prices
MODEL 1: Sidelock in 12 and 20 gauge with special engraving and exhibition quality wood	$7500.00
MODEL 2: Sidelock in 12, 16, 20, 28 gauge and .410 bore	3500.00
MODEL 53: Sidelock in 12, 16 and 20 gauge with 3 locking lugs and side clips	5000.00
MODEL 56: Sidelock in 12 gauge only with 3 locking lugs and side clips	8000.00
MODEL XXV/SL: Sidelock in 12 and 20 gauge only with Churchill-type rib	4000.00

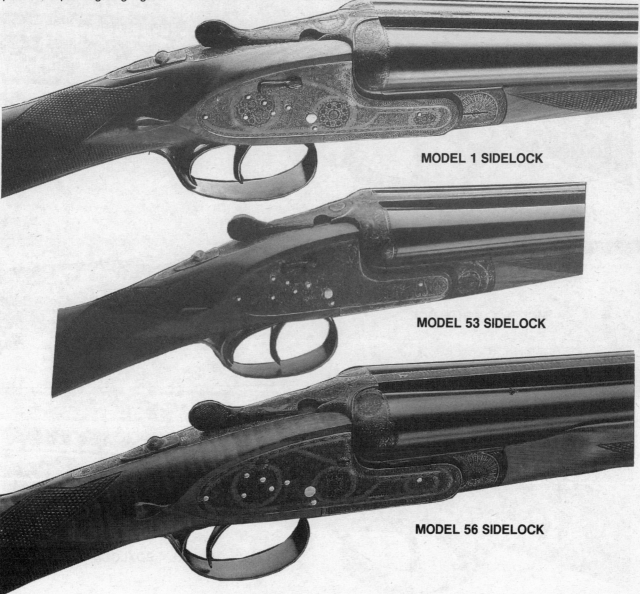

MODEL 1 SIDELOCK

MODEL 53 SIDELOCK

MODEL 56 SIDELOCK

AYA SHOTGUNS

BOXLOCK SHOTGUNS

AYA boxlocks use the Anson & Deeley system with double locking lugs, incorporating detachable cross pin and separate plate to allow easy access to the firing mechanism. Barrels are chopper lump, firing pins are bushed, plus automatic safety and ejectors and metal oval for engraving of initials. Other features include disc set strikers, replaceable hinge pin, split bottom plate.

Barrel lengths: 26″, 27″ and 28″. **Weight:** 5 to 7 pounds, depending on gauge.

Model	Price
MODEL XXV BOXLOCK: 12 and 20 gauge only	$ 3,100.00
MODEL 4 BOXLOCK: 12, 16, 20, 28, .410 ga.	2,000.00
MODEL 4 DELUXE BOXLOCK: Same gauges as above	3,000.00
MODEL 37 SUPER A (12 gauge only)	15,000.00
MODEL AUGUSTA (12 gauge only)	28,000.00

MODEL XXV BOXLOCK
(Close-up)

MODEL XXV BOXLOCK

MODEL 4 BOXLOCK

BENELLI SHOTGUNS

MODEL M1 SUPER 90 SERIES

See table on the following page for all Benelli specifications.

MODEL M1 SUPER 90 DEFENSE (18 1/2" Barrel)
$851.00 (w/Pistol Grip)
$892.00 (w/Ghost Ring Sighting System)

MODEL M1 SUPER 90 SLUG
$819.00 ($860.00 w/Ghost Ring Sighting System)

MODEL M1 SUPER 90 FIELD
$900.00 (26" and 28" barrels w/wood stock)

Also available:
Model M1 Super 90 Sporting Special
   with 18 1/2" barrel . . . . $ 905.00
Model M1 Super 90 Tactical w/18 1/2" bbl. 860.00
   With pistol-grip stock, ghost ring sights 936.00
Model M1 Super 90 Field (polymer stock) w/21", 24", 26", 28" bbl. . . . 884.00
Model M3 Super 90 Pump/Auto Series
   Standard stock, 19 3/4" barrel 1016.00
   w/Ghost Ring Sight and standard stock 1086.00

MONTEFELTRO SUPER 90 VENT RIB
$905.00 (12 Ga.—21", 24", 26", or 28" Barrel)
(20 ga.—24" or 26" barrel only)
$925.00 (Left Hand w/26" or 28" Barrel)

BENELLI SHOTGUNS

EXECUTIVE TYPE III

EXECUTIVE SERIES

These special-order firearms are designed and manufactured with the best materials available. Each Executive Series Shotgun with vent rib has an all-steel tower receiver hand-engraved with gold inlay by Bottega Incisione di Cesare Giovanelli, one of Italy's finest engravers. The highest grade of walnut wood stocks is selected, and each can be custom-fitted with Benelli's drop adjustment kit. The Executive Series is engineered with all the features found on the Black Eagle Series Shotguns plus its many luxury features, including Montefeltro rotating bolt with dual locking lugs.

Prices:
EXECUTIVE TYPE I with 5 screw-in choke tubes and
   21″, 24″, 26″, 28″ vent-rib barrels $4550.00
EXECUTIVE TYPE II 5200.00
EXECUTIVE TYPE III 6032.00

BENELLI SHOTGUN SPECIFICATIONS

	Gauge (Chamber)	Operation	Magazine Capacity*	Barrel Length	Overall Length	Weight (in lbs.)	Choke	Receiver Finish	Stock	Sights
Super Black Eagle	12 (3¹/₂ in.)	semi-auto inertia recoil	3	28 in.	49⁵/₈ in.	7.3	S,IC,M,IM,F**	matte	satin walnut or polymer	front & mid rib bead
Super Black Eagle	12 (3¹/₂ in.)	semi-auto inertia recoil	3	26 in.	47⁵/₈ in.	7.1	S,IC,M,IM,F**	matte or blued	satin walnut or polymer	front & mid rib bead
Super Black Eagle	12 (3¹/₂ in.)	semi-auto inertia recoil	3	24 in.	45⁵/₈ in.	7.0	S,IC,M,IM,F**	matte	polymer	front & mid rib bead
Super Black Eagle Custom Slug	12 (3 in.)	semi-auto inertia recoil	3	24 in.	45¹/₂ in.	7.6	rifled barrel	matte	satin walnut or polymer	scope mount base
Black Eagle Competition Gun	12 (3 in.)	semi-auto inertia recoil	4	28/26 in.	49⁵/₈ or 47⁵/₈ in.	7.3/7	S,IC,M,IM,F**	blued with etched receiver	satin walnut	front & mid rib bead
Black Eagle Executive I, II, III	12 (3 in.)	semi-auto inertia recoil	4	26 in.	47⁵/₈ in	7.3/7	S,IC,M,IM,F**	engraved & gold inlaid rec.	satin high grade walnut	front & mid rib bead
Montefeltro Super 90	12 (3 in.)	semi-auto inertia recoil	4	28/26 in.	49¹/₂ or 47¹/₂ in.	7.4/7	S,IC,M,IM,F**	blued	satin walnut	bead
Montefeltro Super 90	12 (3 in.)	semi-auto inertia recoil	4	24/21 in.	45¹/₂ or 42¹/₂ in.	6.9/6.7	S,IC,M,IM,F**	blued	satin walnut	bead
Montefeltro Left Hand	12 (3 in.)	semi-auto inertia recoil	4	28/26 in.	49¹/₂ or 47¹/₂ in.	7.4/7	S,IC,M,IM,F**	blued	satin walnut	bead
Montefeltro 20 Gauge	20 (3 in.)	semi-auto inertia recoil	4	26/24 in.	47¹/₂ or 45¹/₂ in.	5.75/5.5	S,IC,M,IM,F**	blued	satin walnut	front & mid rib bead
Montefeltro 20 Gauge Limited Edition	20 (3 in.)	semi-auto inertia recoil	4	26 in.	47¹/₂ in.	5.75	S,IC,M,IM,F**	nickel with gold	satin walnut	front & mid rib bead
M1 Super 90 Field	12 (3 in.)	semi-auto inertia recoil	3	28 in.	49¹/₂ in.	7.4	S,IC,M,IM,F**	matte	polymer standard or satin walnut	bead
M1 Super 90 Field	12 (3 in.)	semi-auto inertia recoil	3	26 in.	47¹/₂ in.	7.3	S,IC,M,IM,F**	matte	polymer standard or satin walnut	bead
M1 Super 90 Field	12 (3 in.)	semi-auto inertia recoil	3	24 in.	45¹/₂ in.	7.2	S,IC,M,IM,F**	matte	polymer standard	bead
M1 Super 90 Field	12 (3 in.)	semi-auto inertia recoil	3	21 in.	42¹/₂ in.	7	S,IC,M,IM,F**	matte	polymer standard	bead
M1 Sporting Special	12 (3 in.)	semi-auto inertia recoil	3	18¹/₂ in.	39³/₄ in.	6.5	IC,M,F**	matte	polymer standard	ghost ring
M1 Super 90 Tactical	12 (3 in.)	semi-auto inertia recoil	5	18¹/₂ in.	39³/₄ in.	6.5	IC,M,F**	matte	polymer pistol grip*** or polymer standard	rifle or ghost ring
M1 Super 90 Slug	12 (3 in.)	semi-auto inertia recoil	5	18¹/₂ in.	39³/₄ in.	6.5	Cylinder	matte	polymer standard	rifle or ghost ring
M1 Super 90 Defense	12 (3 in.)	semi-auto inertia recoil	5	18¹/₂ in.	39³/₄ in.	6.8	Cylinder	matte	polymer pistol grip***	rifle or ghost ring
M1 Super 90 Entry	12 (3 in.)	semi-auto inertia recoil	5	14 in.	35¹/₂ in.	6.3	Cylinder	matte	polymer pistol grip*** or polymer standard	rifle or ghost ring
M3 Super 90 Pump/Auto	12 (3 in.)	semi-auto/pump inertia recoil	7	19³/₄ in.	41 in.	7.9	Cylinder	matte	polymer standard	rifle or ghost ring

*Magazine capacity given for 2³/₄ inch shells, size variations among some brands may result in less capacity. **Skeet, Improved Cylinder, Modified, Improved Modified, Full
***CAUTION: Increasing magazine capacity to more than five rounds on M1 shotguns with pistol grip stocks violates provisions of the 1994 Crime Bill.

BENELLI SHOTGUNS

BLACK EAGLE COMPETITION
$1205.00

Benelli's Black Eagle Competition shotgun combines the best technical features of the Montefeltro Super 90 and the classic design of the old SL 80 Series. It comes standard with a specially designed two-piece receiver of steel and aluminum, adding to its reliability and resistance to wear. A premium high-gloss walnut stock and gold-plated trigger are included, along with a Montefeltro rotating bolt. The Black Eagle Competition has no complex cylinders and pistons to maintain. Features include etched receiver, competition stock and mid-rib bead.

SUPER BLACK EAGLE
$1176.00 (24″ or 26″ barrel)
$1192.00 (28″ barrel)

Benelli's Super Black Eagle shotgun offers the advantage of owning one 12-gauge auto that fires every type of 12 gauge currently available. It has the same balance, sighting plane and fast-swinging characteristics whether practicing on the sporting clays course with light target loads or touching off a 3½″ Magnum steel load at a high-flying goose.

The Super Black Eagle also features a specially strengthened steel upper receiver mated to the barrel to endure the toughest shotgunning. The alloy lower receiver keeps the overall weight low, making this model as well balanced and point-able as possible. Distinctive high-gloss or satin walnut stocks and a choice of dull finish or blued metal add up to a universal gun for all shotgun hunting and sports.

Stock: Satin walnut (28″) with drop adjustment kit; high-gloss walnut (26″) with drop adjustment kit; or synthetic stock
Finish: Matte black finish on receiver, barrel and bolt (28″); blued finish on receiver and barrel (26″) with bolt mirror polished
Features: Montefeltro rotating bolt with dual locking lugs
For additional specifications, see table on previous page.

Also available:
Custom Slug Gun with 24″ E.R. Shaw rifled barrel for sabot-type slugs and polymer stock. **Price:** $1220.00

BERETTA SHOTGUNS

MODEL 682 GOLD COMPETITION SKEET O/U

This 12-gauge skeet gun sports a hand-checkered premium walnut stock, forged and hardened receiver w/greystone finish, manual safety with trigger selector, auto ejector, stock with silver oval for initials, silver inlaid on trigger guard. Price includes fitted case.
Action: Low-profile hard chrome-plated boxlock
Trigger: Single adjustable sliding trigger

Barrels: 28″ blued barrels with 2¾″ chambers
Stock dimensions: Length of pull 14¾″; drop at comb 1⅜″; drop at heel 2¼″
Sights: Fluorescent front and metal middle bead
Weight: Approx. 7½ lbs.
Price: $2731.00

BERETTA SHOTGUNS

SERIES 682 GOLD COMPETITION TRAP OVER/UNDER

Available in Competition Mono, Over/Under or Mono Trap Over/Under Combo Set, the 12-gauge 682 trap guns boast hand-checkered walnut stock and forend with International or Monte Carlo left- or right-hand stock.

Features: Adjustable gold-plated, single-selective sliding trigger for precise length of pull fit; fluorescent competition front sight; step-up top rib; Greystone finish (an ultralite, durable, wear-resistant finish in gunmetal grey w/gold accents); low-profile improved boxlock action; manual safety w/barrel selector; 2¾″ chambers; auto ejector; competition recoil pad buttplate; stock with silver oval for initials; silver inscription inlaid on trigger guard; handsome fitted case. **Weight:** Approx. 8 lbs.

Barrel lengths/Chokes
30″ Imp. Mod./Full (Black)
30″ or 32″ Mobilchoke® (Black)
Top Single 32″ or 34″ Mobilchoke®
''Live Bird'' (Flat rib, Silver)
Combo.: 30″ or 32″ Mobilchoke® (Top)
30″ IM/F (Top)
32″ Mobilchoke® (Mono)
30″ or 32″ Mobilchoke® ported

Prices:

Model 682 Gold Trap	$2789.00
Model 682 Gold Trap Combo	3689.00
Ported	3832.00
Model 682 Gold Super Trap Top Combo	4190.00

MODEL 682 GOLD SPORTING

MODELS 682 and 686 SPORTING CLAYS

These competition-style shotguns for sporting clays features 28″ or 30″ barrels with four flush-mounted screw-in choke tubes (Full, Modified, Improved Cylinder and Skeet), plus hand-checkered stock and forend of fine walnut, 2¾″ or 3″ chambers and adjustable trigger. **Model 682 Gold** features greystone finish—an ultra-durable, wear-resistant finish in gunmetal grey w/gold accents. **Model 682 Continental Course Sporting** has tapered rib and schnabel forend. **Model 686 Onyx Sporting** has black matte receiver and **Model 686 Silver Pigeon Sporting** has coin silver receiver with scroll engraving.

Models	Prices
682 Gold Sporting	$2789.00
682 Continental Course Sporting	2431.00
682 Gold Sporting (ported)	2999.00
686 Onyx Sporting	1499.00
686 Silver Pigeon Sporting	1573.00

MODEL 686 ONYX

SPECIFICATIONS
Gauges: 12, 20 **Chambers:** 3″ and 3½″
Barrel lengths: 26″ and 28″
Chokes: Mobilchoke® screw-in system
Weight: 6 lbs. 12 oz. (12 ga.); 6.2 lbs. (20 ga.)

Stock: American walnut with recoil pad (English stock available)
Features: Automatic ejectors; matte black finish on barrels and receiver to reduce glare
Price: $1473.00

BERETTA SHOTGUNS

MODEL 686 ESSENTIAL

SPECIFICATIONS
Gauge: 12 (3″ chamber)
Choke: MC3 Mobilchoke® (F, M, IC)
Barrel length: 26″ or 28″   **Overall length:** 45.7″
Weight: 6.7 lbs.

Stock: American walnut
Drop at comb: 1.4″   **Drop at heel:** 2.2″
Length of pull: 14 1/2″
Features: Matte black receiver
Price: $1186.00

MODEL 686EL GOLD PERDIZ

This 12- or 20-gauge over/under field gun features scroll engraving on sideplates, European walnut stock and forend, hard-chromed bores, and Mobilchoke® interchangeable choke tubes.
Price: $1999.00

MODEL 686 SILVER PIGEON FIELD

SPECIFICATIONS
Gauges: 12, 20 and 28
Barrels/chokes: 26″ and 28″ with Mobilchoke® screw-in choke tubes
Action: Low-profile, improved boxlock
Weight: 6.8 lbs.
Trigger: Selective single trigger, auto safety

Extractors: Auto ejectors
Stock: Choice walnut, hand-checkered and hand-finished with a tough gloss finish
Prices:
Standard $1544.00
Combo 20 or 28 gauge 2259.00

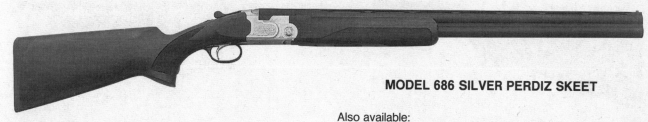

MODEL 686 SILVER PERDIZ SKEET

In 28 gauge with highly polished silver receiver, traditional blued finish , rubber recoil pad and Mobilchoke® choke tubes.
Barrel length: 28″
Price: $1499.00

Also available:
MODEL ULTRALIGHT. 12-ga. over/under in 20-ga. weight (about 5.75 lbs.). Low-profile boxlock, 26″ or 28″ barrels, single selective gold trigger, hand-checkered walnut stock, matte black finish, gold inlayed receiver with P. Beretta signature.
Price: $1574.00

BERETTA SHOTGUNS

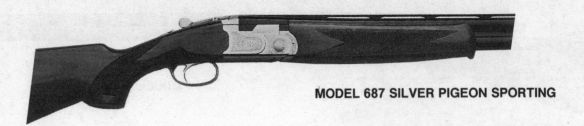

MODEL 687 SILVER PIGEON SPORTING

This sporting over/under features enhanced engraving pattern, schnabel forend and an electroless nickel finished receiver. **Chamber:** 3″. Mobilchoke® screw-in tube system. **Gauges:** 12, 20 and 28 (Field Models)

Prices:
Model 687 Silver Pigeon Sporting $2474.00
Model 687 Silver Pigeon Sporting Combo 3518.00

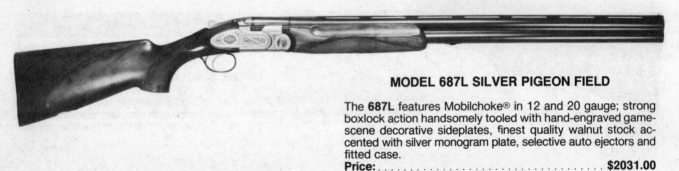

MODEL 687L SILVER PIGEON FIELD

The **687L** features Mobilchoke® in 12 and 20 gauge; strong boxlock action handsomely tooled with hand-engraved game-scene decorative sideplates, finest quality walnut stock accented with silver monogram plate, selective auto ejectors and fitted case.
Price: **$2031.00**

MODEL 687EL GOLD PIGEON FIELD
(not shown)

Features game-scene engraving on receiver with gold highlights. Available in 12, 20 gauge (28 ga. and .410 in small frame).

SPECIFICATIONS
Barrels/chokes: 26″ and 28″ with Mobilchoke®
Action: Low-profile improved boxlock
Weight: 6.8 lbs. (12 ga.)
Trigger: Single selective with manual safety
Extractors: Auto ejectors
Prices:
Model 687EL (12, 20, 28 ga.; 26″ or 28″ bbl.) **$3446.00**
Model 687EL Small Frame (28 ga./.410) 3599.00

MODEL 687EELL DIAMOND PIGEON
$4999.00 (not shown)
Model 687EELL Combo (20 and 28 ga.) $5777.00

In 12, 20 or 28 ga., this model features the Mobilchoke® choke system, a special premium walnut stock and exquisitely engraved sideplate with game-scene motifs.

MODEL 1201 FP RIOT
$715.00

This all-weather semiautomatic shotgun features an adjustable space-age technopolymer stock and forend with recoil pad. Lightweight, it sports a unique weather-resistant matte black finish to reduce glare, resist corrosion and aid in heat dispersion; short recoil action for light and heavy loads. **Gauge:** 12. **Chamber:** 3″ (2³/₄″ or 3″ shells). **Capacity:** 7 rounds w/2³/₄″; 6 rounds w/3″. **Barrel length:** 20″. **Choke:** Cylinder (fixed). **Weight:** 6.3 lbs.

BERETTA SHOTGUNS

PINTAIL

This new 12-gauge semiautomatic shotgun with short-recoil operation is available with 24″ or 26″ barrels and Mobilchoke®. Finish is nonreflective matte on all exposed wood and metal surfaces. Checkered walnut stock and forend; sling swivels.

SPECIFICATIONS
Barrel lengths: 24″, 26″; 24″ Slug
Weight: 7.3 lbs.
Stock: Walnut
Sights: Bead front on vent rib
Price: **$743.00**

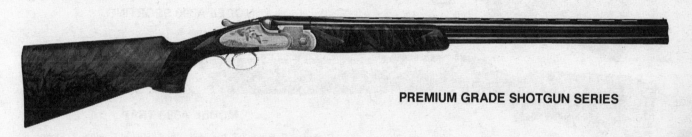

PREMIUM GRADE SHOTGUN SERIES

These hand-crafted over/under and side-by-side shotguns feature custom engraved or game scenes, casehardened, gold-inlay, scroll or floral patterns, all available on receivers. Sidelock action. Stocks are of select European walnut, hand-finished and hand-checkered. Also available in Competition Skeet, Trap, Sporting Clays and Custom Sidelock Side-by-Side models. Barrels are constructed of Boehler high-nickel antinit steel.
Gauges: 12, 20, 28, .410   **Chamber:** 2½″ or 3″

Prices:
SO5 Competition (Sporting Clays, Skeet, Trap) **$13,000.00**
SO6 O/U Competition (Sporting Clays, Skeet, Trap) 17,500.00
SO6 EELL Custom Sidelock (12 gauge only) . . . 28,000.00
SO9 Custom Sidelock (12, 20, 28, .410 ga.) . . . 31,000.00
452 EELL Custom Sidelock Side/Side (12 ga.) 31,000.00

MODEL ASE GOLD

This 12-gauge beauty features drop-out trigger group assembly for ease in cleaning, inspection or in-the-field replacement. Also has wide ventilating top and side rib, hard-chromed bores and a strong competition-style receiver in greystone finish and gold etching with P. Beretta initials.

SPECIFICATIONS
Barrel lengths: 28″ (Pigeon, Skeet, Sporting Clays); 30″ (Trap and Sporting Clays); 30″ and 32″ Combo (Top Combo Trap); 30″ and 34″ Combo (Top Combo Trap)

Chokes: IM/F Trap or MCT (Trap); MC4 (Sporting Clays); SK/SK (Skeet); IM/F (Pigeon)
Prices:
Model ASE Gold Skeet . . . . **$ 8,737.00**
Model ASE Gold Sporting Clays 8,815.00
Model ASE Gold Trap 8,815.00
Model ASE Gold Trap Combo 10,267.00

BERETTA SHOTGUNS

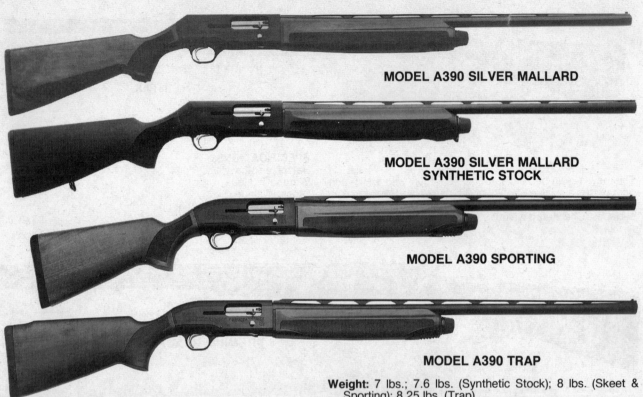

MODEL A390 SILVER MALLARD

MODEL A390 SILVER MALLARD
SYNTHETIC STOCK

MODEL A390 SPORTING

MODEL A390 TRAP

These gas-operated semiautomatics have an innovative gas system that handles a variety of loads. A self-regulating valve automatically adjusts gas pressure to handle anything from 2½" target loads to heavy 3" magnums. Matte finish models for turkey/waterfowl, slug and Deluxe models with gold-engraved receiver and deluxe wood are available. Also offered are **Model A390 Super Trap** and **A390 Super Skeet** with ported barrels and adjustable comb height and length of pull. 390 Trap, Skeet and Sporting models have lower contour, walnut stock. Silver Mallard synthetic stock is matte black w/ anodized aluminum alloy receiver.

SPECIFICATIONS
Gauge: 12 **Action:** Locked breech, gas-operated
Barrel lengths: 24", 26", 28", 30"; 22" Slug

Weight: 7 lbs.; 7.6 lbs. (Synthetic Stock); 8 lbs. (Skeet & Sporting); 8.25 lbs. (Trap)
Sights: Ventilated rib with front bead
Safety: Crossbolt (reversible)
Prices:

A390 Silver Mallard Field	$ 822.00
A390 Silver Mallard Synthetic Stock	822.00
A390 Waterfowl/Turkey Matte Finish (Silver Mallard)	822.00
A390 Gold Mallard	987.00
A390 Trap	865.00
A390 Trap (Ported)	965.00
A390 Super Trap	1256.00
A390 Skeet (3" chamber)	849.00
A390 Skeet (Ported)	949.00
A390 Super Skeet	1199.00
A390 Sporting	865.00
A390 Sporting (Ported)	951.00

MODEL A303 YOUTH GUN

MODEL A303 AUTOLOADERS

SPECIFICATIONS
Gauges: 12 and 20
Barrel lengths: 24", 26", 28"
Weight: 7 lbs. (12 gauge) and 6 lbs. (20 gauge)
Safety: Crossbolt

Action: Locked breech, gas-operated
Sights: Vent rib with front metal bead
Length of pull: 14⅞" (13½" Youth)
Capacity: Plugged to 2 rounds
Prices:

Upland	$772.00
Field (English)	735.00
Youth	772.00
Sporting (MC/F)	822.00

BERNARDELLI SHOTGUNS

Bernardelli shotguns are the creation of the Italian firm of Vincenzo Bernardelli, known for its fine quality firearms and commitment to excellence for more than a century. Most of the long arms featured below can be built with a variety of options, customized for the discriminating sportsman. With the exceptions indicated for each gun respectively, options include choice of barrel lengths and chokes; pistol or straight English grip stock; single selective or non-selective trigger; long tang trigger guard; checkered butt; beavertail forend; hand-cut rib; automatic safety; custom stock dimensions; standard or English recoil pad; extra set of barrels; choice of luggage gun case.

MODEL 112 12 GAUGE
$1770.00 (Single Trigger)
$1625.00 (Double Trigger)
$2135.00 (Ejector & Multichoke)

Features extractors or automatic ejectors, English or half pistol-grip stock and splinter forend. **Barrel length:** 26¾″ (3″ chamber). **Choke:** Improved Cylinder and Improved Modified. **Safety:** Manual. **Weight:** 6½ lbs.

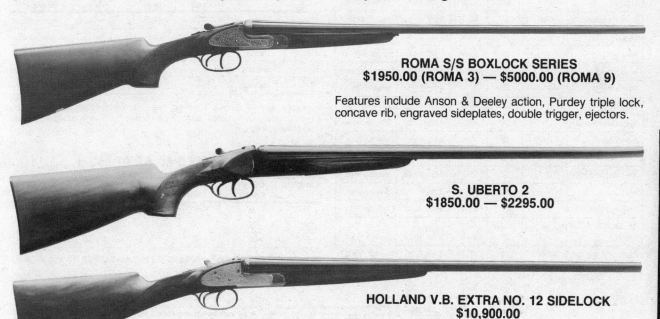

ROMA S/S BOXLOCK SERIES
$1950.00 (ROMA 3) — $5000.00 (ROMA 9)

Features include Anson & Deeley action, Purdey triple lock, concave rib, engraved sideplates, double trigger, ejectors.

S. UBERTO 2
$1850.00 — $2295.00

HOLLAND V.B. EXTRA NO. 12 SIDELOCK
$10,900.00

This 12-gauge Holland & Holland-style side-by-side feature sidelocks with double safety levers, reinforced breech, three-round Purdey locks, automatic ejectors, single or double triggers, right trigger folding, striker retaining plates, best-quality walnut stock and finely chiseled English scroll engraving.

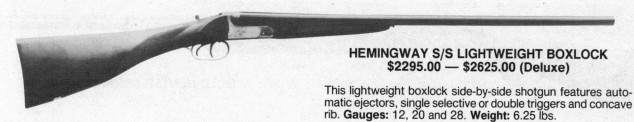

HEMINGWAY S/S LIGHTWEIGHT BOXLOCK
$2295.00 — $2625.00 (Deluxe)

This lightweight boxlock side-by-side shotgun features automatic ejectors, single selective or double triggers and concave rib. **Gauges:** 12, 20 and 28. **Weight:** 6.25 lbs.

SHOTGUNS

BROWNING AUTOMATIC SHOTGUNS

AUTO-5 STALKER

SPECIFICATIONS AUTO-5 SHOTGUNS

Model	Chamber	Barrel Length	Overall Length	Average Weight	Chokes Available
12 GAUGE Light	2³/₄"	30"	49½"	8 lbs. 7 oz.	Invector-Plus
Light	2³/₄"	28"	47½"	8 lbs. 4 oz.	Invector-Plus
Light	2³/₄"	26"	45½"	8 lbs. 1 oz.	Invector-Plus
Lt. Buck Special	2³/₄"	24"	43½"	8 lbs.	Slug/buckshot
Light	2³/₄"	22"	41½"	7 lbs. 13 oz.	Invector-Plus
Magnum	3"	32"	51¼"	9 lbs. 2 oz.	Invector-Plus
Magnum	3"	30"	49¼"	8 lbs. 13 oz.	Invector-Plus
Magnum	3"	28"	47¼"	8 lbs. 11 oz.	Invector-Plus
Magnum	3"	26"	45¼"	8 lbs. 9 oz.	Invector-Plus
Mag. Buck Special	3"	24"	43¼"	8 lbs. 8 oz.	Slug/buckshot
Light Stalker	2³/₄"	28"	47½"	8 lbs. 4 oz.	Invector-Plus
Light Stalker	2³/₄"	26"	45½"	8 lbs. 1 oz.	Invector-Plus
Magnum Stalker	3"	32"	51¼"	8 lbs. 15 oz.	Invector-Plus
Magnum Stalker	3"	30"	49¼"	8 lbs. 13 oz.	Invector-Plus
Magnum Stalker	3"	28"	47¼"	8 lbs. 11 oz.	Invector-Plus
20 GAUGE Light	2³/₄"	28"	47¹/₈"	6 lbs. 10 oz.	Invector-Plus
Light	2³/₄"	26"	45¼"	6 lbs. 8 oz.	Invector-Plus

AUTO-5 MODELS

	Prices
Light 12, Hunting & Stalker, Invector Plus	$839.95
Light 20, Hunting, Invector Plus	839.95
3" Magnum 12, Hunting & Stalker, Invector Plus	865.95
3" Magnum 12, Hunting, Invector Plus	865.95
Light 12, Buck Special	828.95
3" Magnum 12 ga. Buck Special	854.95
Extra Barrels	$296.95–307.95

GOLD HUNTER & STALKER SEMIAUTOMATIC SHOTGUNS
$734.95 $759.95 (Sporting Clays)

SPECIFICATIONS GOLD 12 AND 20

Gauge	Model	Barrel Length	Overall Length	Average Weight	Chokes Available
12	Hunting	30"	50½"	7 lbs. 9 oz.	Invector-Plus
12	Hunting	28"	48½"	7 lbs. 6 oz.	Invector-Plus
12	Hunting	26"	46½"	7 lbs. 3 oz.	Invector-Plus
20	Hunting	28"	48¼"	6 lbs. 14 oz.	Invector
20	Hunting	26"	46¼"	6 lbs. 12 oz.	Invector

Total capacity for 3" loads is 3 shells in magazine, 1 in chamber; with 2½" loads, 4 in magazine, 1 in chamber. Gold 12 ga. models have vent recoil pad; 20 ga. models have solid pad.

SPECIFICATIONS GOLD 10 $1007.95

Chamber	Barrel Length	Overall Length	Average Weight	Chokes
3½"	30"	52"	10 lbs. 13 oz.	Standard Invector
3½"	28"	50"	10 lbs. 10 oz.	Standard Invector
3½"	26"	48"	10 lbs. 7 oz.	Standard Invector

Extra barrels are available for **$261.95** (10 ga.) and **$272.95** (12 and 20 ga.).

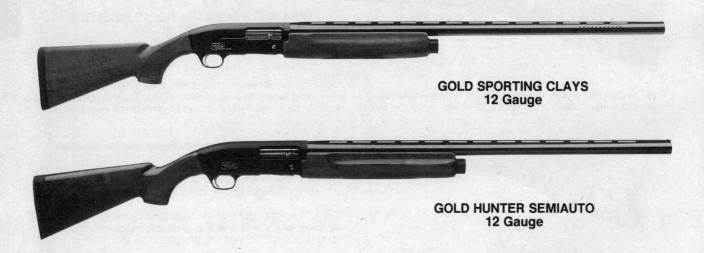

GOLD SPORTING CLAYS
12 Gauge

GOLD HUNTER SEMIAUTO
12 Gauge

BROWNING CITORI SHOTGUNS

CITORI GRADE I HUNTING
12 Gauge 3¹/₂″ Magnum

Grade I = Blued steel w/scroll engraving
Grade III = Grayed steel w/light relief

Grade VI = Blued or grayed w/engraved ringneck pheasants and mallard ducks
GL (Gran Lightning) = High-grade wood w/satin finish

CITORI PRICES (all Invector-Plus chokes unless noted otherwise)

HUNTING MODELS (w/pistol-grip stock, beavertail forearm, high-gloss finish)
12 Ga., 3.5″ Mag., 28″ & 30″
barrels **$1418.00**
Same as above in 12 & 20 Ga. w/3″ chamber
26″, 28″, 30″ barrels **1334.00**
LIGHTNING MODELS (w/classic rounded pistol grip, Lightning-style forearm)
Grade I, 12 & 20 Ga., 3″ chamber 26″ & 28″
barrels **1376.00**
Same as above in Grade
GL **1869.00**
Grade III **2006.00**
Grade VI **2919.00**
MICRO LIGHTNING MODEL (20 Ga.)
Grade I, 2.75″ chamber, 24″
bbl. **1428.00**
SUPERLIGHT MODELS (w/straight-grip stock, slimmed-down Schnabel forearm; 2.75″ chamber, 12 or 20 Ga.)
Grade I **1396.00**
Grade III **2006.00**
Grade VI **2919.00**
CITORI MODELS w/Standard Invector chokes (Lightning models only, 28 and .410 Ga., 2.75″ chamber, 26″ & 28″ barrels)
Grade I **1418.00**
Grade GL **1969.00**
Grade III **2242.00**
Grade VI **3145.00**

SPECIFICATIONS CITORI FIELD MODELS

Gauge	Model	Chamber*	Barrel Length	Overall Length	Average Weight	Chokes Available[1]	Grades Available
12	Hunting	3 1/2″ Mag.	30″	47″	8 lbs. 10 oz.	Invector-Plus	I
12	Hunting	3 1/2″ Mag.	28″	45″	8 lbs. 9 oz.	Invector-Plus	I
12	Hunting	3″	30″	47″	8 lbs. 4 oz.	Invector-Plus	I
12	Hunting	3″	28″	45″	8 lbs. 1 oz.	Invector-Plus	I, III, VI
12	Hunting	3″	26″	43″	7 lbs. 15 oz.	Invector-Plus	I, III, VI
12	Lightning	3″	28″	45″	8 lbs. 1 oz.	Invector-Plus	I, GL, III, VI
12	Lightning	3″	26″	43″	7 lbs. 15 oz.	Invector-Plus	I, GL III, VI
12	Superlight	2 3/4″	28″	45″	6 lbs. 12 oz.	Invector-Plus	I, III, VI
12	Superlight	2 3/4″	26″	43″	6 lbs. 10 oz.	Invector-Plus	I, III, VI
12	Upland Special	2 3/4″	24″	41″	6 lbs. 11 oz.	Invector-Plus	I
20	Hunting	3″	28″	45″	6 lbs. 12 oz.	Invector-Plus	I, III,
20	Hunting	3″	26″	43″	6 lbs. 10 oz.	Invector-Plus	I, III, VI
20	Lightning	3″	28″	45″	6 lbs. 14 oz.	Invector-Plus	I, GL, III, VI
20	Lightning	3″	26″	43″	6 lbs. 9 oz.	Invector-Plus	I, GL, III, VI
20	Lightning	3″	24″	41″	6 lbs. 6 oz.	Invector-Plus	I
20	Micro Lightning	2 3/4″	24″	41″	6 lbs. 3 oz.	Invector-Plus	I, III, VI
20	Superlight	2 3/4″	26″	43″	6 lbs.	Invector-Plus	I, III, VI
20	Upland Special	2 3/4″	24″	41″	6 lbs.	Invector-Plus	I
28	Lightning	2 3/4″	28″	45″	6 lbs. 11 oz.	Invector	I
28	Lightning	2 3/4″	26″	43″	6 lbs. 10 oz.	Invector	I, GL, III, VI
28	Superlight	2 3/4″	26″	43″	6 lbs. 10 oz.	Invector	I, III, VI
.410	Lightning	3″	28″	45″	7 lbs.	Invector	I
.410	Lightning	3″	26″	43″	6 lbs. 14 oz.	Invector	I, GL, III, VI
.410	Superlight	3″	28″	45″	6 lbs. 14 oz.	Invector	I
.410	Superlight	3″	26″	43″	6 lbs. 13 oz.	Invector	I, III, VI

[1]*Full & Modified Choke installed; Improved Cylinder and wrench included. GL=Gran Lightning grade.*

STANDARD INVECTOR (28 & .410 Ga.)
Grade I, 26″ barrel only **1439.00**
Grade III **2242.00**
Grade VI **3145.00**

UPLAND SPECIAL (12 & 20 Ga.)
Grade I only, 24″ barrel **1386.00**

RECOILLESS TRAP
$1995.00

SPECIFICATIONS
Gauge: 12, Standard or Micro; Invector-Plus choke
Chamber: 2³/₄″
Barrel length: 27″ or 30″
Overall length: 48⁵/₈″ (27″ barrel); 51⁵/₈″ (30″ barrel)
Weight: 8 lbs. 10 oz.; 8 lbs. 8 oz. (30″ barrel)

BROWNING CITORI SHOTGUNS

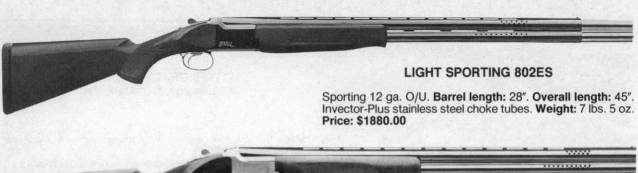

LIGHT SPORTING 802ES

Sporting 12 ga. O/U. **Barrel length:** 28″. **Overall length:** 45″.
Invector-Plus stainless steel choke tubes. **Weight:** 7 lbs. 5 oz.
Price: $1880.00

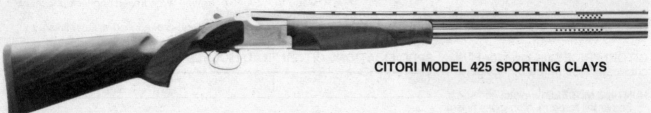

CITORI MODEL 425 SPORTING CLAYS

425 & ULTRA SPORTER

Model	Chamber	Barrel Length	Overall Length	Average Weight	Chokes Available	Grades Available
425						
12 ga.	2 3/4"	32"	49 1/2"	7 lbs. 15 oz.	Invector-Plus	Gr.I, Golden Clays
12 ga.	2 3/4"	30"	47 1/2"	7 lbs. 14 oz.	Invector-Plus	Gr.I, Golden Clays
12 ga.	2 3/4"	28"	45 1/2"	7 lbs. 13 oz.	Invector-Plus	Gr.I, Golden Clays
20 ga.	2 3/4"	30"	47 1/2"	6 lbs. 13 oz.	Invector-Plus	Gr.I, Golden Clays
20 ga.	2 3/4"	28"	45 1/2"	6 lbs. 12 oz.	Invector-Plus	Gr.I, Golden Clays
WSSF 12 ga.	2 3/4"	28"	45 1/2"	7 lbs. 4 oz.	Invector-Plus	Custom WSSF Exclusive
Ultra Sporter						
12 ga. Sporter	2 3/4"	32"	49"	8 lbs. 4 oz.	Invector-Plus	Gr.I, Golden Clays
12 ga. Sporter	2 3/4"	30"	47"	8 lbs. 2 oz.	Invector-Plus	Gr.I, Golden Clays
12 ga. Sporter	2 3/4"	28"	45"	8 lbs.	Invector-Plus	Gr.I, Golden Clays

*Sporting Clays models: One modified, one Improved Cylinder and one Skeet tube supplied.
Other chokes available as accessories.*

SPECIFICATIONS SPECIAL SPORTING CLAYS, TRAP & SKEET AND LIGHTNING SPORTING

Gauge	Model	Chamber	Barrel Length	Overall Length	Average Weight	Chokes	Grades Available
SPECIAL*							
12	Sporting Clays	2 3/4"	32"	49"	8 lbs. 5 oz.	Invector-Plus	I, Golden Clays
12	Sporting Clays	2 3/4"	30"	47"	8 lbs. 3 oz.	Invector-Plus	I, Golden Clays
12	Sporting Clays	2 3/4"	28"	45"	8 lbs. 1 oz.	Invector-Plus	I, Golden Clays
12	Trap (Conv.)	2 3/4"	32"	49"	8 lbs. 11 oz.	Invector-Plus	I, III, Golden Clays
12	Trap (Monte Carlo)	2 3/4"	32"	49"	8 lbs. 10 oz.	Invector-Plus	I, III, Golden Clays
12	Trap (Conv.)	2 3/4"	30"	47"	8 lbs. 7 oz.	Invector-Plus	I, III, Golden Clays
12	Trap (Monte Carlo)	2 3/4"	30"	47"	8 lbs. 6 oz.	Invector-Plus	I, III, Golden Clays
12	Skeet	2 3/4"	28"	45"	8 lbs.	Invector-Plus	I, III, Golden Clays
12	Skeet	2 3/4"	26"	43"	7 lbs. 15 oz.	Invector-Plus	I, III, Golden Clays
20	Skeet	2 3/4"	28"	45"	7 lbs. 4 oz.	Invector-Plus	I, III, Golden Clays
20	Skeet	2 3/4"	26"	43"	7 lbs. 1 oz.	Invector-Plus	I, III, Golden Clays
28	Skeet	2 3/4"	28"	45"	6 lbs. 15 oz.	Invector	I, III, Golden Clays
28	Skeet	2 3/4"	26"	43"	6 lbs. 10 oz.	Invector	I, III, Golden Clays
.410	Skeet	3"	28"	45"	7 lbs. 6 oz.	Invector	I, III, Golden Clays
.410	Skeet	3"	26"	43"	7 lbs. 3 oz.	Invector	I, III, Golden Clays
LIGHTNING SPORTING							
12	Sporting Clays	3"	30"	47"	8 lbs. 8 oz.	Invector-Pus	I, Golden Clays
12	Sporting Clays	3"	28"	45"	8 lbs. 6 oz.	Invector-Plus	I, Golden Clays

MODELS 425 & ULTRA SPORTER
(all Invector-Plus)

MODEL 425 (12 & 20 Ga.)
Grade I, 28″, 30″, 32″ bbls. . **$1775.00**
Grade GC (Golden Clays) . . . 3308.00
For adjustable comb. **add** . . . 210.00
MODEL WSSF*
12 Ga. only, 28″ barrel 1775.00
ULTRA SPORTER (12 Ga. only)
Grade I, Blue or Gray, 28″, 30″,
  32″ bbls. 1722.00
Grade GC 28″, 30″, 32″
  barrels 3203.00
For adjustable comb. **add** . . . 210.00
*WSSF = Women's Shooting Sports Foundation

SPECIAL SPORTING CLAYS   **Prices**
Grade I . . . . $1565.00–$1775.00
Golden Clays 3203.00– 3413.00
SPECIAL TRAP
Grade I 1586.00
Grade III 2179.00
Golden Clays 3239.00
SPECIAL SKEET (12, 20 ga.)
Grade I 1586.00
Grade III 2179.00
Golden Clays 3239.00
SPECIAL SKEET (28, .410 ga.)
Grade I 1549.00
Grade III 2184.00
Golden Clays 3166.00
LIGHTNING SPORTING
Grade I 1496.00– 1775.00
Golden Clays 3092.00– 3413.00

BROWNING CITORI SHOTGUNS

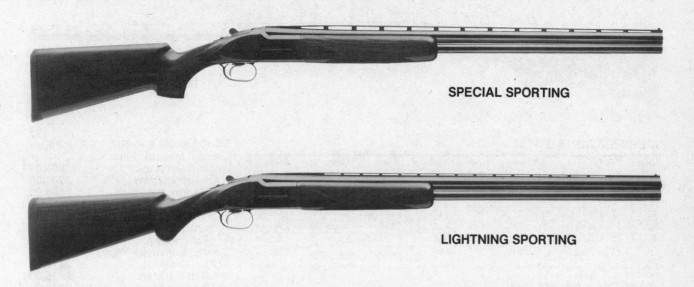

SPECIAL SPORTING

LIGHTNING SPORTING

CITORI SPECIAL SPORTING AND LIGHTNING SPORTING

Prices:

Special Sporting
Grade I, ported barrels $1565.00
Grade I, ported bbls., adj. comb 1775.00
Golden Clays, ported barrels 3203.00
Golden Clays, adj. comb 3413.00

Lightning Sporting
Grade I, high rib, ported bbl., 3″ 1565.00

Lightning Sporting (cont.)
Grade I, high rib, adj. comb $1775.00
Grade I, low rib, ported bbls., 3″ 1496.00
Grade II, low rib, adj. comb 1706.00
Golden Clays, low rib, ported bbls., 3″ 3092.00
Golden Clays, low rib, adj. comb 3302.00
Golden Clays, high rib, ported bbls., 3″ 3203.00
Golden Clays, high rib, adj. comb 3413.00

(See previous page for specifications)

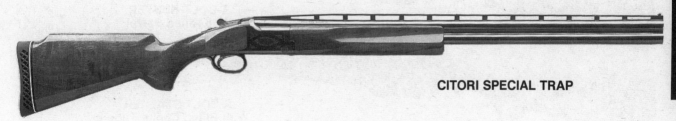

CITORI SPECIAL TRAP

SPECIAL TRAP MODELS

12 Gauge, Invector-Plus, Ported Barrels   Prices
Grade I, Monte Carlo stock $1586.00
Grade I, adj. comb 1796.00
Grade III, Monte Carlo stock 2179.00
Grade III, adj. comb 2389.00
Golden Clays, Monte Carlo stock 3239.00
Golden Clays, adj. comb 3449.00

SPECIAL SKEET MODELS

12 and 20 Gauge, Invector Plus, Ported Barrels   Prices
Grade I, high post rib $1586.00
Grade I, high post rib, adj. comb 1796.00
Grade III, high post rib 2179.00
Grade III, high post rib, adj. comb 2389.00
Golden Clays, high post rib 3239.00
Golden Clays, high post rib, adj. comb 3449.00
28 Ga. and .410 Bore Std. Invector
Grade I, high post rib 1586.00
Grade III, high post rib 2179.00
Golden Clays, high post rib 3239.00

SHOTGUNS

BROWNING SHOTGUNS

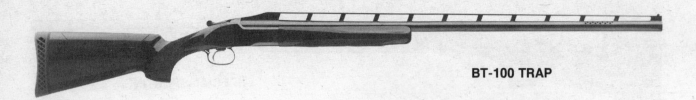

BT-100 TRAP

SPECIFICATIONS BT-100

Gauge	Model	Chamber	Barrel Length	Overall Length	Average Weight	Chokes	Grades Available
12	BT-100	2 3/4"	34"	50 1/2"	8 lbs. 10 oz.	Invector Plus[1]	I, Stainless
12	BT-100	2 3/4"	32"	48 1/2"	8 lbs. 9 oz.	Invector Plus[1]	I, Stainless
12	BT-100 Monte Carlo	2 3/4"	34"	50 1/2"	8 lbs. 10 oz.	Invector Plus	I, Stainless
12	BT-100 Monte Carlo	2 3/4"	32"	48 1/2"	8 lbs. 9 oz.	Invector Plus	I, Stainless
12	BT-100 Thumbhole	2 3/4"	34"	50 3/4"	8 lbs. 8 oz.	Invector Plus	I, Stainless
12	BT-100 Thumbhole	. 2 3/4"	32"	48 3/4"	8 lbs. 6 oz.	Invector Plus	I, Stainless

F=Full, M=Modified, IM=Improved Modified, S=Skeet, Invector=Invector Choke System — Invector-Plus Trap models: Full, Improved Modified, Modified, and wrench included.
[1] Also available with conventional full choke barrel.

STOCK DIMENSIONS BT-100

	Adjustable Conventional	Thumbhole	Monte Carlo
Length of Pull	14 3/8"	14 3/8"	14 3/8"
Drop at Comb	Adj.*	1 3/4"	1 9/16"
Drop at Monte Carlo	—	1 1/4"	1 7/16"
Drop at Heel	Adj.*	2 1/8"	2"

*Adjustable Drop at Comb and Heel.

BT-100 SINGLE BARREL TRAP Prices
Grade I, Invector-Plus

Monte Carlo stock	$1995.00
Adjustable comb	2205.00
Full choke barrel	1948.00
Full choke barrel, adj. comb	2158.00
Thumbhole stock	2270.00
Full choke barrel	2225.00
Stainless, Invector-Plus	
Monte Carlo stock	2415.00
Adjustable comb	2625.00
Full choke barrel	2368.00
Full choke barrel, adj. comb	2578.00
Thumbhole stock	2690.00
Full choke barrel	2645.00
Trigger Assembly Replacement	525.00

A-BOLT HUNTER
With Rifled Barrel

A-BOLT STALKER
With Rifled Choke Tube

A-BOLT SHOTGUNS

	Prices
Hunter	
With choke tube	$828.95
Without sights	804.95
With rifled barrel	881.95
Without sights	856.95
Stalker	
With choke tube	744.95
Without sights	719.95
With rifled barrel	797.95
Without sights	772.95

SPECIFICATIONS A-BOLT SHOTGUNS

Model	Chamber	Magazine Capacity	Barrel Length	Overall Length	Average Weight	Choke/Barrel Available
Hunter/Choke Tube	3"	2[1]	23"	44 3/4"	7 lbs. 2 oz.	Standard Invector*
Hunter/Rifled Barrel	3"	2[1]	22"	43 3/4"	7 lbs.	Fully rifled barrel
Stalker/Choke Tube	3"	2[1]	23"	44 3/4"	7 lbs. 2 oz.	Standard Invector*
Stalker/Rifled Barrel	3"	2[1]	22"	43 3/4"	7 lbs.	Fully rifled barrel

*Standard Invector interchangeable choke tube system: One rifled choke tube and one X-Full Turkey choke tube included.
[1] Total capacity is 2 shells in magazine, one in chamber.

BROWNING SHOTGUNS

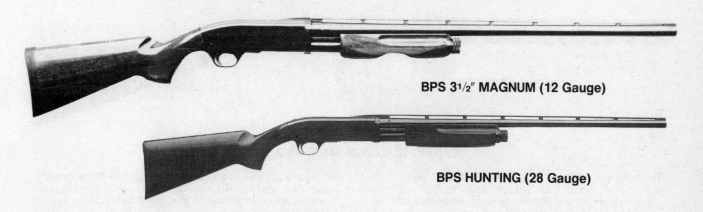

BPS 3¹/₂″ MAGNUM (12 Gauge)

BPS HUNTING (28 Gauge)

SPECIFICATIONS BPS MAGNUMS (Capacity: 4 rounds)

Gauge	Model	Chamber Length	Barrel Length	Overall Weight	Average Available	Chokes
10 Magnum	Hunting & Stalker	3¹/₂″	30″	51³/₄″	9 lbs. 8 oz.	Invector
10 Magnum	Hunting & Stalker	3¹/₂″	28″	49³/₄″	9 lbs. 6 oz.	Invector
10 Magnum	Hunting & Stalker	3¹/₂″	26″	47³/₄″	9 lbs. 4 oz.	Invector
10 Magnum	Hunting & Stalker	3¹/₂″	24″	45³/₄″	9 lbs. 4 oz.	Invector
10 Magnum	Hunting Buck Special	3¹/₂″	24″	45³/₄″	9 lbs. 2 oz.	Slug/Buckshot
12, 3¹/₂″ Mag	Hunting & Stalker	3¹/₂″	30″	51³/₄″	8 lbs. 12 oz.	Invector-Plus
12, 3¹/₂″ Mag	Hunting & Stalker	3¹/₂″	28″	49³/₄″	8 lbs. 9 oz.	Invector-Plus
12, 3¹/₂″ Mag	Hunting & Stalker	3¹/₂″	26″	47³/₄″	8 lbs. 6 oz.	Invector-Plus
12, 3¹/₂″ Mag	Hunting & Stalker	3¹/₂″	24″	45³/₄″	8 lbs. 3 oz.	Invector-Plus
12, 3¹/₂″ Mag	Hunting Buck Special	3¹/₂″	24″	45³/₄″	8 lbs. 7 oz.	Slug/Buckshot

SPECIFICATIONS BPS 12 & 20 GAUGE PUMP (3″)

Model	Barrel Length	Overall Length	Average Weight	Chokes Available
12 GAUGE Hunting	32″	52¹/₂″	7 lbs. 14 oz.	Invector-Plus
Hunting, Stalker	30″	50³/₄″	7 lbs. 12 oz.	Invector-Plus
Hunting, Stalker	28″	48³/₄″	7 lbs. 11 oz.	Invector-Plus
Hunting, Stalker	26″	46³/₄″	7 lbs. 10 oz.	Invector-Plus
Standard Buck Special	24″	44³/₄″	7 lbs. 10 oz.	Slug/Buckshot
Upland Special	22″	42³/₄″	7 lbs. 8 oz.	Invector-Plus
Hunting, Stalker	22″	42¹/₂″	7 lbs. 7 oz.	Invector-Plus
Game Gun Turkey Special	20¹/₂″	40⁷/₈″	7 lbs. 7 oz.	Invector
Game Gun Deer Special	20¹/₂″	40⁷/₈″	7 lbs. 7 oz.	Special Inv./Rifled
20 GAUGE Hunting	28″	48³/₄″	7 lbs. 1 oz.	Invector-Plus
Hunting	26″	46³/₄″	7 lbs.	Invector-Plus
Youth/Ladies	22″	41³/₄″	6 lbs. 11 oz.	Invector-Plus
Upland Special	22″	42³/₄″	6 lbs. 12 oz.	Invector-Plus
28 GAUGE Hunting*	28″	48³/₄″	7 lbs. 1 oz.	Invector
Hunting*	26″	46³/₄″	7 lbs.	Invector

* 2³/₄″ chamber

BPS MAGNUM	**Prices**
10 GAUGE MAGNUM (Standard Invector)	
Hunting & Stalker grades	$671.95
Waterfowl	860.95
Buck Special (cyl. bore)	676.95
12 GAUGE 3.5″ MAGNUM (Invector Plus)	
Hunting & Stalker grades	676.95
FIELD MODELS (12 Ga. Invector Plus)	
Hunting & Stalker grades	534.95
Pigeon grade	713.95
Upland Special grade	534.95
Buck Special grade (cyl. bore)	519.95
GAME GUN MODELS (12 Ga. Standard Invector)	
Deer Special grade (gloss finish w/polished metal)	603.95
Turkey Special	571.95
20 & 28 GAUGE FIELD MODELS (Std./Invector-Plus)	
Hunting/Youth & Ladies	534.95

CONNECTICUT VALLEY CLASSICS

CLASSIC SPORTER

CLASSIC 12 GAUGE SPORTING GUNS

The designers of the CVC "Classic Sporter" and "Classic Waterfowler" trace their lineage back to the well-known "Classic Doubles" and Winchester over/under shotguns. They have used the proven strength and durability of the M-101 design and integrated these qualities with advanced engineering and manufacturing techniques. In addition to the basic specifications listed below, the CVC Classic models feature the following: Frame, monoblock and key integral parts are machined from solid steel bar stock. . . Tang spacer is an integral part of the frame to ensure rigid alignment for solid lockup of buttstock to frame. . . Chrome molybdenum steel barrels; chrome-lined bores and chambers (suitable for steel shot use). . . Barrels have elongated forcing cones for reduced recoil; interchangeable screw-in chokes included. . . Low-luster satin-finished stock and forend are of full, fancy-grade American black walnut and hand-checkered with fine-line engraving.

Grade I: AA grade semi-fancy American walnut; black or claro walnut option available; 20 lines-per-inch hand-checkering; hand-rubbed oil finish

Grade II: AAA grade fancy American walnut; black or claro walnut option available; 22 lines-per-inch hand-checkering; hand-rubbed oil finish; engraving patterns on frame with added scroll design

Grade III: AAA select fancy American walnut; black or claro walnut option available; 22 lines-per-inch hand-checkering with Fleur de lis on Field models; hand-rubbed oil finish; engraving patterns on frame with added scrolls and bird scene panels on Field models; gold inlay of CVC on bottom of frame; gold-plated trigger

CLASSIC SPORTER GRADE III

CONNECTICUT VALLEY CLASSICS SPECIFICATIONS

Model	Barrel Length	Overall Length	Length of Pull	Drop at Comb	Drop at Heel	Nominal Weight (Lbs.)	Price
Classic Sporter Grade I	28"	44⁷/₈"	14¹/₂"	2¹/₈"	7³/₄"	7³/₄	$3195.00
Woman's Classic Sporter	28	44¹/₂	14¹/₈	1¹/₂	2¹/₄	7¹/₂	3195.00
Classic Sporter Grade II	30	46⁷/₈	14¹/₂	1¹/₂	2¹/₄	7³/₄	3795.00
Classic Sporter Grade III	30	46⁷/₈	14¹/₂	1¹/₂	2¹/₈	7⁷/₈	4195.00
Classic Waterfowler	30	46⁷/₈	14³/₈	1¹/₂	2¹/₄	8	2995.00
Classic Field Grade I	27¹/₂	44¹/₄	14¹/₄	1⁵/₈	2³/₈	7¹/₂	3195.00
Classic Field Grade II	27¹/₂	44¹/₄	14¹/₄	1⁵/₈	2³/₈	7¹/₂	3595.00
Classic Field Grade III	27¹/₂	44¹/₄	14¹/₈	1⁵/₈	2³/₈	7¹/₄	4195.00
Classic Skeet	29	45³/₄	14¹/₄	1⁵/₈	2³/₈	7¹/₂	3195.00
Classic Flyer	30	46⁷/₈	14¹/₂	1³/₈	1¹/₂	8	3995.00

COUNTY SHOTGUNS

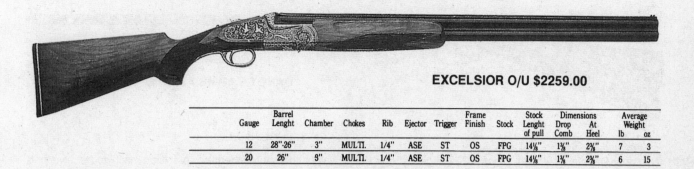

EXCELSIOR O/U $2259.00

Gauge	Barrel Lenght	Chamber	Chokes	Rib	Ejector	Trigger	Frame Finish	Stock	Stock Lenght of pull	Dimensions Drop Comb	At Heel	Average Weight lb	oz
12	28"-26"	3"	MULTI.	1/4"	ASE	ST	OS	FPG	14⅛"	1⅜"	2⅜"	7	3
20	26"	3"	MULTI.	1/4"	ASE	ST	OS	FPG	14⅛"	1⅜"	2⅜"	6	15

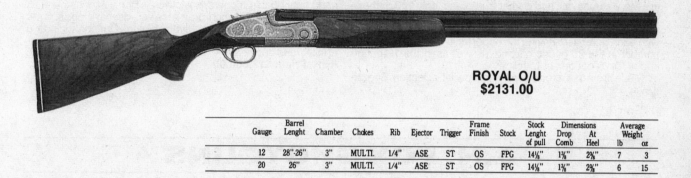

ROYAL O/U
$2131.00

Gauge	Barrel Lenght	Chamber	Chokes	Rib	Ejector	Trigger	Frame Finish	Stock	Stock Lenght of pull	Dimensions Drop Comb	At Heel	Average Weight lb	oz
12	28"-26"	3"	MULTI.	1/4"	ASE	ST	OS	FPG	14⅛"	1⅜"	2⅜"	7	3
20	26"	3"	MULTI.	1/4"	ASE	ST	OS	FPG	14⅛"	1⅜"	2⅜"	6	15

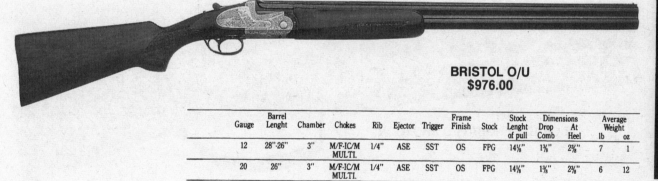

BRISTOL O/U
$976.00

Gauge	Barrel Lenght	Chamber	Chokes	Rib	Ejector	Trigger	Frame Finish	Stock	Stock Lenght of pull	Dimensions Drop Comb	At Heel	Average Weight lb	oz
12	28"-26"	3"	M/F-IC/M MULTI.	1/4"	ASE	SST	OS	FPG	14⅛"	1⅜"	2⅜"	7	1
20	26"	3"	M/F-IC/M MULTI.	1/4"	ASE	SST	OS	FPG	14⅛"	1⅜"	2⅜"	6	12

MODEL FS-300 O/U
$1108.00
w/Monte Carlo Stock and Vent Middle Rib

Gauge	Barrel Lenght	Chamber	Chokes	Rib	Ejector	Trigger	Frame Finish	Stock	Stock Lenght of pull	Dimensions Drop Comb	At Heel	Average Weight lb	oz
12	30"	2¾"	IM/F	3/8"	ASE	ST	OS	FPG	14⁵⁄₁₆"	1⅜"	1½"	8	2

DAKOTA ARMS INC.

DAKOTA ARMS AMERICAN LEGEND

The new Dakota American Legend 20-gauge side-by-side double shotgun is built in the United States and reflects the best fit and finish found on game guns the world over. Cased in a Marvis Huey oak and leather trunk case, only 100 of these world-class double guns will be made. These limited-edition shotguns will be offered on a first come, first served basis, with each purchaser having the opportunity to reserve a serial number in the 20-gauge offering, as well as in the 12-gauge and .410/28-gauge set to follow.

Made from bar stock steel and special selection English walnut, this shotgun features precision-machined receiver and intricate hand checkering. Standard features include custom-fitted stock, full-coverage hand engraving, gold inlays, straight-hand grip, double triggers, selective ejectors, 24-lines-per-inch hand checkering, French gray receiver, concave rib, splinter forend, checkered butt and ivory beads. Options include a single trigger, leather-covered pad, skeleton butt, semi-beavertail forend and screw-in chokes. **Barrel length:** 27". **Weight:** 6 lbs. **Price: $18,000.00**

A.H. FOX SHOTGUNS

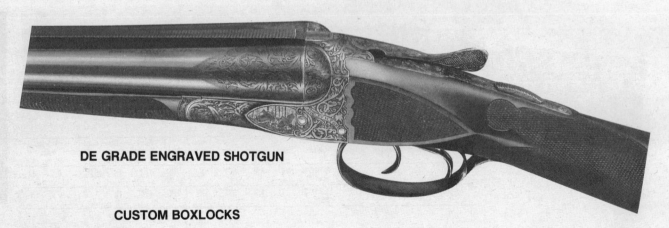

DE GRADE ENGRAVED SHOTGUN

CUSTOM BOXLOCKS

SPECIFICATIONS
Gauges: 16, 20, 28 and .410
Barrel: Any barrel lengths and chokes; rust blued Chromox or Krupp steel barrels
Weight: 5 1/2 to 6 3/4 lbs.
Stock: Custom stock dimensions including cast; hand-checkered Turkish Circassian walnut stock and forend with hand-rubbed oil finish; straight grip, full pistol grip (with cap), or semi-pistol grip; splinter, schnabel or beavertail forend; traditional pad, hard rubber plate, checkered, or skeleton butt
Features: Boxlock action with automatic ejectors; scalloped, rebated and color casehardened receiver; double or Fox single selective trigger; hand-finished and hand-engraved. This is the same gun that was manufactured between 1905 and 1930 by the A.H. Fox Gun Company of Philadelphia,

PA, now manufactured in the U.S. by the Connecticut Shotgun Mfg. Co. (New Britain, CT).
Prices:*
CE Grade (all gauges)	$ 8,200.00
XE Grade (all gauges)	9,700.00
DE Grade (all gauges)	13,800.00
FE Grade (16 and 20 ga.)	17,500.00
FE Grade (28 and .410 ga.)	19,700.00
Exhibition Grade	25,000.00

* Grades differ in engraving and inlay, grade of wood and amount of hand finishing needed.

FRANCOTTE SHOTGUNS

CLOSE-UP OF BOXLOCK S6

"CUSTOM" BOXLOCKS/SIDELOCKS

There are no standard Francotte models, since every shotgun is custom made in Belgium to the purchaser's individual specifications. Features and options include Anson & Deeley boxlocks or Auguste Francotte system sidelocks. All guns have custom-fitted stocks. Available are exhibition-grade stocks as well as extensive engraving and gold inlays. U.S. agent for Auguste Francotte of Belgium is Armes de Chasse (see Directory of Manufacturers and Distributors).

SPECIFICATIONS
Gauges: 12, 16, 20, 28, .410; also 24 and 32
Chambers: 2½", 2¾" and 3"

Barrel length: To customer's specifications
Forend: To customer's specifications
Stock: Deluxe to exhibition grade; pistol, English or half-pistol grip
Prices:
Basic Boxlock $12,000.00
Basic Boxlock (28 & .410 ga.) 13,500.00
Optional sideplates, add 1,400.00
Basic Sidelock 27,000.00
Basic Sidelock (28 & .410 ga.) 30,000.00

GARBI SIDELOCK SHOTGUNS

MODEL 100 SIDELOCK
$4500.00

Like this Model 100 shotgun, all Spanish-made Garbi models featured here are Holland & Holland pattern sidelock ejector guns with chopper lump (demibloc) barrels. They are built to English gun standards with regard to design, weight, balance and proportions, and all have the characteristic "feel" associated with the best London guns. All of the models offer fine 24-line hand-checkering, with outstanding quality wood-to-metal and metal-to-metal fit. The Model 100 is available in 12, 16, 20 and 28 gauge and sports Purdey-style fine scroll and rosette engraving, partly done by machine.
Also available: Model 101 **$5800.00;** Model 103A (**$7100.00**); Model 103B (**$9800.00**).

MODEL 200
$9375.00

The **Model 200** double is available in 12, 16, 20 or 28 gauge; features Holland-pattern stock ejector design, heavy-duty locks, heavy proof, Continental-style floral and scroll engraving, walnut stock.

HARRINGTON & RICHARDSON

SINGLE-BARREL SHOTGUNS

.410 TAMER SHOTGUN
$124.95

This barreled .410 snake gun features single-shot action, transfer-bar safety and high-impact synthetic stock and forend. Stock has a thumbhole design that sports a full pistol grip and a recessed open side, containing a holder for storing ammo. Forend is modified beavertail configuration. Other features include a matte, electroless nickel finish. **Weight:** 5–6 lbs. **Barrel length:** 20″ (3″ chamber). **Choke:** Full.

MODEL SB2-980 ULTRA SLUG HUNTER
$209.95

Features: 12-gauge 24″ barrel, 3″ chamber, fully rifled heavy slug barrel (1:35″ twist); Monte Carlo stock and forend of American hardwood w/dark walnut stain; matte black receiver; transfer-bar safety system; scope rail, swivels and sling.

MODEL SB1-920 ULTRA SLUG GUN
$209.95

Features: Transfer-bar safety system, scope rail, vent recoil pad, matte black receiver, swivels and black nylon sling
Also available:
MODEL SB1-925 ULTRA YOUTH SLUG HUNTER. Features 12-gauge barrel blank underbored to 20 gauge and shortened to 22″; factory-mounted Weaver-style scope base; reduced Monte Carlo stock of American hardwood with dark walnut stain; vent recoil pad, sling swivels and black nylon sling. **Price: $209.05**

SPECIFICATIONS
Gauge: 20 rifled slug (3″ chamber)
Action: 12 gauge action
Barrel length: 24″ heavy target-style
Rate of twist: 1:35″
Finish: Low-luster blue
Stock: American hardwood with dark walnut stain, Monte Carlo style

HARRINGTON & RICHARDSON

SINGLE-BARREL SHOTGUNS

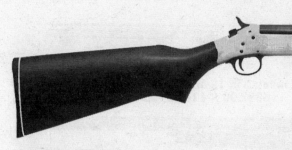

TOPPER MODEL 098
$114.95

Chokes: Modified (12 and 20 ga.); Full (.410 ga.)
Barrel lengths: 26″ and 28″   **Weight:** 5 to 6 lbs.
Action: Break-open; side lever release; automatic ejection
Stock: Full pistol grip; American hardwood; black finish with white buttplate spacer
Length of pull: 14 1/2″

SPECIFICATIONS
Gauges: 12, 20 and .410 (3″ chamber); 16 and 28 ga. (2 3/4″ chamber)

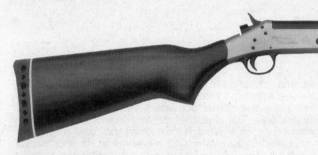

TOPPER JR. YOUTH
$119.95

Barrel length: 22″   **Weight:** 5 to 6 lbs.
Stock: Full pistol grip; American hardwood; black finish; white line spacer; recoil pad
Finish: Satin nickel frame; blued barrel

SPECIFICATIONS
Gauges: 20 and .410 (3″ chamber)
Chokes: Modified (20 ga.); Full (.410 ga.)

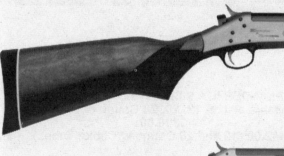

TOPPER CLASSIC YOUTH
$144.95

Same specifications as the Standard Topper, but with 22″ barrel, American black walnut stock and 12 1/2″ pull.

TOPPER DELUXE MODEL 098
$134.95

with semibeavertail forend; white line spacer; ventilated recoil pad
Finish: Satin nickel frame; blued barrel
Also available: TOPPER DELUXE RIFLED SLUG GUN. In gauges 12, 20 and 20 Youth; 24″ compensated choke barrel, 3″ chamber (1:35″ twist); nickel frame; black finished American hardwood stock w/recoil pad and swivel studs; fully adjustable rifle sights; transfer-bar safety system.
Price: $209.95

SPECIFICATIONS
Gauge: 12 (3 1/2″ chamber)
Chokes: Screw-in Modified (Full, Extra-Full Turkey and Steel Shot also available)
Action: Break-open; side lever release; positive ejection
Barrel length: 28″   **Weight:** 5 to 6 lbs.
Stock: American hardwood, black finish, full pistol-grip stock

IGA SHOTGUNS

See table on p. 344 for additional specifications

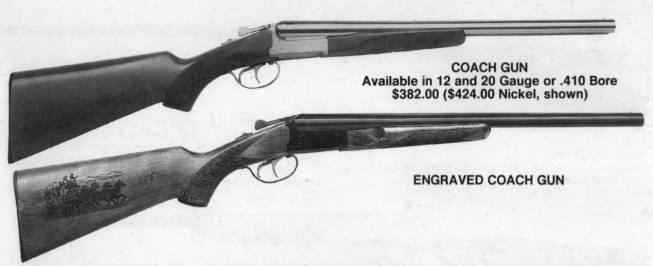

COACH GUN
Available in 12 and 20 Gauge or .410 Bore
$382.00 ($424.00 Nickel, shown)

ENGRAVED COACH GUN

The **IGA CLASSIC SIDE-BY-SIDE COACH GUN** sports a 20-inch barrel. Lightning fast, it is the perfect shotgun for hunting upland game in dense brush or close quarters. This endurance-tested workhorse of a gun is designed from the ground up to give you years of trouble-free service. Two massive underlugs provide a super-safe, vise-tight locking system for lasting strength and durability. The mechanical extraction of spent shells and double-trigger mechanism assures reliability. The automatic safety is actuated whenever the action is opened, whether or not the gun has been fired. The polish and blue is deep and rich, and the solid sighting rib is matte-finished for glare-free sighting. Chrome-moly steel barrels with micro-polished bores give dense, consistent patterns. Nickel finish is now available. The classic stock and forend are of durable hardwood . . . oil finished, hand-rubbed and hand-checkered.

Improved Cylinder/Modified choking and its short barrel make the IGA coach gun the ideal choice for hunting in close quarters, security and police work. Three-inch chambers.

Also available w/Engraved Stagecoach scene on stock: **$412.00**

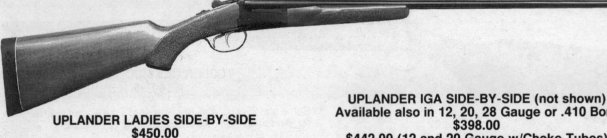

UPLANDER LADIES SIDE-BY-SIDE
$450.00

UPLANDER IGA SIDE-BY-SIDE (not shown)
Available also in 12, 20, 28 Gauge or .410 Bore
$398.00
$442.00 (12 and 20 Gauge w/Choke Tubes)

Crafted specifically with women in mind, IGA's new model features a lightweight 20 gauge with 24″ barrel and is equipped with IC/M choke tubes. The durable 13″ Brazilian hardwood stock is fitted with a ventilated pad to reduce recoil. Standard features include extractors, double triggers and automatic safety.

UPLANDER YOUTH SIDE-BY-SIDE (not shown)
$408.00

IGA's new Youth gun is a lightweight .410 gauge with 24″ barrels bored modified and full. Both barrels will handle 2¹/₂″ or 3″ shells. The 13″ Brazilian hardwood stock includes a recoil pad. Standard features include double triggers, extractors and an automatic safety (activated when the gun is open). This shotgun is easy to load, light to carry and safe to handle with a second shot available when needed.

The **IGA SIDE-BY-SIDE** is a rugged shotgun, endurance-tested and designed to give years of trouble-free service. A vise-tight, super-safe locking system is provided by two massive underlugs for lasting strength and durability. Two design features that make the IGA a standout for reliability are its positive mechanical extraction of spent shells and its traditional double-trigger mechanism. The safety is automatic in that every time the action is opened, whether or not the gun has been fired, the safety is actuated. The polish and bluing are deep and rich. The solid sighting rib carries a machined-in matte finish for glare-free sighting. Barrels are of chrome-moly steel with micro-polished bores to give dense, consistent patterns. The stock and forend are available with either traditional stock or the legendary English-style stock. Both are of durable Brazilian hardwood, oil-finished, hand-rubbed and hand-checkered.

Also available with English stock w/choke tubes (IC/M) and fixed (M/M).

IGA SHOTGUNS

See table on p. 344 for additional specifications.

CONDOR I OVER/UNDER SINGLE TRIGGER
$500.00 (w/Choke Tubes)

The **IGA OVER/UNDER SINGLE TRIGGER** is a workhorse of a shotgun, designed for maximum dependability in heavy field use. The super-safe lock-up system makes use of a sliding underlug, the best system for over/under shotguns. A massive monobloc joins the barrel in a solid one-piece assembly at the breech end. Reliability is assured, thanks to the mechanical extraction system. Upon opening the breech, the spent shells are partially lifted from the chamber, allowing easy removal by hand. IGA barrels are of chrome-moly steel with micro-polished bores to give tight, consistent patterns. They are specifically formulated for use with steel shot where Federal migratory bird regulations require. Atop the barrel is a sighting rib with an anti-glare surface. The buttstock and forend are of durable hardwood, hand-checkered and finished with an oil-based formula that takes dents and scratches in stride.

The IGA **Condor I** over/under shotgun is available in 12 and 20 gauge with 26- and 28-inch barrels with choke tubes and 3-inch chambers; 12 and 20 gauge with 26- and 28-inch barrels choked IC/M and Mod./Full, 3-inch chambers.

Also available:
Condor II O/U in 12 gauge, double trigger, 26″ barrel IC/M or 28″ barrel M/F. **Price:** $415.00

CONDOR SUPREME
$599.00

The IGA Condor Supreme truly complements its name. The stock is selected from upgraded Brazilian walnut, and the hand-finished checkering is sharp and crisp. A matte-laquered finish provides a soft warm glow, while maintaining a high resistance to dents and scratches.

A massive monoblock joins the barrel in a solid one-piece assembly at the breech end. Upon opening the breech, the automatic ejectors cause the spent shells to be thrown clear of the gun. The barrels are of moly-chrome steel with micro-polished bores to give tight, consistent patterns; they are specifically formulated for use with steel shot. Choke tubes are provided. Atop the barrel is a sighting rib with an anti-glare surface with both mid- and front bead. *See* table on the following page for additional specifications.

REUNA SINGLE BARREL
$120.00 ($142.00 w/Choke Tube)

IGA's entry-level single-barrel shotgun features a feeling of heft and quality not found in other shotguns similarly priced. Single mechanical extraction makes for convenient removal of spent shells. For ease of operation and maximum safety, the Reuna is equipped with an exposed hammer, which must be cocked manually before firing.

The Reuna single-barrel shotgun is available with a choke tube in 12 and 20 gauge and with fixed chokes in 12 and 20 gauge or .410 bore. Both the buttstock and semi-beavertail forearm are of durable Brazilian hardwood. The squared-off design of the firearm enhances stability and provides an additional gripping surface for greater comfort.

REUNA YOUTH MODEL SINGLE BARREL (not shown)
$132.00

The Youth Model is designed especially for the young shooter. All the same features of the conventional-sized model are included in the youth version, complemented by an easy-handling shorter barrel (22″), shortened stock and ventilated recoil pad. In 20 gauge and .410 (Full choke).

SHOTGUNS

IGA SHOTGUNS

IGA SHOTGUN SPECIFICATIONS

	Gauge					Bbl. Length					Chokes		Other Specifications				Dimensions			
	12	16	20	28	410	20"	22"	24"	26"	28"	Fixed	Choke tubes	Chamber	Weight (lbs.)	Extractors	Triggers	Length of pull	Drop at comb	Drop at heel	O.A. length
Coach Gun Side by Side	■		■		■	■					IC/M		3"	6¾	■	D.T.	14½"	1½"	2½"	36½"
Uplander Side by Side	■		■						■		IC/M	IC/M	3"	7½	■	D.T.	14½"	1½"	2½"	42"
Uplander Side by Side	■		■							■	M/F	M/F	3"	7½	■	D.T.	14½"	1½"	2½"	44"
Uplander S/S		■							■		IC/M		2¾"	7½	■	D.T.	14½"	.1½"	2½"	42"
Uplander Side by Side				■					■		IC/M		2¾"	6¾	■	D.T.	14½"	1½"	2½"	42"
Uplander Side by Side					■				■		F/F		3"	6¾	■	D.T.	14½"	1½"	2½"	42"
Uplander Ladies		■						■			IC/M	IC/M	3"	6½	■	D.T.	13½"	1½"	2½"	39"
Uplander S/S English**				■				■			M/M		3"	6½	■	D.T.	14½"	1½"	2½"	40"
Uplander S/S Youth**				■				■			M/F		3"	6¼	■	D.T.	13½"	1½"	2½"	40"
English Stock Side by Side		■						■	■		IC/M		3"	6½	■	D.T.	14½"	1⅜"	2⅜"	40"/42"
Condor Supreme*		■							■	■	F, M IC		3"	8	■	S.T.	14½"	1½"	2½"	43½"/45½"
Condor I Over/Under	■		■						■		IC/M	IC/M	3"	8	■	S.T.	14½"	1½"	2½"	43½"
Condor I Over/Under	■		■							■	M/F	M/F	3"	8	■	S.T.	14½"	1½"	2½"	45½"
Condor II Over/Under	■								■		IC/M		3"	8	■	D.T.	14½"	1½"	2½"	43½"
Condor II Over/Under	■									■	M/F		3"	8	■	D.T.	14½"	1½"	2½"	45½"
Reuna Single Barrel	■									■	F	F	3"	6¼	■		14½"	1½"	2½"	44½"
Reuna Single Barrel	■								■		M		3"	6¼	■		14½"	1½"	2½"	42½"
Reuna Single Barrel			■						■		F	F	3"	6¼	■		14½"	1½"	2½"	42½"
Reuna Single Barrel					■				■		F		3"	6	■		14½"	1½"	2½"	42½"
Reuna-Youth Model Single Barrel			■	■	■						F		3"	5	■		13	1½"	2½"	37

* Condor Supreme equipped with automatic ejectors
** Side-by-side Ladies & Youth models supplied with recoil pad

KBI SHOTGUNS

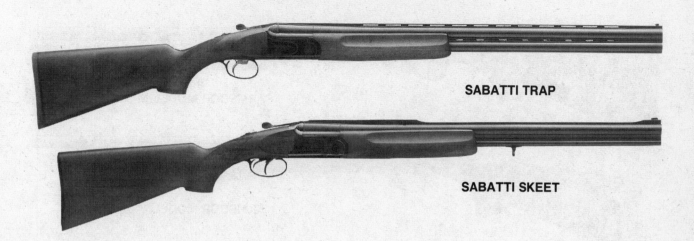

SABATTI TRAP

SABATTI SKEET

SABATTI OVER/UNDER SHOTGUN

SPECIFICATIONS
Gauge: 12 (2³/₄″ and 3″ chambers); 12 ga./.223 Rem. (Combo Model)
Choke: IM&F/SK, 1&2 w/ICT/IM
Barrel lengths: 30″ (Trap); 26″ (Skeet); 28″ (Sport); 25″ (Combo)
Overall length: 47¹/₄″ (28″ barrel); 44″ (26″ and 28″ barrels); 42″ (Combo)
Weight: 8 lbs. (30″ barrel and Combo); 7 lbs. (26″ barrel); 7 lbs. 3 oz. (28″ barrel)

Stock: Walnut
Features: Blued engraved receiver of chrome-moly steel; single selective trigger; automatic ejectors and safeties; 5 interchangeable choke tubes
Prices:
Skeet **$799.00**
Trap 819.00
Sporting Clays 819.00
Combo 879.00

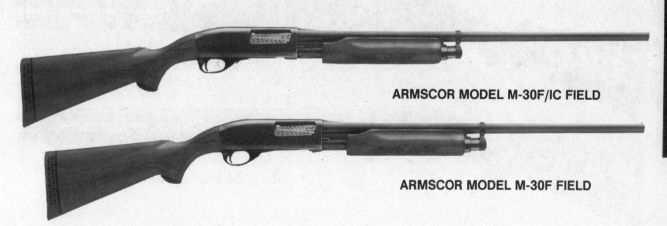

ARMSCOR MODEL M-30F/IC FIELD

ARMSCOR MODEL M-30F FIELD

ARMSCOR FIELD PUMP SHOTGUN

SPECIFICATIONS
Gauge: 12 (3″ chamber)
Capacity: 6 shot
Choke: Modified (Model M-30F); 2-ICT (F/IC, Model M-30F/IC)
Barrel length: 28″
Overall length: 47¹/₂″

Weight: 7.6 lbs.
Stock: Walnut-finished hardwood buttstock and forend
Features: Double slide-action bars; damascened bolt
Prices:
Model M-30F **$209.00**
Model M-30F/IC 259.00

KBI SHOTGUNS

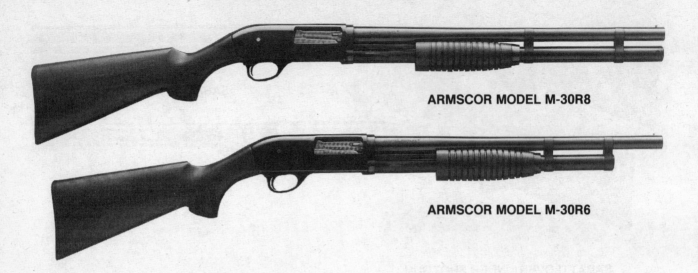

ARMSCOR MODEL M-30R8

ARMSCOR MODEL M-30R6

ARMSCOR MODELS M-30R8/M-30R6 RIOT PUMP SHOTGUNS

SPECIFICATIONS
Gauge: 12 (3″ chamber)
Choke: Cylinder
Capacity: 6-shot (M-30R6); 8-shot (M-30R8)
Barrel lengths: 18½″ (M-30R6); 20″ (M-30R8)
Overall length: 37¾″ and 39¾″

Weight: 7 lbs. and 7.2 lbs.
Stock: Walnut finished hardwood buttstock and forend
Features: Double-action slide bar; damascened bolt; blued finish
Prices:
M-30R6 . . . . $199.00
M-30R8 . . . . 210.00

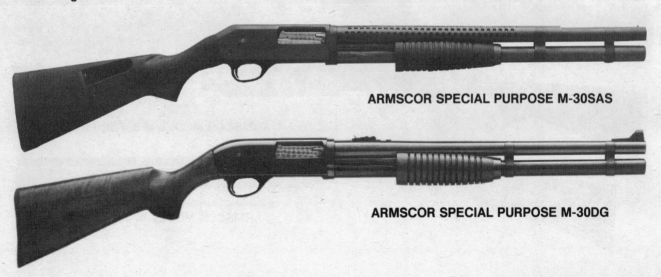

ARMSCOR SPECIAL PURPOSE M-30SAS

ARMSCOR SPECIAL PURPOSE M-30DG

ARMSCOR SPECIAL PURPOSE SHOTGUN

SPECIFICATIONS
Gauge: 12 (3″ chamber)   **Choke:** Cylinder
Barrel length: 20″   **Overall length:** 39¼″
Weight: 7½ lbs.
Stock: Walnut-finished hardwood (Model 30SAS has speed-feed 4-shot capacity buttstock and synthetic forend)

Features: Double-action slide bar; damascened bolt; **Model M-30DG** has 7-shot magazine in traditional stocked/blued pump shotgun with iron sights; **Model M-30SAS** has ventilated shroud and parkerized finish
Prices:
Model M-30DG $249.00
Model M-30SAS 279.00

KRIEGHOFF SHOTGUNS

(See following page for additional Specifications and Prices)

MODEL K-80 SPORTING CLAY

MODEL K-80 TRAP, SKEET, SPORTING CLAY AND LIVE BIRD

Barrels: Made of Boehler steel; free-floating bottom barrel with adjustable point of impact; standard Trap and Live Pigeon ribs are tapered step; standard Skeet, Sporting Clay and International ribs are tapered or parallel flat.
Receivers: Hard satin-nickel finish; casehardened; blue finish available as special order
Triggers: Wide profile, single selective, position adjustable. Removable trigger option available (add'l **$1000.00**)
Weight: 8½ lbs. (Trap); 8 lbs. (Skeet)

Ejectors: Selective automatic
Sights: White pearl front bead and metal center bead
Stocks: Hand-checkered and epoxy-finished Select European walnut stock and forearm; stocks available in seven different styles and dimensions
Safety: Push button safety located on top tang.
Also available:
SKEET SPECIAL (28″ and 30″ barrel; tapered flat or 8mm rib; 5 choke tubes). **Price: $7300.00** (Standard)

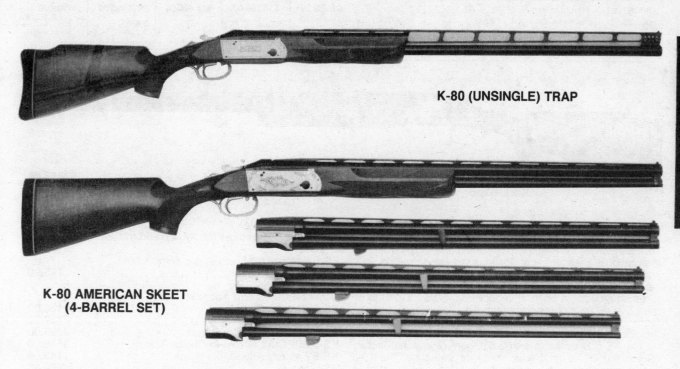

K-80 (UNSINGLE) TRAP

**K-80 AMERICAN SKEET
(4-BARREL SET)**

KRIEGHOFF SHOTGUNS

SPECIFICATIONS AND PRICES MODEL K-80 (see also preceding page)

Model	Description	Bbl. Length	Choke	Standard	Bavaria	Danube	Gold Target	Extra Barrels
TRAP	Over & Under	30″/32″	IM/F	$ 7,375.00	$12,525.00	$23,625.00	$27,170.00	$2900.00
		30″/32″	CT/CT	8,025.00	13,175.00	24,275.00	27,820.00	3550.00
	Unsingle	32″/34″	Full	7,950.00	13,100.00	24,200.00	27,745.00	3575.00
	Combo	30″ + 34″	IM/F&F	10,415.00	15,625.00	26,725.00	30,270.00	
	(Top Single)	32″ + 34″	CT/CT&CT	11,550.00	16,700.00	27,800.00	31,345.00	
	Combo (Unsingle)	30″ + 32″ 30″ + 34″	IM/F+F	9,975.00	15,125.00	26,225.00	29,770.00	2950.00
		32″ + 34″	CT/CT&CT	11,050.00	16,200.00	27,300.00	30,845.00	3375.00

Optional Features:

Screw-in chokes (Top or Unsingle)	$425.00
Single factory release	425.00
Double factory release	750.00

Model	Description	Bbl. Length	Choke	Standard	Bavaria	Danube	Gold Target	Extra Barrels
SKEET	4-Barrel Set	28″/12 ga.	Tula	$16,950.00	$22,100.00	$33,200.00	$36,745.00	$2990.00
		28″/20 ga.	Skeet					2880.00
		28″/28 ga.	Skeet					2990.00
		28″/.410 ga.	Skeet					2880.00
	2-Barrel Set	28″/12 ga.	Tula	11,840.00	18,990.00	28,090.00	31,685.00	4150.00
	Lightweight	28″ + 30″/12 ga.	Skeet	6,900.00	N/A	N/A	N/A	2650.00
	Standardweight	28″/12 ga.	Tula	6,900.00	12,050.00	23,150.00	28,895.00	2650.00
	1-Barrel Set	28″	Skeet	8,825.00	13,975.00	25,075.00	28,620.00	4150.00
	International	28″/12 ga.	Tula	7,825.00	12,975.00	24,075.00	27,620.00	2990.00
	Skeet Special			7,575.00	12,725.00	23,825.00	27,370.00	3300.00
SPORTING CLAYS	Over/Under w/screw-in tubes (5)	28″ + 30″ + 32″/ 12 ga. 30″ Semi-Light	Tubes IC/ICTF	$8,150.00	$13,300.00	$24,400.00	$27,945.00	$2900.00

Optional engravings: Super Scroll **$1995.00**; Gold Super Scroll **$4450.00**   Parcours **$2100.00**   Parcours Special **$3950.00**

MODEL KS-5

Prices:
KS-5 32″ or 34″ barrel, Full choke, case **$3695.00**
KS-5 SPECIAL 32″ or 34″ barrel, Full choke, AR, ADJ, cased **4695.00**

Options Available:
KS-5 Screw-in chokes (M, IM, F), **add** to base price **$425.00**
KS-5 Factory ADJ (adjustable comb stock), **add** to base price **395.00**

Other Features and Accessories:
KS-5 Regular Barrel **$2100.00**
KS-5 SPECIAL Barrel(F) **2750.00**
KS-5 Screw-In Choke Barrel **2525.00**
KS-5 SPECIAL Screw-In Choke Barrel **3175.00**
KS-5 Factory Adjustable Stock **1145.00**
KS-5 Stock **750.00**
KS-5 Forearm **290.00**
KS-5 Release Trigger (installed) **295.00**
KS-5 Fronthanger **70.00**
KS-5 Aluminum Case **425.00**
KS-5 Individual Choke Tubes **75.00**

The KS-5 is a single barrel trap gun made by KRIEGHOFF, Ulm/Germany—the K-80 people—and marketed by Krieghoff International. Standard specifications include: 12 gauge, 2³/₄″ chamber, ventilated tapered step rip, and a casehardened receiver (satin gray finished in electroless nickel). The KS-5 features an adjustable point of impact from 50/50 to 70/30 by means of different optional fronthangers. Screw-in chokes and factory adjustable comb stocks are available options. An adjustable rib (AR) and comb stock (ADJ) are standard features.

The KS-5 is available with pull trigger or optional factory release trigger, adjustable externally for poundage. The KS-5 can be converted to release by the installation of the release parts. To assure consistency and proper functioning, release triggers are installed ONLY by Krieghoff International. Release parts are NOT available separately. These shotguns are available in Standard grade only. Engraved models can be special ordered.

MAGTECH SHOTGUNS

MODEL 586.2VR
Vent Rib

MODEL 586.2VR SERIES

The Magtech 586.2VR Series 12-gauge pump shotguns handle 2³/₄" and 3" magnum shells interchangeably and give the shooter custom features, including: • ordnance-grade, deep-blued steel receiver • double-action slide bars • hand-finished Brazilian Embuia wood stock and forearm • hammer-forged chrome-moly barrel • high-profile steel rib • brass mid-bead and ivory-colored front sight • chrome-plated bolt • screw-in Magchokes in IC, Mod. and Full • crossbolt safety • special magazine release for unloading without cycling round through the chamber.

SPECIFICATIONS
Gauge: 12 (2³/₄" or 3" shells)
Capacity: 5 rounds (8 in Model 586.2P)
Chokes: Magchokes in IC, Mod. & Full (IC only in Model 586.2P)
Barrel: 26" and 28", vent rib (19" plain in Model 586.2P)
Overall length: 46¹/₄" and 48¹/₄" (39¹/₄" in Model 586.2P)
Sights Two beads (one bead in Model 586.2P)
Prices:
MODEL 586.2VR26 and 586.2VR28 . . . . $255.00
MODEL 586.2P 235.00

MARLIN SHOTGUNS

MARLIN MODEL 55 GOOSE GUN
$307.50

High-flying ducks and geese are the Goose Gun's specialty. The Marlin Goose Gun has an extra-long 36-inch full-choked barrel and Magnum capability, making it the perfect choice for tough shots at wary waterfowl. It also features a quick-loading 2-shot clip magazine, a convenient leather carrying strap and a quality ventilated recoil pad.

SPECIFICATIONS
Gauge: 12; 2³/₄" Magnum, 3" Magnum or 2³/₄" regular shells
Choke: Full   **Capacity:** 2-shot clip magazine
Action: Bolt action; positive thumb safety; red cocking indicator
Barrel length: 36"   **Overall length:** 56³/₄"
Sights: Bead front sight and U-groove rear sight
Weight: About 8 lbs.
Stock: Walnut-finish hardwood with pistol grip and ventilated recoil pad; swivel studs; tough Mar-Shield® finish

MODEL 512 SLUGMASTER
$353.50

Overall length: 44.75"
Weight: 8 lbs. (w/o scope and mount)
Sights: Adjustable folding semi-buckhorn rear; ramp front with brass bead and removable cutaway Wide-Scan® hood; receiver drilled and tapped for scope mount
Stock: Walnut finished, press-checkered Maine birch w/pistol grip and Mar-Shield® finish, swivel studs, vent. recoil pad

SPECIFICATIONS
Gauge: 12 (up to 3" shells)
Capacity: 2-shot box magazine (+1 in chamber)
Action: Bolt action; thumb safety; red cocking indicator
Barrel length: 21" rifled (1:28" right-hand twist)

MAROCCHI SHOTGUNS

CONQUISTA SHOTGUNS

CONQUISTA
(12 Gauge, 2³/₄″ Chambers)

CONQUISTA
SPORTING CLAYS GRADE III

The Conquista 12-gauge over/under shotguns feature 2³/₄″ chambers in 28″, 30″ or 32″ barrels with 10mm concave, ventilated upper rib and classic middle rib; competition white front sight, automatic extractors/ejectors, Instajust selective trigger with 3.5–4.0 lbs. trigger pull (weight) and checkered (20 lines/inch) select American walnut stock. Additional specifications appear in the chart below.

Also available:

MODEL 92 CLASSIC DOUBLES. With 3″ chambers, Contrechoke Plus chokes, 30″ barrel, 47″ overall length, 8¹/₈ lbs. weight, 1³/₈″ drop at comb, 2¹/₈″ drop at heel. **Price: $1500.00**

SPECIFICATIONS CONQUISTA SHOTGUNS (all 12 Gauge)

MODEL	Sporting Clays*	Sporting Light	Lady Sport*	Trap	Skeet
Barrel length	28″, 30″, 32″	28″, 30″	28″	30″, 32″	28″
Chokes	Contrechokes	Contrechokes	Contrechokes	Imp. Mod./Full	Skeet
Overall length	45″–49″	44³/₈″–46³/₈″	44³/₈″	47″–49″	45″
Weight approx.	7⁷/₈ lbs.	7¹/₂ lbs.	7¹/₂ lbs.	8¹/₄ lbs.	7³/₄ lbs.
Drop at comb	1⁷/₁₆″	1¹¹/₃₂″	1¹¹/₃₂″	1⁹/₃₂″	1¹/₂″
Drop at heel	2³/₁₆″	2⁹/₃₂″	2⁹/₃₂″	1¹¹/₁₆″	2³/₁₆″
Cast at heel	3/₁₆″ Off	3/₁₆″ Off	3/₁₆″ Off	3/₁₆″ Off	3/₁₆″ Off
Cast at toe	3/₈″ Off	3/₈″ Off	3/₈″ Off	5/₁₆″ Off	5/₁₆″ Off
Pitch	2³/₄″	N/A	2³/₄″	1⁵/₃₂″	2⁵/₁₆″
Prices: **Grade I**	$1895.00	$1945.00	$1945.00	$1895.00	$1895.00
Grade II	2285.00	N/A	N/A	2285.00	2285.00
Grade III	3250.00	N/A	N/A	3250.00	3250.00
Spectrum	N/A	1995.00	1995.00	N/A	N/A

* Left-hand Sporting Clays and Lady Sport have same specifications, except **add $50.00**

MAVERICK BY MOSSBERG

MODEL 88 VENT RIB
$241.00 w/Full or Mod. Barrel
$248.00 w/Threaded Barrel and Mod. Tube

SPECIFICATIONS
Gauge: 12; 3″ chamber
Capacity: 6 shots (2³/₄″ shells)
Barrel length: 28″ **Overall length:** 48″ w/28″ barrel
Weight: 7.2 lbs. w/28″ barrel
Chokes: Threaded for Accu-Choke

Features: Crossbolt safety; rubber recoil pad; synthetic stock and forearm; dual slide bars; accessories interchangeable with Mossberg M500; cablelock included
Also available:
MODEL 88. Same specifications as Model 88 Vent Rib, except fixed, Mod. choke and weight 7.1 lbs. **Price: $221.00**

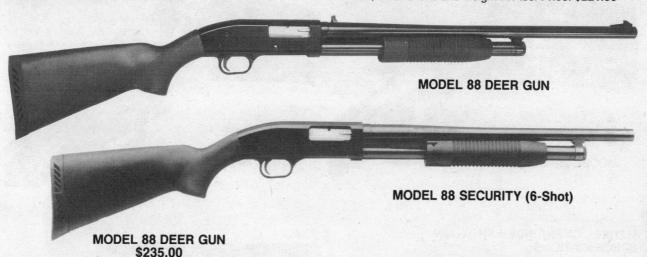

MODEL 88 DEER GUN

MODEL 88 SECURITY (6-Shot)

MODEL 88 DEER GUN
$235.00

SPECIFICATIONS
Gauge: 12; 3″ chamber
Capacity: 6 shots (2³/₄″ shells)
Choke: Cylinder bore
Barrel length: 24″ **Overall length:** 44″
Weight: 7 lbs.
Sights: Adjustable rear leaf and rifle-style front
Features: Crossbolt safety; rubber recoil pad; synthetic stock and forearm; dual slide bars; accessories interchangeable with Mossberg M500; cablelock included

MODEL 88 SECURITY
$213.00 (6-Shot) $246.00 (6-Shot w/P.G. Kit)

SPECIFICATIONS
Gauge: 12; 3″ chamber   **Choke:** Cylinder bore
Barrel length: 18.5″
Overall length: 38.5″ (full stock) or 28″ (pistol grip)
Weight: 6 lbs. 8 oz. (full stock); 5 lbs. 6 oz. (pistol grip)
Features: Synthetic stock and forearm; crossbolt safety; dual slide bars; optional heat shield; accessories interchangeable with Mossberg M500; cablelock included

MODEL 95 BOLT ACTION
$184.00

SPECIFICATIONS
Gauge: 12
Action: Bolt
Choke: Modified, fixed
Barrel length: 25″ **Overall length:** 45.5″

Weight: 6.75 lbs.
Sight: Bead
Features: Synthetic stock with built-in 2-round magazine; rubber recoil pad; gun lock

MERKEL OVER/UNDER SHOTGUNS

Merkel over-and-unders are the first hunting guns with barrels arranged one above the other, and they have since proved to be able competitors of the side-by-side gun. Merkel superiority lies in the following details:
- Available in 12, 16 and 20 gauge (28 ga. in Model 201E with 26¾" barrel)
- Lightweight from 6.4 to 7.28 lbs.
- The high, narrow forend protects the shooter's hand from the barrel in hot or cold climates
- The forend is narrow and therefore lies snugly in the hand to permit easy and positive swinging

- The slim barrel line provides an unobstructed field of view and thus permits rapid aiming and shooting
- The over-and-under barrel arrangement reduces recoil error; the recoil merely pushes the muzzle up vertically

All Merkel shotguns are manufactured by Jagd und Sport-waffen GmbH, Suhl, Thuringia, Germany; imported, distributed and retailed in the U.S. by Gun South Inc. (*see* Directory of Manufacturers and Suppliers).

MODEL 200E BOXLOCK

MODEL 201E BOXLOCK

MERKEL OVER/UNDER SHOTGUN SPECIFICATIONS

Gauges: 12, 16, 20, 28
Barrel lengths: 26¾" and 28" (30" also in Models 200SC, 201E and 203E)
Weight: 6.4 to 7.28 lbs.
Stock: English or pistol grip in European walnut
Features: Models 200E and 201E are boxlocks; Models 202E, 203E and 303E are sidelocks. All models include three-piece forearm, automatic ejectors, Kersten double crossbolt lock, Blitz action and single selective triggers.

Prices:
MODEL 200E Kersten double cross-bolt lock, scroll-engraved casehardened receiver, Blitz action **$ 3,695.00**
MODEL 200ET Trap (Full/Full) 12 ga.
w/30" barrel **5,195.00**
MODEL 200SC Sporting Clays 12 ga.
(30" only) **6,995.00**
Same as above w/Briley choke tubes **7,495.00**
MODEL 201E 12 or 16 ga. 28" IC/Mod, Mod/
Full **5,495.00**
MODEL 201E 20 ga. 26¾" IC/Mod, Mod/Full . . **5,495.00**
MODEL 201E 28 ga. 26¾" IC/Mod, Mod/Full
MODEL 202E Sidelock 12 or 16 ga., 28" IC/Mod,
Mod/Full (w/hunting scenes) **9,295.00**
MODEL 203E Sidelock 12 or 16 ga., 28" IC/Mod,
Mod/Full (w/English-style engraving) **11,295.00**

MODEL 203E SIDELOCK

MODEL 303E Sidelock 12 or 16 ga., 28" IC/Mod, Mod/Full, English-style arabesque engraving in large scrolls on silver-gray sidelocks **$18,995.00**
Also available:
MERKEL O/U SHOTGUN/RIFLE COMBINA-TIONS (Models 210E, 211E, 213E, 313E); 12, 16 & 20 ga. (2¾" chamber) w/22 Hornet (12 ga. only) and 5.6×50R (16 & 20 ga.) . . . . **$6,195.00–$24,595.00**

MERKEL SIDE-BY-SIDE SHOTGUNS

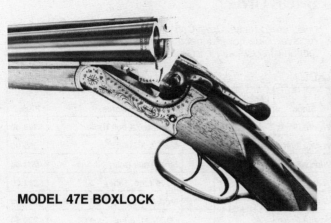

MODEL 47E BOXLOCK

MODEL 147E BOXLOCK

SIDE-BY-SIDE SHOTGUNS

SPECIFICATIONS
Gauges: 12 and 20 (28 ga. and .410 in Models 47S and 147S)
Barrel lengths: 26″ and 28″ (25½″ in Models 47S and 147S)
Weight: 6 to 7 lbs.
Stock: English or pistol grip in European walnut
Features: Models 47E and 147E are boxlocks; Models 47S and 147S are sidelocks. All guns have cold hammer-forged barrels, double triggers, double lugs and Greener crossbolt locking systems and automatic ejectors.

Prices:

MODEL 8	$1695.00
MODEL 47E (Holland & Holland ejectors)	2295.00
MODEL 122 (H&H ejectors, engraved hunting scenes)	4595.00
MODEL 147 (H&H ejectors)	2595.00
MODEL 147E (engraved hunting scenes)	
12, 16 & 20 ga.	2795.00
28 ga.	3595.00
MODEL 47S Sidelock (H&H ejectors)	4895.00
MODEL 147S Sidelock	
12, 16 & 20 ga.	6195.00
28 ga.	6495.00
MODEL 247S (English-style engraving)	6895.00
MODEL 347S (H&H ejectors)	7895.00
MODEL 447S	8995.00

MODEL 47S SIDE-BY-SIDE

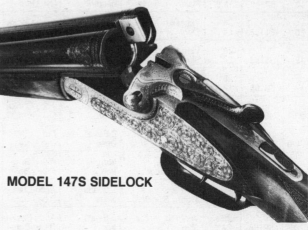

MODEL 147S SIDELOCK

MOSSBERG PUMP SHOTGUNS

MODEL 500 SPORTING

All Mossberg Model 500 pump-action shotguns feature Milspec tough, lightweight alloy receivers with "top thumb safety." Standard models include 6-shot capacity with 2¾" shells, cut-checkered stocks, Quiet Carry forearms, gold trigger, engraved receiver, blued or Marinecote metal finish and the largest selection of accessory barrels.

SPECIFICATIONS & PRICES MODEL 500 CROWN GRADE

Ga.	Stock #	Bbl. Length	Barrel Type	Sights	Chokes	Stock	Length O/A	Wt.	Q.D. Studs	Notes	Prices
12	54120	28"	Vent Rib	2 Beads	Accu-Choke	Walnut Finish	48"	7.2		I.C., Mod. & Full Tubes	$299.00
12	58126	24"	Plain	Iron	Accu-Choke	Walnut Finish	44"	7.0	Y	Mod. & X-Full Tubes	285.00
12	58117	28"	Vent Rib	2 Beads	Accu-Choke	Walnut Finish	48"	7.2		Mod. Tube Only	281.00
12	58116	26"	Vent Rib	2 Beads	Accu-Choke	Walnut Finish	46"	7.1		I.C. & Mod. Tubes	281.00
20	58132	22"	Vent Rib	2 Beads	Accu-Choke	Walnut Finish	42"	6.9		Mod. Tube Only, Bantam Stock	281.00
20	54136	26"	Vent Rib	2 Beads	Accu-Choke	Walnut Finish	46"	7.0		I.C., Mod. & Full Tubes	299.00
20	58137	26"	Vent Rib	2 Beads	Accu-Choke	Walnut Finish	46"	7.0		Mod. Tube Only	281.00
.410	50149	24"	Plain	2 Beads	Full	Synthetic	43"	6.8		Fixed Choke, Bantam Stock	285.00
.410	58104	24"	Vent Rib	2 Beads	Full	Walnut Finish	44"	6.8		Fixed Choke	287.00
12	54032	24"	Trophy Slugster™	None	Rifled Bore	Walnut Finish	44"	7.3	Y	Dual-Comb™ Stock	354.00
12	54044	24"	Slug	Iron	Rifled Bore	Walnut Finish	44"	7.0	Y		326.00
12	58045	24"	Slug	Iron	Cyl. Bore	Walnut Finish	44"	7.0	Y		288.00
12	50308	24"	Slug	Iron	Rifled Bore	Synthetic	44"	7.0	Y		415.00
12	50309	24"	Trophy Slugster™	None	Rifled Bore	Synthetic	44"	7.0	Y		415.00
20	54033	24"	Trophy Slugster™	None	Rifled Bore	Walnut Finish	44"	6.9	Y	Dual-Comb™ Stock	354.00
20	54051	24"	Slug	Iron	Rifled Bore	Walnut Finish	44"	6.9	Y		326.00
20	58050	24"	Slug	Iron	Cyl. Bore	Walnut Finish	44"	6.9	Y		288.00
20	58052	24"	Slug	Iron	Rifled Bore	Walnut Finish	44"	6.9	Y	Bantam Stock	326.00

SPECIFICATIONS MODEL 500 COMBOS

Ga.	Stock #	Bbl. Length	Barrel Type	Sights	Chokes	Stock	Length O/A	Wt.	Q.D. Studs	Notes	Prices
12	54043	28" 24"	Vent Rib Trophy Slugster™	2 Beads None	Accu-Choke Rifled Bore	Walnut Finish	48"	7.2	Y	I.C., Mod. & Full Tubes Dual-Comb™ Stock	$372.00
12	54164	28" 24"	Vent Rib Slug	2 Beads Iron	Accu-Choke Rifled Bore	Walnut Finish	48"	7.2	Y	I.C., Mod. & Full Tubes	356.00
12	58483	28" 18.5"	Plain Plain	Bead Bead	Modified Cyl. Bore	Walnut Finish	48"	7.2		Fixed Choke, Pistol Grip Kit	303.00
20	54182	26" 24"	Vent Rib Slug	2 Beads Iron	Accu-Choke Rifled Bore	Walnut Finish	46"	7.0	Y	I.C., Mod. & Full Tubes	356.00
12	58158	28" 24"	Vent Rib Slug	2 Beads Iron	Accu-Choke Cyl. Bore	Walnut Finish	48"	7.2		Mod. Tube Only	324.00
12	58169	28" 18.5"	Vent Rib Plain	2 Beads Bead	Accu-Choke Cyl. Bore	Walnut Finish	48"	7.2		Mod. Tube Only, Pistol Grip Kit	319.00
20	58186	26" 18.5"	Vent Rib Plain	2 Beads Bead	Accu-Choke Cyl. Bore	Walnut Finish	46"	7.3		Mod. Tube Only, Pistol Grip Kit	319.00
.410	58456	24" 18.5"	Vent Rib Plain	2 Beads Bead	Full Cyl. Bore	Walnut Finish	44"	6.8		Fixed Choke, Pistol Grip Kit	325.00
12	54153	24" 24"	Slug Muzzleloader	Iron Iron	Rifled Bore Rifled Bore	Walnut Finish	44"	7.0		.50 Cal., 1/26" Right Hand Twist	385.00
20	54083	26" 24"	Vent Rib Trophy Slugster	2 Beads None	Accu-Choke Rifled Bore	Walnut Finish	46"	7.0		I.C., Mod., Full Dual-Comb	372.00
20	58188	22" 24"	Vent Rib Slug	2 Beads Iron	Accu-Choke Rifled Bore	Walnut Finish	42"	7.0		Bantam, Mod.	338.00

MOSSBERG PUMP SHOTGUNS

MODEL 500 SPORTING

MODEL 500 TROPHY MARINER

MODEL 500 OFM WOODLAND CAMO

**MODEL 500 OFM WOODLAND CAMO
Ghost Ring Sights/Accu-Choke Barrel**

SPECIFICATIONS MODEL 500 WOODLAND CAMO (6-shot)

12	50197	28"	Vent Rib	2 Beads	Accu-Choke	Synthetic	48"	7.2	Y	Mod. Tube only	**$296.00**
12	50193	28"	Vent Rib	2 Beads	Accu-Choke	Synthetic	48"	7.2	Y	I.C., Mod. & Full Tubes	**325.00**
12	50195	24"	Vent Rib	2 Beads	Accu-Choke	Synthetic	44"	7.1	Y	I.C., Mod., Full & X-Full Tubes	**324.00**
12	50196	24"	Ghost Ring™ Sight	Ghost Ring™	Accu-Choke	Synthetic	44"	7.1	Y	I.C., Mod. Full & X-Full Tubes	**384.00**
20	58135	22"	Vent Rib	2 Beads	Accu-Choke	Synthetic	42"	6.8	Y	X-Full Tubes only	**309.00**
12	50213	28" 24"	Vent Rib Slug	2 Beads Iron	Accu-Choke Rifled Bore	Synthetic	48"	7.2	Y	I.C., Mod. & Full Tubes	**379.00**
12	50214	26" 24"	Vent Rib Slug	2 Beads Iron	Accu-Choke Rifled Bore	Synthetic	46"	6.9	Y	I.C., Mod. & Full Tubes	**379.00**

MODEL 500 AMERICAN FIELD (Pressed Checkered, Blued Barrel)

12	50117	28"	Vent Rib	2 Beads	Accu-Choke	Walnut Finish	48"	7.2		Mod. Tube Only	**$278.00**
20	50137	26"	Vent Rib	2 Beads	Accu-Choke	Walnut Finish	46"	7.1		Mod. Tube Only	**278.00**
.410	50104	24"	Vent Rib	2 Beads	Full	Walnut Finish	44"	7.0		Fixed Choke	**284.00**
12	50044	24"	Slug	Iron	Rifled Bore	Walnut Finish	44"	7.0	Y		**324.00**
12	50045	24"	Slug	Iron	Cyl. Bore	Walnut Finish	44"	7.0	Y		**285.00**
20	50050	24"	Slug	Iron	Cyl. Bore	Walnut Finish	44"	7.0	Y		**285.00**

MOSSBERG PUMP SHOTGUNS

MODEL 500/590 SPECIAL PURPOSE

Since 1979, Mossberg's Special Purpose Models 500 and 590 pump shotguns feature lightweight alloy receivers with ambidextrous "top thumb safety" button, walnut-finished wood or durable synthetic stocks with Quiet Carry™ forearms, rubber recoil pads, dual extractors, two slide bars and twin cartridge stops.

Gauge	Barrel Length	Sight	Stock #	Finish	Stock	Capacity	Overall Length	Weight	Notes	Price
MODEL 500/590 MARINER™										
12	18.5″	Bead	50273	Marinecote™	Synthetic	6	38.5″	6.8	Includes Pistol Grip	$403.00
12	20″	Bead	50299	Marinecote™	Synthetic	9	40″	7.0	Includes Pistol Grip	415.00
12	18.5″	Ghost Ring™	50276	Marinecote™	Synthetic	6	38.5″	6.8		459.00
12	20″	Ghost Ring™	50296	Marinecote™	Synthetic	9	40″	7.0		471.00
12	20″	—	50298	Marinecote™	Synthetic	—	40″	9.0	Line Launcher	999.00
MODEL 500 SPECIAL PURPOSE										
12	18.5″	Bead	50404	Blue	Walnut Finish	6	38.5″	6.8	Includes Pistol Grip	$281.00
12	18.5″	Bead	50411	Blue	Synthetic	6	38.5″	6.8	Includes Pistol Grip	281.00
12	18.5″	Bead	50412*	Blue	Synthetic	6	38.5″	6.8	Mod. Tube only	281.00
12	18.5″	Bead	50521	Parkerized	Synthetic	6	38.5″	6.8	Includes Pistol Grip	315.00
12	18.5″	Bead	50440	Blue	Pistol Grip	6	28″	5.6	Includes Heat Shield	272.00
20	18.5″	Bead	50451	Blue	Walnut Finish	6	38.5″	6.8	Includes Pistol Grip	281.00
20	18.5″	Bead	50452	Blue	Synthetic	6	38.5″	6.8	Includes Pistol Grip	279.00
20	18.5″	Bead	50450	Blue	Pistol Grip	6	28″	5.6		272.00
20	18.5″	Bead	50330	Blue	Pistol Grip	6	28″	5.6	Includes Camper Case	306.00
.410	18.5″	Bead	50455	Blue	Pistol Grip	6	28″	5.3		279.00
.410	18.5″	Bead	50335	Blue	Pistol Grip	6	28″	5.3	Includes Camper Case	312.00
12	20″	Iron	50570	Blue	Walnut Finish	8	40″	7.0	Includes Pistol Grip	304.00
12	20″	Bead	50564	Blue	Walnut Finish	8	40″	7.0	Includes Pistol Grip	281.00
12	20″	Bead	50576*	Blue	Synthetic	8	38.5″	6.9	Includes Mod. tube	281.00
12	20″	Bead	50579	Blue	Synthetic	8	40″	7.0	Includes Pistol Grip	281.00
12	20″	Bead	50580	Blue	Pistol Grip	8	40″	7.0	Includes Heat Shield	272.00
20	20″	Bead	50581	Blue	Synthetic	8	38.5″	6.9	Includes Pistol Grip	279.00
20	20″	Bead	50582	Blue	Pistol Grip	8	28.5″	5.6		272.00
MODEL 590 SPECIAL PURPOSE										
12	20″	Bead	50645	Blue	Synthetic	9	40″	7.2	w/Acc. Lug & Heat Shield	$329.00
12	20″	Bead	50650	Blue	Speed Feed	9	40″	7.2	w/Acc. Lug & Heat Shield	362.00
12	20″	Bead	50660	Parkerized	Synthetic	9	40″	7.2	w/Acc. Lug & Heat Shield	379.00
12	20″	Bead	50665	Parkerized	Speed Feed	9	40″	7.2	w/Acc. Lug & Heat Shield	412.00
MODEL 500/590 GHOST RING™										
12	18.5″	Ghost Ring™	50402	Blue	Synthetic	6	38.5″	6.8		$331.00
12	18.5″	Ghost Ring™	50517	Parkerized	Synthetic	6	38.5″	6.8		384.00
12	20″	Ghost Ring™	50652	Blue	Synthetic	9	40″	7.2	w/Acc. Lug	379.00
12	20″	Ghost Ring™	50662*	Parkerized	Synthetic	9	40″	7.2	w/Acc. Lug & Mod. Tube	454.00
12	20″	Ghost Ring™	50663	Parkerized	Synthetic	9	40″	7.2	w/Acc. Lug	432.00
12	20″	Ghost Ring™	50668	Parkerized	Speed Feed	9	40″	7.2	w/Acc. Lug	465.00
HS 410 HOME SECURITY										
.410	18.5″	Bead	50359	Blue	Synthetic	6	39.5″	6.6	Includes Vertical Foregrip	$295.00

* New models for 1995/6 include Accu-Choke; all others have Cyl. Bore.

MOSSBERG PUMP SHOTGUNS

MODEL 835 ULTI-MAG

Mossberg's Model 835 Ulti-Mag pump action shotgun has a 3½″ 12 gauge chamber but can also handle standard 2¾″ and 3″ shells. Field barrels are backbored for optimum patterns and felt recoil reduction. Cut checkered walnut and walnut-finished stocks and Quiet Carry™ forearms are standard, as are gold triggers and engraved receivers. Camo models are drilled and tapped for scope and feature detachable swivels and sling. All models include a Cablelock™ and 10-year limited warranty.

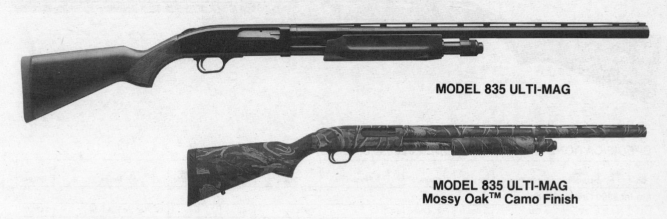

MODEL 835 ULTI-MAG

MODEL 835 ULTI-MAG
Mossy Oak™ Camo Finish

SPECIFICATIONS AND PRICES MODEL 835 ULTI-MAG (12 Gauge, 6 Shot)

Ga.	Stock No.	Barrel Length	Type	Sights	Choke	Finish	Stock	O.A. Length	Wt.	Studs	Notes	Price
Ulti-Mag™ 835 Crown Grade												
12	64110	28″	Vent Rib	2 Beads	Accu-Mag	Blue	Walnut	48.5″	7.7		4 Tubes* & Dual-Comb™ Stock	$412.00
12	64132	24″	Trophy Slugster™	None	Rifled Bore	Blue	Walnut	44.5″	7.3	Y	Dual-Comb™ Stock	434.00
12	64120	28″	Vent Rib	2 Beads	Accu-Mag	Blue	Walnut	48.5″	7.7		4 Tubes*	404.00
12	68120	28″	Vent Rib	2 Beads	Accu-Mag	Blue	Walnut Finish	48.5″	7.7		Mod. Tube Only	316.00
12	68125	24″	Vent Rib	2 Beads	Accu-Mag	Blue	Walnut Finish	44.5″	7.3		Mod. & X-Full Tubes	316.00
12	68144	28″ 24″	Vent Rib Trophy Slugster™	2 Beads None	Accu-Mag Rifled Bore	Blue	Walnut	48.5″	7.7		Mod. Tube only Dual-Comb™ Stock	407.00
12	68123	28″ 24″	Vent Rib Slug	2 Beads Iron	Accu-Mag Rifled Bore	Blue	Walnut	48.5″	7.7		Mod. Tube only	384.00
12	68160	28″ 24″	Vent Rib Slug	2 Beads Iron	Accu-Mag Cyl. Bore	Blue	Walnut Finish	48.5″	7.7		Mod. Tube Only	369.00
Ulti-Mag™ 835 Camo												
12	61034	24″	Vent Rib	2 Beads	Accu-Mag	Realtree®	Synthetic	44.5″	7.3	Y	4 Tube Turkey Pack**	493.00
12	60434	24″	Vent Rib	2 Beads	Accu-Mag	Mossy Oak®	Synthetic	44.5″	7.3	Y	4 Tube Turkey Pack**	493.00
12	61035	28″	Vent Rib	2 Beads	Accu-Mag	Realtree®	Synthetic	48.5″	7.7		4 Tubes*	493.00
12	60016	28″	Vent Rib	2 Beads	Accu-Mag	OFM Woodland	Synthetic	48.5″			4 Tubes*	441.00
12	68130	24″	Vent Rib	2 Beads	Accu-Mag	OFM Woodland	Synthetic	44.5″	7.3	Y	Mod. & X-Full Tubes	344.00
12	61147	24″ 24″	Vent Rib Slug	2 Beads Iron	Accu-Mag Rifled Bore	Realtree®	Synthetic	44.5″	7.3	Y	4 Tube Turkey Pack** Includes Hard Case	601.00
12	60148	28″ 24″	Vent Rib Slug	2 Beads Iron	Accu-Mag Rifled Bore	OFM Woodland	Wood/ Synthetic	48.5″	7.7	Y	4 Tubes* Dual-Comb™ Stock	515.00
Ulti-Mag™ 835 American Field (Pressed Checkering)												
12	61120	28″	Vent Rib	2 Beads	Accu-Mag	Blue	Walnut Finish	48.5″	7.7		Mod. Tube Only	313.00
Viking 835												
12	67120	28″	Vent Rib	2 Beads	Accu-Mag	Matte	Green Synthetic	48.5″	7.7	Y	Mod. Tube Only	301.00

SHOTGUNS

MOSSBERG SHOTGUNS

MODEL 9200 AUTOLOADERS

All Mossberg Model 9200 award-winning autoloader shotguns handle light 2³/₄″ or heavy 3″ magnum loads. Features include cut-checkered walnut stock and forearm, gold trigger, en-graved receiver, top thumb safety, light weight and easy shooting. All models include a Cablelock™ and a 10-year Lim-ited Warranty.

MODEL 9200

SPECIFICATIONS AND PRICES MODEL 9200 (12 Gauge, 5 Shot)

Ga.	Stock #	Bbl. Length	Barrel Type	Sights	Choke	Finish	Stock	Length O.A.	Wt.	Q.D. Studs	Notes	Prices
Model 9200 Crown Grade												
12	49420	28″	Vent Rib	2 Beads	Accu-Choke	Blue	Walnut	48″	7.7		I.C., Mod. & Full Tubes	$478.00
12	49425	24″	Vent Rib	2 Beads	Accu-Choke	Blue	Walnut	44″	7.3		I.C., Mod. & Full Tubes	478.00
12	49432	24″	Trophy Slugster™	None	Rifled Bore	Blue	Walnut	44″	7.3	Y	Dual-Comb™ Stock	500.00
12	49444	24″	Slug	Iron	Rifled Bore	Blue	Walnut	44″	7.3			478.00
12	49403	26″	Vent Rib	2 Beads	Accu-Choke	Blue	Walnut	46″	7.5		USST, I.C., Mod., Full & Skeet	478.00
12	49406	18.5″	Plain	Bead	Mod.	Matte Blue	Synthetic	39.5″	7.0	Y	Fixed Choke	463.00
12	49435	22″	Vent Rib	2 Beads	Accu-Choke	Blue	Walnut	42″	7.2		I.C./Mod., Full Bantam	478.00
12	49487	18.5″	Plain	Bead	Cyl. Bore	Matte	Synthetic	39.5″	7.0	Y	Fixed Choke	390.00
Model 9200 Camo												
12	49434	24″	Vent Rib	2 Beads	Accu-Choke	Mossy Oak®	Synthetic	44″	7.3	Y	I.C., Mod., Full & X-Full Tubes	562.00
12	49134	24″	Vent Rib	2 Beads	Accu-Choke	Realtree®/Matte Blue	Synthetic	44″	7.3	Y	I.C., Mod., Full & X-Full Tubes	562.00
12	49491	28″	Vent Rib	2 Beads	Accu-Choke	OFM Woodland	Synthetic	48″	7.7	Y	I.C., Mod. & Full Tubes	463.00
12	49430	24″	Vent. Rib	2 Beads	Accu-Choke	OFM Woodland	Synthetic	44″	7.3	Y	X-Full Tubes Only	432.00
12	47920	28″	Vent. Rib	2 Beads	Accu-Choke	Matte	Green Synthetic	48″	7.7	Y	Viking Mod. Tube	404.00
12	49466	28″ 24″	Vent Rib Slug	2 Beads Iron	Accu-Choke Rifled Bore	OFM Woodland OFM Woodland	Synthetic	48″	7.7	Y	I.C., Mod. & Full Tubes	535.00
12	49443	28″ 24″	Vent Rib Trophy Slugger™	2 Beads None	Accu-Choke Rifled Bore	Blued	Walnut	48″	7.7		I.C., Mod. & Full Tubes Dual-Comb™ Stock	563.00
12	49464	28″ 24″	Vent Rib Slug	2 Beads Iron	Accu-Choke Rifled Bore	Blued	Walnut	48″	7.7		I.C., Mod., & Full Tubes	546.00

MODEL 9200 OFM WOODLAND CAMO

MOSSBERG SHOTGUNS

MODEL 695

The new 3-inch chambered 12-gauge Model 695 bolt-action shotgun features a 22-inch barrel and rugged new synthetic stock. This combination delivers the fast handling and fine balance of a classic sporting rifle. In addition, every Model 695 comes with a two-round detachable magazine and Weaver-style scope bases to give hunters the advantage of today's specialized slug and turkey optics. The Model 695 Turkey and 695 Rifled Slug guns offer the security of positive extraction for those important follow-up shots.

Rifled slugs deliver tremendous energy. Mossberg's fully rifled slug barrels are specially ported to help soften the recoil and reduce muzzle jump. When combined with the synthetic rifle stock, the result is a fast handling and easier shooting slug gun. Mossberg's pioneering involvement with turkey hunting has also generated the development of the special Extra-full Accu-Choke Tube. The Model 695 Turkey Gun provides the precise pattern placement to make the most of this remarkably tight patterning choke tube. Non-rotating dual claw extractors ensure reliable ejection and feeding.

MOSSBERG MODEL 695 BOLT ACTION

MOSSBERG MODEL 695 OFM CAMO

Ga.	Model No.	Barrel Length	Barrel Type	Sights	Finish	Stock	Choke	Price
12	59001	22″	Rifle	Rifle	Matte	Synthetic	X-Full Turkey Accu-Choke	$293.00
12	59005	22″	Plain	Bead	Woodlands	Synthetic	X-Full Turkey Accu-Choke	276.00

MOSSBERG LINE LAUNCHER
$999.00   ($735.00 Launcher Kit)

The Line Launcher is the first shotgun devoted to rescue and personal safety. It provides an early self-contained rescue opportunity for boaters, police and fire departments, salvage operations or whenever an extra-long throw of line is the safest alternative. This shotgun uses a 12-gauge blank cartridge to propel a convertible projectile with a line attached. With a floating head attached, the projectile will travel 250 to 275 feet. Removing the floating head increases the projectile range to approx. 700 feet. The braided 360-lb. test floating line is highly visible and is supplied inside on an 800' coiled spool.

NEW ENGLAND FIREARMS

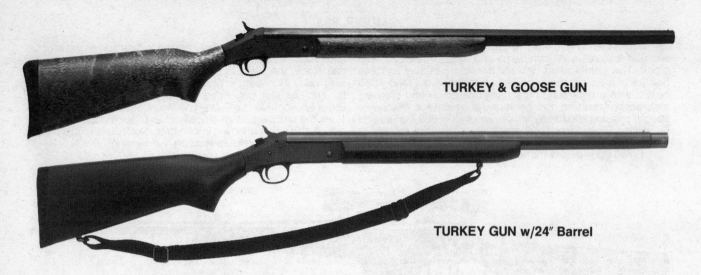

TURKEY & GOOSE GUN

TURKEY GUN w/24″ Barrel

TURKEY & GOOSE GUN
$149.95
($159.95 w/Camo Paint, Swivels & Sling)

SPECIFICATIONS
Gauge: 10 (3¹/₂″ chamber)   **Choke:** Full
Barrel length: 28″   **Overall length:** 44″

Weight: 9¹/₂ lbs.
Sights: Bead sights
Stock: American hardwood; walnut or camo finish; full pistol grip; ventilated recoil pad.   **Length of pull:** 14¹/₂″
Also available:
TURKEY GUN. With 24″ screw-in barrel, turkey Full choke, black matte finish, swivels and sling. **Price: $184.95**

SPECIAL PURPOSE WATERFOWL SINGLE SHOT
$179.95

This sporting shotgun features a 32″ barrel, Modified choke, camo paint finish, swivels and sling.

TRACKER II RIFLED SLUG GUN
$139.95

SPECIFICATIONS
Gauges: 12 and 20 (3″ chamber)   **Choke:** Rifled bore
Barrel length: 24″   **Overall length:** 40″
Weight: 6 lbs.
Sights: Adjustable rifle sights

Length of pull: 14¹/₂″
Stock: American hardwood; walnut or camo finish; full pistol grip; recoil pad; sling swivel studs
Also available:
TRACKER SLUG GUN w/Cylinder Bore: $129.95

NEW ENGLAND FIREARMS

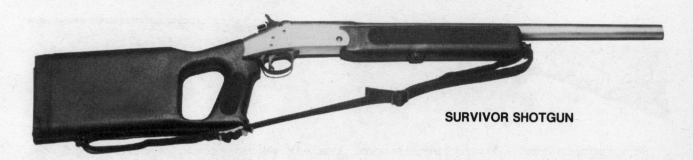

SURVIVOR SHOTGUN

SURVIVOR SERIES

This new series of survival arms is available in 12 and 20 ga. with either a blued or electroless nickel finish. All shotguns feature the New England Firearms action with a patented transfer bar safety and high-impact, synthetic stock and forend. The stock is a modified thumbhole design with a full and secure pistol grip. The buttplate is attached at one end with a large thumbscrew for access to a large storage compartment holding a wide variety of survival gear or extra ammunition. The forend, which has a hollow cavity for storing three rounds of ammunition, is accessible by removing a thumbscrew (also used for takedown).

SPECIFICATIONS
Action: Break open, side-lever release, automatic ejection
Gauge: 12, 20, .410/45 Colt (Combo)
Barrel length: 22″ **Choke:** Modified
Chamber: 3″ (Combo also available w/2½″ chamber)
Overall length: 36″ **Weight:** 6 lbs.
Sights: Bead
Stock: High-density polymer, black matte finish, sling swivels
Prices:
Blued finish **$129.95**
Nickel finish **145.95**
.410/45 Colt Combo **264.95**

PARDNER YOUTH

PARDNER SINGLE-BARREL SHOTGUNS
$99.95   ($104.95 w/32″ Barrel)

SPECIFICATIONS
Gauges: 12, 16, 20, 28 and .410
Barrel lengths: 22″ (Youth); 26″ (20, 28, .410);
   28″ (12 and 16 ga.), 32″ (12 ga.)
Chokes: Full (all gauges, except 28);
   Modified (12, 20 and 28 ga.)

Chamber: 2¾″ (16 and 28 ga.); 3″ (all others)
Also available:
PARDNER YOUTH. With 22″ barrel in gauges 20, 28 and .410.
Price: **$109.95**

SHOTGUNS

PARKER REPRODUCTIONS

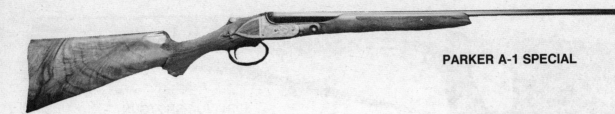

PARKER A-1 SPECIAL

Recognized by the shooting fraternity as the finest American shotgun ever produced, the Parker A-1 Special is again available. Exquisite engraving and rare presentation-grade French walnut distinguish the A-1 Special from any other shotguns in the world. Currently offered in 12 and 20 gauge, each gun is custom-fitted in its own oak and leather trunk case. Two models are offered: Hand Engraved and Custom Engraved. Also available in D Grade.

Standard features: Automatic safety, selective ejectors, skeleton steel butt plate, splinter forend, engraved snap caps, fitted leather trunk case, canvas and leather case cover, chrome barrel interiors, hand-checkering. The A-1 Special also features a 24k gold initial plate or pistol cap, 32 lines-per-inch

checkering, selected wood and fine hand-engraving. Choose from single or double trigger, English or pistol grip stock (all models). Options include beavertail forend, additional barrels.

In addition to the A-1 Special, the D-Grade is available in 12, 20, 16/20 and 28 gauge. A 16-gauge, 28″ barrel can be ordered with a 20-gauge one or two-barrel set. The two-barrel sets come in a custom leather cased with a fitted over cover.

Prices: D-GRADE
One Barrel—12, 20, 28 gauge $3370.00
Two-barrel set **4200.00**
16/20 Combo **4870.00**
20/20/16 Combo **5630.00**

SPECIFICATIONS

Gauge	Barrel Length	Chokes	Chambers	Drop At Comb	Drop At Heel	Length of Pull	Nominal Weight (lbs.)	Overall Length
12	26″	Skeet I & II or IC/M	2³⁄₄″	1³⁄₈″	2³⁄₁₆″	14¹⁄₈″	6³⁄₄	42⁵⁄₈″
12	28″	IC/M or M/F	2³⁄₄ & 3″	1³⁄₈″	2³⁄₁₆″	14¹⁄₈″	6³⁄₄	44⁵⁄₈″
20	26″	Skeet I & II or IC/M	2³⁄₄″	1³⁄₈″	2³⁄₁₆″	14³⁄₈″	6¹⁄₂	42³⁄₈″
20	28″	M/F	3″	1³⁄₈″	2³⁄₁₆″	14³⁄₈″	6¹⁄₂	44⁵⁄₈″
16 on 20 frame	28″	Skeet I & II, IC/M or M/F	2³⁄₄″	1³⁄₈″	2³⁄₁₆″	14³⁄₈″	6¹⁄₄	44⁵⁄₈″
28	26″	Skeet I & II or IC/M	2³⁄₄″	1³⁄₈″	2³⁄₁₆″	14³⁄₈″	5¹⁄₃	42⁵⁄₈″
28	28″	M/F	2³⁄₄ & 3″	1³⁄₈″	2³⁄₁₆″	14³⁄₈″	5¹⁄₃	44⁵⁄₈″

* Note: The 16-gauge barrels are lighter than the 20-gauge barrels.

PERAZZI SHOTGUNS

Today the name *Perazzi* has become synonymous with excellence in competitive shooting. The heart of the Perazzi line is the classic over/under, whose barrels are soldered into a monobloc that holds the shell extractors. At the sides are the two locking lugs that link the barrels to the action, which is machined from a solid block of forged steel. Barrels come with flat, step or raised ventilated rib. The walnut forend, finely checkered, is available with schnabel, beavertail or English styling, and the walnut stock can be of standard, Monte Carlo, Skeet or English design. Double or single nonselective or selective triggers. Sideplates and receiver are masterfully engraved.

OVER/UNDER GAME MODELS

GAME MODEL MX20C

GAME MODELS MX8, MX12, MX20, MX8/20, MX28 & MX410

SPECIFICATIONS
Gauges: 12, 20, 28 & .410
Chambers: 2³/₄″; also available in 3″
Barrel lengths: 26″ and 27¹/₂″
Weight: 6 lbs. 6 oz. to 7 lbs. 4 oz.
Trigger group: Nondetachable with coil springs and selective trigger

Stock: Interchangeable and custom; schnabel forend
Prices:
Standard Grade . . . . $ 8,090.00–$16,170.00
SC3 Grade 13,700.00– 21,780.00
SCO Grade 23,380.00– 31,470.00
SCO Gold Grades 26,320.00– 34,400.00

AMERICAN TRAP COMBO MODELS
(MX6, MX10, MX11, MX14, MX8 SPECIAL, DB81 SPECIAL)

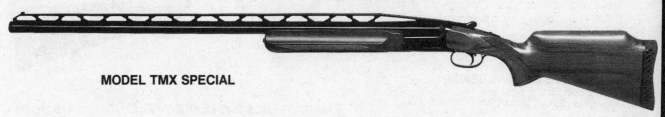

MODEL TMX SPECIAL

COMBO MODEL MX9 (Not Shown)

SPECIFICATIONS
Gauge: 12   **Chamber:** 2³/₄″
Barrel lengths: 29¹/₂″ and 31¹/₂″ (O/U); 32″ and 34″ (single barrel)   **Chokes:** Mod./Full (O/U); Full (single barrel)
Weight (avg.): 8 lbs. 6 oz.
Trigger group: Detachable and interchangeable with flat "V" springs
Stock: Interchangeable and custom; beavertail forend
Prices:
Standard Grade . . . . $ 7,920.00–$13,700.00
SC3 Grade 17,770.00– 19,800.00
SCO Grade 28,380.00– 29,700.00
Gold Grade 31,470.00– 32,650.00

AMERICAN TRAP SINGLE-BARREL MODELS
MX15 & TMX SPECIAL

SPECIFICATIONS
Gauge: 12
Chamber: 2³/₄″
Barrel lengths: 32″ and 34″
Weight: 8 lbs. 6 oz.
Choke: Full
Trigger group: Detachable and interchangeable with coil springs
Stock: Interchangeable and custom made
Forend: Beavertail
Prices:
TMX Special $6590.00
MX15 . . . . 6875.00

SHOTGUNS

PERAZZI SHOTGUNS

COMPETITION OVER/UNDER SHOTGUNS
OLYMPIC, DOUBLE TRAP, SKEET, PIGEON & ELECTROCIBLES

MODEL MX10

MODEL DB81 TRAP

MX8 SKEET

MIRAGE SPORTING

SPECIFICATIONS STANDARD GRADE
Gauges: 12 and 20
Barrel lengths: 27¹/₂″, 28³/₈″, 29¹/₂″, 30³/₄″, 31¹/₂″
Prices:
MX6 12 ga. removable trigger group
   29¹/₂″, 30³/₄″ and 31¹/₂″ barrels . . . . $ 6,270.00
MX8-MIRAGE 12 ga., removable trigger group
   29¹/₂″, 30³/₄″ and 31¹/₂″ barrels 8,090.00
MX8-MIRAGE SPECIAL 12 ga., removable trigger group
   29¹/₂″, 30³/₄″ and 31¹/₂″ barrels 8,570.00–9,160.00
MX10 12 & 20 ga. w/adj. stock and rib
   29¹/₂″, 30³/₄″ and 31¹/₂″ bbl. 10,300.00–11,340.00
MX11 12 ga., removable trigger group
   29¹/₂″, 30³/₄″ and 31¹/₂″ bbl. 7,620.00–8,690.00
MX8/20 20 ga., removable trigger group
   26³/₄″, 27¹/₂″, 28³/₈″, 29¹/₂″, 30³/₄″ and
   31¹/₂″ barrels 8,290.00–9,160.00
MIRAGE SPECIAL 12 ga. w/adj. trigger,
   28³/₈″, 29¹/₂″, 31¹/₂″ barrels 8,570.00
MIRAGE SPECIAL SPORTING 12 ga. w/external
   selector and 5 chokes; 27¹/₂″, 28³/₈″,
   29¹/₂″ and 31¹/₂″ barrels 9,160.00

MIRAGE SPORTING CLASSIC 12 ga. $10,200.00
MX8 SPECIAL 12 ga. w/adjustable trigger
   29¹/₂″ and 31¹/₂″ barrels 9,160.00
DB81 SPECIAL w/adjustable trigger
   29¹/₂″, 30³/₄″ and 31¹/₂″ barrels 8,810.00

NOTE: PIGEON & ELECTROCIBLE MODELS available in MX1B, Mirage, Mirage Special, MX10 & MX11 only w/27¹/₂″, 28³/₄″, 29¹/₂″ & 31¹/₂″ barrels . . . . $7,400.00–$10,300.00
Also available:
SC3 Grade (Models MX8, MX10, MX10/20,
   MX8/20, MX8 Special, Mirage
   Spec., DB81 Spec.) . . . . $13,700.00–$15,600.00
SCO Grade (same models as SC3
   Grade) 23,330.00– 24,650.00
SCO GOLD Grade (same models
   as above) 26,320.00– 27,450.00
SCO Grade Sideplates (same
   models as above) 35,790.00– 36,280.00
SCO GOLD Grade Sideplates (same
   models above) 41,560.00– 42,040.00

PIOTTI SHOTGUNS

One of Italy's top gunmakers, Piotti limits its production to a small number of hand-crafted, best-quality double-barreled shotguns whose shaping, checkering, stock, action and barrel work meets or exceeds the standards achieved in London before WWII. All of the sidelock models exhibit the same overall design, materials and standards of workmanship; they differ only in the quality of the wood, shaping and sculpturing of the action, type of engraving and gold inlay work and other details. The Model Piuma differs from the other shotguns only in its Anson & Deeley boxlock design. Piotti's new over/under model appears below.

SPECIFICATIONS
Gauges: 10, 12, 16, 20, 28, .410
Chokes: As ordered
Barrels: 12 ga., 25″ to 32″; other gauges, 25″ to 30″; chopper lump (demi-bloc) barrels with soft-luster blued finish; level, file-cut rib or optional concave
Action: Boxlock, Anson & Deeley; Sidelock, Holland & Holland pattern; both have automatic ejectors, double triggers with yielding front trigger (non-selective single trigger optional), coin finish or optional color casehardening
Stock: Hand-rubbed oil finish on straight grip stock with checkered butt (pistol grip optional)
Forend: Classic (splinter); optional beavertail
Weight: 5 lbs. 4 oz. (.410 ga.) to 8 lbs. 4 oz. (12 ga.)

SIDELOCK OVER/UNDER
$35,600.00 (and up depending on engraving)

Available in 12 or 20 ga. w/2¾″ or 3″ chambers and 26″ to 32″ barrels. Weight varies from 6 lbs. to 6 lbs. 12 oz. (20 ga.) and 7–8 lbs. (12 ga.). Single or double triggers. Circassion (Turkish) wood

MODEL PIUMA BOXLOCK
$11,800.00

Anson & Deeley boxlock ejector double with chopper lump (demi-bloc) barrels, and scalloped frame. Very attractive scroll and rosette engraving is standard.

MODEL KING NO. 1 SIDELOCK
$20,600.00

Best-quality Holland & Holland pattern sidelock ejector double with chopper lump barrels, choice of rib, very fine, full coverage scroll engraving with small floral bouquets, finely figured wood.

MODEL LUNIK SIDELOCK
$22,200.00

Best-quality Holland & Holland pattern sidelock ejector double with chopper lump (demi-bloc) barrels, choice of rib, Renaissance-style, large scroll engraving in relief, finely figured wood.

MODEL KING EXTRA (not shown)
$26,500.00 (and up depending on engraving)

Best-quality Holland & Holland pattern sidelock ejector double with chopper lump barrels, choice of rib and bulino game-scene engraving or game-scene engraving with gold inlays; engraved and signed by a master engraver.

REMINGTON SHOTGUNS

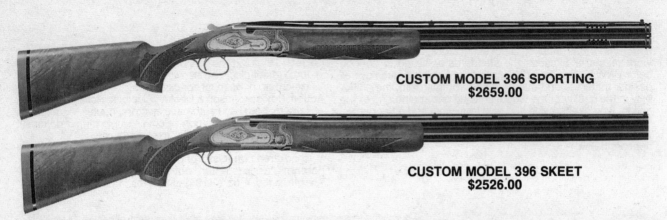

CUSTOM MODEL 396 SPORTING
$2659.00

CUSTOM MODEL 396 SKEET
$2526.00

CUSTOM MODEL 396 OVER/UNDER SHOTGUN (SKEET AND SPORTING CLAYS)

The new Model 396 is produced in 12-gauge Skeet and Sporting Clays versions. Chrome-moly barrels in both versions have lengthened forcing cones, are fitted with side ribs, and have a flat 10-millimeter-wide parallel vent rib. Barrel lengths are 28″ or 30″. All barrels are fitted for the interchangeable Rem Choke system. Skeet and Improved Skeet choke tubes are supplied for the Model 396 Skeet, and four choke tubes—Skeet, Improved Skeet, Improved Cylinder and Modified configurations—for the Model 396 Sporting. The Sporting Clays version also features factory porting on both barrels.

Barrels and side ribs are finished with high-polished deep bluing. The receiver and sideplates, trigger guard, top lever and forend metal are finished with gray nitride coloring.

Extensive scroll work appears on the receiver, trigger guard, tang, hinge pins and forend metal. The sideplates include detailed renditions of a pointer and setter on the left and right sides, respectively. Identifying individual versions of the Model 396 on both sideplates are the words ''Sporting'' or ''Skeet'' in script lettering. Additional scroll work, the Remington logo and the model designation appear on the floorplate.

Stocks on both models are selected from fancy American walnut and given a soft satin finish. Several stock design features are specifically adapted to clay target shooting, including a wider, target-style forend, a comb with larger radius and a universal palm swell on the pistol grip.

SPECIFICATIONS
Gauge: 12   **Chamber:** 2³/₄″
Choke: Rem Choke
Length of pull: 14³/₁₆″
Drop at comb: 1¹/₂″   **Drop at heel:** 2¹/₄″
Barrel lengths: 28″ and 30″
Overall length: 45″ and 47″
Weight: 7¹/₂ lbs. and 7³/₈ lbs.

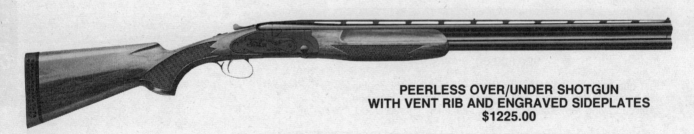

PEERLESS OVER/UNDER SHOTGUN WITH VENT RIB AND ENGRAVED SIDEPLATES
$1225.00

Practical, lightweight, well-balanced and affordable are the attributes of this Remington shotgun. Features include an all-steel receiver, boxlock action and removable sideplates (engraved with a pointer on one side and a setter on the other). The bottom of the receiver has the Remington logo, plus the words ''Peerless, Field'' and the serial number. Cut-checkering appears on both pistol grip and forend (shaped with finger grooves and tapered toward the front). The buttstock is fitted with a black, vented recoil pad. The stock is American walnut.

SPECIFICATIONS
Gauge: 12 (3″ chamber)
Chokes: REM Choke System (1 Full, 1 Mod., 1 Imp. Cyl.)

Barrel lengths: 26″, 28″, 30″ with vent rib
Overall length: 43″ (26″ barrel); 45″ (28″ barrel); 47″ (30″ barrel)
Weight: 7¹/₄ lbs. (26″); 7³/₈ lbs. (28″); 7¹/₂ lbs. (30″)
Trigger: Single, selective, gold-plated
Safety: Automatic safety
Sights: Target gun style with mid-bead and Bradley-type front bead
Length of pull: 14³/₁₆″
Drop at comb: 1¹/₂″   **Drop at heel:** 2¹/₄″
Features: Solid, horseshoe-shaped locking bar with two rectangular lug extensions on either side of the barrel's midbore; fast lock time (3.28 milliseconds)

REMINGTON SHOTGUNS

MODEL 90-T SINGLE-BARREL TRAP GUN
$3199.00
($3992.00 w/High Post, Adj. Rib)

Remington's **Model 90-T Single Barrel Trap** features a top-lever release and internal, full-width, horizontal bolt lockup. Barrel is overbored, with elongated forcing cone, and is available in 34″ length. A medium-high, tapered, ventilated rib includes a white, Bradley-type front bead and stainless steel center bead. Choice of stocks includes Monte Carlo style with 1³/₈″, 1¹/₂″ or 1¹/₄″ drop at comb, or a conventional straight stock with 1¹/₂″ drop. Standard length of pull is 14³/₈″. Stocks and modified beavertail forends are made from semifancy American walnut. Wood finish is low-luster satin with positive, deep-cut checkering 20 lines to the inch. All stocks come with black, vented-rubber recoil pads. **Overall length:** 51″. **Weight:** Approx. 8³/₄ lbs. **Choke:** Full.

MODEL 870 EXPRESS "YOUTH" GUN
20-Gauge Lightweight
$292.00 $325.00 (w/Deer Barrel)

The **Model 870 Express "Youth" Gun** has been specially designed for youths and smaller-sized adults. It's a 20-gauge lightweight with a 1-inch shorter stock and 21-inch barrel. Yet it is still all 870, complete with REM Choke and ventilated rib barrel. Also available with a 20″ fully rifled, rifle-sighted deer barrel. **Barrel length:** 21″. **Stock Dimensions:** Length of pull 12¹/₂″ (including recoil pad); drop at heel; 2¹/₂″ drop at comb 1⁵/₈″. **Overall length:** 39″. **Average Weight:** 6 lbs. **Choke:** REM Choke-Mod. (vent-rib version).

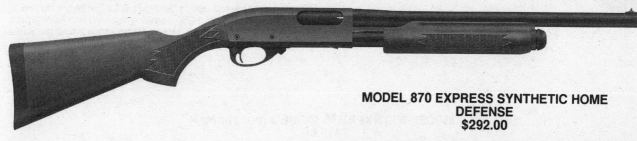

MODEL 870 EXPRESS SYNTHETIC HOME DEFENSE
$292.00

This new shotgun is designed specifically for home defense use. The 12-gauge pump-action shotgun features an 18″ barrel with Cylinder choke and front bead sight. Barrel and action have the traditional Express-style metal finish. The synthetic stock and forend have a textured black, nonreflective finish and feature positive checkering. **Capacity:** 4 rounds.

REMINGTON PUMP SHOTGUNS

MODEL 870 EXPRESS (20 GA.)

MODEL 870 EXPRESS
$292.00 (12 & 20 GA.)
($299.00 w/Black Synthetic Stock & Forend)

Model 870 Express features the same action as the Wing-master and is available with 3″ chamber and 26″ or 28″ vent-rib barrel. It has a hardwood stock with low-luster finish and solid buttpad. Choke is Modified REM Choke tube and wrench. **Overall length:** 48 1/2″ (28″ barrel). **Weight:** 7 1/4 lbs (26″ barrel).

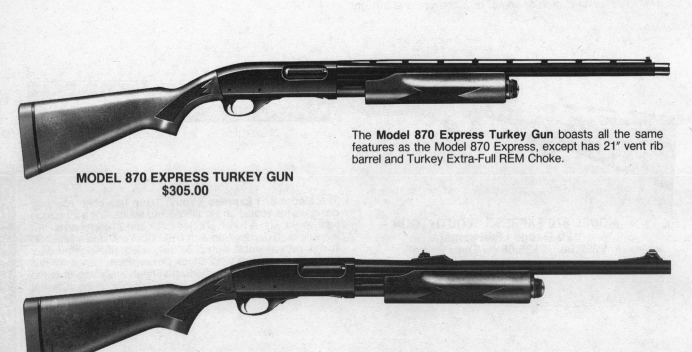

MODEL 870 EXPRESS TURKEY GUN
$305.00

The **Model 870 Express Turkey Gun** boasts all the same features as the Model 870 Express, except has 21″ vent rib barrel and Turkey Extra-Full REM Choke.

MODEL 870 EXPRESS DEER GUN
$287.00 With Rifle Sights
($325.00 Fully Rifled)

This 12-gauge, pump-action deer gun is for hunters who prefer open sights. Features a 20″ barrel, quick-reading iron sights, fixed Imp. Cyl. choke and Monte Carlo stock. Also available with fully rifled barrel.

MODEL 870 EXPRESS COMBO (not shown)
$395.00

The **Model 870 Express** in 12 and 20 gauge offers all the features of the standard Model 870, including twin-action bars, quick-changing 28″ barrels, REM Choke and vent rib plus low-luster, checkered hardwood stock and no-shine finish on barrel and receiver. The Model 870 Combo is packaged with an extra 20″ deer barrel, fitted with rifle sights and fixed, Improved Cylinder choke (additional REM chokes can be added for special applications). The 3-inch chamber handles all 2 3/4″ and 3″ shells without adjustment. **Weight:** 7 1/2 lbs.

REMINGTON PUMP SHOTGUNS

SPECIAL PURPOSE

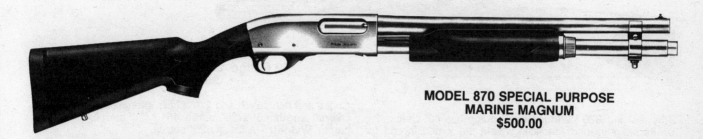

**MODEL 870 SPECIAL PURPOSE
MARINE MAGNUM
$500.00**

Remington's **Model 870 Special Purpose Marine Magnum** is a versatile, multipurpose security gun featuring a rugged synthetic stock and extensive, electroless nickel plating on all metal parts. This new shotgun utilizes a standard 12-gauge Model 870 receiver with a 7-round magazine extension tube and an 18″ cylinder barrel (38½″ overall) with bead front sight.

The receiver, magazine extension and barrel are protected (inside and out) with heavy-duty, corrosion-resistant nickel plating. The synthetic stock and forend reduce the effects of moisture. The gun is supplied with a black rubber recoil pad, sling swivel studs, and positive checkering on both pistol grip and forend. **Weight:** 7½ lbs.

**MODEL 870 SPS-CAMO
$483.00**

This Mossy Oak Bottomland™ Camo version of Model 11-87 and Model 870 Special Purpose Synthetic shotguns features a durable camo finish and synthetic stocks that are immune to the effects of ice, snow and mud. Available with a 26″ vent-rib barrel with twin bead sights and Imp. Cyl., Modified, and Full REM Choke tubes.

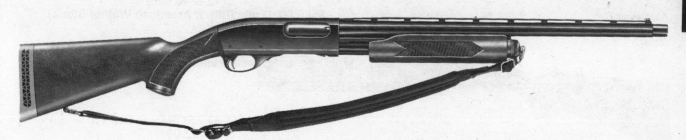

**MODEL 870 SPST ALL BLACK
TURKEY GUN
$412.00**

Same as the Model 870 SPS above, except with a 21″ vent-rib turkey barrel and Extra-Full REM Choke tube.
Also available:
Mossy Oak Greenleaf Camo finish **$497.00**
20″ fully rifled cantilever deer barrel
  (All Black) **483.00**
20″ fully rifled deer barrel, rifle sights **423.00**

REMINGTON SHOTGUNS

MODEL 870 WINGMASTER
12 Gauge, Light Contour Barrel
$505.00

This restyled **870 "Wingmaster"** pump has cut-checkering on its satin-finished American walnut stock and forend for confident handling, even in wet weather. Also available in Hi-Gloss finish. An ivory bead "Bradley"-type front sight is included. Rifle is available with 26″, 28″ and 30″ barrel with REM

Choke and handles 3″ and 2¾″ shells interchangeably.
Overall length: 46½ (26″ barrel), 48½ (28″ barrel), 50½ (30″ barrel). **Weight:** 7¼ lbs. (w/26″ barrel).
Also available:
MODEL 870 WINGMASTER. 20 Ga. Lightweight (6½ lbs.), American walnut stock and forend. **Price:** **$492.00**

MODEL 870 SP (SPECIAL PURPOSE)
ALL BLACK DEER GUN
$423.00

Gauge: 12. **Choke:** Fully rifled with rifle sights, recoil pad.
Barrel length: 20″. **Overall length:** 40½.″ **Average weight:** 7 lbs.

MODEL 870 WINGMASTER
CANTILEVER SCOPE MOUNT DEER GUN
(12 & 20 Ga.)
$585.00 (Fully Rifled, American Walnut Stock)

Also available:
Engraved **Model 870 Wingmaster** in Grade D. Price on request.

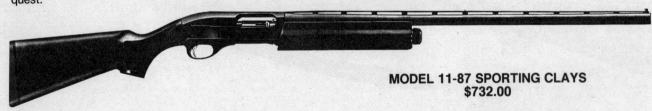

MODEL 11-87 SPORTING CLAYS
$732.00

Remington's new **Model 11-87 Premier Sporting Clays** features a target-grade, American walnut competition stock with a length of pull that is ³/₁₆″ longer and ¼″ higher at the heel. The tops of the receiver, barrel and rib have a nonreflective matte finish. The rib is medium high with a stainless mid-bead and ivory front bead. The barrel (26″ or 28″) has a lengthened

forcing cone to generate greater pattern uniformity; and there are 5 REM choke tubes—Skeet, Improved Skeet, Improved Cylinder, Modified and Full. All sporting clays choke tubes have a knurled end extending .45″ beyond the muzzle for fast field changes. Both the toe and heel of the buttpad are rounded. **Weight:** 7½ lbs. (26″); 7⅝ lbs. (28″)

REMINGTON AUTO SHOTGUNS

MODEL 11-87 PREMIER AUTOLOADER
$670.00 (Light-Contour Barrel)
$720.00 (Left Hand, 28″ Barrel)

Remington's redesigned 12-gauge **Model 11-87 Premier Autoloader** features new, light-contour barrels that reduce both barrel weight and overall weight (more than 8 ounces). The shotgun has a standard 3-inch chamber and handles all 12-gauge shells interchangeably—from 2¾″ field loads to 3″ Magnums. The gun's interchangeable REM choke system includes Improved Cylinder, Modified and Full chokes. Select

American walnut stocks with fine-line, cut-checkering in satin or high-gloss finish are standard. Right-hand models are available in 26″, 28″ and 30″ barrels (left-hand models are 28″ only). A two-barrel gun case is supplied.
Also available: 21″ fully rifled cantilever deer barrel (41″ overall).
Weight: 8½ lbs. **Price:** **$734.00**

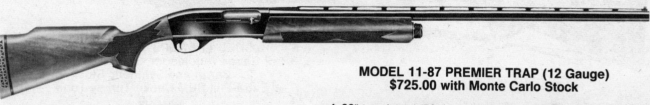

MODEL 11-87 PREMIER TRAP (12 Gauge)
$725.00 with Monte Carlo Stock

A 30″ trap barrel (50½″ overall) offers trap shooters a REM Choke system with three interchangeable choke constrictions: trap full, trap extra full, and trap super full. **Weight:** 8¾ lbs.

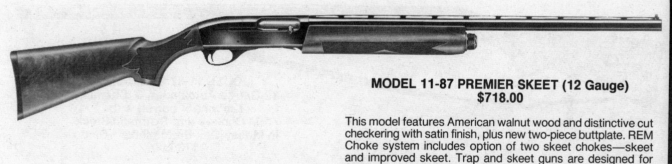

MODEL 11-87 PREMIER SKEET (12 Gauge)
$718.00

This model features American walnut wood and distinctive cut checkering with satin finish, plus new two-piece buttplate. REM Choke system includes option of two skeet chokes—skeet and improved skeet. Trap and skeet guns are designed for 12-gauge target loads and are set to handle 2¾″ shells only.
Barrel length: 26″. **Overall length:** 46″. **Weight:** 8⅛ lbs.

MODEL 11-87 PREMIER DEER GUN
With Cantilever Scope Mount and
Fully Rifled 21″ Barrel
$734.00 (Satin Finish)

REMINGTON AUTO SHOTGUNS

MODEL 11-87 SPS (Special Purpose Synthetic)
12 Gauge Autoloader, 3″ Chamber w/Wood or
Synthetic Stock and REM Chokes
26″ or 28″ Vent-Rib Barrels
$644.00

MODEL 11-87 SPST TURKEY GUN
12 Gauge Autoloader, 3″ Chamber with
21″ Barrel and Synthetic Stock
Extra-Full REM Choke Turkey Tube
$657.00
$744.00 w/Mossy Oak Greenleaf Camo Finish

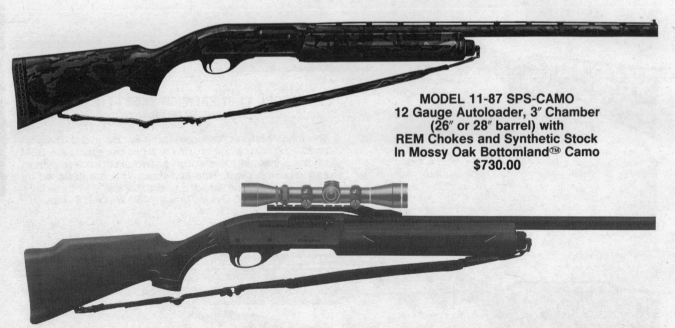

MODEL 11-87 SPS-CAMO
12 Gauge Autoloader, 3″ Chamber
(26″ or 28″ barrel) with
REM Chokes and Synthetic Stock
In Mossy Oak Bottomland™ Camo
$730.00

**MODEL 11-87 SPS SPECIAL PURPOSE
SYNTHETIC ALL-BLACK DEER GUN**
$665.00 (3″ Magnum)
$725.00 (Fully Rifled Cantilever)

Features the same finish as other SP models plus a padded, camo-style carrying sling of Cordura nylon with Q.D. sling swivels. Barrel is 21″ (41″ overall) with rifle sights and rifled and IC choke (handles all 2¾″ and 3″ rifled slug and buckshot loads as well as high-velocity field and magnum loads; does not function with light 2¾″ field loads). **Weight:** 8½ lbs.

REMINGTON AUTO SHOTGUNS

MODEL 1100 AUTOLOADING SHOTGUNS

The Remington **Model 1100** is a 5-shot gas-operated auto-loading shotgun with a gas-metering system designed to reduce recoil effect. This design enables the shooter to use all 2³/₄-inch standard velocity ''Express'' and 2³/₄-inch Magnum loads without any gun adjustments. Barrels, within gauge and versions, are interchangeable. The 1100 is made in gauges of 12, Lightweight 20, 28 and .410. All 12- and 20-gauge versions include REM Choke; interchangeable choke tubes in 26″ and

28″ (12 gauge only) barrels. The solid-steel receiver features decorative scroll work. Stocks come with fine-line checkering in a fleur-de-lis design combined with American walnut and a scratch-resistant finish. Features include white-diamond inlay in pistol-grip cap, white-line spacers, full beavertail forend, fluted-comb cuts, chrome-plated bolt and metal bead front sight. Made in the U.S.A. See also following page for description and specifications of **Model 1100 Sporting 28.**

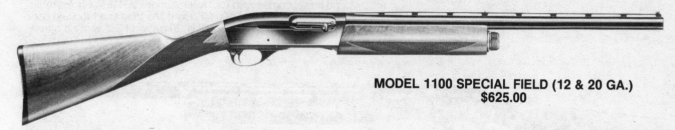

MODEL 1100 SPECIAL FIELD (12 & 20 GA.)
$625.00

The **Model 1100 "Special Field"** shotgun combines traditional, straight-stock styling with its 23-inch vent-rib barrel and slimmed and shortened forend. REM choke. Non-engraved receiver; non-Magnum extra barrels are interchangeable with standard Model 1100 barrels. **Overall length:** 41″. **Stock di-**

mensions: Length of pull 14¹/₈″; drop at comb 1¹/₂″; drop at heel 2¹/₂″. **Weight:** 7¹/₄ lbs. (12 ga.); 6¹/₂ lbs. (20 ga.). Also available w/synthetic stock and forend, black matte metal finish plus positive checkering and black rubber recoil pads.
Price: **$479.00**

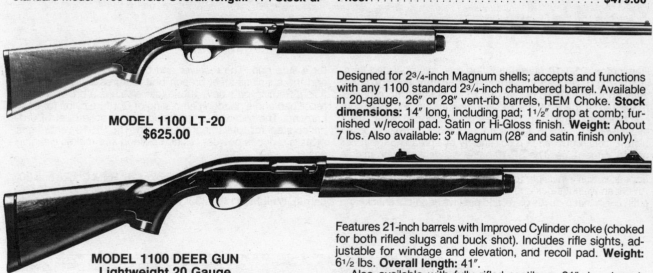

MODEL 1100 LT-20
$625.00

Designed for 2³/₄-inch Magnum shells; accepts and functions with any 1100 standard 2³/₄-inch chambered barrel. Available in 20-gauge, 26″ or 28″ vent-rib barrels, REM Choke. **Stock dimensions:** 14″ long, including pad; 1¹/₂″ drop at comb; furnished w/recoil pad. Satin or Hi-Gloss finish. **Weight:** About 7 lbs. Also available: 3″ Magnum (28″ and satin finish only).

MODEL 1100 DEER GUN
Lightweight 20 Gauge
$584.00

Features 21-inch barrels with Improved Cylinder choke (choked for both rifled slugs and buck shot). Includes rifle sights, adjustable for windage and elevation, and recoil pad. **Weight:** 6¹/₂ lbs. **Overall length:** 41″.

Also available with fully rifled cantilever 21″ deer barrel. **Price: $682.00**

MODEL 1100 LT-20 YOUTH GUN
Lightweight, 20 Gauge Only
$625.00

The Model 1100 LT-20 Youth Gun autoloading shotgun features a shorter barrel (21″) and stock. **Overall length:** 39¹/₂″. **Weight:** 6¹/₂ lbs.

REMINGTON AUTO SHOTGUNS

MODEL 1100 SPORTING 28 GA.
$725.00 (Sporting) $710.00 (Skeet)

Features the original **Model 1100** American walnut tournament-grade stock, gloss finish and sporting recoil pad. The 25″ vent-rib barrel comes with four interchangeable REM Choke tubes in Skeet, Improved Cylinder, Light Modified and Modified constrictions. The Skeet model is 20 ga. with 26″ vent-rib barrel.

SP-10 MAGNUM SHOTGUN

SP-10 MAGNUM SHOTGUN
$1033.00

Remington's **SP-10 Magnum** is the only gas-operated semi-automatic 10-gauge shotgun made today. Engineered to shoot steel shot, the SP-10 delivers up to 34 percent more pellets to the target than standard 12-gauge shotgun and steel shot combinations. This autoloader features a noncorrosive, stainless-steel gas system, in which the cylinder moves—not the piston. This reduces felt recoil energy by spreading the recoil over a longer time. The SP-10 has a 3/8″ vent rib with middle and front sights for a better sight plane. It is also designed to appear virtually invisible to the sharp eyes of waterfowl. The American walnut stock and forend have a protective, low-gloss satin finish that reduces glare, and positive deep-cut checkering

for a sure grip. The receiver and barrel have a matte finish, and the stainless-steel breech bolt features a non-reflective finish. Remington's new autoloader also has a brown-vented recoil pad and a padded camo sling of Cordura nylon for easy carrying. The receiver is machined from a solid billet of ordnance steel for total integral strength. The SP-10 vented gas system reduces powder residue buildup and makes cleaning easier.

Gauge: 10. **Barrel lengths & choke:** 26″ REM Choke and 30″ REM Choke. **Overall length:** 51 1/2″ (30″ barrel) and 47 1/2″ (26″ barrel). **Weight:** 11 lbs. (30″ barrel) and 10 3/4 lbs. (26″ barrel).

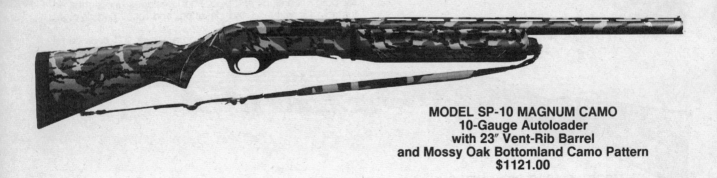

MODEL SP-10 MAGNUM CAMO
10-Gauge Autoloader
with 23″ Vent-Rib Barrel
and Mossy Oak Bottomland Camo Pattern
$1121.00

ROTTWEIL SHOTGUNS

PARAGON OVER/UNDER

ROTTWEIL PARAGON

This concept in shotgun systems, trap, skeet and sporting clays includes the following features: Detachable and interchangeable trigger action with super-imposed hammers • Safety action on trigger and sears • Spring-loaded self-adjusting wedges • Ejector can be turned on and off at will • Top lever convertible for right- and left-handed shooters • Interchangeable firing pins (without disassembly) • Length and weight of barrels selected depending on application (see below) • Module system: Fully interchangeable receiver, barrels, stocks trigger action and forends • Select walnut stocks

Barrel lengths:

Field & Skeet	27¹/₂″	Sporting	28¹/₂″
American Skeet	28″	Trap	29″ & 30″
Parcours	28³/₈″	American Trap Single	32″ & 34″

Prices: . . . . **on request**

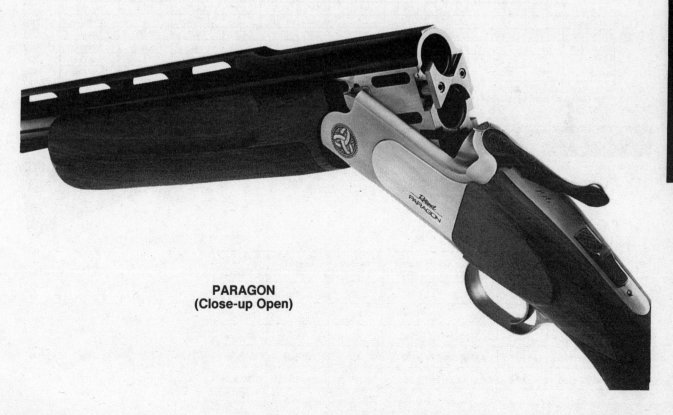

PARAGON
(Close-up Open)

RUGER OVER/UNDER SHOTGUNS

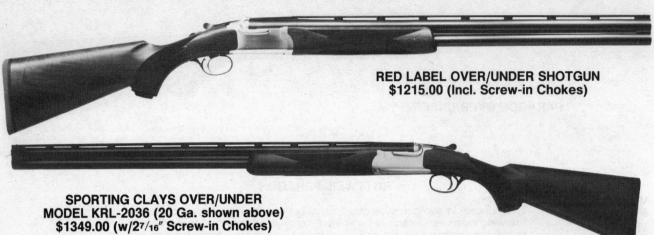

RED LABEL OVER/UNDER SHOTGUN
$1215.00 (Incl. Screw-in Chokes)

SPORTING CLAYS OVER/UNDER
MODEL KRL-2036 (20 Ga. shown above)
$1349.00 (w/2⁷/₁₆″ Screw-in Chokes)

SPECIFICATIONS RED LABEL AND SPORTING CLAYS OVER/UNDERS

Catalog Number	Gauge	Chamber	Choke*	Barrel Length	Overall Length	Length Pull	Drop Comb	Drop Heel	Sights**	Approx. Wt. (lbs.)	Type Stock
KRL-1226	12	3"	F,M,IC,S+	26"	43"	14 1/8"	1 1/2"	2 1/2"	GBF	7 3/4	Pistol Grip
KRL-1227	12	3"	F,M,IC,S+	28"	45"	14 1/8"	1 1/2"	2 1/2"	GBF	8	Pistol Grip
KRLS-1226	12	3"	F,M,IC,S+	26"	43"	14 1/8"	1 1/2"	2 1/2"	GBF	7 1/2	Straight
KRLS-1227	12	3"	F,M,IC,S+	28"	45"	14 1/8"	1 1/2"	2 1/2"	GBF	7 3/4	Straight
KRL-1236	12	3"	M,IC,S+	30"	47"	14 1/8"	1 1/2"	2 1/2"	GBF/GBM	7 3/4	Pistol Grip
KRL-2029	20	3"	F,M,IC,S+	26"	43"	14 1/8"	1 1/2"	2 1/2"	GBF	7	Pistol Grip
KRL-2030	20	3"	F,M,IC,S+	28"	45"	14 1/8"	1 1/2"	2 1/2"	GBF	7 1/4	Pistol Grip
KRLS-2029	20	3"	F,M,IC,S+	26"	43"	14 1/8"	1 1/2"	2 1/2"	GBF	6 3/4	Straight
KRLS-2030	20	3"	F,M,IC,S+	28"	45"	14 1/8"	1 1/2"	2 1/2"	GBF	7	Straight
KRL-2036	20	3"	M,IC,S+	30"	47"	14 1/8"	1 1/2"	2 1/2"	GBF/GBM	7	Pistol Grip
KRLS-2826	28	2 3/4"	F,M,IC,S+	26"	43"	14 1/8"	1 1/2"	2 1/2"	GBF	5 7/8	Straight
KRLS-2827	28	2 3/4"	F,M,IC,S+	28"	45"	14 1/8"	1 1/2"	2 1/2"	GBF	6	Straight
KRL-2826	28	2 3/4"	F,M,IC,S+	26"	43"	14 1/8"	1 1/2"	2 1/2"	GBF	6	Pistol Grip
KRL-2827	28	2 3/4"	F,M,IC,S+	28"	45"	14 1/8"	1 1/2"	2 1/2"	GBF	6 1/8	Pistol Grip

*F-Full, M-Modified, IC-Improved Cylinder, S-Skeet. +Two skeet chokes standard with each shotgun.
**GBF-Gold-Bead Front Sight, GBM-Gold-Bead Middle

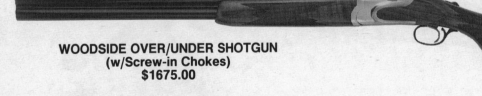

WOODSIDE OVER/UNDER SHOTGUN
(w/Screw-in Chokes)
$1675.00

WOODSIDE SPECIFICATIONS

Catalog Number	Gauge	Choke*	Barrel Length	Overall Length	Approx. Wt.	Stock
KWS-1226	12	F,M,IC,S+	26″	43″	7³/₄ lbs.	Pistol
KWS-1227	12	F,M,IC,S+	28″	45″	8 lbs.	Pistol
KWS-1226	12	F,M,IC,S+	26″	43″	7¹/₂ lbs.	Straight
KWS-1227	12	F,M,IC,S+	28″	45″	7³/₄ lbs.	Straight
KWS-1236	12	F,M,IC,S+	30″	47″	7³/₄ lbs.	Pistol

SKB SHOTGUNS

MODEL 385 SIDE-BY-SIDE
$1695.00

Model 385 features silver nitride receiver with engraved scroll and game scene design; solid boxlock action w/double locking lugs; single selective trigger; selective automatic ejectors; automatic safety; sculpted American walnut stock; pistol or English straight grip; semi-beavertail forend; stock and forend finished w/18-line fine checkering; standard series choke tube system; solid rib w/flat matte finish and metal front bead. For additional specifications, see table below.

SPECIFICATIONS MODEL 385

GAUGE	CHAMBER	BARREL LENGTH	OVERALL LENGTH	INTER-CHOKE**	SIGHTS	RIB WIDTH	STOCK	AVERAGE WEIGHT*	MFR. I.D.
20	3″	26″	42½″	STND	MFB	5/16″	PISTOL	6 lbs. 10 oz.	A3806CFP
20	3″	26″	42½″	STND	MFB	5/16″	ENGLISH	6 lbs. 10 oz.	A3806CFE
28	2¾″	26″	42½″	STND	MFB	5/16″	PISTOL	6 lbs. 13 oz.	A3886CFP
28	2¾″	26″	42½″	STND	MFB	5/16″	ENGLISH	6 lbs. 13 oz.	A3886CFE

* Weights may vary due to wood density. Specifications may vary.
** INTER-CHOKE SYSTEMS: STANDARD SERIES Imp. Cyl., Mod., Skeet
STOCK DIMENSIONS: Length of Pull - 14⅛″; Drop at Comb - 1½″; Drop at Heel - 2½″. MFB = Metal Front Bead

MODEL 505
$999.00

			505 FIELD OVER AND UNDERS						
GAUGE	CHAMBER	BARREL LENGTH	OVERALL LENGTH	INTER CHOKE	SIGHTS	RIB WIDTH	AVERAGE WEIGHT*	MANUFACTURES ID NUMBER
12	3″	28″	45 3/8″	STND-A	MFB	3/8″	7 lb. 12 oz.	N528CFP
12	3″	26″	43 3/8″	STND-B	MFB	3/8″	7 lb. 11 oz.	N526CFP
20	3″	26″	43 3/8″	STND-B	MFB	3/8″	6 lb. 10 oz.	N506CFP

SKB SHOTGUNS

MODEL 585 and 785 SERIES

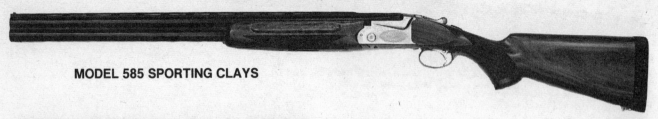

MODEL 585 SPORTING CLAYS

FIELD MODELS

GAUGE	CHAMBER	BARREL LENGTH	OVERALL LENGTH	INTER CHOKE	SIGHTS✓	RIB WIDTH	AVERAGE WEIGHT * 785	585
12	3"	28"	45 3/8"	COMP.	MFB	3/8"	8 lb. 0 oz.	7 lb. 12 oz.
12	3"	26"	43 3/8"	COMP.	MFB	3/8"	8 lb. 0 oz.	7 lb. 11 oz.
20	3"	28"	45 3/8"	STND-A	MFB	5/16"	7 lb. 4 oz.	6 lb. 12 oz.
20	3"	26"	43 3/8"	STND-B	MFB	5/16"	7 lb. 3 oz.	6 lb. 10 oz.
28	2 3/4"	28"	45 3/8"	STND-A	MFB	5/16"	7 lb. 4 oz.	6 lb. 14 oz.
28	2 3/4"	26"	43 3/8"	STND-B	MFB	5/16"	7 lb. 3 oz.	6 lb. 13 oz.
410	3"	28"	45 3/8"	M / F	MFB	5/16"	7 lb. 4 oz.	7 lb. 0 oz.
410	3"	26"	43 3/8"	IC / M	MFB	5/16"	7 lb. 3 oz.	6 lb. 14 oz.

2 BARREL FIELD SETS

GAUGE	CHAMBER	BARREL LENGTH	OVERALL LENGTH	INTER CHOKE	SIGHTS✓	RIB WIDTH	AVERAGE WEIGHT * 785	585
12	3"	28"	45 3/8"	COMP.	MFB	3/8"	8 lb. 1 oz.	7 lb. 11 oz.
20	3"	26"	45 3/8"	STND-B	MFB	3/8"	8 lb. 4 oz.	7 lb. 12 oz.
20	3"	28"	45 3/8"	STND-A	MFB	5/16"	7 lb. 5 oz.	7 lb. 2 oz.
28	2 3/4"	28"	45 3/8"	STND-A	MFB	5/16"	7 lb. 5 oz.	7 lb. 1 oz.
20	3"	26"	43 3/8"	STND-B	MFB	5/16"	7 lb. 3 oz.	7 lb. 1 oz.
28	2 3/4"	26"	43 3/8"	STND-B	MFB	5/16"	7 lb. 3 oz.	7 lb. 0 oz.
28	2 3/4"	28"	45 3/8"	STND-A	MFB	5/16"	7 lb. 6 oz.	7 lb. 1 oz.
410	3"	26"	43 3/8"	IC / M	MFB	5/16"	7 lb. 5 oz.	7 lb. 0 oz.

*Weights may vary due to wood density. Specifications may vary.

*INTER-CHOKE SYSTEMS
 COMP. - Competition series includes Mod., Full, Imp. Cyl.
 STND A - Standard series includes Mod., Full, Imp. Cyl.
 STND B - Standard series includes Imp. Cyl. Mod., Skeet

STOCK DIMENSIONS
Length of Pull - 14 1/8"
Drop at Comb - 1 1/2"
Drop at Heel - 2 3/16"
✓ MFB - Metal Front Bead

MODEL 585

	Prices
Field/Youth (12 & 20 ga.)	$1179.00
Field (28 or .410 ga.)	1229.00
Two-Barrel Field Set (12 & 20 ga.)	1929.00
20/28 ga. or 28/.410 ga.	1989.00
Skeet (12 or 20 ga.)	1279.00
28 or .410 ga.	1319.00
3-Bbl. Set (20, 28, & .410 ga.)	2999.00
Sporting Clays (12 or 20 ga.)	1329.00
28 gauge	1379.00
Trap (Monte Carlo or Std.)	1279.00
2-Barrel Trap Combo	1929.00
Waterfowler	1329.00

SPORTING CLAY MODELS

GAUGE	CHAMBER	BARREL LENGTH	OVERALL LENGTH	INTER CHOKE	SIGHTS✓	RIB WIDTH	AVERAGE WEIGHT * 785	585
12	3"	32"	49 3/8"	COMP.	CP/WFB	15/32" CH/STP	8 lb. 14 oz.	8 lb. 7 oz.
12	3"	30"	47 3/8"	COMP.	CP/WFB	15/32" CH/STP	8 lb. 12 oz.	8 lb. 5 oz.
12	3"	30"	47 3/8"	COMP.	CP/WFB	3/6" SW	8 lb. 9 oz.	8 lb. 1 oz.
12	3"	28"	45 3/8"	COMP.	CP/WFB	15/32" CH/STP	8 lb. 8 oz.	8 lb. 1 oz.
12	3"	28"	45 3/8"	COMP.	CP/WFB	3/8" SW	8 lb. 5 oz.	7 lb. 14 oz.
20	3"	28"	45 3/8"	STND-B	CP/WFB	15/32" CH/STP	7 lb. 6 oz.	6 lb. 14 oz.
28	2 3/4"	28"	45 3/8"	STND-B	CP/WFB	5/16" SW	7 lb. 4 oz.	6 lb. 14 oz.

2 BARREL SPORTING CLAY SET

GAUGE	CHAMBER	BARREL LENGTH	OVERALL LENGTH	INTER CHOKE	SIGHTS✓	RIB WIDTH	AVERAGE WEIGHT * 785	585
12	3"	30"	47 3/8"	COMP.	CP/WFB	15/32" CH/STP	8 lb. 14 oz.	/////
20	3"	28"	45 3/8"	STND-B	CP/WFB	15/32" CH/STP	8 lb. 10 oz.	/////

*Weights may vary due to wood density. Specifications may vary.

*INTER-CHOKE SYSTEMS
 COMP. - Competition series includes SK II/SC III,
 SK I/SC I and MOD/SC IV
 STND B - Standard series includes Mod. Imp. Cyl, Skeet

STOCK DIMENSIONS
Length of Pull - 14 1/4"
Drop at Comb - 1 7/16"
Drop at Heel - 1 7/8"
✓ CP/WFB - Center Post White Front Bead
✓ CH/STP - Center Channeled, Semi Wide Step Up Rib
SW - Semi Wide Step Up Rib

MODEL 585 WATERFOWLER

SKB SHOTGUNS

MODEL 585 and 785 SERIES

MODEL 785 OVER/UNDER

The new SKB 785 Series features chrome-lined oversized chambers and bores, lengthened forcing cones, chrome-plated ejectors and competition choke tube system.

MODEL 785	Prices
Field (12 & 20 ga.)	$1899.00
28 or .410 ga.	1949.00
Two-Barrel Field Set (12 & 20 ga.)	2749.00
20/28 ga. or 28/.410 ga.	2819.00
Skeet (12 or 20 ga.)	1949.00
28 or .410 ga.	1999.00
3-Bbl. Set (20, 28, & .410 ga.)	3929.00
Sporting Clays (12 or 20 ga.)	2029.00
28 gauge	2079.00
2-Barrel Set (12 & 20 ga.)	2889.00
Trap (Monte Carlo or Std.)	1949.00
2-Barrel Trap Combo	2719.00

TRAP MODELS

GAUGE	STOCK	BARREL LENGTH	OVERALL LENGTH	INTER CHOKE	SIGHTS*	785 RIB WIDTH	585 RIB WIDTH	AVERAGE WEIGHT * 785	AVERAGE WEIGHT * 585	MANUFACTURES ID # 785	MANUFACTURES ID # 585
12	STND	30"	47 3/8"	COMP-A	CP/WFB	15/32" CH/STP	3/8" STP	8 lb. 15 oz.	8 lb. 7 oz.	A7820CVTN	A5820CVTN
12	MONTE	30"	47 3/8"	COMP-A	CP/WFB	15/32" CH/STP	3/8" STP	9 lb. 0 oz.	8 lb. 7 oz.	A7820CVTM	A5820CVTM
12	STND	32"	49 3/8"	COMP-A	CP/WFB	15/32" CH/STP	3/8" STP	9 lb. 1 oz.	8 lb. 10 oz.	A7822CVTN	A5822CVTN
12	MONTE	32"	49 3/8"	COMP-A	CP/WFB	15/32" CH/STP	3/8" STP	9 lb. 1 oz.	8 lb. 9 oz.	A7822CVTM	A5822CVTM

TRAP COMBO'S — STANDARD

GAUGE	STOCK	BARREL LENGTH	OVERALL LENGTH	INTER CHOKE	SIGHTS*	785 RIB WIDTH	585 RIB WIDTH	AVERAGE WEIGHT * 785	AVERAGE WEIGHT * 585	MANUFACTURES ID # 785	MANUFACTURES ID # 585
12	STND	O/U-30"	47 3/8"	COMP.	CP/WFB	15/32" CH/STP	3/8" STP	8 lb. 15 oz.	8 lb. 6 oz.	A7820TN / 7822	A5820TN / 5822
12	STND	S/O-32"	49 3/8"	COMP.	CP/WFB	15/32" CH/STP	3/8" STP	9 lb. 0 oz.	8 lb. 6 oz.	A7820TN / 7822	A5820TN / 5822
12	STND	O/U-30"	47 3/8"	COMP.	CP/WFB	15/32" CH/STP	3/8" STP	9 lb. 0 oz.	8 lb. 4 oz.	A7820TN / 7824	A5820TN / 5824
12	STND	S/O-34"	51 3/8"	COMP.	CP/WFB	15/32" CH/STP	3/8" STP	9 lb. 1 oz.	8 lb. 6 oz.	A7820TN / 7824	A5820TN / 5824
12	STND	O/U-32"	49 3/8"	COMP.	CP/WFB	15/32" CH/STP	3/8" STP	9 lb. 0 oz.	8 lb. 7 oz.	A7822TN / 7824	A5822TN / 5824
12	STND	S/O-34"	51 3/8"	COMP.	CP/WFB	15/32" CH/STP	3/8" STP	9 lb. 1 oz.	8 lb. 8 oz.	A7822TN / 7824	A5822TN / 5824

TRAP COMBO'S — MONTE CARLO

12	MONTE	O/U-30"	47 3/8"	COMP.	CP/WFB	15/32" CH/STP	3/8" STP	8 lb. 15 oz.	8 lb. 6 oz.	A7820TM / 7822	A5820TM / 5822
12	MONTE	S/O-32"	49 3/8"	COMP.	CP/WFB	15/32" CH/STP	3/8" STP	9 lb. 0 oz.	8 lb. 6 oz.	A7820TM / 7822	A5820TM / 5822
12	MONTE	O/U-30"	47 3/8"	COMP.	CP/WFB	15/32" CH/STP	3/8" STP	8 lb. 15 oz.	8 lb. 4 oz.	A7820TM / 7824	A5820TM / 5824
12	MONTE	S/O-34"	51 3/8	COMP.	CP/WFB	15/32" CH/STP	3/8" STP	9 lb. 1 oz.	8 lb. 6 oz.	A7820TM / 7824	A5820TM / 5824
12	MONTE	O/U-32"	49 3/8"	COMP.	CP/WFB	15/32" CH/STP	3/8" STP	9 lb. 0 oz.	8 lb. 7 oz.	A7822TM / 7824	A5822TM / 5824
12	MONTE	S/O-34"	51 3/8	COMP.	CP/WFB	15/32" CH/STP	3/8" STP	9 lb. 1 oz.	8 lb. 9 oz.	A7822TM / 7824	A5822TM / 5824

*Weights may vary due to wood density. Specifications may vary.
*INTER-CHOKE SYSTEMS
  COMP. - Competition series includes Full, Mod., Imp. Cyl.
  STND. B - Standard series includes Imp. Cyl., Mod. and Skeet

STOCK DIMENSIONS
Length of Pull - 13 1/2"
Drop at Comb - 1 1/2"
Drop at Heel - 2 1/4"
✓ MFB - Metal Front Bead

YOUTH & LADIES

GAUGE	CHAMBER	BARREL LENGTH	OVERALL LENGTH	INTER CHOKE	SIGHTS*	RIB WIDTH	AVERAGE WEIGHT * 785	AVERAGE WEIGHT * 585	MANUFACTURES ID # 785	MANUFACTURES ID # 585
12	3"	28"	44 1/2"	COMP.	MFB	3/8"		7 lb. 11 oz.		A5828CFY
12	3"	26"	42 1/2"	COMP.	MFB	3/8"		7 lb. 9 oz.		A5826CFY
20	3"	26"	42 1/2"	STND-B	MFB	3/8"		6 lb. 7 oz.		A5806CFY

SKEET MODELS

GAUGE	CHAMBER	BARREL LENGTH	OVERALL LENGTH	INTER CHOKE	SIGHTS*	RIB WIDTH	AVERAGE WEIGHT * 785	AVERAGE WEIGHT * 585	MANUFACTURES ID # 785	MANUFACTURES ID # 585
12	3"	30"	47 1/4"	COMP.	CP/WFB	3/8"	8 lb. 9 oz.	8 lb. 1 oz.	A7820CV	A5820CV
12	3"	28"	45 1/4"	COMP.	CP/WFB	3/8"	8 lb. 6 oz.	7 lb. 12 oz.	A7828CV	A5828CV
20	3"	28"	45 1/4"	STND.	CP/WFB	5/16"	7 lb. 2 oz.	6 lb. 15 oz.	A7808CV	A5808CV
28	2 3/4"	28"	45 1/4"	STND.	CP/WFB	5/16"	7 lb. 5 oz.	6 lb. 15 oz.	A7888CV	A5888CV
410	3"	28"	45 1/4"	SK/SK	CP/WFB	5/16"	7 lb. 5 oz.	7 lb. 0 oz.	A7848V	A5848V

3 BARREL SKEET SETS

20	3"	28"	45 1/4"	STND.	CP/WFB	5/16"	7 lb. 2 oz.	6 lb. 15 oz.		
28	2 3/4"	28"	45 1/4"	STND.	CP/WFB	5/16"	7 lb. 5 oz.	7 lb. 0 oz.	A78088	A58088
410	3"	28"	45 1/4"	SK/SK	CP/WFB	5/16"	7 lb. 5 oz.	7 lb. 0 oz.		

*Weights may vary due to wood density. Specifications may vary.
*INTER-CHOKE SYSTEMS
  COMP. - Competition series includes 2-SKI/SCI, 1-Mod/SCJV
  STND. - Standard series includes Skeet, Skeet and Imp. Cyl.

NOTE: 785's Are Equipped With Step-Up Style Ribs

STOCK DIMENSIONS
Length of Pull - 14 1/8"
Drop at Comb - 1 1/2"
Drop at Heel - 2 3/16"
✓ CP/WFB - Center Post/White Front Bead

SHOTGUNS

TIKKA SHOTGUNS

(Formerly Valmet)

MODEL 512S PREMIUM FIELD

TIKKA 512S OVER/UNDER
PREMIUM FIELD GRADE $1290.00

Designed for the experienced hunter, TIKKA's 512S represents the pride and skill of "Old World" European craftsmanship. The barrels are polished to a mirror finish and deeply blued. Select semi-fancy American walnut stock and forearm highlight fine, deep-cut checkering. Other features include:

Time-proven action: Designed to handle large centerfire calibers for more durability and reliability.

Mechanical trigger: Fires two shots as fast as you can pull the trigger. Does not rely on the inertia from the recoil of the first shot to set the trigger for the second. In the event of a faulty primer or light hit, inertia trigger shotguns cannot function on the second round.

Single selective trigger: Selector button is located on the trigger for fast, easy selection.

Large triggerguard opening: Designed for cold weather shooting; permits easy finger movement when wearing gloves.

Semi-fancy European walnut stock and forearm: Add greatly to overall appearance.

Superior stock design: A palm swell provides additional hand comfort. Length and angle (pitch) can be adjusted for a perfect fit with addition of factory spacers. Fine, deep-cut checkering.

Palm-filling forearm: Rounded and tapered for comfort and smooth, true swing, plus fine, deep-cut checkering.

Automatic ejectors: Select and eject fired rounds. Raise unfired shells for safe removal.

Chrome-lined barrels: For more consistent patterns. Eliminates pitting and corrosion, extends barrel life even with steel shot.

Stainless steel choke tubes: Added strength over regular carbon and alloy materials. Easily handles steel shot. Recessed so as not to detract from appearance. Tight tolerances enable truer patterns and enhance choke versatility.

Sliding locking bolt: Secure lockup between receiver and barrels. Wears in, not loose.

Polished blue receiver: Fully engraved with gold inlay.

Wide vent rib: Cross-file pattern reduces glare. Fluorescent front and middle beads.

Automatic safety: Goes to safe position automatically when gun is opened.

Cocking indicators: Allow shooter to determine (through sight or feel) which barrel has been fired.

Steel receiver: Forged and machined for durability.

Chamber: 3-inch on all models

Two-piece firing pin: For more durability

Versatility: Change from over/under shotgun to shotgun/rifle, trap, skeet or double rifle. Precision tolerances require only minor initial fitting.

SPECIFICATIONS
Gauge: 12
Chambers: 3″
Weight: 7 1/4 lbs. w/26″ barrels; 7 1/2 lbs. w/28″ barrels
Barrel lengths/chokes:
  26″, 5 chokes (F, M, IM, IC & Skeet)
  28″, 5 chokes (F, M, IM, IC & Skeet)

SPORTING CLAYS SHOTGUN (not shown)
$1325.00

Designed to accommodate the specific requirements of the shooter in this, the fastest growing shooting sport in America today. The Sporting Clays shotgun features a specially designed American walnut stock with a double palm swell finished with a soft satin lacquer for maximum protection with minimum maintenance. Available in 12 gauge with a selection of 5 recessed choke tubes. Other features include a 3″ chamber, manual safety, customized sporting clay recoil pad, single selective trigger, blued receiver and 28″ and 30″ barrel with ventilated side and top rib with two iridescent beads. In addition, the shotgun is furnished with an attractive carrying case.

Manufactured in Italy, Tikka is designed and crafted by Sako of Finland, which has enjoyed international acclaim for the manufacture of precision sporting firearms since 1918.

TIKKA SHOTGUNS

(Formerly Valmet)

MODEL 512S SHOTGUN/RIFLE

TIKKA 512S SHOTGUN/RIFLE
$1400.00

TIKKA's unique 512S Shotgun/Rifle combination continues to be the most popular gun of its type in the U.S. Its features are identical to the 512S Field Grade over/under shotguns, including strong steel receiver, superior sliding locking mechanism with automatic safety, cocking indicators, mechanical triggers and two-piece firing pin. In addition, note the other features of this model—

Barrel regulation: Adjusts for windage simply by turning the screw on the muzzle. Elevation is adjustable by regulating the sliding wedge located between the barrels.

Compact: 24-inch barrels mounted on the low-profile receiver limit the overall length to 40 inches (about 5 inches less than most bolt-action rifles with similar 24-inch barrels).

Single selective trigger: A barrel selector is located on the trigger for quick, easy selection. Double triggers are also available.

Choice of rifle calibers: Choose from 222, 30-06, 308 or 9.3×74R for the under barrel to complement the 12-gauge upper barrel with 3″ chamber and Improved Modified choke.

Sighting options: The vent rib is cross-filed to reduce glare. The rear sight is flush-folding and permits rapid alignment with the large blade front sight. The rib is milled to accommodate TIKKA's one-piece scope mount with 1″ rings. The ''quick-release'' design of the scope mount enables the shooter to remove it without altering zero.

European walnut stock: Stock is of semi-Monte Carlo design, available with palm swell for greater control and comfort. Equipped with quick-detachable sling swivels. Length or pitch adjustable with factory spacers.

Interchangeability: Receiver will accommodate TIKKA's over/under shotgun barrels and double-rifle barrels with minor initial fitting.

SPECIFICATIONS
Gauge/Caliber: 12/222, 12/30-06, 12/308 and 12/9.3×74R
Chamber: 3″ with Improved Modified choke
Barrel length: 24″
Overall length: 40″
Weight: 8 lbs.
Stock: European walnut with semi-Monte Carlo design

Extra Barrel Sets:
Over/Under	$710.00
Shotgun/Rifle	775.00
Double Rifle	950.00
Sporting Clays	730.00

SHOTGUNS

WEATHERBY SHOTGUNS

ATHENA GRADE V CLASSIC FIELD

ATHENA GRADE IV $2200.00
ATHENA GRADE V $2527.00

Receiver: The Athena receiver houses a strong, reliable box-lock action, yet it features side lock-type plates to carry through the fine floral engraving. The hinge pivots are made of a special high-strength steel alloy. The locking system employs the time-tested Greener cross-bolt design.

Single selective trigger: It is mechanically rather than recoil operated. This provides a fully automatic switchover, allowing the second barrel to be fired on a subsequent trigger pull, even during a misfire. A flick of the trigger finger and the selector lever, located just in front of the trigger, is all the way to the left, enabling you to fire the lower barrel first, or to the right for the upper barrel. The Athena trigger is selective as well.

Barrels: The breech block is hand-fitted to the receiver, providing closest possible tolerances. Every Athena is equipped with a matted, ventilated rib and bead front sight.

Selective automatic ejectors: The Athena contains ejectors that are fully automatic both in selection and action.

Slide safety: The safety is the traditional slide type located conveniently on the upper tang atop the pistol grip.

Stock: Each stock is carved from specially selected Claro walnut, with fine line hand-checkering and high-luster finish. Trap model has Monte Carlo stock only.

See the Athena and Orion table on the following page for additional information and specifications.

GRADE IV CHOKES
Fixed Choke
Field, .410 Gauge
Skeet, 12 or 20 Gauge
IMC Multi-Choke
Field, 12, 20 or 28 Gauge
Trap, 12 Gauge
Trap, single barrel, 12 Gauge
Trap Combo, 12 Gauge

ORION GRADE II CLASSIC FIELD

ORION GRADES I, II & III OVER/UNDERS

For greater versatility, the Orion incorporates the integral multichoke (IMC) system. Available in Extra-full, Full, Modified, Improved Modified, Improved Cylinder and Skeet, the choke tubes fit flush with the muzzle without detracting from the beauty of the gun. Three tubes are furnished with each gun. The precision hand-fitted monobloc and receiver are machined from high-strength steel with a highly polished finish. The box-lock design uses the Greener cross-bolt locking system and special sears maintain hammer engagement. Pistol grip stock and forearm are carved of Claro walnut with hand-checkered diamond inlay pattern and high-gloss finish. Chrome-moly steel barrels, and the receiver, are deeply blued. The Orion also features selective automatic ejectors, single selective trigger, front bead sight and ventilated rib. The trap model boasts a curved trap-style recoil pad and is available with Monte Carlo stock only. **Weight:** 12 ga. Field, 7½ lbs.; 20 ga. Field, 7½ lbs.; Trap, 8 lbs.

See following page for prices and additional specifications.

ORION CHOKES
Grade I
IMC Multi-Choke, Field, 12 or 20 Gauge
Grade II
Fixed Choke, Field, .410 Gauge
Fixed Choke, Skeet, 12 or 20 Gauge
IMC Multi-Choke, Field, 12, 20 or 28 Gauge
IMC Multi-Choke, Trap, 12 Gauge
Grade II Sporting Clays
12 Gauge only
Grade III
IMC Multi-Choke, Field, 12 or 20 Gauge

WEATHERBY SHOTGUNS

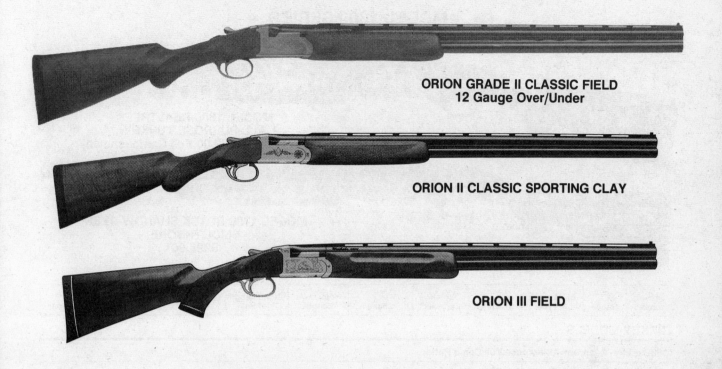

ORION GRADE II CLASSIC FIELD
12 Gauge Over/Under

ORION II CLASSIC SPORTING CLAY

ORION III FIELD

ORION GRADES I, II, III
Prices:
Orion I $1289.00
Orion II Classic Field 1363.00
Orion II Sporting Clays 1460.00
Orion III Field & Classic Field 1626.00

WEATHERBY SHOTGUN SPECIFICATIONS

Model	Gauge	Chamber	Barrel Length	Overall Length	Length of Pull	Drop at Heel	Drop at Comb	Bead Sight	Approx. Weight
Athena Grade V Classic Field	12	3″	28″ or 26″	45″ or 43″	14 1/4″	2.25″	1.5″	Brilliant front	6 1/2–8 lbs.
	20	3″	28″ or 26″	45″ or 43″	14″	2.25″	1.5″	Brilliant front	6 1/2–8 lbs.
Athena Grade IV Field	12	3″	28″ or 26″	45″ or 43″	14 1/4″	2.5″	1.5″	Brilliant front	6 1/2–8 lbs.
	20	3″	28″ or 26″	45″ or 43″	14″	2.5″	1.5″	Brilliant front	6 1/2–8 lbs.
Orion Grade III Classic Field	12	3″	28″	45″	14 1/4″	2.25″	1.5″	Brilliant front	6 1/2–8 lbs.
	20	3″	26″	43″	14″	2.25″	1.5″	Brilliant front	6 1/2–8 lbs.
Orion Grade III Field	12	3″	30″, 28″ or 26″	47″, 45″ or 43″	14 1/4″	2.5″	1.5″	Brilliant front	6 1/2–8 lbs.
	20	3″	28″ or 26″	45″ or 43″	14″	2.5″	1.5″	Brilliant front	6 1/2–8 lbs.
Orion Grade II Classic Field	12	3″	30″, 28″ or 26″	47″, 45″ or 43″	14 1/4″	2.25″	1.5″	Brilliant front	6 1/2–8 lbs.
	20	3″	28″ or 26″	45″ or 43″	14″	2.25″	1.5″	Brilliant front	6 1/2–8 lbs.
	28	2 3/4″	26″	43″	14″	2.25″	1.5″	Brilliant front	6 1/2–8 lbs.
Orion Grade I Field	12	3″	30″, 28″ or 26″	47″, 45″ or 43″	14 1/4″	2.5″	1.5″	Brilliant front	6 1/2–8 lbs.
	20	3″	28″ or 26″	45″ or 43″	14″	2.5″	1.5″	Brilliant front	6 1/2–8 lbs.
Orion Grade II Classic Sporting	12	3″	30″ or 28″	47″ or 45″	14 1/4″	2.25″	1.5″	Midpoint w/white front	7 1/2–8 lbs.
Orion Grade II Sporting	12	3″	30″ or 28″	47″ or 45″	14 1/4″	2.25″	1.5″	Midpoint w/white front	7 1/2–8 lbs.

Weight varies due to wood density.

SHOTGUNS

WINCHESTER SHOTGUNS

MODEL 1300 SERIES

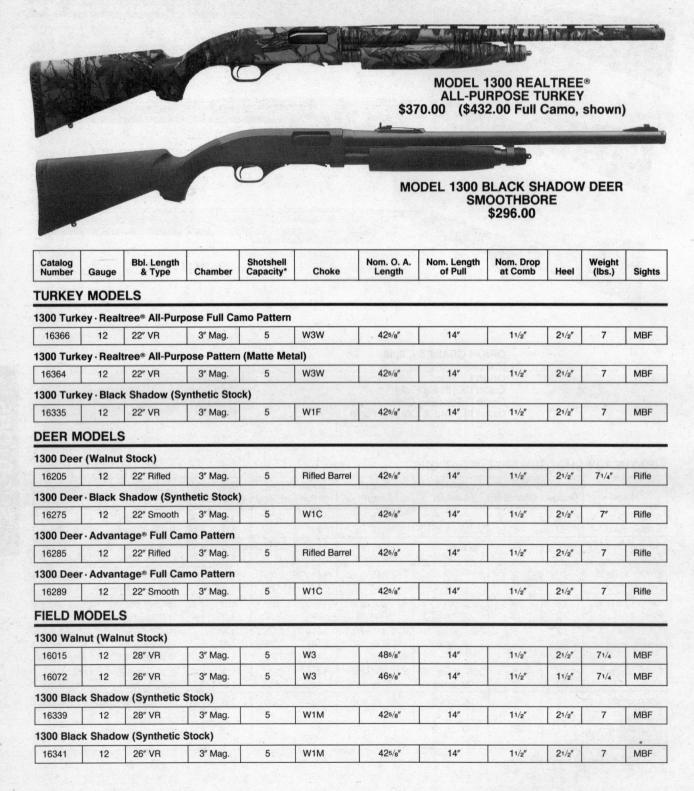

**MODEL 1300 REALTREE®
ALL-PURPOSE TURKEY
$370.00   ($432.00 Full Camo, shown)**

**MODEL 1300 BLACK SHADOW DEER
SMOOTHBORE
$296.00**

Catalog Number	Gauge	Bbl. Length & Type	Chamber	Shotshell Capacity*	Choke	Nom. O. A. Length	Nom. Length of Pull	Nom. Drop at Comb	Heel	Weight (lbs.)	Sights
TURKEY MODELS											
1300 Turkey · Realtree® All-Purpose Full Camo Pattern											
16366	12	22″ VR	3″ Mag.	5	W3W	42⅝″	14″	1½″	2½″	7	MBF
1300 Turkey · Realtree® All-Purpose Pattern (Matte Metal)											
16364	12	22″ VR	3″ Mag.	5	W3W	42⅝″	14″	1½″	2½″	7	MBF
1300 Turkey · Black Shadow (Synthetic Stock)											
16335	12	22″ VR	3″ Mag.	5	W1F	42⅝″	14″	1½″	2½″	7	MBF
DEER MODELS											
1300 Deer (Walnut Stock)											
16205	12	22″ Rifled	3″ Mag.	5	Rifled Barrel	42⅝″	14″	1½″	2½″	7¼″	Rifle
1300 Deer · Black Shadow (Synthetic Stock)											
16275	12	22″ Smooth	3″ Mag.	5	W1C	42⅝″	14″	1½″	2½″	7″	Rifle
1300 Deer · Advantage® Full Camo Pattern											
16285	12	22″ Rifled	3″ Mag.	5	Rifled Barrel	42⅝″	14″	1½″	2½″	7	Rifle
1300 Deer · Advantage® Full Camo Pattern											
16289	12	22″ Smooth	3″ Mag.	5	W1C	42⅝″	14″	1½″	2½″	7	Rifle
FIELD MODELS											
1300 Walnut (Walnut Stock)											
16015	12	28″ VR	3″ Mag.	5	W3	48⅝″	14″	1½″	2½″	7¼	MBF
16072	12	26″ VR	3″ Mag.	5	W3	46⅝″	14″	1½″	1½″	7¼	MBF
1300 Black Shadow (Synthetic Stock)											
16339	12	28″ VR	3″ Mag.	5	W1M	42⅝″	14″	1½″	2½″	7	MBF
1300 Black Shadow (Synthetic Stock)											
16341	12	26″ VR	3″ Mag.	5	W1M	42⅝″	14″	1½″	2½″	7	MBF

WINCHESTER SHOTGUNS

MODEL 1300 RANGER LADIES/YOUTH PUMP-ACTION SHOTGUN
$309.00

Gauge: 20 gauge only; 3″ chamber; 5-shot magazine. **Barrel:** 22″ barrel w/vent rib; Winchoke (Full, Modified, Improved Cylinder). **Weight:** 6½ lbs. **Length:** 41⅝″. **Stock:** Walnut or American hardwood with ribbed forend. **Sights:** Metal bead front. **Features:** Crossbolt safety; black rubber buttpad; twin-action slide bars; front-locking rotating bolt; removable segmented magazine plug to limit shotshell capacity for training purposes

MODEL 1300 RANGER 12 GAUGE DEER COMBO
22″ Rifled w/Sights & 28″ Vent-Rib Barrels
$401.00

SPECIFICATIONS MODEL 1300 RANGER, RANGER DEER & LADIES/YOUTH

Catalog Number	Gauge	Bbl. Length & Type	Chamber	Shotshell Capacity*	Choke	Nom. O. A. Length	Nom. Length of Pull	Nom. Drop at Comb	Heel	Weight (Lbs.)	Sights
1300 Ranger											
16519	12	28″ VR	3″ Mag.	5	W3	48⅝″	14″	1½″	2½″	7¼	MBF
16568	20	28″ VR	3″ Mag.	5	W3	48⅝″	14″	1½″	2½″	7	MBF
16592	12	26″ VR	3″ Mag.	5	W3	46⅝″	14″	1½″	2½″	7¼	MBF
16600	20	26″ VR	3″ Mag.	5	W3	46⅝″	14″	1½″	2½″	7	MBF
1300 Ranger Ladies/Youth											
17111	20	22″ VR	3″ Mag.	5	W3	41⅝″	13″	1½″	2⅜″	6¾	MBF
1300 Ranger Deer											
16770	12	22″ Rifled	3″ Mag.	5	Rifled Barrel	42⅝″	14″	1½″	2½″	7¼	Rifle
1300 Ranger Deer Combo (12 Ga. Extra Vent Rib Barrel)											
16610	12	22″ Smooth	3″ Mag.	5	Cyl.	42⅝″	14″	1½″	2½″	7¼	Rifle
	12	28″ VR	3″ Mag.	5	W1M	48⅝″	14″	1½″	2½″	7¼	MBF
1300 Ranger Deer Combo (Rifled Barrel and 12 Ga. Extra Vent Rib Barrel)											
16630	12	22″ Rifled	3″ Mag.	5	Rifled Barrel	42⅝″	14″	1½″	2½″	7¼	Rifle
	12	28″ VR	3″ Mag.	5	W1M	48⅝″	14″	1½″	2½″	7¼	MBF
1300 Ranger Deer Combo (Smooth Barrel and 20 Ga. Extra Vent Rib Barrel)											
16660	20	22″ Smooth	3″ Mag.	5	Cyl.	42⅝″	14″	1½″	2½″	7	Rifle
	20	28″ VR	3″ Mag.	5	W1M	48⅝″	14″	1½″	2½″	7	MBF

All models have 3″ Mag. chambers and 5-shot shell capacity, including one shotshell in chamber when ready to fire. VR-Ventilated rib. Cyl.-Cylinder Bore, R-Rifled Barrel. MBF-Metal bead front. RT-Rifle type front and rear sights. Model 1300 and Ranger pump-action shotguns have factory-installed plug which limits capacity to three shells. Ladies/Youth has factory-installed plug that limits capacity to one, two or three shells as desired. Extra barrels for Model 1300 and Ranger shotguns are available in 12 gauge, plain or vent rib, in a variety of barrel lengths and chokes; interchangeable with gauge. Winchoke sets with wrench come with gun as follows: W3W-Extra Full, Full, Modified tubes. W3-Full, Modified, Improved Cylinder tubes. W1M-Modified tube. Nominal drop at comb: 1½″; nominal drop at heel: 2½″ (2⅜″-Ladies' models).

WINCHESTER SECURITY SHOTGUNS

These tough 12-gauge shotguns provide backup strength for security and police work as well as all-around utility. The action is one of the fastest second-shot pumps made. It features a front-locking rotating bolt for strength and secure, single-unit lockup into the barrel. Twin-action slide bars prevent binding.

The shotguns are chambered for 3-inch shotshells. They handle 3-inch Magnum, 2³/₄-inch Magnum and standard 2³/₄-inch shotshells interchangeably. They have a crossbolt safety,

walnut-finished hardwood stock and forearm, black rubber buttpad and plain 18-inch barrel with Cylinder Bore choke. All are ultra-reliable and easy to handle.

Special chrome finish on Police and Marine guns are actually triple-plated: first with copper for adherence, then with nickel for rust protection, and finally with chrome for a hard finish. This triple-plating assures durability and quality. Both guns have a forend cap with swivel to accommodate sling.

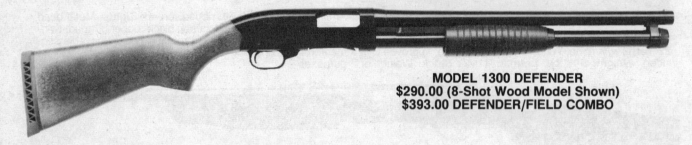

MODEL 1300 DEFENDER
$290.00 (8-Shot Wood Model Shown)
$393.00 DEFENDER/FIELD COMBO

SPECIFICATIONS MODEL 1300 DEFENDER

Model	Gauge	Barrel Length	Chamber	Capacity*	Choke	Overall Length	Length of Pull	Drop At Comb/Heel		Weight (Lbs.)	Sights
Combo, Hardwood Stock and Synthetic Pistol Grip, 5 Shot											
17814	12	18″	3″ Mag	5	Cyl.	38⁵/₈″	14″	1¹/₂″	2¹/₂″	6¹/₂″	MBF
	12	28″ VR	3″ Mag	5	W1M	48⁵/₈″	14″	1¹/₂″	2¹/₂″	7¹/₄″	MBF
Hardwood Stock, 5 Shot											
17665	12	18″	3″ Mag	5	Cyl.	38⁵/₈″	14″	1¹/₂″	2¹/₂″	6¹/₂″	MBF
Hardwood Stock, 8 Shot											
17566	12	18″	3″ Mag	8**	Cyl.	38⁵/₈″	14″	1¹/₂″	2¹/₂″	6¹/₂″	MBF
Synthetic Pistol Grip, 8 Shot											
17616	12	18″	3″ Mag	8**	Cyl.	28⁵/₈″	—	—	—	5³/₄″	MBF
Synthetic Stock, 8 and 5 Shot											
17632	12	18″	3″ Mag	8**	Cyl.	38⁵/₈″	14″	1¹/₂″	2¹/₂″	6¹/₄″	MBF
17673	12	18″	3″ Mag	5	Cyl.	38⁵/₈″	14″	1¹/₂″	2¹/₂″	6¹/₄″	MBF
Synthetic Stock, 5 Shot											
17681	20	18″	3″ Mag	5	Cyl.	38⁵/₈″	14″	1¹/₂″	2¹/₂″	6″	MBF
Hardwood Stock, 8 Shot											
31427	12	24″	3″ Mag	8	Cyl.	44⁵/₈″	14″	1¹/₂″	2¹/₂″	7″	MBF
Synthetic Stock, 8 Shot											
31435	12	24″	3″ Mag	8	Cyl.	44⁵/₈″	14″	1¹/₂″	2¹/₂″	6³/₄″	MBF
Stainless Marine Models											
17475	12	18″	3″ Mag	7**	Cyl.	38⁵/₈″	14″	1¹/₂″	2¹/₂″	6³/₄″	MBF
Stainless Marine with Pistol Grip											
17483	12	18″	3″ Mag	7**	Cyl.	28⁵/₈″	—	—	—	5³/₄″	MBF

* Includes one shotshell in chamber. ** Subtract one for 3-inch shells. VR = Ventilated rib. MBF = Metal bead front. Rifle = Rifle-type front and rear sights. W2 = Modified & Rifled (Sabot) Choke Tube. W3W = WinChoke, Extra Full, Full and Modified Tubes. W3 = WinChoke, Full, Modified and Improved Cylinder Tubes. Cyl. = Non-WinChoke, choked Cylinder Bore. W1M = Modified Tube.
W1C = Cylinder Choke Tube. Walnut and Ranger models are supplied with a removable plug that limits magazine capacity to two shells. Ladies/Youth models are supplied with universal plug for limiting magazine capacity to one, two, or three shells.

Blackpowder

For addresses and phone/fax numbers of manufacturers and distributors included in this section, please turn to DIRECTORY OF MANUFACTURERS AND SUPPLIERS on page 554.

AMERICAN ARMS

1851 COLT NAVY
$165.00 (Brass Frame) $195.00 (Steel Frame)

This replica of the most famous revolver of the percussion era was used extensively during the Civil War and on the Western frontier.

SPECIFICATIONS
Caliber: 36
Capacity: 6 shots
Barrel length: 7½″ octagonal w/hinged loading lever **Overall length:** 13″
Weight: 44 oz.
Features: Solid brass frame, trigger guard and backstrap; one-piece walnut grip; engraved blued steel cylinder

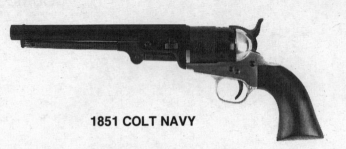

1851 COLT NAVY

1858 ARMY STAINLESS-STEEL TARGET
$375.00

1858 REMINGTON ARMY

1858 REMINGTON ARMY
$179.00 (Brass Frame) $225.00 (Steel Frame)

This replica of the last of Remington's percussion revolvers saw extensive use in the Civil War.

SPECIFICATIONS
Caliber: 44
Capacity: 6 shots

Barrel length: 8″ octagonal w/creeping loading lever
Overall length: 13″
Weight: 38 oz.
Features: Two-piece walnut grips
Also available w/stainless-steel frame, barrel and cylinder, adj. rear target sight and ramp blade.

1860 COLT ARMY
$179.00 (Brass Frame) $225.00 (Steel Frame)

Union troops issued this sidearm during the Civil War and subsequent Indian Wars.

SPECIFICATIONS
Caliber: 44
Capacity: 6 shots
Barrel length: 8″ round w/creeping loading lever
Overall length: 13½″
Weight: 44 oz.
Features: Solid brass or steel frame, trigger guard and backstrap; one-piece walnut grip; engraved blued steel cylinder

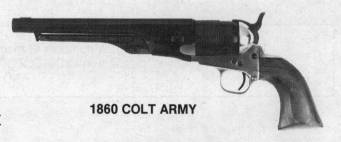

1860 COLT ARMY

ARMSPORT

REPLICA REVOLVERS

MODEL 5133
COLT 1851 NAVY "REB"

A modern replica of a Confederate percussion revolver in 36 or 44 caliber, this has a polished brass frame, rifled blued barrel and polished walnut grips.
Price:.. **$159.00**

MODEL 5136
COLT 1851 NAVY STEEL

This authentic reproduction of the Colt Navy Revolver in 36 or 44 caliber, which helped shape the history of America, features a rifled barrel, casehardened steel frame, engraved cylinder, polished brass trigger guard and walnut grips.
Price:.. **$197.00**

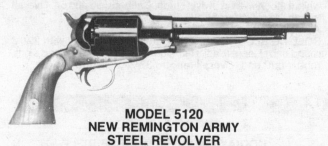

MODEL 5120
NEW REMINGTON ARMY
STEEL REVOLVER

One of the most accurate cap-and-ball revolvers of the 1860s. Its rugged steel frame and top strap made this 44 caliber the favorite of all percussion cap revolvers.
Price:.................................... **$230.00**
Model 5121 with brass frame: 170.00
Also available:
Stainless Target Model 5149 .... 415.00

MODEL 5138
REMINGTON ARMY STAINLESS STEEL

This stainless-steel version of the 44-caliber Remington New Army Revolver is made for the shooter who seeks the best. Its stainless-steel frame assures lasting good looks and durability.
Price:.. **$375.00**

MODEL 5139
COLT 1860 ARMY

This authentic 44-caliber reproduction offers the same balance and ease of handling for fast shooting as the original 1860 Army model.
Price:.................................... **$230.00**
Also available:
Model 5150 Stainless Steel 395.00

MODEL 5140
COLT 1860 ARMY

Same as the Model 5139 Colt Army replica, but with brightly polished brass frame.
Price:.. **$165.00**

CABELA'S RIFLES

HAWKEN RIFLE
$199.99–$224.99

Traditional ''plains rifle'' styling with American walnut stock, brass furniture including patch box, and color-casehardened lockplate. Adjustable double-set trigger, hardened coil-spring three-stage lock with hardened steel sear and tumbler. Screw adjustable rear sight with bead and ramp front. **Calibers:** 45, 50 and 54 percussion (R.H./L.H.); flintlock (R.H. only). **Barrel**

length: 28″ (1:48″ twist and 12 grooves in 45 cal.; 1:48″ twist, 6 grooves in 50 cal.; 1:48″ twist with 5 grooves in 54 caliber). Also available:
SPORTERIZED HAWKEN. Same as standard percussion model except blued steel furniture and fittings, rubber recoil pad, checkered walnut stock and leather sling. Also in carbine and synthetic stock carbine versions (right- and left-hand except in synthetic model). **Price: $219.99-$229.99**

S. HAWKEN PLAINS RIFLE
$1349.00

A true reproduction of a later model rifle built by the legendary Samuel Hawken. The Hawken-style breech plug has an enlarged flash channel for better ignition. Double-set triggers adjust to 3-lb. pull. **Barrel:** 34″ match-grade chrome-moly steel

tapers from 1″ at the breech to ⁷/₈″ at the muzzle; 7 lands/grooves cut to .012 with 1:60″ twist. **Overall length:** 52″. **Weight:** 9 lbs. **Stock:** Premium-grade curly maple with tapered hickory ramrod. **Sights:** Rear has hidden, modern screw adjustment for windage and elevation; front is German silver blade on copper base. ''S. Hawken St. Louis'' stamped on top barrel flat.

ROLLING BLOCK MUZZLELOADER
$359.99

sehardened steel; breech plug is easily removable. American walnut stock w/sling swivel studs. **Calibers:** 50 and 54. **Overall length:** 43¹/₂″. **Weight:** 8¹/₂ lbs.
Also available:
ROLLING BLOCK CARBINE. Same as above, but with 22¹/₄″ round barrel, screw-adj. rear sight and front blade/bead sight, rubber butt pad. **Overall length:** 38³/₄″. **Weight:** 7³/₄ lbs.

The breechblock/firing-pin mechanism on this model completely shrouds the nipple area, keeping caps dry and secure. Features include black engraved receiver, tapered 26¹/₂″ barrel with 1:24″ twist. Block, hammer and buttplate are color-ca-

KODIAK EXPRESS DOUBLE RIFLE
$529.99

sehardened steel buttplate. Ramp-mounted, adjustable folding double rear sights, ramp front sight, drilled and tapped for folding tang sight. Color-casehardened lock, blued top tang and trigger guard are all polished and engraved. **Calibers:** 50, 52, 54. **Barrels:** 28″ with 1:48″ twist (regulated at 75 yards); blued. **Overall length:** 45¹/₄″. **Weight:** 9.3 lbs.

Early explorers of Africa and Asia often had to rely on large-bore express rifles like this handsome sidelock replica featuring oil-finished, hand- checkered European walnut stock with ca-

COLT BLACKPOWDER

SIGNATURE SERIES

COLT WALKER
$442.50

This revolver saw action and extensive service in Mexico and the American West. Built for the U.S. Government, and co-designed by Captain Samuel Walker, this legendary revolver bears the famous Texas Ranger and Indian fight scene designed by W.O. Ormsby in 1847. Color casehardened frame with half-round, half-octagonal barrel

SPECIFICATIONS
Caliber: 44
Barrel length: 9″   **Overall length:** 15.5″
Weight: 73 oz. (empty)
Sights: Fixed blade front sight   **Sight radius:** 12.25″
Stock: One-piece walnut
Finish: Colt blue with color casehardened frame; hammer, lever and plunger

COLT THIRD MODEL DRAGOON
$487.50 ($502.50 Steel)

Easily identified by its round trigger guard, flat mainspring, hammer roller and rectangular bolt cut. Features color case-hardened frame, hammer, loading lever, plunger, blued barrel and cylinder. Brass trigger guard and backstrap or steel trigger guard and backstrap, roll-engraved cylinder and one-piece walnut grip.

SPECIFICATIONS
Caliber: 44 percussion
Barrel length: 7.5″   **Overall length:** 13.75″
Weight: 66 oz. (empty)
Sight: Fixed blade front   **Sight radius:** 10.75″
Stock: One-piece walnut
Finish: Colt blue with color casehardened frame; hammer, lever and plunger

COLT 1849 POCKET REVOLVER
$390.00

A favorite of the Gold Rush and Oregon Trail days and on through the Civil War.

SPECIFICATIONS
Caliber: 31
Barrel length: 4″   **Overall length:** 9.5″
Weight : 24 oz. (empty)
Stock: One-piece walnut
Finish: Colt blue and color casehardened frame

COLT 1851 NAVY
$427.50

Sam Colt's personal favorite and most famous cap-and-ball revolver ever made. Identical to the ones Wild Bill Hickok wore as U.S. Marshall.

SPECIFICATIONS
Caliber: 36
Barrel length: 7.5″   **Overall Length:** 13¹/₈″
Weight: 40.5 oz. (empty)
Sights: Fixed blade front   **Sight Radius:** 10″
Stock: Oiled American walnut
Finish: Colt blue and color casehardened frame

BLACK POWDER

COLT BLACKPOWDER

SIGNATURE SERIES

COLT 1860 ARMY
$427.50

A continuation in production of the famous cap-and-ball revolver used by the U.S. Cavalry with color casehardened frame, hammer and loading lever. Blued backstrap and brass trigger guard, roll-engraved cylinder and one-piece walnut grips

SPECIFICATIONS
Caliber: 44
Barrel length: 8″　**Overall length:** 13.75″
Weight: 42 oz. (empty)
Sights: Fixed blade front　**Sight radius:** 10.5″
Stock: One-piece walnut
Finish: Colt blue with color casehardened frame; hammer, lever and plunger

COLT 1861 NAVY
$465.00

A personal favorite of George Armstrong Custer, who carried a pair of them during the Civil War. Loading lever and plunger; blued barrel, cylinder backstrap and trigger guard; roll-engraved cylinder; one-piece walnut grip.

SPECIFICATIONS
Caliber: 36 percussion
Barrel length: 7.5″　**Overall length:** 13⅛″
Weight: 42 oz. (empty)
Sight: Fixed blade front　**Sight radius:** 10″
Stock: One-piece walnut
Finish: Colt blue with color casehardened frame; hammer, lever and plunger

COLT CAVALRY MODEL 1860 ARMY
FLUTED CYLINDER
$465.00

The first Army revolvers shipped from Hartford were known as the "Cavalry Model"—with fluted cylinder, hardened frame, hammer, loading lever and plunger. Features blued barrel, backstrap and cylinder; brass trigger guard, fluted cylinder, one-piece walnut grip and a 4-screw frame (cut for optional shoulder stock)

SPECIFICATIONS
Caliber: 44 percussion
Barrel length: 8″　**Overall length:** 13.75″
Weight: 42 oz. (empty)
Sight: Fixed blade front　**Sight radius:** 10.5″
Stock: One piece walnut
Finish: Colt blue with color casehardened frame; hammer, lever and plunger

COLT 1861 NAVY

TRAPPER MODEL 1862 POCKET POLICE
$442.50

The first re-issue of the rare and highly desirable Pocket Police "Trapper Model." The Trapper's 3½″ barrel without attached loading lever makes it an ideal backup gun, as well as a welcome addition to any gun collection. Color casehardened frame and hammer; silver-plated backstrap and trigger guard; blued semifluted cylinder and barrel; one-piece walnut grip. Separate 4⅝″ brass ramrod.

SPECIFICATIONS
Caliber: 36
Barrel length: 3.5″　**Overall length:** 8.5″
Weight: 20 oz. (empty)
Sight: Fixed blade front　**Sight radius:** 6″
Stock: One-piece walnut
Finish: Colt blue with color casehardened frame and hammer

TRAPPER MODEL 1862
POCKET POLICE

COLT BLACKPOWDER

COLT MODEL 1861 MUSKET
$615.00

Manufactured to original specifications using modern steels, this re-issue has the authentic Colt markings of its Civil War predecessor. Plus triangular bayonet.

SPECIFICATIONS
Caliber: 58
Barrel length: 40″   **Overall length:** 56″

Weight: 9 lbs. 3 oz. (empty)
Sights: Folding leaf rear; steel blade front   **Sight Radius:** 36″
Stock: One piece
Finish: Bright steel lockplate, hammer, buttplate, bands, ramrod and nipple; blued rear sight

CUMBERLAND MOUNTAIN ARMS

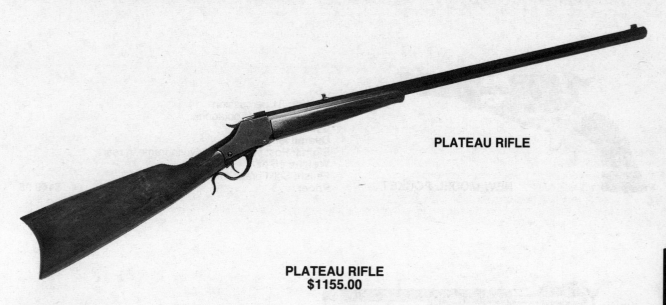

PLATEAU RIFLE

PLATEAU RIFLE
$1155.00

SPECIFICATIONS
Calibers: 40-65, 45-70 (and others as requested)
Action: CMA falling block; 4140 heat-treated steel (regular blue)
Barrel length: Up to 32″ (round)
Weight: 10½ lbs.
Sights: Marble
Stock: Grade #1 walnut stock with lacquer finish; smooth semibeavertail forearm; crescent buttplate

Also available:	Prices
Half-round or half-octagonal barrel	$132.00
Octagonal barrel	112.00
Standard checkering pattern	170.00
Deluxe wood	200.00
Action (unblued)	633.00
Barreled action	957.00
Action kits	430.00
Ebony forend tip	100.00
MOUNTAIN MUZZLELOADER	950.00

CVA REVOLVERS

**1858 ARMY REVOLVER
STEEL FRAME**

Caliber: 44
Cylinder: 6-shot
Barrel length: 8″ octagonal
Overall length: 13″
Weight: 38 oz.
Sights: Blade front; adjustable target
Grip: Two-piece walnut
Prices:
Brass Frame **$149.95**
Steel Frame **199.95**
Also available:
1860 ARMY w/8″ barrel (13½″ overall). **Weight:** 44 oz.
Price: **$139.95**

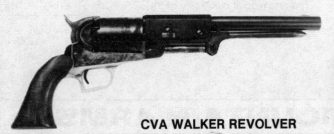

CVA WALKER REVOLVER

Caliber: 44
Barrel: 9″ rounded with hinged-style loading lever
Cylinder: 6-shot engraved
Overall length: 15½″
Weight: 72 oz.
Grip: One-piece walnut
Front sight: Blade
Finish: Solid brass trigger guard
Price: **$279.95**

NEW MODEL POCKET

Caliber: 31 percussion
Barrel length: 4″ octagonal
Cylinder: 5 shots
Overall length: 7½″
Sights: Post in front; groove in frame in rear
Weight: 15 oz.
Finish: Solid brass frame
Price: **$149.95**

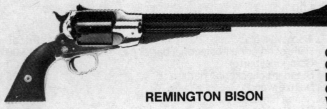

REMINGTON BISON

Caliber: 44
Cylinder: 6-shot
Barrel length: 10¼″ octagonal
Overall length: 18″
Weight: 48 oz.
Sights: Fixed blade front; screw adjustable target rear
Grip: Two-piece walnut
Finish: Solid brass frame
Price: **$199.95**

CVA REVOLVERS/PISTOLS

**1851 NAVY REVOLVER
BRASS FRAME**

Calibers: 36 and 44
Barrel length: 7¹/₂″ octagonal; hinged-style loading lever
Overall length: 13″
Weight: 44 oz.
Cylinder: 6-shot, engraved
Sights: Post front; hammer notch rear
Grip: One-piece walnut
Finish: Solid brass frame, trigger guard and backstrap; blued barrel and cylinder; color casehardened loading lever and hammer
Price: $139.95

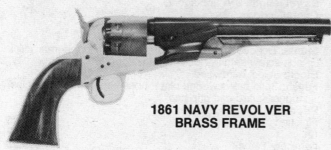

**1861 NAVY REVOLVER
BRASS FRAME**

Caliber: 44
Barrel length: 8″ rounded; creeping style
Overall length: 13″
Weight: 44 oz.
Cylinder: 6-shot, engraved
Sights: Blade front; hammer notch rear
Finish: Solid brass frame, trigger guard and backstrap; blued barrel and cylinder
Grip: One-piece walnut
Price: Finished $139.95

**SHERIFF'S MODEL REVOLVER
BRASS FRAME**

Caliber: 36
Barrel length: 5¹/₂″ (octagonal w/creeping-style loading lever)
Overall length: 11¹/₂″
Weight: 40 oz.
Cylinder: 6-shot semifluted
Grip: One-piece walnut
Sight: Hammer notch in rear
Finish: Solid brass frame, trigger guard and backstrap
Price: $179.95

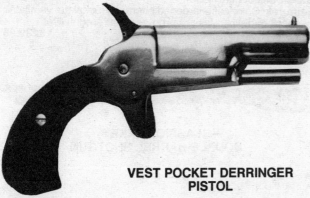

**VEST POCKET DERRINGER
PISTOL**

Caliber: 31 Derringer
Barrel length: 2¹/₂″ (single shot) brass
Overall length: 5″
Weight: 16 oz.
Grip: Two-piece walnut
Frame: Brass
Price: Finished $84.95

POCKET POLICE REVOLVER

Caliber: 36
Capacity: 5-shot cylinder
Barrel length: 5¹/₂″ octagonal, with creeping-style loading lever
Overall length: 10¹/₂″
Weight: 26 oz.
Sights: Post front; hammer notch rear
Price: w/Brass Frame $139.95

CVA PISTOLS/SHOTGUNS

KENTUCKY PISTOL

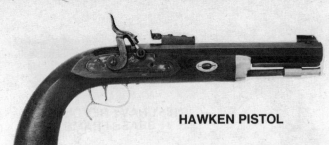

HAWKEN PISTOL

Caliber: 50 percussion
Barrel: 9³/₄", rifled, octagonal
Overall length: 15¹/₂"
Weight: 40 oz.
Finish: Blued barrel, brass hardware
Sights: Brass blade front; fixed open rear
Stock: Select hardwood
Ignition: Engraved, color casehardened percussion lock, screw adjustable sear engagement
Accessories: Brass-tipped, hardwood ramrod; stainless-steel nipple or flash hole liner
Prices:
Finished **$149.95**
Percussion Kit **109.95**

Caliber: 50 percussion
Barrel length: 9³/₄", octagonal
Overall length: 16¹/₂"
Weight: 50 oz.
Trigger: Early-style brass
Sights: Beaded steel blade front; fully adjustable rear (click adj. screw settings lock into position)
Stock: Select hardwood
Finish: Solid brass wedge plate, nose cap, ramrod thimbles, trigger guard and grip cap
Prices:
Finished **$149.95**
Kit **119.95**
Laminated stock **159.95**

TRAPPER SINGLE-BARREL SHOTGUN

Gauge: 12 percussion
Barrel length: 28" round, chrome-lined bore; hooked breech; three Modified interchangeable chokes
Overall length: 46" **Weight:** 6 lbs.
Trigger: Early-style steel
Lock: Color casehardened; engraved with V-type mainspring, bridle and fly

Sights: Brass bead front (no rear sight)
Stock: Select hardwood
Features: Color casehardened engraved lockplate; ventilated recoil pad, fiberglass ramrod and rear sling swivel
Price: **$239.95**

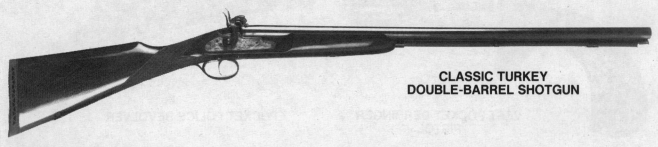

**CLASSIC TURKEY
DOUBLE-BARREL SHOTGUN**

Gauge: 12 percussion
Barrel length: 28" round, chrome-lined bore; double button-style breech, Modified choke
Overall length: 45" **Weight:** 9 lbs.
Triggers: Hinged, gold-tone double triggers
Lock: Color casehardened; engraved with V-type mainspring, bridle and fly

Sights: Brass bead front (no rear sight)
Stock: Select hardwood; wraparound forearm with bottom screw attachment
Features: Ventilated recoil pad; rear sling swivel; fiberglass ramrod
Prices: **$459.95**

CVA RIFLES

VARMINT RIFLE

Caliber: 32 percussion
Barrel length: 24" octagonal; 7/8" across flats
Rifling: 1 in 56"
Overall length: 40"
Weight: 6 3/4 lbs.
Lock: Color casehardened with 45° offset hammer

Trigger: Single trigger
Sights: Steel blade front; Patridge-style click-adjustable rear
Stock: Select hardwood
Features: Brass trigger guard, nose cap, wedge plate, thimble and buttplate
Price: $219.95

LYNX

Calibers: 50 and 54 percussion
Barrel length: 26" (15/16" octagonal)
Rifling: 1:32"
Overall length: 40"
Weight: 6 1/2 lbs.

Sights: Blue beaded blade front; economy rear
Stock: Dura-Grip; checkered forend and trigger; Advantage Camouflage synthetic stock
Finish: RealTree all-purpose gray
Price: $189.95

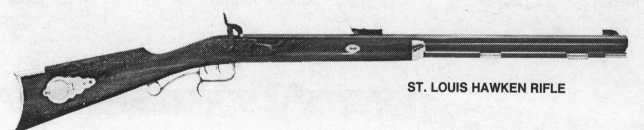

ST. LOUIS HAWKEN RIFLE

Calibers: 50 and 54 percussion or flintlock (50 cal. only)
Barrel: 28" octagonal 15/16" across flats; hooked breech; rifling one turn in 66", 8 lands and deep grooves
Overall length: 44"
Weight: 8 lbs.
Sights: Dovetail, beaded blade front; adjustable open hunting-style dovetail rear
Stock: Select hardwood with beavertail cheekpiece
Triggers: Double set; fully adjustable trigger pull
Finish: Solid brass wedge plates, nose cap, ramrod thimbles, trigger guard and patchbox

Prices:
50 Caliber Flintlock $234.95
50 Caliber Flintlock Left Hand (finished) 249.95
50 Caliber Percussion Left Hand (finished) 234.95
50 Caliber Percussion 219.95
50 Caliber Percussion Kit 169.95
Percussion Combo Kit 234.95

Also available:
ST. LOUIS HAWKEN CLASSIC w/laminated matte finish; 1:48" rifling; brass adjustable trigger. **Price:** $269.95

CVA RIFLES

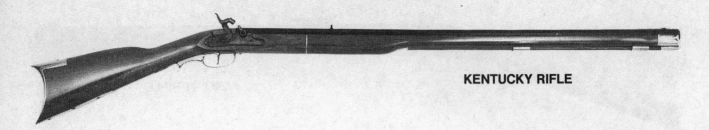

KENTUCKY RIFLE

Caliber: 50 percussion
Barrel length: 33½″ octagonal; ⅞″ across flats
Rifling: 1 in 66″
Overall length: 48″ **Weight:** 7½ lbs.
Lock: Casehardened and engraved with v-type mainspring

Trigger: Early brass-style single trigger
Sights: Brass blade front; fixed open rear
Features: Solid brass trigger guard, buttplate, toe plate, nose cap and thimble; select hardwood stock
Price: Kit $189.95

BOBCAT HUNTER

Calibers: 50 and 54 percussion
Barrel length: 26″ (¹⁵/₁₆″ octagonal)
Rifling: 1:48″
Overall length: 40″ **Weight:** 6½ lbs.
Trigger: Oversized trigger guard

Sights: Blue beaded blade front; economy rear
Stock: Dura-Grip; checkered forend and grip
Finish: RealTree all-purpose gray
Prices: $149.95
With aluminum ramrod 169.95

FRONTIER HUNTER LS CARBINE

Calibers: 50 and 54 percussion
Barrel length: 24″, blued, ¹⁵/₁₆″ octagonal
Overall length: 40″ **Weight:** 7½ lbs.
Sights: Beaded, steel blade front; hunting-style rear, fully click adjustable for windage and elevation

Stock: Laminated hardwood with straight grip; solid rubber recoil pad
Trigger: Early-style blue
Features: Black-chromed nose cap, trigger guard and blued wedge plate
Price: $219.95

CVA RIFLES

IN-LINE MUZZLELOADING RIFLES

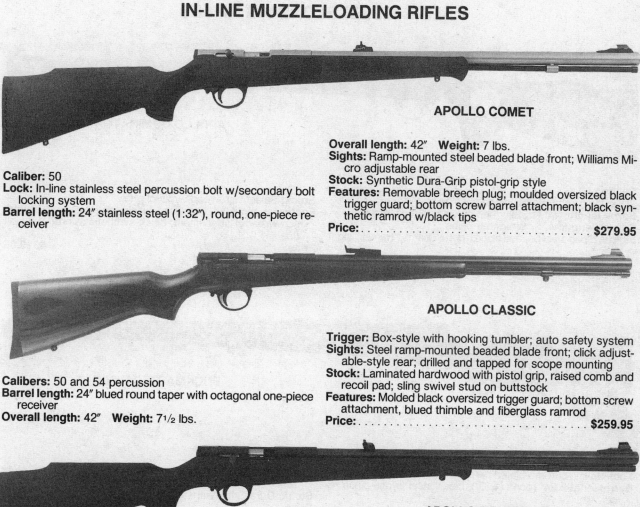

APOLLO COMET

Caliber: 50
Lock: In-line stainless steel percussion bolt w/secondary bolt locking system
Barrel length: 24″ stainless steel (1:32″), round, one-piece receiver
Overall length: 42″ **Weight:** 7 lbs.
Sights: Ramp-mounted steel beaded blade front; Williams Micro adjustable rear
Stock: Synthetic Dura-Grip pistol-grip style
Features: Removable breech plug; moulded oversized black trigger guard; bottom screw barrel attachment; black synthetic ramrod w/black tips
Price: **$279.95**

APOLLO CLASSIC

Calibers: 50 and 54 percussion
Barrel length: 24″ blued round taper with octagonal one-piece receiver
Overall length: 42″ **Weight:** 7½ lbs.
Trigger: Box-style with hooking tumbler; auto safety system
Sights: Steel ramp-mounted beaded blade front; click adjustable-style rear; drilled and tapped for scope mounting
Stock: Laminated hardwood with pistol grip, raised comb and recoil pad; sling swivel stud on buttstock
Features: Molded black oversized trigger guard; bottom screw attachment, blued thimble and fiberglass ramrod
Price: **$259.95**

APOLLO ECLIPSE

Calibers: 50 and 54
Barrel length: 24″, round (1:32″) **Overall length:** 42″
Weight: 6½ lbs.
Features: Weatherproof Dura-Grip synthetic stock; sling swivel studs; sporter adjustable rear sight
Price: **$199.95**

APOLLO BROWN BEAR

Caliber: 50
Barrel length: 24″ round (1:32″); one-piece octagonal receiver
Overall length: 42″ **Weight:** 6½ lbs.
Sights: Blued steel beaded blade front; Williams "Hunter" sight rear
Stock: Select hardwood w/pistol grip
Features: Moulded oversized black trigger guard; bottom screw barrel attachment and swivel studs; black synthetic ramrod w/black tips
Price: **$229.95**

CVA RIFLES

IN-LINE MUZZLELOADING RIFLES

APOLLO DOMINATOR

Caliber: 50
Lock: In-line chrome-plated percussion bolt
Barrel length: 24″ (1:32) w/one-piece octagonal receiver
Overall length: 42″ **Weight:** 8½ lbs.
Sights: Blued steel beaded blade front; Williams "Hunter" sight rear

Stock: Select hardwood w/pistol grip
Features: Moulded oversized black trigger guard; bottom screw barrel attachment; black synthetic ramrod w/black tips
Price: $329.95

BUCKMASTER RIFLE

Caliber: 50
Lock: In-line chrome-plated percussion bolt
Barrel length: 24″ round (1.32″); blued steel w/one-piece receiver
Overall length: 42″ **Weight:** 6½ lbs.

Sights: Blued steel beaded blade front; Williams "Hunter" sight rear
Stock: Dura-Grip synthetic stock w/Advantage camo
Price: $239.95

STAG HORN RIFLE

Calibers: 50 and 54
Lock: In-line chrome-plated steel percussion bolt
Barrel length: 24″ round (1:32″)
Overall length: 42″ **Weight:** 6½ lbs.
Sights: Blued steel beaded blade front; Williams "Hunter" sight rear

Stock: Synthetic Dura-Grip stock w/pistol grip
Features: Removable breech plug; moulded oversized black trigger guard; bottom screw barrel attachment; black synthetic ramrod w/black tips
Price: $179.95

DIXIE

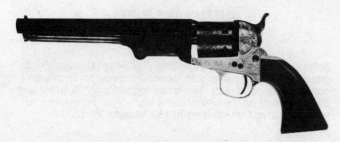

1851 NAVY BRASS-FRAME REVOLVER
Plain Model $135.00
Kit $114.00

This 36-caliber revolver was a favorite of the officers of the Civil War. Although called a Navy type, it is somewhat misnamed since many more of the Army personnel used it. Made in Italy; uses .376 mold or ball to fit and number 11 caps. Blued steel barrel and cylinder with brass frame.

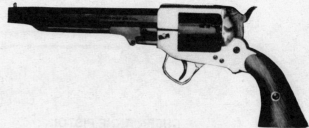

SPILLER & BURR 36 CALIBER BRASS-FRAME REVOLVER
$149.95   Kit $129.95

The 36-caliber octagonal barrel on this revolver is 7 inches long. The six-shot cylinder chambers mike .378, and the hammer engages a slot between the nipples on the cylinder as an added safety device. It has a solid brass trigger guard and frame with backstrap cast integral with the frame, two-piece walnut grips and Whitney-type casehardened loading lever.

REMINGTON 44 ARMY REVOLVER
$169.95

All steel external surfaces finished bright blue, including 8" octagonal barrel (hammer is casehardened). Polished brass guard and two-piece walnut grips are standard.

DIXIE 1860 ARMY REVOLVER
$169.95

The Dixie 1860 Army has a half-fluted cylinder and its chamber diameter is .447. Use .451 round ball mold to fit this 8-inch barrel revolver. Cut for shoulder stock.

"WYATT EARP" REVOLVER
$130.00

This 44-caliber revolver has a 12-inch octagon rifled barrel and rebated cylinder. Highly polished brass frame, backstrap and trigger guard. The barrel and cylinder have a deep blue luster finish. Hammer, trigger, and loading lever are casehardened. Walnut grips. Recommended ball size is .451.

RHO200 WALKER REVOLVER
$225.00   Kit $184.95

This 4½-pound, 44-caliber pistol is the largest ever made. Steel backstrap; guard is brass with Walker-type rounded-to-frame walnut grips; all other parts are blued. Chambers measure .445 and take a .450 ball slightly smaller than the originals.

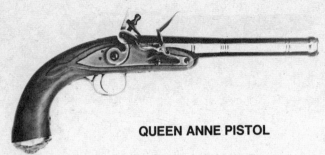

QUEEN ANNE PISTOL

QUEEN ANNE PISTOL
$189.95
Kit $154.95

Named for the Queen of England (1702–1714), this flintlock pistol has a 7½″ barrel that tapers from rear to front with a cannon-shaped muzzle. The brass trigger guard is fluted and the brass butt on the walnut stock features a grotesque mask worked into it. **Overall length:** 13″. **Weight:** 2 ¼ lbs.

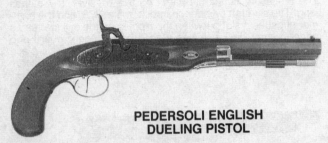

PEDERSOLI ENGLISH DUELING PISTOL

PEDERSOLI ENGLISH DUELING PISTOL
$325.00 (Flint) $275.00 (Percussion)

This reproduction of an English percussion dueling pistol, created by Charles Moore of London, features a European walnut halfstock with oil finish and checkered grip. The 45-caliber octagonal barrel is 11″ with 12 grooves and a twist of 1 in 15″. Nose cap and thimble are silver. Barrel is blued; lock and trigger guard are color casehardened.

PEDERSOLI MANG TARGET PISTOL

PEDERSOLI MANG TARGET PISTOL
$749.00

Designed specifically for the precision target shooter, this 38-caliber pistol has a 10⁷⁄₁₆″ octagonal barrel with 7 lands and grooves. Twist is 1 in 15″. **Sights:** Blade front dovetailed into barrel; rear mounted on breechplug tang, adjustable for windage. **Overall length:** 17¼″. **Weight:** 2½ lbs.

SCREW BARREL PISTOL

SCREW BARREL (FOLDING TRIGGER) PISTOL
$99.95   ($79.95 Kit)

This little gun, only 6½″ overall, has a unique loading system that eliminates the need for a ramrod. The barrel is loosened with a barrel key, then unscrewed from the frame by hand. The recess is then filled with 10 grains of FFFg black powder, the .445 round ball is seated in the dished area, and the barrel is then screwed back into place. The .245×32 nipple uses #11 percussion caps. The pistol also features a sheath trigger that folds into the frame, then drops down for firing when the hammer is cocked. Comes with color casehardened frame, trigger and center-mounted hammer.

DIXIE

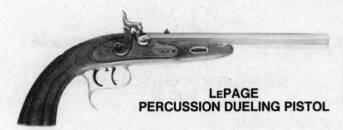

LePAGE
PERCUSSION DUELING PISTOL

DIXIE PENNSYLVANIA PISTOL
Percussion $149.95   Kit $119.95
Flintlock $159.95   Kit $139.95

Available in 44-caliber percussion or flintlock. The bright luster blued barrel measures 10″ long; rifled, 7/8-inch octagonal and takes .430 ball; barrel is held in place with a steel wedge and tang screw; brass front and rear sights. The brass trigger guard, thimbles, nose cap, wedge plates and side plates are highly polished. Locks are fine quality with early styling. Plates measure 4³/₄ inches × ⁷/₈ inch. Percussion hammer is engraved and both plates are left in the white. The flint is an excellent style lock with the gooseneck hammer having an early wide thumbpiece. The stock is walnut stained and has a wide bird's-head-type grip.

LePAGE PERCUSSION DUELING PISTOL
$259.95

This 45-caliber percussion pistol features a blued 10″ octagonal barrel with 12 lands and grooves; a brass-bladed front sight with open rear sight dovetailed into the barrel; polished silver-plated trigger guard and butt cap. Right side of barrel is stamped "LePage á Paris." Double-set triggers are single screw adjustable. **Overall length:** 16″. **Weight:** 2¹/₂ lbs.

DIXIE PENNSYLVANIA PISTOL

DOUBLE-BARREL MAGNUM MUZZLELOADING SHOTGUN (Not Shown)

A full 10, 12 or 20 gauge, high-quality, double-barreled percussion shotgun with 30-inch browned barrels. Will take the plastic shot cups for better patterns. Bores are Choked, Modified and Full. Lock, barrel tang and trigger are casehardened in a light gray color and are nicely engraved.

12 Gauge	$449.00
12 Gauge Kit	375.00
10 Gauge Magnum (double barrel—right-hand = cyl. bore, left-hand = Mod.)	495.00
10 Gauge Magnum Kit	375.00
20 Gauge	495.00

THE KENTUCKIAN RIFLE
Flintlock $269.95
Percussion $259.95

This 45-caliber rifle, in flintlock or percussion, has a 33¹/₂-inch blued octagonal barrel that is ¹³/₁₆ inch across the flats. The bore is rifled with 6 lands and grooves of equal width and about .006″ deep. Land-to-land diameter is .453 with groove-to-groove diameter of .465. Ball size ranges from .445 to .448.

The rifle has a brass blade front sight and a steel open rear sight. The Kentuckian is furnished with brass buttplate, trigger guard, patchbox, sideplate, thimbles and nose cap plus casehardened and engraved lock plate. Highly polished and finely finished stock in European walnut. **Overall length:** 48″. **Weight:** Approx. 6¹/₄ lbs.

SHARPS NEW MODEL 1859 CARBINE
$775.00

About 115,000 Sharps New Model 1859 carbines and its variants were made during the Civil War. Characterized by durability and accuracy, they became a favorite of cavalrymen on both sides. Made in Italy by David Pedersoli & Co.

SPECIFICATIONS
Caliber: 54
Barrel length: 22″ (1 in 48″ twist); blued, round barrel has 7-groove rifling
Overall length: 37½″ **Weight:** 7¾ lbs.
Sights: Blade front; adjustable rear
Stock: Oil-finished walnut
Features: Barrel band, hammer, receiver, saddle bar and ring all color casehardened

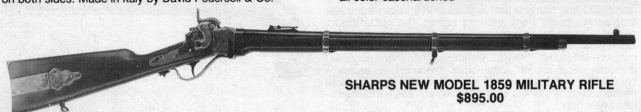

SHARPS NEW MODEL 1859 MILITARY RIFLE
$895.00

Initially used by the First Connecticut Volunteers, this rifle is associated mostly with the 1st U.S. (Berdan's) Sharpshooters. There were 6,689 made with most going to the Sharpshooters (2,000) and the U.S. Navy (2,780). Made in Italy by David Pedersoli & Co.

SPECIFICATIONS
Caliber: 54
Barrel length: 30″ (1 in 48″ twist)

Overall length: 45½″
Weight: 9 lbs.
Sights: Blade front; rear sight adjustable for elevation and windage
Features: Buttstock and forend straight-grained and oilfinished walnut; three barrel bands, receiver, hammer, nose cap, lever, patchbox cover and butt are all color casehardened; sling swivels attached to middle band and butt

1874 SHARPS LIGHTWEIGHT TARGET/ HUNTER RIFLE $895.00

This Sharps rifle in 45-70 Government caliber has a 30″ octagon barrel with blued matte finish (1:18″ twist). It also features an adjustable hunting rear sight and blade front, making it ideal for blackpowder hunters. The tang is drilled and threaded for tang sights. The oil-finished military-style buttstock has a blued metal buttplate. Double-set triggers. Color casehardened receiver and hammer. **Overall length:** 49½″. **Weight:** 10 lbs.

1874 SHARPS SILHOUETTE MODEL
$895.00

This rifle in .40-65 and .45-70 caliber has a shotgun-style buttstock with a pistol grip and a metal buttplate. The 30-inch tapered octagon barrel is blued and has a 1 in 18″ twist. The receiver, hammer, lever and buttplate are color casehardened. Ladder-type hunting rear and blade front sights are standard. Four screw holes are in the tang: two with 10 x 28 threads, two with metric threads, for attaching tang sights. Double set triggers are standard. **Weight** is 10 lbs. 3 oz. without target sights. **Overall length:** 47 ½″. Also available in .45-70

DIXIE RIFLES

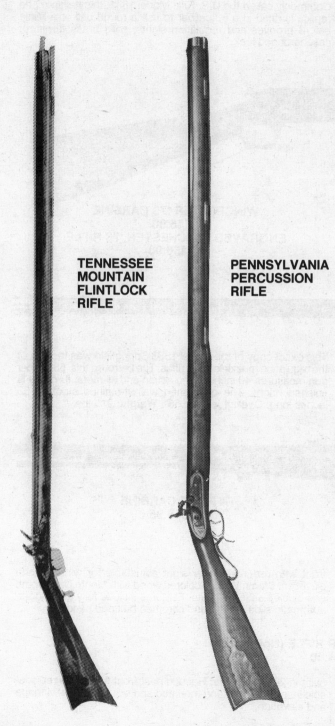

TENNESSEE MOUNTAIN FLINTLOCK RIFLE

PENNSYLVANIA PERCUSSION RIFLE

HAWKEN RIFLE (not shown)
$250.00   Kit $220.00

Blued barrel is 15/16″ across the flats and 30″ in length with a twist of 1 in 64″. Stock is of walnut with a steel crescent buttplate, halfstock with brass nosecap. Double-set triggers, front-action lock and adjustable rear sight. Ramrod is equipped with jag. **Overall length:** 46½″. Average actual **weight:** about 8 lbs., depending on the caliber; shipping weight is 10 lbs. Available in either finished gun or kit. **Calibers:** 45, 50 and 54.

DIXIE TENNESSEE MOUNTAIN RIFLE
$575.00 Percussion or Flintlock

This 50-caliber rifle features double-set triggers with adjustable set screw, bore rifled with 6 lands and grooves, barrel of 15/16 inch across the flats, brown finish and cherry stock. **Overall length:** 41½ inches. Right- and left-hand versions in flint or percussion. **Kit:** $495.00

DIXIE TENNESSEE SQUIRREL RIFLE
$575.00   (not shown)

In 32-caliber flint or percussion, right hand only, cherry stock. **Kit:** $495.00

PENNSYLVANIA RIFLE
Percussion or Flintlock $425.00
Kit (Flint or Perc.) $375.00

A lightweight at just 8 pounds, the 41½″ blued rifle barrel is fitted with an open buckhorn rear sight and front blade. The walnut one-piece stock is stained a medium darkness that contrasts with the polished brass buttplate, toe plate, patchbox, sideplate, trigger guard, thimbles and nose cap. Featuring double-set triggers, the rifle can be fired by pulling only the front trigger, which has a normal trigger pull of 4 to 5 pounds; or the rear trigger can first be pulled to set a spring-loaded mechanism that greatly reduces the amount of pull needed for the front trigger to kick off the sear in the lock. The land-to-land measurement of the bore is an exact .450 and the recommended ball size is .445. **Overall length:** 51½″.

PEDERSOLI WAADTLANDER RIFLE (not shown)
$1295.00

This authentic re-creation of a Swiss muzzleloading target rifle features a heavy octagonal barrel (31″) that has 7 lands and grooves. **Caliber:** 45. Rate of twist is 1 turn in 48″. Double-set triggers are multilever type and are easily removable for adjustment. Sights are fitted post front and tang-mounted Swiss-type diopter rear. Walnut stock, color casehardened hardware, classic buttplate and curved trigger guard complete this reproduction. The original was made between 1839 and 1860 by Marc Bristlen, Morges, Switzerland.

BLACK POWDER

DIXIE

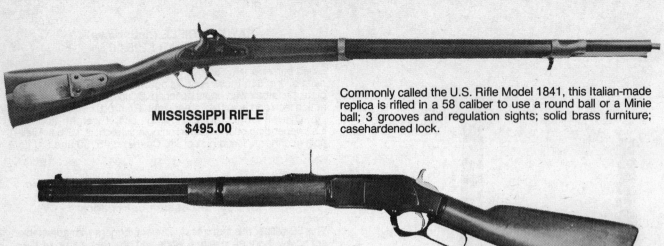

MISSISSIPPI RIFLE
$495.00

Commonly called the U.S. Rifle Model 1841, this Italian-made replica is rifled in a 58 caliber to use a round ball or a Minie ball; 3 grooves and regulation sights; solid brass furniture; casehardened lock.

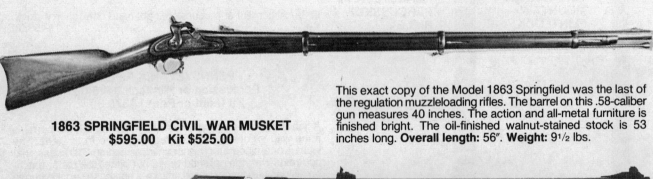

This 44-40 caliber gun can use modern or blackpowder cartridges. **Overall length:** 39″. **Barrel:** 20″ round. Its full tubular magazine will hold 11 shots. The walnut forearm and buttstock complement the high-luster bluing of the all-steel parts such as the frame, barrel, magazine and buttplate. Comes with the trap door in the butt for the cleaning rod; leaf rear sight and blade front sight. This carbine is marked "Model 1873" on the tang and caliber "44-40" on the brass carrier block.

WINCHESTER '73 CARBINE
$745.00
ENGRAVED WINCHESTER '73 RIFLE
$1250.00

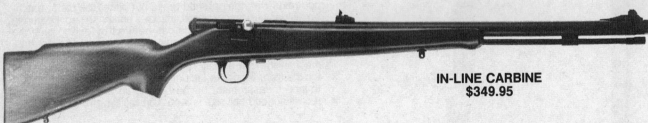

1863 SPRINGFIELD CIVIL WAR MUSKET
$595.00   Kit $525.00

This exact copy of the Model 1863 Springfield was the last of the regulation muzzleloading rifles. The barrel on this .58-caliber gun measures 40 inches. The action and all-metal furniture is finished bright. The oil-finished walnut-stained stock is 53 inches long. **Overall length:** 56″. **Weight:** 9½ lbs.

IN-LINE CARBINE
$349.95

Made in Italy by D. Pedersoli, this rifle in 50 or 54 caliber features a sliding "bolt" that completely encloses cap and nipple, making it the most weatherproof muzzleloader available. **Barrel length:** 24″. **Overall length:** 41″. **Weight:** 6½ lbs. **Sights:** Ramp front with red insert; rear sight adjustable for windage and elevation. **Stock:** Walnut-colored wood with Monte Carlo comb and black plastic buttplate. Features include fully adj. trigger, automatic slide safety, and chromed bolt and handle.

TRYON CREEDMOOR RIFLE (Not Shown)
$625.00

This Tryon rifle features a high-quality back-action lock, double-set triggers, steel buttplate, patchbox, toe plate and curved trigger guard. **Caliber:** 45. **Barrel:** 32¾″, octagonal, with 1 twist in 20.87″. **Sights:** Hooded post front fitted with replaceable inserts; rear is tang-mounted and adjustable for windage and elevation.

DIXIE

U.S. MODEL 1861 SPRINGFIELD PERCUSSION RIFLE-MUSKET
$595.00   Kit $525.00

An exact re-creation of an original rifle produced by Springfield National Armory, Dixie's Model 1861 Springfield .58-caliber rifle features a 40″ round, tapered barrel with three barrel bands. Sling swivels are attached to the trigger guard bow and middle barrel band. The ramrod has a trumpet-shaped head with swell; sights are standard military rear and bayonet-attachment lug front. The percussion lock is marked "1861" on the rear of the lockplate with an eagle motif and "U.S. Springfield" in front of the hammer. "U.S." is stamped on top of buttplate. All furniture is "National Armory Bright." **Overall length:** 55^{13}/$_{16}$″. **Weight:** 8 lbs.

1862 THREE-BAND ENFIELD RIFLED MUSKET
$495.00   Kit $425.00

One of the finest reproduction percussion guns available, the 1862 Enfield was widely used during the Civil War in its original version. This rifle follows the lines of the original almost exactly. The .58-caliber musket features a 39-inch barrel and walnut stock. Three steel barrel bands and the barrel itself are blued; the lockplate and hammer are case colored and the remainder of the furniture is highly polished brass. The lock is marked, "London Armory Co." **Weight:** 10^{1}/$_{2}$ lbs. **Overall length:** 55″.

U.S. MODEL 1816 FLINTLOCK MUSKET
$725.00

The U.S. Model 1816 Flintlock Musket was made by Harpers Ferry and Springfield Arsenals from 1816 until 1864. It had the highest production of any U.S. flintlock musket and after conversion to percussion saw service in the Civil War. It has a .69-caliber, 42″ smoothbore barrel held by three barrel bands with springs. All metal parts are finished in "National Armory Bright." The lockplate has a brass pan and is marked "Harpers Ferry" vertically behind the hammer, with an American eagle placed in front of the hammer. The bayonet lug is on top of the barrel and the steel ramrod has a button-shaped head. Sling swivels are mounted on the trigger guard and middle barrel band. **Overall length:** 56^{1}/$_{2}$″. **Weight:** 9^{3}/$_{4}$ lbs.

1858 TWO-BAND ENFIELD RIFLE
$475.00

This 33-inch barrel version of the British Enfield is an exact copy of similar rifles used during the Civil War. The .58-caliber rifle sports a European walnut stock, deep blue-black finish on the barrel, bands, breech-plug tang and bayonet mount. The percussion lock is color casehardened and the rest of the furniture is brightly polished brass.

EMF REVOLVERS

SHERIFF'S MODEL 1851

SHERIFF'S MODEL 1851 REVOLVER
$140.00 (Brass) $192.00 (Steel)

SPECIFICATIONS
Caliber: 36 Percussion
Ball diameter: .376 round or conical, pure lead
Barrel length: 5″
Overall length: 10½″
Weight: 39 oz.
Sights: V-notch groove in hammer (rear); truncated cone in front
Percussion cap size: #11

MODEL 1860 ARMY REVOLVER
$160.00 (Brass) $207.00 (Engraved, Brass)
$216.00 (Steel) $376.00 (Engraved, Steel)

SPECIFICATIONS
Caliber: 44 Percussion
Barrel length: 8″
Overall length: 13⅝″
Weight: 41 oz.
Frame: Casehardened
Finish: High-luster blue with walnut grips

Also available:
Cased set with steel frame, wood case, flask
  and mould $360.00
  Engraved cased set (brass frame only) 325.00
Fluted cylinder model (steel frame only) 375.00

MODEL 1860 ARMY

SECOND MODEL 44 DRAGOON
$304.00

SPECIFICATIONS
Caliber: 44
Barrel length: 7½″ (round)
Overall length: 14″
Weight: 4 lbs.
Finish: Steel casehardened frame

Also available:
Third Model Dragoon $312.00
Texas Dragoon 309.00
Walker 320.00

SECOND MODEL DRAGOON

MODEL 1862 POLICE REVOLVER
$248.00 (Steel) $184.00 (Brass)

SPECIFICATIONS
Caliber: 36 Percussion
Capacity: 5-shot
Barrel length: 6½″

MODEL 1862 POLICE

EUROARMS OF AMERICA

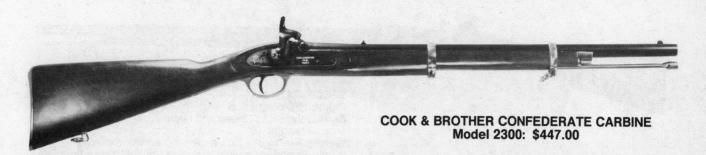

COOK & BROTHER CONFEDERATE CARBINE
Model 2300: $447.00

Classic re-creation of the rare 1861, New Orleans-made Artillery Carbine. The lockplate is marked "Cook & Brother N.O. 1861" and is stamped with a Confederate flag at the rear of the hammer.

SPECIFICATIONS
Caliber: 58 percussion
Barrel length: 24"   **Overall length:** 40⅓"
Weight: 7½ lbs.
Sights: Fixed blade front and adjustable dovetailed rear

Ramrod: Steel
Finish: Barrel is antique brown; buttplate, trigger guard, barrel bands, sling swivels and nose cap are polished brass; stock is walnut
Recommended ball sizes: .575 r.b., .577 Minie and .580 maxi; uses musket caps

Also available:
MODEL 2301 COOK & BROTHER FIELD with 33" barrel
Price: $480.00

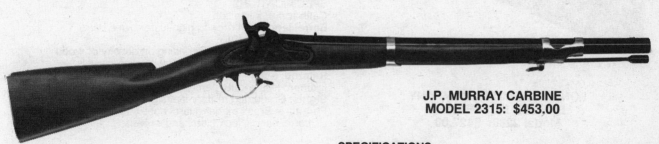

J.P. MURRAY CARBINE
MODEL 2315: $453.00

Replica of an extremely rare CSA Cavalry Carbine based on an 1841 design of parts and lock.

SPECIFICATIONS
Caliber: 58 percussion
Barrel length: 23"
Features: Brass barrel bands and buttplate; oversized trigger guard; sling swivels

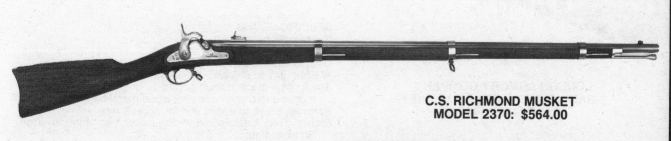

C.S. RICHMOND MUSKET
MODEL 2370: $564.00

SPECIFICATIONS
Caliber: 58 percussion. **Barrel length:** 40" with three bands.

EUROARMS OF AMERICA

LONDON ARMORY COMPANY
2-BAND RIFLE MUSKET
Model 2270: $480.00

SPECIFICATIONS
Caliber: 58 percussion
Barrel length: 33″, blued and rifled
Overall length: 49″
Weight: 8 1/2 to 8 3/4 lbs., depending on wood density
Stock: One-piece walnut; polished "bright" brass buttplate, trigger guard and nose cap; blued barrel bands
Sights: Inverted 'V' front sight; Enfield folding ladder rear
Ramrod: Steel

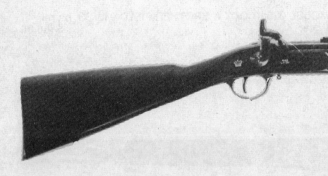

LONDON ARMORY COMPANY
ENFIELD MUSKETOON
Model 2280: $427.00

SPECIFICATIONS
Caliber: 58; Minie ball
Barrel length: 24″; round high-luster blued barrel
Overall length: 40 1/2″
Weight: 7 to 7 1/2 lbs., depending on density of wood
Stock: Seasoned walnut stock with sling swivels
Ramrod: Steel
Ignition: Heavy-duty percussion lock
Sights: Graduated military-leaf sight
Furniture: Brass trigger guard, nose cap and buttplate; blued barrel bands, lock plate, and swivels

LONDON ARMORY COMPANY
3-BAND ENFIELD RIFLED MUSKET
Model 2260: $484.00

SPECIFICATIONS
Caliber: 58 percussion
Barrel length: 39″, blued and rifled
Overall length: 54″
Weight: 9 1/2 to 9 3/4 lbs., depending on wood density
Stock: One-piece walnut; polished "bright" brass buttplate, trigger guard and nose cap; blued barrel bands
Ramrod: Steel; threaded end for accessories
Sights: Traditional Enfield folding ladder rear sight; inverted 'V' front sight
Also available:
MODEL 2261 with white barrel **$507.00**

EUROARMS OF AMERICA

1803 HARPERS FERRY FLINTLOCK RIFLE
Model 2305: $640.00

SPECIFICATIONS
Caliber: 54 Flintlock
Barrel length: 35″, octagonal
Features: Walnut half stock with cheekpiece; browned barrel

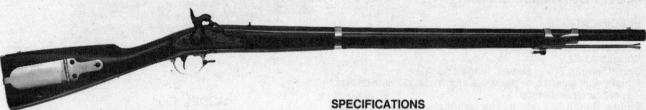

1841 MISSISSIPPI RIFLE
Model 2310: $500.00

SPECIFICATIONS
Calibers: 54 and 58 percussion
Barrel length: 33″, octagonal
Features: Walnut stock; brass barrel bands and buttplate; sling swivels

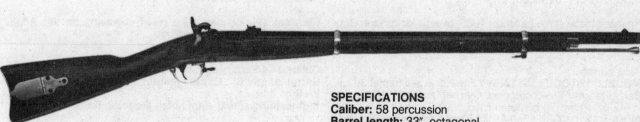

**1863 REMINGTON
ZOUAVE RIFLE (2-Barrel Bands)**
Model 2255: $460.00 (Range Grade)
Model 2250: $387.00 (Field Grade)

SPECIFICATIONS
Caliber: 58 percussion
Barrel length: 33″, octagonal
Overall length: 48$\frac{1}{2}$″
Weight: 9$\frac{1}{2}$ to 9$\frac{3}{4}$ lbs.
Sights: U.S. Military 3-leaf rear; blade front
Features: Two brass barrel bands; brass buttplate and nose cap; sling swivels

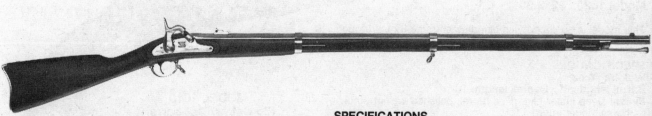

1861 SPRINGFIELD RIFLE
Model 2360: $564.00

SPECIFICATIONS
Caliber: 58 percussion
Barrel length: 40″
Features: 3 barrel bands

EUROARMS OF AMERICA

MODEL 1005

ROGERS & SPENCER ARMY REVOLVER
Model 1006 (Target): $239.00

SPECIFICATIONS
Caliber: 44; takes .451 round or conical lead balls; #11 percussion cap
Weight: 47 oz.
Barrel length: 7¹/₂"   **Overall length:** 13³/₄"
Finish: High gloss blue; flared walnut grip; solid frame design; precision-rifled barrel
Sights: Rear fully adjustable for windage and elevation; ramp front sight

ROGERS & SPENCER REVOLVER
LONDON GRAY (Not shown)
Model 1007: $245.00

Revolver is the same as Model 1005, except for London Gray finish, which is heat treated and buffed for rust resistance; same recommended ball size and percussion caps.

Also available:
MODEL 1120 COLT 1851 NAVY Steel or brass frame. 36 cal. **Barrel length:** 7¹/₂" octagonal. **Overall length:** 13". **Weight:** 42 oz. **Price:** To be determined.
MODEL 1210 COLT 1860 ARMY Steel frame. 44 percussion. **Overall length:** 10⁵/₈" or 13⁵/₈". **Weight:** 41 oz. **Price:** To be determined.

ROGERS & SPENCER REVOLVER
Model 1005: $227.00

SPECIFICATIONS
Caliber: 44 Percussion; #11 percussion cap
Barrel length: 7¹/₂"   **Overall length:** 13³/₄"
Weight: 47 oz.
Sights: Integral rear sight notch groove in frame; brass truncated cone front sight
Finish: High gloss blue; flared walnut grip; solid frame design; precision-rifled barrel
Recommended ball diameter: .451 round or conical, pure lead

MODEL 1006

REMINGTON 1858
NEW MODEL ARMY ENGRAVED (Not shown)
Model 1040: $275.00

Classical 19th-century style scroll engraving on this 1858 Remington New Model revolver.

SPECIFICATIONS
Caliber: 44 Percussion; #11 cap
Barrel length: 8"   **Overall length:** 14³/₄"
Weight: 41 oz.
Sights: Integral rear sight notch groove in frame; blade front sight
Recommended ball diameter: .451 round or conical, pure lead

REMINGTON 1858
NEW MODEL ARMY REVOLVER
Model 1020: $213.00

This model is equipped with blued steel frame, brass trigger guard in 44 caliber.

SPECIFICATIONS
Weight: 40 oz.
Barrel length: 8"   **Overall length:** 14³/₄"
Finish: Deep luster blue rifled barrel; polished walnut stock; brass trigger guard.
Also available:
MODEL 1010. Same as Model 1020, except with 6¹/₂" barrel and in 36 caliber: **$213.00**

MODEL 1010
(36 Cal. w/6¹/₂" barrel)

GONIC ARMS

MODEL GA-87 RIFLE
$870.00 (Open Sights)

SPECIFICATIONS
Calibers: 45 and 50 Mag.
Barrel length: 26″   **Overall length:** 43″
Weight: 6¹/₂ lbs.
Sights: Bead front; open rear (adjustable for windage and elevation); drilled and tapped for scope bases

Stock: American walnut   **Length of pull:** 14″
Trigger: Single stage (4-lb. pull)
Mechanism type: Closed-breech muzzleloader
Features: Ambidextrous safety; nonglare satin finish; newly designed loading system; all-weather performance guaranteed; faster lock time

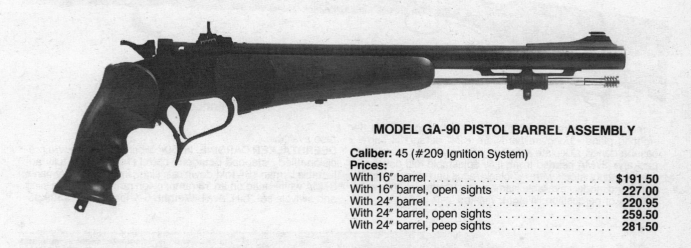

MODEL GA-90 PISTOL BARREL ASSEMBLY

Caliber: 45 (#209 Ignition System)
Prices:
With 16″ barrel **$191.50**
With 16″ barrel, open sights 227.00
With 24″ barrel 220.95
With 24″ barrel, open sights 259.50
With 24″ barrel, peep sights 281.50

MODEL 93 MAGNUM RIFLE
$500.00 (Open Sights)
$603.00 (Stainless w/Open Sights)

Gonic Arms's blackpowder rifle has a unique loading system that produces better consistency and utilizes the full powder charge of the specially designed penetrator bullet (ballistics = 2,650 foot-pounds at 1,600 fps w/465-grain .500 bullet).

SPECIFICATIONS
Caliber: 50 Magnum
Barrel length: 26″   **Overall length:** 43″
Weight: 6 to 6¹/₂ lbs.

Sights: Open hunting sights (adjustable)
Features: Walnut-stained hardwood stock; adjustable trigger; nipple wrench; drilled and tapped for scope bases; ballistics and instruction manual

Also available:
MODEL 93 SAFARI RIFLE w/classic walnut stock, open sights **$1560.00**

LYMAN RIFLES

COUGAR IN-LINE RIFLE
$299.95

The new Lyman Cougar In-Line rifle is designed for the serious blackpowder hunter who wants a rugged and accurate muzzleloader with the feel of a centerfire bolt-action rifle. The Cougar In-Line is traditionally styled with a walnut stock and blued barrel and action. Available in 50 and 54 caliber. Features include a 22″ barrel with 1:24″ twist and shallow rifling grooves; dual safety system (equipped with a bolt safety notch in receiver and a sliding thumb safety that disables the trigger mechanism); drilled and tapped for Lyman 57 WTR receiver sight; fully adjustable trigger; sling swivel studs installed; unbreakable Derlin ramrod; modern folding-leaf rear and bead front sights; rubber recoil pad.

DEERSTALKER RIFLE
Percussion $299.95
Flintlock $324.95

Lyman's Deerstalker rifle incorporates • higher comb for better sighting plane • nonglare hardware • 24″ octagonal barrel • casehardened sideplate • Q.D. sling swivels • Lyman sight package (37MA beaded front; fully adjustable fold-down 16A rear) • walnut stock with 1/2″ black recoil pad • single trigger. Left-hand models available (same price). **Calibers:** 50 and 54, flintlock or percussion. **Weight:** 7 1/2 lbs.

Also available:
DEERSTALKER CARBINE. In .50-caliber percussion w/a precision-rifled "stepped octagon" barrel (1:24″ twist); fully adjustable Lyman 16A fold-down rear sight; front sight is Lyman's 37MA white bead on an 18 ramp; nylon ramrod, modern sling and swivels set. L.H. avail. **Weight:** 6 3/4 lbs. **Price: $309.95**

GREAT PLAINS RIFLE
Percussion $424.95   (Kit $339.95)
Flintlock $449.00   (Kit $364.95)

The Great Plains Rifle has a 32-inch deep-grooved barrel and 1;66″ twist to shoot patched round balls. Blued steel furniture including the thick steel wedge plates and toe plate; correct lock and hammer styling with coil spring dependability; a walnut stock w/o patchbox. A Hawken-style trigger guard protects double-set triggers. Steel front sight and authentic buckhorn styling in an adjustable rear sight. Fixed primitive rear sight also included. Left-hand models available (same price). **Calibers:** 50 and 54.

LYMAN TRADE RIFLE
Percussion $299.95
Flintlock $319.95

The Lyman Trade Rifle features a 28-inch octagonal barrel, rifled 1 turn at 48 inches, designed to fire both patched round balls and the popular maxistyle conical bullets. Polished brass furniture with blued finish on steel parts; walnut stock; hook breech; single spring-loaded trigger; coil-spring percussion lock; fixed steel sights; adjustable rear sight for elevation also included. Steel barrel rib and ramrod ferrrule. **Caliber:** 50 or 54 percussion and flint. **Overall length:** 45″.

MODERN MUZZLELOADING

KNIGHT RIFLES

MK-85 GRAND AMERICAN

MK-85 STALKER

MK-85 KNIGHT RIFLES

The MK-85 muzzleloading rifles (designed by William A. "Tony" Knight) are handcrafted, lightweight rifles capable of 1½-inch groups at 100 yards. They feature a one-piece, in-line bolt assembly, patented double-safety system, Timney featherweight deluxe trigger system, recoil pad, and Green Mountain barrels (1 in 28" twist in 50 and 54 caliber).

Calibers: 50 and 54
Barrel length: 24"   **Overall length:** 43"
Weight: 6 to 7¼ lbs.

Sights: Adjustable high-visibility open sights
Stock: Classic walnut, laminated or composite
Features: Swivel studs installed; hard anodized aluminum ramrod; combo tool; hex keys, and more.
Prices:

MK-85 HUNTER (Walnut)	$ 539.95
MK-85 KNIGHT HAWK (24" Blued barrel)	779.95
Stainless barrel	869.95
MK-85 PREDATOR (Stainless)	729.95
MK-85 STALKER (Laminated)	679.95
MK-85 GRAND AMERICAN (Blued barrel,	
Shadow brown or black)	995.95
In Stainless Steel	1095.95

MODEL BK-92 BLACK KNIGHT
$399.95

Calibers: 50 and 54
Barrel length: 24" (tapered nonglare w/open breech system)
Sights: Adjustable; tapped and drilled for scope mount
Stock: Black composite

Features: Patented double-safety system; in-line ignition system; 1 in 28" twist; stainless-steel breechplug; adjustable trigger; ½" recoil pad; Knight precision loading ramrod; Monte Carlo stock

MAGNUM ELITE
$839.95 (Black Composite Stock)

Calibers: 50 and 54
Barrel length: 24"   **Overall length:** 41"   **Weight:** 6.75 lbs.
Sights: Adjustable high-visibility open sights
Features: "Posi-Fire" ignition system; Knight Double-Safety System; aluminum ramrod; sling swivel studs

MODERN MUZZLELOADING

MODEL LK-93 WOLVERINE
$269.95 (Blued) $349.95 (Stainless)

Calibers: 50 and 54
Barrel length: 22″; blued rifle-grade steel (1:28″ twist)
Overall length: 41″   **Weight:** 6 lbs.

Sights: Adjustable high-visibility rear sight; drilled and tapped for scope mount
Stock: Lightweight Fiber-Lite molded stock
Features: Patented double-safety system; adjustable Accu-Lite trigger; removable breechplug; stainless-steel hammer

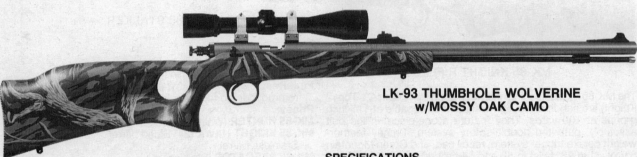

LK-93 THUMBHOLE WOLVERINE
$359.95 (Blued w/Black Stock)
$409.95 (Blued w/Camo Stock)
$449.95 (Stainless Steel w/Black Stock)
$449.95 (Stainless Steel w/Camo Stock)

LK-93 THUMBHOLE WOLVERINE
w/MOSSY OAK CAMO

SPECIFICATIONS
Calibers: 50 and 54
Barrel length: 22″ rifle-grade steel (1:28″ twist)
Overall length: 41″
Weight: 6 lbs. 4 oz.
Features: Patented double safety system; adjustable Accu-Lite trigger; removable breech plug; stainless steel hammer

MOUNTAIN STATE

SILVER CLASSIC
$995.00

SPECIFICATIONS
Caliber: 50 (flint or percussion)
Barrel length: 42″ octagon (1:66″ twist)
Overall length: 59″
Weight: 8 lbs.
Sights: Semi-buckhorn (rear), silver blade (front)
Trigger: Double action, double set
Length of pull: 14″
Drop at heel: 3½″
Features: Nickel-silver (white bronze) furniture; fancy sideplate and chevron nose cap

GOLDEN CLASSIC (not shown)

Same price and specifications as Silver Classic except barrel length is 35 inches and weight is 7½ lbs. Stock is curly maple hand-finished in satin reddish-brown. Also features unbreakable Hunter Super-Rod; polished solid brass or nickel silver buttplate; high relief cheekpiece.

NAVY ARMS REVOLVERS

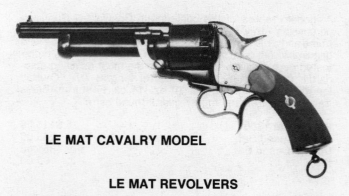

LE MAT CAVALRY MODEL

LE MAT NAVY MODEL

LE MAT ARMY MODEL

LE MAT REVOLVERS

Once the official sidearm of many Confederate cavalry officers, this 9-shot .44-caliber revolver with a central single-shot barrel of approx. 65 caliber gave the cavalry man 10 shots to use against the enemy. **Barrel length:** 7⅝″. **Overall length:** 14″. **Weight:** 3 lbs. 7 oz.

Cavalry Model	$ 595.00
Navy Model	595.00
Army Model	595.00
18th Georgia (engraving on cylinder, display case)	795.00
Beauregard (hand-engraved cylinder and frame; display case and mold)	1000.00

1862 NEW MODEL POLICE

This is the last gun manufactured by the Colt plant in the percussion era. It encompassed all the modifications of each gun, starting from the early Paterson to the 1861 Navy. It was favored by the New York Police Dept. for many years. One-half fluted and rebated cylinder, 36 cal., 5 shot, .375 dia. ball, 18 grains of black powder, brass trigger guard and backstrap. Casehardened frame, loading lever and hammer—balance blue. **Barrel length:** 5½″.

1862 Police	$290.00
Law and Order Set	365.00

ROGERS & SPENCER REVOLVER

This revolver features a six-shot cylinder, octagonal barrel, hinged-type loading lever assembly, two-piece walnut grips, blued finish and casehardened hammer and lever. **Caliber:** 44. **Barrel length:** 7½″. **Overall length:** 13¾″. **Weight:** 3 lbs.

Rogers & Spencer	$245.00
London Gray	270.00
Target Model (w/adjustable sights)	270.00

COLT 1847 WALKER

The 1847 Walker replica comes in 44 caliber with a 9-inch barrel. **Weight:** 4 lbs. 8 oz. Well suited for the collector as well as the blackpowder shooter. Features include: rolled cylinder scene; blued and casehardened finish; and brass guard. Proof tested.

Colt 1847 Walker	$275.00
Single Cased Set	405.00
Deluxe Cased Set	505.00

ROGERS & SPENCER REVOLVER

NAVY ARMS REVOLVERS

REB MODEL 1860

A modern replica of the confederate Griswold & Gunnison percussion Army revolver. Rendered with a polished brass frame and a rifled steel barrel finished in a high-luster blue with genuine walnut grips. All Army Model 60s are completely proof-tested by the Italian government to the most exacting standards. **Calibers:** 36 and 44. **Barrel length:** 7¼″. **Overall length:** 13″. **Weight:** 2 lbs. 10 oz.–11 oz. **Features:** Brass frame, backstrap and trigger guard, round barrel.

Reb Model 1860	$115.00
Single Cased Set	235.00
Double Cased Set	365.00
Kit	90.00

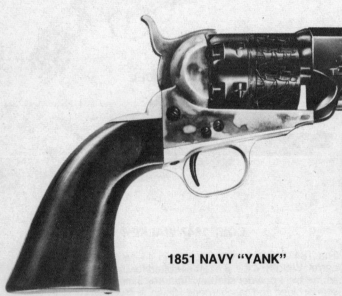

1851 NAVY "YANK"

A favorite of "Wild Bill" Hickok, the 1851 Navy was originally manufactured by Colt from 1850 through 1876. This model was the most popular of the Union revolvers, mostly because it was lighter and easier to handle than the Dragoon. **Barrel length:** 7½″. **Overall length:** 14″. **Weight:** 2 lbs. **Rec. ball diam.:** .375 R.B. (.451 in 44 cal) **Calibers:** 36 and 44. **Capacity:** 6 shot. **Features:** Steel frame, octagonal barrel, cylinder roll-engraved with Naval battle scene, backstrap and trigger guard are polished brass.

1851 Navy "Yank"	$155.00
Kit	125.00
Single Cased Set	280.00
Double Cased Set	455.00

The 1860 Army satisfied the Union Army's need for a more powerful .44-caliber revolver. The cylinder on this replica is roll engraved with a polished brass trigger guard and steel strap cut for shoulder stock. The frame, loading lever and hammer are finished in high-luster color case-hardening. Walnut grips. **Weight:** 2 lbs. 9 oz. **Barrel length:** 8″. **Overall length:** 13⅝″. **Caliber:** 44. **Finish:** Brass trigger guard, steel backstrap, round barrel, creeping lever, rebated cylinder, engraved Navy scene.

1860 Army	$175.00
Single Cased Set	290.00
Double Cased Set	480.00
Kit	155.00

1860 ARMY

NAVY ARMS REVOLVERS

1858 NEW MODEL ARMY REMINGTON-STYLE, STAINLESS STEEL

Exactly like the standard 1858 Remington (below) except that every part except for the grips and trigger guard is manufactured from corrosion-resistant stainless steel. This gun has all the style and feel of its ancestor with all of the conveniences of stainless steel. **Caliber: 44.**

1858 Remington Stainless	$270.00
Single Cased Set	395.00
Double Cased Set	680.00

1858 TARGET MODEL

With its top strap solid frame, the Remington Percussion Revolver is considered the Magnum of Civil War revolvers and is ideally suited to the heavy 44-caliber charges. Based on the Army Model, the target gun has target sights for controlled accuracy. Ruggedly built from modern steel and proof tested.

1858 Target Model	$205.00

1858 NEW MODEL ARMY REMINGTON-STYLE REVOLVER

1858 NEW MODEL ARMY REMINGTON-STYLE REVOLVER

This rugged, dependable, battle-proven Civil War veteran with its top strap and rugged frame was considered the Magnum of C.W. revolvers, ideally suited for the heavy 44 charges. Blued finish. **Caliber: 44. Barrel length: 8″. Overall length: 14¼″. Weight: 2 lbs. 8 oz.**

New Model Army Revolver	$170.00
Single Cased Set	290.00
Double Cased Set	480.00
Kit	150.00

Also available:
Brass Frame	$125.00
Brass Frame Kit	115.00
Single Cased Set	250.00
Double Cased Set	395.00

REB 60 SHERIFF'S MODEL

A shortened version of the Reb Model 60 Revolver. The Sheriff's model version became popular because the shortened barrel was fast out of the leather. This is actually the original snub nose, the predecessor of the detective specials or belly guns designed for quick-draw use. **Calibers: 36 and 44.**

Reb 60 Sheriff's Model	$115.00
Kit	90.00
Single Cased Set	235.00
Double Cased Set	365.00

DELUXE NEW MODEL 1858 REMINGTON-STYLE 44 CALIBER (not shown)

Built to the exact dimensions and weight of the original Remington 44, this model features an 8″ barrel with progressive rifling, adjustable front sight for windage, all-steel construction with walnut stocks and silver-plated trigger guard. Steel is highly polished and finished in rich charcoal blue. **Barrel length: 8″. Overall length: 14¼″. Weight: 2 lbs. 14 oz.**

Deluxe New Model 1858	$415.00

BLACK POWDER

NAVY ARMS PISTOLS

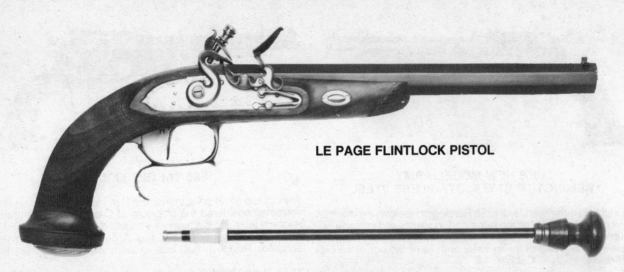

LE PAGE FLINTLOCK PISTOL

LE PAGE FLINTLOCK PISTOL
(44 Caliber)

The Le Page pistol is a beautifully hand-crafted reproduction featuring hand-checkered walnut stock with hinged buttcap and carved motif of a shell at the forward portion of the stock. Single-set trigger and highly polished steel lock and furniture together with a brown-finished rifled barrel make this a highly desirable target pistol. **Barrel length:** 10½″. **Overall length:** 17″. **Weight:** 2 lbs. 2 oz.

Le Page Flintlock (rifled or smoothbore) $625.00

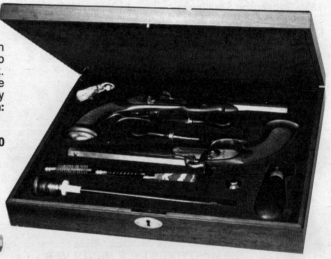

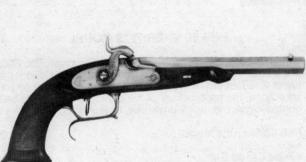

LE PAGE PERCUSSION PISTOL
(44 Caliber)

The tapered octagonal rifled barrel is in the traditional style with 7 lands and grooves. Fully adjustable single-set trigger. Engraved overall with traditional scrollwork. The European walnut stock is in the Boutet style. Spur-style trigger guard. Fully adjustable elevating rear sight. Dovetailed front sight adjustable for windage. **Barrel length:** 9″. **Overall length:** 15″. **Weight:** 2 lbs. 2 oz. **Rec. ball diameter:** 424 R.B.

Le Page Percussion $500.00

CASED LE PAGE PISTOL SETS

The case is French-fitted and the accessories are the finest quality to match.

Double Cased Sets
French-fitted double cased set comprising two Le Page pistols, turn screw, nipple key, oil bottle, cleaning brushes, leather covered flask and loading rod. Rifled or smoothbore barrel.

Double Cased Flintlock Set $1575.00
Double Cased Percussion Set 1300.00

Single Cased Sets
French-fitted single cased set comprising one Le Page pistol, turn screw, nipple key, oil bottle, cleaning brushes, leather covered flask and loading rod. Rifled or smoothbore barrel.

Single Cased Flintlock Set $900.00
Single Cased Percussion Set 775.00

NAVY ARMS

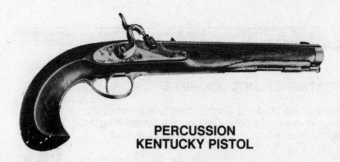

**PERCUSSION
KENTUCKY PISTOL**

**FLINTLOCK
KENTUCKY PISTOL**

KENTUCKY PISTOLS

The Kentucky Pistol is truly a historical American gun. It was carried during the Revolution by the Minutemen and was the sidearm of "Andy" Jackson in the Battle of New Orleans. Navy Arms Company has conducted extensive research to manufacture a pistol representative of its kind, with the balance and handle of the original for which it became famous.

Flintlock	$225.00
Single Cased Flintlock Set	350.00
Double Cased Flintlock Set	580.00
Percussion	215.00
Single Cased Percussion Set	335.00
Double Cased Percussion Set	550.00

**1806 HARPERS FERRY
FLINTLOCK PISTOL**

1806 HARPERS FERRY PISTOL

Of all the early American martial pistols, Harpers Ferry is one of the best known and was carried by both the Army and the Navy. Navy Arms Company has authentically reproduced the Harper's Ferry to the finest detail, providing a well-balanced and well-made pistol. **Weight:** 2 lbs. 9 oz. **Barrel length:** 10″. **Overall length:** 16″. **Caliber:** 58. **Finish:** Walnut stock; casehardened lock; brass-mounted browned barrel.

Harpers Ferry	$310.00
Single Cased Set	355.00

1816 M.T. WICKHAM MUSKET

This version of the French 1777 Charleville musket was chosen by the U.S. Army in 1816 to replace the 1808 Springfield. Manufactured in Philadelphia by M.T. Wickham, it was one of the last contract models. **Caliber:** 69. **Barrel length:** 44½″. **Overall length:** 56¼″. **Weight:** 10 lbs. **Sights:** Brass blade front. **Stock:** European walnut. **Feature:** Brass flashpan.

1816 M.T. Wickham Musket	$810.00

BLACK POWDER

NAVY ARMS RIFLES

MORTIMER FLINTLOCK RIFLE

This big-bore flintlock rifle, a replica of the Mortimer English-style flintlock smoothbore, features a waterproof pan, roller frizzen and external safety. **Caliber:** 54. **Barrel length:** 36″. **Overall length:** 53″. **Weight:** 7 lbs. **Sights:** Blade front; notch rear. **Stock:** Walnut.

Mortimer Flintlock Rifle **$780.00**
 12-gauge drop-in barrel 340.00

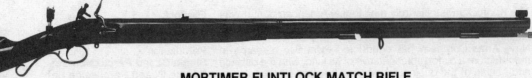

MORTIMER FLINTLOCK MATCH RIFLE

This is the sleek match version of the large-bore rifle above. **Caliber:** .54. **Barrel length:** 36″. **Overall length:** 52¼″. **Weight:** 9 lbs. **Sights:** Precision aperture match rear; globe-style front. **Stock:** Walnut with cheekpiece, checkered wrist, sling swivels. **Features:** Waterproof pan; roller frizzen; external safety.

Mortimer Flintlock Match Rifle **$900.00**

1859 SHARPS CAVALRY CARBINE

This percussion version of the Sharps is a copy of the popular breechloading Cavalry Carbine of the Civil War. It features a patchbox and bar and saddle ring on left side of the stock. **Caliber:** 54. **Barrel length:** 22″. **Overall length:** 39″. **Weight:** 7¾ lbs. **Sights:** Blade front; military ladder rear. **Stock:** Walnut.

Sharps Cavalry Carbine . . . . **$ 885.00**
Also available:
1859 Sharps Infantry Rifle (54 cal.) 1030.00

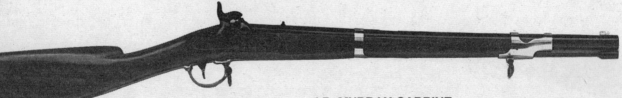

J.P. MURRAY CARBINE

Popular with the Confederate Cavalry, the J.P. Murray percussion carbine was originally manufactured in Columbus, Georgia, during the Civil War. **Caliber:** 58. **Barrel length:** 23½″. **Overall length:** 39¼″. **Weight:** 8 lbs. 5 oz. **Finish:** Walnut stock with polished brass.

J.P. Murray Carbine **$405.00**

NAVY ARMS RIFLES

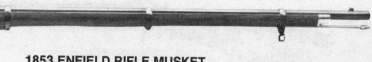

1853 ENFIELD RIFLE MUSKET

The Enfield Rifle Musket marked the zenith in design and manufacture of the military percussion rifle, and this perfection has been reproduced by Navy Arms Company. This and other Enfield muzzleloaders were the most coveted rifles of the Civil War, treasured by Union and Confederate troops alike for their fine quality and deadly accuracy. **Caliber:** 58. **Barrel length:** 39″. **Weight:** 10 lbs. 6 oz. **Overall length:** 55″. **Sights:** Fixed front; graduated rear. **Stock:** Seasoned walnut with solid brass furniture.

1853 Enfield Rifle Musket **$480.00**

1858 ENFIELD RIFLE

In the late 1850s the British Admiralty, after extensive experiments, settled on a pattern rifle with a 5-groove barrel of heavy construction, sighted to 1,100 yards, designated the Naval rifle, Pattern 1858. **Caliber:** 58. **Barrel length:** 33″. **Weight:** 9 lbs. 10 oz. **Overall length:** 48.5″. **Sights:** Fixed front; graduated rear. **Stock:** Seasoned walnut with solid brass furniture.

1858 Enfield Rifle **$450.00**

1861 MUSKETOON

The 1861 Enfield Musketoon was the favorite long arm of the Confederate Cavalry. **Caliber:** 58. **Barrel length:** 24″. **Weight:** 7 lbs. 8 oz. **Overall length:** 40.25″. **Sights:** Fixed front; graduated rear. **Stock:** Seasoned walnut with solid brass furniture.

1861 Musketoon **$405.00**
Kit 365.00

ITHACA/NAVY HAWKEN RIFLE

Features a 31½″ octagonal browned barrel crowned at the muzzle with buckhorn-style rear sight, blade front sight. Color casehardened percussion lock is fitted on walnut stock. **Calibers:** 50 and 54.

Ithaca/Navy Hawken Rifle **$445.00**

NAVY ARMS RIFLES

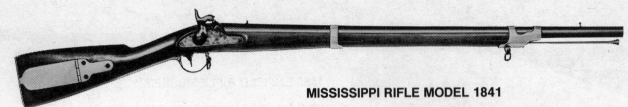

MISSISSIPPI RIFLE MODEL 1841

This historic percussion weapon gained its name because of its performance in the hands of Jefferson Davis' Mississippi Regiment during the heroic stand at the Battle of Buena Vista. Also known as the ''Yager'' (a misspelling of the German Jaeger), this was one of the first percussion rifles adopted by Army Ordnance. The Mississippi is handsomely furnished in brass, including patchbox for tools and spare parts. **Weight:** 9½ lbs. **Barrel length:** 32½". **Overall length:** 48½". **Calibers:** 54 and 58. **Finish:** Walnut finish stock, brass mounted.

Mississippi Rifle Model 1841 . . . . **$465.00**

SMITH CARBINE

The Smith Carbine was considered one of the finest breechloading carbines of the Civil War period. The hinged breech action allowed fast reloading for cavalry units. Available in either the **Cavalry Model** (with saddle ring and bar) or **Artillery Model** (with sling swivels). **Caliber:** 50. **Barrel length:** 21½". **Overall length:** 39". **Weight:** 7¾ lbs. **Sights:** Brass blade front; folding ladder rear. **Stock:** American walnut.

Smith Carbine **$600.00**

1861 SPRINGFIELD RIFLE

One of the most popular Union rifles of the Civil War, the 1861 used the 1855-style hammer. The lockplate on this replica is marked ''1861, U.S. Springfield.'' **Caliber:** 58. **Barrel length:** 40". **Overall length:** 56". **Weight:** 10 lbs. **Finish:** Walnut stock with polished metal lock and stock fitting.

1861 Springfield Rifle **$550.00**

1863 SPRINGFIELD RIFLE

An authentically reproduced replica of one of America's most historical firearms, the 1863 Springfield rifle features a full-size, three-band musket and precision-rifled barrel. **Caliber:** 58. **Barrel length:** 40". **Overall length:** 56". **Weight:** 9½ lbs. **Finish:** Walnut stock with polished metal lock and stock fittings. Casehardened lock available upon request.

1863 Springfield Rifle **$550.00**

NAVY ARMS

PENNSYLVANIA LONG RIFLE

This new version of the Pennsylvania Rifle is an authentic reproduction of the original model. Its classic lines are accented by the long, browned octagon barrel and polished lockplate. **Caliber:** 32 or 45 (flint or percussion. **Barrel length:** 40$\frac{1}{2}$". **Overall length:** 56$\frac{1}{2}$". **Weight:** 7$\frac{1}{2}$ lbs. **Sights:** Blade front; adjustable Buckhorn rear. **Stock:** Walnut.

Pennsylvania Long Rifle Flintlock **$475.00**
   Percussion **460.00**

BROWN BESS MUSKET

Used extensively in the French and Indian War, the Brown Bess Musket proved itself in the American Revolution as well. This fine replica of the "Second Model" is marked "Grice" on the lockplate. **Caliber:** 75. **Barrel length:** 42". **Overall length:** 59". **Weight:** 9$\frac{1}{2}$ lbs. **Sights:** Lug front. **Stock:** Walnut.

Brown Bess Musket **$750.00**
Kit **625.00**

Also available:
Brown Bess Carbine
Caliber: 75. **Barrel length:** 30". **Overall length:** 47". **Weight:** 7$\frac{3}{4}$ lbs.
Price **$750.00**

1803 HARPERS FERRY RIFLE

This 1803 Harpers Ferry rifle was carried by Lewis and Clark on their expedition to explore the Northwest territory. This replica of the first rifled U.S. Martial flintlock features a browned barrel, casehardened lock and a brass patchbox. **Caliber:** 54. **Barrel length:** 35". **Overall length:** 50$\frac{1}{2}$". **Weight:** 8$\frac{1}{2}$ lbs.

1803 Harpers Ferry Rifle **$615.00**

"BERDAN" 1859 SHARPS RIFLE

A replica of the Union sniper rifle used by Col. Hiram Berdan's First and Second U.S. Sharpshooters Regiments during the Civil War. **Caliber:** 54. **Barrel length:** 30". **Overall length:** 46$\frac{3}{4}$". **Weight:** 8 lbs. 8 oz. **Sights:** Military-style ladder rear; blade front. **Stock:** Walnut. **Features:** Double set triggers, casehardened receiver; patchbox and furniture

"Berdan" 1859 Sharps Rifle **$1095.00**
Also available:
Single Trigger Infantry Model **1030.00**

BLACK POWDER

NAVY ARMS RIFLES

1862 C.S. RICHMOND RIFLE

This model was manufactured by the Confederacy at the Richmond Armory utilizing 1855 Rifle Musket parts captured from the Harpers Ferry Arsenal. This replica features the unusual 1855 lockplate, stamped "1862 C.S. Richmond, V.A." **Caliber:** 58. **Barrel length:** 40". **Overall length:** 56". **Weight:** 10 lbs. **Finish:** Walnut stock with polished metal lock and stock fittings.

1862 C.S. Richmond Rifle **$550.00**

TRYON CREEDMOOR RIFLE

This replica of the Tryon Creedmoor match rifle won a Gold Medal at the 13th World Shoot in Germany. It features a blued octagonal heavy match barrel, hooded target front sight, adjustable Vernier tang sight, double-set triggers, sling swivels and a walnut stock. **Caliber:** 451. **Barrel length:** 33". **Overall length:** 48¼". **Weight:** 9½ lbs.

Tryon Creedmoor Rifle **$780.00**

KODIAK DOUBLE RIFLE

The powerful double-barreled Kodiak percussion rifle has fully adjustable sights mounted on blued steel barrels. The lockplates are engraved and highly polished. **Calibers:** 50, 54 and 58. **Barrel length:** 28½". **Overall length:** 45". **Weight:** 11 lbs. **Sights:** Folding notch rear; ramp bead front. **Stock:** Hand-checkered walnut.

Kodiak Double Rifle **$775.00**

"COUNTRY BOY" IN-LINE RIFLE
$175.00

The Navy Arms "Country Boy" incorporates a trap in the buttstock for storage of a takedown tool for removing the breech plug or nipple in the field. It is also capable of replacing the #11 nipple with the hotter musket type. **Caliber:** 50. **Barrel length:** 24" (rate of twist 1:32). **Overall length:** 41". **Weight:** 8 lbs. **Sights:** Bead front, adjustable rear. **Features:** Chrome-lined barrel; weather-resistant synthetic stock; drilled and tapped for scope mount.

NAVY ARMS SHOTGUNS

MORTIMER FLINTLOCK SHOTGUN

This replica of the Mortimer Shotgun features a browned barrel, casehardened furniture, sling swivels and checkered walnut stock. The lock contains waterproof pan, roller frizzen and external safety. **Gauge:** 12. **Barrel length:** 36″. **Overall length:** 53″. **Weight:** 7 lbs.

Mortimer Flintlock Shotgun **$735.00**

STEEL SHOT MAGNUM SHOTGUN

This shotgun, designed for the hunter who must use steel shot, features engraved polished lockplates, English-style checkered walnut stock (with cheekpiece) and chrome-lined barrels. **Gauge:** 10. **Barrel length:** 28″. **Overall length:** 45½″. **Weight:** 7 lbs. 9 oz. **Choke:** Cylinder/Cylinder.

Steel-Shot Magnum Shotgun **$560.00**

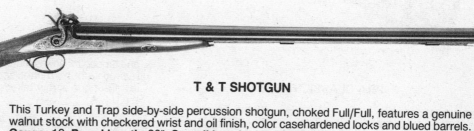

FOWLER SHOTGUN

A traditional side-by-side percussion field gun, this fowler model features blued barrels and English-style straight stock design. It also sports a hooked breech, engraved and color casehardened locks, double triggers and checkered walnut stock. **Gauge:** 12. **Chokes:** Cylinder/Cylinder. **Barrel length:** 28″. **Overall length:** 44½″. **Weight:** 7½ lbs.

Fowler Shotgun **$340.00**
Kit 310.00

T & T SHOTGUN

This Turkey and Trap side-by-side percussion shotgun, choked Full/Full, features a genuine walnut stock with checkered wrist and oil finish, color casehardened locks and blued barrels. **Gauge:** 12. **Barrel length:** 28″. **Overall length:** 44″. **Weight:** 7½ lbs.

T & T Shotgun **$540.00**

BLACK POWDER

PRAIRIE RIVER ARMS

PRA BULLPUP RIFLE

SPECIFICATIONS
Calibers: 50 and 54
Barrel length: 28″ (1:28″ twist) **Overall length:** 31¹/₂″
Weight: 7¹/₂ lbs.
Stock: Hardwood or Black All Weather

Sights: Blade front, open adjustable rear
Features: Bullpup design, thumbhole stock; patented internal percussion ignition system; left-hand model available. Dovetailed for scope mount; two built-in safety positions; introduced 1995. Made in the U.S.A.
Prices:
4140 Alloy barrel, hardwood stock **$375.00**
4140 Alloy barrel, black stock **390.00**
Stainless barrel, hardwood stock **425.00**
Stainless barrel, black stock **440.00**

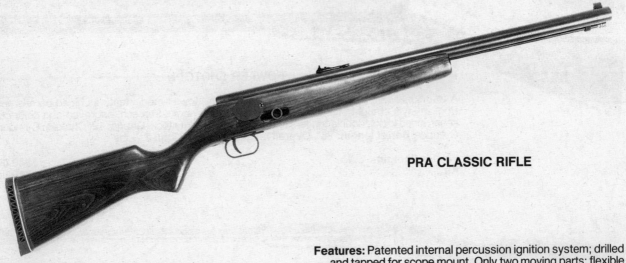

PRA CLASSIC RIFLE

PRA CLASSIC RIFLE

SPECIFICATIONS
Calibers: 50 and 54
Barrel length: 26″ (1:28″ twist) **Overall length:** 40¹/₂″
Stock: Hardwood or Black All Weather
Sights: Blade front, open adjustable rear

Features: Patented internal percussion ignition system; drilled and tapped for scope mount. Only two moving parts; flexible ramrod from hard anodized aluminum; sling swivel studs installed; one screw takedown; introduced 1995. Made in the U.S.A.
Prices:
4140 Alloy barrel, hardwood stock **$375.00**
4140 Alloy barrel, black stock **390.00**
Stainless barrel, hardwood stock **425.00**
Stainless barrel, black stock **440.00**

REMINGTON RIFLES

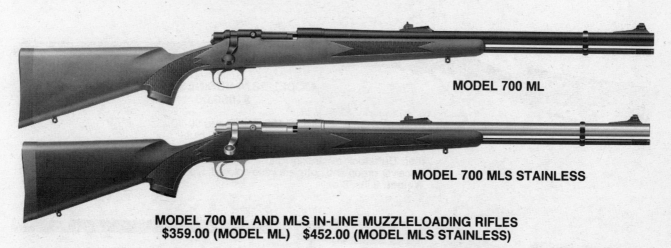

MODEL 700 ML

MODEL 700 MLS STAINLESS

MODEL 700 ML AND MLS IN-LINE MUZZLELOADING RIFLES
$359.00 (MODEL ML) $452.00 (MODEL MLS STAINLESS)

Remington began building flintlock muzzleloaders in 1816. Now as the oldest gunmaker in the country, it is returning to that heritage with two in-line muzzleloading rifles. These have the same cocking action and the same trigger mechanism with an exceptionally fast lock time. The difference comes from a modified bolt and ignition system, plus their method of loading from the muzzle rather than the breech. The Model 700 ML has a traditionally blued carbon-steel barreled action. On the Model 700 MLS the barrel, receiver and bolt are made of 416 stainless steel with a non-reflective, satin finish. Each is set in a strong, fiberglass-reinforced synthetic stock fitted with a Magnum-style recoil pad. One end of the solid aluminum ramrod is recessed into the forend and the outer end is secured by a barrel band. Instead of an open chamber, the breech is closed by a stainless-steel plug and nipple. In the internal

structure of the modified bolt, the firing pin is replaced by a cylindrical rod that is cocked by normal bolt lift. It is released by pulling the trigger to strike a #11 percussion cap seated on the nipple. Lock time is 3.0 milliseconds. Barrels are rifled with a 1 in 28″ twist. Once loaded, a Model 700 ML or MLS handles and shoots like a familiar centerfire bolt-action rifle. The barrels are fitted with standard adjustable iron sights; receivers are drilled and tapped for short-action scope mounts.

SPECIFICATIONS
Barrel length: 24″   **Overall length:** 44$\frac{1}{2}$″
Weight: 7$\frac{3}{4}$ lbs.
Length of pull: 13$\frac{3}{8}$″
Drop at Comb: $\frac{1}{2}$″   **Drop at Heel:** $\frac{3}{8}$″

RUGER

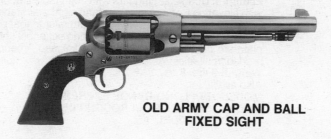

**OLD ARMY CAP AND BALL
FIXED SIGHT**

OLD ARMY CAP AND BALL
$413.00   ($465.00 Stainless Steel)

This Old Army cap-and-ball revolver with fixed sights is reminiscent of the Civil War era martial revolvers and those used by the early frontiersmen in the 1800s. This Ruger model comes in both blued and stainless-steel finishes and features modern materials, technology and design throughout, including steel music-wire coil springs. Fixed or adjustable sights.

SPECIFICATIONS
Caliber: 45 (.443″ bore; .45″ groove)
Barrel length: 7$\frac{1}{2}$″
Rifling: 6 grooves, R.H. twist (1:16″)
Weight: 2$\frac{7}{8}$ lbs.
Sights: Fixed, ramp front; topstrap channel rear
Percussion cap nipples: Stainless steel (#11)

SHILOH SHARPS

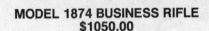

MODEL 1874 BUSINESS RIFLE
$1050.00

Calibers: 45-70, 45-90, 45-120, 50-70 and 50-90.
Barrel: 28-inch heavy-tapered round; dark blue.
Features: Double-set triggers adjustable set. Blade-front sight with sporting-leaf rear. Buttstock is straight grip rifle buttplate, forend sporting schnabel style. Receiver group and buttplate case-colored; wood is American walnut oil-finished.
Weight: 9 lbs. 8 oz.

MODEL 1874 SPORTING RIFLE NO. 1
$1148.00

Calibers: 45-70, 45-90, 45-120, 50-70 and 50-90.
Features: 30-inch tapered octagon barrel. Double-set triggers with adjustable set, blade front sight, sporting rear with elevation leaf and sporting tang sight adjustable for elevation and windage. Buttstock is pistol grip, shotgun butt, sporting forend style. Receiver group and buttplate case colored. Barrel is high-finish blue-black; wood is American walnut oil finish.

MODEL 1874 SPORTING RIFLE NO. 3
$1044.00

Calibers: 45-70, 45-90, 45-120, 50-70 and 50-90.
Barrel: 30-inch tapered octagonal; with high finish blue-black.
Features: Double-set triggers with adjustable set, blade front sight, sporting rear with elevation leaf and sporting tang sight adjustable for elevation and windage. Buttstock is straight grip with rifle buttplate; trigger plate is curved and checkered to match pistol grip. Forend is sporting schnabel style. Receiver group and buttplate are case colored. Wood is oil-finished American walnut, and may be upgraded in all rifles.
Weight: 9 lbs. 8 oz.
Also available:
MODEL 1874 LONG-RANGE EXPRESS $1174.00
MODEL 1874 MONTANA ROUGHRIDER 1044.00
HARTFORD MODEL 1214.00

SHILOH SHARPS RIFLE CARTRIDGE AVAILABILITY

The **Long-Range Express, No. 1 Sporting, No. 3 Sporting, Business, Montana Roughrider** and **Hartford Model** rifles all are available in the following cartridges: 38-55, 40-50 (1^{11}/$_{16}$ B.N.), 40-65 Win, 40-70 (2^1/$_{10}$ B.N.), 40-70 (2^1/$_4$ B.N.), 40-70 (2^1/$_2$ ST), 40-90 (3^1/$_4$ ST), 40-90 (2^5/$_8$ B.N.), 44-77 B.N., 44-90 B.N., 45-70 (2^1/$_{10}$ ST), 45-90 (2^4/$_{10}$ ST), 45-100 (2^6/$_{10}$ ST), 45-110 (2^7/$_8$ ST), 45-120 (3^1/$_4$ ST), 50-70 (1^3/$_4$ ST) and 50-100 (2^1/$_2$ ST). The **1874 Saddle Rifle** is available in all of the above calibers.

STONE MOUNTAIN ARMS

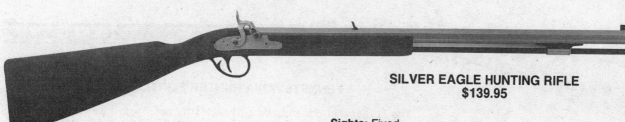

SILVER EAGLE HUNTING RIFLE
$139.95

Sights: Fixed
Stock: Duragrip synthetic stock with checkered grip surfaces
Features: Weatherguard tang, thimble and lock; blued ramp and sights
Also available:
SILVER EAGLE HUNTER. Same specifications as Silver Eagle Hunting Rifle, but includes adjustable sights, sling swivel studs and unbreakable synthetic ramrod; drilled and tapped for scope. **Price: $159.95**

SPECIFICATIONS
Caliber: 50 percussion
Barrel length: 26″ (Weatherguard nickel), octagonal
Overall length: 40″
Rate of twist: 1:48″
Trigger: Single with oversized trigger guard

1853 ENFIELD RIFLE
$550.00

Features: Blued barrel tang, breech plug and bayonet mount; polished brass furniture; color casehardened lock and sideplates
Also available:
1861 SPRINGFIELD RIFLED MUSKET. 50 cal. 40″ barrel fitted with three-tier rear sight. **Overall length:** 56″. **Weight:** 10.5 lbs. **Price:** $599.00

SPECIFICATIONS
Caliber: 58 percussion
Barrel length: 39″ (1:78″ twist) w/3 blued steel bands
Overall length: 54″ **Weight:** 10.5 lbs.
Sights: Folding ladder rear; inverted "V" front
Stock: Walnut

MISSISSIPPI RIFLE
$575.00

SPECIFICATIONS
Caliber: 54
Lock: Color casehardened percussion
Barrel length: 33.5″ round browned (1:66″)
Overall length: 49.5″ **Weight:** 10.5 lbs.
Sights: Brass blade front; fixed open rear
Stock: Oil-finished walnut
Features: Polished brass hardware, patchbox, sling swivels

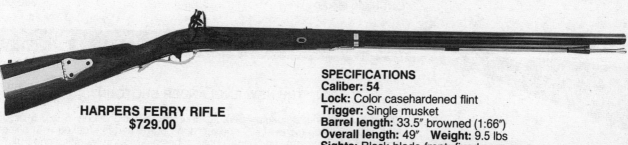

HARPERS FERRY RIFLE
$729.00

SPECIFICATIONS
Caliber: 54
Lock: Color casehardened flint
Trigger: Single musket
Barrel length: 33.5″ browned (1:66″)
Overall length: 49″ **Weight:** 9.5 lbs
Sights: Black blade front; fixed open rear
Stock: Oil-finished walnut; polished brass fixtures; spring-loaded thumb release patch box

THOMPSON/CENTER

PENNSYLVANIA HUNTER FLINTLOCK RIFLE

The 31″ barrel on this model is cut rifled (.010″ deep) with 1 turn in 66″ twist. Its outer contour is stepped from octagon to round. Sights are fully adjustable for both windage and elevation. Stocked with select American black walnut; metal hardware is blued steel. Features a hooked breech system and coil-spring lock, plus T/C's QLA™ Muzzle System for improved accuracy and easier reloading. **Caliber:** 50. **Overall length:** 48″. **Weight:** Approx. 7.6 lbs.

Pennsylvania Hunter Flintlock **$375.00**

PENNSYLVANIA HUNTER FLINTLOCK CARBINE

Thompson/Center's Pennsylvania Hunter Flintlock Carbine is 50-caliber with 1: 66″ twist and cut-rifling. It was designed specifically for the hunter who uses patched round balls only and hunts in thick cover or brush. The 21″ barrel is stepped from octagonal to round. Features T/C's QLA™ Muzzle System. **Overall length:** 38″. **Weight:** 6½ lbs. **Sights:** Fully adjustable open hunting-style rear with bead front. **Stock:** Select American walnut. **Trigger:** Single hunting-style trigger. **Lock:** Color cased, coil spring, with floral design.

Pennsylvania Hunter Flintlock Carbine **$365.00**

THE NEW ENGLANDER RIFLE

This percussion rifle features a 26″ round, 50- or 54-caliber rifled barrel (1 in 48″ twist). Contains T/C's QLA™ Muzzle System. **Weight:** 7 lbs. 15 oz.

New Englander Rifle **$310.00**
    With Composite stock (24″ barrel, right-hand only) 295.00
    12-Gauge Accessory Barrel, IC Choke 170.00
Left-Hand Model 330.00

THE NEW ENGLANDER SHOTGUN

This 12-gauge muzzleloading percussion shotgun weighs only 6 lbs. 8 oz. It features a 27-inch (screw-in IC choke) round barrel and is stocked with select American black walnut. Additional choke tubes available in Modified and Full.

New Englander Shotgun **$330.00**

THOMPSON/CENTER

THE HAWKEN 45, 50 and 54 caliber

Similar to the famous Rocky Mountain rifles made during the early 1800s, the Hawken is intended for serious shooting. Button-rifled for ultimate precision, the Hawken is available in 45-, 50- or 54-caliber percussion or 50- caliber flintlock. It features a hooked breech, double-set triggers, first-grade American walnut stock, adjustable hunting sights, solid brass trim and color casehardened lock. Beautifully decorated; comes equipped with T/C's QLA™ Muzzle System. **Weight:** Approx. 8½ lbs.

Hawken Caplock 45, 50 or 54 caliber	**$415.00**
Hawken Flintlock 50 caliber	425.00
Kit: Caplock (50 and 54 caliber)	315.00
Kit: Flintlock (50 caliber)	335.00

THE RENEGADE

Available in 50- or 54-caliber percussion, the Renegade was designed to provide maximum accuracy and maximum shocking power. It is constructed of superior modern steel with investment cast parts fitted to an American walnut stock, featuring a precision-rifled (26-inch carbine-type) octagonal barrel, hooked-breech system, coil spring lock, double-set triggers, adjustable hunting sights and steel trim. Features T/C's QLA™ Muzzle System. **Weight:** Approx. 8 lbs.

Renegade Caplock 50 and 54 caliber	**$360.00**
Renegade Caplock Left Hand, 50 and 54 caliber	370.00
Renegade Caplock Kit Right Hand, 50 caliber	275.00
Renegade Flintlock Right Hand, 50 caliber	370.00

BLACK POWDER

THOMPSON/CENTER

BIG BOAR CAPLOCK RIFLE
$355.00

This large 58-caliber caplock rifle is designed for the muzzleloading hunter who prefers larger game. The rifle features a 26-inch octagonal barrel with 1 in 48″ twist, rubber recoil pad, leather sling with QD sling swivels, and an adjustable open-style hunting rear sight with bead front sight. Stock is of American black walnut.

FIRE HAWK
$365.00 Blued

This new in-line ignition muzzleloader features a striker that is cocked and held rearward, locked in place when the thumb safety is in the rearward position. By sliding the thumb safety forward, the striker is free to fire the percussion cap when the trigger is pulled. The Fire Hawk's free-floated 24″ barrel is rifled with a 1:38″ twist and is designed for use with modern conical or sabot projectiles. Features T/C's QLA™ Muzzle System. **Calibers:** 32, 50, 54, 58. **Overall length:** 41¾″. **Weight:** 7 lbs. **Sights:** Adj. leaf-style rear; ramp-style white bead front. **Stock:** American black walnut or Composite.
Also available:

Stainless Steel w/Composite stock	**$395.00**
Stainless Steel w/walnut stock	405.00
Stainless Steel w/thumbhole composite stock	425.00
Blued w/walnut stock in all calibers	365.00
Blued w/Advantage camo composite stock	395.00
Deluxe SST w/walnut stock in 50 and 54 cal.	535.00
Deluxe blued w/walnut in 50 and 54 cal.	495.00

FIRE HAWK DELUXE BLUED

FIRE HAWK ADVANTAGE™ CAMO MODEL

THOMPSON/CENTER

SCOUT RIFLE, CARBINE & PISTOL

**SCOUT CARBINE
with Rynite Stock**

Thompson/Center's Scout Carbine & Pistol use the in-line ignition system with a special vented breechplug that produces constant pressures from shot to shot, thereby improving accuracy. The patented trigger mechanism consists of only two moving parts—the trigger and the hammer—thus providing ease of operation and low maintenance. Features T/C's QLA™ Muzzle System. Both the carbine and pistol are available in 50 and 54 caliber. The carbine's 21″ (round) and 24″ (stepped) barrels and the pistol's 12-inch barrel (overall length: 17″) are easily removable for cleaning. Their lines are reminiscent of the saddle guns and pistols of the ''Old West,'' combining modern-day engineering with the flavor of the past. Both are suitable for left- or right--handed shooters.

Scout Rifle w/walnut stock	$435.00
With Composite stock	360.00
Scout Carbine w/walnut stock	425.00
With composite stock	345.00
Scout Pistol (50 and 54 cal.)	350.00

THUNDER HAWK

THUNDER HAWK

Thompson/Center's in-line caplock rifle, the Thunder Hawk, combines the features of an old-time caplock with the look and balance of a modern bolt-action rifle. The in-line ignition system ensures fast, positive ignition, plus an adjustable trigger for a crisp trigger pull. The 21-inch and 24-inch barrels have an adjustable rear sight and bead-style front sight (barrel is drilled and tapped to accept T/C's Thunder Hawk scope rings, Weaver-style base and rings, or Quick-Release Mounting System). The stock is American black walnut with rubber recoil pad and sling swivel studs. Rifling is 1:38″ twist, designed to fire patched round balls, conventional conical projectiles and sabot bullets. Includes T/C's QLA™ Muzzle System. **Weight:** Approx. 6¾ lbs. **Calibers:** 50 and 54.

Thunder Hawk w/21″ barrel, blued w/walnut stock	$315.00
Stainless steel w/composite stock	335.00
Thunder Hawk w/24″ barrel	
Stainless steel with composite stock	345.00
Blued steel with composite stock	305.00
Blued steel with walnut stock	325.00
Thunder Hawk Shadow w/24″ barrel, blued composite	275.00

GREY HAWK

T/C's Grey Hawk is a stainless-steel caplock rifle in 50 and 54 caliber with a composite buttstock and a round 24-inch barrel. It also features a stainless-steel lockplate, hammer, thimble and trigger guard. Adjustable rear sight and bead-style front sight are blued. Includes T/C's QLA™ Muzzle System. **Weight:** Approx. 7 lbs.

Grey Hawk	$330.00

TRADITIONS PISTOLS

PIONEER PISTOL

PIONEER PISTOL
$157.00   ($126.50 Kit)

SPECIFICATIONS
Caliber: 45 percussion
Barrel length: 9⅝" octagonal with tenon; ¹³/₁₆" across flats, rifled 1 in 16"; fixed tang breech
Overall length: 15"   **Weight:** 1 lb. 15 oz.
Sights: Blade front; fixed rear
Trigger: Single
Stock: Beech, rounded
Lock: V-type mainspring
Features: German silver furniture; blackened hardware

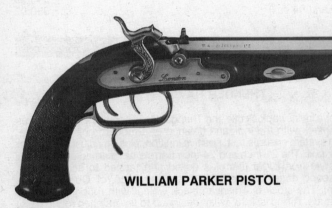

WILLIAM PARKER PISTOL

WILLIAM PARKER PISTOL
$282.00

SPECIFICATIONS
Caliber: 50 percussion
Barrel length: 10⅜" octagonal (¹⁵/₁₆" across flats)
Overall length: 17½"   **Weight:** 2 lbs. 5 oz.
Sights: Brass blade front; fixed rear
Stock: Walnut, checkered at wrist
Triggers: Double set; will fire set and unset
Lock: Adjustable sear engagement with fly and bridle; V-type mainspring
Features: Brass percussion cap guard; polished hardware, brass inlays and separate ramrod

TRAPPER PISTOL

TRAPPER PISTOL
$190.00 Percussion   ($148.00 Percussion Kit)
$207.00 Flintlock

SPECIFICATIONS
Caliber: 50 percussion or flintlock
Barrel length: 9¾"; octagonal (⅞" across flats) with tenon
Overall length: 15½"   **Weight:** 2 lbs. 14 oz.
Stock: Beech
Lock: Adjustable sear engagement with fly and bridle
Triggers: Double set, will fire set and unset
Sights: Primitive-style adjustable rear; brass blade front
Furniture: Solid brass; blued steel on assembled pistol

TRADITIONS PISTOLS

BUCKHUNTER PRO ALL-WEATHER

BUCKHUNTER PRO BLUED
w/Walnut Stock

BUCKHUNTER PRO IN-LINE PISTOLS
$230.00   ($247.00 w/All-Weather Stock)

SPECIFICATIONS
Calibers: 50 and 54 Percussion
Barrel length: 10″ round (removable breech plug); 1:20″ twist
Overall length: 14″
Weight: 3 lbs.
Trigger: Single
Sights: Fold-down adjustable rear; beaded blade front
Stock: Walnut or All-Weather
Features: Blued or C-Nickel furniture; PVC ramrod; drilled and tapped for scope mounting; coil mainspring; thumb safety

BUCKSKINNER PISTOL (not shown)
$165.00   ($180.00 Laminated)

SPECIFICATIONS
Caliber: 50 percussion
Barrel length: 10″ octagonal ($^{15}/_{16}$″ across flats)
Overall length: 15 $^1/_2$″
Weight: 2 lbs. 9 oz.
Trigger: Single
Sights: Fixed rear; blade front
Stock: Beech or laminated
Features: Blackened furniture; PVC ramrod

KENTUCKY PISTOL
$142.00   ($115.00 Kit)

SPECIFICATIONS
Caliber: 50 Percussion
Barrel length: 10″ octagon ($^7/_8$″ flats); fixed tang breech; 1:20″ twist
Overall length: 15″
Weight: 2 lbs. 8 oz.
Trigger: Single
Sights: Fixed rear; blade front
Stock: Beechwood
Features: Brass furniture; wood ramrod; kit available

BLACK POWDER

TRADITIONS

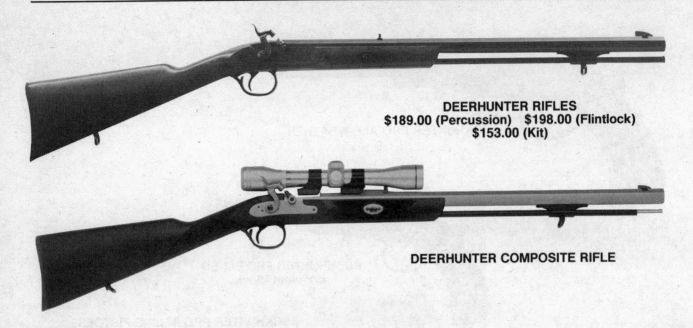

DEERHUNTER RIFLES
$189.00 (Percussion) $198.00 (Flintlock)
$153.00 (Kit)

DEERHUNTER COMPOSITE RIFLE

Tradition's popular Deerhunter Rifle series has added five new models with its Deerhunter Composite stock in both blued and C- Nickel configurations. The new Deer Hunter Composites carry over the fast-handling design of the other Deerhunters into matte black composite stocks with checkering at the wrist and forend to withstand the most rigorous hunting conditions. Offered in 50- and 54-caliber percussion models and a 50-caliber flintlock. The Deerhunter Composite comes with a rubber buttpad, adjustable hunting-style rear sight, an unbreakable PVC ramrod and sling swivels. Drilled and tapped for easy scope mounting.

SPECIFICATIONS (Small Game only)
Calibers: 32 (Hunter Package only), 50 and 54 percussion
Barrel length: 24″ octagonal
Rifling twist: 1:48″ (percussion only); 1:66″ (flint or percussion)
Overall length: 40″
Weight: 6 lbs. (6.25 lbs. in Small Game rifle)
Trigger: Single
Sights: Fixed rear; blade front
Features: PVC ramrod; blackened furniture; inletted wedge plates

Also available:
DEERHUNTER ALL-WEATHER MODEL
Epoxy-covered beech stock and C-Nickel finish.
Flintlock, 1:66″ twist **$214.00**
Percussion, 50 or 54 caliber, 1:48″ twist, drilled and
tapped **198.00**
COMPOSITE STOCK MODELS
Percussion w/blued barrel **172.00**
Percussion w/nickel barrel **189.00**
Flintlock w/nickel barrel and 1:66″ twist **214.00**
SMALL GAME RIFLE w/aluminum ramrod. **190.00**
Percussion Kit **152.75**

DEERHUNTER SCOUT

SPECIFICATIONS
Caliber: 50 percussion
Barrel length: 22″ octagonal
Twist: 1:48″
Overall length: 36½″
Weight: 5 lbs. 10 oz.

DEERHUNTER SCOUT
$239.00

TRADITIONS

HAWKEN WOODSMAN
$247.00 (Percussion)

SPECIFICATIONS
Calibers: 50 and 54 percussion
Barrel length: 28″ (octagonal); hooked breech; rifled 1 turn in 48″ (1 turn in 66″ in 50 caliber also available)
Overall length: 44 1/2″
Weight: 7 lbs. 11 oz.
Triggers: Double set; will fire set or unset
Lock: Adjustable sear engagement with fly and bridle

Stock: Beech
Sights: Beaded blade front; hunting-style rear, fully screw adjustable for windage and elevation
Furniture: Solid brass, blued steel or blackened (50 cal. only); unbreakable ramrod
Also available:
Left-Hand model w/1:48″ twist **$264.00**

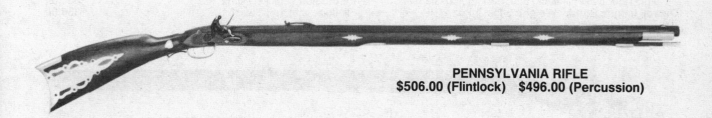

PENNSYLVANIA RIFLE
$506.00 (Flintlock) $496.00 (Percussion)

SPECIFICATIONS
Caliber: 50
Barrel length: 40 1/4″; octagonal (7/8″ across flats) with 3 pins; rifled 1 turn in 66″
Overall length: 57″   **Weight:** 8 lbs. 8 oz.
Lock: Adjustable sear engagement with fly and bridle

Stock: Walnut, beavertail style
Triggers: Double set; will fire set and unset
Sights: Primitive-style adjustable rear; brass blade front
Furniture: Solid brass, blued steel

PIONEER RIFLE

PIONEER RIFLE
$214.00

SPECIFICATIONS
Calibers: 50 and 54 percussion
Barrel length: 28″ (1:48″), octagonal w/tenon
Overall length: 44″
Weight: 6 lbs. 14 oz.

Trigger: Single
Stock: Beech
Sights: Buckhorn rear with elevation ramp, ajustable for windage and elevation; German silver blade front
Lock: Adjustable sear engagement; V-type mainspring
Features: Blackened hardware; German silver furniture; unbreakable ramrod; inletted wedge plates

TRADITIONS

BUCKSKINNER CARBINE
Laminated Stock

BUCKSKINNER CARBINE
$230.00 (Percussion) $264.00 (Flintlock)
$305.00 (Laminated Stock, Percussion)
$330.00 (Laminated Stock, Flintlock)

SPECIFICATIONS
Caliber: 50 percussion or flintlock
Barrel length: 21″ octagonal-to-round with tenon; $15/16$″ across flats; 1:66″ twist (flintlock) and 1:20″ (percussion)
Overall length: $36\frac{1}{4}$″   **Weight:** 5 lbs. 15 oz.

Sights: Hunting-style, click adjustable rear; beaded blade front with white dot
Trigger: Single
Features: Blackened furniture; German silver ornamentation; sling swivels; unbreakable ramrod
Also available:
BUCKSKINNER CARBINE DELUXE
Percussion with 1:20″ twist $305.00
Percussion w/nickel barrel 330.00
Flintlock with 1:66″ twist 330.00

KENTUCKY RIFLE

KENTUCKY RIFLE
$247.00 $($198.00 Kit)

SPECIFICATIONS
Caliber: 50 percussion
Barrel length: $33\frac{1}{2}$″ octagon ($7/8$″ flats); fixed tang; 1:66″ twist
Overall length: 49″
Weight: 7 lbs.

Trigger: Single
Tenons: 2 pins
Stock: Beechwood
Sights: Fixed rear; blade front
Features: Brass furniture; ramrod; inletted wedge plates; toe plate; V-mainspring

TENNESSEE RIFLE

TENNESSEE RIFLE
$313.00 (Flintlock) $297.00 (Percussion)

SPECIFICATIONS
Caliber: 50 flintlock or percussion
Barrel length: 24″ octagon ($15/16$″ across flats); hooked breech; 1:32″ twist (percussion) and 1:66″ (flintlock)
Overall length: $40\frac{1}{2}$″

Weight: 6 lbs.
Sights: Fixed rear; blade front
Stock: Beechwood
Features: Brass furniture; ramrod; inletted wedge plate; stock inlays; toe plate; V-mainspring

TRADITIONS

MODEL 1853 3-BAND ENFIELD RIFLED MUSKET
$595.00

Carried by Northern and Southern troops alike, the 1853 Enfield was noted for its ability to shoot straight and hard. This fine replica captures all the features of the original, from its full-length walnut stock and color casehardened lock to the solid brass buttplate, trigger guard and nose cap. The 1:48″ rifling and V-spring lock mechanism team with the military sights to make this as much a solid shooter today as the original was in its day. Approved by the North-South Skirmish Association.

SPECIFICATIONS
Caliber: 58 percussion
Barrel length: 39″ round; 1:48″ twist; blued finish; 3 barrel bands
Overall length: 55″
Weight: 10 lbs.
Sights: Military
Stock: Walnut
Features: Brass furniture; steel ramrod; sling swivels; V-mainspring

MODEL 1861 U.S. SPRINGFIELD RIFLED MUSKET
$645.00

The Model 1861 Springfield rifled musket was the principal firearm of the Civil War. By the end of 1863, most Federal infantrymen were armed with either this musket or the Enfield 58-caliber rifled barrel. This faithful replica glows ''in the white'' as was the original, with a full-length walnut military stock. The authentic sidelock action is accented by markings of ''1861 U.S. Springfield'' to complement the steel buttplate, wide trigger guard, barrel bands and sling hardware. The steel ramrod, like the original, is of the swelled design. Military-style sights and a long sighting plane make this an accurate long gun approved for use by the North-South Skirmish Association.

SPECIFICATIONS
Caliber: 58 percussion
Barrel length: 40″ round; 1:66″ twist; white steel finish; 3 barrel bands
Overall length: 56″
Weight: 10 lbs.
Trigger: Single
Sights: Military
Stock: Walnut
Features: Steel furniture and ramrod; sling swivels; V-mainspring

SHENANDOAH RIFLE
$366.00 (Flintlock)
$348.00 (Percussion)

The new Shenandoah Rifle captures the frontier styling and steady performance of Tradition's Pennsylvania Rifle in a slightly shorter length and more affordable price. Choice of engraved and color casehardened flintlock or percussion V-type mainspring lock with double-set triggers. The full-length stock in walnut finish is accented by a solid brass curved buttplate, inletted patch box, nose cap, thimbles, trigger guard and decorative furniture.

SPECIFICATIONS
Caliber: 50 (1:66″) flint or percussion
Barrel length: 33 1/2″ octagon
Overall length: 49 1/2″
Weight: 7 lbs. 3 oz.
Sights: Buckhorn rear, blade front
Stock: Beech

BLACK POWDER

TRADITIONS

BUCKHUNTER™ IN-LINE RIFLE SERIES

This family of hunting rifles is designed for serious blackpowder hunters as well as those who are just getting started in muzzleloading. These rifles deliver the balance, fast handling and long-range accuracy of a modern hunting gun. They shoulder naturally, pick up the target quickly, and hold the point of aim. The breech design disperses ignition gases safely to the side.

No special tools are needed for cleaning. All rifles have rubber recoil pads, are drilled and tapped (with 8-40 plug screws) for easy scoping and come with clickadjustable hunting sights and PVC ramrod. Specifications and prices for all models in the series are listed in the table below.

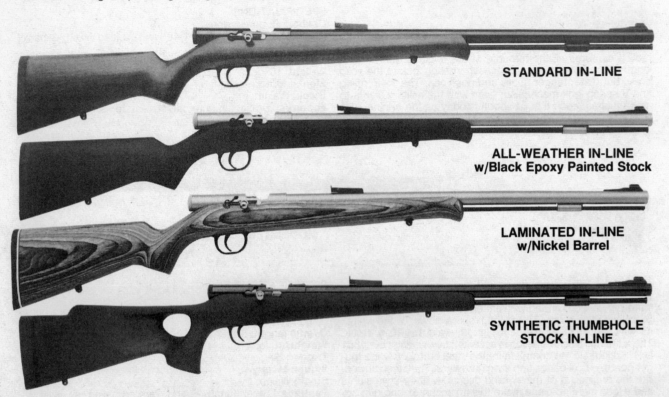

STANDARD IN-LINE

ALL-WEATHER IN-LINE
w/Black Epoxy Painted Stock

LAMINATED IN-LINE
w/Nickel Barrel

SYNTHETIC THUMBHOLE STOCK IN-LINE

SPECIFICATIONS AND PRICES

Buckhunter In-Line Rifles

		Standard	Blackened	Laminated	All-Weather	Thumbhole	Scout
Lock:	ignition	in-line percussion	in-line percussion	in-line percussion	in-line percussion	in-line percussion	in-line percussion
Stock:		beech	epoxied beech	laminated	epoxied beech	composite	epoxied beech
Caliber:	rifling/twist	.50p (1:32") .54p (1:48")	.50p (1:32") .54p (1:48")	.50p (1:32") .54p (1:48")	.50p (1:32") .54p (1:48")	.50p (1:32") .54p (1:48")	.50p (1:32")
Barrel:	length/shape finish breech plug	24" round blued SS removable	24" round blued SS removable	24" round blued or C-Nickel SS removable	24" round C-Nickel SS removable	24" round blued or C-Nickel SS removable	22" C-Nickel SS removable
Sights:	rear front	click adjustable beaded blade	click adjustable beaded blade	click adjustable beaded blade	click adjustable beaded blade	click adjustable beaded blade	click adjustable beaded blade
Features:	furniture ramrod	blackened PVC	blackened PVC	blackened PVC	blackened PVC	blackened PVC	blackened PVC
Overall length:		42"	42"	42"	42"	42½"	39"
Weight:		7 lbs., 10 oz.	7 lbs., 10 oz.	8 lbs.	7 lbs., 10 oz.	7 lbs., 8 oz.	7 lbs., 2 oz.
Models/prices:		R40002 .50p $222 R40048 .54p $222	R41102 .50p $222 R41148 .54p $222	R40202 .50p Br $330 R40248 .54p Br $330 R40302 .50p Bl $314 R40348 .54p Bl $314	R40102 .50p $239 R40148 .54p $239	R42202 .50p B $330 R42248 .54p B $330 R42302 .50p N $345 R42348 .54p N $345	R40702 .50p $239

Br denotes brown laminated/blued. Bl denotes black laminated/C-Nickel.
B denotes blued. N denotes C-Nickel. All models drilled and tapped.

TRADITIONS

BUCKHUNTER PRO™ IN-LINE RIFLES/SHOTGUNS

**BUCKHUNTER PRO™ IN-LINE RIFLE
w/Walnut-Stained Stock**

**BUCKHUNTER PRO™ IN-LINE RIFLE
w/Black Composite Stock, Stainless Barrel,
Optional Scope**

Traditions has upgraded its Buckhunter In-Line ignition rifles and shotguns with the new Buckhunter Pro series. The new guns feature an adjustable trigger, thumb safety and a choice of blued or stainless steel barrels. New slimmed-down matte black composite stocks are available as are two camouflage patterns, laminated, thumbhole or walnut-stained stocks. All Buckhunter Pros have field-removable stainless steel breech plugs and improved adjustable hunting sights. The Buckhunter Pro rifles are available in 50 caliber (1:32″) for use with conical and saboted bullets.

SPECIFICATIONS AND PRICES

		Buckhunter Pro In-Line Rifles & Shotguns				
		Standard & Blackened	**Laminated**	**Composite**	**Thumbhole**	**Shotgun**
Lock:	ignition	in-line percussion	in-line percussion	in-line percussion	in-line percussion	in-line percussion
Stock:		beech or composite	laminated	composite	composite	black or camo
Caliber:	rifling/twist	.50p (1:32″) .54p (1:48″)	.50p (1:32″)	.50p (1:32″) .54p (1:48″)	.50p (1:32″)	12-gauge smoothbore
Barrel:	length/shape finish breech plug	24″ tapered round blued SS removable	24″ tapered round blued/C-Nickel SS removable	24″ tapered round C-Nickel or stainless steel SS removable	24″ tapered round blued or C-Nickel SS removable	24″ round blued SS removable
Sights:	rear front	adjustable (W&E) beaded blade	adjustable (W&E) beaded blade	adjustable (W&E) beaded blade	adjustable (W&E) beaded blade	n/a bead
Features:	furniture ramrod	blackened PVC	blackened PVC	blackened PVC	blackened PVC	blackened PVC
Overall length:		42″	42″	42″	42½″	43″
Weight:		7 lbs., 8 oz.	7 lbs., 8 oz.	7 lbs., 5 oz.	7 lbs., 8 oz.	6 lbs. 4 oz.
Models/prices:		R50002 .50p $255 R51102 .50p Bl $239 R51148 .54p Bl $239 *R51302 .50p Bl $222 **R51302S .50p Bl $272	R50202 .50p Bk $345 R50302 .50p Br $330	R50102 .50p N $272 R50148 .54p N $272 R50802 .50p SS $314 R50848 .54p SS $314	R52202 .50p BlB $340 R52302 .50p BlN $357 R52702 .50p TB $373 R52802 .50p TN $406 R52902 .50p AB $373 R53202 .50p AN $406	S5202 B $313 S5302 T $366 S5402 A $366

All models are drilled and tapped. *. No sights option. ** Scope & mount option. Br denotes brown laminated/blued.
Bk denotes black laminated/C-Nickel. N denotes C-Nickel. SS denotes stainless steel. B denotes blued.
Bl denotes matte black. T denotes Mossy Oak® Treestand camouflage. A denotes Advantage camouflage.

**BUCKHUNTER PRO™ IN-LINE
12 GAUGE SHOTGUN**

The Buckhunter Pro Series all-new 12 Gauge Shotgun for bird and turkey hunters has the same field-removable stainless steel breech plug, thumb safety and slimmed down stock as the Buckhunter Pro In-Line Rifles. The shotgun's 24″ round blued barrel is furnished with a full screw-in choke tube. All shotguns come drilled and tapped, with adjustable trigger and rubber buttpad. Option of matte black composite, Mossy Oak Treestand or Advantage camo stock.

UBERTI

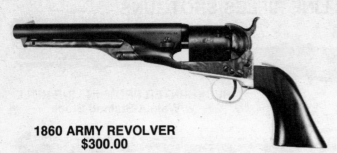

1860 ARMY REVOLVER
$300.00

SPECIFICATIONS
Caliber: 44
Barrel length: 8″ (round, tapered)
Overall length: 13³/₄″
Weight: 2.65 lbs.
Frame: One-piece, color casehardened steel
Trigger guard: Brass
Cylinder: 6 shots (engraved)
Grip: One-piece walnut

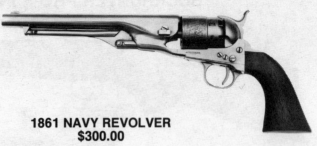

1861 NAVY REVOLVER
$300.00

SPECIFICATIONS
Caliber: 36
Capacity: 6 shots
Barrel length: 7¹/₂″
Overall length: 13″
Weight: 2.75 lbs.
Grip: One-piece walnut
Frame: Color casehardened steel

1851 NAVY REVOLVER
$280.00

SPECIFICATIONS
Caliber: 36
Barrel length: 7¹/₂″ (octagonal, tapered)
Cylinder: 6 shots (engraved)
Overall length: 13″
Weight: 2³/₄ lbs.
Frame: Color casehardened steel
Backstrap and trigger guard: Brass
Grip: One-piece walnut

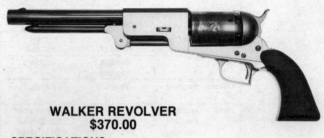

WALKER REVOLVER
$370.00

SPECIFICATIONS
Caliber: 44
Barrel length: 9″ (round in front of lug)
Overall length: 15³/₄″
Weight: 4.41 lbs.
Frame: Color casehardened steel
Backsstrap: Steel
Cylinder: 6 shots (engraved with "Fighting Dragoons" scene)
Grip: One-piece walnut

1st MODEL DRAGOON REVOLVER
$325.00

SPECIFICATIONS
Caliber: 44
Capacity: 6 shots
Barrel length: 7¹/₂″ round forward of lug
Overall length: 13¹/₂″
Weight: 4 lbs.
Frame: Color casehardened steel
Grip: One-piece walnut
Also available:
2nd Model Dragoon w/square cylinder bolt shot . . **$325.00**
3rd Model Dragoon w/loading lever latch, steel
  backstrap, cut for shoulder stock 330.00

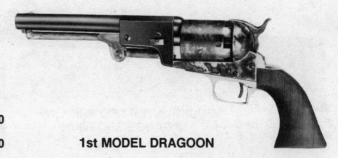

1st MODEL DRAGOON

UBERTI

1858 REMINGTON NEW ARMY 44 REVOLVER

Prices:
8″ barrel, open sights	$285.00
With stainless steel and open sights	385.00
Target Model w/black finish	330.00
Target Model w/stainless steel	420.00

Also available:
1858 New Navy (36 cal.)	280.00
1858 New Army Revolving Carbine (18″ barrel)	425.00

1858 REMINGTON NEW ARMY TARGET MODEL

PATERSON REVOLVER
$399.00
($450.00 w/Lever)

Manufactured at Paterson, New Jersey, by the Patent Arms Manufacturing Company from 1836 to 1842, these were the first revolving pistols created by Samuel Colt. All early Patersons featured a five-shot cylinder, roll-engraved with one or two scenes, octagon barrel and folding trigger that extends when the hammer is cocked.

SPECIFICATIONS
Caliber: 36
Capacity: 5 shots (engraved cylinder)
Barrel length: 7½″ octagonal
Overall length: 11½″
Weight: 2.552 lbs.
Frame: Color casehardened steel
Grip: One-piece walnut

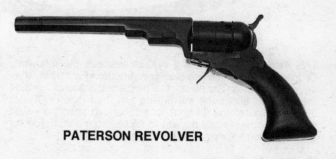

PATERSON REVOLVER

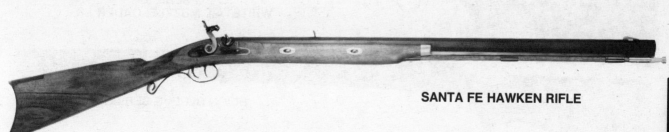

SANTA FE HAWKEN RIFLE

SANTA FE HAWKEN RIFLE
$495.00

SPECIFICATIONS
Calibers: 50 and 54
Barrel length: 32″ octagonal
Overall length: 50″

Weight: 9½ lbs.
Stock: Walnut with beavertail cheekpiece
Features: Brown finish; double-set trigger; color casehardened lockplate; German silver wedge plates

WHITE SYSTEMS

G & W SERIES RIFLES

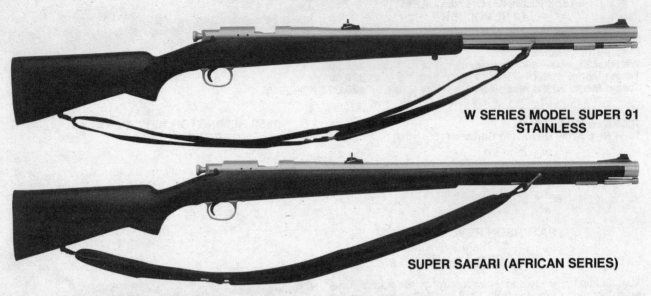

W SERIES MODEL SUPER 91 STAINLESS

SUPER SAFARI (AFRICAN SERIES)

MODEL SUPER 91

This modern muzzleloading system features the following: Ordnance-grade stainless-steel construction • Fast twist, shallow groove rifling • Stainless-steel nipple and breechplug • Side swing safety (locks the striker, not just the trigger) • Classic stock configuration (fits right- or left-handed shooters • Fast second shot and easy access to nipple from either side for quick capping • Fully adjustable trigger

Calibers: 41, 45 and 50
Barrel length: 24″ **Weight:** 7³/₄ lbs.

Rifling: 1 in 20″ (45 cal.); 1 in 24″ (50 cal.)
Sights: Fully adjustable Williams sights
Prices:
Blued **$599.00**
Stainless Steel **659.95**
   w/Black Laminate stock **699.95**
Also available:
SUPER SAFARI SS TAPERED (African Series)
41, 45, 50 caliber Mannlicher **$799.00**
GRAND ALASKAN STAINLESS STEEL BULL
54 caliber, green laminate **699.95**

G SERIES WHITETAIL MUZZLELOADER SS

BISON BLUE (G SERIES)

WHITETAIL AND BISON MUZZLELOADING RIFLES

White's "G Series" rifles feature straight-line action with easy no-tool takedown in the field. A stainless-steel hammer system has an ambidextrous cocking handle that doubles as a sure-safe hammer-lock safety. Other features include the "Insta-

Fire" one-piece nipple/breechplug system (with standard #11 percussion caps); fully adjustable open hunting sights; 22″ bull barrel with integrated ramrod guide and swivel studs.
Calibers: 41, 45, 50 and 54 (Bison only)
Prices:
Bison (50 and 54 cal.) Blued **$399.95**
Whitetail (45 and 50 cal.)
Blued **399.00**
Stainless steel **499.00**
   w/Black Laminate stock **529.95**

Sights & Scopes

For addresses and phone/fax numbers of manufacturers and distributors included in this section, please turn to DIRECTORY OF MANUFACTURERS AND SUPPLIERS on page 554.

AIMPOINT SIGHTS

AIMPOINT 5000 SIGHT
$277.00

SPECIFICATIONS
System: Parallax free
Optical: Anti-reflex coated lenses
Adjustment: 1 click = 1/4-inch at 100 yards
Length: 5 1/2"
Weight: 5.8 oz.
Objective diameter: 36mm
Mounting system: 30mm rings
Magnification: 1X
Material: Anodized aluminum; black or stainless finish
Diameter of dot: 3" at 100 yds. or Mag Dot reticle, 10" at 100 yards.

SERIES 3000 UNIVERSAL
$232.00 (Black or Stainless)

SPECIFICATIONS
System: 100% parallax free
Weight: 5.8 oz.
Length: 6.15"
Magnification: 1X
Scope attachment: 3X
Eye relief: Unlimited
Battery choices: 2X Mercury SP 675 1X Lithium or DL 1/3N
Material: Anodized aluminum, black or stainless finish
Mounting: 1" Rings (Medium or High)

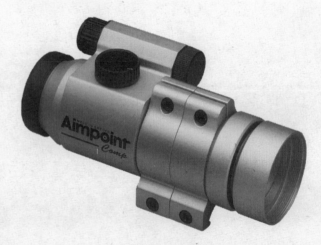

AIMPOINT COMP
$308.00

SPECIFICATIONS
System: 100% Parallax free
Optics: Anti-reflex coated lenses
Eye relief: Unlimited
Batteries: 3 × Mercury SP 675
Adjustment: 1 click = 1/4-inch at 100 yards
Length: 4 3/8"
Weight: 4.75 oz.
Objective diameter: 36mm
Dot diameter: 2" at 30 yds. (7 MOA); 3" at 30 yds. (10 MOA)
Mounting system: 30mm rings
Magnification: 1X
Material: Black, blue or stainless finish
Also available with 3-minute Dot with Flip Up lens covers and captive metal adjustment covers.

AIMPOINT 5000 2-POWER
$367.00

SPECIFICATIONS
System: Parallax free
Optical: Anti-reflex coated lens
Adjustment: clock = 1/4" at 100 yards
Length: 7"
Weight: 9 oz.
Objective diameter: 46mm
Diameter of dot: 1 1/2" at 100 yards
Mounting system: 30mm rings
Magnification: 2X
Material: Anodized aluminum; blue finish

BAUSCH & LOMB RIFLESCOPES

ELITE™ 3000 RIFLESCOPES

Model	Special Features	Actual Magnification	Obj. Lens Aperture (mm)	Field of View ft.@100yds m@100m	Weight (oz/g)	Length (in/mm)	Eye Relief (in/mm)	Exit Pupil (mm)	Click Value in@100yds mm@100m	Adjust Range in.@100yds m@100m	Selection	Suggested Retail
						ELITE® 3000						
30-1545M	Matte Finish	1.5x-4.5x	32	63/21@1.5x 20/7@4.5x	13/368	12.5/318	3.3/84	21-7	.25/7	100/2.8	Low power variable ideal for brush, medium range slug gun hunting.	$434.95
30-1642E	European Reticle Matte Finish	1.5x-6x	42	57.7/19@1.5x 15/5@6x	21/594	14.4/366	3/76	17.6-7	.36/10	60/1.7	Large exit pupil & 30mm tube for max. brightness.	$644.95
30-2028G	Handgun (30-2028S Silver Finish)	2x	28	23/8@2x	6.9/195	8.4/2.13	9-26/ 229-660	14	.25/7	40/1.1	Excellent short to medium range hunting & target scope w/ max. recoil resistance.	30-2028G – $301.95 30-2028S – $321.95
30-2632G	Handgun (30-2632S Silver Finish)	2x-6x	32	10/3@2x 4/1@6x	10/283	9/229	20/508	16-5.3	.25/7	50/1.4	Constant eye relief at all powers w/ max. recoil resistance.	30-2632G – $413.95 30-2632S – $432.95
30-2732G	(30-2732M Matte Finish)	2x-7x	32	44.6/15@2x 12.7/4@7x	12/340	11.6/295	3/76	12.2-4.6	.25/7	50/1.4	Compact variable for close-in brush or medium range shooting. Excellent for shotguns.	30-2732G – $342.95 30-2732M – $361.95
30-3940G	(30-3940M Matte Finish 30-3940S Silver Finish)	3x-9x	40	33.8/11@3x 11.5/4@9x	13/368	12.6/320	3/76	13.3-4.4	.25/7	50/1.4	For the full range of hunting. From varmint to big game. Tops in versatility.	30-3940G – $348.95 30-3940M – $370.95 30-3940S – $370.95
30-3950G	(30-3950M Matte Finish)	3x-9x	50	31.5/10@3x 10.5/4@9x	19/538	15.7/399	3/76	16-5.6	.25/7	50/1.4	All purpose variable with extra brightness.	30-3950G – $434.95 30-3950M – $453.95
30-3955E	European Reticle Matte Finish	3x-9x	50	31.5/10@3x 10.5/4@9x	22/623	15.6/396	3/76	16-5.6	.36/10	70/1.9	Large exit pupil & 30mm tube for max. brightness.	$633.95
30-4124A	Adjustable Objective	4x-12x	40	26.9/9@4x 9/3@12x	15/425	13.2/335	3/76	10-3.33	.25/7	50/1.4	Medium to long-range variable makes a superb choice for varmint or big game.	$421.95

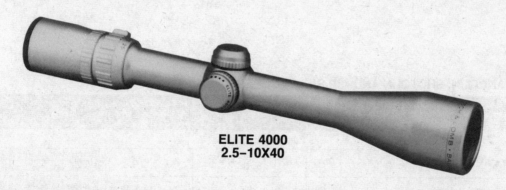

ELITE 4000
2.5–10X40

ELITE™ 4000 RIFLESCOPES

Model	Special Features	Actual Magnification	Obj. Lens Aperture (mm)	Field of View ft.@100yds m@100m	Weight (oz/g)	Length (in/mm)	Eye Relief (in/mm)	Exit Pupil (mm)	Click Value in@100yds mm@100m	Adjust Range in.@100yds m@100m	Selection	Suggested Retail
						ELITE® 4000						
40-1040	Ranging reticle 30mm body tube	10x	40	10.5/3.5@10x	22.1/625	13.8/351	3.6/91	4@10x	.25/7	120/3.3	The ultimate for precise pinpoint accuracy w/parallax focus & target adjustment knobs.	$1745
40-1636G	(40-1636M Matte Finish)	1.5x-6x	36	61.8/20.6@1.5x 16.1/5.4@6x	15.4/436	12.8/325	3/76	14.6@1.5x 6@6x	.25/7	60/1.7	Compact wide angle for close-in & brush hunting. Max. brightness. Execel. for shotguns	40-1636G – $565 40-1636M – $589
40-2104G	(40-2104M Matte Finish 40-2104S Silver Finish)	2.5x-10x	40	41.5/13.8@2.5x 10.8/3.6@10x	16/453	13.5/343	3/76	15.6@2.5x 4@10x	.25/7	50/1.4	All purpose hunting scope w/ 4x zoom range for close-in brush & long range shooting	40-2104G – $606 40-2104M – $632 40-2104S – $632
40-3640A	Adjustable Objective	36x	40	3/1.0@36x	17.6/498	15/381	3.2/81	1.1@36x	.125/3.5	30/.8	Ideal benchrest scope.	$859
40-4165M	Matte Finish	4x-16x	50	26/9@4x 7/2@16x	22/623	15.6/396	3/76	12.5@4x 3.1@16x	.25/7	50/14	The ultimate varmint and precision shooting scope.	$758
40-6244A	Adjustable Objective, Sunshade (40-6244M Matte Finish)	6x-24x	40	18/4.5@6x 6.0/1.5@24x	20.2/572	16.9/429	3/76	6.7@6x 1.7@24x	.125/3.5	26/.7	Varmit, target & silhouette long range shooting. Parallax focus adjust. for pinpoint accuracy.	40-6244A – $702 40-6244M – $726

BAUSCH & LOMB/BUSHNELL

TROPHY RIFLESCOPES

Model	Special Features	Actual Magnification	Obj. Lens Aperature (mm)	Field of View ft.@100yds m@100m	Weight (oz/g)	Length (in/mm)	Eye Relief (in/mm)	Exit Pupil (mm)	Click Value in@100yds mm@100m	Adjust Range in.@100yds m@100m	Selection	Suggested Retail
						TROPHY®						
73-0440	Wide angle	4x	40	36/12	12.5/354	12.5/318	3/76	10	.25/7	100/2.8	General purpose.	$151.95
73-1500	Wide angle	1.75x-5x	32	68/23@1.75x 23/8@5x	12.3/348	10.8/274	3.5/89	18.3@1.75x 6.4@5x	.25/7	120/3.3	Shotgun, black powder or center-fire. Close-in brush hunting.	$258.95
73-2545	45mm objective for maximum light transmission	2.5x-10x	45	39/13@2.5x 10/3@10x	14/396	13.75/349	3/76	18@2.5x 4.5@10x	.25/7	60/1.7	All purpose hunting with 4 times zoom for close-in and long range shooting.	$310.95
73-3940	Wide angle (73-3940S Silver, 73-3948 Matte)	3x-9x	40	42/14@3x 14/5@9x	13.2/374	11.7/297	3/76	13.3@3 4.4@9x	.25/7	60/1.7	All purpose variable, excellent for use from close to long range. Circular view provides a definite advantage over "TV screen" type scopes for running game-uphill or down.	73-3940 – $186.95 73-3940M – $196.95 73-3940S – $196.95
73-3941	Illuminated reticle with back-up crosshairs	3x-9x	40	37/12@3x 12.5/4@9x	16/453	13/330	3/76	13.3@3x 4.4@9x	.25/7	70/1.9	Variable intensity light control Battery Sony CR 2032 or equivalent	$385.95
73-3942	Long mounting length designed for long-action rifles	3x-9x	42	42/14@3x 14/5@9x	13.8/391	12/305	3/76	14@3x 4.7@9x	.25/7	40/1.1	7" mounting length.	$196.95
73-3949	Wide angle ™ with Circle-x Reticle	3x-9x	40	42/14@3x 14/5@9x	13.2/374	11.7/297	3/76	13.3@3x 4.4@9x	.25/7	60/1.7	Matte finish, Ideal low light reticle.	$205.95
73-4124	Wide angle, adjustable objective (73-4124M Matte)	4x-12x	40	32/11@4x 11/4@12x	16.1/456	12.6/320	3/76	10@4x 3.3@12x	.25/7	60/1.7	Medium to long range variable for varmint and big game. Range focus adjustment. Excellent air riflescope.	73-4124 – $288.95 73-4124M – $297.95
73-6184	Semi-turret target adjustments, adjustable objective	6x-18x	40	17.3/6@6x 6/2@18x	17.9/507	14.8/376	3/76	6.6@6x 2.2@18x	.125/3.5	40/1.1	Long-range varmint centerfire or short range air rifle target precision accuracy.	$338.95

TROPHY HANDGUN, SHOTGUN AND AIR RIFLESCOPES

Model	Special Features	Actual Magnification	Obj. Lens Aperature (mm)	Field of View ft.@100yds m@100m	Weight (oz/g)	Length (in/mm)	Eye Relief (in/mm)	Exit Pupil (mm)	Click Value in@100yds mm@100m	Adjust Range in.@100yds m@100m	Selection	Suggested Retail
						TROPHY® HANDGUN SCOPES						
73-0232	(73-0232S Silver)	2x	32	20/7	7.7/218	8.7/221	9-26/ 229-660	16	.25/7	90/2.5	Designed for target and short to medium range hunting. Magnum recoil resistant.	73-0232 – $190.95 73-0232S – $205.95
73-2632	(73-2632S Silver)	2x-6x	32	11/4@2x 4/1@6x	10.9/308	9.1/231	18/457	16@2x 5.3@6x	.25/7	50/1.4	18 inches of eye relief at all powers.	73-2632 – $252.95 73-2632S – $267.95
						TROPHY® SHOTGUN/HANDGUN SCOPES						
73-0130	Illuminated dot reticle	1x	25	61/20	5.5/156	5.25/133	Unltd.	18	1.0/28	80/2.2	30mm tube with rings, ext. tube polarization filter, amber coating. For black powder, shotgun and handgun shooting. Battery 3V DL2032 or equivalent.	$282.95
73-1420	Turkey Scope w/Circle-x™ Reticle	1.75x-4x	32	73/24@1.75x 30/10@4x	10.9/308	10.8/274	3.5/89	18@1.75x 8@4x	.25/7	120/3.3	Ideal for turkey hunting, slug guns or blackpowder guns. Matte finish.	$265.95
73-1421	Brush Scope w/Circle-x™ Reticle	1.75x-4x	32	73/24@1.75x 30/10@4x	10.9/308	10.8/274	3.5/89	18@1.75x 8@4x	.25/7	120/3.3	Ideal for turkey hunting, slug guns or blackpowder guns. Matte finish.	$265.95
						TROPHY® AIR RIFLESCOPES						
73-4124	Wide angle adjustable objective (73-4124M Matte)	4x-12x	40	32/11@4x 11/4@12x	16.1/456	12.6/320	3/76	10@4x 3.3@12x	.25/7	60/1.7	Medium to long range variable for varmint and big game. Range focus adjustment. Excellent air riflescope.	73-4124 – $288.95 73-4124M – $297.95
73-6184	Semi-turret target adjustments, adjustable objective	6x-18x	40	17.3/6@6x 6/2@18x	179/507	14.8/376	3/76	6.6@6x 2.2@18x	.125/3.5	40/1.1	Long-range varmint centerfire or short-range air rifle, target precision accuracy.	$338.95

BAUSCH & LOMB/BUSHNELL

SPORTVIEW RIFLESCOPES

Model	Special Features	Actual Magnification	Obj. Lens Aperature (mm)	Field of View ft.@100yds m@100m	Weight (oz/g)	Length (in/mm)	Eye Relief (in/mm)	Exit Pupil (mm)	Click Value in@100yds mm@100m	Adjust Range in.@100yds m@100m	Selection	Suggested Retail
					SPORTVIEW®							
79-0412	Adjustable objective	4x-12x	40	27/9 @ 4x 9/3@12x	14.6/413	13.1/333	3.2/81	10@4x 3.3@12x	.25/7	60/1.7	Long range.	$132.95
79-0640		6X	40	20.5/7	10.4/294	12.25/311	3/76	6.6	.25/7	50/1.4	Medium range shooting centerfire and rimfire rifles.	$91.95
79-1393	(79-1398 Matte) 79-1393S Matte Silver)	3x-9x	32	38/13@3x 14/5@9x	10/283	11.75/298	3.5/89	10.7@3x 3.6@9x	.25	50/1.4	All purpose variable.	79-1393 – $66.95 79-1398M&S–$69.95
79-1403	(79-1403S Silver)	4x	32	29/10	9.2/260	11.75/298	4/102	8	.25/7	60/1.7	General purpose.	79-1403 – $53.95 79-1403S – $56.95
79-1404	Black powder	4x	32	29/10	9.2/260	11.75/298	4/102	8	.25/7	60/1.7	For black powder guns.	$53.95
79-1545		1.5x-4.5x	21	69/23@1.5x 24/8@4.5x	8.6/243	10.7/272	3/76	14@1.5x 4.7@4.5x	.25/7	60/1.7	Low power variable ideal for close-in brush or medium range shooting.	$88.95
79-2243		4x	32	24/8	9.75/276	9.75/248	5/27	8	.25/7	60/1.7	all purpose .22 scope	$83.95
79-3145	Larger objective	3.5x-10x	45	36/12@3.5x 13/4@10x	13.9/393	12.75/324	3/76	12.9@3.5x 4.5@10x	.25/7	60/1.7	Large objective for low light use.	$145.95
79-3938	Wide Angle	3x-9x	38	42/14@3x 14/5@9x	12.5/354	12.7/323	3/76	12.7@3x 4.2@9x	.25/7	50/1.4	Excellent for use at any range	$105.95
79-3942	Built-in bullet drop compensator	3x-9x	40	40/13@3x 13/4@9x	12/340	12.25/311	3/76	13.3@3x 4.4@9x	.25/7	45/1.3	All purpose	$117.95
79-6184*	Adjustable objective	6x-18x	40	19.1/6@6x 6.8/2@18x	15.9/450	14.5/368	3/76	6.7@6x 2.2@18x	.25/7	50/1.4	Excellent varmint scope	$159.95
					SPORTVIEW® AIR RIFLE SERIES							
79-0004	Adjustable objective, with rings	4x	32	31/10	11.2/317	11.7/297	4/102	8	.25/7	50/1.4	General purpose for air rifle and rimfire. With range focus and target adjustments.	$92.95
79-0039	Adjustable objective, with rings	3x-9x	32	38/13@3x 13/4@9x	11.2/317	10.75/273	3.5/89	10.6@3x 3.5@9x	.25/7	60/1.7	Air rifle, rimfire with range focus adjustments and target adjustments.	$109.95
					SPORTVIEW® RIMFIRE SERIES							
79-1416	3/4" tube	4x	15	17/6	3.6/102	10.7/272	3.5/89	3.8	Friction	60/1.7	General Purpose.	$13.95
79-3720	3/4" tube	3x-7x	20	23/8@3x 11/4@7x	5.7/161	11.3/287	2.6/66	6.7@3x 2.9@7x	Friction	50/1.4	All purpose variable.	$40.95

*We recommend Trophy® airgun scopes for adult spring-loaded airguns which achieve over 800 FPS volocity.

BANNER RIFLESCOPES

Model	Special Features	Actual Magnification	Obj. Lens Aperature (mm)	Field of View ft.@100yds m@100m	Weight (oz/g)	Length (in/mm)	Eye Relief (in/mm)	Exit Pupil (mm)	Click Value in@100yds mm@100m	Adjust Range in.@100yds m@100m	Selection	Suggested Retail
					BANNER®							
71-2520		2.5x	20	44/15	7.5/212	10/254	3.6/91	8	.25/7	80/22	Shotgun use.	$84.95
71-3956	Extra large objective	3x-9x	56	37/12@3x 12/4@9x	17.3/490	13.7/348	3.5/89	10.3@3x 6.2@9x	.25/7	50/1.4	All purpose variable with maximizing brightness.	$288.95
71-4220	With .22 rings	4x	20	28/9	8.1/229	11.7/297	3/76	5	.25/7	60/1.7	All purpose .22 with a 1-inch body tube for increasing brightness	$73.95
71-6102	BDC Wide angle	3x-9x	40	42/14@3x 14/5@9x	13.1/371	12/305	3.3/84	13.3@3x 4.4@9x	.25/7	70/1.9	All purpose variable, excellent for use from close or long range. Circular view provides a definite advantage over "TV screen" type scopes for running game-uphill or down.	$137.95
					LITE-SITE®							
71-3940	Illuminated dot reticle	3x-9x	40	36/12@3x 13/4@9x	15.5/439	12.8/325	3.1/79	13.3@3x 4.4@9x	.25/7	60/1.7	Illuminated dot reticle with back-up cross hairs. All purpose variable. Excellent for use at any range. Battery #2A76 or equivelent	$368.95

BAUSCH & LOMB/BUSHNELL

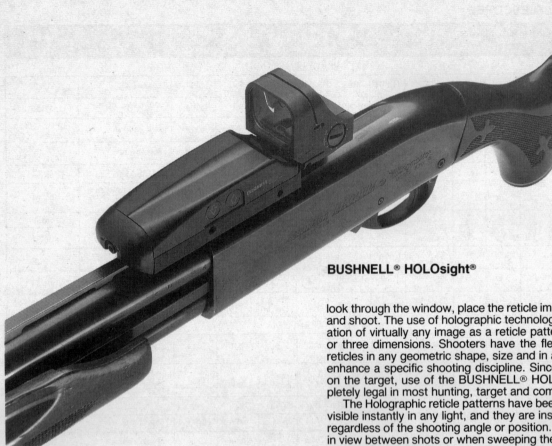

BUSHNELL® HOLOsight®

BUSHNELL® HOLOsight®

The BUSHNELL® HOLOsight® is a revolutionary breakthrough in optical sighting systems. It delivers instant target acquisition, improved accuracy, and can be tailored to virtually any shooting discipline. How does it work? A hologram of a reticle pattern is recorded on a heads-up display window. When illuminated by laser (coherent) light, a holographic image becomes visible at the target plane - where it remains in focus with the target. Critical eye alignment is not required and multi-plane focusing error is eliminated. With the BUSHNELL® HOLOsight®; simply

look through the window, place the reticle image on the target and shoot. The use of holographic technology allows the creation of virtually any image as a reticle pattern, in either two or three dimensions. Shooters have the flexibility to design reticles in any geometric shape, size and in any dimension to enhance a specific shooting discipline. Since no light is cast on the target, use of the BUSHNELL® HOLOsight® is completely legal in most hunting, target and competition areas.

The Holographic reticle patterns have been designed to be visible instantly in any light, and they are instinctive to center regardless of the shooting angle or position. The reticles stay in view between shots or when sweeping the target area. Reticles are designed as large see-through patterns to capture the shooter's eye without covering up the aiming point. With the virtual image of a bright red reticle pattern on the target, absolute concentration on the target is ensured and lighting-quick reticle-to-target acquisition is achieved.

The BUSHNELL® HOLOsight® has a streamlined design that contains no tubes, knobs or batteries to obscure the viewing area. Its unobstructed field of view allows the shooter to use both eyes to gain optimal control of the shooting environment. Through the use of an on-board microprocessor, the HOLOsight® provides a batter indicator feature, programmable auto shut-down modes, and user-selectable auto brightness start-up settings. An all-purpose dovetail mounting arrangement ensures universal adaptability to virtually any gun.

BUSHNELL HOLOSIGHT SPECIFICATIONS

Model	Optics	Magnification @ 100 yds.	Field of View @100 yds	Weight (oz./g)	Length (in./mm)	Eye Relief (in./mm)	Batteries	Click Value in.@100yds. mm@100m	Brightness adjustment settings	Suggested Retail
HOLOSIGHT										
50-0021	Holographic Base with Standard Reticle	1x	Unlimited	8.7/246	6/152	1/2"to 10ft 13 to 3048mm	2 Type N 1.5 Volt	.25 M.O.A./ 7mm @ 100m	20 levels	$599.95
500122	Holosight Dual Rings Reticle									$128.95
500123	Holosight Open Cross Hairs Reticle									$128.95
500131	Holosight Rising Dot Reticle									$128.95

B-SQUARE

MINI-LASERS **$138.95 (Blue) $148.95 (Stainless)**	**BSL-1 LASER SIGHT** **$118.95 (Blue) $128.95 (Stainless)**

SPECIFICATIONS
Power: 5mW max (class IIIA)
Size: 1.1″×1.1″×.6″
Batteries: Common A76 (lithium or alkaline)
Aiming method: Omnidirectional
Visibility: 1″ at 25 yds.
Min. Life: 60 min.
Features: Quick detachable laser allows holstering; moisture proof and shock resistant; "Aim-Lock" screw type; windage and elevation adjustable; no trigger finger interference; cord or integral switch; on-off switch optional; wide selection of mounts available

SPECIFICATIONS
Power: 5mW max (class IIIA)
Size: .75″; dia.×2.65″
Aiming method: Omnidirectional (screw type, lockable)
Visibility: Pulsed dot 1″ at 100 yds.
Features: "Aim-Lock" no-slip mounts; T-Slot cap; cord or integral switch; wide selection of mounts

Also available:
Mini-Laser High Intensity 635 Beam w/cord or integral switch.
   Price: $218.95 (blue finish); $228.95 (stainless)

BURRIS SCOPES

2.75X GUNSITE SCOUT SCOPE
W/Precision Click Adjustments

1.5X GUNSITE SCOUT SCOPE

GUNSITE SCOUT SCOPES

Made for hunters who need a 7- to 14-inch eye relief to mount just in front of the ejection port opening, allowing hunters to shoot with both eyes open. The 15-foot field of view and 2³/₄X magnification are ideal for brush guns and handgunners. Also ideal for the handgunner that uses a "two-handed hold." Rugged, reliable and 100% fog proof.

Models	Prices
1.5X Heavy Plex (black)	$238.00
1.5X Heavy Plex (matte)	257.00
2.75X Heavy Plex (black)	244.00
2.75X Heavy Plex (matte)	263.00
2.75X Plex (black)	235.00

BURRIS SCOPES

SIGNATURE SERIES

All models in the Signature Series have **Hi-Lume** (multi-coated) lenses for maximum light transmission. Also features **Posi-Lock** to prevent recoil and protect against rough hunting use and temperature change. Allows shooter to lock internal optics of scope in position after rifle has been sighted in.

8X-32X SIGNATURE

Models	Prices
4X Plex (black)	$349.00
6X Plex (black)	358.00
6X Plex (matte)	387.00
1.5X-6X Plex (black)	429.00
1.5X-6X Plex (matte)	448.00
1.5X-6X Plex (silver)	457.00
1.5X-6X Heavy Plex (black)	439.00
1.5X-6X Heavy Plex (matte)	457.00
1.5X-6X Plex Posi-Lock (black)	503.00
1.5X-6X Plex Posi-Lock (matte)	521.00
2X-8X Plex (black)	498.00
2X-8X Plex (matte)	517.00
2X-8X Plex Posi-Lock (black)	562.00
2X-8X Plex Posi-Lock (matte)	580.00
3X-9X Plex (black)	509.00
3X-9X Plex (matte)	528.00
3X-9X Plex (silver)	537.00
3X-9X Plex Posi-Lock (black)	573.00
3X-9X Plex Posi-Lock (matte)	591.00
3X-9X Plex Posi-Lock (silver)	600.00
3X-9X LDPX* (black)	599.00
3X-9X LDPX* (matte)	617.00
3X-9X LDPX* Posi-Lock (black)	661.00
3X-9X LDPX* Posi-Lock (matte)	679.00
2.5X-10X Plex Parallax Adjustment (black)	552.00
2.5X-10X Plex Parallax Adjustment (matte)	571.00
2.5X-10X Peep Plex Parallax Adjustment (black)	561.00
2.5X-10X Plex Posi-Lock Parallax Adjustment (black)	624.00
2.5X-10X Plex Posi-Lock Parallax Adjustment (matte)	642.00
2.5X-10X Plex Posi-Lock Parallax Adjustment (silver)	651.00
3X-12X Plex	612.00
3X-12X Plex Parallax Adjustment (matte)	629.00
3X-12X Peep Plex Parallax Adjustment (black)	621.00
3X-12X Peep Plex Parallax Adjustment (matte)	638.00
3X-12X Plex Posi-Lock Parallax Adjustment (black)	683.00
3X-12X Plex Posi-Lock Parallax Adjustment (matte)	701.00
4X-16X Plex Parallax Adjustment (black)	649.00
4X-16X Plex Parallax Adjustment (matte)	667.00
4X-16X Plex Posi-Lock Parallax Adjustment (black)	658.00

*LDPXlectro-Dot Plex

Models	Prices
4X-16X Plex Posi-Lock Parallax Adjustment (matte)	$727.00
6X-24X Plex Parallax Adjustment (black)	664.00
6X-24X Plex Parallax Adjustment (matte)	682.00
6X-24X Fine Flex Target (black)	688.00
6X-24X Fine Plex Target (matte)	706.00
6X-24X Fine Plex Target (silver)	715.00
6X-24X Peep Parallax Adjustment (black)	673.00
6X-24X Peep Plex Parallax Adjustment (matte)	692.00
6X-24X 2"–.5" Dot Target (black)	706.00
6X-24X Plex Posi-Lock Parallax Adjustment (black)	724.00
6X-24XP Plex Posi-Lock Parallax Adjustment (matte)	742.00
6X-24X LDPX* Parallax Adjustment (black)	753.00
6X-24X LDPX* Parallax Adjustment (matte)	772.00
8X-32X Fine Plex Target (black)	727.00
8X-32X Fine Plex Target (matte)	745.00
8X-32X Fine Plex Target (silver)	754.00
8X-32X Peep Plex Target (black)	736.00
8X-32X 2"–5" Dot Target (black)	745.00
8X-32X Fine Plex Posi-Lock Parallax Adjustment (black)	808.00
8X-32X Fine Plex Posi-Lock Parallax Adjustment (matte)	826.00

NEW SIGNATURE SCOPES

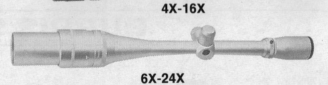

8X-32X

8X-32X

4X-16X

6X-24X

FULLFIELD SCOPES
Fixed Power with Hi-Lume Lenses

12X FULLFIELD

Models	Prices
1X XER Heavy Plex (black)	$259.00
1X XER Heavy Plex (matte)	278.00
1X XER Plex (matte)	297.00
1½X Heavy Plex (black)	268.00

(cont. on next page)

BURRIS SCOPES

FULLFIELD (cont.)

Models	Prices
2¹/₂X Heavy Plex (black)	$282.00
4X Plex (black)	285.00
4X Plex (matte)	310.00
6X Plex (black)	312.00
6X Plex (matte)	330.00
12X Plex Parallax Adjustment (black)	392.00
12X Fine Plex Target (black)	392.00
12X ¹/₂″ Dot Target (black)	422.00
1X-4X XER Heavy Plex (black)	392.00
1X-4X XER Heavy Plex (matte)	360.00
1.75X-5X Plex (black)	340.00
1.75X-5X Plex (matte)	358.00
1.75X-5X Heavy Plex (black)	349.00
1.75X-5X Heavy Plex (matte)	368.00
1.75x-5X Plex Posi-Lock (black)	403.00
1.75X-5X Plex Safari Posi-Lock (matte)	426.00
1.75X-5X Plex Posi-Lock (silver)	430.00
2X-7X Plex (black)	364.00
2X-7X Plex (matte)	383.00
2X-7X Plex (silver)	392.00
2X-7X Post Crosshair (black)	373.00
3X-9X Plex (black)	339.00
3X-9X Plex (matte)	381.00
3X-9X Plex (silver)	390.00
3X-9X Peep Plex (black)	372.00
3X-9X Post Crosshair (black)	372.00
3X-9X 3.″-1.″ Dot (black)	381.00
3X-9X Plex Posi-Lock (black)	425.00
3x-9x Plex Posi-Lock (matte)	443.00
3X-9X Plex Posi-Lock (silver)	452.00
3X-9X Crosshair Plex RAC (black)	404.00
3X-9X Crosshair Plex RAC (matte)	422.00
3X-9X Crosshair Dot (black)	404.00
3X-9X Electro-Dot Plex (black)	462.00
3X-9X Electro-Dot Plex (matte)	470.00
3.5X-10X-50mm Plex (black)	450.00
3.5X-10X-50mm Plex (matte)	480.00
3.5X-10X-50mm Plex (silver)	490.00
3.5X-10X-50mm Peep Plex (black)	471.00
3.5X-10X-50mm Plex Posi-Lock (black)	521.00
3.5X-10X-50mm Plex Posi-Lock (matte)	540.00
3.5X-10X-50mm Plex Posi-Lock (silver)	549.00
4X-12X Plex Parallex Adjustment (black)	458.00
4X-12X Fine Plex Parallex Adjustment (black)	458.00
4X-12X Peep Plex Parallax Adjustment (black) . . .	467.00
6X-18X Plex Parallax Adjustment (black)	479.00
6X-18X Plex Parallax Adjustment (matte)	497.00
6X-18X Fine Plex Parallax Adjustment (black)	479.00
6X-18X Fine Plex Target (black)	$507.00
6X-18X Peep Plex Parallax Adjustment (black)	488.00
6X-18X Peep Plex Parallax Adjustment (matte)	507.00
6X-18X 2.″-.7″ Dot Target (black)	526.00

FULLFIELD SCOPES

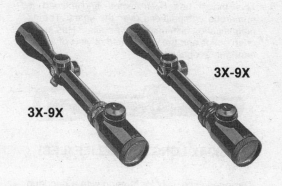

3X-9X

3X-9X

6X-24X

COMPACT SCOPES

4X Plex (black)	$239.00
4X Plex (silver)	268.00
4X Plex Parallax Adjustment (black)	277.00
6X Plex (black)	254.00
6X Plex Target Parallax Adjustment (black)	293.00
6X HBR Fine Plex Target (black)	329.00
6X HBR FCH Target (black)	329.00
6X HBR FCH Target (silver)	358.00
6X HBR .375 Dot Target (black)	348.00
6X HBR .375 Dot Target (silver)	377.00
2X-7X Plex (black)	327.00
2X-7X Plex (matte)	346.00
2X-7X Plex (silver)	356.00
3X-9X Plex (black)	335.00
3X-9X Plex (matte)	354.00
3X-9X Plex (silver)	363.00
4X-12X Plex Parallax Adjustment (black)	442.00
4X-12X Plex Target (black)	471.00

*LDPXlectro-Dot Plex

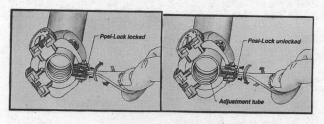

Posi-Lock locked

Posi-Lock unlocked

Adjustment tube

BURRIS POSI-LOCK

BURRIS SCOPES

LONG RELIEF HANDGUN SCOPES

1X LONG EYE RELIEF (LER)

This model has been tested and proved in numerous competitions over the years. The 1X magnification eliminates any parallax. Has super crisp optics and the widest field of view of all our handgun scopes.

1.5X-4X LONG EYE RELIEF (LER)

Designed especially for hunting with a handgun. At 1½X there is a big field of view for those fast, close shots. 4X magnification permits precision, long range shots. Eye relief is 11 inches minimum, 24 inches maximum. Weight is 11 ounces, overall length is 10¼ inches. Burris mounts recommended for this scope.

10X IER P.A.

Designed for the precision shooting handgunner to be shot from a rest or a two handed hold. Handgun should have a 14 inch barrel minimum. Overall length of scope is 13.6 inches. Weight is 14 ounces. Parallax adjustment is 50 yards to infinity.

7X INTERMEDIATE EYE RELIEF (IER)

Developed for the long range, accurate handgunner. Requires a two handed hold. Eye relief is 10 inches minimum, 16 inches maximum. Weight is 10 ounces. Overall length is 11¼ inches. Burris mounts recommended for mounting this scope. Also available with parallax adjustment.

2X-7X LONG EYE-RELIEF (LER)

The perfect handgun scope for varmint or big game hunters. Versatile, compact and available with parallax adjustment.

3X-9X LONG EYE RELIEF (LER)

The highest variable powered handgun scope made. Compact and versatile, this scope is the ultimate for hunting game or testing loads. Fog proof and magnum proof. Also available with parallax adjustment.

HANDGUN LONG EYE RELIEF SCOPE with Plex Reticle:

1X Plex (black)	$228.00
2X Plex (black)	235.00
2X Plex (silver)	264.00
2X Heavy Plex (black)	245.00
2X Heavy Plex (matte)	263.00
2X Plex Posi-Lock (black)	312.00
2X-Plex Posi-Lock (silver)	340.00
3X Plex (black)	252.00
4X Plex (black)	262.00
4X Plex (silver)	293.00
4X Plex Parallax Adjustment (black)	300.00
4X Plex Posi-Lock (black)	339.00
4X Plex Posi-Lock (silver)	369.00
7X Plex Parallax Adjustment (black)	329.00
7X Plex Parallax Adjustment (silver)	356.00
10X Plex Target (black)	388.00
1.5X-4X Plex (black)	365.00
1.5X-4X Plex (silver)	394.00
1.5X-4X Plex Posi-Lock (black)	442.00
1.5X-4X Plex Posi-Lock (silver)	471.00
2X-7X Plex (black)	358.00
2X-7X Plex (matte)	377.00
2X-7X Plex (silver)	386.00
2X-7X Plex Parallax Adjustment (black)	396.00
2X-7X Plex Posi-Lock (black)	434.00
2X-7X Plex Posi-Lock (silver)	463.00
3X-9X Plex (black)	402.00
3X-9X Plex (matte)	421.00
3X-9X Plex (silver)	430.00
3X-9X Peep Plex (black)	411.00
3X-9X Plex Parallax Adjustment (black)	440.00
3X-9X Plex Posi-Lock (black)	478.00
3X-9X Plex Posi-Lock (silver)	507.00

INTERAIMS SIGHTS

RED DOT ELECTRONIC SIGHTS

The following features are incorporated into each model, including the MONO TUBE:

—5 YEAR WARRANTY—

- Sharp Red Dot
- Lightweight
- Compact
- Wide Field of View
- Parallaxfree
- True 1X for Unlimited Eye Relief
- Nitrogen Filled Tube
- Waterproof, Moisture Proof, Shockproof

- Rugged Aluminum Body
- Easy 1″ and 30mm Ring Mounting
- Manually Adjustable Light Intensity
- Windage and Elevation Adjustments
- Dielectrical Coated Lenses
- Battery—Polarized Filter—Extension Tube—Protective Rubber Eye Piece—All included

MONOTUBE CONSTRUCTIONS ONE V

Weight	Length	Battery	Finish
3.9 oz.	4 1/2″	(1) 3 V Lithium	Black or Satin Nickel

ONE V 1″ MODEL
$139.00

Also available:
1″ or 30mm rings in black or satin nickel $11.95

ONE V 30
$159.00

MONOTUBE CONSTRUCTIONS ONE V 30

Weight	Length	Battery	Finish
5.5 oz.	5.4″	(1) 3 V Lithium DL 2032	Black or Satin Nickel

LASERAIM TECHNOLOGIES

MODEL LA16
HOTDOT MIGHTY SIGHT

HOTDOT LASERAIM LASER SIGHTS

Ten times brighter than other laser sights, Laseraim's Hotdot Lasersights include a rechargeable NICad battery and in-field charger. Produce a 2″ dot at 100 yards with a 500-yard range. **Length:** 2″. **Diameter:** .75″. Can be used with handguns, rifles, shotguns and bows. Fit all Laseraim mounts. Available in black or satin.
Prices:
MODEL LA16 HOTDOT MIGHTY SIGHT $169.00
MODEL LA14 HOTDOT TRIGGER GUARD SIGHT
    w/integrated laser, mount, wireless toggle switch 319.00

GI/GI HOT CUSTOM LASERS
$299.00

The all-new GI (standard laser) and GI HOT (Hotdot® laser) have been custom-designed for Glock models 17 to 27. They allow a two-handed shooting grip by locating the laser close to the bottom of the frame. This patented system internalizes the wires, leaving a clean, easy-to-use laser that conforms to the pistol and makes sighting a breeze. A pressure-sensitive pad turns the laser on and off. Four button-cell batteries power it up to one hour continuously. Choose the GI/GI HOT (10 times brighter) for any Glock models 17 to 27. The Easy-lock™ windage & elevation system makes sighting quick and reliable. GI (standard laser) range = 300 yds, GI HOT range = 500 yds. **Length:** 1.5″. **Weight:** 2 oz.

LA3X™ DUALDOT®
LA3XHD™ HOTDOT®
$199.00

Both of these electronic red dot/laser combos can be used in all light conditions—the electronic red dot sight in bright light and the laser in low light conditions. The three-piece sighting system offers the newest technology in red dot scopes and a versatile laser. The 30mm objective lens gives an increased field of view over traditional 1 inch scopes and zero eye relief makes sighting a breeze. The 4 m.o.a. (about 4″ at 100 yards) dot size is ideal for hunting and target. The laser projects a 2″ dot at 100 yards, has up to a 500 yd. range (LA3XHD™ HOT-DOT®) and 300 yd. range (LA3X™), and gives pin-point accuracy with Laseraim's new Easy Lock™ windage & elevation system. The LAEXHD™ HOTDOT® Dualdot laser is 10 times brighter. Fits all rifles, bows, shotguns and handguns with a standard weaver base. **Weight:** 12 oz. **Overall length:** 6 inches.

LA93 ILLUSION III™
RED DOT SCOPE
$139.00

This new two-piece design offers more flexibility in mounting with less added overall weight. The 30mm objective lens gives an increased field of view over traditional 1″ scopes and zero eye relief. The 4 m.o.a. (about 4″ at 100 yards) dot size is ideal for hunting and target. Fits all rifles, bows, shotguns and handguns with a standard weaver base (sold separately). **Weight:** 5 oz. **Overall length:** 6 inches.

LEUPOLD RIFLESCOPES

VARI-X III LINE

The Vari-X III scopes feature a power-changing system that is similar to the sophisticated lens systems in today's finest cameras. Improvements include an extremely accurate internal control system and a sharp sight picture. All lenses are coated with **Multicoat 4**. Reticles are the same apparent size throughout the power range and stay centered during elevation/windage adjustments. Eyepieces are adjustable and fog-free.

VARI-X III 1.5-5X20mm
This selection of hunting powers is for ranges varying from very short to those at which big game is normally taken. The field at 1.5X lets you get on a fast-moving animal quickly. With magnification at 5X, medium and big game can be hunted around the world at all but the longest ranges. Duplex or Heavy Duplex **$551.80**. In black matte finish: **$573.20**.
Also available:
VARI-X III 1.75-6X32mm: $575.00. W/matte finish: **$596.50**

**LEUPOLD VARI-X III 1.75-6X32mm E
(Extended Version)
$596.50**

VARI-X III 2.5-8X36mm
This is an excellent range of powers for almost any kind of game, including varmints. The top magnification provides resolution for practically any situation: **$594.60**. In matte or silver finish: **$616.00**.

VARI-X III 3.5-10X40mm
The extra power range makes these scopes the optimum choice for year-around big game and varmint hunting. The adjustable objective model, with its precise focusing at any range beyond 50 yards, also is an excellent choice for some forms of target shooting: **$616.00**. With matte finish: **$637.50**. With silver: **$637.50**.

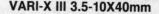

VARI-X III 3.5-10X40mm

VARI-X III 3.5-10X50mm

The hunting scope is designed specifically for low-light situations. The 3.5X10–50mm scope, featuring lenses coated with Multicoat 4, is ideal for twilight hunting (especially whitetail deer) because of its efficient light transmission. The new scope delivers maximum available light through its large 50mm objective lens, which translates into an exit pupil that transmits all the light the human eye can handle in typical low-light circumstances, even at the highest magnification: **$714.50**. With matte or silver finish: **$735.75**.

Also available:
VARI-X III 3.5-10X50mm Adj. Objective: $769.50. With matte finish: **$791.00**.

VARI-X III 3.5-10X50mm

VARI-X III 4.5-14X40mm (Adj. Objective)

This model has enough range to double as a hunting scope and as a varmint scope.
Duplex or Heavy Duplex $691.00
Same as above with 50mm adj. obj., Duplex or
   Heavy Duplex; matte finish only 828.50

**VARI-X III 6.5-20X40mm
(With Adjustable Objective)**

VARI-X III 6.5-20X40mm (Adj. Objective)
This scope has a wide range of power settings, with magnifications useful to hunters of all types of varmints. Can be used for any kind of big-game hunting where higher magnifications are an aid: **$719.50**. With matte or silver finish: **$741.00**.
Also available:
6.5-20X50mm Adj. Obj. w/duplex matte finish $839.50
6.5-20X50mm Adj. Obj. w/European duplex
   matte finish 980.50

LEUPOLD

VARIABLE POWER SCOPES/LASER SIGHTING SYSTEM

VARI-X II 1-4X20mm

VARI-X II 1-4 DUPLEX
This scope, the smallest of Leupold's VARI-X II line, is noted for its large field of view: 70 feet at 100 yards. **$360.75**

VARI-X II 3-9X50mm
This LOV scope delivers a 5.5mm exit pupil for low-light visibility. **$480.50**
With matte finish **501.80**

VARI-X II 2-7X33mm

VARI-X II 2-7 DUPLEX
A compact scope, no larger than the Leupold M8-4X, offering a wide range of power. It can be set at 2X for close ranges in heavy cover or zoomed to maximum power for shooting or identifying game at longer ranges. **$391.00**

SPOTTING SCOPES
Leupold's Golden Ring Armored Spotting Scopes feature extraordinary eye relief and crisp, bright roof prism optics housed in a lightweight, sealed, waterproof body. The Spotting Scopes come complete with a self-storing screw-on sunshade, lens caps, and a green canvas case. Now available in 12-40X60mm variable power with 30.8mm eye relief at 20X.
Prices:
20X50mm Compact Armored . . . . $ 710.75
25X50mm Compact Armored 758.90
30X60mm 782.00
12X40-60mm Variable Power 1089.50

VARI-X II 3-9X40mm DUPLEX
A wide selection of powers offers the right combination of field of view and magnification to fit most hunting conditions. Many hunters use the 3X or 4X setting most of the time, cranking up to 9X for positive identification of game or for extremely long shots. The adjustable objective eliminates parallax and permits precise focusing on any object from less than 50 yards to infinity for extra-sharp definition. **$394.50**
In matte or silver **416.00**

VARI-X II 4-12 MATTE FINISH

LASERLIGHT LASER SIGHTING SYSTEM
$292.90

SPECIFICATIONS
Laser source: Laser emitting diode
Wave length: 670nM
Power output: 5mW
Dot size at 25 yds.: $3/8''$
Battery type: #393 silver oxide (4)
Weight: $1/2$ ounce
Length: $1 3/16''$ **Width:** $3/4''$
Finish: Black matte
Windage/elevation travel: 100 minutes each axis
Adjustment type: Friction

VARI-X II 4-12 (Adj. Objective)
The ideal answer for big game and varmint hunters alike. At 12.25 inches, the 4X12 is virtually the same length as Vari-X II 3X9. . . . . **$542.90**
With matte or silver finish **564.50**

LEUPOLD SCOPES

THE COMPACT SCOPE LINE

The introduction of Leupold Compacts coincides with the increasing popularity of featherweight rifles. Leupold Compact scopes give a balanced appearance atop these scaled-down rifles, offering generous eye relief, magnification and field of view. Fog-free.

M8-4X28mm COMPACT RF SPECIAL
The 4X RF Special is focused to 75 yards and has a Duplex reticle with finer crosshairs................... $335.75

4X COMPACT & 4X RF SPECIAL

2-7X28mm COMPACT
Two ounces lighter and an inch shorter than its full-size counterpart, this 2-X7 is one of the most compact variable power scopes available for today's trend toward smaller and lighter rifles...................................... $421.50

2-7 COMPACT

3-9X28mm COMPACT
The 3X9 Compact is 3½ ounces lighter and 1.3 inches shorter than a standard 3-9. **$435.75**
In black matte finish or silver................... **457.00**

3-9 COMPACT SILVER

SHOTGUN SCOPES (not shown)
Leupold shotgun scopes are parallax-adjusted to deliver precise focusing at 75 yards. Each scope features a special Heavy Duplex reticle that is more effective against heavy, brushy backgrounds. All scopes have matte finish.
Prices:
Vari-X II 1-4 Model Heavy Duplex **$382.00**
M8-4X Heavy Duplex **357.00**
Vari-X III 2-7 Heavy Duplex **412.50**

3-9 COMPACT

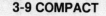

2.5X32mm SCOUT SCOPE

2.5X SCOUT SCOPE
The intermediate eye-relief model for Leupold's line of fixed-power scopes is available in both matte black and silver finish and comes standard with a Duplex-style reticle configuration. At 10″ in length and 7.5 ounces in weight, the 2.5X Scout is one of Leupold's smallest and lightest fixed- power scopes. It was developed for shooters who prefer the simplicity and speed of hunting and shooting with Scout-style lever action or forward-mount rifles. The Scout scope mounts on the barrel forward of the receiver. Eye relief is from 9″ to 17″ (a conventional hunting scope normally has 3″ to 5″ of eye relief). The optical system incorporates fully coated lenses and is computer-optimized for optimal clarity and resolution. Duplex matte or silver:................................... **$353.50**

LEUPOLD SCOPES

HANDGUN SCOPES

M8-2X20mm EER
With an optimum eye relief of 12–24 inches, the 2X EER is suitable for most handguns, carbines and other rifles with top ejection that calls for forward mounting of the scope. Available in black anodized or silver finish to match stainless steel and nickel-plated handguns. **$271.50**
In silver finish **292.90**

LASERLIGHT HANDGUN SIGHT (not shown)
This advanced electronic device projects a laser dot, the result of a collimated coherent laser beam. Micro circuitry pulses the diode thousands of times per second, placing a dot of light where the bullet will impact the target. **$292.90**

2X EER

M8-4X EER
Only 8.4 inches long and 7.6 ounces. Optimum eye relief 12–24 inches. Available in black anodized or silver finish to match stainless steel and nickel-plated handguns. In matte or silver finish **$367.90**
Also available:
VARI-X 2.5-8X32mm EER w/Multicoat 4: **$530.50**
In silver **651.80**

FIXED-POWER SCOPES

M8-4X
The 4X delivers a widely used magnification and a generous field of view. **$335.75**
In black matte finish **357.00**

4X

6X

M8-6X
The 6X extends the range for big-game hunting and doubles in some cases as a varmint scope. **$358.90**

6X42mm

M8-6X42mm W/Multicoat 4
Large 42mm objective lens features increased light-gathering capability and a 7mm exit pupil. Recommended for varmint shooting at night. Duplex or Heavy Duplex: **$444.50**
In matte finish **466.00**

VARMINT SCOPES

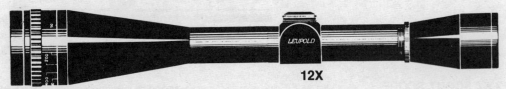

12X

M8-12X40mm STANDARD (Adj. Obj.)
Outstanding optical qualities, resolution and magnification make the 12X a natural for the varmint shooter. Adjustable objective is standard for parallax-free focusing.
Duplex: **$498.25**
With CPC reticle or Dot: **551.80**

Also available:
VARI-X III 6.5-20X40mm VARMINT (Adj. Obj.) Target Dot w/ Multicoat 4 (matte only): **$821.50**

LYMAN SIGHTS

93 MATCH SIGHT

Lyman's globe front sight, the "93 Match," adapts to any rifle with a standard dovetail mounting block. The sight has a diameter of $7/8''$ and comes complete with 7 target inserts. The 93 Match has a special hooked locking bolt and nut to allow quick removal or installation. Bases are available in .860 (European) and .562 (American) hole spacing. The sight height is .550 from the top of the dovetail to the center of the aperture. **$49.50**

90 MJT UNIVERSAL TARGET RECEIVER SIGHT
(Not shown)

Designed to mount on a Marlin Model 2000 Target Rifle using standard Williams FP bases, the Target Sight features target knobs scribed with audible click detents in minute and quarter-minute graduations, plus elevation and windage direction arrows. Adjustable zero scales allow adjustments to be made without disturbing pre-set zero; quick release slide allows slide to be removed with a press of the release button. Large $7/8''$ diameter non-glare .040 target aperture disk is standard. Adjustable from 1.060 to 1.560 above centerline of bore. **$79.95**

20 MJT $7/8''$ DIAMETER GLOBE FRONT SIGHT

Machined from one solid piece of steel designed for use with dovetail slot mounting in the barrel or with Lyman's 25A dovetail base. Height is .700" from bottom of dovetail to center of aperture. Supplied with 7 Anschutz-size steel apertures. **$36.00**

**MODEL
66 SKS**

NO. 16 FOLDING LEAF SIGHT

Designed primarily as open rear sights with adjustable elevation, leaf sights make excellent auxiliary sights for scope-mounted rifles. They fold close to the barrel when not in use, and they can be installed and left on the rifle without interfering with scope or mount. Two lock screws hold the elevation blade adjustments firmly in place. Leaf sights are available in the following heights. **$14.50**

16A—.400" high; elevates to .500"
16B—.345" high; elevates to .445"
16C—.500" high; elevates to .600"

LYMAN NO.2 TANG SIGHT

Recreated for the Special Edition Winchester 1894 100th Anniversary Edition, this version of the tang sight features high index marks on the aperture post with a maximum elevation of .800 for long-range shooting. Comes with both .093 quick-sighting aperture and .040 large disc aperture, plus replacement stock screw and front tang screw.
Prices:
For Winchester 94 Centennial **$77.50**
For Marlin lever actions **82.50**

PEEP SIGHT

The 66-MK "peep" sight fits all versions of the Knight MK-85 rifle with flat-sided receiver. The 57 SME and 57 SMET are designed for White Systems Model 91 and Whitetail models with round receivers. Both sights feature quick release slides, adjustable windage and elevation scales. Also available: **66SKS Receiver sight** w/small large target shooting apertures.
66 MK or 57 SME/57 SMET/66SKS **$69.50**

SHOTGUN SIGHTS (not shown)

No. 10 Front Sight (press fit) for use on double barrel, or ribbed single
-barrel guns **$5.20**
No. 10D Front Sight (screw fit) for use on non-ribbed single-barrel guns;
supplied with a wrench **6.60**
No. 11 Middle Sight (press fit). This small middle sight is intended for use on
double-barrel and ribbed single-barrel guns **5.70**

MILLETT REVOLVER SIGHTS

COLT REVOLVER

The Series 100 Adjustable Sight System offers today's discriminating Colt owner the finest quality replacement sight available. 12 crisp click stops for each turn of adjustment, delivers $5/8''$ of adjustment per click at 100 yards with a 6" barrel. For Colt Python, Trooper, Diamond Back and new Frontier single action army.

Rear Only (White Outline)	CR00001	$49.30
Rear Only (Target Blade)	CR00002	49.30
Rear Only (Silhouette)	CR00003	49.30

Colt owners will really appreciate the high-visability feature of Colt front sights. Easy to install—just drill 2 holes in the new sight and pin on. All steel. Your choice of blaze orange or white bar. Fits 4", 6" & 8" barrels only.

Colt Python & Anaconda (White or Orange Bar)	FB00007-8	$13.60
Diamond Back, King Cobra, Peacemaker	FB00015-16	13.60

SMITH & WESSON

The Series 100 Adjustable Sight System for Smith & Wesson revolvers provides the sight picture and crisp click adjustments desired by the discriminating shooter. $1/2''$ of adjustment per click, at 100 yards on elevation, and $5/8''$ on windage, with a 6" barrel. Can be installed in a few minutes, using factory front sight.

Smith & Wesson N Frame:
N.312—Model 25-5, all bbl., 27-3$1/2''$ & 5", 28-4" & 6"
N.360—Model 25, 27, 29, 57, & 629-4, 6 & 6$1/2''$ bbl.
N.410—Model 27, 29, 57, 629 with 8$3/8''$ bbl.

Smith & Wesson K&L Frame:
K.312—Models 14, 15, 18, 48-4", & 53
K&L360—Models 16, 17, 19, 48-6", 8$3/8''$, 66, 686, 586

Smith & Wesson K&L-Frame $49.30	
Rear Only .312 (White Outline)	SK00001
Rear Only .312 (Target Blade)	SK00002
Rear Only .360 (White Outline)	SK00003
Rear Only .360 (Target Blade)	SK00004
Rear Only .410 (White Outline)	SK00005
Rear Only .410 (Target Blade)	SK00006
Smith & Wesson K&N Old Style $49.30	
Rear Only .312 (White Outline)	KN00001
Rear Only .312 (Target Blade)	KN00002
Rear Only .360 (White Outline)	KN00003
Rear Only .360 (Target Blade)	KN00004
Rear Only .410 (White Outline)	KN00005
Rear Only .410 (Target Blade)	KN00006
Smith & Wesson N-Frame $49.30	
Rear Only .312 (White Outline)	SN00001
Rear Only .312 (Target Blade)	SN00002
Rear Only .360 (White Outline)	SN00003
Rear Only .360 (Target Blade)	SN00001
Rear Only .410 (White Outline)	SN00005
Rear Only .410 (Target Blade)	KN00006

RUGER

The high-visibility white outline sight picture and precision click adjustments of the Series 100 Adjustable Sight System will greatly improve the accuracy and fast sighting capability of your Ruger. $3/4''$ per click at 100 yard for elevation, $5/8''$ per click for windage, with 6" barrel. Can be easily installed, using factory front sight or all-steel replacement front sight which is a major improvement over the factory front. Visibility is greatly increased for fast sighting. Easy to install by drilling one hole in the new front sight.

The Red Hawk all-steel replacement front sight is highly visible and easy to pick up under all lighting conditions. Easy to install. Fits the factory replacement system.

SERIES 100 Ruger Double Action Revolver Sights

Rear Sight (fits all adjustable models)	$49.30
Front Sight (Security Six, Police Six, Speed Six)	13.60
Front Sight (Redhawk)	9.60

TAURUS

Rear, .360 White Outline	$49.30
Rear, .360 Target Blade	49.30

DAN WESSON

This sight is exactly what every Dan Wesson owner has been looking for. The Series 100 Adjustable Sight System provides 12 crisp click stops for each turn of adjustment, with $5/8''$ per click for windage, with a 6" barrel. Can be easily installed, using the factory front or new Millett high-visibility front sights.

Choice of white outline or target blade.

Rear Only (White Outline)	DW00001	$49.30
Rear Only (Target Blade)	DW00002	49.30
Rear Only (White Outline) 44 Mag.	DW00003	49.30
Rear Only (Target Blade) 44 Mag.	DW00004	49.30

If you want super-fast sighting capability for your Dan Wesson, the new Millett blaze orange or white bar front is the answer. Easy to install. Fits factory quick-change system. All steel, no plastic. Available in both heights.

Dan Wesson .44 Mag (White Bar) (high)	FB00009	$13.60
Dan Wesson .44 Mag (Orange Bar) (high)	FB00010	13.60
Dan Wesson 22 Caliber (White Bar) (low)	FB00011	13.60
Dan Wesson 22 Caliber (Orange Bar) (low)	FB00012	13.60

MILLETT AUTO PISTOL SIGHTS

RUGER STANDARD AUTO

The Ruger Standard Auto Combo provides a highly visible sight picture even under low-light conditions. The blaze orange or white bar front sight allows the shooter to get on target fast. Great for target use or plinking. Uses Factory Front Sight on adjustable model guns when using Millett target rear only. All other installations use Millett Front Sight. Easy to install.

Rear Only (White Outline)	$55.60
Rear Only (Silhouette Target Blade)	55.60
Rear Only (Target Blade)	55.60
Front Only (White), Fixed Model	16.00
Front Only (Orange), Fixed Model	16.00
Front Only (Serrated Ramp), Fixed Model	16.00
Front Only (Target-Adjustable Model/White Bar)	16.00
Front Only (Target-Adjustable Model/Orange Bar)	16.00
Front Only Bull Barrel (White or Orange Ramp)	17.60

RUGER P85

Rear (White Outline)	$55.60
Rear (Target Blade)	55.60
Front (White Ramp)	16.00
Front (Orange Ramp)	16.00
Front (Serrated Ramp)	16.00

TAURUS PT92

Rear (White Outline, use Beretta Front)	$55.60
Rear (Target Blade, use Beretta Front)	55.60
Front (White Bar)	25.14
Front (Orange Bar)	25.14
Front (Serrated Ramp)	25.14

GLOCK 17, 17L & 19

Rear (White Outline)	$55.60
Rear (Target Blade)	55.60
Rear (3-Dot)	55.60

GLOCK STAKE-ON FRONT SIGHTS

Front .340 White Bar	$16.00
Front .340 Orange Bar	16.00
Front .340 Serrated Ramp	16.00
Front .340 White Dot	16.00

COLT

Colt Gold Cup Marksman Speed Rear Only (Target .410 Blade)	$49.30
Custom Combat Low Profile Marksman Speed Rear Only (Target .410 Blade)	55.60
Colt Gold Cup Rear (use DC or WS 200 Frt)	49.30
Colt Mark I Fixed Rear Only (use .200 front)	19.75
Colt Mark II Fixed Rear Only (use .200 front)	34.60

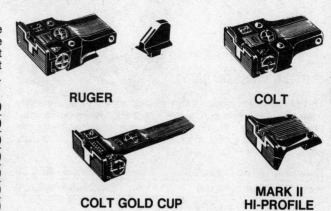

RUGER   **COLT**

COLT GOLD CUP   **MARK II HI-PROFILE**

COLT WIDE STAKE FRONT SIGHTS (POST 6/88) $16.00

.185 WS White Bar
.185 WS Orange Bar
.185 WS Serrated Ramp
.185 WS White Dot
.200 WS White Bar
.200 WS Orange Bare with Skirt
.200 WS Serrated Ramp with Skirt
.200 WS White Dot with Skirt
.312 WS White Bar with Skirt
.312 WS Orange Bar with Skirt
.312 WS Serrated Ramp with Skirt
.312 WS White Dot with Skirt

SIG/SAUER P-220, P-225, P-226, P-228, P-230 (also fits Browning BDA)

Now Sig Pistol owners can obtain a Series-100 adjustable sight system for their guns. Precision click adjustment for windage and elevation makes it easy to zero when using different loads. The high-visibility features assures fast sight acquisition when under the poorest light conditions. Made of high-quality heat-treated nickel steel and built to last. Extremely easy to install on P-225 and P-226. The P-220 and Browning BDA 45 require the Dual-Crimp front sight installation.

Sig P220-25-26 Rear Only (White)*	SP22003	$55.60
Sig P220-25-26 Rear Only (Target)*	SP22004	55.60
Sig P225-6 (White) Dovetail Front*	SP22565	16.00
Sig P225-6 (Orange) Dovetail Front*	SP22566	16.00

The Sig P220 Uses .360 Dual-Crimp Front Sight. The Sig P225-6 Uses a Dovetail Mount Front Sight

MILLETT AUTO PISTOL SIGHTS

SMITH & WESSON 39/59

This sight system provides fast and accurate sighting capability even under low-light conditions. The unique white outline rear blade teamed up with the blaze orange or white bar front sight creates a highly visible sight picture, ideal for match or duty use.

Rear Only (White outline)	SW39595	**$59.30**
Rear Only (Target Blade)	SW39596	59.30

Requires .340 Dual-Crimp Front

SMITH & WESSON 2ND AND 3RD GENERATION
FITS FACTORY ADJUSTABLE $56.80
Rear (3-Dot)
Rear (White Outline)
Rear (Target Blade)
FITS FACTORY FIXED $55.60
Rear (3-Dot)
Rear (White Outline)
Rear (Target Blade)
THIRD GENERATION FRONT SIGHTS $16.00
Front Dovetail White Bar .260
Front Dovetail Orange Bar .260
Front Dovetail Serrated Ramp .260
Front Dovetail White Dot .260
Front Dovetail White Bar .385
Front Dovetail Orange Bar .385
Front Dovetail Serrated Ramp .385
Front Dovetail White Dot .385

BROWNING HI-POWER

The Series 100 Adjustable Sight System for Browning Hi-Power will provide accurate high-visibility sighting for both fixed and adjustable slides with no machine modifications required to the dovetail. Most adjustable slide model Hi-Powers can use the factory front sight as shown in the photo. The fixed slide model requires a new front sight installation. We highly recommend the Dual-Crimp front sight installation on this gun.

BROWNING HI-POWER (Adjustable Slide Model)

Rear Only (White Outline)	BA00009	**$55.60**
Rear Only (Target Blade)	BA00010	55.60

High-Power Requires .340 High Front Sight.

BROWNING HI-POWER (Fixed Slide Model)

Rear Only (White Outline)	BF00009	**$55.60**
Rear Only (Target Blade)	BF00010	55.60

High-Power Requires .340 High Front Sight.

BRUNO CZ75/TZ75/TA90 AUTOPISTOL SIGHTS

Rear Sight (White Outline or Target Blade)	**$55.60**

COLT 45

This Series 100 High Profile Adjustable Sight is rugged, all steel, precision sight which fits the standard factory dovetail with no machine modifications required. This sight provides a highly visible sight picture even under low-light conditions. Blaze orange or white bar front sight, precision click adjustments for windage and elevation makes the Colt .45 Auto Combo the handgunner's choice.

Rear Only (White Outline)	CA00009	**$55.60**
Rear Only (Target Blade)	CA00010	55.60
Rear (Marksman, .410 Blade)	CA00018	55.60

Colt Gov. and Com. Require .312 High Front Sight.

BERETTA ACCURIZER

This amazing new sight system not only provides a highly visible sight picture but also tunes the barrel lockup to improve your accuracy and reduce your group size by as much as 50%. The Beretta Accurizer sight system fits the 92S, 92SB, 84 and 85 models. Easy to install. Requires the drilling of one hole for installation. Your choice of rear blade styles. Front sight comes in white bar, serrated ramp or blaze orange.

Rear Only (White Outline)	BE00005	**$56.40**
Rear Only (Target Blade)	BE00006	56.40
Front Only (White Bar)	BE00007	25.14
Front Only (Orange Bar)	BE00008	25.14
Front Only (Serrated Ramp)	BE00009	25.14

Fits Models 92S, 92SB, 85, 84

NEW BAR-DOT-BAR™ TRITIUM NIGHT SIGHT COMBOS

Ruger P-85, 89, 90 Combo	**$145.00**
Sig Sauer P225/226/228 & New P220 Combo	145.00
Sig Sauer P220 (Prior to 10-90) Combo	145.00
Browning Hi-Power (Fixed Model) Combo	145.00
Browning Hi-Power (Fixed Model Dovetail Front)	145.00
Colt Auto Combo	145.00
CZ-75/TZ-75, TA-90 Combo	145.00
Glock 17, 19, 20, 21, 22, 23 Combo	145.00
S & W 3rd Generation Fixed Combo	145.00
S & W 2nd Generation Fixed Combo	145.00
Beretta 92S, 92SB, 925BF, 92FS	146.00
Taurus PT-92 Combo	146.00

NIKON SCOPES

MONARCH™ UCC SCOPES

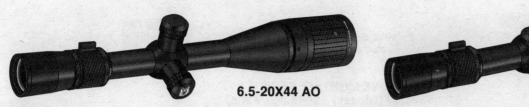

6.5-20X44 AO

2-7X32

Prices:
Riflescopes

Model 6500	$284.00
Model 6520	371.00
Model 6540	476.00
Model 6505	304.00
Model 6525	391.00
Model 6545	496.00
Model 6510	367.00

Model 6530	$554.00
Model 6550	591.00
Model 6515	387.00
Model 6535	572.00
Model 6555	612.00

Handgun Scopes

Model 6560	$213.00
Model 6565	233.00

MONARCH™ UCC RIFLESCOPE SPECIFICATIONS

Model	4x40	2-7x32	3-9x40	3.5-10x50	4-12x40 AO	6.5-20x44 AO	2x20 EER
Lustre	#6500	#6510	#6520	#6530	#6540	#6550	#6560
Matte	#6505	#6515	#6525	#6535	#6545	#6555	-
Silver	-	-	-	-	-	-	#6565
Actual Magnification	4x	2x-7x	3x-9x	3.5x-10x	4x-12x	6.5x-19.46x	1.75x
Objective Diameter	40mm	32mm	40mm	50mm	40mm	44mm	20mm
Exit Pupil	10mm	16-4.6mm	13.3-4.4mm	14.3-5mm	10-3.3mm	6.7-2.2mm	10mm
Eye Relief	89mm 3.5 in.	101-93mm 3.9-3.6 in.	93-90mm 3.6-3.5 in.	100-98mm 3.9-3.8 in.	92-87mm 3.6-3.4 in.	89-81mm 3.5-3.1 in.	670-267mm 26.4-10.5 in.
Field of View at 100 yards	26.9 ft.	44.5-12.7 ft.	33.8-11.3 ft.	25.5-8.9 ft.	25.6-8.5 ft.	16.1-5.4 ft.	22.0 ft.
Tube Diameter	25.4mm 1 in.	25.4mm 1 in.	25.4mm 1 in.	25.4mm 1 in.	25.4mm 1 in.	25.4mm 1 in.	25.4mm 1 in.
Objective Tube Diameter	47.3mm 1.86 in.	39.3mm 1.5 in	47.3mm 1.86 in.	57.3mm 2.2 in.	53.1mm 2.09 in.	54mm 2.13 in.	25.4mm 1 in.
Eyepiece O.D. Diameter	38mm 1.5 in.	38mm 1.5 in.	38mm 1.5 in.	38mm 1.5 in.	38mm 1.5 in.	38mm 1.5 in.	35.5mm 1.4 in.
Length	297mm 11.7 in.	283mm 11.1 in.	312mm 12.3 in.	350mm 13.7 in.	348.5mm 13.7 in.	373mm 14.6 in.	207mm 8.1 in.
Weight	315 g. 11.2 oz.	315 g. 11.2 oz.	355 g. 12.6 oz.	435 g. 15.5 oz.	475 g. 16.9 oz.	565 g. 20.1 oz.	185 g. 6.6 oz.
Adjustment Graduation	¼:1 Click ½:1 Div.	¼:1 Click ¼:1 Div.	¼:1 Click ¼:1 Div.	¼:1 Click ¼:1 Div.	¼:1 Click ¼:1 Div.	⅛:1 Click ⅛:1 Div.	¼:1 Click ½:1 Div.
Max. Internal Adjustment (moa)	120	70	55	45	45	38	120
Parallax Setting (yards)	100	100	100	100	50 to infinity	50 to infinity	100

PENTAX SCOPES

LIGHTSEEKER II RIFLESCOPES

3X-9X LIGHTSEEKER II
$624.00 (Glossy) $648.00 (Matte)

4X-16XAO LIGHTSEEKER II
$804.00 (Glossy) $828.00 (Matte)

6X-24XAO LIGHTSEEKER II
$836.00 (Glossy) $860.00 (Matte)
$884.00 (Satin Chrome)

Features:
- **Scratch-resistant outer tube.** Under ordinary wear and tear, the outer tube is almost impossible to scratch.
- **High Quality cam zoom tube.** No plastics are used. The tube is made of a bearing-type brass with precision machined cam slots. The zoom control screws are precision-ground to 1/2 of one thousandth tolerance.

- **Leak Prevention.** The power rings are sealed on a separate precision-machined seal tube. The scopes are then filled with nitrogen and double-sealed with heavy-duty "O" rings, making them leak-proof and fog-proof.
- **Excellent eyepieces.** The eyepiece lenses have a greater depth of field than most others. Thus, a more focused target at 100, 200 or 500 yards is attainable. Most Pentax Riflescopes are available in High Gloss, Matte or Satin Chrome finish.

LIGHTSEEKER II RIFLESCOPE SPECIFICATIONS

	Lightseeker II 3X-9X	Lightseeker II 4X-16X	Lightseeker II 6X-24X
Tube Dia. (inches)	1.0	1.0	1.0
Objective Dia. (mm)	43	44	44
Eyepiece Dia. (mm)	36	36	36
Exit Pupil (mm)	12.0 - 5.0	10.4 - 2.8	6.9 - 2.3
Eye Relief (inches)	3.5 - 4.0	3.5 - 4.0	3.5 - 4.0
Field of View (ft @ 100 yds.)	36-14	33 - 9	18 - 5.5
Adjust. Grad. (in. @ 100 yds.)	1/4	1/4	1/8
Max. Adjust (in. @ 100 yds.)	50	35	26
Length (inches)	12.7	15.4	16
Weight (ounces)	15.0	23.7	22.7

QUARTON BEAMSHOT SIGHTS

1000 (PLUS RV2 MOUNT)

BEAMSHOT 1000 ULTRA/SUPER

SPECIFICATIONS
Size: ³/₄″×2³/₅″ (overall length)
Weight: 3.8 oz. (incl. battery & mount)
Construction: Aluminum 6061 T6
Finish: Black anodized
Cable length: 5″
Range: 500 yards
Power: <5mW Class IIIA Laser
Wave length: 650nm (Beamshot 1000U-635nm)
Power supply: 3V Lithium battery
Battery life: Approx. 20 hrs. (continuous)
Dot size: 5″ at 10 yds.; 4″ at 100 yds.
Prices:
Standard $69.00
Super 79.00
Ultra 99.00

1000 (PLUS P1A MOUNT)

BEAMSHOT 3000

SPECIFICATIONS
Size: ³/₅″×2″ (overall length)
Weight: 2 oz. (incl. battery)
Construction: Aluminum 6061 T6
Finish: Black
Cable length: 5″
Range: 300 yards
Power: <5mW Class IIIA Laser
Wave length: 670nm
Power supply: 3 SR44 silver oxide watch battery
Battery life: Approx. 4 hrs. (continuous)
Dot size: 0.5″ at 10 yds.; 4″ at 100 yds.
Prices:
Super $75.00
Ultra 95.00

3000 (PLUS P4 MOUNT)

REDFIELD SCOPES

LOW PROFILE WIDEFIELD

The Widefield®, with 25% more field of view than conventional scopes, lets you spot game quicker, stay with it and see other animals that might be missed.

The patented Low Profile design means a low mounting on the receiver, allowing you to keep your cheek tight on the stock for a more natural and accurate shooting stance, especially when swinging on running game.

The one-piece, fog-proof tube is machined with high-tensile strength aluminum alloy and is anodized to a lustrous finish that's rust-free and virtually scratch-proof. Available in seven models.

GOLDEN FIVE STAR TARGET ADJUST KNOBS (6X-18X)

GOLDEN FIVE STAR SCOPES

This series of seven scopes incorporates the latest variable and fixed power scope features, including multicoated and Magnum recoil-resistant optical system, plus maximum light-gathering ability. Positive quarter-minute click adjustments for ease of sighting and optimum accuracy. Anodized finish provides scratch-resistant surface.

Golden Five Star Scopes:

4X Fixed Power	$259.95
6X Fixed Power	282.95
6X Fixed Power Matte	290.95
1X-4X Variable Power	317.95
1X-4X Black Matte Variable Power	326.95
2X-7X Variable Power	333.95
3X-9X Variable Power	357.95
3X-9X Black Matte Variable Power	321.95
3X-9X Nickel Matte Variable Power	331.95
3X-9X Accu-Trac Variable Power	409.95
4X-12X Variable Power (Adj. Objective)	455.95
4X-12X Black Matte	462.95
4X-12X w/Target Knob (AO)	475.95
4X-12X Black Matte Target Knob	480.95
4X-12X Accu-Trac (AO)	505.95
4X-12X Accu-Trac (AO)	512.95
6X-18X Accu-Trac Black Matte	471.95
6X-18X Variable Power (Adj. Objective)	483.95
6X-18X Accu-Trac Variable Power (Adj. Obj.)	533.95
6X-18X Black Matte (AO)	493.95
6X-18X w/Target Knob (AO)	439.95
6X-18X Black Matte w/Targt Knob (AO)	446.95

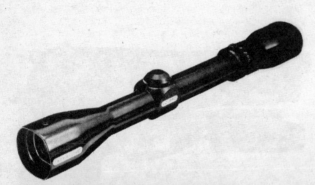

LOW PROFILE WIDEFIELD 3X-9X VARIABLE

WIDEFIELD LOW PROFILE SCOPES

1³/₄X-5X Low Profile Black Matte Variable Power
113807 1³/₄X-5X 4 Plex $397.95
1³/₄X-5X Low Profile Variable Power
113806 1³/₄X-5X 4 Plex 389.95
2X-7X Low Profile Variable Power
111806 2X-7X 4 Plex 400.95
3X-9X Low Profile Variable Power
112806 3X-9X 4 Plex 445.95
3X-9X Low Profile Accu-Trac Variable Power
112810 3X-9X 4 Plex AT 515.95
2³/₄X Low Profile Fixed Power
141807 2³/₄X 4 Plex 283.95
4X Low Profile Fixed Power
143806 4X 4 Plex 317.95
6X Low Profile Fixed Power
146806 6X 4 Plex 340.95
3X-9X Low Profile Nickel Matte Variable Power
112814 4 Plex 404.95
3X-9X Low Profile Black Matte Variable Power
112812 4 Plex 396.95

50mm Golden Five Star Scopes:
3X-9X 50mm Five Star Variable
116500 4 Plex $429.95
3X-9X 50mm Five Star Matte Finish
116508 4 Plex 440.95
3X-9X 50mm Five Star Nickel Matte Finish
116900 4 Plex 394.95

50mm GOLDEN FIVE STAR SCOPE

REDFIELD SCOPES

3X-9X WIDEFIELD® ILLUMINATOR
w/Nickel Matte Finish

THE ILLUMINATOR

With the Illuminator series, you can add precious minutes to morning and evening hunting. These scopes actually compensate for the low light, letting you ''see'' contrasts between field and game.

Optimum resolution, contrast, color correction, flatness of field, edge-to-edge sharpness and absolute fidelity are improved by the unique air-spaced, triplet objective, and the advanced 5-element erector lens system.

The Illuminators also feature a zero tolerance nylon cam follower and thrust washers to provide absolute point of impact hold through all power ranges. The one-piece tube construction is virtually indestructible, tested at 1200g acceleration forces, and fog-free through the elimination of potential leak paths.

Offered in both the Traditional and Widefield® variable power configurations, the Illuminator is also available with the Accu-Trac® feature.

Also offered in 30mm 3X-12X with a 56mm adj. obj.

ILLUMINATOR SCOPES
2X-7X Widefield Variable Power
112910 4 Plex **$539.95**
3X-9X Widefield Variable Power
112886 3X-9X 4 Plex **609.95**
3X-9X Widefield Accu-Trac Variable Power
112880 3X-9X 4 Plex **665.95**
3X9 Widefield Var. Power Black Matte Finish
112888 . . . . **619.95**
3X-9X Widefield Nickel Matte Variable Power
112892 4 Plex AT **629.95**
3X-9X Widefield Accu-Trac Black Matte Variable
112890 4 Plex AT **590.95**
3X-10X Widefield 50mm Black
112700 . . . . **681.95**
3X-10X 50mm Black Matte **689.95**

GOLDEN FIVE STAR EXTENDED EYE RELIEF HANDGUN SCOPES

2X Fixed
140002 4 Plex **$223.95**
2X Nickel Plated Fixed
14003 4 Plex **239.95**
4X Fixed
140005 4 Plex **223.95**
4X Nickel Plated Fixed
140006 4 Plex **239.95**
2-1/2X-7X Variable
140008 4 Plex **303.95**
2½X-7X Nickel Plated Variable
140009 4 Plex **322.95**
2½X-7X Black Matte Variable
140010 4 Plex **322.95**

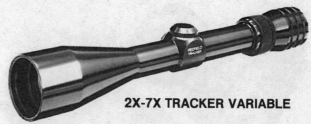

2X-7X TRACKER VARIABLE

THE TRACKER

The Tracker series brings you a superior combination of price and value. It provides the same superb quality, precision and strength of construction found in all Redfield scopes, but at an easily affordable price. Features include the tough, one-piece tube, machined and hand-fitted internal parts, excellent optical quality and traditional Redfield styling.

TRACKER SCOPES:
2X-7X Tracker Variable Power
122300 2X-7X 4 Plex **$239.95**
2X-7X Tracker Nickel Matte Variable Power
122310 4 Plex **226.95**
3X-9X Tracker Variable Power
123300 3X-9X 4 Plex **269.95**
3X-9X Tracker Nickel Matte Variable Power
123320 4 Plex **290.95**
4X Tracker Fixed Power
135300 4X 4 Plex **187.95**
4X 40mm Tracker Nickel Matte Fixed Power
135312 4 Plex **189.95**
4X40mm Black
135310 4 Plex **197.95**
4X 40mm Tracker Black Matte Fixed Power
135320 4 Plex **181.95**
6X Tracker Fixed Power
135600 6X 4 Plex **217.95**
8X40mm Black
135800 . . . . **237.95**
Matte Finish
122308 2X-7X 4 Plex **250.95**
123308 3X-9X 4 Plex **279.95**
135608 6X 4 Plex **226.95**
135308 4X 32mm **197.95**
135808 8X 40mm **246.95**

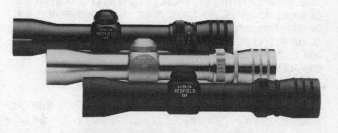

VARIABLE GOLDEN FIVE STAR
(2½X-7X) HANDGUN SCOPES
(Black, Nickel, Black Matte)

SCOPES

SAKO SCOPE MOUNTS

"ORIGINAL" SCOPE MOUNTS

"ORIGINAL" SCOPE MOUNTS

SAKO's "Original" scope mounts are designed and engineered to exacting specifications, which is traditional to all SAKO products. The dovetail mounting system provides for a secure and stable system that is virtually immovable. Unique to this Sako mount is a synthetic insert that provides maximum protection against possible scope damage. It also affords additional rigidity by compressing itself around the scope. Manufactured in Finland.

Prices:
1″ Low, Medium & High (Short, Medium
& Long Action) . . . . $ 94.00
30mm Low, Medium & High (Short, Medium
& Long Action) 113.00
**1″ Medium & High Extended Base Scope
Mounts** 140.00

SCOPE MOUNTS

These SAKO scope mounts are lighter, yet stronger than ever. Tempered steel allows the paring of every last gram of unnecessary weight without sacrificing strength. Like the original mount, these rings clamp directly to the tapered dovetails on Sako rifles, thus eliminating the need for separate bases. Grooves inside the rings preclude scope slippage even under the recoil of the heaviest calibers. Nicely streamlined and finished in a rich blue-black to complement any Sako rifle.

Prices:
Low, medium, or high (1″) $68.00
Medium or high (30mm) 84.00

"NEW" SCOPE MOUNTS

SCHMIDT & BENDER RIFLESCOPES

VARIABLE POWER

2¹/₂-10X56 VARIABLE POWER SCOPE
$1298.00

1¹/₂-6X42 VARIABLE POWER SCOPE
$1073.00

Also available:
1¹/₄-4X20 VARIABLE POWER SCOPE $980.00
3-12X50 VARIABLE POWER SCOPE $1262.00
Note: **All variable power scopes have glass reticles and are available in steel and aluminum**

FIXED POWER

4X36 FIXED POWER SCOPE
(Steel Tube w/o Mounting Rail)
$725.00

6X42 FIXED POWER SCOPE
(Steel Tube w/o Mounting Rail)
$795.00

Also available:
10X42 FIXED POWER SCOPE (Steel Tube w/o Mounting Rail) $910.00

8X56 FIXED POWER SCOPE (Steel Tube w/o Mounting Rail) $915.00

POLICE/MARKSMAN RIFLESCOPES

POLICE/MARKSMAN 3.12X50mm w/Detachable Rubber Sunshade and Bryant P-Rangefinding Reticle

This new line of riflescopes was designed specifically to meet the needs of the precision sharpshooter. It includes fixed-power scopes in 6X42 and 10X42 magnifications and variable-power scopes in 1.5-6X42, 3-12X42 and 3-12X50 configurations. The 3-12X50 is available in two models: Standard (for shooting to 500 yards) and a military version (MIL) designed for ranges up to 1000 yards. Each scope is equipped with two elevation adjustment rings: a neutral ring with ¹/₄″ @ 100-yard clicks, which can be matched to any caliber and bullet weight, and a second ring calibrated for the .308 caliber bullet. The 1.5-6X42 is calibrated for the 150-grain bullet, while all other rings are calibrated for the 168-grain bullet. The military elevation adjustment ring has 1″ @ 100-yard clicks. Windage adjustment rings are set for ¹/₄″ @ 100-yard clicks, except for the MIL scope which has ¹/₂″ @ 100-yard clicks.

SIMMONS SCOPES

AETEC
MODELS 2100/2101/2102
2.8-10X44 WA
Field of view: 44'-14'
Eye relief: 5"
Length: 11.9"
Weight: 15.5 oz.
Reticle: Triplex
Price: $349.95

Also available:
MODEL 2104
3.8-12X44 WA/AO
Aspherical Lens System w/sunshade, black matte
Price: $364.95

AETEC SCOPE
2.8-10X44 WA Aspherical Lens System
w/Sunshade. Black Matte

44 MAG RIFLESCOPES

MODEL M1044
3-10X44mm
Field of view: 38'-12'
Eye relief: 3"
Length: 12.8"
Weight: 16.9 oz.
Price: $259.95

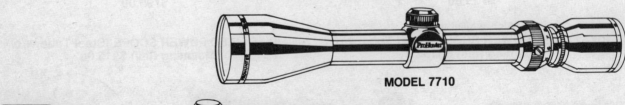

MODEL 1045

MODEL M1045
4-12X44mm
Field of view: 27'-9'
Eye relief: 3"
Length: 12.8"
Weight: 19.5 oz.
Price: $279.95

MODEL M1047
6.5-20X44mm
Field of view: 14'-5'
Eye relief: 2.6"-3.4"
Length: 12.8"
Weight: 19½ oz.
Price: $289.95

Also available:
MODEL M1048
6.5-20X44 Target Turrets
Black Matte (⅛" MOA) $329.95
with Sunshade: $344.90

MODEL M3044
3-10X44mm
Field of view: 38'-11'
Eye relief: 3"
Length: 13.1"
Weight: 16.4 oz.
Price: $269.95

PROHUNTER RIFLESCOPES

MODEL 7710

MODELS 7711/7712

MODEL 7710
3-9X40mm Wide Angle Riflescope
Field of view: 40'-15' at 100 yards
Eye relief: 3"
Length: 12.6"
Weight: 11.6 oz.
Features: Triplex reticle; silver matte finish
Price: $179.95 (Same in black matte or black polish, Models 7711 and 7712)

Also available:
Model 7700/7701 2-7X32 Black Matte or Black
 Polish $169.95
Model 7716 4-12X40 Black Matte 199.95
Model 7720 6-18X40 (adj. obj. Black) 224.95
Model 7721 6-18X40 AO Black Matte 224.95
Model 7740 6X40 Black Matte 144.95

SIMMONS SCOPES

WHITETAIL CLASSIC RIFLESCOPES

Simmons' Whitetail Classic Series features fully coated lenses and glare-proof BlackGranite finish. The Mono-Tube construction means that front bell and tube, saddle and rear tube are all turned from one piece of aircraft aluminum. This system eliminates 3 to 5 joints found in most other scopes in use today, making the Whitetail Classic up to 400 times stronger than comparably priced scopes.

MODEL WTC9
3X28 Lighted Reticle Black Granite
Field of view: 11.5'
Eye relief: 11"-20"
Length: 9"
Weight: 9.2 oz.
Price: $329.95

MODEL WTC11

MODEL WTC11
1.5-5X20mm
Field of view: 80'-23.5'
Eye relief: 3.5"
Length: 9 1/2"
Weight: 9.9 oz.
Price: $184.95

MODEL WTC12

MODEL WTC12
2.5-8X36mm
Field of view: 48'-14.8'
Eye relief: 3"
Length: 12.8"
Weight: 12.9 oz.
Price: $199.95

MODEL WTC13

MODEL WTC13
3.5-10X40mm
Field of view: 35'-12'
Eye relief: 3"
Length: 12.8"
Weight: 16.9 oz.
Price: $219.95

MODEL WTC15/35
3.5-10X50 Black
or Silver Granite
Field of view: 30.3'-11.3'
Eye relief: 3.2"
Length: 12.25"
Weight: 13.6 oz.
Price: $329.95

MODEL WTC16
4X40 Black Granite
Field of view: 36.8'
Eye relief: 4"
Length: 9.9"
Weight: 12 oz.
Price: $149.95

MODEL WTC23
3.5-10X40
Field of view: 34'-11.5'
Eye relief: 3.2"
Length: 12.4"
Weight: 12.8 oz.
Price: $219.95

MODEL WTC33
3.5-10X40 Silver
Same specifications as
Model WTC23
Price: $219.95

MODEL WTC35
3.5-10X50 WA Silver Granite
Field of view: 29.5'-11.5'
Eye relief: 3.2"
Length: 12.75"
Weight: 13.5 oz.
Price: $329.95

MODEL WTC45
4.5-14X40 AO
Field of view: 22.5'-8.6'
Eye relief: 3.2"
Length: 13.2"
Weight: 14 oz.
Price: $269.95

MODEL WTC89D
2X32 Black Granite ProDiamond Reticle
Field of view: 31'
Eye relief: 5.5"
Length: 8.8"
Weight: 8.75 oz.
Price: $159.95

MODEL WTC90D
7X21 Black Granite ProDiamond Reticle
Field of view: 17'
Eye relief: 5.5"
Length: 8.5"
Weight: 8.75 oz.
Price: $169.95

SIMMONS SCOPES

GOLD MEDAL SILHOUETTE/VARMINT SERIES

Simmons Gold Medal Silhouette/Varmint Riflescopes are made of state-of-the-art drive train and erector tube design, a new windage and elevation indexing mechanism, camera-quality 100% multicoated lenses, and a super smooth objective focusing device. High silhouette-type windage and elevation turrets house 1/8 minute click adjustments. The scopes have a black matte finish and crosshair reticle and are fogproof, waterproof and shockproof.

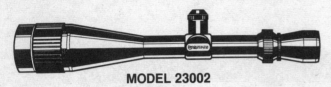

MODEL 23002

MODEL #23002
6-20X44mm
Field of view: 17.4'-5.4'
Eye relief: 3"
Length: 14.5"
Weight: 18.3 oz.
Feature: Truplex reticle, 100% Multi-Coat Lens
System, black matte finish, obj. focus
Price: $529.95 (Crosshair)
          529.95 (Dot Reticle)

MODEL 3006V-TAC

MODEL 3006V-TAC
3-9x40 Black Matte ProDiamond
Field of view: 33'-14.5'
Eye relief: 4.1"-3.0"
Length: 12.5"
Weight: 17 oz.
Price: $699.95

GOLD MEDAL HANDGUN SERIES

Simmons gold medal handgun scopes offer long eye relief, no tunnel vision, light weight, high resolution, non-critical head alignment, compact size and durability to withstand the heavy recoil of today's powerful handguns. In black and silver finishes, all have fully multicoated lenses and a Truplex reticle.

MODEL 22001

MODEL #22001
2.5-7X28mm
Field of view: 9.7'-4.0'
Eye relief: 8.9"-19.4"
Length: 9.2"
Weight: 9 oz.
Feature: Truplex reticle, 100% Multi-Coat
Lens System, black polished finish.
Price: $329.95

MODEL #22002
2.5-7X28mm
Field of view: 9.7'-4.0'
Eye relief: 8.9"-19.4"
Length: 9.2"
Weight: 9 oz.
Feature: Truplex reticle, 100% Multi-Coat
Lens System, black polished finish.
Price: $329.95

Also Available:
MODEL #22003
2X20 . . . . $229.95
MODEL #22004
2X20 . . . . 229.95

SIMMONS SCOPES

MASTER RED DOT SCOPES
$269.95

MODELS 51004/51005
Magnification: 1X30
Finish: Black or silver matte
Field of view: 40'
100 yards
Eye relief: Infinite   **Reticle:** 4 MOA Dot
Length: 5.25"   **Weight:** 4.8 oz.
Also available:
MODELS 51012/51032. Same specifications and price as Models 51004/51005 w/12 MOA Dot reticle

MASTER RED DOT SCOPES

BLACKPOWDER SCOPES

MODELS BP2520M
Magnification: 2.5X20
Finish: Black or silver matte
Field of view: 24'
100 yards
Eye relief: 6"   **Reticle:** Truplex
Length: 7.4"   **Weight:** 7.3 oz.
Price: $109.95

MODEL BP2732M

MODELS BP420M/420S
Magnification: 4X20
Finish: Black or silver matte
Field of view: 19.5'
100 yards
Eye relief: 4"   **Reticle:** Truplex
Length: 7.5"   **Weight:** 8.3 oz.
Price: $109.95

MODELS BP2732M/2732S
Magnification: 2-7X32
Finish: Black or silver matte
Field of view: 57.7'-16.6'
100 yards
Eye relief: 3"   **Reticle:** Truplex
Length: 11.6"   **Weight:** 12.4 oz.
Price: $129.95

Also available:
MODELS BP400M/400S
4X20 Black Matte or Silver Matte, Long Body
Field of view: 28"   **Eye relief:** 5.0"
Length: 10.25"   **Weight:** 8.7 oz.
Reticle: Triplex
Price: $79.95

MODELS BP0420M/420S
4x20 Octagon Body
Field of view: 19.5'
Eye relief: 4"
Length: 7.5"   **Weight:** 8.3 oz.
Reticle: Triplex
Price: $169.95

SHOTGUN SCOPES

MODELS 21004/7790D/7793 DCP
Magnification: 4X32
Finish: Black matte
Field of view: 16' (Model 21004); 17' (Models 7790D/7793 DCP)
Eye relief: 5.5"
Reticle: Truplex (Model 21004); Pro-Diamond (Models 7790D/7793 DCP)
Length: 8.5" (8.8" Model 21004)
Weight: 8.75 oz. (9.1 oz. Models 7790D/7793 DCP)
Prices:
Model 21004 . . . . $109.95
Model 7790D 139.95
Model 7793 DCP 179.95

MODEL 7790D

Also available:
Model 21005 2.5X20 Black matte (Truplex reticle) . . . . $ 99.95
Model 1091 1X20 WA Black matte (Truplex reticle) 119.95
Model 7788 1X32 Black matte (Truplex reticle) 129.95
Model 7789D 2X32 Black matte (ProDiamond reticle) 129.95
Model 7791 1.5-5X20 WA Black matte (ProDiamond reticle) 139.95
Model 7792 DCP 2X32 Black matte w/mount (ProDiamond reticle) . . 179.95

SWAROVSKI RIFLESCOPES

PROFESSIONAL HUNTER PH SERIES

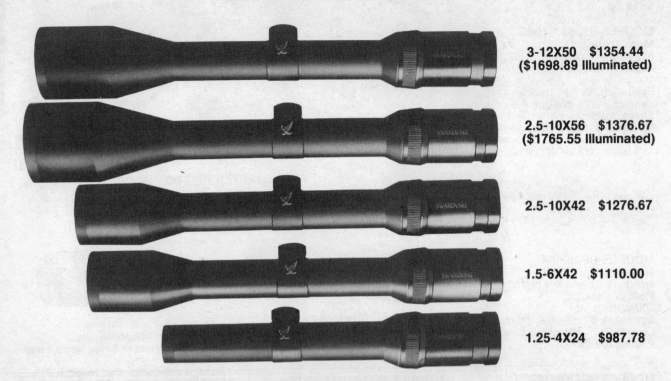

3-12X50 $1354.44
($1698.89 Illuminated)

2.5-10X56 $1376.67
($1765.55 Illuminated)

2.5-10X42 $1276.67

1.5-6X42 $1110.00

1.25-4X24 $987.78

SPECIFICATIONS PROFESSIONAL HUNTER PH SERIES (see following page for additional PH Models)

Type	Maintube	Magnification	Max. effective objective lens ⌀ in/mm	Exit pupil ⌀ in/mm	Exit pupil distance in/mm	Field of view ft/100yds m/100 m	Twilight performance acc. to DIN 58388	Middle tube ⌀ standard in/mm a	Objective lens tube ⌀ in/mm b	Total length in/mm c	1 click in/100 yds mm/100 m	Max. adjustment range in/100 yds m/100 m	Weight S/LS (approx.) oz/g	Licencenumber
1.25-4x24	S L LS	1.25-4	0.94 24	0.49-0.24 12.5-6	3.15 80	10.8-3.5 32.8-10.4	3.5-9.8	1.18 30	1.18 30	10.6 270	0.54 15	119 3.3	450 350 385	15.9 12.3 13.6
1.5-6x42	S L LS	1.5-6	1.65 42	0.52-0.28 13.1-7	3.15 80	7.3-2.3 21.8-7	4.2-15.9	1.18 30	1.89 48	13.0 330	0.36 10	79 2.2	580 450 485	20.5 15.9 17.1
2.5-10x42	S L LS	2.5-10	1.65 42	0.52-0.17 13.1-4.2	3.15 80	4.4-1.4 13.2-4.1	7.1-20.5	1.18 30	1.89 48	13.2 336	0.36 10	47 1.3	550 420 455	19.4 14.8 16.0
2.5-10x56	S L LS	2.5-10	2.20 56	0.52-0.22 13.1-5.6	3.15 80	4.4-1.4 13.2-4.1	7.1-23.7	1.18 30	2.44 62	14.7 374	0.36 10	47 1.3	690 520 560	24.3 18.3 19.8
3-12x50	S L LS	3-12	1.97 50	0.52-0.17 13.1-4.2	3.15 80	3.7-1.2 11-3.5	8.5-24.5	1.18 30	2.20 56	14.3 364	0.36 10	40 1.1	625 470 510	22.0 16.6 18.0

S = steel body, L = light alloy body, LS = light alloy body with mounting rail

SWAROVSKI RIFLESCOPES

6-24X50mm PROFESSIONAL HUNTER "PH" RIFLESCOPE

Swarovski's 6-24X50mm "PH" riflescope was developed for long-range target, big-game and varmint shooting. Its waterproof parallax adjustment system should be popular with White Tail "Bean Field Shooters" and long-range varmint hunters looking for a choice of higher powers in a premium rifle scope and still deliver accuracy. The new scope will also appeal to many bench rest shooters who compete in certain classes where power and adjustment are limited. A non-magnifying, fine plex reticle and an all-new fine crosshair reticle with 1/8"

MOA dot are available in the 6-24X50mm scope. Reticle adjustment clicks are 1/6" (minute) by external, waterproof "target turrets." The internal optical system features a patented coil spring suspension system for dependable accuracy and positive reticle adjustment. The objective bell, 30mm middle tube, turret housing and ocular bell connection are machined from one solid bar of aluminum.

Price: **$1665.50**

3-10X42 AMERICAN RIFLE SCOPE

Swarovski's new 3-10X42mm American style riflescope is an addition to the company's one-inch "A" line of lightweight riflescopes. It offers greater magnification and a larger objective lens for better light gathering ability needed for twilight and "black timber" hunting. Encased in a special one-piece aluminum alloy tube, this scope is waterproof/submersible,

shockproof and carries a limited lifetime warranty. As in all Swarovski's fixed-power scopes, the new 3-10X42 variable riflescope features a variety of popular style reticles, laser-aligned optics and fully multi-coated optics for maximum light transmission and brilliant images

Price: **$776.65**

8X56 (30mm)

8X50 (30mm)

FIXED POWER PH RIFLESCOPES

Swarovski's new fixed-power models—the 1" 6X42 and 30mm 8X50 and 8X56—have been added to the 10 variable-power models introduced in 1994. Among the features of these new additions are an objective bell, 30mm middle tube, turret housing and ocular bell connection machined out of one solid piece of bar stock. The internal optical system uses a patented coil spring suspension that helps to insure dependable accuracy

and positive reticle adjustment. All scopes are purged with nitrogen and tested for accuracy. The scopes come with a wide choice of reticles and an unconditional lifetime warranty.

Prices:
6X42 . . . . **$921.00**
8X50 . . . . **$954.50**
8X56 . . . . **$998.95**

SWAROVSKI RIFLESCOPES

KAHLES Z-95 (6X42)

KAHLES TACTICAL RIFLESCOPES

Both reticles on the Kahles riflescopes (6X42 and 10X42) have a range- finding capability and include a .308 caliber Ballistic Cam Adjustment System. This allows the shooter to estimate range, using known object sizes, downrange. The shooter then dials in a fairly accurate range measurement with the ballistic cam adjustment for predicted bullet drop at that distance. The mil-dot reticle used was developed by the U.S. Marine Corps in the late 1970s. The mil-dots are spaced one mil apart and equal 36″ at 1,000 yards or 18″ at 500 yds. The dots above and below the cross-hair can be used for holdover estimating, while the dots to the right and left can be used to lead a moving target or to compensate for wind drift. The ZF-95 scopes have 1″ steel tubes, a Parkerized matte black finish and externally adjusted turrets.

Prices:

Z-95 6X42 . . . . $1198.95
Z-95 10X42 . . . . 1221.00

KAHLES 30mm RIFLESCOPE

KAHLES 30mm RIFLESCOPE

Three variable-power Kahles riflescopes have been introduced by Swarovski Optik as additions to their "Value Class Optics" line. Produced in Austria, these scopes offer optimum optical clarity and brightness from a 30mm tube using large diameter lenses throughout. The scope selection includes 1.5-6X42, 2.2-9X42 and 3-12X56 models. the optical components are fully multi-coated and the scope tubes are purged with nitrogen. All are shockproof, waterproof and come with an unconditional lifetime warranty.

Prices:

S-6X42 . . . . $776.65
2.2-9X42 . . . . 943.35
3-12X56 . . . . 998.95

AMERICAN LIGHTWEIGHT RIFLESCOPE

This model features precision ground, coated and aligned optics sealed in a special aluminum alloy tube to withstand heavy recoil. Eye relief is 85mm and the recoiling eyepiece protects the eye. Positive click adjustments for elevation and windage change the impact point (approx. 1/4″) per click at 100 yards, with parallax also set at 100 yards. Weight is only 13 ounces.

Prices:

1.5-4.5X20 with duplex reticle $665.56
4X32 with duplex reticle 554.44
6X36 with duplex reticle 610.00
3-9X36 with duplex reticle 698.89
3-10X42 with duplex reticle 776.67

SWIFT RIFLESCOPES

MODEL 650 $80.00
(Matte $99.50 Silver $100.00)

MODEL 653 $101.50

RIFLESCOPE SPECIFICATIONS

MODEL#	DESCRIPTION	FIELD OF VIEW AT 100 YDS. (FT')	ZERO PARALLAX AT	EYE RELIEF (INCH)	TUBE DIAMETER (INCH)	CLICK ADJUST-MENT (INCH)	LENGTH (INCH)	WEIGHT (OZ.)	LENS ELEMENT (PC'E)
650	4x,32mm	26'	100 YDS.	4	1"	1/4"	12"	9.1	9
653	4x,40mm, W.A.	35'	100 YDS.	4	1"	1/4"	12.2"	12.6	11
660	4x,20mm	25'	35 YDS.	4	1"	1/4"	11.8"	9	9
666	1x,20mm	113'	-	3.2	1"	1/4"	7.5"	9.6	-
654	3-9x,32mm	35' @ 3x 12' @ 9x	100 YDS.	3.4 @ 3x 2.9 @ 9x	1"	1/4"	12"	9.8	11
656	3-9x,40mm, W.A.	40' @ 3x 14' @ 9x	100 YDS.	3.4 @ 3x 2.8 @ 9x	1"	1/4"	12.6"	12.3	11
664R	4-12x,40mm	27' / 9'	Adjust-able	3.0 / 2.8	1"	1/4"	13.3"	14.8	-
665	1.5-4.5x,21mm	69' / 24.5'	100 YDS.	3.5 / 3.0	1"	1/4"	10.9"	9.6	-
659	3.5-10x,44mm, W.A.	34' @ 3.5x 12' @ 10x	-	3.0 / 2.8	1"	1/4"	12.8"	13.5	-
649	4-12x,50mm, W.A.	30' @ 4x 10' @ 12x	-	3.2 / 3.0	1"	1/4"	13.2"	14.6	-
658	2-7x,40mm, W.A.	55' @ 2x 18' @ 7x	-	3.3 / 3.0	1"	1/4"	11.6"	12.5	-
667	FIRE-FLY, 1x,30mm	40'	100YDS.	Unlimited	30mm	1/2"	5 3/8"	5	-

Also available:

Model 649	**$216.00**
Model 649M	218.00
Model 654	99.50
Model 656	108.00
Matte	110.00
Silver	110.50
Model 657 Mark I 6X, 40mm .	99.50
Model 658	136.50
Matte	138.00
Model 659	212.00
Matte	213.00
Silver	214.00

MODEL 664R $143.00
(Matte $144.00   Silver $145.00)

MODEL 667 FIRE-FLY SCOPE
1X30 RED-DOT
$215.00

TASCO SCOPES

MODEL WA1.35×20

WORLD CLASS™ WIDE-ANGLE® RIFLESCOPES

Features:
- 25% larger field of view
- Exceptional optics

- Fully coated for maximum light transmission
- Waterproof, shockproof, fogproof
- Non-removable eye bell
- Free haze filter lens caps
- TASCO's unique World Class Lifetime Warranty

This member of Tasco's World Class Wide Angle line offers a wide field of view—103 feet at 1X and 31 feet at 3.5X—and quick sighting without depending on a critical view. The scope is ideal for hunting deer and dangerous game, especially in close quarters or in heavily wooded and poorly lit areas. Other features include ¼-minute positive click stops, fully coated lenses (including Supercon process), nonremovable eyebell and windage/elevation screws. Length is 9¾″, with 1″ diameter tube. Weight is 12 ounces.

WORLD CLASS, WIDE-ANGLE VARIABLE ZOOM RIFLESCOPES

Model No.	Power	Objective Diameter	Finish	Reticle	Field of View @100 Yds.	Eye Relief	Tube Diameter	Scope Length	Scope Weight	Price
WA4X40	4X	40mm	Black Gloss	30/30	36′	3″	1″	13″	11.5 oz.	$135.85
WA6X40	6X	40mm	Black Gloss	30/30	23′	3″	1″	12.75″	11.5 oz.	144.30
WA13.5X20	1X-3.5X	20mm	Black Gloss	30/30	103′-31′	3″	1″	9.6″	12 oz.	168.30
WA1.755X20	1.75X-5X	20mm	Black Gloss	30/30	72′-24′	3″	1″	10.5″	10 oz.	152.80
WA2.58X40	2.5X8X	40mm	Black Gloss	30/30	44′-14′	3″	1″	11.75″	14.25 oz.	178.25
WA27X32	2X-7X	32mm	Black Gloss	30/30	56′-17′	3.25″	1″	11.5″	12 oz.	161.30
DWC39X40	3X-9X	40mm	Black Matte	30/30	41′-15′	3″	1″	12.75″	13 oz.	198.45
WA39X40	3X-9X	40mm	Black Gloss	30/30	41′-15′	3″	1″	12.75″	13 oz.	198.65
WA39X40TV	3X-9X	40mm	Black Gloss	30/30 TV	41′-15′	3″	1″	12.75″	13 oz.	198.65
WA39X40ST	3X-9X	40mm	Stainless	30/30	41′-15′	3″	1″	12.75″	13 oz.	198.65

WORLD CLASS™ 1″ PISTOL SCOPES

Built to withstand the most punishing recoil, these scopes feature a 1″ tube that provides long eye relief to accommodate all shooting styles safely, along with fully coated optics for a bright, clear image and shot-after-shot durability. The 2X22 model is recommended for target shooting, while the 4X28 model and 1.25X-4X28 are used for hunting as well. All are fully waterproof, fogproof, shockproof and include haze filter caps.

SPECIFICATIONS

Model	Power	Objective Diameter	Finish	Reticle	Field of View @ 100 Yds	Eye Relief	Tube Diam.	Scope Length	Scope Weight	Prices
PWC2X22	2X	22mm	Blk Gloss	30/30	25′	11″–20″	1″	8.75″	7.3 oz.	$288.60
PWC2X22MA	2X	22mm	Matte Alum.	30/30	25′	11″–20″	1″	8.75″	7.3 oz.	288.60
PWC4X28	4X	28mm	Blk Gloss	30/30	8′	12″–19″	1″	9.45″	7.9 oz.	399.55
PWC4X28MA	4X	28mm	Matte Alum.	30/30	8′	12″–19″	1″	9.45″	7.9 oz.	339.55
P1.254X28	1.25X-4X	28mm	Blk Gloss	30/30	23′-9′	15″–23″	1″	9.25″	8.2 oz.	339.55
P1.254X28MA	1.25X-4X	28mm	Matte Alum.	30/30	23′-9′	15″–23″	1″	9.25″	8.2 oz.	285.45

TASCO SCOPES

PROPOINT PLUS PDP3CMP

PROPOINT™ MULTI-PURPOSE SCOPES

Tasco's ProPoint is a true 1X-30mm scope with electronic red dot reticle that features unlimited eye relief, enabling shooters to shoot with both eyes open. It is available with a 3X booster and also has application for rifle, shotgun, bow and black powder. The compact version (PDP2) houses a lithium battery pack, making it 1¼ inches narrower than previous models and lighter as well (5.5 oz.). A mercury battery converter is provided for those who prefer standard batteries.

Tasco's 3X booster with crosshair reticle weighs 6.1 oz. and is 5½ inches long. Model PB2 fits the new PDP2/PDP2MA, and because both units include separate windage and elevation systems the electronic red dot is movable within the crosshair. That means it can be set for two different distances, making it the ultimate rangefinder. Another 3X booster—the PB1— has no crosshairs and fits all other Pro-Point models. Specifications and prices are listed below.

SPECIFICATIONS PROPOINT SCOPES

Model	Power	Objective Diameter	Finish	Reticle	Field of View @ 100 Yds.	Eye Relief	Tube Diam.	Scope Length	Scope Weight	Prices
PDP2	1X	25mm	Black Matte	5 M.O.A.Dot	40'	Unlimited	30mm	5"	5.5 oz.	$254.65
PDP2ST	1X	25mm	Stainless	5 M.O.A. Dot	40'	Unlimited	30mm	5"	5.5 oz.	254.65
PDP2BD	1X	25mm	Black Matte	10 M.O.A. Dot	40'	Unlimited	30mm	5"	5.5 oz.	254.65
PDP2BDST	1X	25mm	Stainless	10 M.O.A. Dot	40'	Unlimited	30mm	5"	5.5 oz.	254.65
PDP3	1X	25mm	Black Matte	5 M.O.A. Dot	52'	Unlimited	30mm	5"	5.5 oz.	305.60
PDP3ST	1X	25mm	Stainless	5 M.O.A. Dot	52'	Unlimited	30mm	5"	5.5 oz.	305.60
PDP3BD	1X	25mm	Black Matte	10 M.O.A. Dot	52'	Unlimited	30mm	5"	5.5 oz.	305.60
PDP3BDST	1X	25mm	Stainless	10 M.O.A. Dot	52'	Unlimited	30mm	5"	5.5 oz.	305.60
PDP3CMP	1X	30mm	Black Matte	10 M.O.A. Dot	68'	Unlimited	33mm	4.75"	5.4 oz.	390.45
PDP45	1X	40mm	Black Matte	5 M.O.A. Dot	82'	Unlimited	45mm	4.8"	6.1 oz.	407.45
PDP45ST	1X	40mm	Stainless	5 M.O.A. Dot	82'	Unlimited	45mm	4.8"	6.1 oz.	407.45
PDP410	1X	40mm	Black Matte	10 M.O.A. Dot	82'	Unlimited	45mm	4.8"	6.1 oz.	407.45
PDP410ST	1X	40mm	Stainless	10 M.O.A. Dot	82'	Unlimited	45mm	4.8"	6.1 oz.	407.45
PDP415	1X	40mm	Black Matte	15 M.O.A. Dot	82'	Unlimited	45mm	4.8"	6.1 oz.	407.45
PDP415ST	1X	40mm	Stainless	15 M.O.A. Dot	82'	Unlimited	45mm	4.8"	6.1 oz.	407.45
PDP420	1X	40mm	Black Matte	20 M.O.A. Dot	82'	Unlimited	45mm	4.8"	6.1 oz.	407.45
PDP420ST	1X	40mm	Stainless	20 M.O.A. Dot	82'	Unlimited	45mm	4.8"	6.1 oz.	407.45
PDP420SG	1X	40mm	Black Matte	20 M.O.A. Dot	82'	Unlimited	45mm	4.8"	6.1 oz.	407.45
PDP5	1X	40mm	Black Matte	4, 8, 12 M.O.A.	82'	Unlimited	45mm	5.5"	9.1 oz.	339.55

TASCO RIFLESCOPES

WORLD CLASS PLUS RIFLESCOPES

WORLD CLASS TARGET SCOPE 36X50mm

SPECIFICATIONS WORLD CLASS PLUS RIFLESCOPES

Model	Power	Objective Diameter	Finish	Reticle	Field of View @ 100 Yds.	Eye Relief	Tube Diam.	Scope Length	Scope Weight	Prices
WCP4X44	4X	44mm	Black Gloss	30/30	32'	3¼"	1"	12.75"	13.5 oz.	$392.50
WCP6X44	6X	44mm	Black Gloss	30/30	21'	3¼"	1"	12.75"	13.6 oz.	407.45
WCP39X44	3X-9X	44mm	Black Gloss*	30/30	39'-14'	3½"	1"	12.75"	15.8 oz.	407.45
DWCP39X44	3X-9X	44mm	Black Matte	30/30	39'-14'	3½"	1"	12.75"	15.8 oz.	407.45
WCP39X44ST	3X-9X	44 mm	Stainless	30/30	39'-14'	3½"	1"	12.75"	15.8 oz.	407.45
WCP3.510X50	3.5X-10X	50mm	Black Gloss	30/30	30'-10.5'	3¾"	1"	13"	17.1 oz.	492.35
DWCP3.510X50	3.5X-10X	50mm	Black Matte	30/30	30'-10.5'	3¾"	1"	13"	17.1 oz.	492.35
WCP24X50	24X	50mm	Black Gloss	Crosshair*	4.8'	3½"	1"	13.25"	15.9 oz.	730.00
WCP36X50	36X	50mm	Black Gloss	Crosshair*	3'	3½"	1"	14"	15.9 oz.	760.90

* with ⅛-min. dot

RUBBER ARMORED SCOPES

Model	Power	Objective Diameter	Finish	Reticle	Field of View @ 100 Yards	Eye Relief	Tube Diam.	Scope Length	Scope Weight	Price
RC39X40	3-9X	40mm	Black Rubber	30/30	35'-12'	3¼"	1"	12.5"	14.3 oz.	$254.65

"A" fits standard dove tail base.   "B" fits ⅜" grooved receivers—most 22 cal. and airguns.

MAG IV™ RIFLESCOPES (not shown)

MAG IV scopes yield four times magnification range in a standard size riflescope and one-third more zooming range than most variable scopes. Features include: Fully coated optics and large objective lens to keep target in low light . . . Non-removable eye bell . . . ¼-minute positive click stops . . . Non-removable windage and elevation screws. . . Opticentered 30/30 rangefinding reticle . . . Waterproof, fogproof, shockproof.

SPECIFICATIONS

Model	Power	Objective Diameter	Finish	Reticle	Field of View @ 100 Yds.	Eye Relief	Tube Diam.	Scope Length	Scope Weight	Price
W312X40	3–12	40mm	Black	30/30	35'–9'	3⅛"	1"	12³/₁₆"	12 oz.	$152.80
W416X40†	4–16	40mm	Black	30/30	26'–6'	3⅛"	1"	14⅛"	15.6 oz.	203.75
W624X40†	6–24	40mm	Black	30/30	17'–4'	3"	1"	15⅜"	16.75 oz.	254.65

† Indicates focusing objective.   * Also available: **Model V416X40ST** in stainless. **$203.75**

TASCO RIFLESCOPES

BIG HORN RIFLESCOPES

BIG HORN® RIFLESCOPES
$611.15 (2.5-10X50mm)
$679.05 (4.5-18X50mm)

Tasco's new line of Big Horn® riflescopes features two high-quality models—the 2.5-10X50mm and a 4.5X-18X50mm—with the latter offering a big 18 power and wide-angle optics for fast sighting of running game. Designed with a one-piece body tube for strength and durability, the Big Horn scopes are equipped with 50mm objective lenses that offer greater light transmission for hunting at dawn and dusk when game is most active. Multi-coating on the objective lens and ocular lenses, plus fully coated optics throughout, provide the hunter with sharp detailed images. Big Horn scopes also feature parallax adjustment rings on the objective tube.

MAG-IV
4X-16X50mm

MAG-IV™ RIFLESCOPE LINE EXPANDS
$390.00–$475.00

Tasco's new MAG-IV™ riflescopes feature large 40mm objective lenses that transmit even more light than the MAG-IV with 40mm objectives or the MAG-IV-44 with 44mm objectives and are especially designed for dawn and dusk use. The additions to the MAG-IV line include three high-quality variable scopes: the 4X-16X50mm, the 5X-20X50mm and the 5X-20X50mm with bullet drop compensation. All three models have Super-Con® multi-layered lens coating and fully coated optics. These new MAG-IV scopes feature windage and elevation adjustments with ¼-minute clickstops and an Opti-Centered® 30/30 rangefinding reticle. This adjustment system allows the reticle to remain centered in the field of view (an "image moving" system as opposed to a "reticle moving" system). Finished in black matte.

TITAN™ RIFLESCOPES
$645.10 (3X-9X42mm)
$679.05 (1.5X-6X42mm)
$763.95 (3X-12X52mm)

1.5X-6X42mm

Tasco's new line of Titan™ riflescopes is equipped with unusually large 42mm and 52mm objective lenses that can transmit more light than standard 40mm lenses for dim early morning and dusk conditions. Three variable scopes—the 1.5X-6X42mm, the 3X-9X42mm and the 3X-12X52mm—are available with 30/30 reticles and feature lenses with five-layer multi-coating for greater image contrast and clarity. Titan scopes also have finger-adjustable windage and elevation controls along with fast focusing eyebells. Waterproof, shockproof and fogproof, these scopes feature all-weather lubrication of each moving part for smooth functioning in any climate condition. Finished in matte black.

TASCO SCOPES

HIGH COUNTRY RIFLESCOPES

3X-9X40mm
$195.25

6X-24X40mm
$280.15

4X-16X40mm
$254.65

3.5X-10X40mm
$220.70

SPECIFICATIONS HIGH COUNTRY RIFLESCOPES

Model	Power	Objective Diameter	Field of view @ 100 yds.	Reticle	Eye Relief	Tube Diam.	Finish	Length	Weight
HC416X40	4X-16X	40mm	26'-7'	30/30	3.25"	1"	Black gloss	14.25"	15.6 oz.
HC624X40	6X-24X	40mm	17'-4'	30/30	3"	1"	Black gloss	15.25"	16.8 oz.
HC39X40	3X-9X	40mm	41'-15'	30/30	3"	1"	Black gloss	12.75"	13 oz.
HC3.510X40	3.5X-10X	40mm	30'-10.5'	30/30	3"	1"	Black gloss	11.75"	14.25 oz.

TASCO LUMINA
MODEL 11-6x40wa-1

LUMINA™ RIFLESCOPES
$84.90–152.80

LASER POINT

Tasco's LaserPoint model is the first compact to have a multi-mode red dot (one second continuous followed by one second pulsating), making it the fastest and easiest dot to locate on the target. An index-guided diode designed with minimum astigmatism, maximum efficiency and battery life results in a much improved laser dot. Additional features include adjustable windage and elevation system, waterproofing and several optional mounts that require no gunsmithing.
Price: **$373.50**

Tasco's new line of Lumina riflescopes with Rubicon™ ruby coated objective lenses filter out red light for crisp daylight viewing and are especially suited for use over snow and in other bright conditions. The line offers a mix of five fixed power and variable scopes: 4X21mm, 6X40mm, 3X-12X40mm (all with 30/30 reticles) and a 3X-9X40mm model with a standard round reticle or TV reticle. All but the 3X-12X40mm, which offers a full four times magnification range and focusing objective for parallax correction, are wide angle. All models feature 1/4 minute click stops for windage and elevation adjustments and are completely waterproof, fogproof and shockproof.

WEAVER SCOPES

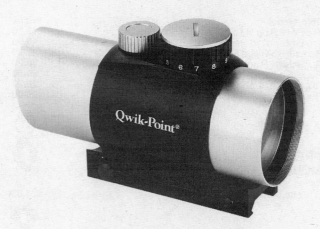

QWIK-POINT 45mm SCOPE

QUIK-POINT 30mm SCOPE

QWIK-POINT™ SCOPE 45MM

The 45mm Quick-Point red dot scope provides a large field of view for shotgun and pistol hunting. A straight-cut objective protects the lens from fragments and powder residue. The objective lock ring keeps lenses aligned and fixed in place. Offers quick MOA dot adjustment, shockproof and waterproof. An 11-setting light adjustment dot for selecting light intensity.

49962 Qwik-Point 45mm 4 MOA Silver **$296.25**
49963 Qwik-Point 45mm 12 MOA Silver **296.25**
49964 Qwik-Point 45mm Variable silver **383.10**
49968 Qwik-Point 45mm Variable Matte **383.10**
49966 Qwik-Point 45mm 12 MOA Matte **296.25**

QWIK-POINT SCOPE 30MM

The 30mm Qwik-Point red dot scope offers shooters the speed and accuracy of point-and-shoot target recognition. The red dot (powered by a low cost camera battery) can be adjusted to 11 different light intensities and is available in 4 or 12 minute-of- angle dot size. Click type windage and elevation adjustments make zeroing easy. The multi-coated optics provide sharp images and the nitrogen filled 30mm tube is fogproof, waterproof and shockproof. Scopes are one power magnification.

49960 Qwik-Point 30mm 4 MOA **$235.95**
49961 Qwik-Point 30mm 12 MOA **235.95**
Also available:
33mm Variable Qwik-Point Scope
Silver **$383.00**
Matte **$382.35**

RIMFIRE 4X MATTE SCOPE

RIMFIRE SCOPE 2.5-7X

Lenses are multi-coated for bright, clear low-light performance and the one-piece tube design is shockproof and waterproof.
49622 2.5-7x Rimfire Matte **$158.75**
49623 2.5-7x Rimfire Silver **158.75**

RIMFIRE SCOPE 4X

Fixed 4x scope is ideal for a variety of shooting applications. It's durable, light-weight and waterproof.
49620 4x Rimfire Matte **$136.00**
49621 4x Rimfire Silver **136.00**

WIDEVIEW SCOPE MOUNTS

PREMIUM SEE-THRU SCOPE MOUNTS

Rifle/Model	Prices
Browning A-Bolt NN	$22.00
Browning Semi-Auto AA	22.00
Browning Lever Action AA	22.00
Browning F.N. Bolt Action CB	22.00
BSA, Medium & Long Action DB	22.00
Glenfield 30 by Marlin GG	22.00
H & R Bolt Action F.N. 300, 301, 317, 330, 370 CB	22.00
Husquvarna F.N. Action CB	22.00
Interarms Mark X CB	22.00
Ithaca Bolt Action DB	22.00
Marlin 336, 62, 36, 444 GG	22.00
Marlin 1893, 1894, 1895, 9, 45 CG	22.00
Marlin 465 F.N. Action CB	22.00
Mauser F.N. 98, 2000, 3000 CB	22.00
Mossberg 800, 500 AA	22.00
Parker Hale 1000, 1000c, 1100, 1200, 1200C CB	22.00
Parker Hale 2100 CB	22.00
Remington 7 JB	22.00
Remington 700, 721, 722, 725 DB	22.00
Remington 740, 742, 600 EB	22.00
Remington 788 FH	22.00
Remington 4, 6, 7400, 7600 EB8	22.00
Remington XP-100 Pistol 600, 660 HB	22.00
Revelation 200 Lever Action GG	22.00
Ruger M-77 Round Receiver DB	22.00
Ruger 44 Rifle QO	22.00
Ruger 10/22 OP	22.00
Savage 99 KM	22.00
Savage 110, 111, 112 IB	22.00
Savage 170 EB	22.00
Smith & Wesson 1500 Bolt DB	22.00
Weatherby Mark V & Vanguard DB	22.00
Western Field 740 GG	22.00
Winchester 88, 100 BB	22.00
Winchester 70, 70A, 670, 770 and ser. #700 (except 375 H & H) FB	22.00
Winchester 94AE Angle Eject 94 AE	24.00
Winchester 94 Side Mount 94	26.00

SHOTGUNS (Must Be Drilled and Tapped)

Ithaca, Remington, Winchester, Mossberg, etc. Note: Remington 1100 and Browning 5 Auto not recommended by Wideview for top mounts. Receivers should be .150 thousands or more in thickness
BB $22.00

FOR WEAVER-STYLE BASES

Savage 24V U-20	$24.00
Straight Cut U-10	22.00
20 Degree Angle Cut U-20	24.00
Straight Cut 30 Millimeter U-1030	24.62
20 Degree Angle Cut 30 Millimeter U-2030	24.62

RING-STYLE MOUNTS

Dove Tail Solid Lock Ring Fits Any Redfield, Tasco or Weaver-Style Base SR	$16.00
Dove Tail Solid Lock 30 Millimeter SR30	18.65
True-Fit Lo Ring L-Ring	16.00

Rifle/Model	Prices
Tru-Fit Hi Ring H-Ring	$16.00
Tru-Fit Grooved Receiver GR-Ring	16.00
Ruger High Rings M77R, M77RS, M77V TU	26.20
Ruger High Rings No. 1-A, RSI., S, H, 3. 77/22 TU	26.20
Ruger Redhawk Hunter UU	26.20
Ruger Mini-14/5R, K-Mini Thirty TU	26.20
Ruger Redhawk, Hunter 30 Millimeter UU30	29.00

PREMIUM FLASHLIGHT MOUNT

Site Lite Mount SL	$26.00

22 RIMFIRE SEE-THRU MOUNT

For All 22-Caliber Rimfire Rifles With Grooved Receiver. Designed for ¼ and 1″ Diameter Scopes. Also Used On Air Rifles 22R .. **$18.00**

BLACK POWDER MOUNTS (See Thru)
Barrels Must Be Drilled and Tapped

CVA Frontier Carbine, Plainsman, Pennsylvania Long Rifle CVA Hawken, GG	$22.00 ea.
CVA Hawken, Hunter Hawken, Mountain Rifle, Blazer GG	22.00 ea.
CVA Squirrel Rifle, Kentucky, Kentucky Hunter & Kit Rifles GG	22.00 ea.
Thompson Center, Renegade, Hawken, White Mountain, New Englander GG	22.00 ea.
Traditions Frontier Carbine, Pioneer Rifle GG	22.00 ea.
Traditions Pennsylvania Rifle, Hawken Woodsman, Frontier Rifle GG	22.00 ea.
Traditions Trapper, Frontier Scout Kits for Hawken GG	22.00 ea.
Woodsman, Frontier Rifle, Frontier Carbine GG	22.00 ea.

BLACK POWDER SEE-THRU MOUNTS
NO DRILLING OR TAPPING

Thompson Center Hawken (Ultra Precision See-Thru Mount Included) TEC	$44.00
Thompson Center Renegade (Ultra Precision See-Thru Mounts Included) TCR	44.00
CVA Stalker Rifle/Carbine ii	22.00 ea.
CVA Apollo 90 Rifle/Carbine ii	22.00 ea.
CVA Apollo Sporter ii	22.00 ea.
CVA Shadow Rifle ii	22.00 ea.
CVA Tracker Carbine ii	22.00 ea.
CVA Hawken Deerslayer Rifle/Carbine ii	22.00 ea.
CVA Trophy Carbine ii	22.00 ea.
CVA Frontier Hunter Carbine ii	22.00 ea.
Knight MK-85, BK-90 ii	22.00 ea.

SHOTGUN MOUNTS (No Drilling or Tapping)

Mossberg 500 500	$34.95
Remington 870 870	34.95
Remington 1100 1100	34.95

WILLIAMS SIGHTS

MODEL WSKS APERTURE SIGHT

MODEL WSKS RIFLE SIGHT
$21.95 (Open Sight)
$23.95 (Aperture Sight)

The WSKS replaces the military rear sight on SKS 7.62X39 rifles. No drilling and tapping required. Fully adjustable for elevation and windage. Open sight comes with 1/4" U blade. Aperture sight includes a special target hole aperture (R 3/8X.150 for enhanced field of view).

FP RECEIVER SIGHTS SERIES
$58.75 $69.95 with Target Knobs

Internal micrometer adjustments have positive internal locks. Alloy used has a tensile strength of 85,000 pounds, yet sights weigh only 1.5 ounces each. Target knobs are available. Options include standard, blade, shotgun/big game aperture. Model shown mounted on a Knight MK-85 (Modern Muzzle-loading).

MODEL FP RECEIVER SIGHT

MODEL WGRS-KN RECEIVER SIGHT

WGRS RECEIVER SIGHTS SERIES
$30.95

These sights (22 in all) offer a compact low profile and in most cases utilize dovetail or existing screws on top of receiver for installation. Made from aluminum alloy (stronger than most steel). Positive windage and elevation locks. Rustproof. Can be converted to open sights by installing a 1/4" WGOS blade (in place of aperture holder).

WGOS OPEN SIGHT BASES (Not Shown)
$15.95

Made from high tensile-strength, rustproof aluminum. Streamlined and lightweight with tough anodized finish. Dovetailed windage and elevation. Interchangeable blades available in four heights and styles. All parts milled.

"SLUGGER" SIGHTS (Not Shown)
$34.95

Williams' own concept in front and rear combinations for ribbed shotgun barrels. Made from tough aircraft aluminum. Fully adjustable rear sight for windage and elevation. No drilling and tapping—installs in minutes without harming gun. 1/4" sight fits most Browning Auto-5's. 5/16" fits most Remington 870, 1100 and 11/87s, Browning BPS, and more. 3/8" fits most Winchester 1200, 1300 and 1400 models.

ZEISS RIFLESCOPES

THE "Z" SERIES

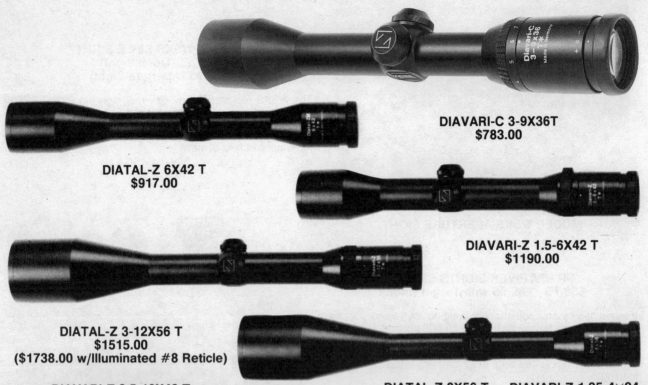

DIAVARI-C 3-9X36T
$783.00

DIATAL-Z 6X42 T
$917.00

DIAVARI-Z 1.5-6X42 T
$1190.00

DIATAL-Z 3-12X56 T
$1515.00
($1738.00 w/Illuminated #8 Reticle)

DIAVARI-Z 2.5-10X48 T
(not shown)
$1407.00

DIATAL-Z 8X56 T
$1092.00

DIAVARI-Z 1.25-4×24
(not shown)
$1041.00

ZM/Z SERIES RIFLESCOPE SPECIFICATIONS

Model	Diatal-ZM/Z 6X42 T	Diavari-ZM/Z 1.5-6X42 T	Diavari-ZM/Z 3-12X56 T	Diatal-ZM/Z 8X56 T	Diavari-ZM/Z 2.5-10X48 T	Diavera-ZM/Z 1.25-4X24	Diavari-C 3-9X36
Magnification	6X	1.5X 6X	3X 12X	8X	2.5X-10X	1.25-4X	3X 9X
Effective obj. diam.	42mm/1.7″	19.5/0.8″ 42/1.7″	38/1.5″ 56/2.2″	56mm/2.2″	33/1.30″ 48/1.89″	NA	30.0/1.2″ 36.0/1.4″
Diameter of exit pupil	7mm	13mm 7mm	12.7mm 4.7mm	7mm	13.2mm 4.8mm	12.6mm 6.3mm	10.0 4.0mm
Twilight factor	15.9	4.2 15.9	8.5 25.9	21.2	7.1 21.9	3.54 9.6	8.5 18.0
Field of view at 100 m/ ft. at 100 yds.	6.7m/20.1′	18/54.0′ 6.5/19.5′	9.2/27.6′ 3.3/9.9′	5m/15.0′	11.0/33.0 3.9/11.7	32 10	12.0/36.0 4.3/12.9
Approx. eye relief	8cm/3.2″	8cm/3.2″	8cm/3.2″	8cm/3.2″	8cm/3.2″	8cm/3.2″	3.5″
Click-stop adjustment 1 click = (cm at 100 m)/ (inch at 100 yds.)	1cm/0.36″	1cm/0.36″	1cm/0.36″	1cm/0.36″	1cm/0.36″	1cm/0.36″	107/0.25″
Max. adj. (elev./wind.) at 100 m (cm)/at 100 yds.	187	190	95	138	110/39.6	300	135/49
Center tube dia.	25.4mm/1″	30mm/1.18″	30mm/1.18″	25.4mm/1″	30mm/1.18″	30mm/1.18″	25.4/1.0″
Objective bell dia.	48mm/1.9″	48mm/1.9″	62mm/2.44″	62mm/2.44″	54mm/2.13″	NA	44.0/1.7
Ocular bell dia.	40mm/1.57″	40mm/1.57″	40mm/1.57″	40mm/1.57″	40mm/1.57″	NA	42.5/1.8
Length	324mm/12.8″	320mm/12.6″	388mm/15.3″	369mm/14.5″	370mm/14.57″	290mm/11.46″	
Approx. weight: ZM	350g/15.3 oz.	586g/20.7 oz.	765g/27.0 oz.	550g/19.4 oz.	715g/25.2 oz.	490g/17.3 oz.	NA
Z	400g/14.1 oz.	562g/19.8	731g/25.8 oz.	520g/18.3 oz.	680g/24 oz.	NA	430g/15.2 oz.

Ammunition

For addresses and phone/fax numbers of manufacturers and distributors included in this section, please turn to DIRECTORY OF MANUFACTURERS AND SUPPLIERS on page 554.

FEDERAL AMMUNITION

Federal's new pistol and rifle cartridges for 1996–97 are featured below. For a complete listing of Federal ammunition, call or write the Federal Cartridge Company (*see* Directory of Manufacturers and Suppliers in the Reference section for address and phone number). *See* also Federal ballistics tables.

NEW BALLISTICLEAN™ PISTOL CARTRIDGES

At public indoor shooting ranges, lead-free, non-toxic ammunition is preferred for the health of both shooters and range staff. On law-enforcement ranges, it's the standard. Federal introduces its BallistiClean™ brand, the first commercially available ammunition that is totally lead-free and non-toxic. BallistiClean loads feature a Toxic-Metal Free™ primer and a zinc core bullet with a copper alloy jacket, forming a totally non-toxic cartridge with no hazard of airborne lead, barrel fouling or hazardous waste disposal problems. This match-grade training round meets the tough environmental standards of the EPA and OSHA. The BallistiClean™ offering currently includes 380 Auto, 9mm Luger, 38 Special, 40 S&W and 45 Auto.

BallistiClean™ features:

- **Non-toxic zinc bullet.** Eliminates hazard of airborne lead or other toxic by-products. No hazardous waste disposal problems.
- **Soft-point bullet.** Retains less than 50% of original weight when fired against steel targets. Minimizes bullet fragment bounce-back and ricochet. Reduces wear and damage to indoor ranges.
- **Copper alloy jacket.** Reduces barrel fouling. Same barrel cleaning as conventional jacketed bullets.
- **Toxic-Metal Free™ primer.** Eliminates hazard of airborne lead created by conventional primers. Equivalent sensitivity to service primers. Clean burning with little or no residue. Moisture resistant.
- **High-performance ballistics.** Reliable, robust function and precision match-grade accuracy.

NEW PREMIUM® HIGH ENERGY RIFLE CARTRIDGES

With velocities up to 200 feet per second faster, Premium High Energy Rifle loads provide higher energy, flatter trajectory, less wind drift and tighter groupings. They can produce the same effective velocity of a larger caliber rifle simply by chambering one of these new loads. A round of 308 Premium High Energy Rifle has the knockdown power of a 30-06. Use High Energy Rifle in a 30-06 Springfield and it's similar to shooting with the power of a 300 Magnum. Premium High Energy Rifle loads are available in **calibers** 308 Win., 30-06 Springfield, 300 Win. Mag. and 338 Win. Mag., in two bullet types:

- **Premium Trophy Bonded Bear Claw®**—The only factory load featuring a 100% fusion-bonded core and jacket that ensures maximum weight retention and penetration.
- **Premium Nosler® Partition®**—A versatile bullet that withstands the impact of high velocity at close range and expands reliably at extreme ranges. Its H-shape design features a front core that expands rapidly and a rear core that retains over half the bullet weight for deep penetrating power.

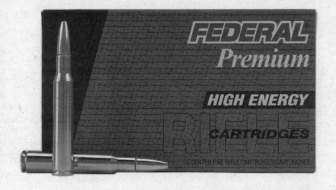

FIOCCHI USA AMMUNITION

GOLDEN PHEASANT HUNTING LOAD

Fiocchi USA's ''GOLDEN PHEASANT®'' hunting load features a 1³/₈ load of nickel-coated lead hauling at 1250 feet per second for reliable patterns. Ignited by the 616 Charger Primer™ with Fiocchi's exclusive multi-seal wad and hull, it provides the best hunting load for harvesting the powerful ring neck. Comes in sizes 4, 5, and 6.

INTERCEPTOR SPORTING CLAYS LOAD

Breaking the sound barrier at over 900 miles per hour, the new one-ounce spreader load—The Interceptor—is designed for low recoil, quick and accurate performance with consistent quality at sporting clays targets. Includes a custom powder blend for top speed of 1300 feet per second with low recoil, a 616 Charger Primer for positive ignition and a multi-seal powder spreader wad. In addition, there's one ounce of low antimony shot for maximum patterns at close ranges. Available in shot sizes 9, 8¹/₂, 8 and 7¹/₂. Designed for use at close ranges with open chokes from cylinder or skeet up to modified.

**GOLDEN PHEASANT
HUNTING LOAD**

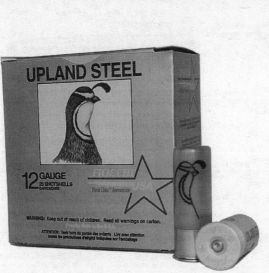

NEW ''UPLAND STEEL'' ALTERNATIVE

As more federal lands require the use of steel for all upland game, the need for new upland loads of steel has grown. Fiocchi's new Upland Steel® hits the air at 1400 feet per second, giving the upland hunter an alternative to heavier steel waterfowl loads. Using the 616 Charger Primers for positive and strong ignition, the combination of Fiocchi's Steel wad, blended powders and custom hull deliver quality and performance in a non-toxic load. Available in steel sizes 4, 6 and 7.

HORNADY AMMUNITION

PISTOL CARTRIDGES

25 AUTO
*35 gr. JHP/XTP........#9001
**35 gr. JHP/XTP.......#9001c

32 AUTO
**71 gr. FMJ-RN........#9007c

380 AUTO
*90 gr. JHP/XTP........#9010

9 x 18 MAKAROV
95 gr. JHP/XTP......#9100c

9MM LUGER
*90 gr. JHP/XTP........#9020
*115 gr. JHP/XTP........#9025
*124 gr. JHP/XTP........#9024
*124 gr. FMJ-RN........#9029
*147 gr. JHP/XTP........#9028

38 SPECIAL
*125 gr. JHP/XTP........#9032
*140 gr. JHP/XTP........#9035
L *148 gr. HBWC (Match)...#9043
*158 gr. JHP/XTP........#9036

357 SIG - NEW!
124 gr. XTP......#9103
147 gr. XTP......#9131

357 MAG.
*125 gr. JHP/XTP........#9050
*125 gr. JFP..........#9053
*140 gr. JHP/XTP........#9055
*158 gr. JHP/XTP........#9056
*158 gr. JFP..........#9058

10MM AUTO
155 gr. JHP/XTP.........#9122
180 gr. JHP/XTP-Full load...#9126
200 gr. JHP/XTP..........#9129

40 S & W
155 gr. JHP/XTP........#9132
180 gr. JHP/XTP........#9136

44 SPECIAL
180 gr. JHP/XTP........#9070

44 REM. MAG.
180 gr. JHP/XTP......#9081
200 gr. JHP/XTP......#9080
240 gr. JHP/XTP......#9085
300 gr. JHP/XTP......#9088

45 ACP
185 gr. JHP/XTP.......#9090
200 gr. JHP/XTP.......#9112
200 gr. + P JHP/XTP.....#9113
230 gr. FMJ-RN......#9097
230 gr. + P JHP/XTP.....#9096
230 gr. FMJ-FP......#9098

**Packed 25 per box.
*Packed 50 per box.

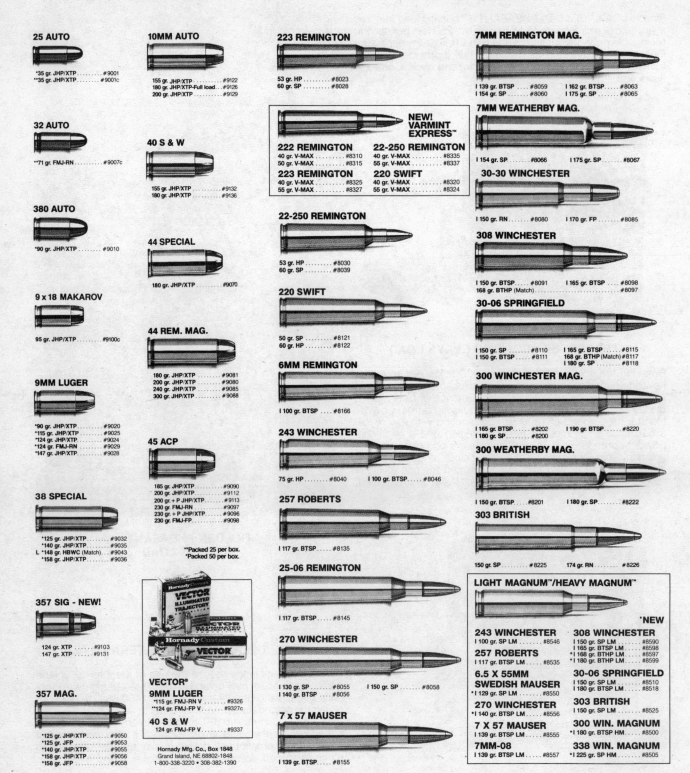

VECTOR®
9MM LUGER
*115 gr. FMJ-RN V.......#9326
**124 gr. FMJ-FP V.....#9327c
40 S & W
124 gr. FMJ-FP V......#9337

Hornady Mfg. Co., Box 1848
Grand Island, NE 68802-1848
1-800-338-3220 • 308-382-1390

RIFLE CARTRIDGES

223 REMINGTON
53 gr. HP.........#8023
60 gr. SP.........#8028

NEW! VARMINT EXPRESS™

222 REMINGTON	22-250 REMINGTON
40 gr. V-MAX......#8310	40 gr. V-MAX......#8335
50 gr. V-MAX......#8315	55 gr. V-MAX......#8337
223 REMINGTON	**220 SWIFT**
40 gr. V-MAX......#8325	40 gr. V-MAX......#8320
55 gr. V-MAX......#8327	55 gr. V-MAX......#8324

22-250 REMINGTON
53 gr. HP.........#8030
60 gr. SP.........#8039

220 SWIFT
50 gr. SP.......#8121
60 gr. HP.......#8122

6MM REMINGTON
I 100 gr. BTSP......#8166

243 WINCHESTER
75 gr. HP.......#8040   I 100 gr. BTSP.....#8046

257 ROBERTS
I 117 gr. BTSP.....#8135

25-06 REMINGTON
I 117 gr. BTSP.....#8145

270 WINCHESTER
I 130 gr. SP......#8055   I 150 gr. SP......#8058
I 140 gr. BTSP......#8056

7 x 57 MAUSER
I 139 gr. BTSP.....#8155

7MM REMINGTON MAG.
I 139 gr. BTSP......#8059   I 162 gr. BTSP.....#8063
I 154 gr. BTSP......#8060   I 175 gr. SP......#8065

7MM WEATHERBY MAG.
I 154 gr. SP......#8066   I 175 gr. SP......#8067

30-30 WINCHESTER
I 150 gr. RN......#8080   I 170 gr. FP......#8085

308 WINCHESTER
I 150 gr. BTSP.....#8091   I 165 gr. BTSP......#8098
168 gr. BTHP (Match)...................#8097

30-06 SPRINGFIELD
I 150 gr. SP......#8110   I 165 gr. BTSP......#8115
I 150 gr. BTSP......#8111   168 gr. BTHP (Match) #8117
                               I 180 gr. SP......#8118

300 WINCHESTER MAG.
I 165 gr. BTSP......#8202   I 190 gr. BTSP......#8220
I 180 gr. SP......#8200

300 WEATHERBY MAG.
I 150 gr. BTSP.....#8201   I 180 gr. SP......#8222

303 BRITISH
150 gr. SP......#8225   174 gr. RN......#8226

LIGHT MAGNUM™/HEAVY MAGNUM™

*NEW

243 WINCHESTER	308 WINCHESTER
I 100 gr. SP LM......#8546	I 150 gr. SP LM......#8590
257 ROBERTS	I 165 gr. BTSP LM......#8598
I 117 gr. BTSP LM......#8535	*I 168 gr. BTHP LM......#8597
6.5 X 55MM	*I 180 gr. BTHP LM......#8599
SWEDISH MAUSER	**30-06 SPRINGFIELD**
*I 129 gr. SP LM......#8550	I 150 gr. SP LM......#8510
270 WINCHESTER	I 180 gr. BTSP LM......#8518
*I 140 gr. SP LM......#8556	**303 BRITISH**
7 X 57 MAUSER	I 150 gr. SP LM......#8525
I 139 gr. BTSP LM......#8555	**300 WIN. MAGNUM**
7MM-08	*I 180 gr. BTSP HM......#8500
I 139 gr. BTSP LM......#8557	**338 WIN. MAGNUM**
	*I 225 gr. SP HM......#8505

REMINGTON AMMUNITION

Remington's new or recent lines of cartridges and shotshells for 1996-97 are featured below. For a complete listing of their ammunition products, call or write Remington whose address/ phone no. is listed in the Directory of Manufacturers and Suppliers in the reference section. *See also* Ballistics Section.

.45 AUTO 185-GR. (+P) LOADING FOR GOLDEN SABER

Remington has expanded its Golden Saber Pistol & Revolver offerings with a .45 Auto, 185-grain (+P) loading. Muzzle velocity is 1140 fps. This combines the increased energy of (+P) velocity with the improved accuracy and exceptional bullet performance of the Golden Saber design, which features extraction, primers pre-inspected five times, and primer and case mouth waterproofing against the effects of weather and long-term storage.

FOUR NEW LOADINGS OF LeadLess™ HANDGUN AMMUNITION

Remington's four new loadings to its line of LeadLess™ pistol and revolver ammunition include 9mm Auto (124-grain), .357 Magnum (158-grain), .38 Special (158-grain) and .380 Auto (95-grain), all utilizing Remington's Lead-Lokt® bullets. Developed specifically for indoor range shooting, this LeadLess ammunition substantially reduces the amount of lead-based residue that can be transferred to the atmosphere. Yet it provides the same performance in terms of trajectories and point of impact as comparable standard ammunition. The two key components are the new lead-free primer mix, and Remington's new Lead-Lokt® bullet that prevents lead vaporization during firing.

NEW HEAVY-DUTY PISTOL AND REVOLVER LOADINGS

Remington's two new pistol and revolver loadings include the .357 SIG and a .45 Auto. The .357 SIG provides performance comparable to the .357 Magnum, but in a semiauto pistol configuration with the benefits of increase cartridge capacity, lower felt recoil and improved gun control. Loaded to a muzzle velocity of 1450 fps with Remington's 125-grain jacketed hollowpoint (JHP) bullet, it delivers uniform expansion and controlled penetration at high velocities. The .45 Auto utilizes Remington's heavyweight 230-grain JHP for maximum penetration, expansion and energy transfer. Nine different specifications are now available for this veteran high-performance caliber.

PREMIER® STS TARGET LOADS

Remington's new 12-gauge Premier® STS Target Load line incorporates the improvements made by last year's Nitro 27 Handicap Trap loads. Specific benefits to reloaders include smoother wad insertion and more responsive crimping with less tool pressure. The case mouths also have a higher crimp memory, which helps to form perfect crimps time after time. Premier STS 12-gauge target loads are available in trap, skeet and sporting clays specifications. Except for the 1-oz. spec, all loads contain 1¹/₈ oz. of high antimony, target-grade shot.

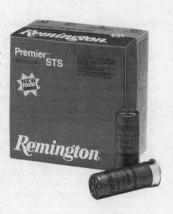

NEW SAFARI GRADE CALIBERS

Two highly regarded big-game calibers have been added to Remington's Safari Grade ammunition line—the flat-shooting .300 Wby. Mag. and the powerful .458 Win. Mag.—both utilizing world-famous Swift A-Frame™, dual-core bullets. The higher ballistic coefficients of these bullets, in weights not previously available in either caliber, retain higher down-range velocities and greater remaining energy at all distances. The 200-grain Swift A-Frame bullet in the .300 Wby. Mag. is loaded to a muzzle velocity of 2925 fps with downrange energy exceeding 2,050 ft.-lbs. at 350 yards. The 450-grain loading for the .458 Win. Mag. is the first time an expanding bullet with the tough, core-retention capabilities of a Swift A-Frame has been commercially available in this caliber. Muzzle velocity is 2150 fps, with an impressive 3609 ft.-lbs. of energy at 100 yards.

CORE-LOKT® BULLETS ADDED TO SIX RIFLE CALIBERS

Remington has expanded the number of Core-Lokt® loadings in its centerfire line with a 28-caliber 140-grain pointed softpoint bullet for the 7mm Mauser, 7×64mm, 7mm-08 Rem., .280 Rem. and 7mm Rem. Mag. Also, it has added both 225- and 250-grain Core-Lokt® bullets to standard .338 Win. Mag. loadings. Many experts agree that the 140-grain bullet weight is the most ballistically efficient choice in 28-caliber cartridges for medium-sized game. Use of a 140-grain Core-Lokt® bullet now brings to these rounds an ideal combination of high velocity and flat trajectory with reliable performance.

WINCHESTER AMMUNITION

NEW DOUBLE X MAGNUM TURKEY LOADS

The Double X Magnum Turkey Load line has been expanded with new introductions in 10 and 12 gauge 3½" Magnum. The new 10 ga. loads feature 2¼ oz. of either #4 or #5 shot (adding to the already available #6) with a 4½ dram equivalent of powder and a muzzle velocity of 1210 fps. Symbol numbers for the #4 and #5 shot are X103XCT4 and X103XCT5, respectively. Winchester is also adding #5 shot to the 12 ga. 3½" round, which now features 2¼ oz. of #5 shot along with the existing #6 and #4. Muzzle velocity is 1150 fps with a magnum dram equivalent of powder. Symbol number is XXT12L5.

NEW OFFERINGS IN SILVERTIP® HOLLOWPOINT COMPONENT HANDGUN BULLETS

Three bullets have been added to the Silvertip Hollowpoint Component Handgun bullet line: an 85-gr. 380 caliber; a 125-gr. 38 Special; and a 185-gr. 45 caliber. Shooters have long enjoyed the performance of the Silvertip Hollowpoint bullet in factory loads; reloaders now have a full line of component bullets to choose from. These bullets feature an aluminum or nickel-plated jacket that enables them to feed smoothly in semiautomatic handguns while still expanding in the target.

NEW BULLET JOINS SUPREME® FAIL SAFE® LINE

A 270-grain component bullet in 375 caliber has been added to the Supreme® FailSafe® bullet line. It features a solid copper hollowpoint front section that expands quickly upon impact and is driven by a heavy lead rear core locked in place by a steel insert. The result is a bullet that expands quickly and penetrates deeply with virtually 100% weight retention. FailSafe® bullets are coated with a Lubalox® coating that adds lubricity to the bullet, reducing pressure and fouling. Symbol number for the 270 gr. is FS375.

Winchester's new or recent lines of cartridges and shotshells for 1996-97 are featured below. For a complete listing of their ammunition products, call or write Winchester whose address/phone no. is listed in the Directory of Manufacturers and Suppliers in the reference section. *See also* Ballistics Section.

SUPER X® SUPER UNLEADED™ PISTOL AMMUNITION LINE EXPANDS

Three new loads have been added to the Super X Super Unleaded Handgun Ammunition line. Among them is a 158-gr. bullet in a 38 Special+P load in Super Unleaded ammunition with a muzzle velocity of 890 fps, matching recoil impulse and bullet impact of other 158 gr. 38 Special Winchester loads: symbol number X38SSU1. In 40 S&W caliber, a 165-gr. load has been added, with a muzzle velocity of 1110 fps to match the velocity of Winchester's Supreme SXT load: symbol number X40SWSU1. A heavier 147-gr. bullet is new to the Super Unleaded 9mm pistol caliber, boasting a muzzle velocity of 990 fps: symbol number Z9MMSU2.

TWO NEW LOADS FOR SUPREME® SXT® HANDGUN AMMO

Owners of 38 Special caliber revolvers now have access to the most consistent performing pistol bullet: a 130-gr. SXT bullet in the 38 Special Supreme handgun ammo line. The new 38 Special+P load drives the 130-gr. bullet at a muzzle velocity of 925 fps and delivers muzzle energy of 247 ft.-lbs. in the proven SXT design: symbol number S38SP. Also new is the 165-gr. bullet weight for the 40 S&W caliber with muzzle velocity of 1110 fps and an impressive muzzle energy of 443 ft.-lbs. It provides handgun enthusiasts a choice of either a 165-gr. SXT or 180-gr. SXT bullet weight in the 40 S&W. Both loads use the patented reverse tapered jacket design and notched hollowpoint nose cavity for uniform expansion/penetration: symbol no.: S40a.

Ballistics

FEDERAL BALLISTICS

PREMIUM® HIGH ENERGY RIFLE

Usage Key: [1] = Varmints, predators, small game

USAGE	FEDERAL LOAD NO.	CALIBER	BULLET WGT. IN GRAINS	GRAMS	BULLET STYLE	FACTORY PRIMER NO.	VELOCITY IN FEET PER SECOND (TO NEAREST 10 FPS) MUZZLE	100 YDS.	200 YDS.	300 YDS.	400 YDS.	500 YDS.	ENERGY IN FOOT-POUNDS (TO NEAREST 5 FOOT-POUNDS) MUZZLE	100 YDS.	200 YDS.	300 YDS.	400 YDS.	500 YDS.
[1] NEW	P308T2	308 Win. (7.62x51mm)	165	10.69	Trophy Bonded Bear Claw	210	2870	2600	2350	2120	1890	1690	3020	2485	2030	1640	1310	1040
[1] NEW	P308G	308 Win. (7.62x51mm)	180	11.66	Nosler Partition	210	2740	2550	2370	2200	2030	1870	3000	2600	2245	1925	1645	1395
[1] NEW	P3006T3	30-06 Spring (7.62x63mm)	180	11.66	Trophy Bonded Bear Claw	210	2880	2630	2380	2160	1940	1740	3315	2755	2270	1855	1505	1210
[1] NEW	P3006R	30-06 Spring (7.62x63mm)	180	11.66	Nosler Partition	210	2880	2690	2500	2320	2150	1980	3315	2880	2495	2150	1845	1570
[1] NEW	P300WT3	300 Win. Mag.	180	11.66	Trophy Bonded Bear Claw	215	3100	2830	2580	2340	2110	1900	3840	3205	2660	2190	1790	1445
[1] NEW	P300WE	300 Win. Mag.	200	12.96	Nosler Partition	215	2930	2740	2550	2370	2200	2030	3810	3325	2885	2495	2145	1840
[1] NEW	P338T2	338 Win. Mag.	225	14.58	Trophy Bonded Bear Claw	215	2940	2690	2450	2230	2010	1810	4320	3610	3000	2475	2025	1640
[1] NEW	P338D	338 Win. Mag	250	16.20	Nosler Partition	215	2800	2610	2420	2250	2080	1920	4350	3775	3260	2805	2395	2035

PREMIUM® HUNTING RIFLE

Usage Key: [1] = Varmints, predators, small game

USAGE	FEDERAL LOAD NO.	CALIBER	BULLET WGT. IN GRAINS	GRAMS	BULLET STYLE*	FACTORY PRIMER NO.	VELOCITY IN FEET PER SECOND (TO NEAREST 10 FPS) MUZZLE	100 YDS.	200 YDS.	300 YDS.	400 YDS.	500 YDS.	ENERGY IN FOOT-POUNDS (TO NEAREST 5 FOOT-POUNDS) MUZZLE	100 YDS.	200 YDS.	300 YDS.	400 YDS.	500 YDS.
[1]	P223E	223 Rem. (5.56x45mm)	55	3.56	Sierra GameKing BTHP	205	3240	2770	2340	1950	1610	1330	1280	935	670	465	315	215
[1]	P22250B	22-250 Rem.	55	3.56	Sierra GameKing BTHP	210	3680	3280	2920	2590	2280	1990	1655	1315	1040	815	630	480
[2]	P243C	243 Win. (6.16x51mm)	100	6.48	Sierra GameKing BTSP	210	2960	2760	2570	2380	2210	2040	1950	1690	1460	1260	1080	925
[1]	P243D	243 Win. (6.16x51mm)	85	5.50	Sierra GameKing BTHP	210	3320	3070	2830	2600	2380	2180	2080	1770	1510	1280	1070	890
[1]	P243F	243 Win. (6.16x51mm)	70	4.54	Nosler Ballistic Tip	210	3400	3070	2760	2470	2200	1950	1795	1465	1185	950	755	590
[2]	P6C	6mm Rem.	100	6.48	Nosler Partition	210	3100	2860	2640	2420	2220	2020	2135	1820	1545	1300	1090	910
[2]	P257B	257 Roberts (High-Velocity + P)	120	7.77	Nosler Partition	210	2780	2560	2360	2160	1970	1790	2060	1750	1480	1240	1030	855
[2] NEW	P257WBA	257 Weatherby Magnum	115	7.45	Nosler Partition	210	3150	2900	2660	2440	2220	2020	2535	2145	1810	1515	1260	1040
[2] NEW	P257WBT1	257 Weatherby Magnum	115	7.45	Trophy Bonded Bear Claw	210	3150	2890	2640	2400	2180	1970	2535	2125	1775	1470	1210	990
[2]	P2506C	25-06 Rem.	117	7.58	Sierra GameKing BTSP	210	2990	2770	2570	2370	2190	2000	2320	2000	1715	1465	1240	1045
[2]	P2506D	25-06 Rem.	100	6.48	Nosler Ballistic Tip	210	3210	2960	2720	2490	2280	2070	2290	1940	1640	1380	1150	955
[2] NEW	P2506E	25-06 Rem.	115	7.45	Nosler Partition	210	2990	2750	2520	2300	2100	1900	2285	1930	1620	1350	1120	915
[2] NEW	P2506T1	25-06 Rem.	115	7.45	Trophy Bonded Bear Claw	210	2990	2740	2500	2270	2050	1850	2285	1910	1590	1310	1075	870
[2]	P270C	270 Win.	150	9.72	Sierra GameKing BTSP	210	2850	2660	2480	2300	2130	1970	2705	2355	2040	1760	1510	1290
[2]	P270D	270 Win.	130	8.42	Sierra GameKing BTSP	210	3060	2830	2620	2410	2220	2030	2700	2320	1980	1680	1420	1190
[2]	P270E	270 Win.	150	9.72	Nosler Partition	210	2850	2590	2340	2100	1880	1670	2705	2225	1815	1470	1175	930
[2]	P270F	270 Win.	130	8.42	Nosler Ballistic Tip	210	3060	2840	2630	2430	2230	2050	2700	2325	1990	1700	1440	1210
[2]	P270T1	270 Win.	140	9.07	Trophy Bonded Bear Claw	210	2940	2700	2480	2260	2060	1860	2685	2270	1905	1590	1315	1080
[2] NEW	P270T2	270 Win.	130	8.42	Trophy Bonded Bear Claw	210	3060	2810	2570	2340	2130	1930	2705	2275	1905	1585	1310	1070
[2]	P270WBA	270 Weatherby Magnum	130	8.42	Nosler Partition	210	3200	2960	2740	2520	2320	2120	2955	2530	2160	1835	1550	1300
[2]	P270WBT1	270 Weatherby Magnum	140	9.07	Trophy Bonded Bear Claw	210	3100	2840	2600	2370	2150	1950	2990	2510	2100	1745	1440	1175
[2]	P730A	7-30 Waters	120	7.77	Sierra GameKing BTSP	210	2700	2300	1930	1600	1330	1140	1940	1405	990	685	470	345
[2]	P7C	7mm Mauser (7x57mm Mauser)	140	9.07	Nosler Partition	210	2660	2450	2260	2070	1890	1730	2200	1865	1585	1330	1110	930
[2]	P764A	7x64 Brenneke	160	10.37	Nosler Partition	210	2650	2480	2310	2150	2000	1850	2495	2180	1895	1640	1415	1215
[2]	P280A	280 Rem.	150	9.72	Nosler Partition	210	2890	2620	2370	2140	1910	1710	2780	2295	1875	1520	1215	970
[2]	P280T1	280 Rem.	140	9.07	Trophy Bonded Bear Claw	210	2990	2630	2310	2040	1730	1480	2770	2155	1655	1250	925	680
[2]	P708A	7mm-08	140	9.07	Nosler Partition	210	2800	2590	2390	2200	2020	1840	2435	2085	1775	1500	1265	1060
[2] NEW	P708B	7mm-08	140	9.07	Nosler Ballistic Tip	215	2800	2610	2430	2260	2100	1940	2440	2135	1840	1590	1360	1165
[2]	P7RD	7mm Rem. Magnum	150	9.72	Sierra GameKing BTSP	215	3110	2920	2750	2580	2410	2250	3220	2850	2510	2210	1930	1690
[3]	P7RE	7mm Rem. Magnum	165	10.69	Sierra GameKing BTSP	215	2950	2800	2650	2510	2370	2230	3190	2865	2570	2300	2050	1825
[3]	P7RF	7mm Rem. Magnum	160	10.37	Nosler Partition	215	2950	2770	2590	2420	2250	2090	3090	2715	2375	2075	1800	1555
[2]	P7RG	7mm Rem. Magnum	140	9.07	Nosler Partition	215	3150	2930	2710	2510	2320	2130	3085	2660	2290	1960	1670	1415
[2] NEW	P7RH	7mm Rem. Magnum	150	9.72	Nosler Ballistic Tip	215	3110	2910	2720	2540	2370	2200	3220	2825	2470	2150	1865	1610
[3]	P7RT1	7mm Rem. Magnum	175	11.34	Trophy Bonded Bear Claw	215	2860	2660	2470	2290	2120	1950	3180	2750	2375	2040	1740	1475
[3]	P7RT2	7mm Rem. Magnum	160	10.37	Trophy Bonded Bear Claw	215	2940	2630	2350	2080	1830	1600	3070	2460	1950	1530	1185	905
[3]	P7WBA	7mm Weatherby Magnum	160	10.37	Nosler Partition	215	3050	2850	2650	2470	2290	2120	3305	2880	2505	2165	1865	1600
[3]	P7WBT1	7mm Weatherby Magnum	160	10.37	Trophy Bonded Bear Claw	215	3050	2730	2420	2140	1880	1640	3305	2640	2085	1630	1255	955
[2]	P3030D	30-30 Win.	170	11.01		210	2200	1900	1620	1380	1190	1060	1830	1355	990	720	535	425
[2]	P308C	308 Win. (7.62x51mm)	165	10.69	Sierra GameKing BTSP	210	2700	2520	2330	2160	1990	1830	2670	2310	1990	1700	1450	1230
[3]	P308E	308 Win. (7.62x51mm)	180	11.66	Nosler Partition	210	2620	2430	2240	2060	1890	1730	2745	2355	2005	1700	1430	1200
[2]	P308F	308 Win. (7.62x51mm)	150	9.72	Nosler Ballistic Tip	210	2820	2610	2410	2220	2040	1860	2650	2270	1935	1640	1385	1155
[2]	P308T1	308 Win. (7.62x51mm)	165	10.69	Trophy Bonded Bear Claw	210	2700	2440	2200	1970	1760	1570	2670	2185	1775	1425	1135	900
[2]	P3006D	30-06 Spring (7.62x63mm)	165	10.69	Sierra GameKing BTSP	210	2800	2610	2420	2240	2070	1910	2870	2490	2150	1840	1580	1340
[3]	P3006F	30-06 Spring (7.62x63mm)	180	11.66	Nosler Partition	210	2700	2500	2320	2140	1970	1810	2915	2510	2150	1830	1550	1350
[2]	P3006G	30-06 Spring (7.62x63mm)	150	9.72	Sierra GameKing BTSP	210	2910	2690	2480	2270	2070	1880	2820	2420	2040	1710	1430	1180
[3]	P3006L	30-06 Spring (7.62x63mm)	180	11.66	Sierra GameKing BTSP	210	2700	2540	2380	2220	2080	1930	2915	2570	2260	1975	1720	1495
[2]	P3006P	30-06 Spring (7.62x63mm)	150	9.72	Nosler Ballistic Tip	210	2910	2700	2490	2300	2110	1940	2820	2420	2070	1760	1485	1245
[2]	P3006Q	30-06 Spring (7.62x63mm)	165	10.69	Nosler Ballistic Tip	210	2800	2610	2430	2250	2080	1920	2870	2495	2155	1855	1585	1350
[3]	P3006T1	30-06 Spring (7.62x63mm)	165	10.69	Trophy Bonded Bear Claw	210	2800	2540	2290	2050	1830	1630	2870	2360	1915	1545	1230	975
[3]	P3006T2	30-06 Spring (7.62x63mm)	180	11.66	Trophy Bonded Bear Claw	210	2700	2460	2220	2000	1800	1610	2915	2410	1975	1605	1290	1035
[3]	P300WC	300 Win. Magnum	200	12.96	Sierra GameKing BTSP	215	2830	2680	2530	2380	2240	2110	3560	3180	2830	2520	2230	1970
[3] NEW	P300WT4	300 Win. Magnum	150	9.72	Trophy Bonded Bear Claw	215	3280	2980	2700	2430	2190	1950	3570	2950	2420	1970	1590	1270
[3] NEW	P35WT1	35 Whelen	225	14.58	Trophy Bonded Bear Claw	210	2500	2300	2110	1930	1770	1610	3120	2650	2235	1870	1560	1290

FEDERAL BALLISTICS

100 YDS.	200 YDS.	WIND DRIFT IN INCHES 10 MPH CROSSWIND 300 YDS.	400 YDS.	500 YDS.	50 YDS.	HEIGHT OF BULLET TRAJECTORY IN INCHES ABOVE OR BELOW LINE OF SIGHT IF ZEROED AT ⊕ YARDS. SIGHTS 1.5 INCHES ABOVE BORE LINE. AVERAGE RANGE 100 YDS.	200 YDS.	300 YDS.	50 YDS.	100 YDS.	LONG RANGE 200 YDS.	300 YDS.	400 YDS.	500 YDS.	TEST BARREL LENGTH INCHES	FEDERAL LOAD NO.
1.0	3.8	9.2	17.0	28.4	-0.2	⊕	-3.6	-13.6	+0.7	+1.8	⊕	-8.2	-24.0	-49.9	24	P308T2
0.7	2.9	6.8	12.6	20.2	-0.1	⊕	-3.8	-13.9	+0.8	+1.9	⊕	-8.2	-23.5	-47.1	24	P308G
0.9	3.6	8.7	16.1	26.6	-0.2	⊕	-3.5	-13.3	+0.7	+1.8	⊕	-8.0	-23.3	-48.2	24	P3006T3
0.7	2.8	6.3	11.7	19.0	-0.2	⊕	-3.3	-12.2	+0.7	+1.7	⊕	-7.2	-21.0	-42.2	24	P3006R
0.8	3.3	7.7	14.5	23.6	-0.3	⊕	-2.9	-10.9	+0.5	+1.4	⊕	-6.6	-19.7	-40.4	24	P300WT3
0.7	2.6	6.0	11.2	18.2	-0.2	⊕	-3.2	-11.6	+0.6	+1.6	⊕	-6.9	-20.1	-40.4	24	P300WE
0.9	3.4	8.1	15.1	24.7	-0.2	⊕	-3.3	-12.4	+0.6	+1.7	⊕	-7.5	-22.0	-45.0	24	P338T2
0.7	2.8	6.6	12.3	19.7	-0.2	⊕	-3.6	-13.1	+0.7	+1.8	⊕	-7.8	-22.5	-44.9	24	P338D

▢ = Medium game   ▢ = Large, heavy game   ▢ = Dangerous game   ▢ = Target shooting, training, practice

100 YDS.	200 YDS.	WIND DRIFT IN INCHES 10 MPH CROSSWIND 300 YDS.	400 YDS.	500 YDS.	50 YDS.	HEIGHT OF BULLET TRAJECTORY IN INCHES ABOVE OR BELOW LINE OF SIGHT IF ZEROED AT ⊕ YARDS. SIGHTS 1.5 INCHES ABOVE BORE LINE. AVERAGE RANGE 100 YDS.	200 YDS.	300 YDS.	50 YDS.	100 YDS.	LONG RANGE 200 YDS.	300 YDS.	400 YDS.	500 YDS.	TEST BARREL LENGTH INCHES	FEDERAL LOAD NO.
1.3	5.8	14.2	27.7	47.6	-0.3	⊕	-2.7	-10.8	+0.4	+1.4	⊕	-6.7	-20.5	-43.4	24	P223E
0.8	3.6	8.4	15.8	26.3	-0.4	⊕	-1.7	-7.6	0	+0.9	⊕	-5.0	-15.1	-32.0	24	P22250B
0.6	2.6	6.1	11.3	18.4	-0.2	⊕	-3.1	-11.4	+0.6	+1.5	⊕	-6.8	-19.8	-39.9	24	P243C
0.7	2.7	6.3	11.6	18.8	-0.3	⊕	-2.2	-8.8	+0.2	+1.1	⊕	-5.5	-16.1	-32.8	24	P243D
0.8	3.4	8.1	15.2	25.1	-0.3	⊕	-2.2	-9.0	+0.2	+1.1	⊕	-5.7	-17.1	-35.7	24	P243F
0.7	2.9	6.7	12.5	20.4	-0.3	⊕	-2.8	-10.5	+0.4	+1.4	⊕	-6.3	-18.7	-38.1	24	P6C
0.8	3.3	7.7	14.3	23.5	-0.1	⊕	-3.8	-14.0	+0.8	+1.9	⊕	-8.2	-24.0	-48.9	24	P257B
0.7	3.0	6.9	12.9	21.1	-0.3	⊕	-2.7	-10.2	+0.4	+1.3	⊕	-6.2	-18.4	-37.5	24	P257WBA
0.7	3.1	7.3	13.7	22.4	-0.3	⊕	-2.7	-10.4	+0.4	+1.4	⊕	-6.3	-18.8	-38.5	24	P257WBT1
0.7	2.8	6.5	12.0	19.6	-0.2	⊕	-3.0	-11.4	+0.5	+1.5	⊕	-6.8	-19.9	-40.4	24	P2506C
0.7	2.9	6.7	12.4	20.2	-0.3	⊕	-2.5	-9.7	+0.3	+1.2	⊕	-6.0	-17.5	-35.8	24	P2506D
0.8	3.2	7.4	13.9	22.6	-0.2	⊕	-3.1	-11.7	+0.6	+1.6	⊕	-7.0	-20.8	-42.2	24	P2506E
0.8	3.4	7.9	14.8	21.4	-0.2	⊕	-3.2	-11.9	+0.6	+1.6	⊕	-7.2	-21.1	-43.2	24	P2506T1
0.7	2.7	6.3	11.6	18.9	-0.2	⊕	-3.4	-12.5	+0.7	+1.7	⊕	-7.4	-21.4	-43.0	24	P270C
0.7	2.8	6.6	12.1	19.7	-0.2	⊕	-2.8	-10.7	+0.5	+1.4	⊕	-6.5	-19.0	-38.5	24	P270D
0.9	3.9	9.2	17.3	28.5	-0.2	⊕	-3.7	-13.8	+0.8	+1.9	⊕	-8.3	-24.4	-50.5	24	P270E
0.7	2.7	6.4	11.9	19.3	-0.2	⊕	-2.8	-10.7	+0.5	+1.4	⊕	-6.5	-18.8	-38.2	24	P270F
0.8	3.2	7.6	14.2	23.0	-0.2	⊕	-3.3	-12.2	+0.6	+1.6	⊕	-7.3	-21.5	-43.7	24	P270T1
0.7	3.2	7.4	13.9	22.5	-0.2	⊕	-2.9	-11.1	+0.5	+1.5	⊕	-6.7	-19.8	-40.5	24	P270T2
0.7	2.7	6.3	11.7	19.0	-0.3	⊕	-2.5	-9.6	+0.3	+1.2	⊕	-5.9	-17.3	-35.1	24	P270WBA
0.8	3.1	7.4	13.7	22.5	-0.3	⊕	-2.8	-10.8	+0.4	+1.4	⊕	-6.6	-19.3	-39.6	24	P270WBT1
1.6	7.2	17.7	34.5	58.1	0	⊕	-5.2	-19.8	+1.2	+2.6	⊕	-12.0	-37.6	-81.7	24	P730A
1.3	3.2	8.2	15.4	23.4	-0.1	⊕	-4.3	-15.4	+1.0	+2.1	⊕	-9.0	-26.1	-52.9	24	P7C
0.7	2.8	6.6	12.3	19.5	-0.1	⊕	-4.2	-14.9	+0.9	+2.1	⊕	-8.7	-24.9	-49.4	24	P764A
0.9	3.8	9.0	16.8	27.8	-0.2	⊕	-3.6	-13.4	+0.7	+1.8	⊕	-8.0	-23.8	-49.2	24	P280A
1.2	4.9	11.8	22.5	37.8	-0.2	⊕	-3.5	-13.7	+0.7	+1.6	⊕	-8.4	-25.4	-54.3	24	P280T1
0.8	3.1	7.3	13.5	21.8	-0.2	⊕	-3.7	-13.5	+0.8	+1.8	⊕	-8.0	-23.1	-46.6	24	P708A
0.7	2.7	6.4	11.9	19.1	-0.2	⊕	-3.6	-13.1	+0.7	+1.8	⊕	-7.7	-14.1	-44.5	24	P708B
0.5	2.2	5.1	9.3	15.0	-0.3	⊕	-2.6	-9.8	+0.4	+1.3	⊕	-5.9	-17.0	-34.2	24	P7RD
0.5	2.0	4.6	8.4	13.5	-0.2	⊕	-3.0	-10.9	+0.5	+1.5	⊕	-6.4	-18.4	-36.6	24	P7RE
0.6	2.5	5.6	10.4	16.9	-0.2	⊕	-3.1	-11.3	+0.6	+1.5	⊕	-6.7	-19.4	-39.0	24	P7RF
0.6	2.6	6.0	11.1	18.2	-0.3	⊕	-2.6	-9.9	+0.4	+1.4	⊕	-6.0	-17.5	-35.6	24	P7RG
0.5	2.3	5.4	9.9	16.2	-0.3	⊕	-2.6	-9.9	+0.4	+1.3	⊕	-6.0	-10.9	-35.0	24	P7RH
0.7	2.8	6.5	12.1	19.6	-0.2	⊕	-3.4	-12.5	+0.7	+1.7	⊕	-7.4	-21.5	-43.3	24	P7RT1
1.0	4.3	10.3	19.5	32.4	-0.2	⊕	-3.5	-13.4	+0.7	+1.8	⊕	-8.1	-24.4	-51.1	24	P7RT2
0.6	2.5	5.8	10.7	17.3	-0.2	⊕	-2.8	-10.5	+0.4	+1.4	⊕	-6.3	-18.4	-37.1	24	P7WBA
1.0	4.2	10.1	19.1	31.9	-0.2	⊕	-3.2	-12.4	+0.6	+1.6	⊕	-7.6	-22.7	-47.8	24	P7WBT1
0.9	8.0	19.4	36.7	59.8	-0.3	⊕	-8.3	-29.8	+2.4	+4.1	⊕	-17.4	-52.4	-109.4	24	P3030D
0.7	3.0	7.0	13.0	21.1	-0.1	⊕	-4.0	-14.4	+0.9	+2.0	⊕	-8.4	-24.3	-49.0	24	P308C
0.8	3.3	7.7	14.3	23.3	-0.1	⊕	-4.4	-15.8	+1.0	+2.2	⊕	-9.2	-26.5	-53.6	24	P308E
0.7	3.1	7.2	13.3	21.7	-0.2	⊕	-3.6	-13.2	+0.7	+1.8	⊕	-7.8	-22.7	-46.0	24	P308F
1.0	4.2	10.0	18.7	31.1	-0.1	⊕	-4.4	-15.9	+1.0	+2.2	⊕	-9.4	-27.7	-57.5	24	P308T1
0.7	2.8	6.6	12.3	19.9	-0.2	⊕	-3.6	-13.2	+0.8	+1.8	⊕	-7.8	-22.4	-45.2	24	P3006D
0.7	3.0	7.3	13.4	27.7	-0.1	⊕	-4.0	-14.6	+0.9	+2.0	⊕	-8.6	-24.6	-49.6	24	P3006F
0.7	3.0	7.1	13.4	22.0	-0.2	⊕	-3.3	-12.4	+0.6	+1.7	⊕	-7.4	-21.5	-43.7	24	P3006G
0.6	2.6	6.0	11.0	17.8	-0.1	⊕	-3.9	-13.9	+0.9	+1.9	⊕	-8.1	-23.1	-46.1	24	P3006L
0.7	2.9	6.8	12.7	20.7	-0.2	⊕	-3.3	-12.2	+0.6	+1.6	⊕	-7.3	-21.1	-42.8	24	P3006P
0.7	2.8	6.6	12.1	19.7	-0.2	⊕	-3.6	-13.2	+0.7	+1.8	⊕	-7.7	-22.3	-45.0	24	P3006Q
1.0	4.0	9.6	17.8	29.7	-0.1	⊕	-3.9	-14.5	+0.8	+2.0	⊕	-8.7	-25.4	-53.1	24	P3006T1
0.9	4.0	9.4	17.7	29.4	-0.1	⊕	-4.3	-15.6	+1.0	+2.2	⊕	-9.2	-27.0	-56.1	24	P3006T2
0.5	2.2	5.0	9.2	14.9	-0.2	⊕	-3.4	-12.2	+0.7	+1.7	⊕	-7.1	-20.4	-40.5	24	P300WC
0.8	3.3	7.8	14.6	24.0	-0.3	⊕	-2.4	-9.6	+0.3	+1.2	⊕	-6.0	-17.9	-37.1	24	P300WT4
0.9	3.8	8.6	16.1	26.6	0.0	⊕	-5.1	-17.9	+1.3	+2.6	⊕	-10.2	-29.9	-61.0	24	P35WT1

FEDERAL BALLISTICS

CENTERFIRE RIFLE

CLASSIC® HUNTING RIFLE

Usage Key: ☐ = Varmints, predators, small game

USAGE	FEDERAL LOAD NO.	CALIBER	BULLET WGT. GRAINS	BULLET WGT. GRAMS	BULLET STYLE**	FACTORY PRIMER NO.	VELOCITY IN FEET PER SECOND (TO NEAREST 10 FPS) MUZZLE	100 YDS.	200 YDS.	300 YDS.	400 YDS.	500 YDS.	ENERGY IN FOOT-POUNDS (TO NEAREST 5 FOOT-POUNDS) MUZZLE	100 YDS.	200 YDS.	300 YDS.	400 YDS.	500 YDS.
☐	222A	222 Rem. (5.56x43mm)	50	3.24	Hi-Shok Soft Point	205	3140	2600	2120	1700	1350	1110	1095	750	500	320	200	135
☐	222B	222 Rem. (5.56x43mm)	55	3.56	Hi-Shok FMJ Boat-tail	205	3020	2740	2480	2230	1990	1780	1115	915	750	610	485	385
☐	223A	223 Rem. (5.56x45mm)	55	3.56	Hi-Shok Soft Point	205	3240	2750	2300	1910	1550	1270	1280	920	650	445	295	195
☐	223B	223 Rem. (5.56x45mm)	55	3.56	Hi-Shok FMJ Boat-tail	205	3240	2950	2670	2410	2170	1940	1280	1060	875	710	575	460
☐	22250A	22-250 Rem.	55	3.56	Hi-Shok Soft Point	210	3680	3140	2660	2220	1830	1490	1655	1200	860	605	410	270
☐ NEW	243AS	243 Win. (6.16x51mm)	80	5.18	Sierra Pro-Hunter SP	210	3350	2960	2590	2260	1950	1670	1995	1550	1195	905	675	495
2	243B	243 Win. (6.16x51mm)	100	6.48	Hi-Shok Soft Point	210	2960	2700	2450	2220	1990	1790	1945	1615	1330	1090	880	710
☐ NEW	6AS	6mm Rem.	80	5.18	Sierra Pro-Hunter SP	210	3470	3060	2690	2350	2040	1750	2140	1665	1290	980	735	540
2	6B	6mm Rem.	100	6.48	Hi-Shok Soft Point	210	3100	2830	2570	2330	2100	1890	2135	1775	1470	1205	985	790
2 NEW	2506BS	25-06 Rem.	117	7.58	Sierra Pro-Hunter SP	210	2990	2730	2480	2250	2030	1830	2320	1985	1645	1350	1100	885
2	6555B	6.5x55 Swedish	140	9.07	Hi-Shok Soft Point	210	2600	2400	2220	2040	1860	1700	2100	1795	1525	1285	1080	900
2	270A	270 Win.	130	8.42	Hi-Shok Soft Point	210	3060	2800	2560	2330	2110	1900	2700	2265	1890	1565	1285	1045
2	270B	270 Win.	150	9.72	Hi-Shok Soft Point RN	210	2850	2500	2180	1890	1620	1390	2705	2085	1585	1185	870	640
2	7A	7mm Mauser (7x57mm Mauser)	175	11.34	Hi-Shok Soft Point RN	210	2440	2140	1860	1600	1380	1200	2315	1775	1340	1000	740	565
2	7B	7mm Mauser (7x57mm Mauser)	140	9.07	Hi-Shok Soft Point	210	2660	2450	2260	2070	1890	1730	2200	1865	1585	1330	1110	930
2	280B	280 Rem.	150	9.72	Hi-Shok Soft Point	210	2890	2670	2460	2260	2060	1880	2780	2370	2015	1695	1420	1180
2	7RA	7mm Rem. Magnum	150	9.72	Hi-Shok Soft Point	215	3110	2830	2570	2320	2090	1870	3220	2670	2200	1790	1450	1160
3	7RB	7mm Rem. Magnum	175	11.34	Hi-Shok Soft Point	215	2860	2650	2440	2240	2060	1880	3180	2720	2310	1960	1640	1370
☐	30CA	30 Carbine (7.62x33mm)	110	7.13	Hi-Shok Soft Point RN	205	1990	1570	1240	1040	920	840	965	600	375	260	210	175
2	76239B	7.62x39mm Soviet	123	7.97	Hi-Shok Soft Point	210	2300	2030	1780	1550	1350	1200	1445	1125	860	655	500	395
2	3030A	30-30 Win.	150	9.72	Hi-Shok Soft Point FN	210	2390	2020	1680	1400	1180	1040	1900	1355	945	650	460	355
2	3030B	30-30 Win.	170	11.01	Hi-Shok Soft Point RN	210	2200	1900	1620	1380	1190	1060	1830	1355	990	720	535	425
☐	3030C	30-30 Win.	125	8.10	Hi-Shok Hollow Point	210	2570	2090	1660	1320	1080	960	1830	1210	770	480	320	260
2	300A	300 Savage	150	9.72	Hi-Shok Soft Point	210	2630	2350	2100	1850	1630	1430	2305	1845	1460	1145	885	685
2	300B	300 Savage	180	11.66	Hi-Shok Soft Point	210	2350	2140	1940	1750	1570	1410	2205	1825	1495	1215	985	800
2	308A	308 Win. (7.62x51mm)	150	9.72	Hi-Shok Soft Point	210	2820	2530	2260	2010	1770	1560	2650	2140	1705	1345	1050	810
2	308B	308 Win. (7.62x51mm)	180	11.66	Hi-Shok Soft Point	210	2620	2390	2180	1970	1780	1600	2745	2290	1895	1555	1270	1030
2	3006A	30-06 Springfield (7.62x63mm)	150	9.72	Hi-Shok Soft Point	210	2910	2620	2340	2080	1840	1620	2820	2280	1825	1445	1130	875
3	3006B	30-06 Springfield (7.62x63mm)	180	11.66	Hi-Shok Soft Point	210	2700	2470	2250	2040	1850	1660	2915	2435	2025	1665	1360	1105
☐ NEW	3006CS	30-06 Springfield (7.62x63mm)	125	8.10	Sierra Pro-Hunter SP	210	3140	2780	2450	2140	1850	1600	2735	2145	1660	1270	955	705
3 NEW	3006HS	30-06 Springfield (7.62x63mm)	220	14.25	Sierra Pro-Hunter SP RN	210	2410	2130	1870	1630	1420	1250	2835	2215	1705	1300	985	760
3 NEW	3006JS	30-06 Springfield (7.62x63mm)	180	11.66	Sierra Pro-Hunter SP RN	210	2700	2350	2020	1730	1470	1250	2915	2200	1630	1190	860	620
3 NEW	300WBS	300 Win. Magnum	180	11.66	Sierra Pro-Hunter SP	215	2960	2750	2540	2340	2160	1980	3500	3010	2580	2195	1860	1565
2 NEW	300WGS	300 Win. Magnum	150	9.72	Sierra Pro-Hunter SP	215	3280	3030	2800	2570	2360	2160	3570	3055	2600	2205	1860	1560
2 NEW	303AS	303 British	180	11.66	Sierra Pro-Hunter SP	210	2460	2230	2020	1820	1630	1460	2420	1995	1625	1315	1060	850
2	303B	303 British	150	9.72	Hi-Shok Soft Point	210	2690	2440	2210	1980	1780	1590	2400	1980	1620	1310	1055	840
2	32A	32 Win. Special	170	11.01	Hi-Shok Soft Point	210	2250	1920	1630	1370	1180	1040	1910	1395	1000	710	520	410
2	*8A	8mm Mauser (8x57mm JS Mauser)	170	11.01	Hi-Shok Soft Point	210	2360	1970	1620	1330	1120	1000	2100	1465	995	670	475	375
2	338C	338 Win. Magnum	225	14.58	Hi-Shok Soft Point	215	2780	2570	2370	2180	2000	1830	3860	3305	2815	2380	2000	1670
2	357G	357 Magnum	180	11.66	Hi-Shok Hollow Point	100	1550	1160	980	860	770	680	960	535	385	295	235	185
2	35A	35 Rem.	200	12.96	Hi-Shok Soft Point	210	2080	1700	1380	1140	1000	910	1920	1280	840	575	445	370
3	375A	375 H&H Magnum	270	17.50	Hi-Shok Soft Point	215	2690	2420	2170	1920	1700	1500	4340	3510	2810	2220	1740	1355
4	375B	375 H&H Magnum	300	19.44	Hi-Shok Soft Point	215	2530	2270	2020	1790	1580	1400	4265	3425	2720	2135	1665	1295
2	44A	44 Rem. Magnum	240	15.55	Hi-Shok Hollow Point	150	1760	1380	1090	950	860	790	1650	1015	640	485	395	330
2 NEW	4570AS	45-70 Government	300	19.44	Sierra Hollow Point FN	210	1880	1650	1430	1240	1110	1010	2355	1815	1355	1015	810	680

FEDERAL BALLISTICS

CENTERFIRE RIFLE

☐ = Medium game   ☐ = Large, heavy game   ☐ = Dangerous game   ☐ = Target shooting, training, practice

| WIND DRIFT IN INCHES 10 MPH CROSSWIND | | | | | HEIGHT OF BULLET TRAJECTORY IN INCHES ABOVE OR BELOW LINE OF SIGHT IF ZEROED AT ⊕ YARDS. SIGHTS 1.5 INCHES ABOVE BORE LINE. | | | | | | | | | | TEST BARREL LENGTH INCHES | FEDERAL LOAD NO. |
| | | | | | AVERAGE RANGE | | | | LONG RANGE | | | | | | | |
100 YDS.	200 YDS.	300 YDS.	400 YDS.	500 YDS.	50 YDS.	100 YDS.	200 YDS.	300 YDS.	50 YDS.	100 YDS.	200 YDS.	300 YDS.	400 YDS.	500 YDS.		
1.7	7.3	18.3	36.4	63.1	-0.2	⊕	-3.7	-15.3	+0.7	+1.9	⊕	-9.7	-31.6	-71.3	24	222A
0.9	3.4	8.5	16.8	26.3	-0.2	⊕	-3.1	-12.0	+0.6	+1.6	⊕	-7.3	-21.5	-44.6	24	222B
1.4	6.1	15.0	29.4	50.8	-0.3	⊕	-3.2	-12.9	+0.5	+1.6	⊕	-8.2	-26.1	-58.3	24	223A
0.8	3.3	7.8	14.5	24.0	-0.3	⊕	-2.5	-9.9	+0.3	+1.3	⊕	-6.1	-18.3	-37.8	24	223B
1.2	5.2	12.5	24.4	42.0	-0.4	⊕	-2.1	-9.1	+0.1	+1.0	⊕	-6.0	-19.1	-42.6	24	22250A
1.0	4.3	10.4	19.8	33.3	-0.3	⊕	-2.5	-10.2	+0.3	+1.3	⊕	-6.4	-19.7	-42.2	24	243AS
0.9	3.6	8.4	15.7	25.8	-0.2	⊕	-3.3	-12.4	+0.6	+1.6	⊕	-7.5	-22.0	-45.4	24	243B
1.0	4.1	9.9	18.8	31.6	-0.3	⊕	-2.2	-9.3	+0.2	+1.1	⊕	-5.9	-18.2	-39.0	24	6AS
0.8	3.3	7.9	14.7	24.1	-0.3	⊕	-2.9	-11.0	+0.5	+1.4	⊕	-6.7	-19.8	-40.6	24	6B
0.8	3.4	8.1	15.1	24.9	-0.2	⊕	-3.2	-12.0	+0.6	+1.6	⊕	-7.2	-21.4	-44.0	24	2506BS
0.8	3.4	8.0	14.8	24.1	-0.1	⊕	-4.5	-16.2	+1.1	+2.3	⊕	-9.4	-27.2	-55.0	24	6555B
0.8	3.2	7.6	14.2	23.3	-0.2	⊕	-2.9	-11.2	+0.5	+1.5	⊕	-6.8	-20.0	-41.1	24	270A
1.2	5.3	12.8	24.5	41.3	-0.1	⊕	-4.1	-15.5	+0.9	+2.0	⊕	-9.4	-28.6	-61.0	24	270B
1.5	6.2	15.0	28.7	47.8	-0.1	⊕	-6.2	-22.6	+1.6	+3.1	⊕	-13.3	-40.1	-84.6	24	7A
1.3	3.2	8.2	15.4	23.4	-0.1	⊕	-4.3	-15.4	+1.0	+2.1	⊕	-9.0	-26.1	-52.9	24	7B
0.7	3.1	7.2	13.4	21.9	-0.2	⊕	-3.4	-12.6	+0.7	+1.7	⊕	-7.5	-21.8	-44.3	24	280B
0.8	3.4	8.1	15.1	24.9	-0.3	⊕	-2.9	-11.0	+0.5	+1.4	⊕	-6.7	-19.9	41.0	24	7RA
0.7	3.1	7.2	13.3	21.7	-0.2	⊕	-3.5	-12.8	+0.7	+1.7	⊕	-7.6	-22.1	-44.9	24	7RB
3.4	15.0	35.5	63.2	96.7	+0.6	⊕	-12.8	-46.9	+3.9	+6.4	⊕	-27.7	-81.8	-167.8	18	30CA
1.5	6.4	15.2	28.7	47.3	+0.2	⊕	-7.0	-25.1	+1.9	+3.5	⊕	-14.5	-43.4	-90.6	20	76239B
2.0	8.5	20.9	40.1	66.1	+0.2	⊕	-7.2	-26.7	+1.9	+3.6	⊕	-15.9	-49.1	-104.5	24	3030A
1.9	8.0	19.4	36.7	59.8	+0.3	⊕	-8.3	-29.8	+2.4	+4.1	⊕	-17.4	-52.4	-109.4	24	3030B
2.2	10.1	25.4	49.4	81.6	+0.1	⊕	-6.6	-26.0	+1.7	+3.3	⊕	-16.0	-50.9	-109.5	24	3030C
1.1	4.8	11.6	21.9	36.3	0	⊕	-4.8	-17.6	+1.2	+2.4	⊕	-10.4	-30.9	-64.4	24	300A
1.1	4.6	10.9	20.3	33.3	+0.1	⊕	-6.1	-21.6	+1.7	+3.1	⊕	-12.4	-36.1	-73.8	24	300B
1.0	4.4	10.4	19.7	32.7	-0.1	⊕	-3.9	-14.7	+0.8	+2.0	⊕	-8.8	-26.3	-54.8	24	308A
0.9	3.9	9.2	17.2	28.3	-0.1	⊕	-4.6	-16.5	+1.1	+2.3	⊕	-9.7	-28.3	-57.8	24	308B
1.0	4.2	9.9	18.7	31.2	-0.2	⊕	-3.6	-13.6	+0.7	+1.8	⊕	-8.2	-24.4	-50.9	24	3006A
0.9	3.7	8.8	16.5	27.1	-0.1	⊕	-4.2	-15.3	+1.0	+2.1	⊕	-9.0	-26.4	-54.0	24	3006B
1.1	4.5	10.8	20.5	34.4	-0.3	⊕	-3.0	-11.9	+0.5	+1.5	⊕	-7.3	-22.3	-47.5	24	3006CS
1.4	6.0	14.3	27.2	45.0	-0.1	⊕	-6.2	-22.4	+1.7	+3.1	⊕	-13.1	-39.3	-82.2	24	3006HS
1.5	6.4	15.7	30.4	51.2	-0.1	⊕	-4.9	-18.3	+1.1	+2.4	⊕	-11.0	-33.6	-71.9	24	3006JS
0.7	2.8	6.6	12.3	20.0	-0.2	⊕	-3.1	-11.7	+0.6	+1.6	⊕	-7.0	-20.3	41.1	24	300WBS
0.7	2.7	6.3	11.5	18.8	-0.3	⊕	-2.3	-9.1	+0.3	+1.1	⊕	-5.6	-16.4	-33.6	24	300WGS
1.1	4.5	10.6	19.9	32.7	0	⊕	-5.5	-19.6	+1.4	+2.8	⊕	-11.3	-33.2	-68.1	24	303AS
1.0	4.1	9.6	18.1	29.9	-0.1	⊕	-4.4	-15.9	+1.0	+2.2	⊕	-9.4	-27.6	-56.8	24	303B
1.9	8.4	20.3	38.6	63.0	+0.3	⊕	-8.0	-29.2	+2.3	+4.0	⊕	-17.2	-52.3	-109.8	24	32A
2.1	9.3	22.9	43.9	71.7	+0.2	⊕	-7.6	-28.5	+2.1	+3.8	⊕	-17.1	-52.9	-111.9	24	8A
0.8	3.1	7.3	13.6	22.2	-0.1	⊕	-3.8	-13.7	+0.8	+1.9	⊕	-8.1	-23.5	-47.5	24	338C
5.8	21.7	45.2	76.1	NA	⊕	-3.4	-29.7	-88.2	+1.7	⊕	-22.8	-77.9	-173.8	-321.4	18	357G
2.7	12.0	29.0	53.5	83.3	+0.5	⊕	-10.7	-39.3	+3.2	+5.4	⊕	-23.3	-70.0	-144.0	24	35A
1.1	4.5	10.8	20.3	33.7	-0.4	⊕	-5.5	-18.4	+1.0	+2.4	⊕	-10.9	-33.3	-71.2	24	375A
1.2	5.0	11.9	22.4	37.1	+0.5	⊕	-6.3	-21.2	+1.3	+2.6	⊕	-11.2	-33.3	-69.1	24	375B
4.2	17.8	39.8	68.3	102.5	⊕	-2.2	-21.7	-67.2	+1.1	⊕	-17.4	-60.7	-136.0	-250.2	20	44A
1.7	7.6	18.6	35.7	NA	⊕	-1.3	-14.1	-43.7	+0.7	⊕	-11.5	-39.7	-89.1	-163.1	24	4570AS

FEDERAL BALLISTICS

CLASSIC® AUTOMATIC PISTOL

Usage Key: ☐ = Varmints, predators, small game   ☐ = Medium game   ☐ = Self-defense   ☐ = Target shooting, training, practice

USAGE	FEDERAL LOAD NO.	CALIBER	BULLET WGT. IN GRAINS	GRAMS	BULLET STYLE*	FACTORY PRIMER NO.	MUZZLE	25 YDS.	50 YDS.	75 YDS.	100 YDS.	MUZZLE	25 YDS.	50 YDS.	75 YDS.	100 YDS.	25 YDS.	50 YDS.	75 YDS.	100 YDS.	TEST BARREL LENGTH INCHES
							VELOCITY IN FEET PER SECOND (TO NEAREST 10 FPS)					ENERGY IN FOOT-POUNDS (TO NEAREST 5 FOOT-POUNDS)					MID-RANGE TRAJECTORY				
☐,☐	25AP	25 Auto (6.35mm Browning)	50	3.24	Full Metal Jacket	200	760	750	730	720	700	65	60	60	55	55	0.5	1.9	4.5	8.1	2
☐,☐	32AP	32 Auto (7.65mm Browning)	71	4.60	Full Metal Jacket	100	910	880	860	830	810	130	120	115	110	105	0.3	1.4	3.2	5.9	4
☐,☐	380AP	380 Auto (9x17mm Short)	95	6.15	Full Metal Jacket	100	960	910	870	830	790	190	175	160	145	130	0.3	1.3	3.1	5.8	3⁹/4
☐	380BP	380 Auto (9x17mm Short)	90	5.83	Hi-Shok JHP	100	1000	940	890	840	800	200	175	160	140	130	0.3	1.2	2.9	5.5	3⁹/4
☐,☐	9AP	9mm Luger (9x19mm Parabellum)	124	8.03	Full Metal Jacket	100	1120	1070	1030	990	960	345	315	290	270	250	0.2	0.9	2.2	4.1	4
☐	9BP	9mm Luger (9x19mm Parabellum)	115	7.45	Hi-Shok JHP	100	1160	1100	1060	1020	990	345	310	285	270	250	0.2	0.9	2.1	3.8	4
☐	9MS	9mm Luger (9x19mm Parabellum)	147	9.52	Hi-Shok JHP	100	980	950	930	900	880	310	295	285	265	255	0.3	1.2	2.8	5.1	4
☐	357S2	357 Sig	125	8.10	Truncated FMJ	100	1350	1270	1190	1130	1080	510	445	395	355	325	0.2	0.7	1.6	3.1	4
☐	40SWA	40 S&W	180	11.06	Hi-Shok JHP	100	990	960	930	910	890	390	365	345	330	315	0.3	1.2	2.8	5.0	4
☐	40SWB	40 S&W	155	10.04	Hi-Shok JHP	100	1140	1080	1030	990	950	445	400	365	335	315	0.2	0.9	2.2	4.1	4
☐	10C	10mm Auto	180	11.06	Hi-Shok JHP	150	1030	1000	970	950	920	425	400	375	355	340	0.3	1.1	2.5	4.7	5
☐	10E	10mm Auto	155	10.04	Hi-Shok JHP	150	1330	1230	1140	1080	1030	605	515	450	400	360	0.2	0.7	1.8	3.3	5
☐	45A	45 Auto	230	14.90	Full Metal Jacket	150	850	830	810	790	770	370	350	335	320	305	0.4	1.6	3.6	6.6	5
☐	45C	45 Auto	185	11.99	Hi-Shok JHP	150	950	920	900	880	860	370	350	335	315	300	0.3	1.3	2.9	5.3	5
☐	45D	45 Auto	230	14.90	Hi-Shok JHP	150	850	830	810	790	770	370	350	335	320	300	0.4	1.6	3.7	6.7	5

*Jacketed Hollow Point   FMJ = Full Metal Jacket

CLASSIC® REVOLVER

Usage Key: ☐ = Varmints, predators, small game   ☐ = Medium game   ☐ = Self-defense   ☐ = Target shooting, training, practice

USAGE	FEDERAL LOAD NO.	CALIBER	BULLET WGT. IN GRAINS	GRAMS	BULLET STYLE**	FACTORY PRIMER NO.	MUZZLE	25 YDS.	50 YDS.	75 YDS.	100 YDS.	MUZZLE	25 YDS.	50 YDS.	75 YDS.	100 YDS.	25 YDS.	50 YDS.	75 YDS.	100 YDS.	TEST BARREL LENGTH INCHES
							VELOCITY IN FEET PER SECOND (TO NEAREST 10 FPS)					ENERGY IN FOOT-POUNDS (TO NEAREST 5 FOOT-POUNDS)					MID-RANGE TRAJECTORY				
☐	32LA	32 S&W Long	98	6.35	Lead Wadcutter	100	780	700	630	560	500	130	105	85	70	55	0.5	2.2	5.6	11.1	4
☐	32LB	32 S&W Long	98	6.35	Lead Round Nose	100	710	690	670	650	640	115	105	100	95	90	0.6	2.3	5.3	9.6	4
☐	32HRA	32 H&R Magnum	95	6.15	Lead Semi-Wadcutter	100	1030	1000	940	930	900	225	210	195	185	170	0.3	1.1	2.5	4.7	4¹/2
☐	32HRB	32 H&R Magnum	85	5.50	Hi-Shok JHP	100	1100	1050	1020	970	930	230	210	195	175	165	0.2	1.0	2.3	4.3	4¹/2
☐	38B	38 Special	158	10.23	Lead Round Nose	100	760	740	720	710	690	200	190	185	175	170	0.5	2.0	4.6	8.3	4-V
☐,☐	38C	38 Special	158	10.23	Lead Semi-Wadcutter	100	760	740	720	710	690	200	190	185	175	170	0.5	2.0	4.6	8.3	4-V
☐,☐	38E	38 Special (High-Velocity+P)	125	8.10	Hi-Shok JHP	100	950	920	900	880	860	250	235	225	215	205	0.3	1.3	2.9	5.4	4-V
☐,☐	38F	38 Special (High-Velocity+P)	110	7.13	Hi-Shok JHP	100	1000	960	930	900	870	240	225	210	195	185	0.3	1.2	2.7	5.0	4-V
☐,☐	38G	38 Special (High-Velocity+P)	158	10.23	Semi-Wadcutter HP	100	890	870	860	840	820	280	265	260	245	235	0.3	1.4	3.3	5.9	4-V
☐,☐	38H	38 Special (High-Velocity+P)	158	10.23	Lead Semi-Wadcutter	100	890	870	860	840	820	270	265	260	245	235	0.3	1.4	3.3	5.9	4-V
☐,☐	38J	38 Special (High-Velocity+P)	125	8.10	Hi-Shok JSP	100	950	920	900	880	860	250	235	225	215	205	0.3	1.3	2.9	5.4	4-V
☐,☐	357A	357 Magnum	158	10.23	Hi-Shok JSP	100	1240	1160	1100	1060	1020	535	475	430	395	365	0.2	0.8	1.9	3.5	4-V
☐,☐	357B	357 Magnum	125	8.10	Hi-Shok JHP	100	1450	1350	1240	1160	1100	580	495	430	370	335	0.1	0.6	1.5	2.8	4-V
☐	357C	357 Magnum	158	10.23	Lead Semi-Wadcutter	100	1240	1160	1100	1060	1020	535	475	430	395	365	0.2	0.8	1.9	3.5	4-V
☐,☐	357D	357 Magnum	110	7.13	Hi-Shok JHP	100	1300	1180	1090	1040	990	410	340	290	260	235	0.2	0.8	1.9	3.5	4-V
☐,☐	357E	357 Magnum	158	10.23	Hi-Shok JHP	100	1240	1160	1100	1060	1020	535	475	430	395	365	0.2	0.8	1.9	3.5	4-V
☐,☐	357G	357 Magnum	180	11.66	Hi-Shok JHP	100	1090	1030	980	930	890	475	425	385	350	320	0.2	1.0	2.4	4.5	4-V
☐,☐	357H	357 Magnum	140	9.07	Hi-Shok JHP	100	1360	1270	1200	1130	1080	575	500	445	395	360	0.2	0.7	1.6	3.0	4-V
☐,☐	41A	41 Rem. Magnum	210	13.60	Hi-Shok JHP	150	1300	1210	1130	1070	1030	790	680	595	540	495	0.2	0.7	1.8	3.3	4-V
☐,☐	44SA	44 S&W Special	200	12.96	Semi-Wadcutter HP	150	900	860	830	800	770	360	330	305	285	260	0.3	1.4	3.4	6.3	6¹/2-V
☐,☐	44A	44 Rem. Magnum	240	15.55	Hi-Shok JHP	150	1180	1130	1080	1050	1010	740	675	625	580	550	0.2	0.9	2.0	3.7	6¹/2-V
☐,☐	44B*	44 Rem. Magnum	180	11.66	Hi-Shok JHP	150	1610	1480	1370	1270	1180	1035	875	750	640	555	0.1	0.5	1.2	2.3	6¹/2-V
☐,☐	45LCA	45 Colt	225	14.58	Semi-Wadcutter HP	150	900	880	860	840	820	405	385	370	355	340	0.3	1.4	3.2	5.8	5¹/2

+P ammunition is loaded to a higher pressure. Use only in firearms so recommended by the gun manufacturer. "V" indicates vented barrel to simulate service conditions.   *Also available in 20-round box (A44820).   **JHP = Jacketed Hollow Point   HP = Hollow Point   JSP = Jacketed Soft Point

CLASSIC® 22

Usage Key: ☐ = Varmints, predators, small game   ☐ = Medium game   ☐ = Large, heavy game   ☐ = Dangerous game   ☐ = Target shooting, training, practice

USAGE	FEDERAL LOAD NO.	CARTRIDGE PER BOX	CALIBER	BULLET WGT. IN GRAINS	BULLET STYLE*	MUZZLE	50 YDS.	100 YDS.	150 YDS.	MUZZLE	50 YDS.	100 YDS.	150 YDS.	50 YDS.	100 YDS.	150 YDS.	50 YDS.	100 YDS.	150 YDS.	50 YDS.	100 YDS.	150 YDS.
						VELOCITY IN FEET PER SECOND (TO NEAREST 10 FPS)				ENERGY IN FOOT-POUNDS (TO NEAREST 5 FOOT-POUNDS)				WIND DRIFT IN INCHES 10 MPH CROSSWIND			HEIGHT OF BULLET TRAJECTORY IN INCHES ABOVE OR BELOW LINE OF SIGHT IF ZEROED AT ⊕ YARDS. SIGHTS 1.5 INCHES ABOVE BORE LINE.					
☐,☐	710	50	22 Long Rifle HV	40	Solid, Copper Plated	1260	1100	1020	940	140	110	90	80	1.5	5.5	11.4	⊕	-6.5	-21.0	+2.7	⊕	-10.8
☐,☐	810	100	22 Long Rifle HV	40	Solid, Copper Plated	1260	1100	1020	940	140	110	90	80	1.5	5.5	11.4	⊕	-6.5	-21.0	+2.7	⊕	-10.8
☐,☐	712	50	22 Long Rifle HV	38	HP Copper Plated	1280	1120	1020	950	140	105	90	75	1.6	5.8	12.1	⊕	-6.3	-20.6	+2.7	⊕	-10.6
☐,☐	NEW 724	50	22 Long Rifle HV	31	HP Copper Plated	1550	1280	1100	980	165	115	85	65	1.7	7.0	15.5	⊕	-3.8	-14.7	+1.9	⊕	-9.0
☐	716	50	22 Long Rifle Bird Shot	25	No. 12 Lead Shot	—	—	—	—	—	—	—	—	—	—	—	—	—	—	—	—	—

*HP = Hollow Point   These ballistic specifications were derived from test barrels 24 inches in length.

CLASSIC® 22 MAGNUM

Usage Key: ☐ = Varmints, predators, small game   ☐ = Medium game   ☐ = Large, heavy game   ☐ = Dangerous game   ☐ = Target shooting, training, practice

USAGE	FEDERAL LOAD NO.	CARTRIDGE PER BOX	CALIBER	BULLET WGT. IN GRAINS	BULLET STYLE*	MUZZLE	50 YDS.	100 YDS.	150 YDS.	MUZZLE	50 YDS.	100 YDS.	150 YDS.	50 YDS.	100 YDS.	150 YDS.	50 YDS.	100 YDS.	150 YDS.	50 YDS.	100 YDS.	150 YDS.
						VELOCITY IN FEET PER SECOND (TO NEAREST 10 FPS)				ENERGY IN FOOT-POUNDS (TO NEAREST 5 FOOT-POUNDS)				WIND DRIFT IN INCHES 10 MPH CROSSWIND			HEIGHT OF BULLET TRAJECTORY IN INCHES ABOVE OR BELOW LINE OF SIGHT IF ZEROED AT ⊕ YARDS. SIGHTS 1.5 INCHES ABOVE BORE LINE.					
☐,☐	757	50	22 Win. Magnum	50	Jacketed HP	1650	1450	1280	1150	300	235	180	145	1.1	4.5	10.3	⊕	-3.6	-12.5	+1.3	⊕	-6.5
☐,☐	737	50	22 Win. Magnum	40	Full Metal Jacket	1910	1600	1330	1140	325	225	155	115	1.3	5.7	13.4	⊕	-2.9	-10.7	+1.0	⊕	-5.8
☐,☐	767	50	22 Win. Magnum	30	Jacketed HP	2200	1750	1380	1120	320	205	125	85	1.4	6.4	15.8	⊕	-1.4	-7.4	+0.7	⊕	-5.3

FEDERAL BALLISTICS

PISTOL/REVOLVER

AMERICAN EAGLE® PISTOL

Usage Key: = Varmints, predators, small game   = Medium game   = Self-defense   = Target shooting, training, practice

USAGE	FEDERAL LOAD NO.	CALIBER	BULLET WGT. GRAINS	IN GRAMS	BULLET STYLE	FACTORY PRIMER NO.	VELOCITY IN FEET PER SECOND (TO NEAREST 10 FPS) MUZZLE	25 YDS.	50 YDS.	75 YDS.	100 YDS.	ENERGY IN FOOT-POUNDS (TO NEAREST 5 FOOT-POUNDS) MUZZLE	25 YDS.	50 YDS.	75 YDS.	100 YDS.	MID-RANGE TRAJECTORY 25 YDS.	50 YDS.	75 YDS.	100 YDS.	TEST BARREL LENGTH INCHES
[T]	AE25AP	25 Auto (6.35mm Browning)	50	3.24	Full Metal Jacket	200	760	750	730	720	700	65	60	60	60	55	0.5	1.9	4.5	8.1	2
[T]	AE380AP	380 Auto (9 x17 short)	95	6.15	Full Metal Jacket	100	960	910	870	830	790	190	175	160	145	130	0.3	1.3	3.1	5.8	3¾
[T]	AE9AP	9mm Luger (9 x 19 Parabellum)	124	8.03	Full Metal Jacket	100	1120	1070	1030	990	960	345	315	290	270	255	0.2	0.9	2.2	4.1	4
[T]	AE9FP	9mm Luger (9 x 19 Parabellum)	147	9.52	Full Metal Jacket Flat Pt.	100	960	930	910	890	870	295	280	270	260	250	0.3	1.3	2.9	5.3	4
[T]	AE9MK	9mm Makarov (9 x 19 Makarov)	90	6.16	Full Metal Jacket	100	990	960	920	900	870	205	190	180	170	160	0.3	1.2	2.8	5.1	3¾
[T]	AE38S1	38 Super High Velocity +P	130	8.42	Full Metal Jacket	200	1200	1140	1100	1050	1020	415	380	350	320	300	0.2	0.8	1.9	3.6	5
[T]	AE38S2	38 Super High Velocity +P	147	9.52	Full Metal Jacket	200	1100	1070	1050	1020	1000	395	375	355	340	325	0.2	0.9	2.2	4	5
[T]	AE40	40 S & W	180	~11.06	Full Metal Jacket	100	990	960	930	910	890	390	365	345	330	315	0.3	1.2	2.8	5	4
[T]	AE40FP	40 S & W	180	11.06	Full Metal Jacket Flat Pt.	100	990	960	930	910	882	390	365	345	330	310	0.3	1.2	2.7	5	4
[T]	AE40T3	40 S & W	165	10.66	Full Metal Jacket	100	980	950	930	920	900	350	335	320	305	295	0.3	1.2	2.7	5	4
[T]	AE10	10mm Auto	180	11.06	Full Metal Jacket	150	1030	1000	970	950	920	425	400	375	355	340	0.3	1.1	2.5	4.7	5
[T]	AE45A	45 Auto	230	14.90	Full Metal Jacket	150	850	830	810	790	770	370	350	335	320	305	0.4	1.6	3.6	6.6	5

GOLD MEDAL® MATCH PISTOL

Usage Key: = Varmints, predators, small game   = Medium game   = Self-defense   = Target shooting, training, practice

USAGE	FEDERAL LOAD NO.	CALIBER	BULLET WGT. GRAINS	IN GRAMS	BULLET STYLE*	FACTORY PRIMER NO.	VELOCITY IN FEET PER SECOND (TO NEAREST 10 FPS) MUZZLE	25 YDS.	50 YDS.	75 YDS.	100 YDS.	ENERGY IN FOOT-POUNDS (TO NEAREST 5 FOOT-POUNDS) MUZZLE	25 YDS.	50 YDS.	75 YDS.	100 YDS.	MID-RANGE TRAJECTORY 25 YDS.	50 YDS.	75 YDS.	100 YDS.	TEST BARREL LENGTH INCHES
[T]	GM9MP	9mm Luger (9x19mm Parabellum)	124	8.03	Truncated FMJ Match	GM100M	1120	1070	1030	990	960	345	315	290	270	255	0.2	0.9	2.2	4.1	4
[T]	GM38A	38 Special	148	9.59	Lead Wadcutter Match	GM100M	710	670	630	600	560	165	150	130	115	105	0.6	2.4	5.7	10.8	4-V
[T]	GM356SW	356 TSW	147	9.52	Truncated FMJ Match	GM100M	1220	1170	1120	1080	1040	485	445	410	380	355	0.2	0.8	1.9	3.5	5
[T]	GM44D	44 Rem. Magnum	250	16.20	MC Profile Match	GM150M	1180	1140	1100	1070	1040	775	715	670	630	600	0.2	0.8	1.9	3.6	6½-V
[T]	GM45B	45 Auto	185	11.99	FMJ-SWC Match	GM150M	780	730	700	660	620	245	220	200	175	160	0.5	2.0	4.8	9.0	5

AMERICAN EAGLE® REVOLVER

Usage Key: = Varmints, predators, small game   = Medium game   = Self-defense   = Target shooting, training, practice

USAGE	FEDERAL LOAD NO.	CALIBER	BULLET WGT. GRAINS	IN GRAMS	BULLET STYLE	FACTORY PRIMER NO.	VELOCITY IN FEET PER SECOND (TO NEAREST 10 FPS) MUZZLE	25 YDS.	50 YDS.	75 YDS.	100 YDS.	ENERGY IN FOOT-POUNDS (TO NEAREST 5 FOOT-POUNDS) MUZZLE	25 YDS.	50 YDS.	75 YDS.	100 YDS.	MID-RANGE TRAJECTORY 25 YDS.	50 YDS.	75 YDS.	100 YDS.	TEST BARREL LENGTH INCHES
[T]	AE38B	38 Special	158	10.23	Lead Round Nose	100	760	740	720	710	690	200	190	185	175	170	0.5	2.0	4.6	8.3	4-V
[M],[S]	AE357A	357 Magnum	158	10.23	Jacketed Soft Point	100	1240	1160	1100	1060	1020	595	475	430	395	365	0.2	0.8	1.0	3.5	4-V
[M],[S]	AE44A	44 Rem. Magnum	240	15.55	Jacketed Hollow Point	150	1180	1130	1080	1050	1010	740	675	625	580	550	0.2	0.9	2.0	3.7	6½-V

AMERICAN EAGLE® RIMFIRE

Usage Key: = Varmints, predators, small game   = Medium game   = Large, heavy game   = Dangerous game   = Target shooting, training, practice

USAGE	FEDERAL LOAD NO.	CARTRIDGES PER BOX	CALIBER	BULLET WGT. IN GRAINS	BULLET STYLE*	VELOCITY IN FEET PER SECOND (TO NEAREST 10 FPS) MUZZLE	50 YDS.	100 YDS.	150 YDS.	ENERGY IN FOOT-POUNDS (TO NEAREST 5 FOOT-POUNDS) MUZZLE	50 YDS.	100 YDS.	150 YDS.	WIND DRIFT IN INCHES 10 MPH CROSSWIND 50 YDS.	100 YDS.	150 YDS.	HEIGHT OF BULLET TRAJECTORY IN INCHES ABOVE OR BELOW LINE OF SIGHT IF ZEROED AT ⊕ YARDS. SIGHTS 1.5 INCHES ABOVE BORE LINE. 50 YDS.	100 YDS.	150 YDS.	50 YDS.	100 YDS.	150 YDS.
[V],[T]	AE22	40	22 Long Rifle High Velocity	38	HP Copper-Plated	1280	1120	1020	950	140	105	90	75	1.6	5.8	12.1	⊕	-6.3	-20.6	+2.7	⊕	-10.6
[V],[T]	AE5022	50	22 Long Rifle High Velocity	40	Solid	1260	1100	1020	940	140	110	90	80	1.5	5.5	11.4	⊕	-6.5	-21.0	+2.7	⊕	-10.8

*Hollow Point

HORNADY BALLISTICS

BALLISTICS INFORMATION

STANDARD AMMO	MUZZLE VELOCITY	VELOCITY FEET PER SECOND					ENERGY FOOT - POUNDS						TRAJECTORY TABLES				
RIFLE CALIBER	Muzzle	100 yds.	200 yds.	300 yds.	400 yds.	500 yds.	Muzzle	100 yds.	200 yds.	300 yds.	400 yds.	500 yds.	100 yds.	200 yds.	300 yds.	400 yds.	500 yds.
223 Rem., 53 gr. HP	3330	2882	2477	2106	1710	1475	1305	978	722	522	369	356	+1.7	-0-	-7.4	-22.7	-49.1
223 Rem., 60 gr. SP	3150	2782	2442	2127	1837	1575	1322	1031	795	603	450	331	+1.6	-0-	-7.5	-22.5	-48.1
22-250 Rem., 53 gr. HP	3680	3185	2743	2341	1974	1646	1594	1194	886	645	459	319	+1.0	-0-	-5.7	-17.8	-38.8
22-250 Rem., 60 gr. SP	3600	3195	2826	2485	2169	1878	1727	1360	1064	823	627	470	+1.0	-0-	-5.4	-16.3	-34.8
220 Swift, 50 gr. SP	3850	3327	2862	2442	2060	1716	1645	1228	909	662	471	327	+0.8	-0-	-5.1	-16.1	-35.3
220 Swift, 60 gr. HP	3600	3199	2824	2475	2156	1868	1727	1364	1063	816	619	465	+1.0	-0-	-5.4	-16.3	-34.8
243 Win., 75 gr. HP	3400	2970	2578	2219	1890	1595	1926	1469	1107	820	595	425	+1.2	-0-	-6.5	-20.3	-43.8
243 Win., 100 gr. BTSP	2960	2728	2508	2299	2099	1910	1945	1653	1397	1174	979	810	+1.6	-0-	-7.2	-21.0	-42.8
6MM Rem., 100 gr. BTSP	3100	2861	2634	2419	2231	2018	2134	1818	1541	1300	1088	904	+1.3	-0-	-6.5	-18.9	-38.5
257 Roberts, 117 gr. BTSP	2780	2550	2331	2122	1925	1740	2007	1689	1411	1170	963	787	+1.9	-0-	-8.3	-24.4	-49.9
25-06 117 gr. BTSP	2990	2749	2520	2302	2096	1900	2322	1962	1649	1377	1141	938	+1.6	-0-	-7.0	-20.7	-42.2
270 Win., 130 gr. SP	3060	2800	2560	2330	2110	1900	2700	2265	1890	1565	1285	1045	+1.8	-0-	-7.1	-20.6	-42.0
270 Win., 140 gr. BTSP	2940	2747	2562	2385	2214	2050	2688	2346	2041	1769	1524	1307	+1.6	-0-	-7.0	-20.2	-40.3
270 Win., 150 gr. SP	2800	2684	2478	2284	2100	1927	2802	2400	2046	1737	1469	1237	+1.7	-0-	-7.4	-21.6	-43.9
7 x 57 Mau., 139 gr. BTSP	2700	2504	2316	2137	1965	1802	2251	1936	1656	1410	1192	1002	+2.0	-0-	-8.5	-24.9	-50.3
7MM Rem. Mag., 139 gr. BTSP	3150	2933	2727	2530	2341	2160	3063	2656	2296	1976	1692	1440	+1.2	-0-	-6.1	-17.7	-35.5
7MM Rem. Mag., 154 gr. SP	3035	2814	2604	2404	2212	2029	3151	2708	2319	1977	1674	1408	+1.3	-0-	-6.7	-19.3	-39.3
7MM Rem. Mag., 162 gr. BTSP	2940	2757	2582	2413	2251	2094	3110	2735	2399	2095	1823	1578	+1.6	-0-	-6.7	-19.7	-39.3
7MM Rem. Mag., 175 gr. SP	2860	2650	2440	2240	2060	1880	3180	2720	2310	1960	1640	1370	+2.0	-0-	-7.9	-22.7	-45.8
7MM Wby. Mag., 154 gr. SP	3200	2971	2753	2546	2348	2159	3501	3017	2592	2216	1885	1593	+1.2	-0-	-5.8	-17.0	-34.5
7MM Wby. Mag., 175 gr. SP	2910	2709	2516	2331	2154	1985	3290	2850	2459	2111	1803	1531	+1.6	-0-	-7.1	-20.6	-41.7
30-30 Win., 150 gr. RN	2390	1973	1605	1303	1095	974	1902	1296	858	565	399	316	-0-	-8.2	-30.0		
30-30 Win., 170 gr. FP	2200	1895	1619	1381	1191	1064	1827	1355	989	720	535	425	-0-	-8.9	-31.1		
308 Win., 150 gr. BTSP	2820	2560	2315	2084	1866	1644	2648	2183	1785	1447	1160	922	+2.0	-0-	-8.5	-25.2	-51.8
308 Win., 165 gr. BTSP	2700	2496	2301	2115	1937	1770	2670	2283	1940	1639	1375	1148	+2.0	-0-	-8.7	-25.2	-51.0
308 Win., 168 gr. BTHP MATCH	2700	2524	2354	2191	2035	1885	2720	2377	2068	1791	1545	1326	+2.0	-0-	-8.4	-23.9	-48.0
30-06 150 gr. SP	2910	2617	2342	2083	1843	1622	2820	2281	1827	1445	1131	876	+2.1	-0-	-8.5	-25.0	-51.8
30-06 150 gr. BTSP	2910	2683	2467	2262	2066	1880	2820	2397	2027	1706	1421	1177	+2.0	-0-	-7.7	-22.2	-44.9
30-06 165 gr. BTSP	2800	2591	2392	2202	2020	1848	2873	2460	2097	1777	1495	1252	+1.8	-0-	-8.0	-23.3	-47.0
30-06 168 gr. BTHP MATCH	2790	2620	2447	2280	2120	1966	2925	2561	2234	1940	1677	1442	+1.7	-0-	-7.7	-22.2	-44.3
30-06 180 gr. SP	2700	2469	2258	2042	1846	1663	2913	2436	2023	1666	1362	1105	+2.4	-0-	-9.3	-27.0	-54.9
300 Wby. Mag., 180 gr. SP	3120	2891	2673	2466	2268	2079	3890	3340	2856	2430	2055	1727	+1.3	-0-	-6.2	-18.1	-36.8
300 Win. Mag., 150 gr. BTSP	3275	2988	2718	2464	2224	1998	3573	2974	2461	2023	1648	1330	+1.2	-0-	-6.0	-17.8	-36.5
300 Win. Mag., 165 gr. BTSP	3100	2877	2665	2462	2269	2084	3522	3033	2603	2221	1887	1592	+1.3	-0-	-6.5	-18.5	-37.3
300 Win. Mag., 180 gr. SP	2960	2745	2540	2344	2157	1979	3501	3011	2578	2196	1859	1565	+1.9	-0-	-7.3	-20.9	-41.9
300 Win. Mag., 190 gr. BTSP	2900	2711	2529	2355	2187	2026	3549	3101	2699	2340	2018	1732	+1.6	-0-	-7.1	-20.4	-41.0
303 British, 150 gr. SP	2685	2441	2210	1992	1787	1598	2401	1984	1627	1321	1064	500	+2.2	-0-	-9.3	-27.4	-56.5
303 British, 174 gr. RN	2500	2181	1886	1669	1387	1201	2414	1837	1374	1012	743	557	+2.9	-0-	-12.8	-39.0	-83.4

LIGHT MAGNUM™	MUZZLE VELOCITY	VELOCITY FEET PER SECOND					ENERGY FOOT - POUNDS						TRAJECTORY TABLES				
RIFLE CALIBER	Muzzle	100 yds.	200 yds.	300 yds.	400 yds.	500 yds.	Muzzle	100 yds.	200 yds.	300 yds.	400 yds.	500 yds.	100 yds.	200 yds.	300 yds.	400 yds.	500 yds.
243 Win., 100 gr. SP LM	3100	2839	2592	2358	2138	1936	2133	1790	1491	1235	1014	832	+1.5	-0-	-6.81	-19.8	-40.2
257 Roberts, 117 gr. BTSP LM	2940	2694	2460	2240	2031	1844	2245	1885	1572	1303	1071	883	+1.7	-0-	-7.6	-21.8	-44.7
7 x 57 Mau., 139 gr. BTSP LM	2830	2620	2450	2250	2070	1910	2475	2135	1835	1565	1330	1115	+1.8	-0-	-7.6	-22.1	-45.0
7MM-08, 139 gr. BTSP LM	3000	2790	2590	2399	2216	2041	2777	2403	2071	1776	1515	1285	+1.5	-0-	-6.7	-19.4	-39.2
308 Win., 150 gr. SP LM	2980	2703	2442	2195	1964	1748	2959	2433	1986	1606	1285	1018	+1.6	-0-	-7.5	-22.2	-46.0
308 Win., 165 gr. BTSP LM	2870	2658	2456	2263	2078	1903	3019	2589	2211	1877	1583	1327	+1.7	-0-	-7.5	-21.8	-44.1
30-06 150 gr. SP LM	3100	2815	2548	2295	2058	1835	3200	2639	2161	1755	1410	1121	+1.4	-0-	-6.8	-20.3	-42.0
30-06 180 gr. BTSP LM	2880	2676	2480	2293	2114	1943	3316	2862	2459	2102	1786	1509	+1.7	-0-	-7.3	-21.3	-43.1
303 British, 150 gr. SP LM	2830	2570	2325	2094	1884	1690	2667	2199	1800	1461	1185	952	+2.0	-0-	-8.4	-24.6	-50.3
6.5 x 55MM, 129 gr. SP LM	2770	2561	2361	2171	1994	1830	2197	1878	1597	1350	1138	959	1.98	-0-	-8.25	-23.16	-47.95
270 Win., 140 gr. BTSP LM	3100	2894	2697	2508	2327	2155	2987	2604	2261	1955	1684	1443	1.37	-0-	-6.32	-18.30	-36.61
308 Win., 168 gr. BTHP LM MATCH	2840	2630	2429	2238	2056	1892	3008	2579	2201	1868	1577	1335	1.84	-0-	-7.83	-22.38	-45.23
308 Win., 180 gr. BTHP LM MATCH	2750	2564	2386	2215	2052	1904	3022	2627	2275	1961	1683	1449	1.98	-0-	-8.15	-23.13	-46.45
300 Win. Mag., 180 gr. BTSP HM	3100	2879	2668	2467	2275	2092	3840	3313	2845	2431	2068	1749	1.39	-0-	-6.45	-18.72	-37.51
338 Win. Mag., 225 gr. SP HM	2920	2678	2449	2232	2027	1843	4259	3583	2996	2489	2053	1697	1.75	-0-	-7.65	-22.01	-45.05

BARREL LENGTH	PISTOL AMMO	MUZZLE VELOCITY	VELOCITY FT. PER SECOND		ENERGY			BARREL LENGTH	PISTOL AMMO	MUZZLE VELOCITY	VELOCITY FT. PER SECOND		ENERGY		
	Caliber	Muzzle	50 yds.	100 yds.	Muzzle	50 yds.	100 yds.		Caliber	Muzzle	50 yds.	100 yds.	Muzzle	50 yds.	100 yds.
2"	25 Auto, 35 gr. JHP/XTP	900	813	742	63	51	43	5"	10MM Auto, 155 gr. JHP/XTP	1265	1119	1020	551	431	358
4"	32 Auto, 71 gr. FMJ	900	845	797	128	112	100	5"	10MM Auto, 180 gr. JHP/XTP Full	1180	1077	1004	556	464	403
3 ³/₄"	380 Auto, 90 gr. JHP/XTP	1000	902	823	200	163	135	5"	10MM Auto, 200 gr. JHP/XTP	1050	994	948	490	439	399
4"	9MM Luger, 90 gr. JHP/XTP	1360	1112	978	370	247	191	4"	40 S&W, 155 gr. JHP/XTP	1180	1061	980	479	388	331
4"	9MM Luger, 115 gr. JHP/XTP	1155	1047	971	341	280	241	4"	40 S&W, 180 gr. JHP/XTP	950	903	862	361	326	297
4"	9MM Luger, 115 gr. FMJ V	1155	1047	971	341	280	241	7 ¹/₂" V	44 Special, 180 gr. JHP/XTP	1000	935	882	400	350	311
4"	9MM Luger, 124 gr. JHP/XTP	1110	1030	971	339	292	259	7 ¹/₂" V	44 Rem. Mag., 180 gr. JHP/XTP	1550	1340	1173	960	717	550
4"	9MM Luger, 147 gr. JHP/XTP	975	935	899	310	285	264	7 ¹/₂" V	44 Rem. Mag., 200 gr. JHP/XTP	1500	1284	1128	999	732	565
4"	9 x 18 Makarov, 95 gr. JHP/XTP	1000	930	874	211	182	161	7 ¹/₂" V	44 Rem. Mag., 240 gr. JHP/XTP	1350	1188	1078	971	753	619
4"V	38 Special, 125 gr. JHP/XTP	900	856	817	225	203	185	7 ¹/₂" V	44 Rem. Mag., 300 gr. JHP/XTP	1150	1084	1031	881	782	708
4"V	38 Special, 140 gr. JHP/XTP	900	850	806	252	225	202	5"	45 ACP, 185 gr. JHP/XTP	950	880	819	371	318	276
4"V	38 Special, 148 gr. HBWC	800	697	610	210	160	122	5"	45 ACP, 200 gr. JHP/XTP	900	938	885	444	391	348
4"V	38 Special, 158 gr. JHP/XTP	800	765	731	225	205	188	5"	45 ACP+P, 200 gr. JHP/XTP	1055	982	925	494	428	380
8"V	357 Mag., 125 gr. JHP/XTP	1500	1314	1166	624	479	377	5"	45 ACP+P, 230 gr. HP/XTP	950	904	865	462	418	382
8"V	357 Mag., 125 gr. JFP/XTP	1500	1311	1161	624	477	374	5"	45 ACP, 230 gr. FMJ/RN	850	809	771	369	334	304
8"V	357 Mag., 140 gr. JHP/XTP	1400	1249	1130	609	485	397	5"	45 ACP, 230 gr. FMJ/FP	850	809	771	369	334	304
8"V	357 Mag., 158 gr. JHP/XTP	1250	1150	1073	548	464	404								
8"V	357 Mag., 158 gr. JFP	1250	1147	1068	548	461	400								

REMINGTON BALLISTICS

HANDGUN

Caliber	Order No.	Primer No.	Weight (grs.)	Bullet Style	Velocity (ft./sec.) Muzzle	Velocity 50 yds.	Velocity 100 yds.	Energy (ft.-lbs.) Muzzle	Energy 50 yds.	Energy 100 yds.	Mid-range Trajectory 50 yds.	Mid-range Trajectory 100 yds.	B.L.
.221 REM. FIREBALL	R221F	7½	50	Pointed Soft Point	2650	2380	2130	780	630	505	0.2"	0.8"	10"
.25 (6.35MM) AUTO. PISTOL	R25AP	1½	50	Metal Case	760	707	659	64	56	48	2.0"	8.7"	2"
6MM BR REM.	R6MMBR	7½	100	Pointed Soft Point	Refer to Remington CF Ballistics Charts								
7MM BR REM.	R7MMBR	7½	140	Pointed Soft Point	Refer to Remington CF Ballistics Charts								
.32 S. & W.	R32SW	1½	88	Lead	680	645	610	90	81	73	2.5"	0.5"	3"
.32 S. & W. LONG	R32SWL	1½	98	Lead	705	670	635	115	98	88	2.3"	10.5"	4"
.32 (7.65MM) AUTO. PISTOL	R32AP	1½	71	Metal Case	905	855	810	129	115	97	1.4"	5.8"	4"
.357 MAG. Vented Barrel Ballistics	R357M7	5½	110	Semi-Jacketed H.P.	1295	1094	975	410	292	232	0.8"	3.5"	4"
	R357M1 ★	5½	125	Semi-Jacketed H.P.	1450	1240	1090	583	427	330	0.6"	2.8"	4"
	GS357MA	5½	125	Brass-Jacketed Hollow Point	1220	1095	1009	413	333	283	0.8"	3.5"	4"
	RH357MA	5½	165	JHP Core-Lokt®	1290	1189	1108	610	518	450	0.7"	3.1"	8⅜"
	LL357MB	5½	130	TEMC, Lead-Lokt™	1400	1239	1116	566	443	360	0.6"	2.8"	4"
Refer to Remington CF Ballistics Charts for test details	LL357MD ★	5½	158	TEMC, Lead-Lokt™	1200	1081	999	505	410	350	0.9"	4.0"	4"
	R357M2	5½	158	Semi-Jacketed H.P.	1235	1104	1015	535	428	361	0.8"	3.5"	4"
	R357M3	5½	158	Soft Point	1235	1104	1015	535	428	361	0.8"	3.5"	4"
	R357M5	5½	158	Semi-Wadcutter	1235	1104	1015	535	428	361	0.8"	3.5"	4"
	R357M9	5½	140	Semi-Jacketed H.P.	1360	1195	1076	575	444	360	0.7"	3.0"	4"
	R357M10	5½	180	Semi-Jacketed H.P.	1145	1053	985	524	443	388	0.9"	3.9"	8⅜"
	R357M11§	5½	125	Semi-Jacketed H.P. (Med. Vel.)	1220	1077	984	413	322	269	0.8"	3.7"	4"
.357 REM. MAXIMUM*	357MX1	7½	158	Semi-Jacketed H.P.	1825	1588	1381	1168	885	669	0.4"	1.7"	10"
.357 SIG.	R357S1	5½	125	Jacketed H.P.	1350	1191	1076	506	394	321	0.7"	3.0"	4"
9MM LUGER AUTO. PISTOL	R9MM1	1½	115	Jacketed H.P.	1155	1047	971	341	280	241	0.9"	3.9"	4"
	R9MM10	1½	124	Jacketed H.P.	1120	1028	960	346	291	254	1.0"	4.1"	4"
	R9MM2	1½	124	Metal Case	1110	1030	971	339	292	259	1.0"	4.1"	4"
	R9MM3	1½	115	Metal Case	1135	1041	973	329	277	242	0.9"	4.0"	4"
	R9MM6	1½	115	Jacketed H.P. (+P)‡	1250	1113	1019	399	316	265	0.8"	3.5"	4"
	R9MM8	1½	147	Jacketed H.P. (Subsonic)	990	941	900	320	289	264	1.1"	4.9"	4"
	R9MM9	1½	147	Metal Case (Match)	990	941	900	320	289	264	1.1"	4.9"	4"
	LL9MMA	1½	115	TEMC, Lead-Lokt™	1135	1041	973	329	277	242	0.9"	4.0"	4"
	LL9MMB ★	1½	124	TEMC, Lead-Lokt™	1110	1030	971	339	292	259	1.0"	4.1"	4"
	LL9MC	1½	147	TEMC, Lead-Lokt™	990	941	900	320	289	264	1.1"	4.9"	4"
	GS9MMB	1½	124	Brass-Jacketed Hollow Point	1125	1031	963	349	293	255	1.0"	4.0"	4"
	GS9MMC	1½	147	Brass-Jacketed Hollow Point	990	941	900	320	289	264	1.1"	4.9"	4"
	GS9MMD	1½	124	Brass-Jacketed Hollow Point (+P)‡	1180	1089	1021	384	327	287	0.8"	3.8"	4"
.380 AUTO. PISTOL	R380AP	1½	95	Metal Case	955	865	785	190	160	130	1.4"	5.9"	4"
	R380A1	1½	88	Jacketed H.P.	990	920	868	191	165	146	1.2"	5.1"	4"
	GS380B	1½	102	Brass-Jacketed Hollow Point	940	901	866	200	184	170	1.2"	5.1"	4"
	LL380B ★	1½	95	TEMC, Lead-Lokt™	955	865	785	190	160	130	1.4"	5.9"	4"
.38 SUPER AUTO. COLT PISTOL (A)	R38SU1	1½	115	Jacketed H.P. (+P)‡	1300	1147	1041	431	336	277	0.7"	3.3"	5"
.38 S. & W.	R38SW	1½	146	Lead	685	650	620	150	135	125	2.4"	10.0"	4"
.38 SPECIAL Vented Barrel Ballistics	R38S10	1½	110	Semi-Jacketed H.P. (+P)‡	995	926	871	242	210	185	1.2"	5.1"	4"
	R38S16	1½	110	Semi-Jacketed H.P.	950	890	840	220	194	172	1.4"	5.4"	4"
	R38S2	1½	125	Semi-Jacketed H.P. (+P)‡	945	898	858	248	224	204	1.3"	5.4"	4"
	LL38SB	1½	130	TEMC, Lead-Lokt™	950	901	859	261	235	213	1.4"	5.0"	4"
	LL38SD ★	1½	158	TEMC, Lead-Lokt™	755	723	692	200	183	168	2.0"	8.3"	4"
	GS38SB	1½	125	Brass-Jacketed Hollow Point (+P)	975	929	885	264	238	218	1.0"	5.2"	4"
	R38S3	1½	148	Targetmaster Lead W.C. Match	710	634	566	166	132	105	2.4"	10.8"	4"
	R38S4	1½	158	Targetmaster Lead	755	723	692	200	183	168	2.0"	8.3"	4"
	R38S5	1½	158	Lead (Round Nose)	755	723	692	200	183	168	2.0"	8.3"	4"
	R38S14	1½	158	Semi-Wadcutter (+P)‡	890	855	823	278	257	238	1.4"	6.0"	4"
	R38S6	1½	158	Semi-Wadcutter	755	723	692	200	183	168	2.0"	8.3"	4"
	R38S12	1½	158	Lead H.P. (+P)‡	890	855	823	278	257	238	1.4"	6.0"	4"
.38 SHORT COLT	R38SC	1½	125	Lead	730	685	645	150	130	115	2.2"	9.4"	6"
.40 S. & W.	R40SW1	5½	155	Jacketed H.P.	1205	1095	1017	499	413	356	0.8"	3.6"	4"
	R40SW2	5½	180	Jacketed H.P.	1015	960	914	412	368	334	1.3"	4.5"	4"
	LL40SWB	5½	180	TEMC, Lead-Lokt™	985	936	893	388	350	319	1.4"	5.0"	4"
	GS40SWA	5½	165	Brass-Jacketed Hollow Point	1150	1040	964	485	396	340	1.0"	4.0"	4"
	GS40SWB	5½	180	Brass-Jacketed Hollow Point	1015	960	914	412	368	334	1.3"	4.5"	4"
10MM AUTO.	R10MM3	2½	180	Jacketed H. P. (Subsonic)	1055	997	951	445	397	361	1.0"	4.6"	5"
	R10MM4	2½	180	Jacketed H. P. (High Vel.)	1160	1079	1017	538	465	413	0.9"	3.8"	5"
.41 REM. MAG. Vented Barrel Ballistics	R41MG1	2½	210	Soft Point	1300	1162	1062	788	630	526	0.7"	3.2"	4"
	R41MG2§	2½	210	Lead	965	898	842	434	376	331	1.3"	5.4"	4"
	R41MG3	2½	170	Semi-Jacketed H.P.	1420	1166	1014	761	513	388	0.7"	3.2"	4"
.44 REM. MAG. Vented Barrel Ballistics	R44MG5	2½	180	Semi-Jacketed H.P.	1610	1365	1175	1036	745	551	0.5"	2.3"	4"
	R44MG2	2½	240	Soft Point	1180	1081	1010	741	623	543	0.9"	3.7"	4"
	R44MG3	2½	240	Semi-Jacketed H.P.	1180	1081	1010	741	623	543	0.9"	3.7"	4"
	R44MG4§	2½	240	Lead (Med. Vel.)	1000	947	902	533	477	433	1.1"	4.8"	6½"
	R44MG6	2½	210	Semi-Jacketed H.P.	1495	1312	1167	1042	803	634	0.6"	2.5"	6½"
	RH44MGA	2½	275	JHP Core-Lokt®	1235	1142	1070	931	797	699	0.8"	3.3"	6½"
.44 S. & W. SPECIAL	R44SW	2½	246	Lead	755	725	695	310	285	265	2.0"	8.3"	6"
	R44SW1	2½	200	Semi-Wadcutter	1035	938	866	476	391	333	1.1"	4.9"	6"
.45 COLT	R45C	2½	250	Lead	860	820	780	410	375	340	1.6"	6.6"	5"
	R45C1	2½	225	Semi-Wadcutter (Keith)	960	890	832	460	395	346	1.3"	5.5"	5"
.45 AUTO.	R45AP1	2½	185	Targetmaster M.C. W.C. Match	770	707	650	244	205	174	2.0"	8.7"	5"
	R45AP2	2½	185	Jacketed H.P.	1000	939	889	411	362	324	1.1"	4.9"	5"
	R45AP4	2½	230	Metal Case	835	800	767	356	326	300	1.6"	6.8"	5"
	R45AP6	2½	185	Jacketed H.P. (+P)‡	1140	1040	971	534	445	387	0.9"	4.0"	5"
	R45AP7 ★	2½	230	Jacketed H.P. (Subsonic)	835	800	767	356	326	300	1.6"	6.8"	5"
	LL45APB	2½	230	TEMC, Lead-Lokt™	835	800	767	356	326	300	1.6"	6.8"	5"
	GS45APA	2½	185	Brass-Jacketed Hollow Point	1015	951	899	423	372	332	1.1"	4.5"	5"
	GS45APB	2½	230	Brass-Jacketed Hollow Point	875	833	795	391	355	323	1.5"	6.1"	5"
	GS45APC ★	2½	185	Brass-Jacketed Hollow Point (+P)	1140	1042	971	534	446	388	1.0"	4.0"	5"

*Will not chamber in 357 Mag. or 38 Special handguns. ‡Ammunition with (+P) on the case headstamp is loaded to higher pressure. Use only in firearms designated for this cartridge and so recommended by the gun manufacturer. §Subject to stock on hand. (A)Adapted only for 38 Colt Super and Colt Commander automatic pistols. Not for use in sporting, military and pocket models.

★ NEW

REMINGTON BALLISTICS

CENTERFIRE RIFLE BALLISTICS

These tables were calculated by computer. A standard scientific technique was used to predict trajectories from the best available data for each round. Trajectories shown typify the ammunition's performance at sea level, but note that they may vary due to atmospheric conditions, and the equipment.

All velocity and energy figures in these charts have been derived by using test barrels of indicated lengths.

Ballistics shown are for 24″ barrels, except those for 30 carbine, 350 Rem. Mag. and .44 Rem. Mag., which are for 20″ barrels, and the 6mm BR Remington and 7mm BR Remington which have a 15″ barrel. These barrel lengths were chosen as representative, as it's impractical to show performance figures for all barrel lengths.

The muzzle velocities, muzzle energies and trajectory data in these tables represent the approximate performance expected of each specified loading. Differences in barrel lengths, internal firearm dimensions, temperature and test procedures can produce actual velocities that vary from those given here.

Specifications are nominal. Ballistics figures established in test barrels. Individual rifles may vary from test-barrel specifications.

* Inches above or below line of sight. Hold low for positive numbers, high for negative numbers.

† 280 Rem. and 7mm Express Rem. are interchangeable.

‡ Interchangeable in 244 Rem.

§ Subject to stock on hand

[1] Bullet does not rise more than 1″ above line of sight from muzzle to sighting in range.

[2] Bullet does not rise more than 3″ above line of sight from muzzle to sighting in range.

Note: 0.0 indicates yardage at which rifle was sighted in.

Caliber	Order No.	Wt. (grs.)	Bullet Style	Primer No.	Muzzle	100 yds.	200 yds.	300 yds.	400 yds.	500 yds.
.17 Remington	R17REM	25	Hollow Point Power-Lokt*	7 ½	4040	3284	2644	2086	1606	1235
.22 Hornet	R22HN1	45	Pointed Soft Point	6 ½	2690	2042	1502	1128	948	840
	R22HN2	45	Hollow Point	6 ½	2690	2042	1502	1128	948	840
.220 Swift	R220S1	50	Pointed Soft Point	9 ½	3780	3158	2617	2135	1710	1357
.222 Remington	R222R1	50	Pointed Soft Point	7 ½	3140	2602	2123	1700	1350	1107
	R222R3	50	Hollow Point Power-Lokt*	7 ½	3140	2635	2182	1777	1432	1172
.222 Remington Mag.	R222M1	55	Pointed Soft Point	7 ½	3240	2748	2305	1906	1556	1272
.223 Remington	R223R1	55	Pointed Soft Point	7 ½	3240	2747	2304	1905	1554	1270
	R223R2	55	Hollow Point Power-Lokt*	7 ½	3240	2773	2352	1969	1627	1341
	R223R3	55	Metal Case	7 ½	3240	2759	2326	1933	1587	1301
	R223R4	60	Hollow Point Match	7 ½	3100	2712	2355	2026	1726	1463
.22-250 Remington	R22501	55	Pointed Soft Point	9 ½	3680	3137	2656	2222	1832	1493
	R22502	55	Hollow Point Power-Lokt*	9 ½	3680	3209	2785	2400	2046	1725
.243 Win.	R243W1	80	Pointed Soft Point	9 ½	3350	2955	2593	2259	1951	1670
	R243W2	80	Hollow Point Power-Lokt*	9 ½	3350	2955	2593	2259	1951	1670
	R243W3	100	Pointed Soft Point Core-Lokt*	9 ½	2960	2697	2449	2215	1993	1786
	ER243WA	105	Extended Range	9 ½	2920	2689	2470	2261	2062	1874
6MM Remington	R6MM1	80	Pointed Soft Point	9 ½	3470	3064	2694	2352	2036	1747
	R6MM4	100	Pointed Soft Point Core-Lokt*	9 ½	3100	2829	2573	2332	2104	1889
	ER6MMRA§	105	Extended Range	9 ½	3060	2822	2596	2381	2177	1982
6MM BR Remington	R6MMBR§	100	Pointed Soft Point	7 ½	2550	2310	2083	1870	1671	1491
.25-20 Win.	R25202	86	Soft Point	6 ½	1460	1194	1030	931	858	797
.250 Savage	R250SV	100	Pointed Soft Point	9 ½	2820	2504	2210	1936	1684	1461
.257 Roberts	R257	117	Soft Point Core-Lokt*	9 ½	2650	2291	1961	1663	1404	1199
	ER257A§	122	Extended Range	9 ½	2600	2331	2078	1842	1625	1431
.25-06 Remington	R25062	100	Pointed Soft Point Core-Lokt*	9 ½	3230	2893	2580	2287	2014	1762
	R25063	120	Pointed Soft Point Core-Lokt*	9 ½	2990	2730	2484	2252	2032	1825
	ER2506A	122	Extended Range	9 ½	2930	2706	2492	2289	2095	1911
6.5x55 Swedish	R65SWE1	140	Pointed Soft Point Core-Lokt*	9 ½	2550	2353	2164	1984	1814	1654
.264 Win. Mag.	R264W2	140	Pointed Soft Point Core-Lokt*	9 ½M	3030	2782	2548	2326	2114	1914
.270 Win.	R270W1	100	Pointed Soft Point	9 ½	3320	2924	2561	2225	1916	1636
	R270W2	130	Pointed Soft Point Core-Lokt*	9 ½	3060	2776	2510	2259	2022	1801
	R270W3	130	Bronze Point	9 ½	3060	2802	2559	2329	2110	1904
	R270W4	150	Soft Point Core-Lokt*	9 ½	2850	2504	2183	1886	1618	1385
	RS270WA	140	Swift A-Frame™ PSP	9 ½	2925	2652	2394	2152	1923	1711
	ER270WB§	135	Extended Range	9 ½	3000	2780	2570	2369	2178	1995
	ER270WA	140	Extended Range Boat Tail	9 ½	2960	2749	2548	2355	2171	1995
7MM BR Remington	R7MMBR§	140	Pointed Soft Point	7 ½	2215	2012	1821	1643	1481	1336
7MM Mauser (7 x 57)	R7MSR1 ★	140	Pointed Soft Point Core-Lokt*	9 ½	2660	2435	2221	2018	1827	1648
7 x 64	R7X641	140	Pointed Soft Point Core-Lokt*	9 ½	2950	2714	2489	2276	2073	1881
	R7X642	175	Pointed Soft Point Core-Lokt*	9 ½	2650	2445	2248	2061	1883	1716
7MM-08 Remington	R7M081 ★	140	Pointed Soft Point Core-Lokt*	9 ½	2860	2625	2402	2189	1988	1798
	R7M083	120	Hollow Point	9 ½	3000	2725	2467	2223	1992	1778
	ER7M08A	154	Extended Range	9 ½	2715	2510	2315	2128	1950	1781
.280 Remington	R280R3 ★	140	Pointed Soft Point Core-Lokt*	9 ½	3000	2758	2528	2309	2102	1905
	R280R1	150	Pointed Soft Point Core-Lokt*	9 ½	2890	2624	2373	2135	1912	1705
	R280R2	165	Soft Point Core-Lokt*	9 ½	2820	2510	2220	1950	1701	1479
	ER280RA	165	Extended Range	9 ½	2820	2623	2434	2253	2080	1915
7MM Remington Mag.	R7MM2	150	Pointed Soft Point Core-Lokt*	9 ½M	3110	2830	2568	2320	2085	1866
	R7MM3	175	Pointed Soft Point Core-Lokt*	9 ½M	2860	2645	2440	2244	2057	1879
	R7MM4 ★	140	Pointed Soft Point Core-Lokt*	9 ½M	3175	2923	2684	2458	2243	2039
	RS7MMA	160	Swift A-Frame™ PSP	9 ½M	2900	2659	2430	2212	2006	1812
	ER7MMA	165	Extended Range	9 ½M	2900	2699	2507	2324	2147	1979
7MM Wby. Mag.	R7MWB1§	140	Pointed Soft Point	9 ½M	3225	2970	2729	2501	2283	2077
	R7MWB2	175	Pointed Soft Point Core-Lokt*	9 ½M	2910	2693	2486	2288	2098	1918
	ER7MWBA§	165	Extended Range	9 ½M	2950	2747	2553	2367	2189	2019
.30 Carbine	R30CAR	110	Soft Point	6 ½	1990	1567	1236	1035	923	842
.30 Remington	R30REM	170	Soft Point Core-Lokt*	9 ½	2120	1822	1555	1328	1153	1036
.30-30 Win. Accelerator*	R3030A	55	Soft Point	9 ½	3400	2693	2085	1570	1187	986
.30-30 Win.	R30301	150	Soft Point Core-Lokt*	9 ½	2390	1973	1605	1303	1095	974
	R30302	170	Soft Point Core-Lokt*	9 ½	2200	1895	1619	1381	1191	1061
	R30303	170	Hollow Point Core-Lokt*	9 ½	2200	1895	1619	1381	1191	1061
	ER3030A	160	Extended Range	9 ½	2300	1997	1719	1473	1268	1116
.300 Savage	R30SV3	180	Soft Point Core-Lokt*	9 ½	2350	2025	1728	1467	1252	1098
	R30SV2	150	Pointed Soft Point Core-Lokt*	9 ½	2630	2354	2095	1853	1631	1432

★ NEW

Muzzle	100 yds.	200 yds.	300 yds.	400 yds.	500 yds.	50 yds.	100 yds.	150 yds.	200 yds.	250 yds.	300 yds.	100 yds.	150 yds.	200 yds.	250 yds.	300 yds.	400 yds.	500 yds.	Barrel Length
		Energy (ft.-lbs.)						Short-range[1] Trajectory*						Long-range[2] Trajectory*					
906	599	388	242	143	85	0.1	0.5	0.0	-1.5	-4.2	-8.5	2.1	2.5	1.9	0.0	-3.4	-17.0	-44.3	24"
723	417	225	127	90	70	0.3	0.0	-2.4	-7.7	-16.9	-31.3	1.6	0.0	-4.5	-12.8	-26.4	-75.6	-163.4	24"
723	417	225	127	90	70	0.3	0.0	-2.4	-7.7	-16.9	-31.3	1.6	0.0	-4.5	-12.8	-26.4	-75.6	-163.4	
1586	1107	760	506	325	204	0.2	0.5	0.0	-1.6	-4.4	-8.8	1.3	1.2	0.0	-2.5	-6.5	-20.7	-47.0	24"
1094	752	500	321	202	136	0.5	0.9	0.0	-2.5	-6.9	-13.7	2.2	1.9	0.0	-3.8	-10.0	-32.3	-73.8	24"
1094	771	529	351	228	152	0.5	0.9	0.0	-2.4	-6.6	-13.1	2.1	1.8	0.0	-3.6	-9.5	-30.2	-68.1	
1282	922	649	444	296	198	0.4	0.8	0.0	-2.2	-6.0	-11.8	1.9	1.6	0.0	-3.3	-8.5	-26.7	-59.5	24"
1282	921	648	443	295	197	0.4	0.8	0.0	-2.2	-6.0	-11.8	1.9	1.6	0.0	-3.3	-8.5	-26.7	-59.6	
1282	939	675	473	323	220	0.4	0.8	0.0	-2.1	-5.8	-11.4	1.8	1.6	0.0	-3.2	-8.2	-25.5	-56.0	24"
1282	929	660	456	307	207	0.4	0.8	0.0	-2.1	-5.9	-11.6	1.9	1.6	0.0	-3.2	-8.4	-26.2	-57.9	
1280	979	739	547	397	285	0.5	0.8	0.0	-2.2	-6.0	-11.5	1.9	1.6	0.0	-3.2	-8.3	-25.1	-53.6	
1654	1201	861	603	410	272	0.2	0.5	0.0	-1.6	-4.4	-8.7	2.3	2.6	1.9	0.0	-3.4	-15.9	-38.9	24"
1654	1257	947	703	511	363	0.2	0.5	0.0	-1.5	-4.1	-8.0	2.1	2.5	1.8	0.0	-3.1	-14.1	-33.4	
1993	1551	1194	906	676	495	0.3	0.7	0.0	-1.8	-4.9	-9.4	2.6	2.9	2.1	0.0	-3.6	-16.2	-37.9	
1993	1551	1194	906	676	495	0.3	0.7	0.0	-1.8	-4.9	-9.4	2.6	2.9	2.1	0.0	-3.6	-16.2	-37.9	24"
1945	1615	1332	1089	882	708	0.5	0.9	0.0	-2.2	-5.8	-11.0	1.9	1.6	0.0	-3.1	-7.8	-22.6	-46.3	
1988	1686	1422	1192	992	819	0.5	0.9	0.0	-2.2	-5.8	-11.0	2.0	1.6	0.0	-3.1	-7.7	-22.2	-44.8	
2139	1667	1289	982	736	542	0.3	0.6	0.0	-1.6	-4.5	-8.7	2.4	2.7	1.9	0.0	-3.3	-14.9	-35.0	24"
2133	1777	1470	1207	983	792	0.4	0.8	0.0	-1.9	-5.2	-9.9	1.7	1.5	0.0	-2.8	-7.0	-20.4	-41.7	
2183	1856	1571	1322	1105	916	0.4	0.8	0.0	-2.0	-5.2	-9.8	1.7	1.5	0.0	-2.7	-6.9	-20.0	-40.4	
1444	1185	963	776	620	494	0.3	0.0	-1.9	-5.6	-11.4	-19.3	2.8	2.3	0.0	-4.3	-10.9	-31.7	-65.1	15"
407	272	203	165	141	121	0.0	-4.1	-14.4	-31.8	-57.3	-92.0	0.0	-8.2	-23.5	-47.0	-79.6	-175.9	-319.4	24"
1765	1392	1084	832	630	474	0.2	0.0	-1.6	-4.7	-9.6	-16.5	2.3	2.0	0.0	-3.7	-9.5	-28.3	-59.5	24"
1824	1363	999	718	512	373	0.3	0.0	-1.9	-5.8	-11.9	-20.7	2.9	2.4	0.0	-4.7	-12.0	-36.7	-79.2	24"
1831	1472	1170	919	715	555	0.3	0.0	-1.9	-5.5	-11.2	-19.1	2.8	2.3	0.0	-4.3	-10.9	-32.0	-66.4	
2316	1858	1478	1161	901	689	0.4	0.7	0.0	-1.9	-5.0	-9.7	1.6	1.4	0.0	-2.7	-6.9	-20.5	-42.7	
2382	1985	1644	1351	1100	887	0.5	0.8	0.0	-2.1	-5.6	-10.7	1.9	1.6	0.0	-3.0	-7.5	-22.0	-44.8	24"
2325	1983	1603	1419	1189	989	0.5	0.9	0.0	-2.2	-5.7	-10.8	1.9	1.6	0.0	-3.0	-7.5	-21.7	-43.9	
2021	1720	1456	1224	1023	850	0.3	0.0	-1.8	-5.4	-10.8	-18.2	2.7	2.2	0.0	-4.1	-10.1	-29.1	-58.7	24"
2854	2406	2018	1682	1389	1139	0.5	0.8	0.0	-2.0	-5.4	-10.2	1.8	1.5	0.0	-2.9	-7.2	-20.8	-42.2	24"
2448	1898	1456	1099	815	594	0.3	0.7	0.0	-1.8	-5.0	-9.7	2.7	3.0	2.2	0.0	-3.7	-16.6	-39.1	
2702	2225	1818	1472	1180	936	0.5	0.8	0.0	-2.0	-5.5	-10.4	1.8	1.5	0.0	-2.9	-7.4	-21.6	-44.3	
2702	2267	1890	1565	1285	1046	0.4	0.8	0.0	-2.0	-5.3	-10.1	1.8	1.5	0.0	-2.8	-7.1	-20.6	-42.0	24"
2705	2087	1587	1185	872	639	0.7	1.0	0.0	-2.6	-7.1	-13.6	2.3	2.0	0.0	-3.8	-9.7	-29.2	-62.2	
2659	2186	1782	1439	1150	910	0.6	0.9	0.0	-2.3	-6.0	-11.5	2.0	1.7	0.0	-3.2	-8.1	-23.8	-48.9	
2697	2315	1979	1682	1421	1193	0.5	0.8	0.0	-2.0	-5.3	-10.1	1.8	1.5	0.0	-2.8	-7.1	-20.4	-41.0	
2723	2349	2018	1724	1465	1237	0.5	0.8	0.0	-2.1	-5.5	-10.3	1.9	1.5	0.0	-2.9	-7.2	-20.7	-41.6	
1525	1259	1031	839	681	555	0.5	0.0	-2.7	-7.7	-15.4	-25.9	1.8	0.0	-4.1	-10.9	-20.6	-50.0	-95.2	15"
2199	1843	1533	1266	1037	844	0.2	0.0	-1.7	-5.0	-10.0	-17.0	2.5	2.0	0.0	-3.8	-9.6	-27.7	-56.3	24"
2705	2289	1926	1610	1336	1100	0.5	0.9	0.0	-2.1	-5.7	-10.7	1.9	1.6	0.0	-3.0	-7.6	-21.8	-44.2	24"
2728	2322	1964	1650	1378	1144	0.2	0.0	-1.7	-4.9	-9.9	-16.8	2.5	2.0	0.0	-3.9	-9.4	-26.9	-54.3	
2542	2142	1793	1490	1228	1005	0.6	0.9	0.0	-2.3	-6.1	-11.6	2.1	1.7	0.0	-3.2	-8.1	-23.5	-47.7	
2398	1979	1621	1316	1058	842	0.5	0.8	0.0	-2.1	-5.7	-10.8	1.9	1.6	0.0	-3.0	-7.6	-22.3	-45.8	24"
2520	2155	1832	1548	1300	1085	0.7	1.0	0.0	-2.5	-6.7	-12.6	2.3	1.9	0.0	-3.5	-8.8	-25.3	-51.0	
2797	2363	1986	1657	1373	1128	0.5	0.8	0.0	-2.1	-5.5	-10.4	1.8	1.5	0.0	-2.9	-7.3	-21.1	-42.9	
2781	2293	1875	1518	1217	968	0.6	0.9	0.0	-2.3	-6.2	-11.8	2.1	1.7	0.0	-3.3	-8.3	-24.2	-49.7	
2913	2308	1805	1393	1060	801	0.2	0.0	-1.5	-4.6	-9.5	-16.4	2.3	1.9	0.0	-3.7	-9.4	-28.1	-58.8	24"
2913	2520	2171	1860	1585	1343	0.6	0.9	0.0	-2.3	-6.1	-11.4	2.1	1.7	0.0	-3.2	-8.0	-22.8	-45.6	
3221	2667	2196	1792	1448	1160	0.4	0.8	0.0	-1.9	-5.2	-9.9	1.7	1.5	0.0	-2.8	-7.0	-20.5	-42.1	
3178	2718	2313	1956	1644	1372	0.6	0.9	0.0	-2.3	-6.0	-11.3	2.0	1.7	0.0	-3.2	-7.9	-22.7	-45.8	24"
3133	2655	2240	1878	1564	1292	0.4	0.7	0.0	-1.8	-4.8	-9.1	2.6	2.9	2.0	0.0	-3.4	-14.5	-32.6	
2987	2511	2097	1739	1430	1166	0.6	0.9	0.0	-2.2	-5.9	-11.3	2.0	1.7	0.0	-3.2	-7.9	-23.0	-46.7	
3081	2669	2303	1978	1689	1434	0.5	0.9	0.0	-2.1	-5.7	-10.7	1.9	1.6	0.0	-3.0	-7.5	-21.4	-42.9	
3233	2741	2315	1943	1621	1341	0.3	0.7	0.0	-1.7	-4.6	-8.8	2.5	2.8	2.0	0.0	-3.2	-14.0	-31.5	
3293	2818	2401	2033	1711	1430	0.5	0.9	0.0	-2.2	-5.7	-10.8	1.9	1.6	0.0	-3.0	-7.6	-21.8	-44.0	24"
3188	2765	2388	2053	1756	1493	0.5	0.8	0.0	-2.1	-5.5	-10.3	1.9	1.6	0.0	-2.9	-7.2	-20.6	-41.3	
967	600	373	262	208	173	0.9	0.0	-4.5	-13.5	-28.3	-49.9	0.0	-4.5	-13.5	-28.3	-49.9	-118.6	-228.2	20"
1696	1253	913	666	502	405	0.7	0.0	-3.3	-9.7	-19.6	-33.8	2.2	0.0	-5.3	-14.1	-27.2	-69.0	-136.9	24"
1412	886	521	301	172	119	0.4	0.8	0.0	-2.4	-6.7	-13.8	2.0	1.8	0.0	-3.8	-10.2	-35.0	-84.4	24"
1902	1296	858	565	399	316	0.5	0.0	-2.7	-8.2	-17.0	-30.0	1.8	0.0	-4.6	-12.5	-24.6	-65.3	-134.9	
1827	1355	989	720	535	425	0.6	0.0	-3.0	-8.9	-18.0	-31.1	2.0	0.0	-4.8	-13.0	-25.1	-63.6	-126.7	
1827	1355	989	720	535	425	0.6	0.0	-3.0	-8.9	-18.0	-31.1	2.0	0.0	-4.8	-13.0	-25.1	-63.6	-126.7	24"
1879	1416	1050	771	571	442	0.5	0.0	-2.7	-7.9	-16.1	-27.6	1.8	0.0	-4.3	-11.6	-22.3	-56.3	-111.9	
2207	1639	1193	860	626	482	0.5	0.0	-2.6	-7.7	-15.6	-27.1	1.7	0.0	-4.2	-11.3	-21.9	-55.8	-112.0	24"
2303	1845	1462	1143	806	685	0.3	0.0	-1.8	-5.4	11.0	18.8	2.7	2.2	0.0	-4.2	-10.7	-31.5	-65.6	

CENTERFIRE RIFLE BALLISTICS (Cont.)

Caliber	Order No.	Wt. (grs.)	Bullet Style	Primer No.	Muzzle	100 yds.	200 yds.	300 yds.	400 yds.	500 yds.
.30-40 Krag	R30402	180*	Pointed Soft Point Core-Lokt*	9 ½	2430	2213	2007	1813	1632	1468
.308 Win.	R308W1	150	Pointed Soft Point Core-Lokt*	9 ½	2820	2533	2263	2009	1774	1560
	R308W2	180	Soft Point Core-Lokt*	9 ½	2620	2274	1955	1666	1414	1212
	R308W3	180	Pointed Soft Point Core-Lokt*	9 ½	2620	2393	2178	1974	1782	1604
	R308W7	168	Boat Tail H.P. Match	9 ½	2680	2493	2314	2143	1979	1823
	ER308WA	165	Extended Range Boat Tail	9 ½	2700	2497	2303	2117	1941	1773
	ER308WB§	178	Extended Range	9 ½	2620	2415	2220	2034	1857	1691
.30-06 Springfield	R30061	125	Pointed Soft Point	9 ½	3140	2780	2447	2138	1853	1595
	R30062	150	Pointed Soft Point Core-Lokt*	9 ½	2910	2617	2342	2083	1843	1622
	R30063	150	Bronze Point	9 ½	2910	2656	2416	2189	1974	1773
	R3006B	165	Pointed Soft Point Core-Lokt*	9 ½	2800	2534	2283	2047	1825	1621
	R30064	180	Soft Point Core-Lokt*	9 ½	2700	2348	2023	1727	1466	1251
	R30065	180	Pointed Soft Point Core-Lokt*	9 ½	2700	2469	2250	2042	1846	1663
	R30066	180	Bronze Point	9 ½	2700	2485	2280	2084	1899	1725
	R30067	220	Soft Point Core-Lokt*	9 ½	2410	2130	1870	1632	1422	1246
	RS3006A	180	Swift A-Frame™ PSP	9 ½	2700	2465	2243	2032	1833	1648
	ER3006A	152	Extended Range	9 ½	2910	2654	2413	2184	1968	1765
	ER3006B	165	Extended Range Boat Tail	9 ½	2800	2592	2394	2204	2023	1852
.300 H&H Mag.	R300HH	180	Pointed Soft Point Core-Lokt*	9 ½ M	2880	2640	2412	2196	1990	1798
.300 Win. Mag.	R300W1	150	Pointed Soft Point Core-Lokt*	9 ½ M	3290	2951	2636	2342	2068	1813
	R300W2	180	Pointed Soft Point Core-Lokt*	9 ½ M	2960	2745	2540	2344	2157	1979
	RS300WA	200	Swift A-Frame™ PSP	9 ½ M	2825	2595	2376	2167	1970	1783
	ER300WB	190	Extended Range Boat Tail	9 ½ M	2885	2691	2506	2327	2156	1993
.300 Wby. Mag.	R300WB1	180	Pointed Soft Point Core-Lokt*	9 ½ M	3120	2866	2627	2400	2184	1979
	ER30WBA§	178	Extended Range	9 ½ M	3120	2902	2695	2497	2308	2126
	ER30WBB	190	Extended Range Boat Tail	9 ½ M	3030	2830	2638	2455	2279	2110
	RS300WBB ★	200	Swift A-Frame™ PSP	9 ½ M	2925	2690	2467	2254	2052	1861
.303 British	R303B1	180	Soft Point Core-Lokt*	9 ½	2460	2124	1817	1542	1311	1137
7.62 x 39MM	R762391	125	Pointed Soft Point	7 ½	2365	2062	1783	1533	1320	1154
.32-20 Win.	R32201	100	Lead	6 ½	1210	1021	913	834	769	712
	R32202	100	Soft Point	6 ½	1210	1021	913	834	769	712
.32 Win. Special	R32WS2	170	Soft Point Core-Lokt*	9 ½	2250	1921	1626	1372	1175	1044
8MM Mauser	R8MSR	170	Soft Point Core-Lokt*	9 ½	2360	1969	1622	1333	1123	997
.338 Win. Mag.	R338W1 ★	225	Pointed Soft Point Core-Lokt*	9 ½ M	2780	2572	2374	2184	2003	1832
	R338W2 ★	250	Pointed Soft Point Core-Lokt*	9 ½ M	2660	2456	2261	2075	1898	1731
	RS338WA	225	Swift A-Frame™ PSP	9 ½ M	2785	2517	2266	2029	1808	1605
.35 Remington	R35R1	150	Pointed Soft Point Core-Lokt*	9 ½	2300	1874	1506	1218	1039	934
	R35R2	200	Soft Point Core-Lokt*	9 ½	2080	1698	1376	1140	1001	911
.350 Remington Mag.	R350M1§	200	Pointed Soft Point Core-Lokt*	9 ½ M	2710	2410	2130	1870	1631	1421
.35 Whelen	R35WH1	200	Pointed Soft Point	9 ½ M	2675	2378	2100	1842	1606	1399
	R35WH3	250	Pointed Soft Point	9 ½ M	2400	2197	2005	1823	1652	1496
.375 H&H Mag.	R375M1	270	Soft Point	9 ½ M	2690	2420	2166	1928	1707	1507
	RS375MA	300	Swift A-Frame™ PSP	9 ½ M	2530	2245	1979	1733	1512	1321
.416 Remington Mag.	R416R1§	400	Solid	9 ½ M	2400	2042	1718	1436	1212	1062
	R416R2	400	Swift A-Frame™ PSP	9 ½ M	2400	2175	1962	1763	1579	1414
	R416R3§	350	Swift A-Frame™ PSP	9 ½ M	2520	2270	2034	1814	1611	1429
.44-40 Win.	R4440W	200	Soft Point	2 ½	1190	1006	900	822	756	699
.44 Remington Mag.	R44MG2	240	Soft Point	2 ½	1760	1380	1114	970	878	806
	R44MG3	240	Semi-Jacketed Hollow Point	2 ½	1760	1380	1114	970	878	806
	R44MG6	210	Semi-Jacketed Hollow Point	2 ½	1920	1477	1155	982	880	802
	RH44MGA	275	JHP Core-Lokt*	2 ½	1580	1293	1093	976	896	832
.444 Mar.	R444M	240	Soft Point	9 ½	2350	1815	1377	1087	941	846
.45-70 Government	R4570G	405	Soft Point	9 ½	1330	1168	1055	977	918	869
	R4570L	300	Jacketed Hollow Point	9 ½	1810	1497	1244	1073	969	895
.458 Win. Mag.	RS458WA ★	450	Swift A-Frame™ PSP	9 ½ M	2150	1901	1671	1465	1289	1150
	R458W1§	500	Metal Case	9 ½ M	2040	1823	1623	1442	1237	1161

★ NEW

REMINGTON BALLISTICS

	Energy (ft.-lbs.)					Short-range¹ Trajectory*						Long-range² Trajectory*							
Muzzle	100 yds.	200 yds.	300 yds.	400 yds.	500 yds.	50 yds.	100 yds.	150 yds.	200 yds.	250 yds.	300 yds.	100 yds.	150 yds.	200 yds.	250 yds.	300 yds.	400 yds.	500 yds.	Barrel Length
2360	1957	1610	1314	1064	861	0.4	0.0	-2.1	-6.2	-12.5	-21.1	1.4	0.0	-3.4	-8.9	-16.8	-40.9	-78.1	24"
2648	2137	1705	1344	1048	810	0.2	0.0	-1.5	-4.5	-9.3	-15.9	2.3	1.9	0.0	-3.6	-9.1	-26.9	-55.7	
2743	2066	1527	1109	799	587	0.3	0.0	-2.0	-5.9	-12.1	-20.9	2.9	2.4	0.0	-4.7	-12.1	-36.9	-79.1	
2743	2288	1896	1557	1269	1028	0.2	0.0	-1.8	-5.2	-10.4	-17.7	2.6	2.1	0.0	-4.0	-9.9	-28.9	-58.8	24"
2678	2318	1998	1713	1460	1239	0.2	0.0	-1.6	-4.7	-9.4	-15.9	2.4	1.9	0.0	-3.5	-8.9	-25.3	-50.6	
2670	2284	1942	1642	1379	1152	0.2	0.0	-1.6	-4.7	-9.4	-16.0	2.3	1.9	0.0	-3.5	-8.9	-25.6	-51.5	
2713	2306	1948	1635	1363	1130	0.2	0.0	-1.7	-5.1	-10.2	-17.2	2.5	2.1	0.0	-3.8	-9.6	-27.6	-55.8	
2736	2145	1662	1269	953	706	0.4	0.8	0.0	-2.1	-5.6	-10.7	1.8	1.5	0.0	-3.0	-7.7	-23.0	-48.5	
2820	2281	1827	1445	1131	876	0.6	0.9	0.0	-2.3	-6.3	-12.0	2.1	1.8	0.0	-3.3	-8.5	-25.0	-51.8	
2820	2349	1944	1596	1298	1047	0.6	0.9	0.0	-2.2	-6.0	-11.4	2.0	1.7	0.0	-3.2	-8.0	-23.3	-47.5	
2872	2352	1909	1534	1220	963	0.7	1.0	0.0	-2.5	-6.7	-12.7	2.3	1.9	0.0	-3.6	-9.0	-26.3	-54.1	
2913	2203	1635	1192	859	625	0.2	0.0	-1.8	-5.5	-11.2	-19.5	2.7	2.3	0.0	-4.4	-11.3	-34.4	-73.7	
2913	2436	2023	1666	1362	1105	0.2	0.0	-1.6	-4.8	-9.7	-16.5	2.4	2.0	0.0	-3.7	-9.3	-27.0	-54.9	24"
2913	2468	2077	1736	1441	1189	0.2	0.0	-1.6	-4.7	-9.6	-16.2	2.4	2.0	0.0	-3.6	-9.1	-26.2	-53.0	
2837	2216	1708	1301	988	758	0.4	0.0	-2.3	-6.8	-13.8	-23.6	1.5	0.0	-3.7	-9.9	-19.0	-47.4	-93.1	
2913	2429	2010	1650	1343	1085	0.2	0.0	-1.6	-4.8	-9.8	-16.6	2.4	2.0	0.0	-3.7	-9.4	-27.2	-55.3	
2858	2378	1965	1610	1307	1052	0.6	0.9	0.0	-2.3	-6.0	-11.4	2.0	1.7	0.0	-3.2	-8.0	-23.3	-47.7	
2872	2462	2100	1780	1500	1256	0.6	1.0	0.0	-2.4	-6.2	-11.8	2.1	1.8	0.0	-3.3	-8.2	-23.6	-47.5	
3315	2785	2325	1927	1583	1292	0.6	0.9	0.0	-2.3	-6.0	-11.5	2.1	1.7	0.0	-3.2	-8.0	-23.3	-47.4	24"
3605	2900	2314	1827	1424	1095	0.3	0.7	0.0	-1.8	-4.8	-9.3	2.6	2.9	2.1	0.0	-3.5	-15.4	-35.5	
3501	3011	2578	2196	1859	1565	0.5	0.8	0.0	-2.1	-5.5	-10.4	1.9	1.6	0.0	-2.9	-7.3	-20.9	-41.9	24"
3544	2989	2506	2086	1722	1412	0.6	1.0	0.0	-2.4	-6.3	-11.9	2.1	1.8	0.0	-3.3	-8.3	-24.0	-48.8	
3511	3055	2648	2285	1961	1675	0.5	0.9	0.0	-2.2	-5.7	-10.7	1.9	1.6	0.0	-3.0	-7.5	-21.4	-42.9	
3890	3284	2758	2301	1905	1565	0.4	0.7	0.0	-1.9	-5.0	-9.5	2.7	3.0	2.1	0.0	-3.5	-15.2	-34.2	
3847	3329	2870	2464	2104	1787	0.4	0.7	0.0	-1.8	-4.8	-9.1	2.6	2.9	2.0	0.0	-3.3	-14.3	-31.8	24"
3873	3378	2936	2542	2190	1878	0.4	0.8	0.0	-1.9	-5.1	-9.6	1.7	1.4	0.0	-2.7	-6.7	-19.2	-38.4	
3799	3213	2701	2256	1870	1538	0.5	0.9	0.0	-2.2	-5.8	-11.0	3.2	3.5	2.4	0.0	-4.0	-17.4	-39.0	
2418	1803	1319	950	687	517	0.4	0.0	-2.3	-6.9	-14.1	-24.4	1.5	0.0	-3.8	-10.2	-19.8	-50.5	-101.5	24"
1552	1180	882	652	483	370	0.4	0.0	-2.5	-7.3	-14.3	-25.7	1.7	0.0	-4.8	-10.8	-20.7	-52.3	-104.0	24"
325	231	185	154	131	113	0.0	-6.3	-20.9	-44.9	-79.3	-125.1	0.0	-11.5	-32.3	-63.8	-106.3	-230.3	-413.3	24"
325	231	185	154	131	113	0.0	-6.3	-20.9	-44.9	-79.3	-125.1	0.0	-11.5	-32.3	-63.6	-106.3	-230.3	-413.3	
1911	1393	998	710	521	411	0.6	0.0	-2.9	-8.6	-17.6	-30.5	1.9	0.0	-4.7	-12.7	-24.7	-63.2	-126.9	24"
2102	1463	993	671	476	375	0.5	0.0	-2.7	-8.2	-17.0	-29.8	1.8	0.0	-4.5	-12.4	-24.3	-63.8	-130.7	24"
3860	3305	2815	2383	2004	1676	0.6	1.0	0.0	-2.4	-6.3	-12.0	2.2	1.8	0.0	-3.3	-8.4	-24.0	-48.4	
3927	3348	2837	2389	1999	1663	0.2	0.0	-1.7	-4.9	-9.8	-16.6	2.4	2.0	0.0	-3.7	-9.3	-26.6	-53.6	24"
3871	3165	2565	2057	1633	1286	0.2	0.0	-1.5	-4.6	-9.4	-16.0	2.3	1.9	0.0	-3.6	-9.1	-26.7	-54.9	
1762	1169	755	494	359	291	0.6	0.0	-3.0	-9.2	-19.1	-33.9	2.0	0.0	-5.1	-14.1	-27.8	-74.0	-152.3	24"
1921	1280	841	577	445	369	0.8	0.0	-3.8	-11.3	-23.5	-41.2	2.5	0.0	-6.3	-17.1	-33.6	-87.7	-176.4	
3261	2579	2014	1553	1181	897	0.2	0.0	-1.7	-5.1	-10.4	-17.9	2.6	2.1	0.0	-4.0	-10.3	-30.5	-64.0	20"
3177	2510	1958	1506	1145	869	0.2	0.0	-1.8	-5.3	-10.8	-18.5	2.6	2.2	0.0	-4.2	-10.6	-31.5	-65.9	
3197	2680	2230	1844	1515	1242	0.4	0.0	-2.2	-6.3	-12.6	-21.3	1.4	0.0	-3.4	-9.0	-17.0	-41.0	-77.8	
4337	3510	2812	2228	1747	1361	0.2	0.0	-1.7	-5.1	-10.3	-17.6	2.5	2.1	0.0	-3.9	-10.0	-29.4	-60.7	24"
4262	3357	2608	2001	1523	1163	0.3	0.0	-2.0	-6.0	-12.3	-21.0	3.0	2.5	0.0	-4.7	-12.0	-35.6	-74.5	
5115	3702	2620	1832	1305	1001	0.4	0.0	-2.5	-7.5	-15.5	-27.0	1.7	0.0	-4.2	-11.3	-21.9	-56.7	-115.1	
5115	4201	3419	2760	2214	1775	0.4	0.0	-2.2	-6.5	-13.0	-22.0	1.5	0.0	-3.5	-9.3	-17.6	-42.9	-82.2	24"
4935	4004	3216	2557	2017	1587	0.3	0.0	-2.0	-5.9	-11.9	-20.2	2.9	2.4	0.0	-4.5	-11.4	-33.4	-68.7	
629	449	360	300	254	217	0.0	-6.5	-21.6	-46.3	-81.8	-129.1	0.0	-11.8	-33.3	-65.5	-109.5	-237.4	-426.2	24"
1650	1015	661	501	411	346	0.0	-2.7	-10.0	-23.0	-43.0	-71.2	0.0	-5.9	-17.6	-36.3	-63.1	-145.5	-273.0	
1650	1015	661	501	411	346	0.0	-2.7	-10.0	-23.0	-43.0	-71.2	0.0	-5.9	-17.6	-36.3	-63.1	-145.5	-273.0	20"
1719	1017	622	450	361	300	0.0	-2.2	-8.3	-19.7	-37.6	-63.2	0.0	-5.1	-15.4	-32.1	-56.7	-134.0	-256.2	
1524	1020	730	582	490	422	1.7	0.0	-6.9	-20.0	-40.1	-68.7	0.0	-6.9	-20.0	-40.1	-68.7	-153.8	-283.0	
2942	1755	1010	630	472	381	0.6	0.0	-3.2	-9.9	-21.0	-38.5	2.1	0.0	-5.6	-15.9	-32.1	-87.8	-187.8	24"
1590	1227	1001	858	758	679	0.0	-4.7	-15.8	-34.0	-60.0	-94.5	0.0	-8.7	-24.6	-48.2	-80.3	-172.4	-305.9	24"
2182	1492	1031	767	625	533	0.0	-2.3	-8.5	-19.4	-35.9	-59.0	0.0	-5.0	-14.8	-30.1	-52.1	-119.5	—	
4618	3609	2789	2144	1659	1321	0.6	0.0	-3.0	-8.8	-17.6	-30.1	2.0	0.0	-4.8	-12.6	-24.0	-59.5	-115.7	24"
4620	3689	2924	2308	1839	1469	0.7	0.0	-3.3	-9.6	-19.2	-32.5	2.2	0.0	-5.2	-13.6	-25.8	-63.2	-121.7	

Specifications are nominal. Ballistics figures established in test barrels.
Individual rifles may vary from test-barrel specifications.
*Inches above or below line of sight. Hold low for positive numbers, high for negative numbers.
† 280 Remington and 7mm Express* Remington are interchangeable.
‡ Interchangeable in 244 Remington
§ Subject to stock on hand.
¹ Bullet does not rise more than one inch above line of sight from muzzle to sighting-in range.
² Bullet does not rise more than three inches above line of sight from muzzle to sighting-in range.
NOTE: 0.0 indicates yardage at which rifle was sighted in.

SAKO RIFLE BALLISTICS

Caliber	Bullet weight Grs Type	Velocity in feet per second						Energy in foot-pounds						Trajectory Inches / Yards					
		Muzzle	100 y	200 y	300 y	400 y	500 y	Muzzle	100 y	200 y	300 y	400 y	500 y	Muzzle	100 y	200 y	300 y	400 y	500 y
22 Hornet	45 SPEEDHEAD	2300	1724	1291	1069	944	861	524	295	165	114	89	74	-1.5	0	-14.3	-47.1	-108.9	-203.5
	45 SP RN	2300	1724	1291	1069	944	861	524	295	165	114	89	74	-1.5	0	-14.3	-47.1	-108.9	-203.5
	42 HP	2700	2193	1764	1419	1161	1011	652	428	277	179	120	91	-1.5	0	-6.6	-24.5	-60.1	-120.9
22 PPC USA	52 HPBT MATCH	3400	2990	2613	2255	1920	1616	1342	1040	795	592	429	304	-1.5	1.2	0	-6.0	-19.1	-41.8
222 Remington	50 SPEEDHEAD	3200	2663	2182	1776	1447	1192	1135	786	528	350	232	158	-1.5	1.7	0	-10.3	-31.1	-67.3
	50 SP P	3200	2663	2182	1776	1447	1192	1135	786	528	350	232	158	-1.5	1.7	0	-10.3	-31.1	-67.3
	55 SP P	3280	2800	2372	1978	1637	1350	1312	958	686	477	326	222	-1.5	1.4	0	-8.0	-24.8	-54.5
	52 HPBT MATCH	3035	2613	2235	1894	1589	1333	1072	795	581	417	294	207	-1.5	1.8	0	-9.0	-27.9	-60.7
222 Remington Mag	50 SPEEDHEAD	3230	2690	2207	1798	1466	1207	1159	803	540	359	238	161	-1.5	1.6	0	-10.0	-30.3	-67.0
	50 SP P	3230	2690	2207	1798	1466	1207	1159	803	540	359	238	161	-1.5	1.6	0	-10.0	-30.3	-67.0
	55 SP P	3330	2848	2414	2016	1671	1378	1352	989	710	495	340	231	-1.5	1.4	0	-7.7	-23.8	-51.9
223 Remington	50 SPEEDHEAD	3230	2690	2207	1798	1466	1207	1159	803	540	359	238	161	-1.5	1.6	0	-10.0	-30.3	-67.0
	50 SP P	3230	2690	2207	1798	1466	1207	1159	803	540	359	238	161	-1.5	1.6	0	-10.0	-30.3	-67.0
	55 SP P	3330	2848	2414	2016	1671	1378	1352	989	710	495	340	231	-1.5	1.4	0	-7.7	-23.8	-51.9
22-250 Remington	50 SPEEDHEAD	3770	3168	2639	2168	1751	1396	1579	1113	773	522	340	216	-1.5	1.0	0	-6.0	-19.5	-44.0
	50 SP P	3770	3168	2639	2168	1751	1396	1579	1113	773	522	340	216	-1.5	1.0	0	-6.0	-19.5	-44.0
	55 SP P	3660	3146	2681	2255	1871	1533	1631	1206	876	620	426	286	-1.5	1.0	0	-5.9	-18.7	-41.3
6PPC USA	70 HPBT MATCH	3100	2740	2407	2090	1793	1527	1481	1156	892	673	495	359	-1.5	1.5	0	-7.2	-22.8	-49.2
243 Winchester	90 SPEEDHEAD	2855	2587	2340	2110	1895	1693	1618	1329	1087	884	713	569	-1.5	1.9	0	-8.2	-24.3	-49.9
	90 SP P	3130	2850	2587	2343	2114	1898	1949	1612	1329	1090	887	715	-1.5	1.5	0	-6.5	-19.5	-40.2
6.5x55 Swedish	100 SPEEDHEAD	2625	2270	1946	1651	1397	1196	1533	1147	842	606	434	319	-1.5	2.6	0	-11.9	-36.0	-76.8
	139 HPBT MATCH	2790	2648	2512	2381	2252	2129	2396	2161	1945	1746	1563	1396	-1.5	1.7	0	-7.2	-20.5	-40.7
	156 SP RN	2625	2384	2156	1941	1740	1554	2382	1966	1607	1303	1047	835	-1.5	2.3	0	-9.8	-28.9	-59.7
270 Winchester	130 SPEEDHEAD	2820	2506	2212	1938	1687	1463	2290	1805	1407	1080	818	616	-1.5	2.0	0	-9.2	-27.5	-58.3
	156 SP RN	2755	2470	2208	1967	1743	1538	2626	2111	1685	1338	1051	818	-1.5	2.2	0	-9.3	-27.6	-57.5
7x33 Sako	78 SPEEDHEAD	2430	1920	1500	1190	1013	906	1029	643	392	247	179	143	-1.5	0	-8.5	-31.0	-78.8	-158.0
	78 SP SP	2430	1920	1500	1190	1013	906	1029	643	392	247	179	143	-1.5	0	-8.5	-31.0	-78.8	-158.0
7 mm Mauser (7x57)	78 SPEEDHEAD	2950	2324	1783	1362	1090	950	1522	943	555	324	208	158	-1.5	2.6	0	-14.9	-50.4	-112.2
	170 SP SP	2495	2283	2086	1901	1728	1567	2342	1962	1638	1361	1125	925	-1.5	2.6	0	-10.8	-31.1	-63.3
7x64	120 SP P	3100	2816	2545	2296	2069	1856	2567	2117	1730	1408	1143	920	-1.5	1.4	0	-7.3	-20.9	-42.6
	170 SP SP	2790	2563	2351	2154	1967	1791	2929	2473	2081	1747	1458	1208	-1.5	1.9	0	-8.2	-23.9	-48.6
7 mm Remington Mag	170 SP SP	2970	2734	2512	2303	2108	1924	3320	2824	2376	1996	1674	1394	-1.5	1.6	0	-7.2	-21.0	-42.5
7.62x39 Russian	123 SPEEDHEAD	2345	2096	1863	1651	1466	1305	1507	1203	951	747	589	466	-1.5	0	-6.5	-23.6	-53.2	-98.5
	123 SP P	2345	2096	1863	1651	1466	1305	1507	1203	951	747	589	466	-1.5	0	-6.5	-23.6	-53.2	-98.5
30-30 Winchester	93 SPEEDHEAD	2970	2354	1818	1400	1126	976	1811	1138	679	403	260	196	-1.5	0	-4.9	-21.8	-56.7	-117.8
	150 SP FP	2310	1982	1681	1439	1240	1096	1777	1304	938	688	510	400	-1.5	0	-8.1	-28.3	-65.6	-125.6
308 Winchester	93 SPEEDHEAD	2970	2354	1818	1400	1126	976	1811	1138	679	403	260	196	-1.5	0	-4.9	-21.8	-56.7	-117.3
	123 SPEEDHEAD	2920	2622	2347	2097	1868	1654	2335	1883	1509	1205	955	749	-1.5	1.8	0	-8.4	-24.5	-50.7
	123 SP P	3035	2734	2455	2194	1958	1738	2523	2047	1650	1318	1050	827	-1.5	1.6	0	-7.6	-22.4	-46.2
	156 SUPER HH	2790	2563	2353	2158	1973	1800	2689	2271	1914	1610	1346	1120	-1.5	2.0	0	-8.2	-23.9	-48.9
	180 HAMMERHEAD	2610	2382	2169	1971	1786	1612	2725	2273	1885	1556	1277	1041	-1.5	2.4	0	-9.9	-28.6	-58.1
	200 HAMMERHEAD	2445	2210	1990	1782	1588	1415	2660	2172	1762	1414	1122	891	-1.5	2.8	0	-11.3	-33.7	-70.1
	168 HPBT MATCH	2690	2500	2321	2159	2004	1857	2701	2328	2010	1739	1499	1286	-1.5	2.3	0	-8.5	-24.5	-49.1
	190 HPBT MATCH	2525	2372	2224	2080	1940	1806	2688	2369	2082	1822	1585	1373	-1.5	2.4	0	-9.0	-26.3	-52.9
7.62x53R	93 SPEEDHEAD	2970	2354	1818	1400	1126	976	1811	1138	679	403	260	196	-1.5	0	-4.9	-21.8	-56.7	-117.3
	123 SPEEDHEAD	2920	2622	2347	2097	1868	1654	2335	1883	1509	1205	955	749	-1.5	1.8	0	-8.4	-24.5	-50.7
	156 SUPER HH	2790	2563	2353	2158	1973	1800	2689	2271	1914	1610	1346	1120	-1.5	2.0	0	-8.2	-23.9	-48.9
	180 HAMMERHEAD	2610	2382	2169	1971	1786	1612	2725	2273	1885	1556	1277	1041	-1.5	2.4	0	-9.9	-28.6	-58.1
	200 HAMMERHEAD	2445	2210	1990	1782	1588	1415	2660	2172	1762	1414	1122	891	-1.5	2.8	0	-11.3	-33.7	-70.1
30-06 Springfield	123 SPEEDHEAD	2920	2622	2347	2097	1868	1654	2335	1883	1509	1205	955	749	-1.5	1.8	0	-8.4	-24.5	-50.7
	123 SP P	3120	2800	2510	2250	2010	1786	2661	2148	1726	1385	1106	873	-1.5	1.6	0	-7.3	-21.3	-43.9
	156 SUPER HH	2900	2670	2454	2255	2070	1893	2915	2466	2083	1759	1481	1240	-1.5	1.8	0	-7.8	-22.2	-44.7
	180 HAMMERHEAD	2700	2465	2242	2042	1857	1682	2935	2433	2013	1670	1381	1133	-1.5	2.3	0	-9.4	-27.0	-54.5
	220 HAMMERHEAD	2410	2200	2000	1826	1664	1517	2847	2369	1963	1632	1356	1126	-1.5	3.3	0	-12.4	-34.7	-69.6
300 Winchester Mag	156 SUPER HH	3150	2905	2673	2453	2243	2044	3430	2918	2470	2080	1740	1445	-1.5	1.3	0	-6.1	-18.1	-37.0
	180 HAMMERHEAD	2950	2700	2467	2243	2031	1833	3493	2926	2438	2015	1653	1345	-1.5	1.6	0	-7.4	-21.7	-44.4
	168 HPBT MATCH	3020	2816	2622	2438	2260	2090	3400	2959	2566	2217	1905	1630	-1.5	1.5	0	-6.5	-18.8	-38.0
8.2x53R	127 SPEEDHEAD	2625	2143	1715	1373	1141	1003	1934	1290	826	529	365	283	-1.5	0	-6.1	-26.2	-64.2	-128.0
	200 HAMMERHEAD	2525	2215	1927	1675	1462	1281	2841	2184	1653	1248	951	731	-1.5	2.8	0	-13.5	-38.6	-79.8
8x57IS (8.2x57)	127 SPEEDHEAD	2625	2143	1715	1373	1141	1003	1934	1290	826	529	365	283	-1.5	0	-6.1	-26.2	-64.2	-128.0
	200 HAMMERHEAD	2525	2215	1927	1675	1462	1281	2841	2184	1653	1248	951	731	-1.5	2.8	0	-13.5	-38.6	-79.8
338 Winchester Mag	250 HAMMERHEAD	2675	2413	2169	1946	1742	1554	3966	3229	2608	2101	1683	1339	-1.5	2.3	0	-10.0	-29.1	-59.7
9.3x53R Finnish	256 SP RN	2330	2000	1695	1439	1236	1091	3010	2211	1593	1148	847	660	-1.5	3.6	0	-16.9	-50.3	-107.0
9.3x62	250 POWERHEAD	2500	2300	2106	1927	1758	1599	3465	2932	2461	2060	1714	1419	-1.5	2.6	0	-10.4	-30.2	-61.3
9.3x74R	250 POWERHEAD	2360	2170	1988	1815	1652	1503	3095	2612	2192	1828	1514	1253	-1.5	3.0	0	-11.8	-34.2	-69.4
375 H&H Mag	270 POWERHEAD	2720	2535	2354	2181	2015	1857	4440	3848	3319	2848	2432	2066	-1.5	1.9	0	-8.3	-23.8	-48.0

SPEEDHEAD = FMJ = Full Metal Jacket
SP P = Soft Point Pointed
SP SP = Soft Point Semi Pointed

SP RN = Soft Point Round Nose
SP FP = Soft Point Flat Point
HP BT = Hollow Point Boat Tail

HAMMERHEAD = Soft Point Bonded Core
SUPER HH = Hollow Point Bonded Core
POWERHEAD = Hollow Point Solid Copper

WEATHERBY BALLISTICS

SUGGESTED USAGE	CARTRIDGE	BULLET Weight Grains	BULLET Type	BALLISTIC COEFFICIENT	VELOCITY Muzzle	100 Yards	200 Yards	300 Yards	400 Yards	500 Yards	ENERGY Muzzle	100 Yards	200 Yards	300 Yards	400 Yards	500 Yards	PATH 100 Yards	200 Yards	300 Yards	400 Yards	500 Yards
V	.224 WM	55	Pt-Ex	.235	3650	3192	2780	2403	2057	1742	1627	1244	944	705	516	370	2.8	3.7	0.0	-9.7	-27.7
V M	.240 WM	87	Pt-Ex	.327	3523	3198	2888	2595	2317	2055	2398	1975	1612	1301	1037	816	2.7	3.4	0.0	-8.6	-23.7
		100	Pt-Ex	.381	3406	3116	2844	2588	2346	2117	2577	2156	1796	1488	1222	996	2.8	3.5	0.0	-8.6	-23.6
		100	Partition	.384	3406	3136	2881	2641	2413	2196	2577	2184	1843	1549	1293	1071	2.7	3.5	0.0	-8.3	-22.7
V M	.257 WM	87	Pt-Ex	.322	3825	3456	3118	2803	2511	2236	2827	2308	1878	1518	1218	966	2.1	2.8	0.0	-7.2	-20.0
		100	Pt-Ex	.357	3602	3280	2980	2701	2438	2190	2882	2389	1973	1620	1320	1065	2.4	3.2	0.0	-7.8	-21.6
		117	Pt-Ex	.391	3402	3134	2878	2632	2397	2173	3007	2552	2151	1799	1493	1227	2.8	3.5	0.0	-8.5	-23.1
		120	Partition	.391	3305	3045	2800	2568	2348	2139	2911	2472	2090	1758	1469	1219	3.0	3.7	0.0	-8.8	-24.0
V M	.270 WM	100	Pt-Ex	.307	3760	3380	3033	2712	2412	2133	3139	2537	2042	1633	1292	1010	2.3	3.0	0.0	-7.8	-21.6
		130	Pt-Ex	.409	3375	3100	2842	2598	2367	2147	3287	2773	2330	1948	1616	1331	2.9	3.6	0.0	-8.7	-23.7
		130	Partition	.416	3375	3127	2893	2670	2458	2257	3287	2822	2415	2058	1714	1470	2.8	3.5	0.0	-8.3	-22.4
		150	Pt-Ex	.462	3245	3019	2803	2598	2402	2215	3507	3034	2617	2248	1922	1634	3.0	3.7	0.0	-8.9	-23.8
		150	Partition	.465	3245	3029	2823	2627	2439	2259	3507	3055	2655	2298	1981	1699	3.0	3.7	0.0	-8.7	-23.3
M	7MM WM	139	Pt-Ex	.392	3340	3082	2838	2608	2389	2180	3443	2931	2486	2099	1761	1467	2.9	3.6	0.0	-8.7	-23.6
		140	Partition	.434	3303	3069	2847	2636	2434	2241	3391	2927	2519	2159	1842	1562	2.9	3.6	0.0	-8.6	-23.1
		154	Pt-Ex	.433	3260	3022	2797	2583	2379	2184	3633	3123	2675	2281	1934	1630	3.0	3.7	0.0	-9.0	-24.1
		160	Partition	.475	3200	2991	2791	2600	2417	2241	3637	3177	2767	2401	2075	1784	3.1	3.8	0.0	-8.9	-23.8
B		175	Pt-Ex	.462	3070	2855	2649	2449	2258	2075	3662	3168	2726	2331	1981	1672	3.5	4.2	0.0	-10.0	-27.0
M	.300 WM	150	Pt-Ex	.349	3600	3297	3016	2751	2502	2266	4316	3621	3028	2520	2084	1709	2.4	3.1	0.0	-7.7	-21.0
		150	Partition	.387	3600	3319	3057	2809	2575	2353	4316	3669	3111	2628	2208	1843	2.4	3.0	0.0	-7.5	-20.1
		165	Boat Tail	.435	3450	3207	2973	2748	2531	2324	4361	3768	3238	2766	2347	1978	2.6	3.3	0.0	-7.9	-21.2
B		180	Pt-Ex	.425	3300	3064	2841	2629	2426	2233	4352	3753	3226	2762	2352	1992	2.9	3.6	0.0	-8.6	-23.2
		180	Partition	.474	3300	3085	2881	2686	2499	2319	4352	3804	3317	2882	2495	2150	2.8	3.5	0.0	-8.3	-22.3
		220	Rn-Ex	.300	2905	2498	2125	1787	1491	1250	4122	3047	2206	1560	1085	763	5.3	6.6	0.0	-17.6	-51.3
B	.340 WM	200	Pt-Ex	.361	3260	2977	2708	2451	2206	1975	4719	3937	3255	2667	2162	1732	3.2	4.0	0.0	-9.8	-26.8
		210	Partition	.400	3250	3000	2763	2539	2325	2122	4924	4195	3559	3004	2520	2098	3.1	3.8	0.0	-9.2	-24.9
		225	Pt-Ex	.307	3105	2854	2614	2385	2166	1957	4816	4070	3414	2841	2343	1914	3.6	4.3	0.0	-10.5	-28.4
		250	Pt-Ex	.291	3002	2672	2365	2079	1814	1574	5002	3963	3105	2399	1827	1375	1.7	0.0	-7.9	-24.0	-50.7
		250	Partition	.473	2980	2780	2588	2404	2228	2059	4931	4290	3719	3209	2756	2354	3.7	4.4	0.0	-10.3	-27.5
B	.378 WM	270	Pt-Ex	.380	3180	2915	2661	2419	2189	1970	6062	5094	4246	3509	2872	2326	1.3	0.0	-6.2	-18.4	-37.9
																	3.4	4.2	0.0	-10.1	-28.0
		300	Rn-Ex	.250	2925	2545	2191	1864	1564	1292	5699	4314	3199	2315	1629	1111	2.0	0.0	-9.3	-28.6	-62.3
A		300	FMJ	.275	2925	2580	2262	1972	1710	1482	5701	4434	3408	2592	1949	1463	1.84	0.0	-8.6	-26.1	-55.9
A	.416 WM	400	Swift A	.391	2650	2411	2185	1971	1770	1585	6239	5165	4242	3450	2783	2233	5.4	6.3	0.0	-15.1	-41.7
																	2.2	0.0	-9.5	-27.7	-57.5
		400	Rn-Ex	.311	2700	2406	2129	1869	1626	1399	6475	5141	4025	3102	2347	1739	5.6	6.6	0.0	-16.7	-46.6
																	2.3	0.0	-10	-30	-63.2
		400	**Mono Solid®	.304	2700	2397	2115	1852	1613	1402	6474	5104	3971	3047	2310	1747	5.7	6.7	0.0	-17.0	-47.4
																	2.3	0.0	-10.1	-30.4	-64.3
A	.460 WM	500	RNSP	.287	2600	2289	1998	1726	1474	1247	7505	5816	4430	3308	2414	1727	2.6	0.0	-11.4	-34.5	-73.7
		500	FMJ	.295	2600	2297	2013	1747	1501	1276	7505	5858	4498	3390	2501	1807	2.6	0.0	-11.2	-33.9	-72.0

VELOCITY in Feet per Second. ENERGY in Foot-Pounds. PATH OF BULLET: Above or below line-of-sight of riflescopes mounted 1.5" above bore.

LEGEND: PT-EX = Pointed Expanding   Rn-Ex = Round nose-Expanding   FMJ = Full Metal Jacket   A = Divided Lead Cavity or "H" Type

NOTE: These tables were calculated by computer using a standard modern scientific technique to predict trajectories and recoil energies from the best available data for each cartridge. The figures shown are expected to be reasonably accurate of ammunition behavior under standard conditions. However, the shooter is cautioned that performance will vary because of variations in rifles, ammunition, atmospheric conditions and altitude.

B.C.: Ballistic Coefficients used for these tables were supplied by the bullet manufacturers.

Listed velocities were determined using 26-inch barrels. Velocities from shorter barrels will be reduced by 30 to 65 feet per second per inch of barrel removed.

Trajectories were computed with the line-of-sight 1.5 inches above the bore centerline.

*Partition is a registered trademark of Nosler, Inc.

**Monolithic Solid is a registered trademark of A-Square, Inc.

USAGE: V-Varmint   M-Medium Game (Deer, Sheep, Pronghorn, Black Bear)   B-Big Game (Elk, Moose, Grizzly)   A-African Big Game (Elephant, Cape Buffalo, Rhino, Lion)

CENTERFIRE RIFLE BALLISTICS

Game Selector	CXP Class	Examples
V-Varmint	1	Prairie dog, coyote, woodchuck
D-Deer	2	Antelope, deer, black bear
O/P-Open or Plains	3	Elk, moose
M-Medium Game	3D	All game in category 3 plus large dangerous game (i.e. Kodiak bear)
L-Large Game	4	Cape Buffalo, elephant
XL-Extra Large Game	M	Match

Acceptable for use in pistols and revolvers also.
Bold type indicates Supreme® product line

*Intended for use in fast twist barrels (e.g., 1 in 7 to 1 in 9).
Slower twist barrels may not sufficiently stabilize bullet.

Cartridge	Symbol	Game Selector Guide	CXP Guide Number	Bullet Wt. Grs.	Bullet Type	Barrel Length (In.)	Velocity in Feet Per Second (fps)						Energy in Foot Pounds (ft-lbs.)						Trajectory, Short Range Yards						Trajectory, Long Range Yards						
							Muzzle	100	200	300	400	500	Muzzle	100	200	300	400	500	50	100	150	200	250	300	100	150	200	250	300	400	500
218 Bee	X218B	V	1	46	Hollow Point	24	2760	2102	1550	1155	961	850	778	451	245	136	94	74	0.3	0	-2.3	-7.2	-15.8	-29.4	1.5	0	-4.2	-12.0	-24.8	-71.4	-155.6
22 Hornet	X22H1	V	1	45	Soft Point	24	2690	2042	1502	1128	948	840	723	417	225	127	90	70	0.3	0	-2.4	-7.7	-16.9	-31.3	1.6	0	-4.5	-12.8	-26.4	-75.6	-163.4
22 Hornet	X22H2	V	1	46	Hollow Point	24	2690	2042	1502	1128	948	841	739	426	230	130	92	72	0.3	0	-2.4	-7.7	-16.9	-31.3	1.6	0	-4.5	-12.8	-26.4	-75.5	-163.3
22-250 Remington	**S22250**	**V**	**1**	**52**	**Hollow Point Boattail**	**24**	**3750**	**3268**	**2835**	**2442**	**2082**	**1755**	**1624**	**1233**	**928**	**689**	**501**	**356**	**0.1**	**0**	**-0.7**	**-2.4**	**-5.1**	**-9.1**	**1.2**	**1.1**	**0**	**-2.1**	**-5.5**	**-16.9**	**-36.3**
22-250 Remington	X222501	V	1	55	Pointed Soft Point	24	3680	3137	2656	2222	1832	1493	1654	1201	861	603	410	272	0.2	0.5	0	-1.6	-4.4	-8.7	2.3	2.6	1.9	0	-3.4	-15.9	-38.9
222 Remington	X222R	V	1	50	Pointed Soft Point	24	3140	2602	2123	1700	1350	1107	1094	752	500	321	202	136	0.5	0.9	0	-2.5	-6.9	-13.7	2.2	1.9	0	-3.8	-10.0	-32.3	-73.8
222 Remington	X222R1	V	1	55	Full Metal Jacket	24	3020	2675	2355	2057	1783	1537	1114	874	677	517	388	288	0.5	0.9	0	-2.2	-6.1	-11.7	2.0	1.7	0	-3.3	-8.3	-24.9	-52.5
223 Remington	X223RH	V	1	53	Hollow Point	24	3330	2882	2477	2106	1770	1475	1305	978	722	522	369	256	0.3	0.7	0	-1.9	-5.3	-10.3	1.7	1.4	0	-2.9	-7.4	-22.7	-49.1
223 Remington	X223R	V	1	55	Pointed Soft Point	24	3240	2747	2304	1905	1554	1270	1282	921	648	443	295	197	0.4	0.8	0	-2.2	-6.0	-11.8	1.9	1.6	0	-3.3	-8.5	-26.7	-59.6
223 Remington	X223R1	V	1	55	Full Metal Jacket	24	3240	2877	2543	2232	1943	1679	1282	1011	790	608	461	344	0.4	0.7	0	-1.9	-5.1	-9.9	1.7	1.4	0	-2.8	-7.1	-21.2	-44.6
223 Remington	X223R2	D	2	64	Power-Point®	24	3020	2656	2320	2009	1724	1473	1296	1003	765	574	423	308	0.1	0.7	0	-2.1	-5.8	-11.4	1.7	1.6	0	-3.2	-8.2	-25.1	-53.6
223 Remington Match	**S223M***	**–**	**M**	**69**	**Hollow Point Boattail**	**24**	**3060**	**2740**	**2442**	**2164**	**1904**	**1665**	**1435**	**1151**	**914**	**717**	**555**	**425**	**-0.2**	**0**	**-0.9**	**-3.1**	**-6.8**	**-12.1**	**1.6**	**1.4**	**0**	**-2.9**	**-7.4**	**-22.3**	**-46.7**
225 Winchester	X2251	V	1	55	Pointed Soft Point	24	3570	3066	2616	2208	1838	1514	1556	1148	836	595	412	280	0.2	0.6	0	-1.7	-4.6	-9.0	2.4	2.8	2.0	0	-3.5	-16.3	-39.5
243 Winchester	X2431	V	1	80	Pointed Soft Point	24	3350	2955	2593	2259	1951	1670	1993	1551	1194	906	676	495	0.3	0.7	0	-1.8	-4.9	-9.4	2.6	2.9	2.1	0	-3.6	-16.2	-37.9
243 Winchester	X2432	D,O/P	2	100	Power-Point	24	2960	2697	2449	2215	1993	1786	1945	1615	1332	1089	882	708	0.5	0.9	0	-2.2	-5.8	-11.0	1.9	1.6	0	-3.1	-7.8	-22.6	-46.3
243 Winchester	**S243**	**D,O/P**	**2**	**100**	**Soft Point Boattail**	**24**	**2960**	**2712**	**2477**	**2254**	**2042**	**1843**	**1946**	**1633**	**1363**	**1128**	**926**	**754**	**0.1**	**0**	**-1.3**	**-3.8**	**-7.8**	**-13.3**	**1.9**	**1.6**	**0**	**-3.0**	**-7.6**	**-22.0**	**-44.8**
6mm Remington	X6MMR2	D,O/P	2	100	Power-Point	24	3100	2829	2573	2332	2104	1889	2133	1777	1470	1207	983	792	0.4	0.8	0	-1.9	-5.2	-9.9	1.7	1.5	0	-2.8	-7.0	-20.4	-41.7
25-06 Remington	X25061	V	1	90	Positive Expanding Point	24	3440	3043	2680	2344	2034	1749	2364	1850	1435	1098	827	611	0.3	0.6	0	-1.7	-4.5	-8.8	2.4	2.7	2.0	0	-3.4	-15.0	-35.2
25-06 Remington	X25062	D,O/P	2	120	Positive Expanding Point	24	2990	2730	2484	2252	2032	1825	2382	1985	1644	1351	1100	887	0.5	0.8	0	-2.1	-5.6	-10.7	1.9	1.6	0	-3.0	-7.5	-22.0	-44.8
25-20 Winchester #	X25202	V	1	86	Soft Point	24	1460	1194	1030	931	858	798	407	272	203	165	141	122	0	-4.1	-14.4	-31.8	-57.3	-92.0	0	-8.2	-23.5	-47.0	-79.6	-175.9	-319.4
25-35 Winchester	X2535	D	2	117	Soft Point	24	2230	1866	1545	1282	1097	984	1292	904	620	427	313	252	0.6	0	-3.1	-9.2	-19.0	-33.1	2.1	0	-5.1	-13.8	-27.0	-70.1	-142.0
250 Savage	X2503	D,O/P	2	100	Silvertip®	24	2820	2467	2140	1839	1569	1339	1765	1351	1017	751	547	398	0.2	0	-1.6	-4.9	-10.0	-17.4	2.4	2.0	0	-3.9	-10.1	-30.5	-65.2
257 Roberts + P	X257P3	D,O/P	2	117	Power-Point	24	2780	2411	2071	1761	1488	1263	2009	1511	1115	806	576	415	0.8	1.1	0	-2.9	-7.8	-15.1	2.6	2.2	0	-4.2	-10.8	-33.0	-70.0
264 Winchester Mag.	X2642	D,O/P	2	140	Power-Point	24	3030	2782	2548	2326	2114	1914	2854	2406	2018	1682	1389	1139	0.5	0.8	0	-2.0	-5.4	-10.2	1.8	1.5	0	-2.9	-7.2	-20.8	-42.2
6.5 x 55 Swedish	X6555	D,O/P	2	140	Soft Point	24	2550	2359	2176	2002	1836	1680	2022	1731	1473	1246	1048	878	0	0	-1.5	-4.8	-9.8	-16.9	2.4	2	0	-3.9	-9.7	-28.1	-56.8
270 Winchester	X2705	D,O/P	2	130	Power-Point	24	3060	2802	2559	2329	2110	1904	2702	2267	1890	1565	1285	1046	0.4	0.8	0	-2.0	-5.3	-10.1	1.8	1.5	0	-2.8	-7.1	-20.6	-42.0
270 Winchester	X2703	D,O/P	2	130	Silvertip	24	3060	2776	2510	2259	2022	1801	2702	2225	1818	1472	1180	936	0.5	0.8	0	-2.0	-5.5	-10.4	1.8	1.5	0	-2.9	-7.4	-21.6	-44.3
270 Winchester	**S270**	**D,O/P**	**2**	**140**	**Silvertip Boattail**	**24**	**2960**	**2753**	**2554**	**2365**	**2183**	**2009**	**2724**	**2356**	**2029**	**1739**	**1482**	**1256**	**0.1**	**0**	**-1.2**	**-3.7**	**-7.5**	**-12.7**	**1.8**	**1.5**	**0**	**-2.9**	**-7.2**	**-20.6**	**-41.3**
270 Winchester	**S270X**	**D,O/P,M**	**3**	**140**	**Fail Safe®**	**24**	**2920**	**2671**	**2435**	**2211**	**1999**	**1799**	**2651**	**2218**	**1843**	**1519**	**1242**	**1007**	**-0.2**	**0**	**-1**	**-3.4**	**-7.2**	**-12.6**	**1.7**	**1.5**	**0**	**-3**	**-7.6**	**-22.3**	**-45.7**
270 Winchester	X2704	D,M	3	150	Power-Point	24	2850	2585	2336	2100	1879	1673	2705	2226	1817	1468	1175	932	0.6	1.0	0	-2.4	-6.4	-12.2	2.2	1.8	0	-3.4	-8.6	-25.0	-51.4
280 Remington	X280R	D,O/P	2	140	Power-Point	24	3050	2705	2428	2167	1924	1698	2799	2274	1833	1461	1151	897	0.5	0.8	0	-2.2	-5.8	-11.1	1.9	1.6	0	-3.1	-7.8	-23.1	-47.8
280 Remington	**S280**	**D,O/P**	**3**	**160**	**Silvertip Boattail**	**24**	**2840**	**2637**	**2442**	**2256**	**2078**	**1909**	**2866**	**2471**	**2120**	**1809**	**1535**	**1295**	**0.1**	**0**	**-1.4**	**-4.1**	**-8.3**	**-14.0**	**2.1**	**1.7**	**0**	**-3.2**	**-7.9**	**-22.6**	**-45.4**
280 Remington	**S280X**	**D,O/P,M**	**3**	**160**	**Fail Safe**	**24**	**2840**	**2600**	**2372**	**2156**	**1951**	**1759**	**2866**	**2402**	**2000**	**1652**	**1353**	**1100**	**-0.2**	**0**	**-1.1**	**-3.7**	**-7.7**	**-13.5**	**1.8**	**1.6**	**0**	**-3.2**	**-8**	**-23.5**	**-48.2**
284 Winchester	X2842	D,O/P,M	3	150	Power-Point	24	2860	2595	2344	2108	1886	1680	2724	2243	1830	1480	1185	940	0.6	1.0	0	-2.4	-6.3	-12.1	2.1	1.8	0	-3.4	-8.5	-24.8	-51.0
7mm Mauser (7x57)	X7MM1	D	2	145	Power-Point	24	2660	2413	2180	1959	1754	1564	2279	1875	1530	1236	990	788	0.2	0	-1.7	-5.1	-10.3	-17.5	1.1	0	-2.8	-7.4	-14.1	-34.4	-66.1
7mm Remington Mag.	X7MMR1	D,O/P,M	2	150	Power-Point	24	3110	2830	2568	2320	2085	1866	3221	2667	2196	1792	1448	1160	0.4	0.8	0	-1.9	-5.2	-9.9	1.7	1.5	0	-2.8	-7.0	-20.5	-42.1
7mm Remington Mag.	**S7MAGA**	**D,O/P,M,L**	**3**	**160**	**Silvertip Boattail**	**24**	**2950**	**2745**	**2550**	**2363**	**2184**	**2012**	**3093**	**2679**	**2311**	**1984**	**1694**	**1439**	**0.1**	**0**	**-1.2**	**-3.7**	**-7.5**	**-12.8**	**1.9**	**1.5**	**0**	**-2.9**	**-7.2**	**-20.6**	**-41.4**
7mm Remington Mag.	**S7MAGX**	**D,O/P,M,L**	**3**	**160**	**Fail Safe**	**24**	**2920**	**2678**	**2449**	**2331**	**2025**	**1830**	**3030**	**2549**	**2131**	**1769**	**1457**	**1190**	**-0.2**	**0**	**-1**	**-3.4**	**-7.1**	**-12.5**	**1.7**	**1.5**	**0**	**-2.9**	**-7.5**	**-22**	**-44.9**
7mm Remington Mag.	X7MMR2	D,O/P,M,L	3	175	Power-Point	24	2860	2645	2440	2244	2057	1879	3178	2718	2313	1956	1644	1372	0.6	0.9	0	-2.3	-6.0	-11.3	2.0	1.7	0	-3.2	-7.9	-22.7	-45.8
7.62 x 39mm Russian	X76239	D,V	2	123	Soft Point	20	2365	2033	1731	1465	1248	1093	1527	1129	818	586	425	327	0.5	0	-2.6	-7.6	-15.4	-26.7	3.8	3.1	0	-6.0	-15.4	-46.3	-98.4
30 Carbine #	X30M1	V	1	110	Hollow Soft Point	20	1990	1567	1236	1035	923	842	967	600	373	262	208	173	0.9	0	-4.5	-13.5	-28.3	-49.9	0	-4.5	-13.5	-28.3	-49.9	-118.6	-228.2
30-30 Winchester	X30301	D	2	150	Hollow Point	24	2390	2018	1684	1398	1177	1036	1902	1356	944	651	461	357	0.5	0	-2.6	-7.7	-16.0	-27.9	1.7	0	-4.3	-11.6	-22.7	-59.1	-120.5
30-30 Winchester	X30306	D	2	150	Power-Point	24	2390	2018	1684	1398	1177	1036	1902	1356	944	651	461	357	0.5	0	-2.6	-7.7	-16.0	-27.9	1.7	0	-4.3	-11.6	-22.7	-59.1	-120.5
30-30 Winchester	X30302	D	2	150	Silvertip	24	2390	2018	1684	1398	1177	1036	1902	1356	944	651	461	357	0.5	0	-2.6	-7.7	-16.0	-27.9	1.7	0	-4.3	-11.6	-22.7	-59.1	-120.5
30-30 Winchester	X30303	D	2	170	Power-Point	24	2200	1895	1619	1381	1191	1061	1827	1355	989	720	535	425	0.6	0	-3.0	-8.9	-18.0	-31.1	2.0	0	-4.8	-13.0	-25.1	-63.6	-126.7
30-30 Winchester	X30304	D	2	170	Silvertip	24	2200	1895	1619	1381	1191	1061	1827	1355	989	720	535	425	0.6	0	-3.0	-8.9	-18.0	-31.1	2.0	0	-4.8	-13.0	-25.1	-63.6	-126.7
30-06 Springfield	X30062	V	1	125	Pointed Soft Point	24	3140	2780	2447	2138	1853	1595	2736	2145	1662	1269	953	706	0.4	0.8	0	-2.1	-5.6	-10.7	1.8	1.5	0	-3.0	-7.7	-23.0	-48.5
30-06 Springfield	X30061	D,O/P	2	150	Power-Point	24	2920	2580	2265	1972	1704	1466	2839	2217	1708	1295	967	716	0.6	1.0	0	-2.4	-6.6	-12.7	2.2	1.8	0	-3.5	-9.0	-27.0	-57.1
30-06 Springfield	X30063	D,O/P	2	150	Silvertip	24	2910	2617	2342	2083	1843	1622	2820	2281	1827	1445	1131	876	0.6	0.9	0	-2.3	-6.3	-12.0	2.1	1.8	0	-3.3	-8.5	-25.0	-51.8
30-06 Springfield	**S3006**	**D,O/P,M**	**2**	**165**	**Silvertip Boattail**	**24**	**2800**	**2597**	**2402**	**2216**	**2038**	**1869**	**2873**	**2421**	**2114**	**1799**	**1522**	**1280**	**0.1**	**0**	**-1.4**	**-4.3**	**-8.6**	**-14.6**	**2.1**	**1.8**	**0**	**-3.3**	**-8.2**	**-23.4**	**-47.0**

The following table reproduces the Winchester centerfire rifle ballistics data on this page. Column groups are:
- **Velocity (ft/sec)** at Muzzle, 100, 200, 300, 400, 500 yds
- **Energy (ft-lbs)** at Muzzle, 100, 200, 300, 400, 500 yds
- **Short‑Range Trajectory (in.)** at 50, 100, 150, 200, 250, 300 yds
- **Long‑Range Trajectory (in.)** at 100, 150, 200, 250, 300, 400, 500 yds

Cartridge	Symbol	Use	Grs.	Bullet Style	Bbl	Vel‑M	V‑100	V‑200	V‑300	V‑400	V‑500	En‑M	E‑100	E‑200	E‑300	E‑400	E‑500	SR50	SR100	SR150	SR200	SR250	SR300	LR100	LR150	LR200	LR250	LR300	LR400	LR500
30‑06 Springfield	S3006XA	D,O/P,M	165	Fail Safe	24	2800	2540	2295	2063	1846	1645	2873	2365	1930	1560	1249	992	−0.1	0	−1.2	−3.9	−8.2	−14.4	2.0	1.7	0	−3.4	−8.6	−25.3	−52.3
30‑06 Springfield	X30065	D,O/PM	165	Pointed Soft Point	24	2800	2573	2357	2151	1956	1772	2873	2426	2036	1696	1402	1151							1.9	1.8	0	−3.6	−8.4	−24.4	−49.6
30‑06 Springfield	S3006X	D,O/P,M,L	180	Fail Safe	24	2700	2486	2283	2089	1904	1731	2914	2472	2083	1744	1450	1198							2.1	1.8	0	−3.5	−8.7	−25.5	−51.8
30‑06 Springfield	X30064	D,O/PM	180	Power‑Point	24	2700	2348	2023	1727	1466	1251	2913	2203	1635	1192	859	625							2.7	2.3	0	−4.4	−11.3	−34.4	−73.7
30‑06 Springfield	X30066	D,O/P,M,L	180	Silvertip	24	2700	2469	2250	2042	1846	1663	2913	2436	2023	1666	1362	1105							2.4	2.0	0	−3.7	−9.3	−27.0	−54.9
30‑06 Springfield	X30069	D,O/P,M,L	220	Silvertip	24	2410	2192	1985	1791	1611	1448	2837	2348	1925	1567	1268	1024									0			−41.8	−79.9
30‑40 Krag	X30401	D	180	Power‑Point	24	2430	2099	1795	1525	1298	1128	2360	1761	1288	929	673	508									0			−51.7	−103.9
300 Winchester Mag.	X30WM1	D,O/P	150	Power‑Point	24	3290	2951	2636	2342	2068	1813	3605	2900	2314	1827	1424	1095							2.6		0			−15.4	−35.5
NEW 300 Winchester Mag.	S300WXA	D,O/P,M	165	Fail Safe	24	3120	2807	2515	2242	1985	1748	3567	2888	2319	1842	1445	1120							1.5	1.3	0			−20.9	−43.6
300 Winchester Mag.	S300WX	M,L	180	Silvertip	24	2960	2732	2514	2307	2110	1923	3503	2983	2528	2129	1780	1478							1.6	1.4	0			−20.7	−42.1
300 Winchester Mag.	X30WM2	O/P,M,L	180	Power‑Point	24	2960	2745	2540	2344	2157	1979	3501	3011	2578	2196	1859	1565							1.9	1.6	0			−20.9	−41.9
300 Winchester Mag.	X30WM3	M,L,XL	220	Power‑Point	24	2680	2448	2228	2020	1823	1640	3509	2928	2425	1994	1624	1314							2.5	2.0	0			−27.5	−56.1
NEW 300 H&H Magnum	S300HX	M,L	180	Fail Safe	24	2880	2628	2390	2165	1952	1752	3316	2761	2284	1874	1523	1227							1.8	1.6	0			−23.2	−47.6
300 H&H Magnum	X300H2	O/P,M,L	180	Silvertip	24	2880	2640	2412	2196	1991	1798	3316	2786	2326	1928	1585	1292							2.1	1.7	0			−23.2	−47.4
300 Savage	X3001	D,O/PM,L	150	Silvertip	24	2630	2354	2095	1853	1631	1434	2305	1846	1462	1144	886	685							2.8	2.3	0			−31.5	−65.5
300 Savage	X3003	D,O/P	150	Power‑Point	24	2630	2311	2015	1743	1500	1295	2305	1779	1353	1012	750	559							2.7	2.2	0			−34.4	−73.0
300 Savage	X3004	D	180	Silvertip	24	2350	2137	1935	1745	1570	1413	2208	1826	1497	1217	985	798									0			−31.5	−65.5
300 Savage	X3032	D	180	Power‑Point	24	2350	2025	1728	1467	1252	1098	2208	1639	1194	860	627	482									0			−55.8	−112.0
303 British	X303B1	D,M	180	Power‑Point	24	2460	2233	2018	1816	1629	1459	2419	1993	1628	1318	1061	851									0			−40.4	−77.4
307 Winchester	X3076	D,M	180	Power‑Point	24	2510	2179	1874	1599	1362	1177	2519	1898	1404	1022	742	554							2.9		0			−47.1	−93.7
308 Winchester	S308	D,O/P	150	Silvertip Boattail	24	2820	2559	2312	2080	1861	1659	2649	2182	1781	1441	1154	917							2.2	1.8	0			−25.5	−54.6
308 Winchester	S308XA	D,O/P,M	150	Fail Safe	24	2820	2533	2263	2010	1775	1561	2649	2138	1706	1346	1049	812							2.0	1.7	0			−26.2	−62.0
308 Winchester	X3085	D,O/P	150	Power‑Point	24	2820	2488	2179	1893	1633	1405	2649	2062	1582	1194	888	657							2.0	1.9	0			−25.1	−55.7
308 Winchester	X3082	D,O/P	150	Silvertip	24	2820	2533	2263	2009	1774	1560	2649	2138	1706	1345	1048	810							2.1	1.8	0			−25.1	−60.7
308 Winchester Match	S308M	–	168	Hollow Point Boattail	M	2680	2485	2297	2118	1948	1786	2680	2304	1969	1674	1416	1190							2.4	2.1	0			−29.4	−60.3
308 Winchester	S308X	D,O/P,M,L	180	Fail Safe	24	2590	2357	2137	1929	1734	1555	2682	2221	1826	1488	1202	967							2.9	2.4	0			−36.9	−79.1
308 Winchester	X3086	D,O/PM	180	Power‑Point	24	2620	2274	1955	1666	1414	1212	2744	2067	1528	1110	799	587							2.9		0			−28.9	−58.8
308 Winchester	X3083	M,L	180	Silvertip	24	2620	2393	2178	1974	1782	1604	2744	2289	1896	1558	1270	1028							2.0		0			−70.9	−144.3
32 Win Special	X32WS2	D	170	Power‑Point	24	2250	1870	1537	1267	1082	971	1911	1320	892	606	442	356							2.0	0		−5.1	−13.8	−27.1	−70.9
32 Win Special	X32WS3	D	170	Silvertip	24	2250	1870	1537	1267	1082	971	1911	1320	892	606	442	356							2.0	0		−5.1	−13.8	−27.1	−70.9
32‑20 Winchester #	X32201	V	100	Lead	1	1210	1021	913	834	769	712	325	232	185	154	131	113								0	−11.5	−32.3	−63.6	−106.3	−230.3
8mm Mauser (8 x 57)	X8MM	D,O/P,M,L	170	Power‑Point	24	2360	1969	1622	1333	1123	997	2103	1464	993	671	476	375							1.8	0		−4.5	−12.4	−24.3	−63.8
338 Winchester Mag.	X3381	M,L,XL	200	Power‑Point	24	2960	2658	2375	2110	1862	1635	3890	3137	2505	1977	1539	1187							2.0	1.7	0			−23.4	−50.4
338 Winchester Mag.	X3383	M,L,XL	225	Soft Point	24	2780	2572	2374	2184	2003	1832	3862	3306	2816	2384	2005	1677							2.7	2.1	0			−25.0	−49.9
338 Winchester Mag.	S338XA	M,L,XL	230	Fail Safe	24	2780	2573	2375	2186	2005	1834	3948	3382	2881	2441	2054	1719							1.9	1.7	0	−3.8		−23.4	−47.4
35 Remington	X35R1	D,M	200	Power‑Point	24	2020	1646	1335	1114	985	901	1812	1203	791	551	431	360							2.7	0		−6.7	−18.3	−35.8	−92.8
356 Winchester	X3561	V,D	200	Power‑Point	24	2460	2114	1797	1517	1284	1113	2688	1985	1434	1022	732	550							1.6	0		−3.8	−10.4	−20.1	−51.2
357 Magnum #	X3575P	D	158	Jacketed Soft Point	20	1830	1427	1138	963	883	809	1175	715	454	337	274	229							0		−12.1	−33.9	−66.4	−110.6	−238.3
358 Winchester	X3581	D,M	200	Silvertip	24	2490	2171	1876	1610	1379	1194	2753	2094	1563	1151	845	633							1.5	0		−3.6	−9.7	−18.6	−47.2
375 Winchester	X375W	D,M	200	Power‑Point	24	2200	1841	1526	1268	1089	980	2150	1506	1034	714	527	427							2.1	0		−5.2	−14.1	−27.4	−70.1
NEW 375 H&H Magnum	S375HX	L,XL	300	Fail Safe	24	2530	2278	2040	1816	1610	1423	4263	3456	2773	2196	1727	1349							2.9	2.4	0	−4.5	−11.5	−33.8	−70.1
375 H&H Magnum	X375H2	M,L,XL	300	Silvertip	24	2530	2171	1843	1551	1307	1126	4263	3139	2262	1602	1138	844							2.9	0		−9.8	−19.1	−49.1	−99.5
375 H&H Magnum	X375H3	XL	300	Full Metal Jacket	24	2530	2171	1843	1551	1307	1126	4263	3139	2262	1602	1138	844							0		−12.1	−33.9	−66.4	−110.6	−238.3
38‑40 Winchester #	X3840	D	180	Soft Point	24	1160	999	901	827	764	710	538	399	325	273	233	201							0		−22.2	−47.3	−83.2	−158.8	−277.4
38‑55 Winchester	X3855	D	255	Soft Point	24	1320	1190	1091	1018	963	917	987	802	674	587	525	476							0		−15.4	−32.7	−57.0	−128.3	−235.8
44 Remington Magnum #	X44MS	V,D	210	Silvertip Hollow Point	20	1580	1198	993	879	795	725	1164	670	460	360	295	245							0	−7.7	−22.4	−44.9	−76.1	−168.0	−305.8
44 Remington Magnum #	X44MHSP2	V,D	240	Hollow Soft Point	20	1760	1362	1094	953	879	789	1650	989	638	484	395	332							0	−6.1	−18.1	−37.4	−65.1	−150.3	−282.5
44‑40 Winchester #	X4440	D	200	Soft Point	24	1190	1006	900	822	756	699	629	449	360	300	254	217							0		−21.6	−46.3	−81.8	−109.5	−237.4
45‑70 Government	X4570H	D,M	300	Jacketed Hollow Point	24	1880	1650	1425	1235	1105	1010	2355	1815	1355	1015	810	680							0		−12.8	−25.4	−44.3	−95.5	–
458 Winchester Magnum	X4581	L,XL	510	Soft Point	24	2040	1770	1527	1319	1157	1046	4712	3547	2640	1970	1516	1239							2.4		0	−5.6	−14.9	−28.5	−71.5	−140.4

WINCHESTER BALLISTICS

CENTERFIRE PISTOL/REVOLVER

	Cartridge	Symbol	Bullet Wt. Grs.	Type	Velocity (fps) Muzzle	50 Yds.	100 Yds.	Energy (ft-lbs.) Muzzle	50 Yds.	100 Yds.	Mid Range Traj. (In.) 50 Yds.	100 Yds.	Barrel Length Inches
	25 Automatic	X25AXP	45	Expanding Point**	815	729	655	66	53	42	1.8	7.7	2
	25 Automatic	X25AP	50	Full Metal Jacket	760	707	659	64	56	48	2.0	8.7	2
	30 Luger (7.65mm)	X30LP	93	Full Metal Jacket	1220	1110	1040	305	255	225	0.9	3.5	4-1/2
	30 Carbine #	X30M1	110	Hollow Soft Point	1790	1601	1430	783	626	500	0.4	1.7	10
	32 Smith & Wesson	X32SWP	85	Lead-Round Nose	680	645	610	90	81	73	2.5	10.5	3
	32 Smith & Wesson Long	X32SWLP	98	Lead-Round Nose	705	670	635	115	98	88	2.3	10.5	4
	32 Short Colt	X32SCP	80	Lead-Round Nose	745	665	590	100	79	62	2.2	9.9	4
	32 Automatic	X32ASHP	60	Silvertip® Hollow Point	970	895	835	125	107	93	1.3	5.4	4
	32 Automatic	X32AP	71	Full Metal Jacket	905	855	810	129	115	97	1.4	5.8	4
	38 Smith & Wesson	X38SWP	145	Lead-Round Nose	685	650	620	150	135	125	2.4	10.0	4
	380 Automatic	X380ASHP	85	Silvertip Hollow Point	1000	921	860	189	160	140	1.2	5.1	3-3/4
	380 Automatic SXT®	**S380**	**95**	**SXT**	**955**	**889**	**835**	**192**	**167**	**147**	**1.3**	**5.5**	**3-3/4**
	380 Automatic	X380AP	95	Full Metal Jacket	955	865	785	190	160	130	1.4	5.9	3-3/4
	38 Special	X38S9HP	110	Silvertip Hollow Point	945	894	850	218	195	176	1.3	5.4	4V
	38 Special Super Unleaded™	X38SSU	130	Full Metal Jacket Encapsulated	775	743	712	173	159	146	1.9	7.9	4V
	38 Special Super Match®	X38SMRP	148	Lead-Wad Cutter	710	634	566	166	132	105	2.4	10.8	4V
	38 Special	X38S1P	158	Lead-Round Nose	755	723	693	200	183	168	2.0	8.3	4V
	38 Special	X38WCPSV	158	Lead-Semi Wad Cutter	755	721	689	200	182	167	2.0	8.4	4V
	38 Special + P	X38SSHP	95	Silvertip Hollow Point	1100	1002	932	255	212	183	1.0	4.3	4V
	38 Special + P#	X38S6PH	110	Jacketed Hollow Point	995	926	871	242	210	185	1.2	5.1	4V
	38 Special + P#	X38S7PH	125	Jacketed Hollow Point	945	898	858	248	224	204	1.3	5.4	4V
	38 Special + P#	X38S8HP	125	Silvertip Hollow Point	945	898	858	248	224	204	1.3	5.4	4V
NEW	**38 Special + P# SXT**	**S38SP**	**130**	**SXT**	**925**	**887**	**852**	**247**	**227**	**210**	**1.3**	**5.5**	**4V**
	38 Special + P Subsonic®	XSUB38S	147	Jacketed Hollow Point	860	830	802	241	225	210	1.5	6.3	4V
NEW	38 Special +P Super Unleaded	X38SSU1	158	Full Metal Jacket-Encapsulated	890	864	839	278	262	249	1.4	5.8	4V
	38 Special + P	X38SPD	158	Lead-Semi Wad Cutter Hollow Point	890	855	823	278	257	238	1.4	6.0	4V
	38 Special + P	X38WCP	158	Lead-Semi Wad Cutter	890	855	823	278	257	238	1.4	6.0	4V
	9mm Luger Super Unleaded	X9MMSU	115	Full Metal Jacket Encapsulated	1155	1047	971	341	280	241	0.9	3.9	4
	9mm Luger	X9LP	115	Full Metal Jacket	1155	1047	971	341	280	241	0.9	3.9	4
	9mm Luger	X9MMSHP	115	Silvertip Hollow Point	1225	1095	1007	383	306	259	0.8	3.6	4
	9mm Luger SXT	**S9**	**147**	**SXT**	**990**	**947**	**909**	**320**	**293**	**270**	**1.2**	**4.8**	**4**
NEW	9mm Luger Super Unleaded	X9MMSU2	147	Full Metal Jacket-Encapsulated	990	945	907	320	292	268	1.2	4.8	4
	9mm Luger Subsonic	XSUB9MM	147	Jacketed Hollow Point	990	945	907	320	292	268	1.2	4.8	4
	9mm Luger	X9MMST147	147	Silvertip Hollow Point	1010	962	921	333	302	277	1.1	4.7	4
	9mm Luger Super Match	X9MMTCM	147	Full Metal Jacket-Truncated Cone-Match	990	945	907	320	292	268	1.2	4.8	4
	38 Super Automatic + P*	X38ASHP	125	Silvertip Hollow Point	1240	1130	1050	427	354	306	0.8	3.4	5
	38 Super Automatic + P*	X38A1P	130	Full Metal Jacket	1215	1099	1017	426	348	298	0.8	3.6	5
	357 Magnum #	X3573P	110	Jacketed Hollow Point	1295	1095	975	410	292	232	0.8	3.5	4V
	357 Magnum #	X3576P	125	Jacketed Hollow Point	1450	1240	1090	583	427	330	0.6	2.8	4V
	357 Magnum #	X357SHP	145	Silvertip Hollow Point	1290	1155	1060	535	428	361	0.8	3.5	4V
	357 Magnum	X3571P	158	Lead-Semi Wad Cutter**	1235	1104	1015	535	428	361	0.8	3.5	4V
	357 Magnum #	X3574P	158	Jacketed Hollow Point	1235	1104	1015	535	428	361	0.8	3.5	4V
	357 Magnum #	X3575P	158	Jacketed Soft Point	1235	1104	1015	535	428	361	0.8	3.5	4V
	40 Smith & Wesson	X40SWSTHP	155	Silvertip Hollow Point	1205	1096	1018	500	414	357	0.8	3.6	4
	40 Smith & Wesson Super Match	X40SWTCM	155	Full Metal Jacket-Truncated Cone-Match	1125	1046	986	436	377	335	0.9	3.9	4
NEW	**40 Smith & Wesson SXT**	**S401**	**165**	**SXT**	**1110**	**1020**	**960**	**443**	**381**	**338**	**1.0**	**4.2**	**4**
NEW	40 Smith & Wesson Super Unleaded	X40SWSU1	165	Full Metal Jacket-Encapsulated	1110	1020	960	443	381	338	1.0	4.2	4
	40 Smith & Wesson Super Unleaded	X40SWSU	180	Full Metal Jacket-Encapsulated	990	933	886	392	348	314	1.2	5.0	4
	40 Smith & Wesson SXT	**S40**	**180**	**SXT**	**1015**	**959**	**912**	**412**	**367**	**333**	**1.1**	**4.7**	**4**
	40 Smith & Wesson Subsonic	XSUB40SW	180	Jacketed Hollow Point	1010	954	909	408	364	330	1.1	4.8	4
	10mm Automatic	X10MMSTHP	175	Silvertip Hollow Point	1290	1141	1037	649	506	418	0.7	3.3	5-1/2
	10mm Automatic Subsonic	XSUB10MM	180	Jacketed Hollow Point	990	936	891	390	350	317	1.2	4.9	5
	41 Remington Magnum #	X41MSTHP2	175	Silvertip Hollow Point	1250	1120	1029	607	488	412	0.8	3.4	4V
	41 Remington Magnum #	X41MHP2	210	Jacketed Hollow Point	1300	1162	1062	788	630	526	0.7	3.2	4V
	44 Smith & Wesson Special #	X44STHPS2	200	Silvertip Hollow Point	900	860	822	360	328	300	1.4	5.9	6-1/2
	44 Smith & Wesson Special	X44SP	246	Lead-Round Nose	755	725	695	310	285	265	2.0	8.3	6-1/2
	44 Remington Magnum #	X44MS	210	Silvertip Hollow Point	1250	1106	1010	729	570	475	0.8	3.5	4V
	44 Remington Magnum #	X44MHSP2	240	Hollow Soft Point	1180	1081	1010	741	623	543	0.9	3.7	4V
	45 Automatic	X45ASHP2	185	Silvertip Hollow Point	1000	938	888	411	362	324	1.2	4.9	5
	45 Automatic Super Match	X45AWCP	185	Full Metal Jacket - Semi Wad Cutter	770	707	650	244	205	174	2.0	8.7	5
	45 Automatic SXT	**S45**	**230**	**SXT**	**880**	**846**	**816**	**396**	**366**	**340**	**1.5**	**6.1**	**5**
	45 Automatic Super Unleaded	X45ASU	230	Full Metal Jacket - Encapsulated	835	800	767	356	326	300	1.6	6.8	5
	45 Automatic Subsonic	XSUB45A	230	Jacketed Hollow Point	880	842	808	396	363	334	1.5	6.1	5
	45 Automatic	X45A1P2	230	Full Metal Jacket	835	800	767	356	326	300	1.6	6.8	5
	45 Colt #	X45CSHP2	225	Silvertip Hollow Point	920	877	839	423	384	352	1.4	5.6	5-1/2
	45 Colt	X45CP2	255	Lead-Round Nose	860	820	780	420	380	345	1.5	6.1	5-1/2
	45 Winchester Magnum #	X45WMA	260	Hollow Soft Point	1250	1137	1053	902	746	640	0.8	3.3	5

+P Ammunition with (+P) on the case head stamp is loaded to higher pressure. Use only in firearms designated for this cartridge and so recommended by the gun manufacturer.

V-Data is based on velocity obtained from 4" vented test barrels for revolver cartridges (38 Special, 357 Magnum, 41 Rem. Mag. and 44 Rem. Mag.)

Specifications are nominal. Test barrels are used to determine ballistics figures. Individual firearms may differ from test barrel statistics.

Specifications subject to change without notice.

**Lubaloy® Coated
*For use only in 38 Super Automatic Pistols.
#Acceptable for use in rifles also.

Reloading

For addresses and phone/fax numbers of manufacturers and distributors included in this section, please turn to DIRECTORY OF MANUFACTURERS AND SUPPLIERS on page 554.

HORNADY BULLETS

RIFLE BULLETS

17 CALIBER (.172)

25 gr. HP
#1710

22 CALIBER (.222)

40 gr. Jet
#2210

22 CALIBER (.223)

45 gr. Hornet
#2220

22 CALIBER (.224)

45 gr. Bee
#2229

45 gr. Hornet
#2230

50 gr. SXSP
#2240

50 gr. SP
#2245

NEW!
40 gr. V-MAX BT
#22241

NEW!
50 gr. V-MAX BT
#22261

NEW!
55 gr. V-MAX
#22271

22 CALIBER MATCH

52 gr. BTHP
#2249

53 gr. HP
#2250

55 gr. SXSP
#2260

55 gr. SP
#2265

55 gr. SP w/c
#2266

55 gr. FMJ-BT w/c
#2267

60 gr. SP
#2270

60 gr. HP
#2275

22 CALIBER MATCH

22 CALIBER (.227)

70 gr. SP
#2280

6MM (.243)

70 gr. SP
#2410

70 gr. SXSP
#2415

75 gr. HP
#2420

80 gr. FMJ
#2430

80 gr. SP
Single Shot Pistol
#2435
InterLock

87 gr. SP
#2440

87 gr. BTHP
#2442

100 gr. SP
#2450
InterLock

100 gr. BTSP
#2453
InterLock

100 gr. RN
#2455
InterLock

25 CALIBER (.257)

60 gr. FP
#2510

75 gr. HP
#2520

87 gr. SP
#2530

100 gr. SP
#2540
InterLock

117 gr. RN
#2550
InterLock

117 gr. BTSP
#2552
InterLock

120 gr. HP
#2560
InterLock

6.5MM (.264)

100 gr. SP
#2610

22 CALIBER (.227)

129 gr. SP
#2620
InterLock

140 gr. SP
#2630
InterLock

6.5MM MATCH

140 gr. BTHP
#2633

160 gr. RN
#2640
InterLock

270 CALIBER (.277)

100 gr. SP
#2710

110 gr. HP
#2720

130 gr. SP
#2730
InterLock

140 gr. BTSP
#2735
InterLock

150 gr. SP
#2740
InterLock

150 gr. RN
#2745
InterLock

7MM (.284)

100 gr. HP
#2800

120 gr. SP
#2810

120 gr. SP
Single Shot Pistol
#2811
InterLock

120 gr. HP
#2815

139 gr. SP
#2820
InterLock

139 gr. FP
#2822
InterLock

HORNADY BULLETS

RIFLE BULLETS

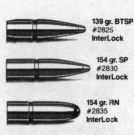

139 gr. BTSP
#2825
InterLock

154 gr. SP
#2830
InterLock

154 gr. RN
#2835
InterLock

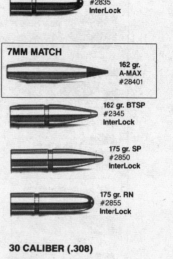

7MM MATCH

162 gr. A-MAX
#28401

162 gr. BTSP
#2345
InterLock

175 gr. SP
#2850
InterLock

175 gr. RN
#2855
InterLock

30 CALIBER (.308)

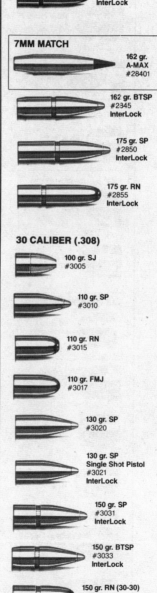

100 gr. SJ
#3005

110 gr. SP
#3010

110 gr. RN
#3015

110 gr. FMJ
#3017

130 gr. SP
#3020

130 gr. SP
Single Shot Pistol
#3021
InterLock

150 gr. SP
#3031
InterLock

150 gr. BTSP
#3033
InterLock

150 gr. RN (30-30)
#3035
InterLock

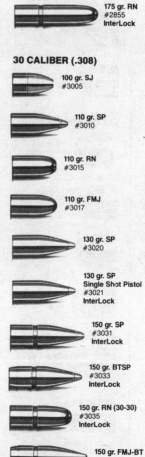

150 gr. FMJ-BT
#3037

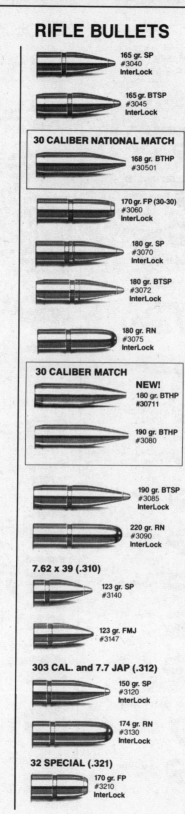

165 gr. SP
#3040
InterLock

165 gr. BTSP
#3045
InterLock

30 CALIBER NATIONAL MATCH

168 gr. BTHP
#30501

170 gr. FP (30-30)
#3060
InterLock

180 gr. SP
#3070
InterLock

180 gr. BTSP
#3072
InterLock

180 gr. RN
#3075
InterLock

30 CALIBER MATCH

NEW!
180 gr. BTHP
#30711

190 gr. BTHP
#3080

190 gr. BTSP
#3085
InterLock

220 gr. RN
#3090
InterLock

7.62 x 39 (.310)

123 gr. SP
#3140

123 gr. FMJ
#3147

303 CAL. and 7.7 JAP (.312)

150 gr. SP
#3120
InterLock

174 gr. RN
#3130
InterLock

32 SPECIAL (.321)

170 gr. FP
#3210
InterLock

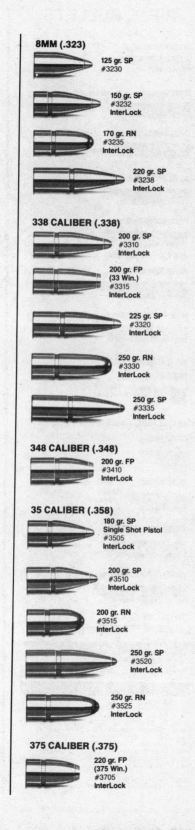

8MM (.323)

125 gr. SP
#3230

150 gr. SP
#3232
InterLock

170 gr. RN
#3235
InterLock

220 gr. SP
#3238
InterLock

338 CALIBER (.338)

200 gr. SP
#3310
InterLock

**200 gr. FP
(33 Win.)**
#3315
InterLock

225 gr. SP
#3320
InterLock

250 gr. RN
#3330
InterLock

250 gr. SP
#3335
InterLock

348 CALIBER (.348)

200 gr. FP
#3410
InterLock

35 CALIBER (.358)

180 gr. SP
Single Shot Pistol
#3505
InterLock

200 gr. SP
#3510
InterLock

200 gr. RN
#3515
InterLock

250 gr. SP
#3520
InterLock

250 gr. RN
#3525
InterLock

375 CALIBER (.375)

**220 gr. FP
(375 Win.)**
#3705
InterLock

HORNADY BULLETS

RIFLE BULLETS

*270 gr. SP
#3710
InterLock

*270 gr. RN
#3715
InterLock

*300 gr. RN
#3720
InterLock

*300 gr. BTSP
#3725
InterLock

*300 gr. FMJ-RN
#3727

416 CALIBER (.416)

*400 gr. RN
#4165
InterLock

*400 gr. FMJ-RN
#4167

44 CALIBER (.430)

265 gr. FP
#4300
InterLock

45 CALIBER (.458)

*300 gr. HP
#4500

*350 gr. RN
#4502
InterLock

*500 gr. RN
#4504
InterLock

*500 gr. FMJ-RN
#4507

50 CALIBER (.510)

**750 gr. A-MAX UHC #5165   **Packed 20 per box.

LEGEND

BBWC . Bevel Base Wadcutter	L . . . . . Swaged Lead Bullet
BT . . . . Boat Tail	LM . . . . Light Magnum™
C/T . . . Combat Target	LRN . . . Lead Round Nose
CL . . . . Crimp Lock™	RN . . . . Round Nose
DEWC . Double End Wadcutter	SIL . . . . Silhouette
FMJ . . . Full Metal Jacket	SJ . . . . Short Jacket
FP . . . . Flat Point	SP . . . . Spire Point
HBWC . Hollow Base Wadcutter	SWC . . . Semi-Wadcutter
HM . . . Heavy Magnum™	UHC . . Ultra-High Coefficient
HP . . . . Hollow Point	V . . . . . VECTOR®
I . . . . . . InterLock™ Bullet	XTP . . . Extreme Terminal
JFP . . . Jacketed Flat Point	Performance™
JHP . . . Jacketed Hollow Point	+P . . . High Pressure

PISTOL BULLETS

25 CALIBER (.251)

35 gr. HP/XTP
#35450

50 gr. FMJ-RN
#3545

32 CALIBER (.311)

71 gr. FMJ-RN
#3200

32 CALIBER (.312)

85 gr. HP/XTP
#32050

100 gr. HP/XTP
#32070

9 x 18 MAKAROV

95 gr. HP/XTP
#36500

9MM (.355)

90 gr. HP/XTP
#35500

100 gr. FMJ-RN
#3552

115 gr. HP/XTP
#35540

115 gr. FMJ-RN
#3555

124 gr. FMJ-FP
#3556

124 gr. FMJ-RN
#3557

124 gr. HP/XTP
#35571

147 gr.
HP-BT/XTP
#35580

147 gr.
FMJ-RN-BT
#3559

CALIBER (.357)

110 gr. HP/XTP
#35700

125 gr. HP/XTP
#35710

125 gr. FP/XTP
#35730

140 gr. HP/XTP
#35740

158 gr. HP/XTP
#35750

158 gr. FP/XTP
#35780

160 gr. CL-SIL
#3572

180 gr. CL-SIL
#3577

180 gr. HP/XTP
35771

10MM (.400)

155 gr. HP/XTP
#40000

180 gr. HP/XTP
#40040

180 gr. FMJ-FP
#40041

200 gr. FMJ-FP
#4007

200 gr. HP/XTP
#40060

41 CALIBER (.410)

210 gr. HP/XTP
#41000

210 gr. CL-SIL
#4105

44 CALIBER (.430)

180 gr. HP/XTP
#44050

200 gr. HP/XTP
#44100

240 gr. HP/XTP
#44200

240 gr. CL-SIL
#4425

*300 gr. HP/XTP
#44280

45 CALIBER (.451)

185 gr. HP/XTP
#45100

45 CALIBER MATCH

185 gr. SWC
#4513

200 gr. HP/XTP
#45140

45 CALIBER MATCH

200 gr. FMJ-C/T
#4515

230 gr. FMJ-RN
#4517

230 gr. FMJ-FP
#4518

230 gr. HP/XTP
45160

45 CALIBER (.452)

250 gr. Long
Colt HP/XTP
#45200

*300 gr. HP/XTP
45230

*Packed 50 per box.
All others packed
100 per box.

NOSLER BULLETS

PISTOL AND REVOLVER BULLETS

Cal. Dia.	HANDGUN Auto	BULLET WEIGHT AND STYLE	SECT. DENS.	BAL. COEF.	PART#
9mm .355"		90 GR. HOLLOW POINT	.102	.086	42050
		115 GR. FULL METAL JACKET	.130	.103	42059
		115 GR. HOLLOW POINT 250 QUANTITY BULK PACK	.130	.110	43009 44848
new ▶		115 GR. HOLLOW POINT IPSC 250 QUANTITY BULK PACK	.129	.110	44835
38 .357"		135 GR. IPSC 250 QUANTITY BULK PACK	.151	.149	44836
		150 GR. IPSC 250 QUANTITY BULK PACK	.168	.157	44839
		135 GR. HOLLOW POINT 250 QUANTITY BULK PACK	.121	.093	44838 44852
		150 GR. HOLLOW POINT	.134	.106	44849
10mm .400"		170 GR. HOLLOW POINT	.152	.137	44844
		180 GR. HOLLOW POINT	.161	.147	44837
45 .451"		185 GR. HOLLOW POINT 250 QUANTITY BULK PACK	.130	.142	42062 44847
		230 GR. FULL METAL JACKET	.162	.183	42064

Cal. Dia.	HANDGUN Revolver	BULLET WEIGHT AND STYLE	SECT. DENS.	BAL. COEF.	PART#
38 .357"		125 GR. HOLLOW POINT 250 QUANTITY BULK PACK	.140	.143	42055 44840
		150 GR. SOFT POINT	.168	.153	42056
		158 GR. HOLLOW POINT 250 QUANTITY BULK PACK	.177	.182	42057 44841
		180 GR. SILHOUETTE 250 QUANTITY BULK PACK	.202	.210	42058 44851
41 .410"		210 GR. HOLLOW POINT	.178	.170	43012
44 .429"		200 GR. HOLLOW POINT 250 QUANTITY BULK PACK	.155	.151	42060 44846
		240 GR. SOFT POINT	.186	.177	42068
		240 GR. HOLLOW POINT 250 QUANTITY BULK PACK	.186	.173	42061 44842
		300 GR. HOLLOW POINT	.233	.206	42069
45 Colt .451"		250 GR. HOLLOW POINT	.176	.177	43013

NOSLER BULLETS

Nosler Partition® Bullets

The Nosler Partition® bullet earned its reputation among professional guides and serious hunters for one reason: it doesn't fail. The patented Partition® design offers a dual core that is unequalled in mushrooming, weight retention and hydrostatic shock.

Cal. Dia.	PARTITION®	BULLET WEIGHT AND STYLE	SECT. DENS.	BAL. COEF.	PART#
270 .277"		130 GR. SPITZER	.242	.416	16322
		150 GR. SPITZER	.279	.465	16323
		160 GR. SEMI SPITZER	.298	.434	16324
7mm .284"		140 GR. SPITZER	.248	.434	16325
		150 GR. SPITZER	.266	.456	16326
		160 GR. SPITZER	.283	.475	16327
		175 GR. SPITZER	.310	.519	35645
30 .308"		150 GR. SPITZER	.226	.387	16329
		165 GR. SPITZER	.248	.410	16330
		170 GR. ROUND NOSE	.256	.252	16333
		180 GR. SPITZER	.271	.474	16331
		180 GR. PROTECTED POINT	.271	.361	25396
		200 GR. SPITZER	.301	.481	35626
		220 GR. SEMI SPITZER	.331	.351	16332
8mm .323"		200 GR. SPITZER	.274	.426	35277
338 .338"		210 GR. SPITZER	.263	.400	16337
		225 GR. SPITZER	.281	.454	16336
		250 GR. SPITZER	.313	.473	35644
35 .358"		225 GR. SPITZER	.251	.430	44800
		250 GR. SPITZER	.279	.446	44801
375 .375"		260 GR. SPITZER	.264	.314	44850
		300 GR. SPITZER	.305	.398	44845

Cal. Dia.	PARTITION®	BULLET WEIGHT AND STYLE	SECT. DENS.	BAL. COEF.	PART#
6mm .243"		85 GR. SPITZER	.206	.315	16314
		95 GR. SPITZER	.230	.365	16315
		100 GR. SPITZER	.242	.384	35642
25 .257"		100 GR. SPITZER	.216	.377	16317
		115 GR. SPITZER	.249	.389	16318
		120 GR. SPITZER	.260	.391	35643
6.5mm .264"		125 GR. SPITZER	.256	.449	16320
		140 GR. SPITZER	.287	.490	16321

SAKO BULLETS

PISTOL AND REVOLVER BULLETS

WC (Wad Cutter)
An accurate, highly popular bullet for target shooting that makes a hole that is easy to interpret. Low recoil.

SWC (Semi Wad Cutter)
Has greater speed and energy than the WC. Also intended for target shooting.

FMJ (Full Metal Jacket)
Good penetration and excellent feeding characteristics with semiautomatic weapons.

NEW!

KPO
Contact-opening special bullet with jacket reliability when feeding from magazine. Electrolytic core will not separate

JSP (Jacketed Soft Point)
A powerful bullet that can be loaded for greater speed without leading the barrel. Better target ballistics than the FMJ.

RIFLE BULLETS

NEW!

SPEEDHEAD FMJ
Intended chiefly for shooting game, the full-metal-jacket bullet is characterized by high accuracy.

SP (Soft Point)
Sako's semijacketed soft-point bullet is the most popular type of bullet for hunting. On hitting the prey the bullet spreads rapidly, immediately producing a fatal shock effect.

HP (Hollow Point)
The ballistic characteristics of the hollow-point bullet make it the ideal choice for target shooting. This bullet is also fast, making it well suited to varmint shooting.

HAMMERHEAD
The Sako Hammerhead is a heavy, lead-tipped bullet especially designed for moose hunting and other big game.

NEW!

SUPER HAMMERHEAD
The famous Hammerhead is designed in a light version for long-range hunting with better ballistic characteristics.

NEW!

POWERHEAD (Hollow Point Copper)
An all-copper opening hollow-point bullet for big-game hunting without fear of core separation.

SP P = Soft Point Pointed
SP SP = Soft Point SemiPointed
SP RN = Soft Point Round Nose
SP FP = Soft Point Flat Point
HP = Hollow Point
HP BT = Hollow Point Boat Tail
HAMMERHEAD = Soft Point Bonded Core
SUPER HH = Hollow Point Bonded Core
POWERHEAD = Hollow Point Solid Copper

SIERRA BULLETS

RIFLE BULLETS

.22 Caliber Hornet
(.223/5.66MM Diameter)

40 gr. Hornet
Varminter #1100

45 gr. Hornet
Varminter #1110

.22 Caliber Hornet
(.224/5.69MM Diameter)

40 gr. Hornet
Varminter #1200

45 gr. Hornet
Varminter #1210

.22 Caliber
(.224/5.69MM Diameter)

40 gr. HP
Varminter #1385

45 gr. SMP
Varminter #1300

45 gr. SPT
Varminter #1310

50 gr. SMP
Varminter #1320

50 gr. SPT
Varminter #1330

50 gr. Blitz
Varminter #1340

52 gr. HPBT
MatchKing #1410

53 gr. HP
MatchKing #1400

55 gr. Blitz
Varminter #1345

55 gr. SMP
Varminter #1350

55 gr. FMJBT
GameKing #1355

55 gr. SPT
Varminter #1360

55 gr. SBT
GameKing #1365

55 gr. HPBT
GameKing #1390

60 gr. HP
Varminter #1375

63 gr. SMP
Varminter #1370

69 gr. HPBT
MatchKing #1380

7"-10" TWST BBLS

6MM .243 Caliber
(.243/6.17MM Diameter)

60 gr. HP
Varminter #1500

70 gr. HPBT
MatchKing #1505

75 gr. HP
Varminter #1510

**80 gr. Blitz
Varminter #1515**

85 gr. SPT
Varminter #1520

85 gr. HPBT
GameKing #1530

90 gr. FMJBT
GameKing #1535

100 gr. SPT
Pro-Hunter #1540

100 gr. SMP
Pro-Hunter #1550

100 gr. SBT
GameKing #1560

107 gr. HPBT
MatchKing #1570

7"-8" TWST BBLS

.25 Caliber
(.257/6.53MM Diameter)

75 gr. HP
Varminter #1600

87 gr. SPT
Varminter #1610

90 gr. HPBT
GameKing #1615

100 gr. SPT
Pro-Hunter #1620

100 gr. SBT
GameKing #1625

117 gr. SBT
GameKing #1630

117 gr. SPT
Pro-Hunter #1640

120 gr. HPBT
GameKing #1650

6.5MM .264 Caliber
(.264/6.71MM Diameter)

85 gr. HP
Varminter #1700

100 gr. HP
Varminter #1710

120 gr. SPT
Pro-Hunter #1720

120 gr. HPBT
MatchKing #1725

6.5MM .264 Caliber (cont.)
(.264/6.71MM Diameter)

140 gr. SBT
GameKing #1730

140 gr. HPBT
MatchKing #1740

160 gr. SMP
Pro-Hunter #1750

.270 Caliber
(.277/7.04MM Diameter)

90 gr. HP
Varminter #1800

110 gr. SPT
Pro-Hunter #1810

130 gr. SBT
GameKing #1820

130 gr. SPT
Pro-Hunter #1830

**135 gr. HPBT
MatchKing #1833**

140 gr. HPBT
GameKing #1835

140 gr. SBT
GameKing #1845

150 gr. SBT
GameKing #1840

150 gr. RN
Pro-Hunter #1850

7MM .284 Caliber
(.284/7.21MM Diameter)

100 gr. HP
Varminter #1895

120 gr. SPT
Pro-Hunter #1900

140 gr. SBT
GameKing #1905

140 gr. SPT
Pro-Hunter #1910

150 gr. SBT
GameKing #1913

150 gr. HPBT
MatchKing #1915

160 gr. SBT
GameKing #1920

160 gr. HPBT
GameKing #1925

168 gr. HPBT
MatchKing #1930

170 gr. RN
Pro-Hunter #1950

175 gr. SBT
GameKing #1940

SIERRA BULLETS

RIFLE BULLETS

.30 (30-30) Caliber
(.308/7.82MM Diameter)

125 gr. HP/FN
Pro-Hunter #2020

150 gr. FN
Pro-Hunter #2000
POWER JACKET

170 gr. FN
Pro-Hunter #2010
POWER JACKET

30 Caliber 7.62MM
(.308/7.82MM Diameter)

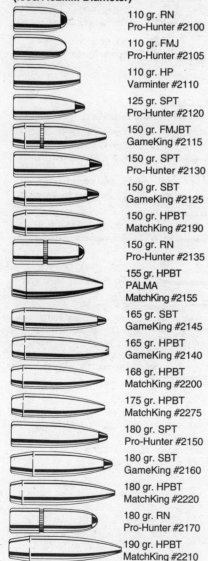

110 gr. RN
Pro-Hunter #2100

110 gr. FMJ
Pro-Hunter #2105

110 gr. HP
Varminter #2110

125 gr. SPT
Pro-Hunter #2120

150 gr. FMJBT
GameKing #2115

150 gr. SPT
Pro-Hunter #2130

150 gr. SBT
GameKing #2125

150 gr. HPBT
MatchKing #2190

150 gr. RN
Pro-Hunter #2135

155 gr. HPBT
PALMA
MatchKing #2155

165 gr. SBT
GameKing #2145

165 gr. HPBT
GameKing #2140

168 gr. HPBT
MatchKing #2200

175 gr. HPBT
MatchKing #2275

180 gr. SPT
Pro-Hunter #2150

180 gr. SBT
GameKing #2160

180 gr. HPBT
MatchKing #2220

180 gr. RN
Pro-Hunter #2170

190 gr. HPBT
MatchKing #2210

30 Caliber 7.62MM (cont.)
(.308/7.82MM Diameter)

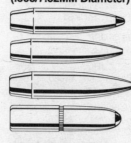

200 gr. SBT
GameKing #2165

200 gr. HPBT
MatchKing #2230

220 gr. HPBT
MatchKing
#2240

220 gr. RN
Pro-Hunter #2180

.303 Caliber 7.7MM
(.311/7.90MM Diameter)

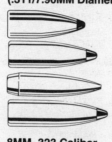

125 gr. SPT
Pro-Hunter #2305

150 gr. SPT
Pro-Hunter #2300

174 gr. HPBT
MatchKing #2315

180 gr. SPT
Pro-Hunter #2310

8MM .323 Caliber
(.323/8.20MM Diameter)

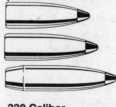

150 gr. SPT
Pro-Hunter #2400

175 gr. SPT
Pro-Hunter #2410

220 gr. SBT
GameKing #2420

.338 Caliber
(.338/8.59MM Diameter)

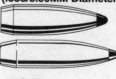

215 gr. SBT
GameKing #2610

250 gr. SBT
GameKing #2600

.35 Caliber
(.358/9.09MM Diameter)

200 gr. RN
Pro-Hunter #2800

225 gr. SBT
GameKing #2850

.375 Caliber
(.375/9.53MM Diameter)

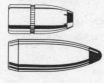

200 gr. FN
Pro-Hunter #2900
POWER JACKET

250 gr. SBT
GameKing #2950

.375 Caliber (cont.)
(.375/9.53MM Diameter)

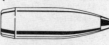

300 gr. SBT
GameKing #3000

.45 Caliber (.45-70)
(.458/11.63MM Diameter)

300 gr. HP/FN
Pro-Hunter #8900

Long Range & Specialty Bullets

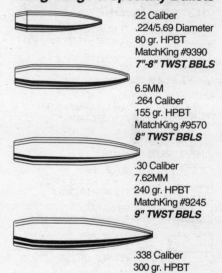

22 Caliber
.224/5.69 Diameter
80 gr. HPBT
MatchKing #9390
7"-8" TWST BBLS

6.5MM
.264 Caliber
155 gr. HPBT
MatchKing #9570
8" TWST BBLS

.30 Caliber
7.62MM
240 gr. HPBT
MatchKing #9245
9" TWST BBLS

.338 Caliber
300 gr. HPBT
MatchKing #9300
10" TWST BBLS

SIERRA BULLETS

HANDGUN BULLETS

Single Shot Pistol Bullets

6MM .243 Dia. 80 gr. SPT
Pro-Hunter #7150

7MM .284 Dia. 130 gr. SPT
Pro-Hunter #7250

.30 cal. .308 Dia. 135 gr. SPT
Pro-Hunter #7350

.25 Caliber
(.251/6.38MM Diameter)

50 gr. FMJ
Tournament Master #8000

.32 Caliber 7.65MM
(.312/7.92MM Diameter)

71 gr. FMJ
Tournament Master #8010

.32 Mag.
(.312/7.92MM Diameter)

90 gr. JHC
Sports Master #8030
POWER JACKET

9MM .355 Caliber
(.355/9.02MM Diameter)

90 gr. JHP
Sports Master #8100
POWER JACKET

95 gr. FMJ
Tournament Master #8105

115 gr. JHP
Sports Master #8110
POWER JACKET

115 gr. FMJ
Tournament Master #8115

125 gr. FMJ
Tournament Master #8120

130 gr. FMJ
Tournament Master #8345

.38 Super
(.356/9.04MM Diameter)

150 gr. FPJ Match
Tournament Master #8250

9MM Makarov
(.363/9.22MM Diameter)

95 gr. JHP
Sports Master #8200
POWER JACKET

100 gr. FPJ
Tournament Master #8210

.38 Caliber
(.357/9.07MM Diameter)

110 gr. JHC Blitz
Sports Master #8300
POWER JACKET

125 gr. JSP
Sports Master #8310

125 gr. JHC
Sports Master #8320
POWER JACKET

140 gr. JHC
Sports Master #8325
POWER JACKET

158 gr. JSP
Sports Master #8340

158 gr. JHC
Sports Master #8360
POWER JACKET

170 gr. JHC
Sports Master #8365
POWER JACKET

170 gr. FMJ Match
Tournament Master #8350

180 gr. FPJ Match
Tournament Master #8370

10MM .400 Caliber
(.400/10.16MM Diameter)

135 gr. JHP
Sports Master #8425
POWER JACKET

150 gr. JHP
Sports Master #8430
POWER JACKET

165 gr. JHP
Sports Master #8445
POWER JACKET

180 gr. JHP
Sports Master #8460
POWER JACKET

190 gr. FPJ
Tournament Master #8480

.41 Caliber
(.410/10.41MM Diameter)

170 gr. JHC
Sports Master #8500
POWER JACKET

210 gr. JHC
Sports Master #8520
POWER JACKET

220 gr. FPJ Match
Tournament Master #8530

.44 Magnum
(.4295/10.91MM Diameter)

180 gr. JHC
Sports Master #8600
POWER JACKET

210 gr. JHC
Sports Master #8620
POWER JACKET

220 gr. FPJ Match
Tournament Master #8605

240 gr. JHC
Sports Master #8610
POWER JACKET

250 gr. FPJ Match
Tournament Master #8615

300 gr. JSP
Sports Master #8630

.45 Caliber
(.4515/11.47MM Diameter)

185 gr. JHP
Sports Master #8800
POWER JACKET

185 gr. FPJ Match
Tournament Master #8810

200 gr. FPJ Match
Tournament Master #8825

230 gr. FMJ Match
Tournament Master #8815

240 gr. JHC
Sports Master #8820
POWER JACKET

300 gr. JSP
Sports Master #8830

SPEER HANDGUN BULLETS

Speer Handgun Bullets

Caliber & Type	25 Gold Dot Hollow Pt.	32 Gold Dot Hollow Pt.	9mm Gold Dot Hollow Point	9mm Gold Dot Hollow Point	9mm Gold Dot Hollow Point	9mm Gold Dot Hollow Point	357 Sig Gold Dot Hollow Point	38 Gold Dot Hollow Point	38 Gold Dot Hollow Point	9mm Makarov Gold Dot Hollow Point	40/10mm Gold Dot Hollow Point	40/10mm Gold Dot Hollow Point	40/10mm Gold Dot Hollow Point	44 Gold Dot Soft Point	45 Gold Dot Hollow Point	45 Gold Dot Hollow Point
Diameter	.251"	.311"	.355"	.355"	.355"	.355"	.355"	.357"	.357"	.364"	.400"	.400"	.400"	.429"	.451"	.451"
Weight (grs.)	35	60	90	115	124	147	125	125	158	90	155	165	180	270	185	230
Ballist. Coef.	.091	.118	0.101	0.125	0.134	0.164	0.141	0.140	0.168	0.107	0.123	.138	0.143	0.193	0.109	0.143
Part Number	3985	3986	3992	3994	3998	4002	4360	4012	4215	3999	4400	4397	4406	4461	4470	4483
Box Count	100	100	100	100	100	100	100	100	100	100	100	100	100	50	100	100

Speer Handgun Bullets

Caliber & Type	25 TMJ	32 JHP	9mm TMJ	9mm JHP	9mm TMJ	9mm JHP	9mm SP	9mm TMJ	9mm TMJ	357 Sig TMJ	38 JHP	38 JSP	38 JHP	38 TMJ	38 JHP	38 JHP-SWC
Diameter	.251"	.312"	.355"	.355"	.355"	.355"	.355"	.355"	.355"	.355"	.357"	.357"	.357"	.357"	.357"	.357"
Weight (grs.)	50		95	100	115	115	124	124	147	125	110	125	125	125	140	146
Ballist. Coef.	0.110	0.167	0.131	0.111	0.177	0.118	0.115	0.114	0.208	0.147	0.122	0.140	0.135	0.146	0.152	0.159
Part Number	3982	3981	4001	3983	3995	3996	3997	4004	4006	4362	4007	4011	4013	4015	4203	4205
Box Count	100	100	100	100	100	100	100	100	100	100	100	100	100	100	100	100

Speer Handgun Bullets

Caliber & Type	38 TMJ	38 JHP	38 JSP	38 JSP-SWC	38 TMJ-Sil.	38 TMJ-Sil.	9mm Makarov TMJ	40/10mm TMJ	40/10mm TMJ	40/10mm TMJ	40/10mm TMJ	41 AE HP	41 JHP-SWC	41 JSP-SWC	41 TMJ-Sil.
Diameter	.357"	.357"	.357"	.357"	.357"	.357"	.364"	.400"	.400"	.400"	.400"	.410"	.410"	.410"	.410"
Weight (grs.)	158	158	158	160	180	200	95	155	165	180	200	180	200	220	210
Ballist. Coef.	0.173	0.158	0.158	0.170	0.230	0.236	0.127	0.125	0.135	0.143	0.208	0.138	0.113	0.137	0.216
Part Number	4207	4211	4217	4223	4229	4231	4375	4399	4410	4402	4403	4404	4405	4417	4420
Box Count	100	100	100	100	100	100	100	100	100	100	100	100	100	100	100

Speer Handgun Bullets

Caliber & Type	44 MAG. JHP	44 JHP-SWC	44 JSP-SWC	44 MAG. JHP	44 MAG. JSP	44 TMJ-Sil.	44 MAG. SP	45 TMJ-Match	45 TMJ-Match	45 JHP	45 MAG. JHP	45 TMJ	45 MAG. JHP	45 SP	50 AE HP
Diameter	.429"	.429"	.429"	.429"	.429"	.429"	.429"	.451"	.451"	.451"	.451"	.451"	.451"	.451"	.500"
Weight (grs.)	200	225	240	240	240	240	300	185	200	200	225	230	260	300	325
Ballist. Coef.	0.122	0.146	0.157	0.165	0.164	0.206	0.213	0.090	0.129	0.138	0.169	0.153	0.183	0.199	0.149
Part Number	4425	4435	4447	4453	4457	4459	4463	4473	4475	4477	4479	4480	4481	4485	4495
Box Count	100	100	100	100	100	100	50	100	100	100	100	100	100	50	50

Speer Handgun Bullets Lead

Caliber & Type	32 HB-WC	9mm RN	38 BB-WC	38 DE-WC	38 HB-WC	38 SWC	38 HP-SWC	38 RN	44 SWC	45 SWC	45 RN	45 SWC
Diameter	.314"	.356"	.358"	.358"	.358"	.358"	.358"	.358"	.430"	.452"	.452"	.452"
Weight (grs.)	98	125	148	148	148	158	158	158	240	200	230	250
Part Number	--	4601	4605	--	4617	4623	4627	4647	4660	4677	4690	4683
Bulk Pkg	4600	4602	4606	4611	4618	4624	4628	4648	4661	4678	4691	4684

Abbreviation Guide: JHP-Jacketed Hollow Point, TMJ-Totally Metal Jacketed, SP-Soft Point, JSP-Jacketed Soft Point, Sil-Silhouette, WC-Wadcutter, SWC-Semi-Wadcutter, HB-Hollow Base, BB-Bevel Base, RN-Round Nose, HP-Hollow Point
Ⓗ-HOT-COR   Ⓤ-UNI-COR

SPEER RIFLE BULLETS

Speer Rifle Bullets

Bullet Caliber & Type	22 Spire Soft Point	22 Spitzer Soft Point	22 Spire Soft Point	22 Spitzer Soft Point	22 218 Bee Flat Soft Point w/Cann.	22 Spitzer Soft Point	22 "TNT" Hollow Point	22 Hollow Point	22 Hollow Point B.T. Match	22 FMJ B.T. w/Cann.	22 Spitzer Soft Point	22 Spitzer S.P. w/Cann.	22 FMJ B.T. w/Cann.	22 Semi-Spitzer Soft Point	6mm "TNT" Hollow Point
Diameter	.223"	.223"	.224"	.224"	.224"	.224"	.224"	.224"	.224"	.224"	.224"	.224"	.224"	.224"	.243"
Weight (grs.)	40	45	40	45	46	50	50	52	52	55	55	55	62	70	70
Ballist. Coef.	0.145	0.166	0.144	0.167	0.094	0.231	0.223	0.225	0.253	0.269	0.255	0.241	0.307	0.214	0.282
Part Number	1005	1011	1017	1023	1024	1029	1030	1035	1036	1044	1047	1049	1050	1053	1206
Box Count	100	100	100	100	100	100	100	100	100	100	100	100	100	100	100

Speer Rifle Bullets

Bullet Caliber & Type	6.5mm Spitzer Soft Point	270 "TNT" Hollow Point	270 Hollow Point	270 Spitzer Soft Point	270 Spitzer Soft Point B.T.	270 Spitzer Soft Point	270 Spitzer Soft Point B.T.	270 Spitzer Soft Point	7mm "TNT" Hollow Point	7mm Hollow Point	7mm Spitzer Soft Point	7mm Spitzer Soft Point	7mm Spitzer Soft Point B.T.	7mm Spitzer Soft Point B.T.	7mm Spitzer Soft Point
Diameter	.263"	.277"	.277"	.277"	.277"	.277"	.277"	.277"	.284"	.284"	.284"	.284"	.284"	.284"	.284"
Weight (grs.)	140	90	100	100	130	130	150	150	110	115	120	130	145	145	145
Ballist. Coef.	0.496	0.275	0.225	0.319	0.449	0.408	0.496	0.481	0.338	0.257	0.386	0.394	0.411	0.502	0.457
Part Number	1441	1446	1447	1453	1458	1459	1604	1605	1616	1617	1620	1623	1624	1628	1629
Box Count	100	100	100	100	100	100	100	100	100	100	100	100	100	100	100

Speer Rifle Bullets

Bullet Caliber & Type	30 Spitzer Soft Point B.T.	30 Spitzer Soft Point	30 Mag-Tip™ Soft Point	30 Round Soft Point	30 Spitzer Soft Point B.T.	30 Spitzer Soft Point	30 Match Hollow Point B.T.	30 Flat Soft Point	30 Round Soft Point	30 Spitzer Soft Point B.T.	30 Spitzer Soft Point	30 Mag-Tip™ Soft Point	30 Match Hollow Point B.T.	30 Spitzer Soft Point	303 Spitzer Soft Point w/Cann.
Diameter	.308"	.308"	.308"	.308"	.308"	.308"	.308"	.308"	.308"	.308"	.308"	.308"	.308"	.308"	.311"
Weight (grs.)	150	150	150	165	165	165	168	170	180	180	180	180	190	200	125
Ballist. Coef.	0.423	0.389	0.301	0.274	0.477	0.433	0.480	0.304	0.304	0.540	0.483	0.352	0.540	0.556	0.292
Part Number	2022	2023	2025	2029	2034	2035	2040	2041	2047	2052	2053	2059	2080	2211	2213
Box Count	100	100	100	100	100	100	100	100	100	100	100	100	50	50	100

SPEER RIFLE BULLETS

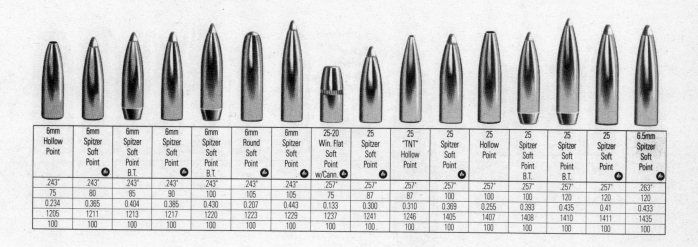

	6mm Hollow Point	6mm Spitzer Soft Point	6mm Spitzer Soft Point B.T.	6mm Spitzer Soft Point	6mm Spitzer Soft Point B.T.	6mm Round Soft Point	6mm Spitzer Soft Point	25-20 Win. Flat Soft Point w/Cann.	25 Spitzer Soft Point	25 "TNT" Hollow Point	25 Spitzer Soft Point	25 Hollow Point	25 Spitzer Soft Point B.T.	25 Spitzer Soft Point B.T.	25 Spitzer Soft Point	6.5mm Spitzer Soft Point
	.243"	.243"	.243"	.243"	.243"	.243"	.243"	.257"	.257"	.257"	.257"	.257"	.257"	.257"	.257"	.263"
	75	80	85	90	100	105	105	75	87	87	100	100	100	120	120	120
	0.234	0.365	0.404	0.385	0.430	0.207	0.443	0.133	0.300	0.310	0.369	0.255	0.393	0.435	0.41	0.433
	1205	1211	1213	1217	1220	1223	1229	1237	1241	1246	1405	1407	1408	1410	1411	1435
	100	100	100	100	100	100	100	100	100	100	100	100	100	100	100	100

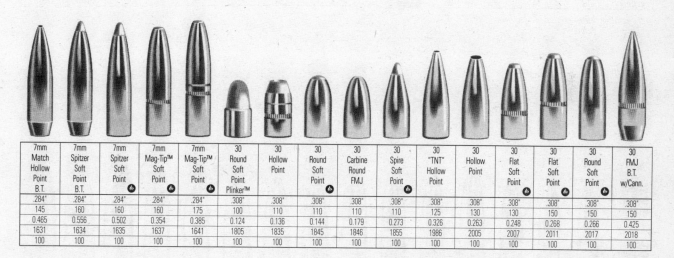

	7mm Match Hollow Point B.T.	7mm Spitzer Soft Point B.T.	7mm Spitzer Soft Point	7mm Mag-Tip™ Soft Point	7mm Mag-Tip™ Soft Point	30 Round Soft Point Plinker™	30 Hollow Point	30 Round Soft Point	30 Carbine Round FMJ	30 Spire Soft Point	30 "TNT" Hollow Point	30 Hollow Point	30 Flat Soft Point	30 Flat Soft Point	30 Round Soft Point	30 FMJ B.T. w/Cann.
	.284"	.284"	.284"	.284"	.284"	.308"	.308"	.308"	.308"	.308"	.308"	.308"	.308"	.308"	.308"	.308"
	145	160	160	160	175	100	110	110	110	110	125	130	130	150	150	150
	0.465	0.556	0.502	0.354	0.385	0.124	0.136	0.144	0.179	0.273	0.326	0.263	0.248	0.268	0.266	0.425
	1631	1634	1635	1637	1641	1805	1835	1845	1846	1855	1986	2005	2007	2011	2017	2018
	100	100	100	100	100	100	100	100	100	100	100	100	100	100	100	100

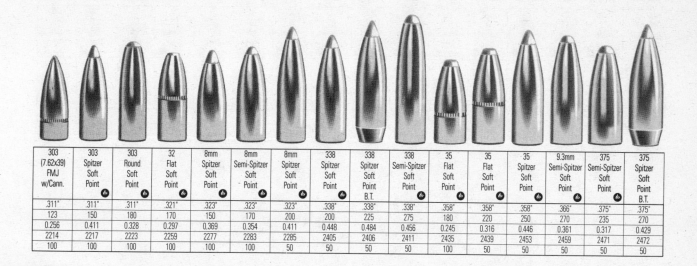

	303 (7.62x39) FMJ w/Cann.	303 Spitzer Soft Point	303 Round Soft Point	32 Flat Soft Point	8mm Spitzer Soft Point	8mm Semi-Spitzer Soft Point	8mm Spitzer Soft Point	338 Spitzer Soft Point	338 Spitzer Soft Point B.T.	338 Semi-Spitzer Soft Point	35 Flat Soft Point	35 Flat Soft Point	35 Spitzer Soft Point	9.3mm Semi-Spitzer Soft Point	375 Semi-Spitzer Soft Point	375 Spitzer Soft Point B.T.
	.311"	.311"	.311"	.321"	.323"	.323"	.323"	.338"	.338"	.338"	.358"	.358"	.358"	.366"	.375"	.375"
	123	150	180	170	150	170	200	200	225	275	180	220	250	270	235	270
	0.256	0.411	0.328	0.297	0.369	0.354	0.411	0.448	0.484	0.456	0.245	0.316	0.446	0.361	0.317	0.429
	2214	2217	2223	2259	2277	2283	2285	2405	2406	2411	2435	2439	2453	2459	2471	2472
	100	100	100	100	100	100	50	50	50	50	100	50	50	50	50	50

SPEER RIFLE BULLETS

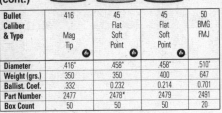

Speer Rifle Bullets (cont.)

Bullet Caliber & Type	416 Mag Tip	45 Flat Soft Point	45 Flat Soft Point	50 BMG FMJ
Diameter	.416"	.458"	.458"	.510"
Weight (grs.)	350	350	400	647
Ballist. Coef.	.332	0.232	0.214	0.701
Part Number	2477	2478*	2479	2491
Box Count	50	50	50	20

*Not intended for lever-action rifles

Speer African Grand Slam®

Bullet Caliber & Type	338 AGS Tungsten Solid	375 AGS Tungsten Solid	416 AGS Soft Point	416 AGS Tungsten Point	45 AGS Soft Point	45 AGS Tungsten Solid
Diameter	.338"	.375"	.416"	.416"	.458"	.458"
Weight (grs.)	275	300	400	400	500	500
Ballist. Coef.	0.291	0.258	0.318	0.262	0.285	0.277
Part Number	2414	2474	2475	2476	2485	2486
Box Count	25	25	25	25	25	25

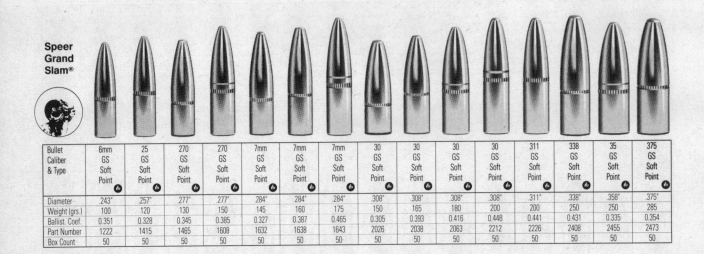

Speer Grand Slam®

Bullet Caliber & Type	6mm GS Soft Point	25 GS Soft Point	270 GS Soft Point	270 GS Soft Point	7mm GS Soft Point	7mm GS Soft Point	7mm GS Soft Point	30 GS Soft Point	30 GS Soft Point	30 GS Soft Point	30 GS Soft Point	311 GS Soft Point	338 GS Soft Point	35 GS Soft Point	375 GS Soft Point
Diameter	.243"	.257"	.277"	.277"	.284"	.284"	.284"	.308"	.308"	.308"	.308"	.311"	.338"	.358"	.375"
Weight (grs.)	100	120	130	150	145	160	175	150	165	180	200	200	250	250	285
Ballist. Coef.	0.351	0.328	0.345	0.385	0.327	0.387	0.465	0.305	0.393	0.416	0.448	0.441	0.431	0.335	0.354
Part Number	1222	1415	1465	1608	1632	1638	1643	2026	2038	2063	2212	2226	2408	2455	2473
Box Count	50	50	50	50	50	50	50	50	50	50	50	50	50	50	50

ALLIANT SMOKELESS POWDERS

Reloder 12

Reloder 15

Reloder 19

Reloder 22

2400

Reloder 7

Bullseye

Herco

Red Dot

Blue Dot

Green Dot

Unique

Power Pistol

American Select

HODGDON SMOKELESS POWDER

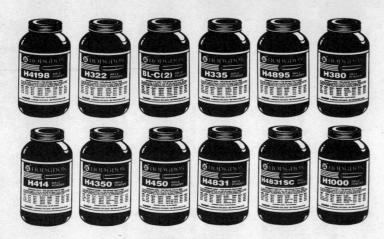

RIFLE POWDER

H4198

H4198 was developed especially for small and medium capacity cartridges.

H322

Any extruded bench rest powder which has proved to be capable of producing fine accuracy in the 22 and 308 bench rest guns. This powder fills the gap between H4198 and BL-C(2). Performs best in small to medium capacity cases.

SPHERICAL BL-C®, Lot No. 2

A highly popular favorite of the bench rest shooters. Best performance is in the 222, and in other cases smaller than 30/06.

SPHERICAL H335®

Similar to BL-C(2), H335 is popular for its performance in medium capacity cases, especially in 222 and 308 Winchesters.

H4895®

4895 may well be considered the most versatile of all propellants. It gives desirable performance in almost all cases from 222 Rem. to 458 Win. Reduced loads, to as low as 3/5 of maximum, still give target accuracy.

SPHERICAL H380®

This number fills a gap between 4320 and 4350. It is excellent in 22/250, 220 Swift, the 6mm's, 257 and 30/06.

SPHERICAL H414®

In many popular medium to medium-large calibers, pressure velocity relationship is better.

H414®

A spherical powder developed especially for 30-06, 220 Swift and 375 H&H.

H4350

This powder gives superb accuracy at optimum velocity for many large capacity metallic rifle cartridges.

H450

This slow-burning spherical powder is similar to H4831. It is recommended especially for 25-06, 7mm Mag., 30-06, 270 and 300 Win. and Wby. Mag.

H4831®

The most popular of all powders. Outstanding performance with medium and heavy bullets in the 6mm's, 25/06, 270 and Magnum calibers. Also available with shortened grains (H4831SC) for easy metering.

H1000 EXTRUDED POWDER

Fills the gap between H4831 and H870. Works especially well in overbore capacity cartridges (1,000-yard shooters take note).

VARGET RIFLE POWDER

HP38

A fast pistol powder for most pistol loading. Especially recommended for mid-range 38 specials.

CLAYS

A powder developed for 12-gauge clay target shooters. Also performs well in many handgun applications, including .38 Special, .40 S&W and 45 ACP. Perfect for 1 1/8 and 1 oz. loads.
Now available:
Universal Clays. Loads nearly all of the straight-wall pistol cartridges as well as 12 ga. 1 1/4 oz. thru 28 ga. 3/4 oz. target loads.
International Clays. Perfect for 12 and 20 ga. autoloaders who want reduced recoil.

HS-6 and HS-7

HS-6 and HS-7 for Magnum field loads are unsurpassed, since they do not pack in the measure. They deliver uniform charges and are dense to allow sufficient wad column for best patterns.

H110

A spherical powder made especially for the 30 M1 carbine. H110 also does very well in 357, 44 Spec., 44 Mag. or .410 ga. shotshell. Magnum primers are recommended for consistent ignition.

H4227

An extruded powder similar to H110, it is the fastest burning in Hodgdon's line. Recommended for the 22 Hornet and some specialized loading in the 45-70 caliber. Also excellent in magnum pistol and .410 shotgun.

IMR SMOKELESS POWDERS

SHOTSHELL POWDER

Hi-Skor 700-X Double-Base Shotshell Powder. Specifically designed for today's 12-gauge components. Developed to give optimum ballistics at minimum charge weight (which means more reloads per pounds of powder). 700-X is dense, easy to load, clean to handle and loads uniformly.

PB Shotshell Powder. Produces exceptional 20 and 28-gauge skeet reloads; preferred by many in 12-gauge target loads, it gives 3-dram equivalent velocity at relatively low chamber pressures.

Hi-Skor 800-X Shotshell Powder. An excellent powder for 12-gauge field loads and 20 and 28-gauge loads.

SR-4756 Powder. Great all-around powder for target and field loads.

SR-7625. A fast-growing favorite for reloading target as well as light and heavy field loads in 4 gauges. Excellent velocity-chamber pressure.

IMR-4227 Powder. Can be used effectively for reloading .410-gauge shotshell ammunition.

RIFLE POWDER

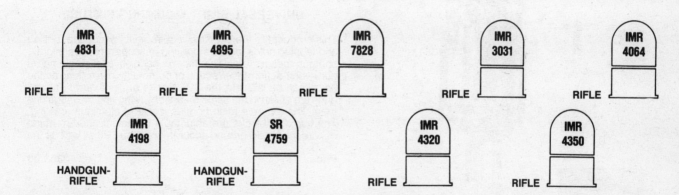

IMR-3031 Rifle Powder. Specifically recommended for medium-capacity cartridges.

IMR-4064 Rifle Powder. Has exceptionally uniform burning qualities when used in medium and large-capacity cartridges.

IMR-4198. Made the Remington 222 cartridge famous. Developed for small and medium-capacity cartridges.

IMR-4227 Rifle Powder. Fastest burning of the IMR Series. Specifically designed for the 22 Hornet class of cartridges.

SR-4759. Brought back by shooter demand. Available for cast bullet loads.

IMR-4320. Recommended for high-velocity cartridges.

IMR-4350 Rifle Powder. Gives unusually uniform results when loaded in Magnum cartridges.

IMR-4831. Produced as a canister-grade handloading powder. Packaged in 1 lb. canister, 8 lb. caddy and 20 lb. kegs.

IMR-4895 Rifle Powder. The time-tested standard for caliber 30 military ammunition; slightly faster than IMR-4320. Loads uniformly in all powder measures. One of the country's favorite powder.

IMR-7828 Rifle Powder. The slowest burning DuPont IMR canister powder, intended for large-capacity and magnum-type cases with heavy bullets.

PISTOL POWDER

PB Powder. Another powder for reloading a wide variety of centerfire handgun ammunition.

IMR-4227 Powder. Can be used effectively for reloading Magnum handgun ammunition.

Hi-Skor 700-X Powder. The same qualities that make it a superior powder contribute to its excellent performance in all the popular handguns.

Hi-Skor 800-X Powder. Good powder for heavier bullet handgun calibers.

SR-7625 Powder. For reloading a wide variety of centerfire handgun ammunition.

SR-4756. Clean burning with uniform performance. Can be used in a variety of handgun calibers.

FORSTER RELOADING

ULTRA BULLET SEATER DIE

Forster's new Ultra Die is available in 51 calibers, more than any other brand of micrometer-style seater. Adjustment is identical to that of a precision micrometer—the head is graduated to .001″ increments with .025″ bullet movement per revolution. The cartridge case, bullet and seating stem are completely supported and perfectly aligned in a close-fitting chamber before and during the bullet seating operation.
Price: **$56.00**

CO-AX LOADING PRESS B-2

UNIVERSAL SIGHT MOUNTING FIXTURE

This product fills the exacting requirements needed for drilling and tapping holes for the mounting of scopes, receiver sights, shotgun beads, etc. The fixture handles any single-barrel gun—bolt-action, lever-action or pump-action—as long as the barrel can be laid into the ''V'' blocks of the fixture. Tubular guns are drilled in the same manner by removing the magazine tube. The fixture's main body is made of aluminum casting. The two ''V'' blocks are adjustable for height and are made of hardened steel ground accurately on the ''V'' as well as the shaft.
Price: **$356.00**

CO-AX® LOADING PRESS MODEL B-2

Designed to make reloading easier and more accurate, this press offers the following features: Snap-in and snap-out die change • Positive spent primer catcher • Automatic self-acting shell holder • Floating guide rods • Working room for right- or left-hand operators • Top priming device seats primers to factory specifications • Uses any standard 7/8″×14 dies • No torque on the head • Perfect alignment of die and case • Three times the mechanical advantage of a ''C'' press
Price: **$287.00**

BENCH REST POWDER MEASURE

BENCH REST POWDER MEASURE

When operated uniformly, this measure will throw uniform charges from 2½ grains Bullseye to 95 grains #4320. No extra drums are needed. Powder is metered from the charge arm, allowing a flow of powder without extremes in variation while minimizing powder shearing. Powder flows through its own built-in baffle so that powder enters the charge arm uniformly.
Price: **$104.00**

FORSTER RELOADING

CO-AX® BENCH REST® RIFLE DIES

Bench Rest Rifle Dies are glass hard for long wear and minimum friction. Interiors are polished mirror smooth. Special attention is given to headspace, tapers and diameters so that brass will not be overworked when resized. Sizing die has an elevated expander button which is drawn through the neck of the case at the moment of the greatest mechanical advantage of the press. Since most of the case neck is still in the die when expanding begins, better alignment of case and neck is obtained.

Bench Rest® Seating Die is of the chamber type. The bullet is held in alignment in a close-fitting channel. The case is held in a tight-fitting chamber. Both bullet and case are held in alignment while the bullet is being seated. Crossbolt lock ring included at no charge.

Bench Rest® Die Set.	**$68.00**
Weatherby Bench Rest Die Set	75.00
Ultra Bench Rest Die Set	84.00
Full Length Sizer	31.50
Bench Rest Seating Die	38.00

PRIMER SEATER
With "E-Z-Just" Shellholder

The Bonanza Primer Seater is designed so that primers are seated Co-Axially (primer in line with primer pocket). Mechanical leverage allows primers to be seated fully without crushing. With the addition of one extra set of Disc Shell Holders and one extra Primer Unit, all modern cases, rim or rimless, from 222 up to 458 Magnum, can be primed. Shell holders are easily adjusted to any case by rotating to contact rim or cannelure of the case.

Primer Seater	**$64.50**
Primer Pocket Cleaner	7.00

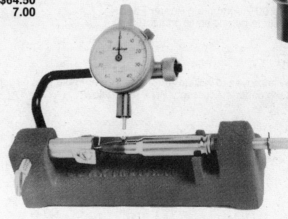

PRIMER SEATER

CO-AX® INDICATOR

Bullets will not leave a rifle barrel at a uniform angle unless they are started uniformly. The Co-Ax Indicator provides a reading of how closely the axis of the bullet corresponds to the axis of the cartridge case. The Indicator features a spring-loaded plunger to hold cartridges against a recessed, adjustable rod while the cartridge is supported in a "V" block. To operate, simply rotate the cartridge with the fingers; the degree of misalignment is transferred to an indicator which measures in one-thousandths.

Price: Without dial		**$52.00**
Indicator Dial		59.00

HORNADY

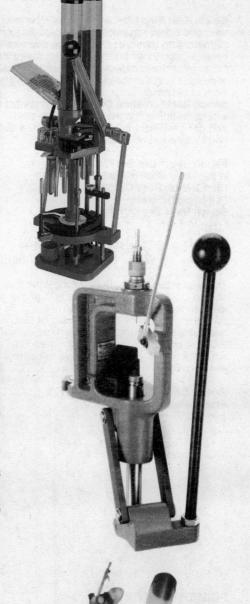

APEX 3.1 AUTO SHOTSHELL RELOADER

This versatile shotshell reloader features a new hold-fast shell plate. Other features include: extra-large shot hopper, short linkage arm, automatic dual-action crimp die, swing-out wad guide, and extra-long shot and powder feed tubes. Also, a new shell-actuated automatic powder shot drop and a new shell retainer system.

Apex 3.0 Shotshell Reloader (Automatic)
In 12 and 20 gauge **$299.95**
In 28 and .410 gauge **329.95**
Apex Shotshell Reloader (Standard)
In 12 and 20 gauge **109.95**
In 28 and .410 gauge **119.95**

00-7 PRESS PACKAGE

- "Power-Pac" linkage multiplies lever-to-arm power.
- Frame of press angled 30° to one side, making the "O" area of press totally accessible.
- More mounting area for rock-solid attachment to bench.
- Special strontium-alloy frame provides greater stress resistance. Won't spring under high pressures needed for full-length resizing.

00-7 Press and 00-7 Automatic Primer Feed
(complete with large and small primer tubes) **$99.95**

THE 00-7 KIT

Expanded and improved to include Automatic Primer Feed, plus all components available in Handloader's Accessory Pack (see below).

00-7 Kit **$259.95**

THE HANDLOADER'S ACCESSORY PACK

Here's everything you need in one money-saving pack. It includes: • Deluxe powder measure • Powder scale • Two non-static powder funnels • Universal loading block • Primer turning plate • Case lube • Chamfering and deburring tool • 3 case neck brushes • Large and small primer pocket cleaners • Accessory handle. Plus one copy of the *Hornady Handbook of Cartridge Reloading.*

Handloader's Accessory Pack No. 030300 . . . . **$184.25**

HORNADY

NEW DIMENSION CUSTOM GRADE RELOADING DIES

Features an Elliptical Expander that minimizes friction and reduces case neck stretch, plus the need for a tapered expander for "necking up" to the next larger caliber. Other recent design changes include a hardened steel decap pin that will not break, bend or crack even when depriming stubborn military cases. A bullet seater alignment sleeve guides the bullet and case neck into the die for in-line benchhrest alignment. All New Dimension Reloading Dies include: collar and collar lock to center expander precisely; one-piece expander spindle with tapered bottom for easy cartridge insertion; wrench flats on die body, Sure-Loc™ lock rings and collar lock for easy tightening; and built-in crimper.

New Dimension Custom Grade Reloading Dies:
Series I Two-die Rifle Set	**$26.95**
Series I Three-die Rifle Set	**28.50**
Series II Three-die Pistol Set (w/Titanium Nitride)	**37.75**
Series III Two-die Rifle Set	**32.25**
Series IV Specialty Die Set	**53.75**

Also available:
50 Caliber BMG Dies (Two-Die Set)	**$260.00**

PROFESSIONAL +P RELOADING

Includes Deluxe Powder Measure and Auto-Powder Drop. Place a case in the shell plate, start a bullet, and pull the handle. Cases are decapped, powder is automatically dispensed with the Auto Powder Drop and Powder Measure, new primers and bullets are seated, the shell plate indexes automatically and a loaded cartridge is ejected into the cartridge catcher. Includes shell plate (dies sold separately).

Pro-Jector Professional +P Reloading Package	**$299.95**

Also available:
Pro-Jector Kit: Includes shell plate, Automatic Powder Drop, wrench, plus all components in Handloader's Accessory Pack (see previous page).**Price** **$394.95**

MODEL 366 AUTO SHOTSHELL RELOADER

The 366 Auto features full-length resizing with each stroke, automatic primer feed, swing-out wad guide, three-stage crimping featuring Taper-Loc for factory tapered crimp, automatic advance to the next station and automatic ejection. The turntable holds 8 shells for 8 operations with each stroke. The primer tube filler is fast. The automatic charge bar loads shot and powder. Right- or left-hand operation; interchangeable charge bushings, die sets and Magnum dies and crimp starters for 6 point, 8 point and paper crimps.

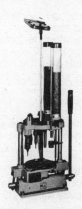

Model 366 Auto Shotshell Reloader:
12, 20, 28 gauge or .410 bore	$340.00
Model 366 Auto Die Set	93.65
Auto Advance	52.95
Swing-out Wad Guide & Shell Drop Combo	131.60

LYMAN BULLET SIZING EQUIPMENT

MAG 20 ELECTRIC FURNACE

The MAG 20 is a new furnace offering several advantages to cast bullet enthusiasts. It features a steel crucible of 20-pound capacity and incorporates a proven bottom-pour valve system and a fully adjustable mould guide. The improved design of the MAG 20 makes it equally convenient to use the bottom-pour valve, or a ladle. A new heating coil design reduces the likelihood of pour spout "freeze." Heat is controlled from "Off" to nominally 825° F by a calibrated thermostat which automatically increases temperature output when alloy is added to the crucible. A pre-heat shelf for moulds is attached to the back of the crucible. Availalbe for 100 V and 200 V systems.

Price: 110 V **$245.00**
220 V **250.00**

BULLET-MAKING EQUIPMENT

Deburring Tool
Lyman's deburring tool can be used for chamfering or deburring of cases up to 45 caliber. For precise bullet seating, use the pointed end of the tool to bevel the inside of new or trimmed cases. To remove burrs left by trimming, place the other end of the deburring tool over the mouth of the case and twist. The tool's centering pin will keep the case aligned . . **$10.75**

Mould Handles
These large hardwood handles are available in three sizes single-, double- and four-cavity.
Single-cavity handles (for small block, black powder and specialty moulds; 12 oz.) **$24.00**
Double-cavity handles (for two-cavity and large-block single-cavity moulds; 12 oz.) **24.00**
Four-cavity handles (1 lb.) **28.00**

Rifle Moulds
All Lyman rifle moulds are available in double cavity only, except those moulds where the size of the bullet necessitates a single cavity (12 oz.) **$48.75**

Hollow-Point Bullet Moulds
Hollow-point moulds are cut in single-cavity blocks only and require single-cavity handles (9 oz.) **$48.75**

Shotgun Slug Moulds
Available in 12 or 20 gauge; do not require rifling. Moulds are single cavity only, cut on the larger double-cavity block and require double-cavity handles (14 oz.) **$48.75**

Pistols Moulds
Cover all popular calibers and bullet designs in double-cavity blocks and, on a limited basis, four-cavity blocks.
Double-cavity mould block **$48.75**
Four-cavity mould block **75.00**

Lead Casting Dipper
Dipper with cast-iron head. The spout is shaped for easy, accurate pouring that prevents air pockets in the finished bullet **$12.95**

Gas Checks
Gas checks are gilding metal caps which fit to the base of cast bullets. These caps protect the bullet base from the burning effect of hot powder gases and permit higher velocities. Easily seated during the bullet-sizing operation. Only Lyman gas checks should be used with Lyman cast bullets.

22 through 35 caliber (per 1000) **$24.75**
375 through 45 caliber (per 1000) **29.75**
Gas check seater **8.00**

Lead Pot
The cast-iron pot allows the bullet caster to use any source of heat. Pot capacity is about 8 pounds of alloy and the flat bottom prevents tipping **$12.95**

Universal Decapping Die
Covers all calibers .22 through .45 (except .378 and .460 Weatherby). Can be used before cases are cleaned or lubricated. Requires no adjustment when changing calibers; fits all popular makes of $7/8 \times 14$ presses, single station or progressive, and is packaged with 10 replacement pins **$10.75**

UNIVERSAL CARBIDE FOUR-DIE SET

Lyman's new 4-die carbide sets allow simultaneous neck expanding and powder charging. They feature specially designed hollow expanding plugs that utilize Lyman's 2-step neck-expansion system, while allowing powder to flow through the die into the cartridge case after expanding. Includes taper crimp die. All popular pistol calibers. **$47.95**

LYMAN RELOADING TOOLS

MODEL 1200 CLASSIC TURBO TUMBLER

Features a redesigned base and drive system, plus a stronger suspension system and built-in exciters for better tumbling action and faster cleaning

Model 1200 Classic	**$104.95**
Model 1200 Auto-Flo	**116.50**
Also available:	
Model 600	**79.95**
Model 2220	**119.95**
Model 2200 Auto-Flo	**129.95**
Model 3200	**164.95**
Model 3200 Auto-Flo	**184.95**
Mag-Flo	**229.95**

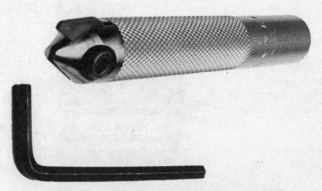

"INSIDE/OUTSIDE" DEBURRING TOOL

This unique new tool features an adjustable cutting blade that adapts easily to any rifle or pistol case from 22 caliber to 45 caliber with a simple hex wrench adjustment. Inside deburring is completed by a conical internal section with slotted cutting edges, thus providing uniform inside and outside deburring in one simple operation. The deburring tool is mounted on an anodized aluminum handle that is machine-knurled for a sure grip.

Deburring Tool **$13.50**

TUBBY TUMBLER

This popular tumbler now features a clear plastic "see thru" lid that fits on the outside of the vibrating tub. The Tubby has a polishing action that cleans more than 100 pistol cases in less than two hours. The built-in handle allows easy dumping of cases and media. An adjustable tab also allows the user to change the tumbling speed for standard or fast action.

Tubby Tumbler **$58.50**

MASTER CASTING KIT

Designed especially to meet the needs of blackpowder shooters, this new kit features Lyman's combination round ball and maxi ball mould blocks. It also contains a combination double cavity mould, mould handle, mini-mag furnace, lead dipper, bullet lube, a user's manual and a cast bullet guide. Kits are available in 45, 50 and 54 caliber.

Master Casting Kit **$149.95**

LYMAN RELOADING TOOLS

FOR RIFLE OR PISTOL CARTRIDGES

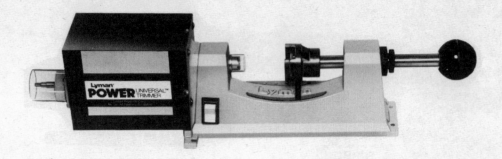

POWER CASE TRIMMER

The new Lyman Power Trimmer is powered by a fan-cooled electric motor designed to withstand the severe demands of case trimming. The unit, which features the Universal™ Chuckhead, allows cases to be positioned for trimming or removed with fingertip ease. The Power Trimmer package includes Nine Pilot Multi-Pack. In addition to two cutter heads, a pair of wire end brushes for cleaning primer pockets are included. Other features include safety guards, on-off rocker switch, heavy cast base with receptacles for nine pilots, and bolt holes for mounting on a work bench. Available for 110 V or 220 V systems.

Prices: 110 V Model **$179.95**
220 V Model **180.00**

ACCULINE OUTSIDE NECK TURNER (not shown)

To obtain perfectly concentric case necks, Lyman's Outside Neck Turner assures reloaders of uniform neck wall thickness and outside neck diameter. The unit fits Lyman's Universal Trimmer and AccuTrimmer. In use, each case is run over a mandrel, which centers the case for the turning operation. The cutter is carefully adjusted to remove a minimum amount of brass. Rate of feed is adjustable and a mechanical stop controls length of cut. Mandrels are available for calibers from .17 to .375; cutter blade can be adjusted for any diameter from .195″ to .405″.

Outside Neck Turner w/extra blade, 6 mandrels . . . **$27.95**
Individual Mandrels **4.00**

ORANGE CRUSHER KIT

Includes "Orange Crusher" Press, loading block, case lube kit, primer tray, Model 500 Pro scale, powder funnel and Lyman Reloading Handbook.

Starter Kit **$149.95**

LYMAN "ORANGE CRUSHER" RELOADING PRESS (see photo below)

The only press for rifle or pistol cartridges that offers the advantage of powerful compound leverage combined with a true Magnum press opening. A unique handle design transfers power easily where you want it to the center of the ram. A 4½-inch press opening accommodates even the largest cartridges.

"Orange Crusher" Press:
With Priming Arm and Catcher **$105.00**

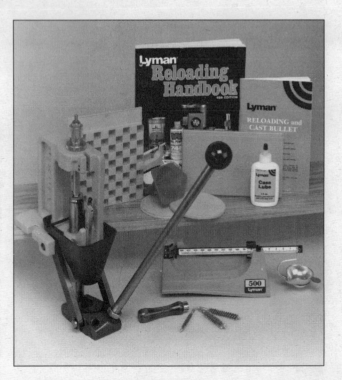

STARTER KIT

LYMAN RELOADING TOOLS

T-MAG II TURRET RELOADING PRESS

With the new T-Mag II you can mount up to six different re-loading dies on our turret. This means you can have all your dies set up, precisely mounted, locked in and ready to reload at all times. The T-Mag works with all 7/8×14 dies. The T-Mag II turret with its quick-disconnect release system is held in rock-solid alignment by a 3/4-inch steel stud.

Also featured is Lyman's Orange Crusher compound leverage system. It has a longer handle with a ball-type knob that mounts easily for right- or left-handed operation.

T-Mag II Press w/Priming Arm & Catcher **$149.95**
   Extra Turret Head **19.95**

Also available:
EXPERT KIT that includes T-MAG II Press, Universal Case Trimmer and pilot Multi-Pak, Model 500 powder scale and Model 50 powder measure, plus accessories and Reloading Manual. Available in calibers 9mm Luger, 38/357, 44 Mag., 45 ACP and 30-06 . . . . **$339.95**

ELECTRONIC SCALE MODEL LE: 1000

Accurate to 1/10 grain, Lyman's new LE: 1000 measures up to 1000 grains of powder and easily converts to the gram mode for metric measurements. The push-botton automatic calibration feature eliminates the need for calibrating with a screwdriver. The scale works off a single 9V battery or AC power adaptor (included with each scale). Its compact design allows the LE: 1000 to be carried to the field easily. A sculpted carrying case is optional. 110 Volt or 220 Volt.

Model LE: 1000 Electronic Scale **$259.95**
Model LE: 300 Electronic Scale **166.50**
Model LE: 500 Electric Scale **183.25**

MODEL LE-500 ELECTRONIC SCALE

PISTOL ACCUMEASURE

Lyman's Pistol AccuMeasure uses changeable brass rotors pre-drilled to drop precise charges of ball and flake pistol propellants (the tool is not intended for use with long grain IMR-type powders). Most of the rotors are drilled with two cavities for maximum accuracy and consistency. The brass operating handle, which can be shifted for left or right hand operation, can be removed. The Pistol AccuMeasure can be mounted on all turret and single station presses; it can also be hand held with no loss of accuracy.

Pistol AccuMeasure w/3-rotor starter kit **$35.00**

Also available:
ROTOR SELECTION SET including 12 dual-cavity rotors and 4 single-cavity units. Enables reloaders to throw a variety of charges for all pistol calibers through 45 . . . . **$46.00**

ELECTRONIC DIGITAL MICROMETER
$84.95

LYMAN RELOADING TOOLS

DRILL PRESS CASE TRIMMER

Intended for competitive shooters, varmint hunters, and other sportsmen who use large amounts of reloaded ammunition, this new drill press case trimmer consists of the Universal© Chuckhead, a cutter shaft adapted for use in a drill press, and two quick-change cutter heads. Its two major advantages are speed and accuracy. An experienced operator can trim several hundred cases in a hour, and each will be trimmed to a precise length.

Drill Press Case Trimmer **$45.00**

AUTO TRICKLER (not shown)

This unique device allows reloaders to trickle the last few grains of powder automatically into their scale powder pans. The Auto-Trickler features vertical and horizontal height adjustments, enabling its use with both mechanical and the new electronic scales. It also offers a simple push-button operation. The powder reservoir is easily removed for cleaning. Handles all conventional ball, stick or flare powder types.

Auto-Trickler **$37.50**

ACCU TRIMMER

Lyman's Accu Trimmer can be used for all rifle and pistol cases from 22 to 458 Winchester Magnum. Standard shellholders are used to position the case, and the trimmer incorporates standard Lyman cutter heads and pilots. Mounting options include bolting to a bench, C-clamp or vise.

Accu Trimmer w/9-pilot multi-pak **$39.95**

UNIVERSAL TRIMMER WITH NINE PILOT MULTI-PACK

This trimmer with patented chuckhead accepts all metallic rifle or pistol cases, regardless of rim thickness. To change calibers, simply change the case head pilot. Other features include coarse and fine cutter adjustments, an oil-impregnated bronze bearing, and a rugged cast base to assure precision alignment and years of service. Optional carbide cutter available. Trimmer Stop Ring includes 20 indicators as reference marks.

Replacement carbide cutter **$39.95**
Trimmer Multi-Pack (incl. 9 pilots: 22, 24, 27, 28/7mm, 30, 9mm, 35, 44 and 45A 64.95
Nine Pilot Multi-Pack 10.50
Power Pack Trimmer 74.95
Universal Trimmer Power Adapter 16.25

UNIVERSAL TRIMMER POWER ADAPTER

ELECTRONIC DIGITAL CALIPER (not shown)

Lyman's 6" electronic caliper gives a direct digital readout for both inches and millimeters and can perform both inside and outside depth measurements. Its zeroing function allows the user to select zeroing dimensions and sort parts or cases by their plus or minus variation. The caliper works on a single, standard 1.5 volt silver oxide battery and comes with a fitted wooden storage case.

Electronic Caliper **$79.95**

LYMAN RELOADING TOOLS

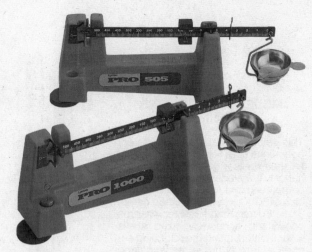

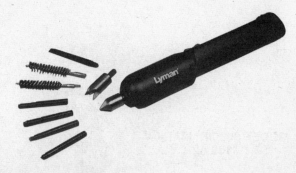

POWER DEBURRING KIT

Features a high torque, rechargeable power driver plus a complete set of accessories, including inside and outside deburr tools, large and small reamers and cleaners and case neck brushes. No threading or chucking required. Set also includes battery recharger and standard flat and phillips driver bits.

Power Deburring Kit $54.95

PRO 1000 & 505 RELOADING SCALES

Features include improved platform system; hi-tech base design of high-impact styrene; extra-large, smooth leveling wheel; dual agate bearings; larger damper for fast zeroing; built-in counter weight compartment; easy-to-read beam.

Pro 1000 Scale $54.95
Pro 505 Scale 39.95

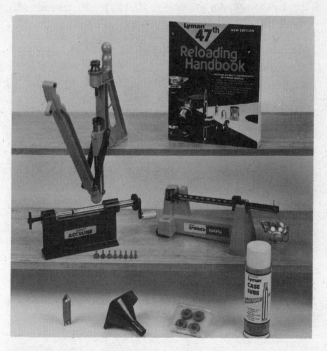

AUTOSCALE

After setting this new autoscale to the desired powder charge, it dispenses the exact amount of powder with the push of a button, over and over again. Features solid-state electronics and is controlled by a photo transistor to ensure accurate powder charges.

Autoscale $296.00

DELUXE RELOADERS PRO KIT

Includes Accupress with compound leverage; Pro 505 Scale; Accutrimmer with 9 popular pilots; ram prime die; deburr tool; powder funnel; Quick Spray case lube; shellholders (4); Lyman's 47th *Reloading Handbook*.

Deluxe Reloaders Pro Kit $132.50

MEC SHOTSHELL RELOADERS

MODEL 600 JR. MARK V
$162.62

This single-stage reloader features a cam-action crimp die to ensure that each shell returns to its original condition. MEC's 600 Jr. Mark 5 can load 6 to 8 boxes per hour and can be updated with the 285 CA primer feed. Press is adjustable for 3″ shells. Die sets are available in 10, 12, 16, 20, 28 and .410 gauges at: **$59.50**

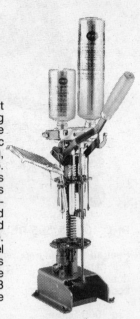

MODEL 8567 GRABBER
$458.78

This reloader features 12 different operations at all 6 stations, producing finished shells with each stroke of the handle. It includes a fully automatic primer feed and Auto-Cycle charging, plus MEC's exclusive 3-stage crimp. The "Power Ring" resizer ensures consistent, accurately sized shells without interrupting the reloading sequence. Simply put in the wads and shell casings, then remove the loaded shells with each pull of the handle. Optional kits to load 3″ shells and steel shot make this reloader tops in its field. Resizes high and low base shells. Available in 12, 16, 20, 28 gauge and .410 bore. No die sets are available.

MODEL 650
$319.80

This reloader works on 6 shells at once. A reloaded shell is completed with every stroke. The MEC 650 does not resize except as a separate operation. Automatic Primer feed is standard. Simply fill it with a full box of primers and it will do the rest. Reloader has 3 crimping stations: the first one starts the crimp, the second closes the crimp, and the third places a taper on the shell. Available in 12, 16, 20 and 28 gauge and .410 bore. No die sets are available.

MODEL 8120
SIZEMASTER
$245.00

Sizemaster's "Power Ring" collet resizer returns each base to factory specifications. This new generation resizing station handles brass or steel heads, both high and low base. An 8-fingered collet squeezes the base back to original dimensions, then opens up to release the shell easily. The E-Z Prime auto primer feed is standard equipment. Press is adjustable for 3″ shells and is available in 12, 16, 20, 28 gauge and .410 bore. Die sets are available at: **$88.65 ($104.00** in 10 ga.).

MEC RELOADING

STEELMASTER SINGLE STAGE

The only shotshell reloader equipped to load steel shotshells as well as lead ones. Every base is resized to factory specs by a precision "power ring" collet. Handles brass or steel heads in high or low base. The E-Z prime auto primer feed dispenses primers automatically and is standard equipment. Separate presses are available for 12 gauge 2³/₄", 3", 12 gauge 3¹/₂" and 10 gauge.

Steelmaster $255.00
In 12 ga. 3¹/₂" only 280.66

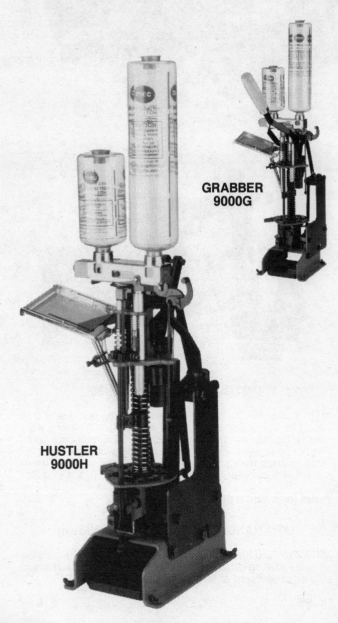

GRABBER 9000G

HUSTLER 9000H

E-Z PRIME "S" AND "V" AUTOMATIC PRIMER FEEDS

From carton to shell with security, these primer feeds provide safe, convenient primer positioning and increase rate of produ.SZ10PT/ction. Reduce bench clutter, allowing more free area for wads and shells.

• Primers transfer directly from carton to reloader, tubes and tube fillers
• Positive mechanical feed (not dependent upon agitation of press)
• Visible supply
• Automatic. Eliminate hand motion
• Less susceptible to damage
• Adapt to all domestic and most foreign primers with adjustment of the cover
• May be purchased separately to replace tube-type primer feed or to update your present reloader

E-Z Prime "S" (for Super 600, 650) or
E-Z Prime "V" (for 600 Jr. Mark V & VersaMEC) . . . **$39.70**

MEC 9000 SERIES SHOTSHELL RELOADER

MEC's 9000 Series features automatic indexing and finished shell ejection for quicker and easier reloading. The factory set speed provides uniform movement through every reloading stage. Dropping the primer into the reprime station no longer requires operator "feel." The reloader requires only a minimal adjustment from low to high brass domestic shells, any one of which can be removed for inspection from any station. Can be set up for automatic or manual indexing.

MEC 9000H Hustler $1386.00
MEC 9000G Series 557.00

MTM RELOADING

GUNSMITH'S MAINTENANCE CENTER

MTM's Gunsmiths Maintenance Center (RMC-5) is designed for mounting scopes and swivels, bedding of actions or for cleaning rifles and shotguns. Multi-positional forks allow for eight holding combinations, making it possible to service firearm level, upright or upside down. The large middle section keeps tools and cleaning supplies in one area. Individual solvent compartments help to eliminate accidental spills. Cleaning rods stay where they are needed with the two built-in holders provided. Both forks (covered with a soft molded-on rubber pad) grip and protect the firearm. The RMC-5 is made of engineering- grade plastic for years of rugged use. **Dimensions:** 29.5″ × 9.5″

Model RMC-5 . . . . **$26.50**

PISTOL REST MODEL PR-30

MTM's new PR-30 Pistol Rest will accommodate any size handgun, from a Derringer to a 14″ Contender. A locking front support leg adjusts up or down, allowing 20 different positions. Rubber padding molded to the tough polypropylene fork protects firearms from scratches. Fork clips into the base when not in use for compact storage. **Dimensions:** 6″ × 11″ × 2.5″

Pistol Rest Model PR-30 . . . . **$15.25**

MTM HANDLOADER'S LOG (not shown)

MTM's revised handloaders log has 150 pages for recording shotshell loading data, firearms inventory, ammo performance, plus an assortment of targets for quick anaylsis.

HL-95 . . . . **$14.99**

MODEL DB-4 STORAGE CASE

MTM'S new DB-4 holds up to four sets of rifle/pistol reloading dies. An extra chamber is provided for the last round off each set of dies. At the end of each row of dies is a shellholder post for storing the shellholder with its dies. Inside/outside labeling is provided (inside label allows recording of dies information). **Dimensions:** 7⁷⁄₈″ × 7⁵⁄₈″ × 5¹⁄₂″

Model DB-4 Storage Case **$10.25**

RCBS RELOADING TOOLS

ROCK CHUCKER PRESS

The Rock Chucker Press, with patented RCBS compound leverage system, delivers up to 200% more leverage than most presses for heavy-duty reloading of even the largest rifle and pistol cases. Rugged, Block "O" Frame prevents press from springing out of alignment even under the most strenuous operations. It case-forms as easily as most presses full-length size; it full-length sizes and makes bullets with equal ease. Shell holders snap into sturdy, all-purpose shell holder ram. Non-slip handle with convenient grip. Operates on downstroke for increased leverage. Standard 7/8-inch×14 thread.

Rock Chucker Press
(Less dies) **$124.35**

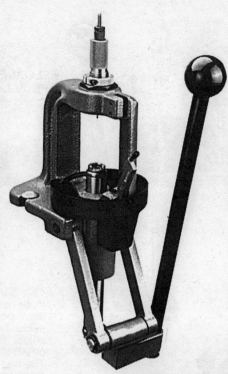

PRIMER POCKET SWAGER COMBO

For fast, precision removal of primer pocket crimp from military cases. Leaves primer pocket perfectly rounded and with correct dimensions for seating of American Boxer-type primers. Will not leave oval-shaped primer pocket that reaming produces. Swager Head Assemblies furnished for large and small primer pockets no need to buy a complete unit for each primer size. For use with all presses with standard 7/8-inch×14 top thread, except RCBS "A-3" Press. The RCBS "A-2" Press requires the optional Case Stripper Washer.

**Primer Pocket
Swager Combo** **$22.99**

ROCK CHUCKER MASTER RELOADING KIT

For reloaders who want the best equipment, the Rock Chucker Master Reloading Kit includes all the tools and accessories needed. Included are the following: • Rock Chucker Press • RCBS 505 Reloading Scale • Speer TrimPro Manual #12 • Uniflow Powder Measure • RCBS Rotary Case Trimmer-2 • deburring tool • case loading block • Primer Tray-2 • Automatic Primer Feed Combo • powder funnel • case lube pad • case neck brushes • fold-up hex ket set.

Rock Chucker Master Reloading Kit **$343.55**

PRIMER POCKET BRUSH COMBO

A slight twist of this tool thoroughly cleans residue out of primer pockets. Interchangeable stainless steel brushes for large and small primer pockets attach easily to accessory handle.

Primer Pocket Brush Combo **$11.45**

RCBS RELOADING TOOLS

RELOADER SPECIAL-5

This RCBS Reloader Special-5 Press is the ideal setup to get started reloading your own rifle and pistol ammo from 12 gauge shotshells and the largest Magnums down to 22 Hornets. This press develops ample leverage and pressure to perform all reloading tasks including: (1) resizing cases their full length; (2) forming cases from one caliber into another; (3) making bullets. Rugged Block "O" Frame, designed by RCBS, prevents press from springing out of alignment even under tons of pressure. Frame is offset 30° for unobstructed front access, and is made of 48,000 psi aluminum alloy. Compound leverage system allows you to swage bullets, full-length resize cases, form 30-06 cases into other calibers. Counter-balanced handle prevents accidental drop. Extra-long ram-bearing surface minimizes wobble and side play. Standard 7/8-inch-14 thread accepts all popular dies and reloading accessories.

Reloader Special-5
(Less dies) $96.85

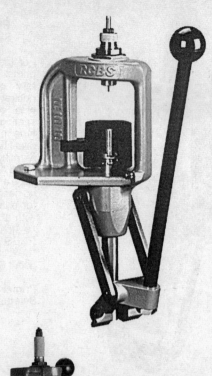

RELOADER SPECIAL-5

RELOADING SCALE MODEL 5-0-5

This 511-grain capacity scale has a three-poise system with widely spaced, deep beam notches to keep them in place. Two smaller poises on right side adjust from 0.1 to 10 grains, larger one on left side adjusts in full 10-grain steps. The first scale to use magnetic dampening to eliminate beam oscillation, the 5-0-5 also has a sturdy die-cast base with large leveling legs for stability. Self-aligning agate bearings support the hardened steel beam pivots for a guaranteed sensitivity to 0.1 grains.

Model 5-0-5 . . . . $70.25

AMMOMASTER SINGLE STAGE

AMMOMASTER AUTO

AMMOMASTER RELOADING SYSTEM

The AmmoMaster offers the handloader the freedom to configure a press to his particular needs and preferences. It covers the complete spectrum of reloading, from single stage through fully automatic progressive reloading, from .32 Auto to .50 caliber. The **AmmoMaster Auto** has all the features of a five-station press.

AmmoMaster Single stage . . $172.50
AmmoMaster Auto 381.65

RELOADING SCALE MODEL 10-10

Up to 1010 Grain Capacity
Normal capacity is 510 grains, which can be increased, without loss in sensitivity, by attaching the included extra weight.

Features include micrometer poise for quick, precise weighing, special approach-to-weight indicator, easy-to-read graduations, magnetic dampener, agate bearings, anti-tip pan, and dustproof lid snaps on to cover scale for storage. Sensitivity is guaranteed to 0.1 grains.

Model 10-10 Scale $111.35

RCBS RELOADING TOOLS

POWDER PRO™ DIGITAL SCALE

The RCBS Powder Pro Digital Scale comes with a limited life-time warranty. With a 1500-grain capacity, powder, bullets, even cases with accuracy up to 0.1 grain, can be weighed.

Powder Pro Digital Scale **$195.00**

POWDER CHECKER (not shown)

Operates on a free-moving rod for simple, mechanical operation with nothing to break. Standard 7/8×14 die body can be used in any progressive loader that takes standard dies. Black oxide finish provides corrosion resistance with good color contrast for visibility.

Powder Checker **$22.59**

ELECTRONIC SCALE

This new RCBS Electronic Scale brings solid state electronic accuracy and convenience to handloaders. The LCD digital readings are ideal for weighing bullets and cases. The balance gives readings in grains, from zero to 500. The tare feature allows direct reading of the sample's weight with or without using the scale pan. The scale can be used on the range, operating on 8 AA batteries (approx. 50 hours).

Electronic Scale **$395.00**

UPM MICROMETER ADJUSTMENT SCREW

Handloaders who want the convenience of a micrometer adjustment on their Uniflow Powder Measure can now add that feature to their powder measure. The RCBS Micrometer Adjustment Screw fits any Uniflow Powder Measure equipped with a large or small cylinder. It is easily installed by removing the standard metering screw, lock ring and bushing, which are replaced by the micrometer unit. Handloaders may then record the micrometer reading for a specific charge of a given powder and return to that setting at a later date when the same charge is used again.

UPM Micrometer Adjustment Screw (lg./sm.) **$31.95**

PRECISION MIC

This "Precisioneered Cartridge Micrometer" provides micrometer readings of case heads to shoulder lengths, improving accuracy by allowing the best possible fit of cartridge to chamber. By allowing comparison of the chamber to SAAMI specifications, it alerts the handloader to a long chamber or excess headspace situation. It also ensures accurate adjustment of seater die to provide optimum seating depth. Available in 19 popular calibers.

Precision MIC **$36.35**

RCBS RELOADING TOOLS

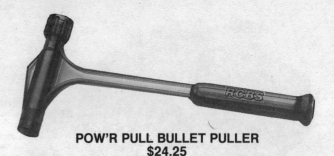

POW'R PULL BULLET PULLER
$24.25

The RCBS Pow'r Pull bullet puller features a three-jaw chuck that grips the case rim—just rap it on any solid surface like a hammer, and powder and bullet drop into the main chamber for re-use. A soft cushion protects bullets from damage. Works with most centerfire cartridges from .22 to .45 (not for use with rimfire cartridges).

HAND-PRIMING TOOL
$24.50

This hand-priming tool features a patented shielding mechanism that separates the seating operation from the primer supply, virtually ending the possibility of primer tray detonation. This tool fits comfortably in the palm of the hand for portable primer seating with a simple squeeze. The primer tray is easily removed, installed and filled, requiring no hand contact with the primers. Uses standard RCBS shell holders. Made of durable cast material and comes with large and small primer feed set-ups.

TRIM PRO™ POWER CASE TRIMMER

CARTRIDGE COUNTER
$17.00

The RCBS Cartridge Counter enables reloaders to compare the number of cartridges actually loaded. It attaches to the RCBS Uniflow powder measure and registers each time the drum dispenses a charge. The cartridge counter also features a reset knob for quick return to zero.

TRIM PRO CASE TRIMMER
$202.35 (Power) $67.45 (Manual)

Cartridge cases are trimmed quickly and easily with a few turns of the RCBS Trim Pro case trimmer. The lever-type handle is more accurate to use than draw collet systems. A flat plate shell holder keeps cases locked in place and aligned. A micrometer fine adjustment bushing offers trimming accuracy to within .001″. Made of die-cast metal with hardened cutting blades. The power model is like having a personal lathe, delivering plenty of torque. Positive locking handle and in-line power switch make it simple and safe.
Also available:
Trim Pro Case Trimmer Stand **$14.25**
Case Holder Accessory 30.35

TRIM PRO™ MANUAL CASE TRIMMER

REDDING RELOADING TOOLS

MODEL 721
"THE BOSS" PRESS

This "O" type reloading press features a rigid cast iron frame whose 36° offset provides the best visibility and access of comparable presses. Its "Smart" primer arm moves in and out of position automatically with ram travel. The priming arm is positioned at the bottom of ram travel for lowest leverage and best feel. Model 721 accepts all standard 7/8-14 threaded dies and universal shell holders.

Model 721 "The Boss" **$129.00**
   With Shellholder and 10A Dies **165.00**
Also available:
Boss Pro-Pak Deluxe Reloading Kit. Includes Boss Reloading Press,
#2 Powder and Bullet Scale, Powder Trickler, Reloading Dies **$336.00**

ULTRAMAG MODEL 700 (Not Shown)

Unlike other reloading presses that connect the linkage to the lower half of the press, the Ultramag's compound leverage system is connected at the top of the press frame. This allows the reloader to develop tons of pressure without the usual concern about press frame deflection. Huge frame opening will handle 50 × 3¼-inch Sharps with ease.

No. 700 Press, complete **$289.50**
No. 700K Kit, includes shell holder and one set of
   dies **324.00**

BENCHREST COMPETITION DIE

TYPE S BUSHING NECK DIE

BUSHING-STYLE NECK-SIZING DIES

Redding introduces two new Bushing Style Neck Sizing Dies— a simplified version (dubbed "Type S") and a Benchrest Competition model—with interchangeable sizing bushings available in .001 increments. The Type S comes in 42 calibers and has an adjustable decapping rod to allow positioning of the bushing to resize only a portion of the neck length, if desired. The Benchrest Competition Model features a cartridge case that is supported and aligned with the interchangeable sizing bushings before the sizing process begins.

Benchrest Competition Bullet Seating Die **$89.50**
Type S Bushing Neck Die **48.00**

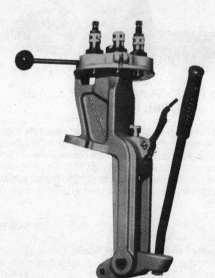

METALLIC TURRET RELOADING PRESS
MODEL 25

Extremely rugged, ideal for production reloading. No need to move shell, just rotate turret head to positive alignment. Ram accepts any standard snap-in shell holder. Includes primer arm for seating both small and large primers.

No. 25 Press, complete **$289.50**
No. 25K Kit, includes press, shell holder, and one set of dies **324.00**

REDDING RELOADING TOOLS

MASTER POWDER MEASURE MODEL 3

Universal- or pistol-metering chambers interchange in seconds. Measures charges from 1/2 to 100 grains. Unit is fitted with lock ring for fast dump with large "clear" plastic reservoir. "See-thru" drop tube accepts all calibers from 22 to 600. Precision-fitted rotating drum is critically honed to prevent powder escape. Knife-edged powder chamber shears coarse-grained powders with ease, ensuring accurate charges.

No. 3 Master Powder Measure
(specify Universal- or Pistol-Metering chamber) **$112.50**
No. 3K Kit Form, includes both
Universal and Pistol
chambers 135.00
Bench Stand 30.00

MATCH GRADE POWDER MEASURE MODEL 3BR

Designed for the most demanding reloaders—bench rest, silhouette and varmint shooters. The Model 3BR is unmatched for its precision and repeatability. Its special features include a powder baffle and zero backlash micrometer.

No. 3BR with Universal or Pistol
Metering Chamber **$150.00**
No. 3 BRK includes both
metering chambers 183.00

COMPETITION MODEL BR-30 POWDER MEASURE (not shown)

This powder measure features a new drum and micrometer that limit the overall charging range from a low of 10 grains (depending on powder density) to a maximum of approx. 50 grains. For serious competitive shooters whose loading requirements are between 10 and 50 grains, this is the measure to choose. The diameter of Model 3BR's metering cavity has been reduced, and the metering plunger on the new model has a unique hemispherical or cup shape, creating a powder cavity that resembles the bottom of a test tube. The result: irregular powder setting is alleviated and charge-to-charge uniformity is enhanced.

Competition Model BR-30 Powder Measure **$172.50**

MASTER CASE TRIMMER MODEL 1400

This unit features a universal collet that accepts all rifle and pistol cases. The frame is solid cast iron with storage holes in the base for extra pilots. Both coarse and fine adjustments are provided for case length.

The case-neck cleaning brush and primer pocket cleaners attached to the frame of this tool make it a very handy addition to the reloading bench. Trimmer comes complete with:
• New speed cutter shaft
• Six pilots (22, 6mm, 25, 270, 7mm and 30 cal.)
• Universal collet
• Two neck cleaning brushes (22 thru 30 cal.)
• Two primer pocket cleaners (large and small)

No. 1400 Master Case Trimmer complete **$93.00**
No. 1500 Pilots 3.90

STANDARD POWDER AND BULLET SCALE MODEL RS-1

For the beginner or veteran reloader. Only two counterpoises need to be moved to obtain the full capacity range of 1/10 grain to 380 grains. Clearly graduated with white numerals and lines on a black background. Total capacity of this scale is 380 grains. An over-and-under plate graduate in 10th grains allows checking of variations in powder charges or bullets without further adjustments.

Model No. RS-1 . . . . **$49.50**

Also available: **Master Powder & Bullet Scale.** Same as standard model, but includes a magnetic dampened beam swing for extra fast readings. 505-grain capacity **$75.00**

THOMPSON/CENTER

BLACKPOWDER TOOLS

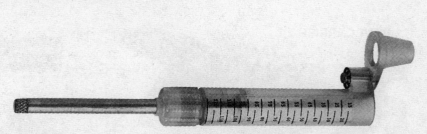

U-VIEW POWDER MEASURE
$16.90

This measure shows the exact level of powder in the tube. Eliminates the guesswork of loading consistent charges. Includes loading spout that swivels out of the way to fill measure. Locking shaft is easy to adjust.

HOT SHOT NIPPLE
$4.75

Allows more even and controlled flow of pressurized gases from cap into ignition channel. Also releases gases through the side ports to prevent gas blowback. Made of hardened stainless steel to tight tolerances. Use with $1/4$-28 threads for T/C caplocks (except T/C Scout).
Also available:
DELUXE NIPPLE WRENCH: $12.90

U-VIEW POWDER FLASK
$21.90

This see-through powder flask makes it easy to monitor powder supply. It's small enough to fit in the pocket yet holds enough powder for a dozen reloads or more. A spring-loaded plunger helps to control dispensing operation.

U-VIEW CAPPER
$22.90

Holds an entire box of 100 caps. Traditional shape makes it easy to use with both inline ignition muzzleloaders and sidelock actions. Simple thumb-actuated mechanism. Rugged construction.

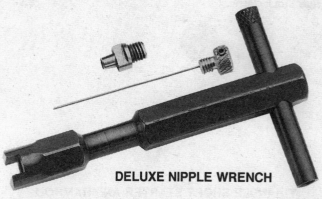

DELUXE NIPPLE WRENCH

MAXI-SHOK BULLET PERFORMANCE TOOLS
$27.95 (not shown)

Seat bullet or round ball with one of 4 tips on the end of the ramrod to improve terminal ballistics. By changing front of the soft lead bullet, maximum energy transfer is assured through increase in projectile expansion. Includes 3 bore guides: .45, .50 & .54 cal., plus $5/16$ adapter.

THOMPSON/CENTER

BLACKPOWDER TOOLS

BELT CARRIER

BUTT STOCK CARRIER

QUICK SHOT CARRIERS

Two new carriers keep Quick Shot reloads accessible on a belt or buttstock. Black nylon Belt Carrier holds 6 Quick Shots in elastic loops, (the black elastic Butt Stock Carrier holds 5).
Belt Carrier **$16.90**
Butt Stock Carrier **9.90**

EXPEDITER CLEANING KIT
$12.50

Cleaning a muzzleloader with the Expediter Cleaning Kit eliminates the mess and saves time by flushing away powder residue so the gun doesn't have to be disassembled. Includes a flush bottle with tube, cleaning patches, nipple tube adapter, all-natural No. 13 Bore Cleaner, and Natural Lube 1000+ Bore Butter.

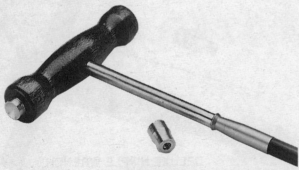

T-HANDLE SHORT STARTER AND RAMROD EXTENSION
$9.00

The T-Handle Short Starter and Ramrod Extension provides extra leverage for firmer, faster, more uniform seating. Removing the seating head and screwing the T-handle onto a standard ramrod extends the length of the ramrod for easier seating of projectiles. Features a hardwood handle with a solid brass rod.

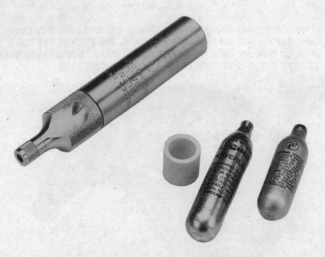

MAGNUM SILENT BALL DISCHARGER
$39.90

Enables reloaders to remove a charge from a muzzleloader without having to sheet the firearm or use a ball and bullet puller. It is especially useful to hunters for unloading their rifles at the end of the day, for removing balls or bullets that were accidentally seated without a powder charge, and for removing charges that fail to ignite due to contamination.

Reference

DIRECTORY OF MANUFACTURERS AND SUPPLIERS

The following manufacturers, suppliers and distributors of firearms, ammunition, reloading equipment, sights, scopes and accessories all appear with their products in the catalog and/or "Manufacturers' Showcase" sections of this SHOOTER'S BIBLE.

AIMPOINT (sights, scopes, mounts)
580 Herndon Parkway, Suite 500
Herndon, Virginia 22070
Tel: 703-471-6828   Fax: 703-689-0575

ALLIANT TECH SYSTEMS (gunpowder)
200 Valley Rd., Suite 305
Mt. Arlington, New Jersey 07856-1320
Tel: 201-770-2526   Fax: 201-770-2529

AMERICAN ARMS (handguns; A. Uberti
  handguns, rifles, blackpowder; Franchi
  shotguns)
715 E. Armour Road
N. Kansas City, Missouri 64116
Tel: 816-474-3161   Fax: 816-474-1225

AMERICAN DERRINGER CORP.
  (handguns)
127 North Lacy Drive
Waco, Texas 76705
Tel: 817-799-9111   Fax: 817-799-7935

AMTEC 2000, INC. (handguns; Erma rifle)
P.O. Box 1191
Gardner, MA 01440
Tel: 508-632-9608

ARCADIA MACHINE & TOOL INC. (AMT
  handguns, rifles)
6226 Santos Diaz Street
Irwindale, California 91702
Tel: 818-334-6629   Fax: 818-969-5247

ARMES DE CHASSE (Francotte rifles,
  shotguns; AyA shotguns)
P.O. Box 86
Hertford, North Carolina 27944
Tel: 919-426-2245   Fax: 919-426-1557

ARMSCOR (handguns, rifles, shotguns)
Available through K.B.I., Inc.

ARMSPORT, INC. (blackpowder arms;
  Bernardelli handguns, shotguns)
3590 NW 49th Street, P.O. Box 523066
Miami, Florida 33142
Tel: 305-635-7850   Fax: 305-633-2877

ARNOLD ARMS CO. INC. (rifles)
P.O. Box 1011
Arlington, Washington 98223
Tel: 206-435-1011   Fax: 206-435-7304

A-SQUARE COMPANY INC. (rifles)
One Industrial Park
Bedford, Kentucky 40006
Tel: 502-255-7456   Fax: 502-255-7657

ASTRA (handguns)
Available through European American
  Armory

AUTO-ORDNANCE CORP. (handguns,
  rifles)
Williams Lane
West Hurley, New York 12491
Tel: 914-679-7225   Fax: 914-679-2698

AYA (shotguns)
Available through Armes de Chasse

BAUSCH & LOMB (scopes)
Sports Optics Division
9200 Cody
Overland Park, Kansas 66214
Tel: 913-752-3433   Fax: 913-752-3489

BENELLI
Handguns avail. through European
  American Armory
Shotguns avail. through Heckler & Koch

BERETTA U.S.A. CORP. (handguns,
  shotguns)
17601 Beretta Drive
Accokeek, Maryland 20607
Tel: 301-283-2191   Fax: 301-375-7677

BERNARDELLI (handguns, shotguns)
Available through Armsport

BERSA (handguns)
Available through Eagle Imports Inc.

BLASER USA, INC. (rifles)
c/o Autumn Sales, Inc.
1320 Lake Street
Fort Worth, Texas 76102
Tel: 817-335-1634   Fax: 817-338-0119

BLUE BOOK PUBLICATIONS (books)
8009 34th Ave. South
Minneapolis, Minnesota 55425

BLOUNT, INC. (RCBS reloading equipment;
  Speer bullets; Weaver scopes)
P.O. Box 856
Lewiston, Idaho 83501
Tel: 208-746-2351   Fax: 208-746-2915

BONANZA (reloading tools)
See Forster Products

BRNO (rifles)
Available through Magnum Research

BROLIN ARMS (handguns)
2755 Thompson Creek Rd.
Pomona, California 91767
Tel: 909-392-2352   Fax: 909-392-2354

BROWN PRECISION, INC. (custom rifles)
7786 Molinos Avenue; P.O. Box 270 W.
Los Molinos, California 96055
Tel: 916-384-2506   Fax: 916-384-1638

BROWNING (handguns, rifles, shotguns)
Route One
Morgan, Utah 84050
Tel: 801-876-2711   Fax: 801-876-3331

B-SQUARE CO. (sights, mounts)
P.O. Box 11281
Fort Worth, Texas 76110
Tel: 817-923-0964   Fax: 817-926-7012

BURRIS COMPANY, INC. (scopes)
331 East Eighth Street, P.O. Box 1747
Greeley, Colorado 80631
Tel: 303-356-1670   Fax: 303-356-8702

BUTLER CREEK CORP. (rifle slings)
290 Arden Drive
Belgrade, Montana 59714
Tel: 406-388-1356   Fax: 406-388-7204

CABELA'S INC. (blackpowder arms)
812 13th Avenue
Sidney, Nebraska 69160
Tel: 308-254-5505   Fax: 308-254-6669

CLIFTON ARMS (custom rifles)
P.O. Box 1471
Medina, Texas 78055
Tel: 210-589-2666

COLT BLACKPOWDER ARMS CO.
  (blackpowder guns)
110 8th Street
Brooklyn, New York 11215
Tel: 718-499-4678   Fax: 718-768-8056

COLT'S MANUFACTURING CO., INC.
  (handguns, rifles)
P.O. Box 1868
Hartford, Connecticut 06144-1868
Tel: 203-236-6311   Fax: 203-244-1449

CONNECTICUT SHOTGUN MFG. CO.
  (A. H. Fox shotguns)
35 Woodland Street, P.O. Box 1692
New Britain, Connecticut 06051-1692
Tel: 860-225-6581   Fax: 860-832-8707

CONNECTICUT VALLEY CLASSICS
  (shotguns)
12 Taylor Lane, P.O. Box 2068
Westport, Connecticut 06880
Tel: 203-254-7864   Fax: 203-254-7866

COONAN ARMS (handguns)
1745 Highway 36E
Maplewood, Minnesota 55109
Tel: 612-777-3156   Fax: 612-777-3683

COOPER FIREARMS (rifles)
P.O. Box 114
Stevensville, Montana 59870
Tel: 406-777-5534

COUNTY (shotguns)
10020 Whitman Lane
Tamarac, Florida 33321
Tel: 954-720-5090   Fax: 954-722-6353

CUMBERLAND MOUNTAIN ARMS
  (blackpowder rifles)
1045 Dinah Shore Blvd., P.O. Box 710
Winchester, Tennessee 37398
Tel: 615-967-8414   Fax: 615-967-9199

CVA (blackpowder guns)
5988 Peachtree Corners East
Norcross, Georgia 30071
Tel: 800-251-9412   Fax: 770-242-8546

CZ (handguns, rifles)
Available through Magnum Research

DAEWOO PRECISION INDUSTRIES, LTD.
   (handguns)
Available through Kimber of America

DAKOTA (handguns)
Available through E.M.F. Co., Inc.

DAKOTA ARMS, INC. (rifles, shotguns)
HC 55, Box 326
Sturgis, South Dakota 57785
Tel: 605-347-4686   Fax: 605-347-4459

DAVIS INDUSTRIES (handguns)
11186 Venture Drive
Mira Loma, California 91752
Tel: 909-360-5598   Fax: 909-360-1749

DeSANTIS HOLSTER & LEATHER GOODS
   (holsters, belts, slings, etc.)
149 Denton Avenue
New Hyde Park, New York 11040
Tel: 516-354-8000   Fax: 516-354-7501

DESERT EAGLE (handguns)
Available through Magnum Research Inc.

DESERT MOUNTAIN MFG. (rifle rests)
P.O. Box 2767
Columbia Falls, Montana 59912-2767
Tel: 800-477-0762

J. DEWEY MFG. CO. (cleaning rods)
P.O. Box 2014
Southbury, Connecticut 06488
Tel: 203-264-3064   Fax: 203-598-3119

DIXIE GUN WORKS (blackpowder guns)
P.O. Box 130, Highway 51 S.
Union City, Tennessee 38261
Tel: 901-885-0561   Fax: 901-885-0440

DYNAMIT NOBEL/RWS (Rottweil shotguns)
81 Ruckman Road
Closter, New Jersey 07624
Tel: 201-767-1995   Fax: 201-767-1589

EAGLE IMPORTS, INC. (Bersa handguns)
1750 Brielle Avenue, Unit B1
Wanamassa, New Jersey 07712
Tel: 908-493-0333   Fax: 908-493-0301

E.M.F. COMPANY, INC. (Dakota handguns;
   A. Uberti handguns, blackpowder arms)
1900 East Warner Avenue 1-D
Santa Ana, California 92705
Tel: 714-261-6611   Fax: 714-756-0133

ERMA
Handguns avail. through Precision Sales
Rifle avail. through H&R 1871, Inc. & Amtec
   2000, Inc.

EUROARMS OF AMERICA INC.
   (blackpowder guns)
1501 Lenoir Drive, P.O. Box 3277
Winchester, Virginia 22601
Tel: 540-662-1863

EUROPEAN AMERICAN ARMORY (Astra
   handguns; Benelli handguns; E.A.A.
   handguns, rifles)
P.O. Box 1299
Sharpes, Florida 32959
Tel: 407-639-4842   Fax: 407-639-7006

FEDERAL CARTRIDGE CO. (ammunition)
900 Ehlen Drive
Anoka, Minnesota 55303-7503
Tel: 612-323-2506   Fax: 612-323-2506

FEG (handguns)
Available through K.B.I., Inc.

FIOCCHI OF AMERICA (ammunition)
5030 Fremont Road
Ozark, Missouri 65721
Tel: 417-725-4118   Fax: 417-725-1039

FLINTLOCKS, ETC. (Pedersoli replica rifles)
160 Rossiter Road
Richmond, Massachusetts 01254
Tel: 413-698-3822   Fax: 413-698-3866

FORSTER PRODUCTS (reloading)
82 East Lanark Avenue
Lanark, Illinois 61046
Tel: 815-493-6360   Fax: 815-493-2371

A. H. FOX (shotguns)
Available thru Connecticut Shotgun Mfg. Co.

FRANCHI (shotguns)
Available through American Arms

FRANCOTTE (rifles, shotguns)
Available through Armes de Chasse

FREEDOM ARMS (handguns)
One Freedom Lane, P.O. Box 1776
Freedom, Wyoming 83120
Tel: 307-883-2468

GARBI (shotguns)
Available through W. L. Moore & Co.

GLASER SAFETY SLUG, INC. (ammunition,
   gun accessories)
P.O. Box 8223
Foster City, California 94404
Tel: 415-345-7677 · Fax: 415-345-8217

GLOCK, INC. (handguns)
6000 Highlands Parkway
Smyrna, Georgia 30082
Tel: 770-432-1202   Fax: 770-433-8719

GONIC ARMS (blackpowder rifles)
134 Flagg Road
Gonic, New Hampshire 03839
603-332-8456   Fax: 603-332-8457

GUN SOUTH INC. (Merkel shotguns; Steyr-
   Mannlicher rifles)
108 Morrow Ave., P.O. Box 129
Trussville, Alabama 35173
Tel: 205-655-8299   Fax: 205-655-7078

GUNLINE TOOLS (gun checkering tools)
P.O. Box 478
Placentia, California 92670
Tel: 714-993-5100   Fax: 714-572-4128

H&R 1871, INC. (Harrington & Richardson
   handguns, rifles, shotguns; Erma rifle)
60 Industrial Rowe
Gardner, Massachusetts 01440
Tel: 508-632-9393   Fax: 508-632-2300

HÄMMERLI U.S.A. (handguns)
19296 Oak Grove Circle
Groveland, California 95321
Tel: 209-962-5311   Fax: 209-962-5931

HARRINGTON & RICHARDSON (handguns,
   rifles, shotguns) See H&R 1871, Inc.

HARRIS ENGINEERING, INC.
Barlow, Kentucky 42024
Tel: 502-334-3633

HARRIS GUNWORKS (rifles)
3840 N. 28th Ave.
Phoenix, Arizona 85017-4733
Tel: 602-230-1414   Fax: 602-230-1422

HECKLER & KOCH (handguns, rifles;
   Benelli shotguns)
21480 Pacific Boulevard
Sterling, Virginia 20166
Tel: 703-450-1900   Fax: 703-450-8160

HERITAGE MANUFACTURING (handguns)
4600 NW 135 St.
Opa Locka, Florida 33054
Tel: 305-685-5966   Fax: 305-687-6721

HI-POINT FIREARMS (handguns)
174 South Mulberry
Mansfield, Ohio 44902
Tel: 419-522-8330

HIGH-STANDARD MFG CO. (handguns)
4601 S. Pinemont, #148B
Houston, Texas 77041
Tel: 713-462-4200   Fax: 713-462-6437

HODGDON POWDER CO., INC.
   (gunpowder)
6231 Robinson, P.O. Box 2932
Shawnee Mission, Kansas 66201
Tel: 913- 362-9455   Fax: 913-362-1307

HORNADY MANUFACTURING COMPANY
   (reloading, ammunition)
P.O. Box 1848
Grand Island, Nebraska 68802-1848
Tel: 308-382-1390   Fax: 308-382-5761

HOWA (rifles)
Available through Interarms

HUNTER CO. INC. (slings, accessories)
3300 West 71st Avenue
Westminster, Colorado 80030
Tel: 303-427-4626   Fax: 303-428-3980

IGA SHOTGUNS
Available through Stoeger Industries

IMR POWDER COMPANY (gunpowder)
1080 Military Turnpike
Plattsburgh, New York 12901
Tel: 518-563-2253

INTERAIMS (sights)
Available through Stoeger Industries

INTERARMS (Rossi handguns, rifles; Howa rifles; Star handguns; Walther handguns)
10 Prince Street
Alexandria, Virginia 22314
Tel: 703-548-1400   Fax: 703-549-7826

JARRETT RIFLES INC. (custom rifles)
383 Brown Road
Jackson, South Carolina 29831
Tel: 803-471-3616

J. O. ARMS, INC. (handguns)
5709 Hartsdale
Houston, Texas 77036
Tel: 713-789-0745   Fax: 713-789-7513

KAHR ARMS (handguns)
P.O. Box 220
Blauvelt, New York 10913
Tel: 914-353-5996

K.B.I., INC. (FEG handguns; Armscor handguns, shotguns)
P.O. Box 6346
Harrisburg, Pennsylvania 17112
Tel: 717-540-8518   Fax: 717-540-8567

KENG'S FIREARMS SPECIALTY, INC. (Lapua ammunition, scopes)
875 Wharton Drive S.W.
P.O. Box 44405
Atlanta, Georgia 30336-1405
Tel: 404-691-7611   Fax: 404-505-8445

KIMBER OF AMERICA, INC. (rifles, handguns; Daewoo handguns)
9039 Southeast Jannsen Road
Clackamas, Oregon 97015
Tel: 503-656-1704   Fax: 503-657-5695

KONGSBERG AMERICA (rifles)
Merwin's Associates
2 Merwin's Lane
Fairfield, Connecticut 06430
Tel: 203-259-0938   Fax: 203-259-2566

KRIEGHOFF INTERNATIONAL INC. (rifles, shotguns)
337A Route 611, P.O. Box 549
Ottsville, Pennsylvania 18942
Tel: 610-847-5173   Fax: 610-847-8691

KNOUFF & KNOUFF, INC. (gun cases)
P.O. Box 9912
Spokane, Washington 99209
Tel: 800-262-3322   Fax: 509-326-5436

L.A.R. MANUFACTURING, INC. (Grizzly handguns, rifles)
4133 West Farm Road
West Jordan, Utah 84084
Tel: 801-255-7106   Fax: 801-569-1972

LASERAIM TECHNOLOGIES INC. (handguns, sights)
P.O. Box 3548
Little Rock, Arkansas 72203
Tel: 501-375-2227   Fax: 501-372-1445

LAZZERONI ARMS CO. (rifles)
P.O. Box 26696
Tucson, Arizona 85726
Tel: 520-571-7500   Fax: 520-624-4250

LEUPOLD & STEVENS, INC. (scopes, mounts)
P.O. Box 688
Beaverton, Oregon 97075
Tel: 503-646-9171   Fax: 503-526-1455

LLAMA (handguns)
Available through SGS Importers Int'l

LOHMAN MFG. CO. (game calls, videos, maintenance equipment, etc.)
4500 Doniphan Drive, P.O. Box 220
Neosho, Missouri 64850
Tel: 417-451-4438   Fax: 417-451-2576

LUGER, American Eagle (pistols)
Available through Stoeger Industries

LYMAN PRODUCTS CORP. (blackpowder guns, sights, reloading tools)
475 Smith Street
Middletown, Connecticut 06457
Tel: 860-632-2020   Fax: 860-632-1699

MAGNUM RESEARCH INC. (Desert Eagle handguns; CZ handguns; Brno rifles)
7110 University Avenue N.E.
Minneapolis, Minnesota 55432
Tel: 612-574-1868   Fax: 612-574-0109

MAGTECH RECREATIONAL PRODUCTS (shotguns)
5030 Paradise Rd., Ste C-211
Las Vegas, Nevada 89119
Tel: 702-795-7191   Fax: 702-795-2769

MARLIN FIREARMS COMPANY (rifles, shotguns)
100 Kenna Drive
North Haven, Connecticut 06473
Tel: 203-239-5621   Fax: 203-234-2991

MAROCCHI (Conquista shotguns)
Available through Precision Sales

MAVERICK OF MOSSBERG (shotguns)
Available through O. F. Mossberg

MEC INC. (reloading tools)
c/o Mayville Engineering Co.
715 South Street
Mayville, Wisconsin 53050
Tel: 414-387-4500   Fax: 414-387-2682

MERIT CORP. (sights)
P.O. Box 9044
Schenectady, New York 12309
Tel: 518-346-1420

MERKEL (shotguns)
Available through Gun South Inc.

MILLETT SIGHTS (sights, mounts)
16131 Gothard Street
Huntington Beach, California 92647
Tel: 714-842-5575   Fax: 714-843-5707

MITCHELL ARMS (handguns, rifles)
3433-B W. Harvard St.
Santa Ana, California 92704
Tel: 714-957-5711   Fax: 714-957-5732

M.O.A. CORP. (handguns)
2451 Old Camden Pike
Eaton, Ohio 45302
Tel: 513-456-3669

MODERN MUZZLE LOADING INC. (blackpowder guns)
P.O. Box 130, 234 Airport Rd.,
Centerville, Iowa 52544
Tel: 515-856-2626   Fax: 515-856-2628

WILLIAM L. MOORE & CO. (Garbi and Piotti shotguns)
31360 Via Colinas, No. 109
Westlake Village, California 91361
Tel: 818-889-4160

O. F. MOSSBERG & SONS, INC. (shotguns)
7 Grasso Avenue; P.O. Box 497
North Haven, Connecticut 06473
Tel: 203-230-5300   Fax: 203-230-5420

MOUNTAIN STATE MUZZLELOADING SUPPLIES (blackpowder guns)
Route 2, Box 154-1
Williamstown, West Virginia 26187
Tel: 304-375-7842

MTM MOLDED PRODUCTS (reloading tools)
P.O. Box 14117
Dayton, Ohio 45413
Tel: 513-890-7461   Fax: 513-890-1747

NAVY ARMS COMPANY, INC. (handguns, rifles; A. Uberti handguns, rifles, blackpowder arms)
689 Bergen Boulevard
Ridgefield, New Jersey 07657
Tel: 201-945-2500

N.C. ORDNANCE (classic grips)
P.O. Box 3254
Wilson, North Carolina 27895

NEW ENGLAND FIREARMS CO., Inc. (handguns, rifles, shotguns)
Industrial Rowe
Gardner, Massachusetts 01440
Tel: 508-632-9393   Fax: 508-632-2300

NIKON INC. (scopes)
1300 Walt Whitman Road
Melville, New York 11747
Tel: 516-547-4381   Fax: 516-547-0309

NORTH AMERICAN ARMS (handguns)
1800 North 300 West
P.O. Box 707
Spanish Fork, Utah 84660
Tel: 800-821-5783   Fax: 801-798-9418

NOSLER BULLETS, INC. (bullets)
P.O. Box 671
Bend, Oregon 97709
Tel: 503-382-3921   Fax: 503-388-4667

NYGORD PRECISION PRODUCTS (Unique handguns, rifles)
P.O. Box 12578
Prescott, Arizona 86304
Tel: 520-717-2315   Fax: 520-717-2198

OLIN/WINCHESTER (ammunition, primers, cases)
427 North Shamrock
East Alton, Illinois 62024
Tel: 618-258-2000

PARA-ORDNANCE (handguns)
3411 McNicoll Avenue #14
Scarborough, Ontario, Canada M1V 2V6
Tel: 416-297-7855   Fax: 416-297-1289

PARKER REPRODUCTIONS (shotguns)
124 River Road
Middlesex, New Jersey 08846
Tel: 908-469-0100   Fax: 908-469-9692

PEDERSOLI, DAVIDE (replica rifles)
Available through Flintlocks Etc.

PELTOR INC. (hearing protection products)
41 Commercial Way
East Providence, Rhode Island 02914
Tel: 401-438-4800   Fax: 401-434-1708

PENTAX (scopes)
35 Inverness Drive East
Englewood, Colorado 80112
Tel: 303-799-8000   Fax: 303-790-1131

PERAZZI U.S.A. (shotguns)
1207 S. Shamrock Ave.
Monrovia, California 91016
Tel: 818-303-0068   Fax: 818-303-2081

PIOTTI (shotguns)
Available through W. L. Moore & Co.

PHOENIX ARMS (handguns)
1420 S. Archibald Ave.
Ontario, California 91761
Tel: 909-947-4843   Fax: 909-947-6798

PRAIRIE RIVER ARMS LTD. (blackpowder
   guns)
1220 North 6th St.
Princeton, Illinois 61356
Tel: 815-875-1616   Fax: 815-875-1402

PRECISION SALES INTERNATIONAL
   (Erma handguns; Marocchi shotguns)
P.O. Box 1776
Westfield, Massachusetts 01086
Tel: 413-562-5055

PRECISION SMALL ARMS (handguns)
155 Carleton Rd.
Charlottesville, Virginia 22902
Tel: 804-293-6124   Fax: 804-295-0780

QUARTON USA (sights)
7042 Alamo Downs Parkway, Suite 250
San Antonio, Texas 78238-4518
Tel: 210-520-8430   Fax: 210-520-8433

RCBS, INC. (reloading tools)
Available through Blount, Inc.

REDDING RELOADING EQUIPMENT
   (reloading tools)
1089 Starr Road
Cortland, New York 13045
Tel: 607-753-3331   Fax: 607-756-8445

REDFIELD (scopes)
5800 East Jewell Avenue
Denver, Colorado 80227
Tel: 303-757-6411   Fax: 303-756-2338

REMINGTON ARMS COMPANY, INC.
   (rifles, shotguns, blackpowder,
   ammunition)
Delle Donne Corporate Center
1011 Centre Rd., 2nd fl.
Wilmington, Delaware 19805-1270
Tel: 800-243-9700   Fax: 302-993-8606

RIFLES, INC. (rifles)
873 West 5400 North
Cedar City, Utah 84720
Tel: 801-586-5995   Fax: 801-586-5996

ROSSI (handguns, rifles)
Available through Interarms

ROTTWEIL (shotguns)
Available through Dynamit Nobel/RWS

RUGER (handguns, rifles, shotguns,
   blackpowder guns). *See* Sturm, Ruger &
   Company, Inc.

SABATTI (shotguns)
Available through K.B.I., Inc.

SAFARI ARMS (rifles)
c/o Olympic Arms, Inc.
624 Old Pacific Highway Southeast
Olympia, Washington 98513
Tel: 360-459-7940   Fax: 360-491-3447

SAKO (rifles, actions, scope mounts,
   bullets)
Available through Stoeger Industries

SAUER (rifles)
c/o Paul Company, Inc.
27385 Pressonville Road
Wellsville, Kansas 66092
Tel: 913-883-4444   Fax: 913-883-2525

SAVAGE ARMS (rifles)
Springdale Road
Westfield, Massachusetts 01085
Tel: 413-568-7001   Fax: 413-562-7764

SCHMIDT AND BENDER (scopes)
Schmidt & Bender U.S.A.
P.O. Box 134
Meriden, New Hampshire 03770
Tel: 800-468-3450   Fax: 603-469-3471

SEGWAY INDUSTRIES (scope mounting
   equipment, etc.)
P.O. Box 783
Suffern, New York 10901-0783
Tel: 914-357-5510

SGS IMPORTERS INTERNATIONAL INC.
   (Llama handguns)
1750 Brielle Avenue
Wanamassa, New Jersey 07712
Tel: 908-493-0302   Fax: 908-493-0301

SHILOH RIFLE MFG. CO., INC. (Shiloh
   Sharps blackpowder rifles)
P.O. Box 279, Industrial Park
Big Timber, Montana 59011
Tel: 406-932-4454   Fax: 406-932-5627

SHOOTING SYSTEMS GROUP, INC. (gun
   holsters, cases)
1075 Headquarters Park
Fenton, Missouri 63026
Tel: 314-343-3575   Fax: 314-349-3311

SHYDA'S SERVICES, INC. (Lincoln traps)
1009 S. Lincoln Ave.
Lebanon, Pennsylvania 17042
Tel: 717-274-8676

SIERRA BULLETS (bullets)
P.O. Box 818
1400 West Henry St.
Sedalia, Missouri 65301
Tel: 816-827-6300   Fax: 816-827-6300

SIGARMS INC. (Sig-Sauer handguns)
Corporate Park
Exeter, New Hampshire 03862
Tel: 603-772-2302   Fax: 603-772-9082

SIMMONS OUTDOOR CORP. (scopes)
2120 Killarney Way
Tallahassee, Florida 32308-3402
Tel: 904-878-5100   Fax: 904-893-5472

SKB SHOTGUNS (shotguns)
4325 South 120th Street
P.O. Box 37669
Omaha, Nebraska 68137
Tel: 800-752-2767   Fax: 402-330-8029

SMITH & WESSON (handguns)
2100 Roosevelt Avenue
Springfield, Massachusetts 01102-2208
Tel: 413-781-8300   Fax: 413-731-8980

SPEER (bullets)
Available through Blount, Inc.

SPRINGFIELD INC. (handguns, rifles)
420 West Main Street
Geneseo, Illinois 61254
Tel: 309-944-5631   Fax: 309-944-3676

STAR (handguns)
Available through Interarms

STEYR-MANNLICHER (rifles)
Available through Gun South Inc.

STOEGER INDUSTRIES (American Eagle
   Luger®; Pro Series handguns, IGA
   shotguns; InterAims sights; Sako bullets,
   actions, mounts, rifles; Tikka rifles,
   shotguns)
5 Mansard Court
Wayne, New Jersey 07470
Tel: 201-872-9500   Fax: 201-872-2230

STONE MOUNTAIN ARMS (blackpowder
   guns)
c/o CVA, 5988 Peachtree Corners East
Norcross, Georgia 30071
Tel: 404-449-4687   Fax: 404-242-8546

STURM, RUGER AND COMPANY, INC.
   (Ruger handguns, rifles, shotguns,
   blackpowder revolver)
Lacey Place
Southport, Connecticut 06490
Tel: 203-259-4537   Fax: 203-259-2167

SWAROVSKI OPTIK NORTH AMERICA
   (scopes)
One Wholesale Way
Cranston, Rhode Island 02920
Tel: 401-942-3380   Fax: 401-946-2587

SWIFT INSTRUMENTS, INC. (scopes, mounts)
952 Dorchester Avenue
Boston, Massachusetts 02125
Tel: 800-446-1116   Fax: 617-436-3232

TASCO (scopes, mounts)
7600 N.W. 26th Street
Miami, Florida 33122
Tel: 305-591-3670   Fax: 305-592-5895

TAURUS INT'L, INC. (handguns)
16175 N.W. 49th Avenue
Miami, Florida 33014
Tel: 305-624-1115   Fax: 305-623-7506

THOMPSON/CENTER ARMS (handguns, rifles, reloading, blackpowder guns)
Farmington Road, P.O. Box 5002
Rochester, New Hampshire 03867
Tel: 603-332-2394   Fax: 603-332-5133

TIKKA (rifles, shotguns)
Available through Stoeger Industries

TRADITIONS, INC. (blackpowder guns)
P.O. Box 776
Old Saybrook, Connecticut 06475
Tel: 860-388-4656   Fax: 860-388-4657

TRIUS PRODUCTS, INC. (traps, targets)
221 South Miami Avenue, P.O. Box 25
Cleves, Ohio 45002
Tel: 513-941-5682   Fax: 513-941-7970

DOUG TURNBULL RESTORATION
(firearms restoration)
6426 County Road 30, P.O. Box 471
Bloomfield, New York 14469
Tel: 716-657-6338

UBERTI USA, INC. (handguns, rifles, blackpowder guns). *See also* American Arms, EMF, Navy Arms
362 Limerock Rd., P.O. Box 469
Lakeville, Connecticut 06039
Tel: 203-435-8068

ULTRA LIGHT ARMS COMPANY (rifles)
214 Price Street, P.O. Box 1270
Granville, West Virginia 26505
Tel: 304-599-5687   Fax: 304-599-5687

UNIQUE (handguns, rifles)
Available thru Nygord Precision Products

U.S.A. MAGAZINES INC. (handgun, rifle magazines)
P.O. Box 39115
Downey, California 90259
Tel: 800-USA-2577   Fax: 310-903-7857

U.S. REPEATING ARMS CO. (Winchester rifles, shotguns)
275 Winchester Avenue
Morgan, Utah 84050
Tel: 801-876-3440   Fax: 801-876-3331

WALTHER (handguns)
Available through Interarms

WEATHERBY, INC. (rifles, shotguns, ammunition)
3100 El Camino Real
Atascadero, California 93422
Tel: 805-466-1767   Fax: 805-466-2527

WEAVER (scopes, mount rings)
Available through Blount, Inc.

WHITE SHOOTING SYSTEMS
(blackpowder rifles)
25 East Highway 40, Box 330-12
Roosevelt, Utah 84066
Tel: 801-277-3085   Fax: 801-722-3054

WICHITA ARMS (handguns)
P.O. Box 11371
Wichita, Kansas 67211
Tel: 316-265-0661

WIDEVIEW SCOPE MOUNT CORP.
(mounts, rings)
13535 S. Hwy. 16
Rapid city, South Dakota 57701
Tel: 605-341-3220   Fax: 605-341-9142

WILDEY INC. (handguns)
P.O. Box 475
Brookfield, Connecticut 06804
Tel: 203-355-9000

WILLIAMS GUN SIGHT CO. (sights, scopes, mounts)
7389 Lapeer Road, P.O. Box 329
Davison, Michigan 48423
Tel: 313-653-2131   Fax: 313-658-2140

WINCHESTER (ammunition, primers, cases)
Available through Olin/Winchester

WINCHESTER (rifles, shotguns)
Available through U.S. Repeating Arms Co.

WINSLOW ARMS CO. (rifles)
P.O. Box 783
Camden, South Carolina 29020
Tel: 803-432-2938

ZEISS OPTICAL, INC. (scopes)
1015 Commerce Street
Petersburg, Virginia 23803
Tel: 804-861-0033   Fax: 804-733-4024

CALIBERFINDER

How to use this guide: To find a 22 LR handgun, look under that heading in the **HANDGUNS** section below. You'll find several models of that description, including the Beretta Model 21 Bobcat Pistol. Next, turn to the **GUNFINDER** section and locate the heading for Pistols—Semiautomatic and go to **Beretta**. The Model 21 appears on p. 105.

HANDGUNS

22 HORNET

Magnum Research Lone Eagle SS Action
MOA Maximum
North American Arms Mini-Revolvers
Thompson/Center Contender Bull Barrel and Super "14"
Uberti 1871 Rolling Block Target

22 LONG RIFLE

American Arms Models PK-22DA Classics, Model P-98 Classic
American Derringer Models 1, 7, 11, 38 DA Derringer
Armscor Model M-200DC/TC
Benelli Model MP95E
Beretta Models 21 Bobcat and 89 Gold Standard Pistols
Bernardelli Model PO10 Target Pistol
Bersa Model Thunder 22
Browning Buck Mark 22 and 5.5 Target Series
Colt .22 Semiauto DA and Target
Daewoo Model DP52
Davis D-Series
EMF/Dakota Hartford Scroll Engraved Revolver
Erma ESP 85A Competition Pistols
European American Armory Windicator DA
FEG SMC-22
Freedom Arms Model 252 Silhouette & Varmint Class
Hämmerli Models 160 Free Pistol, 162 Electronic, 208S Standard Pistol, 280 Target Pistol
Harrington & Richardson Sportsman 999, Models 929 Sidekick, 949 Classic Western and 939 Premier
Heritage Rough Rider SA
High Standard Supermatic Citation, Trophy and Tournament Models; Victor
Magnum Research Mountain Eagle, Target & Compact
Mitchell Arms Target Pistols (Sovereign, Monarch, Baron, Sportster, Medallion); Guardian Angel
New England Firearms Standard Revolver, Ultra/Ultra Mag Revolver
North American Arms Mini-Revolvers and Mini-Master Series; Companion Cap & Ball Mini-Revolver
Rossi Model 518
Ruger Bisley SA Target, New Bearcat, Mark II Pistols, New Model Super Single-Six, Model SP101 Revolver
Smith & Wesson Models 17, 41, 63, 422, 622, 617 (K-22 Masterpiece), 2206, 2206 Target, 2213/2214, Rimfire Sportsman
Stoeger Pro Series 95
Taurus Models 94, 96, PT-22
Thompson/Center Contender Bull Barrel, Octagon Barrel and "Super 14"
Uberti 1871 Rolling Block Target Pistol
Unique Models DES 69U, Int'l Silhouette and Sport
Walther Model TPH DA
Wichita Arms International Pistol

22 RIMFIRE MAGNUM

American Derringer Models 6, 7, 11
AMT 22 Automag II
Armscor Model M-200DC/TC Revolver
Davis D-Series Derringer, Long-Bore D-Series, Big Bore
Freedom Arms Model 252
Heritage Rough Rider Revolver
Mitchell Arms Guardian Angel Pistol
North American Mini-Revolver and Mini-Master Series; Companion Cap & Ball Mini-Revolver
Rossi Model 515 Revolver
Smith & Wesson Model 651 Kit Gun
Taurus Model 941 Revolver
Uberti 1871 Rolling Block Target
Wichita Arms International Pistol

22 SHORT

Harrington & Richardson Model 929 Sidekick, Model 949 Classic Western, 939 Premier Target, Sportsman 999
High Standard Olympic Rapid Fire Pistol
New England Firearms Standard, Ultra/Ultra Mag.
Unique Model DES 2000U Pistol

22 WIN. MAG.

American Derringer Model 6
European American Armory Windicator DA
Davis Long-Bore D-Series, D-Series Derringers
Heritage Rough Rider Revolver
MOA Maximum Single Shot Pistol
New England Firearms Ultra Revolver
North American Mini-Revolvers and Mini-Master Series
Smith and Wesson Model 651
Uberti 1871 Rolling Block Target Pistol
Unique Int'l Silhouette and Sport Pistols

223 REMINGTON

Magnum Research Lone Eagle SS Action
Thompson/Center Contender Bull Barrel, Hunter, "Super 14"

223 REM. COMM. AUTO

American Derringer Model 1

243

Magnum Research Lone Eagle SS Action

25 AUTO

Beretta Model 21 Bobcat, Model 950 Jetfire
Davis D-Series Derringers
Heritage Model H25S Semiauto
KBI Model PSP-25 Pistol
Precision Small Arms Model PSA-25 Pistol
Walther Model TPH Pistol

7mm BR

Magnum Research Lone Eagle SS Action
Wichita Silhouette Pistol

7mm T.C.U.

Thompson/Center Contender Bull Barrel
Unique International Silhouette

7mm SUPER MAG.

Wichita Arms International Pistols

7mm-08

Magnum Research Model Lone Eagle Pistol & Lone Eagle SS Barreled Action

7×30 WATERS

Thompson/Center Contender, Hunter, Super "14"
Wichita Arms International Pistol

30 CARBINE

American Derringer Model 1
AMT Automag III Pistol
Ruger New Model Blackhawk SA Revolver

30-06

Magnum Research Lone Eagle Pistol & Lone Eagle SS Barreled Action

30-30 WIN.

American Derringer Model 1
Magnum Research Lone Eagle SS Action
Thompson/Center Contender Bull Barrel and Hunter, Super "14"
Wichita Arms International Pistol

300 WHISPER

Thompson/Center Contender Super "14" and Bull Barrel

308 WINCHESTER

Magnum Research Lone Eagle Pistol & Lone Eagle SS Barreled Action
Wichita Arms Silhouette Pistol

32 AUTO

Beretta Model 3032 Tomcat
Davis D-Series Derringers, Model P-32
European American Armory SA Compacts
Sig-Sauer Model P230
Walther Model PP DA Pistol

32 H&H MAGNUM

Wichita International Pistol
Davis Big-Bore D-Series Derringer

32 MAGNUM

American Derringer Models 1, 7, 11, Lady Derringer
Ruger Bisley SA Target, Model SP101, New Model Super Single Six

32 S&W LONG

American Derringer Model 7
Hämmerli Model 280 Target Pistol
Ruger New Model Single-Six SSM Revolver

32 S&W WADCUTTER

Erma ESP 85A Competition Pistols, Model 773 Match
European Amer. Armory Benelli Model MP95E
Ruger New Model Single-Six Revolver
Unique Model DES 32U Pistol

32-20

American Derringer Model 1
EMF/Dakota Hartford Model Revolvers
Thompson/Center Contender Bull Barrel Pistol

35 REMINGTON

Magnum Research Lone Eagle SS Action
Thompson/Center Contender Hunter and Super
"14"

357 MAGNUM

American Arms Regulator Revolver
American Derringer Models 1, 4, 6, 38 DA, Lady
Derringer
Colt King Cobra, Python Revolvers
EMF/Dakota Model 1873 Dakota SA, 1875
Outlaw, 1890 Remington Police, Hartford Scroll
Engraved Revolvers
Erma Model 777 Sporting Revolver
European American Armory Big Bore Bounty
Hunter, Windicator DA
Freedom Arms Model 353, Silhouette/
Competition Models
L.A.R. Mark I Grizzly Pistol
Magnum Research Desert Eagle Mark XIX
Component System Pistol
Rossi Model 971 and 971 Compact, 971 VCR
Revolvers
Ruger New Model Blackhawk, Model GP-100,
Model SP101, Bisley SA Target Revolvers
Sig-Sauer Model P229 Pistol
Smith & Wesson Models 13 Military & Police, 19,
60 Chiefs Special Revolvers, 65, 65 LadySmith,
66, 586, 640 Centennial, 686, 686 Plus, 686
Powerport
Taurus Models 65, 66, 605, 607, 669, 689
Revolvers
Thompson/Center Contender Bull Barrel Pistol
Uberti 1871 Rolling Block Target Pistol; 1873
Cattleman & 1875 Remington Army Outlaw
Revolvers
Unique Model Int'l Silhouette Pistol
Wichita Arms International Pistol

357 MAXIMUM

American Derringer Models 1, 4
Magnum Research Lone Eagle SS Action

357 SIG

AMT Backup Pistol
Sig-Sauer Models P226, P239 Pistols

358 WINCHESTER

Magnum Research Lone Eagle SS Action

375 WINCHESTER

Thompson/Center Contender Hunter and Super
"14" Pistols

38 + P

Ruger Model SP101 Spurless

38 S&W

Amtec Model 2000 DA Revolver
Smith and Wesson Models 10, 13, 14, 15, 36, 38
Bodyguard, 49, 60, 64, 65, 67, Model 442,
Model 649, LadySmith Models 36-LS and 60-LS
Revolvers

38 SPECIAL

American Derringer 1, 7, 10, 11, Lady Derringer,
DA 38, Texas Double Derringer Comm.
Colt King Cobra DA, Python Premium DA, Model
38 SF-VI Revolvers
Davis Big-Bore D-Series, Long-Bore D-Series

38 SPECIAL

European American Armory Windicator DA
Heritage Sentry DA Revolver
Rossi Models 68, M88, 851, Lady Rossi
Revolvers
Smith & Wesson Models 10 & 13 Military &
Police, Model 14 K-38 Masterpiece, Model 15
Combat Masterpiece, Model 19 & 66 Combat
Magnum, Models 36 Chiefs Special, Models 36-
LS & 60-LS LadySmith, Models 37 & 637
Chiefs Special Airweight, Model 38 Bodyguard
Airweight, Models 49 & 649 Bodyguard, Model
64 Military & Police, Models 442 & 642
Centenial Airweight, Model 586 Distinguished
Combat Magnum, Model 640 Centennial,
Models 686, 686 Plus, 686 Powerport
Revolvers
Taurus Models 80, 82, 83, 85, 605, 607

38 SUPER

American Derringer Model 1
AMT Backup
Armscor Model M200DC/TC Pistol
Auto-Ordnance Model 1911A1 Thompson,
Competition, Model 1911 "The General"
Colt Combat Commander MKIV Series '80
European American Armory Witness, Gold &
Silver Teams
Sig-Sauer Model 220 "American" Pistol
Springfield Model 1911-A1 Mil-Spec, Factory
Comp, High- Capacity Factory Comp Pistols

38-40

Colt Single Action Army Revolver
EMF/Dakota Model 1873, Hartford Model
Revolvers

380 AUTO

American Arms Escort Pistol
American Derringer Models 1, 7 and 11
AMT Model Backup Pistol
Beretta Cheetah Models 84, 85 and 86 Pistols
Bernardelli PO18 Compact Target Pistol
Bersa Model Thunder 380, Series 95 Pistols
Browning Model BDA-380 Pistol
Colt Government Model, Pocketlite, Mustang,
Mustang Plus II, Mustang PocketLite 380
Pistols
CZ Model 83 Pistol
Daewoo Model DH380 Pistol
Davis P-380 Pistol
European American Armory European SA
Compact
FEG Model SMC-380
Hi-Point 380 Polymer Pistol
Llama Small Frame Automatic
Sig-Sauer Model 230 Pistol
Smith & Wesson Sigma Compact Series
Taurus Model PT 58 Pistol
Walther Model PP DA, Model PPK and PPK/S

9mm MAKAROV

FEG Model SMC-380 Pistol

9mm PARABELLUM (LUGER)

American Arms Aussie Semiauto
American Derringer Model 1, Model DA 38
Double Derringer
Auto-Ordnance Model 1911A1 Thompson
Astra Models A-70, A-75 and A-100
Beretta Cougar Series, Models 92 FS, 92D,
Centurion, Brigadier
Bernardelli Model PO18 Target and Compact
Target Pistols
Bersa Thunder 9 DA Pistol
Browning 9mm Hi-Power, Model BDM DA

9mm PARABELLUM (LUGER)

CZ Model 75 Pistol
Daewoo Model DP51, DP516 (Compact), DP51S
Davis Long-Bore D-Series
European American Armory Witness, Witness
Fab, Witness Gold Team, Witness Silver Team,
Witness Subcompact
Glock Models 17, 17L Competition; Model 19
Compact, Model 26
FEG Model PJK-9HP Pistol
Heckler and Koch Models P7M8, HK USP,
USP45 Universal
Heritage Stealth Compact
Hi-Point Firearms Model 9mm Compact
J.O. Arms Golan DA, Kareen MKII Compact
Kahr Arms Model K9 Pistol
Llama Max-1 Pistol
Magnum Research Baby Eagle
Ruger P-Series Pistols, SP101 Spurless DA
Sig-Sauer Models 220, 225, 226, 228, P229,
P239
Smith & Wesson Model 900 Series, 910, Model
940 Centennial, Model 3900 Compact Series,
5900 and 6900 Compact Series, Sigma Series
Pistols
Springfield Model 1911-A1 Standard &
Lightweight, High Capacity Standard Pistols
Star Models Firestar (incl. M40, M43, M45) and
Ultrastar, Firestar Plus
Stoeger American Eagle Luger
Taurus Models PT92, PT92AFC, PT-92AFC,
PT99, PT-908 Pistols
Walther Model P 5, Compact, P 88 Compact

10mm

American Derringer Model 1
Auto-Ordnance Model 1911A1 Thompson
Colt Delta Elite, Delta Gold Cup
Glock Model 20 Pistol
L.A.R. Mark I Grizzly Pistol
Laseraim Technologies Laseraim Series I, II, III
Pistols

40 AUTO

Beretta Cougar Series
Ruger P-Series Pistols
Safari Arms Cohort, Enforcer, Matchmaster

40 S&W

American Arms Aussie Semiauto
American Derringer Model 1, 38 DA Derringer
AMT Backup
Astra Models A-70, A-75, A-100
Beretta Models 96, 96D, Brigadier, Centurion,
Cougar Series
Bernardelli Model P.018 Compact Target
Daewoo Model DH40
European American Armory Witness, Witness
Fab, Gold & Silver Teams, Subcompact
FEG GKK-45
Glock Models 22, 23, 24, 27 Pistols
Heckler and Koch HK USP, USP 45 Universal
J.O. Arms Golan DA
Magnum Research Baby Eagle Pistol
Para-Ordnance Model P14 & P16 Pistols
Sig-Sauer Model P229 Pistol
Smith & Wesson Model 410, Model 4000
Compact Series and Full Size, Sigma Series
Star Model Firestar M40, M43, M45, UltraStar
Taurus Model 100/101, PT-940

41 MAGNUM

American Derringer Model 1
Ruger Bisley SA Target, New Model Blackhawk
Smith & Wesson Model 657 Stainless

.410

American Derringer Models 4 and 6

44 MAGNUM

American Arms Buckhorn SA
American Derringer Models 1, 4
Colt Anaconda Revolver
European American Armory Big Boar Bounty Hunter
Freedom Arms 454 Casull and Model 555 Premier and Field Grades, Silhouette/ Competition Models
Magnum Research Desert Eagle Mark XIX Component System, Lone Eagle SS Action
Mitchell Arms 44 Magnum Pistol
Ruger Redhawk, Super Redhawk, Super Redhawk Stainless, New Model Super Blackhawk SA, Bisley SA Target, Vaquero SA Revolvers
Smith & Wesson Model 29, Models 629, 629 Classic & Powerport; Series 4500 Compacts
Taurus Model 44 Revolver
Thompson/Center Contender Bull Barrel & Hunter, ''Super 14''
Uberti Buckhorn 1873 SA Target
Unique Int'l Silhouette Pistol

44 SPECIAL

American Derringer Models 1, 7
Colt Anaconda
EMF/Dakota Hartford Model Revolvers
Rossi Model 720, 720 Covert Special DA
Smith & Wesson Model 629, 629 Classic
Taurus Models 431 and 441

44-40

American Arms Regulator SA
Colt Single Action Army
EMF/Dakota Hartford Scroll Engraved SA, Hartford Models, New Hartford Percussion Revolvers (Colt-type 1851 Navy & Sheriff, 1847 Walker, 1848 Dragoon, 1860 Army), Models 1873, 1873 Dakota SA, 1875 Outlaw, 1890 Remington Police
Ruger Vaquero SA Revolver
Uberti Buckhorn SA, 1873 Cattleman, 1875 Outlaw/1890 Police Revolvers

444 MARLIN

Magnum Research Lone Eagle SS Action

45 ACP (AUTO)

American Derringer Models 1, 4, 6, 10
AMT Backup, Longslide, 1911 Government, 1911 Hardballer Models
Armscor Model M1911-A1P
Astra Models A-75, A-100
Auto-Ordnance Model 1911A1 Thompson, Competition, Deluxe, ''The General,'' Pit Bull, WWII Parkerized
Brolin Arms Legend, Patriot and Pro Series Pistols
Colt Anaconda, Combat Commander, Double Eagle, Gold Cup National Match, Government Model, Model 1991A1 (Compact and Commander), Officer's ACP
European American Armory Big Boar Bounty Hunter, Witness, Witness Fab, Gold Team, Subcompact
FEG GKK-45
Glock Model 21 Pistol
Heckler and Koch Model HK USP, USP 45 Universal, Mark 23 Special Operations
Kimber Model Classic Series .45
L.A.R. Mark I Grizzly Pistol
Laseraim Technologies Series I, II and III

45 ACP (AUTO)

Llama Automatic (Compact Frame), Government Model, Max-I
Mitchell Arms Gold Series, Jeff Cooper Signature Models
Para-Ordnance Models P12 and P14
Ruger P-Series Pistols
Safari Arms Cohort, Enforcer, Matchmaster
Sig-Sauer Model 220 American
Smith & Wesson Model 457, Model 625, Model 4500 Series Compact/Full Size
Springfield Champion Series (Compact Mil-Spec, Mil-Spec Champion), PDP Series (Champion Comp, Lightweight Compact Comp, High Capacity Factory Comp) Defender, Factory Comp, Model 1911-A1 Standard, Mil-Spec, Lightweight Compact, High Capacity Series, Trophy Match, Ultra Compact Series
Star Firestar M40, M43, M45
Taurus Model PT-945
Uberti 1873 Cattleman

45 COLT

American Arms Regulator SA
American Derringer Lady Derringer, Models 1, 4, 6, 10, Texas Double Derringer Commemorative, M-4 Alaskan Survival
Colt Single Action Army Revolver
EMF/Dakota Hartford Models (Artillery, Single Action, Cavalry Colt), Models 1873, 1873 Dakota SA, 1875 ''Outlaw,'' Model 1890 Remington Police, Pinkerton Detective SA, Hartford Scroll Engraved SA,
Ruger Model Bisley SA Target, New Model Blackhawk, Vaquero
Thompson/Center Contender Bull Barrel, Super ''16''
Uberti 1871 Rolling Block Target Pistol, 1873 Cattleman

45 WIN. MAG.

AMT Automag IV
American Derringer Model 1
L.A.R. Mark I Grizzly
Wildey Hunter and Survivor Pistols

45-70 GOV'T.

American Derringer Models 1 and 4, M-4 Alaskan Survival

454 CASULL

American Arms Uberti SA
Freedom Arms 454 Casull, Model 555 Field and Premier Grades
Thompson/Center Contender Hunter

475 WILDEY MAG.

Wildey Hunter and Survivor Pistols

50 MAG. AE

AMT Automag V
L.A.R. Grizzly 50 Mark 5
Magnum Research Desert Eagle Mark XIX Component System

RIFLES

CENTERFIRE—BOLT ACTION

STANDARD CALIBERS

17 ACKLEY HORNET

Cooper Arms Model 40 Classic, Custom Classic

17 BEE

Francotte Bolt Action

17 REMINGTON

Cooper Arms Model 21 Varmint Extreme
Kimber Model 84C SuperAmerica & Custom Match
Remington Model 700 ADL, BDL
Sako Deluxe, Super Deluxe; Hunter Lightweight, Varmint
Ultra Light Model 20 Series
Winslow Varmint

17/222, 17/223

Winslow Varmint

22 HORNET

Browning A-Bolt II Micro Medallion
Cooper Arms Model 40 Classic, Custom Classic
CZ Model CZ527
Dakota Arms Model 76 Varmint Grade
KBI Standard 22 Models M-1400SC, M-1500SC, M-1800SC
Ruger Model 77/22RH Hornet, K77/22VH Varmint
Ultra Light Model 20 Series

22 PPC

Cooper Arms Model 21 Benchrest, Varmint Extreme
Dakota Arms Model 76 Varmint Grade
Ruger Model M-77VT HB Target

22-250

AMT Standard & Deluxe Repeaters
A-Square Genghis Khan
Blaser Model R93
Browning A-Bolt II Series (except Gold Medallion)
Dakota 76 Classic, Varmint Grades
Harris Gunworks Classic, Stainless, Standard Sporters; Talon Sporter, Varminter
Howa Lightning
Kimber Swedish Mauser 96 HB SS Varmint
Remington Models 700 ADL, BDL, Varmint LS & Synthetic
Ruger Models M-77VT MKII HB Target, M-77RP MKII All-Weather
Sako Deluxe, Super Deluxe; Hunter Lightweight, Left-Handed Models, Varmint
Savage Models 111G, 111F Classic Hunter; Models 112 BVSS & 112FV Varmint, 112FVSS
Tikka Continental Varmint, Whitetail Hunter
Ultra Light Model 20 Series
Winchester Models 70 Boss Classic and Classic Stainless, Custom Classic, Heavy Barrel Varmint, Sharpshooter II SS, Walnut Classic Featherweight
Winslow Basic

220 SWIFT

Dakota Arms Model 76 Varmint Grade
Kimber Mauser 98 Sporter
Remington Model 700VS Varmint Synthetic
Ruger Model M-77VT MKII HB Target
Winchester Model 70 Heavy Barrel Varmint

221 FIREBALL

Cooper Arms Model 21 Varmint Extreme

222 REMINGTON

Blaser Model R93
Cooper Arms Model 21 Varmint Extreme
CZ Model CZ527
Francotte Bolt Action
Kimber Model 84C Classic, Custom Match, SuperAmerica
Magnum Research Mountain Eagle Varmint
Remington Models 700 ADL, BDL, Varmint LS
Sako Deluxe, Super Deluxe; Hunter Lightweight, Varmint
Steyr-Mannlicher Models Jagd Match, Sporter SL, Varmint
Ultra Light Model 20 Series
Winslow Varmint

223 REMINGTON

AMT Standard & Deluxe Repeaters
Brown Precision High Country Youth and Tactical Elite
Browning A-Bolt II Series (except Gold Medallion)
Cooper Arms Models 21 Benchrest, Varmint Extreme
CZ Model CZ527
Dakota Arms Model 76 Varmint Grade
Harris Gunworks Varminter
Howa Lightning
Kimber Model 84C Classic, Custom Match, SuperAmerica
Magnum Research Mountain Eagle Varmint Edition
Remington Models Seven Lightweight; 700 ADL, BDL; Varmint LS & Synthetic
Ruger Models Mark II M-77R, M-77RL Ultra Light, M-77RP All-Weather, M-77VT HB Target
Sako Deluxe, Hunter Lightweight, Varmint
Savage Models 110FP Tactical, 110CY; 111G, 111F Classic Hunter; 112 BT Competition, 112FV/FVSS, 112BVSS Varmint; 116FCS/116FSS "Weather Warrior"
Steyr-Mannlicher Model Sporter SL
Tikka Continental Varmint, Whitetail Hunter
Ultra Light Model 20 Series
Winchester Models 70 Ranger, HB Varmint
Winslow Varmint

243 WINCHESTER

AMT Standard, Deluxe Repeaters
Arnold Arms African Safari, African Synthetic, African Trophy, Serengeti Synthetic
A-Square Genghis Khan
Blaser Model R93
Brown Precision High Country Youth
Browning A-Bolt II Series (except Eclipse Varmint, Gold Medallion), Euro-Bolt
CZ Model CZ550
Francotte Bolt Action
Harris Gunworks Benchrest; Classic, Stainless, Standard Sporters; Talon Sporter, Varminter
Howa Lightning
Kimber Swedish Mauser 96 Sporter
Kongsberg Hunter 393 Series
Remington Models Seven Lightweight, Stainless Synthetic, Youth; 700 ADL, BDL, BDL (DM), BDL SS, Mountain(DM) , Varmint Laminated
Ruger Models Mark II M-77R, M-77RS, M-77VT HB & All-Weather, Ultra Light; M-77RSI International Mannlicher
Sako Classic, Deluxe, Super Deluxe, Hunter Lightweight, Left-Handed Models, Mannlicher-Style Carbine, Varmint
Sauer Models 90 & 202
Savage Models 110CY; 111G/111F Classic Hunter; 116FCS/116FSS "Weather Warrior"

243 WINCHESTER

Steyr-Mannlicher Jagd Match, Luxus L, Sporter L, SSG
Tikka Whitetail Hunter
Ultra Light Model 20 Series
Unique Model TGC
Winchester Models 70 Boss Classic & Classic Stainless; Heavy Barrel Varmint; Ranger, Ranger Ladies/ Youth; Walnut Classic Featherweight
Winslow Basic

244 REMINGTON

Winslow Basic

6mm BR

Harris Gunworks Benchrest; Classic, Stainless, Standard Sporters; Talon Sporter

6mm PPC

AMT Standard & Deluxe Repeaters
Dakota Arms Model 76 Varmint Grade
Harris Gunworks Benchrest
Ruger M-77VT Mark II HB Target

6mm REMINGTON

A-Square Genghis Khan
Brown Precision High Country Youth
Harris Gunworks Benchrest, Varminter, Classic & Stainless Sporter, Talon Sporter
Remington Model Seven Lightweight, Models 700 BDL SS, BDL DM
Ruger Model M-77R MK II
Ultra Light Model 20 Series

25-06

AMT Standard, Deluxe Repeater
A-Square Hamilcar, Genghis Khan
Browning A-Bolt II Composite & Stainless Stalker, Hunter, Medallion
Harris Gunworks Classic, Stainless, Standard Sporters; Talon Sporter, Varminter
Remington Models 700 ADL, BDL, BDL (DM), BLD SS (DM), Mountain (DM), Sendero
Ruger Models 77RS MKII, M-77VT MKII HB Target
Sako Deluxe, Super Deluxe; Fiberclass, Hunter Lightweight, Left-Handed Models, Long-Range Hunter, TRG-S
Sauer Model 90
Savage Models 110FP, 111G/111F Classic Hunter, 112 FVSS Varmint, 112BVSS Varmint
Steyr-Mannlicher Model MIII Professional
Tikka Whitetail Hunter, Continental Long-Range Hunting
Ultra Light Model 24 Series
Winchester Model 70 Sporter, Ultimate Classic
Winslow Basic

257 ACKLEY

Ultra Light Model 20 Series

257 ROBERTS

Arnold Arms Alaskan Guide, Alaskan Synthetic
Dakota Arms Model 76 Classic
Kimber Swedish Mauser 98 Sporter
Lazzeroni Models 2000 SP-F, ST-F, ST-W
Ruger Model M-77 MKII, M-77RL MKII Ultra Light
Ultra Light Model 20 Series
Winslow Basic

6.5×06

AMT Standard, Deluxe Repeaters
A-Square Hamilcar

6.5×55mm/SWEDISH

A-Square Hamilcar
Kimber Hunter 393 Series, Swedish Mauser 96 Sporter
Ruger M-77R MKII
Sako Model TRG-S Magnum
Steyr-Mannlicher Luxus, Sporter

6.5×57mm   6.5×68mm

Steyr-Mannlicher Luxus, Sporter

264 WINCHESTER

A-Square Hamilcar, Genghis Kahn

270 WINCHESTER

AMT Standard, Deluxe Repeaters
A-Square Hamilcar
Blaser Model R93
Browning A-Bolt II Series (except Micro-Medalliion, Varmint, Eclipse Varmint)
CZ Model CZ550
Dakota Arms Model 76 Classic
Francotte Bolt Action
Harris Gunworks Alaskan; Classic Stainless, Std. Sporters; Talon Sporter, Titanium Mtn.
Howa Lightning
Kimber Mauser 98 Sporter, Model K770 Classic & SuperAmerica
Kongsberg Hunter 393 Series
Magnum Research Mountain Eagle
Marlin Model MR-7
Remington Models 700 ADL, BDL, BDL (DM), BDL SS (DM), BDL Synthetic, Mountain (DM), Sendero
Ruger Models Mark II M-77RP/RSP All-Weather, M-77EXP Express, M-77R/LR, M-77RL Ultra Light, M-77RS; M-77RSI Int'l. Mannlicher
Sako Classic, Deluxe, Super Deluxe; Fiberclass, Hunter Lightweight, L. H. Models, Mannlicher-Style Carbine, Long-Range Hunter, TRG-S
Sauer Models 90, 202
Savage Models 110CY; 111G, 111GC, 111F, 111FC Classic Hunter; 114CE "Classic European," 114CU"Classic Ultra"; 116FCS, 116FSK, 116FSS "Weather Warrior"
Steyr-Mannlicher Luxus, MIII Professional, Sporter
Tikka Continental Long-Range Hunting, Whitetail Hunter
Ultra Light Model 24 Series
Unique Model TGC
Weatherby Models Mark V Euromark, Eurosport, Sporter, Stainless, Synthetic
Winchester Models 70 Classic Series; Classic SM, Ultimate Classic, Classic Super Grade, Classic Sporter, Ranger, Stainless
Winslow Basic

280 REMINGTON

A-Square Hamilcar
Browning A-Bolt II Composite/Stainless Stalker, Hunter, Medallion
Dakota Arms Model 76 Classic
Harris Gunworks Classic, Stainless, Standard Sporters; Alaskan, Talon Sporter, Titanium Mountain
Kimber Mauser 98 Sporter
Magnum Research Mountain Eagle
Remington Models 700 ADL, BDL, BDL (DM), BDL SS (DM), BDL Synthetic, Mountain (DM)
Ruger Model M-77R MKII, M-77RP MKII All-Weather
Sako Deluxe, Fiberclass, Hunter Lightweight, Left-Handed Models
Winchester Models 70 Ultimate Classic, Walnut Classic Featherweight
Winslow Basic

284 WINCHESTER

Harris Gunworks Classic, Stainless, Standard Sporters; Talon Sporter,
Lazzeroni Models L2000 SP-F, ST-F, ST-W
Ultra Light Model 20 Series
Winslow Basic

7mm BR

Harris Gunworks Classic, Stainless, Standard Sporters; Talon Sporter

7mm EXPRESS

Ultra Light Model 24 Series

7mm STW

A-Square Hamilcar
Winchester Models 70 Custom Classic Sporting Sharpshooter II, Ultimate Classic,

7×57mm (ACKLEY/MAUSER)

Ruger Model M-77R MKII
Winslow Basic
Ultra Light Model 20 Series

7×64

Steyr-Mannlicher Luxus, MIII Professional, Sporter

7mm-08

Brown Precision High Country Youth
Browning A-Bolt II Series (except Gold Medallion)
Harris Gunworks Classic, Stainless, Standard Sporters; National Match, Talon Sporter, Varminter
Kimber Swedish Mauser 96 Sporter
Remington Models Seven Lightweight, Stainless Synthetic, Youth; 700 BDL (DM), BDL SS (DM), Mountain (DM)
Sako Deluxe, Super Deluxe; Hunter Lightweight, Left-Handed Models, Varmint
Savage Models 111G/111F Classic Hunters
Ultra Light Model 20 Series
Unique Model TGC
Winchester Model 70 Walnut Classic Featherweight

30-06

AMT Standard, Deluxe Repeaters
A-Square Hamilcar
Blaser Model R 93
Browning A-Bolt II Long Action Std., Euro-bolt
Clifton Arms Scout
CZ Model CZ550
Dakota Arms Model 76 Classic
Francotte Bolt Action
Harris Gunworks Alaskan; Classic, Stainless, Standard Sporters; Talon Sporter, Titanium Mountain
Howa Lightning
Kimber Mauser 98 Sporter, Model K770 Classic & SuperAmerica
Kongsberg Hunter 393 Series, Sporter 393 Thumbhole
Magnum Research Mountain Eagle
Marlin Model MR-7
Remington Models 700 ADL, BDL, BDL (DM), BDL SS (DM), BDL Stainless Synthetic, Mountain (DM)
Ruger Models Mark II M-77EXP Express, M-77R/LR, M-77RL Ultra Light, M-77RP/RSP All-Weather, M-77RS; M-77RSI International Mannlicher
Sako Classic, Deluxe/Super Deluxe, Fiberclass, Hunter Lightweight, Left-Handed Models, Long Range Hunter, Mannlicher-Style Carbine, Model TRG-S

30-06

Sauer Models 90, 202
Savage Models 111F, 111FC, 111G, 111GC Classic Hunters; 114CE "Classic European," 114CU Classic Ultra; 110FP Tactical; 112FVSS, 112BVSS Varmint; 116FCS, 116FSK "Weather Warrior," 116FSS
Steyr-Mannlicher Luxus, MIII Professional, Sporter
Tikka Whitetail Hunter
Ultra Light Model 24 Series
Unique Model TGC
Weatherby Mark V Eurosport, Euromark Sporter, Stainless Synthetic
Winchester Models 70 Classic Featherweight Series; Classic SM/Boss,Stainless SM/Boss, Sporter, Ultimate Classic, Sharpshooter II SS, Ranger, Super Grade
Winslow Basic

300 SAVAGE

Ultra Light Model 20 Series

300 WINCHESTER

A-Square Hamilcar

308 WINCHESTER

AMT Standard, Deluxe Repeaters
Blaser Model R 93
Browning A-Bolt II Short Action, Eurobolt
Brown Precision High Country Youth, Tactical Elite
Clifton Arms Scout
CZ Model CZ550
Francotte Bolt Action
Harrington & Richardson Erma SR-100 Precision
Harris Gunworks Benchrest; Classic, Stainless, Standard Sporters; National Match, Talon Sporter, Varminter
Howa Lightning
Kimber Swedish Mauser 96 Sporter, HBSS Varmint
Kongsberg Hunter 393 Series, Sporter 393 Thumbhole
Lazzeroni Models L2000 SP-F, ST-F, ST-W
Remington Models 700 ADL, BDL, BDL (DM), BDL SS(DM), Varmint, Varmint Synthetic; Models Seven Lightweight, Stainless Synthetic
Ruger Models MarkII M-77 All Weather, M-77R, M-77RL Ultra Light, M-77RS, M-77VT HB Target; M-77RSI International Mannlicher
Sako Deluxe/Super Deluxe, Hunter Lightweight, Left-Handed Models, Mannlicher-Style Carbine, TRG-21, Varmint
Sauer Models 90, 202
Savage Models 110CY; 110FP Tactical, 111G, 111F Classic Hunters; Models 112FVSS & 112BVSS Varmint, 112BT Competition; 116 FSS/FCS "Weather Warrior"
Steyr-Mannlicher Jagd Match, Luxus, Match SPG Series, Sporter, SSG
Tikka Continental Varmint, Whitetail Hunter
Ultra Light Model 20
Unique Model TGC
Winchester Models 70 Classic/Boss Stainless; Custom Classic Sharpshooter II SS; Heavy Barrel Varmint; Ranger Ladies/Youth; Walnut Classic Featherweight
Winslow Basic

8×685S

Steyr-Mannlicher Luxus, Sporter

338-06

A-Square Hamilcar

358 WINCHESTER

Ultra Light Model 20 Series
Winslow Basic

9.3×62mm

A-Square Hamilcar

9.3×64mm

Steyr-Mannlicher Sporter

CENTERFIRE—BOLT ACTION

MAGNUM CALIBERS

17/222 MAG.

Winslow Varmint

222 REM. MAG.

Cooper Arms Model 21 Varmint Extreme
Dakota Arms Model 76 Varmint Grade
Steyr-Mannlicher Model Sporter (SL)
Ultra Light Model 20 Series

240 WBY. MAG.

Weatherby Mark V Deluxe, Euromark, Eurosport, Lazermark, Sporter, Stainless, Synthetic

257 WBY. MAG

A-Square genghis Khan, Hamilcar
Blaser Model R93
Weatherby Models Mark V Accumark, Deluxe, Euromark, Eurosport, Lazermark, Stainless, Sporter, Synthetic
Winslow Basic

264 WIN. MAG.

Blaser Model R93
Ultra Light Arms Model 28 Series
Winchester Models 70 Sporter, Ultimate Classic
Winslow Basic

270 WBY./WIN. MAG.

Sako Hunter Lightweight, TRG-S Magnum
Weatherby Models Mark V Deluxe, Euromark, Eurosport, Lazermark, Sporter, Stainless, Synthetic
Winchester Models 70 Sporter, Ultimate Classic
Winslow Basic

7mm REM. MAG./7mm WBY. MAG.

A-Square Caesar, Hamilcar
Blaser Model R93
Browning A-Bolt II Series (except Eclipse Varmint), Eurobolt
CZ Model CZ550
Dakota Arms Model 76 Classic Grade
Harris Gunworks Alaskan; Classic, Stainless, Standard Sporters; Long Range, Talon Sporter, Titanium Mountain
Howa Lightning
Kimber Mauser 98 Sporter
Kongsberg Hunter 393 Series
Magnum Research Mountain Eagle
Remington Models 700 ADL, BDL, BDL (DM),BDL SS (DM), BDL Synthetic; African Plains, Alaskan Wilderness, Sendero
Ruger Models Mark II M-77EXP Express, M-77R/LR, M-77RS, M-77RS/RSP All-Weather
Sako Classic, Deluxe/Super Deluxe, Fiberclass, Hunter Lightweight, Left-Handed Models, Long-Range Hunter, TRG-S Magnum
Sauer Models 90, 202

7mm REM. MAG./7mm WBY. MAG.

Savage Models 110 FP Tactical; 111GC, 111G, 111F, 111FC Classic Hunters; 112 FVSS, 112BVSS Varmint; 114CE "Classic European," 114CY Classic Ultra, 116 FCS, 116FSK/116FSS "Weather Warrior"
Steyr-Mannlicher Luxus, Sporter
Tikka Continental Long-Range Hunting, Whitetail Hunter
Ultra Light Arms Model 28 Series
Unique Model TGC
Weatherby Mark V Accumark, Deluxe, Euromark, Eurosport, Lazermark, Sporter, Stainless, Synthetic
Winchester Models 70 Classic/Boss SM, Ultimate Classic, Classic/Boss Stainless, Classic Sporter, Classic Laredo, Classic Featherweight/Boss All-Terrain, Classic Super Grade
Winslow Basic

7mm STW

Harris Gunworks Classic, Stainless, Standard Sporters; Talon Sporter
Sako TRG-S Magnum

8mm REM. MAG.

A-Square Caesar and Hannibal
Remington Model 700 Safari, Safari KS

30-338 Wildcat

Remington Model 700 Classic

300 H&H

Harris Gunworks Alaskan; Classic, Stainless, Standard Sporters; Safari, Talon Sporter
Winchester Model 70 Ultimate Classic
Winslow Basic

300 PEGASUS

A-Square Hannibal

300 PHOENIX

Harris Gunworks Long Range, Safari, .300 Phoenix

300 WBY. MAG.

A-Square Caesar, Hamilcar
Blaser Model 93
Harris Gunworks Classic, Stainless, Standard Sporters; Alaskan, Safari, Talon Sporter
Magnum Research Mountain Eagle
Remington Models 700 BDL SS (DM), African Plains, Alaskan Wilderness
Sako Deluxe/Super Deluxe, Hunter Lightweight, Left-Handed Models, Model TRG-S
Sauer Model 90
Ultra Light Arms Model 40 Series
Weatherby Models Mark V Accumark, Deluxe, Euromark, Eurosport, Lazermark, Sporter, Stainless, Synthetic
Winchester Models 70 Classic/Boss Stainless, Classic Sporter, Ultimate Classic
Winslow Basic

300 WIN. MAG.

AMT Deluxe, Standard Repeaters
Arnold Arms Alaskan Rifle, Alaskan Trophy, Grand Alaskan, Serengeti, Synthetic
A-Square Caesar, Hamilcar
Blaser Model R93
Brown Precision Tactical Elite
Browning A-Bolt II Series
CZ Model CZ550
Dakota Arms Model 76 Safari & Classic Grades
Francotte Bolt Action
Harrington & Richardson Erma SR-100 Precision

300 WIN. MAG.

Harris Gunworks Alaskan; Classic, Stainless Sporters; Safari, Talon Sporter, Titanium Mountain
Howa Lightning
Kimber Mauser 98 Sporter
Kongsberg Hunter 393 Series
Magnum Research Mountain Eagle
Remington Models 700 ADL, BDL, BDL (DM), BDL SS, BDL SS (DM) African Plains, Alaskan Wilderness, Classic, Sendero
Ruger Models Mark II M-77R/LR, M-77RS, M-77RS/RSP All-Weather, M-77EXP Express
Sako Deluxe/Super Deluxe, Fiberclass, Hunter Lightweight, Long-Range Hunter, TRG-S Magnum, Left-Handed Models
Sauer Models 90, 202
Savage Models 110 FP Tactical; 111G, 111GC, 111F, 111FC Classic Hunters; 112 FVSS, 112BVSS Varmint; 114CE "Classic European," 114CU Classic Ultra; 116FCS, 116 FSS, 116FSK/FSAK "Weather Warrior"; 116SE Safari Express
Steyr-Mannlicher Luxus, Sporter
Tikka Continental Long-Range Hunting, Whitetail Hunter
Ultra Light Arms Model 28 Series
Unique Model TGC
Weatherby Models Mark V Accumark, Euromark, Eurosport, Sporter, Stainless, Synthetic
Winchester Models 70 Classic/Boss SM, Classic/Boss Stainless, Classic Featherweight/Boss All-Terrain, Classic Laredo, Classic Sporter, Custom Classic Sharpshooter II SS, Sporting Sharpshooter II, Super Grade, Ultimate Classic
Winslow Basic

308 NORMA

Remington Model 700 Classic
Winslow Basic

338 A-SQUARE MAG.

A-Square Caesar, Hannibal

338 LAPUA MAG.

Harrington & Richardson Erma SR-100 Precision
Harris Gunworks Long Range, Safari
Sako Model TRG-S, TRG-41

338 WIN. MAG.

AMT Deluxe, Standard Repeaters
Arnold Arms Alaskan Guide, Alaskan Synthetic, Grand Alaskan
A-Square Caesar, Hannibal
Blaser Model R93
Browning A-Bolt II Series
Dakota Arms Model 76 Safari & Classic Grades
Francotte Bolt Action
Harris Gunworks Classic, Stainless, Standard Sporters; Safari, Talon Sporter
Howa Lightning
Kimber Mauser 98 Sporter
Kongsberg Hunter 393 Series
Lazzeroni Models L2000 SP-F, ST-F, ST-W
Magnum Research Mountain Eagle
Remington Models 700 African Plains, Alaskan Wilderness, BDL (DM), BDL SS (DM), Classic
Ruger Models Mark II M-77R, M-77EXP Express, M-77RP All-Weather, M-77RS
Sako Deluxe/Super Deluxe, Fiberclass, Hunter Lightweight, Left-Handed Models, Mannlicher-Style Carbine, Safari Grade, Model TRG-S Magnum
Savage Model 116FCS; 116FSK, 116FSS "Weather Warrior"; 116SE Safari Express
Tikka Whitetail Hunter
Ultra Light Arms Model 28 Series

338 WIN. MAG.

Weatherby Models Mark V Euromark, Eurosport, Sporter, Stainless, Synthetic
Winchester Models 70 Classic/BOSS SM, Stainless, Sporter, Super Grade, Ultimate Classic
Winslow Basic

340 WBY. MAG.

A-Square Caesar and Hannibal
Harris Gunworks Alaskan; Classic, Stainless, Standard Sporters; Safari, Talon Sporter
Magnum Research Mountain Eagle
Sako Hunter Lightweight, TRG-S Magnum
Weatherby Models Mark V Deluxe, Lazermark, Euromark, Sporter, Accumark, Eurosport, Stainless, Synthetic

35 WHELEN

Clifton Arms Scout
Remington Models 7400 and 7600

350 REM. MAG.

Harris Gunworks Classic, Stainless, Standard Sporters; Talon Sporter, Varminter

357 MAG.

Marlin 1894CS

358 WIN./NORMA

A-Square Caesar, Hannibal
Harris Gunworks Alaskan
Winslow Basic

358 STA | 375 A-SQUARE MAG.

A-Square Caesar, Hannibal

375 H&H

AMT Deluxe, Standard Repeaters
A-Square Caesar, Hannibal
Blaser Model R93, Safari
Browning A-Bolt II Medallion, Stainless Steel
CZ Model ZKK602
Dakota Arms Model 76 Safari, Classic Grades
Francotte Bolt Action
Harris Gunworks Alaskan; Classic, Stainless, Standard Sporters; Safari, Talon Sporter
Magnum Research Mountain Eagle
Remington Models 700 African Plains, Alaskan Wilderness, Classic, Safari, Safari KS
Rifles, Inc. Classic, Lightweight Strata Stainless
Ruger 77RSM MKII Magnum
Sako Deluxe/Super Deluxe, Fiberclass, Hunter Lightweight, Left-Handed Models, Mannlicher-Style Carbine, Safari Grade, Model TRG-S Magnum
Sauer Model 90
Steyr-Mannlicher Models Sporter S, S/T
Weatherby Models Mark V Euromark, Eurosport, Sporter, Stainless, Synthetic
Winchester Models 70 Classic SM, Classic Stainless, Classic Super Express, Custom Classic Express
Winslow Basic

375 J.R.S.

A-Square Caesar, Hannibal
Winchester Model 70 Custom Classic Express

375 WEATHERBY

A-Square Caesar, Hannibal

375 WIN. MAG.

Sauer Model 202

378 WIN./WBY. MAG.

A-Square Hannibal
Harris Gunworks Talon Safari
Weatherby Models Mark V Deluxe, Euromark, Lazermark

404 JEFFERY

A-Square Caesar, Hannibal
Dakota Arms 76 African Grade
Harris Gun Works Safari

416 REM./WBY. MAG.

AMT Deluxe, Standard Repeaters
A-Square Caesar and Hannibal
Blaser Model R93
Clifton Arms Scout
CZ Model ZKK602
Harris Gunworks Alaskan; Classic, Stainless, Std. Sporters; Safari, Talon Safari & Sporter
Magnum Research Mountain Eagle
Remington Model 700 Safari, Safari KS
Sako Deluxe/Super Deluxe, Fiberclass, Hunter Lightweight, Left-Handed Models, Safari Grade, Model TRG-S Magnum
Weatherby Models Mark V Deluxe, Euromark, Lazermark,
Winchester Models 70 Custom Classic Express, Custom Classic Super Express

416 RIGBY/DAKOTA

AMT Deluxe, Standard Repeaters
A-Square Hannibal
CZ Model ZKK602
Dakota Arms 76 African Grade
Francotte Bolt Action
Harris Gunworks Talon Safari
Ruger 77RSM MKII Magnum
Ultra Light Arms Model 40 Series

416 TAYLOR and HOFFMAN

A-Square Caesar, Hannibal

425 EXPRESS

A-Square Caesar, Hannibal

450 ACKLEY/DAKOTA

A-Square Caesar, Hannibal
Dakota Arms 76 African Grade

458 WIN. MAG./LOTT

AMT Deluxe, Standard Repeaters
Arnold Arms African Safari, Synthetic & Trophy; Alaskan Rifle, Trophy; Grand African & Alaskan
A-Square Caesar, Hannibal
CZ Model ZKK602
Dakota Arms Model 76 Classic, Safari Grades
Francotte Bolt Action
Harris Gunworks Safari
Remington Models 700 Safari, Safari KS
Ruger Model M-77RS MKII
Sauer Safari
Savage Model 116SE Safari Express
Steyr-Mannlicher Model Sporter S/T
Winchester Modles 70 Custom Classic Express, Custom Classic Super Express
Winslow Basic

460 SHORT

A-Square Caesar, Hannibal

460 WIN./WBY. MAG.

A-Square Hannibal
Francotte Bolt Action
Harris Gunworks Talon Safari
Weatherby Models Mark V Deluxe, Lazermark

470 CAPSTICK   495 A-SQUARE MAG.

A-Square Caesar, Hannibal

500 A-SQUARE   577 TYRANNOSAUR

A-Square Hannibal

505 GIBBS

Francotte Bolt Action

CENTERFIRE—LEVER ACTION

22-250 REM.   223 REM.

Browning Model Lightning BLR

243 WINCHESTER

Browning Model Lightning BLR
Savage Model 99C

270 WINCHESTER

Browning Model Lightning BLR

7mm REM. MAG.   7mm-08 REM.

Browning Model Lightning BLR

30-06 SPRGFLD.

Browning Model Lightning BLR

30-30 WINCHESTER

Marlin Models 30AS, 336CS
Winchester Models 94 Checkered Walnut, Legacy, Ranger, Standard, Trapper Carbine, Win-Tuff, Wrangler

307 WINCHESTER

Winchester Model 94 Big Bore Walnut

308 WINCHESTER

Browning Model Lightning BLR
Savage Model 99C

35 REMINGTON

Marlin Model 336CS

356 WINCHESTER

Winchester Model 94 Big Bore Walnut

357 MAGNUM

EMF Model 1873 Sporting
Marlin Model 1894CS
Rossi Models M92 SRS and SRC
Uberti 1873 Sporting, Carbine
Winchester Model 94 Trapper Carbine

38 SPECIAL

EMF Model 1866 Yellow Boy Rifle/Carbine
Marlin Model 1894CS
Rossi Model M92 SRC, SRS
Uberti Models 1866 Sporting, Yellowboy Carbine

44 REM. MAG.

Marlin Model 1894S
Winchester Model 94 Trapper Carbine, Wrangler

44 SPECIAL

Marlin Model 1894S
Winchester Model 94 Trapper Carbine, Wrangler

44-40

American Arms 1860 Henry, 1866 Winchester, 1873 Winchester
EMF Model 1860 Henry, 1866 Yellow Boy Rifle/ Carbine, Model 1873 Sporting

44-40

Navy Arms 1866 Yellowboy Rifle/Carbine; Henry Military, Carbine, Iron Frame and Trapper Models, 1873 Winchester-Style and Winchester Sporting
Rossi Model M92
Uberti Model 1866 Yellowboy Carbine, 1873 Sporting & Carbine; Henry Rifle, Carbine, Trapper

444 MARLIN

Marlin Model 444SS

45 COLT

American Arms 1860 Henry, 1866 Winchester, 1873 Winchester
EMF Model 1860 Henry, 1866 Yellow Boy Rifle/ Carbine, 1873 Sporting/Short Rifle, Carbine, Remington Rolling Block Carbine
Marlin Model 1894S, 1894 Cowboy
Navy Arms 1873 Winchester Sporting, Winchester-Style
Rossi Model M92
Uberti Model 1873 Sporting, Carbine; Henry Rifle
Winchester Model 94 Trapper Carbine

45-70 GOV'T.

Marlin Model 1895SS

CENTERFIRE—SEMIAUTOMATIC

5.56mm

Springfield Model SAR-4800 Sporter

223 REMINGTON

Colt Competition H-Bar, Competition H-Bar II; Match Target, Match Target H-Bar and Match Target Lightweight
Ruger K-Mini-14/5, K-Mini-14/5R, Mini-14/5, Mini-14/5R Ranch
Steyr-Mannlicher Aug S.A.

243 WINCHESTER

Browning BAR Mark II Safari
Remington Model 7400
Springfield M1A Standard, M1A-A1 Bush

270 WIN.

Browning BAR Mark II Safari
Remington Model 7400

280 REM

Remington Model 7400

30-06

Browning BAR Mark II Safari
Remington Model 7400

300 WIN. MAG.

Browning BAR Mark II Safari
Harrington & Richardson Erma SR-100 Precision

308 WINCHESTER

Browning BAR Mark II Safari
Harrington & Richardson Erma SR-100 Precision
Heckler and Koch PSG-1 High Precision Marksman's
Remington Model 7400
Springfield Basic M1A, M1A National Match, M1A Standard, M1A-A1 Bush, Super Match; Models SAR-8 & SAR-4800 Sporters

7.62×39

Colt Match Target Lightweight
Ruger Mini-30
Springfield Models SAR-8 and SAR-4800
Sporters
Steyr-Mannlicher M1A Standard, M1A-A1 Bush

338 LAPUA

Harrington & Richardson Erma SR-100 Precision

338 WIN. MAG.

Browning BAR Mark II Safari

35 WHELEN

Remington Model 7400

45 ACP (AUTO)

Auto-Ordnance Thompson Models M1 Carbine,
1927A1, 1927A1C Lightweight
Marlin Model 45

7mm REM. MAG.

Browning BAR Mark II Safari

7mm-08

Springfield M1A Standard, M1A-A1 Bush

9mm

Colt Match Target Lightweight
Marlin Model 9 Camp Carbine
Mitchell Arms Model LW9

CENTERFIRE—DOUBLE RIFLES

308

Krieghoff Model Classic S/S Standard
Tikka Model 512S

30-06

Krieghoff Models Classic S/S Standard
Tikka Model 512S

7×65R

Francotte Sidelock S/S, Boxlock S/S
Krieghoff Classic S/S Standard

8×57JRS

Francotte Sidelock S/S, Boxlock S/S
Krieghoff Classic S/S Standard
Pedersoli Kodiak Mark IV

8×75RS

Krieghoff Classic S/S Standard

9.3×74R

Francotte Sidelock S/S and Boxlock S/S
Krieghoff Classic S/S Standard
Pedersoli Kodiak Mark IV
Tikka Model 512S

375 H&H   375 FLANGED MAG. N.E.

Krieghoff Classic Big Five

416 RIGBY

Krieghoff Classic Big Five

45-70

Navy Arms Deluxe/Kodiak Mark IV
Pedersoli Kodiak Mark IV

458 WIN. MAG.

Krieghoff Model Classic Big Five

470 N.E., 500/416 N.E., 500 N.E.

Krieghoff Classic Big Five

CENTERFIRE/RIMFIRE—PUMP ACTION

22 S, L, LR

Remington Model 572 BDL Deluxe Fieldmaster
Rossi Models M62 SAC and SA

22 MAGNUM

Rossi Model 59

243 WIN./270 WIN. (CF)

Remington Model 7600 (also calibers 280 Rem.,
30-06, 308 Win., 35 Whelen)

CENTERFIRE/RIMFIRE—SINGLE SHOT

17 REMINGTON

Kimber Model 84C Varmint
Thompson/Center Contender Carbine

218 BEE

Ruger No. 1B Standard, No. 1S Medium Sporter

22 HORNET

AMT Single Shot Standard & Deluxe
Browning Model 1885 Low Wall
New England Handi-Rifle
Ruger No. 1B Standard
Thompson/Center Contender Series
Uberti Model 1871 Rolling Block Baby Carbine

22 MAG.

Uberti Model 1871 Rolling Block Baby Carbine

22 PPC

AMT Single Shot Standard & Deluxe
Ruger No. 1V Special Varminter

22 S, L, LR

Dakota Arms Model 10
European American Armory HW 660 Weihrauch
Rimfire Target
KBI Model M-12Y Youth
Kimber Model 82C SVT
Marlin 15YN ''Little Buckaroo,'' Model 2000L
Target
Remington Models 40-XR BR, 40-XR KS Sporter,
Savage Mark I-G
Thompson/Center Contender Series
Uberti Model 1871 Rolling Block Baby Carbine
Ultra Light Arms Model 20RF

22-250 REM.

AMT Single Shot Standard & Deluxe
Browning Model 1885 High Wall
Cooper Arms Black Jack, BR-50 Bench Rest,
Model 22 Pro Varmint Extreme
Ruger No. 1B Standard, No. 1V Special Varminter

220 SWIFT

Cooper Arms Black Jack, BR-50 Bench Rest,
Model 22 Pro Varmint Extreme
Ruger No. 1B Standard, No. 1V Special Varminter
Savage Models 112BVSS Varmint, 112FVSS

222 REMINGTON

AMT Single Shot Deluxe, Standard

223 REMINGTON

AMT Single Shot Deluxe, Standard
Browning Model 1885 Low Wall
Harrington & Richardson Ultra Varmint
New England Handi-Rifle, Survivor
Ruger No. 1B Standard, No. 1V Special Varminter
Thompson/Center Contender Series

243 WINCHESTER

AMT Single Shot Deluxe, Standard
Browning Model 1885 Low Wall
Cooper Arms Black Jack, BR-50 Bench Rest,
Model 22 Pro Varmint Extreme
New England Handi-Rifle
Ruger No. 1A Light Sporter, No. 1B Standard,
No. 1 RSI International

25-06

Cooper Arms Black Jack, BR-50 Bench Rest,
Model 22 Pro Varmint Extreme
Harrington & Richardson Ultra Hunter, Ultra
Single-Shot
Ruger No. 1B Standard, No. 1V Special Varminter

6mm PPC

AMT Single Shot Deluxe, Standard
Cooper Arms Black Jack, BR-50 Bench Rest,
Model 22 Pro Varmint Extreme
Ruger No. 1V Special Varminter

6mm REMINGTON

Ruger No. 1B Standard, No. 1V Special Varminter

257 ROBERTS   270 WBY. MAG.

Ruger No. 1B Standard

270 WINCHESTER

Browning Model 1885 High Wall
New England Handi-Rifle
Ruger No. 1A Light Sporter, No. 1B Standard,
No. 1 RSI International

280 REMINGTON

New England Handi-Rifle
Ruger No. 1B Standard

30-06

Browning Model 1885 High Wall
New England Handi-Rifle
Ruger No. 1A Light Sporter, No. 1B Standard,
No. 1 RSI International

30-30 WIN.

New England Handi-Rifle
Thompson/Center Contender Series

300 WBY. MAG.

Ruger No. 1B Standard

300 WIN. MAG.

Ruger No. 1B Standard, No. 1S Medium Sporter
Savage Model 112 BT Competition

308 WIN.

AMT Single Shot Standard & Deluxe
Cooper Arms Black Jack, BR-50 Bench Rest,
Model 22 Pro Varmint Extreme
Harrington & Richardson Ultra Hunter, Ultra
Single-Shot

7mm REM. MAG.

Browning Model 1885 High Wall
Ruger No. 1S Medium Sporter, No. 1B Standard

7×57mm

Ruger No. 1A Light Sporter

7-30 WATERS

Thompson/Center Contender Series

338 WIN. MAG.

Ruger No. 1S Medium Sporter, No. 1B Standard

35 WHELEN

Harrington & Richardson RMEF Commemorative

357 MAG.

New England Survivor
Pedersoli Calvary, Infantry, Long Range
Creedmoor, Rolling Block Target
Uberti Model 1871 Rolling Block Baby Carbine

357 REM. MAX.

Harrington & Richardson Ultra SS

375 H&H/WIN.

Ruger No. 1H Tropical
Thompson/Center Contender Series

40-65

Browning Model 1885 BPCR

416 REM./RIGBY

Ruger No. 1H Tropical

44 REM. MAG.

New England Handi-Rifle

45-70 GOV'T.

Browning Model 1885 High Wall
Harrington & Richardson Wesson & Harrington
Brand 125™ Anniversary Rifle
Navy Arms Remington Style Rolling Block
Buffalo, Sharps Plains
New England Handi-Rifle
Pedersoli Calvary, Infantry, Long Range
Creemoor, Rolling Block Target
Ruger No. 1S Medium Sporter

458 WIN. MAG.

Ruger No. 1H Tropical

10mm MAGNUM

Dakota 10 Magnum

CENTERFIRE/RIMFIRE— RIFLE/SHOTGUN COMBOS

22 LR, 22 HORNET, 223 REM./12 or 20 Ga.

Savage Model 24F

22 LR/.410 Ga.

Springfield Model M-6 Scout

22 Hornet/.410 Ga.

Springfield Model M-6 Scout

45-70 GOVT./20 Ga.

Pedersoli Kodiak Mark IV

RIMFIRE—BOLT ACTION

22 S, L, LR

Browning Models A-Bolt 22 Grade I & Gold
Medallion
CZ Model ZKM452 Lux, Standard
Dakota Arms Model 22 LR Sporter
KBI M-12 Y Youth, M-1400S/SC, M-1500S/SC,
M1800-S/SC
Kimber Model 82C Series
Magtech Models MT 122.2.S/R/T
Marlin Models 25N, 880, 880SS, 880SQ, 881,
2000 Target
Remington Models 541-T and 581-S
Ruger Model 77/22 Series
Sako Finnfire
Savage Model 900B Biathlon, 900S Silhouette,
900TR Target Repeater
Ultra Light Arms Model 20
Unique Model T Dioptra Sporter, T UIT Standard,
T/SM Silhouette

22 MAGNUM RIMFIRE

KBI M-1400S/SC, M-1500S/SC, M-1800S/SC
Ruger Model 77/22 Series
Unique Model T Dioptera Sporter, Model T/SM
Silhouette

22 WMR

Browning A-Bolt 22 MAG. Grade I
CZ Model ZKM452 Lux, Standard
Marlin Models 25MN, 882, 882L, 882SS, 883,
883SS
Savage Model 93G

RIMFIRE—LEVER ACTION

22 S, L, LR

Browning Model BL-22 (Grades I and II)
Marlin Model Golden 39AS
Uberti Model 1866 Sporting, Yellowboy Carbine
Winchester Model 9422 Series

22 MAG. (WMR)

Uberti Model 1866 Sporting, Yellowboy Carbine
Winchester Models 9422 Walnut, Win-Cam, -Tuff

RIMFIRE—SEMIAUTOMATIC

22 S, L, LR

AMT Challenge Edition
Brown Precision Custom Team Challenger
Browning Model 22 SemiAuto Grades I and VI
Cooper Arms Models 36 Classic, 36RF BR-50,
36RF/CF Featherweight, Custom Classic
European American Armory Sabatti Model
SP1822H
KBI M-2000 S Classic, M-2000SC Super Classic,
Standard M-20P **Marlin** Models 25N, 60/60SS,
70PSS "Papoose," 880, 880SS, 880SQ,
881,995SS
Mitchell Arms Model LW22 Carbine
Remington Model 522 Viper, Model 552 BDL
Deluxe Speedmaster
Ruger Model 10/22 Carbine Series
Savage Models Mark II-G, Youth, 64G

22 WMR

AMT Rimfire Magnum
Brno Model ZKM 611
Marlin Models 25MN, 882, 882L, 882SS, 883
Mag., 883 SS, 922 Mag.

HANDGUNS

30

Gonic Arms Model GA-90

31

Colt Blackpowder Colt 1849 Pocket Pistol
CVA New Model Pocket, Vest Pocket Derringer

36

American Arms 1851 Colt Navy
Armsport Models 5133, 5136
Colt Blackpowder Colt 1851 & 1861 Navy,
Trapper Model 1862 Pocket Police
CVA Model 1851, Pocket Police
Dixie Navy Revolver, Spiller and Burr Revolver
EMF 1851 Sheriff's Model, Model 1862 Police
Euroarms Model 1120 Colt 1851 Navy
Navy Arms 1851 Navy "Yank" Revolver, Reb
Sheriff's Model 1860, 1862 New Model Police
Revolver
Uberti 1851 and 1861 Navy, 1858 New Navy,
Paterson

38

Dixie Pedersoli Mang Target Pistol
Gonic Arms Model GA-90

44

American Arms 1858 Remington Army and Army
SS Target, 1860 Colt Army
Armsport Models 5120, 5133, 5138, 5139, 5140
Colt Blackpowder Colt Third Model Dragoon, Colt
1860 Army, Cavalry Model 1860 Army, Walker
CVA 1851 and 1861 Navy Brass-Framed
Revolvers, Remington Bison, 1858 Remington
Army Revolvers, Walker
Dixie Pennsylvania Pistol, Remington Army
Revolver, Third Model Dragoon, Walker
Revolver, Wyatt Earp Revolver
EMF Model 1860 Army, Second Model 44
Dragoon
Euroarms Rogers and Spencer Models 1005,
1006 and 1007, Remington 1858 New Model
Army, Model 1210 Colt 1860 Army
Navy Arms Colt Walker 1847, 1851 Navy
"Yank", 1858 Target Model, Reb Model 1860
Revolver, 1860 Army Revolver, Reb 60 Sheriff's
Model, Rogers and Spencer Revolver, 1858
Target Remington and Deluxe New Model
Revolvers, Stainless Steel 1858 Remington
New Army, Remington New Model Army, LeMat
Revolvers, Le Page Flintlock/Percussion Pistols
and Cased Sets
Uberti 1st, 2nd and 3rd Model Dragoon, Walker,
1858 Remington New Army, 1860 Army

45

Dixie LePage Dueling Pistol, Pedersoli English
Dueling Pistol
Gonic Arms Model GA-90
Ruger Old Army Cap and Ball
Traditions Pioneer Pistol

50

CVA Kentucky Pistol, Hawken Pistol
Traditions Buckskinner, Buckhunter Pro In-Line,
Kentucky, William Parker, & Trapper Pistols

54

Traditions Buckhunter In-Line Pistol

58

Navy Arms Harpers Ferry Pistol

RIFLES AND CARBINES

32

CVA Varmint
Dixie Tennessee Squirrel
Navy Arms Pennsylvania Long
Thompson/Center Fire Hawk
Traditions Deerhunter

40-65

Browning Model 1885 BPCR Rifle
Cumberland Mountain Arms Plateau Rifle, 1874
 Sharps Silhouette

41

White Systems Model Super 91, Whitetail and
 Bison

44-40

Dixie Winchester '73 Carbine

45

Dixie Hawken, Kentuckian, Pedersoli
 Waadtlander, Tryon Creedmoor, Pennsylvania
Gonic Arms Model GA-87
Navy Arms Pennsylvania Long
Thompson/Center Hawken
White Systems Model Super 91 and ''G'' Series
 (Whitetail & Bison models)

45-70

Browning Model 1885 BPCR
Cumberland Mountain Arms Plateau Rifle
Dixie 1874 Sharps Lightweight Target/Silhouette
Navy Arms Kodiak MK IV Double, No. 2
 Creedmoor Target, 1873 Springfield Calvary
 Carbine, 1874 Sharps Calvary Carbine &
 Infantry Rifle; Sharps Buffalo, Sharps Plains,
 Remington-Style Rolling Block Buffalo
Shiloh Sharps Model 1874 Business, 1874
 Sporting Rifle #1 and #3

45-90

Navy Arms Sharps Buffalo
Shiloh Sharps Model 1874 Business, Sporting
 Rifle #1 and #3

45-120

Shiloh Sharps Model 1874 Business, Sporting
 Rifle #1 and #3

451

Navy Arms Tryon Creedmoor
Traditions Creedmore Match, Hawken Match and
 Henry Match Percussion Rifles

50

CVA In-line Apollo Brown Bear, Classic, Comet,
 Dominator, Eclipse; in-line Buckmaster, Stag
 Horn; Bobcat Hunter, Bushwacker, Express
 Double Rifle and Carbine, Frontier Hunter
 Carbine, Kentucky, Lynx, Panther Carbine,
 Plainsman, St. Louis Hawken, Tracker Carbine,
 Trophy Carbine, Woodsman
Dixie Hawken, In-Line Carbine, Tennessee
 Mountain
Gonic Arms Model GA-87 Rifle, GA-93
Lyman Deerstalker Rifle and Carbine, Great
 Plains, Cougar
Modern Muzzleloading Knight MK-85 Series, BK-
 92 Black Knight, LK-93 Wolverine & Thumbhole
 Wolverine, Magnum Elite
Mountain State Silver & Golden Classics
Navy Arms ''Countryboy'' In-Line, Ithaca-Navy
 Hawken, Kodiak Double, Smith Carbine

50

Prairie River Arms Bullpup & Classic
Remington 1816 Flint Lock Rifle
Stone Mountain Arms Silver Eagle Hunting Rifle
Thompson/Center Fire Hawk, Grey Hawk,
 Hawken, New Englander, Pennsylvania Hunter
 (rifle and carbine), Renegade, Scout Rifle and
 Carbine, Thunder Hawk
Traditions Buckhunter & Buckhunter Pro In-Line
 Rifle Series, Buckskinner Carbine, Deerhunter,
 Hawken Woodsman, Pennsylvania,
 Shenandoah, Pioneer, Whitetail (rifle and
 carbine), Kentucky, Tennessee
Uberti Santa Fe Hawken
White Systems Model Super 91 and ''G'' Series
 (Whitetail & Bison models)

50-70 50-90

Shiloh Sharps 1874 Business, Sporting #1
 and #3

54

CVA In-line Apollo Classic and Eclipse, Stag Horn;
 Bobcat and Frontier Hunters, Lynx, St. Louis
 Hawken
Dixie Hawken, In-Line Carbine, Sharps New
 Model 1859 Carbine and 1859 Military Rifle
Euroarms 1803 Harpers Ferry, 1841 Mississippi
Gonic Arms Model GA-87
Lyman Deerstalker Rifle, Great Plains, Cougar
Modern Muzzleloading Knight MK-85 Series, BK-
 92 Black Knight, LK-93 Wolverine & Thumbhole
 Wolverine, Magnum Elite
Navy Arms 1803 Harpers Ferry, 1841 Mississippi,
 1859 Berdan Sharps, 1859 Sharps Cavalry
 Carbine, Ithaca/Navy Hawken, Mortimer
 Flintlock and Match Flintlock, Kodiak Double
Pedersoli Sharps Carbine Model 766, Sharps
 1859 Military
Prairie Rover Arms Bullpup & Classic
Stone Mountain Harpers Ferry & Mississippi
Thompson/Center Fire Hawk, Grey Hawk,
 Hawken, New Englander, Renegade, Scout
 Carbine and Rifle, Thunder Hawk
Traditions Buckhunter In-Line Rifle Series,
 Hawken Woodsman, Pioneer, Whitetail
Uberti Sante Fe Hawken
White Systems ''G'' Series Bison

58

Colt Blackpowder Colt Model 1861 Musket
Dixie 1858 Two-Band Enfield Rifle, U.S. Model
 1861 Springfield, Mississippi, 1862 Three-Band
 Enfield Rifle Musket, 1863 Springfield Civil War
 Musket
Euroarms Model 2260 London Armory Co. Enfield
 3-Band Rifle Musket, Models 2270 and 2280
 London Armory Co. Enfield Rifled Muskets,
 Model 2300 Cook and Brother Confederate
 Carbine, J. P. Murray Carbine, 1861 Springfield,
 1863 Remington Zouave, C. S. Richmond
 Musket, 1841 Mississippi
Navy Arms Mississippi Model 1841, 1853 Enfield
 Rifle and Musket, 1861 Enfield Musketoon,
 1861 Springfield, 1863 Springfield, J.P. Murray
 Carbine, 1862 C. S. Richmond, Kodiak Double
Stone Mountain 1853 Enfield
Thompson/Center Big Boar Caplock, Firehawk
Traditions Model 1853 3-Band Enfield Rifled
 Musket, Model 1861 U. S. Springfield Rifled
 Musket

69

Dixie U.S. Model 1816 Flintlock Musket
Navy Arms Brown Bess Musket/Carbine, 1816
 M.T. Wickham Musket

DISCONTINUED FIREARMS

The following models have been discontinued or are no longer imported, or are
now listed under a different manufac-
turer/distributor.

HANDGUNS

AMERICAN ARMS Model CX-22 DA Semiauto
AMT Automag V
ANSCHUTZ Exemplar, Exemplar XIV, Exemplar
 Hornet
BENELLI Model MP90S Target Pistol
CHARTER ARMS Bulldog Pug 44 Special, Lady On-
 Duty, Off-Duty, Police Undercover
COLT Detective Special
EMF/DAKOTA Model 1873, Dakota Target
FEATHER Guardian Angel
HÄMMERLI Model 212 Hunter's Pistol
HECKLER & KOCH Models P7K3, P7M10, P7M13
TEXAS ARMS Defender Derringer
WALTHER Model P.38 DA
DAN WESSON 22 Rimfire, 22 Silhouette, Fixed
 Barrel Revolver, 32/32-20 Mag. 6-shot, 357 Super
 Mag., 41/44 Mag. & 45 Colt Revolvers, 445
 Supermag, .45 Pin Gun, Model 738+P ''L'il Dan'',
 Hunter Series, Super Ram Silhouette

RIFLES

BROWNING Model A-Bolt 22 Bolt Action, Model 81
 BLR High Power
COOPER ARMS Model 36 Custom Classic, Model
 40 Classic Varminter
CZ Model ZKK600, Model ZKM 537
EUROPEAN AMERICAN ARMORY Model HW60
 Target/Silhouette Rifle
JARRETT Cowden Rifle
MARLIN Model 39TDS Takedown, Model 70HC,
 Model 1895 CLTD
McMILLAN Signature Rifles (now manufactured and
 distributed by Harris Gunworks)
MITCHELL ARMS Model 15/22 Carbine, Model 20/
 22 Semiauto, Bolt Action Rimfire, Models 9301,
 9302, 9303, 9304 (22LR/Magnum)
SAKO Laminated Stock Models
WINCHESTER Model 70 Lightweight

SHOTGUNS

HARRINGTON & RICHARDSON Turkey Mag and
 Youth Turkey
MAVERICK OF MOSSBERG Model 91 Ulti-Mag
NEW ENGLAND FIREARMS NWTF Turkey
PERAZZI American Trap Single Barrel Models MX8
 Special, DB81 Special; MX7 Sporting
REMINGTON Model 870 Wingmaster Special Field

BLACKPOWDER

AMERICAN ARMS 1847 Walker Revolver
CVA Apollo Shadow SS Rifles, Frontier Carbine,
 Plainsman, PR 412 Express Double-Barrel Rifle,
 Trophy Carbine, Woodsman LS
DIXIE French Charleville Flint Pistol, Third Model
 Dragoon
GONIC ARMS Brown Model GA-87 or Gray
 Laminated Stock
REMINGTON 1816 Commemorative Flint Lock
STONE MOUNTAIN Rogers & Spencer Revolver
THOMPSON/CENTER Custom Rifle, White
 Mountain Carbine
TRADITIONS Frontline Scout, Whitetail Rifle

GUNFINDER

To help you find the model of your choice, the following index includes every firearm found in this Shooter's Bible 1997, listed by type of gun.

PRODUCT INDEX

The Product Index below is intended to give the reader a general overview of the contents of this edition of SHOOTER'S BIBLE. For detailed listings of firearms, see the Gunfinder and Caliberfinder indexes that precede this. For complete addresses and phone/fax numbers of the companies listed below, please turn to the Directory of Manufacturers and Suppliers on page 554.

ACCESSORIES, FIREARM
B-Square (Bipods), 89
Butler Creek (Rifle Sling), 90
DeSantis Holster & Leather Goods (Ankle Holster), 87
DeSantis Holster & Leather Goods (Scabbard), 86
Desert Mountain Mfg. (Rifle Rest), 92
Harris Engineering (Bipods), 96
Hunter Company (Rifle Sling), 85
Keng's Firearms Specialty (Shooting Rest), 93
Knouff & Knouff (Gun Cases), 95
Shooting Systems (Holster), 88
Peltor (Hearing Protector), 88

AMMUNITION
Federal, 492
Fiocchi, 493
Glaser Safety Slug, 95
Hornady, 494
Keng's Lapua Ammo, 86
Remington, 495
U.S.A. Magazines, 88
Winchester, 496

BOOKS, CATALOGS
Blue Book of Gun Values, 93
Lyman Cast Bullet Handbook, 537
Lyman Reloading Handbook, 538, 541
MTM Handloader's Log, 544
Navy Arms Replica Catalog, 90
Stoeger Books, 2

BLACKPOWDER ARMS (see also Gun Kits)
American Arms, 388
Armsport, 389
Cabela's, 390
Colt Blackpowder, 391
Cumberland Mountain, 393
CVA, 394
Dixie, 401
EMF, 408
Euroarms, 409
Gonic Arms, 413
Lyman, 414
Modern Muzzleloading, 415
Mountain State, 416
Navy Arms, 417
Prairie River Arms, 428
Remington, 429
Ruger, 429
Shiloh Sharps, 430
Stone Mountain, 431
Thompson/Center, 432
Traditions, 436
Uberti, 444
White Systems, 446

BULLETS
Hornady, 516
Lyman, 87
Nosler, 519
Sako, 521
Sierra, 522
Speer, 525

CUSTOM RIFLES
Brown Precision, 211
Cooper Arms, 219
Francotte, 225
Jarrett, 231
Kimber, 233
Rifles, Inc., 264
Winchester, 305

CUSTOM SHOTGUNS
AyA, 319
Benelli, 323
Beretta, 326, 327
Bernardelli, 329
Dakota Arms, 338
A.H. Fox, 338
Francotte, 339
Garbi, 339
Krieghoff, 348
Merkel, 352
Parker, 362
Perazzi, 363
Piotti, 365
Remington, 366
Rottweil, 375

CUSTOMIZING (See Repair, Restoration & Customizing)

GUN KITS (Blackpowder/Rifles)
Cumberland Mountain (BP), 393
CVA (BP), 396-398
Dixie (BP), 401-407
Lyman (BP), 414
Navy Arms (BP), 418, 419, 423, 425, 427
Thompson/Center
    Blackpowder Rifle, 433
    Contender Carbine, 294
Traditions (BP), 436-438

GUN MAINTENANCE
B-Square (Choke Tube Speed Wrench), 89
J. Dewey Mfg. Co. (Cleaning Rods), 92
MTM Case-Gard Corp. (Maintenance Center), 94, 544
Thompson/Center (Cleaning Kit), 552

GUNPOWDER
Alliant, 529
Hodgdon, 530
IMR, 531

HANDGUNS
American Arms, 98
American Derringer, 92, 99
AMTEC 2000, 85, 134
AMT, 101
Auto-Ordnance, 103
Beretta, 104
Bernardelli, 108
Bersa, 109
Brolin, 110
Browning, 111
Colt, 114
Coonan Arms, 119
CZ, 120
Daewoo, 121
Davis, 122
EMF/Dakota, 123
Erma, 126
European American Armory, 127
Freedom Arms, 130
Glock, 131
Hämmerli, 133
Harrington & Richardson, 91, 134
Heckler & Koch, 136
Heritage Manufacturing, 137
Hi-Point Firearms, 138
High Standard, 138
J.O. Arms, 140
Kahr Arms, 140
KBI, 141
Kimber, 143
L.A.R. Grizzly, 144
Laseraim Technologies, 145
Llama, 146
Luger, 147
Magnum Research, 148
Mitchell Arms, 150
MOA Maximum, 154
Navy Arms, 154
New England Firearms, 155
North American Arms, 156
Para-Ordnance, 157
Phoenix Arms, 88
Precision Small Arms, 158
Rossi, 158
Ruger, 161
Safari, 169
SIG-Sauer, 170
Smith & Wesson, 172
Springfield, 185
Star, 189
Stoeger, 96, 190
Taurus, 86, 191
Thompson/Center, 197
Uberti, 198
Unique, 199
Walther, 200

Wichita Arms, 202
Wildey, 202

LADIES'/YOUTH GUNS
American Derringer Derringer, 100
Beretta Shotgun, 328
Brown Precision Rifles, 212
Browning Shotguns, 332, 335
Colt Revolver, 118
Conn. Valley Classics Shotgun, 336
Harrington & Richardson
   Revolver, 134
   Shotguns, 340, 341
IGA Shotguns, 342, 343
KBI Armscor Rifles, 232
Marlin Rifle, 242
Marocchi Shotgun, 350
New England Firearms
   Revolvers, 155
   Shotguns, 361
Remington
   Rifle, 261
   Shotguns, 367, 373
Rossi Revolver, 159
Savage Rifles, 287
Smith & Wesson Pistol, 172
   Revolvers, 177, 180
Thompson/Center Carbine, 294
Winchester Carbine, 310
   Shotgun, 385

RELOADING TOOLS
Desert Mountain Mfg., 92
Forster, 532
Hornady, 534
Lyman, 94, 536
MEC, 542
MTM, 544
RCBS, 545
Redding, 549
Thompson/Center, 551

REPAIR, RESTORATION AND CUSTOMIZING
Brown Precision actions, 211
Butler Creek Corp. (Barrel/Stock Combo), 96
Dakota actions, 222
Glaser Safety Slug (Stock Kit), 92
Gunline Tools, 91
Howa actions, 231
N.C. Ordnance (Grips), 90
Sako actions, 281
Doug Turnbull Restoration, 94

REPLICAS (see also Blackpowder Arms)
American Arms Rifles, 204
EMF/Dakota Handguns, 123
EMF Rifles, 223
Navy Arms Revolvers, 154
   Rifles, 249
Pedersoli Rifles, 255
Uberti Handguns, 198
   Rifles, 297

RIFLES
American Arms, 204
AMT, 205
AMTEC 2000, 93, 227
Arnold Arms, 206
A-Square, 208
Auto-Ordnance, 209
Blaser, 210
Brno, 210
Brown Precision, 211
Browning, 213
Clifton Arms, 218
Colt, 218
Cooper Arms, 219
CZ, 221
Dakota Arms, 222
EMF, 223
European American Armory, 224
Francotte, 225
Harrington & Richardson, 87, 226
Harris Gunworks, 227
Heckler & Koch, 230
Howa, 231
Jarrett, 231
KBI, 232
Kimber, 233
Kongsberg, 236
Krieghoff, 237
L.A.R., 237
Lazzeroni, 95, 238
Magnum Research, 239
Magtech, 239
Marlin, 240
Mitchell Arms, 248
Navy Arms, 249
New England Firearms, 254
Pedersoli, 255
Remington, 256
Rifles, Inc., 264
Rossi, 265
Ruger, 266
Sako, 273
Sauer, 282
Savage, 283
Springfield, 289
Steyr-Mannlicher, 291
Thompson/Center, 294
Tikka, 295
Uberti, 297
Ultra Light Arms, 299
Unique, 300
Weatherby, 301
Winchester, 305
Winslow, 314

SCOPES
Bausch & Lomb Riflescopes, 449
Bausch & Lomb/Bushnell, 450
Burris, 453
Kahles (Swarovski), 91
Laseraim Technologies, 458
Leupold, 459
Nikon (Handgun/Rifle), 467
Pentax Riflescopes, 468
Redfield, 470
Schmidt & Bender Riflescopes, 473
Simmons (Handgun/Rifle/Shotgun), 474
Swarovski Riflescopes, 87, 91, 94, 478
Swift Riflescopes, 481
Tasco (Handgun/Riflescopes), 482
Weaver, 487
Zeiss Riflescopes, 490

SCOPE MOUNTS
B-Square, 89
Harrington & Richardson, 134
Sako, 472
Segway Industries (Reticle Leveler), 93
Steyr-Mannlicher, 293
Wideview, 488

SHOTGUNS
American Arms, 316
American Arms/Franchi, 318
AyA, 319
Benelli, 321
Beretta, 323
Bernardelli, 329
Browning, 330
Connecticut Valley Classics, 336
County, 337
Dakota Arms, 338
A.H. Fox, 338
Francotte, 339
Garbi, 339
Harrington & Richardson, 340
IGA, 342
KBI, 345
Krieghoff, 347
Magtech, 349
Marlin, 349
Marocchi, 350
Maverick of Mossberg, 351
Merkel, 352
Mossberg, 354
New England Firearms, 360
Parker Reproductions, 362
Perazzi, 363
Piotti, 365
Remington, 366
Rottweil, 375
Ruger, 376
SKB, 377
Tikka, 380
Weatherby, 382
Winchester, 384

SIGHTS
Aimpoint, 448
Bausch & Lomb/Bushnell, 452
B-Square, 89, 453
Interaims, 457
Laseraim Technologies, 458
Leupold, 460
Lohman Game Call Co. (Sight Vise), 95
Lyman, 463
Millett Handgun Sights, 90, 464
Quarton Handgun Sights, 96, 469
Williams, 489

TARGETS
Trius Products, 91

TRAPS
Shyda's Lincoln Traps, 86
Trius Products, 91